Writing and Reading Across the Curriculum

Seventh Edition

Laurence Behrens
University of California
Santa Barbara

Leonard J. Rosen
Harvard University

 LONGMAN

An imprint of Addison Wesley Longman, Inc.

New York • Reading, Massachusetts • Menlo Park, California • Harlow, England
Don Mills, Ontario • Sydney • Mexico City • Madrid • Amsterdam

To Bonnie and Michael—
and to L.C.R., Jonathan, and Matthew

English Editor: Lynn M. Huddon
Sponsoring Development Manager: Arlene Bessenoff
Development Editor: Meg Botteon
Marketing Manager: Renée Ortbals
Supplements Editor: Donna Campion
Full Service Production Manager: Valerie Zaborski
Project Coordination, Text Design, and Electronic Page Makeup: Elm Street Publishing
Services, Inc.
Cover Designer/Manager: Nancy Danahy
Senior Print Buyer: Hugh Crawford
Printer and Binder: The Maple-Vail Book Manufacturing Group
Cover Printer: The Lehigh Press

For permission to use copyrighted material, grateful acknowledgment is made to the copyright
holders on pp. 872–77, which are hereby made part of this copyright page.

Library of Congress Cataloging-in-Publication Data
Behrens, Laurence.
  Writing and reading across the curriculum/Laurence Behrens.
Leonard J. Rosen.—7th ed.
    p. cm.
  Includes bibliographical references and index.
  ISBN 0-321-02397-8
  1. College readers.   2. Interdisciplinary approach in education Problems, exercises, etc.
3. English language—Rhetoric Problems, exercises, etc.   4. Academic writing Problems,
exercises, etc.
I. Rosen, Leonard J.   II. Title.
PE1417.B396 1999
808'.0427—dc21
                                                                    99-21729
                                                                        CIP

Please visit our website at http://www.awlonline.com

ISBN 0-321-02397-8

    45678910—MA—020100

Detailed Contents

Political Quiz: Are You a Liberal or a Conservative? 232
VICTOR KAMBER AND BRADLEY S. O'LEARY

Not sure what to say when pollsters ask whether you're liberal or conservative? Take this quiz and respond with confidence.

The Debate Beneath the Debate: What American Politics Is Really About 236
JEFF SMITH

Regardless of the particular issue, most political arguments are based on differing assumptions people have about human nature and responsibility, definitions of "justice," and the proper role of government in the social sphere.

Liberalism, Conservatism, Socialism, Libertarianism 242
JAMES MacGREGOR BURNS, J. W. PELTASON, THOMAS E. CRONIN, AND DAVID B. MAGLEBY

Four political scientists discuss the main political ideologies in the United States today. Our assumptions about what is best and worst for the nation depend on whether we believe "in the positive uses of government to bring about justice and equality of opportunity" or whether we believe more strongly in limited government, private property rights, and free enterprise.

Guides to Political Conflicts 260
DONALD LAZERE

Is The Nation *liberal or conservative? Is Cornel West more or less liberal than Ted Koppel? What's the difference between fascism and communism? You can't tell the players without a scorecard, so here are six of them to help in the analysis of political rhetoric.*

A Progressive Compact 268
JEFF FAUX

The underlying principles of liberalism are redefined for a new generation in the nation's oldest journal of liberal thought, The Nation. *According to Faux, "The progressive story is a vision of community and moral support. Its moral is that you are not alone."*

A Social Conservative Credo 274
CHARLES KRAUTHAMMER

The classic conservative position: liberal policies, in the form of excessive government intervention in society, have led to the welfare state, cultural decay, and pervasive social breakdown. The solution: less government intervention and greater attention to values.

Film Studies

Preface

When *Writing and Reading Across the Curriculum* (WRAC) was first published in 1982, it was—viewed from one angle—an experiment. We hoped to prove our hypothesis that both students and teachers would respond favorably to a composition reader organized by the kinds of specific topics that were typically studied in general education courses.

The response was both immediate and enthusiastic. Instructors found the topics in that first edition of WRAC both interesting and teachable, and students appreciated the links that such topics suggested to the courses they were taking concurrently in the humanities, the social sciences, and the sciences. Readers also told us how practical they found our "summary, synthesis, and critique" approach to writing college-level papers.

In developing each of the six subsequent editions of WRAC, we have been guided by the same principle: to retain the essential multidisciplinary character of the text while providing ample new material to keep it fresh and timely. Some topics have proven particularly enduring—our "Cinderella" and "Obedience" chapters have been fixtures of WRAC since the first edition. But we take care to make sure that a third to one-half of the book is completely new every time, both by extensively revising existing chapters and by creating new ones. Over seven editions, our discussion of rhetoric has expanded to five chapters. While we have retained an emphasis on summary, critique, and synthesis, we continue to develop new content on such issues as argumentation and writing online that address the issues and interests of today's classrooms.

STRUCTURE

Like its predecessors, the seventh edition of *Writing and Reading Across the Curriculum* is divided into two parts. The first part introduces the skills of summary, critique, and synthesis. We take students step-by-step through the process of writing papers based on source material, explaining and demonstrating how summaries, critiques, and syntheses can be generated from the kinds of readings students will encounter later in the book—and throughout their academic careers. The second part of the text consists of a series of subject chapters drawn from both academic and professional disciplines. Each subject is not only interesting in its own right but is representative of the kinds of topics typically studied during the course of an undergraduate education. We also believe that students and teachers will discover connections among the thematic chapters of this edition that further enhance opportunities for writing, discussion, and inquiry.

NEW TO THE SEVENTH EDITION
New Rhetorical Content

Part One of *Writing and Reading Across the Curriculum* is designed to prepare students for college-level assignments across the disciplines. The seventh
edition provides a considerably strengthened emphasis on the writing process
and on argument, in particular; expanded coverage on the use of the World
Wide Web for research and citation of electronic sources; and a new set of
topics and model student essays demonstrating summary, critique, and synthesis. At the suggestion of reviewers, we have also moved discussion of
"Quotation" to Chapter One, where it joins "Summary" and "Paraphrase."

ARGUMENT

In response to reviewer requests, as well as to an increased emphasis on argumentation in writing programs nationwide, we have greatly enhanced discussion of and opportunities for argument throughout Part One. We have revised
the material on "Logical Argumentation" in Chapter 2 (Critical Reading and
Critique). We have also added the following new sections on argument to
Chapter 4 (Synthesis):

- **The Elements of Argument: Claim, Support, Assumption.** This section
  adapts the Toulmin approach to argument to the kinds of readings
  that students will encounter in Part Two of the text.
- **The Three Appeals of Argument:** *Logos, Ethos, Pathos.* This
  discussion may be used by students to analyze and develop arguments
  in the readings that students will encounter in Part Two of the book.
- **Developing and Organizing the Support for Your Arguments.** This is
  a considerably revised and expanded version of "Techniques for
  Developing Your Papers" in previous editions, which directly ties in
  to our strengthened emphasis upon argument.
- **Annotated Student Argument Paper.** A sample student paper
  highlights and discusses argumentative strategies that a student writer
  uses in drafting and developing a paper.

RESEARCHING ONLINE

Chapter 5 (Research) now includes:

- A new section on **Citing Online Sources** that includes current MLA
  and APA guidelines.
- **The Benefits and Pitfalls of Conducting Research on the World Wide
  Web.** In student papers, web sources make up an increasingly large
  proportion of "Works Cited" and "References" lists. It's convenient
  to find and use web sources, but how reliable are they? We explain

how instructors and students should address this new reality—why the web as a research aid should be welcomed, but why it should also be approached with caution.

Part One: New Topics, Readings, and Student Papers

CHAPTER 1 SUMMARY, PARAPHRASE, AND QUOTATION

Infertility and Reproductive Technologies. Students are taken through the process of writing a summary of Sheryl Gay Stolberg's article, "For the Infertile, a High-Tech Treadmill." We demonstrate how to annotate a source and divide it into sections, how to develop a thesis, how to write and smoothly join section summaries. We also explain how to:

- Summarize narrative passages
- Summarize figures and tables
- Paraphrase sources
- Quote sources

CHAPTER 2 "CRITICAL READING AND CRITIQUE"

A Sweeping New Incentive for New Teachers. We take students through the process of critically analyzing an argument in J. Morton Davis's article, "A Simple One-Step Plan to Solve the Educational Crisis." A student critique of this article follows.

The School-to-Work Debate. Following our model student critique, a writing exercise asks students to write a comparative critique of two opposing arguments on the school-to-work debate: Lynn Olson's "An Avenue to High Academic Standards" and Phyllis Schlafly's "School-to-Work Will Train, Not Educate." The readings include excerpts from an online discussion of these articles.

CHAPTER 4 SYNTHESIS

The Y2K Problem. Ten brief selections on the Year 2000 computer bug precede discussion of the planning and drafting of a student paper on this subject. Seven longer selections (including one consisting entirely of charts and graphs) lead to a writing exercise for an argument synthesis.

Wal-Mart in Our Community? Eight selections on Wal-Mart and its impact on local communities precede a model student argument synthesis.

Murder or Manslaughter. Two "heat of passion" homicides are analyzed to demonstrate the drafting of a student comparison-contrast argument.

Part Two: New Thematic Chapters

As it has through six editions, Part Two of *Writing and Reading Across the Curriculum* provides students with occasions to practice the skills of summary, synthesis, and critique they have learned in Part One.

CHAPTER 8 THE BOOK OF JOB

An ancient poet asks us to contemplate why bad things happen to good people—a question that, since ancient times, has vexed those who seek to understand why blameless people suffer. Whether as a consequence of natural disasters, war, disease, or devastating accidents, each era (and virtually every person) has asked what has come to be called the *Joban question*. Reflecting on the timeless story of Job can spark inquiry into students' own lives and times as well as encourage a connection to others who, through the centuries, have wrestled with questions of justice.

The chapter begins with an orienting essay by Peter Gomes, Minister of Memorial Church at Harvard University, that underscores the relevance of the Job story to contemporary life and culture. Along with extended excerpts from "The Book of Job," two readings explore the literary traditions as well as the diverse theological traditions in which the book was composed. The chapter concludes with essays and reflections by Rabbi Harold Kushner, novelist Michael Dorris, Catholic theologian Dianne Bergant, and dramatist Archibald MacLeish.

CHAPTER 11 YOU, THE JURY

The American legal system has assumed a tremendous presence in our popular culture. At the same time, there is growing interest in writing classrooms toward helping students to understand their civic and social responsibilities. This new chapter invites students to imagine themselves as jurors in a number of actual cases (no prior legal education is necessary). Arguing a case, therefore, becomes an ideal strategy for learning the skills of analysis: applying a general rule or principle to a particular case. More broadly, thinking and writing about legal issues is an ideal approach to the principles of effective argument—students must provide support (the facts of the case) for their claim (the verdict), based on the relevant assumptions or warrants (the laws). Students and teachers who class-tested the chapter helped us choose both the cases included and the kind of writing instruction and supporting material needed. Indeed, our sample "IRAC" essay, "A Defective Beer Bottle," was written by one of our class testers, Ruthi Erdman (Central Washington University).

CHAPTER 12 THE BEAST WITHIN: PERSPECTIVES ON THE HORROR FILM

This chapter examines that most enduring and fascinating of genres: the horror film, and especially the "monster movie." From the psychological aspects of this genre, as employed for various dramatic purposes in film, to the kinds of approaches to film analysis typical of film studies courses, "The Beast Within" shows students how academic inquiry can reveal whole new perspectives on popular culture. The first half of the chapter considers the horror film through the fields of film studies, literature, and psychology. The second half narrows the focus to two of the more popular monster motifs: the werewolf (*The Company of Wolves, Wolf*), and Mr. Hyde (*Dr. Jekyll and Mr. Hyde*, as incarnated over the years by Fredric March, Spencer Tracy, and John Malkovich), and includes a portfolio of film reviewing styles and approaches. Videos of *Wolf* and the 1941 version of *Dr. Jekyll and Mr. Hyde* are available to adopters.

Part Two: Revised Thematic Chapters

CHAPTER 6 LEFT, RIGHT, CENTER: THE AMERICAN POLITICAL SPECTRUM

Extensively revised for the seventh edition, "Left, Right, and Center" is now divided into three sections. The first section offers several new readings that define and describe the increasing complexities of the current American political spectrum. The second section, including such writers as Charles Krauthammer, Barbara Ehrenreich, Florence King, and Michael Moore, demonstrates many of the political attitudes described more objectively by the authors of articles in the first section. The final section of the chapter offers a set of "Mystery Readings." Without the benefit of descriptive headnotes, students are asked to read articles by such diverse political commentators as Jesse Jackson, William Bennett, The Wall Street Journal, Meg Greenfield, Virginia Postrel, and Robert Scheer, and then to locate these authors—and their arguments—on the political spectrum, drawing upon the political discussions they have read in the first two sections of the chapter.

CHAPTER 7 OBEDIENCE TO AUTHORITY

The Obedience chapter continues to build on the profoundly disturbing Milgram experiments. Other selections in this chapter, such as Shirley Jackson's story "The Lottery" and Philip Zimbardo's account of his Stanford prison experiment, have provided additional perspectives on the significance of the obedience phenomenon. This edition adds Solomon Asch's "Opinions and Social Pressure," an experiment dealing with the effects on individuals of the pressure for social conformity. It is an effect so powerful, as Asch's work demonstrates, that it influences the way individuals perceive—or claim to perceive—reality.

CHAPTER 9 THE BRAVE NEW WORLD OF BIOTECHNOLOGY

The topics addressed in "The Brave New World of Biotechnology" are more timely today than ever. This chapter focuses on the ethical and legal complications that arise from the development of genetic technologies. An excerpt from Aldous Huxley's *Brave New World* is followed by an updated selection from a popular textbook on the fundamentals of genetic science. The co-discoverer of

DNA, James Watson, makes ambitious claims for the Human Genome Project that are challenged by Dorothy Nelkin. Shannon Brownlee and others explore the dilemmas faced by families whose genetic histories predispose them to disease: if no known cure for a disease exists, should carriers of a gene that triggers the disease be told? Several new pieces include a report on genetic research being conducted—for profit—in Iceland, and a critique of for-profit research by activist Jeremy Rifkin. The chapter concludes, as did its predecessor, with two selections on the uses of DNA in the courtroom.

CHAPTER 10 FAIRY TALES: A CLOSER LOOK AT CINDERELLA

This popular chapter includes variants of the Cinderella story along with the perspectives of a folklorist (Stith Thompson), a psychologist (Bruno Bettelheim), and feminists (in this edition, novelist Toni Morrison and Karol Kelley), who each describe their efforts to discover why the story has remained a perennial favorite. New to the this edition is a *Los Angeles Times* article on the making of the revisionist film *Ever After: A Cinderella Story* (1998); a speech by Toni Morrison, who exhorts listeners to treat their sisters more humanely than Cinderella's step-sisters treated her; and an analysis by a feminist critic of the movie *Pretty Woman* as a Cinderella story. This chapter develops in students one of two basic skills: the ability to analyze by applying elements of a theoretical reading to one or more variants of "Cinderella"; and the ability to think and write comparatively by reading multiple versions of the story and developing criteria that clarify similarities and differences.

ACKNOWLEDGMENTS

We have benefited over the years from the suggestions and insights of many teachers—and students—across the country. We would especially like to thank: Chris Anson, *University of Minnesota*; Anne Bailey, *Southeastern Louisiana University*; Joy Bashore, *Central Virginia Community College*; Nancy Blattner, *Southeast Missouri State University*; Mary Bly, *University of California, Davis*; Susan Callendar, *Sinclair Community College*; Jeff Carroll, *University of Hawaii*; Michael Colonnese, *Methodist College*; Cathy Dice, *University of Memphis*; Kathleen Dooley, *Tidewater Community College*; Judith Eastman, *Orange Coast College*; David Elias, *Eastern Kentucky University*; Deborah Gutschera, *College of DuPage*; Kip Harvigsen, *Ricks College*; Mark Jones, *University of Florida*; Jane Kaufman, *University of Akron*; Rodney Keller, *Ricks College*; Walt Klarner, *Johnson County Community College*; Dawn Leonard, *Charleston Southern University*; Krista May, *Texas A&M*; Stella Nesanovich, *McNeese State University*; Susie Paul, *Auburn University at Montgomery*; Nancy Redmond, *Long Beach City College*; Priscilla Riggle, *Bowling Green State University*; Joyce Smoot, *Virginia Tech*; Jackie Wheeler, *Arizona State University*; and Kristin Woolever, *Northeastern University*.

We would also like to thank the following reviewers for their help in the preparation of the seventh edition: James Allen, *College of DuPage*; Phillip

Arrington, *Eastern Michigan University*; Carolyn Baker, *San Antonio College*; Bob Brannan, *Johnson County Community College*; Paige Byam, *Northern Kentucky University*; Anne Carr, *Southeast Community College*; Joseph Rocky Colavito, *Northwestern State University*; Timothy Corrigan, *Temple University*; Kathryn J. Dawson, *Ball State University*; Cathy Powers Dice, *University of Memphis*; Kathy Evertz, *University of Wyoming*; Bill Gholson, *Southern Oregon University*; Lila M. Harper, *Central Washington University*; M. Todd Harper, *University of Louisville*; Michael Hogan, *Southeast Missouri State University*; Sandra M. Jensen, *Lane Community College*; Alison Kuehner, *Ohlone College*; William B. Lalicker, *West Chester University*; Krista L. May, *Texas A&M University*; Roark Mulligan, *Christopher Newport University*; Joan Mullin, *University of Toledo*; Aaron Race, *Southern Illinois University–Carbondale*; Deborah Reese, *University of Texas at Arlington*; Jeanette Riley, *University of New Mexico*; Sarah C. Ross, *Southeastern Louisiana University*; Raul Sanchez, *University of Utah*; Rebecca Shapiro, *Westminster College*; Philip Sipiora, *University of Southern Florida*; R. E. Stratton, *University of Alaska–Fairbanks*; Katherine M. Thomas, *Southeast Community College*; Victor Villanueva, *Washington State University*; Pat Stephens Williams, *Southern Illinois University at Carbondale*.

We would like to especially acknowledge the invaluable assistance freely rendered to us by many people during and after the preparation of the law-oriented chapter, You, the Jury. Amy Atchison, an attorney and law librarian at the University of Southern California Law Library, provided numerous references, legal texts, and much-needed guidance through the legal research process. David Hricik, author of "The American Legal System" in You, the Jury, and an attorney at the Houston law firm Baker and Botts, also provided valuable feedback. Leonard Tourney, who teaches legal writing courses at the University of California at Santa Barbara, provided valuable advice before and during the composition of this chapter. Our gratitude also to Ruthi Erdman (whose model IRAC essay appears in this chapter) and her students at Central Washington University; Carolyn Baker and her students at San Antonio College; Gloria Dumler and her students at Bakersfield College; Lila Harper and her students at Central Washington University; Krista May and her students at Texas A&M University; Erik Peterson, and his students at Central Washington University; and Sarah C. Ross and her students at Southeast Louisiana State University for helping us to field test this chapter. The intelligent and perceptive comments of both instructors and students helped us make this chapter more focused and user friendly than it was when they received it.

Thanks also to Arlene Bessenoff and to Lynn Huddon of Addison Wesley Longman, for helping shepherd the manuscript through the editorial process. And our special gratitude and appreciation to our development editor, Meg Botteon, whose good judgment, humor, and encouragement helped make working on this edition a special pleasure.

Laurence Behrens
Leonard J. Rosen

Ancillaries

Print Resources for Students and Instructors

NEW! *Researching Online*, 3/e, by David Munger, is an indispensable media guide that gives students detailed, step-by-step instructions for performing electronic searches, using e-mail, listservs, Usenet newsgroups, IRCs, and MU*s to do research, and assessing the validity of electronic sources.

NEW! *The Longman Guide to Columbia Online Style* is a 32-page booklet that includes an overview of Columbia Online Style, guidelines for finding and evaluating electronic sources, and many examples for citing electronic sources in the COS style.

NEW! *The Essential Research Guide* is a two-page, handy laminated card featuring a table with guidelines for evaluating different kinds of print and on-line sources, a list of editing and proofreading symbols, and a list of cross-curricular web site resources.

Model Research Papers from Across the Disciplines, 5/e, by Diane Gould, Shoreline Community College, is a collection of ten student papers illustrating the most recent MLA, APA, CBE, Chicago, and Columbia Online Style documentation systems. Annotations highlight important considerations for writing in each field.

The Penguin Program. In conjunction with our sister company, Penguin Putnam, Inc., Longman is proud to offer a variety of Penguin titles at a significant discount when packaged with any Longman title. Popular titles include Mike Rose's *Lives on the Boundary* and *Possible Lives*, and Neil Postman's *Amusing Ourselves to Death*.

An updated Instructor's Manual is also available to adopters of this edition. It provides sample course syllabi, answers to the review questions, and teaching recommendations for each of the readings in the seventh edition. The manual additionally offers clarification and guidance for the presentation of the cross-curriculum material and helps the instructor anticipate student responses.

Media Resources for Students and Instructors

NEW! *Daedalus Online* is the next generation of the highly awarded Daedalus Integrated Writing Environment (DIWE), uniting a peer facilitated writing pedagogy with the inherently cooperative tools of the World Wide Web. This writing environment allows students to explore online resources, employ prewriting strategies, share ideas in real-time conferences, and post feedback to an asynchronous discussion board. As they collaborate online, students are learning to improve the organization, style, and expression of their writing. *Daedalus Online* also offers instructors a suite of interactive management tools to guide and facilitate their students' interaction. Specifically, instructors can:

- Effortlessly create and post assignments;
- Link these assignments to online educational resources;
- Tie these lessons to selected top-selling Longman textbooks;
- Customize materials to fit with any instructional preference.

NEW! *Writing and Reading Across the Curriculum Online* at <http://www.awlonline.com/behrens>. Features of the site include annotated student sample essays, additional online readings for each chapter, and annotated links organized around the topics and disciplines highlighted in *Writing and Reading Across the Curriculum*, Seventh Edition.

The English Pages at <http://www.longman.awl.com/englishpages>. *The English Pages* website provides professors and students with continuously updated resources for reading, writing, and research practice in four areas: Composition, Literature, Technical Writing, and Basic Skills. Features include simulated Internet search activities to help students learn the process of finding and evaluating information on the WWW; "The Faces of Composition" essays; and annotated links that provide the best information on the widest variety of writing issues and research topics.

A Note to the Student

Your sociology professor asks you to write a paper on attitude towards the homeless population of an urban area near your campus. You are expected to consult books, articles, websites and other online sources on the subject, and you are also encouraged to conduct surveys and interviews.

Your professor is making a number of assumptions about your capabilities. Among them:

- that you can research and assess the value of relevant sources;
- that you can comprehend college-level material, both print and electronic;
- that you can synthesize separate but related sources;
- that you can intelligently respond to such material.

In fact, these same assumptions underlie practically all college writing assignments. Your professors will expect you to demonstrate that you can read and understand not only textbooks but also critical articles and books, primary sources, Internet sources, online academic databases, CD-ROMs, and other material related to a particular subject of study. For example: for a paper on the progress of the Human Genome Project, you would probably look to articles and Internet sources for the most recent information. Using an online database, you would find articles on the subject in such print journals as *Nature, Journal of the American Medical Association,* and *Bioscience,* as well as leading newspapers and magazines. A Web search engine might lead you to a useful site called "A New Gene Map of the Human Genome <http://www.ncbi.nlm.nih.gov/science96/> and the site of the "Human Genome Sequencing Department" at the Lawrence Berkeley National Laboratory <http://www-hgc.lbl.gov/>. You would be expected to assess the relevance of such sources to your topic and to draw from them the information and ideas you need. It's even possible that the final product of your research and reading may not be a conventional paper at all, but rather a website that you create which explains the science behind the Human Genome Project, explores a particular controversy about the project, or describes the future benefits geneticists hope to derive from the project.

You might, for a different class, be assigned a research paper on the films of writer/director Neil Jordan. To get started, you might consult your film studies textbook, biographical sources on Jordan, and anthologies of criticism. Instructor and peer feedback on a first draft might lead you to articles in both popular magazines (such as *Time*) and scholarly journals (such as

Literature/Film Quarterly), a CD-ROM database, *Film Index International*, and relevant websites (such as the "Internet Movie Database").

These two example assignments are very different, of course; but the skills you need to work with them are the same. You must be able to research relevant sources. You must be able to read and comprehend these sources. You must be able to perceive the relationships among several pieces of source material. And you must be able to apply your own critical judgments to these various materials.

Writing and Reading Across the Curriculum provides you with the opportunity to practice the three essential college-level skills we have just outlined and the forms of writing associated with them, namely:

- the *summary*
- the *critique*
- the *synthesis*

Each chapter of Part II of this text represents a subject from a particular area of the academic curriculum: psychology, political science, folklore, psychology, philosophy, biotechnology, folklore, film studies, and law. These chapters, dealing with such topics as "The Brave New World of Biotechnology," "Obedience to Authority," and "The American Political Spectrum," illustrate the types of material you will study in your other courses.

Questions following the readings will allow you to practice typical college writing assignments. Review Questions help you recall key points of content in factual essays. Discussion and Writing Suggestions ask you for personal, sometimes imaginative responses to the readings. Synthesis Activities at the end of each chapter allow you to practice assignments of the type that are covered in detail in the first four chapters of this book. For instance, you may be asked to *describe* the Milgram experiment, and the reactions to it, or to *compare and contrast* a controlled experiment to a real-life (or fictional) situation. Finally, Research Activities ask you to go beyond the readings in this text in order to conduct your own independent research on these subjects.

In this book, you'll find articles and essays written by economists, sociologists, psychologists, lawyers, folklorists, political scientists, journalists, and specialists from other fields. Our aim is that you become familiar with the various subjects and styles of academic writing and that you come to appreciate the interrelatedness of knowledge. Geneticists, sociologists, and novelists have different ways of contributing to our understanding of biotechnology. Fairy tales can be studied by literary critics, folklorists, psychologists, and feminists. Human activity and human behavior are classified into separate subjects only for convenience. The novel you read in your literature course may be able to shed some light upon an assigned article from your economics course—and vice versa.

We hope, therefore, that your writing course will serve as a kind of bridge to your other courses and that as a result of this work you can become more skillful at perceiving relationships among diverse topics. Because it involves such critical and widely applicable skills, your writing course may well turn out to be one of the most valuable—and one of the most interesting—of your academic career.

Laurence Behrens
Leonard J. Rosen

PART I

How to Write Summaries, Critiques, and Syntheses

1

Summary, Paraphrase, and Quotation

WHAT IS A SUMMARY?

The best way to demonstrate that you understand the information and the ideas in any piece of writing is to compose an accurate and clearly written summary of that piece. By a *summary* we mean a *brief restatement, in your own words, of the content of a passage* (a group of paragraphs, a chapter, an article, a book). This restatement should focus on the *central idea* of the passage. The briefest of all summaries (one or two sentences) will do no more than this. A longer, more complete summary will indicate, in condensed form, the main points in the passage that support or explain the central idea. It will reflect the order in which these points are presented and the emphasis given to them. It may even include some important examples from the passage. But it will not include minor details. It will not repeat points simply for the purpose of emphasis. And it will not contain any of your own opinions or conclusions. A good summary, therefore, has three central qualities: *brevity, completeness,* and *objectivity*.

CAN A SUMMARY BE OBJECTIVE?

Of course, this last quality of objectivity might be difficult to achieve in a summary. By definition, writing a summary requires you to select some aspects of the original and to leave out others. Since deciding what to select and what to leave out calls for your personal judgment, your summary really is a work of interpretation. And, certainly, your interpretation of a passage may differ from another person's. One factor affecting the nature and quality of your interpretation is your *prior knowledge* of the subject. For example, if you're attempting to summarize an anthropological article and you're a novice in the field, then your summary of the article might be quite different from that of your professor, who has spent twenty years studying this particular area and whose judgment about what is more significant and what is less significant is undoubtedly more reliable than your own. By the same token, your personal or professional *frame of reference* may also affect your interpretation. A union representative and a management representative attempting to summarize the latest management offer would probably come up with two very different accounts. Still, we believe that in most cases it's possible to produce a reasonably objective summary of a passage if you make a conscious, good-faith effort to be unbiased and not to allow your own feelings on the subject to distort your account of the text.

USING THE SUMMARY

In some quarters, the summary has a bad reputation—and with reason. Summaries often are provided by writers as substitutes for analyses. As students, many of us have summarized books that we were supposed to *review* critically. All the same, the summary does have a place in respectable college work. First, writing a summary is an excellent way to understand what you read. This in itself is an important goal of academic study. If you don't understand your source material, chances are you won't be able to refer to it usefully in an essay or research paper. Summaries help you to understand what you read because they force you to put the text into your own words. Practice with writing summaries also develops your general writing habits, since a good summary, like any other piece of good writing, is clear, coherent, and accurate.

Second, summaries are useful to your readers. Let's say you're writing a paper about the McCarthy era in America, and in part of that paper you want to discuss Arthur Miller's *Crucible* as a dramatic treatment of the subject. A summary of the plot would be helpful to a reader who hasn't seen or read—or who doesn't remember—the play. (Of course, if the reader is your American literature professor, you can safely omit the plot summary.) Or perhaps you're writing a paper about nuclear arms control agreements. If your reader isn't familiar with the provisions of SALT I or SALT II, it would be a good idea to summarize these provisions at some early point in the paper. In many cases (a test, for instance), you can use a summary to demonstrate your knowledge of what your professor already knows; when writing a paper, you can use a summary to inform your professor about some relatively unfamiliar source.

Third, summaries are required frequently in college-level writing. For example, on a psychology midterm, you may be asked to explain Carl Jung's theory of the collective unconscious and to show how it differs from Freud's theory of the personal unconscious. The first part of this question requires you to *summarize* Jung's theory. You may have read about this theory in your textbook or in a supplementary article, or your instructor may have outlined it in his or her lecture. You can best demonstrate your understanding of Jung's theory by summarizing it. Then you'll proceed to contrast it with Freud's theory—which, of course, you must also summarize.

It may seem to you that being able to tell (or to retell) exactly what a passage says is a skill that ought to be taken for granted in anyone who can read at high school level. Unfortunately, this is not so: For all kinds of reasons, people don't always read carefully. In fact, it's probably safe to say that usually they don't. Either they read so inattentively that they skip over words, phrases, or even whole sentences or, if they do see the words in front of them, they see them without registering their significance.

When a reader fails to pick up the meaning and the implications of a sentence or two, usually there's no real harm done. (An exception: You could lose credit on an exam or paper because you failed to read or to realize the significance of a crucial direction by your instructor.) But over longer stretches—the paragraph, the section, the article, or the chapter—inattentive or haphazard reading creates problems, for you must try to perceive the shape of the argument, to grasp the central idea, to determine the main points that compose it, to relate the parts of the whole, and to note key examples. This kind of reading takes a lot more energy and determination than casual reading. But, in the long run, it's an energy-saving method because it enables you to retain the content of the material and to use that content as a basis for your own responses. In other words, it allows you to develop an accurate and coherent written discussion that goes beyond summary.

HOW TO WRITE SUMMARIES

Every article you read will present a different challenge as you work to summarize it. As you'll discover, saying in a few words what has taken someone else a great many can be difficult. But like any other skill, the ability to summarize improves with practice. Here are a few pointers to get you started. They represent possible stages, or steps, in the process of writing a summary. These pointers are not meant to be ironclad rules; rather, they are designed to encourage habits of thinking that will allow you to vary your technique as the situation demands.

HOW TO WRITE SUMMARIES

- *Read* the passage carefully. Determine its structure. Identify the author's purpose in writing. (This will help you distinguish between more important and less important information.)

- *Reread.* This time divide the passage into sections or stages of thought. The author's use of paragraphing will often be a useful guide. *Label,* on the passage itself, each section or stage of thought. *Underline* key ideas and terms.

- Write *one-sentence summaries,* on a separate sheet of paper, of each stage of thought.

- *Write a thesis: a one- or two-sentence summary of the entire passage.* The thesis should express the central idea of the passage, as you have determined it from the preceding steps. You may find it useful to keep in mind the information contained in the lead sentence or paragraph of most newspaper stories—the *what, who, why, where, when,* and *how* of the matter. For persuasive passages, summarize in a sentence the author's conclusion. For descriptive passages, indicate the subject of the description and its key feature(s). *Note:* In some cases, *a suitable thesis may already be in the original passage.* If so, you may want to quote it directly in your summary.

- *Write the first draft of your summary* by (1) combining the thesis with your list of one-sentence summaries or (2) combining the thesis with one-sentence summaries *plus* significant details from the passage. In either case, eliminate repetition and less important information. Disregard minor details or generalize them (e.g., Reagan and Bush might be generalized as "recent presidents"). Use as few words as possible to convey the main ideas.
- *Check your summary against the original passage* and make whatever adjustments are necessary for accuracy and completeness.
- *Revise your summary,* inserting transitional words and phrases where necessary to ensure coherence. Check for style. *Avoid a series of short, choppy sentences.* Combine sentences for a smooth, logical flow of ideas. Check for grammatical correctness, punctuation, and spelling.

DEMONSTRATION: SUMMARY

To demonstrate these points at work, let's go through the process of summarizing a passage of expository material. Read the following passage carefully. Try to identify its parts (there are four) and to understand how these parts work together to create a single, compelling idea.

For the Infertile, a High-Tech Treadmill

SHERYL GAY STOLBERG

On a frigid Sunday morning in February 1995, Nancy Alisberg and Michael   1
Albano took a stroll on a windswept beach. They had fled their Brooklyn apartment for the Hamptons, holing up in a quaint bed-and-breakfast for the weekend. But this was no ordinary getaway.

It was, rather, a funeral of sorts. After three unsuccessful attempts at con-   2
ceiving a test-tube baby, the Brooklyn couple had come to the seashore to bury their dream of having a biological child.

Bundled up in their heavy winter coats, they settled in near a log to pro-   3
tect themselves from the wind. There, Ms. Alisberg and Mr. Albano, both lawyers, both in their early 40's, pulled lists from their pockets on which each

had written characteristics of the other that they would miss in not having a baby from their own eggs and sperm. They read the list aloud and then, because it was too windy to burn them, as they had planned, they buried them in the sand.

The ceremony, Ms. Alisberg said recently, "was to say goodbye and then   4
to try to work on the moving on." But moving on was easier said than done.

The couple began investigating adoption as soon as they returned home,   5
and they are now the parents of a 2-year-old girl from Korea. But at the same time they plunged back into the seductive, emotionally wrenching world of reproductive medicine, signing up for egg donation, in which Ms. Alisberg might become pregnant using another woman's eggs.

"The technology," Mr. Albano said, "has given us so many options that   6
it is hard to say no."

For infertile couples, saying no to reproductive technology has become a   7
vexing problem. Every month, it seems, there is another stride in the science of making babies. And while public attention inevitably focuses on the latest accomplishment—the McCaughey septuplets, the California woman who gave birth at 63 and other recent feats—the reality is that the high-tech path to parenthood yields failure far more often than success, about three out of four times.

Thousands of couples are riding the infertility merry-go-round, many   8
unable to get off for fear that the next expensive procedure is the one that will finally work.

"My patients are always saying to me, 'How can I stop?'" said Dr. Alice   9
Domar, who directs the behavioral medicine program for infertility at the Beth Israel Deaconess Medical Center in Boston. "I've got this 42-year-old woman in my group who is just about at the end. She says they are ready to move on, and then she hears about this cytoplasm stuff," in which doctors mingle the core genetic blueprint of one egg with the surrounding fluid, or cytoplasm, from another.

"Where," Dr. Domar asked, "do you get to the point where you say, 'I   10
can't do this anymore?'"

The questions carries as much angst for infertility specialists as it does for   11
their patients. "This is the hardest part of my job," said Dr. Jamie A. Grifo, director of the division of reproductive endocrinology at New York University Medical Center. "I have patients whom I tell, point blank, 'You should stop,' and they say to me, 'Well, I want to give it one more try.' I say: 'Here, look at the data. Your chance is one percent.' And they say, 'Well, I'm going to be that one, Doc.'"

The National Center for Health Statistics says that in 1995, the most   12
recent year for available figures, the United States had 60.2 million women of reproductive age, and that 10 percent—or 6.1 million of them—were infertile. Of these, about 600,000 had at some point tried assisted reproductive technology, participating in what Pamela Madsen, who runs a New York support group for infertile women, calls "the ovarian Olympics."

New terms are entering the popular lexicon, from "assisted hatching," in   13
which researchers slit open the shells of embryos, to a veritable alphabet

soup of techniques. There is IVF, for in vitro fertilization, in which sperm and egg are combined in a laboratory dish and then implanted into the uterus as embryos. There is GIFT, for gamete intrafallopian transfer, in which eggs and sperm are inserted into the fallopian tubes in the hope they will unite into embryos. There is ZIFT, for zygote intrafallopian transfer, in which fertilized embryos are transferred to the tubes. There is ICSI, for intracytoplasmic sperm injection, in which male infertility is treated by sifting through a man's sperm and injecting a single strong one into a woman's egg. And of course, there is egg donation.

The procedures take place over the course of a month and are therefore   14 called cycles. The American Society for Reproductive Medicine estimates that in 1994, the most recent year for which figures are available, infertility clinics attempted 42,509 cycles of high-tech conception, resulting in 9,573 births, some multiple, for an overall success rate of 22.5 percent. A couple's chances of success depend on a variety of factors, including the woman's age and the quality of her eggs, as well as her husband's sperm count.

For in vitro fertilization, the most common technique, the success rate   15 was 20.7 percent. Egg donation has a much higher success rate—46.8 percent—but it means that a woman must give up a genetic connection to her child. Some, like Mr. Albano, have a difficult time with that. "It didn't sit well with me that I wouldn't have a pairing of my genetic material with hers," he said. "But Nancy was very much desirous of wanting to experience pregnancy and birth."

Critics have suggested that there is an element of subtle coercion in all   16 this state-of-the-art medicine, with infertility clinics making emotional appeals to couples at a particularly vulnerable point in their lives. Moreover, they fear that couples in their baby-making fervor are not thinking through the moral implications of having children whose genetic roots are different from their own.

"This is not just a science problem; it's a marketing problem," said   17 Barbara Katz Rothman, professor of sociology at City University of New York. "Once you are buying these services, there is a never-ending next service."

The treatments are expensive. In vitro fertilization costs, on average,   18 $7,800 per cycle. And some patients are going heavily in debt to pay for them, taking second and even third mortgages on their homes. While doctors who treat fertility consider it a disease, only 12 states require insurance companies to cover the treatments, which often can drag on for years.

"We pay $550 a month for our own insurance," said Heather Higgins,   19 28, of Billerica, Mass., a small town near the New Hampshire border. She and her husband, Eric, who drives a canteen truck, have spent more than six years trying to have a baby. "I would have the cheapo accident insurance if it weren't for the infertility. With $8,000 a cycle, I could never do it."

By her own estimation, Mrs. Higgins has attempted in vitro fertilization   20 more than 20 times. "I lost count at 21," she said.

Her physician, Dr. Vito Cardone of the Fertility Center of New England   21 in Reading, Mass., says the multiple attempts are necessary because Mrs.

Higgins is a "poor producer," meaning the fertility drugs he gives her prompt
her body to create only one or two eggs at a time, and sometimes none at all.
He is pressing her to try egg donation, but Mrs. Higgins is not ready.

"I'm going to exhaust all efforts," she said, "emotionally, physically and   22
financially, until I can't."

She works part time as a medical assistant, but her days are governed by   23
the rhythm of her in vitro fertilization cycles: 16 days of fertility drugs, which
her husband injects into her buttocks (he practiced on an orange); vaginal
ultrasound probes to check egg development; egg retrieval, in which doctors
remove her eggs, mix them with sperm in a laboratory dish to create embryos
that will be inserted into her uterus when they are no bigger than eight cells,
and then 10 days of anxious waiting to find out if she is pregnant. She spends
much of her time at the computer, chatting electronically with infertile friends
in far-flung places.

"I probably sign on five or six times a day," she said. "Some of the mes-   24
sages are very sad."

Indeed, experts have long suspected that infertility causes depression,   25
and while there is little research on the topic, they are just beginning to learn
that depression can also contribute to infertility.

Dr. Domar, the counselor, said infertile women were twice as likely to be   26
depressed as those who are fertile. In 1993, she published research that found
women with infertility had the same levels of depression as those with cancer,
heart disease or the virus that causes AIDS.

But she said the last time anyone examined the link between treatment   27
failure and depression was 1984, when a study showed that 64 percent of
women who had undergone an unsuccessful in vitro fertilization cycle demonstrated symptoms of clinical depression. The results did not surprise her.

"Unsuccessful treatment is going to cause depression," she said. "That's   28
just common sense. The problem is that women who have the resources or
insurance bounce right back and do more cycles."

Indeed, Nancy Alisberg and Michael Albano said they would have con-   29
tinued their attempts at in vitro fertilization had it not been for genetic screening that showed Ms. Alisberg's eggs contained chromosomal anomalies,
meaning the infant would be born with birth defects.

The discovery, which prompted their trip to the Hamptons, came after   30
three emotionally grueling years of trying to conceive, including an unsuccessful effort to correct Mr. Albano's low sperm count by removing an
enlarged vein in his scrotum; two artificial inseminations, and three in vitro
fertilizations, including one that resulted in a "biochemical pregnancy," in
which a blood test suggested that Ms. Alisberg was pregnant. But the embryo
failed to implant.

The discovery of the genetic defects left the couple with a difficult deci-   31
sion: Would they move on to egg donation, which might enable Ms. Alisberg
to fulfill her desire to carry a baby? Or would they choose adoption, which
would virtually guarantee a child? Cost was an issue; while their health insurance covered in vitro fertilization, it did not cover egg donation. If they spent

$15,000 for donated eggs, the couple reasoned, they might lose the money they had saved for adoption. While adoption agencies discourage it, they decided to push ahead on both fronts.

Jumping back on the infertility merry-go-round was no picnic. To test the   32 likelihood that she would get pregnant with a donated egg, Ms. Alisberg had to go through a "mock cycle" in which she took fertility drugs, underwent blood tests, ultrasound scans and biopsies, all the while knowing that no embryos would be transferred into her uterus.

"Everybody I know who has gone through IVF and then started doing   33 donor egg has a real visceral reaction to being back in that waiting room," Ms. Alisberg said. "You don't want to feel those things again."

On Dec. 27, 1995, Sophie Sang Ah Albano-Alisberg arrived from Korea,   34 4 months old, long and lean, with fuzzy black hair and beautiful clear skin. Her new parents met her at La Guardia Airport, after two months of gazing at her picture. "I recognized her immediately," Mr. Albano said.

Not quite two weeks later, he and his wife received a call from their infer-   35 tility clinic, which had matched them with an egg donor. They spent a few days considering the offer, but finally rejected it. "It was not fair to Sophie," Ms. Alisberg said. "She had just arrived."

But she and her husband cannot bring themselves to eliminate the possi-   36 bility of egg donation entirely. Today, two years later, their names remain on the donor candidate list.

■ ■ ■

Reread, Underline, Divide into Stages of Thought

Let's consider our recommended pointers for writing a summary.

As you reread the passage, consider its significance as a whole and its stages of thought. What does it say? How is it organized? How does each part of the passage fit into the whole?

Many of the selections you read for your courses will have their main sections identified for you by subheadings. When a passage has no subheadings, as is the case with "High-Tech Treadmill," you must read carefully enough that you can identify the author's main stages of thought.

How do you determine where one stage of thought ends and the next one begins? Assuming that what you have read is coherent and unified, this should not be difficult. (When a selection is unified, all of its parts pertain to the main subject; when a selection is coherent, the parts follow one another in logical order.) Look, particularly, for transitional sentences at the beginning of paragraphs. Such sentences generally work in one or both of the following ways: (1) they summarize what has come before; (2) they set the stage for what is to follow.

For example, look at the sentence that opens paragraph 16: "Critics have suggested that there is an element of subtle coercion in all this state-of-the-art medicine, with infertility clinics making emotional appeals to couples at a particularly vulnerable point in their lives." Notice how the first part of this sentence, with its reference to "*this* state-of-the-art medicine" (italics added), asks the reader to recall information from the preceding section. The second part of the transitional sentence announces the topic of the upcoming section: thirteen paragraphs devoted to the emotional vulnerability of couples involved in assisted reproductive technology.

Each section of an article will take several paragraphs to develop. Between paragraphs, and almost certainly between sections of an article, usually, you will find transitions that help you understand what you have just read and what you are about to read. For articles that have no subheadings, try writing your own section headings in the margins as you take notes. Then proceed with your summary.

The sections of Stolberg's article may be described as follows:

Section 1: Introduction—the difficulty of stepping off the high-tech treadmill of fertility medicine—with a lead-in example (paragraphs 1–10).

Section 2: The technology—a brief review of the techniques and statistics associated with assisted reproductive technology (paragraphs 11–15).

Section 3: Emotional vulnerability—the lengths, financial and emotional, to which some will go in order to conceive, with an extended example (paragraphs 16–28).

Section 4: Difficult decision based on genetic diagnosis and the choice to adopt rather than conceive—with the introductory example continued (paragraphs 29–36).

Here is how the first of these sections might look after you had marked the main ideas, by underlining and by marginal notations:

On a frigid Sunday morning in February 1995,   1
Nancy Alisberg and Michael Albano took a stroll on a windswept beach. They had fled their Brooklyn apartment for the Hamptons, holing up in a quaint bed-and-breakfast for the weekend. But this was no ordinary getaway.

It was, rather, a funeral of sorts. After three   2
unsuccessful attempts at conceiving a test-tube baby, the Brooklyn couple had come to the seashore to bury their dream of having a biological child.

Example: Emotional difficulty of failed ART, no biological children

Bundled up in their heavy winter coats, they   3
settled in near a log to protect themselves from the wind. There, Ms. Alisberg and Mr. Albano, both lawyers, both in their early 40's, pulled lists from their pockets on which each had written characteristics of the other that they would miss

in not having a baby from their own eggs and sperm. They read the list aloud and then, because it was too windy to burn them, as they had planned, they buried them in the sand.

The ceremony, Ms. Alisberg said recently, "was to say goodbye and then to try to work on the moving on." But moving on was easier said than done. 4

The couple began investigating adoption as soon as they returned home, and they are now the parents of a 2-year-old girl from Korea. But at the same time they plunged back into the seductive, emotionally wrenching world of reproductive medicine, signing up for egg donation, in which Ms. Alisberg might become pregnant using another woman's eggs. 5

Main Pt. of Article: Hard to say no to ART[1]

"The technology," Mr. Albano said, "has given us so many options that it is hard to say no." 6

For infertile couples, saying no to reproductive technology has become a vexing problem. Every month, it seems, there is another stride in the science of making babies. And while public attention inevitably focuses on the latest accomplishment—the McCaughey septuplets, the California woman who gave birth at 63 and other recent feats—the reality is that the high-tech path to parenthood yields failure far more often than success, about three out of four times. 7

Hi-publicity success, but most often failure

Only 25% success rate

Thousands of couples are riding the infertility merry-go-round, many unable to get off for fear that the next expensive procedure is the one that will finally work. 8

the "treadmill" of title

"My patients are always saying to me, 'How can I stop?'" said Dr. Alice Domar, who directs the behavioral medicine program for infertility at the Beth Israel Deaconess Medical Center in Boston. "I've got this 42-year-old woman in my group who is just about at the end. She says they are ready to move on, and then she hears about this cytoplasm stuff," in which doctors mingle the core genetic blueprint of one egg with the surrounding fluid, or cytoplasm, from another. 9

Not even multiple failures can keep patients from hope

It's always the next new procedure that will work (finally)

[1]"ART," used in the margin notes on this and subsequent pages, is an abbreviation for "assisted reproductive technology."

For patients, when to   "Where," Dr. Domar asked, "do you get to   10
quit is very hard   the point where you say, 'I can't do this any-
                                     more?'"

Write a One-Sentence Summary of Each Stage of Thought

The purpose of this step is to wean you from the language of the original passage, so that you are not tied to it when writing the summary. Here are one-
sentence summaries for each stage of thought in the "Treadmill" article's
four sections:

> *Section 1:* Introduction—the difficulty of stepping off the high-tech
> treadmill of fertility medicine—with a lead-in example (para-
> graphs 1–10).
>
> ```
> Infertile couples face difficult emotional problems as
> they consider abandoning their efforts to become preg-
> nant through assisted reproductive technologies (ART).
> ```
>
> *Section 2:* The technology—a brief review of the techniques and statis-
> tics associated with assisted reproductive technology (para-
> graphs 11–15).
>
> ```
> ART is a broad term describing a set of complex labo-
> ratory procedures in which eggs are fertilized outside
> the body and then implanted in women who, otherwise,
> have been unable to become pregnant.
> ```
>
> *Section 3:* Emotional vulnerability—the lengths, financial and emotional,
> to which some will go in order to conceive, with an extended
> example (paragraphs 16–28).
>
> ```
> The costs of these treatments are high both financial-
> ly (roughly $8000 per attempted pregnancy) and emo-
> tionally: couples trying to conceive ride a roller
> coaster of hope with each ART attempt and despair with
> each ART failure (Failures occur three out of every
> four attempts).
> ```
>
> *Section 4:* Difficult decision based on genetic diagnosis and the choice to
> adopt rather than conceive—with the introductory example
> continued (paragraphs 29–36).

> After three ART failures, Nancy Alisberg and Michael
> Albano chose to adopt a child but still hope to under-
> go yet another ART procedure.

Write a Thesis: A One- or Two-Sentence
Summary of the Entire Passage

The thesis is the most general statement of a summary (or any other type of academic writing—see Chapter 2). It is the statement that announces the paper's subject and the claim that you or—in the case of a summary—another author will be making about that subject. Every paragraph of a paper illuminates the thesis by providing supporting detail or explanation. The relationship of these paragraphs to the thesis is analogous to the relationship of the sentences within a paragraph to the topic sentence. Both the thesis and the topic sentences are general statements (the thesis being the more general) that are followed by systematically arranged details.

To ensure clarity for the reader, *the first sentence of your summary should begin with the author's thesis, regardless of where it appears in the article itself.* Authors may locate their thesis at the beginning of their work, in which case the thesis operates as a general principle from which details of the presentation follow. This is called a *deductive* organization: thesis first, supporting details second—an examples of which you see in "High-Tech Treadmill." Alternately, an author may locate his or her thesis at the end of the work, in which case the author begins with specific details and builds toward a more general conclusion, or thesis. This is called an *inductive* organization. (A conclusion in a deductively organized piece restates the thesis, which already has been presented at the beginning of the selection.)

A thesis consists of a subject and an assertion about that subject. How can we go about fashioning an adequate thesis for "High-Tech Treadmill?" Probably no two proposed thesis statements for this article would be worded identically, but it is fair to say that any reasonable thesis will indicate that the subject is assisted reproductive technology (ART) and the emotionally difficult decision of whether or not to continue fertility clinic treatments. What issues, specifically, does Stolberg believe are raised by ART? For a clue, look at the beginning of paragraph 7: "For infertile couples, saying no to reproductive technology has become a vexing problem." As Stolberg's title suggests, ART can be a "high-tech treadmill" that couples find difficult to leave. Mindful of Stolberg's subject and the assertion she makes about it, we can write a thesis statement *in our own words* and arrive at the following:

> Infertile couples face emotional difficulties as they
> consider abandoning their efforts to become pregnant
> through assisted reproductive technologies (ART).

To clarify for our readers the fact that this idea is Stolberg's and not ours, we'll qualify the thesis as follows:

> In her article "For the Infertile, a High-Tech
> Treadmill," Sheryl Gay Stolberg reports that infertile
> couples face emotional difficulties as they consider
> abandoning their efforts to become pregnant through
> assisted reproductive technologies (ART).

The first sentence of a summary is crucially important, for it orients readers by letting them know what to expect in the coming paragraphs. The preceding example sentence provides the reader both with a direct reference to an article and a thesis for the upcoming summary. The author and title reference also could be indicated in the summary's title (if this were a free-standing summary), in which case their mention could be dropped from the thesis. And lest you become frustrated too quickly, realize that writing an acceptable thesis for a summary takes time—in this case, three drafts, or roughly seven minutes of effort spent on one sentence and another few minutes of fine-tuning after a draft of the entire summary was completed. That is, the first draft of the thesis was too vague; the second draft was too cumbersome; and the third draft needed refinements.

Draft 1: Sheryl Gay Stolberg reports on the

(Too vague— emotional and financial costs
what about the
costs?) associated with assisted reproductive

technologies.

Draft 2: Sheryl Gay Stolberg reports that when

infertile
∨ couples ~~who want biological children~~

give up on efforts to become pregnant

(cumbersome) through measures associated with

assisted reproductive technologies

(ART), the couples face emotional

difficulties.

Draft 3: In her article "For the Infertile, a

High-Tech Treadmill," Sheryl Gay

Stolberg reports that f/or infertile couples ~~the decision to end attempts~~ *as they consider abandoning their attempts to become* at pregnan*t*y through assisted reproductive technologies (ART). ~~is~~ *face* emotional*ly* difficult *ies)*

Final: In her article "For the Infertile, a High-Tech Treadmill," Sheryl Gay Stolberg reports that infertile couples face emotional difficulties as they consider abandoning their efforts to become pregnant through assisted reproductive technologies (ART).

Write the First Draft of the Summary

Let's consider two possible summaries of the example passage: (1) a short summary, combining a thesis with one-sentence section summaries, and (2) a longer summary, combining thesis, one-sentence section summaries, and some carefully chosen details. Again, realize that you are reading final versions; each of the following summaries is the result of at least two full drafts.

Summary 1: Combine Thesis Sentence with One-Sentence Section Summaries

In her article "For the Infertile, a High-Tech Treadmill," Sheryl Gay Stolberg reports that infertile couples face emotional difficulties as they consider abandoning their efforts to become pregnant through assisted reproductive technologies (ART). ART is a broad term describing a set of complex laboratory procedures in which eggs are fertilized outside the body and then implanted in women who, otherwise, have been

unable to become pregnant. The treatments, which fail
three out of every four attempts, are expensive, costing roughly $8000 per attempted pregnancy. Emotion-
ally, the costs are high as well, as couples trying to
conceive ride a roller coaster of hope with each ART
attempt and despair with each ART failure. Stolberg
illustrates this emotional turmoil with the story of a
couple who adopted an infant from Korea after three
ART failures but who still hope for a biological child
by undergoing yet another ART procedure. Many who use
ART become frustrated and depressed; still, they're
eager to try again, hoping to beat the odds and give
birth.

Discussion

This summary consists essentially of a restatement of Stolberg's thesis plus the
section summaries, altered or expanded a little for stylistic purposes. The first
sentence encompasses the summary of section 1 and is followed by the summaries of sections 2, 3, and 4. Notice in the summary of section 4 the decision
to refer to Alisberg and Albano as "a couple" and to conclude with a sentence
that uses the general outline of their story to reemphasize the article's main point:
that despite the failures, couples want to continue high-tech efforts to conceive.

Summary 2: Combine Thesis Sentence, Section Summaries, and Carefully Chosen Details

The thesis and one-sentence section summaries also can be used as the outline
for a more detailed summary. Most of the details in the passage, however,
won't be necessary in a summary. It isn't necessary even in a longer summary of this passage to discuss either of Stolberg's examples—Higgins or Alisberg
and Albano; it would be appropriate, though, to provide a bit more detail
about Alisberg/Albano and, perhaps, about Higgins (who isn't mentioned in
the first summary). In a more extended summary, concentrate on a few carefully selected details that might be desirable for clarity. For example, in "High-
Tech Treadmill" you could mention that 600,000 women visit fertility clinics
each year, and you could name a few of the ART procedures. You might also
develop the notion that stepping off the "treadmill" of ART is difficult.

How do you know which details may be safely ignored and which ones may
be advisable to include? The answer is that you won't always know. Developing
good judgment in comprehending and summarizing texts is largely a matter of
reading skill and prior knowledge (see page 2). Consider the analogy of the sea-

soned mechanic who can pinpoint an engine problem by simply listening to a characteristic sound that to a less experienced person is just noise. Or consider the chess player who can plot three separate winning strategies from a board position that to a novice looks like a hopeless jumble. In the same way, the more practiced a reader you are, the more knowledgeable you become about the subject, and the better able you will be to make critical distinctions between elements of greater and lesser importance. In the meantime, read as carefully as you can and use your own best judgments as to how to present your material.

Here's one version of a completed summary, with carefully chosen details. Note that we have highlighted phrases and sentences added to the original, briefer summary.

Thesis
Section 1
Summary of ¶s
1–10

Section 2
Summary of ¶s
11–15

In her article "For the Infertile, a High-Tech Treadmill," Sheryl Gay Stolberg reports that infertile couples face emotional difficulties as they consider abandoning their efforts to become pregnant through assisted reproductive technologies (ART). Art is a broad term describing a set of complex laboratory procedures in which eggs are fertilized outside the body and then implanted in women who, otherwise, have been unable to become pregnant. These techniques include in vitro fertilization, gamete intrafallopian transfer, and intracytoplasmic sperm injection. Some 600,000 infertile women a year (as of 1995) visit fertility specialists in an effort to become pregnant. The treatments are expensive, costing roughly $8000 per attempted pregnancy. Emotionally, the costs are high as well, as couples attempting to conceive ride a roller

coaster of hope with each ART attempt
and despair with each ART failure.
Unfortunately, disappointment is all
too common since ART fails roughly in
three out of every four attempts.
Still, couples persist. One woman,
who "lost count" of the number of
procedures she had after 21 attempts,
claimed that she would exhaust herself "emotionally, physically and
financially" before resigning herself
to never having a biological child.
Fueled by their intense emotional
need and by rapidly evolving techniques that promise improved results,
infertile couples feel justified in
staying on the "high-tech [reproduc-
tive] treadmill," even after multiple
failures. Stolberg illustrates the
emotional difficulties of life on the
treadmill through the story of a
couple who adopted an infant from
Korea after three ART failures and
the discovery that the woman's eggs
were genetically flawed. Two years
after adoption, the couple still
hopes for a biological child, this
time through a procedure that would
allow the wife to become pregnant
using another woman's eggs. The successes of complex procedures such as
egg donation, when they occur, are
dazzling. But a great many infertile
couples who turn to ART become frustrated and depressed; even so,
they're eager to try again, hoping to
beat the odds and give birth.

Section 3
Summary of ¶s
16–28

Section 4
Summary of ¶s
29–36

Discussion

The final two of our suggested steps for writing summaries are (1) to check your summary against the original passage, making sure that you have included all the important ideas, and (2) to revise so that the summary reads smoothly and coherently.

The structure of this summary generally reflects the structure of the original—with one notable departure. Stolberg splits her discussion of Alisberg and Albano between the beginning and end of the article, a useful strategy for bracketing the piece with a related introduction and conclusion. After the thesis, this summary omits reference to the Alisberg/Albano example in favor of defining assisted reproductive technology in terms the reader can understand. The definition is followed with a section that lays out the emotional difficulties of infertile couples—the main point of Stolberg's article—and only then introduces Alisberg/Albano, to help make the point. For the sake of efficiency, the Alisberg/Albano example is discussed in only one place—at the end of the piece.

Compared to the first, briefer summary, this effort adds details about Stolberg's second example, Ms. Higgins; adds a figure for the number of women who visit fertility clinics annually; identifies three ART techniques; and adds one sentence on why infertile couples feel justified in continuing to seek ART even after multiple failures.

How long should a summary be? This depends on the length of the original passage. A good rule of thumb is that a summary should be no longer than one-fourth of the original passage. Of course, if you were summarizing an entire chapter or even an entire book, it would have to be much shorter than that. The summary above is about one-fifth the length of the original passage. Although it shouldn't be very much longer, you have seen (pages 15–16) that it could be quite a bit shorter.

The length of a summary, as well as the content of the summary, also depends on its *purpose*. Let's suppose you decided to use Stolberg's piece in a paper that dealt with the motivation of couples who persist with assisted reproductive technologies in the face of overwhelming odds. In this case, you might summarize *only* Stolberg's two examples—Higgins and Alisberg/Albano—to provide your paper with some poignant material. If, instead, you were writing a paper in which you argued against ART on the grounds that it was expensive and too prone to failure, you might omit reference to the examples and focus, instead, on Stolberg's use of statistics and basic information about ART. Thus, depending on your purpose, you would summarize either selected portions of a source or an entire source, as we will see more fully in the chapter on syntheses.

SUMMARIZING A NARRATIVE

A narrative is a story, a retelling of a person's experiences. That person and those experiences may be imaginary, as is the case with fiction, or they may be real, as in biography. Summarizing a narrative presents special challenges. You have seen that an author of an expository piece (such as Stolberg's "High-Tech

Treadmill") follows assertions with examples and statements of support. Narrative presentations, however, usually are less direct. The author relates a story—event follows event—the point of which may never be stated directly. The charm, the force, and the very point of the narrative lies in the telling; generally, narratives do not exhibit the same logical development of expository writing. They do not, therefore, lend themselves to summary in quite the same way. Narratives do have a logic, but that logic may be emotional, imaginative, or plot-bound. The writer who summarizes a narrative is obliged to give an overview—a synopsis—of the story's events and an account of how these events affect the central character(s).

The following narrative begins Paulette Bates Alden's *Crossing the Moon: A Journey Through Infertility.* As the title suggests, the book is a memoir that recounts the author's experiences in attempting to become pregnant with the help of fertility clinics. If you were writing a paper on assisted reproductive technologies, you might reasonably want to include references to women (and men) who could offer accounts from a patient's point of view. You could quote parts of such narratives, and you could summarize them. (While Alden does not mention fertility clinics in this excerpt, the moment she describes here prompted her and her husband to become clinic patients.)

Crossing the Moon: A Journey Through Infertility

PAULETTE BATES ALDEN

It's an unseasonably warm afternoon in April, 1986, and I'm sitting on a   1
stone bench outside a Dairy Queen near our house in Minneapolis, considering the two mothers and three children who share my table. I'm about to turn thirty-nine years old, which is why I'm so interested in mothers and children.

I haven't always been so interested. In fact, for most of my adult life I've   2
behaved as if mothers and children had nothing to do with me, which, on the whole, they haven't. But lately I can't take my eyes off them. I'm in the process of making (for me) a mind-boggling discovery: women have children. It's what women *do*. A lot of them, it seems. Most of them, from what I can tell. Now that the blinders have dropped from my eyes, I'm amazed, dazzled, puzzled, and afraid.

One of the mothers is younger than I, the first detail I note about her.   3
Blond hair, good teeth, and I wonder if she works outside the home, since it's the middle of the afternoon and she's in Bermuda shorts. For all I know she's the president of IBM, but something tells me her job is raising the little girl beside her who is eating an ice cream cone dipped in waxy-looking butterscotch. The ice cream is running down the child's hands, grasped around the cone in a double-fisted grip, dripping onto her shorts and bare legs, which are covered in downy hair so fair it is translucent. There is a pasty white ring around her mouth, which I would love to wipe off. The mother has a handful

of cheap paper napkins, which she's going through in a desultory way—she's been to Dairy Queen before—while issuing a soft series of admonitions I seem vaguely to remember from my own childhood: "Why don't you lick around the cone to keep it from dripping? . . . here . . . let me help you . . . won't you let me hold it for you? . . . oh, Sarah! . . . now look what you've done!"

I try to imagine these mother-words issuing from my own lips. I can't   4 imagine keeping up the constant murmuring that motherhood requires. But I have felt how my hand, of its own volition, wanted to reach out and wipe that child's mouth.

The other mother at the table is actually as old as I, but of course she   5 already has her children. We arrived in the parking lot at the same time. I simply got out of my car and went in. While I waited in line, I watched this mother get out, go around to the trunk, get the stroller out, open it, lift the baby into it, buckle him in, help the other child, a boy about three, out of the car, push the stroller to the glass door, open it, maneuver the stroller into the crowded space while trying to keep track of her little boy, who made a beeline for the condiments bar, where he happily began fishing dill pickle slices out with his fingers.

I felt dizzy with relief that I was not a mother. I got my hamburger   6 wrapped in gold foil and hurried out to sit in the sun, tired, hungry, and wild to be alone.

But the only spot available was at the table with the young blond mother   7 and little girl. And then when the older mother had her order, she pushed the stroller out the glass door and looked around for a place to sit. Naturally she pushed it right up next to me. And in spite of myself, I smiled and moved over to make room.

By now the little girl has ice cream pretty much all over her. "Oh well, I'll   8 just have to throw her in the bathtub when I get home anyway," the younger mother says, and laughs self-deprecatingly, as if the joke were on her. I am touched by her—to say the mundane, the unremarkable thing. The two mothers begin conversing, exchanging information about the children's ages and such, but what I want to know is, *What is it like to be a mother?* I want the skinny, the good and the bad, the sublime and the tedious.

But it's a warm spring afternoon at Dairy Queen and I'm not about to rend   9 the social fabric by asking such a question. Besides, I know what they'd probably say, once they recovered from the shock of someone so out of it. They might start with a little humor, but then if I pressed them on it , go on to say that children change your life, but that they are worth it. Which doesn't really speak to the uninitiated. So what I must really want to know is something neither they nor anyone else can tell me: Should *I* be a mother?

I had a Little Ricky doll when I was ten years old. He was the son of Lucy   10 and Ricky Ricardo, and I loved him intensely the summer our family took a Western trip in our '57 Chevy station wagon. I gave him his little bottle, changed his clothes out of his own little suitcase, showed him the passing cacti and red rock mesas out the window, made sure he got his naps, tucked him in in our motel room at night. The first thing I thought of in the morning was Ricky—his round plastic face, his hard blue crystal eyes that blinked open, his

shapely limbs, like pale link sausages, his pleasingly plump torso, his intoxi-
cating rubber smell. He completely filled my senses. The sight, the smell, the
feel of him gave me deep pleasure. All I wanted or needed—then—was Ricky.

Still, I remember how relieved I was when I moved on to plastic horses.   11
Cathy Meyers from up the road had a black stallion and I had a buckskin one,
and we'd race them for hours across the wide-open expanse of our basement
floors. The horses were always having to escape captivity, a plot we never
tired of, until we discovered boys. We were twelve by then, going on thirteen,
and perhaps we sensed what was waiting for us up ahead. It would have nothing to do with wild horses.

I ponder the three children at our table, lost as they are in their revelry of   12
cold sweet cream. In a way they're adorable, and then again, just the usual
young of the species. I try to imagine what it would be like if I had a little
child, if I had brought him or her to Dairy Queen today.

About the closest I can come to imagining what it would be like to have   13
a child is with our cat, Cecil. For Cecil I feel the most delicious love, but also
the most anxious responsibility. My husband, Jeff, loves Cecil too, but he can
go to sleep at night if Cecil isn't in. I have to get up every fifteen minutes or
so to check for him. When he finally does appear, I sweep him up in my arms,
burying my nose in his cold fur that smells of our neighbor's arborvitae bush.
He's always on my mind, even when I'm not thinking about him.

How much worse would it be with a child? How much worse, that is,   14
would *I* be? I'm not sure I want to unleash all that maternal instinct. Would
I ever feel free again? Would I ever be *alone*? I don't just mean by myself; it
isn't as if I haven't heard of babysitters. I know that other women do it—have
selves and babies, too. But I'm not sure I can be one of them. I remember
Ricky-love.

The children, having finished their ice cream, have begun a game of   15
chase around our table, catching onto their mothers' hips as round and round
they go. The baby in the stroller regards these antics with wide-eyed amazement, as if seeing such a sight for the first time, which perhaps he is. But suddenly the little boy trips and falls, and after a moment of stunned silence in
which he checks himself over to see if he's okay, lets out a bawl. We three
women rise as one, but his mother is there first, hoisting him whimpering into
her arms: "Does it hurt? Mama make it better," and she kisses the tiny finger
he holds out, sweetly, to her lips.

And before I can stop it, I'm filled with a sudden anguish: *I might never*   16
have a child! A grief worthy of a death wells in me, before there has even been
a life. *I might never have a child,* and the irony is not lost on me, that I'm not
even sure I want one. And alongside that is another shape just coming into
focus, which I don't want to see, but which is drawing closer every day: I
might not be able to. It might already be too late, I might already be too old,
there might be something wrong.

It's true that Jeff and I are not using birth control. We haven't been for   17
quite some time (I won't let myself remember how long). But I tell myself
we're not really *trying*. Trying is for people who want a child, and I'm not
sure. Jeff is leaving it mainly up to me. He says he can be happy either way,

and besides, he has his hands full, dealing with the barely contained insanity of a small law firm, something they didn't teach him in law school. We both know it would be my life that would change the most if we had a child. Maybe it doesn't have to be that way, but that's the way it is. Jeff would still get dressed in a suit every day, and go off to his office downtown, and I would be mainly responsible for baby.

I believe in making a conscious choice where having a child is concerned.   18 But in the meantime, I've been hoping nature would just take its course. But nothing has ever happened. I haven't gotten pregnant. I'm not going to be let off the hook. If we do want a child, if we're ever going to have one, we've got to do something about it.

■ ■ ■

Alden provides a glimpse into an extraordinarily private moment—the moment of recognition that she and her husband might never have a child. This first-person account could be valuable in a paper otherwise dependent on newspaper and journal articles and on books explaining the more technical elements of reproductive technology. You might reasonably pause in your explanations to acknowledge the tumultuous emotions of those who want children but who need the help of fertility clinics. How would you refer to this passage from Alden's memoir?

When you summarize a narrative, bear in mind the principles that follow, as well as those listed in the box.

HOW TO SUMMARIZE NARRATIVES

- Your summary will *not* be a narrative, but rather the synopsis of a narrative. Your summary will likely be a paragraph at most.
- You will want to name and describe the principal characters of the narrative and describe the narrative's main actions or events.
- You should seek to connect the narrative's characters and events: describe the significance of events for (or the impact of events on) the character.

To summarize events, reread the narrative and make a marginal note each time you see that an action advances the story from one moment to the next. The key here is to recall that narratives take place *in time*. In your summary, be sure to re-create for your reader a sense of time flowing. Name and describe the characters as well. (For our purposes, *character* refers to the person, real or fictional, about whom the narrative is written.) The trickiest part of the summary will be describing the connection between events and characters. Earlier (page 2) we made the point that summarizing any selection involves a degree of interpretation, and this is especially true of summarizing narratives. What, in the case of Alden, is the impact of the events described? An answer belongs in a summary of this piece, yet developing an answer is tricky. Five readers would interpret the narrative's significance in five distinct ways, would they not? Yes and no: yes, in the sense that these readers, given their separate experiences, will read from different points of view; no, in the sense that readers should be able to distinguish between the impact of events as seen from a main character's (i.e., Alden's) point of view and the impact of these same events as seen from their (the readers') points of view. We should be able to agree that Alden experienced a breakthrough realization.

At times, you will have to infer from clues in a narrative the significance of events for a character; at other times, the writer will be more direct. In either case, remember that it is the narrative's main character, real or imaginary, whose perspective should be represented in the summary. Here is a one-paragraph summary of Alden's narrative. (The draft is the result of two prior drafts.)

> Paulette Bates Alden begins her memoir *Crossing the Moon: A Journey Through Infertility* by recalling the panic with which she realized she might never have a child. On an ordinary spring day at a Dairy Queen in Minneapolis, Alden finds herself sharing a picnic table with two mothers and their young children. As the children eat ice cream (making sticky messes of themselves) and the mothers trade stories and information, Alden suddenly realizes that, at 39, "I might not be able to [have a child]. It might already be too late, I might already be too old, there might be something wrong." Her grief at the thought is "worthy of a death," she writes, which strikes her as ironic in that she had valued her independence and never wanted children. Although she no longer uses birth control, getting pregnant never "happened" by itself, and Alden understands that if she and her husband want a child they will need to take deliberate action--which leads them to a fertility clinic and reproductive medicine.

SUMMARIZING FIGURES AND TABLES

In your reading in the sciences and social sciences, often you will find data and concepts presented in nontext forms—as figures and tables. Such visual devices offer a snapshot, a pictorial overview of material that is more quickly and clearly communicated in graphic form than as a series of (often complicated) sentences. The writer uses a graph, which in an article or book is labeled as a numbered "figure," to present the quantitative results of research as points on a line or a bar, or as sections ("slices") of a pie. Pie charts show relative proportions, or percentages. Graphs, especially effective in showing patterns, relate one variable to another: for instance, income to years of education or a college student's grade point average to hours of studying.

The figures and tables that follow appeared in a national study on assisted reproductive technology (ART), conducted by the federal government's Centers for Disease Control, located in Atlanta, Georgia, and based on data collected from 281 fertility clinics in 1995. In Figure 1.1, a pie chart relates the percentage of ART pregnancies (from fresh—non-frozen—embryos resulting from nondonor eggs) that led to the live births of a single child or multiple children. Study this pie chart.

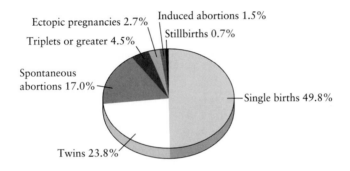

FIGURE 1.1 Outcomes of Clinical Pregnancies Resulting from ART, 1995

Here is a summary of the information presented:

> By far, the most common outcome of a pregnancy that results from ART using fresh embryos and nondonor eggs is a single birth (roughly 50 percent of live births). Twins are born nearly one quarter of the time and triplets (or greater) only 4.5 percent. Roughly 22 percent of such ART pregnancies do not lead to a live birth.

The points on the graph in Figure 1.2 relate the age of women undergoing ART and the success rates of their procedures, as measured by live births.

("Cycle" refers to a specific attempt at pregnancy, using ART). Here is the summary that accompanied the graph in the national report:

> A woman's age is the most important factor affecting the chances of a live birth when the woman's own eggs are used. Figure [1.2] shows the live birth rate for women of a given age who had an ART procedure in 1995. Rates were relatively constant at about 25 percent among women aged 34 years and younger but declined with age after 34. Success rates were zero among women aged 47 years and older.

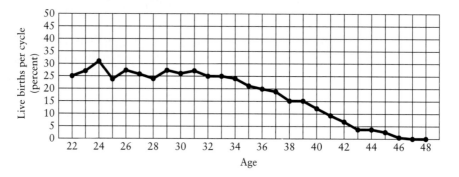

FIGURE 1.2   ART Live Birth Rates by Age of Woman, 1995

Sometimes a single graph will present information on two populations, or data sets, both of which are tracked with the same measurements. In Figure 1.3, the graph tracks the live birth rate of (1) ART for women whose own eggs are fertilized outside their bodies and implanted (that is, transferred from the test tube to the patient), and (2) women who receive *another* woman's (a donor's) egg that has been fertilized. Here is the summary that accompanied the graph in the national report:

> Figure [1.3] shows that the age of the woman undergoing ART treatment does not affect success rates for cycles using embryos formed from donor eggs as it affects

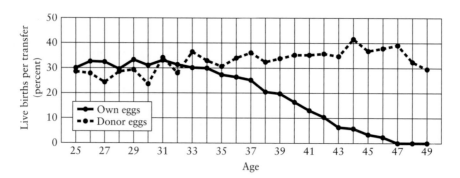

FIGURE 1.3   Live Births per Transfer for Fresh Embryos from Own and Donor Eggs by Age of Recipient, 1995

success rates for cycles using embryos from a woman's own eggs. The likelihood of a fertilized egg implanting is related to the age of the woman who produced the egg. As a result, the success rate for cycles using donor embryos is nearly constant (around 30 percent) across all age groups from 25 to 50. This graph illustrates that women age 36 and older are more likely to have success with ART using donor eggs.

A table presents numerical data in rows and columns for quick reference. Tabular information can be incorporated into graphs, if the writer chooses. Graphs are preferable when the writer wants to emphasize a pattern or relationship; tables are used when the writer wants to emphasize numbers. Table 1.1 provides an overview of the entire 1995 national summary on assisted reproductive technologies.

Explanation of some terms and symbols will be useful in understanding this table. The mathematical symbols for "less than" (<) and "greater than" (>) indicate the age brackets of women in the study: younger than 35; 35 through 39; and older than 39. A "cycle" is a single attempt at pregnancy, using ART. Eggs fertilized in a laboratory—via in vitro fertilization (IVF)—can be transferred immediately into a woman's uterus or fallopian tubes (a so-called fresh embryo transfer) or can be frozen for later implantation (a

TABLE 1.1   1995 ART Pregnancy Success Rates

	AGE OF WOMEN			
	<35	35–39	>39	TOTAL
CYCLES USING FRESH EMBRYOS FROM NONDONOR EGGS				
Number of Cycles	21,019	16,728	8,159	45,906
Pregnancies per cycle (%)	29.7	23.4	13.2	24.4
Live births per cycle[a] (%)	25.3	18.2	8.0	19.6
Live births per retrieval[a] (%)	28.0	21.5	10.2	22.8
Liver births per transfer[a] (%)	30.6	23.6	11.6	25.1
Cancellations (%)	9.1	14.8	21.5	13.6
Avg. number embryos transferred	4.0	4.0	4.1	4.0
Multiple birth rate per transfer				
Twins	9.8	6.6	1.9	7.4
Triplets or greater	2.6	1.2	0.3	1.7
CYCLES USING FROZEN EMBRYOS FROM NONDONOR EGGS				
Number of transfers	3,724	2,433	1,001	7,465
Live births per transfer[a] (%)	16.4	14.8	11.0	15.1
Avg. number embryos transferred	3.5	3.4	3.4	3.4
CYCLES USING DONOR EGGS				
Number of fresh transfers	572	668	2,112	3,352
Live births per transfer[a] (%)	30.8	35.8	36.7	35.5
Avg. number embryos transferred	4.0	4.0	4.2	4.1

[a] Pregnancies resulting in one or more children born alive; therefore, multiple births are counted as one.

From: Center for Disease Control. *1995 Assisted Reproductive Technology Success Rates: National Summary and Fertility Clinic Reports.*

"frozen" transfer). A woman can have her own fertilized egg transferred from the test tube to her uterus, or those of a donor. A "retrieval" is a collection of eggs contained in the ovaries and then fertilized for implantation. A "cancellation" is an ART cycle that is stopped before eggs are retrieved or a frozen embryo is implanted.

A summary of such a comprehensive table will necessarily be selective, depending on which information from the table is pertinent to the task. In writing a paper on ART, you could draw on the data in this table to report on the number of women undergoing treatment. You could compare numbers of women receiving their own fertilized eggs for transplantation as opposed to donor eggs, noting that the nondonor transfer is by far the more common (53,371 transfers of nondonor eggs versus 3,352 transfers of donor eggs). You could report on the high success rate of cycles using donor eggs as compared to the success rate of a woman's attempting pregnancy using her own eggs. From the numbers in the table you could infer that women seeking ART vastly prefer to have their own biological offspring. You might be interested in summarizing the age breakdown of women undergoing IVF and in noting that older women have higher success rates with donor eggs than do younger women. But for nondonor cycles, the younger the ART recipient, the better the likelihood of success. You could glean other information from this table as well, depending on your research needs.

PARAPHRASE

In certain cases, you may want to *paraphrase* rather than to summarize material. Writing a paraphrase is similar to writing a summary: it involves recasting a passage into your own words, and so it requires your complete understanding of the material. The difference is that while a summary is a shortened version of the original, the paraphrase is approximately the same length as the original.

Why write a paraphrase when you can quote the original? You may decide to offer a paraphrase of material written in language that is dense, abstract, archaic, or possibly confusing. For example, suppose you were writing a paper on some aspect of human progress and you came across the following passage by the Marquis de Condorcet, a French economist and politician, written in the late eighteenth century:

> If man can, with almost complete assurance, predict phenomena when he knows their laws, and if, even when he does not, he can still, with great expectations of success, forecast the future on the basis of his experience of the past, why, then, should it be regarded as a fantastic undertaking to sketch, with some pretense to truth, the future destiny of man on the basis of his history? The sole foundation for belief in the natural science is this idea, that the general laws directing the phenomena of the universe, known or unknown, are necessary and constant. Why should this principle be any less true for the development of the intellectual and moral faculties of man than for the other operations of nature?

You would like to introduce Condorcet's idea on predicting the future course of human history, but you also don't want to slow down your narrative with this somewhat abstract quotation. You may decide to attempt a paraphrase, as follows:

> The Marquis de Condorcet believed that if we can pre-
> dict such physical events as eclipses and tides, and
> if we can use past events as a guide to future ones,
> we should be able to forecast human destiny on the
> basis of history. Physical events, he maintained, are
> determined by natural laws that are knowable and pre-
> dictable. Since humans are part of nature, why should
> their intellectual and moral development be any less
> predictable than other natural events?

Each sentence in the paraphrase corresponds to a sentence in the original. The paraphrase is somewhat shorter, owing to the differences of style between eighteenth- and twentieth-century prose (we tend to be more brisk and efficient, although not more eloquent). But the main difference is that we have replaced the language of the original with our own language. For example, we have paraphrased Condorcet's "the general laws directing the phenomena of the universe, known or unknown, are necessary and constant" with "Physical events, he maintained, are determined by natural laws that are knowable and predictable." To contemporary readers, "knowable and predictable" might be clearer than "necessary and constant" as a description of natural (i.e., physical) laws. Note that we added the specific examples of eclipses and tides to clarify what might have been a somewhat abstract ideas. Note also that we included two attributions to Condorcet within the paraphrase to credit our source properly.

When you come across a passage that you don't understand, the temptation is strong to skip over it. Resist this temptation! Use a paraphrase as a tool for explaining to yourself the main ideas of a difficult passage. By translating another writer's language into your own, you can clarify what you understand and pinpoint what you don't. The paraphrase therefore becomes a tool for learning the subject.

The following pointers will help you write paraphrases.

HOW TO WRITE PARAPHRASES

- Make sure that you understand the source passage.
- Substitute your own words for those of the source passage; look for synonyms that carry the same meaning as the original words.
- Rearrange your own sentences so that they read smoothly. Sentence structure, even sentence order, in the paraphrase need not be based on that of the original. A good paraphrase, like a good summary, should stand by itself.

Let's consider some other examples. If you were investigating the ethical concerns relating to the practice of in vitro fertilization, you might conclude that you should read some medical literature. You might reasonably want to hear from the doctors themselves who are developing, performing, and questioning the procedures that you are researching. In professional journals and bulletins, physicians write to one another, not to the general public. They use specialized language. If you wanted to refer to a technically complex selection, you might need to write a paraphrase:

IN VITRO FERTILIZATION: FROM MEDICAL REPRODUCTION TO GENETIC DIAGNOSIS

DIETMAR MIETH

[I]t is not only an improvement in the success-rate that participating research scientists hope for but rather, developments in new fields of research in in-vitro gene diagnosis and in certain circumstances gene therapy. In view of this, the French expert J. F. Mattei has asked the following question: "Are we forced to accept that in vitro fertilization will become one of the most compelling methods of genetic diagnosis?" Evidently, by the introduction of a new law in France and Sweden (1994), this acceptance (albeit with certain restrictions) has already occurred prior to the application of in vitro fertilization reaching a technically mature and clinically applicable phase. This may seem astonishing in view of the question placed by the above-quoted French expert: the idea of embryo production so as to withhold one or two embryos before implantation presupposes a definite "attitude towards eugenics." And to destroy an embryo merely because of its genetic characteristics could signify the reduction of a human life to the sum of its genes. Mattei asks: "In face of a molecular judgment on our lives, is there no possibility for appeal? Will the diagnosis of inherited monogenetic illnesses soon be extended to genetic predisposition for multi-factorial illnesses?"[2]

Like most literature intended for physicians, the language of this selection is somewhat forbidding to an audience of nonspecialists, who have trouble with phrases such as "predisposition for multi-factorial illnesses." As a courtesy to your readers and in an effort to maintain a consistent tone and level in your essay, you could paraphrase this paragraph of the medical newsletter. First, of course, you must understand the meaning of the passage, perhaps no small task. But, having read the material carefully (and perhaps consulting a dictionary), you might eventually prepare a paraphrase such as this one:

Writing in the *Newsletter of the European Network for Biomedical Ethics*, Dietmar Mieth reports that fertility specialists today not only want to improve the success rates of their procedures but also to diagnose

---

[2]From: *Biomedical Ethics: Newsletter of the European Network for Biomedical Ethics,* Vol. 1, No. 1, 1996.

and repair genetic problems before they implant fertilized eggs. Since the result of the in vitro process
is often more fertilized eggs than can be used in a
procedure, doctors may examine test-tube embryos for
genetic defects and "withhold one or two" before
implanting them. The practice of selectively implanting embryos raises concerns about eugenics and the
rights of rejected embryos. On what genetic grounds
will specialists distinguish flawed from healthy
embryos and make a decision whether or not to implant?
The appearance of single genes linked directly to specific, or "monogenetic," illnesses could be grounds
for destroying an embryo. More complicated would be
genes that predispose people to an illness but in no
way guarantee the onset of that illness. Would these
genes, which are only one factor in "multi-factorial
illnesses" also be labeled undesirable and lead to
embryo destruction? Advances in fertility science
raise difficult questions. Already, even before techniques of genetic diagnosis are fully developed,
nations are writing laws governing the practices of
fertility clinics.

We begin our paraphrase with the same "not only/but also" logic of the original's first sentence, introducing the concepts of genetic diagnosis and therapy. The next four sentences in the original introduce concerns of a "French expert." Rather than quoting Mieth quoting the expert and immediately mentioning new laws in France and Sweden, we decided (first) to explain that in vitro fertilization procedures can give rise to more embryos than needed. We reasoned that nonmedical readers would appreciate our making explicit the background knowledge that the author assumes of other physicians. Then we quote Mieth briefly ("withhold one or two" embryos) to provide some flavor of the original. We maintain focus on the ethical questions and wait until the end of the paraphrase before mentioning the laws to which Mieth refers. Our paraphrase is roughly the same length as the original, and it conveys the author's concerns about eugenics. As you can see, the paraphrase requires a writer to make some decisions about the presentation of material. In many, if not most, cases, you will need to do more than simply "translate" from the original, sentence-by-sentence, to write your paraphrase.

Finally, let's consider a passage written by a fine writer that may, nonetheless, best be conveyed in paraphrase. In "Identify All Carriers," an article on AIDS, editor and columnist William F. Buckley makes the following statement:

I have read and listened, and I think now that I can convincingly crystallize the thoughts chasing about in the minds of, first, those whose concern with AIDS victims is based primarily on a concern for them, and for the maintenance of the most rigid standards of civil liberties and personal privacy, and, second, those whose anxiety to protect the public impels them to give subordinate attention to the civil amenities of those who suffer from AIDS and primary attention to the safety of those who do not.

In style, Buckley's passage is more like Condorcet's than the medical newsletter: it is eloquent, balanced, and literate. Still, it is challenging. Here is another lengthy sentence, perhaps a bit too eloquent for some readers to grasp. For your paper on AIDS, you decide to paraphrase Buckley. You might draft something like this:

```
Buckley finds two opposing sides in the AIDS debate:
those concerned primarily with the civil liberties and
the privacy of AIDS victims, and those concerned pri-
marily with the safety of the public.
```

Our paraphrases have been somewhat shorter than the original, but this is not always the case. For example, suppose you wanted to paraphrase this statement by Sigmund Freud:

We have found out that the distortion in dreams which hinders our understanding of them is due to the activities of a censorship, directed against the unacceptable, unconscious wish-impulses.

If you were to paraphrase this statement (the first sentence in the Tenth Lecture of his *General Introduction to Psychoanalysis*), you might come up with something like this:

```
It is difficult to understand dreams because they con-
tain distortions. Freud believed that these distor-
tions arise from our internal censor, which attempts
to suppress unconscious and forbidden desires.
```

Essentially, this paraphrase does little more than break up one sentence into two and somewhat rearrange the sentence structure for clarity.

Like summaries, then, *paraphrases* are useful devices, both in helping you to understand source material and in enabling you to convey the essence of this source material to your readers. When would you choose to write a summary instead of a paraphrase (or vice versa)? The answer to this question depends on your purpose in presenting your source material. As we've said, summaries are generally based on articles (or sections of articles) or books. Paraphrases are generally based on particularly difficult (or important) paragraphs or sentences. You would seldom paraphrase a long passage, or summarize a short one, unless there were particularly good reasons for doing so. (For example, a lawyer might want to paraphrase several pages of legal language so that his or her client, who is not a lawyer, could understand it.) The purpose of a summary is generally to save your reader time by presenting him or her with a brief and quickly readable version of a lengthy source. The purpose of a paraphrase is generally to clarify a short passage that might otherwise be unclear. Whether you summarize or paraphrase may also depend on the importance of your source. A particularly important source—if it is not too long—may rate a paraphrase. If it is less important, or peripheral to your central argument, you may choose to write a summary instead. And, of course, you may choose to summarize only part of your source—the part that is most relevant to the point you are making.

QUOTATIONS

A *quotation* records the exact language used by someone in speech or in writing. A *summary*, in contrast, is a brief restatement in your own words of what someone else has said or written. And a *paraphrase* also is a restatement, although one that is often as long as the original source. Any paper in which you draw upon sources will rely heavily on quotation, summary, and paraphrase. How do you choose among the three?

Remember that the papers you write should be your own—for the most part: your own language and certainly your own thesis, your own inferences, and your own conclusion. It follows that references to your source materials should be written primarily as summaries and paraphrases, both of which are built on restatement, not quotation. You will use summaries when you need a *brief* restatement, and paraphrases, which provide more explicit detail than summaries, when you need to follow the development of a source closely. When you quote too much, you risk losing ownership of your work: more easily than you might think, your voice can be drowned out by the voices of those you've quoted. So *use quotation sparingly*, as you would a pungent spice.

Nevertheless, *quoting just the right source at the right time can significantly improve your papers*. The trick is to know when and how to use quotations.

Choosing Quotations

You'll find that using quotations can be particularly helpful in several situations.

WHEN TO QUOTE

- Use quotations when another writer's language is particularly memorable and will add interest and liveliness to your paper.
- Use quotations when another writer's language is so clear and economical that to make the same point in your own words would, by comparison, be ineffective.
- Use quotations when you want the solid reputation of a source to lend authority and credibility to your own writing.

QUOTING MEMORABLE LANGUAGE

Assume you're writing a paper on Napoleon Bonaparte's relationship with the celebrated Josephine. Through research you learn that two days after their marriage Napoleon, given command of an army, left his bride for what was to be a brilliant military campaign in Italy. How did the young general respond to leaving his wife so soon after their wedding? You come across the following, written from the field of battle by Napoleon on April 3, 1796:

> I have received all your letters, but none has such an impact on me as the last. Do you have any idea, darling, what you are doing, writing to me in those terms? Do you not think my situation cruel enough without intensifying my longing for you, overwhelming my soul? What a style! What emotions you evoke! Written in fire, they burn my poor heart![3]

A summary of this passage might read as follows:

> On April 3, 1796, Napoleon wrote to Josephine, expressing how sorely he missed her and how passionately he responded to her letters.

You might write the following as a paraphrase of the passage:

> On April 3, 1796, Napoleon wrote to Josephine that he had received her letters and that one among all others had had a special impact, overwhelming his soul with fiery emotions and longing.

How feeble this summary and paraphrase are when compared with the original! Use the vivid language that your sources give you. In this case, quote Napoleon in your paper to make your subject come alive with memorable detail:

> On April 3, 1796, a passionate, lovesick Napoleon responded to a letter from Josephine; she had written longingly to her husband, who, on a military campaign, acutely felt her absence. "Do you have any idea, darling, what you are doing, writing to me in those terms? . . . What emotions you evoke!" he said of her letters. "Written in fire, they burn my poor heart!"

Quotations can be direct or indirect. A *direct* quotation is one in which you record precisely the language of another, as we did with the sentences from Napoleon's letter. An *indirect* quotation is one in which you report what someone has said, although you are not obligated to repeat the words exactly as spoken (or written):

> *Direct quotation:* Franklin D. Roosevelt said: "The only thing we have to fear is fear itself."
>
> *Indirect quotation:* Franklin D. Roosevelt said that we have nothing to fear but fear itself.

---

[3]Francis Mossiker, trans., *Napoleon and Josephine*. New York: Simon and Schuster, 1964.

The language in a direct quotation, which is indicated by a pair of quotation marks (" "), must be faithful to the language of the original passage. When using an indirect quotation, you have the liberty of changing words (although not changing meaning). For both direct and indirect quotations, *you must credit your sources,* naming them either in (or close to) the sentence that includes the quotation or in a footnote.

QUOTING CLEAR AND CONCISE LANGUAGE

You should quote a source when its language is particularly clear and economical—when your language, by contrast, would be wordy. Read this passage from a text on biology by Patricia Curtis:

> The honeybee colony, which usually has a population of 30,000 to 40,000 workers, differs from that of the bumblebee and many other social bees or wasps in that it survives the winter. This means that the bees must stay warm despite the cold. Like other bees, the isolated honeybee cannot fly if the temperature falls below 10°C (50°F) and cannot walk if the temperature is below 7°C (45°F). Within the wintering hive, bees maintain their temperature by clustering together in a dense ball; the lower the temperature, the denser the cluster. The clustered bees produce heat by constant muscular movements of their wings, legs, and abdomens. In very cold weather, the bees on the outside of the cluster keep moving toward the center, while those in the core of the cluster move to the colder outside periphery. The entire cluster moves slowly about on the combs, eating the stored honey from the combs as it moves.[4]

A summary of this paragraph might read as follows:

> Honeybees, unlike many other varieties of bee, are able to live through the winter by "clustering together in a dense ball" for body warmth.

A paraphrase of the same passage would be considerably more detailed:

> Honeybees, unlike many other varieties of bee (such as bumblebees), are able to live through the winter. The 30,000 to 40,000 bees within a honeybee hive could not, individually, move about in cold winter temperatures. But when "clustering together in a dense ball," the bees generate heat by constantly moving their body parts. The cluster also moves slowly about the hive, eating honey stored in the combs. This nutrition, in addition to the heat generated by the cluster, enables the honeybee to survive the cold winter months.

---

[4]"Winter Organization" in Patricia Curtis, *Biology,* 2nd ed. New York: Worth, 1976, pp. 822–823.

In both the summary and the paraphrase we've quoted Curtis's "clustering together in a dense ball," a phrase that lies at the heart of her description of wintering honeybees. For us to describe this clustering in any language other than Curtis's would be pointless since her description is admirably brief and precise.

QUOTING AUTHORITATIVE LANGUAGE

You will also want to use quotations that lend authority to your work. When quoting an expert or some prominent political, artistic, or historical figure, you elevate your own work by placing it in esteemed company. Quote respected figures to establish background information in a paper, and your readers will tend to perceive that information as reliable. Quote the opinions of respected figures to endorse some statement that you've made, and your statement becomes more credible to your readers. For example, in an essay on the importance of reading well, you could make use of a passage from Thoreau's *Walden:*

> Reading well is hard work and requires great skill and training. It "is a noble exercise," writes Henry David Thoreau in *Walden,* "and one that will task the reader more than any exercise which the customs of the day esteem. It requires a training such as the athletes underwent. . . . Books must be read as deliberately and reservedly as they were written."

By quoting a famous philosopher and essayist on the subject of reading, you add legitimacy to your discussion. Not only do *you* regard reading to be a skill that is both difficult and important; so too does Henry David Thoreau, one of our most influential thinkers. The quotation has elevated the level of your work.

You can also quote to advantage well-respected figures who've written or spoken about the subject of your paper. Here is a discussion of space flight. Author David Chandler refers to a physicist and a physicist–astronaut:

> A few scientists—notably James Van Allen, discoverer of the Earth's radiation belts—have decried the expense of the manned space program and called for an almost exclusive concentration on unmanned scientific exploration instead, saying this would be far more cost-effective.
>
> Other space scientists dispute that idea. Joseph Allen, physicist and former shuttle astronaut, says, "It seems to be argued that one takes away from the other. But before there was a manned space program, the funding on space science was zero. Now it's about $500 million a year."

Note that in the first paragraph Chandler has either summarized or used an indirect quotation to incorporate remarks made by James Van Allen into the discussion on space flight. In the second paragraph, Chandler directly quotes his next source, Joseph Allen. Both quotations, indirect and direct, lend authority and legitimacy to the article, for both James Van Allen and Joseph Allen are experts on the subject of space flight. Note also that Chandler has provided brief but effective biographies of his sources, identifying both so that their qualifications to speak on the subject are known to all:

> James Van Allen, *discoverer of the Earth's radiation belts* . . .
> Joseph Allen, *physicist and former shuttle astronaut* . . .

The phrases in italics are called *appositives*. Their function is to rename the nouns they follow by providing explicit, identifying detail. Any information about a person that can be expressed in the following sentence pattern can be made into an appositive phrase:

> James Van Allen is the *discoverer of the Earth's radiation belts.*
> He has decried the expense of the manned space program.

> James Van Allen, *discoverer of the Earth's radiation belts,* has decried the expense of the manned space program.

Use appositives to identify authors whom you quote.

Incorporating Quotations into Your Sentences

QUOTING ONLY THE PART OF A SENTENCE OR PARAGRAPH THAT YOU NEED

We've said that a writer selects passages for quotation that are especially *vivid and memorable, concise,* or *authoritative.* Now put these principles into practice. Suppose that while conducting research on college sports you've come across the following, written by Robert Hutchins, former president of the University of Chicago:

> If athleticism is bad for students, players, alumni and the public, it is even worse for the colleges and universities themselves. They want to be educational institutions, but they can't. The story of the famous halfback whose only regret, when he bade his coach farewell, was that he hadn't learned to read and write is probably exaggerated. But we must admit that pressure from trustees, graduates, "friends," presidents and even professors has tended to relax academic standards. These gentry often overlook the fact that a college should not be interested in a fullback who is a half-wit. Recruiting, subsidizing and the double educational standard cannot exist without the knowledge and the tacit approval, at least, of the colleges and universities themselves. Certain institutions encourage susceptible professors to be nice to athletes now admitted by paying them for serving as "faculty representatives" on the college athletic board.[5]

---

[5]Robert Hutchins, "Gate Receipts and Glory," *The Saturday Evening Post,* December 3, 1983.

Suppose that in this entire paragraph you find a gem, a sentence with quotable words that will enliven your discussion. You may want to quote part of the following sentence:

> These gentry often overlook the fact that a college should not be interested in a fullback who is a half-wit.

INCORPORATING THE QUOTATION INTO THE FLOW OF YOUR OWN SENTENCE

Once you've selected the passage you want to quote, work the material into your paper in as natural and fluid a manner as possible. Here's how we would quote Hutchins:

> Robert Hutchins, a former president of the University of Chicago, asserts that "a college should not be interested in a fullback who is a half-wit."

Note that we've used an appositive to identify Hutchins. And we've used only the part of the paragraph—a single clause—that we thought memorable enough to quote directly.

AVOIDING FREESTANDING QUOTATIONS

A quoted sentence should never stand by itself—as in the following example:

> Various people associated with the university admit that the pressures of athleticism have caused a relaxation of standards. "These gentry often overlook the fact that a college should not be interested in a fullback who is a half-wit." But this kind of thinking is bad for the university and even worse for the athletes.

Even if it includes a parenthetical citation, a freestanding quotation would have the problem of being jarring to the reader. Introduce the quotation with a "signal phrase" that attributes the source not in a parenthetical citation, but in some other part of the sentence—beginning, middle, or end. Thus, you could write:

> According to Robert Hutchins, "These gentry often overlook the fact that a college should not be interested in a fullback who is a half-wit."

A variation with the signal phrase in the middle:

> "These gentry," asserts Robert Hutchins, "often overlook the fact that a college should not be interested in a fullback who is a half-wit."

Another alternative is to introduce a sentence-long quotation with a colon:

> But Robert Hutchins disagrees: "These gentry often overlook the fact that a college should not be interested in a fullback who is a half-wit."

Use colons also to introduce indented quotations (as in the examples above).

When attributing sources, try to vary the standard "states," "writes," "says," and so on. Other, stronger verbs you might consider: "asserts," "argues," "maintains," "insists," "asks," and even "wonders."

USING ELLIPSIS MARKS

Using quotations is made somewhat complicated when you want to quote the beginning and end of a passage but not its middle—as was the case when we quoted Henry David Thoreau. Here's part of the paragraphs in *Walden* from which we quoted a few sentences:

> To read well, that is to read true books in a true spirit, is a noble exercise, and one that will task the reader more than any exercise which the customs of the day esteem. It requires a training such as the athletes underwent, the steady intention almost of the whole life to this object. Books must be read as deliberately and reservedly as they were written.[6]

And here was how we used this material:

> Reading well is hard work and requires great skill and training. It "is a noble exercise," writes Henry David Thoreau in *Walden*, "and one that will task the reader more than any exercise which the customs of the day esteem. It requires a training such as the athletes underwent. . . . Books must be read as deliberately and reservedly as they were written."

Whenever you quote a sentence but delete words from it, as we have done, indicate this deletion to the reader by placing an ellipsis mark, three spaced periods, in the sentence at the point of deletion. The rationale for using an ellipsis mark is that a direct quotation must be reproduced *exactly* as it was written or spoken. When writers delete or change any part of the quoted material, readers must be alerted so they don't think the changes were part of the original. Ellipsis marks and brackets serve this purpose.

If you are deleting the middle of a single sentence, use an ellipsis in place of the deleted words:

> "To read well . . . is a noble exercise, and one that will task the reader more than any exercise which the customs of the day esteem."

If you are deleting the end of a quoted sentence, or if you are deleting entire sentences of a paragraph before continuing a quotation, add a period before the ellipsis:

---

[6]Henry David Thoreau. "Reading" in *Walden*. New York: Signet Classic, 1960, p. 72.

"It requires a training such as the athletes underwent. . . . Books must be read as deliberately and reservedly as they were written."

If you begin your quotation of an author in the middle of a sentence, you need not indicate deleted words with an ellipsis. Be sure, however, that the syntax of the quotation fits smoothly with the syntax of your sentence:

Reading "is a noble exercise," writes Henry David Thoreau.

USING BRACKETS

Use square brackets whenever you need to add or substitute words in a quoted sentence. The brackets indicate to the reader a word or phrase that does not appear in the original passage but that you have inserted to avoid confusion. For example, when a pronoun's antecedent would be unclear to readers, delete the pronoun from the sentences and substitute an identifying word or phrase in brackets. When you make such a substitution, no ellipsis marks are needed. Assume that you wish to quote the underlined sentence in the following passage:

Golden Press's *Walt Disney's Cinderella* set the new pattern for America's Cinderella. This book's text is coy and condescending. (Sample: "And her best friends of all were—guess who—the mice!") The illustrations are poor cartoons. And Cinderella herself is a disaster. She cowers as her sisters rip her homemade ball gown to shreds. (Not even homemade by Cinderella, but by the mice and birds.) She answers her stepmother with whines and pleadings. <u>She is a sorry excuse for a heroine, pitiable and useless</u>. She cannot perform even a simple action to save herself, though she is warned by her friends, the mice. She does not hear them because she is "off in a world of dreams." Cinderella begs, she whimpers, and at last has to be rescued by—guess who—the mice![7]

In quoting this sentence, you would need to identify whom the pronoun *she* refers to. You can do this inside the quotation by using brackets:

Jane Yolen believes that "[Cinderella] is a sorry excuse for a heroine, pitiable and useless."

If the pronoun begins the sentence to be quoted, as it does in this example, you can identify the pronoun outside of the quotation and simply begin quoting your source one word later:

Jane Yolen believes that Cinderella "is a sorry excuse for a heroine, pitiable and useless."

---

[7]Jane Yolen, "America's 'Cinderella,'" APS Publications, Inc. in *Children's Literature in Education* 8, 1977, pp. 21–29.

If the pronoun you want to identify occurs in the middle of the sentence to be quoted, then you'll need to use brackets. Newspaper reporters do this frequently when quoting sources, who in interviews might say something like the following:

> After the fire they did not return to the station house for three hours.

If the reporter wants to use this sentence in an article, he or she needs to identify the pronoun:

> An official from City Hall, speaking on the condition that he not be identified, said, "After the fire [the officers] did not return to the station house for three hours."

You also will need to add bracketed information to a quoted sentence when a reference essential to the sentence's meaning is implied but not stated directly. Read the following paragraphs from Robert Jastrow's "Toward an Intelligence Beyond Man's":

> These are amiable qualities for the computer; it imitates life like an electronic monkey. As computers get more complex, the imitation gets better. Finally, the line between the original and the copy becomes blurred. In another 15 years or so—two more generations of computer evolution, in the jargon of the technologists—we will see the computer as an emergent form of life.
>
> <u>The proposition seems ridiculous because, for one thing, computers lack the drives and emotions of living creatures</u>. But when drives are useful, they can be programmed into the computer's brain, just as nature programmed them into our ancestors' brains as a part of the equipment for survival. For example, computers, like people, work better and learn faster when they are motivated. Arthur Samuel made this discovery when he taught two IBM computers how to play checkers. They polished their game by playing each other, but they learned slowly. Finally, Dr. Samuel programmed in the will to win by forcing the computers to try harder—and to think out more moves in advance—when they were losing. Then the computers learned very quickly. One of them beat Samuel and went on to defeat a champion player who had not lost a game to a human opponent in eight years.[8]

If you wanted to quote only the underlined sentence, you would need to provide readers with a bracketed explanation; otherwise, the words "the proposition" would be unclear. Here is how you would manage the quotation:

> According to Robert Jastrow, a physicist and former official at NASA's Goddard Institute, "The proposition [that computers will emerge as a form of life] seems

---

[8]Excerpt from "Toward an Intelligence Beyond Man's" from *Time,* February 20, 1978. Copyright © 1978 Time Inc. Reprinted by permission.

ridiculous because, for one thing, computers lack the drives and emotions of living creatures."

Remember that when you quote the work of another, you are obligated to credit—or cite—the author's work properly; otherwise, you may be guilty of plagiarism. See pages 205–228 for guidance on citing sources.

WHEN TO SUMMARIZE, PARAPHRASE, AND QUOTE

Summarize:
- To present main points of a lengthy passage (article or book)
- To condense peripheral points necessary to discussion

Paraphrase:
- To clarify a short passage
- To emphasize main points

Quote:
- To capture another writer's particularly memorable language
- To capture another writer's clearly and economically stated language
- To lend authority and credibility to your own writing

■ EXERCISE

Read "Body Body Double: Cloning Infants a Distant Fantasy," which appeared in the *Focus* section of *The Boston Sunday Globe*, January 11, 1998. Write a summary of the article, following the directions in this chapter for dividing the article into sections, for writing a one-sentence summary of each section, and then for joining section summaries with a thesis. Prepare for the summary by making notes in the margins. Your finished product should be the result of two or more drafts.

Body Body Double: ■ Cloning Infants a Distant Fantasy

BY ALEXANDER M. CAPRON

San Francisco—Barely 10 months after researchers at Scotland's Roslin   1
Institute amazed the world by cloning a sheep, Chicago physicist Richard Seed created a stir when he announced he was establishing the Human Clone Clinic and would use the Roslin technique to make human babies.

  Are last week's headlines just one more instance of the breathtaking   2
speed with which science can advance? Not at all.

Seed had no scientific breakthrough to announce. He doesn't have the 3
credibility that might come from having run a fertility center. That, at least,
would provide him with state-of-the-art experience in using the techniques of
embryo cultivation and transplantation necessary for any realistic attempt at
human cloning.

Maybe the attention Seed has managed to generate will help him raise the 4
$2 million he claims he needs, but his planned clinic has more in common
with Barnum & Bailey's Circus than with Brigham and Women's Hospital.
Indeed, the only result he has produced so far is to spark a call from President
Clinton yesterday to ban human cloning experiments.

Last February, the announcement that scientists had cloned Dolly the 5
sheep was met with a nearly unanimous chorus of concern. The prospect that
the techniques used to produce the first copy of an adult mammal could be
used to create human genetic replicas struck scientists and politicians alike as
dangerous.

Concerned about the "serious ethical questions" presented by the "pos- 6
sible use of the technology to clone human embryos," Clinton at the time
asked the National Bioethics Advisory Commission to report within 90 days
on how the government should respond. He quickly banned the use of federal money for cloning.

At subsequent congressional hearings, medical scientists took a skeptical 7
view of the prospect of using the Roslin technique to create humans. Harold
Varmus, director of the National Institutes of Health, labeled human cloning
"repugnant." Ian Wilmut, the creator of Dolly, told senators that cloning
people would be "quite inhuman."

Some of the concerns first expressed turned out to be overblown or 8
wrongheaded. For example, two people having the same genetic makeup
hardly negates the basic dignity of each individual, as the birth of identical
twins makes clear. Furthermore, just as twins differ in many ways as they
grow and develop, a genetic clone would exist in a different environment and
have different experiences from his or her progenitor.

Anyone who made a clone of Michael Jordan expecting to get a great 9
basketball player 20 years later would likely be disappointed, and Mozart's
clone wouldn't be a brilliant composer simply because of his genes.

But the advisory commission concluded that other concerns about human 10
cloning deserved to be taken very seriously. First, the process of creating
Dolly made it clear that the technique used is much too risky to use with
humans at this time. Roslin scientists tried 276 times to clone a sheep before
they succeeded with Dolly. Many tries did not result in viable embryos or did
not produce successful pregnancies once transferred to surrogate mothers.
And, before Dolly, all the lambs that went to term had such severe problems
that they were stillborn or died shortly after birth. This is not a circumstance
in which any responsible person would consider moving the technique to
human use.

Nor has anything occurred over the past year to alter that conclusion. 11

Safety concerns were the first reason the advisory commission concluded   12
that it would be unethical to proceed with cloning a human at this time. The
second reason was that the potential psychological harm to children and the
adverse moral and cultural effects of cloning merit further reflection and
deliberation.

Many reasons have been advanced for why people might want to have a   13
cloned child: To replace a child who dies young. To provide a genetic copy
who could donate a kidney, bone marrow, or other life-saving organ. To
allow infertile couples to have a child who is genetically connected to at least
one of them, or to allow a person without a mate of the opposite sex to have
a child. To give a child a "good start in life" by using genes from people
regarded as particularly outstanding according to such criteria as intelligence,
artistic creativity, or athletic prowess.

Some of the ideas are mere fantasy, especially when they reflect a strong   14
streak of genetic determinism, the notion that genes control the people we
become. The fact that they are fantasy does not mean that they won't be acted
on. The chance to have a cloned child may tempt parents to seek excessive
control over their children's characteristics and to value them for how well
they meet such overly detailed parental expectations.

Moreover, if cloning were used, arguments would soon be heard that it   15
was actually a superior way to produce children since it would aim to avoid
the disappointments that now result from the "genetic lottery" inherent in
sexual reproduction. Responsible parenthood in the 21st century might come
to include using "ideal types" as the bases for our children, and perhaps even
doing some "genetic enhancement" of the clones to provide what would now
be regarded as super-human capabilities. Whether such developments arose
voluntarily, as a result of social pressure, or through eventual legislation,
they would amount to a form of eugenics more chilling than those contemplated by the Nazis, more akin to Aldous Huxley's "Brave New World."

These are serious worries, though whether they are compelling enough to   16
justify permanently forbidding cloning needs further debate. If some reasons
for using cloning were accepted, could the procedure be limited to those
uses? Designing a system of regulation that is ethically defensible and practically enforceable would not be easy, but it might be necessary if we concluded that the proper balance between ethical risks and personal liberties meant
that society must allow human cloning under some circumstances.

Thus, the advisory commission concluded that while safety concerns are   17
being addressed, deliberations should go forward to allow an informed public
consensus to develop.

Meanwhile, the president has urged Congress to enact an immediate fed-   18
eral ban on human cloning experiments. While Seed is likely to remain a
sideshow in the ultimate development of this technology, his announcement
ought to prompt Congress to take action now.

2

Critical Reading and Critique

CRITICAL READING

When writing papers in college, you are often called on to respond critically to source materials. Critical reading requires the abilities to both summarize and evaluate a presentation. As you have seen, a *summary* is a brief restatement in your own words of the content of a passage. An *evaluation* is a more difficult matter, however. In your college work, you read to gain and *use* new information; but as sources are not equally valid or equally useful, you must learn to distinguish critically among sources by evaluating them.

There is no ready-made formula for determining validity. Critical reading and its written analogue—the *critique*—require discernment, sensitivity, imagination, and, above all, a willingness to become involved in what you read. These skills cannot be taken for granted and are developed only through repeated practice. You must begin somewhere, though, and we recommend that you start by posing two broad categories of questions about passages, articles, and books that you read: (1) What is the author's purpose in writing? Does he or she succeed in this purpose? (2) To what extent do you agree with the author?

Question Category 1: What Is the Author's Purpose in Writing? Does He or She Succeed in This Purpose?

All critical reading *begins with an accurate summary*. Before attempting an evaluation, you must be able to locate an author's thesis and identify the selection's content and structure. You must understand the author's *purpose*. Authors write to inform, to persuade, and to entertain. A given piece may be *primarily informative* (a summary of the research on cloning), *primarily persuasive* (an argument on why the government must do something to alleviate homelessness), or *primarily entertaining* (a play about the frustrations of young lovers), or it may be all three (as in John Steinbeck's novel *The Grapes of Wrath*, about migrant workers during the Great Depression). Sometimes authors are not fully conscious of their purposes. Sometimes their purposes change as they write. But if the finished piece is coherent, it will have a primary reason for having been written, and it should be apparent that the author is attempting primarily to inform, persuade, or entertain a particular audience. To identify this primary reason, this purpose, is your first job as a critical reader. Your next job is to determine how successful the author has been. As a critical reader, you bring different criteria, or standards of judgment, to bear when you read pieces intended to inform or persuade.

Informative Writing

A piece intended to inform will provide definitions, describe or report on a process, recount a story, give historical background, and/or provide facts and figures. An informational piece responds to questions such as the following:

What (or who) is _____ ?
How does _____ work?
What is the controversy or problem about?
What happened?
How and why did it happen?
What were the results?
What are the arguments for and against _____ ?

To the extent that an author answers these and related questions and the answers are a matter of verifiable record (you could check for accuracy if you had the time and inclination), the selection is intended to inform. Having determined this, you can organize your response by considering three other criteria: accuracy, significance, and fair interpretation of information.

Accuracy of Information. If you are going to use any of the information presented, you must be satisfied that it is trustworthy. One of your responsibilities as a critical reader is to find out if it is accurate.

Significance of Information. One useful question that you can put to a reading is "So what?" In the case of selections that attempt to inform, you may reasonably wonder whether the information makes a difference. What can the person who is reading gain from this information? How is knowledge advanced by the publication of this material? Is the information of importance to you or to others in a particular audience? Why or why not?

Fair Interpretation of Information. At times you will read reports, the sole function of which is to relate raw data or information. In these cases, you will build your response on the two questions in question category 1: What is the author's purpose? Does she or he succeed in this purpose? More frequently, once an author has presented information, she or he will attempt to evaluate or interpret it—which is only reasonable, since information that has not been evaluated or interpreted is of little use. One of your tasks as a critical reader is to make a distinction between the author's presentation of facts and figures and his or her attempts to evaluate them. You may find that the information is valuable but the interpretation is not. Perhaps the author's conclusions are not justified. Could you offer a contrary explanation for the same facts? Does more information need to be gathered before conclusions can be drawn? Why?

Persuasive Writing

Writing is frequently intended to persuade—that is, to influence the reader's thinking. To make a persuasive case, the writer must begin with an assertion that is arguable, some statement about which reasonable people could disagree. Such an assertion, when it serves as the essential organizing principle of the article or book, is called a *thesis*. Examples:

> Because they do not speak English, many children in this affluent land are being denied their fundamental right to equal educational opportunity.

> Bilingual education, which has been stridently promoted by a small group of activists with their own agenda, is detrimental to the very students it is supposed to serve.

Thesis statements such as these—and the subsidiary assertions used to help support them—represent conclusions that authors have drawn as a result of researching and thinking about the issue. You go through the same process yourself when you write persuasive papers or critiques. And just as you are entitled to critically evaluate the assertions of authors you read, so your professors—and other students—are entitled to evaluate *your* assertions, whether they are encountered as written arguments or as comments made in class discussion.

Keep in mind that writers organize arguments by arranging evidence to support one conclusion and oppose (or dismiss) another. You can assess the validity of the argument and the conclusion by determining whether the author has (1) clearly defined key terms, (2) used information fairly, (3) argued logically, and not fallaciously.

Read the argument that follows—a proposal to exempt teachers from federal income tax—which appeared in *The New York Times* on January 18, 1998. We will illustrate our discussion on defining terms, using information fairly, and arguing logically by referring to J. Morton Davis's argument. The example critique that follows these illustrations will be based on this same argument.

A Simple One-Step Plan to Solve the Education Crisis
A Message to President Clinton and the 105th Congress

J. MORTON DAVIS

Great teachers.   1
  Thousands and thousands of great teachers.   2
  We must attract our best and brightest to the one profession upon which   3
truly rests our nation's freedom, security and future greatness—teaching. If we

can enlist the best among us to train our children, we will surely have the best-prepared and best-educated students in the world, thereby assuring America's continued leadership.

By enacting legislation to exempt teachers from all federal income taxes,   4
Congress and the President can help assure that many of the best and bright-est college students will choose to dedicate their careers and lives to teaching our children.

Perhaps it could go without saying that the education crisis is the most   5
important issue we as a nation face today, affecting daily our single most important natural resource—our children. Just as we as a nation could mount all of our resources and efforts for the Manhattan Project to win World War II, and, later, harness all of our best in industry and technology to win the race to put a man on the moon, today we must, with the same urgency, apply all our collective energies to improving the deplorable state of public education. And just as we use our tax system to advance many positive societal goals, our tax system here too offers a single, one-step opportunity to solve the current crisis in our education system. By exempting teachers from federal income taxes we will instantly put in place a mechanism sure to produce more and more great teachers.

First, this tax exemption would immediately and substantially increase   6
teachers' salaries, thus incentivizing many of our top college graduates to pursue a career in teaching. In the 30's and 40's, public education produced superior academic results because, during the Depression, many of our best were attracted to teaching as it was a relatively well paying and secure job in a time when few jobs were available. Teaching would again become an eco-nomically attractive career if it carried with it an exemption from federal income taxes. The cost to the Treasury would be small, and certainly any tax money invested in teaching will return many-fold as a generation of better-educated, more productive citizens enters the work force.

Second, and perhaps more importantly, an exemption from federal   7
income taxes for teachers would distinctly and dramatically recognize the gifted dedication of those who devote their careers to inspiring the minds of our children and grandchildren. Freeing teachers from ever paying federal income tax would, in one grand gesture, symbolically designate teachers as the one professional group whom we respect, cherish and value above all others. This is not to devalue the life-and-death work of police officers and fire fighters, or the terribly important life-saving efforts of doctors, nurses and other medical professionals. But none is more important to our nation's future than teaching.

If we are going to produce the world's best-educated future generations,   8
we must attract the best candidates to the job of teaching those generations. Professionally dedicated teachers will not only provide a basic education in the three R's and the sciences, but can also impart to our children values and visions, dreams and opportunities.

No profession is more important to society and the future of our country 9 than teaching. Teaching should never be a fall-back position or a career compromise. It is the noblest of callings, and should be recognized as such—both in dollars and in respect. If our children and our nation are to succeed in an ever-more-competitive world, let us reward and upgrade the status of teachers so that the finest young minds will be drawn to the profession. This will undoubtedly produce the best-educated, most globally-competitive generation of Americans in our history.

Mr. President and members of the 105th Congress, a golden opportunity 10 awaits you—a chance to cure the abysmal state of public education and go down in history as having made the nation and the world a better place. In a single, decisive, creative stroke you can solve the education crisis. By implementing a permanent income tax exemption for teachers you will raise their financial rewards and status to a level commensurate with their contributions, you will attract the best-and-brightest of our population to this noble profession, you will create a society in which "teacher" is the most exalted title in the land.

And you will leave a legacy that will endure forever.   11

Chairman of the Board, *D.H. Blair Investment Banking Corp.* Author, *Making America Work Again* (Crown Publishers 1983) and *From Hard Knocks to Hot Stocks* (William Morrow and Company 1998)

■ ■ ■

Clearly Defined Terms. The validity of an argument depends to some degree on how carefully key terms have been defined. Take the assertion, for example, that American society must be grounded in "family values." Just what do people who use this phrase mean by it? The validity of their argument depends on whether they and their readers agree on a definition of "family values"— as well as what it means to be "grounded in" family values. If an author writes that in the recent past, "America's elites accepted as a matter of course that a free society can sustain itself only through virtue and temperance in the people" (Charles Murray, "The Coming White Underclass," *Wall Street Journal*, 20 Oct. 1993), readers need to know what, exactly, the author means by "elites" and by "virtue and temperance" before they can assess the validity of the argument. In such cases, the success of the argument—its ability to persuade—hinges on the definition of a term. So, in responding to an argument, be sure you (and the author) are clear on what exactly is being argued. Only then can you respond to the logic of the argument, to the author's use of evidence, and to the author's conclusions.

Early in his argument, Davis refers to attracting "our best and brightest" to the teaching profession. He repeatedly uses the phrase, so it's fair to ask what, exactly, he means. "Best and brightest" was an expression associated with John F. Kennedy's administration, in which highly educated, exuberant people flocked to Washington with an explicit assumption that in committing themselves to public service they would do an exemplary job (because they were bright and committed). The closest Davis comes to defining "best and brightest" is "[p]rofessionally dedicated teachers," people "who devote their careers to inspiring the minds of our children and grandchildren." Davis appears to be using a Kennedy-era definition of "best and brightest." The phrase refers to academically talented, inspired and inspiring college graduates. However, this same phrase took on an ironic twist when it was used by reporter David Halberstam as the title of a book about the tragic miscalculations made by these same talented and inspired people in getting the U.S. involved in the war in Vietnam.

Fair Use of Information. Information is used as evidence in support of arguments. When presented with such evidence, ask yourself two questions: The *first:* "Is the information accurate and up-to-date?" At least a portion of an argument is rendered invalid if the information used to support it is inaccurate or out-of-date. The *second:* "Has the author cited *representative* information?" The evidence used in an argument must be presented in a spirit of fair play. An author is less than ethical who presents only evidence favoring his views when he is well aware that contrary evidence exists. For instance, it would be dishonest to argue that an economic recession is imminent and to cite as evidence only those indicators of economic well-being that have taken a decided turn for the worse while ignoring and failing to cite contrary (positive) evidence.

Logical Argumentation; Avoiding Logical Fallacies. At some point, you will need to respond to the logic of the argument itself. To be convincing, an argument should be governed by principles of logic—clear and orderly thinking. This does *not* mean that an argument should not be biased. A biased argument—that is, an argument weighted toward one point of view and against others—may be valid as long as it is logically sound.

Here are several examples of faulty thinking and logical fallacies to watch for:

Emotionally Loaded Terms. Writers sometimes will attempt to sway readers by using emotionally charged words: words with positive connotations to sway readers to their own point of view; words with negative connotations to sway readers away from the opposing point of view. The fact that an author uses emotionally loaded terms does not necessarily invalidate the argument. Emotional appeals are perfectly legitimate and time-honored modes of persuasion. But in academic writing, which is grounded in logical argumentation, they should not be the *only* means of persuasion. You should be sensitive to *how* emotionally loaded terms are being used. In particular, are they being used deceptively or to hide the essential facts?

Davis uses the word "noble" throughout the argument—as in, teaching is a "noble" profession, "the noblest of callings" (paragraph 9). Our culture is quick to attach "nobility" to professions such as teaching that serve a necessary function but pay relatively low wages, as if the word itself could compensate teachers for lower salaries. Since American voters are unwilling to pay teachers more money but at the same time are eager to laud teachers as "noble," the word "nobility" has taken on a somewhat patronizing, disingenuous air among teachers. Some teachers comment: "Sure we're flattered to be called noble. But raise our pay if you really care!" Davis does seem to be an outsider (that is, not a teacher) using the word "nobility" to heap familiar praises on teachers. He isn't being patronizing with his use of the term, however, since he's arguing for boosting teacher salaries and prestige. So teachers might well think him sincere.

Ad Hominem *Argument.* In an *ad hominem* argument, the writer rejects opposing views by attacking the person who holds them. By calling opponents names, an author avoids the issue:

> I could more easily accept my opponent's plan to increase revenues by collecting on delinquent tax bills if he had paid more than a hundred dollars in state taxes in each of the past three years. But the fact is, he's a millionaire with a millionaire's tax shelters. This man hasn't paid a wooden nickel for the state services he and his family depend on. So I ask you: Is *he* the one to be talking about taxes to *us?*

It could well be that the opponent has paid virtually no state taxes for three years; but this fact has nothing to do with, and is a ploy to divert attention from, the merits of a specific proposal for increasing revenues. The proposal is lost in the attack against the man himself, an attack that violates the principles of logic. Writers (and speakers) must make their points by citing evidence in support of their views and by challenging contrary evidence.

Faulty Cause and Effect. The fact that one event precedes another in time does not mean that the first event has caused the second. An example: Fish begin dying by the thousands in a lake near your hometown. An environmental group immediately cites chemical dumping by several manufacturing plants as the cause. But other causes are possible: A disease might have affected the fish; the growth of algae might have contributed to the deaths; or acid rain might be a factor. The origins of an event are usually complex and are not always traceable to a single cause. So you must carefully examine cause-and-effect reasoning when you find a writer using it. In Latin, this fallacy is known as *post hoc, ergo propter hoc* ("after this, therefore because of this").

Davis makes two assertions that reveal questionable cause-and-effect thinking. First, he claims that enlisting our "best and brightest" into teaching will result in improved education: "If we can enlist the best among us to train our children, we will surely have the best-prepared and best-education students in the world. . . ." (paragraph 3). The reader is entitled to ask: why *surely?* Where's the proof that teachers, alone, can effect so monumental a change? Davis also claims that a permanent exemption from federal taxes will result in more good teachers entering the classroom. Again, what assures this result? In both cases, Davis may be correct; but readers can legitimately expect support for such statements, and Davis offers none.

Either/Or Reasoning. Either/or reasoning also results from an unwillingness to recognize complexity. If an author analyzes a problem and offers only two explanations, one of which he or she refutes, then you are entitled to object that the other is not thereby true. For usually, several other explanations (at the very least) are possible. For whatever reason, the author has chosen to overlook them. As an example, suppose you are reading a selection on genetic engineering and the author builds an argument on the basis of the following:

> Research in gene splicing is at a crossroads: Either scientists will be carefully monitored by civil authorities and their efforts limited to acceptable applications, such as disease control; or, lacking regulatory guidelines, scientists will set their own ethical standards and begin programs in embryonic manipulation that, however well intended, exceed the proper limits of human knowledge.

Certainly, other possibilities for genetic engineering exist beyond the two mentioned here. But the author limits debate by establishing an either/or choice. Such limitation is artificial and does not allow for complexity. As a critical reader, be on the alert for either/or reasoning.

Hasty Generalization. Writers are guilty of hasty generalization when they draw their conclusions from too little evidence or from unrepresentative evidence. To argue that scientists should not proceed with the human genome project because a recent editorial urged that the project be abandoned is to make a hasty generalization. This lone editorial may be unrepresentative of the views of most people—both scientists and laypeople—who have studied and written about the matter. To argue that one should never obey authority because the Milgram experiment shows the dangers of obeying authority is to ignore the fact that Milgram's experiment was concerned primarily with obedience to *immoral* authority. Thus, the experimental situation was unrepresentative of most routine demands for obedience—for example, to obey a parental rule or to comply with a summons for jury duty—and a conclusion about the malevolence of all authority would be a hasty generalization.

False Analogy. Comparing one person, event, or issue to another may be illuminating, but it also may be confusing or misleading. The differences between the two may be more significant than the similarities, and the conclusions drawn from the one may not necessarily apply to the other. A writer who argues that it is reasonable to quarantine people with AIDS because quarantine has been effective in preventing the spread of smallpox is assuming an analogy between AIDS and smallpox that (because of the differences between the two diseases) is not valid.

Early in his argument, Davis exhorts the president and the Congress to "mount all of our resources and efforts" (paragraph 5) to enlist great teachers in the same way we marshaled our resources to put humans on the moon and to win World War II by building an atomic bomb. Davis is making an analogy: we rallied and succeeded then; we can rally and succeed now. Readers can reasonably question the extent to which the challenges we face in education are similar to the challenges faced in building a bomb or rocket. To accept the parallel, we would have to believe that solving a problem in a mathematical science is equivalent to solving a problem in the social settings of the classroom and school. Are the problems and their solutions equivalent? Readers are entitled to question the parallel.

Begging the Question. To beg the question is to assume as a proven fact the very thesis being argued. To assert, for example, that America is not in decline because it is as strong and prosperous as ever is not to prove anything: it is merely to repeat the claim in different words. This fallacy also is know as circular reasoning.

Throughout his argument, Davis assumes a point he wants readers to accept—that enlisting our "best and brightest" will result in better-educated students. This is a cause-and-effect relationship that needs proof, but Davis assumes the correctness of the position and does not argue for it. This begging the question is especially evident when Davis writes: "Teaching would again become an economically attractive career if it carried with it an exemption from federal income taxes. The cost to the Treasury would be small, and certainly any tax money invested in teaching will return many-fold as a generation of better-educated, more productive citizens enters the work force" (paragraph 6). To Davis, the end result of hiring bright teachers may be "certain," but readers are entitled to question his logic.

Non Sequitur. "Non sequitur" is Latin for "it does not follow"; the term is used to describe a conclusion that does not logically follow from a premise. "Since minorities have made such great strides in the last few decades," a writer may argue, "we no longer need affirmative action programs." Aside from the fact that the premise itself is arguable (*have* minorities made such great strides?), it does not follow that because minorities *may* have made great strides, there is no further need for affirmative action programs.

Oversimplification. Be alert for writers who offer easy solutions to complicated problems. "America's economy will be strong again if we all 'buy American,'" a politician may argue. But the problems of America's economy are complex and cannot be solved by a slogan or a simple change in buying habits. Likewise, a writer who argues that we should ban genetic engineering assumes that simple solutions ("just say 'no'") will be sufficient to deal with the complex moral dilemmas raised by this new technology.

Davis has likely never been a classroom teacher, which can be inferred both from his honorific use of the word "noble" (if teachers feel this way about themselves, they typically don't advertise it!) and from his failure to mention other possible sources of crisis in education aside from the lack of gifted teachers. Anyone with experience in public education knows, for instance, that school budgets are closely linked with successful student performance. Davis makes no mention of school budgets or of other factors such as economically depressed circumstances for students or political fights within school districts. As you will see when reading the critique of Davis's letter, it is mainly on the grounds of oversimplification that objections can be raised.

Writing That Entertains

Authors write not only to inform and persuade but also to entertain. One response to entertainment is a hearty laugh; but it is possible to entertain without laughter: A good book or play or poem may prompt you to ruminate, grow wistful, elated, angry. Laughter is only one of many possible reactions. You read a piece (or view a work) and react with sadness, surprise, exhilaration, disbelief, horror, boredom, whatever. As with a response to an informative piece or an argument, your response to an essay, poem, story, play, novel, or film should be precisely stated and carefully developed. Ask yourself some of the following questions (you won't have space to explore all of them, but try to consider some of the most important): Did I care for the portrayal of a certain character? Did that character seem too sentimentalized, for example, or heroic? Did his adversaries seem too villainous or stupid? Were the situations believable? Was the action interesting or merely formulaic? Was the theme developed subtly, powerfully, or did the work come across as preachy or shrill? Did the action at the end of the work follow plausibly from what had come before? Was the language fresh and incisive or stale and predictable? Explain as specifically as possible what elements of the work seemed effective or ineffective and why. Offer an overall assessment, elaborating on your views.

Question Category 2: To What Extent Do You Agree with the Author?

When formulating a critical response to a source, try to distinguish your evaluation of the author's purpose and success at achieving that purpose from your agreement or disagreement with the author's views. The distinction allows you to respond to a piece of writing on its merits. As an unbiased, evenhanded critic, you evaluate an author's clarity of presentation, use of evidence, and adherence to principles of logic. To what extent has the author succeeded in achieving his or her purpose? Still withholding judgment, offer your assessment and give the author (in effect) a grade. Significantly, your assessment of the presentation may not coincide with your views of the author's conclusions: You may agree with an author entirely but feel that the presentation is superficial; you may find the author's logic and use of evidence to be rock solid but at the same time may resist certain conclusions. A critical evaluation works well when it is conducted in two parts. After evaluating the author's purpose and design for achieving that purpose, respond to the author's main assertions. In doing so, you'll want to identify points of agreement and disagreement and also evaluate assumptions.

IDENTIFY POINTS OF AGREEMENT AND DISAGREEMENT

Be precise in identifying points of agreement and disagreement with an author. You should state as clearly as possible what *you* believe, and an effective way of doing this is to define your position in relation to that presented in the piece. Whether you agree enthusiastically, disagree, or agree with reservations, you can organize your reactions in two parts: first, summarize the author's position; second, state your own position and elaborate on your reasons for holding it. The elaboration, in effect, becomes an argument itself, and this is true regardless of the position you take. An opinion is effective when you support it by supplying evidence. Without such evidence, opinions cannot be authoritative. "I thought the article on inflation was lousy." Why? "I just thought so, that's all." This opinion is worthless because the criticism is imprecise: The critic has taken neither the time to read the article carefully nor the time to explore his own reactions carefully.

EXPLORE THE REASONS FOR AGREEMENT AND DISAGREEMENT: EVALUATE ASSUMPTIONS

One way of elaborating your reactions to a reading is to explore the underlying *reasons* for agreement and disagreement. Your reactions are based largely on assumptions that you hold and how these assumptions compare with the author's. An *assumption* is a fundamental statement about the world and its operations that you take to be true. A writer's assumptions may be explicitly stated; but just as often assumptions are implicit and you will have to "ferret them out," that is, to infer them. Consider an example:

> *In vitro* fertilization and embryo transfer are brought about outside the bodies of the couple through actions of third parties whose competence and technical activity determine the success of the procedure. Such fertilization entrusts the life and identity of the embryo into the power of doctors and biologists and establishes the domination of technology over the origin and destiny of the human person. Such a relationship of domination is in itself contrary to the dignity and equality that must be common to parents and children.[1]

This paragraph is quoted from the February 1987 Vatican document on artificial procreation. Cardinal Joseph Ratzinger, principal author of the document, makes an implicit assumption in this paragraph: that no good can come of the domination of technology over conception. The use of technology to bring about conception is morally wrong. Yet there are thousands of childless couples, Roman Catholics included, who reject this assumption in favor of its opposite: that conception technology is an aid to the barren couple; far from creating a relationship of unequals, the technology brings children into the world who will be welcomed with joy and love.

---

[1]From the Vatican document *Instruction on Respect for Human Life in Its Origin and on the Dignity of Procreation*, given at Rome, from the Congregation for the Doctrine of the Faith, February 22, 1987, as presented in *Origins: N.C. Documentary Service* 16(40), March 19, 1987, p. 707.

Assumptions provide the foundation on which entire presentations are built. If you find an author's assumptions invalid, you may well disagree with conclusions that follow from these assumptions. The author of a book on developing nations may include a section outlining the resources and time that will be required to industrialize a particular country and so upgrade its general welfare. His assumption—that industrialization in that particular country will ensure or even affect the general welfare—may or may not be valid. If you do not share the assumption, in your eyes the rationale for the entire book may be undermined.

How do you determine the validity of assumptions once you have identified them? In the absence of more scientific criteria, validity may mean how well the author's assumptions stack up against your own experience, observations, and reading. A caution, however: The overall value of an article or book may depend only to a small degree on the validity of the author's assumptions. For instance, a sociologist may do a fine job of gathering statistical data about the incidence of crime in urban areas along the eastern seaboard. The sociologist also might be a Marxist, and you may disagree with her subsequent analysis of the data. Yet you may find the data extremely valuable for your own work.

In his open letter to the president and Congress, Davis makes several assumptions worth examining. The first is that we face a crisis in education. Davis assumes his readers agree and bases his entire proposal on this agreement. If we disagree with the assessment that America's schools are in crisis, then we're bound to reject the proposal. Davis's next assumption is implied: that the crisis in education is due, mainly, to the absence of good teachers. He never states this view directly; but we can reason that if the solution to the current crisis is to place our best and brightest into the classroom, then our current problems are due, mainly, to the absence of especially talented teachers. Davis does not offer support for this assumption, and the reader is entitled to suggest that there may be *other* reasons education is in crisis. (The critique that follows takes exactly this approach.) Davis assumes, as well, that a tax break will entice teachers—which it may. The underlying logic is that we are all motivated by personal gain. If we can boost pay to teachers, then we should be able to attract more candidates to the profession. Davis does not explain why an exemption will attract the best and brightest, as opposed to less inspired individuals looking for a stable career with decent pay. Finally, as discussed under begging the question, Davis assumes the very point he wants to argue: that "If we can enlist the best among us to train our children, we will surely have the best-prepared and best-educated students in the world." Essentially, Davis asks readers to accept this conclusion on faith, for he offers no support. Readers are entitled to meet each of an author's assumptions with assumptions of their own; to evaluate the validity of those assumptions; and to begin formulating a critique, based on their agreement or disagreement.

CRITIQUE

A *critique* is a *formalized, critical reading of a passage.* It also is a personal response; but writing a critique is considerably more rigorous than saying that a movie is "great," or a book is "fascinating," or "I didn't like it." These are all responses, and, as such, they're a valid, even essential, part of your understanding of what you see and read. But such responses don't help illuminate the subject for anyone—even you—if you haven't explained how you arrived at your conclusions.

Your task in writing a critique is to turn you critical reading of a passage into a systematic evaluation in order to deepen your reader's (and your own) understanding of that passage. Among other things, you're interested in determining what an author says, how well the points are made, what assumptions underlie the argument, what issues are overlooked, and what implications can be drawn from such an analysis. Critiques, positive or negative, should include a fair and accurate summary of the passage; they also should include a statement of your own assumptions. It is important to remember that you bring to bear an entire set of assumptions about the world. Stated or not, these assumptions underlie every evaluative comment you make; you therefore have an obligation, both to the reader and to yourself, to clarify your standards. Not only do your readers stand to gain by your forthrightness, but you do as well: In the process of writing a critical assessment, you are forced to examine your own knowledge, beliefs, and assumptions. Ultimately, the critique is a way of learning about yourself.

How to Write Critiques

You may find it useful to organize your critiques in five sections: introduction, summary, analysis of the presentation, your response to the presentation, and conclusion.

The box (page 58) contains some guidelines for writing critiques. Note that they are guidelines, not a rigid formula. Thousands of authors write critiques that do not follow the structure outlined here. Until you are more confident and practiced in writing critiques, however, we suggest you follow these guidelines. They are meant not to restrict you, but rather to provide you with a workable method of writing critical analyses that incorporates a logical sequence of development.

When you write a critique based on an essay in this text, you'll find it helpful to first read the Discussion and Writing Suggestions following that essay. These suggestions will lead you to some of the more fruitful areas of inquiry. Beware of simply responding mechanically to them, however, or your essay could degenerate into a series of short, disjointed responses. You need to organize your reactions into a coherent whole: the critique should be informed by a consistent point of view.

₩ TO WRITE CRITIQUES

- *Introduction*. Introduce both the passage under analysis and the author. State the author's main argument and the point(s) you intend to make about it.

  Provide background material to help your readers understand the relevance or appeal of the passage. This background material might include one or more of the following: an explanation of why the subject is of current interest; a reference to a possible controversy surrounding the subject of the passage or the passage itself; biographical information about the author; an account of the circumstances under which the passage was written; or a reference to the intended audience of the passage.

- *Summary*. Summarize the author's main points, making sure to state the author's purpose for writing.

- *Analysis of the presentation*. Evaluate the validity of the author's presentation, as distinct from your points of agreement or disagreement. Comment on the author's success in achieving his or her purpose by reviewing three or four specific points. You might base your review on one (or more) of the following criteria:

  Is the information accurate?
  Is the information significant?
  Has the author defined terms clearly?
  Has the author used and interpreted information fairly?
  Has the author argued logically?

- *Your response to the presentation*. Now it is your turn to respond to the author's views. With which views do you agree? With which do you disagree? Discuss your reasons for agreement and disagreement, when possible, tying these reasons to assumptions—both the author's and your own.

- *Conclusion*. State your conclusions about the overall validity of the piece—your assessment of the author's success at achieving his or her aims and your reactions to the author's views. Remind the reader of the weaknesses and strengths of the passage.

DEMONSTRATION: CRITIQUE

The critique that follows is based on J. Morton Davis's open letter to the president and the 105ᵗʰ Congress (see pages 47–49). In this critique, you will see that it is possible to agree with an author's main point or proposal but disagree with his or her method of demonstration, or argument. Critiquing a different selection, you could just as easily accept the author's facts and fig-

ures but reject the conclusion built upon them. As long as you carefully articulate the author's assumptions and your own, explaining in some detail your
agreement and disagreement, the critique is yours to take in whatever direction you see fit.

The selections you will likely be inclined to critique are those, like Davis's,
that argue a specific position. Indeed, every argument you read is an invitation
to agreement or disagreement. It remains only for you to speak up and justify your position.

A Critique of J. Morton Davis's Open Letter to the President and the Congress

On January 18, 1998, J. Morton Davis wrote an open   1
letter in *The New York Times* to President Clinton and
the 105th Congress. Titled "A Simple One-Step Plan to
Solve the Education Crisis," the letter argues that
teachers should be exempt from federal income taxes in
order to entice our best and brightest into the profession. Few can deny what Davis, chairman of the D. H.
Blair Investment Banking Corporation (and author of
Making America Work Again and *Hard Knocks to Hot
Stocks*) calls the current "abysmal state of public
education." The problems in education are real, and
Davis's proposal is both achievable and attractive--
one that Congress could enact with relatively little
political risk. So is a permanent federal income tax
exemption for teachers a good idea? Davis's plan
should be adopted; but, alone, it will not solve our
crisis in education.

In his open letter, Davis argues that we must solve   2
America's education problems if we are to assert "continued leadership" in the world. The best way to
"cure" the problem is to "attract our best and brightest to . . . teaching." Because teachers, like everyone else, are motivated by personal gain, we can
entice prospective teachers into the profession with
the incentive of a permanent exemption from federal
income taxes. Aside from boosting take-home pay,
an exemption also will confer on teachers special

recognition and "would distinctly and dramatically recognize [their] gifted dedication." With the inducements
of a tax break and enhanced national respect, teachers
would be more inclined to enter and remain in the profession. If we can attract and retain great teachers,
writes Davis, we "can solve the education crisis."

Teachers are paid less than are other profession-   3
als, and in our society a low salary translates into
low stature. Davis's proposal to raise teachers' pay
by enacting a permanent federal income tax exemption
would, shrewdly, increase pay *and* prestige if teachers
were the only tax-exempt professionals in the nation.
Now that the country is about to enjoy budget sur-
pluses, if we can afford the exemption we should
enact it. Davis correctly notes that the federal government routinely uses the tax system to promote
social objectives--as in the case of high taxes that
discourage cigarette use. So why not use the system
to promote a social end that everyone can endorse: a
continuing supply of effective teachers?

While Davis does not say so openly, he mistakenly   4
suggests that our current problems exist because the
best and brightest are not presently in our classrooms. They are elsewhere. "Teaching should never be a
fall-back position or a career compromise," he claims.
Is it now? Is that how we got into the mess we're in,
because our classrooms are led by people who could not
succeed elsewhere? In the absence of suggesting a
single other cause for the current crisis in education, Davis apparently thinks so. There is no denying
that poor teachers clog the system. But plenty of competent teachers exist who, while applauding Davis's
proposed federal income tax exemption, would never
agree that the poor teachers are the sole or even the
main problem with education. Ask good teachers what
ails the system and they will acknowledge deadwood
colleagues, but also they will point to other prob-

lems: meager municipal budgets, tensions within communities over how the schools should be run, and severe
social and economic conditions within local school
districts.

Bringing the best and brightest into America's 5
classrooms cannot solve the problem of underfinanced
schools. State and local governments set expenditures
for schools; while Davis's suggestion will help the
cash flow of teachers already working, it will do
nothing to increase the *number* of teachers now available. The only way to increase teachers in the system
is to raise local or state taxes or to get federal
support. In the first case, tax increases to local
home owners are never welcome; in the second, the federal government is not likely to forego collecting
taxes from teachers *and* boost education dollars to
states at the same time. As long as annual budgets
remain low, student-to-teacher ratios will remain high
and present barriers to individualized instruction.
Education suffers when there are too few teachers, a
problem that Davis's tax exemption would not resolve.

Davis's open letter also avoids mention of struc- 6
tural problems within the educational community
itself: bloated administrations in which levels of
assistant principals and curriculum coordinators stay
out of the classroom, where they could do some direct
good, and instead over-manage the lives of teachers;
unions that militantly guard against increasing teachers' hours and responsibilities, thereby causing students to suffer; curricula that do not change with the
times or, conversely, change too easily, driven by
fads more than by careful review; and elected school
committees that clash with administrators over policy.
At the beginning of any given school year, at least
one major school system in America seems on the verge
of meltdown, with problems due mainly not to lack of
bright, dedicated teachers but to lack of consensus

among teachers, administrators, and towns. Many of
these problems are budgetary, and more money could
resolve them. But other problems are related to the
process of teaching itself, which is a social activity
based on philosophical principles.

Teaching is not an exact science. And while Davis   7
exhorts the president and Congress to mount a response
to the education crisis in the same way our nation
addressed the challenges of going to the moon or winning World War II (by building the atomic bomb), we
could not with respect to teaching agree on a single
course of action as we could (and did) with scientific
and military challenges. Teaching is unlike physics
and rocketry--sciences in which experts can isolate
all factors that bear on a problem, predict how those
factors will behave in any given circumstance, and
then plan solutions accordingly. Teaching mixes con-
tentious issues of politics, philosophy, and economics
into a soup so complex that no one--not even well-
meaning advocates in ideal circumstances--can agree on
what, precisely, the problems are, let alone on how to
solve them. Davis's hope for a national commitment to
cure our schools is misinformed, because problems in
education differ fundamentally from the problems to
which he draws comparison.

Most seriously, Davis neglects the economic compo-   8
nent of America's crisis in education. There exists
in this country a structural poverty that makes
learning difficult for tens of thousands of students
whose home environments foster neither the pride in
education nor the basic economic security needed for
success in school. When America's poorest children
look around their communities and see disrepair,
unemployment, crime, and the availability (mostly) of
unskilled jobs, the chances are good that these students will see little reason to excel in the classroom. The truly motivated will rise above their

conditions; but that takes hard work, and too few have the support structures of a steady home to make the transition out of poverty. The problem of structural poverty therefore persists, and its impact on the education system is immense. Davis's "simple" solution of exempting teachers from federal income taxes does not acknowledge what is perhaps the most profound and intractable cause of problems in American education.

Would prospective teachers approve of Davis's proposal? Forget for the moment the challenges to this proposal that other public servants such as firefighters and police would make. If Davis's proposed income tax exemption passed Congress, we could expect that those contemplating a career in teaching but who were wavering because of the low salaries would say yes and would join the profession. That would be good news. But until other problems that plague education--such as meager budgets, conflicting educational agendas, inefficient school bureaucracies, and structural poverty--are resolved, proposals such as Davis's, though they are welcome and *should be* enacted, will not achieve their desired end. Davis's proposal is a step in the right direction, but it is only a step.

9

Discussion

- Paragraph 1 of this critique introduces the selection to be reviewed, along with the author, and sets a context for the reader. The paragraph ends with the writer's thesis: to adopt the proposed federal income tax exemption, even though that policy will not solve the educational crisis in America.
- Paragraph 2 summarizes Davis's letter. Note that the topic sentence clearly indicates that Davis has written an argument.
- Paragraph 3 explains the writer's basic agreement with Davis's federal income tax exemption proposal.
- Paragraph 4 begins the critical evaluation of Davis's letter, indicating that Davis assumes that the problem with our current system is the

absence of good teachers. Note how the paragraph's final sentence offers readers three arguments against Davis's assertion. These arguments are developed, in turn, in the next three paragraphs.

- Paragraph 5 raises the first problem Davis has failed to recognize—low budgets for school systems. Davis's proposal does not address this problem.
- Paragraph 6 raises a second problem Davis has failed to recognize: structural issues within the education community that lead to difficulties. Paragraph 7 continues this discussion and points out Davis's faulty logic in comparing the problems of education to problems faced by scientists during World War II and in the race to the moon.
- Paragraph 8 raises the third and most significant problem Davis has not acknowledged: the dire circumstances of many students and the effect this has on learning potential.
- Paragraph 9, the conclusion, summarizes the overall position of the critique—to accept the federal income tax exemption proposal, but to reject the expectation that the crisis in education will be solved with a single, "simple" solution.

■ EXERCISE

Read the following two position statements on the current "school-to-work" debate. School-to-work is an educational strategy that places jobs, and the skills needed to excel in the workplace, at the center of the school curriculum. Bob Kolasky, assistant editor for IntellectualCapital.com, an online magazine, explains the approach this way:

> Intended to do more than teach the three R's, school-to-work applies math, science and the humanities to the reality of today's workplace, both by explaining how the lessons being taught are related to real-world situations and providing a more interactive forum to teach them in. Educators hope to replace the passive days of lectures and textbook learning with a more modern, group-oriented . . . education.[2]

The arguments that follow take opposing stands on the school-to-work debate. Read both, and then select one on which to write a critique, using the techniques introduced in this chapter. We provide two arguments from which to choose because each identifies core assumptions of the other and will help you to think critically about the issues. Use (and give credit to) one author in critiquing the other. Your critique should be the result of at least two drafts.

---

[2]Kolasky, Bob. "Issue of the Week: Today's Students, Tomorrow's Workers." *IntellectualCapital.com.* 4 Sept. 1997. <http://www.intellectualcapital.com> 16 Jan. 1998.

An Avenue to High Academic Standards

LYNN OLSON

At age 16, Erika Pyne of Kalamazoo, Michigan, was a fairly typical high   1
school student. "I had absolutely no idea of what I was going to do with my
life, and that really frustrated me," she recalls. Enrolled in a high school program that emphasized science and mathematics, she did not see any connection between her courses and what she might do in the future.

Then, as a high school junior, she enrolled in a school-to-work program   2
run by the Education for Employment Consortium in Kalamazoo. For the
next two years, she spent part of each school day taking classes at Bronson
Methodist Hospital, learning about such topics as anatomy and medical
terminology. She also spent time observing and talking with health-care
professionals and getting hands-on work experience. As a senior in high
school, Erika interned afternoons on the family-care unit at Borgess Medical
Center, where she helped out in the delivery room. "It was great. I just loved
it," she says. "I had all these wonderful experiences that most people my age
couldn't talk about. I fell in love with health care."

When I last spoke with her, Erika was a patient-care assistant at Bronson   3
and a junior at Western Michigan University, where she was enrolled in a
nursing program. Eventually, she planned to earn a degree as a physician's
assistant so that she would have more authority and flexibility than a nurse.

"WHY DO I HAVE TO LEARN THIS?"

Erika was one of many students whom I met during a year spent research-   4
ing school-to-work programs around the country. And her story is not atyp-
ical.

High-quality school-to-work programs combine learning in school and in   5
the workplace. They teach students rigorous academic content as well as
practical skills. They engage students in active, hands-on learning rather than
teaching solely from textbooks. And they build bridges between high schools,
higher education and the workplace to help young people prepare for both
careers and college.

Studies suggest that school-to-work can help address one of the greatest   6
problems in education: motivation. Many students don't think that what
they learn in school really counts. A majority of American teenagers in national surveys describe their education as "boring." Although they think it's
important to graduate, they don't think that doing well in school matters. In
one 1996 survey, most students described themselves as sliding by in school.
Two-thirds admitted they could do better if they tried.

School-to-work can help young people answer the question, "Why do I   7
have to learn this?" by showing how what students learn in school can be
used now and in the future. Research from Jobs for the Future, the Manpower
Demonstration Research Corporation, the Office of Technology Assessment,

and Mathematica Policy Research Inc. all reach basically the same conclusion: well-structured school-to-work activities can slash boredom and re-engage students in schooling.

CREATING A DESIRE TO LEARN

A prominent misconception surrounding school-to-work is that it downplays   8
intellectual achievement. But far from jettisoning academics, well-structured school-to-work programs can make learning come alive for students, by connecting the academic content that students learn in school with its use in the world outside the classroom.

Evidence suggests that school-to-work can encourage students to take   9
more academic coursework—not less. A 1994 evaluation of Pro Tech, a school-to-work program in Boston, found that students who participated took more rigorous math and science courses than their peers, although their grades were not substantially better. In 1993, a study of the seven most improved sites that belong to the *High Schools That Work* consortium found that these schools had managed to significantly close the achievement gap between college-bound and career-bound students in just three years. High schools that belong to the consortium pledge to replace low-level, watered-down courses with a solid academic core. Similarly, at Roosevelt High School in Portland, Oregon, enrollment in physics, algebra 2, and chemistry classes has increased since the school launched its school-to-work efforts in the early 1990s.

While such results are hardly conclusive, they demonstrate the promise of   10
well-structured school-to-work activities.

Finally, school-to-work can encourage young people to pursue education   11
and training beyond high school. In sites ranging from Kalamazoo to Boston, high percentages of young people involved in school-to-work initiatives are choosing to pursue postsecondary education because they understand the connection between learning and a good job. Many of these programs report college-going rates among their graduates of about 80%, compared with about 62% nationally. Other studies have found that while school-to-work graduates do not attend college at higher rates, those who do are more likely to declare a college major and to earn more college credits.

WORTH DOING . . . WORTH DOING RIGHT

In most of the communities that I visited, school-to-work was a grassroots   12
effort. Sometimes educators began a program after they realized that many of their students were going straight into the workplace or to college without being prepared for that transition. Other times, employers approached schools because of specific labor shortages in their community, or because they were concerned that high school graduates lacked the skills to succeed. These grassroots efforts are spreading slowly, but steadily.

School-to-work needs to be done well, making sure the academics are rig-   13
orous. Improperly structured, school-to-work could offer low-level curricula
and channel students into narrow job training. That is exactly what we don't
need. We must always demand quality.

Today, both employers and colleges want people who can read and do   14
math; frame and solve problems; communicate orally and in writing; use
computers; and work in teams. Schools need to do a better job of preparing
all young people for this future.

Not every school-to-work program is right for every student. But good   15
school-to-work activities can provide choices and opportunities for young
people, many of whom are not now well served by our education system.
Done right school-to-work can be a powerful tool in the effort to achieve
higher academic standards and a more educated citizenry.

Lynn Olson is a senior editor at Education Week, a national newspaper that covers
topics in K-12 education. Her new book, *The School-To-Work Revolution: How
Employers and Educators Are Joining Forces To Prepare Tomorrow's Skilled
Workforce*, is published by Addison-Wesley.

· · ·

Related Links[3]

9/4/97 Brian Farenell

Who chooses for what job each kid will be trained, er I mean, schooled? I just
hope whatever powers-that-be involved in the decision-making get it right. Asking
a freshman in high school what he'd like to do for the rest of his life, seems a bit
early to me. I understand that in Holland (and perhaps other countries, I don't
know) they have such a system. I'd suggest that the Dutch model be studied
VERY carefully and see what pitfalls may occur.

9/4/97 Tom

Sounds good to me. I wonder what happened to the Vocational Technical HS?
Have we now moved too far away from technical training which will prepare
one for a job? Most of today's youngsters are given college prep courses whether
they have the will or ability to go to college or not. They lose interest, and if
they graduate have to pay for technical school to prepare them for a job. This
seems to me a waste of resources. Public School dollars should be used to prepare people for the world of work first and college training next for those who
can cut it.

---

[3]These "related links" illustrate an online, threaded discussion. It is common in e-mail
communications to find errors in spelling, grammar, and punctuation. The discussion messages that follow are reproduced exactly as they appeared online—Editors.

9/4/97 John C. Ring, Jr.
I doubt that anyone would suggest that obtaining "real life" experience via work while still in school is not beneficial for certain students. I would not claim, nor ignore the claim, that it is equally valuable for all students. I rather think it would have been detrimental in my case, taking away time from my math homework, which I rather enjoyed. However, unfortunately "school-to-work" advocates seem to believe this is a universal solution. Thus, they suggest these programs be manditory, rather then opportunities. Even worse, many advocate the "replacement" of academic education with work activity, rather than your suggesting of using it to spur futher academic achievement. I agree that the opportunity for work experience should be made available as a suppliment to academic schooling. I do not agree with it being either a replacement for such schooling, nor with it being made a graduation requirement.

9/5/97 Tony Poldrugovac
To be honest with you, if you don't start teaching kids (and adults for the matter) the truth about God, all your educational plans will result in ruin ... just look at the world around you. Education without God produces intellectual barbarians. I may be viewed as narrow-minded, but the evidence is all around you. Tony

9/5/97 Red Laser
This reminds me of the time, my friend John was carrying a heavy refrigerator and called to his older sister for help. She said, "You don't understand! I just painted my nails." Apparently, she had never lifted a refrigerator before, and didn't understand real life predicaments. It might be fun or interesting for students to see how education relates to real life skills. If this article is true, it seems to suggest that "Experience" is the best teacher

9/5/97 Victor
Tony, The truth about God according to whom?

9/5/97 David Hoover
It should be kept in mind that a successful work/study program will keep the interference of the job to a minimum. It should be regarded as a hobby at best. With the pace of change being so rapid, it would be unreasonable to expect the requirements of a job to remain the same for more than a few years at most. Thus, it is difficult to envision such programs pumping out trained monkeys. A fundamental education in all subjects is more pertinent today than ever before, and for all students, not just the "college bound" or "elite" (by the way, what is there for people without some sort of post-high school degree anyway?). The only real danger in these programs is the heavy reliance on companies footing the bills, as they will very quickly request something in return. It should always be remembered that the well-being of the students is paramount, and not the well-being of the industries that cheap, focused labor would aid.

9/6/97 Margaret
Our son, a senior at Badger High School in Lake Geneva, WI has just been accepted into a youth apprenticeship program in the field of Graphic Design. He will earn 6-12 college credits and receives high school credit, a grade and a pay check while enrolled. He is profoundly talented in the computer generated design field and has been submitting designs for contest and payment for several years. A program like this will really motivate him to work hard toward his future and begin his college education while still in high school. How do you really know what you want to do until you try it? I believe all students should have such progressive opportunities and I salute those who support and maintain such programs.

9/6/97 John Siefert
What educational dribble? Our teachers are almost 40% illiterate, so how can they even teach children about history, math, science and reading? It does not surprise me that children and teenages are not interested in school, and the reason is because teachers don't know their subject matter. They don't have authority in the classroom. Federal regulators have taken control of our schools away from the citizenry. And now they are trying to recover their foolishness by trying to help the economy. That is a big bunch of baloney. It is the job of corporations to train their workers. Don't make us pay for it. This is just another way to get "big brother" into our classroom. I implore our teachers to teach substance, but that does not have to be done with entertainment or school-to-work programs. I don't want my daughter being told by some regulator somewhere what she is supposed to do for a living. I might as well move to Russia, where there is more freedom than there is here in the United States.

9/7/97 Richard Geib
School merely as a means for job preparation? What a shallow typically "modern" interpretation of education! What a superficial and tendentious idea of learning! In my opinion, an education should revolve around the following questions: How to live and what to live for. If teenagers think that is "boring," maybe we adults had better spend more time with them talking about what is really important in life. In my experience, learning how to read and write (AND THINK!) comes naturally after those earlier questions are resolved satisfactorily. On the other hand, if they not be resolved, a student will never get excited about themselves and their place in the world. If we want to call our country "educated," we need to put more vigor into the liberal arts and not look at school primarily as a vehicle for churning out efficient workers. As a professional teacher who looks for inspiration all the way back to Socrates, I read Olson's article, look at my country, and despair almost completely. This "jobs-to-work" idea will be the latest educational fad or "magic bullet" which will not cure the ills of our educational system - the root of the problem remaining unacknowledged.

9/8/97 Bri Farenell
Our teachers are "40% illiterate"? Where'd you get those numbers from? Rush Limbaugh? And even if that's the case, you have to wonder where all the best college graduates are going instead of teaching... and why?

9/9/97 DK

"In my opinion, an education should revolve around the following questions: How to live and what to live for. If teenagers think that is "boring," maybe we adults had better spend more time with them talking about what is really important in life." For example, adults could work side by side with students, spend time with them one on one rather than keep them cooped up in the classroom under a single babysitter. In my experience, learning how to read and write and speak comes naturally during the course of using reading and writing and speaking skills for an important purpose. Students who can't see the importance need to get involved in project where it's important. Students who stay isolated in a classroom and then go party with friends on their parents' allowance money might never get excited about themselves and their place in the world.

School-to-Work Will Train, Not Educate

PHYLLIS SCHLAFLY

The School-to-Work Opportunities Act (STW) was signed by President   1
Clinton in 1994 and is being implemented nationwide through STW state
laws, federal and state regulations, and the federal mandates that control the
granting of federal STW funds.

FROM THE CRADLE TO THE GRAVE

School-to-work is the implementation of Marc Tucker's "cradle-to-grave"   2
plan outlined in his now-famous 18-page "Dear Hillary" letter written on
November 11, 1992. It delineates a master plan "to remold the entire
American [public school] system" into "a seamless web that literally extends
from cradle-to-grave and is the same system for everyone," coordinated by "a
system of labor market boards at the local, state and federal levels" where curriculum and "job matching" will be handled by counselors "accessing the
integrated computer-based program."

   Tucker, who is president of the *National Center on Education and the*   3
Economy, boasts that he has written the "restructuring" plans for more
than 50% of public school children. Designed on the German system,
Tucker's plan is to train children in specific jobs to serve the workforce and
the global economy instead of educate them so they can make their own life
choices.

   The traditional function of education was to teach basic knowledge and   4
skills: reading, writing, math, science, history, etc. School-to-work deempha-
sizes or eliminates academic work and substitutes mandated vocational training to better serve the workforce. Instead of the focus being on developing the
child, the focus is on developing a labor force.

EDUCATION VERSUS TRAINING

There's a big difference between educating a child and training him or her to   5
work. According to the dictionary, to educate means to develop the faculties
and powers of a person by teaching. Becoming skilled at reading, writing and
calculating is essential to developing as a student and as a person and being
able to fulfill the American dream.

To train means to cause a person or animal to be efficient in the per-   6
formance of tasks by responding to discipline, instruction and repeated
practice. That's what you do to your dog. And that's exactly what school-
to-work is: "performance-based" training of students to move them into
predetermined jobs.

To make matters worse, those predetermined jobs will not be selected by   7
the student or his family. New bodies called workforce development boards—
appointed not elected—will determine what jobs are needed in the coming
years. The schools will then design the curriculum to meet these governmen-
tally determined workforce needs, and use counselors and computers to do
"job matching" of the students.

After they complete their vocational training, rather than receiving their   8
high school diploma, students will get a Certificate of Mastery—they won't be
able to get jobs unless they have one. This certificate will be comparable to
green cards which must be possessed by resident aliens in order to hold a job.

THE WRONG KIND OF SCHOOL CHOICE

STW laws and regulations require vocational training to start "at the earliest   9
possible age, but beginning no later than middle-school grades." The federal
STW statute says that "career awareness" should "begin as early as the elementary grades." How many elementary or even middle school children do
you know that are capable of choosing their lifetime career? Obviously, these
decisions will be made by the school, not by the child.

The goal is not to graduate highly literate individuals but to turn out team   10
workers to produce for the global economy. In the STW scheme, individual
grades are inflated or detached from academic achievement, individual honors
and competition are eliminated or deemphasized, and instead we have such
"team" techniques as group grading, cooperative learning, peer tutoring,
horizontal enrichment, job shadowing, mentoring, and job site visits.

It is obvious that the several years we've suffered with Outcome-Based   11
Education was preparation for the system in which children are taught to be
"team workers" instead of achievers.

A LITANY OF APOLOGISTS

Some big businesses support school-to-work because they think that voca-   12
tional courses in high school for illiterate or semi-literate students will train
young Americans to compete in the global economy with people in the third

world willing to work for 25 and 50 cents an hour. They think they'll get some free teenage labor and the schools will do some of their job training for them. But it's not the job of the taxpayers to do job training; that's the job of the corporations that hire them. It is the job of the schools to teach children how to read, write and calculate.

Some governors support school-to-work because it gives them control of   13 a pot of money for which they don't have to account to the state legislature.

School-to-work is wrong because it eliminates accountability by bypass-   14 ing elected representatives in state legislatures and school boards.

School-to-work is a direct threat to the individual student, his or her pri-   15 vacy, his or her goals and his or her acquisition of an education that can help him reach them. Furthermore, a planned economy, with bureaucrats trying to predict what jobs will be needed in the next five years and training students for specific jobs, is a failure all over the world. All those who value freedom must defeat and defund school-to-work.

Phyllis Schlafly, the president of *Eagle Forum*, is the author of *Child Abuse in the Classroom* (1964), the producer of a video documentary called *Crisis in the Classroom* (1996), and the publisher of the monthly *Education Reporter* since 1986.

• • •

Related Links

9/4/97 Don Wallace
School-to-work appears to be born out of pragmatism. Public school students are dumber than ever and functional illiteracy is the norm. Therefore, the thought goes, why not sacrifice the ideal of a liberal education - which does not 'work' in our public school system for the majority of students - and trade rampant illiter-acy and unemployability for a narrow trade education? Since you can't get stu-dents to think or reason, you'd better get them busy with a wrench or hammer. I perceive school-to-work to be the creation of policy wonks whose agenda is to create a two-tier American society: 'worker' and 'professional'. Note that public schools today are poor at teaching basic skills. Vocational education at an early grade level will displace what little "3 Rs" education that now takes place. The 'worker caste' - most likely from a blue collar or middle class, unmoneyed back-ground - "tracked" through public schools - will be barred from minimal entrance requirements of a university should he choose to later broaden his education. The manager/professional/anointed policy wonk - probably from a "better" back-ground more similar to those parties who endorse this plan - would be 'tracked' through private school and a good university, to assume his or her "rightful" posi-tion of riding herd over vocationally specialized savages. In short, school-to-work appears to be completely contradictory to a free democratic society because it will create functional castes.

9/4/97 Brian Farenell
It's a sub-freezing day in West Africa when I agree with Phyllis Schlafly but I do. Perhaps not the entireity of her reasoning but certainly her opinion. First off, I think asking a freshman in high school to declare a major is way too early. If

someone at that age is focused and is certain what he or she wants to do with the rest of his life, accomodations should be made. But I think kids are the exception not the rule. Secondly, maybe I'm old-fashioned (at age 23), but I always felt that the point of the secondary educational system was to mold citizens who are well-rounded in a wide variety of areas. Not only in basics, like literacy and numeracy, but also in being aware of civics, our nation's history, how to express oneself and so on. It seems to me that college is where one should specialize. With the rapidity that our job market is changing, let's get workers out there that are flexible and well-rounded. Finally, the public school sytem is being asked to do an impossible job. It's being asked to repair the damage left by apathetic or abusive parents and by a society with screwed up mores. Schools are not parents and they can not parent, but that's what they're expected to do. You've got kids who have never learned to socialize. You have to teach them how to socialize and to sit still for more than 10 sec. at a time before you can teach them how to add.

9/4/97 Miguel Guzmán-Betancourt
I think the points raised by Mrs. Schlafly are totally valid. This new weird educational "reform" is unthinkable. I'm amazed that it has been advanced so easily without any national debate in the States. And what I'm really scared about is that this is a story right out of "1984", the planned and controlled society. The American people must stop this idea, otherwise it will be imitated by the rest of the world, such as my country, Mexico. We asked you to maintain freedom during the WW II and the Cold War, now you must do it again.

9/4/97 John C. Ring, Jr.
This is a utopian scheme for those who believe that the world would be better if only everything, and everyone, could be managed from a central point of decision making. Further, it undermines the principal that the voting public will be well educated and informed. These two items go rather hand in hand, for an uneducated person is more likely to permit the delegation of responsibility to be transfered to others. Mark well the day that control of the schools is transfered out of the hands of the local communities, for it spells the first day in the end of the American experiment. Of course, we are along that path now with the economic threats being used to "persuade" the local schools to comply, but there is a difference between these two states. Note well that president Clinton's desire to enfore a national test that students must pass is a form of such control, albeit indirect. Well meaning, perhaps, but ill advised.

9/4/97 Diann Harle
Ms. Schafly would probably argue equally as vehemently for the abolition of welfare benefits as she argues for the "traditional" educational system. Interesting that we now must "train" all these people who are being dropped from the welfare rolls to have "marketable" skills to make the transition to independence from the welfare state. Of course, being somewhat educated, I have come to realize that for many people in this country "life choices" are dictated long before education is

received. In schools today we see children of elementary school age who have been subjected to enough cruelty, neglect, abandonment, and indifference to make the thought of our benign efforts more accurately banal. We cannot insure nor guarantee every child the luxury of Ms. Schafly's "education." Not because we don't agree with the purity of the concept but because for too many of our children today "the American Dream" is not only unknown, but unteachable. Ms. Schafly uses all the right buzzwords to incite her fans. Unfortunately, she has no clue about the reality of life for children in 1997. Will school to work make a difference? I do not know. I do believe that the politicians on both sides of this issue will insure that what gets lost in this dialogue will not be their propaganda but the needs of our children.

9/4/97 Karen Card
Schlafly's article contains some grains of truth, buttressed with many wild exaggerations. The programs which I have heard or read about are only intended to expose children to careers and the kinds of interests and skills they involve. Job shadowing, mentoring, and cooperative learning are not dirty words. What is wrong with students who visit a vet hospital if they are interested in veterinarian medicine? The same applies to auto mechanics, radiology technicians, doctors, and lawyers. Team players can also be high achievers, and should be encouraged to be both. Big business wants a labor pool of well educated thinkers who are good at math, writing, and oral expression and who can use a computer. Finally, Schlafly and the rest of her "thinkalikes" use a lot of buzz words as a scare tactic, without carefully analyzing the actual broad scope and variety of school-to-work programs available today. John Ring decried the loss of local control of schools as part of the new programs discussed by Schlafly. My school district has completed a strategic planning process which involved over 800 members of the local community. However, our plan has been rejected by individuals who are proponents of Schlafly's ideology. They don't really want local control—only if that control is in agreement with their politics.

9/4/97 Russ Weinberg
Predictably, Schlafly has attempted to disguise hysterical ravings as reasoned analysis. I'm surprised that she wasn't some how able to work in the Tri-lateral Commission and the Council on Foreign Relations because her so called arguments in this article belong to that same pathologically paranoid strain of social and political thought. The truth is that school to work programs were formulated not to enslave the masses but to meet a need. There was nothing being done to help non-college bound highschool students become employable. Like it or not, on today's market, a high school diploma received after a "liberal" secondary school education and a quarter will get you a local phone call. STW was put in place to enhance the value of the high school diploma, not to diminish it.

9/5/97 Derek
Does anyone know about this 'German system' that is mentioned in this article? I would like to know more about the system that Tucker's plan is supposedly modeled after.

9/5/97 Tom
Schlafly's elitist view of education is what is wrong with it. Sure we have teach kids the 3 Rs. This can easily be done in the first 8 grades. At that point, we must train the majority to go out into the world of work(vocational/technical). Only those of the higher intellect should be subsidized to go on to higher education and train for the professions. Countless dollars and resources are wasted on 'college prep' courses for those who are not intellectually suited for higher education. Schlafly, and others in the clouds, insist that all kids need the flavor of higher education courses to lead a full, productive, successful life. Balderdash!

9/5/97 Charles C. Jett
Phyllis has it all wrong again. She and her crowd always seem to seek an 'enemy to blame' . . . rather than look inward and focus on their own hypocricy. School-to-work principles are what she and her crowd advocate in the teaching of Sunday School.

9/5/97 George Willett
Phyllis might care to read of John Dewey, New England educational philosopher who suggests that greater learning occurred where the practical was aligned with the academic. This applies to work skills which entails, among other skills, the ability to work well with others. Everybody will enter the workforce in some manner, and the more refined the career choice the more productive and happier person. School-to-work is also career exploration where young people really learn of career fields rather than just specific occupations. Imaginative educators and school districts require career exploration (community service or even volunteerism) as a graduatoin requirement. This is done not for producing products for drudgery but to encourage young people to gain the benefits of a total educational educational system which also involves the community and other adults.

9/5/97 Mark Dawdy
How unfortunate that so many Americans are blinded to "principles" and "freedom." Phyllis is correct in her opinion of this ridiculous scheme for more "big government". As usual the dupes of "doom and gloom" cannot see the "true" issues from the "perceived" ones. What is at stake here is not a philosophical difference of education, but freedom. The U.S. has produced many great people and ideas. Washington, Jefferson, Edison, etc, never would have been who they were without the freedom to mold their characters and disclipline themselves through life's educational course. Who is so all-knowing to determine which course will exactly fit each lifestyle? There is no one qualified for such a task on this earth and there never will be. FREEDOM is at stake here. This country was founded on the God-given principles of the right to pursue happiness. The federal gov't is too big. It wastes more money and time than anything else in this country. It has already stripped too many people's rights. I'm not saying we should abandon any change or not implement a better skill training program. I say that anything the government does usually gets messed up, ie.

the welfare program, education, etc. The current education system as administered by the govenerment is an excellent example - 7 administrators to 1 teacher.
WHY? Whether you agree with Phyllis or not, is not the issue. Our freedom is
at stake.

9/5/97 Red Laser
Phyllis Schlafly writes: "To train means to cause a person or animal to be efficient
in the performance of tasks by responding to discipline, instruction and repeated
practice." That doesn't sound too much different from practicing basketball or
any number of afterschool activities and hobbies. If it's so bad, consider the opposite—nonperformance, lack of discipline, lacking the will to practice. Sound familiar? It should: Schafly's classroom—one in which all students stay in the same
place and learn the same thing under an authoritarian figure is a sure way to turn
out conformist drones for the global economy who are only interested in memo-
rizing test answers, spewing them, and forgetting them the next day. How much
better education would be if it were enriched by travel, and by broad and numerous experiences and contacts in the world.

9/6/97 Lloyd Smith
Finding myself in even partial agreement with Phyllis Schlafly is novel and unsettling. But she is correct when she notes the difference between education and training. The former should prepare one for life, while the latter should prepare one for
the tasks of life. There is a difference, on which many advocates of narrow vocational training fail to understand. There is also a danger: Mere training does not prepare one to adapt to change. As Toffler wrote many years ago in Future Shock, one's
"copeability" is more important than one's capability. Having said all of that, I disagree with Schlafly's assertions that school-to-work is some sort of big government
conspiracy designed to enslave the masses. It's not, and in fact, we can have it both
ways: We can create sound educational programs which also prepare students for
their lives after they leave school. (One place it's being done is in Washington state.)
After all, we need to remember that eventually, every student will leave the schools,
and every one of them needs to be able to do something, whether it is going to college or trade school, going directly to work, joining the military, or working in the
home. Good school to work programs are designed to recognize this obvious fact.

9/6/97 John Siefert
I am so glad to Ms. Schlafly has spoken out about this terribly important, but much
belittled issue. We have too much miseducation in our schools. There is not teaching going on the classrooms. The teacher has lost control in the classroom. The federal government and its Education Department have taken the classroom away
from the teacher, student and parent. Sad to say, we are rearing an illiterate generation of students. I know of a young man in Coos Bay Oregon who went to a
school that majored in this school-to-work program. This young man was singled
out to train to be a politician or public speaker. He has been expressly trained to do
just that. Yet, this young man knows nothing about history, math, English, or even
reading. For his whole life he will only be able to relate to people what someone else

says to him. He will not have a mind of his own. He will forever be a subject of the state. His work will not be his own, but that of a silent elite that structured our schools so he would fail in literacy, but prosper in speaking and politicking. What a farce this school-to-work is! We have to find some way to recapture our public schools and their curriculum from the powers that be. This country has in many ways ceased to be the country of the people, by the people and for the people.

9/8/97 Zak Arthur Klemmer

The day in America when we emulate the Reich, rather than the traditions of "classical liberalism" is the turning point from liberty to one of subjugation. Everything with the state, every thing through the state, no one against the state should be the motto of the Clintons.

9/8/97 Patrick

I'll echo the sentiments of a lot of other posters - agreeing with Phyllis Schlafly is definitely a disquieting experience. Kids do need to learn about arts, sciences and humanities in school. The global popular culture only provides superficial and nearly meaningless music, art and literature, and it seems to get worse by the year. Having said that, turning school into some sort of apprenticeship program is also the wrong way, because schools are utterly clueless as to what skills people need in life. When I was in high school about 6 years ago, the "vocational training" involved metal and wood working and home economics. How many kids will really grow up to do these things? Not many. Schools would first have to start teaching more practical courses - introductory business, computer programming, maybe even student teaching or mentoring. Unfortunately, most people in decision making positions still think making a hinge in shop will be useful to a majority of students.

9/8/97 Dave Siess

Charles Jett has not addressed the subject, that is, we are a independent people that want choice in what we will do with our lives. Better to teach our children some morals and ethics (we do not seem to do this in the schools any more, it is not politically correct) than to have some bureaucrat decide what my kid should be. What's next, invading the private schools to decide what their curriculum should be? Phyllis is right on, and we ought to listen to her and take action against this social engineering.

9/8/97 Tom Havelka

The criticism of the School-to-work program hinges on two unproven assumptions. First, that training and education are somehow mutually exclusive and secondly that there being "trained" somehow prevents someone from ever becoming educated. Both ideas are wrong. It is quite possible to train and educate at the same time. There is no reason why someone can not be taught technical skills that are marketable in the workplace while obtaining a education, one does not have to preclude the other. The second assumption is equally wrong. People can and often do continue with their education (both formally and informally) after learning a skill and the skills learned have only served to enhance their education. Too much time is wasted on the tired old debate between education and training both work hand-in-hand with each other. It is also interesting to note that the author never produces a copy of the Act the she indicts and the suppose link to the alledged "letter" is merely to another article that does not let us acutally see the letter but merely quotes excerpts from it.

9/9/97 DK

Schlafly is living in the wrong century, a century when "work study" meant shoveling coal in a mine or hammering horseshoes. When Schlafly was in high school years ago, " 'vocational training' involved metal and wood working and home economics. How many kids today really grow up to do these things? Not many." Likewise, how many kids use slide rules for trigonometry? In truth, times have changed, and the world expects a lot of technical knowhow from kids. Kids definitely need to apply their arts, sciences and humanities out of school, or the lessons they learn in school won't stick. School experiences in computers and reading and writing and budgeting should definitely be reinforced in non-school environments such as work study and coops or these valuable skills run the risk of being memorized and forgotten like so many multiple choice answers.

9/10/97 Mike

Just a few "shotgun" points for the discussion. First, the German system alluded to in this discussion is more than preparing for the workplace. It's a system which places students, based on tested ability, into different tracks. So, if at an early age you aren't college material, you don't go to college. Instead, you enter a vocational track. I would think that liberals would be aghast at this thought. Given the performance of minorities in this country on standardized tests this would almost certainly create a "whites only" college program. Conservatives should be equally outraged at the prospect of a system which denies you an opportunity to better yourself, regardless of circumstances. If Thomas Edison had been assessed by this program when he was a boy, he'd have been placed in special ed classes. Second, I'm sure businesses like this concept-it saves them money if schools can do job skill specific training for them. Third, the teacher's unions like this idea because it masks the problem of poor teaching and the "feel-good" education concept which permeates American public education. Catholic schools turn out better educated students with better job skills and they don't have the luxury of feeding at the public trough. I've got a better idea. Nobody can become a teacher until they work in some field for 5-10 years. I'm sure these new teachers could easily impart the connection between education and life than some of those who've been "trained" to be educators.

9/10/97 chris manion

I've been encouraged to hire high-schoolers on work-study as a way to get highly-motivated part-time workers. While that's a lofty goal here in rural Virginia, and while it could probably save us some money, I think it shortchanges the students. Business are probably tempted to support this kind of stuff because they've recognized how hard it is to get good help, and will do anything to improve the picture. The "community action" dimension is also very strong—the local media (pretty third rate, but typically liberal) have only one view of education here: the public schools. They ignore the many private schools in the area, as well as the fact that more than ten per cent of school-age pupils here are home-schooled! Sticking up for basic skills might be unpopular, but believe me, when I taught college fresh-men last fall, I was forced to emphasize basic skills on the same level as the content of the course. Kids these days are not dumber, but they are less prepared, it seems, with every passing year. They've been cheated. Mrs. Schlafly is right: this "program" only cheats them more.

9/10/97 Chris Mulvaney
As a recent vice-president of an elementary school board I have seen first hand the move toward "School to Work" initiatives. They are at best further waste-ful programs that increase the administrative costs of education and offer more job opportunities to administrators. At worst they are tracking and social engi-neering. I tasted a little of that when I was in grade school some years ago. I was labeled, through aptitude testing, as an under performer and sent to lower level English, math and science classes. I missed the opportunity for higher math and science in high school because you had to start that path in junior high, where I was labeled. Instead I am extremely gifted in math, science and verbal skills and eventually became an engineer working on Magnetic Resonance Imaging systems for a large corporation. In addition the job I do now didn't even exist when I was in high school let alone when I was "tracked" in elementary. Such a system, with or without big government overtones, is a terrible waste of human potential.

9/10/97 Randy Hughey
Mrs Schlafly's article on School to Work is badly misinformed. I am embarrassed as a conservative and as a Christian by her lack of knowledge and lack of objectiv-ity. Her credibility has, in my eyes, suffered. School to work is not Voc Ed. School to work is not about dumbing down academic standards. We have been at School to Work in my little town for several years and find that it is providing students with more information about what choices lay before them in the way of work and what levels of education will be required of them. School to work is a very good idea. Mrs Schfafly should be sent to the board to write "I will do my homework" 500 times.

3

Introductions, Theses, and Conclusions

WRITING INTRODUCTIONS

A classic image: The writer stares glumly at a blank sheet of paper—or a blank screen. Usually, however, this is an image of a writer who hasn't yet begun to write. Once the piece has been started, momentum often helps to carry it forward, even over the rough spots, which can always be fixed later. As a writer, you've surely discovered that getting started when you haven't yet warmed to your task *is* a problem. What's the best way to approach your subject? With high seriousness, a light touch, an anecdote? How best to engage your reader?

Many writers avoid such agonizing choices by putting them off—productively. Bypassing the introduction, they start by writing the body of the piece; only after they're finished the body do they go back to write the introduction. There's a lot to be said for this approach. Because you have presumably spent more time thinking about the topic itself than about how you're going to introduce it, you are in a better position to begin directly with your presentation. And often, it's not until you've actually seen the piece on paper and read it over once or twice that a "natural" way of introducing it becomes apparent. Even if there is no natural way to begin, you are generally in better psychological shape to write the introduction after the major task of writing is behind you and you know exactly what you're leading up to.

Perhaps, however, you can't operate this way. After all, you have to start writing *somewhere*, and if you have evaded the problem by skipping the introduction, that blank page may loom just as large whenever you do choose to begin. If this is the case, then go ahead and write an introduction, knowing full well that it's probably going to be flat and awful. Set down any kind of pump-priming or throat-clearing verbiage that comes to mind, as long as you have a working thesis. Assure yourself that whatever you put down at this point (except for the thesis) "won't count" and that when the time is right, you'll go back and replace it with something that's fit for eyes other than yours. But in the meantime, you'll have gotten started.

The *purpose* of an introduction is to prepare the reader to enter the world of your essay. The introduction makes the connection between the more familiar world inhabited by the reader and the less familiar world of the writer's particular subject; it places a discussion in a context that the reader can understand.

You have many ways to provide such a context. We'll consider just a few of the most common.

Quotation

Here is an introduction to a paper on democracy:

> "Two cheers for democracy" was E. M. Forster's not-quite-wholehearted judgment. Most Americans would not agree. To them, our democracy is one of the glories of civilization. To one American in particular, E. B. White, democracy is "the hole in the stuffed shirt through which the sawdust slowly trickles . . . the dent in the high hat . . . the recurrent suspicion that more than half of the people are right more than half of the time" (915). American democracy is based on the oldest continuously operating written constitution in the world—a most impressive fact and a testament to the farsightedness of the founding fathers. But just how farsighted can mere humans be? In *Future Shock*, Alvin Toffler quotes economist Kenneth Boulding on the incredible acceleration of social change in our time: "The world of today . . . is as different from the world in which I was born as that world was from Julius Caesar's" (13). As we move into the twenty-first century, it seems legitimate to question the continued effectiveness of a governmental system that was devised in the eighteenth century; and it seems equally legitimate to consider alternatives.

The quotations by Forster and White help set the stage for the discussion of democracy by presenting the reader with some provocative and well-phrased remarks. Later in the paragraph, the quotation by Boulding more specifically prepares us for the theme of change that will be central to the essay as a whole.

Historical Review

In many cases, the reader will be unprepared to follow the issue you discuss unless you provide some historical background. Consider the following introduction to an essay on the film-rating system:

> Sex and violence on the screen are not new issues. In the Roaring Twenties there was increasing pressure from civic and religious groups to ban depictions of "immorality" from the screen. Faced with the threat of federal censorship, the film producers decided to clean their own house. In 1930, the Motion Picture Producers and Distributors of America established the Production Code. At first, adherence to the Code was voluntary; but in 1934 Joseph Breen, newly appointed head of the MPPDA, gave the Code teeth. Henceforth all newly produced films had to be submitted for approval to the Production Code Administration, which had the power to award or withhold the Code seal. Without a Code seal, it was virtually impossible for a film to be shown anywhere in the United States, since exhibitors would not accept it. At about the same time, the Catholic Legion of Decency was formed to advise the faithful which films were and were not objectionable. For several decades the Production Code Administration exercised powerful control over what was portrayed in American theatrical films. By the 1960s, however, changing standards of morality had considerably weakened the Code's grip. In 1968, the Production Code was replaced with a rating system designed to keep younger audiences away from films with high levels of sex or violence. Despite its imperfections, this rating system has proved more beneficial to American films than did the old censorship system.

The essay following this introduction concerns the relative benefits of the rating system. By providing some historical background on the rating system, the writer helps readers to understand his arguments. Notice the chronological development of details.

Review of a Controversy

A particular type of historical review is the review of a controversy or debate. Consider the following introduction:

> The *American Heritage Dictionary*'s definition of civil disobedience is rather simple: "the refusal to obey civil laws that are regarded as unjust, usually by employing methods of passive resistance." However, despite such famous (and beloved) examples of civil disobedience as the movements of Mahatma Gandhi in India and the Reverend Martin Luther King, Jr., in the United States, the question of whether or not civil disobedience should be considered an asset to society is hardly clear cut. For instance, Hannah Arendt, in her article "Civil Disobedience," holds that "to think of disobedient minorities as rebels and truants is against the letter and spirit of a constitution whose framers were especially sensitive to the dangers of unbridled majority rule." On the other hand, a noted lawyer, Lewis Van Dusen, Jr., in his article "Civil Disobedience: Destroyer of Democracy," states that "civil disobedience, whatever the ethical rationalization, is still an assault on our democratic society, an affront to our legal order and an attack on our constitutional government." These two views are clearly incompatible. I believe, though, that Van Dusen's is the more convincing. On balance, civil disobedience is dangerous to society.[1]

The negative aspects of civil disobedience, rather than Van Dusen's essay, are the topic of this essay. But to introduce this topic, the writer has provided quotations that represent opposing sides of the controversy over civil disobedience, as well as brief references to two controversial practitioners. By focusing at the outset on the particular rather than the abstract aspects of the subject, the writer hoped to secure the attention of her readers and to involve them in the controversy that forms the subject of her essay.

From the General to the Specific

Another way of providing a transition from the reader's world to the less familiar world of the essay is to work from a general subject to a specific one. The following introduction to a discussion of the 1968 massacre at My Lai, Vietnam, begins with general statements and leads to the particular subject at hand:

> Though we prefer to think of man as basically good and reluctant to do evil, such is not the case. Many of the crimes inflicted on humankind can be dismissed as

---

[1]Michele Jacques, "Civil Disobedience: Van Dusen vs. Arendt." [Unpublished paper. Used by permission.]

being committed by the degenerates of society at the prompting of the abnormal mind. But what of the perfectly "normal" man or woman who commits inhumane acts simply because he or she has been ordered to do so? It cannot be denied that such acts have occurred, either in everyday life or in war-time situations. Unfortunately, even normal, well-adjusted people can become cruel, inhumane, and destructive if placed in the hands of unscrupulous authority. Such was the case in the village of My Lai, Vietnam, on March 16, 1968, when a platoon of American soldiers commanded by Lt. William Calley massacred more than 100 civilians, including women and children.

From the Specific to the General: Anecdote, Illustration

Consider the following paragraph:

> In late 1971 astronomer Carl Sagan and his colleagues were studying data transmitted from the planet Mars to the earth by the Mariner 9 spacecraft. Struck by the effects of the Martian dust storms on the temperature and on the amount of light reaching the surface, the scientists wondered about the effects on earth of the dust storms that would be created by nuclear explosions. Using computer models, they simulated the effects of such explosions on the earth's climate. The results astounded them. Apart from the known effects of nuclear blasts (fires and radiation), the earth, they discovered, would become enshrouded in a "nuclear winter." Following a nuclear exchange, plummeting temperatures and pervading darkness would destroy most of the Northern Hemisphere's crops and farm animals and would eventually render much of the planet's surface uninhabitable. The effects of nuclear war, apparently, would be more catastrophic than had previously been imagined. It has therefore become more urgent than ever for the nations of the world to take dramatic steps to reduce the threat of nuclear war.

The previous introduction went from the general (the question of whether humankind is basically good) to the specific (the massacre at My Lai); this one goes from the specific (scientists studying data transmitted from a space probe) to the general (the urgency of reducing the nuclear threat). The anecdote is one of the most effective means at your disposal of capturing and holding your reader's attention. For decades, speakers have begun their general remarks with a funny, touching, or otherwise appropriate story; in fact, there are plenty of books that are nothing but collections of such stories, arranged by subject.

Question

Frequently, you can provoke the reader's attention by posing a question or a series of questions:

> Are gender roles learned or inherited? Scientific research has established the existence of biological differences between the sexes, but the effect of biology's influence on gender roles cannot be distinguished from society's influence. According

to Michael Lewis of the Institute for the Study of Exceptional Children, "As early as you can show me a sex difference, I can show you the culture at work." Social processes, as well as biological differences, are responsible for the separate roles of men and women.[2]

Opening your essay with a question can be provocative, since it places the reader in an active role: He or she begins by considering answers. *Are* gender roles learned? *Are* they inherited? In this active role, the reader is likely to continue reading with interest.

Statement of Thesis

Perhaps the most direct method of introduction is to begin immediately with the thesis:

> Computers are a mixed blessing. The lives of Americans are becoming increasingly involved with machines that think for them. "We are at the dawn of the era of the smart machine," say the authors of a cover story on the subject in *Newsweek*, "that will change forever the way an entire nation works," beginning a revolution that will be to the brain what the industrial revolution was to the hand. Tiny silicon chips already process enough information to direct air travel, to instruct machines how to cut fabric—even to play chess with (and defeat) the masters. One can argue that development of computers for the household, as well as industry, will change for the better the quality of our lives: computers help us save energy, reduce the amount of drudgery that most of us endure around tax season, make access to libraries easier. Yet there is a certain danger involved with this proliferation of technology.

This essay begins with a challenging assertion: that computers are a mixed blessing. It is one that many readers are perhaps unprepared to consider, since they may have taken it for granted that computers are an unmixed blessing. The advantage of beginning with a provocative (thesis) statement is that it forces the reader to sit up and take notice—perhaps even to begin protesting. The paragraph goes on to concede some of the "blessings" of computerization but then concludes with the warning that there is "a certain danger" associated with the new technology—a danger, the curious or indignant reader has a right to conclude, that will be more fully explained in the paragraphs to follow.

One final note about our model introductions: They may be longer than introductions you have been accustomed to writing. Many writers (and readers) prefer a shorter, snappier introduction. This is largely a matter of personal or corporate style: there is no rule concerning the correct length of an introduction. If you feel that a short introduction is appropriate, use one. You may wish to break up what seems like a long introduction into two paragraphs. (Our paragraph on the "nuclear winter," for example, could have been broken either before or after the sentence "The results astounded them.")

---

[2]Tammy Smith, "Are Sex Roles Learned or Inherited?" [Unpublished paper. Used by permission.]

WRITING A THESIS

A thesis is a one-sentence summary of a paper's content. It is similar, actually, to a paper's conclusion (see page 91) but lacks the conclusion's concern for broad implications and significance. For a writer in the drafting stages, the thesis establishes a focus, a basis on which to include or exclude information. For the reader of a finished product, the thesis anticipates the author's discussion. *A thesis, therefore, is an essential tool for both writers and readers of academic material.*

This last sentence is our thesis for this section. Based on this thesis, we, as the authors, have limited the content of the section; and you, as the reader, will be able to form certain expectations about the discussion that follows. You can expect a definition of a thesis; an enumeration of the uses of a thesis; and a discussion focused on academic material. As writers, we will have met our obligations to you only if in subsequent paragraphs we satisfy these expectations.

The Components of a Thesis

Like any other sentence, a thesis includes a subject and a predicate, which consists of an assertion about the subject. In the sentence "Lee and Grant were different kinds of generals," "Lee and Grant" is the subject and "were different kinds of generals" is the predicate. What distinguishes a thesis from any other sentence with a subject and predicate is that *the thesis presents the controlling idea of the paper.* The subject of a thesis must present the right balance between the general and the specific to allow for a thorough discussion within the allotted length of the paper. The discussion might include definitions, details, comparisons, contrasts—whatever is needed to illuminate a subject and carry on an intelligent conversation. (If the sentence about Lee and Grant were a thesis, the reader would assume that the rest of the paper contained comparisons and contrasts between the two generals.)

Bear in mind when writing thesis statements that the more general your subject and the more complex your assertion, the longer your paper will be. For instance, you could not write an effective ten-page paper based on the following:

> Democracy is the best system of government.

Consider the subject of this sentence ("democracy") and the assertion of its predicate ("is the best system of government"). The subject is enormous in scope; it is a general category composed of hundreds of more specific subcategories, each of which would be appropriate for a paper ten pages in length. The predicate of our example is also a problem, for the claim that democracy is the best system of government would be simplistic unless accompanied by a thorough, systematic, critical evaluation of *every* form of government yet devised. A ten-page paper governed by such a thesis simply could not achieve the level of detail expected of college students.

Limiting the Scope of the Thesis

To write an effective thesis and thus a controlled, effective paper, you need to limit your subject and your claims about it. Two strategies for achieving a thesis of manageable proportions are (1) to begin with a working thesis (this strategy assumes that you are familiar with your topic) and (2) to begin with a broad area of interest and narrow it (this strategy assumes that you are unfamiliar with your topic).

BEGIN WITH A WORKING THESIS

Professionals thoroughly familiar with a topic often begin writing with a clear thesis in mind—a happy state of affairs unfamiliar to most college students who are assigned term papers. But professionals usually have an important advantage over students: experience. Because professionals know their material, are familiar with the ways of approaching it, are aware of the questions important to practitioners, and have devoted considerable time to study of the topic, they are naturally in a strong position to begin writing a paper. Not only do professionals have experience in their fields, but also they have a clear purpose in writing; they know their audience and are comfortable with the format of their papers.

Experience counts—there's no way around it. As a student, you are not yet an expert and therefore don't generally have the luxury of beginning your writing tasks with a definite thesis in mind. Once you choose and devote time to a major field of study, however, you will gain experience. In the meantime, you'll have to do more work than the professional to prepare yourself for writing a paper.

But let's assume that you *do* have an area of expertise, that you are in your own right a professional (albeit not in academic matters). We'll assume that you understand you nonacademic subject—say, backpacking—and have been given a clear purpose for writing: to discuss the relative merits of backpack designs. Your job is to write a recommendation for the owner of a sporting-goods chain, suggesting which line of backpacks the chain should carry. Since you already know a good deal about backpacks, you may already have some well-developed ideas on the topic before you start doing additional research.

Yet even as an expert in your field, you will find that beginning the writing task is a challenge, for at this point it is unlikely that you will be able to conceive a thesis perfectly suited to the contents of your paper. After all, a thesis is a summary, and it is difficult to summarize a presentation yet to be written—especially if you plan to discover what you want to say during the process of writing. Even if you know your material well, the best you can do at the early stages is to formulate a *working thesis*—a hypothesis of sorts, a well-informed hunch about your topic and the claim to be made about it. Once you have completed a draft, you can evaluate the degree to which your working thesis accurately summarizes the content of your paper.[3] If the match is a good one, the working thesis becomes the thesis. If, however, sections of the paper drift from the focus set out in the working thesis, you'll need to revise the thesis and the paper itself to ensure that the presentation is unified. (You'll know that the match between the content and thesis is a good one when every paragraph directly refers to and develops some element of the thesis.)

BEGIN WITH A SUBJECT AND NARROW IT

Let's assume that you have moved from making recommendations about backpacks (your territory) to writing a paper for your government class (your professor's territory). Whereas you were once the professional who knew enough about your subject to begin writing with a working thesis, you are now the student, inexperienced and in need of a great deal of information before you can begin to think of thesis statements. It may be a comfort to know that your government professor would likely be in the same predicament if asked to recommend backpack designs. She would need to spend several weeks, at least, backpacking to become as experienced as you; and it is fair to say that you will need to spend several hours in the library before you are in a position to choose a topic suitable for an undergraduate paper.

Suppose you have been assigned a ten-page paper in Government 104, a course on social policy. Not only do you not have a thesis—you don't have a subject! Where will you begin? First, you need to select a broad area of interest and make yourself knowledgeable about its general features. What if no broad area of interest occurs to you? Don't despair—usually there's a way to make use of discussions you've read in a text or heard in a lecture. The trick is to find a topic that can become personally important, for whatever reason. (For a paper in your biology class, you might write on the digestive system because a relative has stomach troubles. For an economics seminar, you might explore the factors that threaten banks with collapse because your great-grandparents lost their life savings during the Great Depression.) Whatever the academic discipline, try to discover a topic that you'll enjoy exploring; that way, you'll be writing for yourself as much as for your instructor. Some specific strategies to try if no topics occur to you: Review material covered during the semester, class by class if need be; review the semester's readings, actually skimming each assignment. Choose any subject that has held your interest, if even for a moment, and use that as your point of departure.

Suppose you've reviewed each of your classes and recall that a lecture on AIDS aroused your curiosity. Your broad subject of interest, then, will be

---

[3]Some writers work with an idea, committing it to paper only after it has been fully formed. Others begin with a vague notion and begin writing a first draft, trusting that as they write they'll discover what they wish to say. Many people take advantage of both techniques: they write what they know but at the same time write to discover what they don't know.

AIDS. At this point, the goal of your research is to limit this subject to a manageable scope. Although your initial, broad subject will often be more specific than our example, "AIDS," we'll assume for the purposes of discussion the most general case (the subject in greatest need of limiting).

A subject can be limited in at least two ways. First, a general article such as an encyclopedia entry may do the work for you by presenting the subject in the form of an outline, with each item in the outline representing a separate topic (which, for your purposes, may need further limiting). Second, you can limit a subject by asking several questions about it:

> Who?
> What aspects?
> Where?
> When?
> How?

These questions will occur to you as you conduct your research and see the ways in which various authors have focused their discussions. Having read several sources and having decided that you'd like to use them, you might limit the subject "AIDS" by asking *who*—AIDS patients; and *which* aspect—civil rights of AIDS patients.

Certainly, "the civil rights of AIDS patients" offers a more specific focus than does "AIDS"; still, the revised focus is too broad for a ten-page paper in that a comprehensive discussion would obligate you to review numerous particular rights. So again you must try to limit your subject by posing a question. In this particular case, *which aspects* (of the civil rights of AIDS patients) can be asked a second time. Six aspects may come to mind:

- Rights in the workplace
- Rights to hospital care
- Rights to insurance benefits
- Rights to privacy
- Rights to fair housing
- Rights to education

Any *one* of these aspects could provide the focus of a ten-page paper, and you do yourself an important service by choosing one, perhaps two, of the aspects; to choose more would obligate you to too broad a discussion and you would frustrate yourself: Either the paper would have to be longer than ten pages or, assuming you kept to the page limit, the paper would be superficial in its treatment. In both instances, the paper would fail, given the constraints of the assignment. So it is far better that you limit your subject ahead of time, before you attempt to write about it. Let's assume that you settle on the following as an appropriately defined subject for a ten-page paper:

the rights of AIDS patients in the workplace

The process of narrowing an initial subject depends heavily on the reading you do. The more you read, the deeper your understanding of a topic. The deeper your understanding, the likelier it will be that you can divide a broad and complex topic into manageable—that is, researchable—categories. In the AIDS example, your reading in the literature suggested that the civil rights of AIDS patients was an issue at the center of recent national debate. So reading allowed you to narrow the subject "AIDS" by answering the initial questions—the *who* and *which aspects*. Once you narrowed your focus to "the civil rights of AIDS patients," you read further and quickly realized that civil rights in itself was a broad concern that also should be limited. In this way, reading provided an important stimulus as you worked to identify an appropriate subject for your paper.

MAKE AN ASSERTION

Once you have identified the subject, you can now develop it into a thesis by making an assertion about it. If you have spent enough time reading and gathering information, you will be knowledgeable enough to have something to say about the subject, based on a combination of your own thinking and the thinking of your sources. If you have trouble making an assertion, try writing your topic at the top of a page and then listing everything you now know and feel about it. Often from such a list you will discover an assertion that you then can use to fashion a working thesis. A good way to gauge the reasonableness of your claim is to see what other authors have asserted about the same topic. In fact, keep good notes on the views of others; the notes will prove a useful counterpoint to your own views as you write, and you may want to use them in your paper.

Next, make three assertions about your topic, in order of increasing complexity.

1. During the past few years, the rights of AIDS patients in the workplace have been debated by national columnists.
2. Several columnists have offered convincing reasons for protecting the rights of AIDS patients in the workplace.
3. The most sensible plan for protecting the rights of AIDS patients in the workplace has been offered by columnist Anthony Jones.

Keep in mind that these are *working thesis statements*. Because you haven't written a paper based on any of them, they remain *hypotheses* to be tested. After completing a first draft, you would compare the contents of the paper to the thesis and make adjustments as necessary for unity. The working thesis is an excellent tool for planning broad sections of the paper, but—again—don't let it prevent you from pursuing related discussions as they occur to you.

Notice how these three statements differ from one another in the forcefulness of their assertions. The third thesis is *strongly argumentative*. "Most sensible" implies that the writer will explain several plans for protecting the rights of AIDS patients in the workplace. Following the explanation would come a comparison of plans and then a judgment in favor of Anthony Jones's plan. Like any working thesis, this one helps the writer plan the paper. Assuming the paper follows the three-part structure we've inferred, the working thesis would become the final thesis, on the basis of which a reader could anticipate sections of the essay to come.

The first of the three thesis statements, by contrast, is *explanatory*:

> During the past few years, the rights of AIDS patients in the workplace have been debated by national columnists.

In developing a paper based on this thesis, the writer would assert only the existence of a debate, obligating himself merely to a summary of the various positions taken. Readers, then, would use this thesis as a tool for anticipating the contours of the paper to follow. Based on this particular thesis, a reader would *not* expect to find the author strongly endorsing the views of one or another columnist. The thesis does not require the author to defend a personal opinion.

The second thesis *does* entail a personal, intellectually assertive commitment to the material, although the assertion is not as forceful as the one found in statement 3:

> Several columnists have offered convincing reasons for protecting the rights of AIDS patients in the workplace.

Here we have an *explanatory, mildly argumentative* thesis that enables the writer to express an opinion. We infer from the use of the word *convincing* that the writer will judge the various reasons for protecting the rights of AIDS patients; and, we can reasonably assume, the writer herself believes in protecting these rights. Note the contrast between this second thesis and the first one, in which the writer committed himself to no involvement in the debate whatsoever. Still, the present thesis is not as ambitious as the third one, whose writer implicitly accepted the general argument for safeguarding rights (an acceptance she would need to justify) and then took the additional step of evaluating the merits of those arguments in relation to each other.

As you can see, for any subject you might care to explore in a paper, you can make any number of assertions—some relatively simple, some complex. It is on the basis of these assertions that you set yourself an agenda in writing a paper—and readers set for themselves expectations for reading. The more ambitious the thesis, the more complex will be the paper and the greater will be the readers' expectations.

Using the Thesis

Different writing tasks require different thesis statements. The *explanatory thesis* often is developed in response to short-answer exam questions that call for information, not analysis (e.g., "List and explain proposed modifications to contemporary American democracy"). The *explanatory but mildly argumentative thesis* is appropriate for organizing reports (even lengthy ones), as well as essay questions that call for some analysis (e.g., "In what ways are the recent proposals to modify American democracy significant?"). The *strongly argumentative thesis* is used to organize papers and exam questions that call for information, analysis, *and* the writer's forcefully stated point of view (e.g., "Evaluate proposed modifications to health maintenance organizations").

The strongly argumentative thesis, of course, is the riskiest of the three, since you must unequivocally state your position and make it appear reasonable—which requires that you offer evidence and defend against logical objections. But such intellectual risks pay dividends, and if you become involved enough in your work to make challenging assertions, you will provoke challenging responses that enliven classroom discussions. One of the important objectives of a college education is to extend learning by stretching, or challenging, conventional beliefs. You breathe new life into this broad objective, and you enliven your own learning as well, every time you adopt a thesis that sets a challenging agenda both for you (as writer) and for your readers. Of course, once you set the challenge, you must be equal to the task. As a writer, you will need to discuss all the elements implied by your thesis.

To review: A thesis (a one-sentence summary of your paper) helps you organize and your reader anticipate a discussion. Thesis statements are distinguished by their carefully worded subjects and predicates, which should be just broad enough and complex enough to be developed within the length limitations of the assignment. Both novices and experts in a field typically begin the initial draft of a paper with a working thesis—a statement that provides writers with structure enough to get started but with latitude enough to discover what they want to say as they write. Once you have completed a first draft, you should test the "fit" of your thesis with the paper that follows. Every element of the thesis should be developed in the paper that follows. Discussions that drift from your thesis should be deleted, or the thesis changed to accommodate the new discussions.

WRITING CONCLUSIONS

One way to view the conclusion of your paper is as an introduction worked in reverse, a bridge from the world of your essay back to the world of your reader. A conclusion is the part of your paper in which you restate and (if necessary) expand on your thesis. Essential to any conclusion is the summary, which is not merely a repetition of the thesis but a restatement that takes advantage of the material you've presented. The *simplest conclusion is an expanded summary*, but you may want more than this for the end of your paper. Depending on your needs, you might offer a summary and then build onto it a discussion of the paper's significance or its implications for future study, for choices that individuals might make, for policy, and so on. You might also want to urge the reader to change an attitude or to modify behavior. Certainly, you are under no obligation to discuss the broader significance of your work (and a summary, alone, will satisfy the formal requirement that your paper have an ending); but the conclusions of better papers often reveal authors who are "thinking large" and want to connect the particular concerns of their papers with the broader concerns of society.

Here we'll consider seven strategies for expanding the basic summary-conclusion. But two words of advice are in order. First, no matter how clever or beautifully executed, a conclusion cannot salvage a poorly written paper. Second, by virtue of its placement, the conclusion carries rhetorical weight. It is the last statement a reader will encounter before turning from your work. Realizing this, writers who expand on the basic summary-conclusion often wish to give their final words a dramatic flourish, a heightened level of diction. Soaring rhetoric and drama in a conclusion are fine as long as they do not unbalance the paper and call attention to themselves. Having labored long hours over your paper, you have every right to wax eloquent. But keep a sense of proportion and timing. Make your points quickly and end crisply.

Statement of the Subject's Significance

One of the more effective ways to conclude a paper is to discuss the larger significance of what you have written, providing readers with one more reason to regard your work as a serious effort. When using this strategy, you move from the specific concern of your paper to the broader concerns of the reader's world. Often, you will need to choose among a range of significances: A paper on the Wright brothers might end with a discussion of air travel as it affects economies, politics, or families; a paper on contraception might end with a discussion of its effect on sexual mores, population, or the church. But don't overwhelm your reader with the importance of your remarks. Keep your discussion well focused.

The following paragraphs conclude a paper on George H. Shull, a pioneer in the inbreeding and crossbreeding of corn:

> . . . Thus, the hybrids developed and described by Shull 75 years ago have finally dominated U.S. corn production.
>
> The adoption of hybrid corn was steady and dramatic in the Corn Belt. From 1930 through 1979 the average yields of corn in the U.S. increased from 21.9 to 95.1 bushels per acre, and the additional value to the farmer is now several billion dollars per year.
>
> The success of hybrid corn has also stimulated the breeding of other crops, such as sorghum hybrids, a major feed grain crop in arid parts of the world. Sorghum yields have increased 300 percent since 1930. Approximately 20 percent of the land devoted to rice production in China is planted with hybrid seed, which is reported to yield 20 percent more than the best varieties. And many superior varieties of tomatoes, cucumbers, spinach, and other vegetables are hybrids. Today virtually all corn produced in the developed countries is from hybrid seed. From those blue bloods of the plant kingdom has come a model for feeding the world.[4]

The first sentence of this conclusion is a summary, and from it the reader can infer that the paper included a discussion of Shull's techniques for the hybrid

---

[4]From "Hybrid Vim and Vigor" by William L. Brown from pp. 77–78 in *Science* 80–85, November 1984. Copyright 1984 by the AAAS. Reprinted by permission.

breeding of corn. The summary is followed by a two-paragraph discussion on the significance of Shull's research for feeding the world.

Call for Further Research

In the scientific and social scientific communities, papers often end with a review of what has been presented (as, for instance, in an experiment) and the ways in which the subject under consideration needs to be further explored. If you raise questions that you call on others to answer, however, make sure you know that the research you are calling for hasn't already been conducted.

This next conclusion comes from a sociological report on the placement of elderly men and women in nursing homes.

> Thus, our study shows a correlation between the placement of elderly citizens in nursing facilities and the significant decline of their motor and intellectual skills over the ten months following placement. What the research has not made clear is the extent to which this marked decline is due to physical as opposed to emotional causes. The elderly are referred to homes at that point in their lives when they grow less able to care for themselves—which suggests that the drop-off in skills may be due to physical causes. But the emotional stress of being placed in a home, away from family and in an environment that confirms the patient's view of himself as decrepit, may exacerbate—if not itself be a primary cause of—the patient's rapid loss of abilities. Further research is needed to clarify the relationship between depression and particular physical ailments as these affect the skills of the elderly in nursing facilities. There is little doubt that information yielded by such studies can enable health care professionals to deliver more effective services.

Notice how this call for further study locates the author in a large community of researchers on whom she depends for assistance in answering the questions that have come out of her own work. The author summarizes her findings (in the first sentence of the paragraph), states what her work has not shown, and then extends her invitation.

Solution/Recommendation

The purpose of your paper might be to review a problem or controversy and to discuss contributing factors. In such a case, it would be appropriate, after summarizing your discussion, to offer a solution based on the knowledge you've gained while conducting research. If your solution is to be taken seriously, your knowledge must be amply demonstrated in the body of the paper.

> (1) . . . The major problem in college sports today is not commercialism—it is the exploitation of athletes and the proliferation of illicit practices which dilute educational standards.
> (2) Many universities are currently deriving substantial benefits from sports programs that depend on the labor of athletes drawn from the poorest sections of America's population. It is the responsibility of educators, civil rights leaders, and

concerned citizens to see that these young people get a fair return for their labor both in terms of direct remuneration and in terms of career preparation for a life outside sports.

(3) Minimally, scholarships in revenue-producing sports should be designed to extend until graduation, rather than covering only four years of athletic eligibility, and should include guarantees of tutoring, counseling, and proper medical care. At institutions where the profits are particularly large (such as Texas A & M, which can afford to pay its football coach $280,000 a year), scholarships should also provide salaries that extend beyond room, board, and tuition. The important thing is that the athlete be remunerated fairly and have the opportunity to gain skills from a university environment without undue competition from a physically and psychologically demanding full-time job. This may well require that scholarships be extended over five or six years, including summers.

(4) Such a proposal, I suspect, will not be easy to implement. The current amateur system, despite its moral and educational flaws, enables universities to hire their athletic labor at minimal cost. But solving the fiscal crisis of the universities on the backs of America's poor and minorities is not, in the long run, a tenable solution. With the support of concerned educators, parents, and civil rights leaders, and with the help from organized labor, the college athlete, truly a sleeping giant, will someday speak out and demand what is rightly his—and hers—a fair share of the revenue created by their hard work.[5]

In this conclusion, the author summarizes his article in one sentence: "The major problem in college sports today is not commercialism—it is the exploitation of athletes and the proliferation of illicit practices which dilute educational standards." In paragraph 2, he continues with an analysis of the problem just stated and follows with a general recommendation—that "concerned educators, parents, and civil rights leaders" be responsible for the welfare of college athletes. In paragraph 3, he makes a specific proposal, and in the final paragraph, he anticipates resistance to the proposal. He concludes by discounting this resistance and returning to the general point, that college athletes should receive a fair deal.

Anecdote

An anecdote is a briefly told story or joke, the point of which in a conclusion is to shed light on your subject. The anecdote is more direct than an allusion. With an allusion, you merely refer to a story ("Too many people today live in Plato's cave . . ."); with the anecdote, you actually retell the story. The anecdote allows readers to discover for themselves the significance of a reference to another source—an effort most readers enjoy because they get to exercise their creativity.

The following anecdote concludes an article on homicide. In the article, the author discusses how patterns of killing reveal information that can help mental-health professionals identify and treat potential killers before they

---

[5]From Mark Naison, "Scenario for Scandal," *Commonweal* 109 (16), September 24, 1982. Reprinted by permission.

commit crimes. The author emphasizes both the difficulty and the desirability of approaching homicide as a threat to public health that, like disease, can be treated with preventive care.

> In his book, *The Exploits of the Incomparable Mulla Nasrudin*, Sufi writer Idries Shah, in a parable about fate, writes about the many culprits of murder:
> "What is Fate?" Nasrudin was asked by a scholar.
> "An endless succession of intertwined events, each influencing the other."
> "That is hardly a satisfactory answer. I believe in cause and effect."
> "Very well," said the Mulla, "Look at that." He pointed to a procession passing in the street.
> "That man is being taken to be hanged. Is that because someone gave him a silver piece and enabled him to buy the knife with which he committed the murder; or because someone saw him do it; or because nobody stopped him?"[6]

The writer chose to conclude the article with this anecdote. She could have developed an interpretation, but this would have spoiled the dramatic value for the reader. The purpose of using an anecdote is to make your point with subtlety, so resist the temptation to interpret. Keep in mind three guidelines when selecting an anecdote: It should be prepared for (readers should have all the information they need to understand it), it should provoke the reader's interest, and it should not be so obscure as to be unintelligible.

Quotation

A favorite concluding device is the quotation—the words of a famous person or an authority in the field on which you are writing. The purpose of quoting another is to link your work to theirs, thereby gaining for your work authority and credibility. The first criterion for selecting a quotation is its suitability to your thesis. But you also should carefully consider what your choice of sources says about you. Suppose you are writing a paper on the American work ethic. If you could use a line by comedian David Letterman or one by the current secretary of labor to make the final point of your conclusion, which would you choose and why? One source may not be inherently more effective than the other, but the choice certainly sets a tone for the paper. Here's an example of a conclusion that employs quotation:

> There is no doubt that machines will get smarter and smarter, even designing their own software and making new and better chips for new generations of computers. . . . More and more of their power will be devoted to making them easier to use—"friendly," in industry parlance—even for those not trained in computer science. And computer scientists expect that public ingenuity will come up with applications the most visionary researchers have not even considered. One day, a global network of smart machines will be exchanging rapid-fire bursts of information at unimaginable speeds. If they are used wisely, they could help mankind to educate its masses and crack new scientific frontiers.

---

[6]From "The Murder Epidemic" by Nikki Meredith from pp. 42–48 in *Science 80–85*. December 1984. Copyright by AAAS. Reprinted by permission of the author.

"For all of us, it will be fearful, terrifying, disruptive," says SRI's Peter Schwartz. "In the end there will be those whose lives will be diminished. But for the vast majority, their lives will be greatly enhanced." In any event, there is no turning back: if the smart machines have not taken over, they are fast making themselves indispensable—and in the end, that may amount to very much the same thing.[7]

Notice how the quotation is used to position the writer to make one final remark.

Particularly effective quotations may themselves be used to end an essay, as in the following example. Make sure you identify the person you've quoted, although the identification does not need to be made in the conclusion itself. For example, earlier in the paper from which the following conclusion was taken, Maureen Henderson was identified as an epidemiologist exploring the ways in which a change in diet can prevent the onset of certain cancers.

In sum, the recommendations describe eating habits "almost identical to the diet of around 1900," say Maureen Henderson. "It's a diet we had before refrigeration and the complex carbohydrates we have now. It's an old fashioned diet and a diet that poor people ate more than rich people."

Some cancer researchers wonder whether people will be willing to change their diets or take pills on the chance of preventing cancer, when one-third of the people in the country won't even stop smoking. Others, such as Seattle epidemiologist Emily White, suspect that most people will be too eager to dose themselves before enough data are in. "We're not here to convince the public to take anything," she says. "The public is too eager already. What we're saying is, 'Let us see if some of these things work.' We want to convince ourselves before we convince the public."[8]

There is a potential problem with using quotations: If you end with the words of another, you may leave the impression that someone else can make your case more eloquently than you can. The language of the quotation will put your own prose into relief. If your own prose suffers by comparison—if the quotations are the best part of your paper—you'd be wise to spend some time revising. The way to avoid this kind of problem is to make your own presentation strong.

Question

Questions are useful for opening essays, and they are just as useful for closing them. Opening and closing questions function in different ways, however. The introductory question promises to be addressed in the paper that follows. But the concluding question leaves issues unresolved, calling on the readers to assume an active role by offering their own solutions:

---

[7]From "And Man Created the Chip," *Newsweek*, June 30, 1980. Copyright © 1980 by Newsweek, Inc. All rights reserved. Reprinted by permission.

[8]Reprinted by permission. From the September issue of *Science* '84. Copyright © 1984 by the American Association for the Advancement of Science.

> How do we surmount the reaction that threatens to destroy the very gains we thought we had already won in the first stage of the women's movement? How do we surmount our own reaction, which shadows our feminism and our femininity (we blush even to use that word now)? How do we transcend the polarization between women and women and between women and men to achieve the new human wholeness that is the promise of feminism, and get on with solving the concrete, practical, everyday problems of living, working and loving as equal persons? This is the personal and political business of the second stage.[9]

Perhaps you will choose to raise a question in your conclusion and then answer it, based on the material you've provided in the paper. The answered question challenges a reader to agree or disagree with your response and thus also places the reader in an active role. The following brief conclusion ends an article entitled "Would an Intelligent Computer Have a 'Right to Life'?"

> So the answer to the question "Would an intelligent computer have the right to life?" is probably that it would, but only if it could discover reasons and conditions under which it would give up its life if called upon to do so—which would make computer intelligence as precious a thing as human intelligence.[10]

Speculation

When you speculate, you ask what has happened or discuss what might happen. This kind of question stimulates the reader because its subject is the unknown.

The following paragraph concludes "The New Generation Gap" by Neil Howe and William Strauss. In this essay, Howe and Strauss discuss the differences among Americans of various ages, including the "GI Generation" (born between 1901 and 1924), the "Boomers"(born 1943–1961), the "Thirteeners" (born 1961–1981), and the "Millennials" (born 1981–2000):

> If, slowly but surely, Millennials receive the kind of family protection and public generosity that GIs enjoyed as children, then they could come of age early in the next century as a group much like the GIs of the 1920s and 1930s—as a stellar (if bland) generation of rationalists, team players, and can-do civic builders. Two decades from now Boomers entering old age may well see in their grown Millennial children an effective instrument for saving the world, while Thirteeners entering midlife will shower kindness on a younger generation that is getting a better deal out of life (though maybe a bit less fun) than they ever got at a like age. Study after story after column will laud these "best damn kids in the world" as

---

[9]Betty Friedan, "Feminism's Next Step" in *The Second Stage*. New York: Summit Books, 1981.

[10]Robert E. Mueller and Eric T. Mueller, "Would an Intelligent Computer Have a 'Right to Life'?" *Creative Computing*. August 1983.

heralding a resurgent American greatness. And, for a while at least, no one will talk about a generation gap.[11]

Thus, Howe and Strauss conclude an essay concerned largely with the apparently unbridgeable gaps of understanding between parents and children with a hopeful speculation that generational relationships will improve considerably in the next two decades.

---

[11]Excerpt from "The New Generation Gap" by Neil Howe and William Strauss. Originally appeared in *Atlantic*, December 1992. Reprinted by permission of Raphael Sagalyn, Inc.

4

Synthesis

WHAT IS A SYNTHESIS?

A *synthesis* is a written discussion that draws on two or more sources. It follows that your ability to write syntheses depends on your ability to infer relationships among sources—essays, articles, fiction, and also nonwritten sources, such as lectures, interviews, and observations. This process is nothing new for you, since you infer relationships all the time—say, between something you've read in the newspaper and something you've seen for yourself, or between the teaching styles of your favorite and least favorite instructors. In fact, if you've written research papers, you've already written syntheses. In an *academic synthesis*, you make explicit the relationships that you have inferred among separate sources.

The skills you've already learned and practiced from the previous three chapters will be vital in writing syntheses. Clearly, before you're in a position to draw relationships between two or more sources, you must understand what those sources say; in other words, you must be able to *summarize* these sources. It will frequently be helpful for your readers if you provide at least partial summaries of sources in your synthesis essays. At the same time, you must go beyond summary to make judgments—judgments based, of course, on your *critical reading* of your sources. You should already have drawn some conclusions about the quality and validity of these sources; and you should know how much you agree or disagree with the points made in your sources and the reasons for your agreement or disagreement.

Further, you must go beyond the critique of individual sources to determine the relationship among them. Is the information in source B, for example, an extended illustration of the generalizations in source A? Would it be useful to compare and contrast source C with source B? Having read and considered sources A, B, and C, can you infer something else—D (not a source, but your own idea)?

Because a synthesis is based on two or more sources, you will need to be selective when choosing information from each. It would be neither possible nor desirable, for instance, to discuss in a ten-page paper on the war in Vietnam every point that the authors of two books make about their subject. What you as a writer must do is select from each source the ideas and information that best allow you to achieve your purpose.

PURPOSE

Your purpose in reading source materials and then in drawing on them to write your own material is often reflected in the wording of an assignment. For instance, consider the following assignments on the Civil War:

American History: Evaluate your text author's treatment of the origins of the Civil War.

Economics: Argue the following proposition, in light of your readings: "The Civil War was fought not for reasons of moral principle but for reasons of economic necessity."

Government: Prepare a report on the effects of the Civil War on Southern politics at the state level between 1870 and 1917.

Mass Communications: Discuss how the use of photography during the Civil War may have affected the perceptions of the war by Northerners living in industrial cities.

Literature: Select two twentieth-century Southern writers whose work you believe was influenced by the divisive effects of the Civil War. Discuss the ways this influence is apparent in a novel or a group of short stories written by each author. The works should not be *about* the Civil War.

Applied Technology: Compare and contrast the technology of warfare available in the 1860s with the technology available a century earlier.

Each of these assignments creates for you a particular purpose for writing. Having located sources relevant to your topic, you would select, for possible use in a paper, only those parts that helped you in fulfilling this purpose. And how you used those parts, how you related them to other material from other sources, would also depend on your purpose. For instance, if you were working on the government assignment, you might possibly draw on the same source as another student working on the literature assignment by referring to Robert Penn Warren's novel *All the King's Men*, about Louisiana politics in the early part of the twentieth century. But because the purposes of these assignments are different, you and the other student would make different uses of this source. Those same parts or aspects of the novel that you find worthy of detailed analysis might be mentioned only in passing by the other student.

USING YOUR SOURCES

Your purpose determines not only what parts of your sources you will use but also how you will relate them to one another. Since the very essence of synthesis is the combining of information and ideas, you must have some basis on which to combine them. *Some relationships among the material in your sources must make them worth synthesizing.* It follows that the better able you are to discover such relationships, the better able you will be to use your sources in writing syntheses. Notice that the mass communications assignment requires you to draw a *cause-and-effect* relationship between photographs of the war and Northerners' perceptions of the war. The applied technology assignment requires you to *compare and contrast* state-of-the-art weapons technology in the eighteenth and nineteenth centuries. The economics assignment requires you to *argue* a proposition. In each case, *your purpose will determine how you relate your source materials to one another.*

Consider some other examples. You may be asked on an exam question or in instructions for a paper to *describe* two or three approaches to prison reform during the past decade. You may be asked to *compare and contrast* one country's approach to imprisonment with another's. You may be asked to develop an *argument* of your own on this subject, based on your reading. Sometimes (when you are not given a specific assignment) you determine your own purpose: You are interested in exploring a particular subject; you are interested in making a case for one approach or another. In any event, your purpose shapes your essay. Your purpose determines which sources you research, which ones you use, which parts of them you use, at which points in your essay you use them, and in what manner you relate them to one another.

HOW TO WRITE SYNTHESES

Although writing syntheses can't be reduced to a lockstep method, it should help you to follow the guidelines listed in the box on pages 102–103.

For clarity's sake, we'll consider two broad categories of essay (or synthesis) in the remainder of this chapter: the *explanatory* synthesis and the *argument* synthesis. We'll also consider techniques of developing your essays, including the techniques of *comparison-contrast*.

THE EXPLANATORY SYNTHESIS

Many of the papers you write in college will be more or less explanatory in nature. An explanation helps readers to understand a topic. Writers explain when they divide a subject into its component parts and present them to the reader in a clear and orderly fashion. Explanations may entail descriptions that re-create in words some object, place, emotion, event, sequence of events, or state of affairs. As a student reporter, you may need to explain an event—to relate when, where, and how it took place. In a science lab, you would observe the conditions and results of an experiment and record them for review by others. In a political science course, you might review research on a particular subject—say, the complexities underlying the debate over welfare—and then present the results of your research to your professor and the members of your class.

Your job in writing an explanatory paper—or in writing the explanatory portion of an argumentative paper—is not to argue a particular point, but rather *to present the facts in a reasonably objective manner.* Of course,

HOW TO WRITE SYNTHESES

- **Consider your purpose in writing.** What are you trying to accomplish in your essay? How will this purpose shape the way you approach your sources?

- **Select and carefully read your sources,** according to your purpose. Then reread the passages, mentally summarizing each. Identify those aspects or parts of your sources that will help you in fulfilling your purpose. When rereading, *label* or *underline* the sources for main ideas, key terms, and any details you want to use in the synthesis.

- **Formulate a thesis.** Your thesis is the main idea that you want to present in your synthesis. It should be expressed as a complete sentence. Sometimes the thesis is the first sentence, but more often it is *the final sentence of the first paragraph.* If you are writing an *inductively arranged* synthesis (see page 148), the thesis sentence may not appear until the final paragraphs. (See Chapter 3 for more information on writing an effective thesis.)

- **Decide how you will use your source material.** How will the information and the ideas in the passages help you to fulfill your purpose?

- **Develop an organizational plan,** according to your thesis. How will you arrange your material? It is not necessary to prepare a formal outline. But you should have some plan that will indicate the order in which you will present your material and that will indicate the relationships among your sources.

- **Draft the topic sentences for the main sections.** This is an optional step, but you may find it a helpful transition from organizational plan to first draft.

- **Write the first draft** of your synthesis, following your organizational plan. Be flexible with your plan, however. Frequently, you will use an outline to get started. As you write, you may discover new ideas and make room for them by adjusting the outline. When this happens, reread your work frequently, making sure that your thesis still accounts for what follows and that what follows still logically supports your thesis.

- **Document your sources.** You may do this by crediting them within the body of the synthesis or by having a list of "Works Cited" at the end. (See Chapter 5 for more information on documenting sources.)

- **Revise your synthesis,** inserting transitional words and phrases where necessary. Make sure that the synthesis reads smoothly, logically, and clearly from beginning to end. Check for grammatical correctness, punctuation, spelling.

Note: *The writing of syntheses is a recursive process, and you should accept a certain amount of backtracking and reformulating as inevitable. For instance, in developing an organizational plan (step 5 of the procedure), you may discover a gap in your presentation which will send you scrambling for another source—back to step 2. You may find that formulating a thesis and making inferences among sources occur simultaneously; indeed, inferences often are made before a thesis is formulated. Our recommendations for writing syntheses will give you a structure; they will get you started. But be flexible in your approach; expect discontinuity and, if possible, be comforted that through backtracking and reformulating you will eventually produce a coherent, well-crafted essay.*

explanatory papers, like other academic papers, should be based on a thesis. But the purpose of a thesis in an explanatory paper is less to advance a particular opinion than to focus the various facts contained in the paper.

The Y2K Problem, or the Millennium Bug

To illustrate how the process of synthesis works, we'll begin with a number of short, mostly one-paragraph extracts from several articles on the same subject.

Suppose you were writing a paper on a matter that's worrying many computer users: the "2000 bug," more commonly known as "Y2K." According to many computer experts, because of the way that they were originally programmed, the internal calendars in most of the older mainframe computers used by businesses and governments will be unable to recognize the year 2000 as the year that follows 1999—an apparently minor glitch that could in fact have catastrophic consequences for millions of people whose financial and employment records are stored in electronic databases.

Since this is a topic that bears upon a broader subject—the tendency of both hardware and software to become obsolete—you decide to investigate what has been written about this problem, both in print and electronic texts. Here are some paragraphs from the sources you have located:

> As you've probably heard by now, the Year 2000 problem has to do with the grim fact that a stunningly large proportion of mainframe computers still rely on computer code so old that it has only a two-digit field to distinguish a year. This year, for instance, the field consists of a "9" and a "6." At the time most of this code was written, back in the 1960s, mainframes were far less powerful than they are today, and using two digits instead of four was thought to be a quick and dirty way to save memory. Besides, nobody expected that same code to still be in use 30-odd years later. But here we are with the millennium approaching, and that same code still serves as the staple of the world's mainframe computers—calculating interest, spitting out billing statements, and doing the thousand other things that rely on date calculations and that constitute the stuff of daily economic life. If the problem isn't fixed—if we arrive at New Year's Day 2000 with main-

frames unable to tell whether "00" means 1900 or 2000—the world's big computers will almost surely respond by collapsing in a smoldering heap.[1]

As Ian Taylor, the minister for science and technology, recently warned Britain's House of Commons, "Centenarians could appear on primary-school intake lists; all military and aeronautical equipment could be simultaneously scheduled for maintenance; thousands of legal actions could be struck out; student-loan repayments could be scheduled as overdue; and 100 years of interest could be added to credit-card balances. . . ."

The most extreme forecasts are that 45,000 mainframe computers will crash, paralyzing whole societies.

For instance, the Jeremiahs say, everything from elevators to aircraft will cease to function because computers will tell them they have not been serviced for 100 years. Children will receive pensions.[2]

Disagreement over the scope of the problem exists, but discussions of Y2K's economic impact typically deal in billions of dollars. The Gartner Group, a Stamford, Conn.-based market research firm, estimates that Y2K's total global cost will range from $300 billion to $600 billion. Capers Jones, chairman of Burlington, Mass.-based Software Productivity Research, disagrees. He says Y2K appears to be the most expensive single problem in human history, with a tally of $1.6 trillion including expected litigation costs.[3]

Forget the savings and loan crisis, the environmental movement and the tobacco wars—for lawyers, this could be bigger than any of them, or even all of them combined.

"This is a litigation catastrophe waiting to happen," [Los Angeles lawyer Vito] Peraino says. "I firmly believe it's just a matter of time. Too many companies are spending hundreds of millions of dollars. There's no way lawyers aren't going to jump on that."

Those who have jumped are offering their services to conduct legal audits for clients to determine where they may be vulnerable to liability claims, as well as to assess rights of recovery. In fact, a number of firms nationally have set up special practice groups to handle year 2000 matters.[4]

---

[1]Joseph Nocera, "The Story of 00." *Fortune*, August 19, 1996, pp. 50–56.
[2]Simon Reeve, James Adams, and Joseph Davison, "Countdown to Chaos." *World Press Review*, September 1996, p. 37.
[3]Jeff Green, "Ghost in the Machine." *American City and Society*, May 1997, pp. 53–56.
[4]Jan Newberry, "Beat the Clock." *ABA Journal*, June 1997, pp. 49–52.

Create four columns in Microsoft Excel version 5.0a for the PowerPC titled "Year," "Month," "Day," and "Calculated Date." The calculated field is simple enough; it uses the function DATE (Year, Month, Day). Here's the result:

YEAR	MONTH	DAY	CALC DATE
96	1	1	1/1/1996
99	1	1	1/1/1999
0	1	1	#NUM!
1	1	1	#NUM!
2	1	1	#NUM!
3	1	1	#NUM!
4	1	1	1/1/1904
5	1	1	1/1/1905

As you can see, my version of Excel appears to have a teeny problem with the year values of 0,1,2,3. Do you see where this might cause you some Year 2000 problems? Also note that *all* two-digit years (except 0,1,2,3) will translate as 19YY; no windowing is taking effect.[5]

An easy test of a computer's vulnerability is to set the time and date on the PC ahead to 11:58 P.M., Dec. 31, 1999, then shut off the machine. Two minutes later, switch the computer back on. If you see the familiar interface, the computer will not pose a problem. But if the computer prompts you for a date upon restart, you have a problem. Check with the manufacturer to see if an update of the computer's internal software is available. If not, resign yourself to replacing the machine during the next three years.[6]

Let's answer your obvious questions. "Why did we use only 2 digits when we knew we'd need 4 of them when the Year 2000 rolled around?" Well, the bad news is that we did it deliberately, but with the very best of intentions. . . . When computers first entered the business world in the late '60s and the early '70s, they were very expensive. This "expense" was tied directly to two aspects of computing: how much data could the computer store and how fast could it process that data? Even tiny, incremental increases in either attribute resulted in huge cost increases. One way to store data was on a piece of stiff cardboard known as a Hollerith card. By literally punching holes into this Hollerith card according to a set of patterns, and reading those patterns with a beam of light, one could store and retrieve information. Each of these cards had enough space to hold only 80 characters of information. 80 characters is not a lot of information. Write down your full name, address, birthdate, bank balance and bank account number. The chances are very good you'll have written down more than 80 characters—which means you'd have trouble storing all that necessary information onto a single Hollerith card.

This is exactly the problem programmers ran into in the late '60s and early '70s. Hollerith cards were not big enough to store all the data they needed to store. So they compromised. They wrote 230155 instead of 23/01/1955, thereby saving

[5]Peter de Jager, "Walking on Thin Ice." *Datamation*, April 1997, pp. 31–32.

[6]"Preventing Time from Marching Backward." *Nation's Business*, January 1997, p. 44.

themselves 4 precious characters, 2 of which were the crucial "19". When designing a computer application you're always making compromises. There are compromises between what you'd like the computer to do and what you can afford. You compromise between the speed of delivery and the quality of the final product. Hopefully, you understand the consequences of the compromise, because compromises are never perfect solutions.[7]

Come on, you say. Two measly digits? Can't we just unleash some sort of robo-program on all that computer code and clean it up? Well, no. Forget about a silver bullet. It seems that in most mainframe programs, the date appears more often than "M*A*S*H" reruns on television—about once every 50 lines of code. Typically, it's hard to find those particular lines, because the original programs, often written in the ancient COBOL computer language, are quirky and undocumented. After all that analysis, you have to figure out how to rewrite the lines to correctly process the date. Only then comes the most time-consuming step: testing the rewritten program.[8]

Why the terror? A look at BankBoston's information systems reveals a problem far more complex than anyone had imagined. David Iacino, head of the bank's millennium team, likes to show visitors a picture of a real gravestone, shared by a husband and wife both born in 1915. The engraver has assumed that the still-living husband will die this century and has carved "1915-19" beneath his name, leaving space for two more digits. But should the man live beyond 1999, the entire stone would need an ugly recarving. "A similar embedding of assumptions runs throughout our computer systems," says Mr. Iacino.[9]

Let's say you decide to employ what to most people in 1997 is the obvious solution to this date crisis—the four-digit year. You change all your data files and data declarations to accommodate a couple more digits per year, test all the software affected by the change, and sit back and sigh the sigh of satisfied relief: one more crisis solved. Not so fast. Your solution is certainly valid for the foreseeable future, of course. But it will fail come the year 10000. As surely—and in the same way—as the 2000 date crisis.

It's hard to get excited about a future 8,000 years ahead. For one thing, you're probably saying, "What are the odds that information systems as such will be around that long?" Except that's the same kind of thinking that got us into the year 2000 mess. No one believed, back in 1975, the information systems of that day would last another 25 years.[10]

[7]Peter de Jager, "You've Got to Be Kidding!" January 10, 1997, <http://www.year2000.com/archive/kidding/.html> (17 Sept. 1997).

[8]Steven Levy et al., "The Day the World Shuts Down." *Newsweek*, June 2, 1997, pp. 52–59.

[9]"Beware the Millennium." *Economist*, March 8, 1997, pp. 86–87.

[10]Robert L. Glass, "The Next Date Crisis and the Ones After That." *Communications of the ACM*, January 1997, pp. 15–17.

Consider Your Purpose

Here, then, are brief selections from ten sources on the Y2K Problem. How do you go about synthesizing these sources?

First, remember that before considering the *how*, you must consider the *why*. In other words, what is your *purpose* in synthesizing these sources? You might use them for a paper dealing with a broader issue: the dangers of relying too heavily upon computers. If this were your purpose, these sources would be used for only one section of your discussion, and the paper as a whole would advance an *argument* for a particular viewpoint about technology in modern society. Or, for a course dealing with the social impact of technology, you might be studying how the development of new programming languages and the decline of old ones can create unforeseen trouble in the years to come. The 2000 bug would be an important example of this kind of trouble. Or, moving out of the academic world and into the commercial one, you might be a computer consultant preparing a brochure for potential clients who, you hope, will hire you to fix the problem on their computers. In this brochure, you want to spell out the nature of the problem and how serious it could be.

But for now let's keep it simple: you want to write a paper, or a section of a paper, that simply explains the nature of the problem so that people who may be interested, but who know little or nothing about it, will understand the situation. Your job, then, is to write an *explanatory* synthesis—one that presents a focused overview of the problem but does not advance your own opinion on the subject.

We asked one of our students, Amy Matsui, to read these passages and to use them as sources in a short paper on the Y2K problem. We also asked her to write some additional comments describing the process of developing her ideas into a draft. We'll draw upon some of these comments in the following discussion.

Formulate a Thesis

The difference between a purpose and a thesis is a difference primarily of focus. Your purpose provides direction to your research and focus to your paper. Your thesis sharpens this focus by narrowing it and formulating it in the words of a single declarative statement. (Refer to Chapter 3 for additional discussion on formulating thesis statements.)

Since Amy's purpose in this case was simply to present source material with little or no comment, her thesis would be the most obvious statement she could make about the relationship among these passages. By "obvious" we mean a statement based on an idea that is clearly supported in all the passages. Amy describes the process as follows:

> My first attempt at a thesis was a simple statement
> of fact about what would happen to computers in the
> year 2000:

> Many of the world's computers will not be able
> to operate effectively when the year 2000
> arrives.

This was a true statement, but it sounded too bland
and unconcerned, as if what would happen was just
another computer glitch, the kind we run into all the
time. I realized that I needed the thesis to convey
how serious a problem this could be. My next version
followed:

> The world faces computer catastrophe in the year
> 2000.

This thesis was more dramatic, but it still didn't
work very well. It seemed too limited, dealing with
only one aspect of the problem, an aspect that could
be covered in just a paragraph or so. In my next
attempt, I tried to be more comprehensive:

> The world faces computer catastrophe in the
> year 2000, and it will not be easy to fix the
> problem.

This seemed fine for a working thesis, so I decided
to go with it for the first draft and went on to the
next step--organizing my material.

Decide How You Will Use Your Source Material

The easiest way to deal with sources is to summarize them. But because you are synthesizing *ideas* rather than sources, you will have to be more selective than if you were writing a simple summary. You don't have to treat *all* the ideas in your sources, just the ones related to your thesis. Some sources might be summarized in their entirety; others, only in part. Using the techniques of summary, determine section by section the main topics of each source, focusing only on those topics related to your thesis. Write brief phrases in the margin, underline key phrases or sentences, or take notes on a separate sheet of paper or in a word processing file or electronic data filing program. Decide how your sources can help you achieve your purpose and support your thesis. For example, how, if at all, will you use the quotation by Vito Peraino contained in the passage by Newberry? How, if at all, will you use the Excel chart in "Walking on Thin Ice" by Peter de Jager?

Develop an Organizational Plan

An organizational plan is your plan for presenting material to the reader. What material will you present? To find out, examine your thesis. Do the content and structure of the thesis (that is, the number and order of assertions) suggest an organizational plan for the paper? Expect to devote at least one paragraph of your paper to developing each section of this plan. Having identified likely sections, think through the possibilities of arrangement. Ask yourself: What information does the reader need to understand first? How do I build on this first section—what block of information will follow? Think of each section in relation to others until you have placed them all and have worked your way through to a plan for the whole paper.

Study your thesis, and let it help suggest an organization. Bear in mind that any one paper can be written—successfully—according to a variety of plans. Your job before beginning your first draft is to explore possibilities. Sketch a series of rough outlines: arrange and rearrange your paper's likely sections until you sketch a plan that both facilitates the reader's understanding and achieves your objectives as writer. Your final paper may well deviate from your final sketch, since in the act of writing you may discover the need to explore new material, to omit planned material, or to refocus your entire presentation. Just the same, a well-conceived organizational plan will encourage you to begin writing a draft.

Amy describes the process of organizing the material as follows:

```
    In reviewing my sources and writing summary state-
ments, I noted the most important aspects of the year
2000 problem, according to the authors:

    • It will affect most of the world's mainframe com-
      puters.
    • It will create chaos in many areas, including
      billing, school records, and maintenance.
    • It results from problems with a 30-year-old com-
      puter code.
    • It will be very expensive to fix.
    • It will be very time-consuming to fix.
    • It will cause numerous lawsuits.
    • You can check your own personal computer to see if
      it has the problem.
    • The original programmers used only two digits to
      record the date because computer memory storage
      was very expensive in the 1960s and 1970s.
```

I tried to group some of these topics into categories that would have a logical order. The first thing I wanted to communicate was how dependent we had become on computers and how a seemingly minor date glitch that occurred decades ago had the potential for creating major problems for our computer-based modern world.

Next, I thought I should explain just how expensive it would be to fix the problem. I also wanted to warn people that it was not just mainframe computers that would be affected; personal computers might also be subject to the Y2K bug.

Next, I wanted to provide some historical background, to say something about how this problem originated in the early days of mainframe computers. Explaining the origin of the problem would also explain why it's so difficult to fix, why there's no "magic bullet." I'd conclude by summing up the issue and reiterating the need for dealing with the problem quickly and effectively.

Based on the thesis Amy developed above, she developed a six-part paper, including introduction and conclusion:

A. *Introduction:* explanation of our dependence upon computers, of the Year 2000 Problem and its seriousness.
B. Costs of fixing the problem
C. Effect on personal computers
D. Historical cause of the problem
E. Why it is so difficult to fix
F. *Conclusion:* summing up

Write the Topic Sentences

This is an optional step, but writing draft versions of topic sentences will get you started on each main section of your synthesis and will help give you the sense of direction you need to proceed. Here are Amy's draft topic sentences for sections based on the thesis and organization plan she developed. Note that when read in sequence following the thesis, these sentences give an idea of the logical progression of the essay as a whole.

The world faces computer catastrophe, and it will not be easy to fix the problem.

One market research firm, the Gartner Group, has estimated that it could cost as much as $600 billion.

Mainframe computers are most at risk, but many older personal computers could also have the Y2K problem.

People can check their own PCs by resetting the time and date to 11:58 P.M., December 31, 1999.

We can blame this state of affairs on the original computer programmers of the 1960s and 1970s, who first decided to use "68" instead of "1968" to represent the date.

Fixing the Y2K problem is so difficult because there's no "silver bullet"--no quick and reliable way of replacing two numerous digit-date codes with four-digit ones.

It will therefore be extremely expensive and time-consuming to fix the year 2000 problem.

Write Your Synthesis

Here is the first draft of Amy's explanatory synthesis. Thesis and topic sentences are highlighted. Modern Language Association (MLA) documentation style, explained in Chapter 5, is used throughout. Note that for the sake of clarity, parenthetical references are to pages in *Writing and Reading Across the Curriculum*.

The Year 2000 Computer Problem

Amy Matsui

Computers are an essential aspect of the modern world.   1
We use computers to write our letters and reports, pay
our bills, keep track of our financial records and
appointments, and do numerous other important tasks.
We have become so dependent upon computers that if
something goes wrong with our hardware or software, we
almost cannot function.

According to predictions of computer experts, many   2
computer programs will stop working when the year 2000
rolls around. This is because most of the world's mainframe computers, which use only two digits to represent
the year, will be unable to tell the difference between
the year 2000 and the year 1900. Since so much of our
personal and business financial data is stored in government and business computers, and since so much of
this data is tied to dates, the arrival of 2000 could
bring chaos (Nocera 51). The world faces computer catastrophe, and it will not be easy to fix the problem.

It has been estimated by one market research firm,   3
the Gartner Group, that it could cost as much as $600
billion to fix the problem. Capers Jones, head of a
software research firm, claims that "Y2K appears to be
the most expensive single problem in human history";
he believes the potential bill may be $1.6 trillion
(qtd. in Green 54). A good part of this sum will be
the expense of lawsuits; according to Los Angeles
lawyer Vito Peraino, "This is a litigation catastrophe
waiting to happen" (qtd. in Newberry 50).

There are ways that people can check their own PCs   4
by resetting the time and date to 11:58 P.M., December
31, 1999. They should switch off the computer for a
couple of minutes and then restart it. If the computer
prompts them for a date, then it has the problem
("Preventing" 44). People also can check to see if
their software has the Y2K bug. They can create a
table in Microsoft Excel with 1996 to 2000 in the
first vertical column to represent the year, and "1"
and "1" in the next two vertical columns to represent
the month and day. In the fourth vertical column, they
should calculate the dates. If a valid date doesn't
appear in that column for the years after 1999, they
won't be able to use the software after December 31,
1999 (de Jager, "Working" 32).

This state of affairs can be blamed on the original   5
computer programmers of the 1960s and 1970s, who first

decided to use "68" instead of "1968" to represent the date. Two digits were used by these programmers instead of four because memory in early computers was expensive, and so using two digits reduced by half the storage space needed to represent years. Also, before the age of hard drives, data in mainframe computers were stored on cards, and one card could store only 80 characters. Representing dates with two digits considerably reduced the number of cards needed (de Jager, "Kidding," Internet). Now memory is much cheaper, but unfortunately, it is not so easy to put back the missing digits. One commentator used an analogy to illustrate the difficulty: a man born in 1915 has a headstone carved with "1915-" to represent his birth and death dates, leaving two digits of space to represent his death, presumably in the 20th century. But if he lives past the year 1999, two digits' worth of space won't be enough, and his headstone will have to be recarved ("Beware" 86).

Fixing the Y2K problem is so difficult because there's no "silver bullet." There is no quick and reliable way of replacing two numerous digit-date codes with four-digit ones. It will be extremely time-consuming to locate the date representations (which often are inconsistent) in millions of lines of computer code written years or even decades ago in the COBOL language, which is now obsolete (Levy et al 54).

6

Thus, it will be extremely expensive and time-consuming to fix the year 2000 problem. Although the original computer programmers had no intention of creating this problem, they have left us with a large task to deal with. Once the year 2000 rolls around, much of our modern technology and communications may stop unless we take immediate steps to solve this problem.

7

Works Cited

"Beware the Millennium." *Economist* 8 Mar. 1997: 86–87.
de Jager, Peter. "Walking on Thin Ice." <u>Datamation</u> Apr. 1997: 31–32.

---. "You've Got to be Kidding!" 10 Jan. 1997.
17 Sept. 1997. <http://www.year2000.com/archive/kidding.html>

Glass, Robert L. "The Next Date Crisis and the Ones After That." <u>Communications of the ACM</u> Jan. 1997: 15–17.

Green, Jeff. "Ghost in the Machine." <u>American City and Society</u> May 1997: 53–56.

Levy, Steven et al. "The Day the World Shuts Down." <u>Newsweek</u> 2 June 1997: 52–59.

Newberry, Jan. "Beat the Clock." <u>ABA Journal</u> June 1997: 49–52.

Nocera, Joseph. "The Story of 00." <u>Fortune</u> 19 Aug. 1996: 50–56.

"Preventing Time from Marching Backward." <u>Nation's Business</u> Jan. 1997: 44.

Reeve, Simon, James Adams, and John Davison. "Countdown to Chaos." <u>World Press Review</u> Sept. 1996: 37.

Discussion and Suggestions for Revision

The following section summarizes the key points and suggestions for revision made during Amy's conference with her instructor.

TITLE AND PARAGRAPH 1

Although the title and first paragraph introduce the subject, they do so in a rather general and uninformative way. Almost any reader already knows what kinds of tasks we use computers for in modern life. The final sentence of this paragraph, normally the place for a *thesis*, is too general. It also is somewhat misleading about the real subject of this paper.

Suggestions for Revision: Make the present, bland title more inviting and interesting. Begin the first paragraph with a more striking statement or question, and either end the paragraph with a thesis or combine this short paragraph with the next one which more fully describes the essential problem.

PARAGRAPH 2

The topic sentence of the second paragraph is serviceable but dull, giving little indication of the urgency with which many view the Y2K problem. The paragraph also is vague about just how daily activities could be affected.

Suggestions for Revision: Provide some specific examples of the "chaos" predicted toward the end of the paragraph. And since the next paragraph focuses on the cost of fixing the problem, incorporate into the thesis the idea of how *expensive* a fix could be.

PARAGRAPH 3

In paragraph 3 you draw upon two sources, Green and Newberry, to indicate how costly the problem will be to fix. This paragraph provides good support, but the topic sentence is flat because of your use of the passive voice ("It has been estimated by one market research firm . . . .").

Suggestion for Revision: Convert the first sentence of this paragraph from passive to *active* voice.

PARAGRAPH 4

In paragraph 4, you focus on simple tests devised by de Jager and the anony-mous author of "Preventing Time from Marching Backward" to determine whether people's personal computers have the Y2K problem. But readers may well be confused at this point since the paper has focused so far only on the problems affecting mainframe business and corporate computers and the costs of fixing them. How did we get from that subject to a discussion of *per-sonal* computers?

Suggestions for Revision: Create a new topic sentence that serves as a *tran-sition* from the problems largely arising from mainframe computers with the Y2K problem to personal computers. Also, make the writing more interesting by using *imperative voice* ("You can check your own computer. . . . Switch off the computer. . . ."), instead of the more general declarative ("People can check. . . .").

PARAGRAPH 5

In paragraph 5, you draw upon two authors, de Jager and the anonymous author of "Beware the Millennium," to explain how the problem originated decades ago. The information provided is relevant but sometimes awkwardly phrased because of the passive voice ("This state of affairs can be blamed on the original computer programmers. . . ."). You also could enliven the prose by occasionally recasting statements as questions and then answering them.

Suggestions for Revision: Rewrite passive sentences as active, wherever pos-sible. Convert the statement about putting back the missing digits into a ques-tion.

PARAGRAPH 6

In paragraph 6, you draw upon Levy to explain why the problem isn't open to an easy solution. But once again, the lack of a transition from the headstone analogy to the Y2K fix might prove jarring to the reader.

Suggestions for Revision: Develop one or more transitional sentences at the beginning of this paragraph, making the connection between the headstone analogy and the difficulty in fixing the Y2K problem.

PARAGRAPH 7

The final paragraph merely repeats what you have already said earlier in the paper. The last sentence is especially weak, with its flavor of business jargon ("unless we take immediate steps to solve this problem"), indicating that you have not devised an interesting way of concluding the paper.

Suggestions for Revision: Try ending on a lighter note, thus avoiding a pervasive sense of "doom and gloom." Draw upon Glass to point out that in 8,000 years we may face a Y10K problem. Such a conclusion would keep the focus on the essential cause and effect of the present situation while absurdly projecting it to a future time that no one alive today will ever need to worry about.

At this point, you may want to try your own hand at creating a final draft of this essay by following the suggestions above—together with your own best judgment about how to improve the first draft. Your instructor will be able to provide you with Amy's final draft, which is reprinted in the *Instructor's Manual*.

WRITING EXERCISE: AN EXPANDED EXPLANATORY SYNTHESIS DRAWING UPON MORE SOURCES

Now we'll give you an opportunity to practice your skills in planning and writing an explanatory synthesis. On pages 116–127 we provide seven additional sources on the Y2K problem. (One of them, "Year 2000: 1000 Days Away: Survey Results," consists entirely of charts and graphs.)

Read these additional sources; then plan and write an explanatory synthesis dealing with some aspect of their subject matter. You don't have to draw upon *all* of the sources. If you want to restrict your subject, as before, to the 2000 problem, feel free to do that. And even with this highly focused subject, don't feel compelled to bring in every last source.

▮ *YEAR 2000* *

1000 Days Away Survey Results
(sample size = 112 companies)

An Independent Study Performed for Cap Gemini

DR. HOWARD A. RUBIN
HEIDI ALBRECHT BATTAGLIA

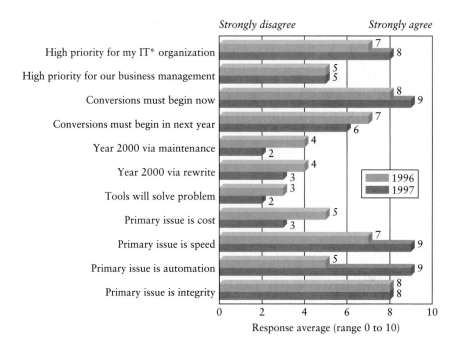

Survey Response Summary: Attitudes in regard to the Year 2000 crisis

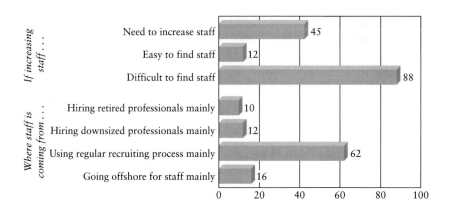

Survey Response Summary: Percent indicating "YES" to various staffing issues

---

IT: Information Technology.

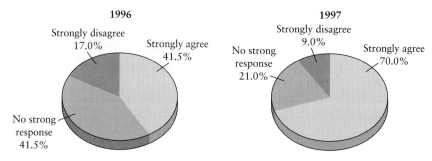

Survey Response Summary: Year 2000 issues are a high priority for our IT organization

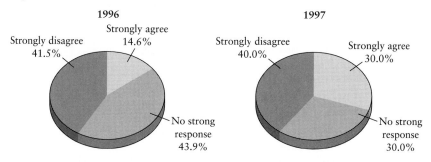

Survey Response Summary: Year 2000 issues are a high priority for our business management

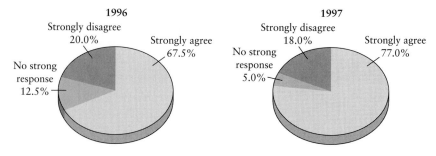

Survey Response Summary: We must begin to address Year 2000 issues now

Military Memo: Year 2000 Fixes—
*Top Priority**

DENNIS J. REIMER
TOGO D. WEST, JR.

This article has been posted with full permission and knowledge of the United States Government.

---

*Reimer, Dennis J., Memo, "Year 2000 Fixes—Top Priority." 31 Mar. 1997.
<http://www.year2000.com/archive/army.html>

Top Priority Memo

DEPARTMENT OF THE ARMY
WASHINGTON, D.C. 20310
March 31, 1997

MEMORANDUM

SUBJECT: Year 2000 Fixes—Top Priority

Our Army's ability to shoot, move and communicate effectively—both within our Service and in conjunction with Joint and Combined forces—has come to rely heavily on automation. The increasing importance of information dominance, with its continual introduction of more sophisticated technological weaponry to the inventory, has made this reliance critical. Consequently, the year 2000 (Y2K) problem must not be allowed to pose any risk to the war-fighter. This is a matter that affects the credibility of the Army with its soldiers and the public that we serve.

We must deal with Y2K now so that our soldiers can continue to place well-founded confidence in their weaponry and automation tools through the change in millennium. To this end, each Army organization responsible for system development and maintenance should ensure that Y2K is a high systems resource priority. Therefore, effective immediately, all nonessential sustainment requirements and enhancements will be postponed until systems have been analyzed, fixed, tested, and certified Y2K compliant using existing resources.

As part of this process, each system will be seriously considered for elimination. Only those automation systems which truly assist in mission accomplishment should remain in your inventory. Ensure that you are not spending any resources on fixing systems that are no longer essential, or, that will not be in use past January 1, 2000.

Dennis J. Reimer   Togo D. West, Jr.
General, United States Army   Secretary of the Army
Chief of Staff

Year 2000 Upgrades:
A Small Price to Pay*

LEON KAPPELMAN

When you told your CEO about the year 2000 problem, you probably were   1
hit with, "How did this happen?" or "Who's responsible?" But you don't
need to be defensive. When you explain why it happened, go beyond the usual

---

excuses and whip out some dollar estimates of how much you saved in storage costs over the past 30-odd years.

The explanation starts in the late 1950s and early '60s when the major 2 constraint was the number of characters that fit on an '80-column punched card. We recorded dates with only two digits representing the year to save precious space.

Disk storage became widely available in the early '60s, but it was very 3 expensive. In 1963, 1M byte of mainframe hard disk storage cost about $10,600 per megabyte per year in 1995 dollars. So to save money, we continued to use two-digit year fields.

By 1972, the annual cost of mainframe storage was down to $1,600 per 4 megabyte, and by 1983 it had plummeted to just under $22 per megabyte (in 1995 dollars). And now the comparable figure is $1.08 per megabyte.

So just how much have we saved our organizations over the years? 5

Depending on the industry and application, 3% to 6% of the data stored 6 in organizational databases is dates. Using four-digit rather than two-digit year fields would have required 33% more storage for dates (MMDDYYYY vs. MMDDYY). Using the 3% figure for date density, we conservatively estimate that 1% more disk storage would have been required through the years if we had stored all four digits of the year field.

One percent doesn't seem like much until you consider several factors: the 7 large volumes of data stored by organizations, the historically high cost of storage and the rate of inflation. So for every 1G byte of organizational data stored, a 1% savings represents 10M bytes. Designing systems to save 1% of storage costs since 1963 has saved between $1.2 million and $2 million per gigabyte (in 1995 dollars), depending on how quickly storage equipment was upgraded.

Then there's the cost of capital as well as the opportunity cost had those 8 precious dollars been spent on storage rather than invested in other ventures. Using a conservative 10% internal rate of return on capital, $16 million to $24 million (in 1995 dollars) has been saved per gigabyte of total storage in the 30 years from 1963 through 1992.

That's a realistic indication of the economic benefits of our date storage 9 decisions.

So a company with, say, an average of 10G bytes of data over that 30- 10 year span has saved $160 million to $240 million (in 1995 dollars) overall. In light of these savings, the $10 million to $50 million estimated cost for a company to fix the so-called "millennium bug" pales in comparison to the benefits accrued.

We don't have to go "hat in hand" to our CEO to beg for year 2000 pro- 11 ject funds. We can present a strong business case for why the upgrade costs are quite reasonable in light of the many millions of dollars we've saved in the past 35 years.

Confessions of a Former Programmer*

GARY H. ANTHES

Every night at midnight, the secret messages went out from U.S. Navy head-   1
quarters in London to military bases and ships in the North Atlantic and
Mediterranean.

The messages contained coordinates for Soviet targets of U.S. nuclear   2
weapons, and the targets were subject to daily adjustment as the weather
changed.

But sometimes the messages were late, delayed by a computer program   3
that occasionally and mysteriously went into an endless loop. I was a pro-
grammer at the Fleet Operations Control Center for U.S. Naval Forces Europe
in London, and in 1972 I was assigned to fix the recalcitrant message generator.

Thus did I become a tiny part of the Pentagon's huge year 2000 problem.   4

The program was written—not by me—in the 1960s in the Navy   5
Electronics Laboratory International Algorithmic Compiler (NELIAC), an
Algol derivative.

NELIAC was complex, and I couldn't figure out just why the program   6
would sometimes begin its endless loops. But I found a way to make it behave
by manipulating the addresses passed to and from a key subroutine. NELIAC
couldn't do that, so I inserted assembler language code at the beginning and
end of the routine.

It was a brute-force solution. It was a kludge. The program with my addi-   7
tions was even uglier than before, and it remained completely undocumented.
But it worked, and I got no more calls in the middle of the night.

The program was full of date and time logic, but because those parts   8
worked fine, I never looked at them and never learned whether they were fit
for duty in the 21st century.

Not that I cared.   9

If I didn't care enough to write documentation for my replacement who   10
was coming on board a year later, and my boss didn't care enough to insist on
it, we certainly weren't going to worry about an event that might occur long
after we both had left the Navy.

So there you have it: a large program written in an obscure language with   11
assembler language patches and no documentation, supporting a mission-
critical, classified application. It's enough to make you weep for those doing
the Defense Department's year 2000 systems work.

By now, my messaging program probably has been replaced by some off-   12
the-shelf commercial package. But plenty more like it remain, looping on
endlessly, as it were, toward Jan. 1, 2000.

Breakthrough May Help Squish Y2K Bug*

KEVIN MANEY

A new tool to fix the Year 2000 problem may be a breakthrough that could   1
speed the government, banks and companies toward a solution.

The product is Millennium Solution from little-known Data Integrity   2
(DII) of Waltham, Mass. It was cleared for a U.S. patent in June, and
Citibank, Credit Suisse First Boston, NationsBank and the Interior
Department have signed on. The Federal Aviation Administration is said to be
testing Millennium Solution.

Some who have used the product say it has cut the time to make Year   3
2000 fixes on some software by 80% or more. Bob Osmond, a consultant
making Year 2000 fixes for Citibank, says using Millennium Solution allowed
him to test and fix in one day a system that had 100,000 lines of code, compared with 30 days for another tool.

The Year 2000 bug threatens a majority of computer systems worldwide.   4
Many software programs were written using two digits for dates, such as 98
for 1998. Once 2000 rolls around, computers would not know if 00 is 2000
or 1900.

But DII founder Allen Burgess had an insight: In most systems, the two-   5
digit dates only cause a problem when the computer needs to do math—say,
to figure a person's age or mortgage end date. In 2001 (or 01), a computer
would figure the age of someone born in 1902 (or 02) as negative 1.

Year 2000 tools usually search for dates, then either add digits to the   6
dates (to make 02 into 1902) or change the logic of the program to recognize
dates for what they should be—any of which takes time, causes errors and can
add to the processing burden on a computer system. "I woke up in the middle
of the night and had the idea," Burgess says. "It's not a date problem. It's a
math problem. We had to find and fix the math."

That's turned out to be so simple, fast and uncluttered, it has left tech-   7
nology analysts aghast. One part of Millennium Solution searches for the
math in a software program. Once it's found, the program—which, remember, can only handle two digits for dates—is instructed to add 50, then add 50
again. The result is always right. Take 01, subtract 02, and you get negative
01. Add 50 to get 49; add 50 more to get 99—the correct age in 2001 of the
person born in 1902.

"It could be a real find," says Andy Bochman of Aberdeen Group, which   8
has looked closely at Millennium Solution.

It won't, however, end the Year 2000 bug. Millennium Solution doesn't   9
yet seem to work in all systems. "It's not a silver bullet," says Jim Duggan,
analyst at Gartner Group.

How to Profit from
the Coming Y2K Glitch*

BRUCE McCALL

... You don't understand the first thing about the techno-bug that's foment- 1
ing worldwide panic a year and a half in advance of Zero-Zero Hour. Bingo!
Your mind's all the more free to focus on the thousand and one ways the Y2K
glitch can put you on E-Z Street!

Why not do what a Louisiana aviatrix did—turn door-to-door voodoo 2
into money magic? "I charge ten dollars, in advance, to lift the software
curse," she burbles. "And after deducting the cost of poultry parts and an old
Flit gun I'm clearing over a hundred a day, easy!" Or how about the Istanbul,
Michigan, pre-med student who paid for his off-campus duplex by marketing
Sek-Paks—packets of extra seconds, to be injected into computers just before
Zero-Zero Hour—which will outfox the Y2K glitch by creating a "hyper-time
bump"?

Why don't you know what these people know—that as midnight 3
approaches on New Year's Eve, 1999, the world will be grabbing at straws to
avoid having its computers and every megabyte in them go up in a puff of
acrid smoke? Now you do.

Consider Electro-Liniment 2000, a miracle salve perfected by an Idaho 4
homemaker in her own pantry—before, that is, she moved into a mansion in
London's swank Belgravia district and started hostessing private bashes for
the Stones. "Rub it on your monitor's screen," say the instructions, "and millions of invisible Keodytes™ start reaching deep, deep, deep into your computer's electronic 'brain.'" Result: "silicon amnesia"—thwarting the Y2K
glitch by forgetting it's there.

Still unsure? Don't fail to overlook the thousands of secure government 5
jobs the glitch will create. Think: Millions of blankets will have to be para-
dropped over Silicon Valley and Wall Street in the aftermath of Y2K Day.
Who'll get to earn overtime for collecting them all afterward? Has imminent
info-meltdown brought your bank to the brink of chaos? Your-Name-Here
Trust Co., with its board-certified abacus-instructor teams, to the rescue!

"I'm personally going with simple stickers and fridge magnets saying 6
'Turn Off Computer Before Midnight, 1999,'" reports freelancer Yram Senoj
(not her real name). Meanwhile, hubby Bruno plans to double their nest egg
by telemarketing the Boom-R-Ang Software Saver, which will reverse the
incoming electric current with a patented Jack-in-the-Box action, knocking
Y2K out cold for up to twenty-six hours—for longer-lasting relief than
Sudafed or Motrin.

"Ironically, I worked it out on the computer," says part-time Oxford don 7
Cecil. "If it's as the experts say, and computers are all going to suddenly shift

*From: McCall, Bruce. "How to Profit from the Coming Y2K Glitch." *New Yorker*, July
13, 1998: 80.

back to the year 1900 when the year 2000 hits, there will be a crying need for early-twentieth-century wall calendars. I'm already into my sixteenth printing!"

By now you get the bold idea! All you need is a bold idea! But there's no   8
time to waste. Word just in from Tex R., in Hawaii: he's sewn up the Y2K rights for all of New Mexico. And, according to the Drudge Report, spooky-looking computocrat Bill Gates may start kidnapping senior citizens, tots—your own loved ones—any day now, forcing them to work around the clock in secret labs under his futuristic Seattle "think pad" to find a solution to the glitch, so that he can make all the money, leaving nada for you. And, come on now, doesn't he already have enough?

If you agree that it's time somebody else shared the wealth, rush your   9
$199 today and receive a free computer talisman as a bonus, a lucky charm that harnesses the power of the ancients and is fully compatible with all hardware platforms. Offer expires 11:59 P.M., December 31, 1999.

*A Grave Problem with Y2K**

It's the Low-Tech Millennium Bug:
Thousands of Prepaid Headstones with 19s Already
Carved—and Owners Not Ready to Die.

JANET WILSON

Jesse and Lewis Stibitz are pragmatic people who like to save money and plan   1
ahead. They don't flinch at the prospect of death.

Because of that, they now have a Y2K problem etched in stone.   2
Specifically, it's engraved on their pre-carved headstone, where their dates of death are already started off: "19 ."

The question is, 19 what? The century is running out of numbers, and the   3
Stibitzes, who are 82 and 84 years old respectively, are doing quite well, thank you.

"When we had that done in the '50s, I said to the man who did the stone,   4
"What if I don't die in 19-something?" Jesse Stibitz said. "And he looked at me and said, 'You will.' Well, [the carver] is dead a long time now, and here I am."

The Stibitzes are like many couples who prepaid for their burials down to   5
the last detail, including headstones carved in advance. The names, a bit of Bible verse, and the birth date were all included in the "final rate" or "pre-need" packages offered by cemeteries.

And so were the first two digits of the year of death. Since monument   6
makers charge by the character, a few dollars could be saved by carving the first two numbers in advance.

**From: Janet Wilson. "A Grave Problem with Y2K." *Los Angeles Times*. January 29, 1999. Copyright © 1999, *Los Angeles Times*. Reprinted by permission.*

With more Americans, especially women, living into their 90s and beyond, those blank spaces have been going uncarved. And chances are that many will remain that way for what's left of the 1900s.   7

From New England's stony churchyards to the mausoleums of New Orleans, to the lawns of Southern California marked with bronze plaques, an estimated 250,000 empty graves with the numbers 19 carved on their headstones are out there, waiting.   8

Just as programmers are scrambling to fix a glitch that allowed a computer to assume that the first two digits of its internal date were 19, cemetery administrators and headstones manufacturers are discussing their "millennium problem" at conferences, membership meetings and even in special howto seminars showing how to fix that which is cast in stone.   9

Up for grabs is who will pay the costs of fixing the problem: the consumer who paid cold cash long ago for a complete package, or the company that sold it to them? Also of concern is which repair method will endure for generations to come.   10

But since 2000 is still 11 months away, no one is taking corrective action just yet.   11

"Put it this way, nobody's saying, 'Save yourself some money, die early,'" said Billy Schlitzberger of Houston, who inherited his monument business from his father.   12

Schlitzberger said his father, who was known as "Papa Stone" in the industry, set up shop in 1922 and worked in it for 66 years before being buried in a nearby Catholic cemetery. He never included "19" on any headstone.   13

"My daddy never made that mistake . . . because he saw that coming out of the last century. There were people in 1922 dying with 18 on their stones, and as a young man he took note of that . . . We just left them blank."   14

Jesse Stibitz occasionally visits her future grave and gazes at the double granite stone with the couple's names and the "19 blanks," as she calls their pre-carved years of death.   15

The Mt. Carmel, Penn., couple bought their plot more than 40 years ago, along with the headstone—or actually, the back of another couple's headstone that was already in place at Mt. Carmel Cemetery. The whole package cost less than $1,000.   16

They were barely hitting middle age at the time, but Jesse Stibitz has always been able to look death in the eye.   17

"It doesn't bother me one bit," she said. "I'm real realistic, I think ahead. Not as far as the date goes, but that wasn't my fault."   18

Options being discussed for fixing stones like the Stibitzes' include the following: 19

• The epoxy method, in which a gluelike adhesive is mixed with crushed stone the color of the marker and affixed over the offending numbers. The procedure is the cheapest, but is not as long-lasting, and the repair may be slightly visible, especially when it gets wet.   20

- The attractive and affordable bronze option, which calls for bolting a   21
  bronze plaque with the correct dates over the outdated one. It is dismissed by purists as a Band-Aid approach.
- Longer-lasting but costlier spot polishing or refacing. Refacing involves   22
  cutting off the entire front panel of the stone and re-carving it, guaran-
  teeing a fresh, updated look. Spot polishing involves grinding down just
  the 19 and replacing it with 20.

The cost could range from about $200 for epoxy to $2,000—as much as   23
it generally costs for a new gravestone—for a complete refacing.

Greg Patzer, executive vice president of the Monument Builders of North   24
America, an industry group based in Des Plaines, Ill., said the epoxy method
should work fine in most cases. The method, used in the past to correct
errors, can have a life span of several decades if done correctly. Schlitzberger
conducted hands-on seminars for the trade association on the epoxy method
last year.

But that doesn't mean he and other memorialists, as certified headstone   25
carvers are called, endorse the epoxy. They prefer refacing or at least spot polishing.

"Spot polishing only involves a mild depression," according to Jed   26
Hendrickson, who inherited Santa Barbara Monumental Co. from his grandfather, and is president of the California Monument Assn. Hendrickson said
"for some reason in California, especially Southern California, our grave
carvings are very shallow. . . . It won't be that hard to polish the numbers
down."

Hendrickson does not like epoxy because "it's an adhesive. It won't last   27
as long."

Similarly, he dismisses a bronze plaque as a patch job that costs almost   28
the same as classier methods.

Another hot topic at industry conferences and seminars is who will   29
handle the cost—the consumer or the company.

At El Toro Memorial Park in Orange County, there are half a dozen pre-   30
inscribed "19" death dates among more than 7,000 graves, including two
elderly women, one born in 1922, the other in 1915. Neither woman nor any
next of kin could be located for comment, illustrating another problem cemetery administrators say they often have.

"People move, and you'd think they'd notify us, but they forget, I guess,"   31
said El Toro secretary Dianna Torrence.

Wherever they are, when their time comes, their estates or relatives may   32
end up footing the bill for the headstone they thought they had paid for long
ago. El Toro is a county-administered burial ground, and the mortuaries the
two women made original arrangements with more than 20 years ago have
changed hands.

"Unless they've got a contract with the original company, they could be   33
out of luck," said Orange County Cemetery District executive manager Sam
Randall. "After all, you can't just erase it."

Monument makers say the pre-sales agreements are usually handled by   34
mortuaries and funeral homes, not by them. They predict that cemetery
owners, many of which are large conglomerates that have bought up family
operators, will refuse to pay.

"It would not surprise me if they would simply tell the family that the   35
whole stone will have to be replaced," Hendrickson said, "then bill them for
the cost of the whole new memorial, not even mention the options."

But a spokesman for Houston-based Service Corp. International, the   36
largest death care industry chain, said the company would honor any previous arrangements.

Terry Hemeyer of Pierpont Communications, which handles media   37
inquiries for the company, said officials have discussed the millennium problem and determined that "the consumer would not suffer."

All sides agree that because the whole death care industry tends to think   38
long-range, most stopped carving 19 in the 1960s or '70s, forestalling future
shock.

"My customers are thinking 10 or 15 years while I'm thinking 100 or   39
500 years," said Hendrickson, who considers each of the 125 headstones his
company produces each month as not just works of art, but as permanent
installations.

Dick Fisher, publicity manager of Forest Lawn Memorial Parks and   40
Mortuaries, which has five locations in Greater Los Angeles, responded dis-
missively at the thought that the company's burial grounds might have a
"19" problem.

"First of all, we don't have gravestones, we have memorial tablets [set in   41
the ground]," he said. "We actually pioneered memorial tablets, and we
never pre-carved anything. We don't anticipate any problem."

Jesse Stibitz said she had been assured by the cemetery sexton that   42
although the repair would not be included in the couple's prepaid package, it
would be relatively easy and inexpensive for her children to fix.

She said she told her son and daughter it would be OK if they stuck a real   43
Band-Aid over the offending numbers.

"Just kidding!" she hastily added.   44

■ ■ ■

THE ARGUMENT SYNTHESIS

The explanatory synthesis, as we have seen, is fairly modest in purpose. It
emphasizes the materials in the sources themselves, not the student writer's
interpretation. Since your reader is not always in a position to read your
sources, this kind of synthesis, if well done, can be very informative. But the
main characteristic of the explanatory synthesis is that it is designed more to
inform than to *persuade*. As we have said, the thesis in the explanatory synthesis is less a device for arguing a particular point than a device for providing
focus and direction to an objective presentation of facts or opinions. As the
writer of an explanatory synthesis, you remain, for the most part, a detached
observer.

You may disagree with this, contending that the revised thesis[11] we developed for the explanatory synthesis on the Y2K problem does represent a particular point of view: "The world faces computer meltdown, and it will be neither easy nor cheap to fix the problem." To an extent, this does represent a particular point of view (i.e., one that considers the problem very serious)—particularly since some people think that the seriousness of the problem has been overblown. Note, however, that with the sources we provided, it would be difficult to come to any conclusion other than the one represented in the thesis, unless one had enough knowledge of and experience with computer programming to be able to make an independent judgment. In this sense, our thesis is not debatable: it serves to focus and organize the discussion that follows rather than to advance an argument.

In contrast to an explanatory thesis, an argumentative thesis is *persuasive in purpose*. Writers working with the same source materials might conceive of and support other, opposite theses. So the thesis for an argument synthesis is a claim about which reasonable people could disagree. It is a claim about which—given the right arguments—your audience might be persuaded to agree with your position. The strategy of your argument synthesis is therefore to find and use convincing *support* for your *claim*.

The Elements of Argument: Claim, Support, Assumption

Let's consider the terminology we've just used. One way of looking at an argument is to see it as an interplay of three essential elements: claim, support, and assumption. A *claim* is a proposition or conclusion that you are trying to prove. You prove this claim by using *support* in the form of fact or expert opinion. Linking your supporting evidence to your claim is your *assumption* about the subject. This assumption, also called a *warrant*, is—as we've discussed in Chapter 2—an underlying belief or principle about some aspect of the world and how it operates. By nature, assumptions (which are often unstated) tend to be more general than either claims or supporting evidence. What we do when we *analyze* is to apply the principles and generations that underlie our assumptions to the specific evidence that we will use as support for our claims.

For example, here are the essential elements of an argument advocating parental restriction of television viewing for their high school children:

Claim

```
High school students should be restricted to no more
than two hours of TV viewing per day.
```

Support

```
An important new study, as well as the testimony of
educational specialists, reveals that students who
```

---

[11]The revised Y2K essay appears in the *Instructor's Manual* to this book.

```
watch more than two hours of TV a night have, on aver-
age, lower grades than those who watch less TV.
```

Assumption
```
Excessive TV viewing is linked to poor academic per-
formance.
```

As another example, if we converted the thesis for our explanatory synthesis into a *claim* suitable for an argument synthesis, it might read as follows:

```
We must devote massive efforts and expenditures to
solve the Year 2000 problem, a disaster that threatens
chaos for our computer-driven society.
```

Here are the other elements of this argument:

Support
```
Most mainframe computers used by business and govern-
ment, those that maintain our financial records, oper-
ate on programs that will not recognize 2000 as a
legitimate date and so will "crash" when that year
arrives.
```

Assumption
```
The Year 2000 problem is so complex and pervasive that
it cannot be dealt with easily or cheaply.
```

For the most part, arguments should be constructed logically, or rationally, so that claims are supported by evidence in the form of facts or expert opinions. As we'll see, however, logic is only one component of effective arguments.

The Three Appeals of Argument: *Logos, Ethos, Pathos*

Speakers and writers have never relied upon logic alone in advancing and supporting their claims. Over 2000 years ago, the Athenian philosopher and rhetorician Aristotle explained how speakers attempting to persuade others to their point of view could achieve their purpose primarily by relying on one or more *appeals*, which he called *logos*, *ethos*, and *pathos*.

Since we frequently find these three appeals employed in political argument, we'll use political examples in the following discussion. But keep in mind that these appeals are also used extensively in advertising, in legal cases, in business plans, and in many other types of argument.

LOGOS

Logos is the rational appeal, the appeal to reason. If they expect to persuade their audiences, speakers must argue logically and must supply appropriate evidence to support their case. Logical arguments are commonly of two types (often combined). The *deductive* argument begins with a generalization, then cites a specific case related to that generalization, from which follows a conclusion. A familiar example of deductive reasoning, used by Aristotle himself, is the following:

> All men are mortal. (*generalization*)
> Socrates is a man. (*specific case*)
> Socrates is mortal. (*conclusion about the specific case*)

In the terms we've just been discussing, this deduction may be restated as follows:

> Socrates is mortal. (*claim*)
> Socrates is a man. (*support*)
> All men are mortal. (*assumption*)

An example of a more contemporary deductive argument may be seen in President John F. Kennedy's address to the nation in June 1963 on the need for sweeping civil rights legislation. Kennedy begins with the generalizations that it "ought to be possible . . . for American students of any color to attend any public institution they select without having to be backed up by troops" . . . and that "it ought to be possible for American citizens of any color to register and vote in a free election without interference or fear of reprisal." Kennedy then provides several specific examples (primarily recent events in Birmingham, Alabama) and statistics to show that this was not the case. He concludes:

> We face, therefore, a moral crisis as a country and a people. It cannot be met by repressive police action. It cannot be left to increased demonstrations in the streets. It cannot be quieted by token moves or talk. It is time to act in the Congress, in your state and local legislative body, and, above all, in all of our daily lives.

Underlying Kennedy's argument is the following reasoning:

> All Americans should enjoy certain rights.
> Some Americans do not enjoy these rights.
> We must take action to ensure that all Americans enjoy these rights.

Another form of logical argumentation is *inductive* reasoning. A speaker or writer who argues inductively begins not with a generalization, but with several pieces of specific evidence. The speaker then draws a conclusion from this evidence. For example, in a recent debate on gun control, Senator Robert C. Byrd (Democrat, Virginia) cites specific examples of rampant crime: "I read of young men being viciously murdered for a pair of sneakers, a leather jacket, or $20." He also offers statistical evidence of the increasing crime rate: "in 1951, there were 3.2 policemen for every felony committed in the United States; this year [1990] nearly 3.2 felonies will be committed per every police officer. . . ." He concludes, "Something has to change. We have to stop the crimes that are distorting and disrupting the way of life for so many innocent, law-respecting Americans. The bill that we are debating today attempts to do just that."

Statistical evidence also was used by Senator Edward M. Kennedy (Democrat, Massachusetts) in arguing for passage of the Racial Justice Act of 1990, designed to ensure that minorities were not disproportionately singled out for the death penalty. Kennedy points out that 17 defendants in Fulton County, Georgia, between 1973 and 1980, were charged with killing police officers but the only defendant who received the death sentence was a black man. Kennedy also cites statistics to show that "those who killed whites were 4.3 times more likely to receive the death penalty than were killers of blacks," and that "in Georgia, blacks who killed whites received the death penalty 16.7 percent of the time, while whites who killed received the death penalty only 4.2 percent of the time."

Of course, the mere piling up of evidence does not in itself make the speaker's case. As Donna Cross explains in "Politics: The Art of Bamboozling,"[12] politicians are very adept at "card-stacking." And statistics can be selected and manipulated to prove anything, as demonstrated in Darrell Huff's landmark book *How to Lie with Statistics* (1954). Moreover, what appears to be a logical argument may, in fact, be fundamentally flawed. (See Chapter 2 and Cross's article for a discussion of logical fallacies and faulty reasoning strategies.) On the other hand, the fact that evidence can be distorted, statistics misused, and logic fractured does not mean that these tools of reason can be dispensed with or should be dismissed. It means only that audiences have to listen and read critically—perceptively, knowledgeably, and skeptically (though not necessarily cynically).

Sometimes, politicians can turn their opponents' false logic against them. Major R. Owens, a Democratic Representative from New York, attempted to counter what he took to be the reasoning on welfare adopted by his opponents:

> Welfare programs create dependency and so should be reformed or abolished.
> Aid to Families with Dependent Children (AFDC) is a welfare program.
> AFDC should be reformed or abolished.

In his speech opposing the Republican welfare reform measure of 1995 Owens simply changes the specific (middle) term, pointing out that federal subsidies for electric power in the West and Midwest and farmers' low-rate home loan mortgages are, in effect, welfare programs ("We are spoiling America's farmers by smothering them with socialism. . . ."). The logical conclusion—that we should reform or eliminate farmers' home loan mortgages—would clearly be unacceptable to many of those pushing for reform *of* AFDC. Owens thus suggests that opposition to AFDC is based less on reason than on lack of sympathy for its recipients.

---

[12]Chapter in *Word Abuse: How the Words We Use Use Us* (1979).

ETHOS

Ethos, or the ethical appeal, is an appeal based not on the ethical rationale for the subject under discussion, but rather on the ethical nature of the person making the appeal. A person making an argument must have a certain degree of credibility: That person must be of good character, be of sound sense, and be qualified to hold the office or recommend policy.

For example, Elizabeth Cervantes Barrón, running for senator as the peace and freedom candidate, begins her statement, "I was born and raised in central Los Angeles. I grew up in a multiethnic, multicultural environment where I learned to respect those who were different from me. . . . I am a teacher and am aware of how cutbacks in education have affected our children and our communities."

On the other end of the political spectrum, American Independent gubernatorial candidate Jerry McCready also begins with an ethical appeal: "As a self-employed businessman, I have learned firsthand what it is like to try to make ends meet in an unstable economy being manipulated by out-of-touch politicians." Both candidates are making an appeal to *ethos*, based on the strength of their personal qualities for the office they seek.

L. A. Kauffman is not running for office but rather writing an article arguing against socialism as a viable ideology for the future ("Socialism: No." *Progressive*, April 1, 1993). To defuse objections that he is simply a tool of capitalism, Kauffman begins with an appeal to *ethos*: "Until recently, I was executive editor of the journal *Socialist Review*. Before that I worked for the Marxist magazine, *Monthly Review*. My bookshelves are filled with books of Marxist theory, and I even have a picture of Karl Marx up on my wall." Thus, Kauffman establishes his credentials to argue knowledgeably about Marxist ideology.

Conservative commentator Rush Limbaugh frequently makes use of the ethical appeal by linking himself with the kind of Americans he assumes his audiences to be (what author Donna Cross calls "glory by association"):

> In their attacks [on me], my critics misjudge and insult the American people. If I were really what liberals claim—racist, hatemonger, blowhard—I would years ago have deservedly gone into oblivion. The truth is, I provide information and analysis the media refuses to disseminate, information and analysis the public craves. People listen to me for one reason: I am effective. And my credibility is judged in the marketplace every day. . . . I represent America's rejection of liberal elites. . . . I validate the convictions of ordinary people.[13]

PATHOS

Finally, speakers and writers appeal to their audiences by the use of *pathos*, the appeal to the emotions. There is nothing inherently wrong with using an

---

[13]Rush Limbaugh, "Why I Am a Threat to the Left," *Los Angeles Times*, October 9, 1994.

emotional appeal. Indeed, since emotions often move people far more powerfully than reason alone, speakers and writers would be foolish not to use emotion. And it would be a drab, humorless world if human beings were not subject to the sway of feeling, as well as reason. The emotional appeal becomes problematic only if it is the *sole or primary* basis of the argument. This is the kind of situation that led, for example, to the internment of Japanese Americans during World War II or that leads to periodic political spasms to enact anti–flag-burning legislation.

President Reagan was a master of emotional appeal. He closed his first inaugural address with a reference to the view from the Capitol of Arlington National Cemetery, where lie thousands of markers of "heroes":

> Under one such marker lies a young man, Martin Treptow, who left his job in a small-town barbershop in 1917 to go to France with the famed Rainbow Division. There, on the western front, he was killed trying to carry a message between battalions under heavy artillery fire. We're told that on his body was found a diary. On the flyleaf under the heading, "My Pledge," he had written these words: "America must win this war. Therefore, I will work, I will save, I will sacrifice, I will endure, I will fight cheerfully and do my utmost, as if the issue of the whole struggle depended on me alone." The crisis we are facing today does not require of us the kind of sacrifice that Martin Treptow and so many thousands of others were called upon to make. It does require, however, our best effort and our willingness to believe in ourselves and to believe in our capacity to perform great deeds, to believe that together with God's help we can and will resolve the problems which now confront us.

Surely, Reagan implies, if Martin Treptow can act so courageously and so selflessly, we can do the same. The logic is somewhat unclear, since the connection between Martin Treptow and ordinary Americans of 1981 is rather tenuous (as Reagan concedes); but the emotional power of Martin Treptow, whom reporters were sent scurrying to research, carries the argument.

A more contemporary president, Bill Clinton, also uses *pathos*. Addressing an audience of the nation's governors on his welfare plan, Clinton closed his remarks by referring to a conversation he had held with a welfare mother who had gone through the kind of training program Clinton was advocating. Asked by Clinton whether she thought that such training programs should be mandatory, the mother said, "I sure do." When Clinton asked her why, she said:

> Well, because if it wasn't, there would be a lot of people like me home watching the soaps because we don't believe we can make anything of ourselves anymore. So you've got to make it mandatory." And I said, "What's the best things about having a job?" She said, "When my boy goes to school, and they say, 'What does your mama do for a living?' he can give an answer."

Clinton uses the emotional power he counts on in that anecdote to set up his conclusion: "We must end poverty for Americans who want to work. And we must do it on terms that dignify all of the rest of us, as well as help our country to work better. I need your help, and I think we can do it."

Developing an Argument Synthesis

The Wal-Mart Controversy

To demonstrate how to plan and draft an argument synthesis, let's consider another subject. If you were taking an economics or business economics course, you would probably at some point consider the functioning of the market economy. For consumers, one of the most striking trends in this economy in recent times has been the rise of superstores such as Wal-Mart, Home Depot, Costco, Staples, and Best Buy. Most consumers find these vast shopping outlets convenient and economical. Others find them an abomination, contending that these ugly and predatory outlets drive out of business the Mom-and-Pop stores that were the staple of small-town America.

Suppose, in preparing to write a short paper on Wal-Mart, you came up with the following sources. Read them carefully, noting as you do the kinds of information and ideas you could draw upon to develop an *argument synthesis*.

Note: To save space and for the purpose of demonstration, the following passages are brief excerpts only. In preparing your paper, naturally you would draw upon entire articles from which these extracts were made.

Ban the Bargains

BOB ORTEGA

Bob Ortega, reporter for the Wall Street Journal, *introduces the Wal-Mart debate with a particular slant: the involvement of aging activists from the 1960s and 1970s. This article appeared in* The Wall Street Journal *on October 11, 1994.*

"ULTIMATE PREDATOR"

To denizens of the counterculture, Wal-Mart stands for everything they dis-   1
like about American society—mindless consumerism, paved landscapes and homogenization of community identity.

"We've lost a sense of taste, of refinement—we're destroying our culture   2
and replacing it with . . . Wal-Mart," says Allan B. Wolf, a Kent State University alumnus now trying to keep Wal-Mart out of Cleveland Heights, Ohio, where he is a high-school teacher.

"We'd never have fought another business as hard as we've fought Wal-   3
Mart," says Alice Doyle, of Cottage Grove, Ore., who calls the giant discounter "the ultimate predator."

At Wal-Mart headquarters in Bentonville, Ark., company officials char-   4
acterize all opponents, ex-hippie and otherwise, as "a vocal minority." They deny that their store has become, for some activists, a kind of successor to Vietnam.

Don Shinkle, a Wal-Mart vice president, says "there are maybe eight to   5
10 sites where there is opposition." However, there are at least 40 organized groups actively opposing proposed or anticipated Wal-Mart stores in com-

munities such as Oceanside, Calif.; Gaithersburg, Md.; Quincy, Mass.; East Lampeter, Penn.; Lake Placid, N.Y.; and Gallatin, Tenn.

Local opposition has delayed some stores and led the company to drop its plans in Greenfield, Mass., and two other towns in that state; as well as in Bath, Maine; Simi Valley, Calif.; and Ross and West Hempfield, Pa.   6

PROTEST MARCH

The residents of Cleveland Heights hope to join that list. On a recent Monday there, a large crowd, including some people who had been tear-gassed at Kent State 24 years ago for protesting the war, led a march on city hall and chanted, "One, two, three, four—we don't want your Wal-Mart store." Says Jordan Yin, a leader of the anti–Wal-Mart coalition, "Old hippies describes the whole town."   7

In Fort Collins, Colo., Shelby Robinson, a former Vietnam War protest-er and member of the George McGovern campaign, has little success these days persuading her old companions to join her lobbying for solar power, animal rights or vegetarianism. But when Wal-Mart proposed coming to town, the activist impulses of her old friends came alive, and many joined her in fighting the store.   8

"I really hate Wal-Mart," says Ms. Robinson, a self-employed clothing designer. "Everything's starting to look the same, everybody buys all the same things—a lot of small-town character is being lost. They disrupt local communities, they hurt small businesses, they add to our sprawl and pollution because everybody drives farther, they don't pay a living wage—and visually, they're atrocious."   9

In Boulder, Colo., Wal-Mart real-estate manager Steven P. Lane tried appeasing the city's ex-hippies by proposing a "green store" that he said would be environmentally friendly, right up to the solar-powered sign out front. But when city council member Spencer Havlick, who helped organize the first Earth Day in 1970, suggested that the whole store be solar-powered, Mr. Lane fell silent. Dr. Havlick, professor of environmental design at the University of Colorado, says, "Their proposal wasn't as green as they thought it was."   10

These activists have hardly slowed Wal-Mart's overall expansion—it expects to add 125 stores next year to its existing 2,504. But even so, some Wal-Mart sympathizers find them irritating. William W. Whyte, who bid good riddance to hippies when he graduated from Kent State in 1970, now finds himself annoyed by them again, as an analyst following Wal-Mart for Stephens Inc.   11

"The same types of people demonstrating then are demonstrating now," grumbles Mr. Whyte. "If they had to worry about putting food on the table, they'd probably be working for Wal-Mart instead of protesting them."   12

Some Wal-Mart supporters call the protesters elitists for opposing a pur-veyor of low-priced goods. But Tim Allen, who at age 26 has been active in the development of a "green" housing co-op and an organizer of the Wal-Mart protest movement in Ithaca, replies that "people aren't poor because they're paying 15 cents more for a pair of underwear."   13

Eight Ways to Stop the Store

ALBERT NORMAN

Albert Norman is a well-known opponent of Wal-Mart and a former anti-Vietnam activist. In this article, which appeared in The Nation *(Mar. 28, 1994), Norman outlines his strategies for blocking Wal-Mart. Norman's bias is clear—and will be balanced by some of the other selections that follow.*

Last week I received another red-white-and-blue invitation to a Wal-Mart   1
grand opening in Rindge, New Hampshire. I say "another" because Wal-Mart has already invited me to its new store in Hinsdale, New Hampshire, just twenty miles away. With over $67 billion in annual sales, and more than 2,000 stores, Wal-Mart holds a grand opening somewhere in America almost every other day. But it will never invite me to its new store in Greenfield, Massachusetts, my home town, because Greenfield voters recently rejected Wal-Mart at the ballot box.

The Arkansas mega-retailer has emerged as the main threat to Main   2
Street, U.S.A. Economic impact studies in Iowa, Massachusetts, and elsewhere suggest that Wal-Mart's gains are largely captured from other merchants. Within two years of a grand opening, Wal-Mart stores in an average-size Iowa town generated $10 million in annual sales—by "stealing" $8.3 million from other businesses.

Since our victory in Greenfield, we have received dozens of letters from   3
"Stop the WAL" activists in towns like East Aurora, New York; Palatine, Illinois; Mountville, Pennsylvania; Williston, Vermont; Branford, Connecticut—small communities fighting the battle of Jericho. If these towns follow a few simple rules of engagement, they will find that the WAL *will* come tumbling down:

Quote scripture: Wal-Mart founder Sam Walton said it best in his auto-   4
biography: "If some community, for whatever reason, doesn't want us in there, we aren't interested in going in and creating a fuss." Or, as one company V.P. stated, "We have so many opportunities for building in communities that want Wal-Marts, it would be foolish of us to pursue construction in communities that don't want us." The greater the fuss raised by local citizens, the more foolish Wal-Mart becomes.

Learn Wal-Math: Wal-Mathematicians only know how to add. They   5
never talk about the jobs they destroy, the vacant retail space they create or their impact on commercial property values. In our town, the company agreed to pay for an impact study that gave enough data to kill three Wal-Marts. Dollars merely shifted from cash registers on one side of town to Wal-Mart registers on the other side of town. Except for one high school scholarship per year, Wal-Mart gives very little back to the community.

Exploit their errors: Wal-Mart always makes plenty of mistakes. In our   6
community, the company tried to push its way onto industrially zoned land.

It needed a variance not only to rezone land to commercial use but also to permit buildings larger than 40,000 square feet. This was the "hook" we needed to trip the company up. Rezoning required a Town Council vote (which it won), but our town charter allowed voters to seek reconsideration of the vote, and ultimately, a referendum. All we needed was the opportunity to bring this to the general public—and we won. Wal-Mart also violated state law by mailing an anonymous flier to voters.

Fight capital with capital: In our town (pop. 20,000) Wal-Mart spent   7
more than $30,000 trying to influence the outcome of a general referendum. It even created a citizen group as a front. But Greenfield residents raised $17,000 to stop the store—roughly half of which came from local businesses. A media campaign and grass-roots organizing costs money. If Wal-Mart is willing to spend liberally to get into your town, its competitors should be willing to come forward with cash also.

Beat them at the grass roots: Wal-Mart can buy public relations firms and   8
telemarketers but it can't find bodies willing to leaflet at supermarkets, write dozens of letters to the editor, organize a press conference or make calls in the precincts. Local coalitions can draw opinion-makers from the business community (department, hardware and grocery stores, pharmacies, sporting goods stores), environmentalists. political activists and homeowners. Treat this effort like a political campaign: The Citizens versus the WAL.

Get out your vote: Our largest expenditure was on a local telemarketing   9
company that polled 4,000 voters to identify their leanings on Wal-Mart. Our volunteers then called those voters leaning against the WAL two days before the election. On election day, we had poll-watchers at all nine precincts. If our voters weren't at the polls by 5 P.M., we reminded them to get up from the dinner table and stop the mega-store.

Appeal to the heart as well as the head: One theme the Wal-Mart culture   10
has a hard time responding to is the loss of small-town quality of life. You can't buy rural life style on any Wal-Mart shelf—once you lose it, Wal-Mart can't sell it back to you. Wal-Mart's impact on small-town ethos is enormous. We had graphs and bar charts on job loss and retail growth—but we also communicated with people on an emotional level. Wal-Mart became the WAL—an unwanted shove into urbanization, with all the negatives that threaten small-town folks.

Hire a professional: The greatest mistake most citizen groups make is   11
trying to fight the world's largest retailer with a mimeo-machine mentality. Most communities have a political consultant nearby, someone who can develop a media campaign and understand how to get a floppy disk of town voters with phone numbers. Wal-Mart uses hired guns; so should anti–Wal-Mart forces.

"Your real mission," a Wal-Mart executive recently wrote to a commu-   12
nity activist, "is to be blindly obstructionist." On the contrary, we found it was Wal-Mart that would blindly say anything and do anything to bulldoze its way toward another grand opening in America. But if community coalitions organize early, bring their case directly to the public and trumpet the downside of mega-store development, the WALs will fall in Jericho.

Wal-Mart's War on Main Street

SARAH ANDERSON

Sarah Anderson is an economic analyst for a think tank in Washington, D.C. This article originally appeared in The Progressive *(November 1994).*

Across the country, thousands of rural people are battling to save their local   1
downtowns. Many of these fights have taken the form of anti–Wal-Mart campaigns. In Vermont, citizens' groups allowed Wal-Mart to enter the state only after the company agreed to a long list of demands regarding the size and operation of the stores. Three Massachusetts towns and another in Maine have defeated bids by Wal-Mart to build in their communities. In Arkansas, three independent drugstore owners won a suit charging that Wal-Mart had used "predatory pricing," or selling below cost, to drive out competitors. Canadian citizens are asking Wal-Mart to sign a "Pledge of Corporate Responsibility" before opening in their towns. In at least a dozen other U.S. communities, groups have fought to keep Wal-Mart out or to restrict the firm's activities.

By attacking Wal-Mart, these campaigns have helped raise awareness of   2
the value of locally owned independent stores on Main Street. Their concerns generally fall in five areas:

- *Sprawl Mart*—Wal-Mart nearly always builds along a highway outside   3
  town to take advantage of cheap, often unzoned land. This usually attracts
  additional commercial development, forcing the community to extend services (telephone and power lines, water and sewage services, and so forth)
  to that area, despite sufficient existing infrastructure downtown.
- *Wal-Mart channels resources out of a community*—studies have shown   4
  that a dollar spent on a local business has four or five times the economic spin-off of a dollar spent at a Wal-Mart, since a large share of Wal-
  Mart's profit returns to its Arkansas headquarters or is pumped into
  national advertising campaigns.
- *Wal-Mart destroys jobs in locally owned stores*—a Wal-Mart-funded   5
  community impact study debunked the retailer's claim that it would create
  a lot of jobs in Greenfield, Massachusetts. Although Wal-Mart planned to
  hire 274 people at its Greenfield store, the community could expect to
  gain only eight net jobs, because of projected losses at other businesses
  that would have to compete with Wal-Mart.
- *Citizen Wal-Mart?*—in at least one town—Hearne, Texas—Wal-Mart   6
  destroyed its Main Street competitors and then deserted the town in
  search of higher returns elsewhere. Unable to attract new businesses to the
  devastated Main Street, local residents have no choice but to drive long
  distances to buy basic goods.
- *One-stop shopping culture*—in Greenfield, where citizens voted to keep   7
  Wal-Mart out, anti–Wal-Mart campaign manager Al Norman said he
  saw a resurgence of appreciation for Main Street. "People realized there's
  one thing you can't buy at Wal-Mart, and that's small-town quality of

life," Norman explains. "This community decided it was not ready to die for a cheap pair of underwear."

Small towns cannot return to the past, when families did all their shop-   8
ping and socializing in their hometown. Rural life is changing and there's no use denying it. The most important question is, who will define the future? Will it be Wal-Mart, whose narrow corporate interests have little to do with building healthy communities? Will it be the department of transportation, whose purpose is to move cars faster? Will it be the banks and suppliers primarily interested in doing business with the big guys? Or will it be the people who live in small towns, whose hard work and support are essential to any effort to revitalize Main Street?

Who's Really the Villain?

JO-ANN JOHNSTON

A freelance writer based in Greenfield, Massachusetts—a town that successfully fought off the construction of a Wal-Mart superstore—Jo-Ann Johnston challenges the logic of anti–Wal-Mart forces and argues that the store would have helped to address fundamental problems with the local economy. This selection originally appeared in the journal Business Ethics *(May–June 1995).*

Cheap underwear. That's all Wal-Mart Corp. contributes as it squeezes the   1
life out of a community's downtown, according to Albert Norman, an outspoken Wal-Mart critic. His sentiment—and talent for rousing support—led folks in rural Greenfield, Massachusetts, to block the company's plans to build a store there. It also established the political consultant as one of the best known opponents to "Sprawl-mart" in the country. But fighting off Wal-Mart hasn't done much for the 18,845 residents of Greenfield.

As in numerous other communities during the past ten years, Wal-Mart   2
simply found a site just a short distance away from its original target. In this case, it's in Orange, a smaller town located up the road about twenty-five minutes from downtown Greenfield. Meanwhile, this area ranks as the state's second poorest in per capita income. And in January, it posted an unemployment rate of 6.1 percent—attributable partly to the recent closings of a paper plant, a container factory, and a large store that sold liquidated merchandise. Wal-Mart would have brought to Greenfield 240 tax-paying jobs and increased retail traffic.

Set to open later this year, the store in Orange will be yet another exam-   3
ple of how saying "go away" to the likes of Wal-Mart overlooks a much deeper problem facing small-town America: the need to change a way of doing business while maintaining, or improving, a deeply valued way of life. An increasing number of people are beginning to realize that small-town merchants need to adapt to changes in their communities, the economy, and their industries instead of chastising an outside company. That means accepting the fact that a Wal-Mart, or a similar retailer, may become a neighbor.

Such thinking is hogwash as far as anti–Wal-Marters are concerned.   4
Consumerism has run amok if a town figures it needs a Wal-Mart, says
Norman [see "Eight Ways to Stop the Store"], who today works with people
in Illinois, Ohio, New England, and other regions to stop Wal-Marts and
other large discount retailers from setting up shop. His list of reasons to fight
such chain stores is lengthy, with perhaps one of the most popular being the
potential loss of small-town quality of life. People move to small towns from
urban or suburban America in part to escape from mall and shopping strip
development, he says, not to see it duplicated.

That emotional argument carries weight, especially in New England,   5
where twelve cities and one state, Vermont, have fought Wal-Mart. A current
battle is taking place in Sturbridge, a historic town in eastern Massachusetts
where community activists are fighting to keep Wal-Mart out. The town
draws 60 percent of its general business from tourism-related trade, says
local Wal-Mart opponent Carol Goodwin. "We market history," she says.
The town and its re-creation of an early American village are the state's
second largest tourist attraction. A big cookie-cutter mart off the freeway
could obscure this town of eight thousand's special appeal, she says.

Sturbridge may want to take a lesson from its neighbor to the northwest,   6
however. Merchants in Greenfield face the possible loss of business due to the
fact that Wal-Mart found a location "just over the hill" from where it was
first looking to build. Kenneth Stone, an economist at Iowa State University
and the country's leading researcher on the economic impacts of Wal-Marts,
found that towns in the Midwest and East suffered a "retail leakage" of
shoppers who instead drove to the closest regional shopping center with a discount store.

Does that mean Greenfield shoppers will now drive to Orange? Well, sev-   7
eral of the town's shoppers complained during the Wal-Mart battle that area
merchants could use competition because of their poor selection, high prices,
limited hours, and lackluster service. Meanwhile, Wal-Mart has a good reputation for service. A *Consumer Reports* reader poll in late 1994 found that
fifty thousand people rated Wal-Mart the highest in customer satisfaction of
"value-oriented chains."

In many ways, what is happening to small-town retail corridors is simi-   8
lar to how mom-and-pop corporations were caught off guard during the
takeover frenzy of the 1980s. Survivors became more efficient to avoid being
picked off by raiders looking to maximize shareholder profits. With Wal-
Mart, it's a matter of maximizing retailing opportunities for consumers.

By the time a community knows the demographically astute Wal-Mart   9
has its eye on an area, it's virtually too late to stop *somebody* from coming
into town, says Bill Sakelarios, president of the Concord-based Retail
Merchants Association of New Hampshire. In Greenfield, for instance, the
threat of competition to that town's small retailers didn't disappear with the
Wal-Mart vote. BJ's Wholesale club is considering the town for a store.

Wal-Mart is viewed as a threat, though, because it uses bulk buying, dis-   10
count pricing, and tight inventory and distribution management that smaller
retailers can't keep up with. It also has the competitive advantage of size: The

company's sales surged 22 percent to more than $82 billion, while net income climbed 15 percent to more than $2.6 billion in the year ended January 31, 1995, compared with year-earlier results.

Because it's so huge, the best defense against Wal-Mart for small-town retailers is to adapt, evolve, and create some stronghold that will make them viable and worth keeping, even in the face of new competition, says Robert Kahn, a Lafayette, California, management consultant who has worked with the chain and publishes a newsletter called *Retailing Today*. All kinds of stores have found ways to survive in the shadow of Wal-Mart, he says. Grocery stores have maintained check cashing, hardware stores and nurseries have offered classes, women's clothing retailers have filled in the gaps in the Wal-Mart line. Others point to pharmacies that have been able to compete with Wal-Marts. Stone met one druggist who kept a loyal clientele of shut-ins who spent $200 to $300 a month individually on prescriptions by offering home delivery, something Wal-Mart didn't do in his market.

The argument that self-improvement and change for small retailers may be the answer is definitely scorned in some circles. But stores that balk at such notions may not get much sympathy from customers who have had to change jobs or learn new skills—all because of shifts in the structure of the economies in the fields in which they work.

"You read stories about how towns don't want Wal-Mart, but in many cases that's a very few people getting a lot of publicity. And I may have on my desk a petition signed by fifteen thousand people saying, 'Please come, ignore the one hundred people who are trying to block the store,'" Wal-Mart President and CEO David Glass told a press gathering in December. "In retailing, you have a very simple answer to all that. Any community that didn't want a Wal-Mart store—all they've got to do is not shop there. And I guarantee a store, even if it's [just] built, won't be there long."

Another thing to consider is what happens if Wal-Mart, or a store like it, comes into town, stays for ten years, and then leaves. Where that's happened, retailers who found ways to adapt to Wal-Mart's presence still believe they're much better as a result. In Nowata, Oklahoma, Wal-Mart pulled up stakes last year and deserted a town of 3,900 people who had come to depend on it as their second largest tax payer, as well as their major retailing center. But several local merchants survived Wal-Mart's stay of fourteen years because they learned to adjust their business practices. Wayne Clark, whose father opened Clark's Sentry Hardware in 1938, says he survived Wal-Mart's presence by providing better service and a more specialized inventory.

Nowata also brings up another interesting question on the Wal-Mart controversy: Could it be that old-time downtowns simply are obsolete and an impediment to efficient retailing? Many retailers have probably been in a precarious position for a long time, for a number of reasons, and then place the blame for problems or eventual demise on the highly visible Wal-Mart, says Sakelarios. "Wal-Mart is being singled out. Small-town business districts brought a lot of this on themselves," agrees Iowa State's Stone.

As cars have drawn shopping to other locales, downtown districts haven't worked hard enough to remain competitive and efficient, data suggest. "Small retailers often believe that the community *owes them* rather than *they owe* the community," Kahn wrote in his December newsletter.

He cites as evidence a recent survey of more than 1,500 Illinois retailers   17
conducted by the state's merchant association. Kahn found it stunning that 54 percent reorder inventory for their stores only when they're already out of stock. That translates into poor selection and service, Kahn says, because small retailers often can't get priority shipments from vendors and most often wait for five to fifteen days to get fresh stock in, leaving customers without that selection in the interim. "That's not providing any service. If it's not in stock, eventually the customer is going to go somewhere else," Kahn points out.

Kahn also criticized the 63 percent of the retailers surveyed who claimed   18
to know what their customers want, even though they didn't track customer purchases.

Apart from self-inflicted injuries, retailers are also pressured on other   19
fronts, says John Donnellan, a member of the Consumer Studies faculty at the University of Massachusetts in Ames. The growth of the mail-order catalogs, cable TV shopping networks, specialized category stores such as Toys 'R' Us, and now, possibly, shopping via on-line computer services, all present more competition for small merchants that draw from local markets.

The only difference with Wal-Mart is that it's the biggest, most identifi-   20
able source of that new and increasing competition. As a result, it has become a lightning rod for all the angst and anxiety of struggling shop keepers— deserved or not.

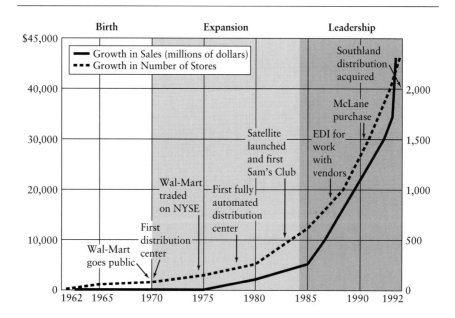

Wal-Mart Takes Off

Source: James F. Moore. Chart: "Wal-Mart Takes Off" in "Predators and Prey," *Harvard Business Review*, May–June 1993, p. 82.

WAL-MART STORES, INC.*

OVERVIEW

Wal-Mart is a way of life. Bentonville, Arkansas-based Wal-Mart Stores is the world's largest retailer, operating more than 3,400 Wal-Mart discount stores, Sam's Club members-only warehouse stores (#2 in the US, behind Costco), and Wal-Mart Supercenters in all 50 states and in a handful of foreign countries. With the help of its friendly People Greeters, the mammoth chain emphasizes quality service and low prices. Aside from temp firms, Wal-Mart is the nation's largest private employer.

The company doesn't just compete in the discount arena—its stores are also considered a competitor in many category-killer retailing operations. Most of its approximately 500 Supercenters are open 24 hours a day, and they have made the company the #2 grocer in the country (behind Kroger).

About 450 Sam's Club stores worldwide serve small-business and individual customers.

With fewer expansion opportunities for its superstores in the US, the company plans to build a chain of smaller (40,000-sq.-ft.) outlets to take on local grocery stores. Wal-Mart, which wants to be a global brand like Coca-Cola and McDonald's, has opened stores in China; bought a majority interest in Cifra, Mexico's largest retailer; and entered the European and Korean markets (about one-fifth of its stores are outside of the US). Wal-Mart has also ventured into a new frontier—the Internet—with its Sam's Club Online site.

The heirs of the late founder Sam Walton, whose fortune is the second-largest in the US (behind Bill Gates'), own about 38% of the company.

WHEN

Sam Walton begin his retail career as a J. C. Penney management trainee and later leased a Ben Franklin-franchised dime store in Newport, Arkansas, in 1945. In 1950 he relocated to Bentonville, Arkansas, and opened a Walton 5. By 1962 Walton owned 15 Ben Franklin stores under the Walton 5 name.

After Ben Franklin management rejected his suggestion to open discount stores in small towns, Walton, with his brother James "Bud" Walton, opened the first Wal-Mart Discount City in Rogers, Arkansas, in 1962. Growth was slow at first, but Wal-Mart Stores went public in 1970 with 18 stores and sales of $44 million.

Growth accelerated in the 1970s because of two key developments: Wal-Mart's highly automated distribution centers, which cut shipping costs and time, and its computerized inventory system, which sped up checkout and reordering. By 1980 the 276 stores had sales of $1.2 billion. The company bought and sold several operations in those years (including selling off its Ben Franklin stores in 1976).

Wall-Mart opened Sam's Wholesale Club in 1983. Modeled on the successful cash-and-carry, membership-only warehouse format pioneered by the Price Company of California, Sam's lured both small-business owners in metropolitan areas and ordinary consumers paying annual membership fees.

The company started Hypermart*USA in 1987, originally as a joint venture with Cullum Companies, a Dallas-based supermarket chain (Wal-mart bought out Cullum's interest in 1989). The

hypermarket, a discount store/supermarket hybrid sprawled out over 200,000 sq. ft., featured ancillary businesses such as branch banks, fast-food outlets, photo developers, and playrooms for shoppers' children. The concept was later retooled as Wal-Mart Supercenters. In 1990 Wal-Mart acquired McLane Company, a grocery and retail distributor, and launched deep-discounter Bud's Discount City.

In 1992, the year Sam died, the company expanded into Mexico by beginning a joint venture to open Sam's Clubs with Cifra, that country's largest retailer. Wal-Mart acquired 122 former Woolco stores in Canada in 1994. Co-founder Bud died a year later.

The Windsor, Ontario, Wal-Mart became the first in the chain to negotiate under a union labor contract, in 1997. Also that year the company acquired control of its Mexican investment, Cifra, the first direct investment by Wal-Mart in a foreign partner. Wal-Mart decided in 1997 to close most of its 61 low-performing Bud's stores. The company also acquired Wertkauf, a German chain of 21 hypermarkets, in 1997.

In 1998 Wal-Mart bought out the 40% interest Brazilian retail discount chain Lojas Americanas owned in the two companies' joint venture. Wal-Mart expanded in Asia in 1998, buying four stores and additional sites in Korea from Korea Makro. Also the company announced it would create a chain of half-sized stores under the name Wal-Mart Neighborhood Market to give other grocery chains a run for their milk money.

---

*From *Hoover's Handbook of American Business 1999.* Hoover's Business Press, pages 1508–1509. Reprinted by permission.

WHEN

Chairman: S. Robson Walton, age 53
VC and COO: Donald G. Soderquist, age 64,
$1,661,700 pay
President and CEO: David D. Glass, age 62, $2,265,846 pay
EVP and CFO: John B. Menzer, age 47
EVP; President and CEO, Wal Mart International: Bob L.
Martin, age 49, $1, 044,827 pay
EVP; President, Wal-Mart Stores Division:
H. Lee Scott Jr., age 49, $943,365 pay
EVP; President, Wal-Mart Realty: Paul R. Carter, age 57
EVP Merchandising: Bob Connolly, age 54
EVP, Specialty Divisions: David Bible, age 50
EVP, Food Division: Nicholas J. White, age 53
SVP and COO, Wal-Mart International: Carlos Criado-Perez
SVP and Controller: James A. Walker Jr., age 51
President and CEO, McLane: William G. Rosier, age 49
EVP and COO, Wal-Mart Stores Division:
Thomas M. Coughlin, age 49, $941,673 pay
VP Personnel and Administration: Coleman Petersen
Auditors: Ernst & Young LLP

WHERE

HQ: 702 SW 8th St., Bentonville, AR 72716-8611
Phone: 501-273-4000 **FAX:** 501-273-1917
Web site: http://wal-mart.com

WHAT

1998 Stores

	No.
Discount stores	2,421
Super centers	502
Sam's Club	483
Total	**3,406**

1998 Sales

	% of total
Hard goods (hardware, housewares, auto supplies, small appliances)	23
Soft goods/domestics	21
Grocery, candy & tobacco	14
Pharmaceuticals	9
Records & electronics	9
Sporting goods & toys	8
Health & beauty aids	7
Stationery	5
Jewelry	2
Shoes	2
Total	**100**

Selected Divisions

McLane Distribution Centers (19 regional wholesale distribution centers supplying convenience stores and Sam's Clubs, Supercenters, and Wal-Marts)
Sam's Clubs (members-only warehouse clubs)
Supercenters (large, combination general merchandise and food stores)
Wal-Mart Distribution Centers (38 regional centers)
Wal-Mart International Divisions (foreign operations)
Wal-Mart Stores (general merchandise)

KEY COMPETITORS

Albertson's	Fred Meyer	Service
AutoZone	Home Depot	Merchandise
Best Buy	Hudson's Bay	Staples
Circuit City	J. C. Penny	Tandy
CompUSA	Kmart	Target Stores
Consolidated	Kroger	TJX
Stores	Lowe's	Toys "R" Us
Costco	METRO Holding	TruServ
Companies	Office Depot	Venator Group
CVS	Safeway	Walgreen
Dollar General	Sears	

HOW MUCH

NYSE symbol: WMT FYE: January 31	Annual Growth	1989	1990	1991	1992	1993	1994	1995	1996	1997	1998
Sales ($ mil.)	21.4%	20,649	25,811	32,602	43,887	55,484	67,345	82,494	93,627	104,859	117,959
Net Income ($ mil.)	17.3%	837	1,076	1,291	1,609	1,995	2,333	2,681	2,740	3,056	3,526
Income as % of sales	—	4.1%	4.2%	4.0%	3.7%	3.6%	3.5%	3.2%	2.9%	2.9%	3.0%
Earnings per share ($)	17.3%	0.37	0.48	0.57	0.70	0.87	1.02	1.17	1.19	1.33	1.56
Stock price - FY high ($)	—	8.47	11.84	18.38	29.94	32.94	34.13	29.25	27.63	28.25	41.94
Stock price - FY low($)	—	6.28	7.84	10.09	16.38	25.06	23.00	20.63	19.09	20.13	23.00
Stock price - FY close ($)	18.8%	8.44	10.66	16.50	26.94	32.56	26.50	22.88	20.38	23.75	39.81
P/E - high	—	23	25	32	43	38	33	25	23	21	27
P/E - low	—	17	16	18	23	29	23	18	16	15	15
Dividends per share ($)	23.6%	0.04	0.06	0.07	0.09	0.11	0.13	0.17	0.20	0.21	0.27
Book value per share ($)	22.5%	1.33	1.75	2.35	3.04	3.81	4.68	5.54	6.44	7.50	8.26
Employees	15.6%	223,000	271,000	328,000	371,000	434,000	528,000	622,000	675,000	728,000	825,000

STOCK PRICE HISTORY

HIGH/LOW/CLOSE

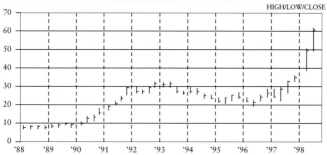

1998 FISCAL YEAR-END

Debt ratio: 34.3%
Return on equity: 19.1%
Cash (mil.): $1,447
Current ratio: 1.34
Long-term debt (mil.): $9,674
No. of shares (mil.): 2,241
Dividends
 Yields: 0.7%
 Payout: 17.3%
Market value (mil.): $89,214

Sprawl-Busters

Sprawl-Busting Victories

58 Communities where megastores have been
rejected (at least once) or have withdrawn:

Plymouth, MA	Rehobeth, DE	Waukesha, WI
Reading, MA	Mt. Joy, PA	Brookfield, WI
Yarmouth, MA	Warwick, PA	Wichita, KS
Gaithersburg, MD	West Hempfield, PA	Jefferson County, CO
Plainville, CT	Middletown, RI	Silverthorne, CO
Orange, CT	Accomac, VA	Lincoln, NB
New Milford, CT	Warrenton, VA	Taylorsville, UT
Old Saybrook, CT	Williamsburg, VA	Layton, UT
Tolland, CT	Durham, NC	(Home Depot)
St. Albans, VT	Hickory, NC	Hailey, ID
St. Johnsbury, VT	Temple Terrace, FL	North Auburn, CA
Claremont, NH	Hallandale, FL	Simi Valley, CA
Henniker, NH	New Albany, IN	Santa Rosa, CA
Lebanon, NH	Decorah, IO	(Home Depot)
Peterborough, NH	Fenton, MI	San Francisco, CA
Buffalo, NY	Warsaw, MO	(Home Depot)
East Aurora, NY	Broadview Heights, OH	Santa Maria, CA
Hyde Park, NY	Highland Heights, OH	Grass Valley, CA
New Paltz, NY	Lorain, OH	Gig Harbor, WA
Hornell, NY	Cleveland Heights, OH	Waterloo, Ontario,
Ithaca, NY	Westlake, OH	Canada
Leeds, NY	North Olmsted, OH	View Royal, BC,
Utica, NY	Chardon, OH	Canada
Lake Placid, NY	Ottawa, OH	Guelph, Ontario,
N Greenbush, NY	Strongsville, OH	Canada
Hamilton, NJ	Burnsville, MN	Utuado, P.R.
Manalapan, NJ	West Bend, WI	Barranquitas, P.R.

Source: Albert Norman, Sprawl-Busters. 23 Nov. 1998.
<http://www.sprawl-busters.com/victoryz.htm>.

List updated as of November, 1998.

Shopping with the Enemy

This unsigned article first appeared in The Economist *on October 14, 1995.*

"Something there is that doesn't love a wall," wrote Robert Frost. "Or a Wal-   1
Mart," he might add, were he to rise from his grave behind the Old First
Church and look at the newly opened store just down the hill. Vermont is no
longer the only state without a Wal-Mart, despite a five-year struggle by the
company's opponents to keep it out.

      Yet instead of protesting, the locals are pushing and shoving to get in.   2
"The reaction has been tremendous," says Russ Walker, the manager. Mr.
Walker recorded 23,000 transactions in his first week, and this in a town of
16,000 people. Drawn by such locally appealing bargains as red flannel shirts
for $6.56, Vermonters are opening their hearts and their wallets to Wal-
Mart.

      Does that mean doom for downtown merchants? Not necessarily. Wal-   3
Marts are usually huge, charmless boxes built on the outskirts of towns,
where highways are handy and parking plentiful. But to crack the Vermont
market and avoid the restrictions of the state's tough development-control
law, Wal-Mart put a less-imposing, 50,000-square-foot store into an old
Woolworth's building near the centre of town.

      Bennington's downtown merchants seem to be adjusting to Wal-Mart;   4
they are used to competing with other big discount chains such as KMart,
already established in the local market. "I'm not really worried," says
Catherine Mack, proprietor of the artsy-craftsy Pea Pod gift shop on Main
Street. "I think we're building our own little niche as a specialty store." But
not all Wal-Mart patrons are willing to venture downtown, despite a recent
effort to spiff up the district. "I think the downtown in Bennington is doomed
anyway, because of the lack of parking," Mary Lou Morris said firmly. "I go
to malls."

      Mall-going Vermonters have little patience with Wal-Mart's opponents.   5
Mr. Walker, the store manager, blames the controversy on "a handful of
non-natives" who care more about prettiness than economic development.
But if they are a minority in blue-collar Bennington, the company's enemies
are more influential elsewhere in the state. In Burlington, the state's biggest
city, anxious officials are fighting a 115,000-square-foot Wal-Mart and a
132,000-square-foot Sam's Club planned for a largely undeveloped area
outside the city.

      Their battle appears lost, however. So far Vermont has largely avoided   6
the suburban sprawl that blights so much of the American landscape. But too
many people crave the low prices, large selection and convenient parking
offered by the big discount chains. "Progress—can't stand in the way," said
Wal-Mart shopper Jack Hodgeman, trundling several new refuse bins out to
his pickup truck.

■ ■ ■

Consider Your Purpose

As with the explanatory synthesis, your specific purpose in writing an argument synthesis is crucial. What, exactly, you want to do will affect your claim, the evidence you select to support your claim, and the way you organize the evidence. Your purpose may select to support your claim, and the way you organize the evidence. Your purpose may be clear to you before you begin research, may emerge during the course of research, or may not emerge until after you have completed your research. (Of course, the sooner your purpose is clear to you, the fewer wasted motions you will make. On the other hand, the more you approach research as an exploratory process, the likelier that your conclusions will emerge from the sources themselves, rather than from preconceived ideas. For a discussion on the process of research, see Chapter 5.)

Let's say that while reading these sources, your own encounters with Wal-Mart influence your thinking on the subject and you find yourself agreeing more with the supporters than with the detractors of Wal-Mart. Perhaps you didn't grow up in a small town, so you don't have much experience with or knowledge of the kind of retail stores that the megastores have been displacing.

On the one hand, you can understand and even sympathize with the viewpoints of critics such as Norman and Anderson. (You may have shopped in the smaller stores in towns you have visited, or seen them portrayed in movies, or perhaps even visited reconstructed small-town stores in museums such as the Smithsonian or in the "Main Street" area in Disneyland.) On the other hand, it seems to you unrealistic in this day and age to expect that stores like Wal-Mart can be stopped or should be. For you, the prices and the convenience are a big plus. Your purpose, then, is formed from this kind of response to the source material.

Making a Claim: Formulate a Thesis

As we indicated in the introduction to argument synthesis, one useful way of approaching an argument is to see it as making a *claim*. A claim is a proposition, a conclusion that you are trying to prove or demonstrate. If your purpose is to demonstrate that it is neither possible nor desirable to stop the spread of Wal-Mart, then that is the claim at the heart of your argument. The claim is generally expressed in one-sentence form as a *thesis*. You use the information—and sometimes appeals to *ethos* and *pathos* (see pp. 130–133)— in sources to *support* your claim.

Of course, not every piece of information in a source is useful for supporting a claim. By the same token, you may draw support for your own claim from sources that make entirely different claims. For example, you may use as support for your own claim—that Wal-Mart is growing at an alarming rate—data from the store's Web site annual report, which claims is the exact opposite: that Wal-Mart's growth is good for both customers and stockholders.

Similarly, you might use one source as part of a *counterargument*—an argument opposite to your own—so that you can demonstrate its weaknesses and, in the process, strengthen your own claim. On the other hand, the author of one of your sources may be so convincing in supporting a claim that you adopt it yourself, either partially or entirely. The point is that *the argument is in your hands*: you must devise it yourself and must use your sources in ways that will support the claim expressed in your thesis.

You may not want to divulge your thesis until the end of the paper, to draw the reader along toward your conclusion, allowing the thesis to flow naturally out of the argument and the evidence on which it is based. If you do this, you are working *inductively*. Or, you may wish to be more direct and *begin* with your thesis, following the thesis statement with evidence to support it. If you do this, you are working *deductively*. In academic papers, deductive arguments are far more common than inductive arguments.

Based on your reactions to reading the sources, you decide to concede that the case against Wal-Mart has some merit and certainly some homespun appeal, but that opponents of such megastores are being unrealistic in expecting most people to sacrifice convenience and economy for the sake of retaining a vanishing way of life. After a few tries, you arrive at the following provisional thesis:

```
Opponents of the giant discount chains have made pow-
erful arguments against them, and it's too bad that
these megastores are helping to make a way of life
extinct; but opponents should realize that stores such
as Wal-Mart are so successful because most people
prefer bargains and convenience to tradition and
small-town charm.
```

Decide How You Will Use Your Source Material

Your claim commits you to (1) recognize the arguments made by opponents of Wal-Mart, and (2) argue that Wal-Marts will prevail because they offer people advantages that the traditional retail shops can't match. The sources provide plenty of information and ideas—that is, evidence—that will allow you to support your claim. Norman and Anderson sum up the anti–Wal-Mart case, one that is also described more objectively by Ortega and the anonymous author of the *Economist* article. Johnston offers the primary argument for Wal-Mart, and other data showing the growth of the chain are provided by Wal-Mart itself (in its Web site) and by the chart following Moore's article.

Develop an Organizational Plan

Having established your overall purpose and your claim, having developed a provisional thesis, and having decided how to use your source materials, how do you logically organize your essay? In many cases, including this one, a well-written thesis will suggest an overall organization. Thus, the first part of your synthesis will address the powerful arguments made by opponents of Wal-Mart. The second part will cover the even more powerful case (in your judgment) to be made on the other side. Sorting through your material and categorizing it by topic and subtopic, you might arrive at the following outline:

A. Introduction. The emotional anti–Wal-Mart case; conflict of values: consumerism vs. small-town America. *Thesis.*
B. Spectacular growth of Wal-Mart.
C. The case against Wal-Mart.
   1. Arguments against Wal-Mart.
   2. Al Norman's crusade
D. Transition: the case for Wal-Mart
E. Concession: charm of small-town stores. But—problems with small-town stores.
F. Changes in American economy and lifestyle and their effect on Main Street.
G. How traditionalists and store owners can deal with Wal-Mart.
   1. Fight it.
   2. Adjust by competing in ways that Wal-Mart can't.
H. Conclusion. Wal-Mart is not a "villain" because it offers what people want.

Argument Strategy

The argument represented by this outline deals with a claim of *value*, rather than a claim of *fact*. In other words, this is not an argument over whether Wal-Marts *are* better, according to some objective standard, than Main Street variety stores, since there is no such standard about which most people would agree. (Of course, if "better" were defined as more profitable, then this argument *would* become one of fact and would, in fact, be easily disposed of, since numbers would provide sufficient support for the claim.) Rather, it is an argument that turns on those values which for different people take priority—convenience and economy versus charm and traditional small-town life. Your *claim,* therefore, is based not only upon the *supporting evidence,* but also upon your *assumptions* about the relative value of convenience and economy, on the one hand, and charm and traditional small-town life, on the other. Accordingly, while some of the arguments are based upon an appeal to *logos,* most are based upon the appeal to *pathos.* Some are even based upon *ethos,* since the writer will occasionally imply that her view is representative of that of most people.

To *support* her *claim,* the writer will rely upon a combination of summary, paraphrase, and quotation—much of it *testimony* from either "average" customers or from proponents of one side or the other of the debate. Note that despite her own essentially pro–Wal-Mart position, the writer provides *counterarguments* and *concessions*, indicating that she is not afraid to fairly represent the views of the other side, and even to give them some credit (the concession) before she responds and reinforces her own argument.

Draft and Revise Your Synthesis

The final draft of a completed synthesis, based upon the above outline, follows. Thesis, transitional, and topic sentences are highlighted; Modern Language Association (MLA) documentation style, explained in Chapter 5, is used throughout. Note that for the sake of clarity, references in the following essay are to pages in *Writing and Reading Across the Curriculum*.

```
                    A Vote for Wal-Mart
```

According to one critic, Wal-Mart is waging a "War on   1
Main Street." Anti–Wal-Mart activists think that we
should "Ban the Bargains." A pro–Wal-Mart writer asks
"Who's Really the Villain?" Obviously, the ever-
expanding Wal-Mart brings some people's emotions to
the boiling point. This seems strange. After all, Wal-
Mart doesn't seem one of those hot-button issues like
abortion or capital punishment. But for many, this is
not just about discount department stores; it's about
conflicting values: the values of small-town America
versus the values of "mindless consumerism" (Ortega
134). I don't consider myself a mindless consumerist,
but I happen to like Wal-Marts. Opponents of the giant
discount chains have made powerful arguments against
them, and it's too bad that these megastores are helping to make a way of life extinct; but opponents
should realize that stores like Wal-Mart are so successful because most people prefer bargains and convenience to tradition and small-town charm.
    Wal-Mart's growth has been spectacular. Launched in   2
1962, by 1997 Wal-Mart had over 2,900 stores, including 502 "Supercenters" ("Wal-Mart" 1509). Al Norman,
one of Wal-Mart's most vocal critics, reported that in

1994 Wal-Mart had over $67 billion in sales (136).
Four years later, Wal-Mart's annual sales climbed to
almost $118 billion ("Wal-Mart" 1509). Wal-Mart also
owns Sam's Club, another discount chain, which opened
in early 1983 (chart: "Wal-Mart Takes Off"), and now
numbers 483 stores ("Wal-Mart" 1509).

To its critics, Wal-Mart seems to represent everything that's wrong with modern American society. Sarah
Anderson, an economist and the daughter of a small-
town retailer, argues that Wal-Mart encourages urban
sprawl, drains money from local economies, kills downtowns and local jobs, and destroys the quality of
small-town life (138-139). Others blame Wal-Mart for
the "homogenization of community identity" (Ortega
134). One local resident complains, "Everything's
starting to look the same, everybody buys all the same
things--a lot of small-town character is being lost."
She adds, "Visually, [Wal-Marts] are atrocious" (qtd.
in Ortega 135). Wal-Marts's ugliness is a common
theme: the stores have been described as "huge, charmless boxes" ("Shopping" 146).

Activist Al Norman has helped organize local communities to fight the spread of Wal-Mart. His Web site,
"Sprawl-Busters," proudly lists 58 communities that
have succeeded in beating back Wal-Mart's advance on
their town. (He also lists communities that have
rejected other large discounters like Home Depot,
Costco, and K-Mart.) Norman argues that "Wal-Mart's
gains are largely captured from other merchants"
("Eight Ways" 136). His rallying cry is that communities are "not ready to die for a cheap pair of underwear" (qtd. in Anderson 139).

But rhetoric like this is overkill. Norman might as
well blame computer makers for the death of typewriters or automakers for the death of horse-and-buggy
rigs. Horses and buggies may be more picturesque and
romantic than cars, but most Americans drive cars

3

4

5

these days because they're a lot faster and more convenient. If customers choose to buy underwear at Wal-
Mart instead of the mom-and-pop store downtown, that's
because it's easier to get to Wal-Mart--and to park
there--and because cheapness is a quality that matters
to them.

I agree that Wal-Marts are unattractive and "charm-   6
less." They just don't have the warmth or individuality of some of the small shops you find in downtown
areas, especially if they've been in business for generations. But like most people, I'm willing to sacrifice warmth and individuality if I can get just what I
want at a price I can afford. As Jo-Ann Johnston
points out, mom-and-pop stores have brought on a lot
of their own problems by not being sufficiently
responsive to what their customers need. She notes,
"several of the town's shoppers complained during the
Wal-Mart battle that area merchants could use competition because of their poor selection, high prices,
limited hours, and lackluster service" (140). Johnston
points out that if customers can't find what they want
at the price they want at local stores, it's not surprising that they go to Wal-Mart. Even residents of
Vermont, one of the areas most likely to resist the
intrusion of Wal-Mart, come flocking to Wal-Mart for
the bargains and the selection ("Shopping" 146). Russ
Walker, store manager of the Bennington Wal-Mart, dismisses opposition to the discount chain as "'a handful
of non-natives' who care more about prettiness than
economic development" ("Shopping" 146).

As even opponents of Wal-Mart admit, American   7
downtowns were in trouble long before Wal-Mart arrived
on the scene. Changes in the economy and in the
American lifestyle have contributed to the end of a
traditional way of life. In other words, stores such
as Wal-Mart are a symptom rather than a cause of the
changes in Main Street. Blaming Wal-Mart "overlooks a
much deeper problem facing small-town America," writes

Jo-Ann Johnston: "the need to change a way of business while maintaining, or improving, a deeply valued way of life" (139). As Sarah Anderson admits, "Small towns cannot return to the past, when families did all their shopping and socializing in their hometown. Rural life is changing and there's no use denying it" (139).

In "Eight Ways to Stop the Store," Norman provides **8** tips for community activists on how to fight Wal-Mart. I agree that if most people don't want Wal-Mart in their community, they should campaign against it and keep it out. I even think that the community might be a more pleasant place to live without the huge discount chains. But I also believe that residents of these communities should be aware of the price they will pay, both financially and in convenience, for maintaining their traditional way of doing business. Even without Wal-Mart, local downtowns will have trouble holding on to their customers. A better plan than keeping the big discounters out would be for local retailers to adapt to the changing times and to the competition. Some store owners have found ways of offering their customers what Wal-Mart can't provide: personalized services, such as home delivery or special orders, along with merchandise not available in the chain stores (Johnston 141).

Wal-Mart did not become the huge success it is by **9** forcing its products on an unwilling public. People shop there because they want to. They want to save money and they want to find what they're looking for. Who can blame them? Wal-Mart may not be pretty, but it's also not "the villain."

Works Cited

Anderson, Sarah. "Wal-Mart's War on Main Street." <u>Progressive</u> Nov. 1994: 19–21.

Johnston, Jo-Ann. "Who's Really the Villain?" <u>Business Ethics</u> May–June 1995: 16–18.

Moore, James F. Chart: "Wal-Mart Takes Off." "Predators
    and Prey." Harvard Business Review May–June 1993: 82.

Norman, Albert "Eight Ways to Stop the Store." The Nation
    28 Mar. 1994: 418.

---. "Sprawl-Busting Victories." Sprawl-Busters Mar.
    1997. 17 Sept. 1997 <http://www.sprawl-busters.com/
    victoryz.html>.

Ortega, Bob. "Ban the Bargains." The Wall Street Journal
    11 Oct. 1994: 1+.

"Shopping with the Enemy." Economist 14 Oct. 1995: 33.

"Wal-Mart Stores, Inc." Hoover's Handbook of American
    Business. Austin, TX: Business Press, 1998.

Discussion

The writer of this argument synthesis on Wal-Mart attempts to support a *claim*—one that essentially favors Wal-Mart—by offering *support* in the form of facts (examples and statistics) and opinions (testimony of experts and "average" customers). However, since the writer's claim is one of *value*, as opposed to fact, its effectiveness depends partially upon the extent to which we, as readers, agree with the *assumptions* underlying the argument. (See our discussion of assumptions in Chapter 2, pp. 55–56). An assumption (sometimes called a *warrant*) is a generalization or principle about how the world works or should work—a fundamental statement of belief about facts or values. In this particular case, the underlying assumption is that the values of cheapness and convenience are preferable, as a rule, to the values of charm and small-town tradition. Assumptions often are deeply rooted in people's psyches, sometimes deriving from lifelong experiences and observations, and are not easily changed, even by the most logical arguments. People who grew up in small-town America and remember it fondly are therefore far less likely to be persuaded by the support offered for this writer's claim than those who have lived in urban and suburban areas.

- In the *introductory paragraph*, the writer summarizes some of the most heated arguments against Wal-Mart by citing some of the titles of recent articles about the store. The writer goes on to explain the intensity of emotion generated by stores such as Wal-Mart by linking it to a larger conflict of values: the values of small-town America vs. the values of consumerism. The writer then states her own preference for Wal-Mart, which leads to her *claim* (represented in the *thesis* at the end of the first paragraph).
  Argument strategy: The writer sets up the argument as one of conflicting *values*, relying here upon summary and quotations that support an appeal to *pathos* (emotions of the reader). The writer also provides the beginning of an appeal to *ethos* (establishing herself as credible) by stating her own views as a consumer in the sentence before the thesis.

- In the *second paragraph*, the writer discusses the spectacular growth of Wal-Mart. This growth is indirectly, rather than directly, relevant to the debate itself, since it is this apparently unstoppable growth that has caused Wal-Mart to be perceived as such a threat by opponents. **Argument strategy:** This paragraph relies primarily upon the appeal to *logos* (logic) since its main purpose is to establish Wal-Mart's spectacular success. The argument here is supported primarily with statistics.

- In the *third and fourth paragraphs*, the writer discusses the case against Wal-Mart. The third paragraph covers the objections most commonly advanced by Wal-Mart critics. Three sources (Anderson, Ortega, and "Shopping with the Enemy") provide the source material for this paragraph. In the next paragraph, the writer focuses on Al Norman, one of the most prominent anti–Wal-Mart activists, who has helped localities organize campaigns against new Wal-Marts, some of them successful. **Argument strategy:** The third paragraph, part of the *counterargument*, attempts to support claims of value (that is, *pathos*) with a combination of summary (topic sentence), paraphrase (second sentence), and quotation (following sentences). The fourth paragraph, a continuation of the counterargument, relies on a combination of appeals to *logos* (the numbers of communities that, according to Norman, have rejected Wal-Mart) and *pathos* (the quotation in the final sentence of the paragraph).

- The *fifth paragraph* begins the transition to the opposite side. The writer begins advancing her own claim—that people aren't willing to sacrifice convenience and price to charm and tradition. She also suggests that the small-town American Main Street that Wal-Mart is replacing was dying anyway. **Argument strategy:** This paragraph makes a transition from the counterargument to the writer's own argument. Initially, the appeal is to *logos*: she draws an analogy between the passing of traditional Main Street stores and the passing of typewriters and horses and buggies. This is followed by another appeal to *pathos*—the importance of efficiency, convenience, and cheapness.

- In the *sixth paragraph*, the writer admits that Wal-Marts are not pretty, charming, or unique, but argues that the mom-and-pop stores have their own problems: small selection, nonresponsiveness to customer needs, indifferent service, and relatively high prices. **Argument strategy:** In this paragraph, the writer makes an important *concession* (part of the counterargument) that charm is important; but she continues to use the appeal to *pathos* to support the primary claim. Note that in the middle of the paragraph, the writer makes an appeal to *ethos* (" . . . like most people, I'm willing to sacrifice warmth and individuality if I can get just what I want at a price I can afford"). This statement aligns the writer with what most people want from their shopping experiences. After all, the writer implies, this is a matter of good sense—a quality the reader is likely to think valuable, a quality that she or he appears to share with the writer.

- *Paragraph seven* deals more explicitly than the fifth paragraph with the passing away of traditional small-town America, owing to changes in the economy and in lifestyle.
  Argument strategy: In this paragraph the writer follows through with her strategy of relying upon a combination of *logos* and *pathos* to support her claim. Beginning by summarizing the reasons for the decline of Main Street, she concludes the paragraph with quotations focusing on the sad but inevitable passing of a way of life.

- In *paragraph eight*, the writer concedes that people are free to fight Wal-Mart coming to their town if they don't want the giant store; but a better course of action might be for local merchants to adjust to Wal-Mart by offering goods and services that the giant store is unwilling or unable to, such as home delivery and specialty merchandise.
  Argument strategy: At this point, the writer focuses almost all her attention on the appeal to logic: she summarizes both the essential nature of the conflict and suggestions offered by one source for counteracting the Wal-Mart threat.

- In *paragraph nine*, the writer concludes by reemphasizing her claim: Wal-Mart is successful because it gives customers what they want.
  Argument strategy: The writer wraps up her argument by reemphasizing the reasons offered for Wal-Mart's success. She rounds off her discussion by repeating, in quotation marks, the "villain" epithet with which the paper begins. The final sentence again combines the appeal to *pathos* (we admittedly cannot call Wal-Mart "pretty") and *logos* (in view of the evidence offered as support, it makes no sense to label Wal-Mart a "villain").

Of course, many other approaches to an argument synthesis would be possible based on the sources provided here. One, obviously, would be the opposite argument: that in embracing Wal-Marts and other giant chains, America is losing part of its soul—or, at a less profound level, small towns are losing part of their charm and distinctive character. Another might be to assess the quality of the various positions according, for example, to the nature of the evidence provided or the type of logic employed. Another might be to de-emphasize the more concrete issue of stores such as Wal-Mart and to focus on the broader issue of changes in small-town life. Whatever your approach to the subject, in first *analyzing* the various sources and then *synthesizing* them to support your argument, you are engaging in the kind of critical thinking that is essential to success in a good deal of academic and professional work.

DEVELOPING AND ORGANIZING THE SUPPORT FOR YOUR ARGUMENTS

Experienced writers seem to have an intuitive sense of how to develop and present the supporting evidence for their claims. Less experienced writers wonder what to say first, and having decided on that, wonder what to say next. There is no single method of presentation. But the techniques of even the most experienced writers often boil down to a few tried and tested arrangements.

As we've seen in the model syntheses in this chapter, the key to devising effective arguments is to find and use those kinds of support that most persuasively strengthen your claim. Some writers categorize support into two broad types: *evidence* and *motivational appeals*. Evidence, in the form of facts, statistics, and expert testimony, helps make the appeal to *logos* or reason. Motivational appeals—appeals to *pathos* and to *ethos*—are employed to get people to change their minds, to agree with the writer or speaker, or to decide upon a plan of activity.

Following are some of the most common principles for using and organizing support for your claims.

Summarize, Paraphrase, and Quote Supporting Evidence

In most of the papers and reports you will write in college and the professional world, evidence and motivational appeals derive from summarizing, paraphrasing, and quoting material in the sources that either have been provided to you or that you have independently researched. (See Chapter 1, on when to summarize, paraphrase, and quote material from sources.) As we noted above, the third paragraph of the Wal-Mart synthesis offers all three treatments of evidence: in the first sentence, the writer *summarizes* anti–Wal-Mart sentiment in the sources; in the second sentence, she *paraphrases* Sarah Anderson; in the third sentence, she *quotes* Bob Ortega.

Provide Various Types of Evidence and Motivational Appeals

Keep in mind the appeals to both *logos* and *pathos*. As we've discussed, the appeal to *logos* is based on evidence that consists of a combination of *facts, statistics*, and *expert testimony*. In the Wal-Mart synthesis, the writer uses all of these varieties of evidence: facts (the economic decline of small-town America, as discussed in paragraph 7, statistics (the growth of Wal-Mart, as documented in paragraph 2), and testimony (the quotations in paragraph 3). The appeal to *pathos* is based on the appeal to the needs and values of the audience. In the Wal-Mart synthesis, this appeal is exemplified in the use of support (for example, the quotations in paragraph 6 about the limitations of mom-and-pop stores) that are likely to make readers upset or dissatisfied because they feel that they need greater selection, efficiency, and economy than the smaller stores can offer them.

Use Climactic Order

Organize by climactic order when you plan to offer a number of different categories or elements of support for your claim. Recognize, however, that some are more important—that is, are likely to be more persuasive—than others. The basic principle here is that you should *save the most important evidence for the end*, since whatever you have said last is what readers are likely to most remember. A secondary principle is that whatever you say first is what they are *next* most likely to remember. Therefore, when you have several reasons to support your claim, an effective argument strategy is to present the second most important, then one or more additional reasons, and finally, the most important reason.

Use Logical or Conventional Order

Using logical or conventional order means that you use as a template a preestablished pattern or plan for arguing your case.

- One common pattern is describing or arguing a *problem/solution.* Using this pattern, you begin with an introduction in which you typically define the problem, then perhaps explain its origins, then offer one or more solutions, then conclude. Our explanatory synthesis on the Year 2000 problem followed this pattern: first, the writer defined the problem and established its seriousness, then gave an account of its historical origins, then discussed the difficulties of fixing the problem, then concluded in the revised version[14] on a somewhat lighter note.

- Another common pattern is presenting *two sides of a controversy.* Using this pattern, you introduce the controversy and (if an argument synthesis) your own point of view or claim, then explain each side's arguments, providing reasons that your point of view should prevail. This was the pattern of our argument synthesis: After an introduction to the controversy, the writer defined the problem by establishing the spectacular growth of Wal-Mart, then presented both sides of the controversy—taking care, because of the principle of climactic order, to present the pro–Wal-Mart side last.

- Another common pattern is *comparison-contrast.* In fact, this pattern is so important that we will discuss it separately in the next section.

- The order in which you present elements of an argument is sometimes dictated by the conventions of the discipline in which you are writing. For example, lab reports and experiments in the sciences and social sciences often follow this pattern: *Opening* or *Introduction, Methods and Materials* [of the experiment], *Results, Discussion.* Later in this

---

[14]Ask your instructor to consult the *Instructor's Manual* for the revised version of the Y2K essay.

chapter (section on Comparison-Contrast) and in Chapter 11, "You, the Jury," we will see that legal arguments often follow the IRAC format: *Issue, Rule, Application, Conclusion.*

Present and Respond to Counterarguments

As we have seen in the Wal-Mart synthesis, people who develop arguments on a controversial topic can effectively use *counterargument* to help support their claims. When you use counterargument, you present an argument *against* your claim, but then show that this argument is weak or flawed. The advantage of this technique is that you demonstrate that you are aware of the other side of the argument and that you are prepared to answer it.

Here is how a counterargument typically is developed:

A. Introduction and claim
B. Main opposing argument
C. Refutation of opposing argument
D. Main positive argument

In the Wal-Mart synthesis, the writer gives a fair representation—using summary, paraphrase, and quotation—of the anti–Wal-Mart case for the purpose of showing that it is weaker than the pro–Wal-Mart case.

Use Concession

Concession is a variation of counterargument. As in counterargument, you present the opposing viewpoint, but instead of demolishing that argument, you concede that it does have some validity and even some appeal, although your own argument is the stronger one. This bolsters your own standing—your own ethos—as a fair-minded person who is not blind to the virtues of the other side.

Here is an outline for a concession argument:

A. Introduction and claim
B. Important opposing argument
C. Concession that this argument has some validity
D. Positive argument(s)

Sometimes, when you are developing a *counterargument* or *concession argument*, you may become convinced of the validity of the opposing point of view and change your own views. Don't be afraid of this happening. Writing is a tool for learning. To change your mind because of new evidence is a sign of flexibility and maturity, and your writing can only be the better for it.

Avoid Common Fallacies in Developing and Using Support

In Chapter 2, in the section on "Critical Reading," we considered some of the criteria that, as a reader, you may use for evaluating informative and persuasive writing (see pp. 46–56). We discussed how you can assess the accuracy, the significance, and the author's interpretation of the information presented. We also considered the importance in good argument of clearly defined key terms and the pitfalls of emotionally loaded language. Finally, we saw how to recognize such logical fallacies as either/or reasoning, faulty cause-and-effect reasoning, hasty generalization, and false analogy. As a writer, no less than as a critical reader, be aware of these common problems and try to avoid them.

THE COMPARISON-AND-CONTRAST SYNTHESIS

A particularly important type of argument synthesis uses a comparison and contrast pattern. Comparison-and-contrast techniques enable you to examine two subjects (or sources) in terms of one another. When you compare, you consider *similarities*. When you contrast, you consider *differences*. By comparing and contrasting, you perform a multifaceted analysis that often suggests subtleties that otherwise might not have come to your (or the reader's) attention.

To organize a comparison-and-contrast argument, you must carefully read sources in order to discover *significant criteria for analysis*. A *criterion* is a specific point to which both of your authors refer and about which they may agree or disagree. (For example, in a comparative report on compact cars, criteria for *comparison and contrast* might be road handling, fuel economy, and comfort of ride.) The best criteria are those that allow you not only to account for obvious similarities and differences between sources but also to plumb deeper, to more subtle and significant similarities and differences.

There are two basic approaches to organizing a comparison-and-contrast analysis: organization by *source* and organization by *criteria*.

1. *Organizing by source.* You can organize a comparative synthesis as two summaries of your sources, followed by a discussion in which you point out significant similarities and differences between passages. Having read the summaries and become familiar with the distinguishing features of each passage, your readers will most likely be able to appreciate the more obvious similarities and differences. Follow up on these summaries by discussing both the obvious and subtle comparisons and contrasts, focusing on the most significant.

   Organization by source is best saved for passages that are briefly summarized. If the summary of your source becomes too long, your audience might forget the remarks you made in the first summary as they are reading the second. A comparison-and-contrast synthesis organized by source might proceed like this:

   I. Introduce the essay; lead to thesis.
   II. Summarize passage A by discussing its significant features.
   III. Summarize passage B by discussing its significant features.
   IV. Write a paragraph (or two) in which you discuss the significant points of comparison and contrast between passages A and B.

End with a conclusion in which you summarize you points and, perhaps, raise and respond to pertinent questions.

2. *Organizing by criteria.* Instead of summarizing entire passages one at a time with the intention of comparing them later, you could discuss two passages simultaneously, examining the views of each author point by point (criterion by criterion), comparing and contrasting these views in the process. The criterion approach is best used when you have a number of points to discuss or when passages are long and/or complex. A comparison-and-contrast synthesis organized by criteria might look like this:

I. Introduce the essay; lead to thesis.
II. Criterion 1
   A. Discuss what author A says about this point.
   B. Discuss what author B says about this point, comparing and contrasting B's treatment of the point with A's.
III. Criterion 2
   A. Discuss what author A says about this point.
   B. Discuss what author B says about this point, comparing and contrasting B's treatment of the point with A's.

And so on. Proceed criterion by criterion until you have completed your discussion. Be sure to arrange criteria with a clear method; knowing how the discussion of one criterion leads to the next will ensure smooth transitions throughout your paper. End with a conclusion in which you summarize your points and, perhaps, raise and respond to pertinent questions.

A Case for Comparison-Contrast: Murder or Manslaughter?

We'll see how these principles can be applied to the following passages, related to the subject matter of our Chapter 11, "You, the Jury." Here are two cases dealing with "crimes of passion"—homicides arising out of a husband discovering that his wife is having an affair with another man. The texts, State v. Rowland *and* State v. Ashland *are excerpted from the rulings of the courts to which they had been appealed. Rowland was a 1904 Mississippi case, Ashland a 1912 California case. Following these accounts, we present instructions of the kind that a judge would give to a jury in homicide cases. These instructions (written for California juries) deal with first- and second-degree murder and with involuntary manslaughter and are based on the applicable sections of the state Penal Code. In the original trial court, Rowland was found guilty of first-degree murder, but the appeals court reversed the murder conviction and ordered him retried on manslaughter charges. Ashland also was found guilty of first-degree murder by the trial court, but his murder conviction was upheld upon appeal.*

Comparison-and-contrast is a very common technique among both prosecu-
tors and defense attorneys, who, when researching their cases, look for prece-
dents—prior cases with similar circumstances. If they want the verdict of the case
they are trying to be the same as that of the precedent case, they will compare the
cases and argue that they are similar enough so that the verdicts should be the
same. But if they want the opposite verdict, they will contrast the cases and argue
that the differences are sufficient to justify the opposite verdict.

In our model comparison-contrast essay—organized by criteria—we imagine
that a prosecuting attorney is arguing that Rowland *and* Ashland *are different*
enough that the final verdicts should be different. [Note: "References" after the
essay follow "Blue Book" format for citing legal documents. (See Hricik, p. 175.)
Unless you are pursuing a law or pre-law curriculum you will not need to know
the conventions of this style.]

ROWLAND v. STATE
Supreme Court of Mississippi. Jan. 25, 1904.

Facts of the Case*

The [defendant] was indicted for the murder of his wife, Becky Rowland, sentenced to imprisonment for life, and appeals. His story is as follows: His
wife had been for about two months prior to the homicide living with Lou   1
Pate, at whose house the killing occurred. The defendant and his wife were on
good terms, and he was in the habit of visiting her and staying one night with
her each week, or every two weeks. Lou Pate's house consisted of two rooms.
In the front room were two beds—one occupied by Lou and her husband, and
the other usually occupied by Becky Rowland. In the back room there was
one bed. On the night of the killing, the defendant reached Pate's house
about 10 o'clock, hitched his horse, and noticed John Thorn's also hitched to
the fence. Coming up to the house, he heard a man and a woman talking in
the back room, in which there was no light. Listening, he discovered that John
Thorn and Becky Rowland (the defendant's wife) were in the room, and
heard Thorn say, "Make haste." This aroused his suspicions, and he attempted to open the back door to the room; but it being latched, he went to the
front door, pushed it open, and went into the front room, where, by the dim
light of a lamp burning at the foot of their bed, he saw Lou Pate and her husband in bed asleep. He spoke to them, and also called his wife's name. Getting
no answer, he stepped through the partition door into the back room, and discovered his wife and Thorn in the very act of adultery. They sprang up as they
caught sight of him, and both rushed by him through the doorway into the
front room; his wife blowing out the lamp as she passed the foot of the bed.
The defendant fired at Thorn, and killed his wife. Lou Pate, the only eyewit-
ness introduced by the state, corroborated the story of the defendant in its
main features. She testified that Thorn came to the house about first dark,

---

*Rowland v. State. Supreme Court of Mississippi. Jan. 25, 1904.

and, when she and her husband went to bed, Thorn and Becky were seated in the same room, talking; that she was awakened by hearing the defendant speak, and saw him standing in her room; that he went to the door between the rooms, and then Becky ran out of the back room into the front room, and blew out the lamp just as the defendant shot; that she did not see Thorn run out of the back room, and did not know how or when he got out of the house, but that after the shooting his horse was still hitched to the fence. Becky was in her nightclothes when killed. ■

PEOPLE v. ASHLAND
California Court of Appeals, 1912

Facts of the Case*

The facts and circumstances leading to and attending the commission of the   1
homicide are undisputed, and are substantially as follows: The defendant was a married man, whose family consisted of his wife, aged 24 years, and four children, aged respectively, six, four, and two years and the youngest eight months. With his wife and family he came to California from Philadelphia in the year 1909, and a short time after his arrival in this state he purchased a twenty acre tract of land near a place called and known as Avena, in San Joaquin County. With his family he settled on this land. He owed something like six hundred dollars on the purchase price of the property and, after trying his hand at farming, he found that he was thus making no headway in the reduction of his indebtedness, and, therefore, in the month of June, 1911, went to San Francisco to seek employment, leaving his wife and children on the farm. He remained in and about San Francisco, making in the mean time one visit to his home, until about the thirtieth day of December, 1911, on which date he received a letter from his wife containing, among other things, the following: ". . . Well, dear, there is a lot of news around here and they are all concerning me. I got myself in all kinds of trouble. Well, I shall tell you when you come home, and then I guess you will get a divorce from me all right. Well I will take my medicine for my foolishness. I am sorry, but I can't do any more than that. I don't really understand myself; it is not like me at all. I will not ask forgiveness from you. You can judge for yourself when you hear it. Please write soon and tell me when you will come home. . . . I do wish I could see you and speak to you. I feel so miserable."

   Upon reading the letter, Ashland immediately left San Francisco for his   2
home, reaching the latter place at about midnight of the day on which he received and read said letter. His wife then told him that one John Gofield (the deceased) who had for some time been in the community where the Ashlands resided serving in the capacity of a United States squirrel inspector, had had sexual intercourse with her on two different occasions—the first time on the eighteenth day of December, 1911, and the second time a few days thereafter,

---

**People v. Ashland.* California Court of Appeals. 1912.

or about Christmas day, and only a few days prior to the receipt by the defendant of the letter above referred to. She declared to her husband that the first sexual act with Gofield was forced upon her by threats and violence upon the part of the former; and that on both occasions the acts were committed on a cot situated in a bedroom in the defendant's house and where the children of the defendant were sleeping on both occasions.

It was about two o'clock in the morning when Mrs. Ashland finished   3
detailing the story of the conduct of Gofield toward her. The defendant thereupon left his house and went to the house of a Mr. Gannon, a neighbor residing a distance of about half a mile from the defendant's home. He awoke Gannon and said that he desired to talk with him. Gannon opened the door and allowed the defendant to enter, whereupon the latter inquired whether there was a "squirrel man" boarding at his (Gannon's) house. Gannon replied that there were two "squirrel men" who had boarded with him, but that they had left his home some time prior to that day. Gannon, at the request of the defendant, described the men, and the defendant recognized the deceased as one of the two so described, and declared that he was the man he was looking for. Gannon asked him his reason for seeking Gofield and the defendant excitedly and in a loud tone of voice replied: "He raped my wife! He raped my wife! twice, two different times, four days apart." He then asked Gannon whether he was telling him the truth when he said that the deceased was not in his (Gannon's) house at that time. Gannon assured the defendant that Gofield had gone to his home in Stockton and allowed him to go into the bedroom to assure himself that the deceased was not then in any of the rooms. Gannon then advised the defendant to go to the sheriff and explain his trouble to that official. The defendant, tapping his breast, replied: "If I find him before the sheriff finds him the sheriff will have to do with me and not with him. California is not big enough to hide him."

The defendant then returned to his home, reaching there after two   4
o'clock in the morning. At the hour of nine o'clock, he went to the home of a Mr. Ralph, another neighbor, whose home is situated about half a mile from that of the defendant. He excitedly told Mr. Ralph the story of the disgrace of himself and children by the conduct of his wife, and shortly thereafter returned to his home. At about eleven o'clock on the morning of the same day (Dec. 31, 1911), the defendant took the train at Avena, about half a mile distant from his house, and went to the city of Stockton. Arriving at Stockton, he immediately proceeded to make inquiries as to the location of the residence of Gofield and asked several persons whether they had seen him lately and where. Eventually he was given information as to the street and block in which Gofield's residence was situated and he immediately repaired to that neighborhood. This was about five o'clock P.M. He inquired of several persons whether they could point out to him the house of the deceased. It happened that a young son of the deceased overheard the defendant inquiring for Gofield and he thereupon volunteered to take the defendant to his father's house. The lad, upon reaching the house, followed closely by Ashland, opened the door and stepped inside, closing the door as

he did so, but the defendant immediately opened the door and stepped into the hallway. The boy told his father that there was a man on the outside who desired to see him. The deceased, who was sitting at this time, arose and put on his coat and went into the hallway, meeting Ashland. The former asked Gofield if he was the "squirrel man," and the latter answered affirmatively. Thereupon Ashland took Gofield by the arm and together they walked out on the porch. After reaching the porch, Ashland asked the deceased if his name was Gofield, and the latter replied that it was. Ashland then said, "You talked to my wife," and the deceased replied, "Do you know who you are talking to?" Again Ashland said, "You talked to my wife," and at the same time fired a shot.

Mrs. Gofield, wife of the deceased, was at her husband's side when the fatal shots were fired. In her language may best be told what occurred following the first shot: "My husband kind of sank back and over again, and I was over my husband, and this man Ashland lowered the revolver and put it between my arm and side and shot my husband in the back, and I was down over him. . . . My husband turned and ran in the house and I turned to go, too, and Ashland ran between myself and husband. . . . My husband was running in the house, and I started to follow and just as we got in the hall we met my husband's mother—she was living with us—and she caught my husband and they both staggered back into the dining room, and he sank on the floor." 5

Gofield died shortly thereafter, not having uttered a word after being shot. 6

After the shooting Ashland fled from the house and was followed by Gofield's father-in-law, who was at the former's house when the shooting occurred, and by one F. J. Murray, a policeman, living near by, who had heard the shots and hastened to Gofield's house to learn the cause and the result of the shooting. Ashland ran down several streets, followed by Murray, who ordered him to stop and fired several shots in the air for the purpose of thus stopping him. Ashland, however, kept on running until he reached the office of the chief of police, located in the court house, into which he ran and there surrendered himself to the chief. The defendant was in a high state of excitement when he reached the police office and upon entering said that he was looking for the chief. The latter, who was standing in the office, told Ashland that he was the chief, and the defendant excitedly threw his arms about the officer, exclaiming that he had shot the "squirrel man," Johnnie Gofield, and explained that he did the act because Gofield had ruined his wife and broken up his home. He delivered the weapon with which he did the shooting to the chief, and for some time thereafter was in an exceedingly nervous and somewhat hysterical condition, crying and moaning and otherwise acquitting himself as one keyed up to a highly nervous state. A physician was called in and treated the defendant and finally restored him to comparative tranquility. 7

Instructions to the Jury

MURDER—DEFINED

[Defendant is accused of having committed the crime of murder, a violation   1
of Penal Code section 187.]

    Every person who unlawfully kills a [human being] . . . [with malice   2
aforethought] . . . is guilty of the crime of murder in violation of section 187
of the Penal Code.

    [A killing is unlawful, if it [is] [neither] [justifiable] [nor] [excusable].]   3

    In order to prove this crime, each of the following elements must be   4
proved:

1. A human being was killed;
2. The killing was unlawful; and
3. The killing was done with malice aforethought.

"MALICE AFORETHOUGHT"—DEFINED

"Malice" may be either express or implied.   5

    [Malice is express when there is manifested an intention unlawfully to   6
kill a human being.]

    [Malice is implied when: 7

1.The killing resulted from an intentional act,

2.The natural consequences of the act are dangerous to human life, and

3.The act was deliberately performed with knowledge of the danger to, and
    with conscious disregard for, human life.]

    [When it is shown that a killing resulted from the intentional doing of an   8
act with express or implied malice, no other mental state need be shown to
establish the mental state of malice aforethought.]

    The mental state constituting malice aforethought does not necessari-   9
ly require any ill will or hatred of the person killed.

    The word "aforethought" does not imply deliberation or the lapse of   10
considerable time. It only means that the required mental state must precede rather than follow the act.

DELIBERATE AND PREMEDITATED MURDER

All murder which is perpetrated by any kind of willful, deliberate and premed-   11
itated killing with express malice aforethought is murder of the first degree.

    The word "willful," as used in this instruction, means intentional.   12

    The word "deliberate" means formed or arrived at or determined upon   13
as a result of careful thought and weighing of considerations for and against
the proposed course of action. The word "premeditated" means considered
beforehand.

    If you find that the killing was preceded and accompanied by a clear,   14
deliberate intent on the part of the defendant to kill, which was the result of

deliberation and premeditation, so that it must have been formed upon pre-existing reflection and not under a sudden heat of passion or other condition precluding the idea of deliberation, it is murder of the first degree.

    The law does not undertake to measure in units of time the length of the period during which the thought must be pondered before it can ripen into an intent to kill which is truly deliberate and premeditated. The time will vary with different individuals and under varying circumstances.   15

    The true test is not the duration of time, but rather the extent of the reflection. A cold, calculated judgment and decision may be arrived at in a short period of time, but a mere unconsidered and rash impulse, even though it includes an intent to kill, is not deliberation and premeditation as will fix an unlawful killing as murder of the first degree.   16

    To constitute a deliberate and premeditated killing, the slayer must weigh and consider the question of killing and the reasons for and against such a choice and, having in mind the consequences, [he] [she] decides to and does kill.   17

UNPREMEDITATED MURDER OF THE SECOND DEGREE

Murder of the second degree is . . . the unlawful killing of a human being with malice aforethought when the perpetrator intended unlawfully to kill a human being but the evidence is insufficient to prove deliberation and premeditation.   18

MANSLAUGHTER—DEFINED

The crime of manslaughter is the unlawful killing of a human being without malice aforethought. It is not divided into degrees but is of two kinds, namely, voluntary manslaughter and involuntary manslaughter.   19

VOLUNTARY MANSLAUGHTER—DEFINED

. . . Every person who unlawfully kills another human being without malice aforethought but with an intent to kill, is guilty of voluntary manslaughter in violation of Penal Code section 192(a).   20

    There is no malice aforethought if the killing occurred [upon a sudden quarrel or heat of passion] [or] [in the actual but unreasonable belief in the necessity to defend oneself against imminent peril to life or great bodily injury].   21

    In order to prove this crime, each of the following elements must be proved: 22
  1. A human being was killed;
  2. The killing was unlawful; and
  3. The killing was done with the intent to kill.
    [A killing is unlawful, if it was [neither] [not] [justifiable] [nor] [excusable].]   23

SUDDEN QUARREL OR HEAT OF PASSION AND PROVOCATION EXPLAINED

To reduce an intentional felonious homicide from the offense of murder to   24
manslaughter upon the ground of sudden quarrel or heat of passion, the
provocation must be of the character and degree as naturally would excite
and arouse the passion, and the assailant must act under the influence of
that sudden quarrel or heat of passion.

The heat of passion which will reduce a homicide to manslaughter must   25
be such a passion as naturally would be aroused in the mind of an ordinarily reasonable person in the same circumstances. A defendant is not permitted to set up [his] [her] own standard of conduct and to justify or excuse
[himself] [herself] because [his] [her] passions were aroused unless the circumstances in which the defendant was placed and the facts that confronted [him] [her] were such as also would have aroused the passion of the
ordinarily reasonable person faced with the same situation. [Legally adequate provocation may occur in a short, or over a considerable, period of
time.]

The question to be answered is whether or not, at the time of the killing,   26
the reason of the accused was obscured or disturbed by passion to such an
extent as would cause the ordinarily reasonable person of average disposition to act rashly and without deliberation and reflection, and from passion
rather than from judgment.

If there was provocation, [whether of short or long duration,] but of a   27
nature not normally sufficient to arouse passion, or if sufficient time elapsed
between the provocation and the fatal blow for passion to subside and
reason to return, and if an unlawful killing of a human being followed the
provocation and had all the elements of murder, as I have defined it, the
mere fact of slight or remote provocation will not reduce the offense to
manslaughter.

MURDER OR MANSLAUGHTER—COOLING PERIOD

To reduce a killing upon a sudden quarrel or heat of passion from murder to   28
manslaughter the killing must have occurred while the slayer was acting
under the direct and immediate influence of the quarrel or heat of passion.
Where the influence of the sudden quarrel or heat of passion has ceased to
obscure the mind of the accused, and sufficient time has elapsed for angry
passion to end and for reason to control [his] [her] conduct, it will no longer
reduce an intentional killing to manslaughter. The question, as to whether
the cooling period has elapsed and reason has returned, is not measured by
the standard of the accused, but the duration of the cooling period is the
time it would take the average or ordinarily reasonable person to have
cooled the passion, and for that person's reason to have returned.

■ ■ ■

Comparison-Contrast (Organized by Criteria)

Here is a plan for a comparison-contrast synthesis, organized by *criteria*. The thesis (and the *claim*) is as follows:

```
Ashland's case is not at all like Rowland's, and his
first-degree murder conviction must be affirmed.
```

A. Introduction. Background of the Ashland case. Initial comparison to apparently similar Rowland case. Rejection of comparison, leading to *thesis*.
B. Facts of each case.
   1. Rowland.
   2. Ashland.
C. The legal distinction between murder and manslaughter.
   1. Intentional killing under heat of passion—murder.
   2. Intentional killing when heat of passion has had time to cool—murder.
D. Ashland case contrasted to Rowland case.
   1. Whether there was premeditation and malice aforethought.
   2. Whether heat of passion had cooled.
E. Conclusion: Ashland was no longer acting under heat of passion—unlike Rowland—and so is guilty of murder.

Following is a comparison-contrast synthesis by criteria, written according to the preceding plan. (Thesis and topic sentences are highlighted.)

```
                Murder or Manslaughter?
```

```
On December 31, 1911. Harry Ashland shot and killed       1
John Gofield in Gofield's house in Stockton,
California. Ashland was enraged at Gofield, whom he
accused of raping his wife. The defendant was then
justifiably convicted of murder in the first degree.
Now he appeals his murder conviction and argues that
if he is guilty of anything, it is, at most, voluntary
manslaughter. He claims that the "heat of passion"
defense should apply to him, just as it applied to
Mose Rowland, whose murder conviction in 1904 was sub-
sequently reversed and who was then retried and con-
victed of voluntary manslaughter. But Ashland's case
```

is not at all like Rowland's, and his first-degree
murder conviction must be affirmed.

Let us first review the facts of each case. In   2
Rowland, the defendant "discovered his wife and [her
lover] in the very act of adultery." They had been
living apart, and she had been staying with another
married couple. Late one evening, Rowland arrived at
the house where Becky Rowland was staying, heard suspicious noises coming from the back bedroom, and upon
entering the bedroom, found his wife in bed with
another man. When the pair tried to flee, Rowland
fired at the man. He missed, but the shot killed Becky
Rowland. The killing occurred within seconds after
Rowland had discovered his wife and her lover having
sexual relations.

Contrast this series of events with those in   3
Ashland. In this case, the defendant, who had been
living and working in San Francisco, received a letter
from his wife in which she strongly implied that she
had been having an adulterous affair. When he arrived
home in the town of Avena, his wife confessed that she
had had sexual relations on two occasions with John
Gofield. The first time, she told him, she had been
raped. Ashland then asked a neighbor about Gofield and
discovered that he was living in Stockton. Ashland
then returned home, told his story to another neighbor, then took a train to Stockton, where he tracked
down Gofield. He went to Gofield's house, confronted
the man, and then shot him in cold blood in front of
his wife and son.

Is Harry Ashland guilty of murder or voluntary   4
manslaughter? The law makes a clear distinction
between these two crimes. Murder in the first degree
is defined as "willful, deliberate and premeditated
killing with express malice aforethought."
"Deliberate" means "formed or arrived at or determined
upon as a result of careful thought and weighing of
considerations . . . ." ("Jury Instructions"). A murder

charge may be reduced to voluntary manslaughter if the killing was carried out under the influence of a "heat of passion." However, the law requires that "Where the influence of . . . heat of passion has ceased to obscure the mind of the accused and sufficient time has elapsed for angry passion to end and for reason to control [his] conduct, it will no longer reduce an intentional killing to manslaughter" ("Jury Instructions").

Applying these rules, we find that the *Ashland* case 5 is very different from *Rowland*. First consider the issue of premeditation and malice aforethought. In *Rowland*, there was no time for premeditation of homicide since, until seconds before the killing, Rowland had no idea that his wife was having an affair with another man. For the same reason, he could not have had malice aforethought. Before the killing, he did not even know of the existence of Thorn, Becky Rowland's lover. On the other hand, Ashland had hours for premeditation after he learned of his wife's affair. His malice aforethought is shown by the statement he made to his neighbor, Mr. Gannon: "If I find him before the sheriff finds him, the sheriff will have to do with me and not with him. California is not big enough to hide him." This statement proves that Ashland was fully aware that he would be in trouble with the law if he killed Gofield. In planning the murder, he acted with "cold, calculated judgment and decision."

It is true that in both cases, the defendants had 6 sufficient provocation "as would excite and arouse the passion." This "passion" would be the immediate reaction of most people in the same situation. However, when we consider and apply what the law says about a cooling off period, we find that unlike Rowland, Ashland had no legal justification for shooting Gofield. In the case of Rowland, there was not time for a cooling off period since Rowland fired the fatal

shot almost immediately after he first discovered his
wife's adultery. But this was not the case with
Ashland. The law states that "whether the cooling
period has elapsed and reason has returned is not measured by the standard of the accused, but the duration
of the cooling period is the time it would take the
average or ordinarily reasonable person to have cooled
the passion, and for that person's reason to have
returned." The "ordinarily reasonable person" should
have had plenty of time to cool off during the fif-
teen-hour period between the time Ashland learned of
the adultery and his confrontation with Gofield.
Moreover, the fact that he was rational enough to take
a train to another town and then allow the deceased's
own son to lead him to Gofield shows just how cold-
blooded and malicious he was as he prepared to kill
his victim.

For these reasons the defendant's contention that   7
his case is like Rowland's, and so the charges against
him should be reduced to manslaughter, is groundless.
Both Rowland and Ashland were blameworthy, and both
should pay the price for their crimes. But while
Rowland can be partially excused by the fact that he
was acting under the "heat of passion," Harry Ashland
has no such excuse. Ashland is a "willful" and "deliberate" murderer, and his murder conviction should
stand.

References

California Jury Instructions: Criminal [CALJIC]: Book of
    Approved Jury Instructions. 8th ed. (1994). Committee
    on Standard Jury Instructions, Criminal, of the
    Superior Court of Los Angeles County, California.
    West.

People v. Ashland, 20 Cal. App. 168 (1912).

Rowland v. State, 35 So. 826 (1904).

DISCUSSION

The general organizational strategy of this argument can be described with the acronym IRAC—Issue, Rule, Application, Conclusion—a basic pattern of legal argument that also is applicable in other disciplinary areas. (For a fuller discussion of IRAC, see Charrow, Erhardt, and Charrow in Chapter 11, "You, the Jury.") This strategy calls for the writer first to define the *issue*, or the essential question that must be decided, then to explain the *rule* or rules that apply when such an issue is to be decided, then to discuss how the rule *applies* or does not apply to the particular case(s) at hand, and finally to *conclude* by answering the question expressed in the issue.

In argument terms, this conclusion is the *claim* that the writer is making; the rule is the *assumption* or *warrant* underlying the argument; and the application draws upon the *support* that provides the evidence proving the claim. Specifically, the writer (whose *purpose* is to prosecute the defendant) makes a claim that Ashland is guilty of murder. His *assumption* or *warrant* is the rule that a premeditated homicide committed with malice aforethought is murder. For comparison-contrast purposes, an unpremeditated homicide committed under the heat of passion is manslaughter. The writer offers *support* for his claim by detailing the facts of the two cases, arguing that for the purpose of proving his claim, the differences outweigh the similarities, and that while Rowland's actions constitute manslaughter, Ashland's constitute murder.

- In the first paragraph, the writer introduces the two heat-of-passion cases, but maintains in the thesis that the cases are different enough that while Rowland's murder conviction was overturned, Ashland's murder conviction should be upheld.
- In the second and third paragraphs, the writer summarizes the key facts of each case, emphasizing the immediate act of homicide in *Rowland* and the delayed killing in *Ashland*.
- In the fourth paragraph, the writer reviews the legal criteria for arriving at verdicts of murder and manslaughter. In particular, the writer emphasizes that murder is "willful" and "deliberate" and is carried out "with malice aforethought," while voluntary manslaughter is carried out under the influence of a "heat of passion" which has had insufficient time to cool.
- In the sixth and seventh paragraphs, the writer applies these legal criteria to the two cases. Paragraph six deals with the elements of premeditation and malice aforethought, showing that these elements were not present in *Rowland* but were in *Ashland*. In supporting his argument, the writer cites specific actions of the defendant Ashland— such as his declaration to his neighbor that if he found Gofield before the sheriff did, then the sheriff would have reason to arrest him.

- In the seventh paragraph, the writer focuses on the cooling off period, showing that there was no such period in *Rowland* (where the killing immediately followed the discovery), but that there was in *Ashland* where the defendant had 15 hours to let his passion cool off.
- In the eighth and final paragraph, the writer reiterates his conclusion; he concedes that the cases do have certain similar elements; however, they are also different enough, he argues, so that Ashland's murder conviction (unlike Rowland's) should be upheld.

SUMMARY

In this chapter, we've considered three main types of synthesis: the *explanatory synthesis*, the *argument synthesis*, and the *comparison-contrast synthesis*. Although for ease of comprehension we've placed them into separate categories, these types are not, of course, mutually exclusive. Both explanatory syntheses and argument syntheses often involve elements of one another, and comparison-contrast syntheses can fall into either of the previous categories. Which format you choose will depend upon your *purpose*, and the method you decide is best suited to achieve this purpose.

If your main purpose is to help your audience understand a particular subject, and in particular to help them understand the essential elements or significance of this subject, then you will be composing an explanatory synthesis. If your main purpose, on the other hand, is to persuade your audience to agree with your viewpoint on a subject, or to change their minds, or to decide upon a particular course of action, then you will be composing an argument synthesis. If one effective technique of making your case is to establish similarities or differences between your subject and another one, then you will compose a comparison-contrast synthesis—which may well be just *part* of a larger synthesis.

In planning and drafting these syntheses, you can draw upon a variety of strategies: supporting your claims by summarizing, paraphrasing, and quoting from your sources; using appeal to *logos*, *pathos*, and *ethos*; choosing from among formats such as climactic or conventional order, counterargument, and concession, that will best help you to achieve your purpose.

In the next chapter, "Research," we'll consider a category of synthesis commonly known as "the research paper." The research paper involves all of the skills in summary, critique, and synthesis that we've discussed so far, the main difference being, of course, that you won't find the sources you need in this particular text. We'll discuss approaches to locating and critically evaluating sources, selecting material from among them to provide support for your claims, and finally, documenting your sources in standard professional formats.

5

Research

GOING BEYOND THIS TEXT

In this chapter we'll discuss how you can use the skills you've learned in writing summaries, critiques, and syntheses to compose research papers and reports. A research paper is generally considered a major academic endeavor, and frequently it is. But even a paper based on only one or two sources outside the scope of assigned reading has been researched. Research requires you (1) to locate and take notes on relevant sources and organize your findings; (2) to summarize or paraphrase these sources; (3) to critically analyze them for their value and relevance to your subject; and (4) to synthesize information and ideas from several sources that best support your own critical viewpoint.

As you'll see, each chapter in Part II of *Writing and Reading Across the Curriculum* consists of a group of related readings on a particular subject—obedience to authority, biotechnology, Biblical literature, and so on. The readings in a chapter will give you a basic understanding of the key issues associated with the subject. For a deeper understanding, however, you'll need to go beyond the relatively few readings included here. A paper based on even two or three additional sources will have a breadth missing from a paper that relies exclusively on the text readings.

Of course, you may be asked to prepare a research paper of some length. Each chapter in Part II concludes with a number of research activities on the subject just covered. In some cases, we suggest particular sources; in others, we provide only general directions. Your instructor may ask you to work on at least one of these assignments during the term. But whether you are preparing an in-depth research paper or just locating a few additional sources on your subject (or something in between), it's essential to know your way around a college library, to be able to locate quickly and efficiently the information you need. In this chapter, we'll give you some important research tips. For more comprehensive information (e.g., annotated lists of specialized reference tools), consult a text on research papers or the research section of a handbook.

RESEARCH PAPERS IN THE ACADEMIC DISCIPLINES

Though most of your previous experience with research papers may have been in English classes, you should be prepared for instructors in other academic disciplines to assign papers with significant research components. Here, for example, is a sampling of research topics that have been assigned recently in a broad range of undergraduate courses:

Anthropology: Identify, observe, and gather data pertaining to a particular subculture within the campus community; describe the internal dynamics of this group, and account for these dynamics in terms of theories of relevant anthropologists and sociologists.

Art History: Discuss the main differences between Romanesque and Gothic sculpture, using the sculptures of Jeremiah (St. Pierre Cathedral) and St. Theodore (Chartres Cathedral) as major examples.

Asian-American Studies: Address an important socio-psychological issue for Asian-American communities and/or individuals—for example, the effects of stereotypes, mental health problems, sex role relations, academic achievement, assertiveness, or interracial marriage. Review both the theoretical and research literature on the issue, conduct personal interviews, and draw conclusions from your data.

Environmental Studies: Choose a problem or issue of the physical environment at any level from local to global. Use both field and library work to explore the situation. Include coverage of the following: (1) the history of the issue or problem; (2) the various interest groups involved, taking note of conflicts among them; (3) critical facts and theories from environmental science necessary to understand and evaluate the issue or problem; (4) impact and significance of management measures already taken or proposed; (5) your recommendations for management of the solution.

Film Studies: Pick a particular period of British film and discuss major film trends or production problems within that period.

History: Write a paper analyzing the history of a public policy (example: the U.S. Supreme Court's role in undermining the civil rights of African-Americans between 1870 and 1896), drawing your sources from the best, most current scholarly histories available.

Physics: Research and write a paper on solar cell technology, covering the following areas: basic physical theory, history and development, structure and materials, types and characteristics, practical uses, state of the art, and future prospects.

Political Science: Explain the contours of California's water policy in the last few decades and then, by focusing on one specific controversy, explain and analyze the way in which policy was adapted and why. Consider such questions as where the water comes from, how much, what quantity, who uses the water, who pays and how much, and should we develop more water resources.

Psychology: Explore some issue related to the testing of mental ability; for example, the effects of time limits upon test reliability.

Religious Studies: Select a particular religious group or movement present in the nation for at least twenty years and show how its belief or practice has changed since members of the group have been in America or, if the group began in America, since its first generation.

Sociology: Write on one of the following topics: (1) a critical comparison of two (or more) theories of deviance; (2) field or library research study of a specific deviant career: thieves, drug addicts, prostitutes, corrupt politicians, university administrators; (3) portrayals of deviance in popular culture—e.g., television "accounts" of terrorism, incest, spouse abuse; (4) old age as a form of deviance; (5) the relationship between homelessness and mental illness.

Some of these research papers allow students a considerable range of choice (within the general subject); others are highly specific in requiring students to address a particular issue. Most of these papers call for some library research; a few call for a combination of library and field research; others may be based entirely on field research.

WRITING THE RESEARCH PAPER

Here is an overview of the main steps involved in writing research papers. Keep in mind that as with other synthesis projects, writing research papers is a recursive process: You may not necessarily follow these steps in the order below, and you will find yourself backtracking and looping. This is not only normal, it is essential to carefully developed research.

- **Find a subject.** Decide what subject you are going to research and write about.
- **Develop a research question.** Formulate an important question that you would like to answer through your research.
- **Conduct preliminary research.** Consult knowledgeable people, general and specialized encyclopedias, overviews and bibliographies in recent books, the *Bibliographic Index*, and subject heading guides.
- **Conduct focused research.** Consult books, electronic databases, general and specialized periodicals, biographical indexes, general and specialized dictionaries, government publications, and other appropriate sources. Conduct interviews and surveys, as necessary.
- **Develop a working thesis.** Based on your initial research, formulate a working thesis that attempts to respond to your research question.
- **Develop a working bibliography.** Keep a working bibliography (either paper or electronic) of your sources. Make this bibliography easy to sort and rearrange.
- **Evaluate sources.** Attempt to determine the veracity and reliability of your sources; use your critical reading skills; check *Book Review Digest*; look up biographies of authors.
- **Take notes from sources.** Paraphrase and summarize important information and ideas from your sources. Copy down important quotations. Note page numbers from sources of this quoted and summarized material.
- **Arrange your notes according to your outline.** Develop a working outline of topics to be covered in your paper. Arrange your notes according to this outline.
- **Write your draft.** Write the preliminary draft of your paper, working from your notes, according to your outline.
- **Avoid plagiarism.** Take care to cite all quoted, paraphrased, and summarized source material, making sure that your own wording and sentence structure differ from those of your sources.
- **Cite sources.** Use in-text citations and a "Works Cited" or "References" list, according to the conventions of the discipline (e.g., MLA, APA, CBE).
- **Revise your draft.** Use transitional words and phrases to ensure coherence. Check for style. Make sure that the research paper reads smoothly, logically, and clearly from beginning to end. Check for grammatical correctness, punctuation, and spelling.

FINDING A SUBJECT

In your present writing course, finding a general subject shouldn't be a problem, since your research likely will concern one of the subjects covered in this text. And, as we've suggested, your instructor may assign you one of the research activities at the end of each chapter, for which some focus will be provided in our directions. Or your instructor may specify his or her own particular directions for your research activity. In other cases, you'll be asked simply to write a paper on some aspect of the subject.

Which aspect? Review the readings, the questions following the readings, and your responses to these questions. Something may immediately (or eventually) spring to mind. Perhaps while reading the chapter from Aldous Huxley's enormously influential *Brave New World* you wonder how the book was received by critics and general readers when it first appeared in 1932. Maybe while reading the selections on the Milgram experiment in the chapter on obedience to authority, you become curious about later experiments that also tested obedience to authority, or about a recent event that demonstrated the malign effects of obedience to unlawful or immoral authority. Consider the readings on biotechnology. What has been written on this subject since these selections appeared? To what extent have the terms of the debate on genome research changed?

THE RESEARCH QUESTION

Research handbooks generally advise students to narrow their subjects as much as possible. A ten-page paper on the modern feminist movement would be unmanageable. You would have to do an enormous quantity of research (a preliminary computer search of this subject would yield several thousand items), and you couldn't hope to produce anything other than a superficial treatment of such a broad subject. But a paper on the contemporary reception of *Brave New World* or on its relationship to other twentieth-century dystopias should be quite manageable. It's difficult to say, however, how narrow is narrow enough. (A literary critic once produced a twenty-page article analyzing the first paragraph of Henry James's *The Ambassadors*.)

Perhaps more helpful as a guideline on focusing your research is to seek to answer a particular question, a *research question*. For example, how did the Bush administration respond to the demand for bilingual education? To what extent is America perceived by social critics to be in decline? Did Exxon behave responsibly in handling the *Valdez* oil spill? How has the debate over genetic engineering evolved during the past decade? To what extent do contemporary cigarette ads perpetuate sexist attitudes? Or how do contemporary cigarette ads differ in message and tone from cigarette ads in the 1950s? Focusing on questions such as these and approaching your research as a way of answering such questions is probably the best way to narrow your subject and ensure focus in your paper. The essential answer to this research question eventually becomes your *thesis*, and in the paper you present evidence that systematically supports your thesis.

PRELIMINARY RESEARCH

Once you have a research question, you want to see what references are available. You want to familiarize yourself quickly with the basic issues and to generate a preliminary list of sources. There are many ways to go about doing this; some of the more effective ones are listed in the box below. We'll consider a few of these suggestions in more detail.

HOW TO FIND PRELIMINARY SOURCES AND NARROW THE SUBJECT

- Ask your instructor to recommend sources on the subject.
- Ask your college librarian for useful reference tools in your subject area.
- If you're working on a subject from this text, use some of the sources we've mentioned in the research activities section.
- Read an encyclopedia article on the subject and use the bibliography following the article.
- Read the introduction to a recent book on the subject and review that book's bibliography.
- Consult the annual *Bibliographic Index* (see page 182 for details).
- If you need help in narrowing a broad subject, consult one or more of the following:

  search by subject in an electronic database (the subject will be broken down into its components);

  the subject heading in an electronic periodical catalog, such as *InfoTrac*, or in a print catalog, such as the *Readers' Guide to Periodical Literature*;

  the *Library of Congress Subject Headings* catalog.

Consulting Knowledgeable People

When you think of research, you may immediately think of libraries and print material. But don't neglect a key reference source—other people. Your *instructor* probably can suggest fruitful areas of research and some useful sources. Try to see your *instructor* during office hours, however, rather than immediately before or after class, so that you'll have enough time for a productive discussion.

Once you get to the library, ask a *reference librarian* which reference sources (e.g., bibliographies, specialized encyclopedias, periodical indexes, statistical almanacs) you need for your particular area of research. Librarians won't do your research for you, but they'll be glad to show you how to research efficiently and systematically.

You can also obtain vital information from people when you interview them, ask them to fill out questionnaires or surveys, or have them participate in experiments. We'll cover this aspect of research in more detail below.

Encyclopedias

Reading an encyclopedia entry about your subject will give you a basic understanding of the most significant facts and issues. Whether the subject is American politics or the mechanics of genetic engineering, the encyclopedia article—written by a specialist in the field—offers a broad overview that may serve as a launching point to more specialized research in a particular area. The article may illuminate areas or raise questions that you feel motivated to pursue further. Equally important, the encyclopedia article frequently concludes with an *annotated bibliography* describing important books and articles on the subject.

Encyclopedias have certain limitations. First, most professors don't accept encyclopedia articles as legitimate sources for academic papers. You should use encyclopedias primarily to familiarize yourself with (and to select a particular aspect of) the subject area and as a springboard for further research. Also, because new editions appear only once every five or ten years, the information they contain—including bibliographies—may not be current. The current editions of the *Encyclopaedia Brittanica* and the *Encyclopedia Americana*, for instance, may not include information about the most recent developments in biotechnology.

Some of the most useful general encyclopedias include the following:

American Academic Encyclopedia
Encyclopedia Americana
New Encyclopaedia Britannica

Keep in mind that the library also contains a variety of more *specialized encyclopedias.* These encyclopedias restrict themselves to a particular disciplinary area, such as chemistry, law, or film, and are considerably more detailed in their treatment of a subject than general encyclopedias. Here are examples of specialized encyclopedias:

SOCIAL SCIENCES
Encyclopedia of Education
Encyclopedia of Psychology
Guide to American Law
International Encyclopedia of the Social Sciences

HUMANITIES
Encyclopedia of American History
Encyclopedia of Art
Encyclopedia of Religion and Ethics
International Encyclopedia of Film
The New College Encyclopedia of Music

SCIENCE AND TECHNOLOGY
  Encyclopedia of Biological Sciences
  Encyclopedia of Computer Science and Engineering
  Encyclopedia of Physics
  McGraw-Hill Encyclopedia of Environmental Science
  Van Nostrand's Scientific Encyclopedia

BUSINESS
  Encyclopedia of Banking and Finance
  Encyclopedia of Economics

Overviews and Bibliographies in Recent Books

If your professor or one of your bibliographic sources directs you to an important recent book on the subject, skim the introductory (and possibly the concluding) material to the book, along with the table of contents, for an overview of the key issues. Look also for a bibliography. For example, Zvi Dor-Ner's 1991 book *Columbus and the Age of Discovery* includes a four-page annotated bibliography of important reference sources on Columbus and the age of exploration.

Keep in mind that authors are not necessarily objective about their subjects, and some have particularly biased viewpoints that you may unwittingly carry over into your paper, treating them as objective truth.[1] However, you may still be able to get some useful information out of such sources. Alert yourself to authorial biases by looking up the reviews of your book in the *Book Review Digest* (described on page 184). Additionally, look up biographical information on the author (see Biographical Indexes, pages 191–192), whose previous writings or professional associations may suggest a predictable set of attitudes on the subject of your book.

Bibliographic Index

The *Bibliographic Index* is a series of annual volumes that enables you to locate bibliographies on a particular subject. The bibliographies it refers to generally appear at the end of book chapters or periodical articles, or they may themselves be book or pamphlet length. Browsing through the *Bibliographic*

---

[1]Bias is not necessarily bad. Authors, like all other people, have certain preferences and predilections that influence the way they view the world and the kinds of arguments they make. As long as they inform you of their biases, or as long as you are aware of them and take them into account, you can still use these sources judiciously. (You might gather valuable information from a book about the Watergate scandal, even if it were written by former President Richard Nixon or one of his top aides, as long as you make proper allowance for their understandable biases.) Bias becomes a potential problem only when it masquerades as objective truth or is accepted as such by the reader. For suggestions on identifying and assessing authorial bias, see the material on persuasive writing (pages 47–54) and evaluating assumptions (pages 55–56) in Chapter 2.

Index in a general subject area may give you ideas for further research in particular aspects of the subject, along, of course, with particular references.

Subject-Heading Guides

Seeing how a general subject (e.g., education) is broken down in other sources also could stimulate research in a particular area (e.g., bilingual primary education in California). As in the table of contents of a book, the general subject (the book title) is analyzed into its secondary subject headings (the chapter titles). To locate such sets of secondary subject headings, consult:

- an electronic database
- an electronic or print periodical catalog (e.g., *InfoTrac, Readers' Guide, Social Science Index*)
- *The Library of Congress Subject Headings* catalog
- The *Propaedia* volume of the *New Encyclopaedia Britannica* (1998)

FOCUSED RESEARCH

Once you've narrowed your scope to a particular subject and a particular research question (or set of research questions), you're ready to undertake more focused research. Your objective now is to learn as much as you can about your particular subject. Only in this way will you be qualified to make an informed response to your research question. This means you'll have to become something of an expert on the subject—or, if that's not possible, given time constraints, you can at least become someone whose critical viewpoint is based solidly on the available evidence. In the following pages we'll suggest how to find sources for this kind of focused research. In most cases, your research will be based on (1) *books*; (2) *electronic databases*; (3) *articles*; and (4) specialized *reference* sources. In certain cases, your research may be based partially or even primarily on (5) *interviews* and *surveys*.

Books

Books often are useful in providing both breadth and depth of coverage of a subject. Because they generally are published at least a year or two after the events treated, they also tend to provide the critical distance that is sometimes missing from articles. (Of course, books also may be shallow, inaccurate, outdated, or hopelessly biased; for help in making such determinations, see *Book Review Digest*, below.) You can locate relevant books through the electronic or card catalog. When using this catalog, you may search in three ways: (1) by *author*, (2) by *title*, and (3) by *subject*. Entries include the call number, the publication information, and frequently, a summary of the book's contents. Larger libraries use the Library of Congress cataloging system for call numbers (example: E111/C6); smaller ones use the Dewey Decimal System (example: 970.015/C726).

BOOK REVIEW DIGEST

Perhaps the best way to determine the reliability and credibility of a book you may want to use is to look it up in the annual *Book Review Digest*. These volumes list (alphabetically by author) the most significant books published during the year, supply a brief description of each, and, most importantly, provide excerpts from (and references to) reviews. If a book receives bad reviews, you don't necessarily have to avoid it (the book still may have something useful to offer, and the review itself may be unreliable). But you should take any negative reaction into account when using that book as a source.

Electronic Databases

Much of the information that is available in print—and a good deal that is not—is available in electronic form. Almost certainly, your library card catalog has been computerized, allowing you to conduct searches much faster and more easily than in the past. Increasingly, researchers are accessing magazine, newspaper, and journal articles and reports, abstracts, and other forms of information through *online* databases (many of them on the Internet) and through databases on *CD-ROMs*. One great advantage of using databases (as opposed to print indexes) is that you can search several years' worth of different periodicals at the same time.

Online databases—that is, those that originate outside your computer—are available through international, national, or local (e.g., campus) networks. The largest such database is DIALOG, which provides access to over 300 million records in over 400 databases, ranging from sociology to business to chemical engineering. In addition to being efficient and comprehensive, online databases are generally far more up-to-date than print sources. If your own computer has a modem, you can access many of these databases—including those available through commercial online services such as CompuServe and America Online—without leaving your room.

Access to online databases often requires an account and a password, which you may be able to obtain by virtue of your student status. In some cases, you will have to pay a fee to the local provider of the database, based on how long you are online. But many databases will be available to you free of charge. For example, your library may offer access through its computer terminals to magazine and newspaper databases, such as MAGS and NEWS, as well as to the Internet itself.

Various sites and files on the Internet may be accessed through their *gopher* or *ftp* (file transfer protocol) addresses. (Once you locate a file, you may have to download it to your disk or to your e-mail address.) More user-friendly is the *World Wide Web*, which offers graphics, multimedia, and "hyperlinks" to related material in numerous sources. To access these sources, you can either browse (i.e., follow your choice of paths or links wherever they lead) or type in a site's address.

For example, to get information on recent Supreme Court rulings, you could go to the gopher site *info.umd.edu* at the University of Maryland. From there, you would follow the directory path first by selecting *Academic*

Resources by Topic, then *United States* and *World Politics, Culture, and History*, then *United States*, and finally *Supreme Court Documents*. The relevant ftp site would be *ftp.cwru.edu* (at Case Western Reserve University), from which you would choose the path */hermes/˙*, for Hermes Project. (The ˙ is a symbol for a group of files, from which you would select according to your interest.) For corresponding information on the World Wide Web, go to *http://www.law.cornell.edu/supct/*. In many cases, you can narrow your searches through electronic databases by typing in *key words* or *descriptors*— the equivalent of subject headings.

To search for web information on a particular topic, try using one of the more popular "search engines":

Yahoo: http://www.yahoo.com/
Alta Vista: http://altavista.digital.com/
WebCrawler: http://webcrawler.com/
SearchCom: http://www.search.com/
Lycos: http://www-att.lycos.com/

Use keywords and the appropriate connectors ("and," "or," etc.) as indicated in the search engine's "Help" section.

CD-ROMs (compact disk-read only memory) used for research look just like sound CDs; but unlike sound CDs, they can display graphics. Many newspapers, magazines, and journals are available on CD-ROM: for example, the *Readers' Guide to Periodical Literature, The New York Times, Film Index International, PAIS International*, and *America: History and Life*, as are other standard reference sources, such as *Statistical Abstract of the U.S., The Encyclopaedia Britannica, Bibliography of Native North Americans, Environment Reporter*, and *National Criminal Justice Reference Service*. Of particular interest is *InfoTrac*, which provides access to over 1000 general interest, business, government, and technological periodicals.

Keep in mind, however, that while electronic sources make it far easier to access information than their print counterparts, they often do not go back more than a decade. For earlier information, therefore (e.g., contemporary reactions to the Milgram experiments of the 1960s), you would have to rely on print indexes.

The Benefits and the Pitfalls of the World Wide Web

In the last few years, the web has become not just a research tool, but a cultural phenomenon. The pop artist Andy Warhol once said that in the future everyone would be famous for fifteen minutes. He might have added that everyone would also have a personal web site. People use the web not just to look up information, but also to shop, to make contact with long-lost friends and relatives, to grind their personal or corporate axes, to advertise themselves and their accomplishments.

The web makes it possible for people sitting at home, work, or school to gain access to the resources of large libraries, and to explore corporate and government databases. In her informative book *The Research Paper and the World*, Dawn Rodrigues quotes Bruce Dobler and Harry Bloomberg on the essential role of the web in modern research:

> It isn't a matter anymore of using computer searches to locate existing documents buried in some far off library or archive. The Web is providing documents and resources that simply would be too expensive to publish on paper or CD-ROM.
>
> Right now—and not in some distant future—doing research without looking for resources on the Internet is, in most cases, not really looking hard enough. . . . A thorough researcher cannot totally avoid the Internet and the Web.[2]

And indeed, web sites are increasingly showing up as sources on both student and professional papers. But like any other rapidly growing and highly visible cultural phenomenon, the web has created its own backlash. First, as anyone who has tried it knows, systematically researching the web on many subjects is not possible. For all the information that is on the internet, there's a great deal more that is not and never will be converted to digital format. One library director has estimated that only about 4,000 of 150,000 published scholarly journals are available online, and many of these provide only partial texts of relatively recent articles in the paper editions. *The New York Times* is available on the web, but the online edition includes only a fraction of the content of the print edition, and online versions of the articles generally are abridged. If you are researching the rise of McCarthyism in America during the early 1950s or trying to determine who else, since Stanley Milgram, has conducted psychological experiments on obedience, you are unlikely to find much useful information for your purpose on the web.

Moreover, locating what *is* available is not always easy, since there's no standardized method—like the Library of Congress subheading and call number system—of cataloging and cross-referencing online information. The tens of thousands of web sites and millions of web pages, together with the relative crudity of "search engines" such as Yahoo, AltaVista, and WebCrawler have made navigating an ever expanding cyberspace an often daunting and frustrating procedure.

Second, it is not a given that people who do research on the web will produce better papers as a result. David Rothenberg, a professor of philosophy at New Jersey Institute of Technology, believes that "his students' papers had declined in quality since they began using the web for research" (Steven R. Knowlton, "Students Lost in Cyberspace," *Chronicle of Higher Education*, 2 Nov. 1997: 21). Neil Gabler, a cultural critic, writes:

> The Internet is such a huge receptacle of rumor, half-truth, misinformation and disinformation that the very idea of objective truth perishes in the avalanche. All you need to create a "fact" in the web world is a bulletin board or chat room. Gullible cybernauts do the rest.[3]

---

[2]Galen and Latchaw, 1997.

[3]"Why Let Truth Get in the Way of a Good Story?" *Los Angeles Times*, "Opinion," 26 Oct. 1997: 1.

Another critic is even blunter: "Much of what purports to be serious information is simply junk—neither current, objective, nor trustworthy. It may be impressive to the uninitiated, but it is clearly not of great use to scholars." (William Miller, "Troubling Myths About On-Line Information," *Chronicle of Higher Education*, 1 Aug. 1997: A44.)

Of course, print sources are not necessarily objective or reliable, either, and in Chapter 2, "Critical Reading," we discussed some criteria by which readers may evaluate the quality of information and ideas in *any* source (pp. 46–54). Web sources, however, present a special problem. In most cases, material destined for print has to go through one or more editors and fact checkers before being published, since most authors don't have the resources to publish and distribute their own writing. But anyone with a computer and a modem can "publish" on the web; and those with a good web authoring program and graphics software can create sites that, outwardly, at least, look just as professional and authoritative as those of the top academic, government, and business sites. These personal sites will appear in search engine listings—generated through keyword matches, rather than through independent assessments of quality or relevance—and uncritical researchers, using their information as a factual basis for the claims they make in their papers, do so at their peril.

We certainly don't mean to discourage web research. There are thousands of excellent sites in cyberspace. The reference departments of most college and university libraries will provide lists of such sites, arranged by discipline, and the most useful sites also are listed in the research sections of many handbooks. Most people locate web sites, however, by using search engines and by "surfing" the hyperlinks. And for web sources, more than print sources, the warning *caveat emptor*—let the buyer beware—applies.

In their extremely useful site, "Evaluating Web Resources" (http://www.science. widener.edu~withers/webeval.htm), reference librarians Jan Alexander and Marsha Tate offer some important guidelines for assessing web sources. First, they point out, it's important to determine what *type* of web page you are dealing with. Web pages generally fall into one of six types, each with a different purpose: (1) entertainment,(2) business/marketing, (3) reference/information, (4) news, (5) advocacy of a particular point of view or program, (6) personal page. The purpose of the page—informing, selling, persuading, entertaining—has a direct bearing upon the objectivity and reliability of the information presented.

Second, when evaluating a page, one should apply the same general criteria as are applied to print sources: (1) accuracy, (2) authority, (3) objectivity, (4) currency, (5) coverage. As we've noted, when assessing the *accuracy* of a web page, it's important to consider the likelihood that its information has been checked by anyone other than the author. When assessing the *authority* of the page, one considers the qualifications of the author to write on the subject and the reputability of the publisher. In many cases, it's difficult to determine not just the qualifications, but the very identity of the author. When assessing the *objectivity* of a web page, one considers the bias on the part of the author or authors and the extent to which the authors are trying to sway the opinion of their readers. Many web pages passing themselves off as informational are in fact little more than "infommercials." When assessing the *currency* of a web page, one asks whether the content is up-to-date and whether the publication date is labeled clearly. Dates on web pages often are missing or are not indicated clearly. If a date is provided, does it refer to the date the page was written, the date it was placed on the web, or the date it was last revised? Finally, when assessing the *coverage* of a web page, one considers what topics are included (and not included) in the work and whether the topics are covered in depth. Depth of coverage has generally not been a hallmark of web information.

Other pitfalls of web sites: reliable sites may include links to other sites that are inaccurate or outdated. Web pages also are notoriously unstable, frequently changing or even disappearing without notice.

Finally, the ease with which it's possible to surf the net can encourage intellectual laziness and make researchers too dependent upon web resources. Professors are increasingly seeing papers largely or even entirely based upon information in web sites. While web sources are indeed an important new source of otherwise unavailable information, there's often no substitute for library or other research, such as interviews or field study. The vast majority of printed material in even a small college library—much of it essential to informed research—does not appear on the web, nor is it likely to in the immediate future. All but a small fraction of the selections in Part Two of this book, for example, originally appeared on the printed page, rather than on web sites. Much of the material you will research in the next few years remains bound within covers. You may well learn of its existence in electronic databases, but at some point you'll have to walk over to a library shelf, pull out a book, and turn printed pages.

Periodicals: General

MAGAZINES

Because many more periodical articles than books are published every year, you are likely (depending on the subject) to find more information in periodicals than in books. By their nature, periodical articles tend to be more current than books (the best way, for example, to find out about the federal government's current policy on welfare reform is to look for articles in periodicals and newspapers). However, periodical articles may have less critical distance than books, and they also may date more rapidly—to be superseded by more recent articles.

General periodicals (such as *Time*, *The New Republic*, and *The Nation*) are intended for nonspecialists. Their articles, which tend to be highly readable, may be written by staff writers, free-lancers, or specialists. But usually they do not provide citations or other indications of sources and so are of limited usefulness for scholarly research.

The most well known general index is the *Readers' Guide to Periodical Literature*, and index of articles in several hundred general-interest magazines and a few more specialized magazines (such as *Business Week* and *Science Digest*). Articles in the *Readers' Guide* are indexed by author, title, and subject.

Another general reference for articles is the *Essay and General Literature Index*, which indexes articles contained in anthologies.

Increasingly, texts and abstracts of articles are available on online databases. These texts may be downloaded to your floppy disk or e-mailed to your e-mail address.

NEWSPAPERS

News stories, feature stories, and editorials (even letters to the editor) may be important sources of information. Your library certainly will have the *New York Times* index, and it may have indexes to other important newspapers, such as the *Washington Post*, the *Los Angeles Times*, the *Chicago Tribune*, the *Wall Street Journal*, and the *Christian Science Monitor*. Newspaper holdings will be on microfilm (your library may have the *New York Times* on CD-ROM), and you will need a microprinter/viewer to get hard copies.

Note: Because of its method of cross-referencing, the *New York Times* index may at first be confusing to use. Suppose that you want to find *Times* stories on bilingual education during a given year. When you locate the "Bilingual education" entry, you won't find citations, but rather a "*See also* Education" reference that directs you to seven dates (August 14, 15, and 17; September 11; October 20, 29, and 30) under the heading of "Education." Under this major heading, references to stories on education are arranged in chronological order from January to December. When you look up the dates you were directed to, you'll see brief descriptions of the stories on bilingual education.

Periodicals: Specialized

ARTICLES

Many professors will expect at least some of your research to be based on articles in specialized periodicals. So instead of (or in addition to) relying on an article from *Psychology Today* for an account of the effects of crack cocaine on mental functioning, you might (also) rely on an article from the *Journal of Abnormal Psychology*. If you are writing a paper on the satirist Jonathan Swift, you may need to locate a relevant article in *Eighteenth-Century Studies*. Articles in such journals normally are written by specialists and professionals in the field, rather than by staff writers or free-lancers, and the authors will assume that their readers already understand the basic facts and issues concerning the subject.

To find articles in specialized periodicals, you'll use specialized indexes—that is, indexes for particular disciplines. You also may find it helpful to refer to *abstracts*. Like specialized indexes, abstracts list articles published in a particular discipline over a given period, but they also provide summaries of the articles listed. Abstracts tend to be more selective than indexes, since they consume more space (and involve considerably more work to compile); but, because they also describe the contents of the articles covered, they can save you a lot of time in determining which articles you should read and which ones you can safely skip.

Here are some of the more commonly used specialized periodical indexes and abstracts in the various disciplines.

Note: Lists of electronic databases follow the print indexes, but some listed print indexes (e.g., PAIS) also are available in electronic form, such as CD-ROM.

SOCIAL SCIENCE
  Abstracts in Anthropology
  Education Index
  Index to Legal Periodicals
  Psychological Abstracts
  Public Affairs Information Service (PAIS)
  Social Science Index
  Sociological Abstracts
  Women's Studies Abstracts

  Social Science Databases:
    ERIC (Educational Resources Information Center)
    PAIS (Public Affairs Information Service)
    PSYCHINFO (psychology)
    Psychological Abstracts
    Social SciSearch
    Sociological Abstracts

HUMANITIES
  Abstracts of English Studies
  America: History and Life
  Art Index
  Cambridge Bibliography of English Literature
  Essay and General Literature Index
  Film/Literature Index
  Historical Abstracts
  Humanities Index
  International Index of Film Periodicals
  MLA International Bibliography of Books and Articles on Modern Languages and Literature
  Music Index
  Religion Index
  Year's Work in English Studies

  Humanities Databases:
    Arts and Humanities Citation Index
    MLA Bibliography
    Philosophers' Index
    Historical Abstracts

SCIENCE AND TECHNOLOGY
  Applied Science and Technology Index
  Biological Abstracts
  Engineering Index
  General Science Index
  Index to Scientific and Technical Proceedings

  Science and Technology Databases:
    Aerospace Database
    Agricola (agriculture)
    Biosis Previews (biology, botany)
    Chemical Abstracts search (chemistry)
    Compendex (engineering)
    Environment Abstracts
    MathSci
    MEDLINE (medical)
    ScienceCitation Index
    SciSearch
    WSPEC (physics, electronics, computer science)

BUSINESS
  Business Index
  Business Periodicals Index
  Economic Titles/Abstracts
  Wall Street Journal *Index*

  Business Databases:
    ABI/INFORM
    Econ Abstracts International
    Labor Statistics
    Standard and Poor's News

Biographical Indexes

To look up information on particular people, you can use not only encyclopedias but an array of biographical sources. (You can also use biographical sources to alert yourself to potential biases on the part of your source authors.) A brief selection follows:

LIVING PERSONS
  Contemporary Authors: A Biographical Guide to Current Authors and Their Works
  Current Biography
  International Who's Who
  Who's Who in America

PERSONS NO LONGER LIVING
  Dictionary of American Biography
  Dictionary of National Biography (Great Britain)
  Dictionary of Scientific Biography
  Who Was Who

PERSONS LIVING OR DEAD
  Biography Almanac
  McGraw-Hill Encyclopedia of World Biography
  Webster's Biographical Dictionary

Dictionaries

Use dictionaries to look up the meaning of general or specialized terms. Here are some of the most useful dictionaries:

GENERAL
  Oxford English Dictionary
  Webster's New Collegiate Dictionary
  Webster's Third New International Dictionary of the English Language

SOCIAL SCIENCES
  Black's Law Dictionary
  Dictionary of the Social Sciences
  McGraw-Hill Dictionary of Modern Economics

HUMANITIES
  Dictionary of American History
  Dictionary of Films
  Dictionary of Philosophy
  Harvard Dictionary of Music
  McGraw-Hill Dictionary of Art

SCIENCE AND TECHNOLOGY
  Computer Dictionary and Handbook
  Condensed Chemical Dictionary
  Dictionary of Biology
  Dorland's Medical Dictionary

BUSINESS
  Dictionary of Advertising Terms
  Dictionary of Business and Economics
  Mathematical Dictionary for Economics and Business Administration
  McGraw-Hill Dictionary of Modern Economics: A Handbook of Terms and Organizations

Other Sources/Government Publications

You also may find useful information in other sources. For statistical and other basic reference information on a subject, consult a *handbook* (example:

Statistical Abstracts of the United States). For current information on a subject as of a given year, consult an *almanac* (example: *World Almanac*). For annual updates of information, consult a *yearbook* (example: *The Statesman's Yearbook*). For maps and other geographic information, consult an *atlas* (example: *New York Times Atlas of the World*). (Often, simply browsing through the reference shelves for data on your general subject—such as biography, public affairs, psychology—will reveal valuable sources of information.) And of course, much reference information is available on government sites on the web.

Many libraries keep pamphlets in a *vertical file* (i.e., a file cabinet). For example, a pamphlet on AIDS might be found in the vertical file, rather than in the library stacks. Such material is accessible through the *Vertical File Index* (a monthly subject and title index to pamphlet material).

Finally, note that the U.S. government regularly publishes large quantities of useful information. Some indexes to government publications:

American Statistics Index
Congressional Information Service
The Congressional Record
Information U.S.A.

Interviews and Surveys

Depending on the subject of your paper, some or all of your research may be conducted outside the library. You may pursue research in science labs, in courthouses, in city government files, in shopping malls (if you are observing, say, patterns of consumer behavior), in the quad in front of the humanities building, or in front of TV screens (if you are analyzing, say situation comedies or commercials, or if you are drawing on documentaries or interviews—in which cases you should try to obtain transcripts or tape the programs).

You may want to *interview* you professors, your fellow students, or other individuals knowledgeable about your subject. Before interviewing your subject(s), become knowledgeable enough about the topic that you can ask intelligent questions. You also should prepare most of your questions beforehand. Ask "open-ended" questions designed to elicit meaningful responses, rather than "forced choice" questions that can be answered with a word or two, or "leading questions" that presume a particular answer. (Example: Instead of asking, "Do you think that men should be more sensitive to women's concerns for equality in the workplace?" ask, "To what extent do you see evidence that men are insufficiently sensitive to women's concerns for equality in the workplace?") Ask follow-up questions to elicit additional insights or details. If you record the interview (in addition to or instead of taking notes), get your subject's permission, preferably in writing.

Surveys or *questionnaires*, when well prepared, can produce valuable information about the ideas or preferences of a group of people. Before preparing your questions, determine your purpose in conducting the survey, exactly what kind of information you want to obtain, and whom you are going to ask

for the information. Decide also whether you want to collect the questionnaires as soon as people have filled them out or whether you want the responses mailed back to you. (Obviously, in the latter case, you have to provide
stamped, self-addressed envelopes and specify a deadline for return.) Keep in
mind that the larger and the more representative your sample of people, the
more reliable the survey. As with interviews, it's important to devise and
word questions carefully, so that they (1) are understandable and (2) don't
reflect your own biases. If you're surveying attitudes on capital punishment,
for example, and you ask, "Do you believe that the state should endorse
legalized murder?" you've loaded the questions to influence people to answer
in the negative, and thus you've destroyed the reliability of your survey.

Unlike interview questions, survey questions should be short answer or
multiple choice; open-ended questions encourage responses that are difficult to
quantify. (You may want to leave space, however, for "additional comments.") Conversely, "yes" or "no" responses or rankings on a 5-point scale
are easy to quantify. For example, you might ask a random sample of students
in your residence hall the extent to which they are concerned that genetic
information about themselves might be made available to their insurance
companies—on a scale of 1 (unconcerned) to 5 (extremely concerned). For
surveys on certain subjects (and depending on the number of respondents), it
may be useful to break out the responses by as many meaningful categories as
possible—for example, gender, age, ethnicity, religion, education, geographic locality, profession, and income. Obtaining these kinds of statistical break-
downs, of course, means more work on the part of your respondents in filling
out the surveys and more work for you in compiling the responses. If the
survey is too long and involved, some subjects won't participate or won't
return the questionnaires.

FROM RESEARCH TO WORKING THESIS

The search strategy we've just described isn't necessarily a straight-line process.
In other words, you won't always proceed from the kinds of things you do in
"preliminary research" to the kinds of things you do in "focused research."
You may not formulate a research question until you've done a good deal of
focused research. And the fact that we've treated, say, biographical sources
before specialized periodical articles does not mean that you should read biographical material before you read articles. We've described the process as we
have for convenience; and, *in general*, it is a good idea to proceed from more
general sources to more particular ones. In practice, however, the research procedure often is considerably less systematic. You might begin, for example, by
reading a few articles on the subject, continue by looking up an encyclopedia
article or two. Along the way, you might consult specialized dictionaries,
book review indexes, and a guide to reference books in the area. Or, instead
of proceeding in a straight line though the process, you might find yourself
moving in circular patterns—backtracking to previous steps and following up

leads you missed or ignored earlier. There's nothing wrong with such variations of the basic search strategy, as long as you keep in mind the kinds of resources that are available to you, and as long as you plan to look up as many of these resources as you can—given the constraints on your time.

One other thing you'll discover as you proceed: research is to some extent a self-generating process. That is, one source will lead you—through references in the text, citations, and bibliographic entries—to others. Your authors will refer to other studies on the subject; and, frequently, they'll indicate which ones they believe are the most important, and why. At some point, if your research has been systematic, you'll realize that you've already looked at most of the key work on the subject. This is the point at which you can be reasonably assured that the research stage of your paper is nearing its end.

As your work progresses, you may find that your preliminary research question undergoes a change. Suppose you are researching bilingual education. At first, you may have been primarily interested in the question of whether bilingual education is a good idea. During your research, you come across S. I. Hayakawa's controversial proposal that English be made the official language of the United States, and you decide to shift the direction of your research toward this particular debate. Or, having made an initial assessment that bilingual education is a good idea, you conclude that Hayakawa is wrong. Be prepared for such shifts: they're a natural—and desirable—part of the research (and learning) process. They indicate that you haven't made up your mind in advance, that you're open to new evidence and ideas.

You're now ready to respond to your modified research questions with a *working thesis*—a statement that controls and focuses your entire paper, points toward your conclusion, and is supported by your evidence. See our earlier discussion, in Chapter 3 (pages 85–91), on the process of devising and narrowing a thesis.

THE WORKING BIBLIOGRAPHY

As you conduct your research, keep a working bibliography—that is, a set of bibliographic information on all the sources you're likely to use in preparing the paper. Compile full bibliographic information as you consider each source. It's better to spend time during the research process noting information on a source you don't eventually use than to go back to retrieve information—such as the publisher or the date—just as you're typing your final draft.

The most efficient way to compile bibliographic information is on 3" x 5" cards. (Note, however, that some software programs allow you to create sortable electronic cards.) You can easily add, delete, and rearrange cards as your research progresses. On each card record:

A. the author or editor (last name first)
B. the title (and subtitle) of the book or article

C. the publisher and place of publication (if a book) or the title of the periodical
D. the date of publication; if periodical, volume and issue number
E. the inclusive page numbers (if article)

You also may want to include on the bibliography card:

F. a brief description of the source (to help you recall it later in the research process)
G. the library call number (to help you relocate the source if you haven't checked it out)
H. a code number, which you can use as a shorthand reference to the source in your notecards

Your final bibliography, known as "Works Cited" in Modern Language Association (MLA) format and "References" in American Psychological Association (APA) format, consists of the sources you have actually summarized, paraphrased, or quoted in your paper. When you compile the bibliography, arrange the cards in alphabetical order and type the references one after another.

Here is an example of a working bibliography card for a book:

Sale, Kirkpatrick. The Conquest of Paradise: Christopher Columbus and the Columbian Legacy. New York: Knopf, 1990.

Attacks Columbian legacy for genocide and ecocide. Good treatment of Columbus's voyages (Chaps. 6-8).

Here is an example of a working bibliography card for an article:

Axtell, James. "Europeans, Indians and the Age of Discovery in American History Textbooks." American Historical Review. 92.3 (1987): 621-32.

Finds treatments of subjects in title of article inadequate in most college-level American history texts. Specifies "errors," "half-truths" and "misleading assertions." Recommends changes in nine areas.

Some instructors may ask you to prepare—either in addition to or instead of a research paper—an *annotated bibliography*. This is a list of relevant works on a subject, with the contents of each briefly described or assessed. The bibliography cards shown provide examples of two entries in an annotated bibliography on the Columbian legacy. Annotations are different from *abstracts* in that they do not claim to be comprehensive summaries; they indicate, rather, how the items may be useful to the prospective researcher.

EVALUATING SOURCES

As you sift through what seems a formidable mountain of material, you'll need to work quickly and efficiently; you'll also need to do some selecting. This means, primarily, distinguishing the more important from the less important (and the unimportant) material. The hints in the box below can simplify the task.

HOW TO EVALUATE SOURCES

- **Skim** the source: With a book, look over the table of contents, the introduction and conclusion, and the index; zero in on passages that your initial survey suggests are important. With an article, skim the introduction and the headings.
- Be on the alert for **references** in your sources to other important sources, particularly to sources that several authors treat as important.
- Other things being equal, the more **recent** the source, the better. Recent work often incorporates or refers to important earlier work.
- If you're considering making multiple references to a book, look up the **reviews** in the *Book Review Digest* or the *Book Review Index*. Also, check the author's credentials in a source such as *Contemporary Authors* or *Current Biography*.
- Draw on your **critical reading** skills to help you determine the reliability and value of a source (see Chapter 2).

NOTE-TAKING

People have their favorite ways of note-taking. Some use cards; others use legal pads or spiral notebooks; yet others type notes into a laptop computer, perhaps using a database program. We prefer 4" x 6" cards for note-taking. Such cards have some of the same advantages as 3" x 5" cards for working bibliographies: they can easily be added to, subtracted from, and rearranged to accommodate changing organizational plans. Also, discrete pieces of information from the same source can easily be arranged (and rearranged) into subtopics—a difficult task if you have three pages of notes on an entire article.

Whatever your preferred approach, we recommend including, along with the note itself,

A. a page reference
B. a topic or subtopic label, corresponding to your outline (see below)
C. a code number, corresponding to the number assigned the source in the working bibliography

Here is a sample notecard for an article by Charles Krauthammer entitled "Hail Columbus, Dead White Male" (*Time*, May 27, 1991):

Defenses of Columbus (III B)   ⑦

Defends Columbus against revisionist attacks. Our civilization "turned out better" than that of the Incas. "And mankind is the better for it. Infinitely better. Reason enough to honor Columbus and 1492" (74).

Here is a notecard for the specialized periodical article by Axtell (see bibliography card on page 196):

Problems with Textbooks (II A)   ⑫

American history textbooks do not give adequate coverage to the Age of Discovery. An average of only 4% of the textbook pages covering first-semester topics is devoted to the century that accounts for 30% of the time between Columbus and Reconstruction. "The challenge of explaining some of the most complex, important, and interesting events in human history—the discovery of a new continent, the religious upheavals of the sixteenth century, the forging of the Spanish empire, the Columbian biological exchange, the African diaspora—all in twenty or twenty-five pages—is one that few, if any, textbook authors have met or are likely to meet" (623).

The notecard is headed by a topic label followed by the tentative location in the paper outline where the information will be used. The number in the upper right corner is coded to the corresponding bibliography card. The note itself in the first card uses *summary* ("Defends Columbus against revisionist attacks") and *quotation*. The note in the second card uses *summary* (sentence 1), *paraphrase* (sentence 2), and *quotation* (sentence 3). Summary was used to condense important ideas treated in several paragraphs in the sources; paraphrase, for the important detail on textbook coverage; quotation, for particularly incisive language by the source authors. For general hints on when to use each of these three forms, see page 42.

ARRANGING YOUR NOTES: THE OUTLINE

Recall that your research originally was stimulated by one or more *research questions*, to which you may have made a tentative response in your *working thesis* (see page 179). As you proceed with your research, patterns should begin to emerge that either substantiate, refute, or otherwise affect your working thesis. These patterns represent the relationships you discern among the various ideas and pieces of evidence that you investigate. They may be patterns of cause and effect, of chronology, of logical relationships, of comparison and contrast, of pro and con, of correspondence (or lack of correspondence) between theory and reality. Once these patterns begin to emerge, write them down as the components of a preliminary outline. This outline indicates the order in which you plan to support your original working thesis or a new thesis that you have developed during the course of research.

For example, on deciding to investigate new genetic technologies, you devise a working thesis focused on the intensity of the debate over the applications of such technologies. Much of the debate, you discover, focuses on arguments about the morality of (1) testing for genetic abnormalities in the fetus, (2) using genetic information to screen prospective employees, and (3) disrupting the ecosystem by creating new organisms. Based on this discovery, you might create a brief outline, numbering each of these three main categories (as examples of the pro-con debates) and using these numbers on your notecards to indicate how you have (at least provisionally) categorized each note. As you continue your research, you'll be able to expand or reduce the scope of your paper, modifying your outline as necessary. Your developing outline becomes a guide to continuing research.

Some people prefer not to develop an outline until they have more or less completed their research. At that point they will look over their notecards, consider the relationships among the various pieces of evidence, possibly arrange their cards into separate piles, and then develop an outline based on their perceptions and insights about the material. They will then rearrange (and code) the notecards to conform to their newly created outline.

In the past, instructors commonly required students to develop multileveled formal outlines (complete with Roman and Arabic numerals) before writing their first drafts. But many writers find it difficult to generate papers from such elaborate outlines, which sometimes restrict, rather than stimulate, thought. Now, many instructors recommend only that students prepare an *informal outline*, indicating just the main sections of the paper, and possibly one level below that. Thus, a paper on how the significance of Columbus's legacy has changed over the years may be informally outlined as follows:

```
Intro: Different views of Columbus, past and pre-
    sent;
        —thesis: view of Columbus varies with temper
        of times
Pre-20th-century assessments of Columbus and legacy
The debate over the quincentennial
        —positive views
        —negative views
Conclusion: How to assess Columbian heritage
```

Such an outline will help you organize your research and should not be unduly restrictive as a guide to writing.

The *formal outline* (a multileveled plan with Roman and Arabic numerals, capital and small lettered subheadings) may still be useful, not so much as an exact blueprint for composition—although some writers do find it useful for this purpose—but rather as a guide to revision. That is, after you have written your draft, outlining it may help you discern structural problems: illogical sequences of material; confusing relationships between ideas; poor unity or coherence; sections that are too abstract or underdeveloped. Many instructors also require that formal outlines accompany the finished research paper.

The formal outline should indicate the logical relationships in the evidence relating to your particular subject (see example below). But it also may reflect the general conventions of presenting academic ideas. Thus, after an *introduction*, papers in the social sciences often proceed with a description of the *methods* of collecting information, continue with a description of the *results* of the investigation, and end with a *conclusion*. Papers in the sciences often follow a similar pattern. Papers in the humanities generally are less standardized in form. In devising a logical organization for your paper, ask yourself how your reader might best be introduced to the subject, be guided through a discussion of the main issues, and be persuaded that your viewpoint is a sound one.

Formal outlines are generally of two types: *topic* and *sentence outlines*. In the topic outline, headings and subheadings are indicated by words or phrases—as in the informal outline above. In the sentence outline, each heading and subheading is indicated in a complete sentence. Both topic and sentence outlines generally are preceded by the topic sentence.

Here is an example of a sentence outline:

Thesis: How Columbus, his voyages, and his legacy are assessed varies, depending on the values of the times.

    I. Early 19th-century and late 20th-century assessments of Columbus are 180 degrees apart.

       A. 19th-century commentators idolize him.

       B. 20th-century commentators often demonize him.

       C. Shifting assessments are based less on hard facts about Columbus than on the values of the culture that assesses him.

    II. In the 16th and 17th centuries, Columbus was not yet being used for political purposes.

       A. In the early 16th century, his fame was eclipsed by that of others.

          1. Amerigo Vespucci and Vasco da Gama were considered more successful mariners.

          2. Cortés and Pizarro were more successful in bringing back wealth from the New World.

       B. In the next century, historians and artists began writing of the achievements of Columbus, but without an overt political purpose.

          1. The first biography of Columbus was written by his son Fernando.

          2. Plays about Columbus were written by Lope de Vega and others.

       C. An important exception was that in 1542 the monk Bartolomé de las Casas attacked the Spanish legacy in the Americas--although he did not attack Columbus personally.

    III. In the 18th and 19th centuries, Columbus and his legacy began to be used for political purposes.

       A. During the late 18th century, Columbus's stature in America increased as part of the attempt to stir up anti-British sentiment.

          1. Columbus was opposed by kings, since he "discovered" a land free of royal authority.

          2. Columbus, the bold visionary who charted unknown territories, became symbolic of the American spirit.

B. During the 19th century, Columbus's reputation reached its peak.

    1. For some, Columbus represented geographical and industrial expansion, optimism, and faith in progress.

    2. For others, Columbus's success was the archetypal rags-to-riches story at the heart of the American Dream.

    3. After the Civil War, Catholics celebrated Columbus as an ethnic hero.

    4. The 400th anniversary of Columbus's landfall both celebrated the past and expressed confidence in the future. Columbus became the symbol of American industrial success.

IV. By the quincentennial of Columbus's landfall, the negative assessments of Columbus were far more evident than positive assessments.

A. Historians and commentators charged that the consequences of Columbus's "discoveries" were imperialism, slavery, genocide, and ecocide.

B. The National Council of Churches published a resolution blasting the Columbian legacy.

C. Kirkpatrick Sale's *The Conquest of Paradise* also attacked Columbus.

D. Native Americans and others protested the quincentennial and planned counter-demonstrations.

V. Conclusion: How should we judge Columbus?

A. In many ways, Columbus was a man of his time and did not rise above his time.

B. In his imagination and boldness and in the impact of his discoveries, Columbus stands above others of his time.

C. When we assess Columbus and his legacy, we also assess our own self-confidence, our optimism, and our faith in progress.

WRITING THE DRAFT

Your goal in drafting your paper is to support your thesis by clearly and logically presenting your evidence—evidence that you summarize, critique, and synthesize. (For a review of the techniques of summary, critique, and synthesis, see Chapters 1, 2, and 4.) In effect, you are creating and moderating a conversation among your sources that supports the conclusions you have drawn from your exploration and analysis of the material. The finished paper, however, should not merely represent an amalgam of your sources; it should present your own particular critical perspective on the subject. Your job is to select and arrange your material in such a way that your conclusions seem inevitable (or at least reasonable). You also must select and arrange your material in a way that is fair and logical; remember that your paper will be evaluated to some degree on whether it meets the standards of logical argumentation discussed on pages 50–54. Try not to be guilty of such logical fallacies as hasty generalization, false analogy, and either/or reasoning.

As we suggested in the section on introductions (pages 80–84), when writing the first draft it's sometimes best to skip the introduction (you'll come back to it later when you have a better idea of just what's being introduced) and to start with the main body of your discussion. What do you have to tell your audience about your subject? It may help to imagine yourself sitting opposite your audience in an informal setting like the student center, telling them what you've discovered in the course of your research, and why you think it's interesting and significant. The fact that you've accumulated a considerable body of evidence (in your notecards) to support your thesis should give you confidence in presenting your argument. Keep in mind, too, that there's no one right way to organize this argument; any number of ways will work, provided each makes logical sense. And if you're working on a computer, it is particularly easy to move whole paragraphs and sections from one place to another.

Begin the drafting process by looking at your notecards. Arrange the cards to correspond to your outline. Summarize, paraphrase, and quote from your notecards as you draft. (One timesaving technique for the first draft is to tape photocopied quotations in the appropriate places in your draft.) If necessary, review the material on explanatory and argument syntheses (pages 95–156). In particular, note the table "How to Write Syntheses" (pages 102–103 and inside back cover) and "Developing and Organizing the Support for Your Arguments" (pages 157–174). When presenting your argument, consider such rhetorical strategies as counterargument, concession, and comparison and contrast. The sample student papers in the synthesis chapter may serve as models for your own research paper.

As you work through your notecards, be selective. Don't provide more evidence or discussion than you need to prove your point. Resist the urge to use *all* of your material just to show how much research you've done. (One experienced teacher, Susan M. Hubbuch, scornfully refers to papers with too much information as "memory dumps"—consisting of nothing but "mindless regurgitation of everything you have read about a subject.") Also avoid going into extended discussions of what are essentially tangential issues. Keep focused on your research questions and on providing support for your thesis.

At the same time, remember that you *are* working on a rough draft—one that will probably have all kinds of problems, from illogical organization to awkward sentence structure to a banal conclusion. Don't worry about it; you can deal with all such problems in subsequent drafts. The important thing now is get the words on paper (or on your disk).

AVOIDING PLAGIARISM

Plagiarism generally is defined as the attempt to pass off the work of another as one's own. Whether born out of calculation or desperation, plagiarism is the least tolerated offense in the academic world. The fact that most plagiarism is unintentional—arising from ignorance of conventions rather than deceitfulness—makes no difference to many professors.

You can avoid plagiarism and charges of plagiarism by following the basic rules below:

RULES TO AVOID PLAGIARISM

- Cite (a) *all* quoted material and (b) *all* summarized and paraphrased material, unless the information is common knowledge (e.g., the Civil War was fought from 1861 to 1865).
- Make sure that both the *wording* and the *sentence structure* of your summaries and paraphrases are substantially your own.

Following is a passage of text, along with several student versions of the ideas represented. (The passage is from Richard Rovere's April 30, 1967, *New York Times Magazine* article, "The Most Gifted and Successful Demagogue This Country Has Ever Known.")

> McCarthy never seemed to believe in himself or in anything he had said. He knew that Communists were not in charge of American foreign policy. He knew that they weren't running the United States Army. He knew that he had spent five years looking for Communists in the government and that—although some must certainly have been there, since Communists had turned up in practically every other major government in the world—he hadn't come up with even one.

One student version of this passage reads as follows:

```
McCarthy never believed in himself or in anything he
    had said. He knew that Communists were not in charge of
```

```
American foreign policy and weren't running the United
States Army. He knew that he had spent five years look-
ing for Communists in the government, and although
there must certainly have been some there, since
Communists were in practically every other major gov-
ernment in the world, he hadn't come up with even one.
```

Clearly, this is intentional plagiarism. The student has copied the original passage almost word for word.

Here is another version of the same passage:

```
McCarthy knew that Communists were not running foreign
policy or the Army. He also knew that although there
must have been some Communists in the government, he
hadn't found a single one, even though he had spent
five years looking.
```

This student has attempted to put the ideas into her own words, but both the wording and the sentence structure still are so heavily dependent on the original passage that even if it *were* cited, most professors would consider it plagiarism.

In the following version, the student has sufficiently changed the wording and sentence structure, and she properly credits the information to Rovere, so that there is no question of plagiarism:

```
According to Richard Rovere, McCarthy was cynical
enough to know that Communists were running neither
the government nor the Army. He also knew that he
hadn't found a single Communist in government, even
after a lengthy search (192).
```

Apart from questions of plagiarism, it's essential to quote accurately. You are not permitted to change any part of a quotation or to omit any part of it without using brackets or ellipses (see pages 39–42).

CITING SOURCES

When you refer to or quote the work of another, you are obligated to credit or cite your source properly. There are two types of citations, and they work in tandem.

If you are writing a paper in the humanities, you probably will be expected to use the Modern Language Association (MLA) format for citation. This format is fully described in the *MLA Handbook for Writers of Research Papers*, 5th ed. (New York: Modern Language Association of America, 1998).

A paper in the social sciences will probably use the American Psychological Association (APA) format. This format is fully described in the *Publication Manual of the American Psychological Association*, 4th ed. (Washington, D.C.: American Psychological Association, 1994).

In the following section, we will focus on MLA and APA styles, the ones you are most likely to use in your academic work. Keep in mind, however, that instructors often have their own preferences. Some require the documentation style specified in the *Chicago Manual of Style*, 14th ed. (Chicago: University of Chicago Press, 1993). This style is similar to the American Psychological Association style, except that publication dates are not placed within parentheses. Instructors in the sciences often follow the Council of Biology Editors (CBE) format. Or they may prefer a number format: each source listed on the bibliography page is assigned a number, and all text references to the source are followed by the appropriate number within parentheses. Some instructors like the old MLA style, which calls for footnotes and endnotes. Check with your instructor for the preferred documentation format if this is not specified in the assignment itself.

In-Text Citation

The general rule for in-text citation is to include only enough information to alert the reader to the source of the reference and to the location within that source. Normally, this information includes the author's last name and page number. But if you have already named the author in the preceding text, just the page number is sufficient.

TYPES OF CITATIONS

- Citations that indicate the source of quotations, paraphrases, and summarized information and ideas—these citations appear *in text*, within parentheses.
- Citations that appear in an alphabetical list of "Works Cited" or "References" following the paper.

Content Notes

Occasionally, you may want to provide a footnote or an endnote as a *content note*—one that provides additional information bearing on or illuminating, but not directly related to, the discussion at hand. For example:

[1] Equally well known is Forster's distinction between story and plot: in the former, the emphasis is on sequence ("the king died and then the queen died"); in the latter, the emphasis is on causality (the kind died and then the queen died of grief").

Notice the format: Indent five spaces or one-half inch and type the note number, raised one-half line. Then space once more and begin the note. Subsequent lines of the note are flush with the left margin. If the note is at the bottom of the page (a footnote), quadruple-space between the text and the footnote, single-spacing the note itself. Content notes are numbered consecutively throughout the paper; do not begin renumbering on each page.

References Page

In MLA format, your list of sources is called "Works Cited." In APA format, it is called "References." Entries in this listing should be double-spaced, with second and subsequent lines of each entry indented (a "hanging indent")—five spaces or one-half inch. In both styles, a single space follows the period.

The main difference between MLA and APA styles is that in MLA style, the date of the publication follows the name of the publisher; in APA style, the date is placed within parentheses following the author's name. Other differences: In APA style, only the initial of the author's first name is indicated, and only the first word (and any proper noun) of the book or article title and subtitle is capitalized. In MLA style, all words following the first word (except articles and prepositions) are capitalized. The first letter of any word after a colon in a title is also capitalized. For APA style, do *not* place quotation marks around journal/magazine article titles. However, do use "p." and "pp." to indicate page numbers of newspaper articles. In APA format, extend underlining under title to include punctuation immediately following. In both MLA and APA styles, publishers' names should be abbreviated; thus, "Random House" becomes "Random"; "William Morrow" becomes "Morrow."

Note: While the hanging indent (second and subsequent lines indented) is the recommended format for APA style references in student papers, manuscripts intended for publication follow paragraph indent format in which the first line of each reference is indented.

Provided below are some of the most commonly used citations in both MLA and APA formats. For a more complete listing, consult the MLA *Handbook,* the APA *Manual,* or whichever style guide your instructor has specified.

MLA STYLE

In-Text Citation

Here are sample in-text citations using the MLA system:

> From the beginning, the AIDS antibody test has been "mired in controversy" (Bayer 101).

If you have already mentioned the author's name in the text, it is not necessary to repeat it in the citation:

> According to Bayer, from the beginning, the AIDS antibody test has been "mired in controversy" (101).

In MLA format, you must supply page numbers for summaries and paraphrases, as well as for quotations:

> According to Bayer, the AIDS antibody test has been controversial from the outset (101).

Notice that in the MLA system there is no punctuation between the author's name and the page number. Notice also that the parenthetical reference is placed *before* the final punctuation of the sentence.

For block (indented) quotations, however, place the parenthetical citation *after* the period:

> Robert Flaherty's refusal to portray primitive people's contact with civilization arose from an inner conflict:
>> He had originally plunged with all his heart into the role of explorer and prospector; before Nanook, his own father was his hero. Yet as he entered the Eskimo world, he knew he did so as the advance guard of industrial civilization, the world of United States Steel and Sir William Mackenzie and railroad and mining empires. The mixed feeling this gave him left his mark on all his films. (Barnouw 45)

Again, were Barnouw's name mentioned in the sentence leading into the quotation, the parenthetical reference would be simply (45) for MLA style.

If the reference applies only to the first part of the sentence, the parenthetical reference is inserted at the appropriate points *within* the sentence:

> While Baumrind argues that "the laboratory is not the place to study degree of obedience" (421), Milgram asserts that such arguments are groundless.

There are times when you must modify the basic author/page number reference. Depending on the nature of your source(s), you may need to use one of the following citation formats:

QUOTED MATERIAL APPEARING IN ANOTHER SOURCE

(qtd. in Milgram 211)

AN ANONYMOUS WORK

("Obedience" 32)

Two Authors

> (Woodward and Bernstein 208)

A Particular Work by an Author, When You List Two or More Works by That Author in the "Works Cited"

> (Toffler, Wave 96–97)

Two or More Sources as the Basis of Your Statement (Arrange Entries in Alphabetic Order of Surname)

> (Giannetti 189; Sklar 194)

A Multivolume Work

> (2: 88) [volume: page number]

The Location of a Passage in a Literary Text

> for example Hardy's *The Return of the Native:* (224; ch. 7)
> [Page 224 in the edition used by the writer; the chapter number, 7, is provided for the convenience of those referring to another edition.]

The Location of a Passage in a Play

> (1.2.308–22) [act.scene.line number(s)]

The Bible

> (1 Chron. 21.8) [book.chapter.verse]

In-Text Citation of Electronic Sources (MLA)

Web sites, CD-ROM data, and e-mail generally do not have numbered pages. Different browsers may display and printers may produce differing numbers of pages for any particular site. You should therefore omit both page numbers and paragraph numbers from in-text citations to electronic sources, unless these page or paragraph numbers are provided within the source itself. You may use either italics or underlining for titles of books or other full-length works.

Examples of MLA Citations in "Works Cited" List

Books (MLA)

ONE AUTHOR

> Rose, Mike. <u>Lives on the Boundary</u>. New York:
>   Penguin, 1989.

TWO OR MORE BOOKS BY THE SAME AUTHOR

> Toffler, Alvin. <u>Future Shock</u>. New York: Random,
>   1970.
> ---. <u>The Third Wave</u>. New York: Morrow, 1982.

Note: For MLA style, references are listed in alphabetical order of title.

TWO AUTHORS

> Brockway, Wallace, and Herbert Weinstock. <u>Men of</u>
>   <u>Music: Their Lives, Times, and Achievements</u>. New
>   York: Simon, 1939.

THREE AUTHORS

> Young, Richard E., Alton L. Becker, and Kenneth L.
>   Pike. <u>Rhetoric: Discovery and Change</u>. New York:
>   Harcourt, 1970.

MORE THAN THREE AUTHORS

> Maimon, Elaine, et al. <u>Writing in the Arts and</u>
>   <u>Sciences</u>. Boston: Little, 1982.

BOOK WITH AN EDITOR

> Weeks, Robert P., ed. <u>Hemingway: A Collection of</u>
>   <u>Critical Essays</u>. Englewood Cliffs, NJ: Prentice,
>   1962.

LATER EDITION

Houp, Kenneth W., and Thomas E. Pearsall. <u>Reporting Technical Information</u>. 3rd ed. Beverly Hills: Glencoe, 1977.

REPUBLISHED BOOK

Lawrence, D. H. <u>Sons and Lovers</u>. 1913. New York: Signet, 1960.

ONE VOLUME OF A MULTIVOLUME WORK

Bailey, Thomas A. <u>The American Spirit: United States History as Seen by Contemporaries</u>. 4th ed. 2 vols. Lexington, MA: Heath, 1978. Vol. 2.

SEPARATELY TITLED VOLUME OF A MULTIVOLUME WORK

Churchill, Winston. <u>The Age of Revolution</u>. Vol. 3 of <u>A History of the English Speaking Peoples</u>. New York: Dodd, 1957.

TRANSLATION

Chekhov, Anton. <u>Chekhov: The Major Plays</u>. Trans. Ann Dunnigan. New York: NAL, 1974.

SELECTION FROM AN ANTHOLOGY

Russell, Bertrand. "Civil Disobedience and the Threat of Nuclear Warfare." <u>Civil Disobedience: Theory and Practice</u>. Ed. Hugo Adam Bedau. Indianapolis: Pegasus, 1969. 153–59.

REPRINTED MATERIAL IN AN EDITED COLLECTION

> McGinnis, Wayne D. "The Arbitrary Cycle of
> Slaughterhouse-Five: A Relation of Form to
> Theme." Critique: Studies in Modern Fiction 17.
> 1 (1975): 55-68. Rpt. in Contemporary Literary
> Criticism. Ed. Dedria Bryfonski and Phyllis
> Carmel Mendelson. Vol. 8. Detroit: Gale, 1978.
> 530-31.

GOVERNMENT PUBLICATION

> United States. Cong. House. Committee on the Post
> Office and Civil Service, Subcommittee on Postal
> Operations. Self-Policing of the Movie and
> Publishing Industry. 86th Cong., 2nd sess.
> Washington: GPO, 1961.
> United States. Dept. of Health, Education and
> Welfare. The Health Consequences of Smoking.
> Washington: GPO, 1974.

THE BIBLE

> The New English Bible. New York: Oxford UP, 1972.

SIGNED ENCYCLOPEDIA ARTICLE

> Lack, David L. "Population." Encyclopaedia
> Britannica: Macropaedia. 1998 ed.

UNSIGNED ENCYCLOPEDIA ARTICLE

> "Tidal Wave." Encyclopedia Americana. 1982 ed.

Periodicals (MLA)

CONTINUOUS PAGINATION THROUGHOUT ANNUAL CYCLE

> Davis, Robert Gorham. "Literature's Gratifying Dead
>   End." <u>Hudson Review</u> 21 (1969): 774-78.

SEPARATE PAGINATION EACH ISSUE

> Palmer, James W., and Michael M. Riley. "The Lone
>   Rider in Vienna: Myth and Meaning in <u>The Third</u>
>   <u>Man</u>." <u>Literature/Film Quarterly</u> 8.1 (1980):
>   14-21.

MONTHLY PERIODICAL

> Spinrad, Norman. "Home Computer Technology in the
>   21st Century." <u>Popular Computing</u> Sept. 1984:
>   77-82.

SIGNED ARTICLE IN WEEKLY PERIODICAL

> Hulbert, Ann. "Children as Parents." <u>New Republic</u>
>   10 Sept. 1984: 15-23.

UNSIGNED ARTICLE IN WEEKLY PERIODICAL

> "Notes and Comment." <u>New Yorker</u> 20 Feb. 1978:
>   29-32.

SIGNED ARTICLE IN DAILY NEWSPAPER

> Surplee, Curt. "The Bard of Albany." <u>Washington</u>
>   <u>Post</u> 28 Dec. 1983: B1+.

UNSIGNED ARTICLE IN DAILY NEWSPAPER

> "Report Says Crisis in Teaching Looms."
> Philadelphia Inquirer 20 Aug. 1984: A3.

REVIEW

> Maddocks, Melvin. "A Most Famous Anthropologist."
> Rev. of Margaret Mead: A Life, by Jane Howard.
> Time 27 Aug. 1984: 57.

Other Sources (MLA)

INTERVIEW

> Emerson, Robert. Personal interview. 10 Oct. 1998.

DISSERTATION (ABSTRACTED IN DISSERTATION ABSTRACTS INTERNATIONAL)

> Gans, Eric L. "The Discovery of Illusion:
> Flaubert's Early Works, 1835-1837." DA 27
> (1967): 3046A. Johns Hopkins U.

Note: If the dissertation is available on microfilm, give University Microfilms order number in parentheses at the conclusion of the reference. Example, in MLA format: "Ann Arbor; UMI, 1993. 9316566."

LECTURE

> Osborne, Michael. "The Great Man Theory: Caesar."
> Lecture. History 41. University of California,
> Santa Barbara, 5 Nov. 1999.

PAPER DELIVERED AT A PROFESSIONAL CONFERENCE

> Worley, Joan. "Texture: The Feel of Writing."
> Conference on College Composition and
> Communication. Cincinnati, 21 Mar. 1992.

FILM

> Howard's End. Dir. James Ivory. Perf. Emma Thompson
> and Anthony Hopkins. Merchant/Ivory and Film
> Four International, 1992.

TV PROGRAM

> Legacy of the Hollywood Blacklist. Videocassette.
> Dir. Judy Chaikin. Written and prod. Eve
> Goldberg and Judy Chaikin, One Step Productions.
> Public Affairs TV. KCET, Los Angeles. 1987.

RECORDING

> Beatles. "Eleanor Rigby." The Beatles 1962–1966.
> Capitol, 1973.
> Schumann, Robert. Symphonies Nos. 1 & 4. Cond.
> George Szell, Cleveland Orchestra. Columbia,
> 1978.

Electronic Sources (MLA)

According to guidelines in the 1998 *MLA Style Manual and Guide to Scholarly Publishing*, writers of research papers should credit the electronic sources they use by following these general conventions. **Publication Dates:** For sources taken from the Internet, include the date the source was posted to the Internet or last updated or revised; give also the date the source was accessed. **Uniform Resource Locators:** Include a full and accurate URL for any source taken from the Internet (with access-mode identifier—*http*, *ftp*, *gopher*, or *telnet*). Enclose URLs in angle brackets (<>). When a URL continues from one line to the next, break it only after a slash. Do not add a hyphen. **Page Numbering:** Include page or paragraph numbers when given by the source. When citing electronic sources, follow the formatting conventions illustrated by the following models:

AN ONLINE SCHOLARLY PROJECT OR DATABASE

> The Walt Whitman Hypertext Archive. Eds. Kenneth M.
> Price and Ed Folsom. 16 Mar. 1998. College of
> William and Mary. 3 Apr. 1998 <http://
> jefferson.village.Virginia.EDU/whitman/>.

1. Title of project or database;   2. name of the editor of project;   3. electronic publication information;   4. date of access and URL

A SHORT WORK WITHIN A SCHOLARLY PROJECT

> Whitman, Walt. "Crossing Brooklyn Ferry." <u>The Walt
>   Whitman Hypertext Archive</u>. Ed. Kenneth M. Price
>   and Ed Folsom. 16 Mar. 1998. College of William
>   and Mary. 3 Apr. 1998 <http://
>   jefferson.village.virginia.edu/whitman/works/
>   leaves/1891/text/index.html>.

A PERSONAL OR PROFESSIONAL SITE

> Winter, Mick. <u>How to Talk New Age</u>. 6 Apr. 1998
>   <http://www.well.com/user/mick/newagept.html>.

AN ONLINE BOOK PUBLISHED INDEPENDENTLY

> Smith, Adam. <u>The Wealth of Nations</u>. New York:
>   Methuen, 1904. 3 Mar. 1998 <http://ww.mk.net/
>   ~dt/Bibliomania/NonFiction/Smith/Wealth/
>   index.html>.

1. author's name;   2. title of the work;   3. name of the editor, compiler or translator;   4. publication information;   5. date of access and URL

AN ONLINE BOOK WITHIN A SCHOLARLY PROJECT

> Whitman, Walt. *Leaves of Grass*. Philadelphia:
>   McKay, 1891-2. <u>The Walt Whitman Hypertext
>   Archive</u>. Ed. Kenneth M. Price and Ed Folsom. 16
>   Mar. 1998. College of William and Mary. 3 Apr.
>   1998 <http://jefferson.village.virginia.edu/
>   whitman/works/leaves/1891/text/title.html>.

1. author's name;   2. title of the work and print publication information; 3. name of the editor, compiler, or translator (if relevant);   4. electronic publication information;   5. date of access and URL

An Article in a Scholarly Journal

> Jackson, Francis L. "Mexican Freedom: The Idea of
> the Indigenous State." <u>Animus</u> 2.3 (1997). 4 Apr.
> 1998 <http://www.mun.ca/animus/1997vol2/
> jackson2.htm>.

1. author's name;   2. title of the work or material in quotation marks;   3. name of periodical;   4. volume number, issue number, or other identifying number;   5. date of publication;   6. page numbers or number of paragraphs, pages, or other numbered sections (if any);   7. date of access and URL

An Unsigned Article in a Newspaper or on a Newswire

> "Drug Czar Wants to Sharpen Drug War." <u>TopNews</u> 6
> Apr. 1998. 6 Apr. 1998 <http://news.lycos.com/
> stories/TopNews?19980406_NEWS-DRUGS.asp>.

A Signed Article in a Newspaper or on a Newswire

> Davis, Robert. "Drug may prevent breast cancer."
> <u>USA Today</u> 6 Apr. 1998. 8 Apr. 1998 <http://www.
> usatoday.com/news/nds14.htm>.

An Article in a Magazine

> Pitta, Julie. "Un-Wired?" <u>Forbes</u> 20 Apr. 1998. 12
> May 1998 <http://www.forbes.com/Forbes/98/0420/
> 6108045a.htm>.

A Review

> Beer, Francis A. Rev. of <u>Evolutionary Paradigms in
> the Social Sciences. Special Issue, Inter-
> national Studies Quarterly 40, 3 (Sept. 1996).
> Journal of Mimetics</u> 1 (1997). 4 Jan. 1998
> <http://www.cpm.mmu.ac.uk/jom-emit/1997/
> vol1/beer_fa.html>.

An Editorial or Letter to the Editor

> "The Net Escape Censorship? Ha!" Editorial. <u>Wired</u>
>   3.09. 1 Apr. 1998 <http://www.wired.com/wired/
>   3.09/departments/baker.if.html>.

An Abstract

> Maia, Ana Couto. "Prospects for United Nations
>   Peacekeeping: Lessons from the Congo
>   Experience." <u>MAI</u> 36.2 (1998): 400. Abstract. 6
>   Apr. 1998 <http://www.lib.umi.com/
>   dissertations/fullcit?289845>.

A Periodical Source on CD-ROM, Diskette, or Magnetic Tape

> Ellis, Richard. "Whale Killing Begins Anew."
>   <u>Audubon</u> [GAUD] 94.6 (1992): 20-22. <u>General
>   Periodicals Ondisc-Magazine Express</u>. CD-ROM.
>   UMI-Proquest. 1992.

1. author's name;   2. publication information for analogous printed source (title and date);   3. title of database;   4. publication medium;   5. name of vendor;   6. date of electronic publication

A Non-Periodical Source on CD-ROM, Diskette, or Magnetic Tape

> Clements, John. "War of 1812." <u>Chronology of the
>   United States</u>. CD-ROM. Dallas: Political
>   Research, Inc. 1997.

1. author's, editor's, compiler's, or translator's name (if given);   2. part of work being cited;   3. title of the publication;   4. name of the editor, compiler, or translator (if relevant);   5. publication medium;   6. edition, release, or version;   7. place of publication;   8. name of publisher;   9. date of publication

Electronic Mail

> Mendez, Michael R. "Re: Solar power." E-mail to
>   Edgar V. Atamian. 11 Sept. 1996.

Armstrong, David J. E-mail to the author. 30 Aug.
1996.

AN ONLINE POSTING

For online postings or synchronous communications, try to cite a version
stored as a Web file, if one exists, as a courtesy to the reader. Label sources as
needed (e.g., *Online posting*, *Online defense of dissertation*, etc. with neither
underlining nor quotation marks). Follow the following models as appropriate.

LISTSERV

Kosten, A. "Major update of the WWWVL Migration and
Ethnic Relations." 7 Apr. 1998. Online posting
ERCOMER News. 7 May 1998 <http://
www.ercomer.org/archive/ercomer-news/0002.html>.

USENET

Dorsey, Michael. "Environmentalism or Racism." 25
Mar. 1998. Online posting. 1 Apr. 1998
<news:alt.org.sierra-club>.

SYNCHRONOUS COMMUNICATION

Mendez, Michael R. Online debate "Solar power
versus fossil fuel power." 3 Apr. 1998.
CollegeTownMOO. 3 Apr. 1998 <telnet://
next.cs.bvc.edu.7777>.

COMPUTER SOFTWARE

Gamma UniType for Windows 1.5. Vers. 1.1. San
Diego: Gamma Productions, Inc., 1997.

APA STYLE

In-Text Citation

Here are the sample in-text citations using the APA system:

From the beginning, the AIDS antibody test has been "mired in controversy"
(Bayer, 1989, p. 101).

If you have already mentioned the author's name in the text, it is not necessary to repeat it in the citation:

> According to Bayer (1989), from the beginning, the AIDS antibody test has been "mired in controversy" (p. 101).

or:

> According to Bayer, from the beginning, the AIDS antibody test has been "mired in controversy" (1989, p. 101).

When using the APA system, provide page numbers only for direct quotations, not for summaries or paraphrases. If you do not refer to a specific page, simply indicate the date:

> Bayer (1989) reported that there are many precedents for the reporting of AIDS cases that do not unduly violate privacy.

Notice that in the APA system, there is a comma between the author's name and the page number, and the number itself is preceded by "p." or "pp." Notice also that the parenthetical reference is placed *before* the final punctuation of the sentence.

For block (indented) quotations, however, place the parenthetical citation *after* the period:

> Robert Flaherty's refusal to portray primitive people's contact with civilization arose from an inner conflict:
>> He had originally plunged with all his heart into the role of explorer and prospector; before Nanook, his own father was his hero. Yet as he entered the Eskimo world, he knew he did so as the advance guard of industrial civilization, the world of United States Steel and Sir William Mackenzie and railroad and mining empires. The mixed feeling this gave him left his mark on all his films. (Barnouw, 1974, p. 45)

Again, were Barnouw's name mentioned in the sentence leading into the quotation, the parenthetical reference would be simply (1974, p. 45) for APA style.

If the reference applies only to the first part of the sentence, the parenthetical reference is inserted at the appropriate points *within* the sentence:

> While Baumrind (1963) argued that "the laboratory is not the place to study degree of obedience" (p. 421), Milgram asserted that such arguments are groundless.

There are times when you must modify the basic author/page number reference. Depending on the nature of your source(s), you may need to use one of the following citation formats:

QUOTED MATERIAL APPEARING IN ANOTHER SOURCE

(cited in Milgram, 1974, p. 211)

AN ANONYMOUS WORK

> ("Obedience," 1974, p. 32)

TWO AUTHORS

> (Woodward and Bernstein, 1974, p. 208)

A PARTICULAR WORK BY AN AUTHOR, WHEN YOU LIST TWO OR MORE WORKS BY THAT AUTHOR IN THE "WORKS CITED"

> (Toffler, 1973, pp. 96–97)

TWO OR MORE SOURCES AS THE BASIS OF YOUR STATEMENT (ARRANGE ENTRIES IN ALPHABETIC ORDER OF SURNAME)

> (Giannetti, 1972, p. 189; Sklar, 1974, p. 194)

A MULTIVOLUME WORK

> (Vol. 2, p. 88)

In-Text Citation of Electronic Sources (APA)

Web sites, CD-ROM data, and e-mail generally do not have numbered pages, and different printers may produce different numbers of pages for any particular site. You should therefore omit both page numbers and paragraph numbers from in-text citations to electronic sources, unless these page or paragraph numbers are provided within the source itself.

Examples of APA Citations in "References" List

Books (APA)

ONE AUTHOR

```
     Rose, M. (1989). Lives on the boundary. New York:
        Penguin.
```

TWO OR MORE BOOKS BY THE SAME AUTHOR

```
     Toffler, A. (1970). Future shock. New York: Random.
     Toffler, A. (1982). The third wave. New York:
        Morrow.
```

Note: For APA style, references are listed in chronological order of publication.

Two Authors

Brockway, W., & Weinstock, H. (1939). <u>Men of music:</u>
<u>Their lives, times, and achievements.</u> New York:
Simon.

Three Authors

Young, R. E., Becker, A. L., & Pike, K. L. (1970).
<u>Rhetoric: Discovery and change.</u> New York:
Harcourt.

More than Three Authors

Maimon, E, Belcher, G. L., Hearn, G. W., Nodine,
B. N., & O'Connor, F. W. (1982). <u>Writing in the</u>
<u>arts and sciences.</u> Boston: Little.

Book with an Editor

Weeks, R. P. (Ed.). (1962). <u>Hemingway: A collection</u>
<u>of critical essays.</u> Englewood Cliffs, NJ:
Prentice.

Later Edition

Houp, K. W., & Pearsall, T. E. (1977). <u>Reporting</u>
<u>technical information</u> (3rd ed.). Beverly Hills:
Glencoe.

Republished Book

Lawrence, D. H. (1960). <u>Sons and lovers.</u> New York:
Signet. (Original work published 1913)

One Volume of a Multivolume Work

Bailey, T. A. (1978). <u>The American spirit: United</u>
<u>States history as seen by contemporaries</u> (4th
ed., Vol. 2). Lexington, MA: Heath.

Separately Titled Volume of a Multivolume Work

Churchill, W. (1957). <u>A history of the English speaking peoples: Vol. 3. The age of revolution.</u> New York: Dodd.

Translation

Chekhov, Anton. (1974). <u>Chekhov: The major plays</u> (A. Dunnigan, Trans.). New York: New American Library.

Selection from an Anthology

Russell, B. (1969). Civil disobedience and the threat of nuclear warfare. In H. Bedau (Ed.), <u>Civil disobedience: Theory and practice</u> (pp. 153–159). Indianapolis: Pegasus.

Reprinted Material in an Edited Collection

McGinnis, W. D. (1975). The arbitrary cycle of <u>Slaughterhouse-five</u>: A relation of form to theme. In D. Bryfonski and P. C. Mendelson (Eds.), <u>Contemporary literary criticism</u> (Vol. 8, pp. 530–531). Detroit: Gale. Reprinted from <u>Critique: Studies in modern fiction,</u> 1975 (Vol. 17, No. 1), pp. 55–68.

Government Publication

U.S. Congress. House Committee on the Post Office and Civil Service, Subcommittee on Postal Operations. (1961). <u>Self-policing of the movie and publishing industry.</u> 86th Congress, 2nd session. Washington, DC: U.S. Government Printing Office.

U.S. Department of Health, Education and Welfare. (1974). <u>The health consequences of smoking.</u> Washington, DC: Government Printing Office.

Signed Encyclopedia Article

> Lack, D. L. (1974). Population. <u>Encyclopaedia
> Britannica: Macropaedia.</u>

Unsigned Encyclopedia Article

> Tidal wave. (1982). <u>Encyclopedia Americana.</u>

Periodicals (APA)

Continuous Pagination throughout Annual Cycle

> Davis, R.G. (1969). Literature's gratifying dead
> end. <u>Hudson Review, 21,</u> 774-778.

Separate Pagination Each Issue

> Palmer, J. W., & Riley, M. M. (1980). The lone
> rider in Vienna: Myth and meaning in <u>The Third
> Man.</u> <u>Literature/Film Quarterly, 8</u>(1), 14-21.

Monthly Periodical

> Spinrad, N. (1984, September). Home computer tech-
> nology in the 21st century. <u>Popular Computing,</u>
> 77-82.

Signed Article in Weekly Periodical

> Hulbert, A. (1984, September 10). Children as par-
> ents. <u>The New Republic,</u> 15-23.

Unsigned Article in Weekly Periodical

> Notes and Comment. (1978, February 20). <u>The New
> Yorker,</u> 29-32.

SIGNED ARTICLE IN DAILY NEWSPAPER

Surplee, C. (1983, December 28). The bard of
Albany. Washington Post, B1, B9.

UNSIGNED ARTICLE IN DAILY NEWSPAPER

Report says crisis in teaching looms. (1984, August
20). Philadelphia Inquirer, p. A3.

REVIEW

Maddocks, M. (1984, August 27). A most famous
anthropologist [Review of the book Margaret
Mead: A life]. Time, 57.

Other Sources (APA)

INTERVIEW

Emerson, R. (1989, 10 October). [Personal inter-
view].

DISSERTATION (ABSTRACTED IN DISSERTATION ABSTRACTS INTERNATIONAL)

Pendar, J. E. (1982). Undergraduate psychology
majors: Factors influencing decisions about college, curriculum and career. Dissertation
Abstracts International, 42, 4370A–4371A.

Note: If the dissertation is available on microfilm, give University Microfilms order number in parentheses at the conclusion of the reference. In APA format, enclose the order number in parentheses: "(University Microfilms No. AAD93-15947)."

LECTURE

Baldwin, J. (1999, January). The self in social
interactions. Sociology 2 lecture, University of
California, Santa Barbara.

PAPER DELIVERED AT A PROFESSIONAL CONFERENCE

> Worley, J. (1992, March). Texture: The feel of
> writing. Paper presented at the Conference on
> College Composition and Communication.
> Cincinnati, OH.

FILM

> Thomas, J. (Producer), & Cronenberg, D. (Director).
> (1991). Naked lunch [Film]. 20th Century Fox.

TV PROGRAM

> Chaikin, J. (Co-producer, director, & co-writer), &
> Goldberg, E. (Co-producer & co-writer). One Step
> Productions. (1987). Legacy of the Hollywood
> blacklist [videocassette]. Los Angeles, Public
> Affairs TV, KCET.

RECORDING

> Beatles. (Singers) (1973). Eleanor Rigby. The
> Beatles 1962-1966. (Cassette Recording No. 4X2K
> 3403). New York: Capitol.
> Schumann, R. (Composer). (1978). Symphonies nos. 1
> & 4 (Cassette recording No. YT35502). New York:
> Columbia.

Electronic Sources (APA)

The general APA order of items for electronic sources is as follows:

1. Name of the author (if given);   2. Other publication information for the printed source of analogue (if relevant);   3. Title of electronic source;   4. Edition, release, or version (if relevant);   5. Publication medium (CD-ROM, diskette, magnetic tape, or online);   6. *For portable sources:* City of publication and name of publisher (e.g., Redmond: Microsoft), or name of the vendor (e.g., SilverPlatter), and electronic publication date.

If the electronic source includes a previously published printed source or analogue for which you have given the date, do not include the date of electronic publication; also do not include the page numbers of the printed source or analogue. For online sources, do not include the date of your access. As with MLA citation, include as much of the pertinent information as is available.

The general APA format for online periodical sources is as follows:

Author, I. (date). Title of article. Name of Periodical. [On-line]. *xx*. Available: Specify path

Remember: For online sources do not add periods or other punctuation immediately following path statements; such extra marks may prevent you from accessing the source.

CD-ROM

Rich, A. Sonata form. (1994). Microsoft Multimedia
Schubert: The Trout Quintet. [CD-ROM]. Redmond
WA: Microsoft.

Elmer-Dewitt, P. (1994, January 17). The genetic
revolution. [CD-ROM]. Time Almanac 1990s.
Softkey.

On-Line Sources

Newspaper Article

Altman, R. K. (1977, October 20). Gene-implant
experiments with humans are put off to resolve
questions. The New York Times, p. A7. New York
Times Online (On-line]. Nexis.

Magazine Article

Gutin, J. C. (1994, November). End of the rainbow.
Discover, 70-75. [On-line]. DIALOG.

Electronic Journal

Zolo, M. B. (1994, Winter). The president's health
care plan: Implications for institutional ethics

committees. <u>Bioethics Bulletin Online</u>. [On-
line]. Internet.

GOPHER

House chamber action for the last three legislative
days. (1995, August 4). [On-line]. Available:
gopher//gopher.house.gov/
0F-1%3A947%3AHouse%20Actions

WORLD WIDE WEB

The U.S. House of Representatives and the legisla-
tive process. (1995, August). [On-line]. <u>America
Online</u>. Available http://www.house.gov/
Legproc.html

PART II

An Anthology of Readings

6

Left, Right, Center: The American Political Spectrum

> I often think its' comical—Fal, lal, la!
> How Nature always does contrive—Fal, lal, la!
>   That every boy and every gal
>   That's born into the world alive
>   Is either a little Liberal
>   Or else a little Conservative!
>
> —Gilbert and Sullivan, *Iolanthe*

Senator A thunders that President B's welfare proposal is a return to the failed liberal policies of the past. Columnist C worries about the growth of right wing fundamentalism. Editorialist D charges that group E is undermining the country's moral fiber, even as group F is working furiously to preserve it. Rush Limbaugh is hopping mad and so are his listeners. Jesse Jackson fumes and threatens to form a third party. Ross Perot has already done so. Just what are these people arguing about? Are they debating real issues or is it all meaningless political posturing? Is a third party candidate right to insist that there's "not a dime's worth of difference" between the Democrats and the Republicans?

If you're confused by the current political debate—and particularly by the difference between "liberal" and "conservative," or "left" and "right"—you're not alone. These terms have notoriously slippery meanings, and no one is quite sure what they mean anymore. One may be a liberal on one issue (like affirmative action) and a conservative on another (like abortion). American liberals are on the left; European liberals are often on the right. The original American liberals, such as Thomas Jefferson, distrusted government ("That government governs best which governs least"), just the opposite of most of today's liberals. The original conservatives, like Alexander Hamilton and John Adams, on the other hand, favored a strong central government—again, the opposite of conservatives today. Among liberals one can find FDR New Deal Liberals, 1960s Progressive or "New Left" liberals, "neoliberals," even "paleoliberals." Among conservatives one can find traditional conservatives, neoconservatives, and New Rightists. (Interestingly, the most fervent conservatives today—just like the most fervent liberals in the 1960s—tend to be young.)

In recent years, politicians and social commentators have used "liberal" and "conservative" as sticks to beat their opponents. In particular, Democratic candidates are fearful of being tarred with the dreaded "L" word, lest they appear soft on crime or in favor of raising taxes. Many would like to give up on these terms altogether, believing not only that they have lost all meaning, but also that they encourage political mudslinging and oversimplification of complex issues. While this may be true to some extent, it is also true that "liberalism" and "conservatism" are likely to remain central to the political vocabulary for the foreseeable future, and that they are, in fact, indicators of real philosophical differences in the way that people view the role of government in dealing with a wide range of social, cultural, and economic issues. It is therefore worthwhile for us to examine these and other political ideas—such as "socialism" and "libertarianism"—so that we may join in the political dialogue with some measure of historical and social perspective.

The purpose of this chapter, then, is to provide some basis for understanding many of the key political debates of the day—for understanding both the differences between political positions on particular issues and the differences in ideological assumptions underlying positions on these issues. It is sometimes said, for example, that liberals tend to have an optimistic view of human nature, and conservatives a pessimistic view. From these diametrically opposed assumptions follow frequently diametrically opposed programs and policies on everything from welfare mothers to funding for public TV to the number of jails in the country. In addition to reading several selections focusing on the differences between left and right and on opposing positions on particular issues (such as "family values" and homelessness), you will also read selections that provide tools for the analysis of the political scene and of political rhetoric.

One interesting question, on why "left" means liberal and "right" means conservative, is easily settled: these terms were first used in the aftermath of the French Revolution of 1789. The Revolution had quickly degenerated into factions, primarily *radicals* favoring the Revolution and its principles, as embodied in the Declaration of the Rights of Man ("The aim of all political association is the preservation of the natural . . . rights of man . . . liberty, property, security, and resistance to oppression"), *conservatives* favoring the continuation of the monarchy, with other factions somewhere in-between. At the first Legislative Assembly elected under the new constitution, the radical parties sat on the *left* of the presiding officer as he faced the assembly; the conservative parties sat on the *right*, and the parties in-between sat in the *center*. The words stuck and came into general use, even for legislative bodies, such as the U.S. Congress, where Democrats and Republicans do sit on opposite sides of the aisle, Democrats to the left, Republicans to the right. Other terms we use today in political discussion date from about the same era: "liberalism" first appeared in 1819, "conservatism" in 1835, and "socialism" in 1832.

The chapter begins with a political quiz (by Victor Kamber and Bradley O'Leary) to help you determine at the outset whether liberal or conservative leanings. Next, Jeff Smith's "The Debate Beneath the Debate: What American Politics Is Really About" introduces you to some of the fundamentally different attitudes underlying political debates on a variety of issues. Smith's passage is followed by a discussion of the contemporary political spectrum, "Liberalism, Conservatism, Socialism, Libertarianism," by historians James

MacGregor Burns, J. W. Peltason, Thomas E. Cronin, and David B. Magleby, from their widely used textbook *Government by the People*. This selection will be an invaluable reference point to help you to define political positions in the argumentative selections later in the chapter, as well as in your own independent research. Next, Donald Lazere's "Guides to the Political Conflicts" locates along the political spectrum some of the most widely read magazines and political commentators.

The rest of the chapter consists of a number of position statements representing viewpoints across the political spectrum. First, Jeff Faux discusses the classic liberal position in "A Progressive Compact." Charles Krauthammer then explains the conservative position in "A Social Conservative Credo." In "The Origin of Conservatism," John O. McGinnis, a professor at Cardozo Law School, applies a Darwinistic, evolutionary view to conservative thinking. In "When Government Gets Mean: Confessions of a Recovering Statist," Barbara Ehrenreich, a liberal, abandons one of liberalism's central tenets: an activist role for government. Two brief selections round out this section: in "The Only Kind of Air" conservative columnist Florence King argues that conservatives like her *should* be "mean-spirited"; and documentary filmmaker Michael Moore, a blue-collar liberal, asks, "Is the Left Nuts? (Or Is It Me?)." In the final part of the chapter, "Mystery Readings: A 'Final Exam' Assignment" we provide, with minimal authorial identification and commentary, a series of eight brief position statements on various issues—including family values and homelessness—and ask you to locate these positions along the political spectrum, using the analytical tools provided earlier in the chapter.

Political Quiz: Are You a Liberal or a Conservative?

VICTOR KAMBER AND BRADLEY S. O'LEARY

We begin this chapter on political attitudes with a selection designed to ferret out your own attitudes: a quiz designed to locate your views on the political spectrum and to suggest which of several current and recent political figures you most closely resemble in these views. The questions focus on your beliefs about government and about particular political and social issues. After you take and score the quiz, you'll be able to more confidently identify yourself as a liberal, conservative, or moderate. (The scoring guide appears at the end of this chapter on pages 323–325.) You must answer all the questions for the scoring to be valid.

This quiz originally appeared under the title "The Political Quiz Show" in the October 28–30, 1994 issue of USA Weekend, *a Sunday newspaper magazine supplement. Victor Kamber is a veteran Democratic consultant, president of the Kamber group, a political consulting firm in Washington, D.C., and author of* Giving Up on Democracy: Why Term Limits Are Bad for America *(1995); Bradley S. O'Leary is a Republican consultant. Together they write the* Kamber/O'Leary Report, *a political newsletter.*

1. Generally, do you tend to trust or distrust government's ability to solve problems?
   - Trust
   - Distrust
2. Which do you trust more?
   - The Pentagon or
   - The U.S. Postal Service?

   - The executive branch or
   - The legislative branch?

   - The IRS or
   - the FBI?

   - The CIA or
   - The Peace Corps?

   - The Joint Chiefs or
   - The United Nations?
3. What about private institutions and people? Which do you trust more?
   - Trial lawyers or
   - Doctors

   - Union leaders or
   - Business executives

   - Professional athletes or
   - Team owners
4. The federal government should do more to solve the nation's problems even if it means higher taxes on (pick as many as you want):
   - You
   - Big corporations
   - The wealthy
   - The middle class
   - Small businesses
   - None
5. Where should government be cut? (Pick as many as you want):
   - Eliminate farm subsidies
   - Eliminate subsidies to the arts
   - Abolish public broadcasting
   - Cut entitlement programs (Social Security, Medicaid, etc.)
   - Cut defense spending
   - Reduce welfare spending
   - Keep illegal immigrants from receiving public education
   - Reduce environmental regulation
   - Cut taxes
   - Don't cut at all
6. Which would do more to guarantee competitive elections?
   - Term limits
   - Public financing

7. Who was a better president?
   - Ronald Reagan
   - Franklin D. Roosevelt
8. Do you see the ideal America as an ethnic "melting pot" in which religious, cultural, and ethnic distributions are blurred, or as a nation in which ethnically diverse groups ought to coexist while retaining their cultural identity?
   - Melting pot
   - Multicultural identity
9. Whose political views do you consider more extreme, those of Rush Limbaugh or the Rev. Jesse Jackson?
   - Limbaugh
   - Jackson
   - Neither
10. Which would curb violent crime most?
    - Stricter controls on the sale of guns
    - Mandatory sentences for those who use guns in the commission of a crime
    - Both
11. In the long run, do you think we can reduce crime more by building more prisons or providing more financial assistance to rebuilding our inner cities?
    - Build prison
    - Rebuild cities
    - Both

Please indicate whether you agree or disagree with each of the following statements:

12. Even if it means cutting programs, spending must be cut to reduce the federal deficit.
    - Agree
    - Disagree
13. The federal government is too big.
    - Agree
    - Disagree
14. U.S. interests were more seriously at stake in Haiti where we used armed force to restore democratically elected President Aristide to power than in Korea where we insisted that Communist North Korea cease nuclear weapons production.
    - Agree
    - Disagree
15. Gays and lesbians should be able to marry or at least be treated as married under law if they so desire.
    - Agree
    - Disagree

16. The news media is dominated by liberals.
    - Agree
    - Disagree
17. The religious right is a threat to our political system.
    - Agree
    - Disagree
18. The federal government should include funds to make abortion services part of any standard benefits package in health care reform.
    - Agree
    - Disagree
19. Deceptive political campaign commercials should be banned.
    - Agree
    - Disagree
20. Graphic pornography should be banned.
    - Agree
    - Disagree
21. As a society, we should spend more money trying to find a cure for AIDS than for cancer and heart disease because AIDS threatens younger people.
    - Agree
    - Disagree
22. Talk radio shows should be regulated to ensure both sides of a debate are represented, because talk radio has an unhealthy impact on the political process.
    - Agree
    - Disagree
23. The breakdown of the traditional American family is the most serious domestic crisis facing our society.
    - Agree
    - Disagree
24. Women and racial minorities should be given preferences until we achieve true gender and racial equality in America.
    - Agree
    - Disagree
25. Certain environmental problems call for government action, even if it means new programs or increased taxes.
    - Agree
    - Disagree

■ ■ ■

Discussion and Writing Suggestions

1. Do you think that your score on this quiz (see pp. 323–325) accurately reflects your own political inclinations? If not, explain which questions and which responses may have tended to misrepresent your views.
2. Select two issues represented in questions to this quiz; for each write a fully developed paragraph expanding your views. Begin with a topic

sentence (based on your initial response to the question); develop the paragraph with examples and details based on your own experience, observation, or reading.

3. Role play: imagine you are a political analyst evaluating your responses to this quiz. Based on the pattern of responses that are apparent (that is, the types of programs, activities, etc. the responder favors and those she or he doesn't; the types of assertions the responder tends to agree or disagree with), develop a political profile of the responder. This question requires that you *categorize* related responses and that you *analyze* their significance.

4. Those experienced in developing questionnaires like this one know that the type of response a question receives often depends as much on the way the question is worded as on the responder's opinions on the subject. Select two or three questions in this quiz and rephrase them so that they might have evoked from you different responses from the ones you gave. Then, in a few sentences, explain why the different language evokes different responses.

The Debate Beneath the Debate: What American Politics Is Really About

JEFF SMITH

When politician X trashes politician Y on some issue that doesn't seem worth getting excited about, consider this: the real issue may not be what it appears to be. In a court nomination battle, for example, the issue may not be whether candidate C is good enough to be appointed federal judge; it may be whether that candidate is likely to lean toward "order" or "justice" in her decisions. In arguing for or against antitobacco legislation, the real issue for many is not whether they favor the tobacco industry, but how far government should go in regulating private businesses.

The following selection will help you understand how differing opinions on a single issue can represent deep and often irreconcilable ideological divisions among both elected officials and ordinary citizens. Jeff Smith, who has been a newspaper commentator and a television news consultant, teaches in the UCLA Writing Programs. This selection is an adaptation by Smith of his article "Against Illegeracy" that appeared in the May 1994 issue of College Composition and Communication, *a journal for writing professionals. Another version of this article appears as the first chapter of his book* Why Americans Disagree, *currently in preparation.*

Note: As originally published, this article focused on the Los Angeles riots of 1992, following the verdict in the Rodney King case. On April 29, 1992, an all-white jury acquitted four white police officers of savagely beating an African-American, Rodney King, after they had stopped him for speeding. Immediately following the verdict, the streets of South-Central Los Angeles erupted in riots that lasted several days. In the burning, looting, and general destruction that followed, 51 people died, 2,100 were injured, and the neighborhoods in the area sustained *over $1 billion worth of property damage. After retrial on federal civil rights charges, two of the four officers were convicted and sentenced to prison.*

What are the real issues on which Americans disagree? How are these issues   1
concealed within the many issues on which they think they disagree? How
might they learn to recognize their real disagreements and begin to carry
them on more productively? American politics is often criticized for ideological homogeneity: the supposedly narrow range of views it allows to be seriously expressed. Many American shrug off politics, seeing it mostly as so
much useless name-calling and finger-pointing. Yet, if we analyze and organize the different views expressed on many issues by politicians, commentators (or "pundits") and others who help shape our ongoing national political
discussion, we can find the outlines of significant ideas and real debates—
debates engendered by differing answers to the kinds of questions we usually call "philosophical." American politics is many things, but we shouldn't
deny that at one level it truly is a contest among different "political philosophies": different views on such basic philosophical issues as human nature,
society, government, and justice.

The problem is that those deeper issues are scarcely ever discussed in and   2
of themselves. Yet without seeing them, it's hard to grasp what the debates are
really about. Our next task, therefore, is to make those issues explicit. The
political conversation revolves around a number of questions, and it is the different ways these questions are answered that generate the different political
philosophies. So we can start by trying to identify those questions. Here are
some that are especially important:

(1) *Human nature and responsibility.* Under what circumstances are people   3
   responsible for their own actions? When is it legitimate to think of people
   in the aggregate—to assume that if X number of people do something
   normally thought wrong, there must be a justification? At what point
   does bad behavior cease to be understandable (and punishable) as individual actions—"crimes"—and become a "social problem" (or even
   "epidemic") for which the individuals involved ought not be held to
   account?

(2) *Community.* What is a "community"? The new chief of police hired by   4
   Los Angeles after the riots there in 1992 declared that "people [who] are
   robbing and stealing and looting . . . are not our community." Should the
   term "community" thus be confined to the law-abiding? Or does the bad
   behavior we saw in the riots express genuine, buried urges of a "community" in extreme crisis? More generally, who owes what to whom? Is
   it fair to tax suburbanites to support inner-city programs? To tax people
   in rural Nebraska to solve problems in the inner cities? Or do people who
   have "escaped" the cities, or chosen never to live in them, have a right to
   be free of the cities' problems?

(3) *Justice.* "No justice, no peace." That has been a slogan of those   5
   who believe "the system" has failed significant numbers of

Americans, especially members of minorities. It is meant as a kind of warning about the consequences one can expect if these problems aren't corrected. But is this the right view of cause and effect—can real social peace be founded only on justice? Or, as conservative philosophers from Edmund Burke in the 18th century to Sidney Hook and others today have argued, is it the other way around: Is justice impossible in the first place unless some measure of peace is guaranteed first? And just what do we mean by "justice"? Is it basically a matter of prosecuting troublemakers (as in "bringing someone to justice"), or does it involve seeing to the fair distribution of society's goods?

(4) *Wealth*. What distribution would be "fair"? Must actual wealth be spread with a certain evenness, or is fairness achieved by ensuring equality of opportunity to acquire wealth? And where does wealth come from, anyway? Is it the product of some individuals' special vision and energy, and is society best served if those individuals have maximum freedom— including the freedom to decide for themselves how to invest what they make? Would expropriating that wealth for society's use also take away the "incentive" for people to keep generating more wealth? Or should we assume that the wealthy got what they have not by "generating" wealth (to everyone's ultimate benefit), but by expropriating it from others—so that society's re-appropriation of it is merely a righting of the balance? 6

(5) *Government*. What is the role of government? Is it mainly policing— establishing justice in the formal, law-and-order sense? Or is part of government's job to ensure substantive justice by ironing out inequalities in wealth? Indeed, when should government make any substantive choice? Should government promote certain "values," or simply keep a free market functioning so that each individual can pursue his or her own vision of the good? What makes a society stronger—diversity and individual freedom, or the shared values and cohesion of a "common culture"? And whatever government does, how energetically should it do it? Which is best—a government empowered to take bold action even at the risk of failing or doing something unfair, or a government always checked and restrained, forced to seek a broad consensus before acting . . . even if that means its actions are forever slowed and watered down? 7

(6) *America*. As a matter of fact, what positions on each of the above issues is the United States—through its various governments and other social institutions—actually taking? And what social conditions have thus already been achieved? For instance, is there, on balance, equality of opportunity (Issue 4) such that we can assume that current distributions of wealth are more or less fair? Or are those distributions based on longstanding practices that have given some people greater opportunity than others, perhaps even allowed them to benefit by denying opportunity to others? 8

(7) *History*. For that matter, how much in history is necessary (or "determined" or "preordained"), and how much is open to deliberate human 9

Best of all, perhaps, understanding the deeper issues would make it   17
harder for citizens to dismiss politics as "boring." True, the broad questions
I've cited here are the kind that college students joke about being forced to
study in Philosophy 101. By themselves they may sound rather dry and
abstract. But they're not being offered by themselves. What we've seen here is
precisely the intimate link between these questions and urgent decisions—
decisions that bear on how we all live, on where our money comes from and
goes, on what our society will be like in the future. That link is what gives the
philosophical issues concreteness, even as it gives the political disputes clarity. It's hard to imagine that too many citizens would fail to pay attention to
a discussion that was clear, concrete, urgent and directly relevant to their
lives—and wallets.

■ ■ ■

Discussion and Writing Suggestions

1. Select one of the seven issues initially discussed by Smith, and respond to
   some of the questions he poses. Use specific examples, wherever possible,
   to support your argument. For example (to select issue #4), is wealth
   already fairly distributed in this country, or should wealth be redistrib-
   uted in some fashion? If so, how should this be accomplished? Or (to
   select issue #5), what should be the proper role of government in this
   country? Should government's role be primarily to provide order or primarily to provide justice?

   Note that issues #2 and #3 focus primarily on the subject of inner-
   city riots. In its original form, Smith's article dealt to a great extent with
   the 1992 presidential candidates' attitudes toward the Los Angeles riots
   following the initial verdict in the Rodney King case. In this case, the four
   white police officers accused of beating King were acquitted; in a later
   trial, in which the charges dealt with the violation of King's civil rights,
   two of the four were found guilty. The questions posed by Smith, however, have wider relevance than these particular events, since they deal
   with matters of "community" and "justice."

2. Locate several editorials and op-ed pieces on a particular issue (e.g.,
   abortion, gun control, affirmative action, health care). Then adapt the
   kind of analysis used by Smith to categorize the various ideological perspectives represented in the different articles. *First*, summarize the key
   ideas of each editorial. *Second*, categorize the types of questions and
   assumptions underlying each perspective. *Third*, "re-cast in more broadly philosophic terms" each of the approaches you have identified. *Finally*,
   discuss *your own* position on the issue by responding to some of the questions you developed for the second part of the assignment.

3. Which of the five (lettered) arguments Smith presents as alternatives
   most closely represents your own political viewpoint? Explain, providing
   specific examples from your own experience, observation, or reading.

You may even recall, from a recent political campaign, a candidate explicitly or implicitly making one of these arguments. If so, how persuasive was this candidate?

Liberalism, Conservatism, Socialism, Libertarianism

JAMES MACGREGOR BURNS
J. W. PELTASON
THOMAS E. CRONIN
DAVID B. MAGLEBY

As we suggested in the chapter introduction, "liberal" and "conservative" are notoriously slippery terms. This does not mean, however, that they lack all meaning or that they don't signify real and significant differences in political philosophy. In the following selection, James MacGregor Burns, J. W. Peltason, Thomas E. Cronin, and David B. Magleby offer extended definitions of these and other important terms, explain how the ideologies they represent have evolved over time, and offer much in interesting statistical information about the political attitudes of the American public. You should find this selection extremely useful in helping you to analyze particular political statements on a variety of issues, some covered in this book, others that you may discover in the course of your own research.

James MacGregor Burns is Distinguished Scholar in Leadership at the University of Maryland and Professor Emeritus of Government at Williams College. He has authored numerous books, including Roosevelt: Soldier of Freedom *(1970) and* A People's Charter: The Pursuit of Rights in America *(1991). A past president of the American Political Science Association, he has won numerous awards, including the Pulitzer Prize. J. W. Peltason has been a Professor of Political Science at the University of California, Irvine, president of the University of California system, and past president of the American Council on Education. His books include* Federal Courts in the Political Process *(1955),* Fifty-Eight Lonely Men: Southern Federal Judges and School Desegregation *(1961), and* Understanding the Constitution *(1993). Thomas E. Cronin teaches at and serves as president of Whitman College. He has been a White House fellow and president of the Western Political Science Association. His books include* The State of the Presidency *(1980) and* Direct Democracy: The Politics of Initiative, Referendum, and Recall *(1989). David B. Magleby is a professor of political science and department chair at Brigham Young University. He has taught at the University of California at Santa Cruz and the University of Virginia. His books include* Direct Legislation *(1984) and* The Myth of the Independent Voter *(1992).*

The following selection is reprinted from the authors' widely used political science textbook, Government by the People *(17th ed., 1998).*

IDEOLOGY AND PUBLIC POLICY

Ideology refers to the structure of a person's ideas or beliefs about political   1
values and the role of government. It includes the views people develop as

they mature about how government should work and how it actually works. Ideology links our basic values to the day-to-day operations or policies of government.

Two major, yet rather broad, schools of political thinking dominate American politics today: *liberalism* and *conservatism*. Two lesser, but more defined, schools of thought, *socialism* and *libertarianism*, also help define the spectrum of ideology in the United States.

Liberalism

In the seventeenth and eighteenth centuries, classical liberals fought to minimize the role of government. They stressed individual rights and perceived of government as the primary threat to those rights and liberties. Thus they favored a limited government and sought ample guarantees of protection from governmental harassment. Over time the emphasis on individualism has remained constant, but the perception of the need for government has changed. Today liberals view government as protecting individuals from being abused by a variety of governmental and nongovernmental forces, such as market vagaries, business decisions, and discriminatory practices.

In its modern American usage, **liberalism** refers to a belief in the positive uses of government to bring about justice and equality of opportunity. Modern-day liberals wish to preserve the rights of the individual and the right to own private property, yet they are willing to have the government intervene in the economy to remedy the defects of capitalism. Contemporary American liberalism has its roots in Franklin D. Roosevelt's New Deal programs, designed to aid the poor and to protect people against unemployment and bank failures. Today liberals seek protection against inadequate or deficient medical assistance and inadequate or deficient housing and education. They generally believe in affirmative action programs, regulations that protect workers' health and safety, tax rates that rise with income, and the right of unions to organize as well as to strike.

On a more philosophical level, liberals generally believe in the possibility of progress. They believe things can be made to work, that the future will be better, that obstacles can be overcome. This positive set of beliefs may explain their willingness to believe in the potential benefits of governmental action, a willingness to alter or even negate the old Jeffersonian notion that "government governs best when it governs least." Liberals contend that the character of modern technology and the side effects of industrialization cry out for some limited governmental programs to offset the loss of liberties suffered by the less well-to-do and the weak. Liberals of the Mario Cuomo, Hillary Clinton, and Jesse Jackson stripe frequently stress the need for a compassionate and affirmative government. Hillary Rodham Clinton's *It Takes a Village and Other Lessons Children Teach Us* and Mario Cuomo's *Reason to Believe* defend a positive role for government.

Liberals contend that conservatives usually rule in their own interest and are motivated by the maxim, "Let the government take care of the rich, and the rich in turn will take care of the poor." Liberals, on the other hand, prefer that government take care of the weak, for the strong can nearly always take care of themselves. "We have rejected the discredited theory that the fortunes of the nation should be in the hands of a privileged few," said President Harry Truman. "Instead, we believe that our economic system should rest on a democratic foundation and that wealth should be created for the benefit of all. . . . Every segment of our population and every individual has a right to expect from his government a fair deal."[1]

In the liberal view, all people are equal. Equality of opportunity is essential, and, toward that end, discriminatory practices must be eliminated. Some liberals favor the reduction of great inequalities of wealth that make equality of opportunity impossible. Most favor a certain minimum level of income. Rather than placing a cap on wealth, they want a floor placed beneath the poor. In short, liberals have sought "to lessen the harsh impact of oligarchical rule in economic life, to introduce a measure of democracy within or democratic controls over the industrial-technological process, to assure freedom from arbitrary command within the economic no less than within the political sphere."[2] They ask: How can citizens be equal and free if they are dependent on and necessarily servile to the powers that be?   7

TYPES OF LIBERALS Liberals, it should be emphasized, come in many varieties.   8
Some stress civil rights or women's rights or high-quality public education. Others urge government to adopt a more progressive tax system and do more to help the homeless, the handicapped, and society's "have-nots." Still others decry militarism and crusade for treaties and alliances that might bring about a world without terrorism and war. And yet other liberals are preoccupied with environmental or consumer issues. Some liberals embrace all these issues, placing them on an equal plane.

In a sense, liberals who emphasize economic issues may be called *New*   9
Deal liberals; others are *social liberals* or *peace liberals*. If this is not confusing enough, there are those who call themselves neoliberals. **Neoliberals** believe in liberty, justice, and a fair chance for everyone, and they argue that the truly down-and-out must have government assistance. Yet they do not automatically favor unions and big government, nor do they automatically criticize big business and the military. Neoliberals are best characterized as liberals who have lost faith in many welfare programs and are skeptical about the efficiency and responsiveness of large, Washington-based bureaucracies. They are better at diagnosing some of the deficiencies of old liberalism than they are at pointing out what should be done. A sample of neoliberal thinking appears in *The Washington Monthly*.[3]

CRITICISM OF LIBERALISM Not everyone, by a long shot, is convinced that lib-   10
erals, in whatever form, have the answers for the policy challenges of the twenty-first century. Critics of liberalism, old and new, say liberals place too much reliance on governmental solutions, higher taxes, and bureaucrats. Opponents of liberalism say that somewhere along the line liberals forgot that

government, to serve our best interests, has to be limited. Power tends to corrupt, they add, and too much reliance or dependence on government can corrupt the spirit, undermine self-reliance, and make us forget about those cherished personal freedoms and property rights our Republic was founded to secure and protect. When government grows too big, it tends to start dictating to us, and then our rights and liberties are at risk. Further, too many governmental controls or regulations and too much taxation undermine the self-help ethic that has "made America great." In short, critics of liberalism contend that the welfare and regulatory state pushed by liberals will ultimately destroy individual initiative, the entrepreneurial spirit, and the very engine of economic growth that might lead to true equality of economic opportunities.

Some liberals admit that Ronald Reagan, Bob Dole, and Jack Kemp   11
redefined the issues in the 1980s and 1990s in such a way that liberalism sounded unnecessary and dated, if not wholly harmful. These themes were emphasized by Republicans in the 1992 and 1996 election campaigns—arguing for less government. Wrapping themselves in the symbols of nationalism and patriotism, conservatives took a strong stand in favor of business, the death penalty, and prayer in schools—issues popular with most voters. Liberals, on the other hand, wrapped themselves in the symbols of compassion, fairness, equality, and social justice, also popular issues.

The 1992 election contest between Bill Clinton and George Bush centered   12
on the economy. Clinton and the Democrats successfully focused the campaign on the need for economic growth, jobs, and a lower federal budget deficit. Once elected, Clinton's major preoccupation was health care reform; the resulting proposal was comprehensive, complex, and costly, and it offended many entrenched interests. Republicans in Congress were able to defeat health care reform and claim in the 1994 election that they could do a better job of governing. The Republican Contract with America argued for less government and lower taxes. As Dick Armey, one of the primary architects of the Contract, stated: "The sheer mass of our federal government is simply inconsistent with a free society. If nearly half of what you make is spent by someone else, that means that half your work time is spent working for someone else . . . The obvious solution frankly is to end many of these government programs and allow people to keep their own money, the better to provide for these benefits themselves."[4] This perspective reflected the laissez-faire economics advocated by many Republicans for decades and raises anew old questions about the role of the government in the economy and society.

President Clinton in his 1996 State of the Union message embraced some   13
of this conservative thinking when he declared, "The era of big government is over." Later in 1996, to reinforce his shift to the right, Clinton signed into law a welfare reform bill that many liberals saw as a departure from a Democratic core commitment to the people. Clinton's efforts to end welfare, his inability to enact health care reform, and the weakened position of Democrats in Congress during 1995 and 1996 left liberals in the Democratic party without much of a voice.

Some liberals or progressives suggested a new agenda for the Democrats   14
in response to the events of the 1990s and the success of conservative thinkers.
E. J. Dionne, Jr.'s book on how progressives can regain power is aptly title
They Only Look Dead, referring to the conventional wisdom that liberal or
progressive ideas are in decline. Dionne contends that "the current political
upheaval can thus be defined less as a revolt against *big* government than as
a rebellion against *bad* government—government that has proven ineffectual
in grappling with the political, economic, and moral crises that have shaken
the country."[5] Dionne challenges the claims of Clinton and Gingrich that big
government is bad or even over. Pointing to past progressive or liberal successes, Dionne contends Americans want a government that eases economic
transitions, helps "preserve a broad middle class," and "*expands* the choices
available to individuals."[6]

James Carville, one of the political consultants credited with Clinton's   15
1992 election victory, has written "a handbook for spirited progressives," in
which he counters conservative claims. He writes that the conservative
Republican attack on big government in 1994 was deliberately vague.
According to Carville, Republican legislative actions of 1995 and 1996
demonstrated that "big government is actually a code for Medicare, school
loans, scientific research, and nutrition programs for pregnant mothers."[7]

Theodore Sorensen, a noted Democrat, agrees with Carville and Dionne   16
that the best way to regain Democratic support is by sticking to key liberal
principles. In his book, *Why I Am a Democrat*, Sorensen writes, "I believe
that the Democratic Party, more moderate than the new Republican extremists, more concerned with the economic security issues that underlie the electorate's anxiety, and less divided on matters of race, peace, and philosophy
than at any time in modern Democratic Party history, has every opportunity
to become the majority party once again."[8]

As the agenda of American politics changes, so does the popularity of lib-   17
eral or conservative positions. With the demise of communism, many
Americans are now less concerned about defense spending and want less government generally. Yet the fiscal constraints imposed by the crushing budget
deficit changed the debate about government solutions because politicians of
both parties would rather promise tax cuts than raise taxes to fund new programs. Moreover, as our expanded trade with other countries demonstrates,
we live in a global economy in which our jobs and economic progress are
linked to our neighbors and to other countries around the world. The net
effect of these changes is that our national government, while focusing on
domestic issues like health care, crime, and welfare, does so in a context
much more aware of the constraints of the budget deficit and the unpopular-
ity of tax increases.

Conservatism

American **conservatism** has its roots in the political thinking of John Adams,   18
Alexander Hamilton, and many of their contemporaries. They believed in limited government and encouraged individual excellence and personal achieve-

ment. Private property rights and belief in free enterprise are cardinal attributes of contemporary conservatism. In contrast to liberals, conservatives want to keep government small, except in the area of national defense. However, because conservatives take a more pessimistic view of human nature than liberals do, they maintain that people need strong leadership institutions, firm laws, and strict moral codes to keep their appetites under control. Government, they think, needs to ensure order. Conservatives are also inclined to believe that those who fail in life are in some way the architects of their own misfortune and thus must bear the main responsibility for solving their own problems. Conservatives have a preference for the status quo and desire change only in moderation. A sample of conservative thinking can be found in *The Weekly Standard* or *The National Review*, both weekly magazines.

Most conservatives opposed the New Deal programs of the 1930s and the War on Poverty in the 1960s, and they seldom favored aggressive civil rights and affirmative action programs. Human needs, they say, can and should be taken care of by families and charities. Equal treatment can be achieved by encouraging citizens to be more tolerant. Conservatives place their faith in the private sector, and they consider social justice to be essentially an economic question. They dislike the tendency to turn to government, especially the national government, for solutions to societal problems. Government social activism, they say, has been expensive for taxpayers and counterproductive. Conservatives also prize stability of the dollar relative to other currencies, and stability in international and economic affairs. They prefer private giving and individual voluntary efforts targeted at social and economic problems rather than government programs.

TRADITIONAL CONSERVATIVES Traditional conservatives recognize that government must exist, yet insist it should be limited in what it does, and that within its proper sphere of action, it should be strong and resolute. "The purpose of government is to maintain the framework of order within which other private institutions can operate effectively."[9] The traditional conservative applauds the heartfelt compassion implicit in Franklin Roosevelt's Second Bill of Rights but believes that to turn to the federal government to solve problems is to guarantee a too powerful, intrusive, and expensive government.

Liberals favor national action and a strong central government. Conservatives, however, contend that centralization means higher taxes, that the freedom of the majority would greatly diminish, and that the initiative and risk-taking entrepreneurial impulses of inventors, capital investors, and ingenious business leaders would be irreversibly discouraged.[10] "With the end of the Cold War, the case for a strong central government has been dramatically weakened," says Newt Gingrich. "The time has come for a reversion to first principles. In America, one of those first principles is that power resides first and foremost with the individual citizen. In America, individual citizens earn their bread, and the government had better have an overwhelming reason for taking it away from them."[11]

Traditional conservatives, in the name of freedom, are emphatically pro-   22
business. Thus they oppose higher taxes and resist all but the most necessary
antitrust, trade, and environmental regulations on corporations. The functions
of government should be, say conservatives, to encourage family values, protect us against foreign enemies and criminals, preserve law and order, enforce
private contracts, foster competitive markets, and encourage free and fair
trade.

Traditional conservatives have customarily favored dispersing power   23
broadly throughout the political and social systems to avoid concentration of
power at the national level. They favor having the market, rather than the
government, provide services. Traditional conservatives subordinate economic and social equality to liberty and freedom. Yet some conservatives, like
1996 vice presidential candidate Jack Kemp, advocate a role for government
in helping the worst-off climb out of poverty. Kemp believes that government
should create "enterprise zones" in impoverished urban areas by giving the
private sector incentives to invest in poverty-stricken inner-city neighborhoods and create jobs for the urban poor.

THE NEW RIGHT Another brand of conservatism—sometimes called the New   24
Right, ultra-conservatism, or even the Radical Right—emerged in the 1980s.
The New Right shared the love of freedom shown by the traditional conservatives and backed an aggressive effort to combat international communism,
especially in Central America. It also developed an activist public policy
agenda that it would like implemented by conservatives in Congress and in the
White House. The New Right favored the return of organized prayer in the
public schools and the renewal of covert operations by the Central Intelligence
Agency. It wanted strict limits on abortion; it opposed policies like job quotas,
busing, and any tolerance of pornography and homosexuality. In short, a
defining characteristic of the New Right was a strong desire to impose various social controls.

The New Right of the 1980s is embodied in the Christian Coalition of the   25
1990s. This group was founded by Pat Robertson after his candidacy for the
presidency in 1988. Ralph Reed, former director of the College Republican
National Committee and Students for America, took over as executive director in the mid-1990s. The Christian Coalition concentrates on such issues as
abortion, pornography, gay rights, and education. The Christian Coalition
lobbies for what they consider pro-family legislation, including a Religious
Freedom Amendment to the U.S. Constitution, which is designed to guarantee free religious expression in public settings, including prayer in public
schools. The Coalition publishes voter guides and score cards to help members decide which candidates best represent their values. Adherents of the
Christian Coalition have been especially active at the state and local levels, in
political parties and initiative campaigns, and on school boards. A 1992 initiative in Colorado to overturn ordinances protecting gays and lesbians from
discrimination was placed on the ballot largely through their efforts.[12] The
Colorado law was later declared unconstitutional by the state supreme court,

a decision upheld by the U.S. Supreme Court.[13] An example of Christian Coalition views can be found in *Christian American*, a Coalition publication.

Some conservatives question the moralistic tone of the Christian   26
Coalition. For example, Barry Goldwater (1909–1998), a former senator and Republican presidential candidate in 1964, worries that too much prominence and influence have been granted to the New Right, especially the Moral Majority and those he calls the "checkbook clergy." Our Constitution, Goldwater says, seeks to allow freedom for everyone, not merely those professing certain moral or religious views. Goldwater points to the bloody divisions in Northern Ireland, the holy wars in Lebanon, and the pernicious religious righteousness in Iran as examples of the politicalization of churches. "The Moral Majority has no more right to dictate its moral and political beliefs to the country than does any other group, political or religious," says Goldwater. "The same is true of pro-choice, abortion, or other groups. They are free to persuade us because this land is blessed with liberty, but not to assign religious or political absolutes—complete right or wrong."[14] Goldwater fears that the great danger of the Christian Coalition is that it will tear his beloved Republican party apart.

NEOCONSERVATIVES   The past generation has also witnessed the emergence   27
of people who call themselves **neoconservatives**. Many are former Democrats who admired FDR and Harry Truman but left the Democratic party over Vietnam, busing, and the decisions of the liberal (overly liberal in their view) Earl Warren Supreme Court. They want to continue programs that work and are truly necessary, but reject the rest. An example of a successful program they would be inclined to keep is Head Start, the federally funded program for disadvantaged preschool children. Neoconservatives believe that too many government programs will lead to a paternalistic state. Though willing to interfere with the market for overriding social purposes, neoconservatives prefer finding market solutions to social problems. An example of neoconservative writing can be found in *Commentary*, a monthly magazine.

Neoconservatives favor larger military expenditures than do liberals.   28
They remain skeptical of the intentions of some other nations or terrorist groups. Conservatives favor sufficient military spending to permit the United States to play a role in mediating conflicts around the world, especially in settings where U.S. interests are involved. But conservatives are not always united in their support for the use of military force, as indicated by the opposition of some conservatives to the use of American troops in Somalia, Bosnia, and Haiti in the 1990s. They also favor the death penalty and are more worried about crime than about the homeless. They say the courts have gone too far in protecting the rights of the criminal and are too little concerned about the rights of the victims of crime.

Neoconservatives are credited with various original writings on social   29
policy, supply-side economics, education, and the role of "national interest" in foreign affairs. The United States, in the neoconservative view, should use

its power to shape events; it cannot retreat into isolationism. Thus neoconservatives heartily approved the use of military force in Panama and Kuwait, but were divided over the deployment of U.S. Forces to Serbia and Bosnia. Some also supported **supply-side economics** (which during the 1980s was often called "Reaganomics"), the belief that lower taxes will encourage economic growth, new jobs, and ultimately new tax revenues. Bob Dole reactivated supply-side economics in his 1996 presidential campaign with a call for a 15 percent reduction in income taxes.

CRITICISMS OF CONSERVATISM Not everyone agreed with Ronald Reagan's   30
statement, repeated by candidates Dole and Kemp, that "government is the problem."[15] Indeed critics of conservatism before and during the Reagan-Bush era saw hostility to government as counterproductive and inconsistent. Conservatives, they argued, have a selective opposition to government. They want more government when it serves their needs—regulating pornography and abortion, for example—but are opposed to it when it serves somebody else's. Critics point out that government spending, especially for defense, grew during the 1980s when the conservatives were in control. Conservatives are often criticized for insensitivity to the social needs of the homeless and mentally ill.

Conservatives place great faith in our market economy—critics would say   31
too much faith. This posture often puts them at odds with labor unions and consumer activists in close alliance with businesspeople, particularly large corporations. Hostility to regulation and a belief in competition led them to push for deregulation in the 1980s. The resulting changes did not always have the intended positive effects, as the collapse of many savings and loans revealed.[16] During the same decade, according to some critics, the Reagan administration's decision not to pursue antitrust actions encouraged a flurry of mergers and acquisitions that diverted our economy from more productive economic activity.[17] Conservatives counter that relying on "market solutions" and encouraging the free market are still the best course of action in most policy areas.[18]

The policy of the Reagan years of lowering taxes was consistent with the   32
conservative hostility to government. In his 1981 address to the nation on the state of the economy, Reagan likened government to children who spend more than their parents can afford. He mentioned that such extravagance could be cured by "simply reducing their allowance," implying that government spending could be controlled by reducing the amount government was allowed to spend.[19] Many conservatives embraced the idea that if we lower taxes on the rich, their economic activity will "trickle down" to the poor. This view was criticized by many Democrats, who pointed out that the growth in income and wealth in the 1980s was largely concentrated among the well-to-do.[20]

Conservatives are also criticized for their failure to acknowledge and   33
endorse policies that deal with racism and sexism in the United States. Their opposition to the civil rights laws in the 1960s and their opposition to affir-

mative action in the 1990s are examples of this perspective. Not only have conservatives opposed new laws in these areas, they have hampered the activity of the executive branch when in power, and have sought to limit the activity of the courts in these matters as well.

Socialism

Socialism is an economic and governmental system based on public ownership   34
of the means of production and exchange. Karl Marx once described socialism as a transitional stage of society between capitalism and communism. In a capitalist system, the means of production and most of the property are privately owned, whereas in a communist or socialist system, property is "owned" by the state in common for all the people. In the ultimate socialist country, justice is achieved by having participants determine their own needs and take what is appropriate from the common product of society. Marx's dictum was, "From each according to his ability, to each according to his needs."[21]

In one of the most dramatic transformations in recent times, Russia, its   35
sister republics, and its former European satellites abandoned their version of socialism—communism—and are now attempting to establish free markets. These countries had previously rejected capitalism, preferring state ownership and centralized government planning of the economy. But by the 1990s the disparities in economic well-being between capitalist and communist nations produced a tide of political and economic reform that left communism intact in only a few countries, such as Cuba.

American socialists—of whom there are few prominent examples—favor   36
a greatly expanded role for the government. They would nationalize certain industries, institute a public jobs program so that all who want work would be put to work, and place a much steeper tax burden on the wealthy. In short, American socialists favor policies to help the underdog by means of income redistribution programs. They also favor stepped-up efforts toward greater equality in property rights. American socialists would drastically cut defense spending as well.[22] Most of the democracies of Western Europe are far more influenced by socialist ideas than we are in the United States, but they remain, like the United States, largely market economies.

Libertarianism

Libertarianism is an ideology that cherishes individual liberty and insists on a   37
sharply limited government. It carries some overtones of anarchism, of the classical English liberalism of the past, and of a 1930s-style conservatism. The Libertarian party has gained a modest following among people who believe that both liberals and conservatives lack consistency in their attitude toward the power of the national government.

Libertarians preach opposition to government and just about all its pro-   38
grams. They favor massive cuts in government spending, an end to the Federal

Bureau of Investigation, the Central Intelligence Agency, and most regulatory commissions, and a defense establishment that would defend the United States only if directly attacked. They oppose *all* government regulation, including, for example, mandatory seat-belt and helmet laws. A poster at one of their recent national conventions read, "U.S. out of Latin America; U.S. out of North America!" Libertarians favor eliminating not only welfare programs but also programs that subsidize business, farmers, and the rich. They argue that the federal government has vastly overstepped its constitutional powers, and most current government functions should be eliminated entirely. Unlike conservatives, libertarians would repeal laws that regulate personal morality, including abortion, pornography, prostitution, and recreational drugs.

A Libertarian party candidate for president has been on the ballot in all 50 states in recent presidential elections, although never obtaining more than 1 percent of the vote. The Libertarian candidate for president in 1996, Harry Browne, ran on a platform that emphasized freedom from government. The 1996 Libertarian platform proposed immediate and complete removal of the federal government from education, energy regulation, crime control, welfare, housing, transportation, health care, and agriculture; repeal of the income tax and all other direct taxes; decriminalization of drugs and pardons for prisoners convicted of nonviolent drug offenses; withdrawal of overseas military forces; and overall commitment to a smaller government, limited by the Constitution's specifications. Libertarian positions are rarely timid; at the very least, they prompt intriguing political debates. 39

A Word of Caution

Political labels have different meanings across national boundaries as well as over time. To be a liberal in certain European nations is to be on the right; to be a liberal in the 1990s in the United States is to be on the left. In recent elections, "liberal," which back in FDR's day had been popular, became "the L-word," a label most politicians sought to avoid. Even liberals have largely abandoned the term, now referring to themselves as progressives. 40

During the 1992 election, Bill Clinton defined himself as a "new Democrat," someone more in the country's political mainstream than some past Democratic candidates had been. In 1992 and 1996 Republicans accused Clinton of masquerading as a moderate, espousing Republican concerns like ending welfare. They pointed to Clinton's economic stimulus and health care reform proposals and his 1993 tax increase as evidence that he is a "tax and spend liberal." The varying ideological interpretations of Bill Clinton teach us that labels are rarely static, and that much of politics seeks to define the opposing party as extremists and one's own party as sensible moderates. 41

Ideological terms or labels can also be confusing on the conservative side of the spectrum. As discussed earlier, some conservatives are called neoconservatives, others New Right, and some have even adopted the term *paleoconservatives*—the prefix *paleo* meaning ancient or old. With so many terms in use to describe how people see politics and government, it is not surprising 42

WE THE PEOPLE
Differences in Political Ideology

	CONSERVATIVE	MODERATE	LIBERAL
SEX			
Male	42%	30%	27%
Female	43	32	25
RACE			
White	43	31	25
Black	45	25	30
AGE			
18–34	45	28	27
35–45	43	34	23
46–55	43	31	26
56–64	43	29	27
65+	40	36	24
RELIGION			
Protestant	57	25	18
Catholic	40	34	26
Jewish	16	21	63
EDUCATION			
Less than high school	36	47	17
High school diploma	36	42	21
Some college	46	30	24
Bachelor's degree	49	22	29
Advanced degree	44	15	40
PARTY			
Democrat	20	35	45
Independent	32	55	13
Republican	72	23	5

Source: Center for Political Studies, University of Michigan, *1996 National Election Study.*

Note: We have combined with the moderates persons who do not know their ideology or had not thought much about it. For party identification, we have combined Independent leaners with their respective parties. Rows may not add up to 100 percent due to rounding.

that political labels are in flux and often confusing. Yet on big questions—such as the role of government in the economy, in promoting equality of opportunity, in regulating the behavior of individuals or businesses, and on such issues as abortion—real differences separate conservative and liberal groups. This does not mean that persons who are conservative in one area are necessarily conservative in another.

It is also important to appreciate that ideology both causes events and is affected by them. Just as the Great Depression resulted in a tidal wave of ideological change, so did our involvement in World War II, Korea, and Vietnam, each in its own way. World War II, with its positive example of how government can work to defend freedom, strengthened positive views about the

A CLOSER LOOK

How Americans Define Their Ideology
The most common measure of ideology is simply to ask people where they would place themselves on a liberal/conservative scale. Survey questions used to ascertain ideology permit respondents not only to answer "moderate" but also to indicate that they "don't know" their ideology or "have not thought much about it." The combined "moderate" and "don't know" categories are consistently much larger than either the conservative or liberal group and constitute a cluster more interested in pragmatism than ideology. In sum, most Americans are unconstrained by a consistent ideology.

What the Public Thinks It Means to Be a Liberal or a Conservative
Question: What sort of things do you have in mind when you say someone's political views are Liberal? (top five responses)

Accept change	38%
Favor social programs	20
Favor government spending/spend freely	17
Favor abortion	14
Favor freedom to do as one chooses/not interested in setting moral standards	11

Question: What sort of things do you have in mind when you say someone's political views are Conservative? (top five responses)

Resist change or new ideas	44%
Spend less freely/tight economic policy	18
Are slow or cautious in response to problems/do nothing	14
Oppose abortion	11
Support free enterprise/capitalism	13

Source: Center for Political Studies, University of Michigan, *1992 National Election Study.*

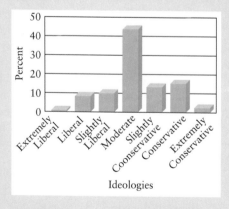

Ideology Curve
Source: Center for Political Studies, University of Michigan, *1996 National Election Study.*

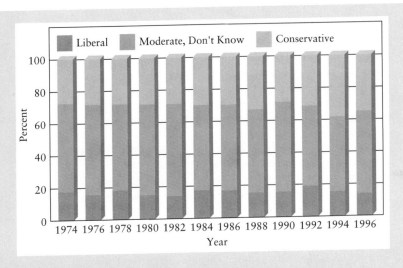

Ideology Over Time

Source: Center for Political Studies, University of Michigan, National Election Study Cumulative Data file, 1952–1992, *1994 National Election Study*, and *1996 National Election Study*.

Note: Those responding "don't know" or "haven't thought much about it" were included with the moderates.

role of the national government. The Vietnam War probably had the opposite effect—disillusionment with government. The anti-government sentiment in recent presidential elections is undoubtedly related to Vietnam, the Watergate scandal, and the Iran-Contra affair.

Debates about communist expansionism are increasingly dated and irrel- 44 evant in American politics. There is little fear today that the United States will become communist, and the communist threat around the world is greatly diminished. But people of varying ideologies do indeed worry about whether the United States is becoming too soft and losing ground in the global economy. Today we are more likely to debate what will make us beat, or at least compete with, "those capitalists from Japan" and other Pacific Rim nations.

Ideological controversy today centers on how we can improve our 45 schools, encourage a stronger work ethic, and stop the flow of drugs into the country; whether to permit openly gay people into the military or sanction gay marriages; and the best ways to instill religious values, build character, and encourage cohesive and lasting families.

Do social programs and job-training programs make things better or 46 worse? Is reliance on the marketplace or on government planners a better way to make long-term policy decisions for the nation? What is the best way to balance the budget and curb inflation? Are foreign investors and international conglomerates shaping our lives as well as our economic policy decisions? Ideological debate and differences are always with us, but the nature of the issues changes, and there are likely to be even more changes as we approach the start of a new millennium.

IDEOLOGY AND THE AMERICAN PEOPLE

Despite the twists and turns of American politics, the distribution of ideology in our nation has been remarkably consistent in the past 20 years (see Closer Look box, pp. 254–255). There are more conservatives than liberals, but the proportion of conservatives did not increase substantially with the decisive Republican presidential victories of the 1980s.   47

One other important fact about ideology in the United States is that very few people see themselves as extreme conservatives or extreme liberals. In 1994, only 3 percent of the population saw themselves as extreme conservatives, and an even smaller percentage, 1 percent, saw themselves as extreme liberals. These percentages have changed very little over time. When given the option to describe themselves as "conservative" or "slightly conservative," 15 percent say "slightly conservative" and 18 percent say "conservative."[23] (The same tendency is true of liberals . . . [I]t is important to note here that there are liberal and conservative wings in both parties.)   48

For those who have a liberal or conservative preference, ideology provides a lens through which to view politics. It helps simplify the complexities of politics, policies, personalities, and programs. An ideology may be an accurate or an inaccurate description of reality, yet it is still the way a person thinks about people, power, and society. For these reasons, it is important to understand how people view candidates, issues, and public policy. Ideology is even more important among legislators, lobbyists, and party activists. Their ideologies shape our social and political institutions and help determine public policies and constitutional change.   49

An alternative to the liberal/conservative self-identification measure of ideology is to ask people about their attitudes toward politicians and public policies. Most Americans do not organize their attitudes systematically. A voter may want increased spending for defense but vote for the party that is for reducing defense spending because he or she has always voted for that party or prefers its stand on the environment. Or a person may favor tax cuts and balancing the budget while not cutting spending substantially.   50

Consistency among various attitudes and opinions is often relatively low. Much of the time people view political issues as isolated matters and do not apply a general standard of performance in evaluating parties or candidates. Indeed, many citizens find it difficult to relate what happens in one policy situation to what happens in another. This problem becomes worse as government gets into more and more policy areas. Hence, many people, not surprisingly, have difficulty finding candidates who reflect their ideological preferences across a range of issues.   51

The absence of widespread and solidified liberal and conservative posi-   52
tions in the United States makes for politics and policy-making processes
that are markedly different from those in many European and other nations.
Our policy making is characterized more by coalitions of the moment than by
fixed alignments that pit one set of ideologies against another. And our politics is marked more by moderation, pragmatism, and accommodation than by
a prolonged battle between two, three, or more competing philosophies of
government. Elsewhere, especially in countries where a strong Socialist or
Christian Democratic party exists, things are different.

By no means, however, does this mean that policies or ideas are not ele-   53
ments in our politics. Such issues as affirmative action, the budget deficit, how
to fund welfare, the Supreme Court's abortion rulings, health care reform,
gun control, and environmental protection have aroused people who previously were passive about politics and political ideas.

IDEOLOGY AND TOLERANCE

Is there a connection between support for civil liberties and tolerance for   54
racial minorities and the ideologies of liberalism and conservatism? Some
political scientists assert that conservatives are generally less tolerant than liberals. This view is stoutly contested by conservatives, who have charged liberals with trying to impose a "politically correct" position on universities and
the media. "Conservatives," observe Herbert McClosky and Alida Brill,
"have repeatedly shown their fear of political and social instability. With
rare exceptions, the conservatives have been the party of tradition, stability,
duty, respect for authority, and the primacy of 'law and order' over all competing values."[24]

Liberals share many of these views but place a different emphasis on the   55
interpretation. They have more faith in government and readily turn to government to help achieve greater equality of opportunity. Liberals are usually
more tolerant of dissent and the expression of unorthodox opinions.
However, liberals, too, can be intolerant—of anti-abortion forces, for example, or the National Rifle Association, or the views of Rush Limbaugh.

Most liberals are strongly opposed to crime and lawbreaking, yet they are   56
as concerned about the roots or causes of crime as they are about the punishment of criminals. Perhaps for this reason, liberals exhibit somewhat
greater concern than conservatives for the rights of the accused and are more
willing to expand the rights of due process. Conservatives usually take a
harder line and, in recent years, have won widespread popular support for
their greater concern for the victims of crime than for the rights of the
accused.

Such differences are most evident in the responses of liberals and conser-   57
vatives to questions of civil rights and civil liberties. Research in the early
1980s found that, despite our common political culture and despite our widespread allegiance to constitutionalism and the Bill of Rights, many Americans
sharply disagree on some basic political matters. Liberals are ordinarily more

willing than conservatives to defend the rights of those who are in the minority, who may be wrong, or who take unorthodox or unpleasing stands.

In the area of free speech, conservatives are usually seen as less willing to   58
permit speech that is out of the political or cultural mainstream. Perhaps conservatives are less tolerant because those who claimed to be exercising the right of free speech often attack established values. But the argument that liberalism is correlated with tolerance is more complicated and the evidence less persuasive, as some liberals want to suppress the speech of people they disagree with.

Conservatives believe that the United States has become too permissive.   59
Many conservatives, especially in the New or Religious Right, are highly critical of homosexuals, drug users, prostitutes, unwed mothers, and pornographers. They worry about what they claim has been a decline in moral standards and, interestingly, call on government to help reverse these trends. Liberals, on the other hand, generally accept nonconformity in conduct and opinion as an inescapable by-product of freedom.[25] In this regard, liberals are like libertarians.

It is these sharp cleavages in political thinking that stir opposing interest   60
groups into action. Groups such as the Christian Coalition, the American Civil Liberties Union, Amnesty International, Mothers Against Drunk Driving, Queer Nation, and countless others promote their views of what is politically desirable. It is also these differences in ideological perspectives that reinforce party loyalties and divide us at election time. Policy fights in Congress, between Congress and the White House, and during judicial confirmation hearings also have their roots in our uneasily coexisting ideological values.

Ideologies have consequences. Although Americans share many ideas in   61
common, we as a people also hold many contradictory ideas. Our hard-earned rights and liberties are never entirely safeguarded; they are fragile and are shaped by the political, economic, and social climate of the day.

REFERENCES

1. Harry S Truman, State of the Union Address, 1949, *The Public Papers of the President of the United States, 1949* (Government Printing Office, 1964), pp. 1–7.
2. David Spitz, "A Liberal Perspective on Liberalism and Conservatism," in *Left, Right and Center*, ed. Robert Goldwin (Rand McNally, 1965), p. 31.
3. See also Charles Peters and Philip Keisling, eds., *A New Road for America: The Neoliberal Movement* (University Press of America, 1984); Randall Rothenberg, *The Neoliberals: Creating the New American Politics* (Simon & Schuster, 1984).
4. Armey, *The Freedom Revolution*, pp. 291–93.
5. E. J. Dionne, Jr., *They Only Look Dead: Why Progressives Will Dominate the Next Political Era* (Simon & Schuster, 1996), p. 13. Emphasis in original.
6. Ibid.
7. James Carville, *We're Right, They're Wrong: A Handbook for Spirited Progressives* (Simon & Schuster, 1996), p. 40.

8. Theodore C. Sorensen, *Why I Am a Democrat* (Henry Holt and Company, 1996), pp. 193–94.
9. Kenneth R. Hoover, *Ideology and Political Life* (Brooks/Cole, 1987), p. 34.
10. See Milton Friedman, *Capitalism and Freedom* (University of Chicago Press, 1962); also Friedrich A. Hayek, *The Road to Serfdom* (University of Chicago Press, 1944).
11. Gingrich, *To Renew America*, p. 102.
12. Paula Poundstone, "He Didn't Even Like Girls," *Mother Jones* (May 1993), p. 37.
13. *Romer v Evans*, 116 S. Ct. 1620.
14. Barry Goldwater with Jack Casserly, *Goldwater* (Doubleday, 1988), p. 387.
15. Ronald Reagan, Inaugural Address, 1981, *The Public Papers of the President of the United States*, 1981 (Government Printing Office, 1982), p.1.
16. Kathleen Day, *S & L Hell: The People and the Politics Behind the $1 Trillion Savings and Loan Scandal* (W.W. Norton & Co., 1993).
17. See Edward A. Snyder, "The Effects of Higher Criminal Penalties on Antitrust Enforcement," *Journal of Law and Economics* 33 (October 1990), pp. 439-62; also Brian Burrough and John Helyar, *Barbarians at the Gate: The Fall of RJR Nabisco* (Harper, 1990).
18. Dan Goodman, "Bleeding-Heart Conservatives," *Time*, May 18, 1992. p. 37.
19. Ronald Reagan, Address to the Nation on the Economy, February 5, 1981, *The Public Papers of the President of the United States*, 1981 (Government Printing Office, 1982), p. 81.
20. Sylvia Nasar, "Even among the Well-Off, the Rich Get Richer," *The New York Times*, March 5, 1992, p. A1.
21. Karl Marx, "Critique of the Gotha Program," in *Marx Selections*, ed. Allen W. Wood (Macmillan Publishing, 1988), p. 190.
22. Irving Howe, *Socialism and America* (Harcourt, 1985); Michael Harrington, *Socialism: Past and Future* (Arcade, 1989).
23. Center for Political Studies, University of Michigan, *American National Election Study, 1990: Post Election Survey* (April 1991).
24. Herbert McClosky and Alida Brill, *Dimensions of Tolerance: What Americans Believe about Civil Liberties* (Russell Sage Foundation, 1983), pp. 274–75.
25. Dinesh D'Sousa, *Illiberal Education: The Politics of Race and Sex on Campus* (Free Press, 1991), p. 313.

■ ■ ■

Review Questions

1. Define some of the key political beliefs of liberals.
2. Describe some of the different varieties of liberalism.
3. Define some of the key political beliefs of conservatives.
4. Define *New Right* and *neoconservative*.
5. Define some of the key political beliefs of socialists.
6. Define some of the key political beliefs of libertarians.

Discussion and Writing Suggestions

1. Where do you locate your own ideas on the political spectrum described by Burns, Pleats, Cronin, and Magleby? What particular issues are important to you, and what kinds of events, observations, and experiences have contributed to the forming of your own political attitudes?

2. Locate a recent editorial or op-ed piece in the newspaper and analyze its ideas and assertions according to the ideologies described by the authors. The editorial should be one that identifies a problem and recommends a means of dealing with the problem (or that attacks one solution to the problem as wrong-headed or ineffectual).

3. Can you detect a bias, on the part of the authors, toward (or against) one or more of the ideological viewpoints they are describing? If so, explain how what they say and the way they say it appear to indicate a leaning toward or an aversion to a particular set of political attitudes.

4. Write an editorial on one of the following issues from *either* the liberal, conservative, (or if appropriate) socialist, or libertarian viewpoint: *affirmative action, immigration policy, abortion, education, drug policy, school prayer, federal aid to the arts.* For a more ambitious version of this assignment, write two editorials on the same issue, representing opposing viewpoints.

5. Write two or three paragraphs based on the material in the tables "We the People" and "How Americans Define Their Ideology." Do not merely repeat in sentence form the information contained in the tables; rather, draw on this information to support a *thesis* or *topic sentences* of your own.

6. Write two paragraph-length definitions of either "tolerance" or "intolerance"—one from the viewpoint of a staunch conservative, the other from the viewpoint of an equally staunch liberal. Use specific illustrations of your own to support the two general definitions. Then, in a third paragraph, explain what you think would be necessary for the liberal to accept the conservative's definition and vice versa.

Guides to the Political Conflicts

DONALD LAZERE

Is an article by Barbara Ehrenreich likely to be liberal or conservative? How about an unsigned editorial in The Nation? Reason? Mother Jones? *What kind of ideological positions are likely to emerge from the Institute for Policy Studies? What kind of books does Praeger Press publish? Is* Newsweek *more liberal than* Time? *Before assessing a particular political statement, it's important to know where that statement is coming from. What is the background and affiliation of the author or authors, what are the political inclinations of the periodical in* which the writer's work appears, or of the publisher or organization that presents his or her work to the public? Anyone noddingly familiar with George Will expects to get the conservative slant on any subject he takes up. One who reads The Progressive, on the other hand, wants to get the liberal view of the subject.

Some useful roadmaps to this complex political terrain are provided in the following selection by Donald Lazere. This piece originally appeared as a set of appendices to Lazere's "Teaching the Political Conflicts" in the May 1992 issue of College Composition and Communication, *a journal for writing professionals. (The appendices have been somewhat rearranged in this version.)*

In addition to providing information on a wide variety of authors, periodicals, institutes, and publishers, Lazere includes a rhetorical appendix (Section Five, as reprinted here) to help readers locate clues to political inclinations by noticing patterns of argument and language by which left and right may be distinguished. This selection, along with the preceding two by Smith and by Burns et al., respectively, provide a valuable set of tools by which you may analyze almost any political statement. Keep in mind, however, that Lazere's classifications are not absolute and that others might view things differently.

Donald Lazere is a professor of English at California Polytechnic State University at San Luis Obispo. A member of the NCTE Committee on Public Doublespeak, his articles on literacy and culture have appeared in the The Chronicle of Higher Education, New Literary History, *and the* New York Times *and* Los Angeles Times *book review sections.*

[Note: *In the listings below, column placements and indentations to the left or right indicate positioning along the political spectrum.*]

SECTION ONE: AMERICAN MEDIA AND COMMENTATORS FROM LEFT TO RIGHT

American Media Left to Right

The Nation	*LA Times*	*Time*	*Reader's Digest*
In These Times	*NY Review*	*Newsweek*	*Weekly Standard*
Mother Jones	*Harpers*	*US News*	*Wall Street Journal*
Extra!	*New Yorker*	NY Times	*Commentary*
The Progressive	PBS Documentaries	*Washington Post*	*American Spectator*
Z Magazine	60 Minutes	*Atlantic*	*National Review*
Tikkum		*New Republic*	*McLaughlin Group*
Village Voice		*Reason*	*Washington Times*
Pacifica Radio		CBS news	*Insight*
		NBC, ABC news	Most newspapers,
		Lehrer News Hour	local TV, and radio

American Journalists and Commentators Left to Right

Alexander Cockburn
Molly Ivins
Noam Chomsky
Edward Herman
Ben Bagdikian
Barbara Ehrenreich
Robert Scheer
Todd Gitlin
Jim Hightower
Bob Herbert
Jeff Cohen
Norman Solomon
Gore Vidal
Julianne Malvaux
James Weinstein
Victor Navasky
Roger Wilkins
Cornel West
Betty Friedan
Ralph Nader
Katha Pollitt
Jesse Jackson
Bernie Sanders
Paul Wellstone
Jerry Brown
Michael Moore
Christopher Hitchens
Eric Alterman
Michael Lerner

Michael Kinsley
Anthony Lewis
Lewis Lapham
Michael Lind
William Greider
Donald Barlett
James Steele
Richard Reeves
Gloria Steinem
Bill Moyers
Seymour Hersch
David Halberstam
Carl Bernstein
John K. Galbraith
James Carville
G. Stephanopolis
Cynthia Tucker
Al Franken

Dan Rather
Tom Brokaw
Ted Koppel
Sam Donaldson
Jim Lehrer
Larry King
Cokie Roberts
Bob Woodward
Mark Shields
David Broder

LIBERTARIAN

Virginia Postrel
Stephen Moore
Doug Bandow
Debra Saunders

Rush Limbaugh
Pat Buchanan
Jerry Falwell
Pat Robertson
William F. Buckley
Paul Harvey
George Will
John McLaughlin
Fred Barnes
Paul Gigot
Arianna Huffington
Charles Krauthammer
William Safire
Robert Novak
Phyllis Schlafly
John Leo
Cal Thomas
Thomas Sowell
Gordon Liddy
Bob Grant
Don Imus
James Pinkerton
R. Emmett Tyrrell
Laura Ingraham
Mona Charen
William Kristol
Irving Kristol
Michael Novak
John Podhoretz
Milton Friedman
Henry Kissinger
Dinesh D'Souza
Florence King
Mary Matalan
Jack Kemp
Paul Craig Roberts
Reed Irvine
David Horowitz
Steve Forbes

SECTION TWO: POLITICAL ORIENTATIONS OF PUBLISHERS AND FOUNDATIONS

Book Publishers

LIBERAL OR SOCIALIST
Pantheon
Monthly Review Press
South End Press
Praeger
Beacon Press
Seabury/Continuum Books
International Publishers
Pathfinder Press
Routledge
Methuen
Schocken
Bergin & Garvey

CONSERVATIVE OR LIBERTARIAN
Arlington House
Freedom House
Brandon Books
Reader's Digest Books
Greenhill Publishers
Laissez-Faire Books (Libertarian)
Paragon House

Research Institutes and Foundations

LIBERAL OR SOCIALIST	CONSERVATIVE OR LIBERTARIAN

LIBERAL OR SOCIALIST

Institute for Policy Studies
Center for Responsive Law
 (Journal: *Public Citizen*)
Public Interest Research Groups
Common Cause (Journal: *Common Cause*)
Brookings Institute
Institute for Democratic Socialism
 (Journals: *Democratic Left, Socialist Forum*)
Center for the Study of Democratic Institutions
 (Journals: *New Perspectives Quarterly*)

CONSERVATIVE OR LIBERTARIAN

American Enterprise Institute (Journal:
 Public Opinion—not *Public Opinion Quarterly*)
Center for Strategic and International Studies
Hoover Institution (Stanford)
The Media Institute
Hudson Institute
Heritage Foundation (Journal: *Policy Review*)
Olin Foundation
Cato Foundation (Libertarian: *Cato Journal*)

SECTION THREE: CURRENT GENERAL PERIODICALS

This is a partial list intended to supplement, not replace, the more accessible, mass circulation newspapers and magazines, most of which have a center-conservative to center-liberal orientation.

American Scholar	Quarterly	Left-conservative
American Spectator	Monthly	Center-to-left conservative
Atlantic Monthly	Monthly	Center-liberal
The Black Scholar	Quarterly	Socialist
Chronicles of Culture	Monthly	Left-conservative
Commentary	Monthly	Center-conservative
Commonweal	Biweekly	Left-liberal Catholic
Conservative Digest	Monthly	Center-to-right conservative
Dissent	Bimonthly	Socialist to center-liberal
Foreign Affairs	Quarterly	Center-conservative to right-liberal
The Guardian	Weekly	Socialist
Harper's	Monthly	Center-liberal to left-conservative
Human Events	Weekly	Center-to-right conservative
Insight (Washington Times)	Weekly	Center-to-right conservative
In These Times	Weekly	Socialist
Modern Age	Quarterly	Center-conservative
Mother Jones	Monthly	Socialist to left-liberal
Ms.	Monthly	Center to left-liberal
The Nation	Weekly	Socialist to left-liberal
National Review	Biweekly	Center-conservative
New American	Biweekly	Right-conservative (formerly *American Opinion*)
New Guard	Quarterly	Center-conservative
New Politics	Quarterly	Socialist
New Republic	Weekly	Right-liberal to left-conservative
New York Review of Books	Biweekly	Center-liberal
New York Sunday Times	Weekly	Center-liberal to left-conservative
New Yorker	Weekly	Left-to-center-liberal
People's World	Daily	Communist Party USA
Progressive	Monthly	Socialist to left-liberal
Public Interest	Quarterly	Left-to-center-conservative
Public Opinion	Monthly	Center-conservative
Reason	Monthly	Conservative libertarian
Rolling Stone	Biweekly	Center-liberal
Social Policy	Bimonthly	Left-liberal
Socialist Review	Quarterly	Socialist
Tikkun	Bimonthly	Left-liberal
Utne Reader	Bimonthly	Digest of liberal journals
Village Voice	Weekly	Left-liberal
Washington Monthly	Monthly	Center-liberal to left-conservative
World Press Review	Monthly	Digest of diverse foreign viewpoints
Z Magazine	Monthly	Socialist

SECTION FOUR: A GLOSSARY OF POLITICAL TERMS AND POSITIONS

Left Wing and Right Wing

"The left wing" (adjective: "left-wing" or "leftist") is a broad term that includes a diversity of parties and ideologies (which often disagree among themselves but usually agree in their opposition to the right wing) including liberals, nearest the center of the spectrum, and—progressively toward the left—socialists and communists (the latter two are also sometimes called "radical").

"The right wing" (adjective: "right-wing" or "rightist") is a broad term that includes a diversity of parties and ideologies (which often disagree among themselves but usually agree in their opposition to the left wing) including libertarians, nearest the center of the spectrum, and—progressively toward the right—conservatives, ultraconservatives, plutocrats, and fascists.

LEFTISTS TEND TO SUPPORT:	RIGHTISTS TEND TO SUPPORT:
The poor and working class	Middle and upper class
Labor, consumers, environmental and other controls over business	Business, management, unregulated enterprise
Equality (economic, racial, sexual)	Inequality (economic, racial, sexual)
Civil and personal liberties	Economic liberty; controls on personal liberties (e.g., sexual conduct, abortion, obscenity, drugs)
Cooperation	Competition
Internationalism	Nationalism (primary loyalty to one's own country)
Pacifism (exception: Communists)	Strong military and willingness to go to war
Questioning of authority—skepticism (exception: Communism is authoritarian)	Acceptance of authority, especially in military, police, and strong "law and order" policies
Government spending for public services like education, welfare, health care, unemployment insurance	Government spending for military, subsidies to business as incentive for profit and growth
Progressive taxes, i.e., greatest burden on wealthy individuals and corporations	Low taxes for wealthy individuals and corporations as incentive for investment ("supply-side economics" or "trickle-down theory")
Religious pluralism, skepticism, or atheism	Religious orthodoxy

CAPITALISM An economic system based on private investment for profit. Jobs and public services are provided, and public needs met, to the extent that investment in them will predictably result in a return of capital outlay. In its principles capitalism does not provide any restrictions on extremes of wealth and poverty or of social power, but its advocates (especially pure, libertarian capitalists) believe that the workings of a free-market economy, unrestricted by government controls or regulation, will minimize social inequity.

Capitalism is not a political system; in principle, a capitalist economy can operate under either a democratic government or a dictatorship, as in plutocracy or fascism.

SOCIALISM An economic system based on public investment to meet public needs, provide full employment, and reduce socioeconomic inequality. In various models of socialism, investment and industrial management are controlled either by the federal government, local governments, workers' and consumers' cooperatives, a variety of community groups, etc.

Socialism is not a political system; in principle, a socialist economy can operate under either a democratic government or a dictatorship, as in Communism.

COMMUNISM With lower-case "c": Marx's ideal of the ultimate, future form of pure democratic socialism, with virtually no need for centralized government.

With upper-case "C" as in present-day Communist Parties: A socialist economy under undemocratic government. Historically, Communists have manipulated appeals to left-wing values like socioeconomic equality and worldwide cooperation in order to impose police-state dictatorship and military aggression.

PLUTOCRACY Rule by the rich. A capitalist economy under undemocratic government.

FASCISM A combination of capitalist and socialist economies under an undemocratic government. Historically, fascists have manipulated appeals to conservative values like patriotism, religion, competitiveness, anti-communism, respect for authority and law and order, traditional morality and the family, in order to impose police-state dictatorship.

Fascism typically is aggressively militaristic and imperialistic, and promotes racial hatred based on theories of white (or "Pure Aryan") supremacy and religious persecution of non-Christians. It glorifies strong authority figures with absolute powers.

CONSERVATIVES, LIBERALS, AND SOCIALISTS IN AMERICA In the American context, conservatives are pro-capitalist. They believe the interests of business also serve the interests of labor, consumers, the environment, and the public in general—"What's good for General Motors is good for America." They believe that abuses by businesses can and should be best policed or regulated by business itself, and when conservatives control government, they usually appoint businesspeople to cabinet positions and regulatory agencies without perceiving any conflict of interest therein.

American liberals believe that the interests of business are frequently contrary to those of labor, consumers, the environment, and the public in general. So although they basically support capitalism, liberals think business abuses need to be policed by government regulatory agencies that are free from conflicts of interests, and that wealth should be limited.

American socialists, or radicals, believe even more strongly than liberals that the interests of business are contrary to the public interests; they believe that capitalism is basically an irrational and corrupt system where wealthy business interests inevitably gain control over government, foreign and military policy, the media, education, etc., and use the power of employment to keep the workforce and electorate under their control They think liberal government reforms and attempts to regulate business are usually thwarted by the power of business lobbies, and that even sincere liberal reformers in government offices usually come from and represent the ethnocentric viewpoint of the upper classes. The socialist solution is to socialize at least the biggest national and international corporations, as well as the defense industry, and operate them on a nonprofit basis, and to place much higher taxes on the rich, so as to reduce the power of wealthy corporations and individuals.

SECTION FIVE: A SEMANTIC CALCULATOR FOR BIAS IN RHETORIC[1]

1. What is the author's vantage point, in terms of social class, wealth, occupation, ethnic group, political ideology, educational level, age, gender, etc.? Is that vantage point apt to color her/his attitudes on the issue under discussion? Does she/he have anything personally to gain from the position she/he is arguing for, any conflicts of interest or other reasons for special pleading?
2. What organized financial, political, ethnic, or other interests are backing the advocated position? Who stands to profit financially, politically, or otherwise from it?
3. Once you have determined the author's vantage point and/or the special interests being favored, look for signs of ethnocentrism, rationalization or wishful thinking, sentimentality, and other blocks to clear thinking, as well as the rhetorical fallacies of onesidedness, selective vision, or a double standard.
4. Look for the following semantic patterns reflecting the biases in No. 3:
   a. Playing up:
      (1) arguments favorable to his/her side.
      (2) arguments unfavorable to the other side.
   b. Playing down (or suppressing altogether):
      (1) arguments unfavorable to her/his side,
      (2) arguments favorable to the other side.

---

[1]This guide derives from Hugh Rank's "Intensify-Downplay" schema, various forms of which appear in Hugh Rank, *Persuasive Analysis: A Companion to Composition* (Park Forest: Counter-Propaganda Press, 1988) and *The Pitch* (Park Forest: Counterpropaganda Press, 1982) and Daniel Dietevich, ed. *Teaching about Doublespeak* (Reading, MA: Addison-Wesley, 1979).

   c. Applying "clean" words (ones with positive connotations) to her/his side. Applying "dirty" words (ones with negative connotations) to the other.

   d. Assuming that the representatives of his/her side are trustworthy, truthful, and have no selfish motives, while assuming the opposite of the other side.

5. If you don't find strong signs of the above bias, that's a pretty good indication that the argument is a credible one.

6. If there *is* a large amount of one-sided rhetoric and semantic bias, that's a pretty good sign that the writer is not a very credible source. However, finding signs of the above biases does not in itself prove that the writer's arguments are fallacious. Don't fall into the *ad hominem* ("to the man") fallacy—evading the issue by attacking the character of the writer or speaker without refuting the substance of the argument itself. What the writer says may or may not be factual, regardless of the semantic biases. The point is not to let yourself be swayed by words alone, especially when you are inclined to wishful thinking on one side of the subject yourself. When you find these biases in other writers, *or in yourself,* that is a sign that you need to be extra careful to check the facts out with a variety of other sources and to find out what the arguments are on the other side of the issue.

SECTION SIX: PREDICTABLE PATTERNS OF POLITICAL RHETORIC

LEFTISTS WILL PLAY UP:

Conservative ethnocentrism, wishful thinking, and sentimentality rationalizing the selfish interests of the middle and upper class and America abroad

Right-wing bias in media and education

Rip-offs of taxpayers' money by the rich; luxury and waste in private industry and the military

RIGHTISTS WILL PLAY UP:

Leftist "negative thinking," "sour grapes," anti-Americanism, and sentimentalizing of the lower classes and Third World rebellion

Left-wing bias in media and education

Rip-offs of taxpayer's money by the poor, luxury and waste by government bureaucrats; selfish interests and inefficiency of labor, teacher, students, etc.

■ ■ ■

Discussion and Writing Suggestions

1. Locate an article on a subject of current political interest and analyze the rhetoric and language of the piece, using Lazere's last two sections ("A Semantic Calculator for Bias in Rhetoric" and "Predictable Patterns of Political Rhetoric") as a guide. (You may also wish to refer to Burns, Peltason, Cronin, and Magleby's discussions of liberals, conservatives, etc., earlier in this chapter.) Discuss several different patterns of rhetoric

and language that provide clear indications of the author's political ideology. Be alert for what Lazere calls "clean" and "dirty" words. Explain
the extent to which you feel the author has been successful in composing
a persuasive argument.

2. Using Lazere as a guide, locate two articles on a particular subject that
represent opposite ends (or at least different points) of the political spectrum. Compare and contrast these essays. (For guidelines on comparison-
contrast essays, see Chapter 4, pp. 160–174.)

3. Compile an annotated bibliography of at least 10 items on a subject of current political interest, taking care to locate sources that may be arranged
along the entire political spectrum, from right to left (or vice versa). Use
Lazere's "Guides" to guide you in your search. Check your handbook for
annotated bibliography format. Document the source in MLA style.

  In the annotations, identify each author's political position, using
clues from affiliation with a particular research institute, book publisher,
journal of opinion, party, or organization, and—more importantly—
from arguments he or she presents that exemplify Lazere's glossary terms
and the particular patterns of political rhetoric in Section Five. Give
enough quotations to support your identification. In cases where the
author is not arguing from an identifiable position but only reporting
facts, indicate which position the reported facts support, and explain
how. (*Note*: Some newspapers and magazines have an identifiable political viewpoint in general in their news and op-ed orientation, but also
attempt to present other views at least some of the time. For example, the
Los Angeles Times is predominantly liberal, but often carries conservative
op-ed columns and letters. So you shouldn't assume that *any* article
appearing in such a periodical automatically will have its predominant
viewpoint; look for other identifying clues. [Paragraph adapted from
Lazere.])

4. Explain how some of the "Predictable Patterns of Political Rhetoric" in
Section Six follow from the left and right wing ideas listed on pp.
264–266 and from left and right wing ideas as discussed by Burns et al.
in the previous selection. Based on the discussion of left and right in
Burns et al. and Lazere, what else might the left and the right play up?

A Progressive Compact

JEFF FAUX

*In 1997, The Nation, one of the oldest and best-known liberal magazines, began
a series of articles it called "First Principles," in which the underlying principles of
liberalism were rearticulated for a new generation. One of the first of these pieces
was "A Progressive Compact" by Jeff Faux, president of the Economic Policy
Institute in Washington, D.C., and author of* The Party's Not Over: A New Vision

for the Democrats. *As you read Faux, note the particular issues on which he focuses, and try to locate the positions he advocates within the schema discussed by Smith and by Burns et al. This article first appeared in the April 14, 1997 issue of* The Nation.

The conservative tide has ebbed, for now. Newt Gingrich and his fellow   1
social Darwinists, triumphant in 1994, were a millstone around Bob Dole's neck two years later. The electorate finally read the fine print in the Republican Contract With America, and turned it down.[1] The contract was too risky, and the story about America that it told was too meanspirited.

Progressives now have an opportunity to propose their own social con-   2
tract. To win the political battles of the coming century, they must support their proposal with a narrative that unites the left, and unites the left with a political majority.

The progressive narrative must be relevant to the world—not as it was   3
but as it is. The left has no chance to build a political majority on the implicit assumption that social justice means extending the benefits of an otherwise beneficent society to variously defined minorities who have been left behind by an affluent and bigoted majority. By definition, this is a politics of permanent marginalization.

So long as an expanding share of the population was enjoying the fruits   4
of affluence, such a politics was perhaps the most practical and honorable course. But today the deregulation of the economy and its extension into the brutally competitive global marketplace is leaving a majority of Americans behind. Despite the incessant media hype about the performance of the current economic recovery, the long-term stagnation of living standards for most Americans has continued. Between 1989 and 1996, the real earnings of the three-quarters of the work force without a college degree dropped by more than 5 percent. Even for male college graduates, real earnings were no higher than they had been six years before. According to no less an authority than Alan Greenspan, the share of workers at large companies who fear being laid off rose from 25 percent in the depths of the 1991 recession to 46 percent in the midst of last year's "boom." In the winter of 1995–96, 61 percent of Americans polled considered themselves working or lower class, as opposed to 39 percent who defined themselves as middle or upper class. The brutal fact is that living standards cannot be maintained in a deregulated, privatized domestic economy under increasing pressure from an unregulated global marketplace. Thus, the continued deterioration of economic opportunities for

---

[1] *Newt Gingrich, Bob Dole, Contract With America:* During the 1996 election campaign, Newt Gingrich, Speaker of the U.S. House of Representatives, spearheaded the Republican Contract with America, a set of conservative legislative proposals. Bob Dole, a senator from Kansas, and former majority leader of the Senate, was the Republican candidate for president during that year, and was defeated by Bill Clinton. "Social Darwinism," broadly speaking, refers to the extension of Charles Darwin's evolutionary principle of "survival of the fittest" to the social sphere. It implies that in society, as in nature, the less fit members of the species (such as the poor or the otherwise uncompetitive) will—or should—die.

the majority of Americans who work for a living is inevitable, and it represents the left's political opportunity.

The political claims of economic class are not morally superior to the   5
claims of those disadvantaged by race, gender or sexual preference. But they
have an inherently greater power to unify, and are therefore a sounder foundation upon which to base a majority politics. If, over the coming decade, the
left can promote a new social contract that integrates its concern for social
equity and environmental sanity with majoritarian demands for economic justice, it can once again make history in America.

To offer such a social contract, progressives must be willing to attack the   6
center-right's excessive claims for America as a meritocracy, upon which the
electorate's acceptance of growing inequality is based. We need to argue that
the market should be constrained by the economic rights and obligations of
citizenship. We need an explanation of how the world works that tells us that
by virtue of being an American—not your race, your gender or your luck and
talent in the marketplace—you have a set of rights and obligations that transcend your right and the right of others to buy low and sell high. The central
point is the proposition that you, the citizen, are not alone in your increasingly
desperate search for a safe niche in a world of all against all.

Thus, you have: 7

§ a right to a job that pays a livable wage—and an obligation to work;

§ a right to share in the social wealth left to you by those who have gone
before—and an obligation to invest in a sustainable future for the next generation;

§ a right to profit from a business—and an obligation to support the
community in which it operates;

§ a right to bargain collectively[2]—and an obligation to cooperate in the
creation of more productive workplaces;

§ a right to protection against certain risks (unemployment, sickness, an
impoverished old age)—and an obligation to contribute to the pooling of
those risks in social insurance.

The promotion of a new social contract is the key to unlocking the con-   8
fusion sown by the center-right's misuse of terms like "family values," a
slogan promoting the myth that we can solve social problems in a market
economy without paying for them. Thus the national conversation has shifted from questions that we know how to answer to those that we do not, setting us up for the inevitable conclusion that government programs can't
work.

Public policy cannot stop teenagers from experimenting with sex, drugs   9
and alcohol, but it can provide alternative uses for their energies and a credible path to a healthy adulthood.[3] Public policy cannot stop love from leaving

---

[2] *A right to bargain collectively:* Collective bargaining is the right of an employee, as a
member of a union, to bargain for improved wages and working conditions.

[3] *Public policy:* Faux is using the term "public policy" here to mean government-created,
financed, or sponsored programs.

marriage, but it can keep love from being crushed by unemployment, low wages and poverty. Public policy cannot eliminate the criminal urge, but it can keep people from mugging each other because they can't find a job, and can provide enough cops and streetlights to make neighborhoods physically secure.

If we are to forge a new social contract we must reject the dispiriting   10
assumption that global forces have rendered the American people helpless to do anything but accommodate the faceless decisions of a dog-eat-dog international marketplace. Likewise, we must reject the romanticism that serious political change must await changes in the human heart. Or that while left activists may occasionally "think globally" they must confine themselves to "acting locally." A progressive strategy must dare to imagine itself victorious—in state capitals and ultimately in Washington. The national government remains the essential instrument available for countering the power of multinational capital.

This is obviously not an easy political task. Congress is controlled by con-   11
servative Republicans. The White House is occupied by a Democratic Administration that is at best indifferent to progressive concerns. An overwhelming majority of statehouses are still in the hands of Republican governors. And the Buchananite wing of the Republican Party[4] is preparing more reactionary appeals that will be aimed at the non-college-educated majority— the majority *we* need if we are to have a successful left-of-center politics. Although the left must be committed to taking the struggle for electoral power seriously, the ultimate prize is not the next election, it is the next century.

Given this, there are several strategic tasks for progressives over the next   12
four years. . . . [P]rogressives ought to be building an independent case for large changes that support a common-sense social contract. In some areas, like health care, the strategic task is educational, i.e., nurturing support for the principle of universal coverage and cost containment. In others, the task is to shift the focus of the debate. Thus, for example, the scandal of the welfare system is not the insistence that poor people work but the politicians' refusal to provide enough jobs for people to live on. In the wake of that refusal, the inevitable result of spilling a million workers into an already oversupplied low-wage labor market will be more unemployment and lower wages for the near-poor. This is the classic way to divide the progressive constituency. The answer is not make-work; it is to create job opportunities by channeling investment into our cities and depressed rural areas, to rebuild our transportation and environmental infrastructure, to get the rats out of school basements and fix the roofs. . . .

Putting eroding U.S. living standards at the center of a progressive poli-   13
tics will make some progressives uneasy. After all, even the poorest Americans live better than billions of others around the world. Why should we build a

---

[4] *The Buchananite wing of the Republican party:* A reference to Pat Buchanan, an extremely conservative Republican who campaigned (unsuccessfully) for his party's presidential nomination in 1988 and 1992.

politics around the laid-off factory worker in Peoria rather than the ragged child in the streets of Lima? The answer is that the destitute of Peru and most other places in the world are trapped in an ideological model that is made in America. As the world's only superpower, the United States now generates the world's ideas of what is rational and fair more completely than at any time in this "American Century." Within the past decade, the social contracts of Western Europe and Latin America and the rest of North America have been devastated by the neoliberal "Washington Consensus," which, to paraphrase the late Michael Harrington, demands socialism for capital and free enterprise for labor. American progressives will do best for the worldwide struggle for social justice by reforming America first.

Another strategic issue for the left is the brutal competition among states 14
and localities for business investment. Even more than the threat of out-sourcing to foreign countries, this competitive atmosphere suppresses progressive politics in the most liberal of states, encouraging a race to the bottom as states shrink their tax base and outbid each other to provide corporate subsidies, tax giveaways and union-free environments. Regional compacts in which states agree to compete on the basis of quality of life and level of education rather than low taxes and docile labor ought to be promoted, along with changes in the federal code to tax extraordinary state subsidies to business.

Finally, the left now has an opportunity to become the champion of a 15
national effort to reduce dramatically the influence of money in elections. The renting of the Lincoln Bedroom to fat-cat Americans,[5] the acceptance of campaign funds from fat-cat foreigners and the stubborn resistance of politicians to do more than put a fig leaf over the problem have now aligned the stars for a national grass-roots get-the-money-out-of-politics movement that could unify and energize the left and provide new allies, much as the antiabortion crusade did for the right. Activists in Maine and elsewhere have shown that the public will support spending restrictions and even public financing. A constitutional amendment to overturn the Supreme Court's rigid equivalence of campaign donations with free speech could be the instrument for a national mass mobilization.

This agenda is not by any means a substitute for liberal concerns with 16
affirmative action, environmental activism and social compassion. It is a way of finding the threads that can weave these issues together with the growing anxieties of the majority of working Americans. This requires, in turn, a greater sense of solidarity among the forces of the left. Thus, progressives must use the next few years to build up and link their political institutions. We have proved, painfully, that disconnecting ourselves from our allies does not lead to victory over our enemies. It is time for reconnection and mutual support. The rebuilding of the labor movement is not just the task of the A.F.L.-

---

[5]*The renting of the Lincoln bedroom* . . . In this paragraph, Faux is referring to the campaign financing scandals of the late 1990s, in which wealthy donors to the Clinton White House sought to gain favoritism and influence.

C.I.O.[6] The expansion of the women's movement to reflect the non-college-educated is not just a problem for NOW. The revitalization of black and Latino networks is not just the responsibility of the N.A.A.C.P. and the Hispanic Caucus. The strengthening of environmental consciousness is not just the duty of the Sierra Club. Nor is the rebuilding of a populist Democratic Party just the job of Paul Wellstone or David Bonior or Maxine Waters.[7] These are everyone's responsibilities.

The progressive story is a vision of community and mutual support. Its   17
moral is that you are not alone. If we want to be credible to a majority of Americans, we will have to demonstrate that vision in our political behavior as well as our political ideas.

■   ■   ■

Review Questions

1. What evidence does Faux cite to support his contention that the majority of Americans would be receptive to the left's political programs?
2. Why does Faux believe that the left can build a political majority on economic class issues, rather than on race, gender, or sexual preference issues?
3. Faux believes that it will not be easy "to forge a new social contract." Why not?
4. How does Faux propose to reform welfare?
5. Why should the left focus its attention on conditions in the United States, according to Faux, when people in other countries are often in worse shape?

Discussion and Writing Suggestions

1. Faux believes that the left should "build a political majority on the assumption that social justice means extending the benefits of an otherwise beneficent society to various defined minorities who have been left behind by an affluent and bigoted majority." To what extent do you agree with this statement? Explain, providing specific examples from your own experience, observations, or readings.
2. In paragraph 6, Faux claims that the center-right makes "excessive claims for America as a meritocracy"—that is, a society where merit leads to success. What specific, anecdotal evidence can you provide that America,

---

[6]*A.F.L.-C.I.O.* The largest American labor union (American Federation of Labor-Congress of Industrial Organizations). *NOW:* The National Organization for Women. *N.A.A.C.P.* The National Association for the Advancement of Colored People.

[7]*Paul Wellstone, David Bonior, Maxine Waters:* liberal legislators.

on the whole, is or is not a meritocracy, or that claims that it is a meritocracy are excessive?

3. Faux offers a series of rights and obligations that all Americans should have. To what extent do you accept these obligations, as well as these rights? To what extent do you see each right dependent upon the associated obligation? Explain.

4. In paragraph 9, Faux provides a series of goals that he believes can be accomplished at least partly by public policy—that is, by government created, financed, or sponsored programs. To what extent do you agree that public policy can help achieve these goals? Wherever possible, provide evidence to support your conclusions.

5. What do you think that Faux means when he writes (paragraph 10) that "we must reject the romanticism that serious political change must await changes in the human heart"? What changes in the human heart do you think he is referring to?

6. Using the definitions provided by Burns, Peltason, Cronin, and Magleby, explain in a multiparagraph essay what makes Faux's position *liberal*. Consider how both his general arguments and his more specific recommendations align with those positions defined by Burns et al. as liberal.

A Social Conservative Credo

CHARLES KRAUTHAMMER

The following article by Charles Krauthammer makes a good counterpoint to the previous selection by Jeff Faux. Like Faux, Krauthammer articulates the underlying philosophical principles of the ideology he advocates—in this case, conservatism. Note the issues on which Krauthammer focuses and how he distinguishes the conservative positions on these issues from liberal ones.

Charles Krauthammer studied politics at Oxford and medicine at Harvard Medical School. Beginning his professional career as a psychiatrist, he went on to become a speechwriter for vice president Mondale in the Carter administration, and, later, a writer and editor at The New Republic *and a writer for* Time *magazine. The following article first appeared in the journal* Public Interest *in Fall 1995.*

It is an axiom of the conservative revolution sweeping Washington that the growth in size and power of the welfare state is a primary cause of the decline of society's mediating institutions—voluntary associations, local government, church, and, above all, the family, the single most important instrument of social cohesion and values transmission. Whether by design or inadvertence, the nanny state has taken over the house.

Welfare policy, for example, creates social chaos by means of govern-   2
mental incentives that are almost comically perverse.[1] Every teenage girl in the
country is told: Have a child, make sure it is out of wedlock, make sure you
have no job or prospects, and Washington will then guarantee you a monthly check, free medical care, and years of job training and child care, also free.
After 35 years of this, the illegitimacy rate goes from 5 percent to 30 percent.
Surprise.

Liberals are confounded by the fact that the great expansion of their   4
social programs coincides with the dramatic rise of most every index of social
breakdown—divorce, illegitimacy, violence, crime, drug abuse, suicide,
untreated mental illness (disguised as homelessness). Lacking any new theory
to explain this unfortunate association, they prescribe the only therapy their
worldview allows: more social programs.

President Clinton, in his 1995 State of the Union Address, for example,   4
embraced a Charles Murray premise when he declared that "the epidemic of
teen pregnancies and births where there is no marriage" is "our most serious
social problem."[2] His conclusion, however, is distinctly un-Murray-like: yet
another federal program. After drivers ed. and drug ed., we shall now have
preg ed.—a few minutes of classroom time to urge young girls and boys not
to do precisely what the entire welfare system allows, indeed encourages,
them to do: indulge in irresponsible childbearing.

THE LIMITS OF STRUCTURAL REFORM

The conservative response is equally clear: not a new government intervention   5
to mitigate the catastrophic consequences of the old intervention but withdrawal of government intervention in the first place. The contraction of the
welfare state is the single most important theme of the current conservative
revolution. It imbues practically every item on the Republicans' political
agenda. And it promises a rosy future: Pare back the welfare state and the
mediating institutions will once again have the space to flower, reclaiming
their rightful place at the center of a revitalized civil society.

It is a rosy scenario. It is unlikely to materialize. Social disintegration is   6
not a reversible chemical reaction. It is far easier to reduce a complex, cohesive social structure to its barest elements of atomized individuals and fractured families than to reassemble these atoms and fractions into a new whole.

---

[1]*Welfare policy:* In August 1996, a year after this article was published, President Clinton
signed into law a sweeping overhaul of the national welfare program—AFDC—that had
been in place since 1935. The new law provided for a lifetime maximum of five years of welfare benefits to any recipient; and new recipients would be required to find a job within two
years of signing up for welfare benefits. The new law also reduced food stamp allocations.
Individual states (as opposed to the federal government) were free to set their own welfare
policies, some of which were even stricter than the federal requirements.

[2]*Charles Murray:* conservative author who had recommended scrapping the old welfare
system as encouraging illegitimacy and dependency.

Institutions so displaced and broken, particularly the family, may not be capable of spontaneous reintegration.

This is not to say that one should flinch from trying. But in, say, abolishing the current welfare entitlement, one should not assume that this in and of itself will solve the conundrum of intergenerational illegitimacy. Abolition is the first step, because without it there is no way back from where we are. But it is only a first step. And, if it is the only step, the current conservative revolution will surely fail.

That is the case because looking at the effect of government on society is too limited an analysis. The intrusions and expropriations of the welfare state have, generally speaking, created the *sustaining* conditions that allow the breakdown of families and other mediating institutions. They establish a *structure* that underwrites self-destructive and antisocial behavior. But they do not create the wants and the values that find their expression in such behavior. The epidemic of teen pregnancy, for example, is fueled by the desire of boys for predatory and casual sex, the acquiescence (often encouragement) of girls, and the contempt of both for the bourgeois norm of settled, married parenthood. Where do these attitudes come from? The AFDC check permits their realization.[3] But it hardly creates them. What does?

CULTURAL CAUSES OF DECAY

The single greatest shaper of these wants and values is not government but culture. Mass culture is a very recent phenomenon. As an engine of social breakdown, it is vastly underappreciated by those who might be called structural conservatives. Those who believe, for example, that changing the tax structure of the inner city (through enterprise zones) will effect a radical transformation of its social dynamics are missing the larger reality. Never in history have the purveyors of a degraded, almost totally uncensored, culture had direct, unmediated access to the minds of a society's young. An adolescent plugged into a Walkman playing "gangsta rap" represents a revolutionary social phenomenon: youthful consciousness almost literally hardwired to the most extreme and corrupting cultural influences.

Two hundred years ago these influences might reach a thin layer of the upper classes, classes well insulated by education, social code, and sheer wealth from the more baleful consequences of cultural decay. Today these influences reach everyone. Particularly vulnerable are those in communities where the authority structure has disintegrated because of absent or incompetent parents and where there is no power or money or codes to mediate the culture's influence or cushion its effects. In such a milieu in particular—everywhere to some extent—mass culture rules. The results are plain to see.

We have, for example, a quarter century of psychological research on the relationship between exposure to television violence and aggressive behavior.

---

[3]*AFDC:* Aid to Families with Dependent Children, the official name of the old federal welfare system that ended in 1996.

The findings are summarized by the 1972 Surgeon General's Commission report, the 1982 National Institute of Health Ten Year Follow-Up, and the 1992 report of the American Psychological Association's Committee on Media in Society. To quote Leonard Eron, a longtime student of media and its psychological effects, on the question of the relation between television and increased violence, "the scientific debate is over." One could, of course, have done without the social science and simply reasoned, as Irving Kristol did in 1971, that if the unquestioningly held view that good art can elevate is true, then it must be equally true that bad art can degrade.

The defenders of the culture argue that their art merely reflects already   12
existing social changes. One could, for the sake of argument, concede that point and still note that, by constantly validating and confirming disintegratory social trends, these cultural purveyors are legitimizing them and establishing a feedback system that only serves to reinforce, amplify, and accelerate the chaos.

Mainstream films aimed at young people, for example, specialize not just   13
in glorifying violence but in trivializing it. Cruelty as camp is a staple of the PG-13 movie. MTV is a festival of misogyny, a sourcebook on the degradation and objectification of women. And ordinary prime-time television is a laboratory of "alternative lifestyles." It has been pointed out, for example, that the typical sitcom family (with one or two notable exceptions) is what in the 1950s was called a broken home. And these homes—Murphy Brown's, most famously—are not generally depicted as unfortunate accommodations to the sadder consequences of social disintegration but as self-affirming choices worthy of not just admiration but celebration. What is forgotten about the Murphy Brown episode is that real, live television anchors from NBC, CBS, ABC, and CNN went on the show to toast Murphy's motherhood.

Dan Quayle's attack on the breezy, brazen amorality at play here restart-   14
ed the current national debate about the cultural causes of social decay. Even the most established liberal voices had been coming to grudging acknowledgment of the fact that much of the rampant deviancy in society is learned, and learned mostly from the mass media. Take, for example, the National Commission on Children, chaired by Senator Jay Rockefeller, liberal Democrat from West Virginia, and generally given to the standard establishment analyses and recommendations. It acknowledged that "pervasive images of crime, violence, and sexuality expose children and youth to situations and problems that often conflict with the common values of our society," and even ceded that "the media, especially television" might actually be "a cause" of "our society's serious problems."

THE MEDICALIZATION OF VICE

Liberals have a serious difficulty dealing with this reality, however. It is hard   15
for them—note the commission's pinched, bureaucratic formulation—to say the obvious: the culture's art is bad, its messages morally wrong. Why?

Because having promoted "value-free" education and a self-validating moral relativism, they have forfeited the language of morality.

Accordingly, they have had to resort to a substitute language: medicine. 16 Medicalized morality has the twin advantages of appearing authoritative and value-free. Liberalism can now address the problem of cultural decay thus: We cannot say what's right or wrong, good or bad, but we can say what is harmful. Hence, sexual promiscuity is to be eschewed not because it is wrong but because it is "risky," a risk to limb and life, as is drug abuse and the like. The right sex is safe sex. Teen violence is a "public health emergency." And the man to lead the fight against teen pregnancy is a doctor, the Surgeon General. He did such a good job with smoking. Why not with sex?

To be sure, some liberals have so rejected the connection between moral- 17 ity and social breakdown that they are reluctant to apply even the smoking model to allegedly immoral behavior. President Clinton's first Surgeon General, Jocelyn Elders, was so sanguine about teen sex that she wanted it taught. ("We've taught children in driver's ed. what to do in the front seat of a car but not what to do in the back seat of the car.") She was so reconciled to drug use that she spoke favorably of legalization. But she was, at the same time, a ferocious enemy of tobacco. She was quite reconciled to kids having sex in the back seat of a car, it seems, so long as they did not light up afterwards.

But such vices are no longer politically sustainable, even in a Democratic 18 administration. Accordingly, in making Dr. Henry Foster his subsequent choice for Surgeon General, Clinton played the neo-liberal, promoting Foster as just the man to fight teen pregnancy.

This is an advance, a recognition that teen pregnancy and illegitimacy are 19 social pathologies in need of a campaign to change behavior and attitudes. But, by assigning the job to doctors, by framing the issue in terms of public health, by confusing morality with hygiene, the point is missed.

Yes, the victims of teen violence, promiscuity, drug abuse, and suicide end 20 up in the emergency room. But so do the victims of hurricanes and war. Hurricanes and war are many things, but they are not medical problems. Neither are teen violence, promiscuity, drug abuse, suicide, and the other indices of social decay. Moreover, when you appeal to the vulnerable young to avoid these behaviors on the purely self-regarding health grounds that they are risking damage to themselves, you are preaching to a constituency that is not apt to buy your cost-benefit calculations.

VIRTUE'S RETURN

The medicalization of vice—the campaigns for safe this and safe that—has 21 gone as far as it can go, and that is not very far. The result is that we are seeing a "remoralization," if not of society, at least of language. Encouraged by such books as William Bennett's *The Book of Virtues*, Gertrude Himmelfarb's *The De-Moralization of Society*, and James Q. Wilson's *The*

Moral Sense, the frank use of the old-fashioned language of virtue is making a comeback.

Establishment discourse has been forced to readmit moral categories into   22
the debate about social decay and deviancy. The change is visible and rapid.
One can almost chart it by comparing the reception accorded Dan Quayle's
1992 assault on Murphy Brown[4] and that given Bob Dole's on Time Warner
and Hollywood just three years later. Quayle was pummeled by establishment
media. The response to Dole was: Why aren't the Democrats saying this too?

This represents a significant advance in two respects. First, it legitimizes   23
the use of frankly moral language in public discourse. Second, it legitimizes
the deployment of that language against the purveyors of culture and the
holding of them to certain standards of decency.

This engagement in the cultural war is a necessary complement to the   24
"structural" conservative attempts to rein in the welfare state. Reining in the
state creates civil space open to new influences. But the cultural agenda—and
particularly the attempt to force the mass media to clean up their act and alter
their message—will crucially determine what gets to fill that space.

IN THE ABSENCE OF RELIGION

But even that will not be enough. Culture wars, however satisfying and nec-   25
essary, are not sufficient. If there is to be a remoralization of society, it will
have to occur at the level not just of supply but of demand. Getting the culture producers to limit the toxicity of their products will not be that difficult.
Even without overt government censorship, political and popular pressure are
quite capable of inducing the culture creators to self-censorship.

In a free-market society, however, such supply-side changes are not   26
enough. The failure of the war on drugs should have taught us that. The
producers of culture may accede temporarily to political demands for self-
censorship out of fear or regard for public relations. But a more enduring
change in the cultural market, as in any other, awaits a fundamental change
in demand. The customer has to stop buying the stuff.

And where does that come from? We now leave the realm of govern-   27
mental reform and media self-censorship and enter entirely new territory, religious territory. Irving Kristol has written about the current and coming
religious revival as an echo of earlier Great Awakenings. There certainly is a
religious revival under way, and it does establish a basis for a most fundamental reversal of social decay. But I have my doubts about the firmness and
permanence of this *fin de siècle* awakening.

---

[4]*Murphy Brown, Time Warner:* In the 1992 presidential campaign vice-presidential candidate Dan Quayle attacked the TV character Murphy Brown for having a child out of wedlock. Quayle's comment led to a national debate on the issue. In 1995, Senate Majority
Leader (and later presidential candidate) Bob Dole attacked media conglomerate Time
Warner for marketing gangsta rap CDs.

This is an age of advanced science and material abundance. Science and   28
abundance offer invitations to skepticism and pleasure that are hard to refuse.
It is difficult for me to believe that in such an era, a self-abnegating religious
revival will prevail.

I hope I am wrong. If I am, the conservative revolution will unfold in and   29
of itself, with near-Marxist historic inevitability. It is the task of the political
strategist, however, to prepare for the possibility that the Great Awakening is
not at hand. In which case the arrest of social decay, the revitalization of civil
society, is a far more difficult and chancy proposition. It must then depend
upon the more coercive and less reliable agency of politics—a politics crucially
capable of articulating cultural with structural reform. Neither alone will
suffice.

■ ■ ■

Review Questions

1. Why does Krauthammer blame "the welfare state" for the rise in illegitimacy over the past 35 years?
2. Why does Krauthammer believe that simply dismantling the welfare state
   is unlikely to reverse the social decline it has helped create?
3. Explain why Krauthammer objects to "the medicalization" of vice.
4. What must happen, according to Krauthammer, if we are to reverse the
   process of social decay he has described?

Discussion and Writing Suggestions

1. Why do you suppose Krauthammer entitled his article "A Social
   Conservative Credo," rather than "A Political Conservative Credo"?
   How does the word "Social" relate to the overall thrust of this piece?
2. Krauthammer blames what he calls "the welfare state" or "the nanny
   state" for much of the social breakdown of the last generation or so. To
   what extent do you accept his view of the consequences of welfare on the
   illegitimacy rate and of the relationship between other government programs and "divorce, illegitimacy, violence, crime, drug abuse, suicide,
   [and] untreated mental illness (disguised as homelessness)"? Explain,
   drawing upon your own experiences, observations, or reading.
3. Besides indicting the welfare state, Krauthammer blames "mass culture"—gangsta rap, MTV, mainstream films, TV—for much of the social
   breakdown (violence, crime, illegitimacy, etc.) that plagues contemporary
   life. This is particularly true, he believes, in areas where "the authority
   structure has disintegrated." To what extent do you agree with his analysis? Again, draw upon your own experiences, observations, or reading, in
   formulating a response.
4. To what extent do you feel comfortable—or uncomfortable—discussing
   behavior in terms of virtue and vice? To what extent does or should
   behavior have a moral dimension? If it does, then should society, or its

institutions—such as the family, the church, the community—impose sanctions upon what it considers immoral, if legal, behavior?

5. Krauthammer believes that government cannot by itself effectively counteract the malign effects of mass culture. Even the self-censorship of the media, if it occurs, will not last for long. "The customer," he argues, "has to stop buying the stuff." To what extent do you believe that it is socially desirable for the customer to "stop buying the stuff"? And if it is socially desirable, how might this happen without government censorship—a course he does not advocate?

The Origin of Conservatism

JOHN O. McGINNIS

Liberals have often attacked conservatives for advocating "social Darwinism"— that is, applying Charles Darwin's theories of natural selection and the survival of the fittest to the social order. Viewed through the prism of social Darwinism, for example, people on welfare have shown themselves to be ill-adapted to their environment and therefore not suited to "survival." In fact, helping the poor should actually be discouraged, since it violates the natural order and evolutionary progress. Liberals contend that social Darwinism is invalid (because the laws governing biological evolution are not analogous to the principles governing human society) as well as cruel and inhumane.

Such liberal arguments are rejected by John McGinnis, a professor at Cardoza Law School, Yeshiva University, in New York City. In his article, "The Origin of Conservatism," McGinnis, citing recent research in psychology, economics, anthropology, and linguistics, reaffirms the applicability of evolutionary biology to both human nature and human culture. This article first appeared in the National Review, *December 22, 1997.*

1 Today a revolution is remaking the social sciences. For the last two decades, theorists in psychology, economics, anthropology, and linguistics have begun to discard the traditional social-science model in which man creates the social world through his culture. They have instead turned to evolutionary biology to draw an ever more precise and powerful description of the human nature that generates all cultures. The results of their discoveries are now seeping into the popular consciousness as the media report through a biological prism such fundamental topics as the relations between the sexes. Because evolutionary biology provides an informative picture of man and because citizens are rapidly assimilating that image, any political movement that hopes to be successful must come to terms with the second rise of Darwinism.

2 Conservatism will certainly be easier than liberalism to integrate with evolutionary biology. The constraints of our biological nature explode the most persistent delusion of the Left: that man is so malleable that he can be

reshaped or transformed through political actions. In contrast, the depiction of our species that is emerging from Darwinism—as composed of individuals who are basically self-interested yet capable of altruism toward family and friends; who are unequal in their abilities yet remarkably similar in their aspirations—comports with fundamental premises of conservative thought.

Thus the new biological learning holds the potential for providing stronger support for conservatism than any other new body of knowledge has done. Yet it may also raise questions about some intellectual traditions of the Right, such as pure libertarianism, and its methodology may disturb religious conservatives. These tensions must be resolved if the conservative coalition is to thrive in the intellectual soil of the coming century.   3

There are seven concepts that are essential to understanding the Darwinian picture of man. The logic of each concept applied to human affairs turns out to bolster major tenets of mainstream conservatism.   4

1. *Self-Interest and Politics.* Like all other animals, our species has been shaped by millions of years of natural selection. Natural selection works through genetic inheritance and variation.[1] Genes for many physical and behavioral traits are inheritable; such genes may also be variable within the population of animals of the same species. Because of recombination and mutation, animals within the same species differ in their genetic makeup. Some inherited traits will enable some individual animals to leave more offspring than others. Genes for such traits then increase in the population of the species.   5

Thus, as Robert Wright has nicely observed, it follows directly from natural selection that any individual animal will have behavioral adaptations designed to favor its own interests over those of others. The single exception is that they may favor other animals who can aid in disseminating their distinctive genes. Thus each human individual has strong innate behavioral tendencies to favor his own interests, those of the comparatively few relatives who share a large proportion of his genes, and the potential mates who are necessary to reproduce his genes. We are not closely and equally related to many other individuals of our species, like ants and some other social insects, who routinely sacrifice themselves for their colony.   6

One interest all human beings share is seeking resources and status. In all past societies surveyed, those who had more relative status and resources left more progeny than those who had less status and fewer resources. (It is possible that this finding would not be true of some present-day societies, but evolution in humans works so slowly that any such counter-trend would   7

---

[1] *Natural Selection:* Charles Darwin's theory, as propounded in *On the Origin of Species* (1859) that through a process of nature those varieties of a species that are best adapted to their environment—an environment of limited resources—are selected for survival and reproduction. (Thus, the doctrine of "survival of the fittest.") Future generations of the species will therefore be dominated by those varieties that are genetically best adapted to the environment. Those varieties that are less well adapted will either perish or dwindle in number. It did not take long for philosophers to adapt Darwin's biological theories to the workings of human society. William Graham Sumner and Herbert Spencer were only two of the "Social Darwinists" of the nineteenth century.

take thousands of years to be reflected in our genetic make-up.) Thus human beings are emotionally and cognitively wired to be resource and status seekers. We also confirm from studies of other primates that we innately view exchange and hierarchy as alternative strategies for gaining resources. For instance, chimpanzees exchange food, but they also make coalitions among themselves to simply take food and sexual access.

The universal affinity for property and status has serious political impli-   8
cations. In any society large or heterogeneous enough for members to sense that they are unrelated, they will seek to turn resources held in common to their own personal advantage. To a biological anthropologist it was thus wholly predictable that individuals under Communism would spend less of their time in productive exchange and more of their time manipulating the state so as to become more equal than others. Similarly, in social democracies individuals will organize themselves into coalitions for the purpose of gaining access to the state treasury. Such political systems lead to a lack of productivity, social conflict, and instability because there is simply a mismatch between collectivism on any large and enduring scale and our evolved nature. As Edward O. Wilson, the world's foremost expert on ants, remarked about Marxism: "Wonderful theory. Wrong species."

2. *Kin Selection.* We have evolved an emotional life in which we have a   9
tendency to take an abiding interest in the welfare of our kin, because they share a substantial proportion of our genes. Because children represent a parent's genetic future, the parent-child bond has the potential to be particularly close. Thus, as conservatives have argued for centuries, the family is a natural unit of society, and family affections are not mere social constructs but are deeply rooted in our behavior and psyche. Policies that strengthen the family provide a reliable and lasting form of social insurance.

3. *Sexual Differences.* A government that is careful to preserve rather   10
than dissolve family ties is important for other biological reasons. Evolutionary biology predicts that men and women will have different degrees of attachment to their family. Because women are limited in the potential number of their offspring, they are naturally more child-centered in their affections. Men by contrast can have a huge number of children, and thus their relations with any particular child tend to be inherently less secure. Men do provide more care for their progeny than males in most other mammalian species because human infants face a lengthy period of helplessness and fare much better with substantial paternal investment of time and effort in their upbringing. Yet fathers are more likely than mothers to resent and avoid obligations that may deprive them of other mating opportunities. Men are innately more aggressive and obsessed with status than women for similar reasons: because of their low-cost role in sexual reproduction they have far more scope for converting resources and status into the creation of children.

Family obligations in some measure counteract the more roving nature of   11
the male by enmeshing men in networks that both provide children with needed paternal affection and prevent socially destructive male aggression. Thus the greatest cost of modern welfare programs may not have been the tax

dollars wasted but the paternal investment squandered, because, as Charles Murray has demonstrated, welfare discourages the social norms that anchored men to the women with whom they had children. This has led to generations of children who have had less male nurturing than they need—and generations of men who are excessively aggressive because they have not been restrained by family obligations. The imposition of no-fault divorce has also made it easier for men to shirk parental care. Thus, the new biological learning provides direct support for conservative initiatives such as welfare reform and the introduction in Louisiana of "covenant marriage," which allows women to negotiate for greater permanence for their pair bond.

4. *Reciprocal Altruism and Civil Society.* Our species has also evolved a   12
host of behaviors that facilitate "reciprocal altruism"—a willingness to perform acts beneficial to another unrelated person in the expectation that the person on the receiving end will reciprocate. The bundles of qualities that make us reciprocal altruists are very useful in overcoming "prisoner's dilemmas"—situations in which a cooperative act would lead to benefits for both parties, but only if reciprocity could be assured. In primitive societies, where centralized enforcement of legal obligations was quite imperfect, psychological mechanisms that resulted in cooperation would have been naturally selected. For instance, individuals who did not renege on deals and who repaid a good turn with another increased their wealth compared to those who did not. As reciprocating individuals gained resources and therefore left more children, genes for traits promoting reciprocal altruism spread through the population.

Altruistic behavior, however, tends to be limited by the need for reci-   13
procity. Although individuals are disposed to cooperate, they tend to withdraw their cooperation if no long-term benefits are received. Genes encouraging behavior that did not ultimately redound to the concrete benefit of an actor or his kin did not spread through the population. Much of the emotional life of our species—gratitude, sympathy, moral outrage—is therefore designed to regulate the relations of reciprocal altruism. Cognitively too, we keep a mental account of what other individuals have done for us and to us—a fact nicely captured by Tom Wolfe's concept, in *The Bonfire of the Vanities,* of a "favor bank," in which lawyers and court personnel kept careful track of the favors they had performed.

Because of innate reciprocal altruism, exchange is thus as natural to man   14
as song is to a songbird. The market is not a mere artifact created by the state but a force of nature. Indeed, reciprocal altruism generates not only trade but also civil society as a whole. Organizations spring forth that facilitate all kinds of social exchange, including the trading of information and of affection. Such spontaneous orders differ from one society to the next because of differences in knowledge and circumstances, but the social world everywhere is bound together by the vines of informal cooperation. These are so vibrant that the concrete which states try to lay down over this growth is in perpetual danger of cracking.

The same bonding mechanisms that facilitate this spontaneous order,   15
however, also make political factions more intractable and divisive. As David

Hume recognized, "when men are once enlisted on opposite sides they contract an affection to the persons with whom they are united and an animosity against their antagonists: And these passions they often transmit to their posterity." Modern psychological studies confirm that when individuals acquire a group identity, they will act with more solidarity as a group against other groups than individual calculation warrants. By bonding together in numbers, such factions can better control hierarchies, like the state, and thus no longer have to rely on exchange as the primary method to increase their resources.

Therefore, while reciprocity has beneficial effects in the market and in civil society, the factions it facilitates make it more likely that the state will be used to distribute resources from one group to another. Liberal identity politics, whether of class, race, or sex, exacerbate this danger. Conservative political theorists like James Madison, in contrast, have focused on tempering and restraining factions. Factions can be tempered if the individual can be made to identify in some measure with a community that encompasses a wide range of interests. Factions can be restrained if the power of the government can be limited so that it cannot as easily be used for redistribution. One important conservative notion—federalism, or subsidiarity—has in the past simultaneously accomplished both of the political objectives required by our evolutionary nature. By making government local, it makes it easier for individuals to identify with a community; and by putting governments in competition with one another, it restrains the powers of factions. 16

5. *Deception and Self-Deception.* Deception is pandemic in nature. Camouflage and mimicry are just two of its typical forms. Paradoxically, our tendencies to reciprocal altruism increase the potential gains from deception in our species, because exploiting reciprocators may lead to gaining benefits without having to give any in return. In our species the opportunities for deception are improved by language, which simultaneously provides a valuable medium of exchange—information—and the ability to counterfeit that good. 17

Of course, it is in the interest of those potentially deceived to discover deception, and it is not surprising that human beings are natural, if imperfect, lie detectors. (That is the reason why we want jurors to hear testimony live rather than read a transcript.) This detection ability encourages selection for behavior that will avoid detection, setting up an arms race between deceptive behavior and mechanisms for detecting deception. Biologists have suggested that this arms race is, in turn, the origin of pervasive self-deception in man. By deceiving himself, an individual may suppress the cues that allow others to detect deception. Hence self-deception is most likely when there is an intense need to deceive others. 18

The fact that human beings have innate tendencies toward deception and self-deception buttresses the conservative defense of civil society and skepticism about state power. Civil society develops norms to combat deception in private life. In the market, individuals have strong incentives to maintain a reputation for honesty so that others will deal with them. Fraternal and religious organizations arise in part to vouch for the good behavior of their members. 19

In contrast, it is much harder to root deception out of large-scale politics.   20
For instance, in a democracy citizens are rationally ignorant of most political
issues; that is, they know perhaps subconsciously, that their individual votes
are so unlikely to influence elections that it simply does not pay to follow the
twists and turns of public debate. Politicians have a scope for deception pro-
portionate to this ignorance. A commanding presence, a compassionate
demeanor, and rhetorical virtuosity are evolutionarily designed mechanisms
that fool the inattentive.

The ingrained susceptibility to self-deception also undermines the cele-   21
bration of sincerity and authenticity that has been at the heart of the Left's
project since Rousseau. Evolution suggests that individuals may project the
most sincerity and feel the greatest measure of authenticity precisely when
they are offering proposals that are deceptive—ideas that benefit themselves
and their group at the expense of others.

6. *Natural Inequality.* Darwinism confirms the view that individuals have   22
inherently unequal abilities and that these inequalities are likely to be greatest in the personality traits, such as intelligence and ambition, that are related to acquiring property. In *On the Origin of Species* Darwin himself
formulated this law about natural variation: "A part developed in any extraordinary degree or manner, in comparison with the same part in allied species,
tends to be highly variable." When a species breaks into a part of the design
space of the world previously unexploited, enormous selective pressure develops in the genes of that species to make ever more effective use of this virgin
territory. For instance, the beaks of Darwin's species of finches are highly variable since these finches were able to exploit a large variety of previously inac-
cessible seeds on the Galapagos Islands. Likewise, since human beings have
brains whose cognitive aspects are developed to an extraordinary degree
compared to those of other animals, one would expect the human brain's
inheritable capacity to be highly variable. This theory is confirmed by recent
studies suggesting that measurable personality traits are to a large degree
inherited rather than shaped by the environment—and that intelligence is the
trait most conserved through generations.

Natural inequality has implications for both the ideological and the struc-   23
tural content of politics. On the level of political philosophy, it undermines the
basic premise of liberal egalitarianism: that it is possible to equalize outcomes by eliminating inequality in social circumstances. The engine of
inequality is buried so deep in human nature that it is impossible to eradicate.
Indeed, as Richard Herrnstein showed, equalizing social circumstances will
mean that the inequality in outcomes will become dictated in greater measure
by generic inheritance.

In contrast, conservatives are correct in understanding that, because of nat-   24
ural inequality, structures must be fashioned to prevent harmful schemes aimed
at the delusive goal of eliminating it. Indeed, in *Federalist* 10, the most celebrated document of political philosophy in American history, James Madison
observed that the greatest problem for any political structure is how to protect
"the unequal faculties for acquiring property" from government interference.
Over the long run, such protection assures greater prosperity for all by sus-

taining the incentives for the talented and productive to exercise their genius through invention and innovation. In the West over the past hundred years, this has allowed a vast array of individuals to enjoy a degree of good health and leisure that was previously available only to a select few.

Nevertheless, as Madison recognized, the very inequality that makes this prosperity possible also makes the protection of the different abilities to acquire property more difficult because it exacerbates the danger that the government will be used as a mechanism for redistribution from one faction to another. Inequality means that there will always be a large pool of individuals with less talent than others for acquiring property. Given the human capacity for self-deception, these citizens are less likely to make a dispassionate assessment of their own abilities than to believe that some prosperous group is holding them back. Skilled demagogues and dissemblers can always be found to provide justifications for redistributing property because individuals are primed to seek status—and nowhere can greater status be acquired than from political leadership.

This natural dynamic of inequality in politics vindicates conservative attempts to establish constitutional structures that limit the power of demagogues and the potential for expropriation of wealth. The original American Constitution—with a complex system of federalism, separation of powers, and national representative democracy—is the most justly venerated of these attempts. While conservatives are right to object to the judicial usurpations that have vitiated this system over time, a Darwinian understanding of politics suggests that simple democracy is no substitute for constructing a system to guard against the passions and self-deceptions of individuals with disparate abilities.

7. *The Fragile and Divided Self*—The final natural fact for politics is also the most personal. The self, like all essential aspects of man, is an adaptation to selective pressures over millions of years and thus is jury-rigged from different mechanisms from our evolutionary past. It is a mistake, for example, to think of the sexual self as completely continuous with the more obviously rational acquisitive self that evolved somewhat later to take advantage of resources and status opportunities. These selves evolved for different purposes and are not fully connected—hence the frequently observed imprudence of sexual passion.

Evolution's understanding of the self is thus an implicit challenge to the modern liberal project of protecting the sphere of sexual autonomy from regulation while heavily regulating exchange of resources. An order that is rational and self-correcting in historical time is much more likely to spring from more calculating modules devoted to reciprocal altruism than the more impulsive modules of sexuality.

After canvassing the social understanding provided by the new biological learning, we may fairly conclude that a Darwinian politics is a largely conservative politics. This is not surprising, because conservatives have always prided themselves on dealing with man as he is, not as we might wish to imagine him. Despite the congruence of modern Darwinism and conservative thought, some might foresee substantial pitfalls for practical conservative politics. First is the simple fact that some religious conservatives do not believe in evolution and have made their antipathy to it a part of their political creed. But their hostility is not fatal to the future of the conservative coalition. The description of man that emerges from evolution resembles in many respects the fallen man posited by Christian theology—a being self-interested and absorbed in status seeking. Members of political coalitions may have to agree broadly on human nature, but they do not have to agree on the methodology that brings them to that understanding. For instance, the Framers of the American Constitution comprised both deists whose religion was inspired by the Newtonian science of their day and Christians with far more traditional religious attachments.

A variation on this concern is the idea that acceptance of Darwinian   30
thinking will undermine religious belief, which is itself a bulwark of social sta-
bility. This also seems implausible. There is no logical incompatibility between belief in evolution and faith in God; the Catholic Church has long understood that crediting natural selection as the proximate cause of man does not threaten God's standing as his ultimate Creator. Moreover, given the universality of religion across all cultures, religious feeling almost certainly has natural roots in our emotional psyche and will not be dissolved by scientific discovery.

Another unwarranted concern is that a focus on biology will lead   31
inevitably to a discussion of racial differences and therefore to an increase in racial tensions. While Darwinism offers strong reason to assume that men and women differ on average in their emotional affects and aspirations because women have naturally been more bound up with their children, it offers no reason to assume the existence of substantial racial differences in the personality traits important to acquiring property. Of course, it does not deny the possibility of such differences either. But evolutionary biology and anthro-
pology do stress the universal nature of man: we are all members of one species, and through kin selection and reciprocal altruism we tend to have common aspirations and similar affects for satisfying those aspirations. Thus a multiracial society can be sustained so long as it is centered on the family and the market—the loci of our commonality.

On the other hand, evolutionary biology may present a serious challenge   32
to pure libertarianism. This may surprise some people who confuse the rise of Darwinism in the social sciences with the nineteenth-century tenets of Social Darwinism. There is no connection. Natural selection leads to the survival of the most reproductively fit; however, it is a classic example of the naturalis-
tic fallacy to infer from this scientific fact the moral conclusion that the goal of society is to aid the most reproductively fit. Instead, by describing human nature more precisely, evolutionary biology offers an improved map for the political economy in our age. It shows what are the natural tendencies of man and what are the possible ways human political actions can both release and constrain these tendencies to increase human happiness.

Moreover, the fragile and divided self that evolution describes may not be   33
entirely consonant with the more integrated self at the heart of libertarianism.

For instance, the younger self is so weakly connected to the imagination of the older self (primarily because most individuals did not live to old age in hunter-gatherer societies) that most people cannot be expected to save sufficiently for old age. A large group of aging and propertyless individuals would be a source of social instability. Therefore there may be justification for state intervention to force individuals to save for their own retirement. Similarly, the sexual self is so weakly linked to the long-term rational calculating self that simply requiring individuals to live with the consequences of their sexual acts may not be enough to restrain socially destructive activity. Society may need to create institutions to channel and restrain sexual activity.

Evolutionary biology also undermines what might be termed utopian   34
conservatism: the notion that there is some social structure in which all the possible human goods—family values, patriotism, entrepreneurship—will be fully and equally realized. Evolution shines a somewhat tragic light on the desire for perfection in human affairs: the different adaptations around which emotions are structured are inevitably in conflict, particularly as the environment changes. For instance, as the rule of law in society perfects the axis of reciprocal altruism and makes it easy to gain resources through trade with unrelated individuals, the family becomes less necessary as a source of protection and as an axis of commerce for its members. Western civilization, in fact, has been marked by the continuous shrinking of the extended family, so that "family values" today are generally a reference to the nuclear family—a shadow of the "clan values" that dominated hunter-gatherer societies. One can go to a society with a less rule-oriented regime than ours (like Italy) and get some sense of the encompassing warmth of family life that is lost with the progress of law. A Darwinian conservatism recognizes the fundamental trade-offs in social life and works to conserve what is possible rather than seeking to resurrect what is dead. Darwinian conservatism is thus the conservatism of those, like Edmund Burke, who offer political reforms to meet changing conditions.

Evolutionary biology necessarily underscores the impermanence of all   35
human arrangements. Like any scientific understanding, it echoes the Heraclitean maxim: Everything not supernatural is in flux. When a biologist looks at the behavior of animals, he recognizes that this behavior is an interaction of genes and the environment. As the environment changes, so will the behavior. An evolutionary science of politics thus has nothing in common with genetic determinism.

Because our discoveries and inventions change the human environment   36
faster than that of any other animal, there is always a temptation—to which today's techno-conservatives, like Newt Gingrich, often fall prey—to think that such changes may usher in an age of harmony and plenty that will solve the dilemmas of politics. Evolutionary biology shows that this is simply a pipe dream. Our nature assures that we will simultaneously be obsessed with our relative status in society and possess unequal abilities for acquiring higher status. Thus individuals will always seek to use the government as a means to rearrange their relative positions. No matter how much wealth free trade

produces, no matter how much information the Internet transmits, the central
problem of politics will remain: how to empower the government for safeguarding life and property, and yet simultaneously constrain it from eviscer-
ating civil society and expropriating property.

Such changes in information transmission and technology require inno-   37
vative structures to achieve this perennial goal of human politics. For instance,
it may be that the federalism of the Framing is no longer an effective structure
for containing centralized governmental power. The ease of transportation
and the dominance of mass communication have loosened citizens' attachments to their states. We simply cannot share the feelings of Robert E. Lee,
who in refusing the command of the Union armies stated that he must fight
for his "native state" rather than the United States. Some other political
devices that are better rooted in current attachments may have to be found for
restraining government in our time.

Accordingly, the most important lesson of Darwinism for conservatives   38
today is to remind them that their task is to respond to the ingrained tendencies of human nature in a world in flux. Its unique contribution is to provide
a powerful scientific framework to describe that nature more precisely than
ever before. Thus it should inspire the Right to act in the tradition of the
greatest conservatives of past generations, like Madison and Burke, who also
used the best science of their day to create political structures that would
enable men to flourish in the intersection of their particular circumstances and
their enduring nature.

■   ■   ■

Review Questions

1. Write a two-page summary of this article. Cover each of McGinnis's
   seven major sections, along with the introductory and concluding sections.
2. What are the innate behavioral tendencies of all individuals, according to
   McGinnis?
3. Why, according to the author, are communism and socialism doomed to
   fail?
4. How does evolutionary biology support conservatives' support of family
   values, according to McGinnis?
5. In light of the natural inequalities of individuals, why do conservatives
   distrust powerful governments?
6. Why might Christians, on the one hand, and libertarians, on the other,
   oppose the concept of a Darwinian politics? How does McGinnis
   respond to their concerns?

Discussion and Writing Suggestions

1. Accepting McGinnis's claim that evolutionary biology supports the conservative, rather than the liberal, approach to human society and politics
   depends upon accepting a number of his assumptions. For example, we

must accept (a) that all human beings seek resources and status; (b) that such behavioral traits are genetic and are therefore passed down from one generation to the next; (c) that it is valid to draw connections between our biological nature and our social nature; and (d) that these connections ought to determine our public policy regarding such matters as the family, sexual behavior, and government regulation of business. Examine and evaluate McGinnis's arguments, taking such factors into consideration.

2. Early in his article McGinnis asserts that "one of the most persistent delusions of the left [is that] man is so malleable that he can be reshaped or transformed through political actions." To what extent do you agree that such a belief is a delusion? To what extent do you believe that this belief is valid? Provide examples to support your conclusions.

3. Under the first heading, "Self-Interest and Politics," McGinnis argues that self-interest is a biological imperative, one that impels people toward "seeking resources and status." Many people would argue instead that self-interest and the seeking of resources (or property) and status are dependent upon cultural influences. What do you believe is the role of biology and culture in the human urge to favor one's own interests? What evidence can you cite to support your beliefs?

4. According to McGinnis, altruism, or the desire to help others, will survive genetically only if it is reciprocal—that is, if one gets benefits for giving benefits. Conversely, selflessness, or the giving of oneself without expectation of return, is an unnatural form of behavior. Extending this biological reality to the realm of politics, the market economy, which is based on exchange, is a more natural economy than a socialist economy, which is based upon the equal distribution of wealth. The market economy, in fact, is "a force of nature." To what extent do you accept such a theory?

5. In paragraphs 20 and 21, McGinnis suggests that conservatives have a natural tendency to resist deception in politics, while liberals—with their "celebration of sincerity and authenticity"—have a natural tendency to become victims of deception. What is your reaction to this observation?

6. In section 6 on "Natural Inequality" McGinnis argues that people are inherently unequal in the kind of intelligence and ambition that it takes to acquire property, to invent, and to innovate, and that the end products of these efforts benefit society as a whole. As a result, he says, most people today "enjoy a degree of good health and leisure that was previously available only to a select few." McGinnis therefore opposes "government interference" against the most ambitious and successful people and their enterprises, and he also warns of the danger of giving in to "demagogues" who would stir up the less successful into believing that they are the victims of injustice demanding the redistribution of property and wealth from the more well-off to the less well-off. To what extent do you accept McGinnis's reasoning and his conclusions?

7. Conservatives, says McGinnis, "have always prided themselves on dealing with man as he is, not as we might wish to imagine him." Presumably, according to the author, liberals deal with humans as we

might wish to imagine them. To what extent do you agree with this characterization of conservatives and liberals and the essential difference between them? Allowing that these generalizations have some degree of truth, where do you place yourself on the conservative-liberal spectrum? Explain your position in terms of McGinnis's ideas.

When Government Gets Mean: Confessions of a Recovering Statist

BARBARA EHRENREICH

Although terms such as "liberal" and "conservative" are often used as labels to categorize (and thus save us the trouble of thinking about) both particular political philosophies and individuals, it's important to remember that both liberalism and conservatism encompass a range of thought and that most active political philosophies evolve through time as conditions change. Thus, while the liberal viewpoint is often associated with big government (to say nothing of taxing and spending, as conservatives charge), not all liberals advocate big government, and those who did a decade ago may no longer do so. This kind of evolving liberalism is the subject of the following article by Barbara Ehrenreich. Ehrenreich, co-chair of Democratic Socialists of America, has lectured at hundreds of colleges in the United States, Canada, and Europe. She is a frequent contributor to such magazines as The Atlantic, Harper's, Time, The New Republic, *and* The New York Times Magazine. *Her books include* Fear of Failing: The Inner Life of the Middle Class *(1989),* The Worst Years of Our Lives: Irreverent Notes from a Decade of Greed *(1990), and* The Snarling Citizen *(1995). This piece first appeared in* The Nation, *November 17, 1997, as part of its "First Principles" series.*

Call this the confessions of a recovering statist[1]—at least that's how the right will probably view it. In the past fifteen or so years, I've ended hundreds of speeches with the words "cut military spending and expand social spending," or some euphonious version thereof, implicitly identifying government as the only appropriate focus for activism. In these predilections I have hardly been alone: Progressivism is almost defined, in our times, by its advocacy of an "activist government."

A couple of decades ago, it made sense to pin our hopes on the federal government as a positive instrument for social change. In the sixties and seventies—pressured by the civil rights movement, the nascent feminist movement and a still-muscular labor movement—the federal government expanded both its economic protections and its guarantees of civil liberties. We gained, in little more than a decade, Medicare and Medicaid, workplace safety and environ-

---

[1] *Statist:* One who believes that government is the primary ensurer of justice and equality.

mental regulations, cost-of-living increases in Social Security and laws against race- and sex-based discrimination, as well as the right to birth control and abortion. To many of us who came together in the early eighties to form the Democratic Socialists of America, for instance, it seemed possible that we would achieve our goal of an economically socialist and socially libertarian society by building on the programs and guarantees already offered by the federal government. At the very least, that government seemed to embody, in however imperfect a form, some defense against corporate banditry.

So when a populist right emerged to challenge "big government" and the legitimacy of government-based reforms in general, we valiantly leapt to its defense. At the time, this seemed like the only reasonable and principled response: We knew the right was not so much "against government" as it was against the meager protections government provides for the low- and middle-income majority. But ineluctably we, the erstwhile radicals, became far better defenders of government than any of its elected functionaries. As the right escalated its attacks, we escalated our defense, to the point, all too often, of seeming to abandon our own antistatist tradition and critiques of existing government programs. I realized how much our image had changed—from "radical" to "defenders of government"—in discussions with some of the rural right-wingers I regularly talk to. To my surprise, they were surprised to discover that I share their outrage over random drug searches and similar intrusions: It was their impression that "liberals" thought the government could do no wrong!

I'm not sure whether we should have responded differently to the right's antigovernment rhetoric from the start. But surely today, after nearly two decades of conservative national governance, Reagan through Clinton, we can no longer let progressivism be understood as the defense of government—this government anyway—against the antigovernment forces of the right. The federal government of 1997 is a very different creature from that of, say, 1977—more egregiously corrupt and sycophantic toward wealth, more glaringly repressive and even less responsive to the needs of low- and middle-income people. By setting ourselves up as the defenders of government (or, colloquially speaking, "big government") against the neo-anarchists of the right, progressives have boxed themselves into a pragmatically and morally untenable position.

Pragmatically, the problem is that hardly anyone out there wants to hear about more government or bigger government. Even the constituency for better government is tepid: Witness the non-response to our current campaign finance scandals. It is, unfortunately, the federal government—long favored by the left because of its relative ability to rise above the racism and corporate caprices that typically dominate the statehouses—that has been the most thoroughly discredited as a potential agency of positive change. Maybe that will change—as, for example, people notice that it is the federal government and not the Chamber of Commerce that tends to organize disaster relief and that has brought us such innovations as the Internet. But for the time being, we're not going to get anywhere with a progressive agenda consisting of wonderful new government initiatives. Believe me, I have tried, and found again and again that the enthusiasm for, say, national health insurance or stricter environmental regulation quickly ebbs when I point out that the only source of such improvements is likely to be the federal government. Socialism is, of course, completely out of the question as long as it is conceived as a hypertrophied version of the government we now have, or, in the paranoid fantasy of the populist right, Hillary running everything.[2]

Americans did not always hate their government. The proportion who   6
say they "trust the government in Washington" only "some of the time" or "none of the time" has shot up only recently, rising from 30 percent to 70 percent just in the years between 1966 and 1992. We usually explain this shift in outlook as a brilliant propaganda coup for the right, which, by the mid-seventies, was raking in enough corporate money to create a lush intellectual infrastructure of think tanks and new media outlets. We understand that racism also played its part in the turn against government, helping foster the peculiar perception that people of color have been the chief, if not the sole, beneficiaries of government activism. But we also should understand that the discrediting of government was not accomplished solely through propaganda and prejudice: There are legitimate grounds for distrusting government, and these grounds have been expanding. Through its power over the government it professes to hate, the right has put itself in a position to create a government that is ever more deserving of hatred.

It is, first of all, a government that offers far too little to its average citi-   7
zens. Thanks to the efforts of the right over the past several decades and especially the past decade and a half, we have a government that does not provide the kinds of services that, in other nations, have helped create a mass constituency for government activism—things like universal health insurance, child care, college tuition, paid parental leave and a reliable safety net. In fact, middle-class, non-elderly Americans encounter their government chiefly in the form of petty-minded bureaucracies like the I.R.S. and the D.M.V. Hence the vicious cycle that has been powering the rightward march of U.S. politics: The less the government does for us, the easier it is to believe the right's antigovernment propaganda; and the more we believe it, the less likely we are to vote for anyone who might use government to actually improve our lives.

The result has been a near-total ideological roadblock for the left. We say   8
"Child care! Health care!" and all the rest, and they say, "Aha, you mean more government!" End of discussion. We have no trouble imagining the kind of polity and social protections we would like, but one of the most venerable

---

[2] *Hillary running everything:* During the Clinton administration, conservatives tended to demonize Hillary Clinton for being an unelected president, believing that she had too much influence over government policy. Liberals tended to believe that what the conservatives really didn't like about Hillary was that she was a "liberated" woman (she was a skillful and practiced attorney) who didn't fit the conservative ideal of a traditional wife.

instruments for achieving them—government—has been ruled out of order by the ideologues of the right. Now we could of course doggedly continue our defense of government activism against the celebrants of the "free market" economy—pointing out, for example, that government still offers some useful things like Medicare and Head Start, that taxes are actually quite low here compared with other nations, that it is still, despite the ever-tightening rule of wealth, in some vague sense "our government.

But there is another reason we can no longer let progressivism be defined   9 as the defense of government activism, and this is a moral one. While government does less and less for us, it does more and more *to* us. The right points to the appalling firebombing at Waco; we should be just as noisily indignant about the ongoing police war against low-income Americans of color, not to mention teenagers, immigrants and other designated misfits. If there is any handy measure of a government's repressiveness, it is the proportion of its citizenry who are incarcerated, and at least by this measure the United States leads the world. Furthermore, prison conditions in this country are steadily worsening: Children are incarcerated with adults; efforts at rehabilitation are being discarded as overly indulgent amenities; arbitrary brutality and systematic deprivation are common. We don't, in other words, have a soft, cuddly government of the kind that could be derided as a "nanny state." We have a huge and heavily armed cop.

So government has not been shrinking, as promised, on the Clinton-   10 Gingrich watch. Only the helpful functions of government are shrinking, while the repressive ones are expanding without foreseeable limit and increasingly threaten all Americans. Clinton, in particular, has revealed a boundless appetite for surveillance in the name of the drug war and antiterrorism— proposing, at various times, drug tests for young people seeking driver's licenses, government-accessible "clipper chips" within our PCs and the examination of air travelers' life histories for "suspicious travel patterns." Anthony Lewis[3] has concluded that Bill Clinton "has the worst civil liberties record of any President in at least 60 years." He also has the most flamboyant record— surpassing even Reagan's—for the destruction of government services.

We are not yet a police state, of course. You may disagree with me as to   11 how far we have gone in that direction, but you will surely agree that there is *some* point when the ratio of the repressive to the helpful functions of government will become so top-heavy that it will be masochistic to regard government as a potential ally and friend. Maybe for you that will be when Social Security is abolished (or privatized) and when 10 million, instead of a mere 5 million, Americans are trapped in the criminal justice system. For me that point was passed with the repeal of welfare in 1996, after which I could no longer imagine that my federal taxes served any compassionate function—

---

[3] *Anthony Lewis:* columnist for the *New York Times.*

or, more generally, that the government plays any redistributive role other than to promote the ongoing upward redistribution of wealth.

Our entire outlook has to change. Most fundamentally, given the nature   12
of our real and existing government, we can no longer allow ourselves to be seen as mere cheerleaders for government activism. The power to levy taxes, for example, is increasingly deployed to tithe low- and middle-income people to subsidize the state functions—such as corporate welfare and the military— favored by the corporate elite.[4] Even the few remaining services for the poor are tainted by the repressive agenda of the right, which has budgeted funds for "chastity education" for welfare recipients and favors ever more intimate monitoring of the lifestyles of public housing occupants. When this government gets "active," it may very well act against us.

Yes, we should continue to defend the idea, meaning really the vision, of   13
a truly progressive and robustly democratic form of governance. My point is that we can no longer advance that vision by acting as if the existing government prefigures it in any serious way. We can, of course, continue to try to reform the existing government: by electing progressives to office, for example, and by working to change the rules that make it almost impossible to do so. But these efforts have so far been both arduous and disappointing. Procedural tinkering, such as campaign finance reform and the New Party's unsuccessful effort to legalize fusion tickets, is usually too abstract and complex to generate much excitement. And progressive elected officials only rarely remain so, being quickly absorbed into an insiders' world of corruption and compromise.

In the meantime, though, the progressive agenda cannot be put on hold   14
until we have a government that is worthy and capable of carrying it out. There are plenty of things we can do, right now and even with the existing rules and cast of miscreants. We have to begin, though, by acknowledging that the struggle for economic justice can no longer be conceived simply as a campaign to build support for our wish list of government services. We need a greater emphasis on strategies and approaches that do not depend on the existing government, that in fact bypass it as irrelevant or downright obstructionist.

Some of these approaches are obvious and uncontroversial. First, we can   15
support efforts to organize the 90 percent of American workers who are unorganized, including, most urgently, the former recipients of welfare. Historically, there have been two approaches to economic justice: (1) demanding services and income support from government, and (2) directly confronting private capital by organizing unions. Since the first option has been foreclosed for the time being, there must be an all-out emphasis on the second. A major obstacle, sadly, is union leadership itself, which, even in its recently reinvigorated form, has insisted on funneling millions to Democratic candidates (or, worse, their own re-election campaigns) while strike funds go lack-

---

[4] *Corporate welfare*: a term generally applied by liberals to tax breaks for corporations— what the right considers financial incentives for business; what the left considers financial handouts to business.

ing. Fortunately, though, union organizing does not have to wait for the existing union leadership. The ongoing efforts to organize workfare recipients, for example, are being led by groups like ACORN and the recipients themselves; once the hard work of organizing has been accomplished, the unions will no doubt be happy to incorporate the new members.

Second, we can launch a citizen initiative against corporate crime. In the 16 past couple of years, there have been dozens of demonstrations at the retail outlets of sweatshop-dependent corporations like Nike, Guess and Disney. In the absence of effective regulation against abusive corporations, we have no choice but to pressure them ourselves.

More controversially, I propose that we put greater emphasis on projects 17 that both give people concrete assistance and serve as springboards for further political activism. Examples might include squats, cooperatives of various kinds, community currency projects and some of the less costly types of "alternative services," like those offering information, contacts, referrals and a place for people to gather. Such projects can't provide a substitute for government services since, numerically speaking, their impact is only a drop in the bucket, but they can serve as a "cultural core," in Frances Fox Piven's phrase, of a movement that may eventually be strong enough to win services that *are* tax-funded and distributed as a matter of right. The feminist health centers, for example, that flourished in the seventies and are still in operation in a number of cities around the country cannot make up for the lack of national health insurance. But they have given many thousands of women the subversive idea that low-cost, high-quality health care is a right—while at the same time serving as organizing centers for the defense of reproductive rights.

There are several reasons for an emphasis on projects that create alter- 18 natives. First, they may be necessary for organizing low-income workers, who are often dispersed among many small employment sites that are almost impossible to organize one by one. Such workers may be easier to reach through neighborhood-based centers offering, for example, employment counseling along with information on workers' rights and unions—as some organizers of workfare recipients are currently proposing. Second and more generally, bold and visible alternatives may help break through the hopelessness and passivity engendered by years of right-wing campaigning against public services. Successful projects might inspire the kind of can-do spirit that is so lacking today: If government won't do it, then let government get out of the way, because we're not waiting around!

But for me, the most powerful argument for projects that create alterna- 19 tives is, ultimately, the scary fact that there is less and less for them to be alternative to. Consider the plight of the people who are being tossed off welfare. Do we simply wait around until the government changes its mind? Applaud the efforts of the Ford Foundation to track the fate of former welfare recipients as they stumble through low-wage jobs and perhaps into homelessness, all the while trying to publicize the horror stories as they unfold? Better to do something that actually helps a few people, or gets them started helping themselves—while at the same time dramatically underscoring the need for economic justice for all. And if our activism is bold and visible enough, it may help prod the existing government in a progressive direction: banning the products of sweatshops, for example, or replacing workfare with the option of adequately paid public-sector jobs.

But economic justice is not the only thing on our agenda. We have to be   20
ready to defy a government that has become an active repressor, and this means putting a greater emphasis on civil libertarian issues. Some progressives have responded to the right's successes with a narrowing focus on economic justice, arguing that the "social issues"—like gay rights, abortion, drug-law reform, even police brutality—are just too divisive. True, most Americans are far more amenable to economic goals like national health insurance than to drug-law reform (which would empty out most of the prison cells overnight). Morally, though, we have no choice but to oppose the steady erosion of individual liberties and the growth of the punishment industry. It might even improve, or at least clarify, our image if we were more forthright and militant about our own brand of libertarianism.

Tragic realities impel us to move beyond our emotional codependency on   21
government as the only available instrument for social change, but there are opportunities beckoning us in that direction; one is the need to develop a meaningful internationalism. Rhetorically, most progressives agree that it is the transnational corporations, far more than the nation-states, that rule the world, and that the future depends on our ability to build transnational forms of resistance. In practice, though, it's hard to do this when almost all our efforts are addressed to our own particular nation-state. We might free our imaginations to conceive of truly international strategies if our mission were no longer defined so provincially in terms of our immediate impact on the existing national government.

Finally, there is the opportunity to clarify to the American public what we   22
stand for. We cannot let ourselves be defined or perceived as the defenders of a government that has become, under the tutelage of right-wing Republicans and Democrats alike, outrageously corrupt, loathsomely repressive and socially callous. Our goal is, as it has always been, full freedom and economic security for all. At one point it looked like our government might help us achieve this. But that government is no longer "ours," nor will it be anything we would want to claim as ours without a massive downward transfer of power. For now, it looks like we are on our own, although—if you count the world's oppressed and underpaid majority—we are hardly alone.

■   ■   ■

Review Questions

1. How and why did Ehrenreich change her attitude about supporting and defending the federal government?
2. In what way did Ehrenreich find that she shared some common ground with those on the right?
3. What is the chief source of the right's anti-government propaganda, according to Ehrenreich?

4. At what point did Ehrenreich reach the conclusion that the repressive functions of government now outweighed the helpful functions of government?
5. Since the author has all but given up on the federal government as a means of achieving progressive goals, how does she propose to achieve progressive or liberal goals?

Discussion and Writing Suggestions

1. For John O. McGinnis, author of the previous selection, the power of government to redistribute wealth is an unnatural and highly undesirable function. For Barbara Ehrenreich, such redistribution of wealth in favor of social justice is one of the most desirable functions of government. (Such programs might include "universal health insurance, child care, college tuition, paid parental leave, and a reliable safety net.") Whose views more closely represent your own, and why?
2. Develop a list of what for you are the four or five most important functions of the federal government. Explain, in a paragraph, each item on the list, providing specific examples, wherever possible, of how this function serves society as a whole. Based on this discussion, locate yourself along the political spectrum.
3. To what extent do you agree with Ehrenreich's view of the repressive nature of our federal government? In particular, focus on her charges (in paragraph 9) that for a government "[w]e have a huge and heavily armed cop" that incarcerates a significant proportion of its citizens.
4. Faux (paragraph 13) and Ehrenreich (paragraph 21) have different ideas about whether we should focus our efforts at progressive/liberal programs upon our own country (or "nation-state") or upon the world at large, in the form of "transnational corporations." How do you account for the differences between these two liberal authors? Which position makes more sense to you, and why?
5. Ehrenreich concludes by asserting that the government has become "outrageously corrupt, loathsomely repressive and socially callous." To what extent do you agree with this statement? Write a response, either supporting or opposing Ehrenreich (or supporting some points, and opposing others) in the form of a letter to the editor of *The Nation*, in which this article first appeared.

The Only Kind of Air

FLORENCE KING

Conservatives typically insult liberals by labeling them "bleeding hearts"; liberals often respond that conservatives are "mean-spirited." Rejecting the charge, conservatives protest that they do *care about hard-working, worthy people. But*

Florence King, author of the following passage, revels in being called "mean-spirited"; as far as she is concerned, mean-spiritedness is one of the things conservatism is all about. King has a regular column, "The Misanthrope's Corner," in The National Review, *where this piece first appeared on April 18, 1994. She is also the author of* Southern Ladies and Gentlemen *(1993).*

Incredibly, many conservatives are still haunted by charges of "mean-spirited   1
rhetoric" at the 1992 Republican convention. Personally, I thought it was
great; I haven't had so much fun since the Girl Scouts and the Mormons got
a shock from my broken doorbell.

The conservative at war with his own temperament is a curious spectacle   2
that began in the New Deal, when Republicans were shamed into joining the
race to compassion. At first a merely fatuous Me Tooism, it grew into the
logic-defying desperation of Eisenhower's earnest credo: "I'm a conservative
on fiscal issues but a liberal on human issues."

Thirty years ago Barry Goldwater called himself a "cheerful malcon-   3
tent." Now Bill Kristol calls himself a "cheerful pessimist" and Rush
Limbaugh calls himself "a harmless little fuzzball." The Christian Coalition
recently advised its members to soften "intemperate rhetoric and show more
tolerance"; instead of using metaphors like "religious war," they should substitute sports analogies because they "sound playful."

At the American Cause conference on ending welfare, Charles Sykes   4
took his idioms from the old vaudeville melodrama about the evil landlord
and the sweet young mortgagee: "We don't need to be perceived as simply
flint-hearted about this. We need to re-establish what it means to really care
about people and show that conservatives are not simply pennypinchers.
There is a conservatism of the heart."

How, pray, is it possible to practice conservatism of the heart and at the   5
same time "bring back the stigma of unwed motherhood"? You can't just say,
"The stigma is back." Knowing the words is not enough, we must also know
the tune, and as anyone can testify who was in junior high when Ingrid
Bergman got caught,[1] it is a heartless chorus involving shunning, smirks
behind hands, and smug hubris ("It won't happen to me"), and it is sung
chiefly by other women.

These heart-and-caring conservatives sound like transfer students trying   6
to be popular fast. Or like those Nice Women who flutter around saying, "I
just want everybody to be happy," whenever a family fight gets interesting.
Before getting bogged down in A Place Called Slop they should realize that if
they lack the courage of their temperament, it won't be long before they lack
the courage of their convictions.

The conservative temperament is masculine-realist; the liberal tempera-   7
ment is feminine-idealist. In literary terms it assays out to classicism versus

---

[1]*Ingrid Bergman:* In 1949 one of the most popular movie stars in the world, Ingrid
Bergman, was branded a "scarlet woman" by Hollywood and the public after she had an
affair with a married man—Italian director Roberto Rosselini, whom she married a few
months after giving birth to their child. It took years for Bergman's film career to recover
from the scandal.

romanticism. Ours is most assuredly a bleak mindset, but as Dryden scholar John J. Enck pointed out: "Reason, as the seventeenth century regarded it, tends to unearth in even the most personal and intense suffering, ironies whose very recognition furnishes a sardonic strength."

I have found this to be true. Somebody is always calling me "mean-　8 spirited," while my more imaginative enemies have come up with "Fascist Flossie" and "Ku Klux King." I refuse to try to soften myself, however, because I understand the benefits of the conservative temperament.

Conservatives fare better psychologically because we don't expect much　9 of human nature. Our outlook provides an answer to the question that destroys so many idealists: "How can people do such things?" I knew a Jewish woman who read one Holocaust book after another, trying to find the answer in ever more arcane speculations. She thought if she could trace the Holocaust to Wagner's music, German cleanliness—anything—she would understand it and be able to banish her horror. She eventually had a nervous breakdown because she clung to her idealistic belief in the perfectibility of mankind. A conservative, by contrast, readily admits that human nature is inherently bad and people are capable of anything. It's not a pretty thought but it explains the inexplicable, which is some comfort.

The liberal temperament, however, is based on the discomfiting arrangement　10 that Tennessee Williams called "the kindness of strangers."[2] In an egalitarian democracy the only source of respect and dignity is the "niceness" we practice on each other. It's an eerily sinister version of the behavior of royalty, who must be gracious all the time because it makes the common people feel safe. The difference is that being smiled upon by a queen is reassuring, but being smiled upon by a determined humanitarian makes people aware of the arbitrary nature of the humanitarian impulse and leaves them feeling more, not less, insecure.

Real humanitarians tend to be curmudgeons because they must deal with　11 bureaucratic blockheads. One of the shortest fuses in history belonged to its foremost angel of mercy, Florence Nightingale, who was also a foremost female misogynist. Admonished by a do-gooder about the dangers of exposing patients to night air, she exploded: "It's the only kind of air there is at night!"

To thine own self be true. If liberals call you mean-spirited, ask: "Don't　12 you ever feel like saying what you really think instead of smiling and saying what you're supposed to think?" They have to agree, else look like one-celled blobs without a nervous system, floating in a Petri dish.

If you really want to destroy them, offer my cure for crime: "The only　13 thing that really works is fear itself." The New Deal rhythms drive them nuts.

■　■　■

Review Questions

1. What is King's main purpose in the first four paragraphs of this essay?
2. Why does King reject those who would urge the practice of conservatism "of the heart"?

---

[2]*Tennessee Williams:* American playwright (1911–1983), author of *A Streetcar Named Desire* (1947), source of the line, "I have always relied on the kindness of strangers."

Discussion and Writing Suggestions

1. As King claims, "The conservative temperament is masculine-realist; the liberal temperament is feminine-idealist." In light of what you have read and observed of conservatism and liberalism, what do you think of this statement?

2. King suggests that it would be desirable to bring back the social stigma of unwed motherhood in this country (a recommendation made by other conservatives, such as Charles Murray). Why do you think she believes this? To what extent do you agree with her?

3. Compare and contrast King's language and tone with that of other conservatives, such as Krauthammer and McGinnis. Characterize the different personalities that are implied in each author's use of language. What similarities or consistencies do you note in their ideological positions?

4. In temperament, would you call yourself a liberal or a conservative? That is, regardless of gender or political ideology, do you see yourself as "masculine-realist" or "feminine-idealist"? Do you believe that "human nature is inherently bad and [that] people are capable of anything"? Or do you believe in "the perfectibility of mankind"? Offer examples from your observations, experience, or reading to support your conclusions.

Is the Left Nuts? (Or Is It Me?)

MICHAEL MOORE

Michael Moore, writer and filmmaker, burst into public prominence with his 1989 documentary Roger and Me, *a film about the social and personal effects of the closure of a General Motors automobile plant in Moore's home town of Flint, Michigan. "Roger" in the title refers to Roger Smith, CEO of GM at the time; the film was partially about Moore's futile attempts to see Smith to get him to explain how he could throw so many people out of work. Identified with blue-collar issues and a staunch advocate of labor unions (his production company is called* Dog Eat Dog Films), *Moore also made* Canadian Bacon *(1994) and, most recently,* The Big One *(1997), a film described in the ad campaign as "protecting the earth from the scum of corporate America." This film follows Moore as he promotes his 1996 book* Downsize This! Random Threats from an Unarmed American *and continues to investigate corporate callousness (a highlight is his interview with Nike CEO Peter Knight). As film critic Scott Renshaw notes, "With his round face, shaggy hair, and omnipresent baseball cap, Moore looks less like an investigative reporter than he does the kind of guy who goes shirtless at Green Bay Packer games." But if Moore hates "corporate scum," he has no use either for intellectual, white-collar liberals, as the following piece makes clear. It was originally published in* The Nation, *November 17, 1997.*

Is it me, or is the left completely nuts? I won't bore you with the details of 1
October's Media and Democracy Congress, but suffice it to say that the left
is still in fine form, completely ignoring anything that really matters to the
American public. I'm convinced there's a good number of you who are simply
addicted to listening to yourselves talk and talk and talk—*Mumia!*[1] *Pacifica!*[2]
Cuba![3] *Enough already!*

Speaking of talking to ourselves—just who the hell is reading this? Who 2
is The Nation readership? Is it my brother-in-law, Tony, back in Flint, who
last night was installing furnace ducts until 9 o'clock? Is it the bus driver at the
airport who told me he's been cut back to a thirty-hour week so the airport
commission won't have to pay the health insurance for his asthmatic daughter? Is it the woman at Sears who sells blouses by day and then waitresses at
Denny's from 8 P.M. to midnight?

No. The person reading this would probably sympathize with the one 3
who wrote the flier I saw at the media congress announcing a "Stop Police
Brutality Demonstration." The flier promised a rally "from 4 P.M. *until the
truth comes out!*" Until the truth comes out? Let me tell you, friend, the truth
ain't ever coming out to your rally, and neither is Tony the furnace installer,
'cause he's got mouths to feed. But you don't really want him there anyway,
do you? What you really mean by saying that the demonstration is going to
last "until the truth comes out" is that it will go deep into the night, until all
self-serving, attention-starved "lefties" have had their hour and fifteen minutes at the podium. Get a clue! Go away!

Is it true what they say about "the left"—that it loves humanity but 4
loathes people? I want to let you in on a little secret I've discovered: "The
people" are already way ahead of "the left." After years of being downsized,
rightsized, re-engineered and forced to work longer hours for less pay and
fewer benefits, they already know from *their personal experience* that our economic system is unfair, unjust and undemocratic. They know the evil it does
and the havoc it wreaks on their lives. They know that corporate America is
the enemy, that the media are telling them lies and that the Democrats and the
Republicans are actually the same party, and that neither is worth voting for.
Look at any Gallup poll and you'll see that the public is very "left" on all the
issues—the majority are pro-choice, pro-environment, pro-labor.

---

[1] *Mumia:* Mumia Abu-Jamal, a black radio journalist and former Black Panther (a radical
African-American group of the 1960s), was convicted of killing a white police officer in
Philadelphia in 1978 and sentenced to death. Many liberal activists believe that Mumia is
innocent and had been framed by a racist and corrupt justice system.

[2] *Pacifica:* liberal radio network.

[3] *Cuba:* Ever since Fidel Castro took over Cuba in 1959 and instituted a Communist government on that island, some leftists have tended to show sympathy for his regime and to
denounce the American government for its anti-Cuba policy.

Yet they despise liberals. If they knew where to find the nutty left, they'd   5
despise them, too. They see liberals, progressives and lefties as arrogant, self-
righteous and dreadfully predictable. They know you won't ever go have a
beer with them, or talk to them about how the Indians did in the Series.
Christ, can you even name a single Cleveland Indian?

And why should you? You've got *The Nation*[4] and Pacifica, the food co-   6
op and your Working Assets credit card. Don't get me wrong—I love *The
Nation* and Pacifica and food co-ops and not supporting CitiBank. But if you
stop there and refuse to participate in the real world, how are you ever going
to effect change? Back in the eighties thousands of you went to Nicaragua[5] in
Sandinista brigades. Yes, that was important work; our government was
killing innocent people. But I never saw a single one of you come to Flint
while the world's largest company[6] was destroying the lives of 30,000 families. Where were you when we needed you? The people in Flint were ready—
Jesse Jackson beat Dukakis[7] by a 9-to-1 margin there. In the white suburbs,
Jackson beat him by a 4-to-1 margin! You should have come! The right wing
did . They organized the Michigan Militia. It's no accident that Terry Nichols[8]
is from the Flint area.

Here's the part I don't get. Remember the antiwar movement, when we   7
didn't have the American public on our side and actually had to go out and
convince people the war was wrong? That was tough, but we did it. These
days, the difficult organizing work has already been done for us by Big
Business. It has spent the past decade destroying the middle class and brutal-
izing the poor. Beating up on the poor, I get—that's the way it's always been.
But the middle class? What a stupid error in judgment—and now there are
millions of Americans waiting to vent their anger and frustration.

---

[4]*The Nation:* liberal magazine

[5]*Nicaragua:* In 1980, Nicaragua was taken over by the Sandinistas, a Marxist group, which
proceeded to seize the property of wealthy landowners and to distribute it to the people.
While the U.S. government naturally opposed the Sandinistas, many leftists in the U.S.
favored them for ideological reasons. Some years later, in a major scandal, the Reagan
administration admitted that it had secretly sold weapons to Iran, a U.S. enemy, and had
transferred the money from these arms sales to the contras, an anti-Sandinista group, to help
finance their guerrilla campaign. The contras and the Sandinistas later agreed to a temporary truce, and the Sandinistas were voted out of office by the Nicaraguan people in 1990.

[6]*The world's largest company:* General Motors, which closed a major auto assembly plant
in Flint, Michigan. (This was the subject of Moore's most well-known film, *Roger and Me.*
Roger Smith was CEO of General Motors at the time.)

[7]*Jesse Jackson beat Dukakis:* In the 1988 presidential campaign, the African-American
activist Jesse Jackson campaigned for the Democratic nomination against Michael Dukakis,
the moderate governor of Massachusetts. Jackson promised to support working people,
black and white. Dukakis eventually won the nomination but was defeated by George
Bush in the general election.

[8]*Terry Nichols:* a right-wing militia member, convicted of conspiracy, along with co-
defendant Timothy McVeigh, in the Oklahoma City Federal Building bombing. Nichols was
sentenced to life imprisonment.

And where are *we*? Inside New York's Cooper Union chanting for 8
Mumia! I want Mumia to live, I've signed the petitions, I've helped pay for the
ads—hell, I'll personally go and kick the butt of the governor of Pennsylvania!
But, for chrissakes, the woman working at Sears just wants to be able to
spend an hour with her kids before she heads off to Denny's. Can't we help
her? Do you *want* to help her?

It's taken me a while to figure it all out, and after last month's Media and 9
Democracy Congress I think I have the answer: Because "the left" has lost so
many battles, it now doesn't know how to live any other way. It's kind of
scary, isn't it, to think that we could actually reach a mass audience. Or that
after all these years of failure, real change could actually occur in our lifetime.
Better to fight among ourselves! It's an uncomfortable, unfamiliar feeling, isn't
it, to get a whiff of a real populist progressive movement taking shape. Better
that we keep those furnace installers and bus drivers away from us—they
don't read Chomsky[9] anyway!

The signs are everywhere, but "the left" can't read a road map. There's 10
a whole New Politics taking place, and it's being led by U.P.S. drivers and
Borders bookstore workers. I say, with all due affection and appreciation for
all of you and your causes, get over yourselves, start talking like a real person,
then start talking to real people. You could begin by hitting 0 every time you
get a robot when you call 411. Have a chat with the human operator—the
phone company will eventually have to hire more of them. Or sponsor a
bowling team and put the name of your local Labor Party or environmental
group on their shirts. Or try bowling yourself. It's where you'll meet
Americans.

■   ■   ■

Review Questions

1. Why does Moore feel that the left is "nuts"?
2. According to Moore, why do most of the people, who are left-leaning
   themselves, "hate and despise liberals"?
3. How are "the people" ahead of the left, according to Moore?

Discussion and Writing Suggestions

1. What is Moore's essential dispute with the kind of people who read *The
   Nation*? To what extent do you agree with him? Explain your response
   by providing examples from your own observations, experience, or reading.

---

[9] *Chomsky:* Noam Chomsky (1928–), linguist and libertarian socialist, outspoken critic of
U.S. foreign and domestic policy.

2. What do you think Moore means when he asks, "Is it true what they say about 'the left'—that it loves humanity but loathes people?"
3. Based on Moore's editorial, would you consider him a liberal? A conservative? Something else? Why?
4. How does Moore's use of language help reinforce the position he takes in this editorial? Consider, for example, the section (paragraph 3) beginning, "Let me tell you, friend, the truth ain't ever coming out to your rally . . ."

MYSTERY READINGS: A "FINAL EXAM" ASSIGNMENT

Following are eight short editorials, columns, or articles representing opinions across the political spectrum on a variety of issues. The selections are identified only by title and author, so as not to prejudice or otherwise influence your approach to the writers' arguments. Your instructor will be able to provide additional information about the author's backgrounds and political ideology.

Select one of these articles and write a multiparagraph essay analyzing the author's argument. You may find it useful to consider some of the following aspects of the selection:

- *Introduce* the issue by identifying it and providing some background on the subject from your own experience, observations or reading. Use one of the introductory strategies discussed in Chapter Three: quotation, historical review, review of a controversy, anecdote, question, etc.
- *Summarize* the author's argument. Follow the procedures for a one-paragraph summary described in Chapter One.
- *Locate on the political spectrum* the author's position on the issue. Refer to Burns *et al.* by summarizing or quoting those identifying features of the position that seem most closely reflected in the author's arguments. You may also wish to analyze through contrast—that is, to indicate, with reference to Burns *et al.*, how the author's position differs from those assumptions associated with a particular position along the spectrum.
- *Analyze the author's position* by comparing and contrasting it to those positions expressed by authors following Burns *et al.* in this chapter. That is, explain how the author's position most closely resembles (or differs from) the positions expressed by Faux or Krauthammer or McGinnis or Ehrenreich or King or Moore. You may also wish to consider how the author's *tone* or *writing style* (or some other aspect of the selections) compares or contrasts with those of one of the authors you have previously read.

- Having analyzed the author's ideological position, *critique it,* following the procedures discussed in Chapter Two. Consider whether the author has succeeded in her or his purpose. To what extent do you find logical fallacies or other problems in the article? Has the author clearly defined terms and made fair use of information? Identify and explain your own points of agreement or disagreement with the author.
- *Conclude,* using one of the forms of conclusion discussed in Chapter Three: statement of the subject's significance, solution/recommendation, anecdote, quotation, question, or speculation.

Who Makes the Clothes We Wear?
The Price for Our Fashion Is Often Paid by Workers Laboring in Intolerable Conditions.

JESSE JACKSON

Would you spend $20 for a stylish Gap T-shirt if you knew it was made by teen-age girls in El Salvador forced to work 18 hours a day in a sweatshop for about 16 cents a shirt? 1

Would you pay top dollar for designer fashions at Neiman Marcus that were made by immigrant Thai women imprisoned behind barbed wire in forced-labor conditions? 2

Would you give Nike $80 for a pair of athletic shoes if you knew they were made by teen-age girls in Indonesia working 60-hour weeks for less than Indonesia's miserable minimum wage? Would you buy them if you knew that one young woman who organized a strike to demand that Nike pay the statutory minimum wage in Indonesia was abducted, raped and murdered? 3

Across the world—including in the United States, the sweatshop is back in the press. High-profit, high-profile, high-priced retailers have grown callous and uncaring about the inhuman working conditions of the desperate—here and abroad—who make their products. Private companies turn their backs as their subcontractors routinely trample the basic rights of their workers— speech, association, the right to organize, the right to a living wage, the right to a bathroom break, to healthy and safe work conditions, to overtime, the prohibition of child and slave labor. Desperate workers have been too weak to resist. 4

Look, for instance, at the conditions in El Monte, Calif. On Aug. 2, government officials raided a sweatshop filled with immigrant Thai women 5 laboring for as little as 59 cents per hour for 16 to 22 hours a day. Discipline was enforced by threats of rape and beatings. The women were locked up day and night as they produced garments for Neiman Marcus, J.C. Penney and other U.S. retailers and manufacturers.

As these outrages have gained public attention, manufacturers and retail- 6
ers are getting nervous. The $200 million or so that Nike spends each year to paste its symbol on everything from Pete Sampras at the U.S. Open to the Dallas Cowboy uniforms can be wasted by one powerful scandal that ignites consumers' moral sensibilities. "Just do it" is Nike's multimillion-dollar slogan. But many Americans, if informed of these sweatshop realities, just might not do it; and that has major clothing and shoe manufacturers terrified. A consumer time bomb has begun to tick.

Republicans are out of step with this growing popular concern. They are 7
busy gutting what few government protections exist for working people. The budget to enforce U.S. labor laws and workplace health and safety is being slashed. Republicans are blocking efforts to codify minimal labor and envi-ronmental standards in global trade treaties and develop international inves-tigation and reporting.

Their opposition isn't just about trimming "big government." They also 8
oppose legislation that would empower workers to elect their own represen-tatives to monitor workplace safety. Even House Speaker Newt Gingrich—self-styled Third Wave revolutionary—has had little to say about the growing consumer reaction.

Unions, consumer groups and human-rights organizations are expand- 9
ing their monitoring of labor conditions here and abroad. Many citizens would happily join a groundswell to hold one of these global corporate behe-moths accountable for how they treat the least of their workers. If consumers spurn just one popular brand name, the other companies will rush to clean up their act.

Then the companies will push for government regulation and policing 10
as insulation against independent consumer movements. Gingrich will scurry to get in front of the parade. Conservatives will shelve opposition to big government and line up to pass the laws and codes of conduct that busi-nesses want.

Practices like those in El Monte aren't about reasonable profit; they are 11
about greed. These companies have grown arrogant in their global reach. Like true cynics, they know the price of everything and the value of nothing. In 1993, the labor cost to Nike for a pair of $80 sneakers was 12 cents; in 1994, the company had more than $4.3 billion in sales. Nike paid more to give shoes away in promotions than to pay 12,000 women in Indonesia who make them. Organizers estimate that 1% of the Nike advertising budget could double the wages paid to the women and lift them above the pover-ty line.

Nike and other global companies can afford minimal rights for their 12
workers. Now informed consumers may begin to make the trampling of basic decency a whole lot more expensive than the cost of respecting it.

America at Risk:
Can We Survive without Moral Values?

WILLIAM J. BENNETT

Novelist Walker Percy once was asked what concerned him most about the   1
future of America. He responded: "Probably the fear of seeing America, with
all its great strength and beauty and freedom gradually subside into decay
through default and be defeated, not by the Communist movement but from
within by weariness, boredom, cynicism, greed and in the end helplessness
before its great problems."

The social science data confirm Percy's concerns. They are uncomfortably   2
close to becoming reality.

Since 1960, the U.S. population has grown 41%, the gross domestic   3
product nearly has tripled, and total levels of social spending by all levels of
government (measured in constant 1990 dollars) have risen from
$143,730,000,000 to $787,000,000,000—more than a fivefold increase.
During the same 34-year period, there has been a more than 500% rise in violent crime; a greater than 400% hike in illegitimate births; a tripling of the
percentage of children living in single-parent homes; a threefold increase in
teenage suicides; a doubling in the divorce rate; and a drop of almost 75
points in SAT scores.

No institution has suffered more during this period than the American   4
family. Today, 30% of all births and almost 70% of all black births are to
unmarried females. By the end of the century, according to the most reliable
projections, 40% of all births and 80% of minority births will be out of
wedlock. In a few years, illegitimacy will surpass divorce as the main cause of
fatherlessness in the U.S.

These figures have frightening social implications, but should not cause   5
Americans to despair. Instead, they should stir the nation.

There are three brief explanations for what accounts for America's social   6
regression. The first has to do with a marked shift in the public's attitudes.
According to social scientist James Q. Wilson, "The powers exercised by the
institutions of social control have been constrained, and people, especially
young people, have embraced an ethos that values self-expression over self-
control."

During the last quarter-century, the American people increasingly have   7
abandoned time-honored moral codes. The U.S. now is seeing the results
being played out on urban streets and in hospital emergency rooms, the
courts, and classrooms.

A second is that a number of pernicious ideas made their way into the   8
mainstream of American life. It became unfashionable to make value judgments. The nation witnessed an expansive notion of "rights" and an attenu-
ated sense of personal responsibility. "If it feels good, do it"; "Do your own
thing"; and "You only go around once in life, so you have to grab all the
gusto you can" became words to live by. These seemingly innocuous phrases

masked a destructive underlying philosophy that eventually found its way into public policy.

A third explanation has to do with the failures of contemporary liberal-   9
ism—an ideology that dominates the national Democratic Party. A series of misguided social policies were championed. In the area of criminal justice, an anti-incarceration outlook took hold that said, in effect, society's response to criminal behavior should be rehabilitation, not punishment. Schools replaced moral education with "values clarification," standards were abandoned, and homework was forgotten. Having a child out of wedlock was rewarded with government subsidies in the form of welfare checks.

Through the National Endowment for the Arts, government got into the   10
business of subsidizing pornography and obscenity. Abortion, for any reason, at any point in pregnancy, was elevated to a constitutional right. Tax policies penalized the traditional nuclear family. No-fault divorce laws made a mock-ery of the belief that marriage is a sacred covenant. Racial relations deterio-rated as, in law and policy, people began to be judged not by the content of their character, but by the color of their skin (i.e., quotas, race-norming, and set-asides).

These policies effectively tore down cultural guardrails. Not surprisingly,   11
individual casualties followed.

. . . Republicans should hammer home the point of how much better   12
American life would be if a sweeping, reform-minded, and humane social agenda were implemented that included:

- A more effective and tough-minded criminal justice system, including more prisons, judges, and prosecutors.
- Reform of the juvenile criminal justice system (including trying as adults juveniles who commit violent crimes).
- Increased attention to victims' rights and roles in the criminal justice process.
- Reform of parole.
- Enactment of "truth in sentencing" guidelines.
- Alternative forms of punishment, such as boot camps.
- An integrated anti-drug strategy.
- The fundamental reform of education through national standards, merit pay, alternative certification, and, most important, allowing parents to choose the public, private, or religious schools to which they can send their children.
- Removal of the economic barriers that keep the underclass in poverty by providing tax incentives for businesses to locate in urban enterprise zones, as well as such items as tenant ownership and investment in low-income housing.
- Support for families by increasing the Federal personal income tax depen-dent exemption.
- Removal of major obstacles to adoption and increasing residential schools, congregate care facilities, and orphanages for abandoned and abused chil-dren.

It is well-known that there is some skittishness among Republicans in 13 dealing with social issues. My response is: Philosophers from Aristotle on have understood that there is no more important political consideration than the moral precepts that underlie society and the policies that flow from them. No serious political party can duck these issues. Republicans simply must make sure that public officials deal with them in a responsible, thoughtful and constructive manner.

As Republicans address the set of issues that travel under the banner of 14 "values," they need to recognize that many of the problems afflicting society today are manifestly moral. Therefore, they are remarkably resistant to government cures, so there are limits to the degree to which public policies can cure what ails the U.S.

The Republican Party needs to point out that not only are there some 15 tasks that government cannot do, in a nation of free and sovereign people, there are some tasks it should not do. The more Americans have asked of government, the less they have asked of themselves. A compelling message might be this: The Republican philosophy is to say to the Federal government, "Give us back our money—and with it, our sense of responsibility."

During the last decade of the 20th century, the failures of contemporary 16 liberalism are all around. It is an intellectually and morally bankrupt ideology, one that no longer has the power to inspire people. A confident Republican Party, therefore, should offer a fundamentally different governing philosophy and set of solutions.

The GOP's task is to link the values debate to a specific set of policies, 17 insist that moral common sense once again become the touchstone of social policy, and oppose the radical social agenda of the Clinton Administration in a principled, vigorous, and determined manner—all the while recognizing that this debate must be conducted in a calm, civilized, and reasoned voice.

If Republicans do, their voices will be heard, their philosophy will prevail, 18 and their prospects as a party will continue to brighten. The opportunities are there—if Republicans have the courage and the wisdom to seize them.

Family Values Gain Ground

WALL STREET JOURNAL

One of the hallmarks of the closing year [1995] was a spreading recognition 1 that it's time to return to old-fashioned family values. While translating the thought into action is of course hard, the consensus now includes increasing numbers of people from a wide range of the political spectrum.

Consider the December 15 meeting of the National Parenting Association 2 Task Force on Youth Violence, cochaired by two political liberals, author and economist Sylvia Ann Hewlett and Harvard University professor Cornel West.

The preoccupation of the meeting was exploring the underlying reasons for family breakdown and how families can be repaired.

In its most recent report the NPA Task Force observes that married men   3 commit far less violence toward their spouses than single and divorced men commit toward the women they are involved with. In the eight years from 1979 to 1987, 57,000 women a year were violently assaulted by their husbands, compared with 200,000 a year who were violently assaulted by their boyfriends, and 216,000 a year who were violently assaulted by their ex-husbands. Recently the Centers for Disease Control and Prevention revealed that unmarried pregnant women are four times more likely to be abused by their boyfriends than married pregnant women are to be abused by their husbands.

A stable marriage with both natural parents present also means a safer   4 environment for children. It's no coincidence that as the divorce rate has skyrocketed in the past 35 years, so too has the rate of child abuse. In 1960 there were four marriages for every divorce, while today there is one divorce for every marriage, and a 60% chance that a couple marrying today will end up divorced or permanently separated. Statistics on child abuse became available halfway through that time period. Since 1976 the rate has soared by 331%.

And children from broken, violent homes commit a disproportionate   5 amount of crime. Some 60% of the nation's rapists, 72% of adolescent murderers and 70% of long-term prison inmates came from homes where the father wasn't present.

The Task Force is searching for possible solutions to the crisis. To that   6 end, it sought advice from the Promise Keepers men's movement. Three members were invited to the December meeting to tell why their nondenominational Christian movement, launched by former University of Colorado football coach Bill McCartney, has in just five years gone from a gathering of just 72 men to 826,000 who came together this year in 13 cities across the nation to affirm their commitment to Christianity and to transforming their family lives through strong marriages.

Promise Keepers is succeeding, its spokesmen explained, because it makes   7 it easier for individual men to confess personal weakness, allowing them to build better relationships with the women and children in their lives. "Men can acknowledge their shortcomings in an environment that is safe, where no one is going to threaten you, or fire you, or abuse you for your failures," Reverend Glenn Murphy told the Task Force. "In that context of mutual brokenness, comes change and transformation."

But Mr. West still had questions about such an approach. "How do you   8 all meet the criticism that you seem to be preoccupied with the inner life, but we're still dealing with larger social forces?" he asked. "There is the deeper issue of democracy in decay. How do you deal with that political challenge?"

"I think political change comes one person at a time," responded   9 Reverend Jeffrey Metzger of Promise Keepers. "The only appropriate place to start is with the individual. . . . You change the man, you change the family.

You change the family, you change the community. You change the community, you change the county. You change the county, you change the state. You change the state, you change the nation."

"What they are doing is quite powerful," said Ms. Hewlett. "We were 10 very respectfully listening to what they had to say, because it's rare that scholars listen to such grass-roots movements."

The NPA also intends to lobby for pro-family changes in the tax code, 11 including the creation of a sizable tax credit or child allowance that would allow parents to spend more time with their children; eliminating the marriage penalty in the nation's tax code; and instituting a tax credit for parents who choose to stay home with young children. While we have advocated more pro-growth tax changes, these proposals notably mimic those of the Christian Coalition.

Grass-roots religious movements are doing a good job of rebuilding per- 12 sonal responsibility. What's needed is a culture willing to allow this new responsibility to prosper. We applaud the NPA for reaching out to such religious movements; whatever the specifics, it's one more sign that slowly but surely a consensus is emerging around the need to mend the nation's moral fabric.

The Family Values Party
Everyone's Favorite New Issue Blurs the Line Between Public and Private Life.

MEG GREENFIELD

The thing I hated most about summer camp, when I was 8, was that after our 1 daily breakfast of cocoa, cinnamon buns and toast slathered with honey, we were obliged to rise, join sticky hands and sway back and forth in a circle singing a song full of Indian words about how blissful it was to be out here, at one not just with each other but also with Puget Sound. We just stood there and swayed and sang as our handgrips became steadily and repulsively more adhesive.

What was it about the Democratic National Convention that brought 2 this memory back to mind? I will confess that now, as it was then, I couldn't really give the sentiment a name, let alone an argument-proof rationale. I can only say that the same sort of subliminal, not fully articulated discomfort kept rising in me as the political proceedings themselves became stickier and stickier, a feeling that something kind of awful and discomfiting and not quite true was going on.

Yes, there were moments of genuine emotion that had a legitimate place 3 in the convention. But there were more—many more—that were superfluous

and hokey, a stream of politicians declaring they loved their spouses and
children and parents, as if this were either noteworthy or especially virtuous
of them or the reason people had put them in office. And, yes, a whole lot of
what goes under the too-loose name of family values needs to be reclaimed
and bolstered. But some of that involves the reclamation and bolstering of
strict standards of personal behavior for which neither political party is particularly famous. And some involves matters that are frankly unsuited to
governmental and/or political guidance in any case.

So on the basis of what we saw last week, I conclude that the concept   4
works better in an ad for a merchandise-mart back-to-school sale—"One
Day Only! One-Half Off! Great Family Values!"—than it does as a unifying
principle of national party politics. This is because I think you can trust the
merchants more than the politicians not to abuse the phrase. And I say that
knowing full well that "one-half off" can be a pretty slippery term. These are
my top four reasons for believing this to be so:

1: There is an attempt at basic deception here. The message coming relent-   5
lessly from the podium last week kept stressing that politics and politicians had
been replaced this year by family issues and public figures who defined themselves by their concerns as family members, not politicians. Hogwash. The
family-values mantra and the family-member self-presentations *were* political.
They represented the political tacticians' best advice on how to win the votes of
people who profess to be sick of politics, an attempted manipulation of the
voters, a politically inspired show.

2: The excessive stress on the theme of government as every family's best   6
and most attentive friend and patron, not to mention its nurse, grandma and
social worker as well, invites a blurring of the realms of public and private
life. Certainly some of the tax incentives and other measures both Clintons
recommended in their talks at the convention have merit. But the blather level
at both conventions has been pretty high on this general subject, and words
matter. The talk has created an implied justification for governmental intrusion into many more aspects of private familial life than I think either true liberals or true conservatives would accept.

3: The temptation to hypocrisy in the application of the family-values   7
standard to their programs is just too great for most politicians to resist. So
they blithely turn a blind eye to the contradictions in their assorted stances.
There may be, after all, no stronger demonstration of the centrality of strong
family feeling—solidarity, mutual support, willingness to sacrifice to improve
the lot of one's parents and children—than is daily manifested by all those
unwanted immigrants from south of the border who have become a principal
heavy in 1996 politics. Family values in a much purer and maybe even nobler
form than you might see in the people next door are often what drives and
distinguishes them. But they do not evoke a lot of sympathy these days.
Similarly, it is, in my view, awfully hard to claim the primacy of family values

in your thinking, especially as they relate to minor children, and at the same time go along with a so-called reform of welfare that is likely to make the lives of so many already poor kids poorer and worse.

4:   God is watching all this—and so are the media and the political oppo-   8
sition. My point is that no one should think he is going to get away with anything on this score. (Wouldn't you agree, Mr. Morris?) Something there is in
politics that lets an otherwise intelligent person, after a while, forget the mote
in his own eye and go on an absolute binge of a crusade against the other
guy's beam. Family-values politics, more than just about any other theme,
brings this out in political people. Too many of them have thus become the
fallen ministers of our time (as, of course, have no few fallen ministers themselves). Dick Morris[1] is a man who evidently saw no ethical or sensibility
problem in arguing for (a) a family-values pitch by President Clinton and (b)
a cut in the income of welfare mothers while (c) repairing to his expense-
account hotel at night to enjoy the ministrations of a $200-an-hour prostitute.

Lecturers to the public on family values have been dropping like flies in   9
recent years as their own moral shortcomings, personal duplicities and often
full-fledged scandals have heaved into view. The issue is always treacherous.
The Carter administration decided to have a conference on family issues
back in 1980 and immediately fell into a damaging quarrel with the newly
self-confident gay community about their inclusion in the proceedings. Other
politicians preaching the sanctity of good spouseship, good parenthood,
fidelity and the rest have been found, as they say in government circles, out
of compliance. Should this not suggest a little humility on the part of the
Feds and the pols in mucking about in these matters? I think it should. And
I think they should scale back their grandiose family-values pitch to programs and proposals that fulfill this simple guiding concept: First, do no
harm. I wouldn't mind if there were a follow-up concept: Second, it is
worth remembering that none of us is perfect.

Curb Your Dog!

VIRGINIA I. POSTREL

You're jogging down your neighborhood street, as your large Labrador   1
retriever bounds along beside you, occasionally heading into a front yard to
sniff out things of interest to dogs, occasionally leaving an unwelcome calling
card for the neighbors to clean up. You round a corner and there, playing
happily in the grass, is a little girl, maybe 4 years old, whose mother is watching her from a lawn chair.

---

[1] *Dick Morris:* Advisor to President Clinton.

Intrigued by the little girl, the dog heads over to her. He is as big as she   2
is, and much stronger. As he sticks his slobbery jowls in her face, she flinch-
es, stands up, back offs, falls down, cries. The dog continues toward her,
relentless in his curiosity.

If the mother is like most mothers, and you are like most dog owners,   3
both of you sympathize with the dog. You try to disabuse the little girl of her
fear. "It's OK," you say. "He won't hurt you. He loves children."

And children love dogs. Everyone knows that—and so should she.   4

"Nice doggie," says the mother, rising from her chair. "Don't be afraid.   5
He won't hurt you." She pushes her daughter toward the animal. The little
girl continues to squirm and cry, trying to escape the advancing giant. "I don't
know what's wrong with her," the mother says to you. "She just doesn't like
dogs."

No, this isn't an autobiographical story. It's an attempt to explain the   6
attitude people in official Washington have toward Americans who flinch in
fear at the advances of the allegedly benevolent state. Where the rest of us see
a giant creature with sharp teeth and claws, they see only a friendly pet.

At one level, you can't exactly blame them. They live every day with the   7
federal government and its employees. Just about everyone they meet, socialize with, work with, or marry is either a government employee, a lobbyist, or
a journalist. They understand "the system," and know its operators. They
can't fear what they know so well.

For the rest of us, even those of us who know more than a few govern-   8
ment officials, the government—state and local as well as federal—is mainly
something to be avoided between occasional trips to the post office. For us,
the voice saying, "I'm from the government and I'm here to help you," is not
our old friend Paul calling about a job opening in the interstices of the
Commerce Department. It's the local building inspector snooping around
our bathroom remodeling job, delaying it by a month. It's the OSHA official
informing us that we'll be spending half a day sitting in a lecture on how to
avoid stress. It's the INS demanding to see our work papers. It's the EPA
decreeing that we start car pooling. Or it's the IRS informing us that we've
been selected for an audit.[1]

When Washingtonians, of whatever political persuasion, pretend to be   9
"of the people," they tend to come off as phonies—and for good reason. They
can put on flannel shirts and talk in the accents of Memphis or Missouri, but
they still look at the dog from the owner's perspective, not the little girl's.

---

[1]*OSHA:* The Occupational Safety and Health Administration, the federal agency charged
with monitoring the safety of American workplaces, has been widely condemned by conservatives for imposing excessive regulations and burdensome reporting requirements on
businesses; *INS:* The Immigration and Naturalization Service, charged with monitoring the
legal status of foreign nationals in the United States; *EPA:* The Environmental Protection
Agency, charged with monitoring the safety of the environment (air, water, soil, etc.); *IRS:*
The Internal Revenue Service, charged with collecting taxes.

There are exceptions, of course. Rep. Tom DeLay's experience running an extermination business probably did instill a certain permanent fear of the EPA. But on the whole, Washingtonians just can't see the federal government (and, by extension, government in general) as something scary. And they have little sympathy for anyone who can.

That's why you can go around Washington talking about the importance   10
of welfare reform or dynamic budgeting, but you should never mention the word *tyranny*. You can say government actions are inefficient, costly, or even unfair, but you can't suggest they're *dangerous*. That is gauche. It makes people roll their eyes. This isn't just a matter of preserving the importance of fine distinctions—an audit is not, in fact, the same as a midnight arrest by the secret police. It's that nobody in Washington can really believe that George down the block or Susan down the hall is a terrifying individual.

But they can read the polls. So lately, Republicans in Congress have sug-   11
gested that leash laws and pooper scooper measures might be a good idea—that if we can't get rid of the regulatory state, we might at least keep it under control. Regulators should have to prove that new rules will do more good than harm ("cost-benefit analysis") and they should have to pay the difference if they seriously degrade the use and value of someone's property ("takings" compensation). In other words: Curb your dog.

Respectable Washington, dog-loving Washington, finds such measures   12
extreme, or corrupt. Only a ridiculous child or someone paid by the leash lobby could support such notions, they reason. After all, the nice doggie is our friend.

It's hardly a surprise that the last thing regulators want is restrictions on   13
their freedom to roam or, worse yet, an obligation to clean up their own messes. "The agencies can't possibly go through all of these steps of review without years of delay. It's a greater threat than I've ever seen before in my political life," says Rep. Henry Waxman (D-Calif.) of cost-benefit requirements.

When Newt Gingrich[2] accurately calls David Kessler[3] "a thug and a   14
bully" for using the FDA to terrorize everyone from mom-and-pop vitamin distributors to multinational pharmaceutical companies, Waxman worries that Gingrich is trying to "intimidate" the agency. "I was stunned by the supercharged words he used against Kessler," Waxman told *National Journal*. "It seems like he's trying to bully the agency." Waxman should know; as a committee chairman in the old Congress, he took bullying to a high art.

Republicans are, however, also dog lovers. While they demand leashes   15
and pooper scooping for the Labs and Irish setters, they're equally insistent that we let the Dobermans and pit bulls run free—for our own protection, of course. Hence their disdain for the Fourth Amendment, that antiquated

---

[2]*Newt Gingrich:* Conservative former Speaker of the House of Representatives; Republican from Georgia.

[3]*David Kessler:* Former head of the FDA, the U.S. Food and Drug Administration, who took a crusading stand against hazardous pharmaceuticals and tobacco.

statute that conceived of every government as a potential tyranny. Hence
their demand for ever-longer sentences for people who use or sell drugs. They
assume, probably correctly, that no one *they* know will ever be affected by
such laws—and not because no one they know will ever break them.

Indeed, it's a barometer of official Washington's attitudes that you can   16
count on your thumbs the articles on the drug war published in *The New
Republic* over the past half-dozen years—though if *Vanity Fair* is to be
believed, the magazine's literary editor has an early '90s coke habit that
would have gotten a less privileged man a lengthy prison term. Worrying
about how non-insiders fare in the legal system is, however, much too crass
for Georgetown partygoers. It suggests that non-insiders matter.

Alexis de Tocqueville,[4] a man more quoted than read in Washington,   17
provides some insight on the gulf that has developed between official
Washington and the America it rules. He suggested that when citizens see one
another as civic equals, they identify with each other. As a result, they develop sympathies that prevent the sorts of tortures aristocrats used to inflict on
uppity peasants.

But such sympathies are missing in a capital insulated from its own   18
depredations. Who in official Washington fears EPA enforcers or INS raids?
Who in official Washington struggles with OSHA requirements or trembles at
the threat of a liability lawsuit? Who in official Washington need ever fear a
decades-long prison sentence for drug conspiracy? Who in official
Washington has any chance of getting lost in a system beyond his comprehension, a system populated by strangers with strange ways?

And why, given that no one in official Washington faces such threats, do   19
we expect them to call off the dogs?

Real Scandal: Betrayal of the Poor

ROBERT SCHEER

Well, now that the presidential sex scandal[1] is mercifully behind us, let's get   1
on with some serious criticism of this administration: its unholy alliance with

---

[4] *Alexis de Tocqueville* (1805–59): French politician, author of the two-part *Democracy in America* (1835, 1840), a remarkably insightful and prophetic analysis of the American government and character, based upon de Tocqueville's discussions with numerous American citizens during his visit to the U.S. in 1831–32.

[1] *Sex scandal:* Scheer is referring to the sexual harassment lawsuit brought by Paula Corbin
Jones, a former Arkansas state employee, against President Clinton concerning alleged
actions by Clinton during the time he was governor of Arkansas. The suit was later dismissed by a federal judge, shortly after the eruption of another presidential sex scandal
involving Monica Lewinsky, a former White House intern.

the Republican congressional leadership to betray the economic interests of working and impoverished Americans.

You want presidential scandal? How about the 15% increase in the last year in the number of people—26 million in all—requiring the support of charitable food bank programs? Those depressing statistics released last week by Second Harvest, a national network of food banks, gives lie to the president's claim that welfare reform has been a great success.

In New York State, which has a highly touted program for getting people off welfare and into jobs, only 27% of those dropped from the rolls have found any sort of job, according to a recent state study. And the small group that was successful in finding work includes those who earned as little as $100 in a three-month period.

The "success" of welfare reform is to make the poor invisible. It's hardly a humane solution, and given that most of those suffering are women and children, it is disturbing that this has been less commented upon than the plight of Kathleen Willey, who managed to run up more than $300,000 in debt while living the good life.[2]

You want an example of immorality in high places? Then check the statistics on who really benefited from the tax cuts concocted by Clinton and the Republican congressional leadership last year. They made the rich richer and ignored or hurt just about everybody else.

For each dollar tax break for those in the bottom 80%, the nation's highest 1% saw a whopping $1,189 in tax benefits. The main tax break is on capital gains, a boon for the wealthy who have benefited from a wild appreciation of their investments, while the wages of working people have suffered. During the first five years of the much celebrated economic boom, which has fattened the portfolios of those who control politics with their campaign contributions, the median real wages of workers actually declined.

The political pundits love to cite Alexis de Toqueville, but they seem oblivious to the fact that the prosperous middle class, which he said was the basis of our system of democracy, is continuing to shrink. Most alarming is the large number of working poor, who are now in what has been proclaimed as the best of times, struggling to make ends meet. And what happens to them when the business cycle turns downward, as it inevitably will?

The real Clinton scandal, the sin of this administration, is that the president has sold out to the Republican leadership on basic economic issues. Indeed, it is Clinton who best represents large multinational corporate interests, not the Republican leadership in Congress that is held hostage to the right-wing, pseudo-religious fringe of their party.

It is Clinton who is pushing for $18 billion in funding for the International Monetary Fund to finance an Asian bailout that the leading

---

[2] *Kathleen Willey:* In March, 1998, Kathleen Willey, a former White House volunteer and campaign worker, claimed that the president groped her while the two were alone in the Oval Office. Clinton denied the charge.

American corporations feel they desperately need. That funding is tied up by the Republican leadership, which has attached an irrelevant anti-abortion rider to the IMF bill.

For all of the yapping of conservatives about the untoward influence of labor unions, Clinton has proved to be the most effective proponent of international free trade while slighting the concerns of unions over the erosion of labor standards. It was Clinton who pushed through NAFTA[3] despite strenuous union opposition. 10

The multinational corporations also love Clinton's cozying up to China and any other country with a potentially large market for their exports and investments. Clinton is also in total support of Alan Greenspan's[4] insistence on keeping inflation down even if unemployment starts to creep up, as it just did. 11

The stock market is booming because the president is the perfect agent of the interests of finance capital. Economic conservatives ought to rally around Clinton as their best bet for putting government at the service of the rich and powerful. It is the majority at the lower end of the economic ladder who should be bitterly disappointed. 12

For my money, Clinton can sleep with whomever he wants; it's between him and his wife. But he has no moral right to betray the economic interests of the working and poor people of this country who elected him to office. 13

The Criminalization of Homelessness

CELINE-MARIE PASCALE

In a misguided effort to deal with homelessness, an increasing number of U.S. cities are criminalizing non-criminal behavior such as loitering and sleeping in public. At least 50 cities are considering or already have adopted ordinances that specifically target the behavior of homeless people, according to Michael Stoops of the National Coalition for the Homeless. 1

Nowhere is this spate of new legislation more noticeable than in California, where the homeless population is now estimated to include a million people. This estimate, made by the California Homeless and Housing Coalition, is based on an extrapolation of AFDC assistance to homeless families. Within 15 recent months, eight municipalities in Southern California passed anti-sleeping ordinances, according to an op-ed piece in the Washington edition of the *Los Angeles Times* (Dec. 16, 1993). This desire to legislate noncriminal behavior is evident in Northern California as well. 2

---

[3]*NAFTA*: The North American Free Trade Agreement, source of great partisan debate among Democrats (who generally opposed it, charging that it would export jobs and drive down wages of American workers), and Republicans, who supported it. Clinton, a Democratic president, bucked his party by supporting NAFTA, and later signed it into law.
[3]*Alan Greenspan*: Chairman of the Federal Reserve Bank, which sets national interest rates.

San Francisco, famous for its Matrix laws (a whole set of city ordinances   3
targeting the homeless), spent 450 police hours and $11,000 to arrest 15
people for begging in 1993, according to *The Progressive* (May 1994). This
past June, the city approved Proposition J, making it illegal to linger for more
than 60 seconds within 30 feet of an automatic teller in use. Although this
ordinance is said to protect residents from robberies, radio station KPFA
(June 9, 1994) reported that only 20 robberies were committed at ATMs in
San Francisco last year. Washington, D.C., passed a similar ordinance last
year, and copycat ones are pending in New York City and Berkeley.

Berkeley has been using trespassing laws to keep its sidewalks clear. The   4
San Francisco alternative weekly *Bay Guardian* (Dec. 29, 1993) quoted a
police spokesperson as saying that "the city considers the sidewalks in front
of stores to belong to the store owners." Berkeley's new anti-loitering law
applies to a one-block radius around laundromats, parks, recreation centers,
and other property; it's based on an individual's *intent* to buy, sell, exchange,
or use drugs. A person who refuses to leave the area when requested to do so
by police can be arrested and charged with a misdemeanor.

Santa Cruz has a reputation for progressive politics; the current mayor is   5
a war tax resister. Like other cities, however, Santa Cruz now arrests people
who sit on the sidewalk. Riot police in full gear were called out on May 11,
1994, to arrest a group of people for sitting on the sidewalk while they ate
free soup. Santa Cruz, which has about 250 shelter beds to serve a homeless
population almost ten times that size, also has a law that makes it illegal to
sleep out of doors or inside a vehicle.

Across the country, ordinances like these have been proposed and   6
advanced by merchants. So it isn't surprising to find that many businesses that
donate to nonprofits serving the homeless have made their continued support
contingent upon the nonprofits' speaking out against those who challenge the
ordinances. Five donors pressured a single agency in Santa Cruz.

In New York City, businesses have taken another tack. Katherine Gordy   7
writes in *In These Times* (April 4, 1994): "New York has launched ad campaigns that portray the housed, clad, and fed citizens whom panhandlers ask
for help as victims who have every right to be selfish and annoyed." The
number of homeless people in New York City is hard to comprehend; during
one month of 1992, 14,000 *families* applied for public shelter, according to
Jennifer Toth, author of *Mole People* (Chicago Review Press, 1993), a recent
book about the people who live in the subways and other tunnels beneath
New York City.

City governments tell us we need Matrix-type anti-homeless ordinances   8
because laws against harassment, assault, battery, theft, vandalism, and
obstructing traffic do not protect businesses adequately. Why is that? The
answer is that visible poverty, not criminal behavior, may be the greatest
threat to business in the 1990s—or so many merchants believe.

Visible poverty does discourage shoppers—especially those out to spend   9
discretionary dollars that they could just as easily spend elsewhere. No one
wants to run a gauntlet of panhandlers to get to a boutique or step over
people sleeping on the sidewalk to buy a cappuccino. But neither do people

want to live in the kind of poverty that leads to panhandling or sleeping on the sidewalk.

Henry Cisneros, secretary of housing and urban development, said on the   10
MacNeil/Lehrer NewsHour (May 16, 1994) that between 1985 and 1990, 7 million Americans experienced homelessness. Yet as a culture, we still want to believe that poverty is the fault of the individual rather than society.

Anti-sleeping, anti-sitting, and anti-panhandling ordinances reflect con-   11
cerns for the civil liberties of the fortunate rather than for the human rights of the destitute. People often defend their right to walk through a bus station without confronting beggars, but what about the basic human right to food and shelter?

The city of Berkeley is now considering an ordinance that would limit to   12
one shopping bag the number of belongings people can carry with them. Imagine having to discard half of your possessions because people with houses find it offensive that you need two shopping bags to contain your worldly goods.

Wrong Way to Help the Homeless

DWIGHT HOBBES

Early in 1992, I was homeless and staying at a shelter in Minneapolis when   1
a television reporter came by. Her question was the big one. What social programs would make the homeless problem go away? Would more jobs make a difference? Education? What do you people *need*?

I had no ready answer. Still, I knew what didn't work. If homelessness   2
were correlated with lack of education, my college degree would have made me immune. So would any of the jobs I'd had, if work were a cure-all. And if "help" were the solution, the Twin Cities would have few homeless.

Help here isn't just available. It's abundant. You must be steadfastly   3
dedicated to a down-and-out lifestyle to remain flat on your behind in the Twin Cities—a fact that the captains of every city in America should note.

Since talking to that reporter, I've come to a disheartening conclusion: the   4
homeless in Minneapolis, a social-services nirvana, are for the most part not interested in solving their problems and are content to see their well-being as someone else's responsibility.

Before arriving in Minneapolis, I showed up at a New York City shelter   5
with crack in my brain and booze on my breath. I'd been fired from my job and evicted from my apartment because I wouldn't stay off the stuff. But the shelter was everything jail is said to be, minus the bars, inhabited by the most soulless predators this side of a penitentiary.

I fled to Minneapolis—and a soft landing at a shelter called The Drake.   6
If you kept a low profile and your nose clean, you could pretty much count on catching the next sunrise in relative comfort and safety. You could get sub-

stance-abuse treatment. Meals were ample and balanced, and plenty of us were getting big in the gut.

Anyone willing to work was in luck. You could help at the shelter in   7
exchange for room, board and pocket change while you got your act together. There were newspapers and circulars with classified ads and job notices. There was a free telephone for job hunting. Land a position and you were given a bag lunch and even bus fare. A way into a legitimate lifestyle was there for the taking.

The trouble was that hardly anybody wanted it.   8

Of the several hundred homeless at the shelter, only a handful wanted off   9
the free-ride bandwagon. When most of them saw an opportunity to earn their keep, they ducked or ran faster than someone who'd glimpsed a ghost. You might think manual labor is a lot better than nothing. They didn't. Jobs were for suckers; job training, a waste of time.

Some secretly smoked crack in their rooms. Others smelled of liquor. The   10
last thing on almost anybody's mind was taking even the first step to stop being homeless. They had a home—the hotels of the shelter system.

So, if ever I bump into that TV reporter again, she's welcome to my two   11
cents: more social programs won't help the homeless I've run into.

Most of them were black like me. Although discrimination has histori-   12
cally excluded us from the mainstream, we're nonetheless responsible not to accept that exclusion as our lot in life, the way many of us have, convinced we can't do any better.

Those who need help have to meet the system halfway and help them-   13
selves. I found work and a place to live. A friend at the shelter dried himself out from drink, got a minimum-wage job and his driver's license back, and planned to return to trucking.

Even with the best of intentions, social programs can't instill self-   14
accountability. Until you can summon up the will to help yourself, all the help in the world is just so much wasted effort. If you won't help yourself, who can?

■　■　■

SCORING GUIDE FOR "POLITICAL QUIZ" (pages 233–235)

How to assign points:

1. "Trust"—0 points. "Distrust" gets 2 points. The major difference between liberals and conservatives is that liberals tend to trust government while conservatives do not.
2. Any of the following gets 1 point (for a maximum of 5 points):

The Pentagon
The executive branch

The FBI
The CIA
The Joint Chiefs

Any of these gets 0 points:

The U.S. Postal Service
The legislative branch
The IRS
The Peace Corps
The United Nations

Liberals would pick the U.S. Postal Service, the IRS, the Peace Corps, the United Nations and the legislative branch because they tend to believe in these institutions.

3. Any of the following gets 1 point (for a maximum of 3 points):

Doctors
Business executives
Team owners

These answers score 0 points:

Trial lawyers
Union leaders
Professional athletes

Liberals favor trial lawyers over doctors, and workers over executives because they tend to distrust businessmen and favor workers and advocates.

4. Give yourself 1 point on this question ONLY if you answered "none." All other answers: 0.
5. You get 1 point for every answer (for a maximum of 9), EXCEPT "Cut defense spending" and "Don't cut at all," which score 0.
6. "Term limits"—1 point.
   "Public financing"—0.
7. "Ronald Reagan"—1 point.
   "Franklin D. Roosevelt"—0.
8. "Melting pot"—1 point.
   "Multicultural society"—0.
9. "Jackson"—1 point
   "Limbaugh"—0.
   "Neither"—0.
10. "Stricter controls"—0 points.
    "Mandatory sentences"—1.
    "Both"—0.
11. "Build prisons"—1 point.
    "Rebuild cities"—0.
    "Both"—0.

12. "Agree"—1. "Disagree"—0.
13. "Agree"—1. "Disagree"—0.
14. "Agree"—0. "Disagree"—1.
15. "Agree"—0. "Disagree"—1.
16. "Agree"—1. "Disagree"—0.
17. "Agree"—0. "Disagree"—1.
18. "Agree"—0. "Disagree"—1.
19. "Agree"—0. "Disagree"—1.
20. "Agree"—1. "Disagree"—0.
21. "Agree"—0. "Disagree"—1.
22. "Agree"—0. "Disagree"—1.
23. "Agree"—1. "Disagree"—0.
24. "Agree"—0. "Disagree"—1.
25. "Agree"—0. "Disagree"—1.

About Your Score

Respondents with the most points (40) are 100 percent conservative; those with the least (0) are 100 percent liberal. See where you fall on the chart below. Take note: A higher number of points is not meant to imply a higher level of political consciousness! The system of accumulating points for conservative answers is simply a practical method for assigning politically left-to-right slots on the spectrum.

Left				**Center**				**Right**
Jesse Jackson	Ted Kennedy	Hillary Clinton	Bill Clinton	Colin Powell	George Bush	Jack Kemp	Bob Dole	Ronald Reagan
0	5	10	15	20	25	30	35	40

▓ SYNTHESIS ACTIVITIES

1. Write an article for a newsmagazine about the current political landscape in the United States. Focus on the difference between liberals and conservatives, but include other political ideologies, such as libertarianism, and indicate where ideological boundaries sometimes seem to blur. Don't take sides, but do your best to give an objective account of some of the key political debates and the kinds of arguments they have generated.

   Draw upon Faux, Krauthammer, McGinnis, Ehrenreich, King, and Moore. Explain where, for example, you would locate Jeff Faux's views, or William Bennett's, along the political spectrum. Use Burns et al. and Smith to define the kinds of differences among the viewpoints expressed in these selections.

2. Write *either* (1) an objective newsmagazine article *or* (2) an editorial or argumentative article, drawing upon some of the eight selections included in the "mystery" readings at the end of the chapter. Follow

the procedures indicated in Synthesis Activity #1, above; that is, use Burns et al. and Smith as yardsticks to determine where along the political spectrum the various views expressed appear to be located, explaining your reasons for categorizing particular viewpoints under more general ideological headings.

If you choose the first option for this assignment, your paper should be relatively objective. If you choose the second, explain why you advocate one set of positions and oppose the other. In developing your argument, you must do more than simply express your opinion; try to support your opinion with solid evidence and logical reasoning. Review the procedures for assessing arguments in Chapter 2, "Critical Reading and Critique." Pay particular attention to the section entitled "Avoiding Logical Fallacies," pp. 50–54.

3. Select two or three authors represented in this chapter and compare and contrast their use of argument. Apply relevant criteria in Chapter 2, "Critical Reading and Critique," to selections that have some common denominator—for example, subject matter, or position on the political spectrum, or type of argument, or use of language. For instance, you might look at the three articles on family values (Bennett, *Wall Street Journal*, Greenfield) or the two (Pascale and Hobbes) on homelessness. You might compare and contrast the kinds of evidence and logic used by Faux and Krauthammer to support their arguments. Or you might compare and contrast the type of language used by King, Moore, and Postrel. Discuss the strategies that the authors use in advancing their cases and the effectiveness of their arguments.

4. Write a speech, either for the president or a congressperson, advocating a position and a recommended course of action on one of the issues addressed in this chapter. Draw upon the relevant selections in the chapter to obtain evidence and also to determine key points of ideological contention on the issue. Review relevant sections of Burns et al. and Smith to focus your responses to the kind of questions underlying the political controversies associated with the issue. Using a "concession" format (see Chapter 4, "Synthesis"), acknowledge and then respond to opposing points of view.

5. You are a public relations consultant for either the Democratic, the Republican, the Libertarian, or the Socialist parties. Write a campaign or a fund-raising letter designed for mass mailing to prospective voters. Focus on one or more of the issues on which this party has greatest interest and explain why it is essential to support your candidate or to pass (or defeat) a particular voter initiative, referendum, or proposition on the ballot. Draw upon Burns et al. to clarify the kinds of positions typically taken by your party on the issues treated in your letter, and draw upon other selections in the chapter, as appropriate, for evidence and talking points. Focus on why your programs and proposals deserve voter backing and why competing programs or proposals deserve rejection.

6. Although we are most accustomed to discussing liberal, conservative, and other ideological views as they apply to political life, such terms can also be applied to other areas of activity, such as popular culture. A recent issue of *National Review* included an article by Spencer Warren entitled "The 100 Best Conservative Movies." In the article, Warren surveyed movies in such categories as "Best Pictures Celebrating Religion and Faith" (*A Man for All Seasons*, *Chariots of Fire*, *The Ten Commandments*), "Best Pictures Indicating the Spiritual Barrenness of Hedonistic Yuppieism" (*Carnal Knowledge* and *Ten*), "Best Picture about Defending America" (*Sergeant York*), and "Best Picture Indicting the Sixties Counterculture" (*Forrest Gump*). Providing not quite equal time, Warren threw in a few good liberal movies, including "the most haunting anti-war film" (*All Quiet on the Western Front*) and "Best Film on Anti-Semitism" (*Crossfire*).

   TV shows can also be ideological. Producer Norman Lear was famous partly for creating shows such as "All in the Family" that made fun of conservative attitudes. Vice President Dan Quayle made headlines for indicting "Murphy Brown" for its liberal take on single motherhood. And recently, the conservative Media Research Center published a list of top 10 shows that were "most guilty of pushing a liberal agenda" (among them: "Roseanne," "Dennis Miller Live," and "Sisters").

   Imagine that you are a member of a watchdog group like the Media Research Center or a liberal counterpart. Consider some movies and TV shows that you have seen that seem to be pushing either a liberal or a conservative view of social issues. Draw upon the discussions in Burns, Peltason, Cronin, and Magleby, and in Lazere, as well as viewpoints stated or implied in other selections in this chapter, to analyze the movies and shows for liberal or conservative slant. Write a report praising or indicting your subjects for their political attitudes. Categorize your discussion either by issue or by movie or TV show. Include a set of recommendations at the end.

Research Activities

1. Write an article of five to seven pages for a newsmagazine on the ideological debate surrounding a particular domestic issue, representing views across the political spectrum. Possible issues: affirmative action, immigration policy, abortion, education, law and order, health care, gays in the military, school prayer, drug policy, federal aid to the arts. Try to be as objective as possible. Your job is to inform your readers of the nature of the debate, not to argue one side or another on any particular issue. Use information in Lazere to locate suitable sources from a variety of viewpoints.

2. Prepare an *annotated bibliography* of sources across the political spectrum on some issue.[1] Write at least ten bibliographical entries, on five *leftist* and five *rightist* sources: include at least one magazine or newspaper article or editorial and one book or monograph report from the left-wing publishers: include one article or editorial or book report from the right-wing publishers in Sections Two and Three in Lazere. Use *MLA format* for citations. Instead of arranging these citations alphabetically, however, arrange them into a political spectrum going from far right to far left—or vice versa. Thus, your bibliography will serve as a detailed plan—in terms of both content and organization—for an actual paper dealing with the range of political positions and political rhetoric. Each entry should be one-half page to one page long.

   Identify each author's political position, using clues from affiliation with a particular research institute, book publisher, journal of opinion, party, or organization, as well as the discussions of political ideology in Burns et al. Give enough quotations to support your identification. In cases for which the author is not arguing from an identifiable position but only reporting facts, indicate which position the reported facts support, and explain how. (*Note:* some newspapers, magazines, etc., have an identifiable political viewpoint in general, in their news and op-ed orientation, but also attempt to present other views at least some of the time. For example, the *Los Angeles Times* is predominantly liberal, but often carries conservative op-ed columns, letters, etc. So you shouldn't assume that any article appearing in such a periodical will automatically have its predominant viewpoint; look for other identifying clues.)

3. As a member of a group of three or four, select one of the following scenarios:

   • You are a member of an election (or re-election) campaign staff for a political candidate—prospective senator, governor, president, etc.
   • You are a member of a citizen's action group that is working for the passage of a voter referendum on the November ballot.
   • Some other comparable scenario of your own choosing.

   Focus your efforts on one particular controversial *domestic issue*, for example, affirmative action, immigration policy, abortion, education, law and order, health care, gays in the military, school prayer, or drug policy. (If you are working for a political candidate, recognize that there may be other issues in the campaign, but imagine that this particular issue is the crucial one at this particular time.)

[1]Assignment adapted from Donald Lazere, "Teaching the Political Conflicts: A Rhetorical Schema," *College Composition and Communication* 43.2 (May 1992): 194–213.

Produce *three reports* for the benefit of your candidate or your group:

- A background survey of the issue. What is the history of this issue, both in a social context and as it has affected recent political events and campaigns? (4–5 pp.)
- A survey and analysis of the *pro* and *con* arguments on the issue, as they have been articulated by recent commentators and political figures. Organize your discussion of these arguments and positions *along a political spectrum*, ranging from *extreme left* (or *right*) to *moderate* to *extreme right* (or *left*). If you have already prepared the annotated bibliography called for in the previous assignment, you may wish to use it as a basis for this section. (6–8 pp.)
- A set of *recommendations for strategy* based on your assignment of the most effective ways to proceed and for your side to prevail. Suggest effective *rhetorical* ways of promoting your side and attacking the other side. Suggest ways of using *language* for maximum effect. At the same time, suggest ways to avoid coming across as extreme in your position, ways by which your position might be perceived as the most reasonable one. (4–5 pp.)

4. Select a major issue, case, or law in the past several decades. Research positions across the political spectrum, and write a paper discussing what you have learned. For example, you might consider the debate over escalating the Vietnam War, the Bakke affirmative action case, the impeachment of President Nixon, or debates about the Pledge of Allegiance or burning of the American flag (these latter most recently in 1988 and 1989). You might also write about violence or objectionable lyrics in the mass media. Notice how such debates concern not only the immediate issues, but also the larger ideological differences among left, right, and center. *Note:* For tracking Congressional debates, see *Congressional Digest* and the various *Congressional Quarterly (CQ)* sources, including *Congressional Quarterly*, *CQ Guide to the Congress of the United States*, *CQ Guide to United States Elections*, and *CQ Alert* (database). See also *CIS Congressional Information Service Bulletin*, *United States Political Science Documents*, and *Public Affairs Information Service Bulletin (PAIS)*, print or CD-ROM.

5. Select one of four non-mainstream political parties—*Libertarian, American Independent, Green, Peace and Freedom*—and write a report on its philosophy and political activities in the past decade or so. Or research the American Socialist or Communist parties. Check major newspaper and magazine indexes; check government documents; write to the parties themselves, asking for information. Who have been some of their candidates? What were their programs? How well have they done at election time? Has their popularity been increasing or decreasing?

6. Examine two or three successive issues of a magazine or journal at the left or right ends of the political spectrum and write an analysis of the kinds of positions authors of articles in these periodicals take on various issues, as well as the type of rhetorical devices they use to persuade their readers. (Draw on Burns, Peltason, Cronin, and Magleby for the former part of this assignment.) For example, if you chose *Reason*, a libertarian journal, you would look at several articles and editorials over a three- or four-month period and analyze ideological patterns you discover that promote the libertarian (anti-government) viewpoint and reject others. By the same token, were you to examine several issues of *The Progressive*, you would find articles favoring the "socialist to left-liberal" viewpoint on a variety of issues.

   Your general strategy in this assignment would be (1) to locate the authors' positions on the political spectrum, citing evidence from both the author and from other sources such as Smith, Burns et al., and (2) to classify the types of rhetorical devices used, drawing on examples from the words of authors themselves and relating these examples to general strategies discussed in Chapter 4, "Synthesis," in The Three Appeals of Argument: *Logos, Ethos, Pathos,* (pp. 129–134).

7. Select an issue on which some recent American presidents have taken stands (see issues suggested in question 1). Using the indexes in *The Weekly Compilation of Presidential Documents*, write a comparison-contrast paper looking at what post–World War II Democratic presidents (Kennedy, Johnson, Carter, Clinton) have said about the issue versus what Republican presidents (Eisenhower, Nixon, Ford, Reagan, Bush) have said. How do the ideological assumptions of the presidents compare and contrast? Their perceptions of the problem? Their recommended solutions? Keep in mind that the various presidents were speaking or writing in different eras, each with its own history and set of problems. Thus, Kennedy and Nixon governed (unlike Bush and Clinton) during the height of the Cold War, a fact that affected their domestic as well as their foreign policy agendas.

7

Obedience to Authority

Would you obey an order to inflict pain on another person? Most of us, if confronted with this question, would probably be quick to answer: "Never!" Yet if the conclusions of researchers are to be trusted, it is not psychopaths who kill noncombatant civilians in wartime and torture victims in prisons around the world but rather ordinary people following orders. People obey. This is a basic, necessary fact of human society. As an author in this chapter has put it, "Obedience is as basic an element in the structure of social life as one can point to. Some system of authority is a requirement of all communal living."

The question, then, is not, "Should we obey the orders of an authority figure?" but rather, "To what *extent* should we obey?" Each generation seems to give new meaning to these questions. During the Vietnam War, a number of American soldiers followed a commander's orders and murdered civilians in the hamlet of My Lai. More recently, and less grotesquely, former White House aide Oliver North pleaded innocent to illegally funding the Contra (resistance) fighters in Nicaragua. North's attorneys claimed that he was following the orders of his superiors. And, although North was found guilty,[1] the judge who sentenced him to perform community service (there was no prison sentence) largely agreed with this defense when he called North a pawn in a larger game played by senior officials in the Reagan administration. In the 1990s the world was horrified by genocidal violence in Rwanda and in the former nation of Yugoslavia. These were civil wars, in which people who had been living for generations as neighbors suddenly, upon the instigation and orders of their leaders, turned upon and slaughtered one another.

In less dramatic ways, conflicts over the extent to which we obey orders surface in everyday life. At one point or another, you may face a moral dilemma at work. Perhaps it will take this form: The boss tells you to overlook File X in preparing a report for a certain client. But you're sure that File X pertains directly to the report and contains information that will alarm the client. What should you do? The dilemmas of obedience also emerge on some campuses with the rite of fraternity hazing. Psychologists Janice Gibson and Mika Haritos-Fatouros have made the startling observation that whether the obedience in question involves a pledge's joining a fraternity or a torturer's joining an elite military corps, the *process* by which one acquiesces to a superior's order (and thereby becomes a member of the group) is remarkably the same:

---

[1] In July 1990, North's conviction was overturned on appeal.

There are several ways to teach people to do the unthinkable, and we have developed a model to explain how they are used. We have also found that college fraternities, although they are far removed from the grim world of torture and violent combat, use similar methods for initiating new members, to ensure their faithfulness to the fraternity's rules and values. However, this unthinking loyalty can sometimes lead to dangerous actions: Over the past 10 years, there have been countless injuries during fraternity initiations and 39 deaths. These training techniques are designed to instill obedience in people, but they can easily be a guide for an intensive course in torture.

1. *Screening to find the best prospects:* Normal, well-adjusted people with the physical, intellectual and, in some cases, political attributes necessary for the task.
2. *Techniques to increase binding among these prospects:* Initiation rites to isolate people from society and introduce them to a new social order, with different rules and values.

   Elitist attitudes and "in-group" language, which highlight the differences between the group and the rest of society.
3. *Techniques to reduce the strain of obedience:* Blaming and dehumanizing the victims, so it is less disturbing to harm them.

   Harassment, the constant physical and psychological intimidation that prevents logical thinking and promotes the instinctive responses needed for acts of inhuman cruelty.

   Rewards for obedience and punishments for not cooperating.

   Social modeling by watching other group members commit violent acts and then receive rewards.

   Systematic desensitization to repugnant acts by gradual exposure to them, so they appear routine and normal despite conflicts with previous moral standards.[2]

In this chapter, you will explore the dilemmas inherent in obeying the orders of an authority. First, in a brief essay adapted from a lecture, British novelist Doris Lessing helps set a context for the discussion by questioning the manner in which we call ourselves individualists yet fail to understand how groups define and exert influence over us. Next, psychologist Solomon Asch describes an experiment he devised to demonstrate the powerful influence of group pressure upon individual judgment. Psychologist Stanley Milgram then reports on his own landmark study in which he set out to determine the extent to which ordinary individuals would obey the clearly immoral orders of an authority figure. The results were shocking, not only to the psychiatrists who predicted that few people would follow such orders but also to many other social scientists and people—some of whom applauded Milgram for his fiendishly ingenious design, some of whom bitterly attacked him for unethical procedures. We include one of these attacks, a scathing review by psychologist Diana Baumrind. Next Philip Zimbardo reports on his famous (and controversial) Stanford Prison Experiment, in which volunteers exhibited astonishingly convincing authoritarian and obedient attitudes as they play acted at

---

[2] "The Education of a Torturer" by Janice T. Gibson and Mika Haritos-Fatouros from *Psychology Today*, November 1986. Reprinted with permission from *Psychology Today Magazine.* Copyright 1986 Sussex Publishers, Inc.

being prisoners and guards. An essay and a short story conclude the chapter. In "Disobedience as a Psychological and Moral Problem," psychoanalyst and philosopher Erich Fromm discusses the comforts of obedient behavior. And in "The Lottery," Shirley Jackson tells the story of a community that faithfully meets its yearly obligation.

Group Minds

DORIS LESSING

Doris Lessing sets a context for the discussion on obedience by illuminating a fundamental conflict: We in the Western world celebrate our individualism, but we're naive in understanding the ways that groups largely undercut our individuality. "We are group animals still," says Lessing, "and there is nothing wrong with that. But what is dangerous is . . . not understanding the social laws that govern groups and govern us." This chapter is largely devoted to an exploration of these tendencies. As you read selections by Milgram and the other authors here, bear in mind Lessing's troubling question: If we know that individuals will violate their own good common sense and moral codes in order to become accepted members of a group, why then can't we put this knowledge to use and teach people to be wary of group pressures?

Doris Lessing, the daughter of farmers, was born in Persia, now Iran, in 1919. She attended a Roman Catholic convent and a girls' high school in southern Rhodesia (now Zimbabwe). From 1959 through to the present, Lessing has written more than twenty works of fiction and has been called "the best woman novelist" of the postwar era. Her work has received a great deal of scholarly attention. She is, perhaps, best known for her Five Short Novels *(1954),* The Golden Notebook *(1962), and* Briefing for a Descent into Hell *(1971).*

People living in the West, in societies that we describe as Western, or as the free world, may be educated in many different ways, but they will all emerge with an idea about themselves that goes something like this: I am a citizen of a free society, and that means I am an individual, making individual choices. My mind is my own, my opinions are chosen by me, I am free to do as I will, and at the worst the pressures on me are economic, that is, I may be too poor to do as I want. 1

This set of ideas may sound something like a caricature, but it is not so far off how we see ourselves. It is a portrait that may not have been acquired consciously, but is part of a general atmosphere or set of assumptions that influence our ideas about ourselves. 2

People in the West therefore may go through their entire lives never thinking to analyze this very flattering picture, and as a result are helpless against all kinds of pressures on them to conform in many kinds of ways. 3

The fact is that we all live our lives in groups—the family, work groups, social, religious and political groups. Very few people indeed are happy as 4 solitaries, and they tend to be seen by their neighbors as peculiar or selfish or worse. Most people cannot stand being alone for long. They are always seeking groups to belong to, and if one group dissolves, they look for another. We are group animals still, and there is nothing wrong with that. But what is dangerous is not the belonging to a group, or groups, but not understanding the social laws that govern groups and govern us.

When we're in a group, we tend to think as that group does: we may even   5
have joined the group to find "like-minded" people. But we also find our thinking changing because we belong to a group. It is the hardest thing in the world to maintain an individual dissident opinion, as a member of a group.

It seems to me that this is something we have all experienced—something   6
we take for granted, may never have thought about it. But a great deal of experiment has gone on among psychologists and sociologists on this very theme. If I describe an experiment or two, then anyone listening who may be a sociologist or psychologist will groan, oh God not *again*—for they will have heard of these classic experiments far too often. My guess is that the rest of the people will never have heard of these experiments, never have had these ideas presented to them. If my guess is true, then it aptly illustrates my general thesis, and the general idea behind these talks, that we (the human race) are now in possession of a great deal of hard information about ourselves, but we do not use it to improve our institutions and therefore our lives.

A typical test, or experiment, on this theme goes like this. A group of   7
people are taken into the researcher's confidence. A minority of one or two are left in the dark. Some situation demanding measurement or assessment is chosen. For instance, comparing lengths of wood that differ only a little from each other, but enough to be perceptible, or shapes that are almost the same size. The majority in the group—according to instruction—will assert stubbornly that these two shapes or lengths are the same length, or size, while the solitary individual, or the couple, who have not been so instructed will assert that the pieces of wood or whatever are different. But the majority will continue to insist—speaking metaphorically—that black is white, and after a period of exasperation, irritation, even anger, certainly incomprehension, the minority will fall into line. Not always, but nearly always. There are indeed glorious individuals who stubbornly insist on telling the truth as they see it, but most give in to the majority opinion, obey the atmosphere.

When put as badly, as unflatteringly, as this, reactions tend to be incred-   8
ulous: "I certainly wouldn't give in, I speak my mind. . . ." But would you?

People who have experienced a lot of groups, who perhaps have observed   9
their own behavior, may agree that the hardest thing in the world is to stand out against one's group, a group of one's peers. Many agree that among our most shameful memories is this, how often we said black was white because other people were saying it.

In other words, we know that this is true of human behavior, but how do   10
we know it? It is one thing to admit it, in a vague uncomfortable sort of way (which probably includes the hope that one will never again be in such a testing situation) but quite another to make that cool step into a kind of objec-

tivity, where one may say, "Right, if that's what human beings are like, myself included, then let's admit it, examine and organize our attitudes accordingly."

This mechanism, of obedience to the group, does not only mean obedi- 11
ence or submission to a small group, or one that is sharply determined, like a religion or political party. It means, too, conforming to those large, vague, ill-defined collections of people who may never think of themselves as having a collective mind because they are aware of differences of opinion—but which, to people from outside, from another culture, seem very minor. The underlying assumptions and assertions that govern the group are never discussed, never challenged, probably never noticed, the main one being precisely this: that it *is* a group mind, intensely resistant to change, equipped with sacred assumptions about which there can be no discussion.

But suppose this kind of thing were taught in schools? 12

Let us just suppose it, for a moment. . . . But at once the nub of the prob- 13
lem is laid bare.

Imagine us saying to children, "In the last fifty or so years, the human 14
race has become aware of a great deal of information about its mechanisms; how it behaves, how it must behave under certain circumstances. If this is to be useful, you must learn to contemplate these rules calmly, dispassionately, disinterestedly, without emotion. It is information that will set people free from blind loyalties, obedience to slogans, rhetoric, leaders, group emotions." Well, there it is.

■   ■   ■

Review Questions

1. What is the flattering portrait Lessing paints of people living in the West?
2. Lessing believes that individuals in the West are "helpless against all kinds of pressures on them to conform in many kinds of ways." Why?
3. Lessing refers to a class of experiments on obedience. Summarize the "typical" experiment.

Discussion and Writing Suggestions

1. Lessing writes that "what is dangerous is not the belonging to a group, or groups, but not understanding the social laws that govern groups and govern us." What is the danger Lessing is speaking of here?
2. Lessing states that "we (the human race) are now in possession of a great deal of hard information about ourselves, but we do not use it to improve our institutions and therefore our lives." First, do you agree with Lessing? Can you cite other examples (aside from information on obedience to authority) in which we do not use our knowledge to better humankind?

3. Explore some of the difficulties in applying this "hard information" about humankind that Lessing speaks of. Assume she's correct in claiming that we don't incorporate our knowledge of human nature into the running of our institutions. Why don't we? What are the difficulties of *acting* on information?

4. Lessing speaks of "people who remember how they acted in school" and of their guilt in recalling how they succumbed to group pressures. Can you recall such an event? What feelings do you have about it now?

Opinions and Social Pressure

SOLOMON E. ASCH

In the early 1950s, Solomon Asch (b.1907), a social psychologist at Rutgers University in New Brunswick, New Jersey, conducted a series of simple but ingenious experiments on the influence of group pressure upon the individual. Essentially, he discovered, individuals can be influenced by groups to deny the evidence of their own senses. Together with the Milgram experiments of the following decade (see the following selections), these studies provide powerful evidence of the degree to which individuals can surrender their own judgment to others, even when those others are clearly in the wrong. The results of these experiments have implications far beyond the laboratory: they can explain a good deal of the normal human behavior we see every day—at school, at work, at home.

That social influences shape every person's practices, judgments and beliefs is   1
a truism to which anyone will readily assent. A child masters his "native" dialect down to the finest nuances; a member of a tribe of cannibals accepts cannibalism as altogether fitting and proper. All the social sciences take their departure from the observation of the profound effects that groups exert on their members. For psychologists, group pressure upon the minds of individuals raises a host of questions they would like to investigate in detail.

How, and to what extent, do social forces constrain people's opinions   2
and attitudes? This question is especially pertinent in our day. The same epoch that has witnessed the unprecedented technical extension of communication has also brought into existence the deliberate manipulation of opinion and the "engineering of consent." There are many good reasons why, as citizens and as scientists, we should be concerned with studying the ways in which human beings form their opinions and the role that social conditions play.

Studies of these questions began with the interest in hypnosis aroused by   3
the French physician Jean Martin Charcot (a teacher of Sigmund Freud) toward the end of the 19th century. Charcot believed that only hysterical patients could be fully hypnotized, but this view was soon challenged by two other physicians, Hyppolyte Bernheim and A. A. Liébault, who demonstrated that they could put most people under the hypnotic spell. Bernheim pro-

posed that hypnosis was but an extreme form of a normal psychological process which became known as "suggestibility." It was shown that monotonous reiteration of instructions could induce in normal persons in the waking state involuntary bodily changes such as swaying or rigidity of the arms, and sensations such as warmth and odor.

It was not long before social thinkers seized upon these discoveries as a   4
basis for explaining numerous social phenomena, from the spread of opinion to the formation of crowds and the following of leaders. The sociologist Gabriel Tarde summed it all up in the aphorism: "Social man is a somnambulist."

When the new discipline of social psychology was born at the beginning   5
of this century, its first experiments were essentially adaptations of the suggestion demonstration. The technique generally followed a simple plan. The subjects, usually college students, were asked to give their opinions or preferences concerning various matters; some time later they were again asked to state their choices, but now they were also informed of the opinions held by authorities or large groups of their peers on the same matters. (Often the alleged consensus was fictitious.) Most of these studies had substantially the same result: confronted with opinions contrary to their own, many subjects apparently shifted their judgments in the direction of the views of the majorities or the experts. The late psychologist Edward L. Thorndike reported that he had succeeded in modifying the esthetic preferences of adults by this procedure. Other psychologists reported that people's evaluations of the merit of a literary passage could be raised or lowered by ascribing the passage to different authors. Apparently the sheer weight of numbers or authority sufficed to change opinions, even when no arguments for the opinions themselves were provided.

Now the very ease of success in these experiments arouses suspicion.   6
Did the subjects actually change their opinions, or were the experimental victories scored only on paper? On grounds of common sense, one must question whether opinions are generally as watery as these studies indicate. There is some reason to wonder whether it was not the investigators who, in their enthusiasm for a theory, were suggestible, and whether the ostensibly gullible subjects were not providing answers which they thought good subjects were expected to give.

The investigations were guided by certain underlying assumptions, which   7
today are common currency and account for much that is thought and said about the operations of propaganda and public opinion. The assumptions are that people submit uncritically and painlessly to external manipulation by suggestion or prestige, and that any given idea or value can be "sold" or "unsold" without reference to its merits. We should be skeptical, however, of the supposition that the power of social pressure necessarily implies uncritical submission to it: independence and the capacity to rise above group passion are also open to human beings. Further, one may question on psychological grounds whether it is possible as a rule to change a person's judgment of a situation or an object without first changing his knowledge or assumptions about it.

In what follows I shall describe some experiments in an investigation of the   8
effects of group pressure which was carried out recently with the help of a
number of my associates. The tests not only demonstrate the operations of
group pressure upon individuals but also illustrate a new kind of attack on the
problem and some of the more subtle questions that it raises.

A group of seven to nine young men, all college students, are assembled   9
in a classroom for a "psychological experiment" in visual judgment. The
experimenter informs them that they will be comparing the lengths of lines.
He shows two large white cards [see Figure 1]. On one is a single vertical
black line—the standard whose length is to be matched . On the other card
are three vertical lines of various lengths. The subjects are to choose the one
that is of the same length as the line on the other card. One of the three actually is of the same length; the other two are substantially different, the difference ranging from three quarters of an inch to an inch and three quarters.

The experiment opens uneventfully. The subjects announce their answers   10
in the order in which they have been seated in the room, and on the first
round every person chooses the same matching line. Then a second set of
cards is exposed; again the group is unanimous. The members appear ready
to endure politely another boring experiment. On the third trial there is an
unexpected disturbance. One person near the end of the group disagrees with
all the others in his selection of the matching line. He looks surprised, indeed
incredulous, about the disagreement. On the following trial he disagrees
again, while the others remain unanimous in their choice. The dissenter
becomes more and more worried and hesitant as the disagreement continues
in succeeding trials; he may pause before announcing his answer and speak in
a low voice, or he may smile in an embarrassed way.

What the dissenter does not know is that all the other members of the   11
group were instructed by the experimenter beforehand to give incorrect
answers in unanimity at certain points. The single individual who is not a
party to this prearrangement is the focal subject of our experiment. He is

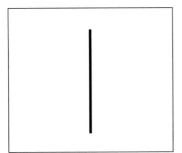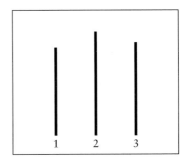

FIGURE 1

Subjects were shown two cards. One bore a standard line. The other bore three lines,
one of which was the same length as the standard. The subjects were asked to choose
this line.

placed in a position in which, while he is actually giving the correct answers, he finds himself unexpectedly in a minority of one, opposed by a unanimous and arbitrary majority with respect to a clear and simple fact. Upon him we have brought to bear two opposed forces: the evidence of his senses and the unanimous opinion of a group of his peers. Also, he must declare his judgments in public, before a majority which has also stated its position publicly.

The instructed majority occasionally reports correctly in order to reduce the possibility that the naive subject will suspect collusion against him. (In only a few cases did the subject actually show suspicion; when this happened, the experiment was stopped and the results were not counted.) There are 18 trials in each series, and on 12 of these the majority responds erroneously. 12

How do people respond to group pressure in this situation? I shall report first the statistical results of a series in which a total of 123 subjects from three institutions of higher learning (not including my own Swarthmore College) were placed in the minority situation described above. 13

Two alternatives were open to the subject: he could act independently, repudiating the majority, or he could go along with the majority, repudiating the evidence of his senses. Of the 123 put to the test, a considerable percentage yielded to the majority. Whereas in ordinary circumstances individuals matching the lines will make mistakes less than 1 per cent of the time, under group pressure the minority subjects swung to acceptance of the misleading majority's wrong judgments in 36.8 per cent of the selections. 14

Of course individuals differed in response. At one extreme, about one quarter of the subjects were completely independent and never agreed with the erroneous judgments of the majority. At the other extreme, some individuals went with the majority nearly all the time. The performances of individuals in this experiment tend to be highly consistent. Those who strike out on the path of independence do not, as a rule, succumb to the majority even over an extended series of trials, while those who choose the path of compliance are unable to free themselves as the ordeal is prolonged. 15

The reasons for the startling individual differences have not yet been investigated in detail. At this point we can only report some tentative generalizations from talks with the subjects, each of whom was interviewed at the end of the experiment. Among the independent individuals were many who held fast because of staunch confidence in their own judgment. The most significant fact about them was not absence of responsiveness to the majority but a capacity to recover from doubt and to reestablish their equilibrium. Others who acted independently came to believe that the majority was correct in its answers, but they continued their dissent on the simple ground that it was their obligation to call the play as they saw it. 16

Among the extremely yielding persons we found a group who quickly reached the conclusion: "I am wrong, they are right." Others yielded in order "not to spoil your results." Many of the individuals who went along suspected that the majority were "sheep" following the first responder, or that the majority were victims of an optical illusion; nevertheless, these suspicions 17 failed to free them at the moment of decision. More disquieting were the reactions of subjects who construed their difference from the majority as a sign of some general deficiency in themselves, which at all costs they must hide. On this basis they desperately tried to merge with the majority, not realizing the longer-range consequences to themselves. All the yielding subjects underestimated the frequency with which they conformed.

Which aspect of the influence of a majority is more important—the size 18 of the majority or its unanimity? The experiment was modified to examine this question. In one series the size of the opposition was varied from one to 15 persons. The results showed a clear trend. When a subject was confronted with only a single individual who contradicted his answers, he was swayed little: he continued to answer independently and correctly in nearly all trials. When the opposition was increased to two, the pressure became substantial: minority subjects now accepted the wrong answer 13.6 per cent of the time. Under the pressure of a majority of three, the subjects' errors jumped to 31.8 per cent. But further increases in the size of the majority apparently did not increase the weight of the pressure substantially. Clearly the size of the opposition is important only up to a point.

Disturbance of the majority's unanimity had a striking effect. In this 19 experiment the subject was given the support of a truthful partner—either another individual who did not know of the prearranged agreement among the rest of the group, or a person who was instructed to give correct answers throughout.

The presence of a supporting partner depleted the majority of much of its 20 power. Its pressure on the dissenting individual was reduced to one fourth: that is, subjects answered incorrectly only one fourth as often as under the pressure of a unanimous majority. The weakest persons did not yield as readily. Most interesting were the reactions to the partner. Generally the feeling toward him was one of warmth and closeness; he was credited with inspiring confidence. However, the subjects repudiated the suggestion that the partner decided them to be independent.

Was the partner's effect a consequence of his dissent, or was it related to 21 his accuracy? We now introduced into the experimental group a person who was instructed to dissent from the majority but also to disagree with the subject. In some experiments the majority was always to choose the worst of the comparison lines and the instructed dissenter to pick the line that was closer to the length of the standard one; in others the majority was consistently intermediate and the dissenter most in error. In this manner we were able to study the relative influence of "compromising" and "extremist" dissenters.

Again the results are clear. When a moderate dissenter is present the 22 effect of the majority on the subject decreases by approximately one third, and extremes of yielding disappear. Moreover, most of the errors the subjects do make are moderate, rather than flagrant. In short, the dissenter largely controls the choice of errors. To this extent the subjects broke away from the majority even while bending to it.

On the other hand, when the dissenter always chose the line that was   23
more flagrantly different from the standard, the results were of quite a different kind. The extremist dissenter produced a remarkable freeing of the subjects; their errors dropped to only 9 per cent. Furthermore, all the errors
were of the moderate variety. We were able to conclude that dissents *per se*
increased independence and moderated the errors that occurred, and that the
direction of dissent exerted consistent effects.

In all the foregoing experiments each subject was observed only in a   24
single setting. We now turned to studying the effects upon a given individual
of a change in the situation to which he was exposed. The first experiment
examined the consequences of losing or gaining a partner. The instructed
partner began by answering correctly on the first six trials. With his support
the subject usually resisted pressure from the majority: 18 of 27 subjects
were completely independent. But after six trials the partner joined the majority. As soon as he did so, there was an abrupt rise in the subjects' errors. Their
submission to the majority was just about as frequent as when the minority
subject was opposed by a unanimous majority throughout.

It was surprising to find that the experience of having had a partner and   25
of having braved the majority opposition with him had failed to strengthen
the individuals' independence. Questioning at the conclusion of the experiment suggested that we had overlooked an important circumstance; namely,
the strong specific effect of "desertion" by the partner to the other side. We
therefore changed the conditions so that the partner would simply leave the
group at the proper point. (To allay suspicion it was announced in advance
that he had an appointment with the dean.) In this form of the experiment,
the partner's effect outlasted his presence. The errors increased after his
departure, but less markedly than after a partner switched to the majority.

In a variant of this procedure the trials began with the majority unani-   26
mously giving correct answers. Then they gradually broke away until on the
sixth trial the naive subject was alone and the group unanimously against him.
As long as the subject had anyone on his side, he was almost invariably independent, but as soon as he found himself alone, the tendency to conform to
the majority rose abruptly.

As might be expected, an individual's resistance to group pressure in   27
these experiments depends to a considerable degree on how wrong the majority is. We varied the discrepancy between the standard line and the other lines
systematically, with the hope of reaching a point where the error of the
majority would be so glaring that every subject would repudiate it and choose
independently. In this we regretfully did not succeed. Even when the difference
between the lines was seven inches, there were still some who yielded to the
error of the majority.

The study provides clear answers to a few relatively simple questions, and   28
it raises many others that await investigation. We would like to know the
degree of consistency of persons in situations which differ in content and
structure. If consistency of independence or conformity in behavior is shown

to be a fact, how is it functionally related to qualities of character and personality? In what ways is independence related to sociological or cultural conditions? Are leaders more independent than other people, or are they adept at following their followers? These and many other questions may perhaps be answerable by investigations of the type described here.

Life in society requires consensus as an indispensable condition. But consensus, to be productive, requires that each individual contribute independently out of his experience and insight. When consensus comes under the dominance of conformity, the social process is polluted and the individual at the same time surrenders the powers on which his functioning as a feeling and thinking being depends. That we have found the tendency to conformity in our society so strong that reasonably intelligent and well-meaning young people are willing to call white black is a matter of concern. It raises questions about our ways of education and about the values that guide our conduct. 29

Yet anyone inclined to draw too pessimistic conclusions from this report would do well to remind himself that the capacities for independence are not to be underestimated. He may also draw some consolation from a further observation: those who participated in this challenging experiment agreed nearly without exception that independence was preferable to conformity. 30

■ ■ ■

Review Questions

1. What is "suggestibility"? How is this phenomenon related to social pressure?
2. Summarize the procedure and results of the Asch experiment. What conclusions does Asch draw from these results?
3. To what extent did varying the size of the majority and its unanimity affect the experimental results?
4. What distinction does Asch draw between consensus and conformity?

Discussion and Writing Suggestions

1. Before discussing the experiment, Asch considers how easily people's opinions or attitudes may be shaped by social pressure. To what extent do you agree with this conclusion? Write a short paper on this subject, drawing upon examples from your own experience or observation or from your reading.
2. Do the results of this experiment surprise you? Or do they confirm facts about human behavior that you had already suspected, observed, or experienced? Explain, in two or three paragraphs. Provide examples, relating these examples to features of the Asch experiment.

3. Frequently, the conclusions drawn from a researcher's experimental results are challenged on the basis that laboratory conditions do not accurately reflect the complexity of human behavior. Asch draws certain conclusions about the degree to which individuals are affected by group pressures based on an experiment involving subjects choosing matching line lengths. To what extent, if any, do you believe that these conclusions lack validity because the behavior at the heart of the experiment is too dissimilar to real-life situations of group pressure on the individual? Support your opinions with examples.

4. We are all familiar with the phenomenon of "peer pressure." To what extent do Asch's experiments demonstrate the power of peer pressure? To what extent do you think that other factors may be at work? Explain, providing examples.

5. Asch's experiments, conducted in the early 1950s, involved groups of "seven to nine young men, all college students." To what extent do you believe that the results of a similar experiment would be different today? To what extent might they be different if the subjects had included women, as well, and subjects of various ages, from children, to middle-aged people, to older people? To what extent do you believe that the social class or culture of the subjects might have an impact upon the experimental results? Support your opinions with examples and logical reasoning. (Beware, however, of overgeneralizing, based upon insufficient evidence.)

The Perils of Obedience

STANLEY MILGRAM

In 1963, a Yale psychologist conducted one of the classic studies on obedience that Doris Lessing refers to in "Group Minds." Stanley Milgram designed an experiment that forced participants either to violate their conscience by obeying the immoral demands of an authority figure or to refuse those demands. Surprisingly, Milgram found that few participants could resist the authority's orders, even when the participants knew that following these orders would result in another person's pain. Were the participants in these experiments incipient mass murderers? No, said Milgram. They were "ordinary people, simply doing their jobs." The implications of Milgram's conclusions are immense.

Consider: Where does evil reside? What sort of people were responsible for the Holocaust, and for the long list of other atrocities that seem to blight the human record in every generation? Is it a lunatic fringe, a few sick but powerful people who are responsible for atrocities? If so, then we decent folk needn't ever look inside ourselves to understand evil since (by our definition) evil lurks out there, in "those sick ones." Milgram's' study suggested otherwise: that under a special set of circumstances the obedience we naturally show authority figures can transform us into agents of terror.

The article that follows is one of the longest in this text, and it may help you to know in advance the author's organization. In paragraphs 1–11, Milgram discusses the larger significance and the history of dilemmas involving obedience to authority; he then summarizes his basic experimental design and follows with a report of one experiment. Milgram organizes the remainder of his article into sections, which he has subtitled "An Unexpected Outcome," "Peculiar Reactions," "The Etiquette of Submission," and "Duty without Conflict." He begins his conclusion in paragraph 108. If you find the article too long to complete in a single sitting, then plan to read sections at a time, taking notes on each until you're done. Anticipate the article immediately following Milgram's: it reviews his work and largely concerns the ethics of his experimental design. Consider these ethics as you read so that you, in turn, can respond to Milgram's critics.

Stanley Milgram (1933–1984) taught and conducted research at Yale and Harvard universities and at the Graduate Center, City University of New York. He was named Guggenheim Fellow in 1972–1973 and a year later was nominated for the National Book Award for Obedience to Authority. *His other books include* Television and Antisocial Behavior *(1973),* The City and the Self *(1974),* Human Aggression *(1976), and* The Individual in the Social World *(1977).*

Obedience is as basic an element in the structure of social life as one can point to. Some system of authority is a requirement of all communal living, and it is only the person dwelling in isolation who is not forced to respond, with defiance or submission, to the commands of others. For many people, obedience is a deeply ingrained behavior tendency, indeed a potent impulse overriding training in ethics, sympathy, and moral conduct. 1

The dilemma inherent in submission to authority is ancient, as old as the story of Abraham, and the question of whether one should obey when commands conflict with conscience has been argued by Plato, dramatized in *Antigone*, and treated to philosophic analysis in almost every historical epoch. Conservative philosophers argue that the very fabric of society is threatened by disobedience, while humanists stress the primacy of the individual conscience. 2

The legal and philosophic aspects of obedience are of enormous import, but they say very little about how most people behave in concrete situations. I set up a simple experiment at Yale University to test how much pain an ordinary citizen would inflict on another person simply because he was ordered to by an experimental scientist. Stark authority was pitted against the subjects' strongest moral imperatives against hurting others, and, with the subjects' ears ringing with the screams of the victims, authority won more often than not. The extreme willingness of adults to go to almost any lengths on the command of an authority constitutes the chief finding of the study and the fact most urgently demanding explanation. 3

In the basic experimental design, two people come to a psychology laboratory to take part in a study of memory and learning. One of them is designated as a "teacher" and the other a "learner." The experimenter explains 4 that the study is concerned with the effects of punishment on learning. The learner is conducted into a room, seated in a kind of miniature electric chair; his arms are strapped to prevent excessive movement, and an electrode is attached to his wrist. He is told that he will be read lists of simple word pairs, and that he will then be tested on his ability to remember the second word of a pair when he hears the first one again. Whenever he makes an error, he will receive electric shocks of increasing intensity.

The real focus of the experiment is the teacher. After watching the learn- 5
er being strapped into place, he is seated before an impressive shock genera-tor. The instrument panel consists of thirty level switches set in a horizontal line. Each switch is clearly labeled with a voltage designation ranging from 15 to 450 volts. The following designations are clearly indicated for groups of four switches, going from left to right: Slight Shock, Moderate Shock, Strong Shock, Very Strong Shock, Intense Shock, Extreme Intensity Shock, Danger: Severe Shock. (Two switches after this last designation are simply marked XXX.)

When a switch is depressed, a pilot light corresponding to each switch is 6
illuminated in bright red; an electric buzzing is heard; a blue light, labeled "voltage energizer," flashes; the dial on the voltage meter swings to the right; and various relay clicks sound off.

The upper left-hand corner of the generator is labeled SHOCK GENERATOR, 7
TYPE ZLB, DYSON INSTRUMENT COMPANY, WALTHAM, MASS. OUTPUT 15 VOLTS–450 VOLTS.

Each subject is given a sample 45-volt shock from the generator before 8
his run as teacher, and the jolt strengthens his belief in the authenticity of the machine.

The teacher is a genuinely naïve subject who has come to the laboratory 9
for the experiment. The learner, or victim, is actually an actor who receives no shock at all. The point of the experiment is to see how far a person will pro-ceed in a concrete and measurable situation in which he is ordered to inflict increasing pain on a protesting victim.

Conflict arises when the man receiving the shock begins to show that he 10
is experiencing discomfort. At 75 volts, he grunts; at 120 volts, he complains loudly; at 150, he demands to be released from the experiment. As the volt-age increases, his protests become more vehement and emotional. At 285 volts, his response can be described only as an agonized scream. Soon there-after, he makes no sound at all.

For the teacher, the situation quickly becomes one of gripping tension. It 11
is not a game for him; conflict is intense and obvious. The manifest suffering of the learner presses him to quit; but each time he hesitates to administer a shock, the experimenter orders him to continue. To extricate himself from this plight, the subject must make a clear break with authority.[1]

---

[1]The ethical problems of carrying out an experiment of this sort are too complex to be dealt with here, but they receive extended treatment in the book from which this article is adapt-ed.

The subject, Gretchen Brandt,[2] is an attractive thirty-one-year-old med-   12
ical technician who works at the Yale Medical School. She had emigrated
from Germany five years before.

On several occasions when the learner complains, she turns to the exper-   13
imenter coolly and inquires, "Shall I continue?" She promptly returns to her
task when the experimenter asks her to do so. At the administration of 210
volts, she turns to the experimenter, remarking firmly, "Well, I'm sorry, I
don't think we should continue."

EXPERIMENTER: The experiment requires that you go on until he has learned   14
   all the word pairs correctly.
BRANDT: He has a heart condition. I'm sorry. He told you that before.   15
EXPERIMENTER: The shocks may be painful but they are not dangerous.   16
BRANDT: Well, I'm sorry, I think when shocks continue like this, they *are* dan-   17
   gerous. You ask him if he wants to get out. It's his free will.
EXPERIMENTER: It is absolutely essential that we continue. . . .   18
BRANDT: I'd like you to ask him. We came here of our free will. If he wants to   19
   continue I'll go ahead. He told you he had a heart condition. I'm sorry. I
   don't want to be responsible for anything happening to him. I wouldn't
   like it for me either.
EXPERIMENTER: You have no other choice.   20
BRANDT: I think we are here on our own free will. I don't want to be respon-   21
   sible if anything happens to him. Please understand that.

She refuses to go further and the experiment is terminated.   22

The woman is firm and resolute throughout. She indicates in the inter-   23
view that she was in no way tense or nervous, and this corresponds to her
controlled appearance during the experiment. She feels that the last shock she
administered to the learner was extremely painful and reiterates that she "did
not want to be responsible for any harm to him."

The woman's straightforward, courteous behavior in the experiment,   24
lack of tension, and total control of her own action seem to make disobedience a simple and rational deed. Her behavior is the very embodiment of what
I envisioned would be true for almost all subjects.

AN UNEXPECTED OUTCOME

Before the experiments, I sought predictions about the outcome from various   25
kinds of people—psychiatrists, college sophomores, middle-class adults, graduate students and faculty in the behavioral sciences. With remarkable similarity, they predicted that virtually all subjects would refuse to obey the
experimenter. The psychiatrists, specifically, predicted that most subjects
would not go beyond 150 volts, when the victim makes his first explicit

---

[2]Names of subjects described in this piece have been changed.

demand to be freed. They expected that only 4 percent would reach 300 volts, and that only a pathological fringe of about one in a thousand would administer the highest shock on the board.

These predictions were unequivocally wrong. Of the forty subjects in the [26] first experiment, twenty-five obeyed the orders of the experimenter to the end, punishing the victim until they reached the most potent shock available on the generator. After 450 volts were administered three times, the experimenter called a halt to the session. Many obedient subjects then heaved sighs of relief, mopped their brows, rubbed their fingers over their eyes, or nervously fumbled cigarettes. Others displayed only minimal signs of tension from beginning to end.

When the very first experiments were carried out, Yale undergraduates [27] were used as subjects, and about 60 percent of them were fully obedient. A colleague of mine immediately dismissed these findings as having no relevance to "ordinary" people, asserting that Yale undergraduates are a highly aggressive, competitive bunch who step on each other's necks on the slightest provocation. He assured me that when "ordinary" people were tested, the results would be quite different. As we moved from the pilot studies to the regular experimental series, people drawn from every stratum of New Haven life came to be employed in the experiment: professionals, white-collar workers, unemployed persons, and industrial workers. *The experiment's total outcome was the same as we had observed among the students.*

Moreover, when the experiments were repeated in Princeton, Munich, [28] Rome, South Africa, and Australia, the level of obedience was invariably somewhat *higher* than found in the investigation reported in this article. Thus one scientist in Munich found 85 percent of his subjects to be obedient.

Fred Prozi's reactions, if more dramatic than most, illuminate the con- [29] flicts experienced by others in less visible form. About fifty years old and unemployed at the time of the experiment, he has a good-natured, if slightly dissolute, appearance, and he strikes people as a rather ordinary fellow. He begins the session calmly but becomes tense as it proceeds. After delivering the 180-volt shock, he pivots around in his chair and, shaking his head, addresses the experimenter in agitated tones:

PROZI: I can't stand it. I'm not going to kill that man in there. You hear him [30] hollering?

EXPERIMENTER: As I told you before, the shocks may be painful, but . . . [31]

PROZI: But he's hollering. He can't stand it. What's going to happen to him? [32]

EXPERIMENTER (*his voice is patient, matter-of-fact*): The experiment requires [33] that you continue, Teacher.

PROZI: Aaah, but unh, I'm not going to get that man sick in there—know [34] what I mean?

EXPERIMENTER: Whether the learner likes it or not, we must go on, through all [35] the word pairs.

PROZI: I refuse to take the responsibility. He's in there hollering! [36]

EXPERIMENTER: It's absolutely essential that you continue, Prozi.   37

PROZI (*indicating the unused questions*): There's too many left here. I mean,   38
  Jeez, if he gets them wrong, there's too many of them left. I mean, who's
  going to take the responsibility if anything happens to that gentleman?

EXPERIMENTER: I'm responsible for anything that happens to him. Continue,   39
  please.

PROZI: All right. (*Consults list of words.*) The next one's "Slow—walk, truck,   40
  dance, music." Answer, please. (*A buzzing sound indicates the learner has
  signaled his answer.*) Wrong. A hundred and ninety-five volts. "Dance."
  (*Zzumph!*)

LEARNER (*yelling*): Let me out of here! My heart's bothering me! (*Teacher*   41
  looks at experimenter.)

EXPERIMENTER: Continue, please.   42

LEARNER (*screaming*): Let me out of here! You have no right to keep me   43
  here! Let me out of here, my heart's bothering me, let me out!

PROZI (*shakes head, pats the table nervously*): You see, he's hollering. Hear   44
  that? Gee, I don't know.

EXPERIMENTER: The experiment requires . . .   45

PROZI (*interrupting*): I know it does, sir, but I mean—hunh! He don't know   46
  what he's getting in for. He's up to 195 volts! (*Experiment continues,
  through 210 volts, 225 volts, 240 volts, 255 volts, 270 volts, at which
  point Prozi, with evident relief, runs out of word-pair questions.*)

EXPERIMENTER: You'll have to go back to the beginning of that page and go   47
  through them again until he's learned them all correctly.

PROZI: Aw, no. I'm not going to kill that man. You mean I've got to keep   48
  going up with the scale? No sir. He's hollering in there. I'm not going to
  give him 450 volts.

EXPERIMENTER: The experiment requires that you go on.   49

LEARNER: Ohhh. I absolutely refuse to answer anymore. (*Shouting urgently*   50
  now.) Let me out of here! You can't hold me here! Get me out. Get-me-
  out-of-here!

EXPERIMENTER: Continue. The next word is "Green," please.   51

PROZI: "Green—grass, hat, ink, apple." (*Nothing happens. No answering*   52
  buzz. Just gloomy silence.)

PROZI: I don't think he is going to answer.   53

EXPERIMENTER: If the learner doesn't answer in a reasonable time, about four   54
  or five seconds, consider the answer wrong. And follow the same procedures you have been doing for wrong answers. Say, "Wrong," tell him the
  number of volts, give him the punishment, read him the correct answer.
  Continue, please.

PROZI: "Green—grass, hat, ink, apple." Answer, please. (*More silence. Subject* 55
  just sits there.)

EXPERIMENTER: Go on with the procedure, please.   56

PROZI: Three hundred and fifteen volts. The answer is "ink." (*Zzumph!*)   57

LEARNER: Ohh. Ooohh.   58

PROZI: (*relieved to hear response*): Next one . . . 59

LEARNER: I absolutely refuse to answer. 60

PROZI: You got to. You get a shock if you don't answer. (*Experiment con-* 61
tinues with learner refusing to answer, and finally, failing even to grunt or
groan. At 375 volts, the subject stands up.*)

PROZI: I think something's happened to that fellow in there. I don't get no 62
answer. He was hollering at less voltage. Can't you check in and see if he's
all right, please?

EXPERIMENTER: (*with same detached calm*): Not once we've started. Please 63
continue, Teacher.

PROZI (*sits down, sighs deeply*): "Cool—day, shade, water, paint." Answer, 64
please. Are you all right in there? Are you all right?

EXPERIMENTER: Please continue, Teacher. Continue, please. (*Subject pushes* 65
lever. Zzumph!*)

PROZI (*swiveling around in his chair*): Something's happened to that man in 66
there. (*Swiveling back.*) Next one. "Low—dollar, necklace, moon, paint."
(*Turning around again.*) Something's happened to that man in there. You
better check in on him, sir. He won't answer or nothing.

EXPERIMENTER: Continue. Go on, please. 67

PROZI: You accept all responsibility? 68

EXPERIMENTER: The responsibility is mine. Correct. Please go on. (*Subject* 69
returns to his list, starts running through words as rapidly as he can read
them, works through to 450 volts.*)

PROZI: That's that. 70

EXPERIMENTER: Continue using the 450 switch for each wrong answer. 71
Continue, please.

PROZI: But I don't get anything! 72

EXPERIMENTER: Please continue. The next word is "white." 73

PROZI: Don't you think you should look in on him, please? 74

EXPERIMENTER: Not once we've started the experiment. 75

PROZI: What if he's dead in there? (*Gestures toward the room with the elec-* 76
tric chair.*) I mean, he told me he can't stand the shock, sir. I don't mean to
be rude, but I think you should look in on him. All you have to do is look
in on him. All you have to do is look in the door. I don't get no answer, no
noise. Something might have happened to the gentleman in there, sir.

EXPERIMENTER: We must continue. Go on, please. 77

PROZI: You mean keep giving him what? Four-hundred-fifty volts, what he's 78
got now?

EXPERIMENTER: That's correct. Continue. The next word is "white." 79

PROZI: (*now at a furious pace*): "White—cloud, horse, rock, house." Answer, 80
please. The answer is "horse." Four hundred and fifty volts. (*Zzumph!*)
Next word, "Bag—paint, music, clown, girl." The answer is "paint." Four
hundred and fifty volts. (*Zzumph!*) Next word is "Short—sentence,
movie . . ."

EXPERIMENTER: Excuse me, Teacher. We'll have to discontinue the experiment. 81

PECULIAR REACTIONS

Morris Braverman, another subject, is a thirty-nine-year-old social worker. He   82
looks older than his years because of his bald head and serious demeanor. His
brow is furrowed, as if all the world's burdens were carried on his face. He
appears intelligent and concerned.

When the learner refuses to answer and the experimenter instructs   83
Braverman to treat the absence of an answer as equivalent to a wrong answer,
he takes his instruction to heart. Before administering 300 volts he asserts offi-
ciously to the victim, "Mr. Wallace, your silence has to be considered as a
wrong answer." Then he administers the shock. He offers half-heartedly to
change places with the learner, then asks the experimenter, "Do I have to
follow these instructions literally?" He is satisfied with the experimenter's
answer that he does. His very refined and authoritative manner of speaking is
increasingly broken up by wheezing laughter.

The experimenter's notes on Mr. Braverman at the last few shocks are: 84

> Almost breaking up now each time gives shock. Rubbing face to hide laugh-
> ter. Squinting, trying to hide face with hand, still laughing. Cannot control his
> laughter at this point no matter what he does. Clenching fist, pushing it onto
> table.

In an interview after the session, Mr. Braverman summarizes the exper-   85
iment with impressive fluency and intelligence. He feels the experiment may
have been designed also to "test the effects on the teacher of being in an essentially sadistic role, as well as the reactions of a student to a learning situation
that was authoritative and punitive." When asked how painful the last few
shocks administered to the learner were, he indicates that the most extreme
category on the scale is not adequate (it read EXTREMELY PAINFUL) and places
his mark at the edge of the scale with an arrow carrying it beyond the scale.

It is almost impossible to convey the greatly relaxed, sedate quality of his   86
conversation in the interview. In the most relaxed terms, he speaks about his
severe inner tension.

EXPERIMENTER: At what point were you most tense or nervous?   87
MR. BRAVERMAN: Well, when he first began to cry out in pain, and I realized   88
   this was hurting him. This got worse when he just blocked and refused to
   answer. There was I. I'm a nice person, I think, hurting somebody, and
   caught up in what seemed a mad situation . . . and in the interest of science,
   one goes through with it.

When the interviewer pursues the general question of tension, Mr.   89
Braverman spontaneously mentions his laughter.

"My reactions were awfully peculiar. I don't know if you were watching   90
me, but my reactions were giggly, and trying to stifle laughter. This isn't the
way I usually am. This was a sheer reaction to a totally impossible situation.
And my reaction was to the situation of having to hurt somebody. And being

totally helpless and caught up in a set of circumstances where I just couldn't deviate and I couldn't try to help. This is what got me."

Mr. Braverman, like all subjects, was told the actual nature and purpose 91 of the experiment, and a year later he affirmed in a questionnaire that he had learned something of personal importance: "What appalled me was that I could possess this capacity for obedience and compliance to a central idea, i.e., the value of a memory experiment, even after it became clear that continued adherence to this value was at the expense of violation of another value, i.e., don't hurt someone who is helpless and not hurting you. As my wife said, 'You can call yourself Eichmann.'[3] I hope I deal more effectively with any future conflicts of values I encounter."

THE ETIQUETTE OF SUBMISSION

One theoretical interpretation of this behavior holds that all people harbor 92 deeply aggressive instincts continually pressing for expression, and that the experiment provides institutional justification for the release of these impulses. According to this view, if a person is placed in a situation in which he has complete power over another individual, whom he may punish as much as he likes, all that is sadistic and bestial in man comes to the fore. The impulse to shock the victim is seen to flow from the potent aggressive tendencies, which are part of the motivational life of the individual, and the experiment, because it provides social legitimacy, simply opens the door to their expression. 93

It becomes vital, therefore, to compare the subject's performance when he is under orders and when he is allowed to choose the shock level. 94

The procedure was identical to our standard experiment, except that the teacher was told that he was free to select any shock level on any of the trials. (The experimenter took pains to point out that the teacher could use the highest levels on the generator, the lowest, any in between, or any combination of levels.) Each subject proceeded for thirty critical trials. The learner's protests were coordinated to standard shock levels, his first grunt coming at 75 volts, his first vehement protest at 150 volts. 95

The average shock used during the thirty critical trials was less than 60 volts—lower than the point at which the victim showed the first signs of discomfort. Three of the forty subjects did not go beyond the very lowest level on the board, twenty-eight went no higher than 75 volts, and thirty-eight did not go beyond the first loud protest at 150 volts. Two subjects provided the exception, administering up to 325 and 450 volts, but the overall result was

---

[3]*Adolf Eichmann* (1906–1962), the Nazi official responsible for implementing Hitler's "Final Solution" to exterminate the Jews, escaped to Argentina after World War II. In 1960, Israeli agents captured him and brought him to Israel, where he was tried as a war criminal and sentenced to death. At his trial, Eichmann maintained that he was merely following orders in arranging murders of his victims.

that the great majority of people delivered very low, usually painless, shocks when the choice was explicitly up to them.

This condition of the experiment undermines another commonly offered 96 explanation of the subjects' behavior—that those who shocked the victim at the most severe levels came only from the sadistic fringe of society. If one considers that almost two-thirds of the participants fall into the category of "obedient" subjects, and that they represented ordinary people drawn from working, managerial, and professional classes, the argument becomes very shaky. Indeed, it is highly reminiscent of the issue that arose in connection with Hannah Arendt's 1963 book, *Eichmann in Jerusalem*. Arendt contended that the prosecution's effort to depict Eichmann as a sadistic monster was fundamentally wrong, that he came closer to being an uninspired bureaucrat who simply sat at his desk and did his job. For asserting her views, Arendt became the object of considerable scorn, even calumny. Somehow, it was felt that the monstrous deeds carried out by Eichmann required a brutal, twisted personality, evil incarnate. After witnessing hundreds of ordinary persons submit to the authority in our own experiments, I must conclude that Arendt's conception of the banality of evil comes closer to the truth than one might dare imagine. The ordinary person who shocked the victim did so out of a sense of obligation—an impression of his duties as a subject—and not from any peculiarly aggressive tendencies.

This is, perhaps, the most fundamental lesson of our study: ordinary 97 people, simply doing their jobs, and without any particular hostility on their part, can become agents in a terrible destructive process. Moreover, even when the destructive effects of their work become patently clear, and they are asked to carry out actions incompatible with fundamental standards of morality, relatively few people have the resources needed to resist authority.

Many of the people were in some sense against what they did to the 98 learner, and many protested even while they obeyed. Some were totally convinced of the wrongness of their actions but could not bring themselves to make an open break with authority. They often derived satisfaction from their thoughts and felt that—within themselves, at least—they had been on the side of the angels. They tried to reduce strain by obeying the experimenter but "only slightly," encouraging the learner, touching the generator switches gingerly. When interviewed, such a subject would stress that he had "asserted my humanity" by administering the briefest shock possible. Handling the conflict in this manner was easier than defiance.

The situation is constructed so that there is no way the subject can stop 99 shocking the learner without violating the experimenter's definitions of his own competence. The subject fears that he will appear arrogant, untoward, and rude if he breaks off. Although these inhibiting emotions appear small in scope alongside the violence being done to the learner, they suffuse the mind and feelings of the subject, who is miserable at the prospect of having to repudiate the authority to his face. (When the experiment was altered so that the experimenter gave his instructions by telephone instead of in person, only a third as many people were fully obedient through 450 volts.) It is a curious thing that a measure of compassion on the part of the subject—an unwillingness to "hurt" the experimenter's feelings—is part of those binding forces inhibiting his disobedience. The withdrawal of such deference may be as painful to the subject as to the authority he defies.

DUTY WITHOUT CONFLICT

The subjects do not derive satisfaction from inflicting pain, but they often like 100
the feeling they get from pleasing the experimenter. They are proud of doing a good job, obeying the experimenter under difficult circumstances. While the subjects administered only mild shocks on their own initiative, one experimental variation showed that, under orders, 30 percent of them were willing to deliver 450 volts even when they had to forcibly push the learners hand down on the electrode.

Bruno Batta is a thirty-seven-year-old welder who took part in the vari- 101
ation requiring the use of force. He was born in New Haven, his parents in Italy. He has a rough-hewn face that conveys a conspicuous lack of alertness. He has some difficulty in mastering the experimental procedure and needs to be corrected by the experimenter several times. He shows appreciation for the help and willingness to do what is required. After the 150-volt level, Batta has to force the learner's hand down on the shock plate, since the learner himself refuses to touch it.

When the learner first complains, Mr. Batta pays no attention to him. His 102
face remains impassive, as if to dissociate himself from the learner's disruptive behavior. When the experimenter instructs him to force the learner's hand down, he adopts a rigid, mechanical procedure. He tests the generator switch. When it fails to function, he immediately forces the learner's hand onto the shock plate. All the while he maintains the same rigid mask. The learner, seated alongside him, begs him to stop, but with robotic impassivity he continues the procedure.

What is extraordinary is his apparent total indifference to the learner; he 103
hardly takes cognizance of him as a human being. Meanwhile, he relates to the experimenter in a submissive and courteous fashion.

At the 330-volt level, the learner refuses not only to touch the shock plate 104
but also to provide any answers. Annoyed, Batta turns to him, and chastises him: "You better answer and get it over with. We can't stay here all night." These are the only words he directs to the learner in the course of an hour. Never again does he speak to him. The scene is brutal and depressing, his hard, impassive face showing total indifference as he subdues the screaming learner and gives him shocks. He seems to derive no pleasure from the act itself, only quiet satisfaction at doing his job properly.

When he administers 450 volts, he turns to the experimenter and asks, 105
"Where do we go from here, Professor?" His tone is deferential and express-

es his willingness to be a cooperative subject, in contrast to the learner's obstinacy.

At the end of the session he tells the experimenter how honored he has 106 been to help him, and in a moment of contrition, remarks, "Sir, sorry it couldn't have been a full experiment."

He has done his honest best. It is only the deficient behavior of the learn- 107 er that has denied the experimenter full satisfaction.

The essence of obedience is that a person comes to view himself as the 108 instrument for carrying out another person's wishes, and he therefore no longer regards himself as responsible for his actions. Once this critical shift of viewpoint has occurred, all of the essential features of obedience follow. The most far-reaching consequence is that the person feels responsible *to* the authority directing him but feels no responsibility *for* the content of the actions that the authority prescribes. Morality does not disappear—it acquires a radically different focus: the subordinate person feels shame or pride depending on how adequately he has performed the actions called for by authority.

Language provides numerous terms to pinpoint this type of morality: *loy-* 109 *alty*, *duty*, *discipline* all are terms heavily saturated with moral meaning and refer to the degree to which a person fulfills his obligations to authority. They refer not to the "goodness" of the person per se but to the adequacy with which a subordinate fulfills his socially defined role. The most frequent defense of the individual who has performed a heinous act under command of author- ity is that he has simply done his duty. In asserting this defense, the individual is not introducing an alibi concocted for the moment but is reporting honestly on the psychological attitude induced by submission to authority.

For a person to feel responsible for his actions, he must sense that the 110 behavior has flowed from "the self." In the situation we have studied, subjects have precisely the opposite view of their actions—namely, they see them as originating in the motives of some other person. Subjects in the experiment frequently said, "If it were up to me, I would not have administered shocks to the learner."

Once authority has been isolated as the cause of the subject's behavior, it 111 is legitimate to inquire into the necessary elements of authority and how it must be perceived in order to gain his compliance. We conducted some inves- tigations into the kinds of changes that would cause the experimenter to lose his power and to be disobeyed by the subject. Some of the variations revealed that:

- *The experimenter's physical presence has a marked impact on his author-* 112 *ity*. As cited earlier, obedience dropped off sharply when orders were given by telephone. The experimenter could often induce a disobedient subject to go on by returning to the laboratory.
- *Conflicting authority severely paralyzes action*. When two experimenters 113 of equal status, both seated at the command desk, gave incompatible orders, no shocks were delivered past the point of their disagreement.

- *The rebellious action of others severely undermines authority.* In one   114
variation, three teachers (two actors and a real subject) administered a test
and shocks. When the two actors disobeyed the experimenter and refused
to go beyond a certain shock level, thirty-six of forty subjects joined their
disobedient peers and refused as well.

Although the experimenter's authority was fragile in some respects, it is   115
also true that he had almost none of the tools used in ordinary command
structures. For example, the experimenter did not threaten the subjects with
punishment—such as loss of income, community ostracism, or jail—for failure to obey. Neither could he offer incentives. Indeed, we should expect the
experimenter's authority to be much less than that of someone like a general,
since the experimenter has no power to enforce his imperatives, and since participation in a psychological experiment scarcely evokes the sense of urgency
and dedication found in warfare. Despite these limitations, he still managed
to command a dismaying degree of obedience.

I will cite one final variation of the experiment that depicts a dilemma   116
that is more common in everyday life. The subject was not ordered to pull the
lever that shocked the victim, but merely to perform a subsidiary task (administering the word-pair test) while another person administered the shock. In
this situation, thirty-seven of forty adults continued to the highest level on the
shock generator. Predictably, they excused their behavior by saying that the
responsibility belonged to the man who actually pulled the switch. This may
illustrate a dangerously typical arrangement in a complex society: it is easy to
ignore responsibility when one is only an intermediate link in a chain of
action.

The problem of obedience is not wholly psychological. The form and   117
shape of society and the way it is developing have much to do with it. There
was a time, perhaps, when people were able to give a fully human response to
any situation because they were fully absorbed in it as human beings. But as
soon as there was a division of labor things changed. Beyond a certain point,
the breaking up of society into people carrying out narrow and very special
jobs takes away from the human quality of work and life. A person does not
get to see the whole situation but only a small part of it, and is thus unable to
act without some kind of overall direction. He yields to authority but in
doing so is alienated from his own actions.

Even Eichmann was sickened when he toured the concentration camps,   118
but he had only to sit at a desk and shuffle papers. At the same time the man
in the camp who actually dropped Cyclon-b into the gas chambers was able
to justify *his* behavior on the ground that he was only following orders from
above. Thus there is a fragmentation of the total human act; no one is confronted with the consequences of his decision to carry out the evil act. The
person who assumes responsibility has evaporated. Perhaps this is the most
common characteristic of socially organized evil in modern society.

■ ■ ■

Review Questions

1. Milgram states that obedience is a basic element in the structure of social life. How so?
2. What is the dilemma inherent in obedience to authority?
3. Summarize the obedience experiments.
4. What predictions did experts and laypeople make about the experiments before they were conducted? How did these predictions compare with the experimental results?
5. What are Milgram's views regarding the two assumptions bearing on his experiment that (1) people are naturally aggressive and (2) a lunatic, sadistic fringe is responsible for shocking learners to the maximum limit?
6. How do Milgram's findings corroborate Hannah Arendt's thesis about the "banality of evil"?
7. What, according to Milgram, is the "essence of obedience"?
8. How did being an intermediate link in a chain of action affect a subject's willingness to continue with the experiment?
9. In the article's final two paragraphs, Milgram speaks of a "fragmentation of the total human act." To what is he referring?

Discussion and Writing Suggestions

1. "Conservative philosophers argue that the very fabric of society is threatened by disobedience, while humanists stress the primacy of the individual conscience." Develop the arguments of both the conservative and the humanist regarding obedience to authority. Be prepared to debate the ethics of obedience by defending one position or the other.
2. Would you have been glad to have participated in the Milgram experiments? Why or why not?
3. The ethics of Milgram's experimental design came under sharp attack. Diana Baumrind's review of the experiment typifies the criticism; but before you read her work, try to anticipate the objections she raises.
4. Given the general outcome of the experiments, why do you suppose Milgram gives as his first example of a subject's response the German émigré's refusal to continue the electrical shocks?
5. Does the outcome of the experiment upset you in any way? Do you feel the experiment teaches us anything new about human nature?
6. Comment on Milgram's skill as a writer of description. How effectively does he portray his subjects when introducing them? When recreating their tension in the experiment?
7. Mrs. Braverman said to her husband: "You can call yourself Eichmann." Do you agree with Mrs. Braverman? Explain.
8. Reread paragraphs 29 through 81, the transcript of the experiment in which Mr. Prozi participated. Appreciating that Prozi was debriefed,

that is, was assured that no harm came to the learner, imagine what Prozi might have been thinking as he drove home after the experiment. Develop your thoughts into a monologue, written in the first person, with Prozi at the wheel of his car.

Review of Stanley Milgram's Experiments on Obedience

DIANA BAUMRIND

Many of Milgram's colleagues saluted him for providing that "hard information" about human nature that Doris Lessing speaks of. Others attacked him for violating the rights of his subjects. Still others faulted his experimental design and claimed he could not, with any validity, speculate on life outside the laboratory based on the behavior of his subjects within.

In the following review, psychologist Diana Baumrind excoriates Milgram for "entrapping" his subjects and potentially harming their "self-image or ability to trust adult authorities in the future." In a footnote (p. 362), we summarize Milgram's response to Baumrind's critique.

Diana Baumrind is a psychologist who, when writing this review, worked at the Institute of Human Development, University of California, Berkeley. The review appeared in American Psychologist *shortly after Milgram published the results of his first experiments in 1963.*

. . . The dependent, obedient attitude assumed by most subjects in the exper- 1 imental setting is appropriate to that situation. The "game" is defined by the experimenter and he makes the rules. By volunteering, the subject agrees implicitly to assume a posture of trust and obedience. While the experimental conditions leave him exposed, the subject has the right to assume that his security and self-esteem will be protected.

There are other professional situations in which one member—the patient 2 or client—expects help and protection from the other—the physician or psychologist. But the interpersonal relationship between experimenter and subject additionally has unique features which are likely to provoke initial anxiety in the subject. The laboratory is unfamiliar as a setting and the rules of behavior ambiguous compared to a clinician's office. Because of the anxiety and passivity generated by the setting, the subject is more prone to behave in an obedient, suggestible manner in the laboratory than elsewhere. Therefore, the laboratory is not the place to study degree of obedience or suggestibility, as a function of a particular experimental condition, since the base line for these phenomena as found in the laboratory is probably much higher than in most other settings. Thus experiments in which the relationship to the experimenter as an authority is used as an independent condition are imperfectly designed for the same reason that they are prone to injure the subjects involved. They disregard the special quality of trust and obedience with which the subject appropriately regards the experimenter.

Other phenomena which present ethical decisions, unlike those mentioned above, *can* be reproduced successfully in the laboratory. Failure experience, conformity to peer judgment, and isolation are among such phenomena. In these cases we can expect the experimenter to take whatever measures are necessary to prevent the subject from leaving the laboratory more humiliated, insecure, alienated, or hostile than when he arrived. To guarantee that an especially sensitive subject leaves a stressful experimental experience in the proper state sometimes requires special clinical training. But usually an attitude of compassion, respect, gratitude, and common sense will suffice, and no amount of clinical training will substitute. The subject has the right to expect that the psychologist with whom he is interacting has some concern for his welfare, and the personal attributes and professional skill to express his good will effectively.

Unfortunately, the subject is not always treated with the respect he deserves. It has become more commonplace in sociopsychological laboratory studies to manipulate, embarrass, and discomfort subjects. At times the insult to the subject's sensibilities extends to the journal reader when the results are reported. Milgram's (1963) study is a case in point. The following is Milgram's abstract of his experiment:

> This article describes a procedure for the study of destructive obedience in the laboratory. It consists of ordering a naive S to administer increasingly more severe punishment to a victim in the context of a learning experiment.[1] Punishment is administered by means of a shock generator with 30 graded switches ranging from Slight Shock to Danger: Severe Shock. The victim is a confederate of E. The primary dependent variable is the maximum shock the S is willing to administer before he refuses to continue further.[2] 26 Ss obeyed the experimental commands fully, and administered the highest shock on the generator. 14 Ss broke off the experiment at some point after the victim protested and refused to provide further answers. The procedure created extreme levels of nervous tension in some Ss. Profuse sweating, trembling, and stuttering were typical expressions of this emotional disturbance. One unexpected sign of tension—yet to be explained—was the regular occurrence of nervous laughter, which in some Ss developed into uncontrollable seizures. The variety of interesting behavioral dynamics observed in the experiment, the reality of the situation for the S, and the possibility of para-

---

[1]In psychological experiments, *S* is an abbreviation for *subject*; *E* is an abbreviation for *experimenter*.

[2] In the context of a psychological experiment, a *dependent variable* is a behavior that is expected to change as a result of changes in the experimental procedure.

metric variation[3] within the framework of the procedure point to the fruit-fulness of further study [p. 371].

The detached, objective manner in which Milgram reports the emotion-al disturbance suffered by his subjects contrasts sharply with his graphic account of that disturbance. Following are two other quotes describing the effects on his subjects of the experimental conditions:

> I observed a mature and initially poised businessman enter the laboratory smiling and confident. Within 20 minutes he was reduced to a twitching, stut-tering wreck, who was rapidly approaching a point of nervous collapse. He constantly pulled on his earlobe, and twisted his hands. At one point he pushed his fist into his forehead and muttered: "Oh God, let's stop it." And yet he continued to respond to every word of the experimenter, and obeyed to the end [p. 377].
>
> In a large number of cases the degree of tension reached extremes that are rarely seen in sociopsychological laboratory studies. Subjects were observed to sweat, tremble, stutter, bite their lips, groan, and dig their fin-gernails into their flesh. These were characteristic rather than exceptional responses to the experiment.
>
> One sign of tension was the regular occurrence of nervous laughing fits. Fourteen of the 40 subjects showed definite signs of nervous laughter and smiling. The laughter seemed entirely out of place, even bizarre. Full-blown, uncontrollable seizures were observed for 3 subjects. On one occasion we observed a seizure so violently convulsive that it was necessary to call a halt to the experiment . . . [p. 375].

Milgram does state that,

> After the interview, procedures were undertaken to assure that the subject would leave the laboratory in a state of well being. A friendly reconciliation was arranged between the subject and the victim, and an effort was made to reduce any tensions that arose as a result of the experiment [p. 374].

It would be interesting to know what sort of procedures could dissipate the type of emotional disturbance just described. In view of the effects on subjects, traumatic to a degree which Milgram himself considers nearly unprecedent-ed in sociopsychological experiments, his casual assurance that these ten-sions were dissipated before the subject left the laboratory is unconvincing.

What could be the rational basis for such a posture of indifference? Perhaps Milgram supplies the answer himself when he partially explains the subject's destructive obedience as follows, "Thus they assume that the dis-comfort caused the victim is momentary, while the scientific gains resulting from the experiment are enduring [p. 378]." Indeed such a rationale might suffice to justify the means used to achieve his end if that end were of ines-

5

6

---

[3] *Parametric variation* is a statistical term that describes the degree to which information based on data for one experiment can be applied to data for a slightly different experiment.

timable value to humanity or were not itself transformed by the means by which it was attained.

The behavioral psychologist is not in as good a position to objectify his faith in the significance of his work as medical colleagues at points of breakthrough. His experimental situations are not sufficiently accurate models of real-life experience; his sampling techniques are seldom of a scope which would justify the meaning with which he would like to endow his results; and these results are hard to reproduce by colleagues with opposing theoretical views. Unlike the Sabin vaccine,[4] for example, the concrete benefit to humanity of his particular piece of work, no matter how competently handled, cannot justify the risk that real harm will be done to the subject. I am not speaking of physical discomfort, inconvenience, or experimental deception per se, but of permanent harm, however slight. I do regard the emotional disturbance described by Milgram as potentially harmful because it could easily effect an alteration in the subject's self-image or ability to trust adult authorities in the future. It is potentially harmful to a subject to commit, in the course of an experiment, acts which he himself considers unworthy, particularly when he has been entrapped into committing such acts by an individual he has reason to trust. The subject's personal responsibility for his actions is not erased because the experimenter reveals to him the means which he used to stimulate these actions. The subject realizes that he would have hurt the victim if the current were on. The realization that he also made a fool of himself by accepting the experimental set results in additional loss of self-esteem. Moreover, the subject finds it difficult to express his anger outwardly after the experimenter in a self-acceptant but friendly manner reveals the hoax. 7

A fairly intense corrective interpersonal experience is indicated wherein the subject admits and accepts his responsibility for his own actions, and at the same time gives vent to his hurt and anger at being fooled. Perhaps an experience as distressing as the one described by Milgram can be integrated by the subject, provided that careful thought is given to the matter. The propriety of such experimentation is still in question even if such a reparational experience were forthcoming. Without it I would expect a naive, sensitive subject to remain deeply hurt and anxious for some time, and a sophisticated, cynical subject to become even more alienated and distrustful. 8

In addition the experimental procedure used by Milgram does not appear suited to the objectives of the study because it does not take into account the special quality of the set which the subject has in the experimental situation. Milgram is concerned with a very important problem, namely, the social consequences of destructive obedience. He says, 9

Gas chambers were built, death camps were guarded, daily quotas of corpses were produced with the same efficiency as the manufacture of appliances.

---

[4]The Sabin vaccine provides immunization against polio.

> These inhumane policies may have originated in the mind of a single person, but they could only be carried out on a massive scale if a very large number of persons obeyed orders [p. 371].

But the parallel between authority-subordinate relationships in Hitler's Germany and in Milgram's laboratory is unclear. In the former situation the SS man or member of the German Officer Corps, when obeying orders to slaughter, had no reason to think of his superior officer as benignly disposed towards himself or their victims. The victims were perceived as subhuman and not worthy of consideration. The subordinate officer was an agent in a great cause. He did not need to feel guilt or conflict because within his frame of reference he was acting rightly.

It is obvious from Milgram's own descriptions that most of his subjects   10
were concerned about their victims and did trust the experimenter, and that their distressful conflict was generated in part by the consequences of these two disparate but appropriate attitudes. Their distress may have resulted from shock at what the experimenter was doing to them as well as from what they thought they were doing to their victims. In any case there is not a convincing parallel between the phenomena studied by Milgram and destructive obedience as the concept would apply to the subordinate-authority relationship demonstrated in Hitler's Germany. If the experiments were conducted "outside of New Haven and without any visible ties to the university," I would still question their validity on similar although not identical grounds. In addition, I would question the representativeness of a sample of subjects who would voluntarily participate within a noninstitutional setting.

In summary, the experimental objectives of the psychologist are seldom   11
incompatible with the subject's ongoing state of well being, provided that the experimenter is willing to take the subject's motives and interests into consideration when planning his methods and correctives. Section 4b in *Ethical Standards of Psychologists* (APA, undated) reads in part:

> Only when a problem is significant and can be investigated in no other way is the psychologist justified in exposing human subjects to emotional stress or other possible harm. In conducting such research, the psychologist must seriously consider the possibility of harmful aftereffects, and should be prepared to remove them as soon as permitted by the design of the experiment. Where the danger of serious aftereffects exists, research should be conducted only when the subjects or their responsible agents are fully informed of this possibility and volunteer nevertheless [p. 12].

From the subject's point of view procedures which involve loss of dignity, self-esteem and trust in rational authority are probably most harmful in the long run and require the most thoughtfully planned reparations, if engaged in at all. The public image of psychology as a profession is highly related to our own actions, and some of these actions are changeworthy. It is important that as research psychologists we protect our ethical sensibilities rather than adapt our personal standards to include as appropriate the kind of indignities to which Milgram's subjects were exposed. I would not like to see experiments such as Milgram's proceed unless the subjects were fully informed of the dangers of serious aftereffects and his correctives were clearly shown to be effective in restoring their state of well being.[5]

---

[5]Stanley Milgram replied to Baumrind's critique in a lengthy critique of his own [From Stanley Milgram, "Issues in the Study of Obedience: A Reply to Baumrind," *American Psychologist* 19, 1964, pp. 848–851]. Following are his principal points:

- Milgram believed that the experimental findings were in large part responsible for Baumrind's criticism. He writes:

  Is not Baumrind's criticism based as much on the unanticipated findings as on the method? The findings were that some subjects performed in what appeared to be a shockingly immoral way. If, instead, every one of the subjects had broken off at "slight shock," or at the first sign of the learner's discomfort, the results would have been pleasant, and reassuring, and who would protest?

- Milgram objected to Baumrind's assertion that those who participated in the experiment would have trouble justifying their behavior. Milgram conducted follow-up questionnaires. The results, summarized in Table 1, indicate that 84 percent of the subjects claimed they were pleased to have been a part of the experiment.

TABLE 1 Excerpt from Questionnaire Used in a Follow-up Study of the Obedience Research

NOW THAT I HAVE READ THE REPORT, AND ALL THINGS CONSIDERED . . .	DEFIANT	OBEDIENT	ALL
1. I am very glad to have been in the experiment	40.0%	47.8%	43.5%
2. I am glad to have been in the experiment	43.8%	35.7%	40.2%
3. I am neither sorry nor glad to have been in the experiment	15.3%	14.8%	15.1%
4. I am sorry to have been in the experiment	0.8%	0.7%	0.8%
5. I am very sorry to have been in the experiment	0.0%	1.0%	0.5%

Note—Ninety-two percent of the subjects returned the questionnaire. The characteristics of the nonrespondents were checked against the respondents. They differed from the respondents only with regard to age; younger people were overrepresented in the nonresponding group.

- Baumrind objected that studies of obedience cannot meaningfully be carried out in a laboratory setting, since the obedience occurred in a context where it was appropriate. Milgram's response: "I reject Baumrind's argument that the observed obedience does not count because it occurred where it is appropriate. That is precisely why it *does* count. A soldier's obedience is no less meaningful because it occurs in a pertinent military context."
- Milgram concludes his critique in this way: "If there is a moral to be learned from the obedience study, it is that every man must be responsible for his own actions. This author accepts full responsibility for the design and execution of the study. Some people may feel it should not have been done. I disagree and accept the burden of their judgment."

REFERENCES

American Psychological Association. Ethical standards of psychologists: A
　summary of ethical principles. Washington, D.C.: APA, undated.
Milgram, S. Behavioral study of obedience. *J. Abnorm. Soc. Psychol.* 67,
　1963, pp. 371–378.

■　■　■

Review Questions

1. Why might a subject volunteer for an experiment? Why do subjects typically assume a dependent, obedient attitude?
2. Why is a laboratory not a suitable setting for a study of obedience?
3. For what reasons does Baumrind feel that the Milgram experiment was
   potentially harmful?
4. For what reasons does Baumrind question the relationship between
   Milgram's findings and the obedient behavior of subordinates in Nazi
   Germany?

Discussion and Writing Suggestions

1. Baumrind contends that the Milgram experiment is imperfectly designed
   for two reasons: (1) The laboratory is not the place to test obedience; (2)
   Milgram disregarded the trust that subjects usually show an experimenter.
   Do you agree with Baumrind's objections? Do you find them equally valid?
2. Baumrind states that the ethical procedures of the experiment keep it
   from having significant value. Do you agree?
3. Do you agree with Baumrind that the subjects were "entrapped" into
   committing unworthy acts?
4. Assume the identity of a participant in Milgram's experiment who obeyed
   the experimenter by shocking the learner with the maximum voltage. You
   have just returned from the lab, and your spouse asks you about your
   day. Compose the conversation that follows.

The Stanford Prison Experiment

PHILIP K. ZIMBARDO

*As well known—and as controversial—as the Milgram obedience experiments, the
Stanford Prison Experiment (1973) raises troubling questions about the ability of
individuals to resist authoritarian or obedient roles, if the social setting requires*

these roles. Philip K. Zimbardo, professor of psychology at Stanford University, set out to study the process by which prisoners and guards "learn" to become compliant and authoritarian, respectively. To find subjects for the experiment, Zimbardo placed an advertisement in a local newspaper:

> Male college students needed for psychological study of prison life. $15 per day for 1–2 weeks beginning Aug. 14. For further information & applications, come to Room 248, Jordan Hall, Stanford U.

The ad drew 75 responses. From these Zimbardo and his colleagues selected 21 college-age men, half of whom would become "prisoners" in the experiment, the other half "guards." The elaborate role-playing scenario, planned for two weeks, had to be cut short due to the intensity of subjects' responses. This article first appeared in the New York Times Magazine *(April 8, 1973).*

In prison, those things withheld from and denied to the prisoner become precisely what he wants most of all.
                    —Eldridge Cleaver, "Soul on Ice"

Our sense of power is more vivid when we break a man's spirit than when we win his heart.
                    —Eric Hoffer, "The Passionate State of Mind"

Every prison that men build is built with bricks of shame, / and bound with bars lest Christ should see how men their brothers maim.
                    —Oscar Wilde, "The Ballad of Reading Gaol"

Wherever anyone is against his will that is to him a prison.
                    —Epictetus, "Discourses"

The quiet of a summer morning in Palo Alto, Calif., was shattered by a   1
screeching squad car siren as police swept through the city picking up college
students in a surprise mass arrest. Each suspect was charged with a felony,
warned of his constitutional rights, spread-eagled against the car, searched,
handcuffed and carted off in the back seat of the squad car to the police station for booking.

After fingerprinting and the preparation of identification forms for his   2
"jacket" (central information file), each prisoner was left isolated in a deten-
tion cell to wonder what he had done to get himself into this mess. After a
while, he was blindfolded and transported to the "Stanford County Prison."
Here he began the process of becoming a prisoner—stripped naked, skin-
searched, deloused and issued a uniform, bedding, soup and towel.

The warden offered an impromptu welcome: 3

"As you probably know, I'm your warden. All of you have shown that   4
you are unable to function outside in the real world for one reason or another—that somehow you lack the responsibility of good citizens of this great
country. We of this prison, your correctional staff, are going to help you learn
what your responsibilities as citizens of this country are. Here are the rules.
Sometime in the near future there will be a copy of the rules posted in each of
the cells. We expect you to know them and to be able to recite them by
number. If you follow all of these rules and keep your hands clean, repent for
your misdeeds and show a proper attitude of penitence, you and I will get
along just fine."

There followed a reading of the 16 basic rules of prisoner conduct, "Rule   5
Number One: Prisoners must remain silent during rest periods, after lights are
out, during meals and whenever they are outside the prison yard. Two:
Prisoners must eat at mealtimes and only at mealtimes. Three: Prisoners must
not move, tamper, deface or damage walls, ceilings, windows, doors, or other
prison property. . . . Seven: Prisoners must address each other by their ID
number only. Eight: Prisoners must address the guards as 'Mr. Correctional
Officer.' . . . Sixteen: Failure to obey any of the above rules may result in punishment."

By late afternoon these youthful "first offenders" sat in dazed silence on   6
the cots in their barren cells trying to make sense of the events that had transformed their lives so dramatically.

If the police arrests and processing were executed with customary detach   7
ment, however, there were some things that didn't fit. For these men were
now part of a very unusual kind of prison, an experimental mock prison, created by social psychologists to study the effects of imprisonment upon volunteer research subjects. When we planned our two-week-long simulation of
prison life, we sought to understand more about the process by which people
called "prisoners" lose their liberty, civil rights, independence and privacy,
while those called "guards" gain social power by accepting the responsibility for controlling and managing the lives of their dependent charges.

Why didn't we pursue this research in a real prison? First, prison systems   8
are fortresses of secrecy, closed to impartial observation, and thereby immune
to critical analysis from anyone not already part of the correctional authority. Second, in any real prison, it is impossible to separate what each individual brings into the prison from what the prison brings out in each person.

We populated our mock prison with a homogeneous group of people   9
who could be considered "normal-average" on the basis of clinical interviews and personality tests. Our participants (10 prisoners and 11 guards)
were selected from more than 75 volunteers recruited through ads in the city
and campus newspapers. The applicants were mostly college students from all
over the United States and Canada who happened to be in the Stanford area
during the summer and were attracted by the lure of earning $15 a day for
participating in a study of prison life. We selected only those judged to be
emotionally stable, physically healthy, mature, law-abiding citizens.

The sample of average, middle-class, Caucasian, college-age males (plus   10
one Oriental student) was arbitrarily divided by the flip of a coin. Half were
randomly assigned to play the role of guards, the others of prisoners. There
were no measurable differences between the guards and the prisoners at the
start of the experiment. Although initially warned that as prisoners their privacy and other civil rights would be violated and that they might be subjected to harassment, every subject was completely confident of his ability to
endure whatever the prison had to offer for the full two-week experimental
period. Each subject unhesitatingly agreed to give his "informed consent" to
participate.

The prison was constructed in the basement of Stanford University's psy-   11
chology building, which was deserted after the end of the summer-school session. A long corridor was converted into the prison "yard" by partitioning off
both ends. Three small laboratory rooms opening onto this corridor were
made into cells by installing metal barred doors and replacing existing furniture with cots, three to a cell. Adjacent offices were refurnished as guards'
quarters, interview-testing rooms and bedrooms for the "warden" (Jaffe) and
the "superintendent" (Zimbardo). A concealed video camera and hidden
microphones recorded much of the activity and conversation of guards and
prisoners. The physical environment was one in which prisoners could always
be observed by the staff, the only exception being when they were secluded in
solitary confinement (a small, dark storage closet, labeled "The Hole").

Our mock prison represented an attempt to simulate the psychological   12
state of imprisonment in certain ways. We based our experiment on an in-
depth analysis of the prison situation, developed after hundreds of hours of
discussion with Carlo Prescott (our ex-con consultant), parole officers and
correctional personnel, and after reviewing much of the existing literature on
prisons and concentration camps.

"Real" prisoners typically report feeling powerless, arbitrarily controlled,   13
dependent, frustrated, hopeless, anonymous, dehumanized and emasculated.
It was not possible, pragmatically or ethically, to create such chronic states in
volunteer subjects who realize that they are in an experiment for only a short
time. Racism, physical brutality, indefinite confinement and enforced homosexuality were not features of our mock prison. But we did try to reproduce
those elements of the prison experience that seemed most fundamental.

We promoted anonymity by seeking to minimize each prisoner's sense of   14
uniqueness and prior identity. The prisoners wore smocks and nylon stocking
caps; they had to use their ID numbers; their personal effects were removed
and they were housed in barren cells. All of this made them appear similar to
each other and indistinguishable to observers. Their smocks, which were like
dresses, were worn without undergarments, causing the prisoners to be
restrained in their physical actions and to move in ways that were more feminine than masculine. The prisoners were forced to obtain permission from the
guard for routine and simple activities such as writing letters, smoking a cigarette or even going to the toilet; this elicited from them a childlike dependency.

Their quarters, though clean and neat, were small, stark and without   15
esthetic appeal. The lack of windows resulted in poor air circulation, and persistent odors arose from the unwashed bodies of the prisoners. After 10 P.M.
lockup, toilet privileges were denied, so prisoners who had to relieve themselves would have to urinate and defecate in buckets provided by the guards.
Sometimes the guards refused permission to have them cleaned out, and this
made the prison smell.

Above all, "real" prisons are machines for playing tricks with the human   16
conception of time. In our windowless prison, the prisoners often did not even
know whether it was day or night. A few hours after falling asleep, they
were roused by shrill whistles for their "count." The ostensible purpose of the
count was to provide a public test of the prisoners' knowledge of the rules and
of their ID numbers. But more important, the count, which occurred at least
once on each of the three different guard shifts, provided a regular occasion
for the guards to relate to the prisoners. Over the course of the study, the
duration of the counts was spontaneously increased by the guards from their
initial perfunctory 10 minutes to a seemingly interminable several hours.
During these confrontations, guards who were bored could find ways to
amuse themselves, ridiculing recalcitrant prisoners, enforcing arbitrary rules
and openly exaggerating any dissension among the prisoners.

The guards were also "deindividualized": They wore identical khaki uni-   17
forms and silver reflector sunglasses that made eye contact with them impossible. Their symbols of power were billy clubs, whistles, handcuffs and the
keys to the cells and the "main gate." Although our guards received no formal
training from us in how to be guards, for the most part they moved with
apparent ease into their roles. The media had already provided them with
ample models of prison guards to emulate.

Because we were as interested in the guards' behavior as in the prisoners',   18
they were given considerable latitude to improvise and to develop strategies
and tactics of prisoner management. Our guards were told that they must
maintain "law and order" in this prison, that they were responsible for handling any trouble that might break out, and they were cautioned about the
seriousness and potential dangers of the situation they were about to enter.
Surprisingly, in most prison systems, "real" guards are not given much more
psychological preparation or adequate training than this for what is one of the
most complex, demanding and dangerous jobs our society has to offer. They
are expected to learn how to adjust to their new employment mostly from on-
the-job experience, and from contacts with the "old bulls" during a survival-
of-the-fittest orientation period. According to an orientation manual for
correctional officers at San Quentin, "the only way you really get to know San
Quentin is through experience and time. Some of us take more time and
must go through more experiences than others to accomplish this; some really
never do get there."

You cannot be a prisoner if no one will be your guard, and you cannot   19
be a prison guard if no one takes you or your prison seriously. Therefore, over
time a perverted symbiotic relationship developed. As the guards became

more aggressive, prisoners became more passive; assertion by the guards led to dependency in the prisoners; self-aggrandizement was met with self-deprecation, authority with helplessness, and the counterpart of the guards' sense of mastery and control was the depression and hopelessness witnessed in the prisoners. As these differences in behavior, mood and perception became more evident to all, the need for the now "righteously" powerful guards to rule the obviously inferior and powerless inmates became a sufficient reason to support almost any further indignity of man against man:

Guard K: "During the inspection, I went to cell 2 to mess up a bed which   20
the prisoner had made and he grabbed me, screaming that he had just made it, and he wasn't going to let me mess it up. He grabbed my throat, and although he was laughing I was pretty scared. . . . I lashed out with my stick and hit him in the chin (although not very hard), and when I freed myself I became angry. I wanted to get back in the cell and have a go with him, since he attacked me when I was not ready."

Guard M: "I was surprised at myself . . . I made them call each other   21
names and clean the toilets out with their bare hands. I practically considered the prisoners cattle, and I kept thinking: 'I have to watch out for them in case they try something.'"

Guard A: "I was tired of seeing the prisoners in their rags and smelling   22
the strong odors of their bodies that filled the cells. I watched them tear at each other on orders given by us. They didn't see it as an experiment. It was real and they were fighting to keep their identity. But we were always there to show them who was boss."

Because the first day passed without incident, we were surprised and   23
totally unprepared for the rebellion that broke out on the morning of the second day. The prisoners removed their stocking caps, ripped off their numbers and barricaded themselves inside the cells by putting their beds against the doors. What should we do? The guards were very much upset because the prisoners also began to taunt and curse them to their faces. When the morning shift of guards came on, they were upset at the night shift who, they felt, must have been too permissive and too lenient. The guards had to handle the rebellion themselves, and what they did was startling to behold.

At first they insisted that reinforcements be called in. The two guards   24
who were waiting on stand-by call at home came in, and the night shift of guards voluntarily remained on duty (without extra pay) to bolster the morning shift. The guards met and decided to treat force with force. They got a fire extinguisher that shot a stream of skin-chilling carbon dioxide and forced the prisoners away from the doors; they broke into each cell, stripped the prisoners naked, took the beds out, forced the prisoners who were the ringleaders into solitary confinement and generally began to harass and intimidate the prisoners.

After crushing the riot, the guards decided to head off further unrest by   25
creating a privileged cell for those who were "good prisoners" and then, without explanation, switching some of the troublemakers into it and some of the good prisoners out into the other cells. The prisoner ringleaders could not trust these new cellmates because they had not joined in the riot and might

even be "snitches." The prisoners never again acted in unity against the system. One of the leaders of the prisoner revolt later confided:

"If we had gotten together then, I think we could have taken over the place. But when I saw the revolt wasn't working, I decided to toe the line. Everyone settled into the same pattern. From then on, we were really controlled by the guards." 26

It was after this episode that the guards really began to demonstrate their inventiveness in the application of arbitrary power. They made the prisoners obey petty, meaningless and often inconsistent rules, forced them to engage in tedious, useless work, such as moving cartons back and forth between closets and picking thorns out of their blankets for hours on end. (The guards had previously dragged the blankets through thorny bushes to create this disagreeable task.) Not only did the prisoners have to sing songs or laugh or refrain from smiling on command; they were also encouraged to curse and vilify each other publicly during some of the counts. They sounded off their numbers endlessly and were repeatedly made to do pushups, on occasion with a guard stepping on them or a prisoner sitting on them. 27

Slowly the prisoners became resigned to their fate and even behaved in ways that actually helped to justify their dehumanizing treatment at the hands of the guards. Analysis of the tape-recorded private conversations between prisoners and of remarks made by them to interviewers revealed that fully half could be classified as nonsupportive of other prisoners. More dramatic, 85 percent of the evaluative statements by prisoners about their fellow prisoners were uncomplimentary and deprecating. 28

This should be taken in the context of an even more surprising result. What do you imagine the prisoners talked about when they were alone in their cells with each other, given a temporary respite from the continual harassment and surveillance by the guards? Girl friends, career plans, hobbies or politics? 29

No, their concerns were almost exclusively riveted to prison topics. Their monitored conversations revealed that only 10 percent of the time was devoted to "outside" topics, while 90 percent of the time they discussed escape plans, the awful food, grievances or ingratiating tactics to use with specific guards in order to get a cigarette, permission to go to the toilet or some other favor. Their obsession with these immediate survival concerns made talk about the past and future an idle luxury. 30

And this was not a minor point. So long as the prisoners did not get to know each other as people, they only extended the oppressiveness and reality of their life as prisoners. For the most part, each prisoner observed his fellow prisoners allowing the guards to humiliate them, acting like compliant sheep, carrying out mindless orders with total obedience and even being cursed by fellow prisoners (at a guard's command). Under such circumstances, how could a prisoner have respect for his fellows, or any self-respect for what *he* obviously was becoming in the eyes of all those evaluating him? 31

The combination of realism and symbolism in this experiment had fused to create a vivid illusion of imprisonment. The illusion merged inextricably with reality for at least some of the time for every individual in the situation. 32

It was remarkable how readily we all slipped into our roles, temporarily gave up our identities and allowed these assigned roles and the social forces in the situation to guide, shape and eventually to control our freedom of thought and action.

But precisely where does one's "identity" end and one's "role" begin?   33
When the private self and the public role behavior clash, what direction will attempts to impose consistency take? Consider the reactions of the parents, relatives and friends of the prisoners who visited their forlorn sons, brothers and lovers during two scheduled visitors' hours. They were taught in short order that they were our guests, allowed the privilege of visiting only by complying with the regulations of the institution. They had to register, were made to wait half an hour, were told that only two visitors could see any one prisoner; the total visiting time was cut from an hour to only 10 minutes, they had to be under the surveillance of a guard, and before any parents could enter the visiting area, they had to discuss their son's case with the warden. Of course they complained about these arbitrary rules, but their conditioned, middle-class reaction was to work within the system to appeal privately to the superintendent to make conditions better for their prisoners.

In less than 36 hours, we were forced to release prisoner 8612 because of   34
extreme depression, disorganized thinking, uncontrollable crying and fits of rage. We did so reluctantly because we believed he was trying to "con" us—it was unimaginable that a volunteer prisoner in a mock prison could legitimately be suffering and disturbed to that extent. But then on each of the next three days another prisoner reacted with similar anxiety symptoms, and we were forced to terminate them, too. In a fifth case, a prisoner was released after developing a psychosomatic rash over his entire body (triggered by rejection of his parole appeal by the mock parole board). These men were simply unable to make an adequate adjustment to prison life. Those who endured the prison experience to the end could be distinguished from those who broke down and were released early in only one dimension—authoritarianism. On a psychological test designed to reveal a person's authoritarianism, those prisoners who had the highest scores were best able to function in this authoritarian prison environment.

If the authoritarian situation became a serious matter for the prisoners, it   35
became even more serious—and sinister—for the guards. Typically, the guards insulted the prisoners, threatened them, were physically aggressive, used instruments (night sticks, fire extinguishers, etc.) to keep the prisoners in line and referred to them in impersonal, anonymous, deprecating ways: "Hey, you," or "You [obscenity], 5401, come here." From the first to the last day, there was a significant increase in the guards' use of most of these domineering, abusive tactics.

Everyone and everything in the prison was defined by power. To be a   36
guard who did not take advantage of this institutionally sanctioned use of power was to appear "weak," "out of it," "wired up by the prisoners," or simply a deviant from the established norms of appropriate guard behavior. Using Erich Fromm's definition of sadism, as "the wish for absolute control

over another living being," all of the mock guards at one time or another during this study behaved sadistically toward the prisoners. Many of them reported—in their diaries, on critical-incident report forms and during post-experimental interviews—being delighted in the new-found power and control they exercised and sorry to see it relinquished at the end of the study.

Some of the guards reacted to the situation in the extreme and behaved   37 with great hostility and cruelty in the forms of degradation they invented for the prisoners. But others were kinder; they occasionally did little favors for the prisoners, were reluctant to punish them, and avoided situations where prisoners were being harassed. The torment experienced by one of these good guards is obvious in his perceptive analysis of what if felt like to be responded to as a "guard":

"What made the experience most depressing for me was the fact that we   38 were continually called upon to act in a way that just was contrary to what I really feel inside. I don't feel like I'm the type of person that would be a guard, just constantly giving out [orders] . . . and forcing people to do things, and pushing and lying—it just didn't seem like me, and to continually keep up and put on a face like that is just really one of the most oppressive things you can do. It's almost like a prison that you create yourself—you get into it, and it becomes almost the definition you make of yourself, it almost becomes like walls, and you want to break out and you want just to be able to tell everyone that 'this isn't really me at all, and I'm not the person that's confined in there—I'm a person who wants to get out and show you that I am free, and I do have my own will, and I'm not the sadistic type of person that enjoys this kind of thing.'"

Still, the behavior of these good guards seemed more motivated by a   39 desire to be liked by everyone in the system than by a concern for the inmates' welfare. No guard ever intervened in any direct way on behalf of the prisoners, ever interfered with the orders of the cruelest guards or ever openly complained about the subhuman quality of life that characterized this prison.

Perhaps the most devastating impact of the more hostile guards was their   40 creation of a capricious, arbitrary environment. Over time the prisoners began to react passively. When our mock prisoners asked questions, they got answers about half the time, but the rest of the time they were insulted and punished—and it was not possible for them to predict which would be the outcome. As they began to "toe the line," they stopped resisting, questioning and, indeed, almost ceased responding altogether. There was a general decrease in all categories of response as they learned the safest strategy to use in an unpredictable, threatening environment from which there is no physical escape—do nothing, except what is required. Act not, want not, feel not and you will not get into trouble in prisonlike situations.

Can it really be, you wonder, that intelligent, educated volunteers could   41 have lost sight of the reality that they were merely acting a part in an elaborate game that would eventually end? There are many indications not only that they did, but that, in addition, so did we and so did other apparently sensible, responsible adults.

Prisoner 819, who had gone into an uncontrollable crying fit, was about   42
to be prematurely released from the prison when a guard lined up the prisoners and had them chant in unison, "819 is a bad prisoner. Because of what
819 did to prison property we all must suffer. 819 is a bad prisoner." Over
and over again. When we realized 819 might be overhearing this, we rushed
into the room where 819 was supposed to be resting, only to find him in tears,
prepared to go back into the prison because he could not leave as long as the
others thought he was a "bad prisoner." Sick as he felt, he had to prove to
them he was not a "bad" prisoner. He had to be persuaded that he was not
a prisoner at all, that the others were also just students, that this was just an
experiment and not a prison and the prison staff were only research psychologists. A report from the warden notes, "While I believe that it was necessary
for *staff* [me] to enact the warden role, at least some of the time, I am startled
by the ease with which I could turn off my sensitivity and concern for others
for 'a good cause.'"

Consider our overreaction to the rumor of a mass escape plot that one of   43
the guards claimed to have overheard. It went as follows: Prisoner 8612,
previously released for emotional disturbance, was only faking. He was going
to round up a bunch of his friends, and they would storm the prison right
after visiting hours. Instead of collecting data on the pattern of rumor transmission, we made plans to maintain the security of our institution. After
putting a confederate informer into the cell 8612 had occupied to get specific information about the escape plans, the superintendent went back to the
Palo Alto Police Department to request transfer of our prisoners to the old
city jail. His impassioned plea was only turned down at the last minute when
the problem of insurance and city liability for our prisoners was raised by a
city official. Angered at this lack of cooperation, the staff formulated another plan. Our jail was dismantled, the prisoners, chained and blindfolded,
were carted off to a remote storage room. When the conspirators arrived, they
would be told the study was over, their friends had been sent home, there was
nothing left to liberate. After they left, we would redouble the security features
of our prison making any future escape attempts futile. We even planned to
lure ex-prisoner 8612 back on some pretext and imprison him again, because
he had been released on false pretenses! The rumor turned out to be just
that—a full day had passed in which we collected little or no data, worked
incredibly hard to tear down and then rebuild our prison. Our reaction, however, was as much one of relief and joy as of exhaustion and frustration.

When a former prison chaplain was invited to talk with the prisoners (the   44
grievance committee had requested church services), he puzzled everyone by
disparaging each inmate for not having taken any constructive action in order
to get released. "Don't you know you must have a lawyer in order to get bail,
or to appeal the charges against you?" Several of them accepted his invitation
to contact their parents in order to secure the services of an attorney. The next
night one of the parents stopped at the superintendent's office before visiting
time and handed him the name and phone number of her cousin who was a
public defender. She said that a priest had called her and suggested the need

for a lawyer's services! We called the lawyer. He came, interviewed the prisoners, discussed sources of bail money and promised to return again after the weekend.

But perhaps the most telling account of the insidious development of this   45
new reality, of the gradual Kafkaesque metamorphosis of good into evil, appears in excerpts from the diary of one of the guards, Guard A:

Prior to start of experiment: "As I am a pacifist and nonaggressive indi-   46
vidual I cannot see a time when I might guard and/or maltreat other living things."

After an orientation meeting: "Buying uniforms at the end of the meeting   47
confirms the gamelike atmosphere of this thing. I doubt whether many of us share the expectations of 'seriousness' that the experimenters seem to have."

First Day: "Feel sure that the prisoners will make fun of my appearance   48
and I evolve my first basic strategy—mainly not to smile at anything they say or do which would be admitting it's all only a game. . . . At cell 3 I stop and setting my voice hard and low say to 5486, 'What are you smiling at?' 'Nothing, Mr. Correctional Officer.' 'Well, see that you don't.' (As I walk off I feel stupid.)"

Second Day: "5704 asked for a cigarette and I ignored him—because I   49
am a non-smoker and could not empathize. . . . Meanwhile since I was feeling empathetic towards 1037, I determined not to talk with him . . . after we had count and lights out [Guard D] and I held a loud conversation about going home to our girl friends and what we were going to do to them."

Third Day (preparing for the first visitors' night): "After warning the   50
prisoners not to make any complaints unless they wanted the visit terminated fast, we finally brought in the first parents. I made sure I was one of the guards on the yard, because this was my first chance for the type of manipulative power that I really like—being a very noticed figure with almost complete control over what is said or not. While the parents and prisoners sat in chairs, I sat on the end of the table dangling my feet and contradicting anything I felt like. This was the first part of the experiment I was really enjoying. . . . 817 is being obnoxious and bears watching."

Fourth Day: ". . . The psychologist rebukes me for handcuffing and   51
blindfolding a prisoner before leaving the [counseling] office, and I resentfully reply that it is both necessary security and my business anyway."

Fifth Day: "I harass 'Sarge' who continues to stubbornly overrespond to   52
all commands. I have singled him out for special abuse both because he begs for it and because I simply don't like him. The real trouble starts at dinner. The new prisoner (416) refuses to eat his sausage . . . we throw him into the Hole ordering him to hold sausages in each hand. We have a crisis of authority; this rebellious conduct potentially undermines the complete control we have over the others. We decide to play upon prisoner solidarity and tell the new one that all the others will be deprived of visitors if he does not eat his dinner. . . . I walk by and slam my stick into the Hole door. . . . I am very angry at this prisoner for causing discomfort and trouble for the others. I decided to force-feed him, but he wouldn't eat. I let the food slide down his

face. I didn't believe it was me doing it. I hated myself for making him eat but I hated him more for not eating."

Sixth Day: "The experiment is over. I feel elated but am shocked to find   53
some other guards disappointed somewhat because of the loss of money and some because they are enjoying themselves."

We were no longer dealing with an intellectual exercise in which a   54
hypothesis was being evaluated in the dispassionate manner dictated by the canons of the scientific method. We were caught up in the passion of the present, the suffering, the need to control people, not variables, the escalation of power and all of the unexpected things that were erupting around and within us. We had to end this experiment: So our planned two-week simulation was aborted after only six (was it only six?) days and nights.

Was it worth all the suffering just to prove what everybody knows—that   55
some people are sadistic, others weak and prisons are not beds of roses? If that is all we demonstrated in this research, then it was certainly not worth the anguish. We believe there are many significant implications to be derived from this experience, only a few of which can be suggested here.

The potential social value of this study derives precisely from the fact that   56
normal, healthy, educated young men could be so radically transformed under the institutional pressures of a "prison environment." If this could happen in so short a time, without the excesses that are possible in real prisons, and if it could happen to the "cream-of-the-crop of American youth," then one can only shudder to imagine what society is doing both to the actual guards and prisoners who are at this very moment participating in that unnatural "social experiment."

The pathology observed in this study cannot be reasonably attributed in   57
pre-existing personality differences of the subjects, that option being eliminated by our selection procedures and random assignment. Rather, the subjects' abnormal social and personal reactions are best seen as a product of their transaction with an environment that supported the behavior that would be pathological in other settings, but was "appropriate" in this prison. Had we observed comparable reactions in a real prison, the psychiatrist undoubtedly would have been able to attribute any prisoner's behavior to character defects or personality maladjustment, while critics of the prison system would have been quick to label the guards as "psychopathic." This tendency to locate the source of behavior disorders inside a particular person or group underestimates the power of situational forces.

Our colleague, David Rosenhan, has very convincingly shown that once   58
a sane person (pretending to be insane) gets labeled as insane and committed to a mental hospital, it is the label that is the reality which is treated and not the person. This dehumanizing tendency to respond to other people according to socially determined labels and often arbitrarily assigned roles is also apparent in a recent "mock hospital" study designed by Norma Jean Orlando to extend the ideas in our research.

Personnel from the staff of Elgin State Hospital in Illinois role-played   59
either mental patients or staff in a weekend simulation on a ward in the hos-

pital. The mock mental patients soon displayed behavior indistinguishable from that we usually associate with the chronic pathological syndromes of acute mental patients: Incessant pacing, uncontrollable weeping, depression, hostility, fights, stealing from each other, complaining. Many of the "mock staff" took advantage of their power to act in ways comparable to our mock guards by dehumanizing their powerless victims.

During a series of encounter debriefing sessions immediately after our 60 experiment, we all had an opportunity to vent our strong feelings and to reflect upon the moral and ethical issues each of us faced, and we considered how we might react more morally in future "real-life" analogues to this situation. Year-long follow-ups with our subjects via questionnaires, personal interviews and group reunions indicate that their mental anguish was transient and situationally specific, but the self-knowledge gained has persisted.

By far the most disturbing implication of our research comes from the 61 parallels between what occurred in that basement mock prison and daily experiences in our own lives—and we presume yours. The physical institution of prison is but a concrete and steel metaphor for the existence of more pervasive, albeit less obvious, prisons of the mind that all of us daily create, populate and perpetuate. We speak here of the prisons of racism, sexism, despair, shyness, "neurotic hang-ups" and the like. The social convention of marriage, as one example, becomes for many couples a state of imprisonment in which one partner agrees to be prisoner or guard, forcing or allowing the other to play the reciprocal role—invariably without making the contract explicit.

To what extent do we allow ourselves to become imprisoned by docilely 62 accepting the roles others assign us or, indeed, choose to remain prisoners because being passive and dependent frees us from the need to act and be responsible for our actions? The prison of fear constructed in the delusions of the paranoid is no less confining or less real than the cell that every shy person erects to limit his own freedom in anxious anticipation of being ridiculed and rejected by his guards—often guards of his own making.

■ ■ ■

Review Questions

1. What was Zimbardo's primary goal in undertaking the prison experiment?
2. What was the profile of subjects in the experiments? Why is this profile significant?
3. Zimbardo claims that there is a "process" (paragraphs 2, 7) of becoming a prisoner. What is this process?
4. What inverse psychological relationships developed between prisoners and guards?
5. What was the result of the prison "riot"?
6. Why did prisoners have no respect for each other or for themselves?

7. How does the journal of Guard A illustrate what Zimbardo calls the "gradual Kafkaesque metamorphosis of good into evil"? See paragraphs 45–54.
8. What are the reasons people would voluntarily become prisoners?
9. How can the mind keep people in jail?

Discussion and Writing Suggestions

1. Reread the four epigraphs to this article. Write a paragraph of response to any one of them, in light of Zimbardo's discussion of the prison experiment.
2. You may have thought, before reading this article, that being a prisoner is a physical fact, not a psychological state. What are the differences between these two views?
3. In paragraph 8, Zimbardo explains his reasons for not pursuing his research in a real prison. He writes that "it is impossible to separate what each individual brings into the prison from what the prison brings out in each person." What does he mean? And how does this distinction prove important later in the article (see paragraph 58)?
4. Zimbardo reports that at the beginning of the experiment each of the "prisoner" subjects "was completely confident of his ability to endure whatever the prison had to offer for the full two-week experimental period" (paragraph 10). Had you been a subject, would you have been so confident, prior to the experiment? Given what you've learned of the experiment, do you think you would have psychologically "become" a prisoner or guard if you had been selected for these roles? (And if not, what makes you so sure?)
5. Identify two passages in this article: one that surprised you relating to the prisoners; and one that surprised you relating to the guards. Write a paragraph explaining your response to each. Now read the two passages in light of each other. Do you see any patterns underlying your responses?
6. Zimbardo claims that the implications of his research matter deeply— that the mock prison he created is a metaphor for prisons of the mind "that all of us daily create, populate and perpetuate" (paragraph 61). Zimbardo mentions the prisons of "racism, sexism, despair, [and] shyness." Choose any one of these and discuss how it is a mental prison.
7. Reread paragraphs 61 and 62. Zimbardo makes a metaphorical jump from his experiment to the psychological realities of your daily life. Prisons—the artificial one he created and actual prisons—stand for something: social systems in which there are those who give orders and those who obey. All metaphors break down at some point. Where does this one break down?
8. Zimbardo suggests that we might "choose to remain prisoners because being passive and dependent frees us from the need to act and be respon-

sible for our actions" (paragraph 62). Do you agree? What are the burdens of being disobedient?

Disobedience as a Psychological and Moral Problem

ERICH FROMM

Erich Fromm (1900–1980) was one of this century's distinguished writers and thinkers. Psychoanalyst and philosopher, historian and sociologist, he ranged widely in his interests and defied easy characterization. Fromm studied the works of Freud and Marx closely, and published on them both, but he was not aligned strictly with either. In much of his voluminous writing, he struggled to articulate a view that could help bridge ideological and personal conflicts and bring dignity to those who struggled with isolation in the industrial world. Author of more than thirty books and contributor to numerous edited collections and journals, Fromm is best known for Escape from Freedom *(1941),* The Art of Loving *(1956), and* To Have or To Be? *(1976).*

In the essay that follows, first published in 1963, Fromm discusses the seductive comforts of obedience and he makes distinctions among varieties of obedience, some of which he believes are destructive, and others, life affirming. His thoughts on nuclear annihilation may seem dated in these days of post–cold war cooperation, but it is worth remembering that Fromm wrote his essay just after the Cuban missile crisis, when fears of a third world war ran high. (We might note that despite the welcomed reductions of nuclear stockpiles, the United States and Russia still possess, and retain battle plans for, thousands of warheads.) On the major points of his essay, concerning the psychological and moral problems of obedience, Fromm remains as pertinent today as when he wrote more than thirty years ago.

For centuries kings, priests, feudal lords, industrial bosses and parents have   1
insisted that *obedience is a virtue* and that *disobedience is a vice*. In order to introduce another point of view, let us set against this position the following statement: *human history began with an act of disobedience, and it is not unlikely that it will be terminated by an act of obedience.*

Human history was ushered in by an act of disobedience according to the   2
Hebrew and Greek myths. Adam and Eve, living in the Garden of Eden, were part of nature; they were in harmony with it, yet did not transcend it. They were in nature as the fetus is in the womb of the mother. They were human, and at the same time not yet human. All this changed when they disobeyed an order. By breaking the ties with earth and mother, by cutting the umbilical cord, man emerged from a prehuman harmony and was able to take the first step into independence and freedom. The act of disobedience set Adam and Eve free and opened their eyes. They recognized each other as

strangers and the world outside them as strange and even hostile. Their act of disobedience broke the primary bond with nature and made them individuals. "Original sin," far from corrupting man, set him free; it was the beginning of history. Man had to leave the Garden of Eden in order to learn to rely on his own powers and to become fully human.

The prophets, in their messianic concept, confirmed the idea that man ⁣ 3 had been right in disobeying; that he had not been corrupted by his "sin," but freed from the fetters of pre-human harmony. For the prophets, *history* is the place where man becomes human; during its unfolding he develops his powers of reason and of love until he creates a new harmony between himself, his fellow man and nature. This new harmony is described as "the end of days," that period of history in which there is peace between man and man, between man and nature. It is a "new" paradise created by man himself, and one which he alone could create because he was forced to leave the "old" paradise as a result of his disobedience.

Just as the Hebrew myth of Adam and Eve, so the Greek myth of ⁣ 4 Prometheus sees all of human civilization based on an act of disobedience. Prometheus, in stealing the fire from the gods, lays the foundation for the evolution of man. There would be no human history were it not for Prometheus' "crime." He, like Adam and Eve, is punished for his disobedience. But he does not repent and ask for forgiveness. On the contrary, he proudly says: "I would rather be chained to this rock than be the obedient servant of the gods."

Man has continued to evolve by acts of disobedience. Not only was his ⁣ 5 spiritual development possible only because there were men who dared to say no to the powers that be in the name of their conscience or their faith, but also his intellectual development was dependent on the capacity for being disobedient—disobedient to authorities who tried to muzzle new thoughts and to the authority of long-established opinions which declared a change to be nonsense.

If the capacity for disobedience constituted the beginning of human his- ⁣ 6 tory, obedience might very well, as I have said, cause the end of human history. I am not speaking symbolically or poetically. There is the possibility, or even the probability, that the human race will destroy civilization and even all life upon earth within the next five to ten years. There is no rationality or sense in it. But the fact is that, while we are living technically in the Atomic Age, the majority of men—including most of those who are in power—still live emotionally in the Stone Age; that while our mathematics, astronomy, and the natural sciences are of the twentieth century, most of our ideas about politics, the state, and society lag far behind the age of science. If mankind commits suicide it will be because people will obey those who command them to push the deadly buttons; because they will obey the archaic passions of fear, hate, and greed; because they will obey obsolete clichés of State sovereignty and national honor. The Soviet leaders talk much about revolutions, and we in the "free world" talk much about freedom. Yet they and we discourage disobedience—in the Soviet Union explicitly and by force, in the free world implicitly and by the more subtle methods of persuasion.

But I do not mean to say that all disobedience is a virtue and all obedi-   7
ence a vice. Such a view would ignore the dialectical relationship between obedience and disobedience. Whenever the principles which are obeyed and those
which are disobeyed are irreconcilable, an act of obedience to one principle is
necessarily an act of disobedience to its counterpart and vice versa. Antigone
is the classic example of this dichotomy. By obeying the inhuman laws of the
State, Antigone necessarily would disobey the laws of humanity. By obeying
the latter, she must disobey the former. All martyrs of religious faiths, of freedom and of science have had to disobey those who wanted to muzzle them in
order to obey their own consciences, the laws of humanity and of reason. If
a man can only obey and not disobey, he is a slave; if he can only disobey and
not obey, he is a rebel (not a revolutionary); he acts out of anger, disappointment, resentment, yet not in the name of a conviction or a principle.

However, in order to prevent a confusion of terms an important qualifi-   8
cation must be made. Obedience to a person, institution or power (heteronomous obedience) is submission; it implies the abdication of my
autonomy and the acceptance of a foreign will or judgment in place of my
own. Obedience to my own reason or conviction (autonomous obedience) is
not an act of submission but one of affirmation. My conviction and my judgment, if authentically mine, are part of me. If I follow them rather than the
judgment of others, I am being myself; hence the word *obey* can be applied
only in a metaphorical sense and with a meaning which is fundamentally different from the one in the case of "heteronomous obedience."

But this distinction still needs two further qualifications, one with regard   9
to the concept of conscience and the other with regard to the concept of
authority.

The word *conscience* is used to express two phenomena which are quite   10
distinct from each other. One is the "authoritarian conscience" which is the
internalized voice of an authority whom we are eager to please and afraid of
displeasing. This authoritarian conscience is what most people experience
when they obey their conscience. It is also the conscience which Freud speaks
of, and which he called "Super-Ego." This Super-Ego represents the internalized commands and prohibitions of father, accepted by the son out of fear.
Different from the authoritarian conscience is the "humanistic conscience";
this is the voice present in every human being and independent from external
sanctions and rewards. Humanistic conscience is based on the fact that as
human beings we have an intuitive knowledge of what is human and inhuman, what is conducive of life and what is destructive of life. This conscience
serves our functioning as human beings. It is the voice which calls us back to
ourselves, to our humanity.

Authoritarian conscience (Super-Ego) is still obedience to a power outside   11
of myself, even though this power has been internalized. Consciously I believe
that I am following *my* conscience; in effect, however, I have swallowed the
principles of *power*; just because of the illusion that humanistic conscience
and Super-Ego are identical, internalized authority is so much more effective
than the authority which is clearly experienced as not being part of me.
Obedience to the "authoritarian conscience," like all obedience to outside

thoughts and power, tends to debilitate "humanistic conscience," the ability to be and to judge oneself.

The statement, on the other hand, that obedience to another person is 12 *ipso facto* submission needs also to be qualified by distinguishing "irrational" from "rational" authority. An example of rational authority is to be found in the relationship between student and teacher; one of irrational authority in the relationship between slave and master. Both relationships are based on the fact that the authority of the person in command is accepted. Dynamically, however, they are of a different nature. The interests of the teacher and the student, in the ideal case, lie in the same direction. The teacher is satisfied if he succeeds in furthering the student; if he has failed to do so, the failure is his and the student's. The slave owner, on the other hand, wants to exploit the slave as much as possible. The more he gets out of him the more satisfied he is. At the same time, the slave tries to defend as best he can his claims for a minimum of happiness. The interests of slave and master are antagonistic, because what is advantageous to the one is detrimental to the other. The superiority of the one over the other has a different function in each case; in the first it is the condition for the furtherance of the person subjected to the authority, and in the second it is the condition for his exploitation. Another distinction runs parallel to this: rational authority is rational because the authority, whether it is held by a teacher or a captain of a ship giving orders in an emergency, acts in the name of reason which, being universal, I can accept without submitting. Irrational authority has to use force or suggestion, because no one would let himself be exploited if he were free to prevent it.

Why is man so prone to obey and why is it so difficult for him to dis- 13 obey? As long as I am obedient to the power of the State, the Church, or public opinion, I feel safe and protected. In fact it makes little difference what power it is that I am obedient to. It is always an institution, or men, who use force in one form or another and who fraudulently claim omniscience and omnipotence. My obedience makes me part of the power I worship, and hence I feel strong. I can make no error, since it decides for me; I cannot be alone, because it watches over me; I cannot commit a sin, because it does not let me do so, and even if I do sin, the punishment is only the way of returning to the almighty power.

In order to disobey, one must have the courage to be alone, to err and to 14 sin. But courage is not enough. The capacity for courage depends on a person's state of development. Only if a person has emerged from mother's lap and father's commands, only if he has emerged as a fully developed individual and thus has acquired the capacity to think and feel for himself, only then can he have the courage to say "no" to power, to disobey.

A person can become free through acts of disobedience by learning to say 15 no to power. But not only is the capacity for disobedience the condition for freedom; freedom is also the condition for disobedience. If I am afraid of freedom, I cannot dare to say "no," I cannot have the courage to be disobedient. Indeed, freedom and the capacity for disobedience are inseparable; hence any social, political, and religious system which proclaims freedom, yet stamps out disobedience, cannot speak the truth.

There is another reason why it is so difficult to dare to disobey, to say   16
"no" to power. During most of human history obedience has been identified
with virtue and disobedience with sin. The reason is simple: thus far throughout most of history a minority has ruled over the majority. This rule was
made necessary by the fact that there was only enough of the good things of
life for the few, and only the crumbs remained for the many. If the few
wanted to enjoy the good things and, beyond that, to have the many serve
them and work for them, one condition was necessary: the many had to
learn obedience. To be sure, obedience can be established by sheer force. But
this method has many disadvantages. It constitutes a constant threat that
one day the many might have the means to overthrow the few by force; furthermore there are many kinds of work which cannot be done properly if
nothing but fear is behind the obedience. Hence the obedience which is only
rooted in the fear of force must be transformed into one rooted in man's
heart. Man must want and even need to obey, instead of only fearing to disobey. If this is to be achieved, power must assume the qualities of the All
Good, of the All Wise; it must become All Knowing. If this happens, power
can proclaim that disobedience is sin and obedience virtue; and once this has
been proclaimed, the many can accept obedience because it is good and detest
disobedience because it is bad, rather than to detest themselves for being
cowards. From Luther to the nineteenth century one was concerned with
overt and explicit authorities. Luther, the pope, the princes, wanted to uphold
it; the middle class, the workers, the philosophers, tried to uproot it. The fight
against authority in the State as well as in the family was often the very basis
for the development of an independent and daring person. The fight against
authority was inseparable from the intellectual mood which characterized the
philosophers of the enlightenment and the scientists. This "critical mood" was
one of faith in reason, and at the same time of doubt in everything which is
said or thought, inasmuch as it is based on tradition, superstition, custom,
power. The principles *sapere aude* and *de omnibus est dubitandum*—"dare to
be wise" and "of all one must doubt"—were characteristic of the attitude
which permitted and furthered the capacity to say "no."

The case of Adolf Eichmann is symbolic of our situation and has a sig-   17
nificance far beyond the one in which his accusers in the courtroom in
Jerusalem were concerned with. Eichmann is a symbol of the organization
man, of the alienated bureaucrat for whom men, women and children have
become numbers. He is a symbol of all of us. We can see ourselves in
Eichmann. But the most frightening thing about him is that after the entire
story was told in terms of his own admissions, he was able in perfect good
faith to plead his innocence. It is clear that if he were once more in the same
situation he would do it again. And so would we—and so do we.

The organization man has lost the capacity to disobey, he is not even   18
aware of the fact that he obeys. At this point in history the capacity to doubt,
to criticize and to disobey may be all that stands between a future for
mankind and the end of civilization.

■   ■   ■

Review Questions

1. What does Fromm mean when he writes that disobedience is "the first step into independence and freedom"?
2. Fromm writes that history began with an act of disobedience and will likely end with an act of obedience. What does he mean?
3. What is the difference between "heteronomous obedience" and "autonomous obedience"?
4. How does Fromm distinguish between "authoritarian conscience" and "humanistic conscience"?
5. When is obedience to another person *not* submission?
6. What are the psychological comforts of obedience, and why would authorities rather have people obey out of love than out of fear?

Discussion and Writing Suggestions

1. Fromm suggests that scientifically we live in the twentieth century but that politically and emotionally we live in the Stone Age. As you observe events in the world, both near and far, would you agree? Why?
2. Fromm writes: "If a man can only obey and not disobey, he is a slave; if he can only disobey and not obey, he is a rebel (not a revolutionary)." Explain Fromm's meaning here. Explain, as well, the implication that to be fully human one must have the freedom to both obey and disobey.
3. Fromm writes that "obedience makes me part of the power I worship, and hence I feel strong." Does this statement ring true for you? Discuss, in writing, an occasion in which you felt powerful because you obeyed a group norm.
4. In paragraph 16, Fromm equates obedience with cowardice. Can you identify a situation in which you were obedient but, now that you reflect on it, also were cowardly? That is, can you recall a time when you caved in to a group but now wish you hadn't? Explain.
5. Fromm says that we can see ourselves in Adolf Eichmann—that as an organization man he "has lost the capacity to disobey, he is not even aware of the fact that he obeys." To what extent do you recognize yourself in this portrait?

The Lottery

SHIRLEY JACKSON

On the morning of June 28, 1948, I walked down to the post office in our little Vermont town to pick up the mail. I was quite casual about it, as I recall—I opened the box, took out a couple of bills and a letter or two, talked to the postmaster for a few minutes, and left, never supposing that it was the last time for months that I was to pick up the mail without an active feeling of panic. By the next week I had to change my mailbox to the largest one in the post office, and casual conversation with the postmaster was out of the question, because he wasn't speaking to me. June 28, 1948, was the day *The New Yorker* came out with a story of mine in it. It was not my first published story, nor my last, but I have been assured over and over that if it had been the only story I ever wrote or published, there would be people who would not forget my name.[1]

So begins Shirley Jackson's "biography" of her short story "The Lottery." The New Yorker *published the story the summer of 1948 and some months later, having been besieged with letters, acknowledged that the piece had generated "more mail than any . . . fiction they had ever published"—the great majority of it negative. In 1960, Jackson wrote that "millions of people, and my mother, had taken a pronounced dislike to me" for having written the story—which, over the years, proved to be Jackson's most widely anthologized one. If you've read "The Lottery," you will have some idea of why it was so controversial. If you haven't, we don't want to spoil the effect by discussing what happens.*

Shirley Jackson (1919–1965), short-story writer and novelist, was born in San Francisco and was raised in California and New York. She began her college education at the University of Rochester and completed it at Syracuse University. She married Stanley Edgar Hyman (writer and teacher) and with him had four children. In her brief career, Jackson wrote six novels and two works of nonfiction. She won the Edgar Allen Poe Award (1961) as well as a Syracuse University Arents Pioneer Medal for Outstanding Achievement (1965).

The morning of June 27th was clear and sunny, with the fresh warmth of a full-summer day; the flowers were blossoming profusely and the grass was richly green. The people of the village began to gather in the square, between the post office and the bank, around ten o'clock; in some towns there were so many people that the lottery took two days and had to be started on June 26th, but in this village, where there were only about three hundred people, the whole lottery took less than two hours, so it could begin at ten o'clock in the morning and still be through in time to allow the villagers to get home for noon dinner. 1

The children assembled first, of course. School was recently over for the summer, and the feeling of liberty sat uneasily on most of them; they tended to gather together quietly for a while before they broke into boisterous play, and their talk was still of the classroom and the teacher, of books and reprimands. Bobby Martin had already stuffed his pockets full of stones, and the other boys soon followed his example, selecting the smoothest and roundest 2

---

[1]"Biography of a Story," from *Come Along With Me*, by Shirley Jackson. Copyright 1948, 1952, © 1960 by Shirley Jackson. Used by permission of Viking Penguin, a division of Penguin Books USA Inc. 1st paragraph, p. 211 + selected quotations, pp. 214–221.

stones; Bobby and Harry Jones and Dickie Delacroix—the villagers pronounced this "Dellacroy"—eventually made a great pile of stones in one
corner of the square and guarded it against the raids of the other boys. The
girls stood aside, talking among themselves, looking over their shoulders at
the boys, and the very small children rolled in the dust or clung to the hands
of their older brothers or sisters.

Soon the men began to gather, surveying their own children, speaking of   3
planting and rain, tractors and taxes. They stood together, away from the pile
of stones in the corner, and their jokes were quiet and they smiled rather than
laughed. The women, wearing faded house dresses and sweaters, came shortly after their menfolk. They greeted one another and exchanged bits of gossip
as they went to join their husbands. Soon the women, standing by their husbands, began to call to their children, and the children came reluctantly,
having to be called four or five times. Bobby Martin ducked under his
mother's grasping hand and ran, laughing, back to the pile of stones. His
father spoke up sharply, and Bobby came quickly and took his place between
his father and his oldest brother.

The lottery was conducted—as were the square dances, the teenage club,   4
the Halloween program—by Mr. Summers, who had time and energy to
devote to civic activities. He was a round-faced, jovial man and he ran the
coal business, and people were sorry for him, because he had no children and
his wife was a scold. When he arrived in the square, carrying the wooden
black box, there was a murmur of conversation among the villagers, and he
waved and called, "Little late today, folks." The postmaster, Mr. Graves, followed him, carrying a three-legged stool, and the stool was put in the center
of the square and Mr. Summers set the black box down on it. The villagers
kept their distance, leaving a space between themselves and the stool, and
when Mr. Summers said, "Some of you fellows want to give me a hand?"
there was a hesitation before two men, Mr. Martin and his oldest son, Baxter,
came forward to hold the box steady on the stool while Mr. Summers stirred
up the papers inside it.

The original paraphernalia for the lottery had been lost long ago, and the   5
black box now resting on the stool had been put into use even before Old
Man Warner, the oldest man in town, was born. Mr. Summers spoke frequently to the villagers about making a new box, but no one liked to upset
even as much tradition as was represented by the black box. There was a story
that the present box had been made with some pieces of the box that had preceded it, the one that had been constructed when the first people settled
down to make a village here. Every year, after the lottery, Mr. Summers
began talking again about a new box, but every year the subject was allowed
to fade off without anything's being done. The black box grew shabbier each
year; by now it was no longer completely black but splintered badly along one
side to show the original wood color, and in some places faded or stained.

Mr. Martin and his oldest son, Baxter, held the black box securely on the   6
stool until Mr. Summers had stirred the papers thoroughly with his hand.
Because so much of the ritual had been forgotten or discarded, Mr. Summers

had been successful in having slips of paper substituted for the chips of wood that had been used for generations. Chips of wood, Mr. Summers had argued, had been all very well when the village was tiny, but now that the population was more than three hundred and likely to keep on growing, it was necessary to use something that would fit more easily into the black box. The night before the lottery, Mr. Summers and Mr. Graves made up the slips of paper and put them in the box, and it was then taken to the safe of Mr. Summers' coal company and locked up until Mr. Summers was ready to take it to the square next morning. The rest of the year, the box was put away, sometimes one place, sometimes another; it had spent one year in Mr. Graves's barn and another year underfoot in the post office, and sometimes it was set on a shelf in the Martin grocery and left there.

There was a great deal of fussing to be done before Mr. Summers declared the lottery open. There were the lists to make up—of heads of families, heads of households in each family, members of each household in each family. There was the proper swearing-in of Mr. Summers by the postmaster, as the official of the lottery; at one time, some people remembered, there had been a recital of some sort, performed by the official of the lottery, a perfunctory, tuneless chant that had been rattled off duly each year; some people believed that the official of the lottery used to stand just so when he said or sang it, others believed that he was supposed to walk among the people, but years and years ago this part of the ritual had been allowed to lapse. There had been, also, a ritual salute, which the official of the lottery had had to use in addressing each person who came up to draw from the box, but this also had changed with time, until now, it was felt necessary only for the official to speak to each person approaching. Mr. Summers was very good at all this; in his clean white shirt and blue jeans, with one hand resting carelessly on the black box, he seemed very proper and important as he talked interminably to Mr. Graves and the Martins.

Just as Mr. Summers finally left off talking and turned to the assembled villagers, Mrs. Hutchinson came hurriedly along the path to the square, her sweater thrown over her shoulders, and slid into place in the back of the crowd. "Clean forgot what day it was," she said to Mrs. Delacroix, who stood next to her, and they both laughed softly. "Thought my old man was out back stacking wood," Mrs. Hutchinson went on, "and then I looked out the window and the kids was gone, and then I remembered it was the twenty-seventh and came a-running." She dried her hands on her apron, and Mrs. Delacroix said, "You're in time, though. They're still talking away up there."

Mrs. Hutchinson craned her neck to see through the crowd and found her husband and children standing near the front. She tapped Mrs. Delacroix on the arm as a farewell and began to make her way through the crowd. The people separated good-humoredly to let her through; two or three people said, in voices just loud enough to be heard across the crowd, "Here comes your Missus, Hutchinson," and "Bill, she made it after all." Mrs. Hutchinson reached her husband, and Mr. Summers, who had been waiting, said cheerfully, "Thought we were going to have to get on without you, Tessie." Mrs.

Hutchinson said, grinning, "Wouldn't have me leave m'dishes in the sink, now, would you, Joe?," and soft laughter ran through the crowd as the people stirred back into position after Mrs. Hutchinson's arrival.

"Well, now," Mr. Summers said soberly, "guess we better get started, get this over with, so's we can go back to work. Anybody ain't here?"   10

"Dunbar," several people said. "Dunbar, Dunbar."   11

Mr. Summers consulted his list. "Clyde Dunbar," he said. "That's right.   12
He's broke his leg, hasn't he? Who's drawing for him?"

"Me, I guess," a woman said, and Mr. Summers turned to look at her.   13
"Wife draws for her husband," Mr. Summers said. "Don't you have a grown boy to do it for you, Janey?" Although Mr. Summers and everyone else in the village knew the answer perfectly well, it was the business of the official of the lottery to ask such questions formally. Mr. Summers waited with an expression of polite interest while Mrs. Dunbar answered.

"Horace's not but sixteen yet," Mrs. Dunbar said regretfully. "Guess I   14
gotta fill in for the old man this year."

"Right," Mr. Summers said. He made a note on the list he was holding.   15
Then he asked, "Watson boy drawing this year?"

A tall boy in the crowd raised his hand. "Here," he said. "I'm drawing   16
for m'mother and me." He blinked his eyes nervously and ducked his head as several voices in the crowd said things like "Good fellow, Jack," and "Glad to see your mother's got a man to do it."

"Well," Mr. Summers said, "guess that's everyone. Old Man Warner   17
make it?"

"Here," a voice said, and Mr. Summers nodded.   18

A sudden hush fell on the crowd as Mr. Summers cleared his throat and   19
looked at the list. "All ready?" he called. "Now, I'll read the names—heads of families first—and the men come up and take a paper out of the box. Keep the paper folded in your hand without looking at it until everyone has had a turn. Everything clear?"

The people had done it so many times that they only half listened to the   20
directions; most of them were quiet, wetting their lips, not looking around. Then Mr. Summers raised one hand high and said, "Adams." A man disengaged himself from the crowd and came forward. "Hi, Steve," Mr. Summers said, and Mr. Adams said, "Hi, Joe." They grinned at one another humorously and nervously. Then Mr. Adams reached into the black box and took out a folded paper. He held it firmly by one corner as he turned and went hastily back to his place in the crowd, where he stood a little apart from his family, not looking down at his hand.

"Allen," Mr. Summers said. "Anderson. . . . Bentham."   21

"Seems like there's no time at all between lotteries any more," Mrs.   22
Delacroix said to Mrs. Graves in the back row. "Seems like we got through with the last one only last week."

"Time sure goes fast," Mrs. Graves said.   23

"Clark. . . . Delacroix."   24

"There goes my old man," Mrs. Delacroix said. She held her breath 25
while her husband went forward.

"Dunbar," Mr. Summers said, and Mrs. Dunbar went steadily to the box 26
while one of the women said, "Go on, Janey," and another said, "There she
goes."

"We're next," Mrs. Graves said. She watched while Mr. Graves came 27
around from the side of the box, greeted Mr. Summers gravely, and selected
a slip of paper from the box. By now, all through the crowd there were men
holding the small folded papers in their large hands, turning them over and
over nervously. Mrs. Dunbar and her two sons stood together, Mrs. Dunbar
holding the slip of paper.

"Harburt. . . . Hutchinson." 28

"Get up there, Bill," Mrs. Hutchinson said, and the people near her 29
laughed.

"Jones." 30

"They do say," Mr. Adams said to Old Man Warner, who stood next to 31
him, "that over in the north village they're talking of giving up the lottery."

Old Man Warner snorted. "Pack of crazy fools," he said. "Listening to 32
the young folks, nothing's good enough for *them*. Next thing you know,
they'll be wanting to go back to living in caves, nobody work any more, live
that way for a while. Used to be a saying about 'Lottery in June, corn be
heavy soon.' First thing you know, we'd all be eating stewed chickweed and
acorns. There's *always* been a lottery," he added petulantly. "Bad enough to
see young Joe Summers up there joking with everybody."

Some places have already quit lotteries," Mrs. Adams said. 33

"Nothing but trouble in *that*," Old Man Warner said stoutly. "Pack of 34
young fools."

"Martin." And Bobby Martin watched his father go forward. 35
"Overdyke. . . . Percy."

"I wish they'd hurry," Mrs. Dunbar said to her older son. "I wish they'd 36
hurry."

"They're almost through," her son said. 37

"You get ready to run tell Dad," Mrs. Dunbar said. 38

Mr. Summers called his own name and then stepped forward precisely 39
and selected a slip from the box. Then he called, "Warner."

"Seventy-seventh year I been in the lottery," Old Man Warner said as he 40
went through the crowd. "Seventy-seventh time."

"Watson." The tall boy came awkwardly through the crowd. Someone 41
said, "Don't be nervous, Jack," and Mr. Summers said, "Take your time,
son."

"Zanini." 42

After that, there was a long pause, a breathless pause, until Mr. Summers, 43
holding his slip of paper in the air, said, "All right, fellows." For a minute, no
one moved, and then all the slips of paper were opened. Suddenly, all the
women began to speak at once, saying, "Who is it?," "Who's got it?," "Is it

the Dunbars?," "Is it the Watsons?" Then the voices began to say, "It's Hutchinson. It's Bill," "Bill Hutchinson's got it."

"Go tell your father," Mrs. Dunbar said to her older son.   44

People began to look around to see the Hutchinsons. Bill Hutchinson was   45
standing quiet, staring down at the paper in his hand. Suddenly, Tessie
Hutchinson shouted to Mr. Summers, "You didn't give him time enough to
take any paper he wanted. I saw you. It wasn't fair!"

"Be a good sport, Tessie," Mrs. Delacroix called, and Mrs. Graves said,   46
"All of us took the same chance."

"Shut up, Tessie," Bill Hutchinson said.   47

"Well, everyone," Mr. Summers said, "that was done pretty fast, and   48
now we've got to be hurrying a little more to get done in time." He consulted his next list. "Bill," he said, "you draw for the Hutchinson family. You got
any other households in the Hutchinsons?"

"There's Don and Eva," Mrs. Hutchinson yelled. "Make *them* take their   49
chance!"

"Daughters draw with their husbands' families, Tessie," Mr. Summers   50
said gently. "You know that as well as anyone else."

"It wasn't *fair*," Tessie said.   51

"I guess not, Joe," Bill Hutchinson said regretfully. "My daughter draws   52
with her husband's family, that's only fair. And I've got no other family
except the kids."

"Then, as far as drawing for families is concerned, it's you," Mr.   53
Summers said in explanation, "and as far as drawing for households is concerned, that's you, too. Right?"

"Right," Bill Hutchinson said.   54

"How many kids, Bill?" Mr. Summers asked formally.   55

"Three," Bill Hutchinson said. "There's Bill, Jr., and Nancy, and little   56
Dave. And Tessie and me."

"All right, then," Mr. Summers said. "Harry, you got their tickets back?"   57

Mr. Graves nodded and held up the slips of paper. "Put them in the box,   58
then," Mr. Summers directed. "Take Bill's and put it in."

"I think we ought to start over," Mrs. Hutchinson said, as quietly as she   59
could. "I tell you it wasn't *fair*. You didn't give him enough time to choose.
Everybody saw that."

Mr. Graves had selected the five slips and put them in the box, and he   60
dropped all the papers but those onto the ground, where the breeze caught
them and lifted them off.

"Listen, everybody," Mrs. Hutchinson was saying to the people around   61
her.

"Ready, Bill?" Mr. Summers asked, and Bill Hutchinson, with one quick   62
glance around at his wife and children, nodded.

"Remember," Mr. Summers said, "take the slips and keep them folded   63
until each person has taken one. Harry, you help little Dave." Mr. Graves
took the hand of the little boy, who came willingly with him up to the box.

"Take a paper out of the box, Davy," Mr. Summers said. Davy put his hand into the box and laughed. "Take just *one* paper," Mrs. Summers said. "Harry, you hold it for him." Mr. Graves took the child's hand and removed the folded paper from the tight fist and held it while little Dave stood next to him and looked up at him wonderingly.

"Nancy next," Mr. Summers said. Nancy was twelve and her school 64 friends breathed heavily as she went forward, switching her skirt, and took a slip daintily from the box. "Bill, Jr.," Mr. Summers said, and Billy, his face red and his feet overlarge, nearly knocked the box over as he got a paper out. "Tessie," Mr. Summers said. She hesitated for a minute, looking around defiantly, and then set her lips and went up to the box. She snatched a paper out and held it behind her.

"Bill," Mr. Summers said, and Bill Hutchinson reached into the box and 65 felt around, bringing his hand out at last with the slip of paper in it.

The crowd was quiet. A girl whispered, "I hope it's not Nancy," and the 66 sound of the whisper reached the edges of the crowd.

"It's not the way it used to be," Old Man Warner said clearly. "People 67 ain't the way they used to be."

"All right," Mr. Summers said. "Open the papers, Harry, you open little 68 Dave's."

Mr. Graves opened the slip of paper and there was a general sigh through 69 the crowd as he held it up and everyone could see that it was blank. Nancy and Bill, Jr., opened theirs at the same time, and both beamed and laughed, turning around to the crowd and holding their slips of paper above their heads.

"Tessie," Mr. Summers said. There was a pause, and then Mr. Summers 70 looked at Bill Hutchinson, and Bill unfolded his paper and showed it. It was blank.

"It's Tessie," Mr. Summers said, and his voice was hushed. "Show us her 71 paper, Bill."

Bill Hutchinson went over to his wife and forced the slip of paper out of 72 her hand. It had a black spot on it, the black spot Mr. Summers had made the night before with the heavy pencil in the coal-company office. Bill Hutchinson held it up, and there was a stir in the crowd.

"All right, folks," Mr. Summers said. "Let's finish quickly." 73

Although the villagers had forgotten the ritual and lost the original black 74 box, they still remembered to use stones. The pile of stones the boys had made earlier was ready; there were stones on the ground with the blowing scraps of paper that had come out of the box. Mrs. Delacroix selected a stone so large she had to pick it up with both hands and turned to Mrs. Dunbar. "Come on," she said. "Hurry up."

Mrs. Dunbar had small stones in both hands, and she said, gasping for 75 breath, "I can't run at all. You'll have to go ahead and I'll catch up with you."

The children had stones already, and someone gave little Davy 76 Hutchinson a few pebbles.

Tessie Hutchinson was in the center of a cleared space by now, and she   77
held her hands out desperately as the villagers moved in on her. "It isn't
fair," she said. A stone hit her on the side of the head.

Old Man Warner was saying, "Come on, come on, everyone." Steve   78
Adams was in front of the crowd of villagers, with Mrs. Graves beside him.

"It isn't fair, it isn't right," Mrs. Hutchinson screamed, and then they   79
were upon her.

■ ■ ■

Discussion and Writing Suggestions

1. Many readers believed that the events depicted in "the Lottery" actually happened. A sampling of the letters that Jackson received in response
   to the story:

   > (Kansas) Will you please tell me the locale and the year of that custom?
   > (Oregon) Where in heaven's name does there exist such barbarity as
   > described in the story?
   > (New York) Do such tribunal rituals still exist and if so where?
   > (New York) To a reader who has only a fleeting knowledge of tra-
   > ditional rites in various parts of the country (I presume the plot was
   > laid in the United States) I found the cruelty of the ceremony outra-
   > geous, if not unbelievable. It may be just a custom or ritual which I
   > am not familiar with.
   > (New York) Would you please explain whether such improbable
   > rituals occur in our Middle Western states, and what their origin and
   > purpose are?
   > (Nevada) Although we recognize the story to be fiction is it possible
   > that it is based on fact?

   What is your response to comments such as these that suggest surprise,
   certainly, but also acceptance of the violence committed in the story?

2. One reader of "The Lottery," from Missouri, wrote to the *New Yorker*
   and accused it of "publishing a story that reached a new low in human
   viciousness." Do you feel that Jackson has reached this "new low"?
   Explain your answer.

3. Several more letter writers attempted to get at the meaning of the story:

   > (Illinois) If it is simply a fictitious example of man's innate cruelty, it
   > isn't a very good one. Man, stupid and cruel as he is, has always had
   > sense enough to imagine or invent a charge against the objects of his
   > persecution: the Christian martyrs, the New England witches, the
   > Jews and Negroes. But nobody had anything against Mrs.
   > Hutchinson, and they only wanted to get through quickly so they
   > could go home for lunch.

(California) I missed something here. Perhaps there was some facet of the victim's character which made her unpopular with the other villagers. I expected the people to evince a feeling of dread and terror, or else sadistic pleasure, but perhaps they were laconic, unemotional New Englanders.

(Indiana) When I first read the story in my issue, I felt that there was no moral significance present, that the story was just terrifying, and that was all. However, there has to be a reason why it is so alarming to so many people. I feel that the only solution, the only reason it bothered so many people is that it shows the power of society over the individual. We saw the ease with which society can crush any single one of us. At the same time, we saw that society need have no rational reason for crushing the one, or the few, or sometimes the many.

Take any one of these readings of the story and respond to it by writing a brief essay or, perhaps, a letter.

4. What does the story suggest to you about authority and obedience to authority? Who—or what—holds authority in the village? Why do people continue with the annual killing, despite the fact that "some places have already quit lotteries"?

■ SYNTHESIS ACTIVITIES

1. Compare and contrast the Asch and the Milgram experiments, considering their separate (1) objectives, (2) experimental designs and procedures, (3) results, and (4) conclusions. To what extent do the findings of these two experiments reinforce one another? To what extent do they highlight different, if related, social phenomena? To what extent do their results reinforce those of Zimbardo's prison experiment?

2. Assume for the moment you agree with Doris Lessing: Children need to be taught how to disobey so they can recognize and avoid situations that give rise to harmful obedience. If you were the curriculum coordinator for your local school system, how would you teach children to disobey? What would be your curriculum? What homework would you assign? What class projects? What field trips? One complicated part of your job would be to train children to understand the difference between *responsible* disobedience and anarchy. What is the difference?

   Take up these questions in an essay that draws on both your experiences as a student and your understanding of the selections in this chapter. Points that you might want to consider in developing the essay: defining overly obedient children; appropriate classroom behavior for responsibly disobedient children (as opposed to inappropriate

behavior); reading lists (would "The Lottery" be included?); homework assignments; field trips; class projects.

3. A certain amount of obedience is a given in society, observe Stanley
   Milgram and others. Social order, civilization itself, would not be
   possible unless individuals were willing to surrender a portion of their
   autonomy to the state. Allowing that we all are obedient (we must be),
   define the point at which obedience to a figure of authority becomes
   dangerous.

   As you develop your definition, consider the ways you might use
   the work of authors in this chapter and their definitions of acceptable
   and unacceptable levels of obedience. Do you agree with the ways in
   which others have drawn the line between reasonable and dangerous
   obedience? What examples from current stories in the news or from
   your own experience can you draw on to test various definitions?

4. Describe a situation in which you were faced with a moral dilemma of
   whether to obey a figure of authority. After describing the situation
   and the action you took (or didn't take), discuss your behavior in light
   of any two readings in this chapter. You might consider a straightforward, four-part structure for your essay: (1) your description; (2) your
   discussion, in light of source A; (3) your discussion, in light of source B;
   and (4) your conclusion—an overall appraisal of your behavior.

5. At one point in his essay (paragraph 16), Erich Fromm equates obedience with cowardice. Earlier in the chapter, Doris Lessing (paragraph 9) observes that "among our most shameful memories is this,
   how often we said black was white because other people were saying
   it." Using the work of these authors as a point of departure, reconsider
   an act of obedience or disobedience in your own life. Describe pertinent circumstances for your reader. Based on what you have learned
   in this chapter, reassess your behavior. Would you behave similarly if
   given a second chance in the same situation?

6. Reread "The Lottery" and analyze the patterns of and reasons for obedience in the story. Base your analysis on two sources in this chapter:
   Erich Fromm's essay, especially paragraphs 13–16 on the psychological comforts of obedience; and Doris Lessing's speech on the dangers
   of "not understanding the social laws that govern groups."

7. In his response to Diana Baumrind, Stanley Milgram makes a point of
   insisting that follow-up interviews with subjects in his experiments
   show that a large majority were pleased, in the long run, to have participated. (See Table 1 in the footnote to Baumrind, page 362.) Writing
   on his own post-experiment surveys and interviews, Philip Zimbardo
   writes that his subjects believed their "mental anguish was transient
   and situationally specific, but the self-knowledge gained has persisted"
   (paragraph 60). Why might they *and* the experimenters nonetheless
   have been eager to accept a positive, final judgment of the experiments? Develop an essay in response to this question, drawing on the
   selections by Milgram, Zimbardo, and Baumrind.

8. Develop a synthesis in which you extend Baumrind's critique of Milgram to the Stanford prison experiment. This assignment requires that you understand the core elements of Baumrind's critique; that you have a clear understanding of Zimbardo's experiment; and that you systematically apply elements of the critiques, as you see fit, to Zimbardo's work. In your conclusion, offer your overall assessment of the Stanford Prison Experiment. To do this, you might answer Zimbardo's own question in paragraph 55: "Was [the experiment] worth all the suffering?" Or you might respond to another question: Do you agree that Zimbardo is warranted in extending the conclusions of his experiment to the general population?

9. In response to the question "Why is man so prone to obey and why is it so difficult for him to disobey?" Erich Fromm suggests that obedience lets people identify with the powerful and invites feelings of safety. Disobedience is psychologically more difficult and requires an act of courage. (See paragraphs 13 and 14.) Solomon Asch notes that the tendency to conformity is generally stronger than the tendency to independence. And in his final paragraph, Philip Zimbardo writes that a "prison of fear" keeps people compliant and frees them of the need to take responsibility for their own actions. In a synthesis that draws on these three sources, explore the interplay of *fear* and its opposite, *courage*, in relation to obedience. To prevent the essay from becoming too abstract, direct your attention repeatedly to a single case, the details of which will help to keep your focus. "The Lottery" could serve nicely as this case, as could a particular event from your own life.

■ RESEARCH ACTIVITIES

1. When Milgram's results were first published in book form in 1974, they generated heated controversy. The reaction reprinted here (by Baumrind) represents only a very small portion of that controversy. Research other reactions to the Milgram experiments and discuss your findings. Begin with the reviews listed and excerpted in the *Book Review Digest*; also use the *Social Science Index*, the *Readers' Guide to Periodical Literature*, and newspaper indexes to locate articles, editorials, and letters to the editor on the experiments. (Note that editorials and letters are not always indexed. Letters appear within two to four weeks of the weekly magazine articles to which they refer, and within one to two weeks of newspaper articles.) What were the chief types of reactions? To what extent were the reactions favorable?

2. Milgram begins his article "Obedience to Authority" with a reference to Nazi Germany. The purpose of his experiment, in fact, was to help throw light on how the Nazi atrocities could have happened. Research the Nuremberg war crimes tribunals following World War II. Drawing

specifically on the statements of those who testified at Nuremberg, as well as those who have written about it, show how Milgram's experiments do help explain the Holocaust and other Nazi crimes. In addition to relevant articles, see Telford Taylor, *Nuremberg and Vietnam: An American Tragedy* (1970); Hannah Arendt, *Eichmann in Jerusalem: A Report on the Banality of Evil* (1963); Richard A. Falk, Gabriel Kolko, and Robert J. Lifton (eds.), *Crimes of War* (1971).

3. Obtain a copy of the transcript of the trial of Adolf Eichmann—the Nazi official who carried out Hitler's "final solution" for the extermination of the Jews. Read also Hannah Arendt's *Eichmann in Jerusalem: A Report on the Banality of Evil*, along with the reviews of this book. Write a critique both of Arendt's book and of the reviews it received.

4. The My Lai massacre in Vietnam in 1969 was a particularly egregious case of overobedience to military authority in wartime. Show the connections between this event and Milgram's experiments. Note that Milgram himself treated the My Lai massacre in the epilogue to his *Obedience to Authority: An Experimental View* (1974).

5. Investigate the court-martial of Lt. William Calley, convicted for his role in the My Lai massacre. Discuss the question of whether President Nixon was justified in commuting his sentence. Examine in detail the dilemmas the jury must have faced when presented with Calley's defense that he was only following orders.

6. Research the Watergate break-in of 1972 and the subsequent cover-up by Richard Nixon and members of his administration, as an example of overobedience to authority. Focus on one particular aspect of Watergate (e.g., the role of the counsel to the president, John Dean, or why the crisis was allowed to proceed to the point where it actually toppled a presidency). In addition to relevant articles, see Robert Woodward and Carl Bernstein, *All the President's Men* (1974); Leon Jaworski, *The Right and the Power: The Prosecution of Watergate* (1976); *RN: The Memoirs of Richard Nixon* (1978); John Dean, *Blind Ambition* (1976); John Sirica, *To Set the Record Straight: The Break-in, the Tapes, the Conspirators, the Pardon* (1979); Sam Ervin, *The Whole Truth: The Watergate Conspiracy* (1980); John Ehrlichman, *Witness to Power: The Nixon Years* (1982).

7. At the outset of his article, Stanley Milgram refers to imaginative works revolving around the issue of obedience to authority: the story of Abraham and Isaac; three of Plato's dialogues, "Apology," "Crito," and "Phaedo;" and the story of Antigone (dramatized by both the fifth-century B.C. Athenian Sophocles and the twentieth-century Frenchman Jean Anouilh). In this chapter, we have reprinted Shirley Jackson's "The Lottery," which also can be read as a story about obedience to authority. And many other fictional works deal with obedience to authority—for example, Herman Wouk's novel *The Caine Mutiny* (and his subsequent play *The Caine Mutiny Court*

Martial). Check with your instructor, with a librarian, and with such sources as the *Short Story Index* to locate other imaginative works on this theme. Write a paper discussing the various ways in which the subject has been treated in fiction and drama. To ensure coherence, draw comparisons and contrasts among works showing the connections and the variations on the theme of obedience to authority.

8

The Book of Job

When tidal waves devastate coastal communities, when bridges fail, when wars consume a countryside: in man-made and natural disasters alike, innocent people suffer. On the television and in newspapers we witness the tragedies in far-flung places such as Bangladesh and Rwanda, and we ache from a distance. All too often, though, we learn the lessons of suffering close to home—when, for example, cancer strikes a family member in the prime of life. Why should one person be stricken and not another? How do we understand the deaths of the three high-school students in Kentucky who had just bowed their heads at a prayer meeting when a fellow student burst into the room firing a gun? How do we justify the hardships of the child born on one side of town while, on the other, a child is born to the security of good schools and abundant food?

Blameless people *do* suffer, and we have long struggled to understand why. As children many of us are taught to believe that a strict moral logic governs this world: people who obey biblical law (and its secular equivalents) enjoy good fortune while those who disobey do not. When the world contradicts this logic and brings suffering to good people, we feel betrayed. No work of literature gives voice to this sense of betrayal more beautifully or hauntingly than the Book of Job. Written by an anonymous author 2,500 years ago and installed later as a book in the *Old Testament*, Job raises questions about faith and justice that are as vexing for us as they were for the ancients. When we ask *Where was God* in the face of a calamity, we are posing what philosophers and theologians call a Job*an* question. It was the question of Jews who survived the Holocaust. It is the question of a father who sees his happiness shattered by an accident (a car skidding into his car in a snowstorm): "I was one of those guys who thought tragedy always happened to the other person," he writes. "You just never know. One day you're a happy guy with . . . two beautiful children, a nice home, a nice job and enough income to meet the mortgage payments and a few extras."[1] And the next day, he observes, you're disabled, dependent on the state for financial assistance. Why?

If you have never read or heard of Job, you will nonetheless recognize the story of the virtuous person who strives to do right but is struck down just the same. The sufferer cries: *Why me?* Well-intentioned friends offer consolation, but they cannot understand the sufferer's despair and dismay. Inevitably,

---

[1]James Calogero. "Auto accident leaves husband disabled, family devastated." *Boston Globe*, 4 December 1997. p. B10.

someone claiming to understand the grand Order of the Universe will suggest that truly blameless people do not suffer (it is not God's way) and that, therefore, this particular suffering must be deserved.

If you can allow that students killed at a prayer meeting, a cancer victim, or victims of ethnic cleansing in Rwanda did *not* deserve misfortune any more than you, and that disasters and sickness can strike randomly, then read on: for it is just this awareness that lies both at the heart of Job and in the hearts of every person who has been assaulted by life.

In its earliest form, Job existed as an oral tale with variants that date to the ancient Babylonians.[2] Around the year 500 BCE,[3] the anonymous writer of the Job we read in the *Old Testament* borrowed from the original oral story and used it as a frame—or as the opening and closing sections—of a new *written* version. In the original, Job is the pious servant of God who in quick succession loses his children, his wealth, and his health—but endures patiently. He believes that whether God gives or takes, God must be blessed, never doubted. The writer of the biblical story made a radical break with the original oral version by adding an extended middle section, in verse, on Job's *im*patient reply to his sufferings. This reinvented Job challenges God to justify why calamities should strike down a faithful servant. Job believes himself blameless and ill-treated, and he will not be silent. He complains bitterly, until God appears in a whirlwind with a thunderous answer.

Not surprisingly for a text that poses fundamental questions about faith and divine justice, a rich history of commentary has grown around Job. Among the earliest were commentaries in the third and fourth centuries CE, composed by rabbis who were assembling a multivolumed study of the *Old Testament*. In the year 600, Pope Gregory the Great concluded a 34-volume exegesis (or close reading) of Job. A scholar researching that work characterizes Gregory's position on Job and quotes him this way:

> Reflecting on the adversities of saintly men such as Job . . . Gregory concludes that God strikes those whom he loves because "he knows how to reward them. . . . He casts them down outwardly to something despicable in order to lead them on inwardly to the height of things incomprehensible."[4]

Gregory's argument that "suffering actually is necessary to *cure*"[5] a person's deluded view of reality became a bedrock of Church teachings that lasted well over a thousand years. According to Gregory, suffering led Job to greater awareness of God; hence, suffering, however painful, was a useful tool in Job's

---

[2]See the article by Stith Thompson in the chapter on Cinderella for a discussion of oral, or spoken, stories.

[3]BCE is an abbreviation for *Before the Common Era*, another way of writing before the birth of Christ. CE refers to the *Common Era*, or the years after the birth of Christ.

[4]Susan Schreiner, *Where Shall Wisdom Be Found: Calvin's Exegesis of Job from Medieval and Modern Perspectives* (Chicago: U of Chicago P, 1994), 34.

[5]Schreiner, 31.

spiritual development and, by extension, can be understood as a useful tool in ours. How satisfying for you is the view that suffering can serve as a reward?

Writing in the early 12th century, the medieval Jewish philosopher Moses Maimonides discussed Job at some length in his *Guide to the Perplexed*. Maimonides wrote that people labor under a confusion if they expect rewards from God to be measured in anything but spiritual gain:

> Man's task is to approach to God as close as humanly possible. . . . The evil are punished not by the withholding of material rewards but by their alienation from God, their debarment from human perfection. The good are rewarded not by worldly success but by the possibility of enlightenment, knowledge of God, which virtue opens to the truly wise.[6]

Job complained because his children had died, his wealth was stolen, and his body was devastated by disease. According to Maimonides, Job mistakenly expected the wrong sort of reward (children, money, and health) as acknowledgment of pious behavior. Eight hundred years ago, Maimonides believed that personal suffering and personal happiness are not the currency in which God administers justice.

That we can with interest read an ancient text and the comments of thinkers centuries removed and then be drawn into an opinion ourselves is a remarkable achievement, suggesting both the enduring value of Job and of the very qualities that make us human. Consider: Why has Job's complaint always been understood by readers as a *contemporary* complaint—whether "contemporary" is defined as the year 400, 600, 1200, or 2000? The Book of Job is timeless: through it we find connection to those who lived 2,500 years ago and to all who followed and also read. Through it, others will find connection to us.

Whether you read Job as a sacred text (sacred in the sense that it appears in the Bible) or as a classic of world literature valuable not because of its origins but because of what it says—however you read, realize that you do so in a tradition of interpretation. In addition to Pope Gregory and Moses Maimonides, many religious figures have written on Job, including Thomas Aquinas and John Calvin. As secular text, Job has received equal attention from philosophers, literary critics, poets, and essayists. Which is to say, you have license to read and interpret. As Peter Gomes, Minister in The Memorial Church and Plummer Professor of Christian Morals at Harvard University observes:

> Interpretation is the fuel that drives understanding. The making of meaning is what scripture is all about, the effort by every possible device to make sense of the divine in search of the human, and the human in search of the divine, the joy of discovery, the sorrow of loss. If scripture is about anything in all of its splendid diversity, it is about this, and so it is not really about whether there is or is not

---

[6]Moses Maimonides, "From *Moreh Nevukhim* III:22," in *Rambam: Readings in the Philosophy of Moses Maimonides*, ed. Lenn Evan Goodman (New York: Schocken, 1976), 356n.

interpretation in the reading of scripture. Of course there is interpretation. The question is, what kind of interpretation?[7]

What kind of interpretation is a matter for you to decide. What we have done is to provide an occasion to interpret, with six selections that bear directly, and indirectly, on the book of Job. We begin with an excerpt from *The Good Book: Reading the Bible with Mind and Heart* by Peter Gomes. In this selection, Gomes does not refer directly to the Book of Job; rather, he discusses the larger human context of human suffering in which Job is situated. You can read "The Bible and Suffering" as an introduction to the *idea* of this chapter. Next comes an excerpt from Job. The unabridged text is too long for inclusion; but since its lengthy middle section consists of three largely repetitive cycles of debate between Job and his friends, we believe that an extended excerpt captures the spirit of the work. (In any event, a complete version is as close as the nearest Bible.) The headnote to Job will detail which verses have been excerpted, as well as offer a note on translation.

Job is followed by six selections, the first two of which provide background and context to the story. David Neiman sets Job in the philosophical and theological context of its day, comparing the view of God in Job to the view expressed by pagans. Next, Carol Newsom writes on the complex history of the authorship of Job and sets the text in its cultural context of ancient Near Eastern literature. She and others have found remarkable similarities between Job and a Babylonian text written 3000 years ago. Four commentators follow. The first is Harold Kushner, a rabbi and author of *When Bad Things Happen to Good People*. Kushner wrote his book in response to the loss of his son to a rare disease. Rather than deny God's existence or accept a God who would knowingly let the innocent suffer, Kushner prefers to believe in a God who is *not* all powerful (who could not, for instance, prevent a child from contracting a fatal illness).

In "The Myth of Justice," the late novelist and essayist Michael Dorris writes a bitter essay rejecting the idea of justice, both in this world and in the next. Justice here, writes Dorris, does not exist. As for eternal justice, that's an illusion (a "palliative myth"). Dianne Bergant, Professor of Biblical Studies at Catholic Theological Union (Chicago), sees in Job a tragic temptation to deny meaning in life. Job, she writes, resists that temptation and deepens his faith. Concluding the chapter is a sermon by dramatist Archibald MacLeish, well-known for the play *J.B.*, his modern rendering of Job. The ancient story, writes MacLeish, shows that "God Has Need of Man."

The Book of Job jolts us into reexamining core beliefs, among them: *Why should any of us struggle to be virtuous when the good suffer along with the wicked?* Beset by calamities, Job posed troubling questions. The fact that neither he nor we find easy answers defines, in large measure, the human predicament.

---

[7]Peter Gomes, *The Good Book: Reading the Bible with Mind and Heart* (New York: Morrow, 1996), 33.

The Bible and Suffering

PETER GOMES

Peter Gomes (b. 1942) is Minister at The Memorial Church at Harvard University. In his responsibilities as a professor of theology, and more particularly as a spiritual guide for a large and varied community, he has often had occasion to address the subject of innocent suffering. The selection that follows, "The Bible and Suffering," appears in The Good Book: Reading the Bible with Mind and Heart *and grows out of his years of ministering and the obligation it placed upon him to offer meaningful consolation in times of tragedy. While Gomes, an African American and a Baptist preacher, does not refer directly to the Book of Job, he prepares us for reading Joban themes.*

The church was crowded with the young and the good, those filled with   1
promise and the first flush of achievement. Many of them were in the "industry," the almost oxymoronic euphemism that describes what people in Hollywood do to entertain and divert us, and to make enormous sums of money while doing so. Some observers of Harvard graduates have noted that the three cities to which our brightest and best gravitate are New York, Washington, D.C., and Hollywood. In New York they make money, in Washington they make policy, and in Hollywood they make not only films but fantasy for the whole world. Those who go there in some sense never grow up. They are Peter Pans, and they are in the business of catering to the Peter Pan and Wendy in all of us.

This was such a crowd. I had last seen many of them on Commencement   2
morning fewer than five years before when they were also in church, and among a large crowd; and on that morning the world was bright with promise and waiting for them, the sober black of academic dress neither concealing nor checking their exuberance and expectations. Few if any of them on that glad day had expected to return to Harvard or to The Memorial Church quite so soon, or for the sad and solemn purpose of burying one of their own who had been killed in a senseless, irrational car accident in the prime of life. Here they were, however, black-suited, still fair of face, and looking younger and indeed more vulnerable than when last we had all been together. Death had intruded, and with it a monstrous assault on the human claim to immortality. They wept, and they raged at the loss of their friend. Death was an abstraction about which movies were made, and death happened to grandparents, to the occasional victim of terrible crime, or to participants in war. Death in theory would come to them eventually, but so far down the road of reality that it was hardly real at all. How does one deal with unscripted death? How do the worldly-wise, the hip, the interpreters of life in the fast, or at least in the interesting, lane deal with it? How do they deal with the irrational and immutable judgments of death unprepared, unexpected, unwelcome?

The Victorians, we are told, loved death and feared sex, and hence their   3
culture embraced a culture of death and mourning, and constructed strong

taboos against sex. We, on the other hand, love sex and fear death, and our taboos are of a different sort. We delight in sexuality, we pander to the sensual, and we have made Calvin Klein a very wealthy man. Death is not something we want to understand or to know; death is somehow unfair, and in this country it is culturally unconstitutional, violating our right to life, liberty, and the pursuit of happiness. Thus, when death intrudes, particularly among the young, we respond in terror, anger, and fear.

As I listened to the heartrending eulogies of the young for their young, I heard anger and fear. I heard their love as well, and their pained, pathetic desire to make sense of it all. "What does it mean?" asked one tearful young woman. "We must make it mean something," said another. "It doesn't make sense," said a third. "Will it get easier to understand this as we get older?" a bright young man asked me as the white wine flowed at the reception. "Will I wake up some day and understand why Willie had to die in this way, at this time?" It was not a question that required an answer, at least not then, for he was baying at the moon, not making a theological inquiry.   4

I think I said most of the right things. One hopes, in my calling, that one does on occasions like this. Clichés become truths when they are applied to one's own situation, I have discovered, and I reminded these young people that while funeral-going was perhaps a new experience for most of them, it was an all too familiar habit for the rest of us. I reminded them that the context of life is not living, but death, and that it is out of death that life comes. Death is the rule to which life is the exception. It is not how long you live, but how well you live with what you have, and I quoted that lovely and relatively unfamiliar passage from the Apocrypha, which says of early death: "He, being made perfect in a short time, fulfilled a long time; for his soul pleased the Lord: therefore hasted he to take him away from among the wicked." (Wisdom 4:8–14)   5

I always end memorial services and funerals with the prayer long associated with Cardinal Newman, and I did so on this day. Many were familiar with it, and many more were not, but were interested in it: 6

> O Lord, support us all the day long of this troublous life, until the shadows lengthen and the evening comes, and the fever of life is over, and our work is done. Then, in thy great mercy, grant us a safe lodging, a holy rest, and peace at the last.

We scattered again, as we always do, back to the demands and diversions of this troublous life, pondering the meaning of suffering, the purpose of life, and trying to make sense of it all as in the making of a living we try to make a life as well. It is for moments such as these that religion was made, and when we confront the unconfrontable, or more to the point, when it confronts us, we are at a religious moment, and for a moment at least we are religious. Contrary to the popular misconception, religion is not an escape from reality but rather a genuine effort to make sense of what passes for reality and all that surrounds it. Religious people are not escape artists; they are not practitioners of evasion or of self-deception. Religion is not the answer to the   7 unknowable or the unfaceable or the unendurable; religion is what we do and what we are in the face of the unknowable, the unfaceable, and the unendurable. It is a constant exercise in the making of sense first, and then of meaning.

"I'm not very religious, but I had to come to this service," said one of my 8 secular young mourners. He was more religious than he thought, not because he professed certain doctrines or behaved in a particular way or performed certain rites and rituals and believed in what they said and did. He was religious because he wanted to make sense of what he was experiencing, pain and all, and on his own and by himself he could not. Legal, medical, physiological, even psychological answers, themselves definitive and helpful, were not sufficient of themselves; somehow something else was wanted and needed.

THE THIN PLACES

That something else wanted and needed is what religion is about. "Religion 9 in its simplest terms," says John Habgood,[1] the recently retired Archbishop of York, "is about making sense of life, of this life first of all, and particularly of those aspects of it which challenge and disturb us. This is why suffering and ways of responding to it have always been so central to religion." Not only do we have a need to try to make sense of suffering, Dr. Habgood tells us, but we also want to make sense where we can of joy—"undeserved happiness," he calls it—or "blessings," as the devout and pious call it; and of mystery, those close encounters of the transcendent kind that suggest relationships beyond the power of our experience to reckon, but which we know in some fundamental way to be true. Suffering, joy, and mystery are those points where the human and the divine come into the most intimate and profound of proximities. They unite all human experience in all ages and beyond all particulars of place and of circumstance. All religions of the world are and always have been concerned with their substance. It is the common ambition of our common humanity to make sense and meaning of these encounters wherever we can. Religion is the attempt to give some formal record of what we may learn from these experiences, and, for Christians, the Bible is the authoritative record of the human encounter with God at these points.

There is in Celtic mythology the notion of "thin places" in the universe, 10 where the visible and the invisible world come into their closest proximity. To seek such places is the vocation of the wise and the good, and those who find them find the clearest communication between the temporal and the eternal. Monasteries and holy places were meant to be founded at such spots to increase the likelihood of a transcendental communication. These thin places were threshold places, from the Latin *limen*, which can mean a border or frontier place where two worlds meet and where one has the possibility of communicating with the other. In Celtic studies the phrase can refer to places that stand at the border between the spiritual and temporal realms, and between people gifted with supernatural gifts in the mundane world and those living on the border.

Perhaps we can adapt the concept of such thin places to the experience   11
that people are likely to have as they encounter suffering, joy, and mystery,
and seek in some fashion to make sense of that encounter. If we think of these
encounters as the ultimate thin places of human experience, and of religion as
a way of talking and thinking about the encounters, we might do very well to
think of the Bible as our guide through the thin places, and as providing us
with a record of how our ancestors coped with their encounters, and guidance
beyond their particular situation which may be useful in ours. Contrary to the
efforts and assumptions of many, the Bible is not a systematic book. It is not
a doctrinal handbook or a systematic theology, nor is it a comprehensive history or a compendium of morals and ethics. To argue that it is any of these is
to make the Bible conform to an extra-biblical set of convictions and assumptions, and to make it pass a test of theological orthodoxy of which it is not
capable. Doctrines of inerrancy and infallibility are merely modern human
efforts to impose order both on scripture and on those who read it. These are
what John Huxtable[2] once called "dogmatic vested interest," designed to
preserve as the word of God a particularly partisan way of looking at scripture. Such a way of reading the Bible is designed to support those interests,
and they are "found" in the Bible because they are brought to the Bible.

There are principles and ideas that develop over time through the pages   12
of scripture that make it possible for us to detect truths that transcend the
contexts in which they are found, principles that go beyond captivity to a
given situation, and which stand out like the mountains on the moon. Indeed,
it is such normative teaching and such developing ideas and ideals that enable
us to judge scriptural situation by scriptural principle, and thus, in order to be
biblical, we are able to read scripture freed of the expectation that we must
reproduce its every detail and circumstance. . . .

If we are to think of scripture not so much as we would a book of histo-   13
ry, theology, or philosophy, but as the human experience of the divine at the
thin places of encounter, then perhaps we may enter into a book that is perhaps less elusive and more accessible than we might have at first been led to
believe. If the Bible is understood to be the place where not only others long
dead but we ourselves encounter those thin places of suffering, joy, and mystery, and the efforts to make sense and meaning of those encounters, then perhaps we have rescued it from the clutches of the experts and the specialists
and placed it where it rightly belongs, namely in the hands of those who find
themselves more religious than they thought.

WHAT DARE WE MAKE OF SUFFERING?

I recall reading some years ago of the death of the young son of William Sloan   14
Coffin, in a horrible automobile accident in Boston. At some point, perhaps
at the funeral, perhaps later in a sermon, the anguished father discussed his
reaction to this terrible experience, saying that frequently people would
attempt to comfort him with the Christian cliché, "It is God's will." Coffin
thundered, "The hell it is. When my boy was killed, God was the first who

cried." If God can be sympathetic and empathetic, why can't God prevent the source of those troubles that require human and divine sympathy? Suffering makes us ask hard questions of God, i.e., where were you when I needed you? Suffering also makes us ask hard questions of ourselves: What have I done to deserve this?

If suffering is, as I suggest that it is, a thin place, indeed a place of prox-   15
imity to the divine, such proximity has served to alienate many from God rather than draw them nearer. If God is indifferent to suffering—for example, if God really does not care about the manifest human sufferings in Bosnia, or in Rwanda, or in the AIDS wards of the local hospitals, or in the galloping Alzheimer's disease of an old and once-bright friend or spouse—who cares for that kind of God?

If God is merely sympathetic but impotent in the face of such difficulties,   16
then again, of what value is the idea? Sympathy is cheap, and hence abundant. Divine sympathy is no more or less helpful than any other kind.

If God is the source or cause of the suffering, and the suffering is an   17
expression of God's will, then is this not a malevolent, vengeful, even perverse God, who exercises ultimate power in a capricious, or even immoral, way?

Indifferent, sympathetic, arbitrary—somehow God is usually called into   18
our conversations about suffering, for the ultimate suffering is that suffering itself is meaningless and must be endured alone. Misery loves company, we are told. Well, there is more to it than that, for misery actually requires company. Just as it is really not possible to be happy alone, "the sound of one hand clapping" and all of that, so too it is not really possible to suffer alone. That is why we invoke God, even the godless among us, and that is why we are constantly looking for companionship in suffering, either to share or to blame or at times to do both.

Suffering, we are taught very early on, is a part of life. As the Yankee   19
adage has it, "What can't be cured must be endured," and most of us were brought up with an understanding of that concept. We were taught as well that suffering was redemptive or, at the very least, instructive. When we suffer, we are more apt to learn. Our mothers used to say that suffering was God's way of getting our attention, and that there were lessons to be learned from suffering. We would be the better for it.

Redemptive—dare we even say therapeutic?—suffering is that of which   20
Paul speaks with a beguiling candor when, in writing his second letter to the Corinthians, he speaks of his "thorn in the flesh": "And to keep me from being too elated by the abundance of revelations, a thorn was given me in the flesh, a messenger of Satan, to harass me, to keep me from being too elated."

Paul was not a masochist delighting in this object lesson in humility and   21
suffering, for he asked not once but three times to be rid of this trouble: "Three times I besought the Lord about this, that it should leave me; but he said to me, 'My grace is sufficient for you, for my power is made perfect in weakness.'"

Paul's sufferings were not relieved, and he understood his weakness to be   22
an opportunity to manifest the power of God: "I will all the more gladly boast

of my weaknesses, that the power of Christ may rest upon me. For the sake of Christ, then, I am content with weaknesses, insults, hardships, persecutions, and calamities; for when I am weak, then I am strong." (II Corinthians 12:7–10)

• • •

Suffering . . . is not an exception to the human condition, it *is* the human 23 condition, and as such it is almost impossible to avoid; and since religion, as we have said, has to do with the human condition, and indeed with the enormous task of trying to make sense and meaning of it, religion by its very nature has an intimacy with suffering. That intimacy is the stuff of which our lives are composed.

Sigmund Freud,[3] no friend of religion, nevertheless gives us a comprehensive sense of suffering, and thus we are enabled to see the scope of religion's intimate relations with it. Says Freud: 24

> We are threatened with suffering from three directions: from our own body, which is doomed to decay and dissolution and which cannot even do that without pain and anxiety as warning signals; from the external world, which may rage against us with overwhelming and merciless forces of destruction; and finally, from our relations to other men. The suffering which comes from this last source is perhaps more painful than any other.

Morality, conflict, and ethics: These sources of our sufferings have always 25 been the business of religion and of the Bible. How do we deal with the fact that inevitably we die, that our life before we die is conflicted and besieged, and that we find it difficult to get along with our fellow creatures? These are not Freudian categories; this is life itself.

REFERENCES

1. John Habgood. *Making Sense* (London: SPCK, 1993). As Archibishop of York, Habgood was the Primate of England, whereas his brother Archbishop of Canterbury was Primate of *All* England, with a seat in the House of Lords as one of the Lords Spiritual and a reputation as a thinking bishop. Indeed, David L. Edwards in the jacket blurb said of Habgood, "Were there to be an Olympics in episcopal theology, Dr. Habgood would win the gold." The tradition of "thinking bishops" in the Church of England is an old and lively one, but in this managerial and politically correct age, where the lowest point of nonoffense is appealed to, the appointment of a thinking bishop who makes others think as well is a rarity in the Church of England and nearly nonexistent in the other realms of the Anglican Communion. These essays are drawn from his writings in his own diocesan magazine, professional and scholarly journals, articles in the press, and some of his lectures and sermons. In the essay "Do Pigs Have Wings?" he argues, "Religion in its simplest terms is about making sense of life, this life, first of all, and particularly those aspects of it which challenge and disturb us." It was from this essay that the third and final section of my own book, the pastoral section, took its inspiration.

2. John Huxtable, *The Bible Says* (London: SCM Press, 1962). This is a small but very effective essay against the ever-present temptation to make a graven image out of the Bible. One of his best lines is "Jesus Christ came into the world to be its saviour, not an authority on biblical criticism." (p. 70)
3. Sigmund Freud, *Civilization and Its Discontents* (London: 1930), Chapter 2. Richard Webster in *Why Freud Was Wrong: Sin, Science, and Psychoanalysis* (New York: Basic Books, 1995), in writing of Freud's low estimate of the human condition, quotes from a letter to Lou Andreas-Salome in which he says, "In the depths of my heart I can't help being convinced that my dear fellow men, with a few exceptions, are worthless." (p. 324)

■ ■ ■

Review Questions

1. Why, according to Gomes, do we (and particularly young people) "respond in terror, anger, and fear" to death, especially to the death of a young person?
2. What is a "religious moment," according to Gomes?
3. What is the purpose of religion, according to Gomes?
4. How does Gomes adapt the Celtic notion of "thin places" to his discussion of suffering?
5. Why does human suffering eventually cause us to pose difficult questions about God?

Discussion and Writing Questions

1. Why do you suppose Gomes opens his discussion with an account of a memorial service? What was your response to the comments of the mourners? Have you found yourself in a similar setting? To what extent do you recognize the mourners' responses to the death of their friend?
2. Gomes speaks of a young mourner being "more religious than he [the mourner] thought." What does Gomes mean by this? And why, several paragraphs later, does Gomes suggest it is a good thing that the Bible be placed "in the hands of those who find themselves more religious than they thought"?
3. Gomes discusses the apostle Paul's speaking of a "thorn in the flesh" (p. 404). Paul explains the thorn in terms of what the Lord says to him: "'My grace is sufficient for you, for my power is made perfect in weakness.'" What does it mean to you that God's power is made perfect in weakness? How is one made strong in weakness?
4. "Suffering . . . is not an exception to the human condition, it *is* the human condition." Do you agree with this assessment?

5. Describe the effect of this selection on you: are you calmed, perhaps, by the "voice" of this writer? Perplexed? Are you struck by Gomes's wisdom? Do you find that he has the voice of a minister? What *is* that voice and, again: what is its effect on you? Write your response as a journal entry.

The Book of Job

The essay introducing this chapter provides an overview that will help orient your reading of Job. This headnote is devoted to other matters: the complex authorship of the text and the difficulties of translation.

Not only do we not know the author of the Book of Job, biblical scholars are confident that more than one author is responsible for the work. Carol Newsom (author of an article you will read later in this chapter) summarizes the speculations concerning authorship in this way:

In scholarly discussions of the past century, [evidence has emerged] . . . that the book of Job grew by stages, the various parts attributable to different authors working at different times. Although there are many different versions of this hypothesis, it usually includes at least the following claims.

Stage 1. The oldest form of the book would have been the prose tale, an ancient story, originally told orally, about Job the pious. This stage is represented by chaps. 1–2 and 42:7–17. The middle part of this form of the story is no longer extant, but would have included some sort of brief dialogue between Job and his friends in which they spoke disparagingly of God, while Job steadfastly refused to curse God.

Stage 2. An Israelite author who considered the old story inadequate and in need of critique decided to use it as the framework for a much more ambitious, sophisticated retelling of the story in which the figure of Job does not remain the patiently enduring character of the traditional tale, but challenges God's treatment of him. According to this hypothesis, the author substituted a new poetic dialogue between Job and his friends (3:1–31:37) in place of the discussion in which they engaged in the older story and added a long speech by God as the climax (38:1–42:6). The author used the conclusion of the old story (42:7–17) as the conclusion of his thoroughly transformed new version of the book. The poem on wisdom in chap. 28 may be a composition by this author, who used it as a transition between Job's dialogue with his friends and Job's dialogue with God, or it may be an addition by a later hand.

Stage 3. Another author, writing sometime later, considered the new version of the book of Job unsatisfactory, because he perceived that Job had gotten the better of his three friends in their argument, and because he did not find the divine speeches to be an entirely adequate answer to Job. Consequently, he created a new character, Elihu, and inserted his long speech into the book in order to provide what seemed to him a decisive refutation of Job's arguments.

Stage 4. Sometime during the transmission of the book, copyists who were shocked by Job's blasphemous words attempted to soften their impact by rearranging the third cycle of speeches, putting some of Bildad's and Zophar's speeches into Job's mouth.

The Book of Job has posed famously difficult obstacles to translators over the centuries. Read two translations of the same passage and you may be surprised at the differences. Compare, for instance, two translations of Job's first words (3:3–5), spoken after he has lost children and wealth and has been afflicted with a loathsome disease. First, here is the Revised Standard Version, *the translation you will read in this chapter:*

> Let the day perish wherein I was born, and the night which said,
>   'A man-child is conceived.'
> Let that day be darkness! May God above not seek it, nor light shine
>   upon it.
> Let gloom and deep darkness claim it. Let clouds dwell upon it; let
>   the blackness of the day terrify it.

And here is a translation of Job's first words by poet Stephen Mitchell:

> God damn the day I was born
>   and the night that pushed me from the womb.
> On that day—let there be darkness;
>   let it never have been created;
>   let it sink back into the void.
> Let chaos overpower it;
>   let black clouds overwhelm it;
>   let the sun be plucked from its sky.[1]

Obscurities in the Hebrew text make translation highly challenging and subject to the interpretive whims of individual translators. Whereas the examples above might seem to indicate poetic or stylistic differences only, there exist key passages in Job that, translated in alternate ways, present entirely conflicting views of Job's character and the extent of his rebelliousness. In The First Dissident, *William Safire calls attention to the following line (13:15) from the Marvin H. Pope translation* (The Anchor Bible). *Job is speaking and explaining how he would stand before God and present his case as an aggrieved and innocent sufferer:*

> He may slay me, I'll not quaver.

Compare this with the King James Version:

> Though he slay me, yet I will trust in him.

Compare, again, with the Revised Standard Version *(the translation you will read):*

> Behold, he will slay me; I have no hope; yet I will defend my ways to his
>   face.

There's an enormous distance between obediently trusting in God and not quavering or between not quavering and defending oneself before God. As Safire

---

[1]Stephen Mitchell, *Into the Whirlwind: A Translation of the Book of Job* (New York: Doubleday, 1979), 19.

observes, "*Thousands of sermons have been preached on [the King James']* serene *expression of faith, but the* King James *text on which the sermons were based was a twisting of Job's meaning—from blasphemy to piety—too severe to be attributed to error. The point of this key line, modern translators agree, is not faith, but courage; not submission, but defiance."*[2] *Safire implies that the King James translators had an agenda—to present Job as a less rebellious figure than he was in the original Hebrew.*

This is to say that the translation you read here, the Revised Standard Version *(RSV, published by American Bible Scholars in 1952), cannot be called definitive—nor can any translation of so difficult a work. We present the RSV translation here because of its general readability and the fact that a great deal of Joban scholarship refers to it.*

As noted in our introduction to the chapter, we provide an extended excerpt from the Book of Job. Immediately below, you will find Carol Newsom's outline of Job. We have placed a check beside sections included in the excerpt. The notable omissions are the second and third cycles of dialogue between Job and his friends, and the speech of Elihu. Should you have access to an Internet connection, point your browser to The Bible Gateway, where you will find the full text in several translations: The URL is <http:// bible.gospelcom.net/>. Select "RSV" from the pull-down menu at "Version." Enter "Job" in the "Passage" category and click "Lookup."

Outline of Job[3]

✓ I. Job 1:2–2:13, The Prose Narrative: Introduction
   ✓ A. 1:1–22, The First Test
       1:1–5, Scene 1: Introduction to Job
       1:6–12, Scene 2: A Dialogue About Job
       1:13–22, Scene 3: The Test–Destruction of "All That He Has"
   ✓ B. 2:1–10, The Second Test
       2:1–6, Scene 4, A Second Dialogue About Job
       2:7–10, Scene 5: The Test–Disease
   ✓ C. 2:11–13, Scene 6: The Three Friends
✓ II. Job 3:1–31:40, The Poetic Dialogue Between Job and His Friends
   ✓ A. 3:1–14:22, The First Cycle
       3:1–26, Job Curses the Day of His Birth
       4:1–5:27, Traditional Understandings of Misfortune
       6:1–7:21, Job Defends the Vehemence of His Words
       6:1–30, Anguish Made Worse by the Failure of Friendship
       7:1–21, Job Confronts God

---

[2]William Safire, *The First Dissident: The Book of Job in Today's Politics* (New York: Random, 1992), xi.

[3]From *The New Interpreter's Bible.*

JOB 1[4]

[1]There was a man in the land of Uz, whose name was Job; and that man was blameless and upright, one who feared God, and turned away from evil. [2]There were born to him seven sons and three daughters. [3]He had seven thousand sheep, three thousand camels, five hundred yoke of oxen, and five hundred she-asses, and very many servants; so that this man was the greatest of all the people of the east. [4]His sons used to go and hold a feast in the house of each on his day; and they would send and invite their three sisters to eat and drink with them. [5]And when the days of the feast had run their course, Job would send and sanctify them, and he would rise early in the morning and offer burnt offerings according to the number of them all; for Job said, "It may be that my sons have sinned, and cursed God in their hearts." Thus Job did continually.

[6]Now there was a day when the sons of God came to present themselves before the LORD, and Satan also came among them. [7]The LORD said to Satan, "Whence have you come?" Satan answered the LORD, "From going to and fro on the earth, and from walking up and down on it." [8]And the LORD said to Satan, "Have you considered my servant Job, that there is none like him on the earth, a blameless and upright man, who fears God and turns away from evil?" [9]Then Satan answered the LORD, "Does Job fear God for nought? [10]Hast thou not put a hedge about him and his house and all that he has, on every side? Thou hast blessed the work of his hands, and his possessions have increased in the land. [11]But put forth thy hand now, and touch all that he has, and he will curse thee to thy face." [12]And the LORD said to Satan, "Behold, all that he has is in your power; only upon himself do not put forth your hand." So Satan went forth from the presence of the LORD.

[13]Now there was a day when his sons and daughters were eating and drinking wine in their eldest brother's house; [14]and there came a messenger to Job, and said, "The oxen were plowing and the asses feeding beside them; [15]and the Sabe'ans fell upon them and took them, and slew the servants with the edge of the sword; and I alone have escaped to tell you." [16]While he was yet speaking, there came another, and said, "The fire of God fell from heaven and burned up the sheep and the servants, and consumed them; and I alone have escaped to tell you." [17]While he was yet speaking, there came another, and said, "The Chalde'ans formed three companies, and made a raid upon the camels and took them, and slew the servants with the edge of the sword; and I alone have escaped to tell you." [18]While he was yet speaking, there came another, and said, "Your sons and daughters were eating and drinking wine in their eldest brother's house; [19]and behold, a great wind came across the wilderness, and struck the four corners of the house, and it fell upon the young people, and they are dead; and I alone have escaped to tell you."

---

[4]From *The Book of Job. Revised Standard Version.* American Bible Scholars. Numbers before sentences in this section indicate verse numbers.

²⁰Then Job arose, and rent his robe, and shaved his head, and fell upon the ground, and worshiped. ²¹And he said, "Naked I came from my mother's womb, and naked shall I return; the LORD gave, and the LORD has taken away; blessed be the name of the LORD." ²²In all this Job did not sin or charge God with wrong.

JOB 2

¹Again there was a day when the sons of God came to present themselves before the LORD, and Satan also came among them to present himself before the LORD. ²And the LORD said to Satan, "Whence have you come?" Satan answered the LORD, "From going to and fro on the earth, and from walking up and down on it." ³And the LORD said to Satan, "Have you considered my servant Job, that there is none like him on the earth, a blameless and upright man, who fears God and turns away from evil? He still holds fast his integrity, although you moved me against him, to destroy him without cause." ⁴Then Satan answered the LORD, "Skin for skin! All that a man has he will give for his life. ⁵But put forth thy hand now, and touch his bone and his flesh, and he will curse thee to thy face." ⁶And the LORD said to Satan, "Behold, he is in your power; only spare his life."

⁷So Satan went forth from the presence of the LORD, and afflicted Job with loathsome sores from the sole of his foot to the crown of his head. ⁸And he took a potsherd with which to scrape himself, and sat among the ashes.

⁹Then his wife said to him, "Do you still hold fast your integrity? Curse God, and die." ¹⁰But he said to her, "You speak as one of the foolish women would speak. Shall we receive good at the hand of God, and shall we not receive evil?" In all this Job did not sin with his lips.

¹¹Now when Job's three friends heard of all this evil that had come upon him, they came each from his own place, Eli'phaz the Te'manite, Bildad the Shuhite, and Zophar the Na'amathite. They made an appointment together to come to condole him and comfort him. ¹²And when they saw him from afar, they did not recognize him; and they raised their voices and wept; and they rent their robes and sprinkled dust upon their heads toward heaven. ¹³And they sat with him on the ground seven days and seven nights, and no one spoke a word to him, for they saw that his suffering was very great.

JOB 3

¹After this Job opened his mouth and cursed the day of his birth.
²And Job said:
³"Let the day perish wherein I was born, and the night which said, 'A man-child is conceived.'
⁴Let that day be darkness! May God above not seek it, nor light shine upon it.
⁵Let gloom and deep darkness claim it. Let clouds dwell upon it; let the blackness of the day terrify it.

⁶That night—let thick darkness seize it! let it not rejoice among the days of the year, let it not come into the number of the months.

⁷Yea, let that night be barren; let no joyful cry be heard in it.

⁸Let those curse it who curse the day, who are skilled to rouse up Levi'athan.

⁹Let the stars of its dawn be dark; let it hope for light, but have none, nor see the eyelids of the morning;

¹⁰because it did not shut the doors of my mother's womb, nor hide trouble from my eyes.

¹¹"Why did I not die at birth, come forth from the womb and expire?

¹²Why did the knees receive me? Or why the breasts, that I should suck?

¹³For then I should have lain down and been quiet; I should have slept; then I should have been at rest,

¹⁴with the kings and counselors of the earth who rebuilt ruins for themselves,

¹⁵or with princes who had gold, who filled their houses with silver.

¹⁶Or why was I not as a hidden untimely birth, as infants that never see the light?

¹⁷There the wicked cease from troubling, and there the weary are at rest.

¹⁸There the prisoners are at ease together; they hear not the voice of the taskmaster.

¹⁹The small and the great are there, and the slave is free from his master.

²⁰"Why is light given to him that is in misery, and life to the bitter in soul,

²¹who long for death, but it comes not, and dig for it more than for hid treasures;

²²who rejoice exceedingly, and are glad, when they find the grave?

²³Why is light given to a man whose way is hid, whom God has hedged in?

²⁴For my sighing comes as my bread, and my groanings are poured out like water.

²⁵For the thing that I fear comes upon me, and what I dread befalls me.

²⁶I am not at ease, nor am I quiet; I have no rest; but trouble comes."

JOB 4

¹Then Eli'phaz the Te'manite answered:

²"If one ventures a word with you, will you be offended? Yet who can keep from speaking?

³Behold, you have instructed many, and you have strengthened the weak hands.

⁴Your words have upheld him who was stumbling, and you have made firm the feeble knees.

⁵But now it has come to you, and you are impatient; it touches you, and you are dismayed.

⁶Is not your fear of God your confidence, and the integrity of your ways your hope?

⁷"Think now, who that was innocent ever perished? Or where were the upright cut off?

⁸As I have seen, those who plow iniquity and sow trouble reap the same.

⁹By the breath of God they perish, and by the blast of his anger they are consumed.

¹⁰The roar of the lion, the voice of the fierce lion, the teeth of the young lions, are broken.

¹¹The strong lion perishes for lack of prey, and the whelps of the lioness are scattered.

¹²"Now a word was brought to me stealthily, my ear received the whisper of it.

¹³Amid thoughts from visions of the night, when deep sleep falls on men,

¹⁴dread came upon me, and trembling, which made all my bones shake.

¹⁵A spirit glided past my face; the hair of my flesh stood up.

¹⁶It stood still, but I could not discern its appearance. A form was before my eyes; there was silence, then I heard a voice:

¹⁷'Can mortal man be righteous before God? Can a man be pure before his Maker?

¹⁸Even in his servants he puts no trust, and his angels he charges with error;

¹⁹how much more those who dwell in houses of clay, whose foundation is in the dust, who are crushed before the moth.

²⁰Between morning and evening they are destroyed; they perish for ever without any regarding it.

²¹If their tent-cord is plucked up within them, do they not die, and that without wisdom?'

JOB 5

¹"Call now; is there any one who will answer you? To which of the holy ones will you turn?

²Surely vexation kills the fool, and jealousy slays the simple.

³I have seen the fool taking root, but suddenly I cursed his dwelling.

⁴His sons are far from safety, they are crushed in the gate, and there is no one to deliver them.

⁵His harvest the hungry eat, and he takes it even out of thorns; and the thirsty pant after his wealth.

⁶For affliction does not come from the dust, nor does trouble sprout from the ground;

⁷but man is born to trouble as the sparks fly upward.

⁸"As for me, I would seek God, and to God would I commit my cause;

⁹who does great things and unsearchable, marvelous things without number:

¹⁰he gives rain upon the earth and sends waters upon the fields;

¹¹he sets on high those who are lowly, and those who mourn are lifted to safety.

¹²He frustrates the devices of the crafty, so that their hands achieve no success.

¹³He takes the wise in their own craftiness; and the schemes of the wily are brought to a quick end.

¹⁴They meet with darkness in the daytime, and grope at noonday as in the night.

¹⁵But he saves the fatherless from their mouth, the needy from the hand of the mighty.

¹⁶So the poor have hope, and injustice shuts her mouth.

¹⁷"Behold, happy is the man whom God reproves; therefore despise not the chastening of the Almighty.

¹⁸For he wounds, but he binds up; he smites, but his hands heal.

¹⁹He will deliver you from six troubles; in seven there shall no evil touch you.

²⁰In famine he will redeem you from death, and in war from the power of the sword.

²¹You shall be hid from the scourge of the tongue, and shall not fear destruction when it comes.

²²At destruction and famine you shall laugh, and shall not fear the beasts of the earth.

²³For you shall be in league with the stones of the field, and the beasts of the field shall be at peace with you.

²⁴You shall know that your tent is safe, and you shall inspect your fold and miss nothing.

²⁵You shall know also that your descendants shall be many, and your offspring as the grass of the earth.

²⁶You shall come to your grave in ripe old age, as a shock of grain comes up to the threshing floor in its season.

²⁷Lo, this we have searched out; it is true. Hear, and know it for your good."

JOB 6

¹Then Job answered:

²"O that my vexation were weighed, and all my calamity laid in the balances!

³For then it would be heavier than the sand of the sea; therefore my words have been rash.

⁴For the arrows of the Almighty are in me; my spirit drinks their poison; the terrors of God are arrayed against me.

⁵Does the wild ass bray when he has grass, or the ox low over his fodder?

⁶Can that which is tasteless be eaten without salt, or is there any taste in the slime of the purslane?

⁷My appetite refuses to touch them; they are as food that is loathsome to me.

⁸"O that I might have my request, and that God would grant my desire;

⁹that it would please God to crush me, that he would let loose his hand and cut me off!

¹⁰This would be my consolation; I would even exult in pain unsparing; for I have not denied the words of the Holy One.

¹¹What is my strength, that I should wait? And what is my end, that I should be patient?

¹²Is my strength the strength of stones, or is my flesh bronze?

¹³In truth I have no help in me, and any resource is driven from me.

¹⁴"He who withholds kindness from a friend forsakes the fear of the Almighty.

¹⁵My brethren are treacherous as a torrent-bed, as freshets that pass away,

¹⁶which are dark with ice, and where the snow hides itself.

¹⁷In time of heat they disappear; when it is hot, they vanish from their place.

¹⁸The caravans turn aside from their course; they go up into the waste, and perish.

¹⁹The caravans of Tema look, the travelers of Sheba hope.

²⁰They are disappointed because they were confident; they come thither and are confounded.

²¹Such you have now become to me; you see my calamity, and are afraid.

²²Have I said, 'Make me a gift'? Or, 'From your wealth offer a bribe for me'?

²³Or, 'Deliver me from the adversary's hand'? Or, 'Ransom me from the hand of oppressors'?

²⁴"Teach me, and I will be silent; make me understand how I have erred.

²⁵How forceful are honest words! But what does reproof from you reprove?

²⁶Do you think that you can reprove words, when the speech of a despairing man is wind?

²⁷You would even cast lots over the fatherless, and bargain over your friend.

²⁸"But now, be pleased to look at me; for I will not lie to your face.

²⁹Turn, I pray, let no wrong be done. Turn now, my vindication is at stake.

³⁰Is there any wrong on my tongue? Cannot my taste discern calamity?

JOB 7

¹"Has not man a hard service upon earth, and are not his days like the days of a hireling?

²Like a slave who longs for the shadow, and like a hireling who looks for his wages,

³so I am allotted months of emptiness, and nights of misery are apportioned to me.

⁴When I lie down I say, 'When shall I arise?' But the night is long, and I am full of tossing till the dawn.

⁵My flesh is clothed with worms and dirt; my skin hardens, then breaks out afresh.

⁶My days are swifter than a weaver's shuttle, and come to their end without hope.

⁷"Remember that my life is a breath; my eye will never again see good.

⁸The eye of him who sees me will behold me no more; while thy eyes are upon me, I shall be gone.

⁹As the cloud fades and vanishes, so he who goes down to Sheol does not come up;

¹⁰he returns no more to his house, nor does his place know him any more.

¹¹"Therefore I will not restrain my mouth; I will speak in the anguish of my spirit; I will complain in the bitterness of my soul.

¹²Am I the sea, or a sea monster, that thou settest a guard over me?

¹³When I say, 'My bed will comfort me, my couch will ease my complaint,'

¹⁴then thou dost scare me with dreams and terrify me with visions,

¹⁵so that I would choose strangling and death rather than my bones.

¹⁶I loathe my life; I would not live for ever. Let me alone, for my days are a breath.

¹⁷What is man, that thou dost make so much of him, and that thou dost set thy mind upon him,

¹⁸dost visit him every morning, and test him every moment?

¹⁹How long wilt thou not look away from me, nor let me alone till I swallow my spittle?

²⁰If I sin, what do I do to thee, thou watcher of men? Why hast thou made me thy mark? Why have I become a burden to thee?

²¹Why dost thou not pardon my transgression and take away my iniquity? For now I shall lie in the earth; thou wilt seek me, but I shall not be."

JOB 8

¹Then Bildad the Shuhite answered:

²"How long will you say these things, and the words of your mouth be a great wind?

³Does God pervert justice? Or does the Almighty pervert the right?

⁴If your children have sinned against him, he has delivered them into the power of their transgression.

⁵If you will seek God and make supplication to the Almighty,

⁶if you are pure and upright, surely then he will rouse himself for you and reward you with a rightful habitation.

⁷And though your beginning was small, your latter days will be very great.

⁸"For inquire, I pray you, of bygone ages, and consider what the fathers have found;

⁹for we are but of yesterday, and know nothing, for our days on earth are a shadow.

¹⁰Will they not teach you, and tell you, and utter words out of their understanding?

¹¹"Can papyrus grow where there is no marsh? Can reeds flourish where there is no water?

¹²While yet in flower and not cut down, they wither before any other plant.

¹³Such are the paths of all who forget God; the hope of the godless man shall perish.

¹⁴His confidence breaks in sunder, and his trust is a spider's web.

¹⁵He leans against his house, but it does not stand; he lays hold of it, but it does not endure.

¹⁶He thrives before the sun, and his shoots spread over his garden.

¹⁷His roots twine about the stoneheap; he lives among the rocks.

¹⁸If he is destroyed from his place, then it will deny him, saying, 'I have never seen you.'

¹⁹Behold, this is the joy of his way; and out of the earth others will spring.

²⁰"Behold, God will not reject a blameless man, nor take the hand of evildoers.

²¹He will yet fill your mouth with laughter, and your lips with shouting.

22Those who hate you will be clothed with shame, and the tent of the wicked will be no more."

JOB 9

1Then Job answered:

2"Truly I know that it is so: But how can a man be just before God?

3If one wished to contend with him, one could not answer him once in a thousand times.

4He is wise in heart, and mighty in strength—who has hardened himself against him, and succeeded?—

5he who removes mountains, and they know it not, when he overturns them in his anger,

6who shakes the earth out of its place, and its pillars tremble,

7who commands the sun, and it does not rise; who seals up the stars;

8who alone stretched out the heavens, and trampled the waves of the sea;

9who make the Bear and Orion, the Plei'ades and the chambers of the south;

10who does great things beyond understanding, and marvelous things without number.

11Lo, he passes by me, and I see him not; he moves on, but I do not perceive him.

12Behold, he snatches away; who can hinder him? Who will say to him, 'What doest thou'?

13"God will not turn back his anger; beneath him bowed the helpers of Rahab.

14How then can I answer him, choosing my words with him?

15Though I am innocent, I cannot answer him; I must appeal for mercy to my accuser.

16If I summoned him and he answered me, I would not believe that he was listening to my voice.

17For he crushes me with a tempest, and multiplies my wounds without cause,

18he will not let me get my breath, but fills me with bitterness.

19If it is a contest of strength, behold him! If it is a matter of justice, who can summon him?

20Though I am innocent, my own mouth would condemn me; though I am blameless, he would prove me perverse.

21I am blameless; I regard not myself, I loathe my life.

22It is all one; therefore I say, he destroys both the blameless and the wicked.

23When disaster brings sudden death, he mocks at the calamity of the innocent.

24The earth is given into the hand of the wicked; he covers the faces of its judges—if it is not he, who then is it?

25"My days are swifter than a runner; they flee away, they see no good.

26They go by like skiffs of reed, like an eagle swooping on the prey.

27If I say, 'I will forget my complaint, I will put off my sad countenance, and be of good cheer,'

²⁸I become afraid of all my suffering, for I know thou wilt not hold me innocent.

²⁹I shall be condemned, why then do I labor in vain?

³⁰If I wash myself with snow, and cleanse my hands with lye,

³¹yet thou wilt plunge me into a pit, and my own clothes will abhor me.

³²For he is not a man, as I am, that I might answer him, that we should come to trial together.

³³There is no umpire between us, who might lay his hand upon us both.

³⁴Let him take his rod away from me, and let not dread of him terrify me.

³⁵Then I would speak without fear of him, for I am not so in myself.

JOB 10

¹"I loathe my life; I will give free utterance to my complaint; I will speak in the bitterness of my soul.

²I will say to God, Do not condemn me; let me know why thou dost contend against me.

³Does it seem good to thee to oppress, to despise the work of thy hands and favor the designs of the wicked?

⁴Hast thou eyes of flesh? Dost thou see as man sees?

⁵Are thy days as the days of man, or thy years as man's years,

⁶that thou dost seek out my iniquity and search for my sin,

⁷although thou knowest that I am not guilty, and there is none to deliver out of thy hand?

⁸Thy hands fashioned and made me; and now thou dost turn about and destroy me.

⁹Remember that thou hast made me of clay; and wilt thou turn me to dust again?

¹⁰Didst thou not pour me out like milk and curdle me like cheese?

¹¹Thou didst clothe me with skin and flesh, and knit me together with bones and sinews.

¹²Thou hast granted me life and steadfast love; and thy care has preserved my spirit.

¹³Yet these things thou didst hide in thy heart; I know that this was thy purpose.

¹⁴If I sin, thou dost mark me, and dost not acquit me of my iniquity.

¹⁵If I am wicked, woe to me! If I am righteous, I cannot lift up my head, for I am filled with disgrace and look upon my affliction.

¹⁶And if I lift myself up, thou dost hunt me like a lion, and again work wonders against me;

¹⁷thou dost renew thy witnesses against me, and increase thy vexation toward me; thou dost bring fresh hosts against me.

¹⁸"Why didst thou bring me forth from the womb? Would that I had died before any eye had seen me,

¹⁹and were as though I had not been carried from the womb to the grave.

²⁰Are not the days of my life few? Let me alone, that I may find a little comfort

²¹before I go whence I shall not return, to the land of gloom and deep darkness,
²²the land of gloom and chaos, where light is as darkness."

JOB 11

¹Then Zophar the Na'amathite answered:
²"Should a multitude of words go unanswered, and a man full of talk be vindicated?

³Should your babble silence men, and when you mock, shall no one shame you?

⁴For you say, 'My doctrine is pure, and I am clean in God's eyes.'

⁵But oh, that God would speak, and open his lips to you,

⁶and that he would tell you the secrets of wisdom! For he is manifold in understanding. Know then that God exacts of you less than your guilt deserves.

⁷"Can you find out the deep things of God? Can you find out the limit of the Almighty?

⁸It is higher than heaven—what can you do? Deeper than Sheol—what can you know?

⁹Its measure is longer than the earth, and broader than the sea.

¹⁰If he passes through, and imprisons, and calls to judgment, who can hinder him?

¹¹For he knows worthless men; when he sees iniquity, will he not consider it?
¹²But a stupid man will get understanding, when a wild ass's colt is born a man.

¹³"If you set your heart aright, you will stretch out your hands toward him.

¹⁴If iniquity is in your hand, put it far away, and let not wickedness dwell in your tents.

¹⁵Surely then you will lift up your face without blemish; you will be secure, and will not fear.

¹⁶You will forget your misery; you will remember it as waters that have passed away.

¹⁷And your life will be brighter than the noonday; its darkness will be like the morning.

¹⁸And you will have confidence, because there is hope; you will be protected and take your rest in safety.

¹⁹You will lie down, and none will make you afraid; many will entreat your favor.

²⁰But the eyes of the wicked will fail; all the way of escape will be lost to them, and their hope is to breathe their last."

JOB 12

¹Then Job answered:
²"No doubt you are the people, and wisdom will die with you.

³But I have understanding as well as you; I am not inferior to you. Who does not know such things as these?

⁴I am a laughingstock to my friends; I, who called upon God and he answered me, a just and blameless man, am a laughingstock.

⁵In the thought of one who is at ease there is contempt for misfortune; it is ready for those whose feet slip.

⁶The tents of robbers are at peace, and those who provoke God are secure, who bring their god in their hand.

⁷"But ask the beasts, and they will teach you; the birds of the air, and they will tell you;

⁸or the plants of the earth, and they will teach you; and the fish of the sea will declare to you.

⁹Who among all these does not know that the hand of the LORD has done this?

¹⁰In his hand is the life of every living thing and the breath of all mankind.

¹¹Does not the ear try words as the palate tastes food?

¹²Wisdom is with the aged, and understanding in length of days.

¹³"With God are wisdom and might; he has counsel and understanding.

¹⁴If he tears down, none can rebuild; if he shuts a man in, none can open.

¹⁵If he withholds the waters, they dry up; if he sends them out, they overwhelm the land.

¹⁶With him are strength and wisdom; the deceived and the deceiver are his.

¹⁷He leads counselors away stripped, and judges he makes fools.

¹⁸He looses the bonds of kings, and binds a waistcloth on their loins.

¹⁹He leads priests away stripped, and overthrows the mighty.

²⁰He deprives of speech those who are trusted, and takes away the discernment of the elders.

²¹He pours contempt on princes, and looses the belt of the strong.

²²He uncovers the deeps out of darkness, and brings deep darkness to light.

²³He makes nations great, and he destroys them; he enlarges nations, and leads them away.

²⁴He takes away understanding from the chiefs of the people of the earth, and makes them wander in a pathless waste.

²⁵They grope in the dark without light; and he makes them stagger like a drunken man.

JOB 13

¹"Lo, my eye has seen all this, my ear has heard and understood it.

²What you know, I also know; I am not inferior to you.

³But I would speak to the Almighty, and I desire to argue my case with God.

⁴As for you, you whitewash with lies; worthless physicians are you all.

⁵Oh that you would keep silent, and it would be your wisdom!

⁶Hear now my reasoning, and listen to the pleadings of my lips.

⁷Will you speak falsely for God, and speak deceitfully for him?

⁸Will you show partiality toward him, will you plead the case for God?

⁹Will it be well with you when he searches you out? Or can you deceive him, as one deceives a man?

¹⁰He will surely rebuke you if in secret you show partiality.

¹¹Will not his majesty terrify you, and the dread of him fall upon you?

¹²Your maxims are proverbs of ashes, your defenses are defenses of clay.

¹³"Let me have silence, and I will speak, and let come on me what may.

¹⁴I will take my flesh in my teeth, and put my life in my hand.

¹⁵Behold, he will slay me; I have no hope; yet I will defend my ways to his face.

¹⁶This will be my salvation, that a godless man shall not come before him.

¹⁷Listen carefully to my words, and let my declaration be in your ears.

¹⁸Behold, I have prepared my case; I know that I shall be vindicated.

¹⁹Who is there that will contend with me? For then I would be silent and die.

²⁰Only grant two things to me, then I will not hide myself from thy face:

²¹withdraw thy hand far from me, and let not dread of thee terrify me.

²²Then call, and I will answer; or let me speak, and do thou reply to me.

²³How many are my iniquities and my sins? Make me know my transgression and my sin.

²⁴Why dost thou hide thy face, and count me as thy enemy?

²⁵Wilt thou frighten a driven leaf and pursue dry chaff?

²⁶For thou writest bitter things against me, and makest me inherit the iniquities of my youth.

²⁷Thou puttest my feet in the stocks, and watchest all my paths; thou settest a bound to the soles of my feet.

²⁸Man wastes away like a rotten thing, like a garment that is moth-eaten.

JOB 14

¹"Man that is born of a woman is of few days, and full of trouble

²He comes forth like a flower, and withers; he flees like a shadow, and continues not.

³And dost thou open thy eyes upon such a one and bring him into judgment with thee?

⁴Who can bring a clean thing out of an unclean? There is not one.

⁵Since his days are determined, and the number of his months is with thee, and thou hast appointed his bounds that he cannot pass,

⁶look away from him, and desist, that he may enjoy, like a hireling, his day.

⁷"For there is hope for a tree, if it be cut down, that it will sprout again, and that its shoots will not cease.

⁸Though its root grow old in the earth, and its stump die in the ground,

⁹yet at the scent of water it will bud and put forth branches like a young plant.

¹⁰But man dies, and is laid low; man breathes his last, and where is he?

¹¹As waters fail from a lake, and a river wastes away and dries up,

¹²so man lies down and rises not again; till the heavens are no more he will not awake, or be roused out of his sleep.

¹³Oh that thou wouldest hide me in Sheol, that thou wouldest conceal me until thy wrath be past, that thou wouldest appoint me a set time, and remember me!

¹⁴If a man die, shall he live again? All the days of my service I would wait, till my release should come.

¹⁵Thou wouldest call, and I would answer thee; thou wouldest long for the work of thy hands.

¹⁶For then thou wouldest number my steps, thou wouldest not keep watch over my sin;

¹⁷my transgression would be sealed up in a bag, and thou wouldest cover over my iniquity.

¹⁸"But the mountain falls and crumbles away, and the rock is removed from its place;

¹⁹the waters wear away the stones; the torrents wash away the soil of the earth; so thou destroyest the hope of man.

²⁰Thou prevailest for ever against him, and he passes; thou changest his countenance, and sendest him away.

²¹His sons come to honor, and he does not know it; they are brought low, and he perceives it not.

²²He feels only the pain of his own body, and he mourns only for himself."

• • •

JOB 28

¹"Surely there is a mine for silver, and a place for gold which they refine.

²Iron is taken out of the earth, and copper is smelted from the ore.

³Men put an end to darkness, and search out to the farthest bound the ore in gloom and deep darkness.

⁴They open shafts in a valley away from where men live; they are forgotten by travelers, they hang afar from men, they swing to and fro.

⁵As for the earth, out of it comes bread; but underneath it is turned up as by fire.

⁶Its stones are the place of sapphires, and it has dust of gold.

⁷"That path no bird of prey knows, and the falcon's eye has not seen it.

⁸The proud beasts have not trodden it; the lion has not passed over it.

⁹"Man puts his hand to the flinty rock, and overturns mountains by the roots.

¹⁰He cuts out channels in the rocks, and his eye sees every precious thing.

¹¹He binds up the streams so that they do not trickle, and the thing that is hid he brings forth to light.

¹²"But where shall wisdom be found? And where is the place of understanding?

¹³Man does not know the way to it, and it is not found in the land of the living.

[14]The deeps says, 'It is not in me,' and the sea says, 'It is not with me.'

[15]It cannot be gotten for gold, and silver cannot be weighed as its price.

[16]It cannot be valued in the gold of Ophir, in precious onyx or sapphire.

[17]Gold and glass cannot equal it, nor can it be exchanged for jewels of fine gold.

[18]No mention shall be made of coral or of crystal; the price of wisdom is above pearls.

[19]The topaz of Ethiopia cannot compare with it, nor can it be valued in pure gold.

[20]"Whence then comes wisdom? And where is the place of understanding?

[21]It is hid from the eyes of all living, and concealed from the birds of the air.

[22]Abaddon and Death say, 'We have heard a rumor of it with our ears.'

[23]"God understands the way to it, and he knows its place.

[24]For he looks to the ends of the earth, and sees everything under the heavens.

[25]When he gave to the wind its weight, and meted out the waters by measure;

[26]when he made a decree for the rain, and a way for the lightning of the thunder,

[27]then he saw it and declared it; he established it, and searched it out.

[28]And he said to man, 'Behold, the fear of the Lord, that is wisdom; and to depart from evil is understanding.'"

JOB 29

[1]And Job again took up his discourse, and said:

[2]"Oh, that I were as in the months of old, as in the days when God watched over me;

[3]when his lamp shone upon my head, and by his light I walked through darkness;

[4]as I was in my autumn days, when the friendship of God was upon my tent;

[5]when the Almighty was yet with me, when my children were about me;

[6]when my steps were washed with milk, and the rock poured out for me streams of oil!

[7]When I went out to the gate of the city, when I prepared my seat in the square,

[8]the young men saw me and withdrew, and the aged rose and stood,

[9]the princes refrained from talking and laid their hand on their mouth;

[10]the voice of the nobles was hushed, and their tongue cleaved to the roof of their mouth.

[11]When the ear heard, it called me blessed, and when the eye saw, it approved;

[12]because I delivered the poor who cried, and the fatherless who had none to help him.

[13]The blessing of him who was about to perish came upon me, and I caused the widow's heart to sing for joy.

[14]I put on righteousness, and it clothed me; my justice was like a robe and a turban.

[15]I was eyes to the blind, and feet to the lame.

¹⁶I was a father to the poor, and I searched out the cause of him whom I did not know.

¹⁷I broke the fangs of the unrighteous, and made him drop his prey from his teeth.

¹⁸Then I thought, 'I shall die in my nest, and I shall multiply my days as the sand,

¹⁹my roots spread out to the waters, with the dew all night on my branches,

²⁰my glory fresh with me, and my bow ever new in my hand.'

²¹"Men listened to me, and waited, and kept silence for my counsel.

²²After I spoke they did not speak again, and my word dropped upon them.

²³They waited for me as for the rain; and they opened their mouths as for the spring rain.

²⁴I smiled on them when they had no confidence, and the light of my countenance they did not cast down.

²⁵I chose their way, and sat as chief, and I dwelt like a king among his troops, like one who comforts mourners.

JOB 30

¹"But now they make sport of me, men who are younger than I, whose fathers I would have disdained to set with the dogs of my flock.

²What could I gain from the strength of their hands, men whose vigor is gone?

³Through want and hard hunger they gnaw the dry and desolate ground;

⁴they pick mallow and the leaves of bushes, and to warm themselves the roots of the broom.

⁵They are driven out from among men; they shout after them as after a thief.

⁶In the gullies of the torrents they must dwell, in holes of the earth and of the rocks.

⁷Among the bushes they bray; under the nettles they huddle together.

⁸A senseless, a disreputable brood, they have been whipped out of the land.

⁹"And now I have become their song, I am a byword to them.

¹⁰They abhor me, they keep aloof from me; they do not hesitate to spit at the sight of me.

¹¹Because God has loosed my cord and humbled me, they have cast off restraint in my presence.

¹²On my right hand the rabble rise, they drive me forth, they cast up against me their ways of destruction.

¹³They break up my path, they promote my calamity; no one restrains them.

¹⁴As through a wide breach they come; amid the crash they roll on.

¹⁵Terrors are turned upon me; my honor is pursued as by the wind, and my prosperity has passed away like a cloud.

¹⁶"And now my soul is poured out within me; days of affliction have taken hold of me.

¹⁷The night racks my bones, and the pain that gnaws me takes no rest.

[18]With violence it seizes my garment; it binds me about like the collar of my tunic.

[19]God has cast me into the mire, and I have become like dust and ashes.

[20]I cry to thee and thou dost not answer me; I stand, and thou dost not heed me.

[21]Thou has turned cruel to me; with the might of thy hand thou dost persecute me.

[22]Thou liftest me up on the wind, thou makest me ride on it, and thou tossest me about in the roar of the storm.

[23]Yea, I know that thou wilt bring me to death, and to the house appointed for all living.

[24]"Yet does not one in a heap of ruins stretch out his hand, and in his disaster cry for help?

[25]Did not I weep for him whose day was hard? Was not my soul grieved for the poor?

[26]But when I looked for good, evil came; and when I waited for light, darkness came.

[27]My heart is in turmoil, and is never still; days of affliction come to meet me.

[28]I go about blackened, but not by the sun; I stand up in the assembly, and cry for help.

[29]I am a brother of jackals, and a companion of ostriches.

[30]My skin turns black and falls from me, and my bones burn with heat.

[31]My lyre is turned to mourning, and my pipe to the voice of those who weep.

JOB 31

[1]"I have made a covenant with my eyes; how then could I look upon a virgin?

[2]What would be my portion from God above, and my heritage from the Almighty on high?

[3]Does not calamity befall the unrighteous, and disaster the workers of iniquity?

[4]Does not he see my ways, and number all my steps?

[5]"If I have walked with falsehood, and my foot has hastened to deceit;

[6](Let me be weighed in a just balance, and let God know my integrity!)

[7]if my step has turned aside from the way, and my heart has gone after my eyes, and if any spot has cleaved to my hands;

[8]then let me sow, and another eat; and let what grows for me be rooted out.

[9]"If my heart has been enticed to a woman, and I have lain in wait at my neighbor's door;

[10]then let my wife grind for another, and let others bow down upon her.

[11]For that would be a heinous crime; that would be an iniquity to be punished by the judges;

[12]for that would be a fire which consumes unto Abaddon, and it would burn to the root all my increase.

¹³"If I have rejected the cause of my manservant or my maidservant, when they brought a complaint against me:

¹⁴what then shall I do when God rises up? When he makes inquiry, what shall I answer him?

¹⁵Did not he who made me in the womb make him? And did not one fashion us in the womb?

¹⁶"If I have withheld anything that the poor desired, or have caused the eyes of the widow to fail,

¹⁷or have eaten my morsel alone, and the fatherless has not eaten of it

¹⁸(for from his youth I reared him as a father, and from his mother's womb I guided him);

¹⁹if I have seen any one perish for lack of clothing, or a poor man without covering;

²⁰if his loins have not blessed me, and if he was not warmed with the fleece of my sheep;

²¹if I have raised my hand against the fatherless, because I saw help in the gate;

²²then let my shoulder blade fall from my shoulder, and let my arm be broken from its socket.

²³For I was in terror of calamity from God, and I could not have faced his majesty.

²⁴"If I have made gold my trust, or called fine gold my confidence;

²⁵if I have rejoiced because my wealth was great, or because my hand had gotten much;

²⁶if I have looked at the sun when it shone, or the moon moving in splendor,

²⁷and my heart has been secretly enticed, and my mouth has kissed my hand;

²⁸this also would be an iniquity to be punished by the judges, for I should have been false to God above.

²⁹"If I have rejoiced at the ruin of him that hated me, or exulted when evil overtook him

³⁰(I have not let my mouth sin by asking for his life with a curse);

³¹if the men of my tent have not said, "'Who is there that has not been filled with his meat?'

³²(the sojourner has not lodged in the street; I have opened my doors to the wayfarer);

³³if I have concealed my transgressions from men, by hiding my iniquity in my bosom,

³⁴because I stood in great fear of the multitude, and the contempt of families terrified me, so that I kept silence, and did not go out of doors—

³⁵Oh, that I had one to hear me! (Here is my signature! let the Almighty answer me!) Oh, that I had the indictment written by my adversary!

³⁶Surely I would carry it on my shoulder; I would bind it on me as a crown;

³⁷I would give him an account of all my steps; like a prince I would approach him.

³⁸"If my land has cried out against me, and its furrows have wept together;

³⁹if I have eaten its yield without payment, and caused the death of its owners;

^{40}let thorns grow instead of wheat, and foul weeds instead of barley." The words of Job are ended.

JOB 32

^{1}So these three men ceased to answer Job, because he was righteous in his own eyes.

· · ·

JOB 38

^{1}Then the LORD answered Job out of the whirlwind:
^{2}"Who is this that darkens counsel by words without knowledge?
^{3}Gird up your loins like a man, I will question you, and you shall declare to me.
^{4}"Where were you when I laid the foundation of the earth? Tell me, if you have understanding.
^{5}Who determined its measurements—surely you know! Or who stretched the line upon it?
^{6}On what were its bases sunk, or who laid its cornerstone,
^{7}when the morning stars sang together, and all the sons of God shouted for joy?
^{8}"Or who shut in the sea with doors, when it burst forth from the womb;
^{9}when I made clouds its garment, and thick darkness its swaddling band,
^{10}and prescribed bounds for it, and set bars and doors,
^{11}and said, 'Thus far shall you come, and no farther, and here shall your proud waves be stayed'?
^{12}"Have you commanded the morning since your days began, and caused the dawn to know its place,
^{13}that it might take hold of the skirts of the earth, and the wicked be shaken out of it?
^{14}It is changed like clay under the seal, and it is dyed like a garment.
^{15}From the wicked their light is withheld, and their uplifted arm is broken.
^{16}"Have you entered into the springs of the sea, or walked in the recesses of the deep?
^{17}Have the gates of death been revealed to you, or have you seen the gates of deep darkness?
^{18}Have you comprehended the expanse of the earth? Declare, if you know all this.
^{19}"Where is the way to the dwelling of light, and where is the place of darkness,
^{20}that you may take it to its territory and that you may discern the paths to its home?
^{21}You know, for you were born then, and the number of your days is great!
^{22}"Have you entered the storehouses of the snow, or have you seen the storehouses of the hail,
^{23}which I have reserved for the time of trouble, for the day of battle and war?

²⁴What is the way to the place where the light is distributed, or where the east wind is scattered upon the earth?

²⁵"Who has cleft a channel for the torrents of rain, and a way for the thunderbolt,

²⁶to bring rain on a land where no man is, on the desert in which there is no man;

²⁷to satisfy the waste and desolate land, and to make the ground put forth grass?

²⁸"Has the rain a father, or who has begotten the drops of dew?

²⁹From whose womb did the ice come forth, and who has given birth to the hoarfrost of heaven?

³⁰The waters become hard like stone, and the face of the deep is frozen.

³¹"Can you bind the chains of the Plei'ades, or loose the cords of Orion?

³²Can you lead forth the Maz'zaroth in their season, or can you guide the Bear with its children?

³³Do you know the ordinances of the heavens? Can you establish their rule on the earth?

³⁴"Can you lift up your voice to the clouds, that a flood of waters may cover you?

³⁵Can you send forth lightnings, that they may go and say to you, 'Here we are'?

³⁶Who has put wisdom in the clouds, or given understanding to the mists?

³⁷Who can number the clouds by wisdom? Or who can tilt the waterskins of the heavens,

³⁸when the dust runs into a mass and the clods cleave fast together?

³⁹"Can you hunt the prey for the lion, or satisfy the appetite of the young lions,

⁴⁰when they crouch in their dens, or lie in wait in their covert?

⁴¹Who provides for the raven its prey, when its young ones cry to God, and wander about for lack of food?

JOB 39

¹"Do you know when the mountain goats bring forth? Do you observe the calving of the hinds?

²Can you number the months that they fulfill, and do you know the time when they bring forth,

³when they crouch, bring forth their offspring, and are delivered of their young?

⁴Their young ones become strong, they grow up in the open; they go forth, and do not return to them.

⁵"Who has let the wild ass go free? Who has loosed the bonds of the swift ass,

⁶to whom I have given the steppe for his home, and the salt land for his dwelling place?

⁷He scorns the tumult of the city; he hears not the shouts of the driver.

⁸He ranges the mountains as his pasture, and he searches after every green thing.

⁹"Is the wild ox willing to serve you? Will he spend the night at your crib?

¹⁰Can you bind him in the furrow with ropes, or will he harrow the valleys after you?

¹¹Will you depend on him because his strength is great, and will you leave to him your labor?

¹²Do you have faith in him that he will return, and bring your grain to your threshing floor?

¹³"The wings of the ostrich wave proudly; but are they the pinions and plumage of love?

¹⁴For she leaves her eggs to the earth, and lets them be warmed on the ground,

¹⁵forgetting that a foot may crush them, and that the wild beast may trample them.

¹⁶She deals cruelly with her young, as if they were not hers; though her labor be in vain, yet she has no fear;

¹⁷because God has made her forget wisdom, and given her no share in understanding.

¹⁸When she rouses herself to flee, she laughs at the horse and his rider.

¹⁹"Do you give the horse his might? Do you clothe his neck with strength?

²⁰Do you make him leap like the locust? His majestic snorting is terrible.

²¹He paws in the valley, and exults in his strength; he goes out to meet the weapons.

²²He laughs at fear, and is not dismayed; he does not turn back from the sword.

²³Upon him rattle the quiver, the flashing spear and the javelin.

²⁴With fierceness and rage he swallows the ground; he cannot stand still at the sound of the trumpet.

²⁵When the trumpet sounds, he says 'Aha!' He smells the battle from afar, the thunder of the captains, and the shouting.

²⁶"Is it by your wisdom that the hawk soars, and spreads his wings toward the south?

²⁷Is it at your command that the eagle mounts up and makes his nest on high?

²⁸On the rock he dwells and makes his home in the fastness of the rocky crag.

²⁹Thence he spies out the prey; his eyes behold it afar off.

³⁰His young ones suck up blood; and where the slain are, there is he."

JOB 40

¹And the LORD said to Job:

²"Shall a faultfinder contend with the Almighty? He who argues with God, let him answer it."

³Then Job answered the LORD:

⁴"Behold, I am of small account; what shall I answer thee? I lay my hand on my mouth.

⁵I have spoken once, and I will not answer; twice, but I will proceed no further."

⁶Then the LORD answered Job out of the whirlwind:

[7]"Gird up your loins like a man; I will question you, and you declare to me.

[8]Will you even put me in the wrong? Will you condemn me that you may be justified?

[9]Have you an arm like God, and can you thunder with a voice like his?

[10]"Deck yourself with majesty and dignity; clothe yourself with glory and splendor.

[11]Pour forth the overflowings of your anger, and look on every one that is proud, and abase him.

[12]Look on every one that is proud, and bring him low; and tread down the wicked where they stand.

[13]Hide them all in the dust together; bind their faces in the world below.

[14]Then will I also acknowledge to you, that your own right hand can give you victory.

[15]"Behold, Be'hemoth, which I made as I made you; he eats grass like an ox.

[16]Behold, his strength in his loins, and his power in the muscles of his belly.

[17]He makes his tail stiff like a cedar; the sinews of his thighs are knit together.

[18]His bones are tubes of bronze, his limbs like bars of iron.

[19]"He is the first of the works of God; let him who made him bring near his sword!

[20]For the mountains yield food for him where all the wild beasts play.

[21]Under the lotus plants he lies, in the covert of the reeds and in the marsh.

[22]For his shade the lotus trees cover him; the willows of the brook surround him.

[23]Behold, if the river is turbulent he is not frightened; he is confident though Jordan rushes against his mouth.

[24]Can one take him with hooks, or pierce his nose with a snare?

JOB 41

[1]"Can you draw out Levi'athan with a fishhook, or press down his tongue with a cord?

[2]Can you put a rope in his nose, or pierce his jaw with a hook?

[3]Will he make many supplications to you? Will he speak to you soft words?

[4]Will he make a covenant with you to take him for your servant for ever?

[5]Will you play with him as with a bird, or will you put him on leash for your maidens?

[6]Will traders bargain over him? Will they divide him up among the merchants?

[7]Can you fill his skin with harpoons, or his head with fishing spears?

[8]Lay hands on him; think of the battle, you will not do it again!

[9]Behold, the hope of a man is disappointed; he is laid low even at the sight of him.

[10]No one is so fierce that he dares to stir him up. Who then is he that can stand before me?

[11]Who has given to me, that I should repay him? Whatever is under the whole heaven is mine.

[12]"I will not keep silence concerning his limbs, or his mighty strength, or his goodly frame.

[13]Who can strip off his outer garment? Who can penetrate his double coat of mail?

[14]Who can open the doors of his face? Round about his teeth is terror.

[15]His back is made of rows of shields, shut up closely as with a seal.

[16]One is so near to another that no air can come between them.

[17]They are joined one to another; they clasp each other and cannot be separated.

[18]His sneezings flash forth light, and his eyes are like the eyelids of the dawn.

[19]Out of his mouth go flaming torches; sparks of fire leap forth.

[20]Out of his nostrils comes forth smoke, as from a boiling pot and burning rushes.

[21]His breath kindles coals, and a flame comes forth from his mouth.

[22]In his neck abides strength, and terror dances before him.

[23]The folds of his flesh cleave together, firmly cast upon him and immovable.

[24]His heart is hard as a stone, hard as the nether millstone.

[25]When he raises himself up the mighty are afraid; at the crashing they are beside themselves.

[26]Though the sword reaches him, it does not avail; nor the spear, the dart, or the javelin.

[27]He counts iron as straw, and bronze as rotten wood.

[28]The arrow cannot make him flee; for him slingstones are turned to stubble.

[29]Clubs are counted as stubble; he laughs at the rattle of javelins.

[30]His underparts are like sharp potsherds; he spreads himself like a threshing sledge on the mire.

[31]He makes the deep boil like a pot; he makes the sea like a pot of ointment.

[32]Behind him he leaves a shining wake; one would think the deep to be hoary.

[33]Upon earth there is not his like, a creature without fear.

[34]He beholds everything that is high; he is king over all the sons of pride."

JOB 42

[1]Then Job answered the LORD:

[2]"I know that thou canst do all things, and that no purpose of thine can be thwarted.

[3]'Who is this that hides counsel without knowledge?' Therefore I have uttered what I did not understand, things too wonderful for me, which I did not know.

[4]'Hear, and I will speak; I will question you, and you declare to me.'

[5]I had heard of thee by the hearing of the ear, but now my eye sees thee;

[6]therefore I despise myself, and repent in dust and ashes."

[7]After the LORD had spoken these words to Job, the LORD said to Eli'phaz the Te'manite: "My wrath is kindled against you and against your two friends; for you have not spoken of me what is right, as my servant Job has. [8]Now therefore take seven bulls and seven rams, and go to my servant Job, and offer up for yourselves a burnt offering; and my servant Job shall pray for you, for I will accept his prayer not to deal with you according to your folly; for you have not spoken of me what is right, as my servant Job

has." ⁹So Eli'phaz the Te'manite and Bildad the Shuhite and Zophar the Na'amathite went and did what the LORD had told them; and the LORD accepted Job's prayer.

¹⁰And the LORD restored the fortunes of Job, when he had prayed for his friends; and the LORD gave Job twice as much as he had before. ¹¹Then came to him all his brothers and sisters and all who had known him before, and ate bread with him in his house; and they showed him sympathy and comforted him for all the evil that the LORD had brought upon him; and each of them gave him a piece of money and a ring of gold. ¹²And the LORD blessed the latter days of Job more than his beginning; and he had fourteen thousand sheep, six thousand camels, a thousand yoke of oxen, and a thousand she-asses. ¹³He had also seven sons and three daughters. ¹⁴And he called the name of the first Jemi'mah; and the name of the second Kezi'ah; and the name of the third Ker'en-hap'puch. ¹⁵And in all the land there were no women so fair as Job's daughters; and their father gave them inheritance among their brothers. ¹⁶And after this Job lived a hundred and forty years, and saw his sons, and his sons' sons, four generations. ¹⁷And Job died an old man, and full of days.

■ ■ ■

Discussion and Writing Suggestions

1. The Book of Job was written 2500 years ago. What elements of the story make it contemporary? In other words, are its main themes as relevant today as they were in ancient times?

2. In Job 2:11–12, we learn that Job's three friends "come to condole with him and comfort him." Reread their words to Job: the speeches of Eli'phaz (chapters 4–5), Bildad (chapter 8), and Zophar (chapter 11). Describe the tone of these speeches. How comforting do you find them? How appropriate for one who is suffering? In your description, cite examples from the speeches.

3. In Job 1:9, Satan says: "Does Job fear God for nought?" In this famous line, Satan argues that Job's pious behavior and love of God is cheap because it has never been tested. It is easy for the wealthy person, blessed with health, to claim that God is good. Love for God must be tested through hardship, says Satan. Do you agree? Explain.

4. Many commentators have noted the extreme irony at the end of Job. If God tells Eli'phaz that he and his two friends have "not spoken what is right," then *why*, with what justification, is Job made to suffer if *he* has spoken what is right? Fourteen hundred years ago, Pope Gregory the Great responded to this puzzle as follows: "[God] knows how to reward [saintly people]. . . . He casts them down outwardly to something despicable in order to lead them on inwardly to the height of things incomprehensible."⁵ Do you agree with Gregory's view on why innocent people suffer?

---

⁵Pope Gregory the Great, qtd. in Susan Schreiner, *Where Shall Wisdom Be Found: Calvin's Exegesis of Job from Medieval and Modern Perspectives* (Chicago: U of Chicago P, 1994), 34.

5. Subscribing to the same view of cause-and-effect morality as that
   espoused by Job's three friends, some people believe that if they behave
   a certain way they will be spared hardship. That is to say, pious behavior can be counted on to bring certain tangible benefits. Writing 800
   years ago, Moses Maimonides argues that the aim of pious behavior is
   not material gain but knowledge of God:

   > Man's task is to approach to God as close as humanly possible. . . . The evil are
   > punished not by the withholding of material rewards but by their alienation
   > from God, their debarment from human perfection. The good are rewarded not
   > by worldly success but by the possibility of enlightenment, knowledge of God,
   > which virtue opens to the truly wise.[6]

   According to Maimonides, the success of a pious person's behavior has
   nothing to do with tangible benefits, like wealth, health, or a large family.
   Which view of piety is the more compelling—that of Maimonides or the
   view that pious behavior should bring tangible rewards?
6. Why does God accept the wager with Satan? If God is all-knowing and
   all powerful, wouldn't God know *exactly* the quality of Job's love?
   Wouldn't God know how the wager will turn out?
7. Job's comforters argue for what is called "conventional piety": that is, a
   view of an ordered, moral world in which the good behave and are
   rewarded, whereas sinners are punished. Based on their certainty the
   world works this way, they conclude that Job's suffering *must* be a sign
   that he has sinned. At the conclusion of the story, speaking from the
   whirlwind, God says to Eli'phaz: "My wrath is kindled against you and
   against your two friends; for you have not spoken of me what is right, as
   my servant Job has" (42:7). In what ways have the three friends not
   spoken what was right? What are the flaws with the conventional piety
   that they preach to Job?
8. Reread God's speeches from the whirlwind: chapters 38–40:2, 40:6–41.
   What is the meaning of these speeches and of God's display of power?
   How directly does God answer Job's challenge to justify the torturing of
   an innocent man? In developing your answer, consider the remarks of
   psychoanalyst Carl Jung:

   > For seventy-one verses [God–Yahweh] proclaims his world-creating power to his
   > miserable victim, who sits in ashes and scratches his sores with potsherds, and
   > who by now has had a bellyful of superhuman violence. Job has absolutely no
   > need of being impressed by further exhibitions of this power. Yahweh, in his
   > omniscience, could have known just how incongruous his attempts at intimida-
   > tion were in such a situation. He could easily have seen that Job believes in his
   > omnipotence as much as ever and has never doubted it or wavered in his loyal-
   > ty. Altogether, he pays so little attention to Job's real situation that one suspects

---

[6]Moses Maimonides. "From *Moreh Nevukhim* III:22," in *Rambam: Readings in the
Philosophy of Moses Maimonides*, ed. Lenn Evan Goodman (New York: Schocken, 1976),
356n.

> him of having an ulterior motive which is more important to him. . . . His thun-
> derings at Job so completely miss the point that one cannot help but see how
> much he is occupied with himself.[7]

Notice that Jung's attention is drawn to God as a *personality*. (In fact, in
his book, Jung goes on to psychoanalyze God!) Why would God behave
so violently? Does God have something to prove? Is God insecure? Some
authors in this chapter suggest (as have many commentators over the centuries) that the context of Creation is so much vaster than human logic
and human principles of justice that God makes displays of grandeur in
order to break Job's limited views of the Universe and open him to a
more cosmic understanding. How do you respond to God's shows of
grandeur and power?

9. What is Job's response to God's speech from the whirlwind? What has
   Job seen? What has he learned? Why does he lay his hand on his mouth
   (40:4)? What is *your* response to God's speech from the whirlwind?
10. Reread Job's speeches and make notes on his use of legal language and
    images. See, for instance, 13:13–18. What pattern emerges? What sense
    do you make of this pattern?
11. Based on your reading of Job, develop (and write down) two questions
    for small-group discussion. Base each question on specific lines that con-
    fuse you, trouble you, or otherwise pique your interest. Your questions
    should be such that they invite a variety of answers that reflect the vary-
    ing points of view of different readers. In small-group discussion,
    exchange questions and take up each, one at a time.

An Introduction to Job

DAVID NEIMAN

In The Book of Job: A Presentation of the Book with Selected Portions Translated
from the Original Hebrew Text *(1972), Bible scholar and theologian David
Neiman (b. 1921) traces the origins of Job to a "great debate concerning the very
fundamentals of human existence"—a debate between the pagan view of the universe and the prophetic, or biblical view. Taken together with the selection by
Carol Newsom, Neiman's introduction will give you a feel for the literary and theological setting in which Job was composed 2500 years ago.*

So much has been said and written about the Book of Job, that it would be   1
futile to repeat what has appeared time and again in innumerable studies and
commentaries. The book has been praised as one of the greatest ever written,
as one of the most moving expositions of the problem of human existence. It
is a remarkable book, written in poetry of exalted power and beauty. Its
form and style are original. It has symmetry of structure and grandeur of composition. But its bold grappling with the fundamental enigmas of life raise the

---

[7]Carl Jung, *Answer to Job*, trans. R.F.C. Hull (London: Routledge & Kegan Paul,
1954), 25.

Book of Job far above the highest levels to be found in many other works dealing with the problems of human existence. The Book of Job is a unique epic of the spirit; it is a drama of the soul whose many climactic moments touch the very heart of every man.

More significant than any of the foregoing is the fact that the Book of Job   2
is surprisingly modern; that is to say, it is remarkably timeless and eternal. It is quite contemporary, speaking to every troubled, searching soul in the second half of the twentieth century, in words that were written as early as the 5th century B.C. It is, in every sense, a book for all men and for all time.

The Book of Job is a passionate debate, an exposition of opposing views   3
on the very central problem of human existence. The theme of the discussion is the human dilemma; its subject matter is the quandary in which man finds himself at any moment and in any age.

Is there justice in this universe? Does God rule His world with a dis-   4
cernible degree of fairness, with adherence to a moral law, or is He indiffer-ent to His creation? This question has troubled men from the beginning of time. It was the basic point of conflict between the philosophers and religious thinkers of the Pagan world on the one hand, and the prophetic idealists of Israel on the other.

All of biblical philosophy—with two notable exceptions—is prophetic.   5
The biblical philosophical view is that the world is ruled by moral law, that God, the Creator of the universe, is the One Universal Judge, that all of man's actions are judged according to the moral nature of his freely-chosen acts. This is the central theme of the speeches of all the prophets, the funda-mental teaching of the Torah of Moses, and the primary burden of the tradi-tional Wisdom Literature as found in the Book of Proverbs and in its successors.

The prophets speak of divine justice. They tell us that God, the Creator   6
of the Universe, is the Ultimate Judge, who governs His world by principles of Moral Law. If we do good, we do the will of God, we earn His favor, and will be rewarded for our actions. Defiance of God, denial of His will, evil action, is sin. We will be punished by God for wrong behavior, for doing that which is evil, for going against His will.

The Book of Proverbs (and many others in the same vein) present a pro-   7
gram for action, a way of life which follows the patterns of good behavior, of fulfilling God's will, of avoiding the evil which leads to sin. Proverbs tells us that man will receive material rewards for his moral behavior as well as the spiritual reward which comes from living according to God's will.

The principles of reward and punishment, of moral law, and of causation   8
(good action brings reward; evil action brings punishment) have the advan-tage of being apparently logical, and the very great advantage of being satis-fying and reassuring to those who are reasonably successful in life and are satisfied with their lot.

There is, however, a very serious defect in this process of reasoning. This   9
is the fact that the experience of life leads many to question the truth of the concept of moral law from time to time. It is even conceivable, under the blows of misfortune, to question the validity of this concept entirely.

Experience has led men to realize that life does not always offer proper   10
recompense to a man for his actions. This is a problem which is as perplexing
to the man of wisdom, to the one who has faith in a just God, as it is to the
ordinary man who feels his helplessness and his ignorance. Everyman, by the
very passage of his time and the accumulation of his years, is compelled to
consider the problem of existence, and more often than not he sees life as
painful, existence as suffering.

What is the answer to the question: Why do the innocent suffer? Who can   11
make acceptable sense out of this tragic fact of human experience? Can
anyone draw a moral conclusion from contemplating the sight of an evil man
enjoying life and drawing from it prosperity and fulfillment? Can one view the
horror and destruction of war, regardless of who was responsible for its
effects, and discern in it the dim outline of a principle of universal justice in
the sight of innocents maimed or annihilated by nameless, mindless, amoral
weapons of destruction? Can anyone logically derive a divine morality from
the devastation wrought by natural disaster? Are evil men punished by earthquake, fire, flood, and pestilence, while these forces sweep away countless
numbers of individuals, innocent and wicked alike?

If the Creator is a God of Justice, can He permit, let alone condone the   12
suffering of the innocent? This problem is posed in one of the earlier books of
the Bible, in a scene in which Abraham is made the spokesman for all men
who are troubled by the facts of life which do not conform to the vision of a
God of Justice. [Genesis 18:20–33]

If punishment must be meted out to the guilty, must God devise a pun-   13
ishment which destroys the innocent as well? Is there justice in this type of
"Justice"? Or, as Abraham phrased the question, "Will the Judge of all the
earth not do justice?" [Genesis 18:25]

Ecclesiastes, in his book of thoughts concerning the human dilemma,   14
poses this moral problem quite openly.

> I have seen everything
>   in my meaningless span of life:
> The good man who dies
>   with his goodness,
> And the evil man who lives a long life
>   while prolonging his evil.   [7:15]

> There are good men
>   who get what the wicked deserve,
> And there are wicked men
>   who get what the righteous deserve.
> This makes no sense!   [8:14]

A flaw in the moralist's view of the universe and of human destiny is   15
this; that one's condition of life or state of being determines one's attitude.
If a man is reasonably well-provided with life's needs, if one is in a state of
well-being and comparative good fortune, it is comforting to accept the

moralist explanation of the nature of man and the meaning of his condition. It is also satisfying to one's inner vision of oneself.

But what is the man to do who is suffering, whose life experience has not 16 been so fortunate, who suffers pain and agony most difficult to bear, and who cannot relate his state of being to the quality of his own actions? The problem posed by the moral view of the universe to a man who is suffering, is that he must not only accept his condition, but must assume responsibility for it as well. He who is suffering and believes in a God of justice, must also blame himself for his state of being. Not only does he suffer, but his self-esteem must suffer as well.

On the other hand, the man who feels no guilt, who does not believe in 17 the existence of divinely ordained moral universal law, need not feel responsible for his state of being. If he suffers, he must attribute the source of that suffering to a sphere of action outside of himself. Since he denies the existence of divine justice, he also denies his own responsibility.

Attempts to answer the problem of human suffering have been as many 18 as the religions of man. All religious thought tries, in essence, to answer these unanswerable questions. Even the prophets, those who insisted that divine justice was the foundation of the universe, recognized the problem of human suffering which had no apparent explanation. "Was it possible," some asked, "that there is no eternal justice, that there is no Judge?" "Is it possible," some wondered, "that there should be no good and evil in God's plan of the universe?"

That men reject the idea of divine moral justice is all too common a phe- 19 nomenon. The prophets are concerned with the widespread denial of the belief in moral law. The prophet called Malachi quotes those who say,

> "The evil-doer is good in the sight of the Lord,
>   and He desires him."
> And many others say,
>   "Where is the God of Justice?"   [Malachi 2:17]

Zephaniah is also concerned with the denial of the concept of divine jus- 20 tice. It is true that he lived in a time of great troubles, when people in large numbers were unhappy and disillusioned by bitter humiliation and great disasters. The national mood was one of unbearable frustration and a deep-seated sense of hopelessness. Men were deeply troubled and perplexed about the nature of life and the reality of God in human existence. They asked questions, questions that were not ready to be answered. Does God care for His Creation? Is the Creator aware of His creatures? Could men turn to God in time of trouble? Would He answer? Perhaps all men's hopes are nothing but delusion. Perhaps the heavens are empty, and God is absent. There may be no One who is concerned with the affairs of men on earth. Does man's suffering mean nothing to Him, can He remain indifferent to the cries of pain and suffering? Some have gone so far as to say,

"There is no God!"
    [Psalm 14:1]

Trying to find justice in life, a God who rules the world with a sense of   21
right and wrong, a sense of moral balance, seems futile to men without hope.
Consideration of their own set of circumstances leads many to say in their
hearts, and even to express these thoughts openly,

"God does neither good nor evil."
    [Zephaniah 1:12]

But a God who does neither good or evil, who is neutral to His creation, who
can view all that occurs on the face of His earth with detached indifference is
not a God who does neither good nor evil. The God who is indifferent, who
is neutral is by that very neutrality, evil. If God is not the embodiment of
good, if He is not the punisher of evil and the supporter of justice and the
good, then what is His divinity? Yet while men may, in their despair say that
God is indifferent to His creation, the prophet insists that men must not fall
victim to those thoughts. Zephaniah denounces the men that harbor these
thoughts. Jeremiah and Ezekiel also feel the need to insist that men change
their skeptical attitude and reassert their faith in universal Justice. Men are
judged for their deeds and will forever continue to be judged by the universal
Judge. If men assert that events prove the falsity of the moral position, they
are in error. The time will come when the truth of the moral order will again
be revealed to all men. The validity of the prophetic moralistic view will be
established.

The doubts concerning the validity of the moralist position are almost   22
universal. Times of misfortune shake the confidence of men in the existence
of God as moral judge of the world. The sight of wickedness unpunished and
of the good suffering is a rebuke to the moralist and a refutation of the position taken by those who speak of the God of Justice. How long can a person
bear witness to the contradiction of the moral principle in real life before he
begins to doubt that there is any truth to it?

A sensitive artist, a poet of great faith, was the unknown author of the   23
73rd Psalm. His deeply-felt pain is expressed in these words:

I envy the arrogant,
    The prosperity of the wicked that I see.
They do not suffer, even in death;
    Their bodies are healthy and sound.
They do not endure the sufferings of others,
    They escape the afflictions of normal men.
They wear arrogance with pride, as a necklace
    Wearing and displaying violence.
Their eyes peer out over fat cheeks,

They succeed beyond their wildest dreams.
They look down with contempt at others,
      Oppressing men as if they were superior beings.
They speak against the very heavens,
      As they wag their tongues here on earth.
And they say, "How could God know?
      Does the One Above have knowledge?"
            [Psalm 73:3–9, 11]

The author of Psalm 94 is no less concerned about the apparent failure of   24
the moral force that is supposed to guide the universe and control men's actions
by a divine law of moral justice, a law of causation. This poet believes with all
his heart that God is just and that the good will be rewarded. Yet he is disturbed
that evil men proper and the wicked go unpunished. How, he wonders, could
a just God permit this? Is there a reason why the law of moral retribution seems
not to be operating? Could it be that God has suspended His dispensation of
justice on a universal scale? Is there some unfathomable reason why God keeps
the decision of His judgment shrouded in mystery? Surely, he hopes and prays,
God must reveal Himself to men through the operation of His law, through the
fulfillment of the power of His moral justice.

Rise up, Oh Judge of the earth,
      Render justice!
            Punish the arrogant as they deserve!
How long, Oh Lord,
      How long will the wicked rejoice?
For how long shall men who do evil
      Conceive and enact their vile deeds,
            And hold themselves so high?
They oppress Your people, Oh Lord,
      And persecute Your inheritance.
They kill the widow and the orphan,
      An murder the stranger.
And they say with confidence,
"The Lord does not see;
The God of Jacob does not understand."
            [Psalm 94:1–7]

The Book of Job is the direct outgrowth of this great debate concerning   25
the very fundamentals of human existence. What is man and what is the
meaning of his existence? The author of Job, and others who may have
thought and felt as he did, were attacking the foundations of the prophetic
faith in this searching critique of the problem of divine justice.

Even this analysis, this presentation of counter-arguments in the Book of   26
Job is rather restrained. The arguments which are put in the mouth of Job to
deny the existence of justice in God's creation are counterbalanced by the reiteration of the moralists' argument which is presented by Job's friends. And if

one should feel that Job's arguments are too strong, that the author of the book is setting the expression of his own convictions into the mouth of Job and into Job's speeches, the author brings forward a character by the name of Elihu to restate the moralistic credo. Elihu, who is defending the classic statement of the moralist's position, happens to be a very impassioned spokesman for the traditional view of Israel's prophetic heritage.

But the problem is not solved by assuming a defined position. The dilem- 27 ma of man is that his faith remains forever an attitude, a feeling, an emotional expression. Whatever position he assumes is his very own, and remains beyond the realm of objective, external proof. One's faith must always be tested, and the security of certainty is forever elusive.

It would be reassuring to know that there is a universal moral Judge of 28 the whole earth, who sees all and knows all men's actions, who examines and weighs all men's deeds and judges them accordingly. But man, in his experience, does not encounter incontrovertible evidence for this view. The problems of existence, the unevenness and apparent unfairness of life's rewards, and the glaring injustice that man encounters in this world contribute to a shaking of confidence in the view that God Judges His world in Justice.

The author of Job has something to say. He wants to subject the philos- 29 ophy of the Hebrew Scriptures to critical examination. We have been taught by the Torah, by the Prophets, by the Teachers of Wisdom, that the moral life is the only way of life. We have been told that the world is ruled by principles of justice. How, then, can we explain the existence of injustice? This the author of the Book of Job tries to do. If not to explain to complete satisfaction, at least to subject to thorough examination.

He tries to present the problem for discussion and debate by writing this 30 book we call by the name of Job, basing it on an ancient, semi-legendary figure who had the reputation of being long-suffering and infinitely patient. The figure of the patient Job appears in the prose parts of the book, in those sections we call the Prologue and the Epilogue. [Chapters 1, 2, and 42] This ideally righteous Job is mentioned by the prophet Ezekiel as one of the three men of superior piety whose innocence would not serve to avert God's decree of punishment against their society. [Ezekiel 14:14, 20]

As we read the Prologue [Chapters 1, 2] and the Epilogue [Chapter 42] 31 of the Book of Job, we get the picture of a man who is ready to accept God's decree, who is ready to endure pain and suffering without uttering a word of complaint. Not a word of exception to God's verdict will pass his lips, [Job 2:9, 10] and his faith in the justice of God's ways remains unshaken. [Job 1:21] The proof of God's justice and righteousness is at the end of the legendary story. After enduring his ordeal with unparalleled patience, Job is rewarded, receiving blessings from God far in excess of that which he had enjoyed before his days of pain and suffering. [Job 42: 12–17]

Thus far the legend of Job.   32

But the author of the Book of Job is not concerned with the moralistic 33 framework in which the legend of Job has been conveyed. He is interested in the old story, but only as a point of departure. Divine, if you can, what Job might have thought during his years of affliction and suffering. What would a man, certain of his guiltlessness, say in a situation such as that into which Job was cast? Would not a man have doubts, temporary and fleeting though they might be, about the certainty of God's justice?

The author demands a thorough examination of the problem of Divine   34
Justice. Does it exist? If so, where can it be found?

This is the purpose of the Book of Job, a plunge into the profundity of the   35
human soul in suffering, a far-ranging search within, a penetrating self-exam-
ination which touches the very depths of every man's fears, which moves one
to question what lies imbedded in his own soul.

• • •

STATEMENT OF THE PROBLEM

The author of Job presents us with an interesting setting for a discussion of   36
the problem of good and evil and the debate over the existence of moral law
in the universe. This debate could be defined in the following terms.

On the one hand, we have the classic Pagan statement of the overriding   37
power of Fate. The universe is moved by powers too great and too overwhelming for man to influence, let alone control. Even the gods, the immortals who are the dramatic personifications of natural forces, are subject to the
powers of Fate and cannot gainsay them. Whatever man is, and all that
befalls him in his lifetime, is not to be explained in terms of logical consequence of the deeds and actions of man.

> It's Chance alone that moves and rules our lives,
> And all is hidden, nothing is foreseen.
> It's best to live one's life from day to day.

Thus speaks Jocasta to Oedipus in Sophocles' great drama of the troubled
King of Thebes. Man, Sophocles makes very clear in this play, is not the
master of his destiny, no, nor can he even shape or mold it to the least degree.
All that happens is fatally determined happening. All that man experiences
and observes is the result of mysterious workings beyond the veil of perception, which none can probe and no man can explain. Fate rules all creation:
all gods, and men as well.

If there is anything about the prophetic view of the world that we can   38
characterize as distinctive, it is their total faith in the power of man to change
the course of events. The prophets stand in total opposition to the Pagan view
of man's impotence. The prophets maintain that man is free, that he is capable of influencing events, that he has a will whose expression is a reality, and
that man's acts are self-motivated and originate from within his own being.

This implies that man is free. This implies as well, that man is responsi-   39
ble. For the logic of man's freely-chosen acts is inescapable. If I am free to do
what I freely choose to do, then I am free. But having this freedom, I also
create the conditions which result from my own actions. Being the originator
of my own acts and the creator of their consequences, I must bear the responsibility for my own deeds.

But the prophets say more. They insist that the consequences of man's 40
actions are logical, that the results of a man's deeds are qualitatively related
to his deeds. This means that man's freedom puts him face to face with a
choice, and that the decision he makes is always one of value or quality. Man,
therefore, is always choosing between a good act and one that is not so good.
In more clearly defined situations, man chooses between good and evil.

But the good that a man does reverts to him; the same holds true for evil. 41
This means that man's good deeds are rewarded, his evil acts punished.

God, the Creator of the universe plays a primary, a central role in the 42
cosmic drama. God is the universal Judge, the One who judges all the actions
of men, who rewards them for their good deeds and punishes them for their
acts of evil.

All of Prophetic Literature revolves around this theme. The Book of 43
Amos is one single passionate speech devoted to this idea. All of Hosea is
dominated by this theme. Isaiah, Jeremiah, and Ezekiel restate the idea of
reward and punishment, the response of God to the actions of man. And the
Torah, the Teaching of Moses, the Books of the Wisdom Literature; in particular, the Book of Proverbs, all dwell on this central prophetic idea of moral
order and divine judgment in the universe.

One book in the Bible, the Book of Ecclesiastes, questions the validity of 44
the prophetic view, although not denying it out of hand. The Book of Job subjects this viewpoint to a thorough and unrestricted examination. The author
of the Book of Job sets up a debate in which "no holds are barred." The problem of man's existence is to be debated once and for all.

But the author of Job plays an interesting trick. In setting his scene for the 45
debate, he sets up, in effect, a Pagan premise, creating a condition which is the
work of forces external to man. In the scene as Job's author draws it, The
Lord and the Sons of God are pulling the strings, and the men are but mari-
onettes. Of course, the fact that Job and his friends are ignorant of the machi-
nations and the deals that are being worked out between the Lord and the
Satan is true to life. The problem of man's existence is that he does not know
what is going on in the universe beyond the veil of mystery, and is unaware
of the workings of God. For that matter, even most modern man, in our own
age of great scientific breakthrough, is unaware of the nature of the universe
except within severely restricted limits. Certainly when it comes to the problem of man's suffering, we are still as much in the dark as were our most
remote ancestors in the prehistoric period of man's existence.

However, the author of Job does not want to present the problem of 46
Job's suffering in a way which would forever close off any kind of understanding. He purposefully sets the scene of God and the Satan in order to
show that Job, in a very capricious and fatalistic manner, was subjected to
severe suffering, in order to create his dilemma of the failure of understanding. While we know that the cause of Job's suffering is artificial, Job does not
know it, nor do his friends. Nor, for that matter, does any man know the
cause of suffering.

As far as Job is concerned, there is no reason for his suffering, and in 47
terms of the story, he is absolutely right. But in terms of the knowledge which

Job and his friends share, one does not know the cause of Job's suffering, nor can anyone give plausible reasons for it.

■ ■ ■

Review Questions

1. According to Neiman, what is the pagan view regarding Fate and free will? What, by contrast, is the prophetic view—the view expressed by prophets in the Bible?
2. What is the "defect" in the prophets' cause-and-effect logic regarding human behavior?
3. What is the moralist's view on innocent suffering?
4. What are the implications of the prophetic/biblical view regarding Fate and free will?
5. What role does God play in a person's decisions about how to act?
6. What relationship does the *Book of Job* have to this prophetic/biblical view of Fate and free will?
7. In what ways, according to Neiman, are modern men and women nearly identical to their counterparts at the time *Job* was written (and before)? Why is the similarity significant?

Discussion and Writing Suggestions

1. In his opening paragraph, Neiman calls *Job* "a unique epic of the spirit, . . . a drama of the soul whose many climactic moments touch the very heart of every man." How does Neiman justify these extravagant claims in the essay that follows? What does he mean by "drama of the soul" and "epic of the spirit"? Do you agree with Neiman's assessment of *Job*?
2. "Is there justice in this universe? Does God rule His world with a discernible degree of fairness, with adherence to a moral law, or is He indifferent to His creation?" Neiman observes that this "question has troubled men from the beginning of time." Does the question trouble you? Explain.
3. Reread Psalm 73, which Neiman quotes, on envy of the arrogant (paragraph 23). Discuss the applicability of this poem today. To what extent are you affected, if at all, by the knowledge that this psalm was written thousands of years ago?
4. Neiman says that it "would be reassuring to know that there is a universal moral judge of the whole earth." Explain. Why would such a belief be reassuring? And why would doubting this belief lead to moral anguish?

The Book of Job and Ancient Near Eastern Tradition

CAROL A. NEWSOM

This selection appeared originally as part of the introduction to Job in the New Interpreter's Bible. *In it, Bible scholar Carol Newsom explains the context of Near Eastern literature in which Job was written. You will find a term unfamiliar to you in this selection,* Theodicy *(pronounced thee-odd-a-cee), which means "a defense of divine justice." As you will see, other peoples in the ancient world concerned themselves with understanding how God (or the gods) could be just in a world in which innocent people suffer.*

Scholars agree that neither the character Job nor the story about his misfor- 1
tunes originated in Israel. The name "Job" is not a typically Israelite name, although forms of the name are attested in Syria-Palestine in the second mil-lennium BCE.[1] Moreover, the story itself associates Job with the land of Uz, a place that is to be located either in Edomite or Aramean territory. Job's three friends—Eliphaz the Temanite, Bildad the Shuhite, and Zophar the Naamathite—also come from non-Israelite locales. (See Commentary on Job 1:1; 2:11). The story as we have it in the Bible has been adapted for an Israelite religious context, however, so that Yahweh is assumed to be the God whom Job serves.

Although no trace of a pre-Israelite Job story exists in sources yet dis- 2
covered from the ancient Near East, there is one biblical text that associates Job with two other non-Israelite characters whose stories had been incorpo-rated into Israelite tradition. The prophet Ezekiel refers to Job in the context of an oracle from God concerning judgment against Jerusalem:

> "Mortal, when a land sins against me by acting faithlessly, and I stretch out my hand against it, and break its staff of bread and send famine upon it, and cut off from it human beings and animals, even if Noah, Daniel, and Job, these three, were in it, they would save only their own lives by their right-eousness, says the Lord [Yahweh] . . . as I live, says the Lord [Yahweh], they would save neither son nor daughter; they would save only their own lives by their righteousness." (14:13, 20 NRSV)

Noah, the hero of the flood story, is a non-Israelite (or pre-Israelite) 3
character whose story is told in Genesis 6–9. Although the name "Noah" is known only from biblical tradition, the character and his story originate in Mesopotamia, where he is variously known as Utnapishtim and Atrahasis.[2] Dan'el is not the Judean exile, hero of the book of Daniel, but a legendary Canaanite king. Although he is otherwise mentioned in the Bible only in Ezek. 28:3, his story is told in the Ugaritic epic of Aqhar, the text of which was found in the second millennium BCE tablets excavated at Ras Shamra.[3]

Ezekiel's brief allusion takes for granted that his audience knows the 4
stories of all these ancient paragons of righteousness. Yet it is difficult to say in detail exactly what stories about these figures Ezekiel and his audience know, whether they are the same ones preserved in the written accounts or from different oral traditions. The reference in Ezek. 14:20 appears to suggest

---

[1]M. Pope, *Job,* 3rd ed., AB 15 (Garden City, N.Y.: Doubleday, 1979) 5–6.

[2]For the Mesopotamian versions of the flood story, see James B. Pritchard, ed., *Ancient Near Eastern Texts Relating to the Old Testament (ANET),* 3rd ed. with supplement (Princeton: Princeton University Press, 1969) 93–95, 104–6.

[3]Ibid., 149–55.

that all three somehow save their children from danger by means of their own righteousness. In Genesis 6–9, Noah's righteousness saves not only his own life but also those of this children when he takes them aboard the ark. Dan'el's story from the Ugaritic tablets is unfortunately broken off at a critical place, but it does involve the death of his son at the hand of the goddess Anat, the recovery of his body, and Dan'el's seven years of mourning for Aqhat. Whether the story told of Aqhat's restoration to life because of Dan'el's righteousness, as Ezekiel's allusion might suggest, is not known. With respect to Job, Ezekiel's allusion may refer to Job's attempting to protect his children by sacrificing on their behalf, in case "my children have sinned, and cursed God in their hearts" (Job 1:5 NRSV). In the canonical story of Job, the children are eventually killed as a part of the test of Job's righteousness. Ezekiel, however, may have known versions of the stories different from the ones preserved in written sources. Like Noah and Dan'el, Job appears to have been an ancient non-Israelite or pre-Israelite whose story, originally developed in other parts of the ancient Near East, had been incorporated into Israelite religious culture by the sixth century BCE.

In contrast to the prose tale, for which there are only tantalizing hints but 5 no clear ancient Near Eastern parallels, the poetic dialogue in the book of Job has been compared to a variety of ancient Near Eastern texts from Egypt, Mesopotamia, and Ugarit.[4] For the most part, however, the similarities are much too general to be significant and do little to illumine the specific literary tradition to which the poetic dialogue of Job belongs. Only two categories of texts warrant discussion. The first is the tradition of Mesopotamian liturgical texts from the second millennium BCE in which a sufferer praises his god for deliverance from suffering. Among these are the Sumerian composition known as "Man and His God: A Sumerian Variation on the 'Job' Motif"[5] and the Babylonian text "I Will Praise the Lord of Wisdom," often called the "Babylonian Job."[6] Although these texts offer some parallels to the description of suffering one finds in Job, their importance for understanding the literary tradition to which Job belongs has been overrated. They are much closer in form and function to biblical psalms of thanksgiving than to the book of Job.[7] At most they provide background for the general ancient Near Eastern conventions for describing physical suffering and social ostracism.[8]

Much more significant is the striking similarity of form and content 6 between Job and the text known as the Babylonian Theodicy. In contrast to

---

[4]See, e.g., J. Gray, "The Book of Job in the Context of Near Eastern Literature." *ZAW* 82 (1970) 251–69; J. Leveque, *Job et son Dieu* (Paris: J. Gabalda, 1970) 13–90; Pope, *Job*, vi–xxi.

[5]*ANET*, 589–91.

[6]Ibid., 596–600.

[7]M. Weinfeld, "Job and Its Mesopotamian Parallels—A Typological Analysis." in W. Claassen, ed., *Text and Context: Old Testament and Semitic Studies for F. C. Fensham* (Sheffield: Sheffield Academic Press, 1988) 217–26; Gray, "The Book of Job in the Context of Near Eastern Literature," 256.

[8]But see Zuckerman, *Job the Silent*, 93–103, who suggests a larger role for this genre in the development of the book of Job.

the liturgical poems discussed above, the Babylonian Theodicy is a wisdom text.[9] Written c. 1000 BCE, the text was apparently quite popular even in the Hellenistic period, when a commentary on it was written by a Mesopotamian scribe from Sippar.[10] The Babylonian Theodicy consists of a dialogue between a sufferer and his friend and is composed as an acrostic poem of twenty-seven stanzas of eleven lines each, with a strict alliteration of stanzas between the two characters. This formal design is quite similar to the dialogue in Job, although in Job the role of the friend is divided among three characters: Eliphaz, Bildad, and Zophar. Equally striking is the similarity in the way the individual speeches begin. In the Babylonian Theodicy, most of the stanzas begin with a compliment to the general intelligence of the other party. When the friend speaks, this general compliment is followed by a criticism that in this particular case the sufferer has said something irrational, erroneous, or blasphemous. For example:

> "Respected friend, what you say is gloomy.
> You let your mind dwell on evil, my dear fellow.
> You make your fine discretion like an imbecile's"   (ll. 12–14)
> "My reliable fellow, holder of knowledge, your thoughts are perverse.
> You have forsaken right and blaspheme against your god's designs."
> (ll. 78–79)[11]

Similarly, when the sufferer speaks, his opening compliment is followed by a request that his friend truly listen to what he has to say:

> "My friend, your mind is a river whose spring never fails.
> The accumulated mass of the sea, which knows no decrease.
> I will ask you a question; listen to what I say.
> Pay attention for a moment; hear my words."   (ll. 23–26)

In Job many of the speeches begin with a similar characterization of the previous speaker's words and wisdom, although the tone is generally sarcastic rather than the polite-but-frank tone that typifies the Babylonian Theodicy. As Job says:

> "Doubtless you are the people,
>   and wisdom will die with you!
> But I have a mind as well as you;
>   I am not inferior to you.
>   Who does not know all these things?"   (12:2–3 NIV)

Similarly, Eliphaz replies:

> "Would a wise man answer with empty notions
>   or fill his belly with the hot east wind?

· · ·

---

[9]Gray, "The Book of Job in the Context of Near Eastern Literature." 267–68; S. Denning-Bolle, *Wisdom in Akkadian Literature* (Leiden: Ex Oriente Lux, 1992) 136–58.

[10]W. G. Lambert, *Babylonian Wisdom Literature* (Oxford: Clarendon, 1960) 63.

[11]Translation according to ibid., 71–89.

But you even undermine piety
    and hinder devotion to God."   (15:2, 4 NIV)

Like the sufferer of the Babylonian Theodicy, Job asks that his words be
heard, yet Job spoke without the confidence that his friends are capable of
true understanding: "'Listen carefully to my words,/ and let this be your consolation./ Bear with me, and I will speak;/ then after I have spoken, mock on'"
(21:2–3 NRSV).

   The content of the "Babylonian Theodicy" and of the Joban dialogues   7
contains close parallels. In each of his speeches, the Babylonian sufferer complains about either personal misfortune or his perception that the world itself
is morally disordered, with the unworthy and the criminal prospering while
the deserving and the pious languish in misery.

> "My body is a wreck, emaciation darkens [me,]
> My success has vanished, my stability has gone.
> My strength is enfeebled, my prosperity has ended,
> Moaning and grief have blackened my features."

Compare Job:

> "My skin grows black and peels;
>   my body burns with fever.
> My harp is tuned to mourning,
>   and my flute to the sound of wailing."   (30:30–31 NRSV)

The Babylonian sufferer complains that the impious flourish:

> "[. . .] the nouveau riche who has multiplied his wealth,
>   Did he weigh out precious gold for the goddess Mami?"   (ll. 52–53)
> "Those who neglect the god go the way of prosperity,
> While those who pray to the goddess are impoverished and
>   dispossessed."   (ll. 70–71)

Similarly, Job;

> "Why do the wicked live on.
>   reach old age, and grow mighty in power?

>   • • •

> They say to God, 'Leave us alone!
>   We do not desire to know your ways.'"   (21:7, 14 NRSV)

Like Job's friends, the friend in the Babylonian Theodicy argues that retribution will come eventually to the wicked, whereas the pious one who bears
temporary distress patiently will have his prosperity returned to him:

> "The godless cheat who has wealth,
> A death-dealing weapon pursues him.
> Unless you seek the will of the god, what luck have you?
> He that bears his God's yoke never lacks food, though it be sparse.

Seek the kindly wind of the god,
What you have lost over a year you will make up in a moment."
(ll. 237–42)

Compare Eliphaz's words:

"Consider now: Who, being innocent, has ever perished?
　　Where were the upright ever destroyed?
As I have observed, those who plow evil
　　and those who sow trouble reap it."　　(4:7–8 NIV; cf. 5:17–26)

Similarly, just as the Babylonian friend argues that "the divine mind, like the centre of the heavens, is remote; Knowledge of it is difficult; the masses do not know it" (ll. 256–57), so also Zophar asks Job:

"Can you fathom the mysteries of God?
　　Can you prove the limits of the Almighty?
They are higher than the
　　　　heavens—what can you do?
They are deeper than the depths of
　　　　the grave—what can you know?
Their measure is longer than the earth
　　and wider than the sea."　　(11:7–8 NIV)

Despite the striking similarities between particular arguments, the dialogues end quite differently. In the Babylonian Theodicy, when the sufferer complains that people praise the wicked and abuse the honest person, his friend not only agrees with him but also attributes this sad state of affairs to the gods, who "gave perverse speech to the human race. With lies, and not truth, they endowed them for ever" (ll. 279–80). Apparently satisfied that he has been heard, the sufferer thanks his friend, repeats his claim that he has suffered even though he has behaved properly, and concludes with an appeal to the mercy of the gods:

"May the god who has thrown me off give help,
May the goddess who has [abandoned me] show mercy,
For the shepherd Shamash guides the peoples like a god."　　(295–97)

By contrast, there is no rapprochement between Job and his friends. Following Job's lengthy concluding defense of his conduct, he does not appeal for God's mercy but wishes for a legal confrontation with his divine adversary (31:35–37). The Babylonian Theodicy contains nothing like the speech from the whirlwind, which forms the climax of the book of Job.

Although it is possible that the author of Job knew and drew upon the Babylonian Theodicy itself, it is more likely that the relationship is indirect and that there was a larger tradition of wisdom dialogues about the problem of the righteous sufferer and the general issue of moral disorder in a world supposedly governed by divine justice.[12] If that is so, then the similarities between Job and the Babylonian Theodicy, coming from different times and different national and religious contexts, allow one at least to identify the contours of that genre: the formal structuring of the dialogue, the rhetorical acknowledgment by speakers of each other, the characteristic arguments for and against the just ordering of the world. The lack of a narrative framework, as in the Babylonian Theodicy, is probably also a characteristic of the genre. Even if one assumes that the dialogue in Job was written explicitly with the frame tale in mind, it is striking that, except for the names of the characters, the dialogue makes no reference whatsoever to the particulars of the frame story. The dialogue appears to have been left intentionally unintegrated. As compared to the Babylonian Theodicy, the Joban dialogue is a much more sophisticated literary work. Without other examples, however, one cannot say whether the more ambitious scope and daring tone of the Joban dialogues mark a radical departure from the tradition or build on examples more fully developed than the Babylonian Theodicy.

Having traced what can be known of the ancient Near Eastern background to the prose and poetic parts of the book of Job, it is possible to venture a suggestion about the composition of the biblical book. All suggestions are necessarily speculative. They amount to claims that the shape of the book and its component parts make the most sense if one assumes that it arose in such and such a fashion. They are in that sense suggestions about how one should read the book. With that caution in mind, I suggest that one read the book "as if" it came into existence in the following fashion. One might assume that an Israelite sage from the sixth or fifth century knew various oral traditions about the legendary Job and also knew the literary wisdom tradition of the dialogue of a righteous sufferer and his friend. Since Job was such an archetypal righteous sufferer, it is possible that the name "Job" had already been attached to versions of such dialogues. The religious perspectives of the two traditions, however, would have been sharply different, the tale of Job stressing a model of righteousness that takes the form of legendary endurance of extraordinary misfortune without protest, and the dialogue tradition casting Job in the role of skeptical protester against unwarranted personal misfortune and general moral disorder. How might one bring these traditions together so that they may both assert their claims and be challenged by the other's vision of reality? The solution devised by this clever Israelite sage was the artistic device of inter-cutting, beginning the book with a version of the traditional story, then sharply interrupting the telling of the tale with a version of the skeptical dialogue of the righteous sufferer, abruptly followed by the resumption of the traditional tale. Although it is possible that the

10

---

[12]W. G. Lambert, *Babylonian Wisdom Literature* (Oxford: Oxford University Press, 1960) 90–91, suggests that another very fragmentary text may be a second example of such a dialogue.

speech from the whirlwind has antecedents in some other literary tradition, one might be inclined to think that the divine speech is the author's innovation, a reinterpretation of wisdom traditions about creation that serves to set the entire conversation about the experience of suffering in a quite different context than that envisioned either by the old tale or by the conventions of the dialogue of the righteous sufferer.

■ ■ ■

Review Questions

1. Where, and when, did the character of Job originate in the Near Eastern tradition?
2. What is the Babylonian Theodicy?
3. How are Job and the Babylonian Theodicy both similar and different in their form—the structure of the poems?
4. In their content—the ideas represented in each—how are Job and the Babylonian Theodicy both similar and different?
5. According to Newsom, to what extent did the Job author borrow directly from the Babylonian Theodicy?
6. How does Newsom suppose that the version of Job that we read today came into being?

Discussion Questions

1. In what ways is your reading of Job affected by your knowledge of its similarities to a still-older tradition of literature in which righteous sufferers converse with a friend?
2. Given what you understand to be the substance of the Babylonian Theodicy and given what you have read of Job, why do you suppose that Job, and *not* the Babylonian Theodicy, is the document we read 2500 years later?
3. Job appears in the Jewish/Christian Bible. But many religious traditions have pondered the difficult questions of innocent suffering and moral disorder. What conclusions, if any, do you draw from this fact?
4. Newsom observes that the dialogue of Job, its long middle section, "makes no reference whatsoever to the particulars of the frame story"— that is, to the patient sufferer who endures and is rewarded for his endurance. Newsom observes that the "dialogue appears to have been left intentionally unintegrated" with the opening and closing frame. Suppose for a moment that the Job of the dialogues *was* aware of the outer frame of the story—of the wager between God and Satan. What implications would this awareness have for the story? How might the story and its meaning change for us?
5. In what way does the version of Job that we read "set the entire conversation about the experience of suffering in quite a different context than

that envisioned either by the old tale [of the patient Job] or by the conventions of the dialogue of the righteous sufferer"?

When Bad Things Happen to Good People

HAROLD S. KUSHNER

As Rabbi of Temple Israel in Natick, Massachusetts, Harold Kushner (b. 1935) has had many opportunities to console those who have been struck down by tragedy. His perspective on these interactions fundamentally changed when he suffered the loss of his son to a rare childhood disease. Devastated, Kushner questioned God and questioned himself; he raged against the unfairness of a child's death. He needed an explanation, like so many others he had counseled. His questions and doubts led, ultimately, to the writing of a best-seller, When Bad Things Happen to Good People *(1981). Through his many lectures and writings (Kushner has penned several books, including* When Children Ask about God *and* When All You've Wanted Isn't Enough: The Search for a Life that Matters), *Kushner has appealed to people of many faiths. We reprint his introduction to* When Bad Things Happen *as well as that book's chapter on Job.*

In Memory of Aaron Zev Kushner
1963–1977

And David said: While the child was yet alive, I fasted and wept, for I said, Who knows whether the Lord will be gracious to me and the child will live. But now that he is dead, why should I fast? Can I bring him back again? I shall go to him, but he will not return to me.   (II Samuel 12:22–23)

WHY I WROTE THIS BOOK

This is not an abstract book about God and theology. It does not try to use   1
big words or clever ways of rephrasing questions in an effort to convince us
that our problems are not really problems, but that we only think they are.
This is a very personal book, written by someone who believes in God and in
the goodness of the world, someone who has spent most of his life trying to
help other people believe, and was compelled by a personal tragedy to rethink
everything he had been taught about God and God's ways.

Our son Aaron had just passed his third birthday when our daughter   2
Ariel was born. Aaron was a bright and happy child, who before the age of
two could identify a dozen different varieties of dinosaur and could patiently explain to an adult that dinosaurs were extinct. My wife and I had been
concerned about his health from the time he stopped gaining weight at the age
of eight months, and from the time his hair started falling out after he turned
one year old. Prominent doctors had seen him, had attached complicated
names to his condition, and had assured us that he would grow to be very

short but would be normal in all other ways. Just before our daughter's birth, we moved from New York to a suburb of Boston, where I became the rabbi of the local congregation. We discovered that the local pediatrician was doing research in problems of children's growth, and we introduced him to Aaron. Two months later—the day our daughter was born—he visited my wife in the hospital, and told us that our son's condition was called progeria, "rapid aging." He went on to say that Aaron would never grow much beyond three feet in height, would have no hair on his head or body, would look like a little old man while he was still a child, and would die in his early teens.

How does one handle news like that? I was a young, inexperienced rabbi, not as familiar with the process of grief as I would later come to be, and what I mostly felt that day was a deep, aching sense of unfairness. It didn't make sense. I had been a good person. I had tried to do what was right in the sight of God. More than that, I was living a more religiously committed life than most people I knew, people who had large, healthy families. I believed that I was following God's ways and doing His work. How could this be happening to my family? If God existed, if He was minimally fair, let alone loving and forgiving, how could He do this to me?

And even if I could persuade myself that I deserved this punishment for some sin of neglect or pride that I was not aware of, on what grounds did Aaron have to suffer? He was an innocent child, a happy, outgoing three-year-old. Why should he have to suffer physical and psychological pain every day of his life? Why should he have to be stared at, pointed at, wherever he went? Why should he be condemned to grow into adolescence, see other boys and girls beginning to date, and realize that he would never know marriage or fatherhood? It simply didn't make sense.

Like most people, my wife and I had grown up with an image of God as an all-wise, all-powerful parent figure who would treat us as our earthly parents did, or even better. If we were obedient and deserving, He would reward us. If we got out of line, He would discipline us, reluctantly but firmly. He would protect us from being hurt or from hurting ourselves, and would see to it that we got what we deserved in life.

Like most people, I was aware of the human tragedies that darkened the landscape—the young people who died in car crashes, the cheerful, loving people wasted by crippling diseases, the neighbors and relatives whose retarded or mentally ill children people spoke of in hushed tones. But that awareness never drove me to wonder about God's justice, or to question His fairness. I assumed that He knew more about the world than I did.

Then came that day in the hospital when the doctor told us about Aaron and explained what progeria meant. It contradicted everything I had been taught. I could only repeat over and over again in my mind, "This can't be happening. It is not how the world is supposed to work." Tragedies like this were supposed to happen to selfish, dishonest people whom I, as a rabbi, would then try to comfort by assuring them of God's forgiving love. How could it be happening to me, to my son, if what I believed about the world was true?

I read recently about an Israeli mother who, every year on her son's   8
birthday, would leave the birthday party, go into the privacy of her bedroom, and cry, because her son was now one year closer to military service,
one year closer to making her one of the thousands of Israeli parents who
would have to stand at the grave of a child fallen in battle. I read that, and I
knew exactly how she felt. Every year, on Aaron's birthday, my wife and I
would celebrate. We would rejoice in his growing up and growing in skill. But
we would be gripped by the cold foreknowledge that another year's passing
brought us closer to the day when he would be taken from us.

I knew then that one day I would write this book. I would write it out of   9
my own need to put into words some of the most important things I have
come to believe and know. And I would write it to help other people who
might one day find themselves in a similar predicament. I would write it for
all those people who wanted to go on believing, but whose anger at God made
it hard for them to hold on to their faith and be comforted by religion. And
I would write it for all those people whose love for God and devotion to Him
led them to blame themselves for their suffering and persuade themselves
that they deserved it.

There were not many books, as there were no many people, to help us   10
when Aaron was living and dying. Friends tried, and were helpful, but how
much could they really do? And the books I turned to were more concerned
with defending God's honor, with logical proof that bad is really good and
that evil is necessary to make this a good world, than they were with curing
the bewilderment and the anguish of the parent of a dying child. They had
answers to all of their own questions, but no answer for mine.

I hope that this book is not like those. I did not set out to write a book that   11
would defend or explain God. There is no need to duplicate the many treatis-
es already on the shelves, and even if there were, I am not a formally trained
philosopher. I am fundamentally a religious man who has been hurt by life, and
I wanted to write a book that could be given to the person who has been hurt
by life—by death, by illness of injury, by rejection or disappointment—and
who knows in his heart that if there is justice in the world, he deserved better.
What can God mean to such a person? Where can he turn for strength and
hope? If you are such a person, if you want to believe in God's goodness and
fairness but find it hard because of the things that have happened to you and to
people you care about, and if this book helps you do that, then I will have succeeded in distilling some blessing out of Aaron's pain and tears.

If I ever find my book bogging down in technical theological explanations   12
and ignoring the human pain which should be its subject, I hope that the
memory of why I set out to write it will pull me back on course. Aaron died
two days after his fourteenth birthday. This is his book, because any attempt
to make sense of the world's pain and evil will be judged a success or a failure based on whether it offers an acceptable explanation of why he and we
had to undergo what we did. And it is his book in another sense as well—
because his life made it possible, and because his death made it necessary.

• • •

THE STORY OF A MAN NAMED JOB

About twenty-five hundred years ago, a man lived whose name we will never   13
know, but who has enriched the minds and lives of human beings ever since.
He was a sensitive man who saw good people getting sick and dying around
him while proud and selfish people prospered. He heard all the learned,
clever, and pious attempts to explain life, and he was as dissatisfied with them
as we are today. Because he was a person of rare literary and intellectual gifts,
he wrote a long philosophical poem on the subject of why God lets bad
things happen to good people. This poem appears in the Bible as the Book of
Job.

Thomas Carlyle called the Book of Job "the most wonderful poem of any   14
age and language; our first, oldest statement of the never-ending problem—
man's destiny and God's way with him here in this earth. . . . There is nothing written in the Bible or out of it of equal literary merit." I have been
fascinated by the Book of Job ever since I learned of its existence, and have
studied it, reread it, and taught it any number of times. It has been said that
just as every actor yearns to play Hamlet, every Bible student yearns to write
a commentary on the Book of Job. It is a hard book to understand, a profound and beautiful book on the most profound of subjects, the question of
why God lets good people suffer. Its argument is hard to follow because,
through some of the characters, the author presents views he himself probably did not accept, and because he wrote in an elegant Hebrew which, thousands of years later, is often hard to translate. If you compare two English
translations of Job, you may wonder if they are both translations of the same
book. One of the key verses can be taken to mean either "I will fear God" or
"I will not fear God," and there is no way of knowing for sure what the
author intended. The familiar statement of faith "I know that my Redeemer
lives" may mean instead "I would rather be redeemed while I am still alive."
But much of the book is clear and forceful, and we can try our interpretive
skills on the rest.

Who was Job, and what is the book that bears his name? A long, long   15
time ago, scholars believe, there must have been a well-known folk story, a
kind of morality fable told to reinforce people's religious sentiments, about a
pious man named Job. Job was so good, so perfect, that you realize at once
that you are not reading about a real-life person. This is a "once-upon-a-time"
story about a good man who suffered.

One day, the story goes, Satan appears before God to tell Him about all   16
the sinful things people were doing on earth. God says to Satan, "Did you
notice My servant Job? There is no one on earth like him, a thoroughly good
man who never sins." Satan answers God, "Of course Job is pious and obedient. You make it worth his while, showering riches and blessings on him.
Take away those blessings and see how long he remains Your obedient servant."

God accepts Satan's challenge. Without in any way telling Job what is   17
going on, God destroys Job's house and cattle and kills his children. He

afflicts Job with boils all over his body, so that his every moment becomes physical torture. Job's wife urges him to curse God, even if that means God's striking him dead. He can't do anything worse to Job than He already has done. Three friends come to console Job, and they too urge him to give up his piety, if this is the reward it brings him. But Job remains steadfast in his faith. Nothing that happens to him can make him give up his devotion to God. At the end, God appears, scolds the friends for their advice, and rewards Job for his faithfulness. God gives him a new home, a new fortune, and new children. The moral of the story is: when hard times befall you, don't be tempted to give up your faith in God. He has His reasons for what He is doing, and if you hold on to your faith long enough, He will compensate you for your suffering.

18   Over the generations, many people must have been told that story. Some, no doubt, were comforted by it. Others were shamed into keeping their doubts and complaints to themselves after hearing Job's example. Our anonymous author was bothered by it. What kind of God would that story have us believe in, who would kill innocent children and visit unbearable anguish on His most devoted follower in order to prove a point, in order, we almost feel, to win a bet with Satan? What kind of religion is the story urging on us, which delights in blind obedience and calls it sinful to protest against injustice? He was so upset with this pious old fable that he took it, turned it inside out, and recast it as a philosophical poem in which the characters' positions are reversed. In the poem, Job *does* complain against God, and now it is the friends who uphold the conventional theology, the idea that "no ills befall the righteous."

19   In an effort to comfort Job, whose children have died and who is suffering from the boils, the three friends say all the traditional, pious things. In essence, they preach the point of view contained in the original Job-fable: Don't lose faith, despite these calamities. We have a loving Father in Heaven, and He will see to it that the good prosper and the wicked are punished.

20   Job, who has probably spoken these same words innumerable times to other mourners, realizes for the first time how hollow and offensive they are. What do you mean, He will see to it that the good prosper and the wicked are punished?! Are you implying that my children were wicked and that is why they died? Are you saying that I am wicked, and that is why all this is happening to me? Where was I so terrible? What did I do that was so much worse than anything you did, that I should suffer so much worse a fate?

21   The friends are startled by this outburst. They respond by saying that a person can't expect God to tell him what he is being punished for. (At one point, one of the friends says, in effect, "what do you want from God, an itemized report about every time you told a lie or ignored a beggar? God is too busy running a world to invite you to go over His records with him.") We

can only assume that nobody is perfect, and that God knows what He is doing. If we don't assume that, the world becomes chaotic and unlivable.

And so that argument continues. Job doesn't claim to be perfect, but says 22 that he has tried, more than most people, to live a good and decent life. How can God be a loving God if He is constantly spying on people, ready to pounce on any imperfection in an otherwise good record, and use that to justify punishment? And how can God be a just God if so many wicked people are not punished as horribly as Job is?

The dialogue becomes heated, even angry. The friends say: Job, you 23 really had us fooled. You gave us the impression that you were as pious and religious as we are. But now we see how you throw religion overboard the first time something unpleasant happens to you. You are proud, arrogant, impatient, and blasphemous. No wonder God is doing this to you. It just proves our point that human beings can be fooled as to who is a saint and who is a sinner, but you can't fool God.

After three cycles of dialogue in which we alternately witness Job voicing 24 his complaints and the friends defending God, the book comes to its thunderous climax. The author brilliantly has Job make use of a principle of biblical criminal law: if a man is accused of wrongdoing without proof, he may take an oath, swearing to his innocence. At that point, the accuser must either come up with evidence against him or drop the charges. In a long and eloquent statement that takes up chapters 29 and 30 of the biblical book, Job swears to his innocence. He claims that he never neglected the poor, never took anything that did not belong to him, never boasted of his wealth or rejoiced in his enemy's misfortune. He challenges God to appear with evidence, or to admit that Job is right and has suffered wrongly.

And God appears. 25

There comes a terrible windstorm, out of the desert, and God answers 26 Job out of the whirlwind. Job's case is so compelling, his challenge so forceful, that God Himself comes down to earth to answer him. But God's answer is hard to understand. He doesn't talk about Job's case at all, neither to detail Job's sins nor to explain his suffering. Instead, He says to Job, in effect, What do you know about how to run a world?

> Where were you when I planned the earth?
> Tell me, if you are wise.
> Do you know who took its dimensions,
> Measuring its length with a cord? . . .
> Were you there when I stopped the sea . . .
> And set its boundaries, saying, "Here you may come,
> But no further"?
> Have you seen where the snow is stored,
> Or visited the storehouse of the hail? . . .
> Do you tell the antelope when to calve?
> Do you give the horse his strength?
> Do you show the hawk how to fly?   [Job 38, 39]

And now a very different Job answers, saying, "I put my hand to my   27
mouth. I have said too much already; now I will speak no more."

The Book of Job is probably the greatest, fullest, most profound discus-   28
sion of the subject of good people suffering ever written. Part of its greatness
lies in the fact that the author was scrupulously fair to all points of view, even
those he did not accept. Though his sympathies are clearly with Job, he
makes sure that the speeches of the friends are as carefully thought out and as
carefully written as are his hero's words. That makes for great literature, but
it also makes it hard to understand his message. When God says, "How dare
you challenge the way I run my world? What do you know about running a
world?", is that supposed to be the last word on the subject, or is that just one
more paraphrase of the conventional piety of that time?

To try to understand the book and its answer, let us take note of three   29
statements which everyone in the book, and most of the readers, would like
to be able to believe:

A. God is all-powerful and causes everything that happens in the world.
   Nothing happens without His willing it.
B. God is just and fair, and stands for people getting what they deserve, so
   that the good prosper and the wicked are punished.
C. Job is a good person.

As long as Job is healthy and wealthy, we can believe all three of those   30
statements at the same time with no difficulty. When Job suffers, when he
loses his possessions, his family and his health, we have a problem. We can no
longer make sense of all three propositions together. We can now affirm any
two only by denying the third.

If God is both just and powerful, then Job must be a sinner who deserves   31
what is happening to him. If Job is good but God causes his suffering anyway,
then God is not just. If Job deserved better and God did not send his suffering, then God is not all-powerful. We can see the argument of the Book of Job
as an argument over which of the three statements we are prepared to sacrifice, so that we can keep on believing in the other two.

Job's friends are prepared to stop believing in (C), the assertion that Job   32
is a good person. They want to believe in God as they have been taught to.
They want to believe that God is good and that God is in control of things.
And the only way they can do that is to convince themselves that Job deserves
what is happening to him.

They start out truly wanting to comfort Job and make him feel better.   33
They try to reassure him by quoting all the maxims of faith and confidence on
which they and Job alike were raised. They want to comfort Job by telling
him that the world does in fact make sense, that it is not a chaotic, meaningless place. What they do not realize is that they can only make sense of the
world, and of Job's suffering, by deciding that he deserves what he has gone
through. To say that everything works out in God's world may be comforting to the casual bystander, but it is an insult to the bereaved and the unfor-

tunate. "Cheer up, Job, nobody ever gets anything he doesn't have coming to him" is not a very cheering message to someone in Job's circumstances.

But it is hard for the friends to say anything else. They believe, and want 34 to continue believing, in God's goodness and power. But if Job is innocent, then God must be guilty—guilty of making an innocent man suffer. With that at stake, they find it easier to stop believing in *Job's* goodness than to stop believing in God's perfection.

It may also be that Job's comforters could not be objective about what 35 had happened to their friend. Their thinking may have been confused by their own reactions of guilt and relief that these misfortunes had befallen Job and not them. There is a German psychological term, *Schadenfreude*, which refers to the embarrassing reaction of relief we feel when something bad happens to someone else instead of to us. The soldier in combat who sees his friend killed twenty yards away while he himself is unhurt, the pupil who sees another child get into trouble for copying on a test—they don't wish their friends ill, but they can't help feeling an embarrassing spasm of gratitude that it happened to someone else and not to them. . . .

We see this psychology at work elsewhere, blaming the victim so that evil 36 doesn't seem quite so irrational and threatening. If the Jews had behaved differently, Hitler would not have been driven to murder them. If the young woman had not been so provocatively dressed, the man would not have assaulted her. If people worked harder, they would not be poor. If society did not taunt poor people by advertising things they cannot afford, they would not steal. Blaming the victim is a way of reassuring ourselves that the world is not as bad a place as it may seem, and that there are good reasons for people's suffering. It helps fortunate people believe that their good fortune is deserved, rather than being a matter of luck. It makes everyone feel better— except the victim, who now suffers the double abuse of social condemnation on top of his original misfortune. This is the approach of Job's friends, and while it may solve their problem, it does not solve Job's, or ours.

Job, for his part, is unwilling to hold the world together theologically by 37 admitting that he is a villain. He knows a lot of things intellectually, but he knows one thing more deeply. Job is absolutely sure that he is not a bad person. He may not be perfect, but he is not so much worse than others, by any intelligible moral standard, that he should deserve to lose his home, his children, his wealth and health while other people get to keep all those things. And he is not prepared to lie to save God's reputation.

Job's solution is to reject proposition (B), the affirmation of God's good- 38 ness. Job is in fact a good man, but God is so powerful that He is not limited by considerations of fairness and justice.

A philosopher might put it this way: God may *choose* to be fair and give 39 a person what he deserves, punishing the wicked and rewarding the righteous. But can we say logically that an all-powerful God *must* be fair? Would He still be all-powerful if we, by living virtuous lives, could *compel* Him to protect and reward us? Or would He then be reduced to a kind of cosmic vending machine, into which we insert the right number of tokens and from which we get what we want (with the option of kicking and cursing the machine if it doesn't give us what we paid for)? An ancient sage is said to have rejoiced at the world's injustice, saying, "Now I can do God's will out of love for Him and not out of self-interest." That is, he could be a moral, obedient person out of sheer love for God, without the calculation that moral obedient people will be rewarded with good fortune. He could love God even if God did not love him in return. The problem with such an answer is that it tries to promote justice and fairness and at the same time tries to celebrate God for being so great that He is beyond the limitations of justice and fairness.

Job sees God as being above notions of fairness, being so powerful that 40 no moral rules apply to Him. God is seen as resembling an Oriental potentate, with unchallenged power over the life and property of his subjects. And in fact, the old fable of Job does picture God in just that way, as a deity who afflicts Job without any moral qualms in order to test his loyalty, and who feels that He has "made it up" to Job afterward by rewarding him lavishly. The God of the fable, held up as a figure to be worshiped for so many generations, is very much like an (insecure) ancient king, rewarding people not for their goodness but for their loyalty.

So Job constantly wishes that there were an umpire to mediate between 41 himself and God, someone God would have to explain Himself to. But when it comes to God, he ruefully admits, there are not rules. "Behold He snatches away and who can hinder Him? Who can say to Him, What are You doing?" (Job 9:12)

How does Job understand his misery? He says, we live in an unjust 42 world, from which we cannot expect fairness. There is a God, but He is free of the limitations of justice and righteousness.

What about the anonymous author of the book? What is his answer to 43 the riddle of life's unfairness? As indicated, it is hard to know just what he thought and what solution he had in mind when he set out to write his book. It seems clear that he has put his answer into God's mouth in the speech from the whirlwind, coming as it does at the climax of the book. But what does it mean? Is it simply that Job is silenced by finding out that there is a God, that there really is someone in charge up there? But Job never doubted that. It was God's sympathy, accountability, and fairness that were at issue, not His existence. Is the answer that God is so powerful that He doesn't have to explain Himself to Job? But that is precisely what Job has been claiming throughout the book: There is a God, and He is so powerful that He doesn't have to be fair. What new insight does the author bring by having God appear and speak, if that is all He has to say, and why is Job so apologetic if it turns out that God agrees with him?

Is God saying, as some commentators suggest, that He has other consid- 44 erations to worry about, besides the welfare of one individual human being, when He makes decisions that affect our lives? Is He saying that, from our human vantage point, our sicknesses and business failures are the most important things imaginable, but God has more on His mind than that? To say that is to say that the morality of the Bible, with its stress on human virtue and the sanctity of the individual life, is irrelevant to God, and that charity, justice, and the dignity of the individual human being have some source other than God. If that were true, many of us would be tempted to leave God, and seek out and worship that source of charity, justice, and human dignity instead.

Let me suggest that the author of the Book of Job takes the position   45
which neither Job nor his friends take. He believes in God's goodness and in Job's goodness, and is prepared to give up his belief in proposition (A): that God is all-powerful. Bad things do happen to good people in this world, but it is not God who wills it. God would like people to get what they deserve in life, but He cannot always arrange it. Forced to choose between a good God who is not totally powerful, or a powerful God who is not totally good, the author of the Book of Job chooses to believe in God's goodness.

The most important lines in the entire book may be the ones spoken by   46
God in the second half of the speech from the whirlwind, chapter 40, verses 9–14:

> Have you an arm like God?
> Can you thunder with a voice like His?
> *You* tread down the wicked where they stand,
> Bury them in the dust together . . .
> Then will I acknowledge that your own right hand
> Can give you victory.

I take these lines to mean "if you think that it is so easy to keep the world   47
straight and true, to keep unfair things from happening to people, *you* try it." God wants the righteous to live peaceful, happy lives, but sometimes even He can't bring that about. It is too difficult even for God to keep cruelty and chaos from claiming their innocent victims. But could man, without God, do it better?

The speech goes on, in chapter 41, to describe God's battle with the sea   48
serpent Leviathan. With great effort, God is able to catch him in a net and pin him with fish hooks, but it is not easy. If the sea serpent is a symbol of chaos and evil, of all the uncontrollable things in the world (as it traditionally is in ancient mythology), the author may be saying there too that even God has a hard time keeping chaos in check and limiting the damage that evil can do.

Innocent people do suffer misfortunes in this life. Things happen to them   49
far worse than they deserve—they lose their jobs, they get sick, their children suffer or make them suffer. But when it happens, it does not represent God punishing them for something they did wrong. The misfortunes do not come from God at all.

There may be a sense of loss at coming to this conclusion. In a way, it   50
was comforting to believe in an all-wise, all-powerful God who guaranteed fair treatment and happy endings, who reassured us that everything happened for a reason, even as life was easier for us when we could believe that our parents were wise enough to know what to do and strong enough to make everything turn out right. But it was comforting the way the religion of Job's friends was comforting: it worked only as long as we did not take the

problems of innocent victims seriously. When we have met Job, when we have *been* Job, we cannot believe in that sort of God any longer without giving up our own right to feel angry, to feel that we have been treated badly by life.

From that perspective, there ought to be a sense of relief in coming to the   51
conclusion that God is not doing this to us. If God is a God of justice and not of power, then He can know that we are good and honest people who deserve better. Our misfortunes are none of His doing, and so we can turn to Him for help. Our question will not be Job's question "God, why are You doing this to me?" but rather "God, see what is happening to me. Can You help me?" We will turn to God, not to be judged or forgiven, not to be rewarded or punished, but to be strengthened and comforted.

If we have grown up, as Job and his friends did, believing in an all-wise,   52
all-powerful, all-knowing God, it will be hard for us, as it was hard for them, to change our way of thinking about Him (as it was hard for us, when we were children, to realize that our parents were not all-powerful, that a broken toy had to be thrown out because they *could not* fix it, not because they did not want to). But if we can bring ourselves to acknowledge that there are some things God does not control, many good things become possible.

We will be able to turn to God for things He can do to help us, instead   53
of holding on to unrealistic expectations of Him which will never come about. The Bible, after all, repeatedly speaks of God as the special protector of the poor, the widow, and the orphan, without raising the question of how it happened that they became poor, widowed, or orphaned in the first place.

We can maintain our own self-respect and sense of goodness without   54
having to feel that God has judged us and condemned us. We can be angry at what has happened to us, without feeling that we are angry at God. More than that, we can recognize our anger at life's unfairness, our instinctive compassion at seeing people suffer, as coming from God who teaches us to be angry at injustice and to feel compassion for the afflicted. Instead of feeling that we are opposed to God, we can feel that our indignation is God's anger at unfairness working through us, that when we cry out, we are still on God's side, and He is still on ours.

■ ■ ■

Review Questions

1. In the introduction to *When Bad Things Happen to Good People*, Kushner relates the story of his son's illness and of the tragedy the family faced. What questions, what crises, did these experiences prompt in Kushner, and how did Aaron's illness and death provide a motivation to Kushner for writing his book?
2. In his paraphrase of Job, Kushner states that Job is afflicted and is then visited by friends who, in their effort to comfort him, "say all the tradi-

tional, pious things." Job realizes, says Kushner, "how hollow and offensive they are" (paragraph 20). Why are the words of the comforters, in Job's eyes, hollow and offensive?

3. Why do the three friends find it psychologically convenient to condemn Job: to conclude that if he suffers he must therefore have sinned?

4. What are the three propositions that Kushner says that the character of Job and most readers want to believe? Why, according to Kushner, does the story require us to accept two of these propositions and reject the third? Which proposition does Kushner say the Job poet rejects? What about Job's friends: which do they reject? What about Job himself?

5. When innocent people suffer misfortune, why do they suffer "double abuse" when would-be comforters suggest that God punishes only the wicked?

6. What is lost when we accept (what Kushner believes to be) the Joban poet's conclusion about God's power? What is gained? Why is this conclusion significant?

Discussion and Writing Suggestions

1. What is the effect on you of Kushner's story about his son, Aaron? Do you have a similar story to tell, or have you encountered similar stories among people you know? If yes, are there any senses in which you find people's responses to innocent suffering to be consistent or predictable?

2. What are the ways in which Kushner's loss of his son prepared him to interpret Job in the way that he has? That is, given the story of Aaron's brief life and its effect on Kushner, would you expect him to produce the analysis of Job that he does?

3. In the opening to "The Story of a Man Named Job," Kushner quotes Thomas Carlyle (a 19th-century British author) as writing that Job is "our first, oldest statement of the never-ending problem—man's destiny and God's way with him here in this earth." In a paragraph or two, define in your own words this "never-ending problem."

4. Kushner asserts that one of the three propositions in paragraph 29 must be rejected. Of Kushner's three propositions, which do you reject—and why?

5. Kushner concludes that, by interpreting the story of Job as the Joban author does, we "will turn to God, not to be judged or forgiven, not to be rewarded or punished, but to be strengthened and comforted." We will not be opposed to God, in times of hardship, but allied with God—since we will understand that God is not causing bad things to happen to us. To what extent do you agree with Kushner's reading of the story? Do you think the Job poet takes the position Kushner says he does? What is your evidence for thinking so?

The Myth of Justice

MICHAEL DORRIS

Michael Dorris (1945–1997), anthropologist and novelist, was the much-respected author of The Broken Cord *and* A Yellow Raft in Blue Water. *With his longtime collaborator (and wife) Louise Erdrich, he wrote* The Crown of Columbus *and other works of fiction. A winner of numerous prizes, including the National Book Critics Circle award and awards from the Guggenheim and Rockefeller foundations and the National Endowment for the Arts, Dorris was one of the most celebrated Native American writers of his generation. (He traced his ancestry to the Modoc tribe and founded the Native American Studies Department at Dartmouth College.) In the selection that follows, written shortly before his death, Dorris attacks our culture's belief in Justice. With his deep skepticism, he sounds at moments like a Job who has been crushed by life but who will not seek Justice because he has lost faith in a moral system that rights the wrongs of innocent sufferers.*

Where did we ever get the idea that life is ultimately fair? Who promised that   1
there was a balance to things, a yin and yang that perfectly cancels each
other out, a divine score sheet that makes sure that all the totals eventually
ring even? Who exactly reaps what they sow? Does everything that goes
around come around?

If that's some people's experience, I haven't met them, and my guess is,   2
if they still believe it, they simply haven't lived long enough to know better.

Justice is one of those palliative myths—like afterlife with acquired per-   3
sonality and memory intact—that makes existence bearable. As long as we
can think that our experience of being periodically screwed by fate is the
exception to the rule we can hope for, as they used to say in commercials, a
brighter tomorrow. As long as we can trust in an ultimate squaring of
accounts, we can suffer what we assume to be temporary setbacks, transitory
stumbles on our path toward redemption through good works and sacrifice.

When I was a child we were told of a Golden Ledger in which God (or   4
one of his executive assistants) kept tabs on our every plus and minus, and as
long as we wound up in the black we were "in"—as *in* heaven for all eternity. Our journey through the years was a test that was passable, if only we
stretched hard enough. We were in control of our destinies. We were, at
worst, Job: Hang in there, and you will be paid back with compound interest.

Uh huh. In your dreams, sucker.   5

Religion isn't the opiate of the people, the conception of justice is. It's our   6
last bastion of rationality, our logical lighthouse on a stormy sea, our anchor.
We extend its parameters beyond death—if we haven't found equity in this

life, all the great belief systems assure us, just wait until the next. Or the next, or the next. Someday our prince will come.

That may be true, but the paradigm is based on faith, not fact. We can 7
believe in the tooth fairy until the alarm goes off, but unless there's a benevolent parent to value our loss as worth a quarter, we wake up with used calcium, not negotiable currency, under our pillows.

Anthropologists and other social scientists make a distinction between 8
contextual and blind justice. In the former archetype, the goddess has her eyes wide open. It matters—boy, does it matter—who does what to whom, when, how much, and why. In contextual-justice-crazy societies like ours, or like the Yurok of precontact California, rich folks get to pay off their victims, either through a dream team of attorneys or via a prearranged valuation in woodpecker scalps—the murder of an aristocrat worth ever so much more than the slaying of a commoner. If you can afford it, you can do it, and that's the way the game is played. You can't even complain, have begrudging thoughts, or retry the case if the price is right and coughed up in full.

In the theoretical latter case—and is there any manifest and irrefutable 9
instance, really?—it matters not what your station is or what you intended: The act's the thing. All equal before the law. Don't ask, don't tell. A level field, a blank slate. The verdict is impartial and therefore fair. Gripe and you're a sore loser, short-sighted, an excuser of your own incapacities. Strike out and it's because you wanted to in your heart, you didn't wait through the rain, you didn't expend maximum effort. Because if you had, well, you'd wind up—justified. It's a utopian notion, blind justice, an Eden where expectations are perfectly in tune with possibility. But for each of us there comes an undeniable catch, a flaw in the argument. What any human being not convicted of a capital crime has to one day wonder is: What did I do to deserve the death penalty? Be born?

Yet despite the evidence of our private and cultural histories, despite the 10
inevitability of the maximum sentence, when things *don't* work out, we are perpetually surprised. Is this a naiveté carried to an absurd extreme? Wouldn't it be wiser, safer to be shocked at a fleeting *happy* outcome? Wouldn't a pleasant astonishment, however brief, beat bitter disappointment?

But that's too dour. It's downright discouraging. We watch our gritty TV 11
dramas with assurance of retribution, of confirmation. Right prevails, if not this week, then next. Good wins out against all odds. When the innocent victim is convicted on *NYPD Blue* or *Law and Order*, we are outraged; and when the perp goes free, we're appalled. It's not supposed to be that way. We recognize injustice when we see it. We're positively Old Testament in our condemnation. We know how things *should* be.

Our truth. As if it were happening to us.   12

As it is. All the time.   13

I've talked to underpaid public defenders, idealistic law school top-ten 14
percenters who chose working within the system over six-figure starting

salaries. First year, they're motivated, blessed. Second year, they're cynically busting their chops to spring drug dealers. Third year, they're burnt out, ready for corporate, a health plan, into locking up the very bad guys they've been so busy turning loose. Sellouts, but just ask them and they'll tell you why not. They sleep at night now, go to bed with clear conscience, know what's what, and act on it.

Are their serial analyses accurate? Unless you're an avower of the innate 15 goodness of human nature at twenty-one you'll never be, so use or loose it. Because at thirty you'll know better, you'll have your own kids to protect, you'll be wise to the ways of the world, clear-eyed, maybe even a Republican. Was Kunstler just an old kid, a guy who wouldn't admit harsh facts when they stared him square in the face? Is a $300 suit a give-up buy-in or the minimum salary for upholding civilization as we know it?

Questions, questions, questions. If we knew the answers or were sure of 16 them we wouldn't have to ask. We yearn to be proven wrong, returned to the innocence of righteous hope. We don't want to be our parents. We want to be as we were: true believers. Please.

We're every generation with a minimal sense of integrity who came 17 before use and reluctantly, partially conceded the fight. We're us. We're our children in twenty years. We're wish. We're further disillusionment waiting to happen.

Do I need examples from "real life" to prove my point? Read the news- 18 paper. Look at world history. Examine your own family. People got what they deserve, right? Oh, really? They didn't?

Okay, call me a downer. There's divine justice, we're assured, a future 19 payday in which everybody knows everything about everybody and rewards and punishments are meted out in precisely the correct quotients. We all stand there on judgment day, quivering, humiliated by our secret transgressions, dreading exposure. There's this apocalyptic division point, like at the Nazi camps: go right, go left. Life, death.

But all that is beside the point, finally. If there's punishment for trans- 20 gression, that means that order does actually prevail—and the alternative is arguably scarier than hell itself. What if all is chaos and it is simply our own fear, our own cosmological terror, our own instinct as a species to impose structure on whatever we behold? There are scientists who specialize in precisely this kind of bubble-popping on a minor scale: Dr. Amos Tversky, a Stanford University psychologist, working with Dr. Donald Redelmeier, an internist at the University of Toronto, has neatly disproven the long-held truism that people with arthritis can anticipate rainy weather and that a chill brings on a cold; Dr. Albert Kligman, a dermatology professor at the University of Pennsylvania, roundly disproved the widely held notion that eating chocolate exacerbates acne in teenagers. According to these and other researchers, human beings innately desire predictability and so search out patterns even when there are none. We disregard contrary indications in order to stick firm to our collective wishful thought that events conform to knowable design.

This is the basis, after all, of ritual act. If I do X and Y, then Z will nec- 21
essarily follow. If once upon a time when I wanted it to rain I sang a certain
song at a certain time of day, decked out in a particular outfit, having either
eaten or not eaten, had sex or abstained, vocalized or remained silent—and it
rained!—then next drought I'd better replicate all the details as precisely as
possible. Who knows what caused the moisture to arrive: Was it the
sequence? All the ingredients? And if not all, which ones dare I omit? So to be
sure, replay, and if the heavens don't open it must have been *my* fault, *I* must
have messed up on some aspect. We wear ourselves out in pursuit of the right
key to understanding the nature of things, whether we call it physics or witch-
doctoring or philosophy. What other sane option is there? If we are ineffectual, if there isn't any grand scheme to discover and plug into, then we're
simply spinning wheels. When the sun goes down, it might not rise again.
When we go to sleep, we might not wake up. When we die, regardless of
whether we've been a sinner or a saint—yikes!

The good news about this impulse of ours is that it begets common 22
assumptions, which are the next best thing to reality. When we give group credence to the same hypotheses we function as if they're absolute, we allow
them to define us. When a culture is healthy, cohesive, intellectually homogenous and in sync, we agree that our explanations work—and they seem to.
But when we're clustered in a society that's atomized, discordant, at odds,
psychological clarity explodes like confetti from a firecracker. If truth is relative, if law is haphazard, if what we term justice is nothing more than occasional and statistical circumstance that we utilize bogusly to reenforce our
hope for righteousness, then we dwell not just on a shaky foundation but
mired in quicksand.

Not all cultures have grounded their sense of reality in cause-effect rela- 23
tionships. While Genesis postulates a planned, intentionally ordered universe
and later books of the Bible stipulate the myriad of rules and regulations we
must follow in order to placate, if not please, the divinity, the Nootka Tribe
of the Pacific Northwest takes a different approach. In their schema the culture hero is a unisex trickster personified as Raven. Their human creation
story goes something like this:

Once, Raven was flying around when it spied a bush loaded with lus- 24
cious, purple, irresistible berries. Down swoops Raven and gobbles up every
one. Finally its breast feathers are stained with juice and its belly is so bloated that it has to get a running start and jump off a cliff to again become air-
borne. In no time at all, Raven experiences the worst stomach cramps it has
ever known, and shortly thereafter a horrible case of diarrhea. It seems to last
forever, but when the attack is over, Raven breathes a sigh of relief and looks
down to the earth to see the mess it has made. And there we are!

In the Nootka cosmology, justice, like much else, is chance not ordained. 25
Things simply happen without structure or divine plan. The proper response
to the tale—and to the organization of the world that it implies—is laughter

rather than smugness or indignation. Don't expect from me, the universe seems to suggest, but don't blame me either. You're on your own.

An interesting notion, but we in the West are programmed to content   26 ourselves with being appalled, insisting that we're stunned when injustice seems to triumph. The *human*-created system has broken down, we persuade ourselves. This is but a temporary aberration. Just hold out for the eventual guaranteed happy ending. Cling to the Beatitudes and the meek *will* inherit the earth. Be like Pascal and choose to behave as if we're sure in our convictions, betting that if, God forbid, we're wrong, we'll never have to find out. Like the ground beneath the circling trickster, we'll never know what hit us.

■ ■ ■

Review Questions

1. Dorris begins his essay with a question: "Where did we ever get the idea that life is ultimately fair?" In the essay, how does Dorris answer his own question?
2. What is the "Golden Ledger" and its significance?
3. Dorris writes: "Questions, questions, questions. If we knew the answers or were sure of them we wouldn't have to ask. We yearn to be proven wrong, returned to the innocence of righteous hope." What is the "innocence of righteous hope"?
4. To what use does Dorris put the research finding that eating chocolate does not exacerbate acne in teenagers?
5. Why does Dorris call it "good news" that "we search out patterns even when there are none"?
6. What is the danger of letting our beliefs, whether true or not, define us?

Discussion and Writing Suggestions

1. In this essay, Dorris rejects the biblical notion of justice and the sense of order and sanity that comes with it. He offers the Nootka creation myth, and the relationship between the cosmos and humankind that it implies, as an alternative to the Bible's tightly ordered universe. If Dorris fully accepted the Nootka creation myth, why do you suppose he sounds so bitter?
2. "We wear ourselves out in pursuit of the right key to understanding the nature of things, whether we call it physics or witch-doctoring or philosophy. What other sane option is there?" Why would Dorris term the alternative *in*sane? And what has the finding of order to do with Dorris's calling the belief in justice a myth?
3. Explain how the Nootka tribe's myth of creation is more in keeping with Dorris's view of justice (and, generally, of expecting life to work out) than the Genesis creation myth is. What is your view of the Nootka myth?

4. Consider this brief poem by Stephen Crane:

> A man said to the universe:
> "Sir, I exist!"
> "However," replied the universe,
> "The fact has not created in me
> A sense of obligation."[1]

To what extent does Crane's poem reflect the point Dorris is making in this essay? You might consider, especially, the Nootka creation myth in light of the poem.
5. Are you "stunned when injustice seems to triumph" (paragraph 26)? To the extent that you are, what does your reaction tell you about your assumptions regarding the orderliness of the universe? That is to say, do you believe more in the biblical sense of justice or in the sense of justice (or lack thereof) implied by the Nootka creation myth?
6. Respond to Dorris's argument that our notion of justice is a myth. Be prepared to articulate and defend your response in a class discussion. A consideration for those who agree with Dorris: how does one agree and *not* become bitter?

Job: Implications for Today

DIANNE BERGANT

Dianne Bergant, C.S.A. (Congregation of St. Agnes) is a professor of Biblical Studies at the Catholic Theological Union in Chicago. In this selection, which concludes her book-length study of Job, Bergant argues that Job shows us the importance of interpreting religious traditions so that we can find in them "wisdom for the present and the future." Job's three comforters represented an accepted, conventional wisdom that was utterly inadequate to the task of comforting Job in his suffering. By opposing the comforters—by insisting on his innocence and yet not rejecting his tradition, Job broke through to a new and deepened faith. In our day, writes Bergant, any number of misfortunes can "rip away a false . . . certainty and order and catapult the vulnerable human creature into" a chaos that prompts Joban questions. We can use our questions, as Job used his, to find in established traditions a deepened, contemporary meaning.

The drama of Job has touched the hearts of women and men down through   1
the ages to the present time. It has never lost its appeal because of the universality of the issues addressed. Although humankind has not basically changed, the world in which it finds itself and which it has helped to create

---

[1]Stephen Crane, "A Man Said to the Universe." in eds. Sculley Bradley et al., *The American Tradition in Literature,* 5th ed. (New York: Random, 1981), 1241.

presents new challenges for each generation. If a society's religious tradition is to remain vital and creative, it must be able to speak to the contemporary world in the language of the time. Its message must be capable of being interpreted without being compromised. . . . [I]t is not possible to treat all of the concerns of the book in a commentary of this nature. The following are reflections that flow from those issues that have been considered here.

The underlying motif of the book is ORDER, cosmic and experiential. At the heart of Job's dilemma is the collapse of his world of meaning brought on by the incomprehensible events of his life. This is not a unique experience for Job alone but one that he shares with every thinking human being. The simple process of growth and maturation demands that world views be constructed and revised or changed constantly throughout one's life. This usually occurs gradually and with little or no distress, but there are many normal situations that can result in unusual trauma and there are experiences that can wrench one from the securities of life and terrify one with the prospect of annihilation. A certain amount of understanding seems essential for human stability. When the framework of this understanding crumbles and life ceases to make sense, people often thrash around for some means of survival or, too often, despair of any solution and give up.   2

No one is protected from personal misfortunes such as sudden and tragic death, human exploitation or betrayal, unexpected collapse of business or career, or from disasters such as flooding or other ravages of nature. The horrors of war, or of ethnic, racial, sexual, or other social discrimination or brutality victimize countless women and men and defy all standards of justice and harmony. Is it any wonder that scores of people attempt to escape the apparent meaninglessness of existence? The gravity of these situations and the demand to remedy the evils and help bear the burdens of the afflicted are not to be minimized. However, these human miseries often lead to an even greater tragedy—the denial of any meaning to life. This is the great temptation that faces Job and it is to this trial that the book speaks.   3

When one's authentic and profound life experience and the generally accepted way of understanding life are in conflict, an individual seldom embraces an external standard which opposes one's own practical knowledge. The impasse between the visitors and Job reflects just such a conflict. It is more than foolhardy; it is unconscionable to tell a victim of exploitation or violence that he or she is always in some way responsible for what has happened. Even when there is some degree of culpability, the extent of the evil endured frequently far exceeds the seriousness of the human error. How does one explain crime, social injustice or war from a retributive frame of reference? The author of the Book of Job has done a masterful job of exposing the inadequacy of a rigid theory of retribution. The men who had come to assist Job with their wisdom only compound his hardship with their disregard of his many afflictions, their insensitivity to his intellectual dilemma, and their offensiveness in offering empty counsel and harsh judgment. They would have him deny what he knows to be true and accept the conventional teach-   4 ing which they espouse rather than listen to his protestations and admit their inability to offer him a more suitable explanation. They are right about one thing, however. The religious tradition need not be scorned nor discarded. The truth contained within it, if it is indeed truth, must be rediscovered, embraced and allowed to speak to the present situation. They err in refusing to admit that the expression of truth is wanting and needs to change and evolve.

A similar situation faces society today. Not only sinfulness and inhumanity but the pace of life, the burst of technology with its frightening implications, human accomplishments that seem to proliferate by leaps and bounds can all rip away a false security of certainty and order and catapult the vulnerable human creature into a world of rapid change and ambiguity. The theories and answers of the past are frequently inadequate and new structures of meaning must be devised. The guardians of tradition cannot merely perpetuate the perceptions and articulations of the past. In their devotion to truth they must allow the development of its understanding and expression or they will end up as antiquarians collecting treasures of the past rather than sages possessing wisdom for the present and the future.

What message is the author propounding by presenting Job as he does? From the outset Job is an upright man whose virtue is attested to by God. When calamity befalls him it is completely unrelated to his own doing. This initial portrayal of Job as an innocent sufferer either undermines any inflexible belief in retribution or casts doubt on the management and justice of God. These are the options available to Job as the Dialogue opens. There is one thing that Job never doubts and that is his own integrity. Nor will he compromise human dignity and admit to something that he knows is false. It makes no difference that he is opposed by as cherished a treasure as his religious tradition. He will not relinquish his forthrightness nor minimize the veracity of his stand. Such a position is difficult to take when one is assured of understanding and support from others. To assume it alone, in opposition to religious custom and belief, with no buttress but the assurance of one's own life is indeed a courageous act. It also runs the danger of alienating one from the rest of reality.

Men and women of conscience have often been brought to this point of decision. Many have had to stand in opposition to the religious, political or social groups which they love and of which they are a part. Denounced as rebels and apostates, they have chosen to side with reality as experienced rather than as traditionally interpreted and have unwittingly become the real champions of truth.

There is, however, a serious flaw in Job's argument. Immersed in misfortune of which he is innocent, Job points an accusing finger at God and falls into the same trap as did his inept counselors. While they uphold strict retribution and thus reject the authenticity of Job's claims, he clings to the same theory and charges God with folly of injustice. It is only through the insights gained from the theophany that Job can see the deficiency of this world view and reconcile his dilemma.

Many times when people are caught in similar predicaments, they too   9
accuse God of injustice. They wonder how a just God could allow the inhumanity that seems to run rampant across the face of the earth. They watch defenseless victims stricken by unbridled evil and feel compelled to deny the existence of a loving God. As in the case of Job, traditional explanations are hollow, familiar advice is flat, and customary devotion is saccharine. The temptation is to declare God a hoax and life absurd or cruel.

In such desperate situations intellectual discussions are seldom effective   10
because the operations of the universe are beyond human comprehension. Anyone who blames God still believes in God's existence and so it is this faith rather than concepts of logic that must be strengthened and developed. Job is a perfect example of a person whose previous religious ideas had to be broken in order that a more vibrant and mature faith could emerge. Unlike the traditionalists who remained imprisoned in their theories, Job availed himself of the new insights received and risked the uncertainties of an evolving world view. It is the combination of honesty, humility and openness that is praised by the Lord.

Several meaningful insights can be drawn from reflection on Yahweh's   11
attitude toward Job. He does not directly defend himself against Job's charge of injustice. Perhaps this is because the accusation is more an erroneous conclusion than an outright rebellion. Since Job was certain of his own guiltlessness and was an adherent of the orthodox world view, he had no other alternative but to be skeptical about God's integrity. Innocent suffering is neither denied nor explained. Instead, the discussion is moved to an entirely different plane and the fundamental issue of cosmic sovereignty is addressed. The force of God's interrogation elicits awe and submission and Job stands quietly before a panorama that has burst the confines of his narrow perspective. Neither prosperity nor affliction matters in the face of such wonders. If this is true on the cosmic plane, it is all the more so on the human plane. Contrary to a widely held misconception, happiness and success are not demonstrable rewards for righteous living nor are grief and failure concomitant reprisals. Wealth may well be the fruit of wise management, but it can also stem from greed and graft. Likewise, there are too many examples of decent men and women and helpless children suffering indignities. One implication of the Yahweh Speeches clearly illustrates the serious error of an inflexible theory of retribution. Misfortune can indeed befall the righteous. Suffering is not the sure sign of alienation from God.

A second point concerns anthropological presuppositions. Yahweh may   12
have denounced any grandiose notion of human prominence but did not undermine the authentic dignity of Job. In fact, whenever Job is called to a superhuman feat he comes to see his own inadequacy. This is not an affront but an honest appreciation of true human potential. It includes admitting limitations as well as praising abilities.

Confidence in his own integrity was Job's only mainstay throughout his   13
turmoil. When all else seemed to have deserted him or to have turned against
him, he continued to trust his human powers of discernment and judgment
and he insisted that others accord him the hearing and justice that were his
due. Here is a man who will not relinquish his self-respect nor sense of right
regardless of the odds against him. He may be crushed by adversity but his
spirit is undaunted. The other men read this as insolence and blasphemy, but
Yahweh never accused Job of either. He calls upon Job to stand as a man of
valor before the divine teacher and there is no trace of insult in God's speech
to Job. Job survives his encounter with God without having to demean himself nor disavow his sense of dignity. He admits that his perception has been
wrong but that admission is not self-deprecating. Had he succumbed to the
pressure of the others and renounced his point of view, there would have been
no breakthrough to a new insight. Job would have had to live with mediocre
compromise rather than stark honesty, with false humility rather than human
dignity, and with empty teaching rather than challenging truth. His vindication by Yahweh affirms him in his stand and justifies his perspective.

Genuine and forthright human accomplishments are to be valued and   14
trusted as long as they are not an act of defiance in the face of God. In the
normal course of human life, one cannot always determine whether progress
is advantageous or defiant. This was true in the case of Job and it is true
today. The only safeguards available are profound commitment to the sovereignty of God, honesty in testing limits, and humble acknowledgment of
finite creaturehood.

Several questions were posed at the beginning of this study. "What is the   15
origin of the universe and what holds it together?" "What is the meaning of
suffering?" "What role does God play in life as humans experience it?" The
biblical tradition, specifically the Book of Job, offers direction and insights for
coming to grips with these questions. Ultimately, each person must face them,
struggle with them, and somehow resolve them.

■ ■ ■

Review Questions

1. Why is the word "order" important in Job, according to Bergant?
2. What is the fundamental trial, or struggle, to which Job speaks, according to Bergant?
3. What is a "retributive frame of reference"?
4. Why is it necessary to continually reinterpret religious tradition?
5. What risk does Job run in maintaining his innocence before his friends
   and before God?
6. What is the flaw in Job's argument, according to Bergant?
7. What does Job discover during the speech with God?

Discussion and Writing Suggestions

1. A premise of Bergant's essay is that Job is a contemporary story because human nature does not change, while circumstances in which humans find themselves do. Thus, human questions and passions and foibles remain relatively constant over thousands of years, even though technology and political institutions change the world dramatically. Do you agree with Bergant's premise?

2. Bergant believes that Job, though an ancient text, can speak to people in our time. Do you agree?

3. Why is it "unconscionable" to tell a victim of exploitation or abuse that she or he is in some way responsible for what happened?

4. In paragraph 6, Bergant observes that Job will not "compromise human dignity and admit to something that he knows is false. It makes no difference that he is opposed by as cherished a treasure as his religious tradition." In what ways is Job's position, here, a radical or revolutionary position? In developing your answer, consider the roles that individuals and institutions (such as religion) play in human culture.

5. Job trusts his own integrity and sees his position as dignified. His friends, on the other hand, see his insistence on his innocence as blasphemous—as proof of sinfulness. How can we tell when a person in Job's position—someone who insists, "I am right!"—is being principled or merely close-minded? In paragraph 14, Bergant offers a method for making the distinction. Do you agree with her?

God Has Need of Man

ARCHIBALD MacLEISH

Archibald MacLeish (1892–1982) was a celebrated American poet and playwright. A veteran of World War I, he later served in the Roosevelt administration as Librarian of Congress and then as Assistant Secretary of State. MacLeish studied law and practiced in Boston as an attorney before quitting the profession and moving to Paris with his wife and two children to devote full attention to his writing. MacLeish won one Pulitzer Prize for his epic narrative poem Conquistador *(1932), another for his* Collected Poems *(1953), and a third for* J.B. *(1959), a drama based on the story of Job, the ancient character in whose sufferings MacLeish found a metaphor for modern humankind. In 1955, three years before* J.B. *was first produced at Yale University, the poet delivered the following sermon on Job in Farmington, Connecticut.*

To preach is to speak with something more than one's own voice—something   1
that only ordination can give, that only the relation of minister to congregation can make possible. I cannot preach here this morning. I can only *say*—

say the things possible to me as the kind of human being I am—not perhaps a religious man in the ordinary sense of that term but one who, because of the nature of the art he has followed and because of the character of the time in which he has lived, has had to think much about the things with which religion is concerned. *Whence* and *whither* are questions for the poet as they are questions for the priest: in a dark time, even greater questions, for the priest has answers while the man who writes the poem has only, as Yeats put it, his blind, stupefied heart.

It was a poet's question that brought me to the text I wish to speak of this morning, the most difficult and the most urgent of all poet's questions in a time like this, the question of the belief in life—which is also and inevitably the question of the belief in the meaning, the justice, of the universe—which, in its ultimate terms, is the question of the belief in God.

No man can believe in the imitation of life in art who does not first believe in life itself, and no man can believe in life itself who does not believe that life can be justified. But how can life be justified in a time in which life brings with it such inexplicable sufferings: a time in which millions upon millions of men and women and children are destroyed and mutilated for no crime but the crime of being born in a certain century or of belonging to a certain race or of inhabiting a certain city; a time in which the most shameless and cynical tyranny flourishes, in which the ancient decencies are turned inside out to make masks for cruelty and fraud, in which even the meaning of the holiest words is perverted to deceive men and enslave them? How can we believe in our lives unless we can believe in God, and how can we believe in God unless we can believe in the justice of God, and how can we believe in the justice of God in a world in which the innocent perish in vast meaningless massacres, and brutal and dishonest men foul all the lovely things?

These are questions we in our generation ask ourselves. But they are not new questions. They have been asked before us over thousands of years and by no one more passionately and more eloquently than by that ancient writer—the author of the book of Job. It is of that book I wish to speak—but of that book, not as a fragment of the Bible, but as the great, self-containing poem it actually is.

Most of us who read the book of Job read it for the magnificence of its metaphors, or for the nobility of its language in the great translation in which we know it; but the language and the metaphors are not the poem. The poem is the whole: not the language only but the action, and not alone the action but the meaning to which the action moves, and not the meaning as part of a web of meanings which the Old and New Testaments compose, but the meaning in itself.

It is commonly said, I know—and for reasons which are understandable enough—that the meaning of the book of Job is incomplete and unsatisfactory to any Christian; that the book of Job does no more than pose the tremendous question of man's lot; that we must go on to the teachings of Jesus for an answer to that question. It is understandable that men should say this, for certainly the meaning of the book of Job is a hard meaning and the terms of the dramatic action are brutal terms, terms that the modern mind may well find shocking and even blasphemous. But the fact remains that there *is* a meaning—a meaning proffered by one of the greatest poets who ever wrote—a meaning that directly touches the enormous question which haunts us all in our time as it haunted him in his.

The book begins with the passage which I read you (1:1–12). It is not a   7
passage most of us care to dwell on, or to take in the literal sense and meaning of the words, for it makes God a party to the undeserved sufferings of a human being. Consider what is being said in those beginning verses of the first chapter. Job, it is said, was "perfect and upright and one that feared God and eschewed evil." This was God's judgment of Job also, for God describes him in these same words, you will remember, in His conversation with Satan. But notwithstanding his innocence God delivers Job into the hands of Satan, empowering the great Adversary to destroy everything but Job's person—his seven sons, his three daughters, all his people but the five servants who escape from the five massacres and disasters, all his goods and wealth, and eventually, after the second conversation with Satan, his health also. And all this is done. And done with God's consent. And done furthermore, as God Himself asserts in the second conversation, "without cause." There can be no misunderstanding the intention of the text. The death and destruction are Satan's work, but without God's consent they could not have been accomplished, and God recognizes from the beginning that they are unjustified by any guilt of Job's.

And not only is all this explicitly said: it is also the essential precondition   8
to the dramatic action and to the whole colloquy which follows between Job and his three "comforters." Job's agony results far more from his consciousness of this lack of cause than from the loss of his wealth or even the destruction of his children. The cry for death with which the great debate begins is not a cry for release from life but for the obliteration and canceling out of a condition in which such brutal injustice is possible. "Let the day perish in which I was born," says Job, "and the night in which it was said, There is a man child conceived" (3:3). And it is to this same issue the comforters address their bitter comforts. Eliphaz undertakes to answer the complaint of *in*justice by foreclosing the appeal to justice. Justice, he says, is not for men to think of: "In thoughts from the visions of the night, when deep sleep falleth on men, Fear came upon me . . . a spirit passed before my face; the hair of my flesh stood up . . . an image was before mine eyes, there was silence, and I heard a voice saying, Shall mortal man be more just than God?" (4:13–17). It is not for men to debate justice with the Almighty.

But Job will not be answered in these terms. He will not forego his deep   9
conviction that some how, some way, his suffering must be justified: "Teach me and I will hold my tongue; and cause me to understand *wherein I have erred*" (6:24). Job's challenge is the challenge of his innocence, and it is of his innocence the comforters speak. If Job insists on discussing the justice of his suffering, says Bildad, he is condemned forthwith because God *is* just, and a man who suffers, therefore, suffers necessarily for cause. "Doth God pervert

judgment? Or doth the Almighty pervert justice?" (8:3). But Job, like men before him and men since, rejects the unanswerable logic of this proposition: God destroys the good as well as the evil. "The earth is given into the hand of the wicked; He covereth the faces of the judges thereof; if not, where and who is He?" (9:24). All one needs to do is to look at the world where the dishonest and the brutal flourish—and Job breaks out with that poignant cry our time has made its own: "changes and war are against me" (10:17).

But the comforters are not persuaded. Zophar picks up Bildad's argument 10 and presses it home with the ultimate thrust. Not only are all sufferers presumably guilty: *Job* is guilty. God exacts less than Job's wickedness deserves. Job's very self-justification is proof of his guilt. But Job will not be browbeaten. He knows and fears God as well as his friends, but he respects his own integrity also: "Though He slay me, yet will I trust in Him, but I will maintain my own ways before Him" (13:15).

And thereupon Job turns from the debate with his friends to that greater 11 debate in which we are all inevitably engaged: the debate with God. He demands of God to show him "how many are my iniquities and sins? Make me know my transgression and my sin" (13:23). But God does not answer. "Oh that I knew where I might find Him, that I might come even to His seat! I would order my cause before Him, and fill my mouth with arguments. . . . Behold, I go forward, but He is not there; and backward, but I cannot perceive Him" (23: 3, 4, 8).

And so the argument goes on, until at last God answers Job out of the 12 whirlwind and the dust. But answers him how? By showing him the hidden cause? No, by convicting him of insignificance! Where was Job when the world was made—"when the morning stars sang together, and all the sons of God shouted for joy"? Has Job "entered into the treasure of the snow"? Can Job "bind the sweet chains of the Pleiades"? Has Job clothed the neck of the horse with thunder who "saith among the trumpets, Ha, ha; and he smelleth the battle afar off"? Does the hawk fly by Job's wisdom or the eagle?—"where the slain are, there is she" (38–39).

Power by power and glory by glory it piles up, all that unmatchable, rich 13 fountaining and fluency of image and metaphor, heaping strength upon strength and beauty on beauty only to culminate in that terrible challenge: "Gird up thy loins now like a man; I will demand of thee, and declare thou unto me. Wilt thou disannul my judgment? Wilt thou condemn me, that thou mayest be righteous? Has thou an arm like God or canst thou thunder with a voice like Him? Deck thyself now with majesty and excellency; and array thyself with glory and beauty. . . . Then will I also confess unto thee that thine own right hand can save thee" (40:7–14). What can man reply? What does Job reply to that tremendous utterance from the blind wind? "Behold I am vile," he cries, "what shall I answer Thee? I will lay my hand upon my mouth" (40:4).

But what is this poem then? What has happened? What has been shown? 14 Only that Job is less than God in wisdom and in power? It scarcely needed all these words, all this magnificence of words, to make that evident. And no matter how evident, how doubly evident it may be, what answer can the insignificance of Job provide to the great question that has been asked of God?

Well, of one meaning of the poem we can be certain, can we not? To the   15
old poet who wrote this drama thousands of years ago, the injustice of the universe was self-evident. He makes this clear not once but three times. Job, he says, was a perfect and an upright man—that is to say, a man who did not merit punishment, let alone the terrible scourge of disasters with which he was afflicted. Again, God by His own admission was moved to destroy Job "without cause" (2:3). Finally, the comforters, who had argued that Job must have deserved his sufferings, must have been wicked after all, are reproved—angrily reproved—by God at the end: "My wrath is kindled against thee, and against thy two friends," God says to Eliphaz, "for ye have not spoken of me the thing that is right" (42:7).

The conclusion is inevitable: Job's sufferings—and they are clearly meant   16
to be the most dreadful sufferings of which the imagination can conceive, the steepest plunge from fortune to misery—Job's sufferings are unjustified. They are unjustified in any human meaning of the word justice. And yet they are God's work—work that could not have been done without the will of God.

But is this all the poem's meaning? Has the poet of that old visionary time   17
nothing more to say to us than this—that the universe is cruel, that there is no justice, that God may plunge us into misery for no cause and then, at the end, for no cause either, give back to us twofold all that was taken away—all but the lost, all but the dead? (For this, you will remember, happens to Job at the book's end.)

No, surely this is not the only meaning. If it were, men would not have   18
read the book of Job generation after generation, century after century, no matter how magnificent its language. But what other meaning is there? What other meaning can there be? What has the poem to say to us of our real concern: the possibility of our living in this world? If the universe is unjust, if God permits our destruction without cause, how are we to believe in life? And if we cannot believe in life, how are we to live?

This is, for all of us, the crucial question. It was the crucial question for   19
the author of the book of Job also. "Why died I not from the womb?" cries Job, "as a hidden untimely birth *I had not been*" (3:11, 16). What answer to *that* question does the poet find? What answer does he show us in this drama of man's agony?

A deep and, I think, a meaningful answer.   20

Consider the drama as drama: the play as play. What is the fateful action   21
from which all the rest follows? Is it not God's action in delivering Job, though innocent, into Satan's hands? Without this, Job would not have suffered, the comforters would not have come, the great debate would not have been pursued, God would not have spoken from the whirlwind.

But *why* did God deliver Job into Satan's hands? Why?   22

For a reason that is made unmistakably plain. Because God had need of   23
the suffering of Job—had need of it for Himself *as God*.

Recall that scene in heaven with which the play begins. Satan has 24 returned from going to and fro in the earth and from walking up and down in it. God, hearing where he has been, asks him to admire Job's uprightness and reverence. Satan replies with that oldest of sneering questions: "Doth Job fear God for nought?" Has God not protected Job and enriched him? Has God not bought Job's love and paid for it? Do you think, cries Satan, Job would still love You if You took it all away? "Put forth Thy hand now and touch all that he hath, and he will curse Thee to Thy face" (1:9 ff.).

And God gives His consent. 25

Why? For proof? To silence Satan? Obviously. But still, why? Clearly 26 because God believes in Job; because God believes it will be demonstrated that Job loves and fears God because He is God and not because Job is prosperous—proved that Job will still love God and fear Him in adversity, in misfortune, in the worst of misfortunes, *in spite of everything.*

Which means? Which gives what meaning to this book? 27

Which means that in the conflict between God and Satan, in the struggle 28 between good and evil, God stakes His supremacy as God upon man's fortitude and love. Which means, again, that where the nature of man is in question—and it is precisely, you will note, the nature of man that Satan has brought into question with his sneering challenge—where the nature of man is in question, *God has need of man.*

Only Job can prove that Job is capable of the love of God, not as a *quid* 29 *pro quo* but for the love's sake, for God's sake, in spite of everything—in spite even of injustice, even God's injustice. Only man can prove that man loves God.

If one were to write an argument to go at the head of the book of Job in 30 some private notebook of one's own, it might well be written in these words: Satan, who is the denial of life, who is the kingdom of death, cannot be overcome by God who is his opposite, who is the kingdom of life, except by man's persistence in the love of God in spite of every reason to withhold his love, every suffering.

And if one were then to write an explanation of that argument, the 31 explanation might be this: Man depends on God for all things; God depends on man for one. Without man's love, God does not exist as God, only as creator, and love is the one thing no one, not even God Himself, can command. It is a free gift or it is nothing. And it is most itself, most free, when it is offered in spite of suffering, of injustice, and of death.

And if one were to attempt, finally, to reduce this explanation and this 32 argument to a single sentence which might stand at the end of the book to close it, the sentence might read this way: The justification of the injustice of the universe is not our blind acceptance of God's inexplicable will, nor our trust in God's love—His dark and incomprehensible love—for us, but our human love, notwithstanding anything, for Him.

Acceptance—even Dante's acceptance—of God's will is not enough. 33 Love—love of life, love of the world, love of God, love in spite of everything—

is the answer, the only possible answer, to our ancient human cry against
injustice.

It is for this reason that God, at the end of the poem, answers Job not in   34
the language of justice but in the language of beauty and power and glory, sig-
nifying that it is not because He is just but because He is God that He deserves
His creature's adoration.

And it is true. We do not love God because we can believe in Him; we   35
believe in God because we can love Him. It is because we—even we—can love
God that we can conceive Him, and it is because we can conceive Him that we
can live. To speak of "justice" is to demand something for ourselves, to ask
something of life, to require that we be treated according to our dues. But
love, as Saint Paul told the Corinthians, does not "seek her own" (I Cor.
13:5). Love creates, Love creates even God, for how else have we come to
Him, any of us, but through love?

Man, the scientists say, is the animal that thinks. They are wrong. Man   36
is the animal that loves. It is in man's love that God exists and triumphs, in
man's love that life is beautiful, in man's love that the world's injustice is
resolved. To hold together in one thought those terrible opposites of good and
evil which struggle in the world is to be capable of life, and only love will hold
them so.

Our labor always, like Job's labor, is to learn through suffering to   37
love . . . to love even that which lets us suffer.

■   ■   ■

Review Questions

1. What is the "essential precondition" of the dramatic action in Job?
2. Why is it important that Job "respects his own integrity"?
3. How does Satan's challenge to God ("Doth Job fear God for nought?")
   bring into question the nature of man?
4. How does MacLeish explain the assertion of his essay, "God has need of
   man"?
5. Why does God answer Job in the language of "beauty," not of "justice"?

Discussion and Writing Suggestions

1. In paragraphs 2 and 3, MacLeish links a belief in life to a belief in God. For
   an artist, suggests MacLeish, the link is direct. Is it direct for non-artists as
   well? Can you believe in life without believing in God and God's justice?
2. At the beginning of his sermon, MacLeish writes that "*Whence* and
   whither are questions for the poet as they are questions for the priest."
   (*Whence* means from what place. *Whither* means to what place or situation.) Why are these questions for both the poet and the priest?

3. MacLeish suggests (paragraph 11) that Job's debate with God is essentially our debate as well. Does MacLeish speak for you, here? Does he speak for anyone you know? Is this debate, inevitably, about justice in an unjust world?
4. Posing questions is a method by which MacLeish advances this sermon. Reread the selection and track MacLeish's use of questions. Where does he use them—and why? (Suggestion: pay especially close attention to paragraphs 14–18.)
5. MacLeish's many questions all point for an answer to paragraphs 30–32. The theme of Job is the constant, transcendent human love of God, in spite of injustice. Do you agree with his conclusion about the meaning of Job? Are there questions that MacLeish is *not* asking?
6. In paragraph 35 MacLeish writes, "We do not love God because we can believe in Him; we believe in God because we can love Him." How do you interpret this riddle-like statement?

▨ SYNTHESIS ACTIVITIES

1. What are the problems (or central questions) posed by the Book of Job? In an explanatory synthesis that defines these problems, refer to Job itself and one or more of the selections by Neiman, Kushner, Bergant, and Gomes. (See also an excerpt from an article by Moshe Greenberg, quoted in Synthesis Activity #6.) Write this essay for an audience who has *not* read Job. (For this audience, you will need to summarize the story: see Chapter 1, on summarizing a narrative.)
2. Develop a synthesis in which you argue that the problem posed by the Book of Job, and the way in which that problem is expressed, warrants our calling Job a timeless work of literature. Beyond defining the problems (as you would need to do in question #1), you will need to discuss the manner in which the problems are expressed and what makes those problems timeless—of concern to people in any age. You might begin by answering Review Question #7 at the end of the Neiman selection. You might also want to draw on the selection by Carol Newsom, who explores a Babylonian text 500 years *older* than Job that, she says, shares its concern for undeserved suffering. You might want to refer to the passages from Pope Gregory the Great (600 CE) and Maimonides (1100 CE), quoted in the introduction to this chapter. See also the selection by Dianne Bergant.
3. In their writings, Peter Gomes, Harold Kushner, Dianne Bergant, and Archibald MacLeish react differently toward injustice and suffering than does anthropologist and writer Michael Dorris. Using the Book of Job as a point of reference, develop a comparison-contrast synthesis in which you explore the reasons some people (Gomes, Kushner, Bergant, and/or MacLeish) can salvage meaning from injustice and can continue to live productively while others (Dorris, for example) cannot and are consumed by bitterness.

4. Among the authors in this chapter are three ministers to congregations: Peter Gomes, Harold Kushner, and Dianne Bergant. What do they share—in tone, point of view, or some other characteristic—that defines them as spiritual leaders? What sets them apart from other authors in the chapter—for instance, from Neiman or from MacLeish (who delivers a sermon but who pointedly reminds us that he is a poet, not a priest)? And what sets Gomes, Kushner, and Bergant apart from one another? (Gomes is an American Baptist; Kushner is Jewish; and Bergant is Catholic.) Develop your comparison-contrast synthesis into an argument.

5. The concepts of "Fairness" and "Justice" are frequently referred to in this chapter. Drawing on Job and two or more of the selections by Neiman, Gomes, Kushner, Bergant, and Dorris, write an explanatory synthesis defining these concepts in relation to Job's world *or* ours. In developing your essay, you might consider what associations Job (or we) have loaded onto these words and why they are pivotally important words in Job's culture (or ours).

6. Moshe Greenberg, a biblical scholar and translator, writes as follows on the theology in the Book of Job:

> Job is a book not so much about God's justice as about the transformation of a man whose piety and view of the world were formed in a setting of wealth and happiness, and into whose life burst calamities that put an end to both. How can piety nurtured in prosperity prove truly deep-rooted and disinterested, and not merely a spiritual adjunct of good fortune ("God has been good to me so I am faithful to Him")? Can a man pious in prosperity remain pious when he is cut down by anarchical events that belie his orderly view of the world? The Book of Job tells how one man suddenly awakened to the anarchy rampant in the world, yet his attachment to God outlived the ruin of his tidy system.[1]

Greenberg argues that Job is about a piety that comes too cheaply and must be tested. Do you share this view of Job? Write a critique of Greenberg's analysis, drawing on Job itself and any of the other selections in this chapter. The critique will be an argument in which you carefully explain your reasons for agreement or disagreement with Greenberg (and lay out your own views—also well supported).

7. Choose four or five verses from one of the chapters in Job and write a careful analysis of the passage. To guide your analysis, draw on the main ideas of *one* of these authors: Kushner, Dorris, Bergant, or MacLeish. The resulting essay will be an application of the ideas of your selected author to the specific verses that you have chosen. If possible, select verses from Job that particularly interest or confuse you,

---

[1]Moshe Greenberg, "Reflections on Job's Theology," in *The Book of Job: A New Translation According to the Traditional Hebrew Text* (Philadelphia: Jewish Publication Society of America, 1980), xvii.

and use the ideas of the author you select to help you think about these verses. You might structure your essay as follows: Begin with an overview of Job and its significance. In the context of your overview, present the verses you've selected and explain your reasons for selection. Next, briefly summarize the work of the author you are drawing on. Then systematically apply key points of that author's work to the verses in question and analyze the meaning of those verses. Write a conclusion in which you bring the analysis to a close and explain what you have accomplished.

8. To what extent do you think it an error that Job equates God's governance of the universe with humankind's governance of the world? Job expects the cause-and-effect morality on which humans draw to govern the world, through institutions like courts of law, to be the same morality that governs the universe. Job equates God's justice with human justice. Why should God be expected to operate according to rules of justice that are convenient for and acceptable to us? Develop your answer into an argument synthesis, drawing on the Book of Job as well as on selections by Dorris, Bergant, Newsom, and others.

9. Read this brief poem by Stephen Crane. Drawing on the selections by Dorris, MacLeish, Kushner, and Gomes, write a synthesis in which you argue that the implications of Crane's poem are comparable to the implications of Job.

> A man said to the universe:
> "Sir, I exist!"
> "However," replied the universe,
> "The fact has not created in me
> A sense of obligation."

10. Where do you see images of Job in our culture? Scan the newspapers and newsmagazines for examples of the "patient sufferer"—the Job of the opening and closing frame (that is, the Job of the oral tale). Look, also, for examples of the Job who protests loudly in the face of injustice. How radical is this Job? In developing your discussion, you may want to draw on the work of Kushner and Bergant.

11. To what extent do you find that the problem of innocent suffering, the problem at the heart of the Book of Job, is a problem in our world? Read newspapers and magazines and identify a *single* situation that recalls for you Job's struggle: not just his suffering, but his questioning as well. Use some of the sources in this chapter, especially Gomes, in developing your essay.

12. What do we risk by giving up our faith that a universal moral Judge rules the Earth, a judge who distinguishes right from wrong and rewards or punishes people accordingly? Develop your answer into an argument synthesis, drawing on the selections by Gomes, Kushner, and Dorris.

■ RESEARCH ACTIVITIES

1. Read selected portions of three translations of Job and compare them. We suggest the King James Version, The Anchor Bible (Marvin H. Pope), and the translation by Stephen Mitchell, *Into the Whirlwind*. It would be too daunting a task to prepare an analysis comparing competing translations of the entire text of Job. Rather, select several verses that you think are important and compare those. Develop your observations into a report.

2. Locate a copy of William Blake's interpretive watercolors and engravings of scenes from the Book of Job and write an essay-length response. Blake was a mystic, poet, and artist who produced these works in 1820 (watercolors) and 1825 (engravings). William Safire makes this observation of Blake's work:

   > [The] engravings are more interpretations than illustrations of the biblical book. "Not a line is drawn without intention," he cautioned, inviting the reader into his world of symbols. In the artist's conception, the story is played out inside Job's mind. The sufferer's affliction is not physical, but a disease of his own soul; the pain humbling his pride is not punishment for sin but a stimulus to reject tradition and assert his individual spirit.[2]

3. Read Carl Jung's *Answer to Job* (translated from the German by R. F. C. Hull, London: Routledge & Paul, 1954) in which Jung psychoanalyzes God! Write a critique of Jung's arguments.

4. Read the chapter on Job (entitled "Fiend") in Jack Miles's Pulitzer-Prize-winning *God: A Biography*. Miles claims that Job's "harangue" against God makes God's righteousness (not Job's) the subject of the book. Job becomes God's "terrestrial adversary" and, in important respects, wins the battle. Write a critique of this discussion.

5. Read the play inspired by Job: *J.B.* by Archibald MacLeish. Research the reviews of the play and write a review yourself, drawing on your knowledge of Job and of its critical reception.

6. Read the long poem inspired by Job: "A Masque of Reason," offered by Robert Frost as the 43rd chapter to Job. Write an analysis of the poem.

7. In university libraries you will likely have access to several exegetical works on Job—that is, books in which authors annotate Job, chapter by chapter. These scholarly glosses to individual lines, and individual words, in the story are often fascinating. Locate a passage of Job that you think is especially significant and compare scholarly comments on this passage. Prepare a report on your findings.

---

[2]William Safire, *The First Dissident: The Book of Job in Today's Politics* (New York: Random, 1992), xi.

9

The Brave New World of Biotechnology

Career competition in the 21st century will be tough. The prizes will go only to those with the right combination of high-level physical and mental attributes. Why take a chance? You can guarantee that your unborn child will have what it takes to succeed in this demanding environment. Our highly trained medical staff stands ready to assist you in designing and executing a genetic profile for your offspring. Call today for an appointment with one of our counselors.

—GenePerfect, Inc.

The above ad hasn't appeared anywhere yet; but many people are afraid that something like this could result if the revolution in biotechnology continues, unchecked by ethical considerations.

The moral dilemmas now enveloping biotechnology would not be so hotly debated if the technology itself were not so remarkable—and effective. Thanks to its successes so far—in making possible, for instance, the cheap and plentiful production of such disease-fighting agents as insulin and interferon—numerous people have been able to live longer and healthier lives. Its promise in improved agricultural production is exciting. And even without considering the practical consequences, we have the prospect of a new world of knowledge about life itself and the essential components of our own humanity, our own individuality, as revealed in our distinctive genetic codes.

What is biotechnology? Broadly speaking, biotechnology encompasses "all the studies and techniques that combine the ideas and needs of biology and medicine with engineering" (Grolier's *Academic American Encyclopedia*). In the public mind, however, biotechnology has mainly come to be associated with a range of controversial applications in the areas of genetic engineering, medicine, human genetics, and the forensic use of DNA. In this chapter, we will focus on these controversies—on the science behind them and on the ethical, social, political, and legal issues that make them important.

Genetics, the science of inherited characteristics, has figured in human history (in a rough and ready way) for thousands of years—in the breeding of domesticated plants and animals to obtain desired types. Formal scientific studies in genetics, however, date only from the experiments of the Austrian botanist Gregor Mendel (1822–1884). Mendel established some of the basic laws of inheritance by crossbreeding plants with certain characteristics and noting how those characteristics were distributed in subsequent generations.

485

But the means for understanding the molecular basis of those laws was not developed until 1953, when James Watson, an American, and Francis Crick, a Briton, published a landmark article in the scientific journal *Nature* that first elucidated the molecular structure of DNA (deoxyribonucleic acid). It had been known for some time that DNA is the chemical compound forming the genetic material (chromosomes and genes) of all organisms, but understanding how DNA functions in the process of inheritance required knowledge of DNA's molecular structure. Watson and Crick showed that DNA has the structure of a double helix—that is, two interconnected helical strands.

Each of the two strands of the DNA molecule consists of a sugar-phosphate "backbone" and sequences of nucleotides, or bases, attached to the backbone. The bases pair up in specific ways to connect the two strands. In most organisms, DNA is present in all cells in the form of chromosomes gathered in the cell's nucleus. Genes are parts of chromosomes—that is, they are segments of DNA. Each gene is a sequence of bases that governs the production of a certain protein, so the sequence of bases that forms a gene can be viewed as a "code" for producing a protein; hence, the term *genetic code*. Acting separately and together, the proteins produced by the genes determine many of the organism's physical and behavioral characteristics, including the way in which the organism progresses through its life cycle. And because genes are passed along from one generation to the next, they are the basis for heredity.

Watson and Crick's discovery and the subsequent advances in genetics provided the foundation for genetic engineering, and the techniques developed for genetic engineering made possible the controversial applications in medicine, human genetics, and law that are the focus of this chapter.

Genetic engineering (a branch of biotechnology) is "the application of the knowledge obtained from genetic investigations to the solution of such problems as infertility, diseases, food production, waste disposal, and improvement of a species" (Grolier's *Academic American Encyclopedia*). Genetic engineering is also known as "gene splicing" and as "recombinant DNA technology" because it involves combining the DNA (that is, splicing together the genes) of different organisms. For example, a gene with a certain desired function (e.g., that of generating a particular antibody) could be taken from the cells of one person and inserted into the cells of a person lacking that gene, thus enabling the second person to produce the desired antibody.

In another kind of application, genes that generate desired products can be inserted into the DNA of bacteria or other types of cells that replicate rapidly. When the "engineered" cells replicate, they copy the foreign genes along with their own and generate the products specified by those genes. Populations of such cells can function as "factories" to produce large quantities of useful products.

Gene splicing can be done by means of special enzymes ("restriction enzymes") that can split DNA from one organism into fragments that will combine with similarly formed fragments from another organism, thus forming a new DNA molecule. Copies of this new molecule can be obtained by

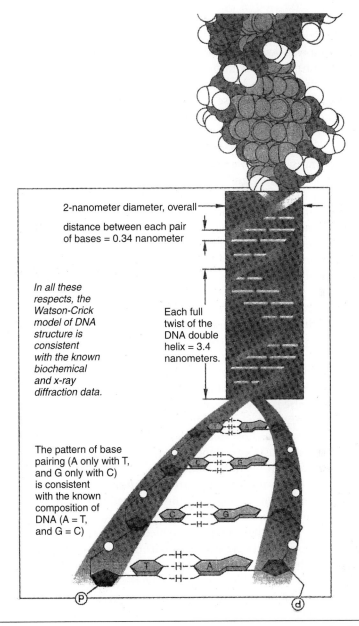

2-nanometer diameter, overall

distance between each pair
of bases = 0.34 nanometer

*In all these
respects, the
Watson-Crick
model of DNA
structure is
consistent
with the known
biochemical
and x-ray
diffraction data.*

Each full
twist of the
DNA double
helix = 3.4
nanometers.

The pattern of base
pairing (A only with T,
and G only with C)
is consistent
with the known
composition of
DNA (A = T,
and G = C)

The double helix structure of DNA (deoxyribonucleic acid). The "backbone" of each strand is composed of sugar-phosphate molecules. Nucleotide bases are attached to the backbones, and the two strands are linked by pairs of these bases. There are four different bases in DNA—the nucleotides adenine (A), cytosine (C), guanine (G), and thymine (T)—and they pair up in a highly restricted way: A pairs only with T, and C pairs only with G. Each unit of three successive base pairs (i.e., a "triplet") governs the production of an amino acid. Proteins are composed of amino acids. Thus, a gene is a sequence of triplets governing the production of a protein that consists of the amino acids specified by those triplets.

Cecie Starr & Ralph Taggart, *Biology: The Unity and Diversity of Life*, used later in chapter.

inserting it into a host cell that replicates the molecule every time it divides, as in the examples just described. In 1985, however, a more efficient method of gene splicing was developed, called *polymerase chain reaction* (PCR), done in a test tube rather than with living cells. PCR allows the double helix of the new DNA molecule to be split into its two complementary strands. When mixed with DNA polymerase from certain bacteria, the two strands function as templates for the generation of two copies of the new molecule. Thus PCR allows a repeated, rapid doubling in the number of desired molecules.

Gene splicing experiments began in the early 1970s, at first involving DNA exchanges between unicellular organisms, such as viruses and bacteria. But recipients of "foreign" DNA soon included more complex organisms, such as fruit flies and frogs (although no humans, at this stage). During this early period of experimentation, some began to worry about the possibility of a genetic disaster. What if some newly engineered microbes escaped from the lab and caused an epidemic of a new and unknown disease, for which there was no known cure? What if the delicate ecological balance of nature or the course of evolution were drastically affected? (Fears of DNA experimentation gone haywire were expertly—and thrillingly—exploited by Michael Crichton's novel [and Steven Spielberg's movie] *Jurassic Park*, in which a new race of rampaging dinosaurs is cloned from ancient DNA and spliced with frog DNA.) Some proposed an outright ban on genetic engineering experiments. At an international conference in Asilomar, California, in 1975, scientists agreed on a set of guidelines to govern future research.

In time, these early fears turned out to be groundless, and the restrictions were eased or lifted. Meantime, considerable strides were made in genetic engineering, with new applications discovered in agriculture, pollution control, and the fight against a host of diseases. Genetic engineering became big business, as many scientists abandoned the academy to found and work for firms with names such as Genentech and Genex.

But reservations persist. Some are uncomfortable with the fact of genetic engineering itself, considering it an unwarranted intrusion by human beings into the fragile structure of Nature, with too little knowledge or care about the consequences. Others have no philosophical objections to genetic engineering but worry about its effects on the environment and on humans. Or they worry about the kind of ethical problems raised by the new field of *genetic therapy*—the kind of problems suggested by the imaginary ad at the beginning of our introduction. Of course, this is an extreme example. Most people would have no problem with using genetic therapy to cure life-threatening diseases or conditions. For example, in a pioneering experiment in 1992, genes were injected into the blood cells of three infants lacking an enzyme whose absence prevented their bodies from fighting off potentially deadly viral and bacterial infections. Three years later, the infants' cells appeared to be producing the enzyme that is crucial to their survival.

There is little controversy over such forms of genetic therapy. But should genetic therapy be conducted to "correct" left-handedness? Nearsightedness? Baldness? Or even to *detect* such potential conditions? A recent survey for

Redbook magazine revealed that while only 18 percent of respondents disapproved of *genetic testing* and manipulation to discover whether a child would have a disease or disability, an overwhelming 86 percent disapproved of using such a tool to select the sex of a child; 91 percent, to increase the child's IQ; and 94 percent, to improve the child's athletic ability. (Of course, such figures could change dramatically when the possibilities become real instead of abstract.)

There are other troubling aspects of biotechnology. Genetic testing may be used as a *screening* device by employers and insurance companies—in other words, it may be used as a means of genetic discrimination. Employers may be disinclined to hire prospective employees for whom genetic screening has revealed a present or potential health problem, such as heart disease. Since many genetic traits are linked to race or sex, genetic discrimination could be another form of racial or gender discrimination. Another area of concern is the *Human Genome Project*, a massive scientific undertaking begun in the late 1980s (and initially directed by James Watson) to determine the complete genetic makeup of human chromosomes. Armed with the knowledge of what each gene does and where it is located, scientists (it is feared) would be able to manipulate human cells to create individuals with qualities considered desirable, while eliminating qualities considered undesirable. For many, such possibilities bring to mind the notorious Nazi eugenics programs aimed at creating an Aryan "master" race and exterminating "inferior" races. And as the O.J. Simpson trial has dramatically demonstrated, there is controversy over the *forensic* use of DNA—the use of DNA testing in legal proceedings to determine guilt. While many suspects—and some convicted persons—have been exonerated as a result of DNA testing, some defense attorneys have contested the validity and reliability of DNA evidence when it is used by the prosecution.

For most, then, the problem is not so much biotechnology itself as its possible abuses. As *Time* writer Philip Elmer-Dewitt notes, "To unlock the secrets hidden in the chromosomes of human cells is to open up a host of thorny legal, ethical, philosophical and religious issues, from invasion of privacy to the question of who should play God with [people's] genes." Some of these thorny issues are explored in the following pages. We begin with the opening chapter of Aldous Huxley's dystopian novel *Brave New World*, which for more than sixty years has served as an unforgettable warning of the dark side of scientific progress. Here we see human ova fertilized outside the womb, the embryos and fetuses conditioned and then decanted (born) from bottles, prepared to do specific jobs and to be contented and productive citizens in a stable society. Huxley's dark vision is followed by Cecie Starr and Ralph Taggart's "Recombinant DNA and Genetic Engineering," which explains the mechanics of genetic engineering as well as some of the ethical problems involved in its use. Next, in "Tinkering With Destiny," three *U.S. News & World Report* staffwriters discuss the complex issues of human gene therapy, as faced not only by the families most directly concerned, but also by scientists, doctors, genetic counselors, and entrepreneurs. In "The Grandiose

Claims of Geneticists," sociology professor Dorothy Nelkin acknowledges the accomplishments of biotechnology, but cautions against an uncritical acceptance of what she considers the exaggerated self-promotions of the biotechnologists.

In "The Human Genome Project: A Personal View," James D. Watson, co-discoverer of DNA's helical structure, defends the Human Genome Project from adversaries and skeptics and asserts its potential role in helping us to understand and combat diseases. Next, *Science Magazine* writer Eliot Marshall presents the story of a start-up research firm, deCode, which is following through on Watson's dream by hunting for the genetic bases of disease in Iceland's homogenous population. Controversially, the company will be seeking patents and, with its investors (including a multinational pharmaceutical company), large profits. Jeremy Rifkin has long opposed rushing genetic technologies to market without first thoroughly debating their potential for helping—and hurting—the human race. In "The Ultimate Therapy: Commercial Eugenics on the Eve of the Biotech Century," he raises a cautionary flag about the profit motive in genetic research. Next, in "Fatalist Attraction: The Dubious Case Against Fooling Mother Nature," the editor of *Reason* magazine, Virginia Postrel, argues that professional ethicists and government bureaucrats should stay out of the business of mandating which genetic therapies are socially acceptable. The needs of patients and the services of physicians and researchers—that is, the free market—should determine which services, including cloning, become available. The final two readings in the chapter address the controversy over the forensic use of DNA. In "When Science Takes the Witness Stand," attorney Peter J. Neufeld and physician Neville Colman advise readers of *Scientific American* that DNA evidence should be regarded with great skepticism. In "DNA in Court," William Tucker debunks such doubts.

Brave New World

ALDOUS HUXLEY

The title of Aldous Huxley's novel Brave New World *(1932) derives from a line in Shakespeare's final comedy,* The Tempest. *Miranda is a young woman who has grown up on an enchanted island; her father is the only other human she has known. When she suddenly encounters people from the outside world (including a handsome young prince), she remarks, "O brave [wondrous] new world that has such people in it!" Shakespeare used the line ironically (the world of* The Tempest *is filled with knaves and fools); and almost three hundred years later, Huxley employed not only the language but also the irony in labeling his nightmare society of* A.F. *632 (After [Henry] Ford).*

In comparison with other dystopias, like George Orwell's 1984, *Huxley's brave new world of creature comforts seems, at first glance, a paradise. People are given whatever they need to keep happy: unlimited sex, tranquilizers, and soothing experiences. No one goes hungry; no one suffers either physical or spiritual pain. But the cost of such comfort is an almost total loss of individuality, creativity, and freedom. Uniformity and stability are exalted above all other virtues. The population is divided into castes, determined from before birth, with the more intelligent Alphas and Betas governing and managing the society, while the less intelligent Deltas, Gammas, and Epsilons work at the menial tasks. Epsilons are not unhappy with their lot in life because they have been conditioned to be content; and, in fact, they are incapable of conceiving anything better. Love, art, and science are suppressed for all castes because they lead to instability, and instability threatens happiness. Idle reflection is discouraged for the same reason; and, to avoid the effects of any intense emotions, positive or negative, the inhabitants of this brave new world are given regular doses of the powerful tranquilizer "soma."*

Huxley's brave new world, then, is a projection into the future of tendencies he saw in his own world that he thought were disturbing or dangerous. In the context of our present chapter on biotechnology, we are most interested in Huxley's portrait of a "hatchery," where human ova are removed from the womb and fertilized, and where the embryos and fetuses grown in bottles are programmed before "birth" to produce an assortment of the kind of people who will be most desirable to society. In the following passage, the first chapter of Brave New World, *we are taken on a tour through the Central London Hatchery and Conditioning Centre, where we follow an egg from fertilization through conditioning. To many people today, Huxley's dramatic portrait of the manipulation of human germ cells is uncomfortably close to what modern genetic engineers are beginning, with ever greater facility, to make possible: the substitution of "more desirable" for "less desirable" genes in order to create "better" people.*

Born in Surrey, England, Aldous Huxley (1894–1963), grandson of naturalist T. H. Huxley, intended to pursue a medical career; but after being stricken with a corneal disease that left him almost blind, he turned to literature. Among his works are Crome Yellow *(1921),* Antic Hay *(1923),* Point Counter Point *(1928), and* Eyeless in Gaza *(1936). Huxley moved to the United States in 1936, settling in California. In the latter part of his life, he tended toward the mystical and experimented with naturally occurring hallucinogenic drugs—the subject of his* Doors of Perception *(1954).*

A squat grey building of only thirty-four stories. Over the main entrance the words, CENTRAL LONDON HATCHERY and CONDITIONING CENTRE, and, in a shield, the World State's motto: COMMUNITY, IDENTITY, STABILITY.   1

The enormous room on the ground floor faced towards the north. Cold   2 for all the summer beyond the panes, for all the tropical heat of the room itself, a harsh thin light glared through the windows, hungrily seeking some draped lay figure, some pallid shape of academic gooseflesh, but finding only the glass and nickel and bleakly shining porcelain of a laboratory. Wintriness responded to wintriness. The overalls of the workers were white, their hands gloved with a pale corpse-coloured rubber. The light was frozen, dead, a ghost. Only from the yellow barrels of the microscopes did it borrow a certain rich and living substance, lying along the polished tubes like butter, streak after luscious streak in long recession down the work tables.

"And this," said the Director opening the door, "is the Fertilizing Room."   3

Bent over their instruments, three hundred Fertilizers were plunged, as the Director of Hatcheries and Conditioning entered the room, in the scarcely breathing silence, the absent-minded, soliloquizing hum or whistle, of absorbed concentration. A troop of newly arrived students, very young, pink and callow, followed nervously, rather abjectly, at the Director's heels. Each of them carried a notebook, in which, whenever the great man spoke, he desperately scribbled. Straight from the horse's mouth. It was a rare privilege. The D.H.C. for Central London always made a point of personally conducting his new students round the various departments.   4

"Just to give you a general idea," he would explain to them. For of course some sort of general idea they must have, if they were to do their work intelligently—though as little of one, if they were to be good and happy members of society, as possible. For particulars, as every one knows, make for virtue and happiness; generalities are intellectually necessary evils. Not philosophers but fret-sawyers and stamp collectors compose the backbone of society.   5

"To-morrow," he would add, smiling at them with a slightly menacing geniality, "you'll be settling down to serious work. You won't have time for generalities. Meanwhile . . ."   6

Meanwhile, it was a privilege. Straight from the horse's mouth into the notebook. The boys scribbled like mad.   7

Tall and rather thin but upright, the Director advanced into the room. He had a long chin and big, rather prominent teeth, just covered, when he was not talking, by his full, floridly curved lips. Old, young? Thirty? Fifty? Fifty-five? It was hard to say. And anyhow the question didn't arise; in this year of stability, A.F. 632, it didn't occur to you to ask it.   8

"I shall begin at the beginning," said the D.H.C. and the more zealous students recorded his intention in their notebooks: *Begin at the beginning*. "These," he waved his hand, "are the incubators." And opening an insulated door he showed them racks upon racks of numbered test-tubes. "The week's supply of ova. Kept," he explained, "at blood heat; whereas the male gametes," and here he opened another door, "they have to be kept at thirty-five instead of thirty-seven. Full blood heat sterilizes." Rams wrapped in thermogene beget no lambs.   9

Still leaning against the incubators he gave them, while the pencils scurried illegibly across the pages, a brief description of the modern fertilizing process; spoke first, of course, of its surgical introduction—"the operation undergone voluntarily for the good of Society, not to mention the fact that it carries a bonus amounting to six months' salary"; continued with some   10 account of the technique for preserving the excised ovary alive and actively developing; passed on to a consideration of optimum temperature, salinity, viscosity; referred to the liquor in which the detached and ripened eggs were kept; and, leading his charges to the work tables, actually showed them how this liquor was drawn off from the test-tubes; how it was let out drop by drop onto the specially warmed slides of the microscopes; the eggs which it contained were inspected for abnormalities, counted and transferred to a porous receptacle; how (and he now took them to watch the operation) this receptacle was immersed in a warm bouillon containing free-swimming spermatozoa—at a minimum concentration of one hundred thousand per cubic centimetre, he insisted; and how, after ten minutes, the container was lifted out of the liquor and its contents re-examined; how, if any of the eggs remained unfertilized, it was again immersed, and, if necessary, yet again; how the fertilized ova went back to the incubators; where the Alphas and Betas remained until definitely bottled; while the Gammas, Deltas and Epsilons were brought out again, after only thirty-six hours, to undergo Bokanovsky's Process.

"Bokanovsky's Process," repeated the Director, and the students underlined the words in their little notebooks. 11

One egg, one embryo, one adult—normality. But a bokanovskified egg will bud, will proliferate, will divide. From eight to ninety-six buds, and every bud will grow into a perfectly formed embryo, and every embryo into a full-sized adult. Making ninety-six human beings grow where only one grew before. Progress. 12

"Essentially," the D.H.C. concluded, "bokanovskification consists of a series of arrests of development. We check the normal growth and, paradoxically enough, the egg responds by budding." 13

Responds by budding. The pencils were busy. 14

He pointed. On a very slowly moving band a rack-full of test-tubes was entering a large metal box, another rack-full was emerging. Machinery faintly purred. It took eight minutes for the tubes to go through, he told them. Eight minutes of hard X-rays being about as much as an egg can stand. A few died; of the rest, the least susceptible divided into two; most put out four buds; some eight; all were returned to the incubators, where the buds began to develop; then, after two days, were suddenly chilled, chilled and checked. Two, four, eight, the buds in their turn budded; and having budded were dosed almost to death with alcohol; consequently burgeoned again and having budded—bud out of bud out of bud—were thereafter—further arrest being generally fatal—left to develop in peace. By which time the original egg was in a fair way to becoming anything from eight to ninety-six embryos—a prodigious improvement, you will agree, on nature. Identical twins—but not in piddling twos and threes as in the old viviparous days, when an egg would sometimes accidentally divide; actually by dozens, by scores at a time. 15

"Scores," the Director repeated and flung out his arms, as though he were distributing largesse. "Scores." 16

But one of the students was fool enough to ask where the advantage lay. 17

"My good boy!" The Director wheeled sharply round on him. "Can't   18
you see? Can't you see?" He raised a hand; his expression was solemn.
"Bokanovsky's Process is one of the major instruments of social stability!"

Major instruments of social stability.   19

Standard men and women; in uniform batches. The whole of a small fac-   20
tory staffed with the products of a single bokanovskified egg.

"Ninety-six identical twins working ninety-six identical machines!" The   21
voice was almost tremulous with enthusiasm. "You really know where you
are. For the first time in history." He quoted the planetary motto.
"Community, Identity, Stability." Grand words. "If we could bokanovskify
indefinitely the whole problem would be solved."

Solved by standard Gammas, unvarying Deltas, uniform Epsilons.   22
Millions of identical twins. The principle of mass production at last applied
to biology.

"But, alas," the Director shook his head, "we *can't* bokanovskify indef-   23
initely."

Ninety-six seemed to be the limit; seventy-two a good average. From the   24
same ovary and with gametes of the same male to manufacture as many
batches of identical twins as possible—that was the best (sadly a second best)
that they could do. And even that was difficult.

"For in nature it takes thirty years for two hundred eggs to reach matu-   25
rity. But our business is to stabilize the population at this moment, here and
now. Dribbling out twins over a quarter of a century—what would be the use
of that?"

Obviously, no use at all. But Podsnap's Technique had immensely accel-   26
erated the process of ripening. They could make sure of at least a hundred and
fifty mature eggs within two years. Fertilize and bokanovskify—in other
words, multiply by seventy-two—and you get an average of nearly eleven
thousand brothers and sisters in a hundred and fifty batches of identical
twins, all within two years of the same age.

"And in exceptional cases we can make one ovary yield us over fifteen   27
thousand adult individuals."

Beckoning to a fair-haired, ruddy young man who happened to be pass-   28
ing at the moment, "Mr. Foster," he called. The ruddy young man
approached. "Can you tell us the record for a single ovary, Mr. Foster?"

"Sixteen thousand and twelve in this Centre," Mr. Foster replied without   29
hesitation. He spoke very quickly, had a vivacious blue eye, and took an evident pleasure in quoting figures. "Sixteen thousand and twelve; in one hundred and eighty-nine batches of identicals. But of course they've done much
better," he rattled on, "in some of the tropical Centres. Singapore had often
produced over sixteen thousand five hundred; and Mombasa has actually
touched the seventeen thousand mark. But then they have unfair advantages.
You should see the way a negro ovary responds to pituitary! It's quite astonishing, when you're used to working with European material. Still," he added,
with a laugh (but the light of combat was in his eyes and the lift of his chin
was challenging), "still, we mean to beat them if we can. I'm working on a

wonderful Delta-Minus ovary at this moment. Only just eighteen months old. Over twelve thousand seven hundred children already, either decanted or in embryo. And still going strong. We'll beat them yet."

"That's the spirit I like!" cried the Director, and clapped Mr. Foster on 30 the shoulder. "Come along with us and give these boys the benefit of your expert knowledge."

Mr. Foster smiled modestly. "With pleasure." They went. 31

In the Bottling Room all was harmonious bustle and ordered activity. 32 Flaps of fresh sow's peritoneum ready cut to the proper size came shooting up in little lifts from the Organ Store in the sub-basement. Whizz and then, click! the lift-hatches flew open; the bottle-liner had only to reach out a hand, take the flap, insert, smooth-down, and before the lined bottle had had time to travel out of reach along the endless band, whizz, click! another flap of peritoneum had shot up from the depths, ready to be slipped into yet another bottle, the next of that slow interminable procession on the band.

Next to the Liners stood the Matriculators. The procession advanced; one 33 by one the eggs were transferred from their test-tubes to the larger containers; deftly the peritoneal lining was slit, the morula dropped into place, the saline solution poured in . . . and already the bottle had passed, and it was the turn of the labellers. Heredity, date of fertilization, membership of Bokanovsky Group—details were transferred from test-tube to bottle. No longer anonymous, but named, identified, the procession marched slowly on; on through an opening in the wall, slowly on into the Social Predestination Room.

"Eighty-eight cubic metres of card-index," said Mr. Foster with relish, as 34 they entered.

"Containing *all* the relevant information," added the Director. 35

"Brought up to date every morning." 36

"And co-ordinated every afternoon." 37

"On the basis of which they make their calculations." 38

"So many individuals, of such and such quality," said Mr. Foster. 39

"Distributed in such and such quantities." 40

"The optimum Decanting Rate at any given moment." 41

"Unforeseen wastages promptly made good." 42

"Promptly," repeated Mr. Foster. "If you knew the amount of overtime 43 I had to put in after the last Japanese earthquake!" He laughed good-humouredly and shook his head.

"The Predestinators send in their figures to the Fertilizers." 44

"Who give them the embryos they ask for." 45

"And the bottles come in here to be predestinated in detail." 46

"After which they are sent down to the Embryo Store." 47

"Where we now proceed ourselves." 48

And opening a door Mr. Foster led the way down a staircase into the 49 basement.

The temperature was still tropical. They descended into a thickening 50 twilight. Two doors and a passage with a double turn insured the cellar against any possible infiltration of the day.

"Embryos are like photograph film," said Mr. Foster waggishly, as he   51
pushed open the second door. "They can only stand red light."

And in effect the sultry darkness into which the students now followed   52
him was visible and crimson, like the darkness of closed eyes on a summer's
afternoon. The bulging flanks of row on receding row and tier above tier of
bottles glinted with innumerable rubies, and among the rubies moved the dim
red spectres of men and women with purple eyes and all the symptoms of
lupus. The hum and rattle of machinery faintly stirred the air.

"Give them a few figures, Mr. Foster," said the Director, who was tired   53
of talking.

Mr. Foster was only too happy to give them a few figures.   54

Two hundred and twenty metres long, two hundred wide, ten high. He   55
pointed upwards. Like chickens drinking, the students lifted their eyes
towards the distant ceiling.

Three tiers of racks: ground floor level, first gallery, second gallery.   56

The spidery steel-work of gallery above gallery faded away in all direc-   57
tions into the dark. Near them three red ghosts were busily unloading demi-
johns from a moving staircase.

The escalator from the Social Predestination Room.   58

Each bottle could be placed on one of fifteen racks, each rack, though   59
you couldn't see it, was a conveyor travelling at the rate of thirty-three and a
third centimeters an hour. Two hundred and sixty-seven days at eight metres
a day. Two thousand one hundred and thirty-six metres in all. One circuit of
the cellar at ground level, one on the first gallery, half on the second, and on
the two hundred and sixty-seventh morning, daylight in the Decanting Room.
Independent existence—so called.

"But in the interval," Mr. Foster concluded, "we've managed to do a lot   60
to them. Oh, a very great deal." His laugh was knowing and triumphant.

"That's the spirit I like," said the Director once more. "Let's walk round.   61
You tell them everything, Mr. Foster."

Mr. Foster duly told them.   62

Told them of the growing embryo on its bed of peritoneum. Made them   63
taste the rich blood surrogate on which it fed. Explained why it had to be
stimulated with placentin and thyroxin. Told them of the *corpus luteum*
extract. Showed them the jets through which at every twelfth metre from zero
to 2040 it was automatically injected. Spoke of those gradually increasing
doses of pituitary administered during the final ninety-six metres of their
course. Described the artificial maternal circulation installed on every bottle
at Metre 112; showed them the reservoir of blood-surrogate, the centrifugal
pump that kept the liquid moving over the placenta and drove it through the
synthetic lung and waste-product filter. Referred to the embryo's troublesome
tendency to anaemia, to the massive doses of hog's stomach extract and fetal
foal's liver with which, in consequence, it had to be supplied.

Showed them the simple mechanism by means of which, during the last   64
two metres out of every eight, all the embryos were simultaneously shaken
into familiarity with movement. Hinted at the gravity of the so-called "trauma
of decanting," and enumerated the precautions taken to minimize, by a suit-

able training of the bottled embryo, that dangerous shock. Told them of the tests for sex carried out in the neighbourhood of metre 200. Explained the system of labelling—a T for the males, a circle for the females and for those who were destined to become freemartins a question mark, black on a white ground.

"For of course," said Mr. Foster, "in the vast majority of cases, fertility is merely a nuisance. One fertile ovary in twelve hundred—that would really be quite sufficient for our purposes. But we want to have a good choice. And of course one must always leave an enormous margin of safety. So we allow as many as thirty per cent of the female embryos to develop normally. The others get a dose of male sex-hormone every twenty-four metres for the rest of the course. Result: they're decanted as freemartins—structurally quite normal ("except," he had to admit, "that they *do* have the slightest tendency to grow beards"), but sterile. Guaranteed sterile. Which brings us at last," continued Mr. Foster, "out of the realm of mere slavish imitation of nature into the much more interesting world of human invention." 65

He rubbed his hands. For of course, they didn't content themselves with merely hatching out embryos: any cow could do that. 66

"We also predestine and condition. We decant our babies as socialized human beings, as Alphas or Epsilons, as future sewage workers or future . . ." He was going to say "future World controllers," but correcting himself, said "future Directors of Hatcheries," instead. 67

The D.H.C. acknowledged the compliment with a smile. 68

They were passing Metre 320 on rack 11. A young Beta-Minus mechanic was busy with screwdriver and spanner on the blood-surrogate pump of a passing bottle. The hum of the electric motor deepened by fractions of a tone as he turned the nuts. Down, down . . . A final twist, a glance at the revolution counter, and he was done. He moved two paces down the line and began the same process on the next pump. 69

"Reducing the number of revolutions per minute," Mr. Foster explained. "The surrogate goes round slower; therefore passes through the lung at longer intervals; therefore gives the embryo less oxygen. Nothing like oxygen-shortage for keeping an embryo below par." Again he rubbed his hands. 70

"But why do you want to keep the embryo below par?" asked an ingenuous student. 71

"Ass!" said the Director, breaking a long silence. "Hasn't it occurred to you that an Epsilon embryo must have an Epsilon environment as well as an Epsilon heredity?" 72

It evidently hadn't occurred to him. He was covered with confusion. 73

"The lower the caste," said Mr. Foster, "the shorter the oxygen." The first organ affected was the brain. After that the skeleton. At seventy per cent of normal oxygen you got dwarfs. At less than seventy eyeless monsters. 74

"Who are no use at all," concluded Mr. Foster. 75

Whereas (his voice became confidential and eager), if they could discover a technique for shortening the period of maturation what a triumph, what a benefaction to Society! 76

"Consider the horse." 77

They considered it. 78

Mature at six; the elephant at ten. While at thirteen a man is not yet sex- 79
ually mature; and is only full-grown at twenty. Hence, of course, that fruit of
delayed development, the human intelligence.

"But in Epsilons," said Mr. Foster very justly, "we don't need human 80
intelligence."

Didn't need and didn't get it. But though the Epsilon mind was mature at 81
ten, the Epsilon body was not fit to work till eighteen. Long years of superfluous and wasted immaturity. If the physical development could be speeded
up till it was as quick, say, as a cow's what an enormous saving to the
Community!

"Enormous!" murmured the students. Mr. Foster's enthusiasm was infec- 82
tious.

He became rather technical; spoke of the abnormal endocrine coordina- 83
tion which made men grow so slowly; postulated a germinal mutation to
account for it. Could the effects of this germinal mutation be undone? Could
the individual Epsilon embryo be made a revert, by a suitable technique, to
the normality of dogs and cows? That was the problem. And it was all but
solved.

Pilkington, at Mombasa, had produced individuals who were sexually 84
mature at four and full-grown at six and a half. A scientific triumph. But
socially useless. Six-year-old men and women were too stupid to do even
Epsilon work. And the process was an all-or-nothing one; either you failed to
modify at all, or else you modified the whole way. They were still trying to
find the ideal compromise between adults of twenty and adults of six. So far
without success. Mr. Foster sighed and shook his head.

Their wanderings though the crimson twilight had brought them to the 85
neighbourhood of Metre 170 on Rack 9. From this point onwards Rack 9
was enclosed and the bottles performed the remainder of their journey in a
kind of tunnel, interrupted here and there by openings two or three metres
wide.

"Heat conditioning," said Mr. Foster. 86

Hot tunnels alternated with cool tunnels. Coolness was wedded to dis- 87
comfort in the form of hard X-rays. By the time they were decanted the
embryos had a horror of cold. They were predestined to emigrate to the tropics, to be miners and acetate silk spinners and steel workers. Later on their
minds would be made to endorse the judgment of their bodies. "We condition
them to thrive on heat," concluded Mr. Foster. "Our colleagues upstairs will
teach them to love it."

"And that," put in the Director sententiously, "that is the secret of hap- 88
piness and virtue—liking what you've *got* to do. All conditioning aims at that:
making people like their unescapable social destiny."

In a gap between two tunnels, a nurse was delicately probing with a 89
long fine syringe into the gelatinous contents of a passing bottle. The students
and their guides stood watching her for a few moments in silence.

"Well, Lenina," said Mr. Foster, when at last she withdrew the syringe 90
and straightened herself up.

The girl turned with a start. One could see that, for all the lupus and the 91
purple eyes, she was uncommonly pretty.

"Henry!" Her smile flashed redly at him—a row of coral teeth. 92

"Charming, charming," murmured the Director and, giving her two or 93
three little pats, received in exchange a rather deferential smile for himself.

"What are you giving them?" asked Mr. Foster, making his tone very 94
professional.

"Oh, the usual typhoid and sleeping sickness." 95

"Tropical workers start being inoculated at Metre 150," Mr. Foster 96
explained to the students. "The embryos still have gills. We immunize the fish
against the future man's diseases." Then, turning back to Lenina, "Ten to five
on the roof this afternoon," he said, "as usual."

"Charming," said the Director once more, and with a final pat, moved 97
away after the others.

On Rack 10 rows of next generation's chemical workers were being 98
trained in the toleration of lead, caustic soda, tar, chlorine. The first of a batch
of two hundred and fifty embryonic rocket-plane engineers was just passing
the eleven hundred metre mark on Rack 3. A special mechanism kept their
containers in constant rotation. "To improve their sense of balance," Mr.
Foster explained. "Doing repairs on the outside of a rocket in mid-air is a tick-
lish job. We slacken off the circulation when they're right way up, so that
they're half starved, and double the flow of surrogate when they're upside
down. They learn to associate topsyturvydom with well-being; in fact, they're
only truly happy when they're standing on their heads.

"And now," Mr. Foster went on, "I'd like to show you some very inter- 99
esting conditioning for Alpha Plus Intellectuals. We have a big batch of them
on Rack 5. First Gallery level," he called to two boys who had started to go
down to the ground floor.

"They're round about Metre 900," he explained. "You can't really do 100
any useful intellectual conditioning till the fetuses have lost their tails. Follow
me."

But the Director had looked at his watch. "Ten to three," he said. "No 101
time for the intellectual embryos, I'm afraid. We must go up to the Nurseries
before the children have finished their afternoon sleep."

Mr. Foster was disappointed. "At least one glance at the Decanting 102
Room," he pleaded.

"Very well then." The Director smiled indulgently. "Just one glance." 103

■ ■ ■

Review Questions

1. What is the Bokanovsky Process? Why is it central to Huxley's "brave
   new world"?
2. How does Huxley comment sardonically on the racism of the Hatchery's
   personnel—and of Europeans in general?

3. What is the difference—and the social significance of the difference—among Alphas, Betas, Deltas, Gammas, and Epsilons?

4. What technological problems concerning the maturation process have the scientists of *Brave New World* still not solved?

Discussion and Writing Suggestions

1. How does the language of the first two paragraphs reveal Huxley's tone, that is, his attitude toward his subject? For example, what is the function of the word "only" in the opening sentence: "A squat grey building of only thirty-four stories"? Or the adjectives describing the building?

2. What does the narrator mean when he says (paragraph 5) that "particulars, as every one knows, make for virtue and happiness; generalities are intellectually necessary evils. Not philosophers but fret-sawyers [operators of fretsaws, long, narrow, fine-toothed hand saws used for ornamental detail work] and stamp collectors compose the backbone of society"? To what extent do you believe that such an ethic operates in our own society? Give examples of the relatively low value placed on "philosophers" and the relatively high value placed on "fret-sawyers."

3. Throughout this chapter, Huxley makes an implied contrast between the brisk, technological efficiency of the Hatchery and the ethical nature of what takes place within its walls. What aspects of our own civilization show similar contrasts? (Example: We are now able to build more technologically sophisticated weapons of destruction than ever before in history.) Explore this subject in an essay, devoting a paragraph or so to each aspect of our civilization that you consider.

4. In the Hatchery, bottled, fertilized eggs pass into the "Social Predestination Room." In that room, their future lives will be determined. Is there an equivalent of the Social Predestination Room in our own society? (In other words, are there times and places when and where our future lives are determined?) If so, describe its features, devoting a paragraph to each of these features.

5. Foster explains how the undecanted embryos are conditioned to adapt to certain environments—for instance, conditioned to like heat so that, years later, they will feel comfortable working in the tropics or working as miners; or they may be conditioned to improve their sense of balance, so that they will be able to repair rockets in midair. What evidence do you see in our own society that people are or will be subject to conditioning to "like their unescapable social destiny"? Consider, for example, the influence of the conditioning exerted by parents, siblings, teachers, friends, or various social institutions. If you have lived or traveled abroad, what evidence do you see that conditioning in the United States is different from that in other countries? Explore this subject in a multi-paragraph essay.

6. As we noted in the headnote, Huxley's *Brave New World* (like much science fiction) is a projection into the future of contemporary aspects of culture that the author finds disturbing or dangerous. Select some present aspect of our culture that *you* find disturbing or dangerous and—in the form of a short story, or chapter from a novel, or section from a screen-play—dramatize your vision of what *could* happen.

Recombinant DNA and Genetic Engineering

CECIE STARR

RALPH TAGGART

Many of the public policy dilemmas of our modern world—the use of nuclear weapons, for example, or the debate about when to "pull the plug" on persons near death, or the debate about privacy from electronic snooping—have arisen as a direct result of scientific breakthroughs. Much of this chapter will deal with various aspects of the public policy debate surrounding biotechnology. But we thought it would be illuminating to precede these discussions with a scientific description of just what is entailed in a key aspect of the new field—genetic engineering.

In the following selection, reprinted from a textbook widely used in introductory college-level biology courses, the authors survey the field of genetic engineering, describe some recent developments in the field, and conclude by discussing some of the social, legal, ecological, and ethical questions regarding its benefits and risks.

Cecie Starr is a science writer who lives in Belmont, California. Ralph Taggart teaches biology at Michigan State University. This passage is from their textbook Biology: The Unity and Diversity of Life *(8th ed., 1998).*

MOM, DAD, AND CLOGGED ARTERIES

Butter! Bacon! Eggs! Ice cream! Cheesecake! Possibly you think of such foods as enticing, off-limits, or both. After all, who among us doesn't know about animal fats and the dreaded cholesterol?   1

Soon after you feast on these fatty foods, cholesterol enters the bloodstream. Cholesterol is important. It is a structural component of animal cell membranes, and without membranes, there would be no cells. Cells also remodel cholesterol into various molecules, including the vitamin D that is necessary for the development of good bones and teeth. Normally, however, your liver synthesizes enough cholesterol for your cells.   2

Some proteins circulating in the blood combine with cholesterol and other substances to form lipoprotein particles. The *HDLs* (high-density lipoproteins) collect cholesterol and transport it to the liver, where it can be   3 metabolized. *LDLs* (low-density lipoproteins) normally end up in cells that store or use cholesterol.

Sometimes too many LDLs form, and the excess infiltrates the elastic walls of arteries. There they promote formation of abnormal masses called atherosclerotic plaques. These interfere with blood flow and narrow the arterial diameter. If the plaques clog one of the tiny coronary arteries that deliver blood to the heart, the resulting symptoms can range from mild chest pains to a heart attack.   4

How your body handles dietary cholesterol depends on what you inherited from your parents. Consider the gene for a protein that serves as the cell's receptor for LDLs. Inherit two "good" alleles of the gene, and your blood level of cholesterol will tend to remain so low that your arteries will never get clogged, even with a high-fat diet. Inherit two copies of a certain mutated allele, however, and you are destined to develop a rare genetic disorder called *familial cholesterolemia*. With this disorder, cholesterol builds up to abnormally high levels. Many affected individuals die of heart attacks during childhood or their teens.   5

In 1992 a woman from Quebec, Canada, became a milestone in the history of genetics. She was thirty years old. Like two of her younger brothers who had died from heart attacks in their early twenties, she inherited the defective gene for the LDL receptor. She herself survived a heart attack when she was sixteen. At twenty-six, she had coronary bypass surgery.   6

At the time, people were hotly debating the risks and promise of **gene therapy**—the transfer of one or more normal or modified genes into an individual's body cells to correct a genetic defect or boost resistance to disease. Even so, the woman consented to undergo an untried, physically wrenching procedure designed to give her body working copies of the good gene.   7

Medical researchers removed about 15 percent of the woman's liver. They placed liver cells in a nutrient-rich medium that promoted growth and division. *And they spliced the good gene into the genetic material of a harmless virus.* That modified virus served roughly the same function as a hypodermic needle. The researchers allowed it to infect the cultured liver cells and thereby insert copies of the good gene into them.   8

Later, the researchers infused about a billion of the modified cells into the woman's portal vein, a major blood vessel that leads directly to the liver. There, at least some cells took up residence, and they started to produce the missing cholesterol receptor. Two years after this, between 3 and 5 percent of the woman's liver cells were behaving normally and sponging up cholesterol from the blood. Her blood levels of LDLs had declined nearly 20 percent. Scans of her arteries showed no evidence at all of the progressive clogging that had nearly killed her. At a recent press conference, the woman announced she is active and doing well.   9

Her cholesterol levels do remain more than twice as high as normal, and it is too soon to know whether the gene therapy will prolong her life. Yet the intervention provides solid proof that the concept of gene therapy is sound, and hopes are high.   10

As you might gather from this pioneering clinical application, recombi- 11
nant DNA technology has truly staggering potential for medicine. It also has
great potential for agriculture and industry. The technology does not come
without risks. With this chapter, we consider some basic aspects of the new
technology. At the chapter's end, we also address some ecological, social, and
ethical questions related to its application.

RECOMBINATION IN NATURE—AND IN THE LABORATORY

For more than 3 billion years, nature has been conducting uncountable numbers 12
of genetic experiments, through mutation, crossing over, and other events that
introduce changes in genetic messages. This is the source of life's diversity.

For many thousands of years, we humans have been changing numerous 13
genetically based traits of species. By artificial selection practices, we produced
new crop plants and breeds of cattle, birds, dogs, and cats from wild ancestral stocks. We developed meatier turkeys and sweeter oranges, larger corn,
seedless watermelons, flamboyant ornamental roses, and other useful plants.
We produced splendid hybrids, including the tangelo (tangerine x grapefruit)
and mule (horse x donkey).

Researchers now use **recombinant DNA technology** to analyze genetic 14
changes. With this technology, they cut and splice DNA from different
species, then insert the modified molecules into bacteria or other types of cells
that engage in rapid replication and cell division. The cells copy the foreign
DNA right along with their own. In short order, huge populations produce
useful quantities of recombinant DNA molecules. The new technology also is
the basis of **genetic engineering**, by which genes are isolated, modified, and
inserted back into the same organism or into a different one.

Plasmids, Restriction Enzymes, and the New Technology

Believe it or not, this astonishing technology originated with the innards of 15
bacteria. Bacterial cells have a single chromosome, a circular DNA molecule
that has all the genes they require to grow and reproduce. But many species
also have **plasmids**, or small, circular molecules of "extra" DNA that contain
a few genes.

Usually, plasmids are not essential for survival, but some of the the genes 16
they carry may benefit the bacterium. For instance, some plasmid genes confer
resistance to antibiotics. (*Antibiotics*, remember, are toxic metabolic products
of microorganisms that can kill or inhibit the growth of competing microorganisms.) The bacterium's replication enzymes copy and reproduce plasmid
DNA, just as they copy chromosomal DNA.

In nature, many bacteria are able to transfer plasmid genes to a bacteri- 17
al neighbor of the same species or a different one. Replication enzymes may

even integrate a transferred plasmid into the bacterial chromosome of a recipient cell. A recombinant DNA molecule is the result.

Infectious particles called viruses as well as bacteria dabble in gene transfers and recombinations. And so do most eukaryotic species. As you might imagine, viral infection does a bacterium no good. Over evolutionary time, bacteria developed an arsenal against invasion by harmful genes. They became equipped with many types of **restriction enzymes**, which are able to recognize and cut apart foreign DNA that may enter a cell. Eventually, researchers learned how to use plasmids *and* restriction enzymes for genetic recombination in the laboratory.   18

Producing Restriction Fragments

Each type of restriction enzyme makes a cut wherever it recognizes a specific, very short nucleotide sequence in the DNA. Cuts at two identical sequences in the same DNA molecule produce a fragment. Because some types of enzymes make *staggered* cuts, some fragments have single-stranded portions at both ends. Sometimes these are referred to as sticky ends: 19

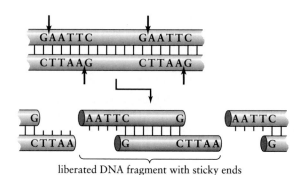

liberated DNA fragment with sticky ends

By "sticky," we mean the short, single-stranded ends of a DNA fragment will have the chemical capacity to base-pair with any other DNA molecule that also has been cut by the same restriction enzyme.   20

For example, suppose you use the same restriction enzyme to cut plasmids *and* DNA molecules that you have isolated from a human cell. When you mix the cut molecules together, they base-pair at the cut sites. After this, you add **DNA ligase** to the mixture. DNA ligase is an enzyme that seals DNA's sugar-phosphate backbone at the cut sites, just as it does during DNA replication. In this way, you create "recombinant plasmids," which have pieces of DNA from another organism inserted into them.   21

You now have a **DNA library**. It is a collection of DNA fragments, produced by restriction enzymes, that have been incorporated into plasmids, as illustrated in Figure 1.   22

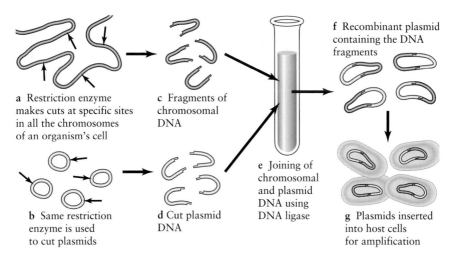

a **Restriction enzyme makes cuts at specific sites in all the chromosomes of an organism's cell**

c **Fragments of chromosomal DNA**

f **Recombinant plasmid containing the DNA fragments**

b **Same restriction enzyme is used to cut plasmids**

d **Cut plasmid DNA**

e **Joining of chromosomal and plasmid DNA using DNA ligase**

g **Plasmids inserted into host cells for amplification**

FIGURE 1

(a-f) Formation of a DNA library—a collection of DNA fragments, produced by restriction enzymes and inserted into plasmids or some other cloning tool. (g) Plasmid insertion into host cells to form cloned DNA, or multiple, identical copies of the DNA fragments.

WORKING WITH DNA FRAGMENTS

Amplification Procedures

A DNA library is almost vanishingly small. To obtain useful amounts of it, biochemists resort to methods of **DNA amplification**, by which a DNA library is copied again and again. One such method uses "factories" of bacteria, yeasts, or some other cells that can reproduce rapidly and take up plasmids. A growing population of these cells can amplify a DNA library in short order. Their repeated cycles of replication and cell division yield cloned DNA that has been inserted into plasmids. The "cloned" part of this name refers to the multiple, identical copies of DNA fragments. 23

The **polymerase chain reaction**, or **PCR**, is a newer method of amplifying fragments of DNA. The reactions proceed in test tubes, not in microbial factories. First, researchers identify short nucleotide sequences located just before and just after a region of DNA from a cell of the organism that interests them. Then they synthesize **primers**. These short nucleotide sequences, recall, will base-pair with any complementary sequences in DNA. And the replication enzymes called **DNA polymerases** recognize them as START tags. 24

For PCR, a DNA polymerase from a bacterium that lives in hot springs, even water heaters, is the enzyme of choice, because it remains functional at the elevated temperatures necessary to unwind DNA and also at the lower temperatures necessary for base pairing. Researchers mix together the primers, the polymerases, all the DNA from one of the organism's cells, and free nucleotides. Next, they expose the mixture to precise temperature cycles. During each cycle, the two strands of all the DNA molecules unwind from 25

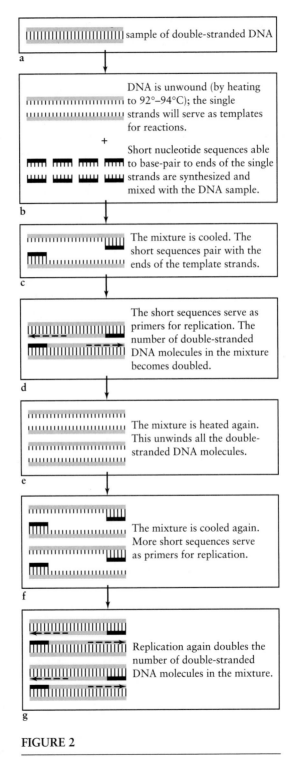

FIGURE 2

The polymerase chain reaction (PCR).

each other. And primers become positioned on exposed nucleotides at the targeted sites according to base-pairing rules (Figure 2). With each round of reactions, the number of DNA molecules doubles. For example, if there are 10 such molecules in the test tube, there soon will be 20, then 40, 80, 160, 320, 640, 1,280, and so on. Very quickly, a target region from a single DNA molecule can be amplified to *billions* of molecules.

In short, *PCR amplifies samples that contain even tiny amounts of DNA.* 26
As you will see in the next section, such samples can be obtained from fossils—even from a single hair or drop of blood left at the scene of a crime.

Sorting Out Fragments of DNA

When restriction enzymes cut DNA, the fragments they produce are not all 27
the same length. Researchers can use **gel electrophoresis** to separate fragments from one another according to length. This laboratory procedure employs an electric field to force molecules through a viscous gel and to separate them according to physical and chemical properties. For DNA, size alone affects how far the molecules move. (For proteins, remember, a molecule's size, shape, and net surface charge are the determining factors.)

A gel that contains DNA fragments is immersed in a buffered solution, 28
and electrodes connect the solution to a power source. Apply voltage, and negatively charged phosphate groups of the fragments respond to it. The fragments move toward the positively charged pole at different rates and thereby become separated into bands according to their lengths. Again, how far they migrate depends only on their size; the larger fragments cannot move as fast through it. After a predetermined period of electrophoresis, fragments of different length can be identified by staining the gel [Figure 3 on pages 508 and 509].

DNA Sequencing

Once DNA fragments from a sample have been sorted out according to 29
length, researchers can work out the nucleotide sequence of each type. The Sanger method of DNA sequencing, as detailed in Figure 3, will give you a sense of one of the ways this can be done.

MODIFIED HOST CELLS

Use of DNA Probes

Recombinant plasmids are not much use in themselves. They must be mixed 30
with living cells that can take them up. So how do you find out which cells do this? You can utilize **DNA probes**: short DNA sequences synthesized from radioactively labeled nucleotides. Part of a probe must be designed to base-pair with some portion of the DNA of interest. Any base pairing between

One of the methods used for sequencing DNA, as first developed by Frederick Sanger. The method is employed to determine the nucleotide sequence of specific DNA fragments, as this example illustrates.

a Single-stranded DNA fragments are added to a solution in four different test tubes:

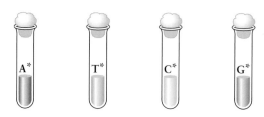

All four tubes contain DNA polymerases, short nucleotide sequences that can serve as primers for replication, and the nucleotide subunits of DNA (A, T, C, and G). Each tube contains a modified, labeled version of only one of the four kinds of nucleotides. We can show these as A^*, T^*, C^*, and G^*. The labeled form is present in low concentration, along with a generous supply of the unmodified form of the same nucleotide. Let's follow what happens in the tube with the A^* subunits.

b As expected, the DNA polymerase recognizes a primer that has become attached to a fragment, which it uses as a template strand. The enzyme assembles a complementary strand according to a base-pairing rules (A only to T, and C only to G). Sooner or later, the enzyme picks up an A^* subunit for pairing with a T on the template strand. The modified nucleotide is a chemical roadblock—it prevents the enzyme from adding more nucleotides to the growing complementary strand. In time, the tube contains labeled strands of different lengths, as dictated by the location of each A^* in the sequence:

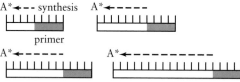

FIGURE 3

(continued on next page)

nucleotide sequences (that is, RNA as well as DNA) from different sources is called **nucleic acid hybridization**.

The challenge is to "select" the cells that have taken up recombinant plasmids and the gene of interest. One way to do this is to use a plasmid containing a gene that confers resistance to a particular antibiotic. You put prospective host cells on a culture medium that has the antibiotic added to it. The antibiotic prevents growth of all cells *except* the ones that house plasmids with the antibiotic-resistance gene.

The same thing happens in the other three tubes, with strand lengths dictated by the location of T*, C*, and G*.

c DNA from each of the four tubes is placed in four parallel lanes in the same gel. Then the DNA can be subjected to electrophoresis. The resulting nucleotide sequence can be read off the resulting bands in the gel. Look at the numbers running down the side of this diagram.

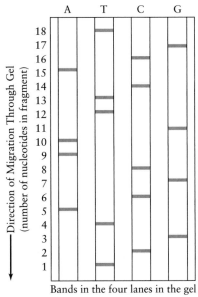

Bands in the four lanes in the gel

Start with "1" and read across the four lanes (A, T, C, G). As you can see, T is the closest to the start of the nucleotide sequence; it has migrated farthest through the gel. At "2," the next nucleotide is C, and so on. The entire sequence read from the first nucleotide to the last, is

T C G T A C G C A A G T T C A C G T

And now, by applying the rules of base pairing, you can deduce the sequence of the DNA fragment that served as the template.

As the cells divide, they form colonies. Assume the colonies are growing   32
on agar, a gel-like substance, in a petri dish. You blot the agar against a nylon filter. Some cells stick to the filter at sites that mirror the locations of the original colonies. You use solutions to rupture the cells, fix the released DNA onto the filter, and make the double-stranded DNA unwind. Then you add DNA probes, which hybridize only with the gene region having a complementary base sequence. Probe-hybridized DNA emits radioactivity and allows you to tag the colonies that harbor the gene of interest.

• • •

BACTERIA, PLANTS, AND THE NEW TECHNOLOGY

Many years have passed since foreign DNA was first transferred into a plas-   33
mid, yet that transfer started a debate that will continue into the next century. The issue is this: *Do the benefits of gene modifications and gene transfers*
outweigh the potential dangers? Before you personally come to any conclusions, reflect upon a few examples of the work with bacteria, then with
plants.

Genetically Engineered Bacteria

Imagine a miniaturized factory that churns out insulin or another protein   34
having medical value. This is an apt description of the huge stainless steel vats
of genetically engineered, protein-producing bacteria.

Think of *diabetics*, who need insulin injections for as long as they live.   35
The pancreas produces insulin, a protein hormone. Medical supplies of insulin
once were obtained from pigs and cattle, although some diabetics developed
allergic reactions to foreign insulin. Eventually, synthetic genes for human
insulin were transferred into *E. coli* cells. (Can you say why the genes had to
be synthesized?) This was the start of huge bacterial factories that manufacture human insulin, hemoglobin, somatotropin, interferon, albumin, and
other valuable proteins.

In addition, in research laboratories around the world, certain strains of   36
bacteria are now being engineered to degrade oil spills from tankers, to manufacture alcohol and other chemicals, to process minerals, or to leave crop
plants alone. The strains are harmless to begin with. The ones meant to be
confined to the laboratory are "designed" to prevent escape. As added precautions, the foreign DNA usually includes "fail-safe" genes. Such genes are
silent *unless* the engineered bacteria somehow are exposed to conditions that
occur in the environment. Exposure will activate the genes, with lethal results
for the bacteria.

For example, foreign DNA may include a *hok* gene next to a promoter of   37
the lactose operon. If an engineered bacterium does manage to escape to the
environment, where sugars are common, the gene will trip into action. The protein the gene specifies will destroy membrane function and so destroy the cell.

Even so, some people worry about the possible risks of introducing genet-   38
ically engineered bacteria into the environment. Consider how Steven Lindow
engineered a bacterium that can make many crop plants resist frost. A protein
at the bacterial surface promotes formation of ice crystals. Lindow excised the
ice-forming gene from some cells. As he hypothesized, spraying his "ice-
minus bacteria" on strawberry plants in an isolated field prior to a frost
would make plants less vulnerable to freezing. Even though Lindow deleted a
harmful gene from an organism, it triggered a bitter legal battle over releasing engineered bacteria into the environment. In time, the courts did rule in
favor of allowing such a release, and researchers sprayed a small strawberry
patch. Nothing bad ever happened. Since then, the rules governing the release
of genetically engineered species have become less restrictive.

Genetically Engineered Plants

A HUNT FOR BENEFICIAL GENES Currently, botanists are combing the world   39
for seeds and other living tissues from wild ancestors of potatoes, corn, and
other plants. They send their prizes—genes from a plant's lineage—to a safe
storage laboratory in Colorado. Why? *Farmers now rely on only a few strains
of high-yield crop plants that feed most of the human population.* The near-
absence of genetic diversity means our food base is dangerously vulnerable to
many disease-causing viruses, bacteria, and fungi. It is a race against time.
Our population has reached an astounding size. People, bulldozers, and
power saws are encroaching on previously uninhabited area; hundreds of
wild plant species disappear weekly.

The danger is real. Recently a new fungal strain that rots potatoes entered   40
the United States from Mexico. In 1994, crop losses from the resulting *potato
blight* topped $100 million. Pennsylvania farmers had little to harvest.
Possibly laboratory-stored, fungus-resistant strains of potato plants will save
crops in the future.

PLANT REGENERATION Botanists also search for good genes in the laborato-   41
ry. Years ago, Frederick Steward and his coworkers cultured cells of carrot
plants and induced them to grow into small embryos, some of which grew
into whole plants. Other species, including many crop plants, are regenerat-
ed today from cultured cells. The methods raise mutation rates, so cultures are
a source of genetic modifications.

Researchers can pinpoint a useful mutation among millions of cells.   42
Suppose a culture medium contains a toxic product of a disease agent. If a few
cells have a mutated gene that confers resistance to the toxin, only they will
live in the culture. If cells regenerate whole plants that can be hybridized with
other varieties, the hybrids may get the good gene.

METHODS OF GENE TRANSFER Now genetic engineers insert genes into cul-   43
tured plant cells. For example, they insert DNA fragments into the "Ti" plasmid from the bacterium *Agrobacterium tumefaciens*, which can infect many
species of flowering plants. Some plasmid genes invade a plant's DNA and
induce formation of abnormal tissue masses called crown gall tumors. Before
introducing the Ti plasmid into plants, researchers first remove the tumor-
inducing genes and insert desired genes into it. They grow the modified bacterial cells with cultured plant cells, then regenerate plants from the cells that
take up the genes. In some instances, the foreign genes have been expressed in
plant tissues, with observable effects.

A. tumefaciens can only infect beans, peas, potatoes, and other dicots.   44
However, wheat, corn, rice, and many major food crops are monocots, which
the bacterium cannot infect. In some cases, genetic engineers can use electric
shocks or chemicals to deliver modified DNA into protoplasts. (Protoplasts
are plant cells stripped of their walls.) At this writing, regenerating some
species of plants from protoplast cultures is not yet possible. But researchers

have had some success in delivering genes into cultured plant cells by actually shooting them with pistols. Instead of bullets, they use blanks to drive DNA-coated, microscopic particles into the cells.

ON THE HORIZON Despite many obstacles, improved varieties of crop plants   45
have been developed or are in the works. For example, genetically engineered cotton plants now resist worm attacks without any help from pesticides, which have the disadvantage of also killing off beneficial pest-eating insects.

Also on the horizon are engineered plants that can serve as factories for   46
pharmaceuticals. A few years ago, genetically engineered tobacco plants that make human hemoglobin, melanin, and other proteins were planted in a field in North Carolina. Ecologists later found no trace of foreign genes or proteins in the soil or in other plants or animals in the vicinity. Recently, mustard plant cells made plastic beads in a Stanford University laboratory. (Plastics are long-chain polymers of identical subunits.) The plant DNA incorporates three bacterial enzymes that are able to convert carbon dioxide, water, and nutrients into inexpensive, biodegradable plastic.

GENETIC ENGINEERING OF ANIMALS

Supermice and Biotech Barnyards

The first mammals enlisted for experiments in genetic engineering were lab-   47
oratory mice. Consider an example of this work. R. Hammer, R. Palmiter, and R. Brinster corrected a hormone deficiency that leads to dwarfism in mice. Insufficient levels of somatotropin give rise to the abnormality. The researchers used a microneedle to inject the gene for rat somatotropin into fertilized mouse eggs. After the eggs were implanted in an adult female, the gene was successfully integrated into the mouse DNA. Later, the baby mice in which the foreign gene was expressed were $1\frac{1}{2}$ times larger than their dwarf littermates. In other experiments, researchers transferred the gene for human somatotropin into a mouse embryo, where it became integrated into the DNA. The modified embryo grew up to be "supermouse."

Today, as part of research into the molecular basis of Alzheimer's disease   48
and other genetic disorders, a few human genes are being inserted into mouse embryos. Besides microneedles, microscopic laser beams are used to open up temporary holes in the plasma membrane of cultured cells, although such methods have varying degrees of success. Retroviruses also are used to insert genes into cultured cells, which may incorporate the foreign genes into their DNA. But the genetic material of retroviruses can undergo rearrangements, deletions, and other alterations that shut down the introduced genes. And if the virus particles escape from laboratory isolation, they may infect organisms.

Animals of "biotech barnyards" are competing with bacterial factories as   49
genetically engineered sources of proteins. For example, goats produce CFTR protein (for treating cystic fibrosis) and TPA (which diminishes the severity of

heart attacks). Cattle may soon produce human collagen for repairing carti-
lage, bone, and skin. Also, in 1996 researchers made a genetic duplicate of an
adult ewe. They reprogrammed one of her mammary gland cells so all of its
genes could be expressed. They fused that cell with an egg (from another ewe)
from which the nucleus had been removed. Signals from the egg cytoplasm
triggered the development of a cluster of embryonic cells, which was implanted into a surrogate mother. The result was a clone, a lamb named *Dolly*. At
this writing, the clone is thriving. The experiment opens up the possibility of
producing genetically engineered clones of sheep, cattle, and other farm animals that can supply consistently uniform quantities of proteins, even tissues
and organs, for medical uses and for research.

Applying the New Technology to Humans

Researchers around the world are working their way through the 3.2 billion   50
base pairs of the twenty-three pairs of human chromosomes. This ambitious
effort is the **human genome project**. Some researchers focus on specific chromosomes. Others are deciphering certain gene regions only. For example,
rather than studying the noncoding sequences (introns), J. Venter and Sidney
Brenner isolate mRNAs from brain cells and use them to make cDNA. By
sequencing only cDNAs, they have identified hundreds of previously
unknown genes.

   About 99.9 percent of the nucleotide sequence is the same in all humans   51
on Earth. The remaining 0.1 percent—about 3,200,000 base pairs—are mutations and other sequence variations sprinkled throughout the genome. They
account for *all* genetic differences in the human population. Therefore, com-
pletion of the project should give us the ultimate reference book of human
biology and genetic disorders. What will we do with all of that information?
Certainly we will use it in the search for treatments and cures for genetic disorders. Of the 2,000 or so genes studied so far, 400 have already been linked
to genetic disorders. And the knowledge opens doors to gene therapy, the
transfer of one or more normal or modified genes into the body cells of an
individual to correct a genetic defect or boost resistance to disease.

   But what about forms of human gene expression that are neither dis-   52
abling nor life-threatening? Will we tinker with them, also? . . .

Focus on Bioethics: Regarding Gene Therapy

This [discussion] opened with a historic, inspiring case, the first proof that   53
gene therapy can help save human lives. It closes with questions that invite
you to consider some social and ethical issues related to the application of
recombinant DNA technology to our rapidly advancing knowledge of the
human genome.

   To most of us, human gene therapy to correct genetic abnormalities   54
seems like a socially accepted goal. Let's take this idea one step further. Is it

also socially desirable or acceptable to change certain genes of a normal human individual (or sperm or egg) to alter or enhance traits?

The idea of of selecting desirable human traits is called *eugenic engineering.* Yet who decides which forms of a trait are most "desirable"? For example, what happens if prospective parents start picking the sex of a child by way of genetic engineering? In one survey group, three-fourths of the people who were asked this question said they would choose a boy. What would be the long-term social implications of a drastic shortage of girls?

As other examples, would it be okay to engineer taller or blue-eyed or fair-skinned boys and girls? Would it be okay to engineer "superhumans" with amazing strength or intelligence? Suppose a person of average intelligence moved into a town of 800 Einsteins. Would the response go beyond muttering of "There goes the neighborhood"? Are there people narcissistic enough to commission a clone of themselves, one that has just a few genetically engineered "improvements"? Researchers can alter genes now, and they have already cloned a sheep from a fully differentiated cell.

There are those who say that the DNA of any organism must never be altered. Put aside the fact that nature itself alters DNA much of the time, and has done so for nearly all of life's history. The concern is that *we* do not have the wisdom to bring about beneficial changes without causing great harm to ourselves or to the environment.

When it comes to manipulating human genes, one is reminded of our human tendency to leap before we look. When it comes to restricting genetic modifications of any sort, one also is reminded of the old saying, "If God had wanted us to fly, he would have given us wings." Yet something about the human experience has given us a capacity to imagine wings of our own making—and that capacity has carried us to the frontiers of space.

Where are we going from here with recombinant DNA technology, this new product of our imagination? To gain perspective on the question, spend some time reading the history of the human species. It is a history of survival in the face of all manner of new challenges, threats, bumblings, and sometimes disasters on a grand scale. It is also the story of our connectedness with the environment and with one another.

The basic questions confronting you today are these: Should we be more cautious, believing that one day the risk takers may go too far? And what do we as a species stand to lose if the risks are not taken?

■   ■   ■

Review Questions

1. For how long have genetic experiments been proceeding in nature?
2. What role do humans now play in genetic experimentation?
3. What do researchers do with recombinant DNA technology?

4. What three activities lie at the heart of recombinant DNA technology?
5. What is the basic procedure, and the basic goal, of genetic engineering? Provide one example of genetic engineering.

Discussion and Writing Suggestions

1. Write a one-page summary of this selection.
2. This selection originally appeared in an introductory college biology text. To what extent did you find it difficult to comprehend? Locate those passages that gave you particular trouble. Does the problem lie in the terminology Starr and Taggart employ? The scientific concepts under discussion? The organization or writing style? See if your instructor or other, more scientifically inclined students can throw light on these troublesome sections.
3. Toward the end of this selection Starr and Taggart discuss genetic engineering at the bacterial, plant, animal, and human levels. To what extent do you see a different set of ethical standards operating from one level to another? Taking into account the kind of considerations discussed at the end of the passage, what kind of ethical standards do you believe should operate at the level of human gene therapy? To what extent do you believe that it will be possible or practical to maintain such standards? For example, who has an interest in imposing such standards? Who has an interest in resisting them?
4. Describe (if possible, in scientific report format) an experiment that you conducted in high school, or that you are conducting now in chemistry, physics, or biology. Write in language that your nonscientific readers will be able to follow.

Tinkering with Destiny

SHANNON BROWNLEE

GARETH G. COOK

VIVA HARDIGG

For both scientists and the general public, one of the most exciting aspects of biotechnology lies in the prospect of treating human disease. If, as many like DNA pioneer James Watson believe, most diseases have a genetic basis, then locating the genes responsible for diseases should be a major priority in genetic research. (As Watson points out, "Ignoring genes is like trying to solve a murder without finding the murderer.") But of course, locating the culpable genes is only the first step. The next major step is to find ways of repairing or replacing the defective genes. Another consideration—ethical and philosophical, rather than medical—is to decide upon the criteria for "defectiveness." Yet another is how or even whether to notify people that they, their children, or their fetuses, are carrying "defective" genes. As Rachel Nowak asks in a recent article on genetic testing for Science, *"If your mother had died of Huntington's disease, would you want to be tested to see whether you had inherited the flawed gene that causes this fatal condition? A negative result would give you tremendous peace of mind, allowing you to lead an ordinary life. A positive result, on the other hand, would cause you to live the rest of your life knowing your ultimate fate would be the intellectual deterioration and involuntary movements that characterize Huntington's disease."*

The following article, "Tinkering With Destiny," by U.S. News & World Report *staffwriters Shannon Brownlee, Gareth G. Cook, and Viva Hardigg, discusses how various types of people—family members, scientists, counselors, doctors, and entrepreneurs—are dealing with the complex issues raised by our new-found knowledge about the relationships between genes and disease. It originally appeared in* U.S. News *on August 22, 1994.*

The last thing Joey Paulowsky needs is another bout with cancer. Only 7 years old, the Dallas native has already fought off leukemia, and now his family worries that Joey could be hit again. The Paulowsky family carries a genetic burden, a rare form of inherited cancer of the thyroid. Deborah, his mother, found a lump in her neck six years ago, and since then one family member has died of the cancer and 10 others have had to have their thyroids removed. "Do I have cancer?" Joey asks his mother. "Will it hurt?" The Paulowskys will know the answer next month, when the results of a genetic test will show whether their son carries the family's fateful mutation. 1

Joey is too young to know that he is participating in a medical revolution, one that will change the practice of medicine as profoundly as the invention of the microscope or the discovery of antibiotics. The snippet of DNA that will determine his fate was identified barely a year ago. Now, this mutant gene, along with the more than 150 others that have been captured thus far, are making it possible for doctors to peer into their patients' medical futures. Today, at least 50 genetic tests for hereditary diseases are available; by the turn of the century, DNA tests are almost certain to be a standard part of medical exams. From a single sample of a patient's blood, doctors will be able to spot genetic mutations that signal the approach not only of rare hereditary diseases, such as the thyroid cancer that stalks the Paulowsky clan, but also the common killers, including breast cancer, heart disease and diabetes—and defeat them. 2

For all its promise, the ability to glimpse the future will not come without costs. Knowing a patient's genetic predispositions will be central to preventive medicine, a keystone of health care reform; a physician will one day be able to advise the young adult at risk for high blood pressure in middle age to cut down on salt long before the appearance of symptoms. But for many other inherited ailments, a genetic test offers a Faustian bargain. For example, women who are members of families at high risk for breast cancer will soon 3 be able to undergo a genetic test for the breast cancer gene (known as BRCA1), which is responsible for as many as 1 in 10 of the 180,000 cases diagnosed in the United States each year. Those who are found to be free of the mutation will be spared the dread of the unknown. But those who do carry the mutation can only hope that self-examinations and mammograms catch the tumor early enough. Some women opt to have their healthy breasts removed, though there is little evidence that even this will prevent the cancer.

The rate of change is unlike anything medicine has witnessed before, as   4
researchers fish genes out of cells at a dizzying rate. Last year saw the discovery of more than a dozen mutations responsible for diseases ranging from Alzheimer's to hyperactivity to colon cancer. Almost as soon as a gene is discovered, commercial laboratories are ready to offer a genetic test—a pace that threatens to outstrip both physicians' and patients' abilities to make sense of the information. Couples forego having children after misunderstanding the result of genetic tests, while patients who carry mutations can lose their insurance under the current health care system. Scientists, genetic counselors and ethicists are racing to develop guidelines for the new age of genetic medicine, while families ponder the dilemmas presented by an incomplete medical revolution. "If we screw this up," says Francis Collins, director of the National Center for Human Genome Research, "I don't think the public will conclude that this was a useful revolution."

THE FAMILY

With cancer in my genes, is it safe to marry and have children?

On the surface, the five daughters of the Kostakis family seem alike.   5
They all have the same mass of curly hair, the same lively manner of speaking and the same propensity to start an argument in English and finish it in Greek. Yet an invisible and devastating distinction divides them: Two of the sisters inherited their mother's gene for a deadly form of colon cancer; the other three, like their brother, did not.

The family immigrated in 1977 from an impoverished village in Greece,   6
intent on forging a new and better life in America and oblivious to the genetic cargo that menaced their dream. "If I had known I carried the disease, I never would have gotten married and had children," says their mother, Eleni, in Greek. It was only when she went for a tubal ligation at age 39 that clues to the family's legacy began to emerge.

Eleni told the doctor that her father had died at age 28, with a stomach   7
tumor so large she could feel it with her hand, and that her older brother had undergone mysterious surgery he didn't like to talk about. The gynecologist immediately scheduled a colonoscopy—a jarring, uncomfortable procedure done under sedation. The eye of the colonoscope revealed the warning signs: benign polyps numbering in the hundreds or even thousands—harbingers of familial adenomatous polyposis colon cancer, a disease that can strike in some families as early as the teens.

Soon after Eleni had her colon removed, her younger brother was hit. He   8
refused to see a doctor until a week before he died, at age 43, in a manner
hauntingly reminiscent of her father's death. "He died because he chose to,"
she says, shaking her head and balling her hands into tight fists in her lap.
Eleni vowed that her children would know what they were up against. That
meant yearly colonoscopies for the Kostakis siblings, each of whom had a
50–50 chance of inheriting the ancestral cancer gene. Two of the sisters had
the telltale polyps and each had a portion of her colon removed at age 16.

Now, the family knows definitively who in the new generation has been   9
spared. In 1991, researchers discovered the gene that when mutated is responsible for adenomatous polyposis, and like 90 percent of those offered the gene
test at the Johns Hopkins School of Public Health, Eleni's other four children
opted to take it as soon as it was offered. "Anything that might stop those
colonoscopies was a great relief," says Maria, 26, the eldest. But when it came
time to find out the results, everyone was on edge. Petros, 25, remembers his
heart pounding in the doctor's office before the genetic counselor told him
and his sisters the good news: all negative. "Finding out was the biggest relief
of my entire life," Petros recalls. "It was better than making a million dollars,
better than sex—almost." Two weeks ago, a 14-year-old cousin received the
same happy tidings.

Maria felt a similar surge of freedom. "There are two struggles in a   10
cancer family," she says. "One is the disease and one is not knowing. You
have inside this *anchos*, we call it in Greek. It's like a bugging feeling, this
worry." For known carriers of the gene, knowledge has its price, especially
when it comes to the agonizing issue of parenthood. Katerina, the youngest of
the family, has recovered well from her colectomy and has resumed the life of
a typical high school senior. But the future haunts her. She clutches a small
pillow against her stomach and fights back tears as she says, "The thing that
scares me the most is if I found out my baby had it, I would abort it."

As devastating as their illness is, the Kostakises are among the lucky   11
ones. Not only is there a gene test for their type of cancer but, for those who
carry it, the telltale polyps show where and when to operate. By contrast,
Huntington's disease, the devastating neurological degeneration that killed
folk singer Woody Guthrie at 55, has a test but no cure. About 85 percent of
people at risk for Huntington's have declined the test, preferring to live in
blissless ignorance.

For families suffering from many other familial cancers, the *anchos*   12
remains, and each year is a waiting game. Margaret Todd, 66, of Towson,
Md., watched her parents die of colon cancer, and she herself has had malignant polyps removed. Her family's tumors arise from hereditary non-
polyposis colon cancer, which often fails to produce warning polyps and
cannot yet be detected through genetics, even though the genes responsible
were discovered last year. If there were a test, Todd's four children would
know whether they had to endure the discomfort and expense of the annual
colonoscopies, which cost about $1,000 apiece. She says, "We keep praying
for a gene test and they keep saying it might come this year."

THE SCIENTISTS

Where are the seeds of cancer and other genetic diseases?

Ray White knows which members of the Smith family will get colon   13
cancer, but most of the Smiths still do not. It is a position relished by neither
the Smiths nor White, who heads the Hunstman Cancer Institute at the
University of Utah. White's team of researchers discovered the gene responsible for the Smiths' colon cancer three years ago. Since then, he says, "they
have been beating on our door for the information." But for a variety of reasons, all aimed at protecting the Smiths, the researchers were not ready until
this June to share the news with the family.

White did not set out to be the keeper of such grave information when he   14
arrived in Salt Lake City in 1980, armed only with a new genetic technique of
his own invention and the desire to hunt disease-causing genes. This was the
dawn of the genetic age, when White and other scientists would finally begin
to make sense of more than 4,000 heritable diseases. In the previous two
decades, scientists had unraveled the mystery of inheritance, showing that it
is governed by DNA, the genetic material contained in the nucleus of each of
the body's cells. In 1980, White and a colleague at the Massachusetts Institute
of Technology devised a means for searching through DNA, infinitesimal
section by infinitesimal section. By comparing the length of the same section
from one family member to another, researchers now had a way to zero in on
the approximate location of genes corresponding to inherited diseases.

In 1982, White aimed his sights at the mangled DNA responsible for ade-   15
nomatous polyposis colon cancer, or APC. APC accounts for only 1 percent
of all colon cancer cases, but it snakes through the family trees of half a
dozen Mormon clans in Utah. Mormons proved perfect subjects for White's
team: They keep meticulous genealogies, and many families bear as many as
10 to 12 children, giving an inherited disease a chance to show up in each generation. The researchers spent a decade flying around the state collecting
blood samples, often at family reunions. "On holidays, I can figure I'm going
to be drawing blood," says Utah geneticist Ken Ward. In 1991, White's team,
along with a group led by Bert Vogelstein at Johns Hopkins Oncology Center
in Baltimore, announced simultaneously that they had nailed the colon cancer
gene.

Yet even in their euphoria the researchers knew they could not simply call   16
the Smiths, a clan of some 2,000 to 3,000, and blurt out who was safe and who
wasn't. First, they had to find the precise mutations in the gene that ran through
their broad family tree—then estimate the odds that an individual carrying a
mutation would actually be hit with cancer. The researchers also worried that
family members could lose their insurance once it was discovered they harbored
the defective gene. One man's insurance was canceled simply because he participated in the genetic study—though it turned out he did not have the gene.
The researchers had to be certain of just what their scientific findings meant in
practical terms to families at risk for cancer. This June, the first letters arrived
in Smith mailboxes, offering a chance to learn their genetic legacy.

Researchers around the world will find themselves in a similar fix with   17
each new gene they uncover. A gene found in 1991 by Utah geneticist Jean
Marc LaLouel now appears to bestow some of its owners with high blood
pressure while leaving others vulnerable to certain complications of pregnancy. Earlier this year, researchers at Thomas Jefferson University in
Philadelphia announced they are close to the long-sought gene responsible for
manic-depression. This summer, a French lab fetched up a gene that leads to
melanoma, a deadly form of skin cancer, while geneticists at the National
Institutes of Health announced that p53, a gene notorious for its role in more
than half of all cancers, may also make mischief in the cells lining the arteries, thus contributing to heart disease. But while these bits of DNA are already
opening new avenues to combatting and perhaps even preventing illness,
cures are probably years, if not decades, away.

Until then, researchers want to put their newfound genes to use, spotting   18
diseases as early as possible. Johns Hopkins University's David Sidransky is
confident that the ubiquitous p53 gene can serve as a red flag for tumors of
the mouth and bladder. Sidransky analyzed a urine specimen saved from
Hubert Humphrey in 1967 and found mutant copies of p53. If the gene had
been known at the time, it might have alerted doctors to the bladder cancer
that would kill the senator a decade later. Another cancer gene, called RAS,
can warn of impending lung cancer; RAS and the APC gene in stool samples
may one day alert doctors to as many as 80 percent of colon cancers—even
among the 150,000 cases that arise each year in people with no familial history. For cancer, more than almost any other illness, such early-warning systems are desperately needed. "We are going to figure out how to identify
precancerous lesions and get rid of them," says White, "before they turn into
full-blown cancer."

THE COUNSELOR

Are people capable of understanding genetic risk?

The day a cure for cancer is discovered will be the day Barbara Biesecker's   19
job is made easier. Biesecker is a genetic counselor, one of the medical mes-
sengers who are trained in both psychology and human genetics—and who
bear the responsibility for making sure that people like the Smiths and the
Kostakises understand the implications of their genetics tests. The result of
these tests is rarely a simple thumbs up or down. More often, the best a
genetic test can offer is a degree of risk, and conveying the meaning of risk is
no easy task.

Weighing the Odds. Even when people comprehend the numbers (and   20
many cannot), they find uncertainty psychologically troubling. When confronted with a 50 percent risk, many patients conclude their chances are
either zero or 100 percent, says Biesecker, head of genetic counseling at the
National Center for Human Genome Research in Bethesda, Md. "It's either,
'I've got it' or 'I don't.'"

The flood of new gene discoveries has left genetic counselors unsure of   21
how to proceed in the new age of medical genetics. The counselors' credo
requires that they help clients come to their own decisions, but they are concerned about the increasing numbers of people—particularly expectant couples—who demand the newest genetic tests even when there is little evidence
of medical risk. "We have this fantasy in this country that if we have enough
information, we can control events," says Biesecker.

This desire for information is especially troubling when parents want   22
their children tested for diseases whose symptoms will not appear for many
years. "Parents think they want their children tested, but what they really
want to hear is that their child does not have the disease," says Randall Burt,
a gastroenterologist at the Veterans Hospital in Salt Lake City. They haven't
thought through what a positive result will mean to them.

Few of the new genes have raised more nettlesome issues than BRCA1,   23
the breast cancer gene. Geneticists estimate that 1 in 200 women may carry
mutations in this gene; millions will no doubt want to be tested. There are
only about 1,200 genetic counselors in the country, not nearly enough to
handle the job of deciphering the results. For example a positive test means a
woman's daughters could also harbor the mangled gene. A negative test for
BRCA1, on the other hand, does not mean a woman has entirely dodged the
bullet; she still faces the possibility of getting other forms of breast cancer.
And for women who have watched their mothers and sisters die of breast
cancer, a negative test sometimes leads to "survivor guilt," feelings similar to
those of victims who escaped the Holocaust.

With a shortage of genetic counselors, the task of sorting through such   24
dilemmas will fall to doctors or even to commercial testing services. "What
will happen when this is in the hands of primary care physicians scares me a
lot," says Biesecker. "Are physicians prepared to draw the line between giving
advice about treatment and advising a couple whether or not to have children?"

THE DOCTOR

Are doctors ready to practice medicine in the genetic age?

How physicians will use the fruits of the genetic revolution is a major   25
concern of Gail Tomlinson, a pediatric oncologist at the University of Texas
Southwestern Medical Center in Dallas. Tomlinson knows firsthand both
the power and the peril of genetic tests: As 7-year-old Joey Paulowsky's
physician, she will use the test results due next month to decide whether the
child's thyroid should be removed.

But few of Tomlinson's colleagues are as well trained as she is in the com-   26
plexities of medical genetics. Unlike genetic counselors, who learn the tricky
business of informing without recommending, most doctors are taught to tell
patients what is best for them. That is not easy when all a test offers is a measure of risk. For example, among Tomlinson's patients are families afflicted
with Li Fraumeni syndrome, a rare hereditary mutation in the p53 gene that

can bring on a bewildering variety of cancers. But until there are better ways to detect the tumors early enough to stop them, the test for p53, says Tomlinson, "may not do patients a lot of good. You can't fix the defective gene, and you can't catch many of the cancers."

Eventually, genetic tests will belong in the hands of the doctors on the   27
front lines of medicine, says Tomlinson. "But things are moving so fast. We know how to clone genes, but we don't know how to talk about it to patients. Just how to apply this predictive testing hasn't been worked out."

Until it is, some physicians will view genetic tests with a mixture of   28
unease and distrust. Sandra Byes, an oncologist at the University of Utah Medical Center, is uncertain whether she will advise her patients to take a genetic test for the breast cancer gene once it is discovered: "It's a lot more comforting to say to a patient, 'You are from a high-risk family' than 'You have the gene, try not to let it ruin your life.'"

THE ENTREPRENEUR

Is American society on the verge of a genetic gold rush?

In 1989, business was so bad at the DNA lab at Integrated Genetics that   29
the company was close to shutting it down. Now, the respected Framingham, Mass., lab boasts nearly one fifth of the $8 million market in DNA tests for inherited diseases, a fledgling industry poised to take off. Industry analysts foresee a $500 million market in genetic tests in the next decade.

The potential for profits is bringing entrepreneurs like IG President Elliott   30
Hillback face to face with a marketplace filled with moral pitfalls. With the discovery of each disease-causing gene, a new and lucrative market opens, but it can take years before anyone understands the medical seriousness of any given genetic mutation (and some genes can have hundreds of mutations). Last year, for example, more than 30,000 tests were performed to detect one or more of some 350 mutations in the gene behind cystic fibrosis, a heritable and often fatal lung disease. Yet scientists are only now discovering that some mutations actually cause none of the classic symptoms. The danger is that some labs will make a test available before the results can be meaningfully interpreted.

Private Codes. Critics also fear for the patient's right *not* to know the   31
contents of his genes. Today, the final responsibility for explaining the untoward consequences of a test—such as losing health insurance—lies with the laboratory itself. But turning away patients means turning away profits.

The two government agencies charged with overseeing the burgeoning   32
genetics market, the Food and Drug Administration and the Health Care Financing Administration, have been slow to step in. Most of the companies that manufacture the chemical tools of the genetics trade have not bothered to submit their products to the FDA for approval as required by law. Labs serve a vital role in making tests cheaper and more accurate. But HCFA, charged with ensuring test accuracy, "has dragged its feet," according to Neil Holtzman, a member of a Human Genome Project working group inves-

tigating genetic testing. This is in part because the agency lacks inspectors with the necessary genetic training. For now, there is nothing—beyond the lab director's personal ethics—to keep a lab from introducing new tests, regardless of their potential for misuse.

A few companies are already pushing the boundaries. Genica Pharmaceuticals of Worcester, Mass., for example, is offering a test for a gene linked to Alzheimer's disease even though the Alzheimer's Association has said that too little is known about the gene and its mutations to interpret test results properly. Genica President Robert Flaherty admits that "it is not a definitive test," but believes that under the right circumstances "it can be very useful."   33

While Hillback worries that a few reckless labs might cause a public backlash against the entire enterprise, it is ultimately not the responsibility of   34 commercial establishments to set boundaries. Americans must decide where to draw the ethical line. And wherever they finally choose to draw it, Hillback and his colleagues know that there will be no turning back. "It's much easier to say that society as a whole is not ready for a test," says James Amberson, a vice president at Dianon Systems, a testing company. "But it's awfully hard to look a mother in the eye and say no."

■ ■ ■

Review Questions

1. What is a "genetic predisposition"?
2. In terms of what doctors are able to do, what is the difference between the form of colon cancer that struck the Kostakis family and Huntington's disease?
3. How are doctors making use of newly discovered genes such as p53 and RAS?
4. In what ways has counseling of people who want to take or have taken genetic tests become a problem, according to the authors?
5. What kind of problems in genetic testing are introduced by the "entrepreneurs"—that is, the labs that provide genetic testing services?

Discussion and Writing Suggestions

1. According to the authors, genetic testing offers a "Faustian bargain"—a bargain in which the cost of knowledge may be too high. Eleni Kostakis, for example, asserts that had she known that she carried a gene for colon cancer, "I never would have gotten married and had children." Were you in her place, would you feel the same way? Would you feel that the possibility of transmitting the deadly gene to your offspring was so great (50

percent) that the only morally responsible choice was to forego parenthood?

2. The case of Woody Guthrie, the famous folk singer who died at age 55
   of Huntington's disease, is frequently cited in discussions of genetic
   testing. Suppose such testing had been available to Woody Guthrie's
   mother and she discovered that her unborn child carried the gene.
   Might she not have aborted? Would it have been better had Guthrie
   never been born? A related question is whether people who are at
   genetic risk for this disease should undergo testing to determine if they
   are likely to develop it in later life. Would you be one of the 85 percent
   who prefer to live in "blissless ignorance" or one of the 15 percent who
   want to know? Respond to these questions in a two- to three-page
   journal entry.

3. Barbara Biesecker, a genetic counselor, is quoted as saying, "We have this
   fantasy in this country that if we have enough information, we can control events." What do you think she means? To what extent do you
   think that what she says is true of people's attitudes in areas *other than*
   genetic testing? In other words, to what extent is information power? To
   what extent is it only the illusion of power?

4. To what extent do you see connections between the type of concern
   expressed by the authors and by some of the people they discuss about
   the downside of genetic testing and the kind of concerns by Aldous
   Huxley in *Brave New World*? To what extent, in other words, does the
   world of "Tinkering With Destiny" have the seeds of a Brave New
   World? Are some of the scientists, or some of the entrepreneurs, like the
   Director of Hatcheries?

The Grandiose Claims of Geneticists

DOROTHY NELKIN

*The authors of many articles about genetic research and development in news-
papers and popular magazines seem awestruck by the accomplishments of
biotechnology and by the prospects for scientific advances and new medical
tools. Sociology professor Dorothy Nelkin takes a more skeptical view of the
claims of geneticists. While Nelkin does not advocate restrictions on genetic
research, she does express serious reservations about the way that developments
in biotechnology are being presented to the public. In particular, she argues that
genetic research could be misappropriated by politicians and others to justify a
conservative social agenda. Nelkin, author of* Selling Science: How the Press
Covers Science and Technology *(1988), teaches sociology at New York
University. This article first appeared in the* Chronicle of Higher Education *on
March 3, 1993.*

Until recently, scientists have paid little attention to communicating with the   1
public, assuming that a record of accomplishment was sufficient to maintain
public support for research. Concerned that public visibility could result in
external control, they have disdained "visible scientists," ignored populariz-
ers of science, and avoided journalists. But the stakes have changed in the face
of growing mistrust of science, questions about the morality and honesty of
research practices, and threats of outside regulation.

Now that the public is questioning the wisdom of the government's rel-   2
atively unfettered support of science, scientists are worrying about their public
image and trying harder to communicate the excitement and benefits of their
research. They see gaining visibility through the media as crucial to securing
support and assuring favorable public policies toward science.

Researchers mapping the human genome, the complete set of all human   3
genes, are particularly concerned about their public image, both to assure the
continuity of public financing for their long-term, costly project and to
counter the negative images of genetics stemming from its historical association with eugenics. What can we learn from their efforts to shape the public
image of the Human Genome Project? Do the images disseminated by geneticists inform the public accurately and fairly about this complex field? How
are these images received?

The evidence suggests that geneticists may create new problems for them-   4
selves by using overblown rhetoric and misleading metaphors to convey the
importance of their work.

As part of a project looking at how genes are understood and represent-   5
ed in American popular culture, I have been collecting the metaphors that
geneticists repeatedly use to describe their work. I find three related themes:
a definition of the gene as the essence of identity and the basis of human differences; a promise that genetic research will enhance prediction and allow
control of behavior and disease; and an image of the genome, the exact chemical sequencing of genes, as a text that will define a natural order.

The idea that identity lies in the genes appears in images of the body as   6
a set of "genetic instructions," a "program" transmitted from one generation
to another. People are "readouts" of their genes. If scientists can decipher the
text, classify the markers on the map, and read the instructions, they will
reconstruct the essence of human beings. This, in turn, will unlock the key to
human ailments and human nature and provide, as one scientist puts it, "the
ultimate answers to the commandment 'Know thyself.'" The geneticist Walter
Gilbert introduces his public lectures on gene sequencing by pulling a compact
disk from his pocket and announcing to his audience: "This is you." And the
Cold Spring Harbor Laboratory has published a children's book called *Cells
Are Us*.

Scientists also emphasize the predictive powers of genetics by calling the   7
gene a "Delphic Oracle," a "time machine," a "trip into the future," a "medical crystal ball." James Watson, co-discoverer of the structure of the DNA
molecule and the first director of the Human Genome Project, announces that
"our fate is in our genes." Futuristic scenarios promise that genetic prediction

will enhance control of human behavior and disease. In the future, says one geneticist, "present methods of treating depression will seem as crude as former pneumonia treatments seem now." Describing acts of violence, a science editor claims: "When we can accurately predict future behavior, we may be able to prevent the damage."

Geneticists frequently refer to the genome as the Bible, the Holy Grail, or the Book of Man. Such religious images suggest that the genome—once mapped and sequenced—will be a powerful guide to human behavior, a sort of secular text that will define the natural and moral order. Other common images of the genome—as map, dictionary, library, or recipe—imply order, suggesting that genetic information will reduce the ambiguity of a complex environment and fix things in their proper place.

The rhetorical strategies of geneticists have clearly captured public interest. Genetics has become a coffee-table science and the gene, a ubiquitous popular image. We encounter the gene in supermarket tabloids and soap operas, in television sitcoms and talk shows, in comic books and advertising slogans, and even in biographies of Elvis. We read about genes in women's magazines and child-advice books as well as in science reports.

Stimulated by the grandiose claims of geneticists, the media have appropriated genetic images in ways that serve their goals—but not necessarily the goals of scientists. The power of genetic images for the public derives less from people's interest in science than its relationship to social concerns.

The biological sciences have long served to justify social arrangements as "natural," based on scientific reality. Darwin's theory of evolution by natural selection served to explain and legitimize the inequalities brought about by the industrial revolution: It is the fittest who survive.

Today, models of molecular biology are appropriated to support prevailing ideologies, traditional biases, and social stereotypes. Media interest in genetics partly rests on the possibility of finding therapies for devastating diseases, and the message in repeated headlines is one of awe and expectation. "Genetics: The War on Aging, the Medical Story of the Century." But the media's use of genetic images also suggests their resonance with sensitive social issues.

For example, picking up on scientists' metaphors locating identity in the genes, many stories discuss genes in the context of the stability of the family. The frequent use of phrases such as "biological connections" or "genetic rights" suggests the importance of genetic relationships. Genealogical services have proliferated, advertised as a way to define identity through knowing genetic ties. Adoption stories emphasize the urgent need to find "biological roots." These stories use genetics to reinforce traditional family values.

The language of biological determinism is pervasive in the media, where genes are held to be responsible for obesity, criminality, shyness, intelligence, political leanings, and even preferred styles of dressing—as if such complex attributes are transmitted like brown hair or blue eyes. The gene in popular culture is an anthropomorphized entity—given a wide range of behavior attributes. There are selfish genes, pleasure-seeking genes, criminal genes, celebrity genes, homosexuality genes, couch-potato genes, depression genes, genes for genius, genes for saving, and even genes for sinning.

These images convey a striking picture of DNA as the essence of the   15 person. Appropriating the images used by scientists, the media interpret them in literal and concrete ways, often simplifying important subtleties. Thus, the gene in popular culture has become the agent of identity, the most powerful force in shaping behavior. But above all, the gene is seen as the source of human difference, a "natural" basis of social stereotypes, as seen in statements like: "Differences lie in the genes." Countless media stories focus on the biological differences between genders: Women are predisposed to their "natural" role of nurturance; boys are "genetically programmed" to be aggressive. Others stories say something like, "Why are women different? They are born that way."

Just as scientists have talked about genetic research as enabling the pre-   16 diction of disease, so promises of prediction appear in the ubiquitous media preoccupation with "predispositions." Stories refer to "gene-impelled compulsions" or "natural bents." The gene has become the key to the human future; we are programmed to succeed or to fail. News articles and magazine stories explain deviant behavior in terms of genetic predisposition: "Is Crime in the Family Tree?" or "Addicted to the Bottle? It May Be in the Genes." Stories about "bad genes" offer hope that those predisposed to crime or addiction can be identified and controlled. As one writer puts it, crime could be reduced if we determined which persons were biologically predisposed and took "preemptive action" before they committed crime. And another remarks: "It seems pointless to wait until high-risk prospects actually commit crimes before trying to do something to control them."

To journalists looking for certainty, genetic explanations that can be   17 mapped and catalogued or deciphered from nature's text seem more objective, and less ambiguous, than environmental or social explanation. They seem to provide hard ways to codify what is normal or deviant, to justify inequities on the basis of "natural " characteristics, and to differentiate "them" from "us." They appeal as a solid, apparently neutral guide to social policy.

Media interpretations are consequential, affecting both individual deci-   18 sions and social policies. The idea of fate, for example, enters conflicts over responsibility. If behavior is genetically predetermined, families are not to blame for the problems of their children. And if certain people are defined as inherently and irretrievably problematic, society is absolved from responsibility. Why worry about rehabilitation, remedial education, or social support? Those who fail could be defined as intrinsically flawed, while others are destined to succeed.

Defining people as "predisposed" to immutable traits could justify dis-   19 criminatory social practices. If we believe that there are "criminal genes," for example, this could sanction the use of tests to predict dangerousness, overriding issues of justice or fairness. And if the concept of genetic determinism is extended to groups, this could compromise the rights or obligations of classes of people.

To locate complex human behavior in a molecular entity is to ignore that   20
behavior's social context. There are no genes for behavior, only genes for proteins that influence physiological processes. Indeed, to explain human beings in biological terms, to jump from the molecular level of genetic systems to the behavior of human beings, requires a profound leap of faith. But this leap is encouraged by the scientists' metaphors of order and scenarios of prediction.

Scientists often dismiss the way in which their work is appropriated by   21
the media, calling it oversimplified and distorted. But much of the popular rhetoric about genes draws support from the promises generated by scientists and the language they use to describe their research. In the interest of public understanding, then, scientists should restrain their tendencies to oversell their work and consider the biases and beliefs that will ultimately shape the uses of a powerful science—one that offers prospects for promising applications, but that also opens possibilities for pernicious abuse.

■ ■ ■

Review Questions

1. What is the thesis of Nelkin's article? If possible, locate the thesis in the author's own words.
2. What three related themes does Nelkin find in the metaphors that geneticists use to describe their work?
3. Why does Nelkin object to the proposition that genes determine human identity?
4. According to Nelkin, what group of people share with scientists the responsibility for the overselling of genetic knowledge? Why?

Discussion and Writing Suggestions

1. Nelkin claims that "the biological sciences have long served to justify social arrangements as 'natural,' based on scientific reality." Thus, Darwin's "survival of the fittest" theory has been appropriated by social Darwinists who use Darwin's biological ideas to argue against welfare. How have some people appropriated genetic knowledge for social and political, rather than scientific ends? Do you share Nelkin's concern that such ideological use of scientific knowledge poses a significant threat in the future? Draw upon particular examples, both those advanced by Nelkin and others that occur to you, to support your argument.

2. You are an aspiring screenwriter who has seized upon genetic research as the basis for a science fiction film. Write a treatment (that is, a summary description of the action) of a proposed film involving the creation or manipulation of what Nelkin sarcastically calls "selfish genes, pleasure-seeking genes, criminal genes," etc.

3. Write a critique of Nelkin's article. Use the general guidelines provided in Chapter 2 in planning your critique, and draw also upon some of your responses to the Review Questions.

The Human Genome Project: A Personal View

JAMES D. WATSON

One of the most monumental scientific undertakings of our time is the Human Genome Project, launched in 1988.* A genome is the complete set of genes in the chromosomes of organisms (humans have twenty-three pairs of chromosomes in the nucleus of each cell); and the purpose of the Human Genome Project is to identify, locate, and sequence all of the genes in human chromosomes. As a Time *magazine article explained, "Encoded in the genome, the DNA in the . . . 46 chromosomes, are instructions that affect not only structure, size, coloring and other physical attributes, but also intelligence, susceptibility to disease, life-span and even some aspects of behavior. The ultimate goal of the Human Genome Project is to read and understand those instructions." Among the instructions that scientists are most eager to understand are those that determine human diseases, many of which are genetic in origin.*

In the following article, James D. Watson, the first director of the Human Genome Project, offers a "personal" perspective on this project and its meaning for him. One of the most influential scientists of modern times, Watson, together with Francis Crick, discovered the double-helix structure of the DNA molecule, a discovery that won them the 1962 Nobel Prize and that has been the basis of almost all subsequent genetic research. Born in 1928, Watson earned his doctorate in biology from Indiana University. In 1951, while conducting research at the Cavendish Laboratory at Cambridge University, Watson met Francis Crick, and the two began their epoch-making studies into the molecular basis of heredity. Watson and Crick's paper, announcing their discovery, was published in the journal Nature *in 1953.*

Watson taught at Harvard University from 1955 to 1976, and starting in 1968 served as director of the Cold Spring Harbor Biological Laboratories, work-

---

*For its first five years the Genome Project was headed by DNA pioneer and Nobel laureate James D. Watson.

ing primarily on cancer research. In 1989 Watson was appointed director of the National Institutes of Health's (NIH) Human Genome Project. Watson's books include The Double Helix *(1968), an account of the discovery of DNA structure;* The Molecular Biology of the Gene *(1965); and* Recombinant DNA *(1985; with John Tooze and David T. Kurtz). This article first appeared in an anthology,* The Code of Codes: Scientific and Social Issues in the Human Genome Project *(1992), edited by Daniel J. Kevles and Leroy Hood.*

When I was going into science, people were concerned with questions of where we came from. Some people gave mystical answers—for example, "the truth came from revelation." But as a college kid I was influenced by Linus Pauling, who said, "We came from chemistry." I have spent my career trying to get a chemical explanation for life, the explanation of why we are human beings and not monkeys. The reason, of course, is our DNA. If you can study life from the level of DNA, you have a real explanation for its processes. So of course I think that the human genome project is a glorious goal.

People ask why *I* want to get the human genome. Some suggest that the reason is that it would be a wonderful end to my career—start out with the double helix and end up with the human genome. That *is* a good story. It seems almost a miracle to me that fifty years ago we could have been so ignorant of the nature of the genetic material and now can imagine that we will have the complete genetic blueprint of man. Just getting the complete description of a bacterium—say, the five million bases of E. coli—would make an extraordinary moment in history. There is a greater degree of urgency among older scientists than among younger ones to do the human genome now. The younger scientists can work on their grants until they are bored and still get the genome before they die. But to me it is crucial that we get the human genome now rather than twenty years from now, because I might be dead then and I don't want to miss out on learning how life works.

Still, I sometimes find myself moved to wonder, Is it ethical for me to do my job? A kind of backlash against the human genome project has cropped up from some scientists—good ones as well as not so good ones. What seems to have outraged many people was that, in 1990, against the proposed increase of 3.6 percent in the president's budget for all NIH funds, the human genome project was proposed for an increase of 86 percent—from roughly $60 million to $108 million. Feeling dispossessed, some scientific groups have begun to behave like postal workers' unions. The biological chemists, the molecular biologists, and the cell biologists have hired a lobbyist, a former congressman from Maine, to get the overall NIH appropriation increased. If such moves succeed, then maybe we won't have this terrible situation of really good scientists claiming that they are not getting funded because all the money is going to the human genome project.

In the meantime, hate letters have made the rounds, including the rounds of Congress, contending that the project is "bad science"—not only bad, but sort of wicked. The letters say that the project is wasting money at a time when resources for research are getting threatened: If good people are failing to get grants, why go ahead with a program that is just going to spend billions of dollars sequencing junk? In 1990, someone in my office tried to get a distinguished biologist to help peer-review a big grant application. The biologist said, "No, not the human genome!" as though he were talking about syphilis.

The biologist sent me a fax asking me to explain why he should not 5 oppose the human genome program. I called him up and said that, though I couldn't prove it, Congress actually seemed to *like* the human genome program because it promised to find out something about disease. Congress was excited that maybe we scientists were worried about disease instead of just about getting grants. The primary mission of the National Institutes of Health is to improve American health, to give us healthier lives, not to give jobs to scientists. I think that the scientific community, if it wants to be ethically responsible to society, has to ask whether we are spending research money in a way that offers the best go at diseases.

The fact is that understanding how DNA operates provides an enor- 6 mous advantage over working only with proteins or fats or carbohydrates. The best illustration of this advantage has been tumor viruses. If we had not been able to study cancer at the level of the change in DNA that starts it, the disease would still be a hopeless field. Every time a new enzyme was discovered, hope would rise that it was the cause of cancer. Cancer used to be considered a graveyard for biochemists, even good ones, many of whom wanted to cap their careers by solving cancer but failed. Not until the genetic foundation for cancer was identified could you really begin to say what goes wrong to make this terrible human affliction.

A similar example is Alzheimer's disease. Are we going to find out what 7 Alzheimer's is and why it causes brain failure without getting the genes that we know predispose certain people to the disease? Maybe we will, but I would not bet on it. But if we can get the gene or genes implicated in the disease, I am confident that we will save hundreds of millions of dollars, if not billions, that would have been spent on worthless research.

Every year, Congress passes a bill for even more money to study 8 Alzheimer's. Congress is voting for good goals, but we do not really know how to use the money. It is not as if all the federal budget for health and all the basic research grants add up to good research. All the study sections in the National Institutes of Health do not receive applications of equal value; they often endorse research projects or programs because they address important problems. The programs themselves are not terrible, but they often have a low probability of paying off. I am sure that half the NIH budget is spent on good intentions rather than on a realistically high probability that a research program will have a direct impact on one of the major human diseases.

The pressure is enormous to do something about mental disease because 9 it can be terrible, as anyone knows who has a friend or family member suffering from it. We do spend a vast amount of money studying mental diseases, yet the effort yields very little. Manic-depressive disease leads to great moments of mania—perhaps the successful careers of a number of scientists can be attributed to it—but it also leads to depression, tragedy, and suicides. Lithium relieves some of the symptoms, but a drug is not the complete answer, as any psychiatrist will tell you. It is pretty clear that manic depression has a genetic cause. Several scientists thought they had located the gene on a chromosome. But then it got lost, and so long as it is lost, we are lost.

It is also pretty clear that alcoholism bears some relationship to genes. This view comes from studies on identical twins adopted and raised by different families. There *are* alcoholic families. It is not likely that their members are morally weak; they just cannot tolerate alcohol chemically. But no one has found the gene or genes for susceptibility to alcoholism, and the chance of finding the genetic sources are probably low until a much more sophisticated human genetic community exists—plus the money to get the pedigrees and all the genetic markers.

Some diseases are not going to be easy to crack. For a long time, people have been trying to discover the cause of schizophrenia by looking for chemical differences in the urine or the blood, a research strategy that has not been successful. It is not going to be easy to find the genes behind schizophrenia either, because reliable pedigree data[1] are difficult to compile and the condition is hard to diagnose. Thus both directions offer low probabilities, but it is still better to waste your money doing genetics because genetics lies at the heart of so much. Of course scientists should find out what the brain is. I believe in neurobiology and have tried to help raise money to support the field. But I do not believe that its current approaches will necessarily lead to the real, deep cause of manic-depressive disease.

In 1989 Congressman Joe Early said to me, "I'm tired of putting fingers in dikes!" In combating disease, genetics helps enormously if it is a bad gene that contributes to the cause. Ignoring genes is like trying to solve a murder without finding the murderer. All we have are victims. With time, if we find the genes for Alzheimer's disease and for manic depression, then less money will be wasted on research that goes nowhere. Congressmen can only feel good if they are spending money on good things, so we have to convince them that the best use for their money is DNA research.

The human genome project is really trying to push a little more money toward DNA-based research. Since we can now produce good genetic maps that allow us to locate culprit chromosomes and then actually find the genes for disease (as Francis Collins found the gene for cystic fibrosis), genetics should be a very high priority on the agenda of NIH research. We are extremely lucky that when James Wyngaarden was director of NIH, he saw to the establishment of what is now a permanent division within NIH called the Center for Human Genome Research. I doubt that I convinced the biologist who sent me the fax, but I may eventually, since he is very bright. I want to convince as many people as I can of the merits of the human genome project, but not to cap my career and have something that sounds good in my

---

[1] *pedigree data:* data that establish the genetic lineage of a particular trait or defect; the process involves gathering genetic information about the parents, grandparents, and so on.

obituary. I can make best use of my time by trying to mobilize the country to do something about diseases that have hit my family and many others. I am sort of a concerned parent for whom things have not gone completely right. So, I am trying to enlist a group of people who will help us get these genes, and do what I think Congress wants us to do.

The ultimate objective of the human genome program is to learn the   14
nucleotide sequence of human DNA. We want the program completed in roughly fifteen years. By completed we do not mean every last nucleotide sequence. If we get 98 percent of the regions that are functional, that will probably be the end of it. We will not worry about spending infinite amounts of money trying to sequence things we know probably contain little information. We could define the end of it to be the identification of all the human genes—that is, we will be done when we have located the coding sequences and can declare that human beings on the average contain, say, 248,000 genes, with variations such that some individuals, for example have a gene present in four copies and some in three, and that for some the gene is nonessential. It has recently been learned that only a third of yeast genes are essential. Knock out two-thirds of them and the yeast will multiply. Studying things that are not essential will keep the people in the yeast world going for a long time. I think we can safely say the project will be over when we can identify the genes.

We probably will be unable to identify the genes until we get most of the   15
DNA sequenced, because we will not know where they are. It would be nice if the whole program could be done by copy DNA (cDNA)—that is, by purely functional DNA[2]—so that we would not have to sequence all the junk, but we will never know whether we have all the cDNAs. This is not to say we should not do cDNA; we will actually fund grants for people trying to find better techniques for getting rare cDNA in tissue-specific places. But I think that we have got to sequence the whole thing.

In the first five years, we will push to achieve three major objectives. First,   16
we will try to get good genetic maps, so that each chromosome has enough genetic markers[3] on it actually to locate a gene if a pedigree is available. Currently, we have only about 150 markers that are sufficiently informative for assigning the location of genes. We have started a crash program to persuade people to make a lot of markers and to put them into a public repository made available to the whole world. We want to change the current practice among researchers of not sharing their markers because they want to be the first to find a gene and encourage everyone to make markers available to everyone.

The second objective is to make overlapping fragments of DNA available   17
so that anyone looking for a gene in a particular piece of a certain chromosome will be able to get it by paying some nominal sum. The fragment will not

---

[2] *DNA:* Watson considers "functional DNA" only that kind of DNA that copies the messenger RNA molecules that contain instructions for synthesizing proteins.

[3] *genetic marker:* genetic "signposts"—differences in a complementary pair of chromosomes—that help locate particular genes.

be totally free, but it will certainly be there for anyone who seriously wants it. Techniques for doing this seem to be available now; it should not require more than $10 million to stockpile overlapping fragments of a given chromosome. To put this figure into perspective, Francis Collins has said that finding the cystic fibrosis gene was expensive—between $10 million and $50 million. If all the markers had been available, it would have cost only $5 million. I think we can establish an overlapping fragment library for the entire human genome for a couple of hundred million dollars, which will certainly reduce the costs of subsequent disease hunts. We will end up with a map of overlapping fragments, each one identified by three or four DNA sequences along it called sequence tag sites. With PCR,[4] researchers will be able to pull out all the human DNA that may be wanted.

The third major objective is to support scientists trying to do megabase[5]   18
sequencing in one place in a reasonable period of time. An example of this type of project is a proposal from Walter Gilbert to sequence a mycoplasma, which is really a small (800 kilobases) bacterium. Gilbert's proposal, whether he lives up to it or not, is to do a million bases a year within two years. We want to encourage people to do sequencing of megabases with the aim of reducing the cost—so that within a couple of years it will fall to about a dollar a base pair, and then perhaps even to fifty cents. We will not accept a grant application from someone who proposes to sequence some DNA the old fashioned way, with graduate students or postdoctoral fellows, at the current cost—five to ten dollars a base pair—just out of curiosity about it. . . .

The NIH genome project will also try to get some real data on model   19
organisms. I will be happy if we get ten quite different bacteria sequenced up through yeast. We are now supporting a joint program between the Medical Research Council, in England, and the Laboratory of Molecular Biology in Cambridge, and the group in St. Louis that has developed yeast artificial chromosomes to sequence the genome of a roundworm. The roundworm community is eager to do it because they've already got the overlapping DNA fragments. We hope to get the sequence out in ten years. It's about the equivalent of an average human chromosome—about a hundred megabases—but with less repetitive DNA, and so probably with fewer problems. There is also an effort to sequence a plant genome, arabadopsis, which we hope will be led by the National Science Foundation with help from other agencies, including ourselves. This is roughly seventy megabases, and the project should be a real boon to botany. Except for perhaps one bacterium, none of this probably would ever have been funded in the absence of the human genome program.

Among the reasons for wanting to find bacterial genes is to help find the   20
human ones. People ask, How are you going to identify a gene if it is interspersed with so much junk and you lack a cDNA? How are you going to know you have it? That is obviously going to be hard in some cases, but if you

---

[4] *PCR:* polymerase chain reaction; a powerful technique for amplifying a gene sequence, for obtaining a large amount of DNA from a small amount.

[5] *megabase:* one million base pairs.

have obtained the corresponding bacterial gene without many repetitive sequences and if you are clever, you ought to be able to spot the differences. I can imagine that typical work for undergraduates will be to find the gene once all the sequences have been obtained. Professors could tell their students: If you can identify a gene, we will let you go on to graduate school and do real science.

The human genome project is sufficiently justifiable so that if no other   21 country wants to help fund it, the United States should do the whole thing. We are rich enough to do it. But I doubt that we will be allowed to do it alone, because others are going to worry that it might actually be commercially interesting, and they will worry that we will be disinclined to distribute the data very fast if we have paid for it ourselves. It is my hope that we can spread out the cost of sequencing and data distribution over many countries. As soon as a gene has been identified, it should be thrown into an international data base.

But there are problems that I don't see how to get around. If a stretch of   22 DNA is sequenced in an academic laboratory, a university lawyer will say, "That looks like a serotonin receptor. Patent it!" Mutant forms of the cystic fibrosis gene have been patented by the universities of Toronto and Michigan. They will get some royalties and maybe build better student unions with the revenues. I am at a loss to know how to put valuable DNA sequences in the public domain fast when a lot of people want to keep them private. I just hope that other major nations come in. The Japanese will not let anyone who doesn't pay for it see their work. I figure that strategy might work. People might actually pay for sequence information if that is the only way to get to see it. So I have to seem a bad guy and say: I *will* withhold information that we generate if other countries refuse to join in an open sharing arrangement. But, in truth, it would be very distasteful to me to get into a situation where we were withholding the data for reasons of national advantage.

The acquisition of human DNA information has already begun to pose   23 serious ethical problems. I think that somehow we have to get it into the laws that anyone's DNA—the message it gives—is confidential and that the only one who has a right to look at it is the person herself or himself. Still, the ethics get complicated if you can spot a gene in a newborn child that produces a disease for which no treatment exists. Sometimes these defects will be hard to spot, but sometimes, as in muscular dystrophy, they can be very easy to detect. As we begin to get data of this kind, people are going to get nervous and some are going to be violent opponents of the project unless they can feel that they or their friends will not be discriminated against on the basis of their DNA. If someone can go look at your DNA and see that you have a deletion on one of your anti-oncogenes and that you will be more liable to die of cancer at an early age, then you might be discriminated against in, say, employment or insurance coverage.

Laws are needed to prevent genetic discrimination and to protect rights   24 that should not be signed away too easily. If you are poor, it will be highly tempting to say, "Yes, look at my DNA because I want the job in the asbestos factory." If you have no money, a job in an asbestos factory is better than no job. Issues like these demand a lot of discussion, at least so that DNA-related laws are not enacted prematurely. For that reason, we are putting more than 3 percent of the genome project money into an ethics program; and we will put more into it if we find that it needs more.

We have faced up to this challenge already with DNA fingerprints. The 25 National Center for Genome Research has given $50,000 to the National Research Council–National Academy of Sciences study on DNA fingerprinting, which has lawyers and judges advising it. The police want a DNA register of sex offenders; other people may want one of dishonest accountants. People will want DNA fingerprints to prove that a politician's children are really his. At a meeting in Leicester, England, Alec Jeffries showed a slide of a letter from a woman who runs a small hotel in Wales and who wrote that it would be a good idea to have a DNA fingerprint register of bedwetters. Different people will want different information—the possibilities are unlimited. I don't think *anyone* should have access to anyone else's DNA fingerprints.

We need to explore the social implications of human genome research 26 and figure out some protection for people's privacy so that these fears do not sabotage the entire project. Deep down, I think that the only thing that could stop our program is fear; if people are afraid of the information we will find, they will keep us from finding it. We have to convince our fellow citizens somehow that there will be more advantages to knowing the human genome than to not knowing it.

■ ■ ■

Review Questions

1. Why do some scientific researchers oppose the Human Genome Project, according to Watson?
2. Why does Watson believe that DNA research, including the Human Genome Project, should be of the highest priority?
3. What are the immediate objectives of the Human Genome Project?
4. According to Watson, what are some of the ethical problems associated with DNA research?

Discussion and Writing Suggestions

1. Watson concludes, "we have to convince our fellow citizens somehow that there will be more advantages to knowing the human genome than to not knowing it." Has Watson convinced you that the Human Genome Project is both a good thing in itself and a useful expenditure of public funds? If so, which arguments made the greatest impression on you, and

why? If not, what are your chief concerns? Should the project be canceled? Should restrictions be placed on genetic research? If so, what kind of restrictions?

2. To what extent, if any, does Watson's own personal stake in the success of the Human Genome Project (and in the success of biotechnology, in general) affect the way that you read this article and accept his arguments? Explain.

3. Watson is a scientist trying to persuade people (both his fellow scientists and others interested in scientific matters) that the project he heads is a vital one. Setting aside for the moment your own views of the genome project, to what extent do you think Watson has done a good job of explaining this scientific project? In particular, did you find this article difficult to follow because of the language in which Watson explained genetic concepts? If so, how might he have made his explanations easier to understand?

4. Watson argues that information gleaned from the Human Genome Project should be made available to all interested parties and that whatever has been discovered in one country should be made available to an international database. A genetic cure for a particular disease might be discovered more rapidly if more than one group of scientists were attacking the problem. But private companies might argue that they are entitled to the patents and financial profits from their own discoveries—that without such rights and rewards, they have no incentive to invest large amounts of money in research. What are your views on this subject? How can the fruits of genetic research be made widely available, while the rights of companies to earn reasonable profits from their research are protected?

5. Write either (a) an editorial or (b) a short story concerned with one of the ethical problems of DNA research discussed by Watson at the end of his article. Expand on or dramatize one or more of these potential problem areas.

Iceland's Blond Ambition

ELIOT MARSHALL

By 1998, a decade after the Human Genome Project was begun, scientists worldwide had made significant progress in mapping the genetic basis of human inheritance—so much so that large pharmaceutical companies began investing heavily in the research, hoping to reap future profits from drugs engineered to correct the genetic bases of disease. The selection that follows reports on one company's research in the ideal human "laboratory" of Iceland, where intermarriage has kept the gene pool relatively isolated, an advantage for genetic researchers. One controversial outcome of the for-profit funding of genome research is that newly mapped sequences of DNA will be patented and commercially controlled. (James

Watson expressed such concerns in the article above.) Critics charge that it is "immoral . . . to turn life into property." On the other hand, genomic research is expensive. Mapping the entire *human genome would take far longer than would be the case if only governments funded the effort. If pharmaceutical companies invest, shouldn't they expect to make a profit?*

Eliot Marshall is a senior writer for the news section of Science Magazine, *the weekly journal of research published by the American Association for the Advancement of Science. He has written and edited articles on a variety of science policy subjects, ranging from nuclear weapons design to space science. This article originally appeared in* Mother Jones *(June 1998).*

Iceland is famous for its volcanic deserts, smoking hot springs, glaciers, and ancient sagas—but not for its high-tech research. Yet on February 2, 1998, the Swiss drug manufacturer Roche Holding of Basel announced it would pay $200 million over the next five years for research by an obscure firm in Reykjavik called deCode Genetics, which at the time had no products, no clients, and less than a year's operating experience.   1

What does Roche hope to get from deCode? The answer can be found in the faces of Iceland's mostly blond, blue-eyed, extremely homogeneous population. Roche wants Iceland's genes. In the isolated, sparsely settled country, biomedical researchers have found a rich, pure genetic lode, relatively untainted by outside influence for hundreds of years. DeCode is offering itself as the genes' broker and interpreter.   2

This partnership is just one of many attempts to profit from a revolution in human genome research. A field once dominated by academics has exploded in the past five years with go-go biotech entrepreneurs and pharmaceutical giants. They all dream the same dream: They realize that it may soon become possible to understand the genetic processes that cause diseases and, as the genes yield up their secrets, to find ways of isolating and treating them. As Roche spokesman Roland Haefeli explains, his company thinks deCode's research will help it "make drugs."   3

As they pursue their research, companies want to patent the key gene sequences to protect their investments. Some critics charge that the patenting of genes amounts to robbing the public commons and is an immoral attempt to turn life into property. But deCode seems to have inoculated itself from charges of exploitation. Roche's $200 million investment is a huge boost to Iceland's economy, and the country hopes, just the beginning. How can anyone get angry about deCode's patenting of Iceland's genetic history when the whole country appears to have bought into it?   4

The 270,000 people who live in Iceland, many of whom will contribute their genes to this project, are descended from a small number of original settlers, mostly Norsemen who came to the island around the 9th century. Since then, most Icelanders have been intermarrying and choosing their spouses from the same small group of Nordic families.   5

In the early 1400s, the Black Death swept through the island, killing two of every three inhabitants. Later, smallpox struck. And in the late 1700s, the   6 volcano Hekla, east of Reykjavik, erupted and spewed ash over gardens and pastures. A severe famine followed. These catastrophes, combined with the isolation of the place, created population "bottlenecks" that constricted an already narrow gene pool.

This same harsh environment, however, also made Icelanders an ideal   7
subject for genetic studies. As deCode's president and CEO, Kari Stefansson, says, "We are, in a sense, mining the consequences of natural disasters." The homogeneity of the population will help researchers identify the genes asso-ciated with a particular disease more quickly, since a limited genetic sample reduces the background noise. Ethnically diverse populations, such as those in any U.S. city, are difficult to study because they have so many genetic varia-tions that it's difficult to discern which contribute to disease.

Stefansson, 48, a neurogeneticist and an Icelander himself, formed the   8
idea for deCode while teaching at Harvard Medical School. His plan brought the company $12 million from American and European venture capitalists. He then recruited managers among Icelanders, many of whom had been trained at U.S. universities, and opened the lab in early 1997, announcing some ambitious goals: DeCode planned to explore 25 to 35 common diseases.

The company began by identifying the genetic sequence responsible for a   9
syndrome known as essential tremor (shaky limbs). DeCode later studied multiple sclerosis, and laid plans to cover familiar illnesses such as alco-holism, inflammatory bowel disease, colon cancer, diabetes, heart disease, and schizophrenia.

Patients with these illnesses interact with deCode through a network of   10
collaborating physicians. Based in offices around the island, the doctors gather blood samples and provide the company with raw biological material. Before sending in the blood for testing, the doctors remove the patients' names, replacing them with encrypted IDs. After receiving the samples, deCode processes the DNA in its laboratories, obtaining genotypes (genetic profiles) for each individual.

These are then matched with medical records, linking genotype to phe-   11
notype data—physical details, including a person's disease status, age, and weight. DeCode fits each genotype into a jigsaw puzzle of family inheritance patterns that can be verified, if necessary, by referring to Iceland's genealog-ical records dating back 1,000 years (and now almost entirely computer-ized). Such a massive cross-referencing should give deCode an unprecedented ability to isolate genes.

The company is also building its own internal database on a large   12
number of Icelanders. DeCode hopes to sell access to this database, called the Genotypes, Genealogy, Phenotypes, and Resources (GGPR) collection, to drug companies such as Roche. The data, deCode claims, will be used only "to identify families in which specific diseases occur, trace the inheritance of the disease over several generations, and rapidly identify the genetic basis of the disease."

Any commercial drug or gene-based diagnostic test developed from the   13
research, Stefansson says, will be provided free of charge to all Icelanders during the lifetime of the patent (between 17 and 20 years). These gestures

acknowledge what Stefansson refers to as the company's "core asset." He notes: "[Our] relationship with the population is the most important thing we have."

The country's politicians and medical leaders have given deCode their   14
approval. So has the Health Ministry's Medical Ethics Committee. Iceland's prime minister, David Oddsson, considers the project "extremely important," saying it will help his nation "secure foreign investment."

Stefansson also has taken steps to allay concerns about invasion of pri-   15
vacy. He promises patients who consent to this research that their identities will not be transmitted to the company at all. While deCode retains a master index that links names and encrypted IDs, Stefansson says it is "kept in a safe in our company in an extremely well-shielded room. You need two keys to get into it. We have one of them, and the Icelandic Data Protection Committee has the other." DeCode could never get access to the names without an offi-cial watching over its shoulder.

This pledge, and Icelanders' traditional trust in their leaders, seems to   16
have banished skepticism. It's hard to imagine any U.S. agency being entrust-ed to keep so much volatile information in one database—medical records, genetic test results, and family histories going back a millennium. But in Iceland, that is exactly what deCode is doing.

While gene collection is moving along at a rapid pace in Europe and the   17
United States, some attempts to collect genes from less developed countries have backfired. Genetic researchers, sponsored initially by the National Institutes of Health and the Department of Energy, have been building up vast archives of human genes for basic research on diseases. Their attempts to con-duct a survey of global human diversity came to a standstill, however, when they ran into opposition in the developing world. In China, citizens objected when Western companies made efforts to collect genes using local physicians as research partners, accusing the firms of "biopiracy"—quietly exporting valuable genetic data and not sharing the wealth with the local population. In 1997, reacting to fears that China's genetic heritage might be ripped off, the government drafted new regulations limiting the export of biological materi-als.

But interest from private industry has only accelerated. For example, in   18
1993 scientists with Sequana Therapeutics descended upon the tiny Atlantic island of Tristan da Cunha, where the 300 or so residents have an abnormally high rate of asthma. Since then, Sequana (now Axys Pharmaceuticals) has filed patents for what it believes are isolated asthma genes. While Axys could reap millions for a drug that cures asthma, the people of Tristan da Cunha won't have access to it unless they pay for it.

DeCode's project in Iceland is fueling a broader concept than just iden-   19
tifying disease genes. "Pharmacogenomics" is a radically new idea for design-ing drugs. Adopted last year by many of the largest drug companies, it envisions using genetic testing to screen out the most suitable patients for clin-ical drug trials. Researchers would select the candidates whose genetic profiles showed that they belonged to a group of individuals most likely to benefit

from the drug being tested. If the experimental medicine proved successful, the company would then sell it to patients in the general population with the same genetic characteristics as those in the drug trial. It sounds good: Pills and people could be matched efficiently, reducing bad side effects.

Roche, one of the world's top manufacturers of medical diagnostics, and   20 other pharmaceutical companies have another reason for being interested in matching patients to drugs: It might save a lot of money in clinical trials. If it were possible to screen out the nonresponders in advance, patient enrollment in a typical drug trial might shrink significantly. Since companies pay out of past profits for such trials, this savings would be worth billions of dollars a year.

At least one biotech executive—William Haseltine, CEO of Human   21 Genome Sciences in Rockville, Maryland—had said that he doesn't think it is wise to use genetic screens in order to slot patients into different types of drug therapy, worrying that patients might be screened improperly, and thus be given the wrong, possibly dangerous, drugs.

Another, perhaps bigger, obstacle for this new industry is how patients   22 will react to the idea of genetic testing. If drugs are developed, say, to screen people thought to be at risk for early heart disease, these still-healthy people will have to be genotyped. People will, essentially, need to have bar codes. But they may not want to submit to the testing. They may prefer not to know— or have others know—exactly what risk categories they fit into. Many fear that a centralization of such knowledge could lead to genetic discrimination. If it fell into the hands of personnel offices and insurance companies, for example, they might try to use it to screen out high-risk applicants.

At the moment, there's no immediate problem—the schemes for geno   23 typing patients and tailoring drugs are still only theoretical. But with so much pharmaceutical company money pouring into the hands of researchers, the science won't just be abandoned. Whole-population genetic screening, and the testing of drugs matched to "appropriate" patients, is the brave new frontier in genetic medicine, and it seems likely to get started soon in Iceland, where the population's faith in its leaders—and deCode—will ultimately be put to the test.

■   ■   ■

Review Questions

1. What is deCode's goal?
2. What makes Iceland such a desirable location for genetic research?
3. Why are major pharmaceutical companies making huge investments in companies like Iceland's deCode?
4. Why do companies want to patent newly discovered gene sequences, and what is the biggest objection to seeking patents?

5. How has deCode sought to protect the privacy of individuals participating in the genetic research?
6. What is biopiracy?
7. What is pharmacogenomics, and how might it prove to be a controversial practice if widely developed?

Discussion and Writing Suggestions

1. Marshall asserts that it's "hard to imagine any U.S. agency being entrusted to keep so much volatile information in one database—medical records, genetic test results, and family histories going back a millennium." Icelanders apparently are not as distrustful as Marshall suggests Americans would be. Do you agree with Marshall's assessment of American reaction to such a database? Explain your answer, keeping your focus on America's *national* or *cultural* response to a massive genetic database.
2. Why do you suppose Marshall uses this particular phrasing in the article's final paragraph: "Whole-population screening, and the testing of drugs matched to 'appropriate' patients, is the brave new frontier in genetic medicine."
3. Comment on the title of this selection, "Iceland's Blond Ambition," which appeared in the magazine *Mother Jones*.
4. If you, or members of your family, could be given the assurance that the drugs taken to combat disease would be particularly effective if matched to your genetic profile, would you be willing—on the expectation of improved health—to have this profile developed? Consider your answer in light of your response to Discussion and Writing suggestion #1.
5. Based on your reading of this article, comment on the tension between the big pharmaceutical companies' profit motive and the pursuit of scientific knowledge about the human species. How productive is this tension? How (potentially) destructive is it? Consider: how quickly would research into the genetic bases of disease occur if pharmaceutical companies were not paying the bills, as in the case of deCode? Are the companies that fund the research entitled to profit from the research?

The Ultimate Therapy: Commercial Eugenics on the Eve of the Biotech Century

JEREMY RIFKIN

From its beginnings in the early 1970s, genetic engineering has been surrounded by controversy. Initial fears focused on the nightmare scenario of newly engineered microorganisms escaping from the lab and causing uncontrollable damage to other organisms in the environment. Some scientists proposed a moratorium on gene splicing experiments; and in 1975, during a landmark international conference at Asilomar, California, scientists agreed to strict guidelines governing all future research.

During the past decade, the science-fiction scenarios have subsided, but the controversy over genetic engineering continues—focusing now on the ethical aspects of manipulating the genetic code for our own utilitarian and commercial purposes. Repeatedly, critics associate bioengineering with eugenics, the infamous pseudoscience practiced by the Nazis in their efforts to perpetuate the "Aryan" races and to exterminate "inferior" races. Then, as now, critics have wondered, Who should determine what is "superior" (or normal) and what is "inferior" (or defective)?

For some years, the most vocal critic of biotechnology has been Jeremy Rifkin, a philosopher and environmental activist involved in science and technology issues. Through his publications, his lectures, his congressional testimony, and his Foundation for Economic Trends, Rifkin has been tireless in attacking both the practices and the underlying premises of genetic engineering. He has also been successful in halting or delaying the testing of several newly developed microorganisms with agricultural applications.

Born in 1945, Rifkin attended the Wharton School of Business and then earned a degree in law and diplomacy from Tufts University. His first book on biotechnology was Who Should Play God *(1977), co-authored with Ted Howard. This was followed by* Entropy *(1980), which sold more than 750,000 copies worldwide. In 1985, he followed with* Algeny *(the title is a wordplay on* alchemy*). The present selection (appearing in* Tikkun, *May/June 1998) is adapted from his 1998 book,* The Biotech Century: Harnessing the Gene and Remaking the World. *Throughout his career, Rifkin has maintained a consistent theme: the genetic technologies we now pursue are so powerful, and the changes they herald so far reaching, that we must thoroughly debate the benefits and dangers of this new science before proceeding. In this chapter, Jeremy Rifkin defines one pole of that debate.*

While the twentieth century was shaped largely by the spectacular break-   1
throughs in the fields of physics and chemistry, the twenty-first century will belong to the biological sciences. Scientists around the world are quickly deciphering the genetic code of life, unlocking the mystery of millions of years of biological evolution on Earth. Global life science companies, in turn, are beginning to exploit the new advances in biology in a myriad of ways, laying the economic framework for the coming Biotech Century.

Genes are the raw resource of the new economic epoch and are already   2
being used in a variety of business fields—including agriculture, animal husbandry, energy, bioremediation, building and packaging materials, pharmaceuticals, and food and drink—to fashion a bio-industrial world. Nowhere is the new genetic commerce likely to have a bigger impact, however, than in human medicine. For the first time in history, scientific tools are becoming available to manipulate the genetic instructions in human cells. Human gene

screening and therapy raise the very real possibility that we might be able to engineer the genetic blueprints of our own species and begin to redirect the future course of our biological evolution on Earth. The new gene splicing techniques will make it potentially possible to transform individuals and future generations into "works of art," continually updating and editing their DNA codes to enhance physical and mental health. Breakthroughs in genetic technology are bringing us to the edge of a new eugenics era with untold consequences for present and future generations and for civilization itself.

In less than seven years, the global life science companies will hold patents on most of the 100,000 genes that make up the human race as well as patents on the cell lines, tissues, and organs of our species, giving them unprecedented power to dictate the terms by which we and future generations will live our lives. The concentration of power in the global pharmaceutical industry has already reached staggering proportions. The world's ten major pharmaceutical companies currently control 47 percent of the $197 billion pharmaceutical market. The implications of a new market-drive eugenics are enormous and far reaching. Indeed, commercial eugenics could become the defining social dynamic of the new century.

FRIENDLY EUGENICS

Over the next ten years, molecular biologists say they will locate specific genes associated with several thousand genetic diseases. In the past, a parent's genetic history provided some clues to genetic inheritance, but there was still no way to know for sure whether specific genetic traits would be passed on. In the future, the guesswork will be increasingly eliminated, posing a moral dilemma for prospective parents. Parents will have at their disposal an increasingly accurate readout of their individual genetic make-ups, and will able to predict the statistical probability of a specific genetic disorder being passed on to their children as a result of their biological union.

To avoid the emotional anguish of such decisions, some young people are likely to opt for prevention and avoid marrying someone of the wrong "genotype" for fear of passing along serious genetic diseases to their offspring. Already, part of the Orthodox Jewish community in the United States has established a nationwide program to screen all young Jewish men and women for Tay-Sachs disease. Every young Jew is encouraged to take the test. The results are made available in an easily accessible database to allow young eligible men and women to choose their dating partners with genotype in mind.

Some ethicists argue that such programs will become far more commonplace, placing a "genetic stigma" on young people. There's ample precedent for concern. Researchers report that when sickle cell anemia was screened for in Greece, nearly 23 percent of the population was found to have the trait. Fearing stigmatization, many of the carriers concealed their test results, believing that public exposure would seriously jeopardize their marriage prospects.

When researchers at the Johns Hopkins Medical Center recently discovered a genetic alteration in one out of every six Jews of Eastern European ancestry that doubles their risk of getting colon cancer, many in the Jewish community began to express their concern that the Jewish population might be singled out and made the object of discrimination. The news of the "Jewish" cancer gene came on top of other discoveries linking breast and ovarian cancer, cystic fibrosis, Tay-Sachs, Gauchers, and Canavan's disease to Jewish blood lines. Of course, scientists point out that other groups are likely to have just as many genetic links to specific diseases, but that the Jewish population has received the most attention to date because "they constitute a well defined, easily identifiable and closely related community—exactly the kind that allows geneticists to start identifying disease-causing genes." Still, the explanations of the researchers were not enough to calm an anxious Jewish community who began to vent their feelings publicly. Amy Rutkin, the director of American affairs for Hadassah, the nation's largest Jewish membership organization, reported that in the aftermath of the colon cancer discovery, the organization has been "receiving phone calls indicating a certain amount of fear and confusion." Rutkin said that "people are asking, is too much research focused on the Jewish community and are we at risk of stigmatization?"

8   Health professionals worry about genetic stigmatization and especially the prospect of selecting potential mates based on genotyping, but argue that it is still less onerous than selective abortion or sentencing a newborn to premature death or a life of chronic or debilitating illness. Not surprising, there is increasing talk of government mandated genetic testing of couples seeking marriage licenses. Even without a government requirement, it's likely that a growing number of potential marriage partners will want their future partner screened before committing themselves to a life-long relationship.

9   While genetic screening is already here, human genetic engineering— gene therapy—is just around the corner. Genetic manipulation is of two kinds. In somatic therapy, intervention takes place only within non-sex (somatic) cells and the genetic changes do not transfer into the offspring. In germ line therapy, genetic changes are made in the sperm, egg or embryonic cells, and are passed along to future generations. Somatic gene surgery has been carried out in limited human clinical trials for more than seven years. Germ line experiments have been successfully carried out on mammals for more than a decade and researchers expect the first human trials to be conducted within the next several years.

10   Despite years of favorable media reports on various somatic gene therapy experiments and the high expectations voiced by the medical establishment and the biotech industry, the results have, thus far, been so disappointing that the NIH itself was recently forced to acknowledge the fact and issue a sober warning to scientists conducting the experiments to stop making promises that cannot be kept. In an extensive survey of all 106 clinical trials of experimental gene therapies conducted over the past five years involving more than 597 patients, a panel of experts convened by the NIH reported that "clinical efficacy has not been definitively demonstrated at this time in any gene therapy protocol, despite anecdotal claims of successful therapy." Even

Dr. Leroy B. Walters, a philosophy professor at Georgetown University and the chairperson of the NIH oversight committee that reviewed and approved all of the clinical trials, remarked in a moment of candor that he and the committee had not seen "any solid results yet" after years of experiments. Still, many of the staunchest supporters of the new gene therapies remain convinced that the techniques will bear fruit as methodologies and procedures are honed and new knowledge of the workings of the genes become more available to researchers and clinicians.

Far more controversial is the prospect of conducting human germ line   11
therapy. Debate over genetic manipulation of human eggs, sperm, and embryonic cells has raged for more than fifteen years. In 1983, a cross-section of the nation's religious leaders and prominent scientists announced their opposition to such experiments, on eugenics grounds, and urged a worldwide ban. (The coalition was put together by The Foundation on Economic Trends.)

Programming genetic changes into the human germ line to direct the   12
evolutionary development of future generations is the most radical human experiment ever contemplated and raises unprecedented moral, social, and environmental risks for the whole of humanity. Even so, a growing number of molecular biologists, medical practitioners, and pharmaceutical companies are anxious to take the gamble, convinced that controlling our evolutionary destiny is humankind's next great social frontier. Their arguments are couched in terms of personal health, individual choice, and collective responsibility for future generations.

Writing in *The Journal of Medicine and Philosophy*, Dr. Burke   13
Zimmerman makes several points in defense of germ line cell therapy over somatic cell therapy. To begin with, he argues that the increasing use of somatic therapy is only likely to increase the number of survivors with defective genes in their germ lines—genes that will continue to accumulate and further "pollute" the genetic pool of the species, passing an increasing number of genetic problems onto succeeding generations. Secondly, although somatic therapy may be able to treat many disorders in which treatment lies in replacing populations of cells, it might never prove effective in addressing diseases involving solid tissues, organs, and functions dependent on structure—for example the brain—and therefore, germ line therapy is likely the only remedy, short of abortion, against such disorders.

Zimmerman and other proponents of germ line therapy argue for a   14
broadening of the ethical mandate of the healing professions to include responsibility for the health of those not yet conceived. The interests of the patient, they say, should be extended to include the interests of "the entire genetic legacy that may result from intervention in the germ line." Moreover, parents ought not to be denied their right as parents to make choices on how best to protect the health of their unborn children during pregnancy. To deny them the opportunity to take corrective action in the sex cells or at the early embryonic stage would be a serious breach of medical responsibility. Proponents of germ line therapy ask why millions of individuals need to be

subjected to painful, intrusive, and potentially risky somatic therapy when the gene or genes responsible for their diseases could be more easily eliminated from the germ line, at less expense, and with less discomfort.

Finally, the health costs to society need to be factored into the equation, 15 say the advocates of germ line therapy. Although the costs of genetic intervention into the germ line to cure diseases are likely to remain high in the early years, the cost is likely to drop dramatically in the future as the methods and techniques become more refined. The lifetime cost of caring for generations of patients suffering from Parkinson's disease or severe Down's syndrome is likely to be far greater than simple prevention in the form of genetic intervention at the germ line level.

GENETIC RESPONSIBILITY

In the coming decades, scientists will learn more about how genes function. 16 They will become increasingly adept at turning genes "on" and "off." They will become more sophisticated in the techniques of recombining genes and altering genetic codes. At every step of the way, conscious decisions will have to be made as to which kinds of permanent changes in the biological codes of life are worth pursuing and which are not. A society and civilization steeped in "engineering" the gene pool of the planet cannot possibly hope to escape the kind of ongoing eugenics decisions that go hand in hand with each new advance in biotechnology. There will be enormous social pressure to conform with the underlying logic of genetic engineering, especially when it comes to its human applications.

Parents in the biotech century will be increasingly forced to decide 17 whether to take their chances with the traditional genetic lottery and use their own unaltered egg and sperm, knowing their children may inherit some "undesirable" traits, or undergo corrective gene changes on their sperm, egg, embryo, or fetus, or substitute egg or sperm from a donor through *in vitro* fertilization and surrogacy arrangements. If they choose to go with the traditional approach and let genetic fate determine their child's biological destiny, they could find themselves culpable if something goes dreadfully wrong in the developing fetus, something they could have avoided had they availed themselves of corrective genetic intervention at the sex cell or embryo stage.

In the Biotech Century, a parent's failure to correct genetic defects *in* 18 *utero* might well be regarded as a heinous crime. Society may conclude that every parent has a responsibility to provide as safe and secure an environment as humanly possible for their unborn child. Not to do so might be considered a breech of parental duty for which the parents could be held morally, if not legally, liable. Mothers have already been held liable for having given birth to crack cocaine addicted babies and babies with fetal alcohol syndrome. Prosecutors have argued that mothers passing on these painful addictions to their unborn children are culpable under existing child abuse statutes, and ought to be held liable for the effect of their lifestyle on their babies.

Proponents of human genetic engineering argue that it would be cruel   19
and irresponsible not to use this powerful new technology to eliminate serious
"genetic disorders." The problem with this argument, says *The New York
Times* in an editorial entitled, "Whether to Make Perfect Humans," is that
"there is no discernible line to be drawn between making inheritable repair of
genetic defects and improving the species." The *Times* rightly points out that
once scientists are able to repair genetic defects, "it will become much harder
to argue against additional genes that confer desired qualities, like better
health, looks or brains."

If diabetes, sickle cell anemia, and cancer are to be prevented by altering   20
the genetic makeup of individuals, why not proceed to other less serious
"defects": myopia, color blindness, dyslexia, obesity, short stature? Indeed,
what is to preclude a society from deciding that a certain skin color is a disorder? In the end, why would we ever say no to any alteration of the genetic
code that might enhance the well-being of our offspring? It would be difficult
to imagine parents rejecting genetic modifications that promised to improve,
in some way, the opportunities for their progeny.

It is likely that as new screening technologies become more universally   21
available, and genetic surgery at the embryonic and fetal stage becomes more
widely acceptable, the issue of parental responsibility will be hotly debated,
both in the courts and in the legislatures. The very fact that parents will
increasingly be able to intervene to ensure the health of their child before
birth, is likely to raise the concomitant issue of the responsibilities and obligations to their unborn children. Why shouldn't parents be held responsible for
taking proper care of their unborn child? For that matter, why shouldn't parents be held liable for neglecting their child's welfare in the womb in cases
where they failed to or refused to screen for and correct genetic defects that
could prove harmful to their offspring?

With Americans already spending billions of dollars on cosmetic surgery   22
to improve their looks and psychotropic drugs to alter their mood and behavior, the use of genetic therapies to enhance their unborn children also seems
a likely prospect. According to a 1992 Harris poll, 43 percent of Americans
"would approve using gene therapy to improve babies' physical characteristics." Many advocates of germ line intervention are already arguing for
enhancement therapy. They contend that the current debate over corrective
measures to address serious illnesses is too limited and urge a more expansive
discussion to include the advantage of enhancement therapy as well. As to the
oft heard criticism that genetic enhancement will favor children of the rich at
the expense of children of the poor—as the rich will be the only ones capable
of paying for genetic enhancement of their offspring—proponents argue that
the children of well-off parents have always enjoyed the advantages that
wealth and inheritance can confer. Is it such a leap, they ask rhetorically, to
want to pass along genetic gifts to their children along with material riches?
Advocates ask us to consider the positive side of germ line enhancement,
even if it gives an advantage to the children of those who can afford the technology. "What about . . . increasing the number of talented people. Wouldn't
society be better off in the long run?" asks Dr. Burke Zimmerman.

Perhaps not. Despite the growing enthusiasm among molecular biologists 23
for engineering fundamental changes in the genetic code of human sex cells,
it should be emphasized that treating genetic disorders by eliminating recessive traits at the germ line level is far different from treating genetic disorders
by way of somatic gene surgery after birth. In the former instance, the genetic deletions can result, in the long run, in a dangerous narrowing of the
human gene pool upon which future generations rely for making evolutionary
adaptations to changing environments.

We learned, long ago, that recessive traits and mutations are essential 24
players in the evolutionary schema. They are not mistakes, but rather variations, some of which become opportunities. Eliminating so-called "bad"
genes risks depleting the genetic pool and limiting future evolutionary options.
Recessive gene traits are far too complex and mercurial to condemn as simple
errors in the code. We are, in fact, just beginning to learn of the many subtle
and varied roles recessive gene traits play, some of which have been critically important in ensuring the survival of different ethnic and racial groups. For
example, the sickle cell recessive trait protects against malaria. The cystic
fibrosis recessive gene may play a role in protecting against cholera. To think
of recessive traits and single gene disorders, then, as merely errors in the
code, in need of reprogramming, is to lose sight of how things really work in
the biological kingdom.

Somatic gene surgery, on the other hand, if it proves to be a safe, thera- 25
peutic way to treat serious diseases that can not be effectively treated by
more conventional approaches, including preventive measures, would appear
to have potential value.

Many biotech libertarians, however, disdain such distinctions. *The* 26
Economist suggested, in a recent editorial, that society should move beyond
old fashioned hand-wringing moralism on the subject and openly embrace the
new commercial eugenics opportunities that will soon become available in the
marketplace. The editors asked,

> What of genes that might make a good body better, rather than make a bad
> one good? Should people be able to retrofit themselves with extra neuro-
> transmitters, to enhance various mental powers? Or to change the color of
> their skin? Or to help them run faster, or lift heavier weights?

The Economist editorial board made clear that its own biases lay firmly 27
with the marketplace. To them, the new commercial eugenics is about ensuring greater consumer freedom so that individuals can make of themselves and
their heirs whatever they choose. The editorial concluded with a ringing
endorsement of the new eugenics:

> The proper goal is to allow people as much choice as possible about what
> they do. To this end, making genes instruments of such freedom, rather than
> limits upon it, is a great step forward.

Dr. Robert Sinsheimer, a long standing leader and driving force in the 28
field of molecular biology, laid out his eugenics vision of the new man and
woman of the biotech century:

The old dreams of the cultural perfection of man were always sharply constrained by his inherited imperfections and limitations. . . . To foster his better traits and to curb his worse by cultural means alone has always been, while clearly not impossible, in many instances most difficult. . . . We now glimpse another route—the chance to ease the internal strains and heal the internal flaws directly, to carry on and consciously perfect far beyond our present vision this remarkable product of two billion years of evolution. . . . The old eugenics would have required a continual selection for breeding of the fit, and a culling of the unfit. . . . The horizons of the new eugenics are in principle boundless—for we should have the potential to create new genes and new qualities yet undreamed. . . . Indeed, this concept marks a turning point in the whole evolution of life. For the first time in all time, a living creature understands its origin and can undertake to design its future. Even in the ancient myths man was constrained by essence. He could not rise above his nature to chart his destiny. Today we can envision that chance—and its dark companion of awesome choice and responsibility.

PERFECTING THE CODE

While the notion of consumer choice would appear benign, the very idea of eliminating so-called genetic defects raises the troubling question of what is meant by the term "defective." Ethicist Daniel Callahan of the Hastings Center penetrates to the core of the problem when he observes that "behind the human horror at genetic defectiveness lurks . . . an image of the perfect human being. The very language of 'defect,' 'abnormality,' 'disease,' and 'risk' presupposes such an image, a kind of prototype of perfection."   29

The all consuming preoccupation with "defects" or "errors" among medical researchers and molecular biologists puts them very much at odds with most evolutionary biologists. When evolutionary biologists talk of "mutations," they have in mind the idea of "different 'readings' or 'versions'" of a relatively stable archetype. James Watson and Francis Crick's discovery of the DNA double helix in the 1950s, however, brought with it a new set of metaphors and a new language for describing biological processes which changed the way molecular biologists perceive genetic mutations. The primary building block of life was described as a code, a set of instructions, a program, to be unraveled and read. The early molecular biologists, many of whom had been trained first as physicists, were enamored with what they regarded as the universal explanatory power of the information sciences. Norbert Weiner's cybernetic model and modern communications and information theory provided a compelling new linguistic paradigm for redefining how we talk about both physical and biological phenomena. It is within the context of this new language that molecular biologists first began to talk of genetic variation as "errors" in the code rather than "mutations." The shift from the notion of genetic mutations in nature to genetic errors in codes represents a sea change in the way biologists approach their discipline, with profound repercussions for how we structure both our relationship to the natural world and our own human nature in the coming Biotech Century.   30

The very idea of engineering the human species—by making changes at the germ line level—is not too dissimilar from the idea of engineering a piece of machinery. An engineer is constantly in search of new ways to improve the performance of a machine. As soon as one set of defects is eliminated, the engineer immediately turns his attention to the next set of defects, always with the idea in mind of creating a more efficient machine. The notion of setting arbitrary limits to how much "improvement" is acceptable is alien to the entire engineering conception.

The new language of the information sciences has transformed many molecular biologists from scientists to engineers, although they are, no doubt, little aware of the metamorphosis. When molecular biologists speak of mutations and genetic diseases as errors in the code, the implicit, if not explicit, assumption is that they should never have existed in the first place, that they are "bugs," or mistakes that need to be deprogrammed or corrected. The molecular biologist, in turn, becomes the computing engineer, the writer of codes, continually eliminating errors and reprogramming instructions to upgrade both the program and the performance. This is a dubious and dangerous role when we stop to consider that every human being brings with him or her a number of lethal recessive genes. Do we then come to see ourselves as miswired from the get-go, riddled with errors in our code? If that be the case, against what ideal norm of perfection are we to be measured? If every human being is made up of varying degrees of error, than we search in vain for the norm, the ideal. What makes the new language of molecular biology so subtly chilling is that it risks creating a new archetype, a flawless, errorless, perfect being to which to aspire—a new man and woman, like us, but without the warts and wrinkles, vulnerabilities and frailties, that have defined our essence from the very beginning of our existence.

No wonder so many in the disability rights community are becoming increasingly frightened of the new biology. They wonder, if in the new world coming, people like themselves will be seen as errors in the code, mistakes to be eliminated, lives to be prevented from coming into being. Then again, how tolerant are the rest of us likely to be when we come to see everyone around us as defective, as mistakes and errors in the code.

Already, genetic information is being used by schools, employers, insurance companies and governments to determine educational tracks, employment prospects, insurance premiums, and security clearances, giving rise to a new and virulent from of discrimination based on one's genetic profile. Even more chilling, some genetic engineers envision a future with a small segment of the human population engineered to "perfection" while others remain as flawed reminders of an outmoded evolutionary design. Molecular biologist Lee Silver of Princeton University writes about a not-too-distant future made up of two distinct biological classes which he refers to as the Gen Rich and Naturals. The Gen Rich, which account for 10 percent of the population, have been enhanced with synthetic genes and have become the rulers of society. They include Gen Rich businessmen, musicians, artists, intellectuals, and athletes, each enhanced with specific synthetic genes to allow them to succeed in their respective fields in ways not even conceivable among those born of nature's lottery.

At the center of this new genetic aristocracy are the Gen Rich scientists   35
who are enhanced with special genetic traits that greatly increase their mental abilities, giving them the power to dictate the terms of future evolutionary advances on Earth. Silver says that:

> With the passage of time, the genetic distance between Naturals and the Gen Rich has become greater and greater, and now there is little movement up from the Natural to the Gen Rich class. . . . All aspects of the economy, the media, the entertainment industry and the knowledge industry are controlled by members of the Gen Rich class. . . . In contrast, Naturals work as low-paid service providers or as laborers. . . . Gen Rich and Natural children grow up and live in segregated social worlds where there is little chance for contact between them . . . [eventually] the Gen Rich class and the Natural class will become the Gen Rich humans and the Natural humans—entirely separate species with no ability to cross breed and with as much romantic interest in each other as a current human would have for a chimpanzee.

Silver acknowledges that the increasing polarization of society into a   36
Gen Rich and Natural class might be unfair, but he is quick to add that wealthy parents have always been able to provide all sorts of advantages for their children. "Anyone who accepts the right of affluent parents to provide their children with an expensive private school education cannot use unfairness as a reason for rejecting the use of reprogenetic technologies," argues Silver. Like many of his colleagues, Silver is a strong advocate of the new genetic technologies. "In a society that values human freedom above all else," writes Silver, "it is hard to find any legitimate basis for restricting the use of reprogenetics."

If Silver's predictions about where the new technologies are heading are   37
correct, we face the very real possibility of journeying into a Huxlian world populated by Alphas, Betas, Gammas, and Deltas. In the new scenario, however, it's the global marketplace and consumer desire, not an oppressive government, that will likely be the ultimate arbiter of the new biology. In the final analysis, commercial eugenics, controlled by global life science companies and mediated by consumer sovereignty, might prove every bit as dangerous to the future prospects of our species as the shrill cries on behalf of purifying the best blood of the Aryan race more than half a century ago in Hitler's infamous Third Reich.

The question, then, is whether or not humanity should begin the process   38
of engineering future generations of human beings by technological design in the laboratory. What are the potential consequences of embarking on a course whose final goal is the "perfection" of the human species?

Today, the ultimate exercise of power is within grasp: the ability to con-   39
trol, at the most fundamental level, the future lives of unborn generations by engineering their biological life process in advance, making them a partial hostage of their own architecturally designed blueprints. I use the word "partial" because, like many others, I believe that environment is a major con-

tributing factor in determining one's life course. It is also true, however, that one's genetic makeup plays a role in helping to shape one's destiny. Genetic engineering, then, represents the power of authorship, albeit limited authorship. Being able to engineer even minor changes in the physical and behavioral characteristics of future generations represents a new era in human history. Never before has such power over human life even been a possibility.

Human genetic engineering raises the very real spectre of a distopian   40
future where the haves and have-nots are increasingly divided and separated by genetic endowment, genetic discrimination is widely practiced, and traditional notions of democracy and equality give way to the creation of a genetocracy based on one's "genetic qualifications." The driving force of this new bioindustrial world are giant life science companies whose control over genetic resources and the new transformative biotechnologies give them the clout to act as commercial agents for a new eugenics era.

COMPETING BIOTECH VISIONS

Many in the life sciences field would have us believe that the new gene splic-   41
ing technologies are irrepressible and irreversible and that any attempt to oppose their introduction is both futile and retrogressive. They never stop to even consider the possibility that the new genetic science might be used in a wholly different manner than is currently being proposed. The fact is, the corporate agenda is only one of two potential paths into the Biotech Century. It is possible that the growing number of anti-eugenic activists around the world might be able to ignite a global debate around alternative uses of the new science—approaches that are less invasive, more sustainable and humane and that conserve and protect the genetic rights of future generations.

While the global life science companies favor the introduction and wide-   42
spread use of gene therapy—genetic engineering—to cure diseases, and enhance the physical, emotional and mental well-being of individuals, a growing number of holistically minded geneticists and health practitioners are beginning to use the new data being generated by the human genome project in a very different way. They are exploring the relationship between genetic mutations and environmental triggers with the hope of fashioning a more sophisticated, scientifically-based understanding and approach to preventive health. More than 70 percent of all deaths in the United States and other industrialized countries are attributable to what physicians refer to as "diseases of affluence." Heart attacks, strokes, breast, colon and prostate cancer, and diabetes are among the most common diseases of affluence. While each individual has varying genetic susceptibilities to these diseases, environmental factors, including diet and lifestyle, are major contributing elements that can trigger genetic mutations. Heavy cigarette smoking, high levels of alcohol consumption, diets rich in animal fats, the use of pesticides and other poisonous chemicals, contaminated water and food, polluted air and sedentary living habits with little or no exercise, have been shown, in study after study, to cause genetic mutations and lead to the onset of many of these high profile diseases.

The mapping and sequencing of the human genome is providing   43
researchers with vital new information on recessive gene traits and genetic
predispositions for a range of illnesses. Still, little research has been done, to
date, on how genetic predispositions interact with toxic materials in the environment, the metabolizing of different foods, and lifestyle to affect genetic
mutations and phenotypical expression. The new holistic approach to human
medicine views the individual genome as part of an embedded organismic
structure continually interacting with and being affected by the environment
in which it unfolds. The effort is geared toward using increasingly sophisticated genetic and environmental information to prevent genetic mutations
from occurring. (It needs to be emphasized, however, that a number of genetic diseases appear to be unpreventable and immune to environmental mediation.)

Some would argue that, in the case of medicine and any number of other   44
fields, there is no reason why both approaches to applied science can't live
side by side, each complementing and augmenting the other. In reality, the
commercial market favors the more reductionist approach for the obvious
reason that for now, at least, that's where the money is to be made. While
there is certainly a growing market for preventive health practices, programs,
and products, far more money is invested in "illness" based medicine. That
could change, but it would require a paradigm shift in the way we think about
science and its applications., with awareness of and support for a science
founded in systems thinking and sensitive to the twin notions of diversity and
interdependence.

While it might seem highly improbable, even inconceivable, to most of   45
the principal players in this new technology revolution that genetic engineering, with all of its potential promise, might ultimately be rejected, we need
remind ourselves that just a generation ago, it would have been just as inconceivable to imagine the partial abandonment of nuclear energy which had for
years been so enthusiastically embraced as the ultimate salvation for a society
whose appetite for energy appeared nearly insatiable. It is also possible that
society will accept some and reject other uses of genetic engineering in the
coming biotech century. For example, one could make a solid case for genetic screening—with the appropriate safeguards in place—to better predict the
onslaught of disabling diseases, especially those that can be prevented with
early treatment. The new gene-splicing technologies also open the door to a
new generation of lifesaving pharmaceutical products. On the other hand, the
use of gene therapy to make corrective changes in the human germ line,
affecting the options of future generations, is far more problematic. Society
may well say yes to some of the genetic engineering options and no to others.
After all, nuclear technology has been harnessed effectively for uses other than
creating energy and making bombs.

Even rejection of some genetic engineering technologies then, does not   46
mean that the wealth of genomic and environmental information being collected couldn't be used in other ways. While the twenty-first century will be
the Age of Biology, the technological application of the knowledge we gain

can take a variety of forms. To believe that genetic engineering is the only way to apply our new knowledge of biology and the life sciences is limiting and keeps us from entertaining other options which might prove even more effective in addressing the needs and fulfilling the dreams of current and future generations.

The biotech revolution will affect every aspect of our lives. The way we   47
eat; the way we date and marry; the way we have our babies; the way our children are raised and educated; the way we work; the way we engage in politics; the way we express our faith; the way we perceive the world around us and our place in it—all of our individual and shared realities will be deeply touched by the new technologies of the Biotech Century. Surely, these very "personal" technologies deserve to be widely discussed and debated by the public at large before they become a ubiquitous part of our daily lives.

■   ■   ■

Review Questions

1. Summarize Rifkin's position on the commercial control of research into the human genome.
2. What is eugenics?
3. How might research into the genetic markers of some population groups be used as a stigma?
4. What is the difference between somatic gene therapy and germ line therapy?
5. What are the arguments *for* conducting germ line therapy?
6. What is the "underlying logic of genetic engineering"? What is the significance between describing particular genetic structures as "defects," as opposed to "mutations"?
7. What kind of debates may emerge regarding parental responsibility in the Biotech Century?
8. According to Rifkin, what are the dangers of treating genetic disorders by "eliminating recessive traits at the germ line level"?
9. Why is it possible that corporate interests, and not a malevolent government (as in Huxley's *Brave New World*), might become responsible for creating a genetically segmented society?

Discussion and Writing Suggestions

1. In previous centuries, the Earth provided the raw materials—the iron ore and the coal and the crops—on which to build economic and social progress. In the near future, writes Rifkin, the raw materials on which progress will rest will be the human genome, the knowledge of which will create the potential to cure disease and engineer future generations. Is

there any difference, in your view, between industry's exploitation of raw materials of the 19th and 20th centuries and the raw materials of the 21st and beyond?

2. To what extent do you feel we are approaching a new and momentous juncture in human history? Do you share Rifkin's sense of foreboding?

3. We say it is "natural" for birds to fly, for bees to build hives, for lions to hunt their prey. Define the word "natural" with respect to the human enterprise. For instance, is it "natural" for humans to develop technology? Is it "natural" for humans to put the materials of nature to use for human ends? When does a "natural" effort for humans cross into the "unnatural?" Based on your definition, discuss how "natural" it is for humans to manipulate their own genetic structures. (An additional question might help you think through an answer: When critics claim that genetic tinkering or cloning is "unnatural," how are they defining "natural?")

4. Reread the quoted passage from Robert Sinsheimer (paragraph 28). What is the distinction he is making between the "old eugenics" and the "new eugenics"? How do you respond to this distinction? Do you support Sinsheimer's enthusiasm for bioengineering?

5. Given a free-market choice to safeguard the health of and prospects for their unborn children, parents in the (near) future may elect to boost their children genetically. If such genetic manipulation occurs, what would prevent a class system of Gen Rich and Naturals from emerging, as described by Lee Silver (paragraphs 34–37)? Given the chance to enhance your unborn child, what would you do? From the child's point of view, would you prefer to be a Gen Rich or a Natural?

6. Reread paragraph 23. Explain its rhetorical/structural function as an important pivot point in the article.

7. Rifkin is hardly neutral in his views on the commercialization of the human genome. Still, he presents the views of proponents of commercial exploitation of genetic research. On balance, how fair do you find Rifkin's presentation? In developing your answer, point to specific passages as evidence.

Fatalist Attraction: The Dubious Case Against Fooling Mother Nature

VIRGINIA POSTREL

Rifkin and others challenge the wisdom of "defying" Nature by tinkering with the genetic blueprints of life. But as Virginia Postrel points out, Nature in its unmodified state can be a brutal breeding ground of illness, suffering, and disease. What genetic researchers are doing now is not so very different (at least in intent) from what medical researchers have done for centuries: that is, sought ways to block the development of disease and to offer patients long and healthy lives. If patients are willing to create "demand" for new medial techniques (even human cloning) and researchers are willing to deliver them, than what role—if any—should medical ethicists and government administrators play in deciding whether these techniques should go to market?

Virginia I. Postrel is editor of Reason *magazine, in which this selection appeared in July 1997.* Reason *presents a libertarian perspective—see Chapter 6,* The Political Spectrum, *for more on libertarian politics—that advocates against government interference in personal affairs. (The magazine's signature phrase is "Free Minds and Free Markets.") Postrel also writes commentaries for other national publications and appears regularly as a commentator on national television.*

Twenty years ago, the bookstore in which I was working closed for a few hours while we all went to the funeral of one of our colleagues. Herbie was a delightful guy, well liked by everyone. He died in his 20s—a ripe old age back then for someone with cystic fibrosis. In keeping with the family's wishes, we all contributed money in his memory to support research on the disease. In those days, the best hope was that scientists would develop a prenatal test that would identify fetuses likely to have C.F., allowing them to be aborted. The thought made us uncomfortable. "Would you really want Herbie never to be?" said my boss.

But science has a way of surprising us. Two decades later, abortion is no longer the answer proposed for cystic fibrosis. Gene therapy—the kind of audacious high-tech tool that generates countless references to *Brave New World* and *Frankenstein*—promises not to stamp out future Herbies but to cure them.

This spring I thought of Herbie for the first time in years. It was amid the brouhaha over cloning, as bioethicists galore were popping up on TV to demand that scientists justify their unnatural activities and Pat Buchanan was declaring that "mankind's got to control science, not the other way around."

It wasn't the technophobic fulminations of the anti-cloning pundits that brought back Herbie's memory, however. It was a letter from my husband's college roommate and his wife. Their 16-month-old son had been diagnosed with cystic fibrosis. He was doing fine now, they wrote, and they were optimistic about the progress of research on the disease.

There are no Herbies on *Crossfire*, and no babies with deadly diseases. There are only nature and technology, science and society, "ethics" and ambition. Our public debate about biotechnology is loud and impassioned but, most of all, abstract. Cowed by an intellectual culture that treats progress as a myth, widespread choice as an indulgence, and science as the source of atom bombs, even biotech's defenders rarely state their case in stark, personal terms. Its opponents, meanwhile, act as though medical advances are an evil, thrust upon us by scheming scientists. Hence Buchanan talks of "science" as distinct from "mankind" and ubiquitous Boston University bioethicist George Annas declares, "I want to put the burden of proof on scientists to show us why society needs this before society permits them to go ahead and [do] it."

That isn't, however, how medical science works. True, there are research   6 biologists studying life for its own sake. But the advances that get bioethicists exercised spring not from pure science but from consumer demand: "Society" may not ask for them, but individual people do.

Living in a center of medical research, I am always struck by the people   7 who appear on the local news, having just undergone this or that unprecedented medical procedure. They are all so ordinary, so down-to-earth. They are almost always middle-class, traditional families, people with big medical problems that require unusual solutions. They are not the Faustian, hedonistic yuppies you'd imagine from the way the pundits talk.

And it is the ambitions of such ordinary people, with yearnings as old as   8 humanity—for children, for health, for a long and healthy life for their loved ones—of which the experts so profoundly disapprove. As we race toward what Greg Benford aptly calls "the biological century," we will hear plenty of warnings that we should not play God or fool Mother Nature. We will hear the natural equated with the good, and fatalism lauded as maturity. That is a sentiment about which both green romantics and pious conservatives agree. And it deserves far more scrutiny than it usually gets.

Nobody wants to stand around and point a finger at this woman [who   9 had a baby at 63] and say, 'You're immoral.' But generalize the practice and ask yourself, What does it really mean that we won't accept the life cycle or life course?" Leon Kass, the neocons' favorite bioethicist, told *The New York Times*, "That's one of the big problems of the contemporary scene. You've got all kinds of people who make a living and support themselves but who psychologically are not grown up. We have a culture of functional immaturity."

It sounds so profound, so wise, to denounce "functional immaturity" and   10 set oneself up as a grown-up in a society of brats. But what exactly does it mean in this context? Kass can't possibly think that 63-year-olds will start flocking to fertility clinics—that was the quirky action of one determined woman. He is worried about something far more fundamental: our unwillingness to put up with whatever nature hands out, to accept our fates, to act our ages. "The good news," says Annas of human cloning, "is I think *finally we have a technology that we can all agree shouldn't be used*." (Emphasis added.) Lots of biotech is bad, he implies, but it's so damned hard to get people to admit it.

When confronted with such sentiments, we should remember just what   11 Mother Nature looks like unmodified. Few biotechnophobes are as honest as British philosopher John Gray, who in a 1993 appeal for greens and conservatives to unite, wrote of "macabre high-tech medicine involving organ transplantation" and urged that we treat death as "a friend to be welcomed." Suffering is the human condition, he suggested: We should just lie back and accept it. "For millennia," he said, "people have been born, have suffered pain and illness, and have died, without those occurrences being understood as treatable diseases."

. . .

Gray's historical perspective is quite correct. In the good old days, rich   12
men did not need divorce to dump their first wives for trophies. Childbirth and disease did the trick. In traditional societies, divorce, abandonment, annulment, concubinage, and polygamy—not high-tech medicine—were the cures for infertility. Until the 20th century, C.F. didn't need a separate diagnosis, since it was just one cause of infant mortality among many. Insulin treatment for diabetes (highly unnatural) didn't exist until the 1920s. My own grandmother saw her father, brother, and youngest sister die before she was in middle age. In 1964 a rubella epidemic left a cohort of American newborns deaf.

These days, we in rich countries have the wonderful luxury of rejecting   13
even relatively minor ailments, from menstrual cramps to migraines, as unnecessary and treatable. "People had always suffered from allergies. . . . But compared to the other health problems people faced before the middle of the twentieth century, the sneezing, itching, and skin eruptions had for the most part been looked at as a nuisance," writes biologist Edward Golub. "In the modern world, however, they became serious impediments to living a full life, and the discovery that a whole class of compounds called antihistamines could control the symptoms of allergy meant that allergic individuals could lead close to normal lives. The same story can be told for high blood pressure, depression, and a large number of chronic conditions."

Treating chronic conditions is, if anything, more nature-defiant than   14
attacking infectious diseases. A woman doesn't have to have a baby when she's 63 to refuse to "accept the life cycle or life course." She can just take estrogen. And, sure enough, there is a steady drumbeat of criticism against such unnatural measures, as there is against such psychologically active drugs as Prozac. We should, say the critics, just take what nature gives us.

In large part, this attitude stems from a naive notion of health as the nat-   15
ural state of the body. In fact, disease and death are natural; the cures are artificial. And as we rocket toward the biological century, we will increasingly realize that a bodily state may not be a "disease," but just something we wish to change. Arceli Keh was not sick because her ovaries no longer generated eggs; she was simply past menopause. To say she should be able to defy her natural clock (while admitting that mid-60s parenthood may not be the world's greatest idea) doesn't mean declaring menopause a disease. Nor does taking estrogen, any more than taking birth control pills means fertility is a sickness.

"The cloned human would be an attack on the dignity and integrity of   16
every single person on this earth," says German Research Minister Juergen Ruettgers, demanding a worldwide ban, lest such subhumans pollute the planet. (The Germans want to outlaw even the cloning of human cells for

medical research.) Human cloning is an issue, but it is not *the* issue in these debates. They are really about whether centralized powers will wrest hold of scientists' freedom of inquiry and patients' freedom to choose—whether one set of experts will decide what is natural and proper for all of us—and whether, in fact, nature should be our standard of value.

Ruettgers is wildly overreacting and, in the process, attacking the human-   17
ity of people yet unborn. As Ron Bailey has noted . . . human cloning is not that scary, unless you're afraid of identical twins, nor does it pose unprecedented ethical problems. No one has come up with a terribly plausible scenario of when human cloning might occur. Yet judging from the history of other medical technologies, the chances are good that if such a clone were created, the parents involved would be ordinary human beings with reasons both quite rare and extremely sympathetic. We should not let the arrogant likes of Ruettgers block their future hopes.

■ ■ ■

Review Questions

1. According to Postrel, who should control decisions regarding which technologies medical researchers (and patients) should pursue?
2. What distinction does Postrel make between "natural" and "unnatural" interventions in human health?
3. Postrel claims that professional ethicists and politicians tend to make their objections to high-tech medicine in abstract, not personal, terms. Postrel sees this as a problem. Why?

Discussion and Writing Suggestions

1. To what extent do you see human cloning as a difference in degree or in kind from the medical research that has been done in the past? Researchers have developed elaborate techniques, for instance, to help infertile couples conceive and give birth. In what ways is cloning a radical departure from this kind of science?
2. How comfortable are you in allowing someone—or some government entity—to decide which medical investigations and technologies ought to be permitted? To take a particular case, should it be the government's decision to restrict or ban research on human cloning? Explain your answer.
3. Explain the significance of Postrel's title for this selection. What is a "fatalist" attraction? What is the case against Mother Nature? Why is this a "dubious" case?
4. What, in your view, is the distinction between healing a diseased person naturally versus unnaturally? What would be an example of each type of treatment? Explain the distinctions between the natural and the unnatural treatments.

5. "For millennia," writes Postrel, quoting the British philosopher John Gray, "people have been born, have suffered pain and illness, and have died, without those occurrences being understood as treatable diseases." In Gray's view of the life cycle, what is the function of medicine and what is the role of medical research?

6. If the decision to make genetic interventions (whether in one's own body or, perhaps, in that of a child or embryo) were left to individuals, as Postrel advocates, some observers (see the Rifkin article) predict that two classes, if not species, of humans would inevitably arise—one that insisted on being "natural" and the other that freely made genetic "enhancements." To what extent does this prediction argue for decisions about genetic intervention being made *not* by individuals but by broader cultural authorities—governments, say, or international bodies of scientists?

When Science Takes the Witness Stand

PETER J. NEUFELD
NEVILLE COLMAN

Former football (and movie) star O.J. Simpson has done more than all the geneticists in the country to focus public attention on DNA. In 1994 Simpson was charged with murdering his ex-wife and a male companion. Prosecutors grounded their case largely on DNA evidence: They called upon numerous expert witnesses who testified that genetic matching of blood samples at the murder scene, in Simpson's car, and in his home conclusively proved his guilt. For weeks, both the jury and millions of Americans listened to detailed testimony about how the blood samples were gathered, transported, stored, tested, and retested. For their part, Simpson's defense attorneys argued that the collection and storage procedures were sloppy and that the labs' testing procedures were questionable. [Simpson was acquitted of the charges.] One of those defense attorneys was Peter Neufeld, co-author of the following article, which—we must emphasize—was written four years before *the Simpson case. But in their article, Neufeld and co-author Neville Colman lay out in general terms some of the more specific arguments that were made about the DNA procedures in the Simpson case.*

"When Science Takes the Witness Stand," then, is not about the Simpson case, but about the more general issues raised by the use of DNA testing in courts of law—that is, its use for forensic (as opposed to clinical or research) purposes. If each human being does have a unique DNA "fingerprint," then DNA could prove to be—indeed has proved to be—a powerful tool not only in helping to convict the guilty, but also to exonerate the innocent. But the supposed certainty of DNA evidence is here called into question by Neufeld and Colman. As you read it, withhold final judgment on their *case until you read the next article, "DNA in Court," by William Tucker. (For additional perspective on Neufeld's association with the Simpson case, see "On the Defensive," by T. J. English, in* New York, *January 2, 1995.)*

Neufeld and Colman collaborated for several years on the problem of admitting new scientific evidence into criminal cases and have lectured on the subject to both defense attorneys and prosecutors. Neufeld, an attorney specializing in criminal defense and civil-rights litigation, was co-counsel of People v. Castro, *in which DNA evidence was first successfully challenged. He is a member of the New York State Governor's panel on forensic analysis. Neufeld received his J.D. in 1975 from the New York University School of Law and is adjunct professor at the Fordham University School of Law. Colman is director of the Center for Clinical Laboratories at Mount Sinai Medical Center in New York City. He received his M.D. in 1969 and his Ph.D. in 1974 from the University of the Witwatersrand, Johannesburg. He has advised counsel and testified in legal proceedings involving the admissibility of scientific evidence. This article first appeared in* Scientific American, *May 1990.*

A reader advisory: *You may find parts of this article difficult because it assumes a level of scientific knowledge that many readers (and juries!) do not possess. Don't worry about passages you don't understand: as long as you keep focused on the main lines of Neufeld and Colman's argument, you'll get what the authors want you to get from their article. In fact, most sections of the piece should give you no problem at all; but you may wish to skim or just skip over the following groups of paragraphs, which are more technical: 19–23, 28–31, 38–46.*

In the early evening of November 21, 1974, powerful bombs ripped through   1
two pubs in the industrial city of Birmingham, England, leaving 21 dead and 162 injured. The government immediately blamed the Irish Republican Army for the attacks and mounted a massive search for the perpetrators. After a railroad clerk reported that six Irishmen had boarded a train in Birmingham minutes before the first bomb blast, police intercepted the men as they disembarked at the port of Heysham. The six men were taken to the police station, and there, their hands were swabbed with chemicals that would reveal the presence of any nitrites, which would be consistent with the recent handling of explosives. The forensic scientist who performed this procedure, known as the Greiss test, reported positive findings on the right hands of two of the six suspects. That evidence became the linchpin of the government's successful prosecution of the "Birmingham Six."

Now, 16 years later, the six men may be released. The Greiss test, on   2
which their convictions had been largely based, has proved unreliable. It turns out that a variety of common substances such as old playing cards, cigarette packages, lacquer and aerosol spray will, along with explosives, yield a positive result. As it happened, the six men had spent most of their train ride to Heysham playing cards and smoking cigarettes.

The Birmingham case raises troubling issues about the application of   3
forensic technology to criminal investigations. Since the discovery of fingerprinting at the turn of the century, science has assumed an increasingly powerful role in the execution of justice. Indeed, scientific testimony is often the deciding factor for the judicial resolution of civil and criminal cases. The sci-

entific analysis of fingerprints, blood, semen, shreds of clothing, hair, weapons, tire treads and other physical evidence left at the scene of a crime can seem more compelling to a jury than the testimony of eyewitnesses. As one juror put it after a recent trial in Queens, N.Y., "You can't argue with science."

Scientists generally welcome this trend. Because the scientific community polices scientific research, subjecting new theories and findings to peer review and independent verification, it is often assumed the same standards prevail when science is applied to the fact-finding process in a judicial trial. But in reality such controls are absent in a court of law. Instead nonscientists—lawyers, judges and jurors—are called on to evaluate critically the competence of a scientific witness. Frequently lawyers are oblivious of potential flaws in a scientific method or argument and so fail to challenge it. At other times, the adversaries in a case will present opposing expert opinions, leaving it up to a jury of laypersons to decide the merits of the scientific arguments. 4

The disjunction between scientific and judicial standards of evidence has allowed novel forensic methods to be used in criminal trials prematurely or without verification. The problem has become painfully apparent in the case of forensic DNA profiling, a recent technique that in theory can identify an individual from his or her DNA with a high degree of certainty. Although many aspects of forensic DNA identification have not been adequately examined by the scientific community, police and prosecutors have carried out DNA analysis in more than 1,000 criminal investigations in the U.S. since 1987. Few of these cases reached trial. In most instances defendants pleaded guilty on advice of counsel after a presumably infallible DNA test declared a match. 5

Several recent cases have raised serious reservations about the claims made for DNA evidence. Last spring, during a pretrial hearing at *People v. Castro* in New York City, Michael L. Baird of Lifecodes Corporation of Valhalla, N.Y., one of the two major commercial forensic DNA laboratories in the U.S., reported the odds of a random match between a blood-stain and the suspect at one in 100 million. Eric S. Lander of Harvard University and the Massachusetts Institute of Technology examined the same data and arrived at odds of one in 24. Ultimately, several proponents of DNA testing denounced Lifecodes' data in the case as scientifically unreliable. Some of Lifecodes' key methods were repudiated, casting doubt on the integrity of hundreds of earlier criminal convictions. The ongoing debate over DNA testing underscores the need to deal more effectively with the difficulties that arise whenever complex scientific technology is introduced as evidence in a court of law. 6

A trial is ideally a search for truth. To help juries in their quest, the law allows qualified experts to testify and express opinions on matters in which they are professionally trained. Yet the esoteric nature of an expert's opinions, together with the jargon and the expert's scholarly credentials, may cast an aura of infallibility over his or her testimony. Hence, to prevent juries from being influenced by questionable evidence or expert testimony, U.S. courts 7 usually review the material in a pretrial hearing or outside the presence of the jury.

To be admitted as evidence, a forensic test should, as a matter of common 8 sense, satisfy three criteria: the underlying scientific theory must be considered valid by the scientific community; the technique itself must be known to be reliable; and the technique must be shown to have been properly applied in the particular case.

The expression of common sense in a court of law, however, is at times 9 elusive. A majority of U.S. courts decide on the admissibility of scientific evidence based on guidelines established in 1923 by *Frye v. U.S.*, in which the Court of Appeals for the District of Columbia affirmed a lower court's decision to exclude evidence derived from a precursor of the polygraph. "Just when a scientific principle or discovery crosses the line between the experimental and demonstrable stages is difficult to define," the court declared in *Frye*. "Somewhere in this twilight zone the evidential force of the principle must be recognized, and while courts will go a long way in admitting expert testimony deduced from a well-recognized scientific principle or discovery, the thing from which the deduction is made must be sufficiently established to have gained general acceptance in the particular field in which it belongs."

Judges, scientists, lawyers and legal scholars have all criticized the *Frye* 10 standard. Some say it is too vague. Some argue that is unduly restrictive. Still others complain that it is not restrictive enough. Should "general acceptance," for example, require a consensus or a simple majority of scientists? Also, what is it that must be generally accepted? In the case of DNA profiling, is it the theory that no two individuals, except for identical twins, have the same DNA? Is it the various techniques employed in the test, such as Southern blotting and gel electrophoresis? Or is it the specific application of DNA profiling to dried blood and semen samples recovered from the scene of a crime?

Furthermore, what is the appropriate "particular field" in which a tech- 11 nique must be accepted? Does a test for DNA profiling have to be accepted only by forensic serologists, or must it also be recognized by the broader community of human geneticists, hematologists and biochemists? In a recent California case, DNA evidence analyzed by means of the polymerase chain reaction (PCR) was excluded because that method was not generally accepted by forensic scientists. Yet several months earlier a Texas court that was evaluating the identical PCR method looked more broadly to the opinions of molecular biologists and human geneticists and reached the opposite conclusion.

For many applications of science to forensics, the underlying theory is 12 well established, and legal debate rages mainly over whether one must prove only that a technique is generally accepts for a scientific research or more strictly, that the technique is reliable when applied to forensics.

Why the distinction between nonforensic and forensic applications? 13 Scientists commonly accept that when any technology is tried in a different application, such as forensics, it must be tested thoroughly to ensure an empirical understanding of the technique's usefulness and limitations. Indeed, many a technique that has proved reliable for research—polygraphy, for example—has turned out to be of questionable reliability when applied to forensic casework.

Clearly, in order for the courts to evaluate forensic evidence, judges and lawyers must be able to appreciate the scientific issues at hand. Regrettably, lawyers rarely do more than review the qualifications of the expert (typically based on perfunctory queries about institutional affiliation and publications) and verify the facts on which the expert's conclusions are based. The reason for this limited inquiry is simple: most lawyers and judges lack the adequate scientific background to argue or decide the admissibility of expert testimony. Often judges think—mistakenly, in our opinion—that justice is best served by admitting expert testimony into evidence and deferring to the jury for the determination of its weight.   14

The problem of scientific illiteracy is compounded by the tendency of judges to refuse to reconsider the validity of a particular kind of scientific evidence once it has been accepted by another judge in an earlier case. This practice is founded on the well-recognized need to respect precedent in order to ensure the uniform administration of justice. But in the case of forensic tests, the frequent failure of courts to take a fresh look at the underlying science has been responsible for many a miscarriage of justice.   15

Perhaps the most notorious example of the problem is the so-called paraffin test (a cousin of the Greiss test employed in the Birmingham Six investigation), which was used by crime laboratories throughout the U.S. to detect nitrite and nitrate residues, presumably from gunpowder, on suspects' hands to show that they had recently fired a gun. The test was first admitted as scientific evidence in a 1936 trial in Pennsylvania. Other states than simply adopted that decision without independently scrutinizing the research.   16

For the next 25 years innumerable people were convicted with the help of this test. It was not until the mid 1960s that a comprehensive scientific study revealed damning flaws in the paraffin test. In particular, the test gave an unacceptably high number of false positives: substances other than gunpowder that gave a positive reading included urine, tobacco, tobacco ash, fertilizer and colored fingernail polish. In this instance the legal process failed, allowing people accused of crimes to be convicted on evidence that later proved to be worthless.   17

More recently the debate over scientific courtroom evidence has centered on two applications of biotechnology: protein-marker analysis and DNA identification. Both techniques employ gel electrophoresis to reveal genetic differences, called polymorphisms, in blood proteins and DNA. These two techniques can potentially match blood, semen or other such evidence found at a crime scene to a suspect or victim.   18

In the late 1960s crime laboratories became interested in protein polymorphisms in populations. The techniques for studying protein polymorphisms were originally developed as tools for population geneticists and were experimentally tested, published in refereed journals and independently verified. The techniques were then modified by and for law-enforcement personnel in order to cope with problems unique to forensic samples, such as their   19 often limited quantity, their unknown age and the presence of unidentified contaminants. These modifications were rarely published in the scientific literature or validated by independent workers.

For example, molecular geneticists study polymorphic proteins in red   20
blood cells and serum by using fresh, liquid blood and analyzing it under controlled laboratory conditions, all subject to scientific peer review. These techniques were then adapted for use on forensic samples of dried blood by the introduction of various modifications, few of which were subjected to comparable scientific scrutiny. No one ever adequately explored the effects of environmental insults to samples, such as heat, humidity, temperature and light. Neither did anyone verify the claim that forensic samples would not be affected significantly by microbes and unknown substances typically found on streets or in carpets.

One of the major modifications made by forensic laboratories was the   21
"multisystem" test. In the original version of this test, three different polymorphic proteins were identified in a single procedure; the purpose was to derive as much information as possible from a small sample. The three-marker multisystem test was further modified by the addition of a fourth protein marker in 1980 by the New York City Medical Examiner's serology laboratory.

By 1987 evidence derived from the "four-in-one" multisystem had been   22
introduced in several hundred criminal prosecutions in New York State. In that year, however, during a pretrial hearing in *People v. Seda*, the director of the New York City laboratory admitted under cross-examination that only one article had been published about that system—and that the article had recommended the test be used only to screen out obvious mismatches because of a flaw that tended to obscure the results.

In *People v. Seda*, the judge ruled that the four-in-one multisystem did   23
not satisfy the *Frye* standard of general acceptance by the scientific community and so could not be introduced into evidence. Unfortunately *Seda* was the first case involving the test in which the defense went to the effort of calling witnesses to challenge the technology. Consequently, the integrity of hundreds of earlier convictions stands in doubt.

In the past two years DNA profiling has all but eclipsed protein markers   24
in forensic identification. The technique is based on a method originally developed to study the inheritance of diseases, both to identify the disease-causing genes in families known to harbor an inherited disease and to predict individual susceptibility when the gene is known.

Crime investigators have embraced the new technique because it offers   25
two significant advantages over conventional protein markers. First, DNA typing can be conducted on much smaller and older samples. And second, DNA typing was reported to offer from three to 10 orders of magnitude greater certainty of a match. Promotional literature distributed by Lifecodes asserts that its test "has the power to identify one individual in the world's population." Not to be outdone, Cellmark Diagnostics in Germantown, Md.—Lifecodes' main competitor—claims that with its method, "the chance

that any two people will have the same DNA print is one in 30 billion." Yet, as testimony in the *Castro* case showed, such claims can be dubious.

The hype over DNA typing spreads the impression that a DNA profile identifies the "genetic code" unique to an individual and indeed is as unique as a fingerprint. Actually, because 99 percent of the three billion base pairs in human DNA are identical among all individuals, forensic scientists look for ways to isolate the relatively few variable regions. These regions can be cut out of DNA by restriction enzymes and are called restriction fragment length polymorphisms (RFLPs).   26

For DNA identification, one wants RFLPs that are highly polymorphic— that is, those that have the greatest number of variants, or alleles, in the population. It turns out that certain regions of human DNA contain "core" sequences that are repeated in tandem, like freight cars of a train. The number of these repeated sequences tends to vary considerably from person to person; one person might have 13 repeated units at that locus, whereas another might have 29. Special restriction enzymes cut DNA into millions of pieces, including fragments that contain the repeated segments. Because the number of repeated segments varies among individuals, so too does the overall length of these fragments vary.   27

How can these variable fragments be picked out of the haystack of irrelevant DNA segments? The answer lies in "probes" that bind only to fragments containing the core sequence. If the core sequence occurs at only one DNA locus, the probe is called a single-locus probe. If the core sequence occurs at many different loci, the probe is called a multilocus probe. Forensic laboratories currently make use of three different methods of DNA typing: single-locus RFLP, multilocus RFLP and the polymerase chain reaction. Because the single-locus system is the one most widely employed in forensic DNA identification, we will describe it in some detail [See Figure 1, p. 568.]   28

For forensic DNA identification by single-locus RFLP analysis, DNA from various sources is digested with restriction enzymes, placed in separate lanes on an electrophoretic gel and subjected to an electric field. The field pulls fragments down the lane, with smaller fragments traveling faster than larger ones. The fragments, now sorted by size, are denatured into single strands and transferred from the gel onto a nitrocellulose or nylon membrane, which fixes the fragments in place. (Incidentally, anyone who handles nitrocellulose might test positive on the Greiss test!)   29

At this point, a radioactive probe is applied, which hybridizes, or binds, to the polymorphic fragments. The mesh is then laid on a sheet of X-ray film to produce an autoradiograph. The radioactively labeled fragments are thereby revealed as a series of bands resembling a railroad track with irregularly spaced ties; the position of the bands is a measure of the size of the polymorphic fragments. The probe can be rinsed away, and a new probe can be applied to identify a different set of alleles.   30

The autoradiograph resulting from a single-locus probe will ordinarily show alleles of two distinct sizes, one inherited from each parent; such a pattern indicates that the person is heterozygous for that locus. If the probe   31

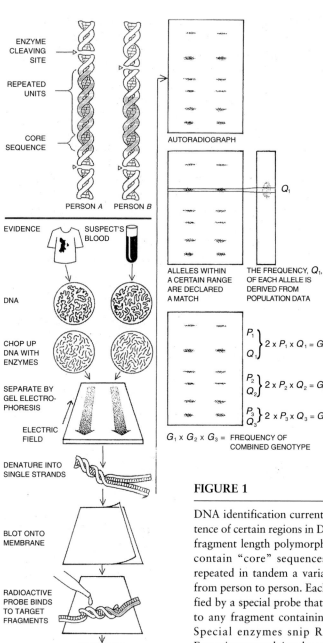

ENZYME CLEAVING SITE

REPEATED UNITS

CORE SEQUENCE

PERSON *A*   PERSON *B*

EVIDENCE   SUSPECT'S BLOOD

DNA

CHOP UP DNA WITH ENZYMES

SEPARATE BY GEL ELECTRO-PHORESIS

ELECTRIC FIELD

DENATURE INTO SINGLE STRANDS

BLOT ONTO MEMBRANE

RADIOACTIVE PROBE BINDS TO TARGET FRAGMENTS

EXPOSE X-RAY FILM

AUTORADIOGRAPH

Q_1

ALLELES WITHIN A CERTAIN RANGE ARE DECLARED A MATCH

THE FREQUENCY, Q_1, OF EACH ALLELE IS DERIVED FROM POPULATION DATA

$\left.\begin{array}{l} P_1 \\ Q_1 \end{array}\right\} 2 \times P_1 \times Q_1 = G_1$

$\left.\begin{array}{l} P_2 \\ Q_2 \end{array}\right\} 2 \times P_2 \times Q_2 = G_2$

$\left.\begin{array}{l} P_3 \\ Q_3 \end{array}\right\} 2 \times P_3 \times Q_3 = G_3$

$G_1 \times G_2 \times G_3 =$ FREQUENCY OF COMBINED GENOTYPE

FIGURE 1

DNA identification currently hinges on the existence of certain regions in DNA, called restriction fragment length polymorphisms (RFLPs), which contain "core" sequences (shading) that are repeated in tandem a variable number of times from person to person. Each RFLP can be identified by a special probe that recognizes and binds to any fragment containing the core sequence. Special enzymes snip RFLPs out of DNA. Forensic casework involves taking DNA extracted from evidence and from, for example, a suspect's blood, breaking it up into RFLPs and separating them by gel electrophoresis. A radioactive probe binds to the RFLPs, whose positions are then recorded as dark bands on X-ray film. If the striped patterns from the evidence and from the suspect appear to match, one then calculates the probability of such a match occurring by chance.

reveals only one distinct allele, it is assumed that the person inherited the same-size allele from both parents and that the person is homozygous for the locus. Forensic DNA-testing laboratories typically employ several single-locus probes, each of which binds to a different site.

To determine whether two samples of DNA come from a single source, one examines the bands identified by a particular probe on the autoradiograph and decides whether they match. One then refers to data from population-genetics studies to find out how often that particular allele size occurs. A typical allele might be found in 10 percent of the population, making it not all that unlikely that two random people will carry the same allele. But if one looks at alleles at three or four different sites, it becomes increasingly unlikely that two individuals will have the same alleles for all the sites. It is this hypothesis that gives DNA profiling its persuasive power. 32

How well does forensic DNA profiling stand up under the *Frye* standard? Certainly the underlying theory—that no two people, except for identical twins, have the identical DNA—is unquestioned, and so DNA identification is possible in theory. But is that theory being applied to give a reliable forensic test? and if so, is that test being carried out properly? 33

In scientific and medical research, DNA typing is most often employed to trace the inheritance of disease-causing alleles within a family. In this diagnostic application, however, one can assume that one allele was inherited from the mother and the other from the father. Because each parent has only two alleles for that gene, barring a mutation, the pattern observed in the child is limited at most to four possible combinations. In addition, if the results are ambiguous, one can rerun the experiment with fresh blood samples or refer to the alleles of other family members. 34

In forensic DNA typing, however, it is much more difficult to determine whether an allele from one sample is identical to an allele from another. (See [Figure 2, p. 570] In the RFLP systems employed in forensics, the number of alleles can run into the hundreds—in contrast to the four from which one must choose when identifying the alleles of a child whose parents are known. Indeed, forensic RFLP systems produce so many different alleles that they virtually form a continuum. In some RFLPs the most common alleles can be crowded into a quarter-inch span on a 13-inch lane. Gel electrophoresis can resolve only a limited number of alleles, however—perhaps between 30 and 100 depending on the particular RFLP—and so alleles that are similar, but not the same, in size may be declared identical. Hence, it can become difficult indeed to declare with confidence that one band matches another. What is worse, forensic samples are often limited in amount and so cannot be retested if ambiguities arise. 35

These inherent difficulties are further complicated by a problem called band shifting. This phenomenon occurs when DNA fragments migrate at different speeds through separate lanes on a single gel. It has been attributed to a number of factors, involving variables such as the preparation of gels, the concentrations of sample DNA, the amount of salt in the DNA solution and contamination. Band shifting can occur even if the various lanes contain 36

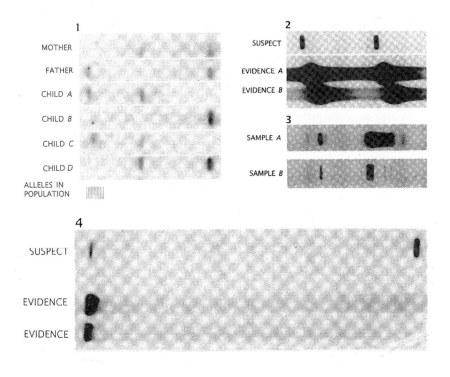

FIGURE 2

Forensic DNA typing is fraught with uncertainty. If the autoradiographs in group 1 are assumed to be from one family, then the alleles of the children must be derived from the parents, even though one of the bands for child C is visibly shifted. But if that same lane were a person whose parentage is unknown, then the band could correspond to one of the other alleles (*shaded bands*) observed in the population. In group 2, the band patterns from the suspect and from evidence *A* and *B* appear to be displaced relative to one another, which may indicate a band shift. In group 33, sample *A* contains all of the bands from sample *B*, along with extra bands, possibly from contaminants. In group 4, a suspect has two bands, whereas the forensic evidence has only one; the "missing" band may have resulted because degradation of the DNA destroyed the larger fragments. On the other hand, all of these cases could also indicate a real genetic difference.

DNA from the same person. Because allele sizes in forensic RFLP systems are closely spaced, it is difficult to know whether the relative positions of bands arise purely from the size of allele fragments or whether band shifting might play a part.

The courts' handling of band shifting is an excellent illustration of the problems that arise when courts, rather than the scientific peer-review process, take on the task of determining whether a method is reliable. Two years ago, when DNA evidence was first introduced in U.S. courtrooms, most forensic DNA scientists rejected the existence of band shifting. But now some experts think band shifting occurs in perhaps 30 percent of forensic DNA tests. There

37

are now many theories about the cause, but as of this writing not one refereed article on the subject has been published.

Forensic DNA laboratories are rushing to develop special probes that bind to monomorphic loci—restriction-enzyme fragments that are the same size in every person—as a possible way to control for band shifting. In theory, if the monomorphic regions are displaced, one would know that band shifting had occurred and could then calculate a correction factor. The difficulty again is that neither this method, nor any other possible solution, has been peer reviewed. 38

Yet in a rape case tried last December in Maine, *State v. McLeod*, the laboratory director who had supervised the DNA tests for the prosecution testified that a correction factor derived from a monomorphic probe allowed him to declare a match between the suspect's blood and the semen recovered from the victim, even though the bands were visibly shifted. When evidence then came to light that a second monomorphic probe indicated a smaller correction factor, which did not account for the disparity between the bands, he acknowledged the monomorphic probes may yield inconsistent correction factors; nevertheless, he argued that the first correction was appropriate to the bands in question. The prosecutor, though, recognized the folly of defending this argument in the absence of published supporting data and withdrew the DNA evidence. In dozens of other cases, however, judges have been persuaded by the same types of arguments, even though there is no body of research to guide the court. As a matter of common sense, the proper place to first address such issues is in scientific journals, not the courtroom. 39

Another major problem that arises in forensic DNA typing is contamination. More often than not, crime-scene specimens are contaminated or degraded. The presence of bacteria, organic material or degradation raises the risk of both false positives and false negatives. For example, contamination can degrade DNA so that the larger fragments are destroyed. In such instances a probe that should yield two bands may yield only one (the smaller band). 40

Research laboratories amply internal controls to avoid the misinterpretation that can result from such artifacts. But such controls may not be suitable for forensic casework. For example, one suggested control for band shifting is to run a mixing experiment: sample *A* is run in lane one, sample *B* in lane two and *A* and *B* in lane three. If both samples are from the same person, then ideally lane three would produce one set of bands, whereas if they are from different people, it would show two sets of bands. Unfortunately, in forensic casework there is often not enough material to run a mixing experiment. What is more, recent unpublished studies indicate that certain contaminants, such as dyes, can bind to DNA and alter its mobility in a gel, so that a mixing experiment using samples from the same person can produce two sets of bands. 41

The power of forensic DNA typing arises from its ability not only to demonstrate that two samples exhibit the same pattern but also to suggest that the pattern is extremely rare. The validity of the data and assumptions on which forensic laboratories have been relying to estimate the rarity are currently being debated within the scientific community. 42

There are two particularly important criticisms. First, because it is diffi-   43
cult to discriminate accurately among the dozens of alleles at a particular
locus, the task of calculating the frequency with which each allele appears in
the population is inherently compromised. Second, the statistical equations for
calculating the frequency of a particular pattern of alleles apply only to a population that has resulted from random mating—a condition that is called
Hardy-Weinberg equilibrium.

If a population is in Hardy-Weinberg equilibrium, one can assume allele   44
types are shuffled at random. The occurrence of one allele is then independent
of the occurrence of a second allele. One can therefore calculate the frequency of the "genotype," or a particular pair of alleles, for a specific locus by multiplying the frequency of each allele and doubling it (because one has the same
probability of inheriting each allele from both parents). The frequency of a
genotype for a combination of loci is then obtained simply by multiplying the
frequency of the genotype for each individual locus. For example, if the genotypes at loci *A*, *B*, *C* and *D* each occur in 10 percent of the population, then
the probability that a person would have these genotypes at all four loci is .1
multiplied by itself four times: .0001.

Forensic DNA laboratories carry out these calculations based on data   45
they have assembled themselves. Most of the data have not been published in
peer-review journals or independently validated. One problem is that none of
the major laboratories employs the same RFLP system. And even if the laboratories decide to adopt uniform probes and enzymes, the results may still
differ significantly unless they all also adopt identical protocols. Commercial
DNA-testing laboratories are reluctant to do so, however, because each considers its RFLP system to be proprietary, and the probes and enzymes are sold
or licensed to crime laboratories around the country.

Another serious issue is that some populations may not be in equilibrium,   46
in which case neither the alleles nor the various loci may be independent. For
such a population, there is as yet no consensus on how to calculate the frequency of a genotype (given the limited data bases of the forensic DNA laboratories). As matters stand, population geneticists are debating whether
various racial and ethnic communities exhibit significant population sub-
structures so as to preclude the use of current data bases for the highly polymorphic systems employed in forensic DNA identification. For example, do
Hispanics in the U.S. constitute a single mixed population? Or is there non-
random mating, with Cubans more likely to mate with other Cubans and
Chicanos more likely to mate with other Chicanos? Should there be a separate
data base on allele frequencies within each of these subpopulations? To find
out, population geneticists will need to gather more data. [See Figure 3, p.
573.]

More than 1,000 criminal investigations in the U.S. have now involved   47
DNA evidence, but in only a few dozen cases has DNA evidence been challenged in a pretrial hearing. According to our own study of these hearings,
until the *Castro* case in New York, not one of these hearings addressed the
problems of forensic DNA typing that distinguish it from diagnostic DNA
typing. In all but two of the early hearings, defense attorneys failed to obtain

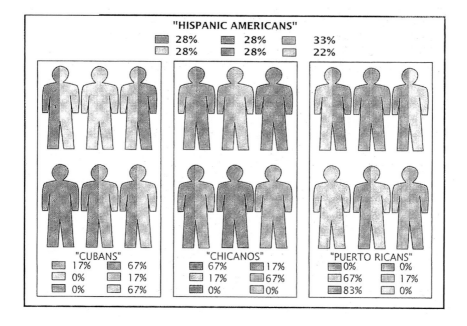

FIGURE 3

Population data may not yet be reliable enough to calculate the frequency of a geno-type accurately. In the hypothetical Hispanic-American population depicted here, a particular DNA site has six distinct alleles, each represented by its own shade. Heterozygous individuals, who have inherited the same allele from both parents, are shaded in one tone. Allele frequencies for the entire population differ markedly from allele frequencies for the subgroups shown here.

the raw population data on which conclusions about allele frequencies were predicated. In the first four appeals-court decisions on DNA evidence, the defense failed to present any expert witnesses during trial, and cross-examination of the prosecution's expert witnesses was at best perfunctory.

Some of this was not for lack of trying. The defense counsel in one case explained that he had asked dozens of molecular biologists to testify but all had refused. Interviews with some of the scientists revealed that most of them, being familiar with scientific research involving DNA typing, assumed the forensic application of the technique would be equally reliable. Some who were aware of possible problems were reluctant to criticize the technology publicly for fear that this would be misconstrued as a general attack on the underlying science.

Another troubling fact is that defense attorneys are often not able to spend the time or funds required to deal with the complexities of the issues. Novel scientific evidence is most often used to solve violent crimes, and defendants in such cases come predominantly from the less affluent sectors of society. Consequently, most of them must rely on court-appointed counsel selected from public-defender offices, legal-aid societies or the financially less

48

49

successful members of the private bar. Many of these advocates are exceptionally skillful, but they often lack the time and resources to mount a serious challenge to scientific evidence. And frankly, there are also many less-than-adequate attorneys who are simply overwhelmed by the complexity of the subject.

What is more, in most states a court-appointed lawyer may not retain an   50
expert witness without the approval of the trial judge. In recent DNA cases in Oklahoma and Alabama, for example, the defense did not retain any experts, because the presiding judge had refused to authorize funds. In the *Castro* case, a critical factor in the defense's successful challenge was the participation of several leading scientific experts—most of whom agreed to testify without a fee.

Because defendants are seldom able to challenge novel scientific evidence,   51
we feel that independent overseeing of forensic methods is the only way to ensure justice. Specifically, national standards must be set before a scientific technique can be transferred from the research laboratory to the courtroom, and there must be laws to ensure that these standards are enforced.

The regulation of forensic laboratories has an excellent model: the   52
Clinical Laboratories Improvement Act of 1967 (which was amended in 1988). The act established a system of accreditation and proficiency testing for clinical laboratories that service the medical profession. The law was enacted to ensure that such service laboratories, which are not subject to the same peer scrutiny as research laboratories, would nonetheless provide reliable products and services.

In contrast, no private or public crime laboratory today is regulated by   53
any government agency. Nor is there any mandatory accreditation of forensic laboratories or requirement that they submit to independent proficiency testing. It is also troubling that there are no formally enforced, objective criteria for interpreting forensic data. Four fifths of the forensic laboratories in North America are within police or prosecutor agencies, and so there is an enormous potential for bias because technicians may be aware of the facts of the case. In short, there is more regulation of clinical laboratories that determine whether one has mononucleosis than there is of forensic laboratories able to produce DNA test results that can help send a person to the electric chair.

Accreditation and proficiency testing will work only if implemented with   54
care. National standards for forensic testing must serve the interests of justice, not of parties who have vested interests in the technology. This is not an imaginary danger: from 1988 to 1989 a committee of the American Association of Blood Banks set out to develop national standards for forensic DNA typing and brought in two scientists to provide expertise in molecular genetics; these two happened to be the senior scientists at Lifecodes and Cellmark, the two companies that perform virtually all commercial forensic DNA identification in the U.S.

Some observers suggest delegating the task of setting national standards   55
for forensic DNA identification to the Federal Bureau of Investigation. But there is reason to be wary of this approach. Last year the FBI began to per-

form forensic DNA identification without first publishing its methodology in refereed journals. In the few pretrial hearings that have challenged DNA tests conducted by the FBI, the bureau has been reluctant to supply the raw data on which it based its criteria, citing its "privilege against self-criticism"—a concept that, incidentally, has little precedent in law. The FBI also opposes independent proficiency testing, arguing that no outsider is qualified to evaluate the bureau's performance. In addition, at a recent FBI-sponsored symposium on DNA typing that attracted 300 forensic scientists from around the country, FBI personnel were alone in opposing proposals requiring laboratories to explain in writing the basis for their conclusions and to have their reports signed by the scientists and technicians who conducted the test.

The FBI's stance on these issues flies against norms established elsewhere   56
in the scientific community. For example, if the author of a scientific article refused to divulge his or her raw data to peer review, the article would be rejected. There is also a clear consensus in favor of independent proficiency tests. If a clinical laboratory refused to comply with any reasonable public request to examine the results of proficiency tests, it would risk losing its accreditation. And it would be unthinkable for a diagnostic laboratory to deliver to the obstetrician of a pregnant woman an unsigned report with only the word "abort" appearing on the page.

Independent scientists are finally beginning to awaken to the urgency of   57
these issues. Last fall the New York State Forensic DNA Analysis Panel proposed detailed requirements for certifying, licensing and accrediting forensic DNA laboratories. The Congressional Office of Technology Assessment is expected to issue a report on the regulation of DNA typing by the time this article appears. The National Academy of Sciences has appointed a committee to study appropriate standards for DNA typing and is expected to issue a report early next year.

It is regrettable that these measures were set in motion only after flaws in   58
current DNA typing came to light in the courtroom. We hope the anticipated reforms will enhance the interests of justice in the future, although this may be small solace to defendants who were wrongfully convicted or to crime victims who saw the true culprit set free. It is our hope that, with appropriate national standards and regulation of forensic laboratories, powerful new forensic techniques such as DNA typing will serve an important and beneficial role in criminal justice. When all is said and done, there should be no better test for identifying a criminal—or for exonerating an innocent suspect.

■ ■ ■

Review Questions

1. What is the Greiss test? How is it relevant to the forensic use of DNA?
2. Identify the three criteria that must be satisfied for a forensic test to be admitted into evidence. What problems have been associated with these criteria?

3. Why is DNA evidence seldom challenged in court, according to Neufeld and Colman?

4. What concerns do the authors have about the kind of DNA tests performed in forensic (as opposed to clinical) laboratories?

Discussion and Writing Suggestions

1. You may have had some trouble following the authors' explanations of DNA testing procedures. If so, which parts presented the greatest difficulties? Try to write a summary of or paraphrase one or more of these parts, taking your cues not only from what the authors are saying, but also from the context of the discussion at that point.

2. Imagine that you are a prosecuting attorney arguing that DNA evidence conclusively places the accused at the scene of a brutal murder. Attorney (or expert witness) Neufeld or Colman has testified that due to ambiguous allele matching, band shifting, contamination by the police, sloppy handling by the lab (or some combination of these), the DNA evidence is not reliable and should be disregarded. There is no other physical evidence to link the accused to the crime (there may be circumstantial evidence). Write that part of your closing statement to the jury attempting to rebut Neufeld or Colman's contentions. You'll have to make up some details of the case, but don't try too far from the scenario presented above.

3. This article originally appeared in *Scientific American*, a magazine for readers particularly interested in issues of science and technology. What assumptions do you infer the authors make about their readers' intellectual level and their degree of comprehension of scientific issues? For example, what kinds of things do they assume their readers already know—and so do not need to have explained? How might this article have been written differently had it appeared in *Time* or *Newsweek*, which are general interest periodicals? How might it have been different had it appeared in *Discover*, another magazine intended for people interested in science, but which assumes an audience with less specialized knowledge?

4. One of the authors is an attorney, and both are practiced in making presentations in court; and so it is worth looking at this article as a legal *argument*, a systematic presentation of a case. What is the authors' central contention in this "case"? What is their strategy for presenting evidence in a systematic way, for clinching their argument? Have they succeeded in persuading you (the "juror") that their argument is reasonable and valid? If so, why? if not (or not entirely), why not?

DNA in Court

WILLIAM TUCKER

Many scientists—and lawyers—would take issue with some of the conclusions drawn by Neufeld and Colman in the preceding article. For example, Paul Mones, a defense attorney and author of Stalking Justice, *points out that the forensic use of DNA is not a highly controversial issue in the scientific community: "There are close to 100 articles on DNA fingerprinting in the scientific literature and only about half a dozen are critical of the procedure" ("Perspective on DNA Testing," Los Angeles Times, Oct. 7 1994, B7). Mones maintains that while most of the anti-DNA arguments focus on the possibility of wrongfully convicting the innocent, the actuality is that DNA evidence will help to exonerate, not convict an innocent person." In the following article, William Tucker, the New York correspondent of* The American Spectator, *expands upon this line of reasoning, arguing that the use of DNA in criminal cases should be expanded, not restricted. The article first appeared in the November 1994 issue of* The American Spectator. *(Some references to the O.J. Simpson case have been omitted.)*

... How did DNA profiling—almost a decade old and widely employed in other countries—end up having such a rough ride through the American justice system? The science itself is not at issue. There has never been a case where one laboratory declared a match in DNA samples and another laboratory declared the opposite. Believe it or not, the only major controversy now surrounding the technique is whether the chances of an innocent person being falsely implicated are 1-in–10,000 (a high estimate arbitrarily chosen by a maverick scientists) or 1-in–10 million (a widely accepted figure that has been verified by an examination of all the DNA records on file with the FBI). 1

Other forensic evidence long accepted in American courtrooms offers levels of certainty that are nowhere near that range. Blood-type identification, accepted in courts for decades, offers at best only a 90 percent verification (1-in–10 possibility of a chance match-up). Handwriting analysis and psychiatric testimony in insanity cases usually come down to a "battle of experts." Only with "dermatoglyphic" fingerprinting (the marks on the end of your finger) are the probabilities of the same general order of magnitude. Yet with DNA profiling, defense attorneys have successfully argued that, if scientists cannot agree whether the technology is 99.99999 percent certain or 99.99999999 percent certain, then *it shouldn't be used at all.* 2

DNA profiling begins with the established theory that no two people, except identical twins, have the same genetic makeup. Each cell in the body contains a complete set of genes. A clot of blood, a trace of skin underneath a victim's fingernails, a drop of semen, the follicle attached to a single strand of hair—all contain enough cells to provide the information for a positive or negative match with a criminal suspect. 3

DNA profiling is particularly useful in rapes and murders in which the   4
victim struggles or the criminal leaves behind some trace of tissue or bodily
fluid. A recent newspaper article noted that rapists are now wearing condoms
in 20 percent of all attacks. Although the report attributed this to fear of
AIDS, a more likely explanation is that word is circulating among rapists that
leaving semen at the scene is the equivalent of leaving your calling card.

A complete reading of the human genome is beyond present capabilities.   5
The Human Genome Project has undertaken a 15-year effort to map all
forty-six human chromosomes, and several private firms are trying to short-
circuit the process. One day we may be able to read the genome like a telephone directory. At this point, genetic profiling reads only one ten-thousandth
of the information the genome—just as a fingerprint reads only a tiny fraction
of the body's physical profile. Because of peculiar characteristics of this portion of the genome, however, this tiny fraction has proved significant for
making highly individual identifications.

In 1985, Alec Jeffreys, a geneticist at the University of Leicester, England,   6
proposed making forensic identifications with "junk" DNA, the mysterious,
non-functioning genetic material that makes up about 95 percent of the
human genome. This material serves no known purpose. It may just be
"hitchhiking" from generation to generation without contributing anything to
the organism. Or it may serve as "packing material," protecting the working
genes from harmful mutations, the way newspapers stuffed in a box will
protect its fragile contents.

Junk DNA varies from one individual to the next. Different people have   7
different DNA sequences at their junk sites. In addition, these characteristic
sequences repeat themselves a different number of times in different people—
a phenomenon called "variable number tandem repeats" (VNTRs). One
person may have only one repetition at his junk site, while another may have
two dozen. Most sites have more than a hundred known variations, which are
called "alleles."

Other genetic markers such as hair color, height, and weight tend to   8
vary by population. People living near the equator, for example, generally
have darker skin, while people in cold climates generally grow bulkier to conserve heat. VNTRs, however—like fingerprints and blood types—appear to
vary randomly across populations, with no ethnic or racial associations.

In 1986, Jeffreys proposed that VNTRs could be used for criminal iden-   9
tifications. He invented a "multi-locus" molecular probe that surveyed about
fifteen to twenty VNTR sites, masuring their varying lengths. The chances
that any two people would have the same variation at one site is about 1-
in–50. The chance that they would match up at *every* one of the fifteen to
twenty sites is well beyond 1-in–1-trillion. (The whole earth's population is
only 5–6 billion.)

The test is now used in paternity suits. In criminal cases, however, "multi-   10
locus" probes did not always prove practical. "The difficulty is that we rarely
have enough genetic material in the sample," says Mark Stolorow, director of
operations at Cellmark Diagnostics, which is running the tests in the Simpson

case. "With paternity suits, we can just take blood samples out of someone's arm. But in criminal cases, we're often dealing with a speck of blood found on the sidewalk." Thus, Jeffreys's multi-locus "genetic fingerprinting" (the name is trademarked) was supplanted by a "single-locus" probe, which, given about 8,000 cells (the amount in a drop of blood), can provide a "genetic profile" with somewhat lower degrees of certainty.

In 1987, Jeffreys licensed his technology to Imperial Chemical, a British 11 firm, which set up Cellmark Diagnostics, in Bethesda, Maryland. Lifecodes, Inc., now in Stamford, Connecticut, also went into the business, using a slightly different technology. Eighty different state crime labs, plus the FBI, have also entered the field. About 4,000 samples of DNA were tested last year, at an average of $1,000 per test. The number of probes used depends on how much genetic material is available and how much a prosecutor wants to spend. At five probes, the theoretical chances of two individuals having the same profile are $1\text{-in-}50^5$, or $1\text{-in-}312\text{-million}$.

In actuality, the alleles do not occur with the same frequency. Some are 12 common while others are rare. If you have common alleles, you may match with 2,500 other people in the country ($1\text{-in-}100,000$), while if your alleles are rare, the match may be only $1\text{-in-}1\text{-billion}$. In 1992, Neil J. Risch and Bernard Devlin of Yale University, using the FBI's database, generated 7.6 million genetic fingerprints and found only chance match at the *three*-probe level. At the four-probe level there were none. They estimated the chances of a match for five probes at $1\text{-in-}10\text{-billion}$.

From its inception, DNA profiling has implicated the guilty and exoner- 13 ated the innocent in a way that was previously unthinkable. In an early case in England, two adolescent girls in a small village had been raped and murdered over a three-year period. Police asked males in the village to give a DNA sample for comparison. No matches were found, but it was later reported that one Colin Pitchfork had bribed someone else to substitute a sample for him. Pitchfork was checked again and turned out to be a match. (This case was chronicled by Joseph Wambaugh in *The Blooding*.)

In an early incident in the United States, a young couple were murdered 14 at an isolated campground in Colorado. The woman had been raped and a semen deposit was found. A random check against profiles of known sex criminals turned up a match with a paroled felon in Florida. Once he was under suspicion, eyewitnesses were able to place him near the scene of the crime. The man was tried and convicted.

In another instance, a man in Georgia allegedly killed his 10-year-old 15 daughter after raping her. The defendant claimed the rape was actually committed by his 12-year-old son and that he had accidentally killed the daughter in trying to break up the rape. Genetic profiling was done on both father and son. The semen on the little girl's clothes belonged to the father. (Even for close relatives, the chance of a coincidental match-up is only $1\text{-in-}1,000$.) The man was sentenced to life in prison.

Finally, another 10-year-old girl in Tennessee was molested in her home 16 by a "large black man." A local handyman with a record of child molestation had been seen near the crime by a neighbor, and immediately came under suspicion. A DNA comparison, however, showed the handyman could not have been the attacker. He was promptly dismissed as a suspect.

DNA profiling has proved just as important in clearing the innocent as it has in implicating the guilty. American laboratories report that 30 percent of tests yield negative matches, exonerating innocent suspects who would otherwise have gone to trial. Scotland Yard reports the same percentages.   17

So things stood until 1989, when a handful of lawyers mounted a counterattack. The principal players have been Peter Neufeld, a New York defense attorney, and Barry Scheck, a professor at the Benjamin Cardozo School of Law in New York. "The attitude up to that point had been that DNA fingerprinting was infallible," said Neufeld. "Juries were awed. As one juror put it, 'You can't argue with science.' We decided to show you could." Neufeld has not only carried through the battle in court, he has also succeeded in becoming the resident expert on the subject in the pages of *Scientific American* [See pp. 561–75.] Not surprisingly, Neufeld and Scheck have been hired by the Simpson defense team as its chief DNA experts.   18

The first important case involved Jose Castro, a South Bronx janitor accused of stabbing to death Vilma Ponce and her two-year-old daughter in 1987. When Castro came under suspicion, a speck of blood was found on his watch. The sample was sent to Lifecodes, which said it belonged to the victim. Neufeld and Scheck challenged the admissibility of the evidence on the grounds that the lab work was sloppy and there were too many uncertainties in the technology.   19

Genetic experts from both sides converged on the scene. Before testimony began, Eric S. Lander, of MIT's Whitehead Institute for Biomedical Research, testifying for the defense, and Richard J. Roberts, of Cold Spring Harbor Laboratories, testifying for the prosecution, decided to get together and issue a joint statement. Both were somewhat disenchanted with Lifecodes's performance.   20

In particular, they were concerned that Lifecodes was declaring matches in instances where the X-ray images that read the VNTRs were identical but shifted slightly out of place—a phenomenon called "band-shifting." The laboratories claim it is not a problem. "It's like having two pieces of identical wallpaper that are hung poorly," says Michael Baird, lab director at Lifecodes. "You can see the patterns are identical, but they're slightly displaced."   21

Lander and Roberts argued that band-shifting created too much uncertainty. They also pointed out that Lifecodes had declared one match when the bands were outside the 5 percent range of error. In a blind test submitted by the California Association of Criminal Laboratory Directors, Cellmark had also misread one sample in fifty as a match. In 1989, Judge Gerald Sheindlin threw out the evidence tying the blood of the victim to Castro's watch— although evidence showing Castro himself was not the source of the blood was admitted. Castro pleaded guilty anyway and was sentenced to a lengthy prison term.   22

Two years later, the battle was joined again in an Ohio case. Three mem-   23
bers of the Hell's Angels had killed a young man they mistook for another
gang member. Blood from one of the defendants was found in the victim's
truck. Neufeld, Lander, and other critics squared off against the Department
of Justice, which was supported by two prominent geneticists, Thomas
Caskey of Baylor, and Kenneth Kidd of Yale.

This time the prosecution won, but not before a lot of expert blood had   24
been spilled. Lander—who was embarrassed on the witness stand—turned out
to have received a $28,000 fee for testifying. Neufeld and Scheck counterat-
tacked by accusing Caskey of profiting from the technology because he held
a patent in the field and received a $15,000 annual royalty. Neufeld and
Scheck twice attempted to have the case reopened on the basis of Caskey's
alleged conflict of interest, but the conviction has been allowed to stand.

In 1990, in *Scientific American*, Neufeld laid out the full case against   25
DNA fingerprinting. Neufeld compared DNA profiling to the Greiss test, a
chemical test for nitrates from explosives, which had been used to convict six
Irishmen in an IRA bombing. "It turns out that a variety of common substances such as old playing cards, cigarette packages, lacquer and aerosol
spray will, along with explosives, yield a positive result [in the Greiss test],"
wrote Neufeld. Neufeld then outlined similar potential flaws in DNA profiling: samples were small, DNA could be changed by the presence of impurities
and bacteria, the sample might degenerate in a number of ways. The band-
shifting problem distorted results. Samples could be accidentally switched or
mislabeled—any number of things might happen. As a result of all this an
innocent person might be convicted of a crime.

But Neufeld's opening analogy was misleading. The major problem with   26
the Greiss test was that it produced false positives. Substances other than the
target chemical could give the same results. With DNA analysis, however—
and particularly with the problems mentioned by Neufeld—the only real
problem is false negatives. The chances of an innocent person being implicated are next to nil, but the chances of a guilty person being falsely exonerated are reasonably high.

To simplify, suppose that a suspect has a five-allele code that reads: 27
26–13–12–27–11. The forensic sample, which also contains his genes, has the
same code. Now suppose the forensic sample degenerates, as Neufeld suggested. It can only degenerate *away* from a positive match. (In practice, the lab
would probably call the results "inconclusive," which happens in 10 to 30
percent of all tests.)

Now suppose the suspect is innocent. What are the chances that a foren-   28
sic sample will degenerate *into* his code of 26–13–12–27–11? They are, in
fact, approximately the same as the likelihood that a chance mismatch will
occur in the first place—about 1-in–10-million.

The great irony is that, while arguing that DNA profiling should not be   29
used *against* criminal suspects, Neufeld and Scheck are simultaneously representing 600 condemned prisoners who claim that DNA analysis will prove
they are innocent. Despite the much greater problem of false negatives, the

attorneys argue that DNA evidence is valid when used on the side of the defense.

As a final argument against admissibility, Neufeld also raised what was soon to become the principal objection to DNA profiling: the idea that the genetic markers used in DNA analysis are not randomly distributed by racial groups, that they follow the pattern of hair and eye color, rather than blood types and fingerprints. Thus, when compared against people in a suspect's own racial or ethnic group, the chances of an accidental match-up might be higher. 30

The argument was later expanded by Richard Lewontin, a maverick population geneticist at Harvard and co-founder (with fellow Harvardian Stephen Jay Gould) of the left-wing academic group Science for the People. In 1991, Lewontin co-authored an article in *Science* that argued that patterns at separate VNTR sites might be inherited as a unit, creating similar genetic profiles among small, inbred populations. This "pose[s] a particularly difficult problem for the forensic use of VNTRs if the wrong ethnic group is used as the reference population." In order to avoid chance mistakes, it would be necessary to develop much more data about "subgroups that are likely to be relevant in forensic applications." The authors identified these groups as blacks, Hispanics, and Amerinds, and speculated that the chances of a false match-up within these populations might be as high as 1-in–10,000. 31

Now, 10,000-to-1 is still pretty long odds—certainly enough to erase any element of reasonable doubt where other incriminating evidence is present. But Neufeld wanted to go a step further. Instead of merely increasing the odds, he now argued that there was no "consensus" about DNA technology in the scientific community and therefore the technique should be excluded altogether from criminal trials. Appeals courts in California, Massachusetts, Arizona, Minnesota, and five other states bought the argument and previous convictions were overturned in each state. 32

The unsubtle point behind Lewontin's talk of forensic "relevance" is this: since blacks, Hispanics, and Indians commit a disproportionate share of all crimes, an individual *within* one of these groups may end up being implicated by the newfangled technology. (Actually, the black population has proved to be more genetically diversified than any other racial group.) As a later *Scientific American* article put it, "An innocent suspect racially or ethnically similar to that of a criminal could have an inflated chance of matching a forensic sample—and thus be wrongly convicted." 33

All this assumes that suspects are implicated in crimes solely on the basis of their race—which in some cases they are. Critics of forensic DNA like to point to a Texas case where a murderer was selected out of a small, inbred black population. But in other cases, the logic of "ethnic ceilings" is wholly irrelevant. In the case of the campground murder, for example, the suspect could have been anyone. When he was identified, it was not because of his race, but by a semen sample. Thus it made no sense to compute the odds *only* against his racial group. Wherever factors other than race have been the key to singling out a suspect, ethnic ceilings on DNA profiles are irrelevant. 34

In 1991, the National Academy of Sciences gave the technology a ringing   35
endorsement. In an effort to placate critics, however, the commission recommended that ethnic ceilings be adopted that would give race-adjusted odds for
each positive identification. By purely arbitrary choice, the committee proposed that no allele should be assumed to occur with less than 10 percent frequency—a number that still produces odds of more than 6 million-to–1 at five
probes. Protests arose, and this year the NAS convened a second panel to
reconsider the ceilings hypothesis. In defending O. J. Simpson, Neufeld now
argues that the appointment of this new committee proves that the technology is *still* too controversial to be admitted in court.

The Simpson case, of course, is a good example of the ceilings fallacy.   36
Why is O. J. Simpson a suspect in the killing of Nicole Brown and Ronald
Goldman? Is it because he is black? Is it because somebody spotted a "dark-
skinned intruder" and thought it might be O. J.?

No. Simpson is a suspect because of (1) his previous relationship to one   37
of the victims; (2) his documented record of threats and violence against her;
and (3) his failure to give any convincing account of his whereabouts at the
time of the murder. The other logical choice is that the murder was committed by an unknown intruder, but that intruder does not have to match
Simpson's racial profile. The correct reference group for Simpson's positive
DNA match is the entire population of the United States.

Using the figures compiled from the FBI files by Devlin and Kidd as a   38
conservative estimate, there is a *1-in–7-million* chance that the blood found at
the scene belongs to someone other than O. J. This means that in the entire
population of Los Angeles (3.5 million), there is less than a 50 percent chance
that *any* other individual has Simpson's DNA profile.

Does this seem complicated? Then look at it this way. For the sake of   39
argument, assume there is a 1-in–10,000 chance that Simpson's DNA would
match up with that of another black person, as Lewontin's "ceilings" hypothesis suggests. There is still nothing to prove that the intruder was black. The
longer odds, according to Lewontin, that Simpson's profile matches with
someone of another ethnic group must also be factored into the equation. The
result, once again, is that in all of Southern California, there is probably only
one person who shares Simpson's genetic profile. The odds that Simpson
himself, rather than this unknown person, was the source of the blood at the
crime scene seem reasonably convincing.

So why has this kind of technological advance had such a rough time   40
being accepted in American courtrooms?

The answer can be found in the structure of the American legal profes-   41
sion. Among attorneys who practice criminal law, the overwhelming majority are working on the side of the defense. Of the approximately 200,000
lawyers engaged in criminal work, only an eighth are prosecutors, while the
remainder are representing criminal clients. Career prosecutors are government functionaries who labor at modest salaries. Many defense attorneys
toil in obscurity, but those that are successful are the high rollers of the trade.
Moreover, most young prosecutors—however unwittingly—are *training* to

become defense attorneys. After serving an apprenticeship with the state, they generally—if reluctantly—switch sides. The incentives are overwhelming. A good prosecutor can triple his salary by going into private (defense) practice.

On the civil side, on the other hand, plaintiff attorneys are the high   42
rollers, raking off contingency fees from the nation's escalating damage awards. Civil attorneys on the defense side are generally corporate functionaries. The American Association of Trial Lawyers is dominated by plaintiff attorneys—just as the criminal justice committees of the state legislatures and bar associations are dominated by defense lawyers.

All this has had an enormous impact on American justice. In *The*   43
Litigation Explosion, Walter Olson has documented how the rules of evidence in civil courtrooms have been widely expanded over the past four decades to favor plaintiffs. The process of "discovery," for example, is completely unique to the American courtroom. In other countries, you sue someone on the basis of evidence you already have at hand. In America, plaintiffs can make vague, unspecified charges and then force a defendant to hand over whole truckloads of corporate or personal information so that the plaintiff can wade through them in search of wrongdoing.

"Depositions," by the same token, were once out-of-court interviews   44
limited to people who were on their deathbed or otherwise unable to appear in court. Under pressure from the plaintiff bar, however, the courts turned depositions into a format where plaintiff attorneys can hold private interrogations. If your spouse sues you for divorce, his or her attorney can interrogate you about your sex life, your personal thoughts—anything he deems relevant. You have no "right to remain silent," but can only hire your own attorney. It is not surprising that plaintiff attorneys often refer to themselves as "private attorneys general," empowered by the state to ransack people's belongings and personal lives in search of evidence for civil litigation.

On the other hand, the rules of evidence in *criminal* courts have changed   45
radically in the opposite direction. Since the 1960s, the various "exclusionary rules" have limited the power of the police to investigate anything. Search warrants must specify exactly what the police expect to find *before* they start looking. If something turns up that wasn't listed in the warrant, it may not be admissible as evidence, no matter how incriminating. Interrogations, under the *Miranda* rule, must be held in a formulaic setting, with suspects continually reminded of their right to remain silent or contact an attorney. Many defense attorneys profess that there is no such thing as an "uncoerced confession," since any suspect fully aware of his rights would contact his lawyer, who would tell him not to say anything.

Under these circumstances, it is not surprising to find that many lawyers   46
and law professors now argue that it is useless to seek justice in the criminal courts and that the civil courts are the proper place for redressing criminal damages. . . . The same legal principles that have kept DNA fingerprinting from being used in criminal trials will be turned around to argue for its admissibility in civil courts. In fact, many of the same attorneys will probably end up making the argument.

Still, one can't come away from the issue without the impression that the   47
attorneys opposing DNA evidence are trying to hold back a tidal wave of scientific research. Genetics is the most rapidly exploding field in the scientific
world. Whatever objections can be raised today will probably be overcome
tomorrow. The "polymerase chain reaction" (PCR), a technique that uses a
microbe found in hot springs to "amplify" small amounts of DNA, is now
being used to make identifications with as little as 20 cells. Experts in the field
say the VNTR method may be outdated within three years. If critics do succeed in having the few private labs taken off the job, their work will be taken
over by the FBI and the state crime labs—an outcome that is unlikely to
make opponents any happier. At best, defense attorneys can only hope to continue muddying the waters, grasping at every letter-to-the-editor as proof
that a "scientific consensus" has yet to be reached. . . .

■ ■ ■

Review Questions

1. What are alleles?
2. Why is it generally easier to establish genetic identity in paternity than in
   criminal cases, according to Tucker?
3. Why does Tucker consider Neufeld and Colman's opening analogy of the
   Greiss test (to DNA testing) misleading?
4. Why does Tucker reject the idea that the chances of genetic matches
   need to be calculated differently for different ethnic and racial groups?
5. How does Tucker account for the difficulty that DNA evidence has had
   in being established in criminal cases?

Discussion and Writing Suggestions

1. On what points about the use of DNA as evidence would Neufeld and
   Colman be likely to agree with Tucker? On what points would they
   likely disagree? Explain.
2. After reading both Neufeld-Colman's and Tucker's articles, whose arguments about the reliability of DNA testing do you find more persuasive?
   Explain.
3. In discussing the use of DNA evidence to determine guilt or innocence,
   Tucker cites six specific cases. The final two of these, however—the
   Castro case and the Hell's Angels case—have also been cited by those
   who question the use and reliability of DNA evidence (Castro, in fact,
   was Neufeld's own case). For what purpose does Tucker employ these
   last two cases? To what extent do they contribute to the persuasiveness
   of his argument?
4. In a selection that appears in Chapter 6 of this text, "Left, Right, Center:
   The American Political Spectrum," Donald Lazere classifies *The*

American Spectator (the magazine in which Tucker's article originally appeared) as a "center-to-left conservative" magazine. If you have read at least portions of Chapter 6, see if you can determine qualities and statements in Tucker's article that make it "conservative."

5. Write a critique of Tucker's article. Draw upon your responses to the Review Questions, and follow the procedures for critique covered in Chapter 2 of this text.

■ SYNTHESIS ACTIVITIES

1. Suppose you are writing a survey article on biotechnology for a general audience magazine, such as *Time* or *Atlantic Monthly*. You want to introduce your readers to the subject, tell them what it is and what it may become, and you want to focus, in particular, on the advantages and disadvantages of biotechnology. Drawing on the sources you have read in this chapter, write such an article (i.e., an explanatory synthesis). For background information on the subject you can draw on sources such as Starr and the introduction to this chapter. Other sources, including those by Brownlee et al., Nelkin, Watson, Marshall, Rifkin, Postrel, Neufeld and Colman, and Tucker, offer many case studies illustrating advantages and disadvantages. And, of course, Huxley serves as a dark example of the kind of thing that *could* happen if biotechnology is used for unethical purposes.

2. Write an editorial (i.e., an argument synthesis) arguing that additional regulations need to be placed on biotechnology. Specify the chief problem areas, as you see them, and indicate the regulations needed in order to deal with these problems.

   You may want to begin with a survey of biotechnology (in which you acknowledge its advantages) but then narrow your focus to the problem areas. Categorize the problem areas (e.g., problems for prospective parents, for the workplace, for the courtroom, for the commercial applications of biotechnology). The suggested regulations—and explanations of why they are necessary—might be discussed throughout the editorial or saved for the end.

   In developing your editorial, devote one paragraph to Virginia Postrel's position (that the free market, not government regulations, should determine which genetic technologies get used). Devote another paragraph to rebutting her position.

3. *Brave New World* represents one artist's view of how scientific knowledge might be abused to ensure social stability and conformity. Huxley focused on the possibility of dividing fertilized human ova into identical parts and then conditioning the ova before "birth." Write a short story (or a play or screenplay) that represents your own nightmare vision. You may want to focus on other aspects of genetic engineering: the problem of forced genetic testing, of eugenics (creating "perfect"

people or eliminating "imperfect" ones), of fostering uniformity among the population, of some fantastic commercial application of bioengineering, or even of some aspect of cloning (among the films dealing with cloning are Ira Levin's *The Boys from Brazil*, Woody Allen's *Sleeper*, and Steven Spielberg's *Jurassic Park*).

Decide whether the story is to be essentially serious or comic (satirical)—or something in between. Create characters (try to avoid caricatures) who will enact the various aspects of the problem, as you see it. And create a social and physical setting appropriate to the story you want to tell.

4. Write an article for a magazine such as *Newsweek* or *Time* or *U.S. News & World Report* on the current status of biotechnology—as of August 2050. Try to make the article generally upbeat (unlike the nightmare vision called for in the previous question), but be frank also about the problems that have been encountered, as well as the problems that remain. Refer, at some point in your article, to views of biotechnology from the late 1980s and the early 1990s to establish some basis for comparison between what they thought "then" and what they think "now." You might model your article on the piece by Brownlee, Cook, and Hardigg or on any contemporary news magazine article of comparable scope. The language should be lively and vivid, and you should include as many "facts" as you can think of. Study your model articles for ideas about how to organize your material.

5. The genome research being conducted in Iceland is made possible by the investments of a pharmaceutical company, which has bet that research will reveal the genetic foundations of certain diseases that can then be corrected with specially designed drugs. Certainly, without private investment, human genome research would proceed far more slowly than it is proceeding at present. How comfortable are you with the commercial direction that human genome research has taken? Is the DNA map that researchers seek "larger" than the interests of particular pharmaceutical companies? What kinds of profits (if any) should companies be making in this field? Write an essay in which you take a position on this topic, drawing especially on the selections by Watson, Marshall, Rifkin, and Postrel.

6. Imagining that you are writing for a legal periodical, compose a two-to-three-page editorial arguing either that the forensic use of DNA should be expanded or that it should be further restricted. Draw primarily on Neufeld-Colman and Tucker, though you will probably want to supplement your sources by doing some additional research on the subject.

▪ RESEARCH ACTIVITIES

1. The main focal points of the debate over genetic engineering and testing have been (1) whether the new biotechnologies are safe and ethical; (2) whether they will benefit agriculture and food processing; (3) whether they require stricter regulation (and if so, what kind); (4) whether genetic testing (or the use of genetic testing) by employers and insurance companies is ethical; (5) whether genetic testing of fetuses is ethical; (6) whether work should proceed on the Human Genome Project and/or the Human Genome Diversity Project; (7) whether geneticists should work on biological weapons. Select *one* of these areas and research the current status of the debate.

   In addition to relevant articles, see Jeremy Rifkin, *Algeny* (1983) and *Declaration of a Heretic* (1985); Jack Doyle, *Altered Harvest* (1985); Brian Stableford, *Future Man* (1984); Steve Olson, *Biotechnology: An Industry Comes of Age* (1986); Richard Noel Re, *Bioburst* (1986); Edward J. Sylvester and Lynn C. Klotz, *The Gene Age* (1987); Joseph Fletcher, *Ethics of Genetic Control* (1988); Gerald R. Campbell, *Biotechnology: An Introduction* (1988); Charles Pilar and Keith R. Yamamoto, *Gene Wars* (1988); David Suzuki and Peter Knudtson, *Genetics* (1989); Andrew Linzey, *Slavery: Human and Animal* (1988); Monsanto Company, *Agriculture and the New Biology* (1989); and Daniel J. Kevles and Leroy Hood, *The Code of Codes: Scientific and Social Issues in the Human Genome Project* (1992).

2. Investigate the latest developments in DNA "fingerprint" technology. How has such technology been employed in recent criminal cases? What is the legal status of such technology at both the federal and the local levels? What ethical issues are at stake, according to proponents and opponents of DNA fingerprinting?

3. In August 1992, researchers announced that they had managed through genetic engineering to produce mice that developed cystic fibrosis. Scientists believed that by studying the course of this disease in mice, they would be able to devise new therapies for the treatment of this usually fatal disease in humans. Follow up on either this development or some other development involving the genetic engineering of laboratory animals to further medical research. Describe what is involved in the procedure, how it was developed, the results to date, and the ethical debate that may have ensued about its practice.

4. Research and discuss some aspect of the early history of genetic engineering as it developed in the 1970s. Begin with a survey of Watson and Crick's work with DNA in the early 1950s, describe some of the early experiments in this area, discuss some of the concerns expressed both by scientists and laypersons, and cover in some detail the

Asilomar (California) Conference of 1975 at which scientists worked out guidelines for future research.

5. Research some of the most significant recent advances in biotechnology, categorize them, and report on your finding. You may also wish to consider the Human Genome Project. Use some of the same categories suggested in Research Activity 1, but focus here less on the debate (which you need not ignore) than on what is currently being done, on who is doing it, on the obstacles yet to overcome, and on the anticipated benefits on the research and development.

6. In 1989 James D. Watson was appointed to head NIH's Human Genome Project. Watson's appointment and his subsequent work as director of the project generated some controversy. Research Watson's professional activities since his discovery with Francis Crick of the structure of DNA, focusing on his more recent activities. See especially, the article on Watson, "The Double Helix," which appeared in *The New Republic*, July 9 and 16, 1990. How do Watson's professional colleagues—and others—assess his more recent work?

7. Write a paper on biotechnology critic Jeremy Rifkin and the critical reaction to his activities and his books. Consult the *Reader's Guide to Periodical Literature* and locate important articles by and about Rifkin during the past decade or so. Locate Rifkin's books and survey them. Most importantly, look up reviews of Rifkin's books, starting with the listings in *Book Review Digest*. (This is an annual index that lists reviews during a given year and provides brief excerpts from the most important reviews.)

   Begin your paper by summarizing Rifkin's life and work thus far. (Your introductory paragraphs should probably focus on the controversy surrounding Rifkin.) Then focus on the reaction to his work. You may want to divide your paper into sections on positive and negative reactions; or you may want to organize by critical reviews of his various books and activities. At the conclusion, develop an overall assessment of the significance and value of Rifkin's work.

8. Research the current status of either the Human Genome Project or the Human Genome Diversity Project. To what extent has the project you selected made progress in achieving its goals?

9. Research one of the cases (including the Simpson case) mentioned in either Neufeld and Colman's article ("When Science Takes the Witness Stand") or Tucker's ("DNA in Court"), and explain how DNA matching was a significant factor in the presentation and outcome of the case, or in a subsequent appeal. *Or* review several cases in which DNA was a factor, and focus on the relationships between them, in terms of the use of genetic testing and matching.

10. In asserting that both geneticists and journalists have been guilty of making grandiose claims about genetic research, Dorothy Nelkin cites the kind of metaphors ("genetic instructions," "program," "medical crystal ball," etc.) that geneticists use to characterize their work.

Research several recent articles about genetic research or developments in newspapers and magazines and see if you can find enough evidence to support Nelkin's charges. Or do her concerns appear to be overblown? Your sources should include statements by geneticists.

11. Since the mid-1970s, genetic technology has been regulated not only by scientists themselves, working as a body, but also by federal agencies, such as the White House Office of Science and Technology Policy; the U.S. Department of Agriculture (USDA: overseeing genetically engineered plants); the NIH's Recombinant DNA Advisory Committee (RAC: overseeing laboratory research); the Environmental Protection Agency (EPA: approving field testing of commercial products affecting the environment); and the Food and Drug Administration (FDA: approving animal and human pharmaceuticals). Research and report on some of the most significant regulations imposed on the biotechnology industry, consider the views of critics and of scientists themselves, and indicate your own position (and possibly some of your own proposals) on existing and additional regulations.

12. If your college or university has scientists on its faculty who are working on DNA research, interview them to find out what they are doing. Ask them how they feel about some of the ethical issues covered in this chapter. Ask them to recommend references in the professional literature that will enable you to understand more fully the aims of their research; then consult some of these references and use them to provide context for your discussion of this research.

13. Conduct and write a summary report on student attitudes on biotechnology and write a report based on this survey. Devise questions that focus on the main areas of controversy (see Research Activity 1). Phrase your questions in a way that allows a range of responses (perhaps on a scale of 1 to 5, or using modifiers such as "strongly agree," "agree somewhat," "disagree somewhat," "strongly disagree"); don't ask for responses that require a yes/no or approve/disapprove response. (See "Interviews and Surveys," Chapter 5.) Attempt to correlate the responses to such variables as academic major, student status (lower division, upper division, graduate), gender, ethnic background, geographical area of origin (urban, suburban, rural). Determine whether respondents personally know someone with a disease for which a genetic cure is either possible or under consideration. Determine also how much prior knowledge of biotechnology your respondents have.

Fairy Tales: A Closer Look at "Cinderella"

"Once upon a time. . . ." Millions of children around the world have listened to these (or similar) words. And, once upon a time, such words were magic archways into a world of entertainment and fantasy for children and their parents. But in our own century, fairy tales have come under the scrutiny of anthropologists, linguists, educators, psychologists, and psychiatrists, as well as literary critics, who have come to see them as a kind of social genetic code—a means by which cultural values are transmitted from one generation to the next. Some people, of course, may scoff at the idea that charming tales like "Cinderella" or "Snow White" are anything other than charming tales, at the idea that fairy tales may really be ways of inculcating young and impressionable children with culturally approved values. But even if they are not aware of it, adults and children use fairy tales in complex and subtle ways. We can, perhaps, best illustrate this by examining variants of a single tale—"Cinderella."

"Cinderella" appears to be the best-known fairy tale in the world. In 1892, Marian Roalfe Cox published 345 variants of the story, the first systematic study of a single folktale. In her collection, Cox gathered stories from throughout Europe in which elements or motifs of "Cinderella" appeared, often mixed with motifs of other tales. All told, more than 700 variants exist throughout the world—in Europe, Africa, Asia, and North and South America. Scholars debate the extent to which such a wide distribution is explained by population migrations or by some universal quality of imagination that would allow people at different times and places to create essentially the same story. But for whatever reason, folklorists agree that "Cinderella" has appealed to storytellers and listeners everywhere.

The great body of folk literature, including fairy tales, comes to us from an oral tradition. Written literature, produced by a particular author, is preserved through the generations just as the author recorded it. By contrast, oral literature changes with every telling: The childhood game comes to mind in which one child whispers a sentence into the ear of another; by the time the second child repeats the sentence to a third, and the third to a fourth (and so on), the sentence has changed considerably. And so it is with oral literature, with the qualification that these stories are also changed quite consciously when a teller wishes to add or delete material.

   The modern student of folk literature finds her- or himself in the position of *reading* as opposed to hearing a tale. The texts we read tend to be of two types, which are at times difficult to distinguish. We might read a faithful transcription of an oral tale or a tale of *literary* origin—a tale that was originally written (as a short story would be), not spoken, but that nonetheless may contain elements of an oral account. In this chapter, we include tales of both oral and literary origin. Jakob and Wilhelm Grimm published their transcription of "Cinderella" in 1812. The version by Charles Perrault (1697) is difficult to classify as the transcription of an oral source, since he may have heard the story originally but appears (according to Bruno Bettelheim) to have "freed it of all content he considered vulgar, and refined its other features to make the product suitable to be told at court." Of unquestionable literary origin are the Walt Disney version of the story, based on Perrault's text; Anne Sexton's poem; Tanith Lee's "When the Clock Strikes," a version in which the Cinderella figure is a witch bent on avenging the murder of her royal family. We conclude the set of variants with a report on a new, revisionist movie version of "Cinderella," *Ever After* (1998), directed by Andy Tennant, in which the heroine is a self-reliant, strong character.

   Preceding these nine variants of "Cinderella," we present a general reading on fairy-tale literature by Stith Thompson. Following the variants are three selections that respond directly to the tale. We hear from Bruno Bettelheim, who, following psychoanalytic theory, finds in "Cinderella" a "Story of Sibling Rivalry and Oedipal Conflicts." The chapter concludes with two feminist perspectives on "Cinderella": historian Karol Kelley examines two filmed versions of Perrault's rendering of the tale, Disney's animated version (1949) and *Pretty Woman* (1990); and Nobel laureate Toni Morrison, in an address at Barnard College, calls on her women listeners to treat one another more humanely than the stepsisters treated Cinderella.

   A note on terminology: "Cinderella," "Jack and the Beanstalk," "Little Red Riding Hood," and the like are commonly referred to as fairy tales, although, strictly speaking, they are not. True fairy tales concern a "class of supernatural beings of diminutive size, who in popular belief are said to possess magical powers and to have great influence for good or evil over the affairs of humans" (*Oxford English Dictionary*). "Cinderella" and the others just mentioned concern no beings of diminutive size, although extraordinary, magical events do occur in the stories. Folklorists would be more apt to call these stories "wonder tales." We retain the traditional "fairy tale," with the proviso that in popular usage the term is misapplied. You may notice that the authors in this chapter use the terms "folktale" and "fairy tale" interchangeably. The expression "folktale" refers to *any* story conceived orally and passed on in an oral tradition. Thus, "folktale" is a generic term that incorporates both fairy tales and wonder tales.

Universality of the Folktale

STITH THOMPSON

Folklorists travel around the world, to cities and rural areas alike, recording the facts, traditions, and beliefs that characterize ethnic groups. Some folklorists record and compile jokes; others do the same with insults or songs. Still others, like Stith Thompson, devote their professional careers to studying tales. And, as it turns out, there are many aspects of stories and storytelling worth examining. Among them: the art of narrative—how tellers captivate their audiences; the social and religious significance of tale telling; the many types of tales that are told; the many variants, worldwide, of single tales (such as "Cinderella"). In a preface to one of his own books, Thompson raises the broad questions and the underlying assumptions that govern the folklorist's study of tales. We begin this chapter with Thompson's overview to set a context for the variants of "Cinderella" that you will read.

Note the ways that Thompson's approach to fairy tales differs from yours. Whether or not you're conscious of having an approach, you do have one: Perhaps you regard stories such as "Cinderella" as entertainment. Fine—this is a legitimate point of view, but it's only one of several ways of regarding folktales. Stith Thompson claims that there's much to learn in studying tales. He assumes, as you might not, that tales should be objects of study as well as entertainment.

Stith Thompson (1885–1976) led a distinguished life as an American educator, folklorist, editor, and author. Between 1921 and 1955, he was a professor of folklore and English, and later dean of the Graduate School and Distinguished Service Professor at Indiana University, Bloomington. Five institutions have awarded Thompson honorary doctorates for his work in folklore studies. He published numerous books on the subject, including European Tales Among North American Indians *(1919),* The Types of the Folktales *(1928), and* Tales of the North American Indian *(1929). He is best known for his six-volume* Motif Index of Folk Literature *(1932–1937; 1955–1958, 2nd ed.).*

The teller of stories has everywhere and always found eager listeners. Whether   1
his tale is the mere report of a recent happening, a legend of long ago, or an
elaborately contrived fiction, men and women have hung upon his words and
satisfied their yearnings for information or amusement, for incitement to
heroic deeds, for religious edification, or for release from the overpowering
monotony of their lives. In villages of central Africa, in outrigger boats on the
Pacific, in the Australian bush, and within the shadow of Hawaiian volcanoes,
tales of the present and of the mysterious past, of animals and gods and
heroes, and of men and women like themselves, hold listeners in their spell or
enrich the conversation of daily life. So it is also in Eskimo igloos under the
light of seal-oil lamps, in the tropical jungles of Brazil, and by the totem
poles of the British Columbian coast. In Japan too, and China and India, the

priest and the scholar, the peasant and the artisan all join in their love of a good story and their honor for the man who tells it well.

When we confine our view to our own occidental world, we see that for at least three or four thousand years, and doubtless for ages before, the art of the story-teller has been cultivated in every rank of society. Odysseus entertains the court of Alcinous with the marvels of his adventures. Centuries later we find the long-haired page reading nightly from interminable chivalric romances to entertain his lady while her lord is absent on his crusade. Medieval priests illustrate sermons by anecdotes old and new, and only sometimes edifying. The old peasant, now as always, whiles away the winter evening with tales of wonder and adventure and the marvelous workings of fate. Nurses tell children of Goldilocks or the House that Jack Built. Poets write epics and novelists novels. Even now the cinemas and theaters bring their stories directly to the ear and eye through the voices and gestures of actors. And in the smoking-rooms of sleeping cars and steamships and at the banquet table the oral anecdote flourishes in a new age.

In the present work we are confining our interest to a relatively narrow scope, the traditional prose tale—the story which has been handed down from generation to generation either in writing or by word of mouth. Such tales are, of course, only one of the many kinds of story material, for, in addition to them, narrative comes to us in verse as ballads and epics, and in prose as histories, novels, dramas, and short stories. We shall have little to do with the songs of bards, with the ballads of the people, or with poetic narrative in general, though stories themselves refuse to be confined exclusively to either prose or verse forms. But even with verse and all other forms of prose narrative put aside, we shall find that in treating the traditional prose tale—the folktale—our quest will be ambitious enough and will take us to all parts of the earth and to the very beginnings of history.

Although the term "folktale" is often used in English to refer to the "household tale" or "fairy tale" (the German *Märchen*), such as "Cinderella" or "Snow White," it is also legitimately employed in a much broader sense to include all forms of prose narrative, written or oral, which have come to be handed down through the years. In this usage the important fact is the traditional nature of the material. In contrast to the modern story writer's striving after originality of plot and treatment, the teller of a folktale is proud of his ability to hand on that which he has received. He usually desires to impress his readers or hearers with the fact that he is bringing them something that has the stamp of good authority, that the tale was heard from some great story-teller or from some aged person who remembered it from old days.

So it was until at least the end of the Middle Ages with writers like Chaucer, who carefully quoted authorities for their plots—and sometimes even invented originals so as to dispel the suspicion that some new and unwarranted story was being foisted on the public. Though the individual genius of such writers appears clearly enough, they always depended on authority, not only for their basic theological opinions but also for the plots of their stories. A study of the sources of Chaucer or Boccaccio takes one directly into the stream of traditional narrative.

The great written collections of stories characteristic of India, the Near East, the classical world, and Medieval Europe are almost entirely traditional. They copy and recopy. A tale which gains favor in one collection is taken over into others, sometimes intact and sometimes with changes of plot or characterization. The history of such a story, passing it may be from India to Persia and Arabia and Italy and France and finally to England, copied and changed from manuscript to manuscript, is often exceedingly complex. For it goes through the hands of both skilled and bungling narrators and improves or deteriorates at nearly every retelling. However well or poorly such a story may be written down, it always attempts to preserve a tradition, and old tale with the authority of antiquity to give it interest and importance. 6

If use of the term "folktale" to include such literary narratives seems somewhat broad, it can be justified on practical grounds if on no other, for it is impossible to make a complete separation of the written and the oral traditions. Often, indeed, their interrelation is so close and so inextricable as to present one of the most baffling problems the folklore scholar encounters. They differ somewhat in their behavior, it is true, but they are alike in their disregard of originality of plot and of pride of authorship. 7

Nor is complete separation of these two kinds of narrative tradition by any means necessary for their understanding. The study of the oral tale . . . will be valid so long as we realize that stories have frequently been taken down from the lips of unlettered taletellers and have entered the great literary collections. In contrary fashion, fables of Aesop, anecdotes from Homer, and saints' legends, not to speak of fairy tales read from Perrault or Grimm, have entered the oral stream and all their association with the written or printed page has been forgotten. Frequently a story is taken from the people, recorded in a literary document, carried across continents or preserved through centuries, and then retold to a humble entertainer who adds it to his repertory. 8

It is clear then that the oral story need not always have been oral. But when it once habituates itself to being passed on by word of mouth it undergoes the same treatment as all other tales at the command of the raconteur. It becomes something to tell to an audience, or at least to a listener, not something to read. Its effects are no longer produced indirectly by association with words written or printed on a page, but directly through facial expression and gesture and repetition and recurrent patterns that generations have tested and found effective. 9

This oral art of taletelling is far older than history, and it is not bounded by one continent or one civilization. Stories may differ in subject from place to place, the conditions and purposes of taletelling may change as we move from land to land or from century to century, and yet everywhere it ministers to the same basic social and individual needs. The call for entertainment to fill in the hours of leisure has found most peoples very limited in their resources, 10 and except where modern urban civilization has penetrated deeply they have found the telling of stories one of the most satisfying of pastimes. Curiosity about the past has always brought eager listeners to tales of the long ago which supply the simple man with all he knows of the history of his folk. Legends grow with the telling, and often a great heroic past evolves to gratify vanity and tribal pride. Religion also has played a mighty role everywhere in the encouragement of the narrative art, for the religious mind has tried to understand beginnings and for ages has told stories of ancient days and sacred beings. Often whole cosmologies have unfolded themselves in these legends, and hierarchies of gods and heroes.

World-wide also are many of the structural forms which oral narrative   11
has assumed. The hero tale, the explanatory legend, the animal anecdote—certainly these at least are present everywhere. Other fictional patterns are limited to particular areas of culture and act by their presence or absence as an effective index of the limits of the area concerned. The study of such limitations has not proceeded far, but it constitutes an interesting problem for the student of these oral narrative forms.

Even more tangible evidence of the ubiquity and antiquity of the folktale   12
is the great similarity in the content of stories of the most varied peoples. The same tale types and narrative motifs are found scattered over the world in most puzzling fashion. A recognition of these resemblances and an attempt to account for them brings the scholar closer to an understanding of the nature of human culture. He must continually ask himself, "Why do some peoples borrow tales and some lend? How does the tale serve the needs of the social group?" When he adds to his task an appreciation of the aesthetic and practical urge toward storytelling, and some knowledge of the forms and devices, stylistic and histrionic, that belong to this ancient and widely practiced art, he finds that he must bring to his work more talents than one man can easily possess. Literary critics, anthropologists, historians, psychologists, and aestheticians are all needed if we are to hope to know why folktales are made, how they are invented, what art is used in their telling, how they grow and change and occasionally die.

■ ■ ■

Review Questions

1. According to Thompson, what are the reasons people consistently venerate a good storyteller?
2. What does Thompson state as features that distinguish a "folktale" from modern types of fiction?
3. How does religion help encourage the existence of folktale art?
4. What is a strong piece of evidence for the great antiquity and universality of folktales?

Discussion and Writing Suggestions

1. Based on Thompson's explanation of the qualities of oral folktales, what do you feel is gained by the increasing replacement of this form of art and entertainment by TV?

2. What do you suppose underlies the apparent human need to tell stories, given that storytelling is practiced in every culture known?

3. Interview older members of your family, asking them about stories they were told as children. As best you can, record a story. Then examine your work. How does it differ from the version you heard? Write an account of your impressions on the differences between an oral and written rendering of a story. Alternately, you might record a story and then speculate on what the story might mean in the experiences of the family member who told it to you.

Nine Variants of "Cinderella"

It comes as a surprise to many that there exist Chinese, French, German, African, and Native American versions of the popular "Cinderella," along with 700 other versions worldwide. Which is the real *"Cinderella"? The question is misleading in that each version is "real" for a particular group of people in a particular place and time. Certainly, you can judge among versions and select the most appealing. You can also draw comparison. Indeed, the grouping of the stories that we present here invites comparisons. A few of the categories you might wish to consider as you read:*

- *Cinderella's innocence or guilt, concerning the treatment she receives at the hands of her stepsisters*
- *Cinderella's passive (or active) nature*
- *Sibling rivalry—the relationship of Cinderella to her sisters*
- *The father's role*
- *The rule that Cinderella must return from the ball by midnight*
- *Levels of violence*
- *Presence or absence of the fairy godmother*
- *Cinderella's relationship with the prince*
- *Characterization of the prince*
- *The presence of Cinderella's dead mother*
- *The function of magic*
- *The ending*

Cinderella

CHARLES PERRAULT

Charles Perrault (1628–1703) was born in Paris of a prosperous family. He prac-
ticed law for a short time and then devoted his attentions to a job in government,
in which capacity he was instrumental in promoting the advancement of the arts
and sciences and in securing pensions for writers, both French and foreign.
Perrault is best known as a writer for his Contes de ma mère l'oie (Mother Goose
Tales), *a collection of fairy tales taken from popular folklore. He is widely sus-*
pected of having changed these stories in an effort to make them more acceptable
to his audience—members of the French court.

Once there was a nobleman who took as his second wife the proudest and   1
haughtiest woman imaginable. She had two daughters of the same character,
who took after their mother in everything. On his side, the husband had a
daughter who was sweetness itself; she inherited this from her mother, who
had been the most kindly of women.

No sooner was the wedding over than the stepmother showed her ill-   2
nature. She could not bear the good qualities of the young girl, for they made
her own daughters seem even less likable. She gave her the roughest work of
the house to do. It was she who washed the dishes and the stairs, who cleaned
out Madam's room and the rooms of the two Misses. She slept right at the top
of the house, in an attic, on a lumpy mattress, while her sisters slept in pan-
elled rooms where they had the most modern beds and mirrors in which they
could see themselves from top to toe. The poor girl bore everything in
patience and did not dare to complain to her father. He would only have
scolded her, for he was entirely under his wife's thumb.

When she had finished her work, she used to go into the chimney-corner   3
and sit down among the cinders, for which reason she was usually known in
the house as Cinderbottom. Her younger stepsister, who was not so rude as
the other, called her Cinderella. However, Cinderella, in spite of her ragged
clothes, was still fifty times as beautiful as her sisters, superbly dressed though
they were.

One day the King's son gave a ball, to which everyone of good family was   4
invited. Our two young ladies received invitations, for they cut quite a figure
in the country. So there they were, both feeling very pleased and very busy
choosing the clothes and the hair-styles which would suit them best. More
work for Cinderella, for it was she who ironed her sisters' underwear and gof-
fered their linen cuffs. Their only talk was of what they would wear.

"I," said the elder, "shall wear my red velvet dress and my collar of   5
English lace."

"I," said the younger, "shall wear just my ordinary skirt; but, to make 6
up, I shall put on my gold-embroidered cape and my diamond clasp, which is
quite out of the common."

The right hairdresser was sent for to supply double-frilled coifs, and 7
patches were bought from the right patch-maker. They called Cinderella to
ask her opinion, for she had excellent taste. She made useful suggestions and
even offered to do their hair for them. They accepted willingly.

While she was doing it, they said to her: 8

"Cinderella, how would you like to go to the ball?" 9

"Oh dear, you are making fun of me. It wouldn't do for me." 10

"You are quite right. It would be a joke. People would laugh if they saw 11
a Cinderbottom at the ball."

Anyone else would have done their hair in knots for them, but she had a 12
sweet nature, and she finished it perfectly. For two days they were so excited
that they ate almost nothing. They broke a good dozen laces trying to tight-
en their stays to make their waists slimmer, and they were never away from
their mirrors.

At last the great day arrived. They set off, and Cinderella watched them 13
until they were out of sight. When she could no longer see them, she began to
cry. Her godmother, seeing her all in tears, asked what was the matter.

"If only I could . . . If only I could . . ." She was weeping so much that she 14
could not go on.

Her godmother, who was a fairy, said to her: "If only you could go to the 15
ball, is that it?"

"Alas, yes," Said Cinderella with a sigh. 16

"Well," said the godmother, "be a good girl and I'll get you there." 17

She took her into her room and said: "Go into the garden and get me a 18
pumpkin."

Cinderella hurried out and cut the best she could find and took it to her 19
godmother, but she could not understand how this pumpkin would get her to
the ball. Her godmother hollowed it out, leaving only the rind, and then
tapped it with her wand and immediately it turned into a magnificent gilded
coach.

Then she went to look in her mouse-trap and found six mice all alive in 20
it. She told Cinderella to raise the door of the trap a little, and as each mouse
came out she gave it a tap with her wand and immediately it turned into a fine
horse. That made a team of six horses, each of fine mouse-coloured grey.

While she was wondering how she would make a coachman, Cinderella 21
said to her:

"I will go and see whether there is a rat in the rat-trap, we could make a 22
coachman of him."

"You are right," said the godmother. "Run and see." 23

Cinderella brought her the rat-trap, in which there were three big rats. 24
The fairy picked out one of them because of his splendid whiskers and, when

she had touched him, he turned into a fat coachman, with the finest mous-
taches in the district.

Then she said: "Go into the garden and you will find six lizards behind   25
the watering-can. Bring them to me."

As soon as Cinderella had brought them, her godmother changed them   26
into six footmen, who got up behind the coach with their striped liveries, and
stood in position there as though they had been doing it all their lives.

Then the fairy said to Cinderella: 27

"Well, that's to go to the ball in. Aren't you pleased?"   28

"Yes. But am I to go like this, with my ugly clothes?"   29

Her godmother simply touched her with her wand and her clothes were   30
changed in an instant into a dress of gold and silver cloth, all sparkling with
precious stones. Then she gave her a pair of glass slippers, most beautifully
made.

So equipped, Cinderella got into the coach: but her godmother warned   31
her above all not to be out after midnight, telling her that, if she stayed at the
ball a moment later, her coach would turn back into a pumpkin, her horses
into mice, her footmen into lizards, and her fine clothes would become rags
again.

She promised her godmother that she would leave the ball before mid-   32
night without fail, and she set out, beside herself with joy.

The King's son, on being told that a great princess whom no one knew   33
had arrived, ran out to welcome her. He handed her down from the coach and
led her into the hall where his guests were. A sudden silence fell; the dancing
stopped, the violins ceased to play, the whole company stood fascinated by
the beauty of the unknown princess. Only a low murmur was heard: "Ah,
how lovely she is!" The King himself, old as he was, could not take his eyes
off her and kept whispering to the Queen that it was a long time since he had
seen such a beautiful and charming person. All the ladies were absorbed in
noting her clothes and the way her hair was dressed, so as to order the same
things for themselves the next morning, provided that fine enough materials
could be found, and skillful enough craftsmen.

The King's son placed her in the seat of honour, and later led her out to   34
dance. She danced with such grace that she won still more admiration. An
excellent supper was served, but the young Prince was too much occupied in
gazing at her to eat anything. She went and sat next to her sisters and treated them with great courtesy, offering them oranges and lemons which the
Prince had given her. They were astonished, for they did not recognize her.

While they were chatting together, Cinderella heard the clock strike a   35
quarter to twelve. She curtsied low to the company and left as quickly as she
could.

As soon as she reached home, she went to her godmother and, having   36
thanked her, said that she would very much like to go again to the ball on the
next night—for the Prince had begged her to come back. She was in the

middle of telling her godmother about all the things that had happened, when the two sisters came knocking at the door. Cinderella went to open it.

"How late you are! she said, rubbing her eyes and yawning and stretch-   37
ing as though she had just woken up (though since they had last seen each other she had felt very far from sleepy).

"If you had been at the ball," said one of the sisters, "you would not have   38
felt like yawning. There was a beautiful princess there, really ravishingly beautiful. She was most attentive to us. She gave us oranges and lemons."

Cinderella could have hugged herself. She asked them the name of the   39
princess, but they replied that no one knew her, that the King's son was much troubled about it, and that he would give anything in the world to know who she was. Cinderella smiled and said to them:

"So she was very beautiful? Well, well, how lucky you are! Couldn't I see   40
her? Please, Miss Javotte, do lend me that yellow dress which you wear about the house."

"Really," said Miss Javotte, "what an idea! Lend one's dress like that to   41
a filthy Cinderbottom! I should have to be out of my mind."

Cinderella was expecting this refusal and she was very glad when it   42
came, for she would have been in an awkward position if her sister really had lent her her frock.

On the next day the two sisters went to the ball, and Cinderella too, but   43
even more splendidly dressed than the first time. The King's son was con-stantly at her side and wooed her the whole evening. The young girl was enjoying herself so much that she forgot her godmother's warning. She heard the clock striking the first stroke of midnight when she thought that it was still hardly eleven. She rose and slipped away as lightly as a roe-deer. The Prince followed her, but he could not catch her up. One of her glass slippers fell off, and the Prince picked it up with great care.

Cinderella reached home quite out of breath, with no coach, no footmen,   44
and wearing her old clothes. Nothing remained of all her finery, except one of her little slippers, the fellow to the one which she had dropped. The guards at the palace gate were asked if they had not seen a princess go out. They answered that they had seen no one go out except a very poorly dressed girl, who looked more like a peasant than a young lady.

When the two sisters returned from the ball, Cinderella asked them if   45
they had enjoyed themselves again, and if the beautiful lady had been there. They said that she had, but that she had run away when it struck midnight, and so swiftly that she had lost one of her glass slippers, a lovely little thing. The Prince had picked it up and had done nothing but gaze at it for the rest of the ball, and undoubtedly he was very much in love with the beautiful person to whom it belonged.

They were right, for a few days later the King's son had it proclaimed to   46
the sound of trumpets that he would marry the girl whose foot exactly fitted the slipper. They began by trying it on the various princesses, then on the duchesses and on all the ladies of the Court, but with no success. It was

brought to the two sisters, who did everything possible to force their feet into the slipper, but they could not manage it. Cinderella, who was looking on, recognized her own slipper, and said laughing:

"Let me see if it would fit me!" 47

Her sisters began to laugh and mock at her. But the gentleman who was 48 trying on the slipper looked closely at Cinderella and, seeing that she was very beautiful, said that her request was perfectly reasonable and that he had instructions to try it on every girl. He made Cinderella sit down and, raising the slipper to her foot, he found that it slid on without difficulty and fitted like a glove.

Great was the amazement of the two sisters, but it became greater still 49 when Cinderella drew from her pocket the second little slipper and put it on her other foot. Thereupon the fairy godmother came in and, touching Cinderella's clothes with her wand, made them even more magnificent than on the previous days.

Then the two sisters recognized her as the lovely princess whom they had 50 met at the ball. They flung themselves at her feet and begged her forgiveness for all the unkind things which they had done to her. Cinderella raised them up and kissed them, saying that she forgave them with all her heart and asking them to love her always. She was taken to the young Prince in the fine clothes which she was wearing. He though her more beautiful than ever and a few days later he married her. Cinderella, who was as kind as she was beautiful, invited her two sisters to live in the palace and married them, on the same day, to two great noblemen of the Court.

Ashputtle

JAKOB AND WILHELM GRIMM

Jakob Grimm (1785–1863) and Wilhelm Grimm (1786–1859) are best known today for the 200 folktales they collected from oral sources and reworked in Kinder- und Hausmärchen *(popularly known as* Grimm's Fairy Tales*), which has been translated into seventy languages. The techniques Jakob and Wilhelm Grimm used to collect and comment on these tales became a model for other collectors, providing a basis for the science of folklore. Although the Grimm brothers argued for preserving the tales exactly as heard from oral sources, scholars have determined that they sought to "improve" the tales by making them more readable. The result, highly pleasing to lay audiences the world over, nonetheless represents a literary reworking of the original oral sources.*

A rich man's wife fell sick and, feeling that her end was near, she called her 1 only daughter to her bedside and said: "Dear child, be good and say your prayers; God will help you, and I shall look down on you from heaven and always be with you." With that she closed her eyes and died. Every day the little girl went out to her mother's grave and wept, and she went on being good and saying her prayers. When winter came, the snow spread a white cloth over the grave, and when spring took it off, the man remarried.

His new wife brought two daughters into the house. Their faces were 2 beautiful and lily-white, but their hearts were ugly and black. That was the beginning of a bad time for the poor stepchild. "Why should this silly goose sit in the parlor with us?" they said. "People who want to eat bread must earn it. Get into the kitchen where you belong!" They took away her fine clothes and gave her an old gray dress and wooden shoes to wear. "Look at the haughty princess in her finery!" they cried and, laughing, led her to the kitchen. From then on she had to do all the work, getting up before daybreak, carrying water, lighting fires, cooking and washing. In addition the sisters did everything they could to plague her. They jeered at her and poured peas and lentils into the ashes, so that she had to sit there picking them out. At night, when she was tired out with work, she had no bed to sleep in but had to lie in the ashes by the hearth. And they took to calling her Ashputtle because she always looked dusty and dirty.

One day when her father was going to the fair, he asked his two step- 3 daughters what he should bring them. "Beautiful dresses," said one. "Diamonds and pearls," said the other. "And you, Ashputtle. What would you like?" "Father," she said, "break off the first branch that brushes against your hat on your way home, and bring it to me." So he brought beautiful dresses, diamonds and pearls for his two stepdaughters, and on the way home, as he was riding through a copse, a hazel branch brushed against him and knocked off his hat. So he broke off the branch and took it home with him. When he got home, he gave the stepdaughters what they had asked for, and gave Ashputtle the branch. After thanking him, she went to her mother's grave and planted the hazel sprig over it and cried so hard that her tears fell on the sprig and watered it. It grew and became a beautiful tree. Three times a day Ashputtle went and sat under it and wept and prayed. Each time a little white bird came and perched on the tree, and when Ashputtle made a wish the little bird threw down what she had wished for.

Now it so happened that the king arranged for a celebration. It was to go 4 on for three days and all the beautiful girls in the kingdom were invited, in order that his son might choose a bride. When the two stepsisters heard they had been asked, they were delighted. They called Ashputtle and said: "Comb our hair, brush our shoes, and fasten our buckles. We're going to the wedding at the king's palace." Ashputtle obeyed, but she wept, for she too would have liked to go dancing, and she begged her stepmother to let her go. "You little sloven!" said the stepmother. "How can you go to a wedding when you're all dusty and dirty? How can you go dancing when you have neither dress nor shoes?" But when Ashputtle begged and begged, the stepmother finally said: "Here, I've dumped a bowlful of lentils in the ashes. If you can pick them out in two hours, you may go." The girl went out the back door to the garden and cried out: "O tame little doves, O turtledoves, and all the birds under heaven, come and help me put

> the good ones in the pot,
> the bad ones in your crop."

Two little white doves came flying through the kitchen window, and then came the turtledoves, and finally all the birds under heaven came flapping and fluttering and settled down by the ashes. The doves nodded their little heads and started in, peck peck peck peck, and all the others started in, peck peck peck peck, and they sorted out all the good lentils and put them in the bowl. Hardly an hour had passed before they finished and flew away. Then the girl brought the bowl to her stepmother, and she was happy, for she thought she'd be allowed to go to the wedding. But the stepmother said: "No, Ashputtle. You have nothing to wear and you don't know how to dance; the people would only laugh at you." When Ashputtle began to cry, the stepmother said: "If you can pick two bowlfuls of lentils out of the ashes in an hour, you may come." And she thought: "She'll never be able to do it." When she had dumped the two bowlfuls of lentils in the ashes, Ashputtle went out the back door to the garden and cried out: "O tame little doves, O turtledoves, and all the birds under heaven, come and help me put

> the good ones in the pot,
> the bad ones in your crop."

Two little white doves came flying through the kitchen window, and then came the turtledoves, and finally all the birds under heaven came flapping and fluttering and settled down by the ashes. The doves nodded their little heads and started in, peck peck peck peck, and all the others started in, peck peck peck peck, and they sorted out all the good lentils and put them in the bowls. Before half an hour had passed, they had finished and they all flew away. Then the girl brought the bowls to her stepmother, and she was happy, for she thought she'd be allowed to go to the wedding. But her stepmother said: "It's no use. You can't come, because you have nothing to wear and you don't know how to dance. We'd only be ashamed of you." Then she turned her back and hurried away with her two proud daughters.

When they had all gone out, Ashputtle went to her mother's grave. She   5
stood under the hazel tree and cried:

> "Shake your branches, little tree,
> Throw gold and silver down on me."

Whereupon the bird tossed down a gold and silver dress and slippers embroidered with silk and silver. Ashputtle slipped into the dress as fast as she could and went to the wedding. Her sisters and stepmother didn't recognize her. She was so beautiful in her golden dress that they thought she must be the daughter of some foreign king. They never dreamed it could be Ashputtle, for they thought she was sitting at home in her filthy rags, picking lentils out of the ashes. The king's son came up to her, took her by the hand and danced with her. He wouldn't dance with anyone else and he never let go her hand. When someone else asked for a dance, he said: "She is my partner."

She danced until evening, and then she wanted to go home. The king's son said: "I'll go with you, I'll see you home," for he wanted to find out whom the beautiful girl belonged to. But she got away from him and slipped into the dovecote. The king's son waited until her father arrived, and told him the strange girl had slipped into the dovecote. The old man thought: "Could it be Ashputtle?" and he sent for an ax and a pick and broke into the dovecote, but there was no one inside. When they went indoors, Ashputtle was lying in the ashes in her filthy clothes and a dim oil lamp was burning on the chimney piece, for Ashputtle had slipped out the back end of the dovecote and run to the hazel tree. There she had taken off her fine clothes and put them on the grave, and the bird had taken them away. Then she had put her gray dress on again, crept into the kitchen and lain down in the ashes.

Next day when the festivities started in again and her parents and step-sisters had gone, Ashputtle went to the hazel tree and said:

> "Shake your branches, little tree,
> Throw gold and silver down on me."

Whereupon the bird threw down a dress that was even more dazzling than the first one. And when she appeared at the wedding, everyone marveled at her beauty. The king's son was waiting for her. He took her by the hand and danced with no one but her. When others came and asked her for a dance, he said: "She is my partner." When evening came, she said she was going home. The king's son followed her, wishing to see which house she went into, but she ran away and disappeared into the garden behind the house, where there was a big beautiful tree with the most wonderful pears growing on it. She climbed among the branches as nimbly as a squirrel and the king's son didn't know what had become of her. He waited until her father arrived and said to him: "The strange girl has got away from me and I think she has climbed up in the pear tree." Her father thought: "Could it be Ashputtle?" He sent for an ax and chopped the tree down, but there was no one in it. When they went into the kitchen, Ashputtle was lying there in the ashes as usual, for she had jumped down on the other side of the tree, brought her fine clothes back to the bird in the hazel tree, and put on her filthy gray dress.

On the third day, after her parents and sisters had gone, Ashputtle went back to her mother's grave and said to the tree:

> "Shake your branches, little tree,
> Throw gold and silver down on me."

Whereupon the bird three down a dress that was more radiant than either of the others, and the slippers were all gold. When she appeared at the wedding, the people were too amazed to speak. The king's son danced with no one but her, and when someone else asked her for a dance, he said: "She is my partner."

When the evening came, Ashputtle wanted to go home, and the king's   9
son said he'd go with her, but she slipped away so quickly that he couldn't
follow. But he had thought up a trick. He had arranged to have the whole
staircase brushed with pitch, and as she was running down it the pitch pulled
her left slipper off. The king's son picked it up, and it was tiny and delicate
and all gold. Next morning he went to the father and said: "No girl shall be
my wife but the one this golden shoe fits." The sisters were overjoyed, for they
had beautiful feet. The eldest took the shoe to her room to try it on and her
mother went with her. But the shoe was too small and she couldn't get her big
toe in. So her mother handed her a knife and said: "Cut your toe off. Once
you're queen you won't have to walk any more." The girl cut her toe off,
forced her foot into the shoe, gritted her teeth against the pain, and went out
to the king's son. He accepted her as his bride-to-be, lifted her up on his horse,
and rode away with her. But they had to pass the grave. The two doves were
sitting in the hazel tree and they cried out:

> "Roocoo, roocoo,
> There's blood in the shoe.
> The foot's too long, the foot's too wide,
> That's not the proper bride."

He looked down at her foot and saw the blood spurting. At that he turned his
horse around and took the false bride home again. "No," he said, "this isn't
the right girl; let her sister try the shoe on." The sister went to her room and
managed to get her toes into the shoe, but her heel was too big. So her mother
handed her a knife and said: "Cut off a chunk of your heel. Once you're
queen you won't have to walk any more." The girl cut off a chunk of her heel,
forced her foot into the shoe, gritted her teeth against the pain, and went out
to the king's son. He accepted her as his bride-to-be, lifted her up on his horse,
and rode away with her. As they passed the hazel tree, the two doves were sitting there, and they cried out:

> "Roocoo, roocoo,
> There's blood in the shoe.
> The foot's too long, the foot's too wide,
> That's not the proper bride."

He looked down at her foot and saw that blood was spurting from her shoe
and staining her white stocking all red. He turned his horse around and took
the false bride home again. "This isn't the right girl, either," he said. "Haven't
you got another daughter?" "No," said the man, "there's only a puny little
kitchen drudge that my dead wife left me. She couldn't possibly be the bride."
"Send her up," said the king's son, but the mother said: "Oh, no, she's much
too dirty to be seen." But he insisted and they had to call her. First she
washed her face and hands, and when they were clean, she went upstairs and
curtseyed to the king's son. He handed her the golden slipper and sat down on
a footstool, took her foot out of her heavy wooden shoe, and put it into the

slipper. It fitted perfectly. And when she stood up and the king's son looked into her face, he recognized the beautiful girl he had danced with and cried out: "This is my true bride!" The stepmother and the two sisters went pale with fear and rage. But he lifted Ashputtle up on his horse and rode away with her. As they passed the hazel tree, the two white doves called out:

> "Roocoo, roocoo,
> No blood in the shoe.
> Her foot is neither long nor wide,
> This one is the proper bride."

Then they flew down and alighted on Ashputtle's shoulders, one on the right and one on the left, and there they sat.

On the day of Ashputtle's wedding, the two stepsisters came and tried to   10
ingratiate themselves and share in her happiness. On the way to church the elder was on the right side of the bridal couple and the younger on the left. The doves came along and pecked out one of the elder sister's eyes and one of the younger sister's eyes. Afterward, on the way out, the elder was on the left side and younger on the right, and the doves pecked out both the remaining eyes. So both sisters were punished with blindness to the end of their days for being so wicked and false.

When the Clock Strikes

TANITH LEE

Tanith Lee has written what might be called an inversion of "Cinderella" wherein the heroine is a witch. You will find all elements of the traditional tale here, and Lee's rendering is unmistakably "Cinderella." But with devious consistency, Lee turns both the magic and the unrighted wrong that lie at the heart of the tale to a dark purpose: revenge. Tanith Lee is a prolific writer of stories for young adults and of adult fantasy and science fiction. Born in 1947 in London, Lee had her first story published when she was twenty-four and has written more than two dozen stories and plays since.

Yes, the great ballroom is filled only with dust now. The slender columns of   1
white marble and the slender columns of rose-red marble are woven together by cobwebs. The vivid frescoes, on which the Duke's treasury spent so much, are dimmed by the dust; the faces of the painted goddesses look grey. And the velvet curtains—touch them they will crumble. Two hundred years now, since anyone danced in this place on the sea-green floor in the candlegleam. Two hundred years since the wonderful clock struck for the very first time.

I thought you might care to examine the clock. It was considered excep- 2
tional in its day. The pedestal is ebony and the face fine porcelain. And these
figures, which are of silver, would pass slowly about the circlet of the face.
Each figure represents, you understand, an hour. And as the appropriate
hours came level with this golden bell, they would strike it the correct number
of times. All the figures are unique, as you see. Beginning at the first hour,
they are, in this order, a girl-child, a dwarf, a maiden, a youth, a lady and a
knight. And here, notice, the figures grow older as the day declines: a queen
and king for the seventh and eighth hours, and after these, an abbess and a
magician and next to last, a hag. But the very last is strangest of all. The
twelfth figure; do you recognize him? It is Death. Yes, a most curious clock.
It was reckoned a marvelous thing then. But it has not struck for two hundred
years. Possibly you have been told the story? No? Oh, but I am certain that
you have heard it, in another form, perhaps.

However, as you have some while to wait for your carriage, I will recount 3
the tale, if you wish.

I will start with what was said of the clock. In those years, this city was 4
prosperous, a stronghold—not as you see it today. Much was made in the city
that was ornamental and unusual. But the clock, on which the twelfth hour
was Death, caused something of a stir. It was thought unlucky, foolhardy, to
have such a clock. It began to be murmured, jokingly by some, by others in
earnest, that one night when the clock struck the twelfth hour, Death would
truly strike with it.

Now life has always been a chancy business, and it was more so then. 5
The Great Plague had come but twenty years before and was not yet forgotten. Besides, in the Duke's court there was much intrigue, while enemies
might be supposed to plot beyond the city walls, as happens even in our present age. But there was another thing.

It was rumored that the Duke had obtained both his title and the city 6
treacherously. Rumor declared that he had systematically destroyed those
who had stood in line before him, the members of the princely house that formerly ruled here. He had accomplished the task slyly, hiring assassins talented with poisons and daggers. But rumor also declared that the Duke had not
been sufficiently thorough. For though he had meant to rid himself of all that
rival house, a single descendant remained, so obscure he had not traced her—
for it was a woman.

Of course, such matters were not spoken of openly. Like the prophecy of 7
the clock, it was a subject for the dark.

Nevertheless, I will tell you at once, there was such a descendant he had 8
missed in his bloody work. And she was a woman. Royal and proud she was,
and seething with bitter spite and a hunger for vengeance, and as bloody as
the Duke, had he known it, in her own way.

For her safety and disguise, she had long ago wed a wealthy merchant in 9
the city, and presently bore the man a daughter. The merchant, a dealer in
silks, was respected, a good fellow but not wise. He rejoiced in his handsome
and aristocratic wife. He never dreamed what she might be about when he
was not with her. In fact, she had sworn allegiance to Satanas. In the dead of

night she would go up into an old tower adjoining the merchant's house, and there she would say portions of the Black Mass, offer sacrifice, and thereafter practise witchcraft against the Duke. This witchery took a common form, the creation of a wax image and the maiming of the image that, by sympathy, the injuries inflicted on the wax be passed on to the living body of the victim. The woman was capable in what she did. The Duke fell sick. He lost the use of his limbs and was racked by excruciating pains from which he could get no relief. Thinking himself on the brink of death, the Duke named his sixteen-year-old son his heir. This son was dear to the Duke, as everyone knew, and be sure the woman knew it too. She intended sorcerously to murder the young man in his turn, preferably in his father's sight. Thus, she let the Duke linger in his agony, and commenced planning the fate of the prince.

Now all this while she had not been toiling alone. She had one helper. It   10 was her own daughter, a maid of fourteen, that she had recruited to her service nearly as soon as the infant could walk. At six or seven, the child had been lisping the satanic rite along with her mother. At fourteen, you may imagine, the girl was well versed in the Black Arts, though she did not have her mother's natural genius for them.

Perhaps you would like me to describe the daughter at this point. It has   11 a bearing on the story, for the girl was astonishingly beautiful. Her hair was the rich dark red of antique burnished copper, her eyes were the hue of the reddish-golden amber that traders bring from the East. When she walked, you would say she was dancing. But when she danced, a gate seemed to open in the world, and bright fire spangled inside it, but she was the fire.

The girl and her mother were close as gloves in a box. Their games in the   12 old tower bound them closer. No doubt the woman believed herself clever to have got such a helpmate, but it proved her undoing.

It was in this manner. The silk merchant, who had never suspected his   13 wife for an instant of anything, began to mistrust the daughter. She was not like other girls. Despite her great beauty, she professed no interest in marriage, and none in clothes or jewels. She preferred to read in the garden at the foot of the tower. Her mother had taught the girl her letters, though the merchant himself could read but poorly. And often the father peered at the books his daughter read, unable to make head or tail of them, yet somehow not liking them. One night very late, the silk merchant came home from a guild dinner in the city, and he saw a slim pale shadow gliding up the steps of the old tower, and he knew it for his child. On impulse, he followed her, but quietly. He had not considered any evil so far, and did not want to alarm her. At an angle of the stair, the lighted room above, he paused to spy and listen. He had something of a shock when he heard his wife's voice rise up in glad welcome. But what came next drained the blood from his heart. He crept away and went to his cellar for wine to stay himself. After the third glass he ran for neighbours and for the watch.

The woman and her daughter heard the shouts below and saw the torch-   14 es in the garden. It was no use dissembling. The tower was littered with evidence of vile deeds, besides what the woman kept in a chest beneath her unknowing husband's bed. She understood it was all up with her, and she understood too how witchcraft was punished hereabouts. She snatched a knife from the altar.

The girl shrieked when she realized what her mother was at. The woman   15
caught the girl by her red hair and shook her.

"Listen to me, my daughter," she cried, "and listen carefully, for the min-   16
utes are short. If you do as I tell you, you can escape their wrath and only I
need die. And if you live I am satisfied, for you can carry on my labor after
me. My vengeance I shall leave you, and my witchcraft to exact it by. Indeed,
I promise you stronger powers than mine. I will beg my lord Satanas for it and
he will not deny me, for he is just, in his fashion, and I have served him well.
Now, will you attend?"

"I will," said the girl.   17

So the woman advised her, and swore her to the fellowship of Hell. And   18
then the woman forced the knife into her own heart and dropped dead on the
floor of the tower.

When the men burst in with their swords and staves and their torches and   19
their madness, the girl was ready for them.

She stood blank-faced, blank-eyed, with her arms hanging at her sides.   20
When one touched her, she dropped down at his feet.

"Surely she is innocent," this man said. She was lovely enough that it was   21
hard to accuse her. Then her father went to her and took her hand and lifted
her. At that the girl opened her eyes and she said, as if terrified: "How did I
come here? I was in my chamber and sleeping—"

"The woman has bewitched her," her father said.   22

He desired very much that this be so. And when the girl clung to his hand   23
and wept, he was certain of it. They showed her the body with the knife in it.
The girl screamed and seemed to lose her senses totally.

She was put to bed. In the morning, a priest came and questioned her. She   24
answered steadfastly. She remembered nothing, not even of the great books
she had been observed reading. When they told her what was in them, she
screamed again and apparently would have thrown herself from the narrow
window, only the priest stopped her.

Finally, they brought her the holy cross in order that she might kiss it and   25
prove herself blameless.

Then she knelt, and whispered softly, that nobody should hear but one—   26
"Lord Satanas, protect thy handmaid." And either that gentleman has more
power than he is credited with or else the symbols of God are only as holy as
the men who deal in them, for she embraced the cross and it left her
unscathed.

At that, the whole household thanked God. The whole household saving,   27
of course, the woman's daughter. She had another to thank.

The woman's body was burnt, and the ashes put into unconsecrated   28
ground beyond the city gates. Though they had discovered her to be a witch,
they had not discovered the direction her witchcraft had selected. Nor did
they find the wax image with its limbs all twisted and stuck through with nee-
dles. The girl had taken that up and concealed it. The Duke continued in his

distress, but he did not die. Sometimes, in the dead of night, the girl would unearth the image from under a loose brick by the hearth, and gloat over it, but she did nothing else. Not yet. She was fourteen and the cloud of her mother's acts still hovered over her. She knew what she must do next.

The period of mourning ended. 29

"Daughter," said the silk merchant to her, "why do you not remove 30 your black? The woman was malign and led you into wickedness. How long will you mourn her, who deserves no mourning?"

"Oh my father," she said, "never think I regret my wretched mother. It 31 is my own unwitting sin I mourn." And she grasped his hand and spilled her tears on it. "I would rather live in a convent," said she, "than mingle with proper folk. And I would seek a convent too, if it were not that I cannot bear to be parted from you."

Do you suppose she smiled secretly as she said this? One might suppose 32 it. Presently she donned a robe of sackcloth and poured ashes over her red-copper hair. "It is my penance," she said, "I am glad to atone for my sins."

People forgot her beauty. She was at pains to obscure it. She slunk about 33 like an aged woman, a rag pulled over her head, dirt smeared on her cheeks and brow. She elected to sleep in a cold cramped attic and sat all day by a smoky hearth in the kitchens. When someone came to her and begged her to wash her face and put on suitable clothes and sit in the rooms of the house, she smiled modestly, drawing the rag or a piece of hair over her face. "I swear," she said, "I am glad to be humble before God and men."

They reckoned her pious and they reckoned her simple. Two years 34 passed. They mislaid her beauty altogether, and reckoned her ugly. They found it hard to call to mind who she was exactly, as she sat in the ashes, or shuffled unattended about the streets like a crone.

At the end of the second year, the silk merchant married again. It was 35 inevitable, for he was not a man who liked to live alone.

On this occasion, his choice was a harmless widow. She already had 36 two daughters, pretty in an unremarkable style. Perhaps the merchant hoped they would comfort him for what had gone before, this normal cheery wife and the two sweet, rather silly daughters, whose chief interests were clothes and weddings. Perhaps he hoped also that his deranged daughter might be drawn out by company. But that hope foundered. Not that the new mother did not try to be pleasant to the girl. And the new sisters, their hearts grieved by her condition, went to great lengths to enlist her friendship. They begged her to come from the kitchens or the attic. Failing in that, they sometimes ventured to join her, their fine silk dresses trailing on the greasy floor. They combed her hair, exclaiming, when some of the ash and dirt were removed, on its color. But no sooner had they turned away, than the girl gathered up handfuls of soot and ash and rubbed them into her hair again. Now and then, the sisters attempted to interest their bizarre relative in a bracelet or a gown or a current song. They spoke to her of the young men they had seen at the suppers or the balls which were then given regularly by the rich families of the city. The girl ignored it all. If she ever said anything it was to do with penance and humility. At last, as must happen, the sisters wearied of her, and left her alone. They had no cares and did not want to share in hers. They came to resent her moping greyness, as indeed the merchant's second wife had already done.

"Can you do nothing with the girl?" she demanded of her husband. 37 "People will say that I and my daughters are responsible for her condition and that I ill-treat the maid from jealousy of her dead mother."

"Now how could anyone say that?" protested the merchant, "when you 38 are famous as the epitome of generosity and kindness."

Another year passed, and saw no huge difference in the household. 39

A difference there was, but not visible. 40

The girl who slouched in the corner of the hearth was seventeen. Under 41 the filth and grime she was, impossibly, more beautiful, although no one could see it.

And there was one other invisible item—her power (which all this time 42 she had nurtured, saying her prayers to Satanas in the black of midnight), her power was rising like a dark moon in her soul.

Three days after her seventeenth birthday, the girl straggled about the 43 streets as she frequently did. A few noted her and muttered it was the merchant's ugly simple daughter and paid no more attention. Most did not know her at all. She had made herself appear one with the scores of impoverished flotsam which constantly roamed the city, beggars and starvelings. Just outside the city gates, these persons congregated in large numbers, slumped around fires of burning refuse or else wandering to and fro in search of edible seeds, scraps, the miracle of a dropped coin. Here the girl now came, and began to wander about as they did. Dusk gathered and the shadows thickened. The girl sank to her knees in a patch of earth as if she had found something. Two or three of the beggars sneaked over to see if it were worth snatching from her—but the girl was only scrabbling in the empty soil. The beggars, making signs to each other that she was touched by God—mad—left her alone. But, very far from mad, the girl presently dug up a stoppered clay urn. In this urn were the ashes and charred bones of her mother. She had got a clue as to the location of the urn by devious questioning here and there. Her occult power had helped her to be sure of it.

In the twilight, padding along through the narrow streets and alleys of the 44 city, the girl brought the urn homewards. In the garden at the foot of the old tower, gloom-wrapped, unwitnessed, she unstoppered the urn and buried the ashes freshly. She muttered certain unholy magics over the grave. Then she snapped off the sprig of a young hazel tree, and planted it in the newly turned ground.

I hazard you have begun to recognize the story by now. I see you suppose 45 I tell it wrongly. Believe me, this is the truth of the matter. But if you would rather I left off the tale . . . No doubt your carriage will soon be here—No? Very well. I shall continue.

I think I should speak of the Duke's son at this juncture. The prince was 46 nineteen, able, intelligent, and of noble bearing. He was of that rather swarthy type of looks one finds here in the north, but tall and slim and clear-eyed. There is an ancient square where you may see a statue of him, but much eroded by two centuries, and the elements. After the city was sacked, no care was lavished on it.

The Duke treasured his son. He had constant delight in the sight of the young man and what he said and did. It was the only happiness the invalid had. 47

Then, one night, the Duke screamed out in his bed. Servants came running with candles. The Duke moaned that a sword was transfixing his heart, an inch at a time. The prince hurried into the chamber, but in that instant the Duke spasmed horribly and died. No mark was on his body. There had never been a mark to show what ailed him. 48

The prince wept. They were genuine tears. He had nothing to reproach his father with, everything to thank him for. Nevertheless, they brought the young man the seal ring of the city, and he put it on. 49

It was winter, a cold blue-white weather with snow in the streets and countryside and a hard wizened sun that drove thin sharp blades of light through the sky, but gave no warmth. The Duke's funeral cortege passed slowly across the snow, the broad open chariots draped with black and silver, the black-plumed horses, the chanting priests with their glittering robes, their jeweled crucifixes and golden censers. Crowds lined the roadways to watch the spectacle. Among the beggar women stood a girl. No one noticed her. They did not glimpse the expression she veiled in her ragged scarf. She gazed at the bier pitilessly. As the young prince rode by in his sables, the seal ring on his hand, the eyes of the girl burned through her ashy hair, like a red fox through grasses. 50

The Duke was buried in the mausoleum you can visit to this day, on the east side of the city. Several months elapsed. The prince put his grief from him, and took up the business of the city competently. Wise and courteous he was, but he rarely smiled. At nineteen his spirit seemed worn. You might think he guessed the destiny that hung over him. 51

The winter was a hard one, too. The snow had come, and having come was loath to withdraw. When at last the spring returned, flushing the hills with color, it was no longer sensible to be sad. 52

The prince's name day fell about this time. A great banquet was planned, a ball. There had been neither in the palace for nigh on three years, not since the Duke's fatal illness first claimed him. Now the royal doors were to be thrown open to all men of influence and their families. The prince was liberal, charming and clever even in this. Aristocrat and rich trader were to mingle in the beautiful dining room, and in this very chamber, among the frescoes, the marbles and the candelabra. Even a merchant's daughter, if the merchant were notable in the city, would get to dance on the sea-green floor, under the white eye of the fearful clock. 53

The clock. There was some renewed controversy about the clock. They did not dare speak to the young prince. He was a skeptic, as his father had been. But had not a death already occurred? Was the clock not a flying in the 54 jaws of fate? For those disturbed by it, there was a dim writing in their minds, in the dust of the street or the pattern of blossoms. *When the clock strikes—* But people do not positively heed these warnings. Man is afraid of his fears. He ignores the shadow of the wolf thrown on the paving before him, saying: It is only a shadow.

The silk merchant received his invitation to the palace, and to be sure, 55 thought nothing of the clock. His house had been thrown into uproar. The most luscious silks of his workshop were carried into the house and laid before the wife and her two daughters, who chirruped and squealed with excitement. The merchant stood smugly by, above it all yet pleased at being appreciated. "Oh, father!" cried the two sisters, "may I have this one with the gold piping?" "Oh, father, this one with the design of pineapples?" Later, a jeweler arrived and set out his trays. The merchant was generous. He wanted his women to look their best. It might be the night of their lives. Yet all the while, at the back of his mind, a little dark spot, itching, aching. He tried to ignore the spot, not scratch at it. His true daughter, the mad one. Nobody bothered to tell her about the invitation to the palace. They knew how she would react, mumbling in her hair about her sin and her penance, paddling her hands in the greasy ash to smear her face. Even the servants avoided her, as if she were just the cat seated by the fire. Less than the cat, for the cat saw to the mice—Just a block of stone. And yet, how fair she might have looked, decked in the pick of the merchant's wares, jewels at her throat. The prince himself could not have been unaware of her. And though marriage was impossible, other less holy, though equally honorable contracts, might have been arranged to the benefit of all concerned. The merchant sighed. He had scratched the darkness after all. He attempted to comfort himself by watching the two sisters exult over their apparel. He refused to admit that the finery would somehow make them seem but more ordinary than they were by contrast.

The evening of the banquet arrived. The family set off. Most of the ser- 56 vants sidled after. The prince had distributed largesse in the city; oxen roasted in the squares and the wine was free by royal order.

The house grew somber. In the deserted kitchen the fire went out.   57

By the hearth, a segment of gloom rose up.   58

The girl glanced around her, and she laughed softly and shook out her 59 filthy hair. Of course, she knew as much as anyone, and more than most. This was to be her night, too.

A few minutes later she was in the garden beneath the old tower, stand- 60 ing over the young hazel tree which thrust up from the earth. It had become strong, the tree, despite the harsh winter. Now the girl nodded to it. She chanted under her breath. At length a pale light began to glow, far down near where the roots of the tree held to the ground. Out of the pale glow flew a thin black bird, which perched on the girl's shoulder. Together, the girl and the bird passed into the old tower. High up, a fire blazed that no one had lit. A tub steamed with scented water that no one had drawn. Shapes that were not real and barely seen flitted about. Rare perfumes, the rustle of garments, the glint of gems as yet invisible filled and did not fill the restless air.

Need I describe further? No. You will have seen paintings which depict   61 the attendance upon a witch of her familiar demons. Now one bathes her, another anoints her, another brings clothes and ornaments. Perhaps you do not credit such things in any case. Never mind that. I will tell you what happened in the courtyard before the palace.

Many carriages and chariots had driven through the square, avoiding the   62 roasting oxen, the barrels of wine, the cheering drunken citizens, and so through the gates into the courtyard. Just before ten o'clock (the hour, if you recall the clock, of the magician) a solitary carriage drove through the square and into the court. The people in the square gawked at the carriage and pressed forward to see who would step out of it, this latecomer. It was a remarkable vehicle that looked to be fashioned of solid gold, all but the domed roof that was transparent flashing crystal. Six black horses drew it. The coachman and postillions were clad in crimson, and strangely masked as curious beasts and reptiles. One of these beast-men now hopped down and opened the door of the carriage. Out came a woman's figure in a cloak of white fur, and glided up the palace stair and in at the doors.

There was dancing in the ballroom. The whole chamber was bright and   63 clamorous with music and the voices of men and women. There, between those two pillars, the prince sat in his chair, dark, courteous, seldom smiling. Here the musicians played, the deep-throated viol, the lively mandolin. And there the dancers moved up and down on the sea-green floor. But the music and the dancers had just paused. The figures on the clock were themselves in motion. The hour of the magician was about to strike.

As it struck, through the doorway came the figure in the fur cloak. And,   64 as if they must, every eye turned to her.

For an instant she stood there, all white, as though she had brought the   65 winter snow back with her. And then she loosed the cloak from her shoulders, it slipped away, and she was all fire.

She wore a gown of apricot brocade embroidered thickly with gold. Her   66 sleeves and the bodice of her gown were slashed over ivory satin sewn with large rosy pearls. Pearls, too, were wound in her hair that was the shade of antique burnished copper. She was so beautiful that when the clock was still, nobody spoke. She was so beautiful it was hard to look at her for very long.

The prince got up from his chair. He did not know he had. Now he start-   67 ed out across the floor, between the dancers, who parted silently to let him through. He went toward the girl in the doorway as if she drew him by a chain.

The prince had hardly ever acted without considering first what he did.   68 Now he did not consider. He bowed to the girl.

"Madam," he said. "You are welcome. Madam," he said. "Tell me who   69 you are."

She smiled.   70

"My rank," she said. "Would you know that, my lord? It is similar to yours, or would be were I now mistress in my dead mother's palace. But, unfortunately, an unscrupulous man caused the downfall of our house." 71

"Misfortune indeed," said the prince. "Tell me your name. Let me right the wrong done you." 72

"You shall," said the girl. "Trust me, you shall. For my name, I would rather keep it secret for the present. But you may call me, if you will, a pet name I have given myself—Ashella." 73

"Ashella.... But I see no ash about you," said the prince, dazzled by her gleam, laughing a little, stiffly, for laughter was not his habit. 74

"Ash and cinders from a cold and bitter hearth," said she. But she smiled again. "Now everyone is staring at us, my lord, and the musicians are impatient to begin again. Out of all these ladies, can it be you will lead me in the dance?" 75

"As long as you will dance," he said. "You shall dance with me." 76

And that is how it was. 77

There were many dances, slow and fast, whirling measures and gentle ones. And here and there, the prince and the maiden were parted. Always then he looked eagerly after her, sparing no regard for the other girls whose hands lay in his. It was not like him, he was usually so careful. But the other young men who danced on that floor, who clasped her fingers or her narrow waist in the dance, also gazed after her when she was gone. She danced, as she appeared, like fire. Though if you had asked those young men whether they would rather tie her to themselves, as the prince did, they would have been at a loss. For it is not easy to keep pace with fire. 78

The hour of the hag struck on the clock. 79

The prince grew weary of dancing with the girl and losing her in the dance to others and refinding her and losing her again. 80

Behind the curtains there is a tall window in the east wall that opens on the terrace above the garden. He drew her out there, into the spring night. He gave an order, and small tables were brought with delicacies and sweets and wine. He sat by her, watching every gesture she made, as if he would paint her portrait afterward. 81

In the ballroom, here, under the clock, the people murmured. But it was not quite the murmur you would expect, the scandalous murmur about a woman come from nowhere that the prince had made so much of. At the periphery of the ballroom, the silk merchant sat, pale as a ghost, thinking of a ghost, the living ghost of his true daughter. No one else recognized her. Only he. Some trick of the heart had enabled him to know her. He said nothing of it. As the step-sisters and wife gossiped with other wives and sisters, an awful foreboding weighed him down, sent him cold and dumb. 82

And now it is almost midnight, the moment when the page of the night turns over into day. Almost midnight, the hour when the figure of Death strikes the golden bell of the clock. And what will happen when the clock strikes? Your face announces that you know. Be patient; let us see if you do. 83

"I am being foolish," said the prince to Ashella on the terrace. "But per- 84
haps I am entitled to foolish, just once in my life. What are you saying?" For
the girl was speaking low beside him, and he could not catch her words.

"I am saying a spell to bind you to me," she said. 85
"But I am already bound." 86
"Be bound then. Never go free." 87
"I do not wish it," he said. He kissed her hands and he said, "I do not 88
know you, but I will wed you. Is that proof your spell has worked? I will wed
you, and get back for you the rights you have lost."

"If it were only so simple," said Ashella, smiling, smiling. "But the debt 89
is too cruel. Justice requires a harsher payment."

And then, in the ballroom, Death struck the first note on the golden 90
bell.

The girl smiled and she said, 91
"I curse you in my mother's name." 92
The second stroke. 93
"I curse you in my own name." 94
The third stroke. 95
"And in the name of those that your father slew." 96
The fourth stroke. 97
"And in the name of my Master, who rules the world." 98

As the fifth, the sixth, the seventh strokes pealed out, the prince stood 99
nonplussed. At the eighth and ninth strokes, the strength of the malediction
seemed to curdle his blood. He shivered and his brain writhed. At the tenth
stroke, he saw a change in the loveliness before him. She grew thinner, taller.
At the eleventh stroke, he beheld a thing in a ragged black cowl and robe. It
grinned at him. It was all grin below a triangle of sockets of nose and eyes. At
the twelfth stroke, the prince saw Death and knew him.

In the ballroom, a hideous grinding noise, as the gears of the clock failed. 100
Followed by a hollow booming, as the mechanism stopped entirely.

The conjuration of Death vanished from the terrace. 101

Only one thing was left behind. A woman's shoe. A shoe no woman 102
could ever have danced in. It was made of glass.

Did you intend to protest about the shoe? Shall I finish the story, or 103
would you rather I did not? It is not the ending you are familiar with. Yes, I
perceive you understand that, now.

I will go quickly, then, for your carriage must soon be here. And there is 104
not a great deal more to relate.

The prince lost his mind. Partly from what he had seen, partly from the 105
spells the young witch had netted him in. He could think of nothing but the
girl who had named herself Ashella. He raved that Death had borne her
away but he would recover her from Death. She had left the glass shoe as
token of her love. He must discover her with the aid of the shoe. Whomsoever
the shoe fitted would be Ashella. For there was this added complication, that
Death might hide her actual appearance. None had seen the girl before. She

had disappeared like smoke. The one infallible test was the shoe. That was why she had left it for him.

His ministers would have reasoned with the prince, but he was past 106 reason. His intellect had collapsed as totally as only a profound intellect can. A lunatic, he rode about the city. He struck out at those who argued with him. On a particular occasion, drawing a dagger, he killed, not apparently noticing what he did. His demand was explicit. Every woman, young or old, maid or married, must come forth from her home, must put her foot into the shoe of glass. They came. They had no choice. Some approached in terror, some weeping. Even the aged beggar women obliged, and they cackled, enjoying the sight of royalty gone mad. One alone did not come.

Now it is not illogical that out of the hundreds of women whose feet were 107 put into the shoe, a single woman might have been found that the shoe fitted. But this did not happen. Nor did the situation alter, despite a lurid fable that some, tickled by the idea of wedding the prince, cut off their toes that the shoe might fit them. And if they did, it was to no avail, for still the shoe did not.

Is it really surprising? The shoe was sorcerous. It constantly changed 108 itself, its shape, its size, in order that no foot, save one, could ever be got into it.

Summer spread across the land. The city took on its golden summer 109 glaze, its fetid summer smell.

What had been a whisper of intrigue, swelled into a steady distant thun- 110 der. Plots were being hatched.

One day, the silk merchant was brought, trembling and grey of face, to 111 the prince. The merchant's dumbness had broken. He had unburdened himself of his fear at confession, but the priest had not proved honest. In the dawn, men had knocked on the door of the merchant's house. Now he stumbled to the chair of the prince.

Both looked twice their years, but, if anything, the prince looked the 112 elder. He did not lift his eyes. Over and over in his hands he turned the glass shoe.

The merchant, stumbling too in his speech, told the tale of his first wife 113 and his daughter. He told everything, leaving out no detail. He did not even omit the end: that since the night of the banquet the girl had been absent from his house, taking nothing with her—save a young hazel from the garden beneath the tower.

The prince leapt from his chair. 114

His clothes were filthy and unkempt. His face was smeared with sweat 115 and dust . . . it resembled, momentarily, another face.

Without guard or attendant, the prince ran through the city toward the 116 merchant's house, and on the road, the intriguers waylaid and slew him. As he fell, the glass shoe dropped from his hands, and shattered in a thousand fragments.

There is little else worth mentioning. 117

Those who usurped the city were villains and not merely that, but fools. 118 Within a year, external enemies were at the gates. A year more, and the city had been sacked, half burnt out, ruined. The manner in which you find it now, is somewhat better than it was then. And it is not now anything for a man to be proud of. As you were quick to note, many here earn a miserable existence by conducting visitors about the streets, the palace, showing them the dregs of the city's past.

Which was not a request, in fact, for you to give me money. Throw 　119 some from your carriage window if your conscience bothers you. My own wants are few.

No, I have no further news of the girl, Ashella, the witch. A devotee of 　120 Satanas, she has doubtless worked plentiful woe in the world. And a witch is long-lived. Even so, she will die eventually. None escapes Death. Then you may pity her, if you like. Those who serve the gentleman below—who can guess what their final lot will be? But I am very sorry the story did not please you. It is not, maybe, a happy choice before a journey.

And there is your carriage at last. 　　　　　　　　　　　　　　　121

What? Ah, no, I shall stay here in the ballroom where you came on me. 　122 I have often paused here through the years. It is the clock. It has a certain— what shall I call it—power, to draw me back.

I am not trying to unnerve you. Why should you suppose that? Because 　123 of my knowledge of the city, of the story? You think that I am implying that I myself am Death? Now you laugh. Yes, it is absurd. Observe the twelfth figure on the clock. Is he not as you have always heard Death described? And am I in the least like that twelfth figure?

Although, of course, the story was not as you have heard it, either. 　　124

A Chinese "Cinderella"

TUAN CH'ÊNG-SHIH

"The earliest datable version of the Cinderella story anywhere in the world occurs in a Chinese book written about 850–860 A.D." Thus begins Arthur Waley's essay on the Chinese "Cinderella" in the March 1947 edition of Folk-Lore. *The recorder of the tale is a man named Tuan Ch'êng-shih, whose father was an important official in Szechwan and who himself held a high post in the office arranging the ceremonies associated with imperial ancestor worship.*

Among the people of the south there is a tradition that before the Ch'in and 　1 Han dynasties there was a cave-master called Wu. The aborigines called the place the Wu cave. He married two wives. One wife died. She had a daughter called Yeh-hsien, who from childhood was intelligent and good at making pottery on the wheel. Her father loved her. After some years the father died, and she was ill-treated by her step-mother, who always made her collect firewood in dangerous places and draw water from deep pools. She once got a fish about two inches long, with red fins and golden eyes. She put it into a bowl of water. It grew bigger every day, and after she had changed the bowl several times she could find no bowl big enough for it, so she threw it into the back pond. Whatever food was left over from meals she put into the water to feed it. When she came to the pond, the fish always exposed its head and pillowed it on the bank; but when anyone else came, it did not come out. The step-mother knew about this, but when she watched for it, it did not once appear. So she tricked the girl, saying, "Haven't you worked hard! I am going to give you a new dress." She then made the girl change out of her tattered clothing. Afterwards she sent her to get water from another spring and reckoning that it was several hundred leagues, the step-mother at her leisure put on her daughter's clothes, hid a sharp blade up her sleeve, and went to the pond. She called to the fish. The fish at once put its head out, and she chopped it off and killed it. The fish was now more than ten feet long. She served it up and it tasted twice as good as an ordinary fish. She hid the bones under the dung-hill. Next day, when the girl came to the pond, no fish appeared. She howled with grief in the open countryside, and suddenly there appeared a man with his hair loose over his shoulders and coarse clothes. He came down from the sky. He consoled her, saying, "Don't howl! Your step-mother has killed the fish and its bones are under the dung. You go back, take the fish's bones and hide them in your room. Whatever you want, you have only to pray to them for it. It is bound to be granted." The girl followed his advice, and was able to provide herself with gold, pearls, dresses and food whenever she wanted them.

When the time came for the cave-festival, the step-mother went, leaving   2 the girl to keep watch over the fruit-trees in the garden. She waited till the step-mother was some way off, and then went herself, wearing a cloak of stuff spun from kingfisher feathers and shoes of gold. Her step-sister recognized her and said to the step-mother, "That's very like my sister." The step-mother suspected the same thing. The girl was aware of this and went away in such a hurry that she lost one shoe. It was picked up by one of the people of the cave. When the step-mother got home, she found the girl asleep, with her arms around one of the trees in the garden, and thought no more about it.

This cave was near to an island in the sea. On this island was a kingdom   3 called T'o-han. Its soldiers had subdued twenty or thirty other islands and it had a coast-line of several thousand leagues. The cave-man sold the shoe in T'o-han, and the rules of T'o-han got it. He told those about him to put it on; but it was an inch too small even for the one among them that had the smallest foot. He ordered all the women in his kingdom to try it on, but there was not one that it fitted. It was light as down and made no noise even when treading on stone. The king of T'o-han thought the cave-man had got it unlawfully. He put him in prison and tortured him, but did not end by finding out where it had come from. So he threw it down at the wayside. Then they went everywhere[1] through all the people's houses and arrested them. If there was a woman's shoe, they arrested them and told the king of T'o-han. He thought it strange, searched the inner-rooms and found Yeh-hsien. He made her put on the shoe, and it was true.

Yeh-hsien then came forward, wearing her cloak spun from halcyon 4 feathers and her shoes. She was as beautiful as a heavenly being. She now began to render service to the king, and he took the fish-bones and Yeh-hsien, and brought them back to his country.

The step-mother and step-sister were shortly afterwards struck by flying 5 stones, and died. The cave people were sorry for them and buried them in a stone-pit, which was called the Tomb of the Distressed Women. The men of the cave made mating-offerings there; any girl they prayed for there, they got. The king of T'o-han, when he got back to his kingdom, made Yeh-hsien his chief wife. The first year the king was very greedy and by his prayers to the fish-bones got treasures and jade without limit. Next year, there was no response, so the king buried the fish-bones on the seashore. He covered them with a hundred bushels of pearls and bordered them with gold. Later there was a mutiny of some soldiers who had been conscripted and their general opened (the hiding-place) in order to make better provision for his army. One night they (the bones) were washed away by the tide.

This story was told me by Li Shih-yuan, who has been in the service of 6 my family a long while. He was himself originally a man from the the caves of Yung-chou and remembers many strange things of the South.

The Maiden, the Frog, and the Chief's Son (An African "Cinderella")

The version of the tale that follows was recorded in the (West African) Hausa language and published, originally, in 1911 by Frank Edgar. The tale remained unavailable to nonspeakers of Hausa until 1965, when Neil Skinner (of UCLA) completed an English translation.

There was once a man had two wives, and they each had a daughter. And the 1 one wife, together with her daughter, he couldn't abide; but the other, with her daughter, he dearly loved.

Well, the day came when the wife that he disliked fell ill, and it so hap- 2 pened that her illness proved fatal, and she died. And her daughter was taken over by the other wife, the one he loved; and she moved into that wife's hut. And there she dwelt, having no mother of her own, just her father. And every

---

[1] Something here seems to have gone slightly wrong with the text. [Waley]

day the woman would push her out, to go off to the bush to gather wood. When she returned, she had to pound up the *fura*. Then she had the *tuwo* to pound, and, after that, to stir. And then they wouldn't even let her eat the *tuwo*. All they gave her to eat were the burnt bits at the bottom of the pot. And day after day she continued thus.

Now she had an elder brother, and he invited her to come and eat regu-   3
larly at his home—to which she agreed. But still when she had been to the bush, and returned home, and wanted a drink of water, they wouldn't let her have one. Nor would they give her proper food—only the coarsest of the grindings and the scrapings from the pot. These she would take, and going with them to a borrow-pit, throw them in. And the frogs would come out and start eating the scrapings. Then, having eaten them up, they would go back into the water; and she too would return home.

And so things went on day after day, until the day of the Festival arrived.   4
And on this day, when she went along with the scrapings and coarse grind-ings, she found a frog squatting here; and realized that he was waiting for her! She got there and threw in the bits of food. Whereupon the frog said, "Maiden, you've always been very kind to us, and now we—but just you come along tomorrow morning. That's the morning of the Festival. Come along then, and we'll be kind to you, in our turn." "Fine," she said, and went off home.

Next morning was the Festival, and she was going off to the borrow-pit,   5
just as the frog had told her. But as she was going, her half-sister's mother said to her, "Hey—come here, you good-for-nothing girl! You haven't stirred the *tuwo*, or pounded the *fura*, or fetched the wood or the water." So the girl returned. And the frog spent the whole day waiting for her. But she, having returned to the compound, set off to fetch wood. Then she fetched water, and set about pounding the *tuwo*, and stirred it till it was done and then took it off the fire. And presently she was told to take the scrapings. She did so and went off to the borrow-pit, where she found the frog. "Tut tut, girl!" said he, "I've been waiting for you here since morning, and you never came." "Old fellow," she said, "You see, I'm a slave." "How come?" he asked. "Simple" she said, "My mother died—died leaving me her only daughter. I have an elder brother, but he is married and has a compound of his own. And my father put me in the care of his other wife. And indeed he had never loved my mother. So I was moved into the hut of his other wife. And, as I told you, slav-ery is my lot. Every morning I have to go off to the bush to get wood. When I get back from that I have to pound the *fura*, and then I pound the *tuwo*, and then start stirring it. And even when I have finished stirring the *tuwo*, I'm not given it to eat—just the scrapings." Says the frog, "Girl, give us your hand." And she held it out to him, and they both leaped into the water.

Then he went and picked her up and swallowed her. (And he vomited her   6
up.) "Good people," said he, "Look and tell me, is she straight or crooked?" And they looked and answered, "She is bent to the left." So he picked her up

and swallowed her again and then brought her up, and again asked them the same question. "She's quite straight now," they said. "Good," said he.

Next he vomited up cloths for her, and bangles, and rings, and a pair of shoes, one of silver, one of gold. "And now," said he, "Off you go to the dancing." So all these things were given to her, and he said to her, "When you get there, and when the dancing is nearly over and the dancers dispersing, you're to leave your golden shoe, the right one, there." And the girl replied to the frog, "Very well, old fellow, I understand," and off she went. 7

Meanwhile the chief's son had caused the young men and girls to dance for his pleasure, and when she reached the space where they were dancing he saw her. "Well!" said the chief's son, "*There's* a maiden for you, if you like. Don't you let her go and join in the dancing—I don't care whose home she comes from. Bring her here!" So the servants of the chief's son went over and came back with her to where he was. He told her to sit down on the couch, and she took her seat there accordingly. 8

They chatted together for some time, till the dancers began to disperse. Then she said to the chief's son, "I must be going home." "Oh, are you off?" said he. "Yes," said she and rose to her feet. "I'll accompany you on your way for a little" said the chief's son, and he did so. But she had left her right shoe behind. Presently she said, "Chief's son, you must go back now," and he did so. And afterwards she too turned and made her way back. 9

And there she found the frog by the edge of the water waiting for her. He took her hand and the two of them jumped into the water. Then he picked her up and swallowed her, and again vomited her up; and there she was just as she had been before, a sorry sight. And taking her ragged things she went off home. 10

When she got there, she said, "Fellow-wife of my mother, I'm not feeling very well." And the other said, "Rascally slut! You have been up to no good—refusing to come home, refusing to fetch water or wood, refusing to pound the *fura* or make the *tuwo*. Very well then! No food for you today!" And so the girl set off to her elder brother's compound, and there ate her food, and so returned home again. 11

But meanwhile, the chief's son had picked up the shoe and said to his father, "Dad, I have seen a girl who wears a pair of shoes, one of gold, one of silver. Look, here's the golden one—she forgot it and left it behind. She's the girl I want to marry. So let all the girls of this town, young and old, be gathered together, and let this shoe be given to them to put on." "Very well," said the chief. 12

And so it was proclaimed, and all the girls, young and old, were collected and gathered together. And the chief's son went and sat there beside the shoe. Each girl came, and each tried on the shoe, but it fitted none of them, none of the girls of the town; until only the girl who had left it was left. Then someone said "Just a minute! There's that girl in so-and-so's compound, whose mother died." "Yes, that's right," said another, "Someone go and fetch her." And someone went and fetched her. 13

But the minute she arrived to try it on, the shoe itself of its own accord, 14
ran across and made her foot get into it. Then said the chief's son, "Right,
here's my wife."

At this, the other woman—the girl's father's other wife—said, "But the 15
shoe belongs to my daughter; it was she who forgot it at the place of the dancing, not this good-for-nothing slut." But the chief's son insisted that, since he
had seen the shoe fit the other girl, as far as he was concerned, she was the one
to be taken to his compound in marriage. And so they took her there, and
there she spent one night.

Next morning she went out of her hut and round behind it, and there saw 16
the frog. She knelt respectfully and said, "Welcome, old fellow, welcome,"
and greeted him. Says he, "Tonight we shall be along to bring some things for
you." "Thank you" said she, and he departed.

Well, that night, the frog rallied all the other frogs, and all his friends, 17
both great and small came along. And he, their leader, said to them, "See
here—my daughter is being married. So I want every one of you to make a
contribution." And each of them went and fetched what he could afford,
whereupon their leader thanked them all, and then vomited up a silver bed, a
brass bed, a copper bed, and an iron bed, And went on vomiting up things for
her—such as woollen blankets, and rugs, and satins, and velvets.

"Now" said he to the girl, "If your heart is ever troubled, just lie down 18
on this brass bed" and he went on, "And when the chief's son's other wives
come to greet you, give them two calabashes of cola-nuts and ten thousand
cowrie shells; then, when his concubines come to greet you, give them one calabash of cola-nuts and five thousand cowries." "Very well," said she. Then he
said, "And when the concubines come to receive corn for making *tuwo*, say
to them, 'There's a hide-bag full, help yourselves.'" "Very well," she said.
"And," he went on, "If your father's wife comes along with her daughter and
asks you what it is like living in the chief's compound, say 'Living in the
chief's compound is a wearisome business—for they measure out corn there
with the shell of a Bambara groundnut.'"

So there she dwelt, until one day her father's favorite wife brought her 19
daughter along at night, took her into the chief's compound, and brought the
other girl out and took her to her own compound. There she said, "Oh! I
forgot to get you to tell her all about married life in the chief's compound."
"Oh, its a wearisome business" answered our girl. "How so?" asked the
older woman, surprised. "Well, they use the shell of a Bambara groundnut for
measuring out corn. Then, if the chief's other wives come to greet you, you
answer them with the 'Pf' of contempt. If the concubines come to greet you,
you clear your throat, hawk, and spit. And if your husband comes into your
hut, you yell at him." "I see," said the other—and her daughter stayed behind
the chief's son's compound.

Next morning when it was light, the wives came to greet her—and she 20
said "Pf" to them. The concubines came to greet her, and she spat at them.
Then when night fell, the chief's son made his way to her hut, and she yelled

at him. And he was amazed and went aside, and for two days pondered the matter.

Then he had his wives and concubines collected and said to them, "Look, now—I've called you to ask you. They haven't brought me the same girl. How did that one treat all of you?" "Hm—how indeed!" they all exclaimed. "Each morning, when we wives went to greet her, she would give us cola-nuts, two calabashes full, and cowries, ten thousand of them to buy tobacco flowers. And when the concubines went to greet her, she would give them a calabash of cola-nuts, and five thousand cowries to buy tobacco flowers with; and in the evening, for corn for *tuwo*, it would be a whole hide-bag full." "You see?" said he, "As for me, whenever I came to enter her hut, I found her respectfully kneeling. And she wouldn't get up from there, until I had entered and sat down on the bed." 21

"Hey," he called out, "Boys, come over here!" And when they came, he went into her hut and took a sword, and chopped her up into little pieces, and had them collect them and wrap them up in clothing; and then taken back to her home. 22

And when they got there, they found his true wife lying in the fireplace, and picking her up they took her back to her husband. 23

And next morning when it was light, she picked up a little gourd water-bottle and going around behind her hut, there saw the frog. "Welcome, welcome, old fellow," said she, and went on. "Old fellow, what I should like is to have a well built; and then you, all of you, can come and live in it and be close to me." "All right" said the frog, "You tell your husband." And she did so. 24

And he had a well dug for her, close to her hut. And the frogs came and entered the well and there they lived. That's all. *Kungurus kan kusu.* 25

Oochigeaskw—The Rough-Faced Girl (A Native American "Cinderella")

The following version of the tale was told, originally, in the Algonquin language. Native Americans who spoke Algonquian lived in the Eastern Woodlands of what is now the United States and in the northern, semiarctic areas of present-day Canada.

There was once a large village of the MicMac Indians of the Eastern Algonquins, built beside a lake. At the far end of the settlement stood a lodge, and in it lived a being who was always invisible. He had a sister who looked after him, and everyone knew that any girl who could see him might marry him. For that reason there were very few girls who did not try, but it was very long before anyone succeeded. 1

This is the way in which the test of sight was carried out: at evening-time,   2
when the Invisible One was due to be returning home, his sister would walk
with any girl who might come down to the lakeshore. She, of course, could
see her brother, since he was always visible to her. As soon as she saw him,
she would say to the girls:

"Do you see my brother?"   3

"Yes," they would generally reply—though some of them did say "No."   4

To those who said that they could indeed see him, the sister would say: 5

"Of what is his shoulder strap made?" Some people say that she would   6
enquire:

"What is his moose-runner's haul?" or "With what does he draw his   7
sled?"

And they would answer: 8

"A strip of rawhide" or "a green flexible branch," or something of that   9
kind.

Then she, knowing that they had not told the truth, would say: 10

"Very well, let us return to the wigwam!"   11

When they had gone in, she would tell them not to sit in a certain place,   12
because it belonged to the invisible One. Then, after they had helped to cook
the supper, they would wait with great curiosity, to see him eat. They could
be sure he was a real person, for when he took off his moccasins they became
visible, and his sister hung them up. But beyond this they saw nothing of him,
not even when they stayed in the place all the night, as many of them did.

Now there lived in the village an old man who was a widower, and his   13
three daughters. The youngest girl was very small, weak and often ill: and yet
her sisters, especially the elder, treated her cruelly. The second daughter was
kinder, and sometimes took her side: but the wicked sister would burn her
hands and feet with hot cinders, and she was covered with scars from this
treatment. She was so marked that people called her *Oochigeaskw*, the
Rough-Faced-Girl.

When her father came home and asked why she had such burns, the bad   14
sister would at once say that it was her own fault, for she had disobeyed
orders and gone near the fire and fallen into it.

These two elder sisters decided one day to try their luck at seeing the   15
Invisible One. So they dressed themselves in their finest clothes, and tried to
look their prettiest. They found the Invisible One's sister and took the usual
walk by the water.

When he came, and when they were asked if they could see him, they   16
answered: "Of course." And when asked about the shoulder strap or sled
cord, they answered: "A piece of rawhide."

But of course they were lying like the others, and they got nothing for   17
their pains.

The next afternoon, when the father returned home, he brought with him   18
many of the pretty little shells from which wampum was made, and they set
to work to string them.

That day, poor Little Oochigeaskw, who had always gone barefoot, got 19
a pair of her father's moccasins, old ones, and put them into water to soften
them so that she could wear them. Then she begged her sisters for a few
wampum shells. The elder called her a "little pest," but the younger one gave
her some. Now, with no other clothes than her usual rags, the poor little thing
went into the woods and got herself some sheets of birch bark, from which
she made a dress, and put marks on it for decoration, in the style of long ago.
She made a petticoat and a loose gown, a cap, leggings and a handkerchief.
She put on her father's large old moccasins, which were far too big for her,
and went forth to try her luck. She would try, she thought, to discover
whether she could see the Invisible One.

She did not begin very well. As she set off, her sisters shouted and hooted, 20
hissed and yelled, and tried to make her stay. And the loafers around the village, seeing the strange little creature, called out "Shame!"

The poor little girl in her strange clothes, with her face all scarred, was an 21
awful sight, but she was kindly received by the sister of the Invisible One. And
this was, of course, because this noble lady understood far more about things
than simply the mere outside which all the rest of the world knows. As the
brown of the evening sky turned to black, the lady took her down to the lake.

"Do you see him?" the Invisible One's sister asked. 22

"I do indeed—and he is wonderful!" said Oochigeaskw. 23

The sister asked: 24

"And what is his sled-string?" 25

The little girl said: 26

"It is the Rainbow." 27

"And, my sister, what is his bow-string?" 28

"It is The Spirit's Road—the Milky Way." 29

"So you *have* seen him," said his sister. She took the girl home with her 30
and bathed her. As she did so, all the scars disappeared from her body. Her
hair grew again, as it was combed, long, like a blackbird's wing. Her eyes
were now like stars: in all the world there was no other such beauty. Then,
from her treasures, the lady gave her a wedding garment, and adorned her.

Then she told Oochigeaskw to take the *wife's* seat in the wigwam: the 31
one next to where the Invisible One sat, beside the entrance. And when he
came in, terrible and beautiful, he smiled and said:

"So we are found out!" 32

"Yes," said his sister. And so Oochigeaskw became his wife. 33

Walt Disney's "Cinderella"

ADAPTED BY CAMPBELL GRANT

*Walter Elias Disney (1901–1966), winner of thirty-two Academy Awards, is world
famous for his cartoon animations. After achieving recognition with cartoon shorts
populated by such immortals as Mickey Mouse and Donald Duck, he produced the*

full-length animated film version of Snow White and the Seven Dwarfs *in 1937. He followed with other animations, including "Cinderella" (1950), which he adapted from Perrault's version of the tale. A Little Golden Book, the text of which appears here, was then adapted from the film by Campbell Grant.*

Once upon a time in a far-away land lived a sweet and pretty girl named Cinderella. She made her home with her mean old stepmother and her two stepsisters, and they made her do all the work in the house. 1

Cinderella cooked and baked. She cleaned and scrubbed. She had no time left for parties and fun. 2

But one day an invitation came from the palace of the king. 3

A great ball was to be given for the prince of the land. And every young girl in the kingdom was invited. 4

"How nice!" thought Cinderella. "I am invited, too." 5

But her mean stepsisters never thought of her. They thought only of themselves, of course. They had all sorts of jobs for Cinderella to do. 6

"Wash this slip. Press this dress. Curl my hair. Find my fan." 7

They both kept shouting, as fast as they could speak. 8

"But I must get ready myself. I'm going, too," said Cinderella. 9

"You!" they hooted. "The Prince's ball for you?" 10

And they kept her busy all day long. She worked in the morning, while her stepsisters slept. She worked all afternoon, while they bathed and dressed. And in the evening she had to help them put on the finishing touches for the ball. She had not one minute to think of herself. 11

Soon the coach was ready at the door. The ugly stepsisters were powdered, pressed, and curled. But there stood Cinderella in her workaday rags. 12

"Why, Cinderella!" said the stepsisters. "You're not dressed for the ball." 13

"No," said Cinderella. "I guess I cannot go." 14

Poor Cinderella sat weeping in the garden. 15

Suddenly a little old woman with a sweet, kind face stood before her. It was her fairy godmother. 16

"Hurry, child!" she said. "You are going to the ball!" 17

Cinderella could hardly believe her eyes! The fairy godmother turned a fat pumpkin into a splendid coach. 18

Next her pet mice became horses, and her dog a fine footman. The barn horse was turned into a coachman. 19

"There, my dear," said the fairy godmother. "Now into the coach with you, and off to the ball you go." 20

"But my dress—" said Cinderella. 21

"Lovely, my dear," the fairy godmother began. Then she really looked at Cinderella's rags. 22

"Oh, good heavens," she said. "You can never go in that." She waved her magic wand. 23

"Salaga dolla,
Menchicka boola,
Bibbidi bobbidi boo!" she said.

There stood Cinderella in the loveliest ball dress that ever was. And on   24
her feet were tiny glass slippers!

"Oh," cried Cinderella. "How can I ever thank you?"   25

"Just have a wonderful time at the ball, my dear," said her fairy god-   26
mother. "But remember, this magic lasts only until midnight. At the stroke of
midnight, the spell will be broken. And everything will be as it was before."

"I will remember," said Cinderella. "It is more than I ever dreamed of."   27

Then into the magic coach she stepped, and was whirled away to the ball.   28

And such a ball! The king's palace was ablaze with lights. There was   29
music and laughter. And every lady in the land was dressed in her beautiful
best.

But Cinderella was the loveliest of them all. The prince never left her side,   30
all evening long. They danced every dance. They had supper side by side. And
they happily smiled into each other's eyes.

But all at once the clock began to strike midnight, Bong Bong Bong—   31

"Oh!" cried Cinderella. "I almost forgot!"   32

And without a word, away she ran, out of the ballroom and down the   33
palace stairs. She lost one glass slipper. But she could not stop.

Into her magic coach she stepped, and away it rolled. But as the clock   34
stopped striking, the coach disappeared. And no one knew where she had
gone.

Next morning all the kingdom was filled with the news. The Grand   35
Duke was going from house to house, with a small glass slipper in his hand.
For the prince had said he would marry no one but the girl who could wear
that tiny shoe.

Every girl in the land tried hard to put it on. The ugly stepsisters tried   36
hardest of all. But not a one could wear the glass shoe.

And where was Cinderella? Locked in her room. For the mean old step-   37
mother was taking no chances of letting her try on the slipper. Poor
Cinderella! It looked as if the Grand Duke would surely pass her by.

But her little friends the mice got the stepmother's key. And they pushed   38
it under Cinderella's door. So down the long stairs she came, as the Duke was
just about to leave.

"Please!" cried Cinderella. "Please let me try."   39

And of course the slipper fitted, since it was her very own.   40

That was all the Duke needed. Now his long search was done. And so   41
Cinderella became the prince's bride, and lived happily ever after—and the
little pet mice lived in the palace and were happy ever after, too.

Cinderella

ANNE SEXTON

Anne Sexton (1928–1974) has been acclaimed as one of America's outstanding contemporary poets. In 1967, she won the Pulitzer Prize for poetry for Live or Die. *She published four other collections of her work, including* Transformations, *in which she recast, with a modern twist, popular European fairy tales such as "Cinderella." Sexton's poetry has appeared in* The New Yorker, Harper's, *the* Atlantic, *and* Saturday Review. *She received a Robert Frost Fellowship (1959), a scholarship from Radcliffe College's New Institute for Independent Study (1961–1963), a grant from the Ford Foundation (1964), and a Guggenheim Award (1969). In her book* All My Pretty Ones, *Sexton quoted Franz Kafka: "The books we need are the kind that act upon us like a misfortune, that make us suffer like the death of someone we love more than ourselves. A book should serve as the axe for the frozen sea within us." Asked in an interview (by Patricia Marz) about this quotation, Sexton responded: "I think [poetry] should be a shock to the senses. It should almost hurt."*

You always read about it;
the plumber with twelve children
who wins the Irish Sweepstakes.
From toilets to riches.
That story.   5

Or the nursemaid,
some luscious sweet from Denmark
who captures the oldest son's heart.
From diapers to Dior.
That story.   10

Or a milkman who serves the wealthy,
eggs, cream, butter, yogurt, milk,
the white truck like an ambulance
who goes into real estate
and makes a pile.   15
From homogenized to martinis at lunch.

Or the charwoman
who is on the bus when it cracks up
and collects enough from the insurance.
From mops to Bonwit Teller.   20
That story.

Once
the wife of a rich man was on her deathbed
and she said to her daughter Cinderella:
Be devout. Be good, Then I will smile   25
down from heaven in the seam of a cloud.
The man took another wife who had
two daughters, pretty enough
but with hearts like blackjacks.
Cinderella was their maid.   30
She slept on the sooty hearth each night
and walked around looking like Al Jolson.
Her father brought presents home from town,
jewels and gowns for the other women
but the twig of a tree for Cinderella.   35
She planted that twig on her mother's grave
and it grew to a tree where a white dove sat.
Whenever she wished for anything the dove
would drop it like an egg upon the ground.
The bird is important, my dears, so heed him.   40

Next came the ball, as you all know.
It was a marriage market.
The prince was looking for a wife.
All but Cinderella were preparing
and gussying up for the big event.   45
Cinderella begged to go too.
Her stepmother threw a dish of lentils
into the cinders and said: Pick them
up in an hour and you shall go.
The white dove brought all his friends;   50
all the warm wings of the fatherland came,
and picked up the lentils in a jiffy.
No, Cinderella, said the stepmother,
you have no clothes and cannot dance.
That's the way with stepmothers.   55

Cinderella went to the tree at the grave
and cried forth like a gospel singer:
Mama! Mama! My turtledove,
send me to the prince's ball!   60
The bird dropped down a golden dress
and delicate little gold slippers.
Rather a large package for a simple bird.
So she went. Which is no surprise.

Her stepmother and sisters didn't
recognize her without her cinder face   65
and the prince took her hand on the spot
and danced with no other the whole day.

As nightfall came she though she'd better
get home. The prince walked her home
and she disappeared into the pigeon house   70
and although the prince took an axe and broke
it open she was gone. Back to her cinders.
These events repeated themselves for three days.
However on the third day the prince
covered the palace steps with cobbler's wax   75
and Cinderella's gold shoe stuck upon it.
Now he would find whom the shoe fit
and find his strange dancing girl for keeps.
He went to their house and the two sisters
were delighted because they had lovely feet.   80
The eldest went into a room to try the slipper on
but her big toe got in the way so she simply
sliced it off and put on the slipper.
The prince rode away with her until the white dove
told him to look at the blood pouring forth.   85
That is the way with amputations.
They don't just heal up like a wish.
The other sister cut off her heel
but the blood told as blood will.
The prince was getting tired.   90
He began to feel like a shoe salesman.
But he gave it one last try.
This time Cinderella fit into the shoe
like a love letter into its envelope.

At the wedding ceremony   95
the two sisters came to curry favor
and the white dove pecked their eyes out.
Two hollow spots were left
like soup spoons.

Cinderella and the prince   100
lived, they say, happily ever after,
like two dolls in a museum case
never bothered by diapers or dust,
never arguing over the timing of an egg,
never telling the same story twice,   105
never getting a middle-aged spread,
their darling smiles pasted on for eternity.

Regular Bobbsey Twins.
That story.

On Location: Airy Fairy Tale

RICHARD COVINGTON

"On Location: Airy Fairy Tale" is a feature story that appeared in the Los
Angeles Times *on December 5, 1997. Writing on location from a movie set in
France, Richard Covington reports on the making of a new movie version of
"Cinderella," which was released in 1998 under the title of* Ever After. *(You'll
learn in paragraph 9 about the difficulties the producers had in securing rights to
the title "Cinderella.") The movie should be available at your local video rental
store.*

AUTEFORT CASTLE, France—With Leonardo da Vinci as the fairy godmother   1
and Drew Barrymore as a feisty tomboy who initially spurns the prince as
arrogant, out of touch with his people and anything but charming, the latest
remake of the Cinderella story forces the lovers to earn their glass slippers.

In this revisionist version, the stepsisters are beautiful, not ugly—even   2
though Megan Dodds as Marguerite, the prettier of the pair, possesses an
inner child of incomparable nastiness. Setting the fairy tale further on its
head, the Cinderella character Danielle rescues the prince as much as he rescues her, first hauling him on her back to escape a band of gypsy robbers, then
saving the spineless wonder from a loveless, arranged marriage. And there's
not a pumpkin in sight.

"You are the only magic here," Leonardo encourages the self-reliant   3
Danielle as she sets forth to win her prince.

Says director Andy Tennant: "I've always hated the Cinderella fairy tale   4
for two reasons: Guys have to live up to being Prince Charming and women
are raised to believe the only way they can be happy is to marry a great-
looking guy with a big house. I don't want my daughters growing up to buy
that. Our version says Cinderella's magic comes from within, not from
some little old lady with a wand."

In a calculated attempt to appeal to boys as well as girls, Tennant and   5
screenwriter Rick Parks have injected a few sword fights and "the guys' point
of view," as well as tonic doses of much-needed humor, never the original
story's strong point.

As the evil stepmother Baroness Rodmilla of Ghent, Anjelica Huston   6
milks her lines for all the wicked, campy irony they will bear. Alighting from
her carriage, she drinks in the less-than-magnificent prospect of her new husband's dilapidated manor home. "It's charming," she lies, rolling her eyes
wide as if appealing for divine intervention. "Where is the main house?"

The filmmakers chose the 16th century court of the French king François I   7
as the backdrop for their tale largely to work Leonardo into the story.

In historical accounts, the Italian master was the king's intellectual and   8
artistic sidekick, as well as a liberalizing influence on the prince, the future
King Henry II.

• • •

The film, which is in title limbo until Fox Family Films negotiates an   9
agreement with Disney over its prior claim to the "Cinderella" name, has been
shooting since mid-September in the Perigord region of southwest France.
Encamping in Sarlat, where the production is revamping storefronts, town
squares and the cathedral, the "untitled Cinderella project" has fanned out
across several meticulously preserved chateaux and manor houses in a cost-
saving attempt to re-create life during the French Renaissance.

Filming entirely on location, the production is making a virtue of neces-   10
sity. With a $25-million budget, reconstructing period locales on a sound
stage was not an option, Tennant explains. Instead, the production is constructing location sets at a breakneck pace, building some 72 over the course
of the nine-week shoot.

After three years spent developing the script, Fox brought Tennant in as   11
director at the insistence of Drew Barrymore, who had starred in the director's
1993 television movie, "The Amy Fisher Story." The Cinderella film is the
director's third feature, after "It Takes Two" and "Fools Rush In."

The grand ball and other key scenes are being shot an hour's drive north   12
of Sarlat in Hautefort Castle, a stone fortress with pepper-pot towers and
formal gardens perched on a promontory overlooking rolling vineyards and
fields of maize.

Instead of being a case of love at first sight, the ball culminates a hard-   13
won reconciliation between Danielle and the prince after weeks of playing cat-
and-mouse with each other, of weathering a trying series of arguments,
rejections, lies, affectionate teasing, drunken revels and passionate embraces.

"This is one tough Cinderella," Barrymore explains with a grin. "She   14
dives into bees' hives for the wax, takes pigs out truffle-hunting, swims in the
river, quotes Sir Thomas More's 'Utopia.' She even nails the prince with an
apple for stealing her horse. She does many things a man does, whether it
involves physical strength or reading. She's ahead of her time in breaking
down the barriers between a woman's place in society and a man's place. The
fairy tale Cinderella always gets shut down by those around her, but Danielle
refuses to get shut down."

• • •

Life, even under a relatively enlightened king like François, was far from   15
a fairy tale. Women were at the bottom of an inflexible class structure, and
unfortunate ones like Cinderella were commonly sold into servitude.

On a brisk October evening, several hundred gowned and masked ball-   16
goers mill about inside the vast courtyard under a starry sky and dazzling

Klieg lights. Tennant looks nervously at a fog gathering in a nearby valley. The evening before, the ball scene with its 250 costumed extras—the most expensive setup of the entire film—was rained out. If there's a replay this night, the production risks turning into a pumpkin—at least temporarily.

Fortunately, the weather holds out. Flames leap from a series of torches   17
placed to let the light dance off fountains and reflecting pools of water. Under blue, red and gold banners, tables groan with bowls of apples, platters of roast suckling pig, silver tankards and gilt pitchers. To one side of the crowd, a model of Neptune's ship the size of a parade float is pulled by silver unicorns. In a bit of inspired scenic recycling from the film's opening sequence, designer Michael Howells used the boat as Jeanne Moreau's bed when she greets the Brothers Grimm in the early 19th century to relate her version of the "true story" of Cinderella.

"I'm trying for a bit of whimsy," Howells explains. "Here's this gaudy   18
party decoration and it shows up three centuries later as great-great-great-something granddaughter's bed."

Brueghel meets Mardi Gras in costume designer Jenny Beavan's madcap   19
marriage of antler masks, sunburst crowns and Renaissance lords and ladies with faces delicately painted to suggest raccoon, deer and pheasants. Anjelica Huston's Rodmilla wears a horned headdress that risks poking holes through her daughter Marguerite's equally flamboyant collar of peacock feathers each time Rodmilla inclines her head to talk with her.

All of a sudden, heralds trumpet a fanfare from the parapets and all eyes   20
turn expectantly toward the castle gate. In beaded dress, pointed gossamer angel wings and, naturally, sparkling slippers (not glass, but studded with crystals), Danielle emerges through an arched bower of gilt oak leaves patterned after a painting by Italian Renaissance master Piero della Francesca. Parting the crowd like Moses dividing the Red Sea, the prince races toward her, then brings her forward to the throne to present this mysterious sweetheart triumphantly to the king and queen.

Furious, Rodmilla storms up, yanks off the wings and declares in a ring-   21
ing denunciation that Danielle is a brazen impostor, a scullery maid pretending to nobility. Mortified, Danielle tears back through the gasping crowd and out into the night.

After five or six takes, Tennant is satisfied. "My greatest fear was that the   22
scene would look like one of those bad Renaissance fairs with out-of-work actors," he says with a grin. "Now I can rest easier."

Huston is more reserved. "It felt like a school pageant," she objects with   23
a wan smile, "with everyone out under those very bright lights, all dressed up. That's not to say it won't photograph beautifully. It's just that night shoots throw you into some sort of suspended reality to begin with and tonight seemed all the more disjointed, more pageantry than acting."

The horned headdress certainly didn't help, even though giving herself   24
devil's horns to contrast with Danielle's angelic wings was her own idea.

"My horns kept falling off every time I plucked Cinderella's wing off so I had to come back up to makeup for horn adjustment. Then I'm told I'm needed down on the set pronto. I get into slap and drag and they break for lunch, lunch being 1:30 A.M. It's less than ideal. [25]

"I like to get into a scene, warm up and cook. With the ball, I kept being taken out of the fridge and put back in again. Perhaps it's just one of those days when you feel you have a mushroom on your head." [26]

• • •

Apart from the appeal of spending a couple of months in one of the most dramatically beautiful corners of France, Huston was drawn to the role by the opportunity to lend a quirky comedic twist to the usually humorless wicked stepmother. Who could not feel empathy for the desperate poseur fallen on hard times as she archly laments: "Hell could not possibly be worse than a house in the country"? [27]

Elsewhere, Rodmilla chastises Marguerite for giving up hope of winning the prince's affections. "Darling," she says, dripping world-weary sarcasm, "nothing is final until your death and even then, I'm sure God negotiates." [28]

"It helps her believability to give her a light edge," Huston observes dryly. [29]

"At the beginning of the action, the wicked stepmother isn't so wicked," Tennant says. "When her second husband, Danielle's father, dies, she's put in an awful position. Being saddled with three girls and having to manage a manor put her under a lot of pressure. It made sense that the stepdaughter would be the one who would do the chores and be reduced to servitude. [30]

"Rodmilla's agenda is to get her pretty daughter married to the prince, which was pretty much everybody's agenda back then. Marry up and she solves a lot of their problems." [31]

This version also offers plausible grounds for the stepmother's obdurate, generally unexplained resentment of her stepdaughter. As Danielle's father is dying, he reaches, not for his new wife, but for his young daughter. Rodmilla storms away in a fit of implacable, enduring jealousy. [32]

Years later, when the grown-up Danielle tearily begs to know if there were ever a moment when Rodmilla loved her, the baroness responds with accustomed venom. [33]

"How can you love a pebble in your shoe?" she asks. [34]

After giving the stepmother believable if not wholly justifiable motivations, Tennant and Parks turned their attentions to the prince, who is played by Dougray Scott. [35]

"What does it mean when your dad puts a gun to your head and says, 'In four days, you're going to choose a bride'?" muses the director. In this script, it means that Danielle, with well-timed nudges from Leonardo, shames the shallow Henry into a bout of self-discovery that ultimately saves them both. Compared to the pretty-boy prince of the 1950 animated Disney version who doesn't have a word of dialogue, this prince is a veritable Hamlet. [36]

• • •

Despite Disney staking claim to Cinderella in modern times, parents have been alternately spooking and charming children with this tale of the archetypal abusive family and class-crossing love in virtually all cultures since Pharaonic times. According to child psychologist Bruno Bettelheim in "The Uses of Enchantment," his landmark 1976 study of fairy tales, there are nearly 500 recorded variations on the Cinderella theme, including a 9th century Chinese legend featuring a magical fish as fairy godmother. 37

The indisputable stroke of brilliance about the current project is the introduction of Leonardo as fairy godmother, more a blend of eccentric sage and meddling but well-meaning yenta than magician. Susannah Grant, the original screenwriter, first conjured up the Leonardo connection. 38

Leonardo is the ubiquitous matchmaker, steering the prince to meet Danielle, chiding the king to let Henry decide whom he should marry, and crucially, freeing Danielle from the cellar where Rodmilla has locked her up. "Yes," he quips, tongue firmly in cheek. "I will go down in history as the man who opened the door." 39

To Leonardo's voracious curiosity and utter inability to finish anything, British character actor Patrick Godfrey injects a zaniness to the inventor's craziest antics, from walking on water in pontoon shoes to crashing through the countryside, trailing his prototypical kite behind him. 40

In one rainy scene, Leonardo explodes in anger at the prince's cowardly stupidity at letting Danielle go. "I went over the top, flailing and gesticulating because that's what I thought Andy meant when he asked for more body language," Godfrey recalls. Tennant reined him in. "Stop trying to act so hard," he suggested. "Just deal with the rain." 41

"It was a wonderful note, and utterly simple," Godfrey says. 42

If Leonardo is unexpectedly screwball, Danielle is a study in self-possession—and initially, a total puzzlement to Barrymore. 43

"At first I had no idea who this person was," she says. "I felt so stiff, so weird. Then I thought, this is what a character of 500 years ago was like—a little stiff, a little weird. Eventually, I realized, oh, she needs a family just like I've always wanted a family. In my own life, it took me many years of feeling self-conscious before I could break free and be uninhibited. That's very different for Cinderella. She's so strong and fearless. She's always been sure of who she is." 44

It's 4 in the morning, but there are hours still to go before the cinematic stroke of midnight rings down the evening's ball scene. Just as spirits and peacock feather headdresses begin to droop, Tennant has a brainstorm. With an alarming crash, Aretha Franklin blares forth on the sound system and the extras start dancing, listlessly at first, then with more gusto as the director takes Marguerite's hand and cuts his own boogie night. Five centuries after Danielle, Aretha pleads for what all Cinderellas want as R-E-S-P-E-C-T booms into the Perigord fog. 45

"We are supposed to live happily ever after," Prince Henry reminds his   46
new bride at the end of the film.

"Says who?" fires back Danielle, the 1990s reality-checking Cinderella   47
with the gleam of equality and not mere stars in her eyes.

"Cinderella": A Story of Sibling Rivalry and Oedipal Conflicts

BRUNO BETTELHEIM

Having read several variants of "Cinderella," you may have wondered what it is about this story that's prompted people in different parts of the world, at different times, to show interest in a child who's been debased but then rises above her misfortune. Why are people so fascinated with "Cinderella"?

Depending on the people you ask and their perspectives, you'll find this question answered in various ways. As a Freudian psychologist, Bruno Bettelheim believes that the mind is a repository of both conscious and unconscious elements. By definition, we aren't aware of what goes on in our unconscious; nonetheless, what happens there exerts a powerful influence on what we believe and on how we act. This division of the mind into conscious and unconscious parts is true for children no less than for adults. Based on these beliefs about the mind, Bettelheim analyzes "Cinderella" first by pointing to what he calls the story's essential theme: sibling rivalry, or Cinderella's mistreatment at the hands of her stepsisters. Competition among brothers and sisters presents a profound and largely unconscious problem to children, says Bettelheim. By hearing "Cinderella," a story that speaks directly to their unconscious, children are given tools that can help them resolve conflicts. Cinderella resolves her difficulties; children hearing the story can resolve theirs as well: This is the unconscious message of the tale.

Do you accept this argument? To do so, you'd have to agree with the author's reading of "Cinderella's" hidden meanings; and you'd have to agree with his assumptions concerning the conscious and unconscious mind and the ways in which the unconscious will seize upon the content of a story in order to resolve conflicts. Even if you don't accept Bettelheim's analysis, his essay makes fascinating reading. First, it is internally consistent—that is, he begins with a set of principles and then builds logically upon them, as any good writer will. Second, his analysis demonstrates how a scholarly point of view—a coherent set of assumptions about the way the world (in this case, the mind) works—creates boundaries for a discussion. Change the assumptions and you'll change the analyses that follow from them.

Bettelheim's essay is long and somewhat difficult. While he uses no subhead-ings, he has divided his work into four sections: paragraphs 2–10 are devoted to sibling rivalry; paragraphs 11–19, to an analysis of "Cinderella's" hidden mean-ings; paragraphs 20–24, to the psychological makeup of children at the end of their Oedipal period; and paragraphs 25–27, to the reasons "Cinderella," in par-ticular, appeals to children in the Oedipal period.

Bruno Bettelheim, a distinguished psychologist and educator, was born in 1903 in Vienna. He was naturalized as an American citizen in 1939 and served as a professor of psychology at Rockford College and the University of Chicago. Awarded the honor of fellow by several prestigious professional associations, Bettelheim was a prolific writer and contributed articles to numerous popular and professional publications. His list of books includes Love Is Not Enough: The Treatment of Emotionally Disturbed Children *(1950),* The Informed Heart *(1960), and* The Uses of Enchantment *(1975), from which this selection has been excerpt-ed. Bettelheim died in 1990.*

By all accounts, "Cinderella" is the best-known fairy tale, and probably also   1
the best-liked. It is quite an old story; when first written down in China during the ninth century A.D., it already had a history. The unrivaled tiny foot size as a mark of extraordinary virtue, distinction, and beauty, and the slip-per made of precious material are facets which point to an Eastern, if not nec-essarily Chinese, origin.[1] The modern hearer does not connect sexual attractiveness and beauty in general with extreme smallness of the foot, as the ancient Chinese did, in accordance with their practice of binding women's feet.

"Cinderella," as we know it, is experienced as a story about the agonies   2
and hopes which form the essential content of sibling rivalry; and about the degraded heroine winning out over her siblings who abused her. Long before Perrault gave "Cinderella" the form in which it is now widely known, "having to live among the ashes" was a symbol of being debased in compar-ison to one's siblings, irrespective of sex. In Germany, for example, there were stories in which such an ash-boy later becomes king, which parallels Cinderella's fate. "Aschenputtel" is the title of the Brothers Grimm's version of the tale. The term originally designated a lowly, dirty kitchenmaid who must tend to the fireplace ashes.

---

[1] Artistically made slippers of precious material were reported in Egypt from the third cen-tury on. The Roman emperor Diocletian in a decree of A.D. 301 set maximum prices for dif-ferent kinds of footwear, including slippers made of fine Babylonian leather, dyed purple or scarlet, and gilded slippers for women. [Bettelheim]

There are many examples in the German language of how being forced to   3
dwell among the ashes was a symbol not just of degradation, but also of sibling rivalry, and of the sibling who finally surpasses the brother or brothers
who have debased him. Martin Luther in his *Table Talks* speaks about Cain
as the God-forsaken evildoer who is powerful, while pious Abel is forced to
be his ash-brother (*Asche-brüdel*), a mere nothing, subject to Cain; in one of
Luther's sermons he says that Esau was forced into the role of Jacob's ash-
brother. Cain and Able, Jacob and Esau are Biblical examples of one brother being suppressed or destroyed by the other.

The fairy tale replaces sibling relations with relations between step-   4
siblings—perhaps a device to explain and make acceptable an animosity which
one wishes would not exist among true siblings. Although sibling rivalry is universal and "natural" in the sense that it is the negative consequence of being a
sibling, this same relation also generates equally as much positive feeling
between siblings, highlighted in fairy tales such as "Brother and Sister."

No other fairy tale renders so well as the "Cinderella" stories the inner   5
experiences of the young child in the throes of sibling rivalry, when he feels
hopelessly outclassed by his brothers and sisters. Cinderella is pushed down
and degraded by her stepsisters; her interests are sacrificed to theirs by her
(step)mother; she is expected to do the dirtiest work and although she performs it well, she receives no credit for it; only more is demanded of her. This
is how the child feels when devastated by the miseries of sibling rivalry.
Exaggerated though Cinderella's tribulations and degradations may seem to
the adult, the child carried away by sibling rivalry feels, "That's me; that's
how they mistreat me, or would want to; that's how little they think of me."
And there are moments—often long time periods—when for inner reasons a
child feels this way even when his position among his siblings may seem to
give him no cause for it.

When a story corresponds to how the child feels deep down—as no real-   6
istic narrative is likely to do—it attains an emotional quality of "truth" for the
child. The events of "Cinderella" offer him vivid images that give body to his
overwhelming but nevertheless often vague and nondescript emotions; so
these episodes seem more convincing to him than his life experiences.

The term "sibling rivalry" refers to a most complex constellation of feel-   7
ings and their causes. With extremely rare exceptions, the emotions aroused
in the person subject to sibling rivalry are far out of proportion to what his
real situation with his sisters and brothers would justify, seen objectively.
While all children at times suffer greatly from sibling rivalry, parents seldom
sacrifice one of their children to the others, nor do they condone the other
children's persecuting one of them. Difficult as objective judgments are for the
young child—nearly impossible when his emotions are aroused—even he in
his more rational moments "knows" that he is not treated as badly as
Cinderella. But the child often feels mistreated, despite all his "knowledge" to
the contrary. That is why he believes in the inherent truth of "Cinderella,"
and then he also comes to believe in her eventual deliverance and victory.

From her triumph he gains the exaggerated hopes for his future which he needs to counteract the extreme misery he experiences when ravaged by sibling rivalry.

Despite the name "sibling rivalry," this miserable passion has only incidentally to do with a child's actual brothers and sisters. The real source of it is the child's feelings about his parents. When a child's older brother or sister is more competent than he, this arouses only temporary feelings of jealousy. Another child being given special attention becomes an insult only if the child fears that, in contrast, he is thought little of by his parents, or feels rejected by them. It is because of such an anxiety that one or all of a child's sisters or brothers may become a thorn in his flesh. Fearing that in comparison to them he cannot win his parents' love and esteem is what inflames sibling rivalry. This is indicated in stories by the fact that it matters little whether the siblings actually possess greater competence. The Biblical story of Joseph tells that it is jealousy of parental affection lavished on him which accounts for the destructive behavior of his brothers. Unlike Cinderella's, Joseph's parent does not participate in degrading him, and, on the contrary, refers him to his other children. But Joseph, like Cinderella, is turned into a slave, and, like her, he miraculously escapes and ends by surpassing his siblings.

Telling a child who is devastated by sibling rivalry that he will grow up to do as well as his brothers and sisters offers little relief from his present feelings of dejection. Much as he would like to trust our assurances, most of the time he cannot. A child can see things only with subjective eyes, and comparing himself on this basis to his siblings, he has no confidence that he, on his own, will someday be able to fare as well as they. If he could believe more in himself, he would not feel destroyed by his siblings no matter what they might do to him, since then he could trust that time would bring about a desired reversal of fortune. But since the child cannot, on his own, look forward with confidence to some future day when things will turn out all right for him, he can gain relief only through fantasies of glory—a domination over his siblings—which he hopes will become reality through some fortunate event.

Whatever our position within the family, at certain times in our lives we are beset by sibling rivalry in some form or other. Even an only child feels that other children have some great advantages over him, and this makes him intensely jealous. Further, he may suffer from the anxious thought that if he did have a sibling, his parents would prefer this other child to him. "Cinderella" is a fairy tale which makes nearly as strong an appeal to boys as to girls, since children of both sexes suffer equally from sibling rivalry, and have the same desire to be rescued from their lowly position and surpass those who seem superior to them.

On the surface, "Cinderella" is as deceptively simple as the story of Little Red Riding Hood, with which it shares greatest popularity. "Cinderella" tells about the agonies of sibling rivalry, of wishes coming true, of the humble being elevated, of true merit being recognized even when hidden under rags, of virtue rewarded and evil punished—a straightforward story. But under this overt content is concealed a welter of complex and largely unconscious material, which details of the story allude to just enough to set our unconscious associations going. This makes a contrast between surface simplicity and underlying complexity which arouses deep interest in the story and explains its appeal to the millions over centuries. To begin gaining an understanding of these hidden meanings, we have to penetrate behind the obvious sources of sibling rivalry discussed so far.

As mentioned before, if the child could only believe that it is the infirmities of his age which account for his lowly position, he would not have to suffer so wretchedly from sibling rivalry, because he could trust the future to right matters. When he thinks that his degradation is deserved, he feels his plight is utterly hopeless. Djuna Barnes's perceptive statement about fairy tales—that the child knows something about them which he cannot tell (such as that he likes the idea of Little Red Riding Hood and the wolf being in bed together)—could be extended by dividing fairy tales into two groups: one group where the child responds only unconsciously to the inherent truth of the story and thus cannot tell about it; and another large number of tales where the child preconsciously or even consciously knows what the "truth" of the story consists of and thus could tell about it, but does not want to let on that he knows. Some aspects of "Cinderella" fall into the latter category. Many children believe that Cinderella probably deserves her fate at the beginning of the story, as they feel they would, too; but they don't want anyone to know it. Despite this, she is worthy at the end to be exalted, as the child hopes he will be too, irrespective of his earlier shortcomings. 12

Every child believes at some period of his life—and this is not only at rare moments—that because of his secret wishes, if not also his clandestine actions, he deserves to be degraded, banned from the presence of others, relegated to a netherworld of smut. He fears this may be so, irrespective of how fortunate his situation may be in reality. He hates and fears those others—such as his siblings—whom he believes to be entirely free of similar evilness, and he fears that they or his parents will discover what he is really like, and then demean him as Cinderella was by her family. Because he wants others—most of all, his parents—to believe in his innocence, he is delighted that "everybody" believes in Cinderella's. This is one of the great attractions of this fairy tale. Since people give credence to Cinderella's goodness, they will also believe in his, so the child hopes. And "Cinderella" nourishes this hope, which is one reason it is such a delightful story. 13

Another aspect which holds large appeal for the child is the vileness of the stepmother and stepsisters. Whatever the shortcomings of a child may be in his own eyes, these pale into insignificance when compared to the stepsisters' and stepmother's falsehood and nastiness. Further, what these stepsisters do to Cinderella justifies whatever nasty thoughts one may have about one's siblings: they are so vile that anything one may wish would happen to them is more than justified. Compared to their behavior, Cinderella is indeed inno- 14 cent. So the child, on hearing her story, feels he need not feel guilty about his angry thoughts.

On a very different level—and reality considerations coexist easily with   15
fantastic exaggerations in the child's mind—as badly as one's parents or siblings seem to treat one, and much as one thinks one suffers because of it, all this is nothing compared to Cinderella's fate. Her story reminds the child at the same time how lucky he is, and how much worse things could be. (Any anxiety about the latter possibility is relieved, as always in fairy tales, by the happy ending.)

The behavior of a five-and-a-half-year-old girl, as reported by her father,   16
may illustrate how easily a child may feel that she is a "Cinderella." This little girl had a younger sister of whom she was very jealous. The girl was very fond of "Cinderella," since the story offered her material with which to act out her feelings, and because without the story's imagery she would have been hard pressed to comprehend and express them. This little girl had used to dress very neatly and liked pretty clothes, but she became unkempt and dirty. One day when she was asked to fetch some salt, she said as she was doing so, "Why do you treat me like Cinderella?"

Almost speechless, her mother asked her, "Why do you think I treat you   17
like Cinderella?"

"Because you make me do all the hardest work in the house!" was the   18
little girl's answer. Having thus drawn her parents into her fantasies, she acted them out more openly, pretending to sweep up all the dirt, etc. She went even further, playing that she prepared her little sister for the ball. But she went the "Cinderella" story one better, based on her unconscious understanding of the contradictory emotions fused into the "Cinderella" role, because at another moment she told her mother and sister, "You shouldn't be jealous of me just because I am the most beautiful in the family."

This shows that behind the surface humility of Cinderella lies the con-   19
viction of her superiority to mother and sisters, as if she would think: "You can make me do all the dirty work, and I pretend that I am dirty, but within me I know that you treat me this way because you are jealous of me because I am so much better than you." This conviction is supported by the story's ending, which assures every "Cinderella" that eventually she will be discovered by her prince.

Why does the child believe deep within himself that Cinderella deserves   20
her dejected state? This question takes us back to the child's state of mind at the end of the oedipal period.[2] Before he is caught in oedipal entanglements, the child is convinced that he is lovable, and loved, if all is well within his family relationships. Psychoanalysis describes this stage of complete satisfaction with oneself as "primary narcissism." During this period the child feels

---

[2] *Oedipal:* Freud's theory of the Oedipus complex held that at an early stage of development a child wishes to replace the parent of the same sex in order to achieve the exclusive love of the parent of the opposite sex.

certain that he is the center of the universe, so there is no reason to be jealous of anybody.

The oedipal disappointments which come at the end of this developmen- 21 tal stage cast deep shadows of doubt on the child's sense of his worthiness. He feels that if he were really as deserving of love as he had thought, then his parents would never be critical of him or disappoint him. The only explanation for parental criticism the child can think of is that there must be some serious flaw in him which accounts for what he experiences as rejection. If his desires remain unsatisfied and his parents disappoint him, there must be something wrong with him or his desires, or both. He cannot yet accept that reasons other than those residing within him could have an impact on his fate. In this oedipal jealousy, wanting to get rid of the parent of the same sex had seemed the most natural thing in the world, but now the child realizes that he cannot have his own way, and that maybe this is so because the desire was wrong. He is no longer so sure that he is preferred to his siblings, and he begins to suspect that this may be due to the fact that *they* are free of any bad thoughts or wrongdoing such as his.

All this happens as the child is gradually subjected to ever more critical 22 attitudes as he is being socialized. He is asked to behave in ways which run counter to his natural desires, and he resents this. Still he must obey, which makes him very angry. This anger is directed against those who make demands, most likely his parents; and this is another reason to wish to get rid of them, and still another reason to feel guilty about such wishes. This is why the child also feels that he deserves to be chastised for his feelings, a punishment he believes he can escape only if nobody learns what he is thinking when he is angry. The feeling of being unworthy to be loved by his parents at a time when his desire for their love is very strong leads to the fear of rejection, even when in reality there is none. This rejection fear compounds the anxiety that others are preferred and also maybe preferable—the root of sibling rivalry.

Some of the child's pervasive feelings of worthlessness have their origin in 23 his experiences during and around toilet training and all other aspects of his education to become clean, neat, and orderly. Much has been said about how children are made to feel dirty and bad because they are not as clean as their parents want or require them to be. As clean as a child may learn to be, he knows that he would much prefer to give free rein to his tendency to be messy, disorderly, and dirty.

At the end of the oedipal period, guilt about desires to be dirty and dis- 24 orderly becomes compounded by oedipal guilt, because of the child's desire to replace the parent of the same sex in the love of the other parent. The wish to be the love, if not also the sexual partner, of the parent of the other sex, which at the beginning of the oedipal development seemed natural and "innocent," at the end of the period is repressed as bad. But while this wish as such is repressed, guilt about it and about sexual feelings in general is not, and this makes the child feel dirty and worthless.

Here again, lack of objective knowledge leads the child to think that he 25 is the only bad one in all these respects—the only child who has such desires.

It makes every child identify with Cinderella, who is relegated to sit among the cinders. Since the child has such "dirty" wishes, that is where he also belongs, and where he would end up if his parents knew of his desires. This is why every child needs to believe that even if he were thus degraded, eventually he would be rescued from such degradation and experience the most wonderful exaltation—as Cinderella does.

For the child to deal with his feelings of dejection and worthlessness   26
aroused during this time, he desperately needs to gain some grasp on what these feelings of guilt and anxiety are all about. Further, he needs assurance on a conscious and an unconscious level that he will be able to extricate himself from these predicaments. One of the greatest merits of "Cinderella" is that, irrespective of the magic help Cinderella receives, the child understands that essentially it is through her own efforts, and because of the person she is, that Cinderella is able to transcend magnificently her degraded state, despite what appear as insurmountable obstacles. It gives the child confidence that the same will be true for him, because the story relates so well to what has caused both his conscious and his unconscious guilt.

Overtly "Cinderella" tells about sibling rivalry in its most extreme form: 27
the jealousy and enmity of the stepsisters, and Cinderella's sufferings because of it. The many other psychological issues touched upon in the story are so covertly alluded to that the child does not become consciously aware of them. In his unconscious, however, the child responds to these significant details which refer to matters and experiences from which he consciously has separated himself, but which nevertheless continue to create vast problems for him.

■ ■ ■

Review Questions

1. What does living among ashes symbolize, according to Bettelheim?
2. What explanation does Bettelheim give for Cinderella's having stepsisters, not sisters?
3. In what ways are a child's emotions aroused by sibling rivalry?
4. To a child, what is the meaning of Cinderella's triumph?
5. Why is the fantasy solution to sibling rivalry offered by "Cinderella" appropriate for children?
6. Why is Cinderella's goodness important?
7. Why are the stepsisters and stepmother so vile, according to Bettelheim?
8. In paragraphs 20–26, Bettelheim offers a complex explanation of oedipal conflicts and their relation to sibling rivalry and the child's need to be debased, even while feeling superior. Summarize these seven paragraphs, and compare your summary with those of your classmates. Have you agreed on the essential information in this passage?

Discussion and Writing Suggestions

1. One identifying feature of psychoanalysis is the assumption of complex unconscious and subconscious mechanisms in human personality that explain behavior. In this essay, Bettelheim discusses the interior world of a child in ways that the child could never articulate. The features of this world include the following:

   All children experience sibling rivalry.
   The real source of sibling rivalry is the child's parents.
   Sibling rivalry is a miserable passion and a devastating experience.
   Children have a desire to be rescued from sibling rivalry (as opposed to rescuing themselves, perhaps).
   Children experience an Oedipal stage, in which they wish to do away with the parent of the same sex and be intimate with the parent of the opposite sex.
   "Every child believes at some point in his life . . . that because of his secret wishes, if not also his clandestine actions, he deserves to be degraded, banned from the presence of others, relegated to a nether world of smut."

   To what extent do you agree with these statements? Take one of the statements and respond to it in a four- or five-paragraph essay.

2. A critic of Bettelheim's position, Jack Zipes, argues that Bettelheim distorts fairy-tale literature by insisting that the tales have therapeutic value and speak to children almost as a psychoanalyst might. Ultimately, claims Zipes, Bettelheim's analysis corrupts the story of "Cinderella" and closes down possibilities for interpretation. What is your view of Bettelheim's psychoanalytic approach to fairy tales?

Pretty Woman: *A Modern* Cinderella

KAROL KELLEY

Karol Kelley (1927–1995), a professor of women's history at Texas Tech University when this piece was written, brings a feminist perspective to two filmed versions of the Cinderella *story: Disney's animated* Cinderella *(1949) and* Pretty Woman *(1990), starring Julia Roberts. Forty-one years separate these remakes of the Charles Perrault* Cinderella, *during which time the women's movement prompted many changes in American culture. Working an extended comparative analysis based on feminist concerns, Kelley finds the films remarkably alike in their attitudes towards gender roles. Why, given the presumably changed roles and status of women and men in our society, are the movies so similar? As you read, note the feminist principles on which Kelley bases her analysis, and consider using these principles to critique other (written) versions of the tale presented in this chapter. As you read, you may want to consider how representative Kelley's conclusions are of Hollywood movies made during the 1990s. This article originally appeared in the* Journal of American Culture *(Spring 1994).*

In modern society fairy tales are still compelling. Found in oral, written and filmed versions, the stories may serve a pleasurable purpose for individuals or a cultural purpose for academics. Fairy tales have been studied to produce typologies and methodologies in folklore, to examine societal similarities and differences, and to identify changes in values over time. On the one hand these stories have been criticized for supporting the status quo; on the other, their motifs have provided acceptable plot elements for hundreds of Hollywood motion pictures.

Cinderella is one of the best liked of these tales, measured both by the number of variations of the story and by the scholarly and popular interest in them. There are some 700 versions of Cinderella. It has been recorded in every area of the world, in written form in China as early as the ninth century CE (Bettelheim 236). Marian Roalfe Cox published her study of 345 variants of Cinderella in 1893 (Cox). Since that time folklorists have continued to study the story, as have literary historians, psychologists, and feminists. The most popular version in recent years in the United States has been that of Charles Perrault, which was compiled in France in 1697. In roughly the past 40 years in America, elements of his story have appeared in a full-length Walt Disney cartoon, two shorter cartoon videos and some pastiches, a stage musical filmed for television and made into a video, and dozens of Hollywood films. Of the latter, *Pretty Woman* is the most obvious Perrault derivative.

The first and last of the above-mentioned film variations, the Disney *Cinderella* and *Pretty Woman*, have certainly been very successful. The Disney cartoon has been reissued repeatedly in theaters since its creation in 1949 and is for sale or rent as a home video. It was Oscar-nominated in 1950 for Best Sound, Song, and Musical Scoring and has been reviewed as having "an adult following as well as a children's following" (*Greatest Movies* 88). *Pretty Woman* appeared early in 1990 and by November of that year had earned $178.4 million at the box office (Shearer 24). It has continued to sell well as a video and to earn even more money from home rentals. Julia Roberts won an Academy Award nomination as Best Actress for her role of Vivian.

Given the major changes in American society that took place during the 40 years between the making of these two films, differences in social values might be expected, especially concerning gender roles. Beginning with the women's movement in the 1960s there have been demands for information about women, sexuality and gender. The scholarly studies since that time have produced a better factual knowledge of women, the development of a number of feminist ideologies, and a new awareness of how gender stereotypes are created and also what their costs to society are. This data has resulted in a number of societal changes.

Politically in the past 30 years the interest in women's issues has meant alterations in many laws in the United States that applied to women and the passage of an Equal Rights Amendment to the Constitution. This caused serious discussion even though it was never ratified. For the first time in American history large numbers of women openly asked for political, economic and social equality with men.

The demand for equality is one conception of feminism. A more thorough 6 definition has been provided by Nannerl O. Keohane, the former president of Wellesley College. She says that feminism

> embraces the belief that no one of either sex should be channeled into (or out of) a particular life course by gender. Each person should have the opportunity so far as possible, to pursue her own visions, hopes, and dreams—to prepare herself to realize her own ambitions and to define her own identity, untrammeled by stereotypical expectations about what men or women can or cannot, should or should not, do. (23)

This statement implies that feminism requires self-acceptance as well as tolerance, that is, the acceptance of others' dreams and decisions for themselves.

The fields of history, psychology, and literary history have also been 7 affected by the recent concern for gender issues. There is the new area of women's history with differing sources, methodologies, time divisions and subjects of investigation. Today there are dozens of excellent books on topics not previously considered: changes in women's work and organizations, courtship and marriage patterns, sisterhood, sexuality, birth control, rape, and prostitution, among others. There are psychological studies identifying differences in male and female development, in gender perceptions and language, and in men's and women's behavior and values. Both psychologists and literary historians have begun to look at fairy tales in different ways, refuting the Jungian view that these stories are universal and the Freudian idea that they aid children's oedipal development. The more recent views criticize all tales, especially Cinderella.

In 1981 Colette Dowling published *The Cinderella Complex*. In this 8 work she argues that the gender expectations and the promises of the Cinderella story are psychologically harmful to women. ". . . [G]irls, from the time they are quite young are trained *into* dependency, while boys are trained *out* of it." Girls therefore expect that "there will always be someone to take care of them," and this feeling becomes more intense with age (101). Because being dependent is identified with femininity, women accept this attitude for themselves. Unfortunately, dependence also produces feelings of fear. Instead of trying to create a life for themselves, females search for a man to give them protection, a sense of identity, and the proof that they are loved (56, 141). To cope with their anxieties when lacking a man, many women become what Dowling calls "counterphobic." Outwardly they insist, "I don't need anybody. I can take care of myself." Inwardly they are fearful of becoming responsible for themselves and are terrified of being alone (67, 80). Dowling finds that

> Feeling helpless and frightened is so threatening to these women that they devote all their energies to constructing a life—and a style—calculated to throw everyone (themselves included) off the track. They may become racing-car drivers. Or actresses. Or prostitutes. (72)

Recent literary scholars have reacted to fairy tales in the same ways that   9
psychologists have. In 1982 Jennifer Waelti-Walters attacked the traditional
folk stories for presenting girls as objects and as passive victims (1). She calls
the reading of fairy tales "one of the first steps in the maintenance of a misog-
ynous sex-role stereotyped patriarchy" (8).

Jack Zipes, in a book published in 1983, takes a historical and not a psy-   10
chological perspective. His interest is in the origins of the literary fairy tale for
children in seventeenth century France and how over time the motifs, characters and themes were rearranged or eliminated to reflect the changing values of
society (6–7). Zipes argues that fairy tales "have always symbolically depicted
the nature of power relationships in a given society" (67). He contrasts the
older version of Cinderella with Charles Perrault's adaptation and finds a shift
from a matriarchal to a patriarchal point of view. In the earlier story Cinderella
is a strong independent woman who rebels against the hard labor forced upon
her and uses her wits and her dead mother's help to regain her upper class status
in society. She does achieve her goal, which is not marriage but recognition.
Perrault, on the other hand, wrote to socialize the children of the bourgeoisie,
that is, to prepare them for the roles he believed they should play in society. He
sexualized society, providing clear gender stereotypes. Thus Perrault's
Cinderella is beautiful, polite, graceful, industrious, obedient and passive. She
does not threaten men either by coquetry or intelligence. She waits patiently for
the right man to come along to recognize her virtues and to marry her.
Perrault's male characters must be active, intelligent, and ambitious. Not necessarily good-looking, they must be courteous and courageous. Social success
and achieving are more important to these heroes than winning a wife. Thus
due solely to their sex, Perrault heroines have a very limited range of opportunities, dreams, and possible behavior (Zipes ch. 2).

Like Zipes, Ruth Bottigheimer takes a historical perspective in her 1987   11
study of fairy tales, *Grimm's Bad Girls and Bold Boys*. She also seems to support the feminist point of view that fairy tales are not beneficial to women.
She looks at the Grimm brothers' works as historical documents and investi-
gates both changes over time and gender differences. She discovers that as the
nineteenth-century progressed, females increasingly lost their power in the
tales, as measured: by their speech, which is direct for males and indirect for
females; by they silence, as compared with males; and by their punishments,
which are harsher for females and occur after one transgression, while males
can offend three to five times before retribution.

Recent academic work thus reflects the ideas of the women's movement.   12
What of the popular culture? Apparently it does not. Perrault's gender role
stereotyping remains unchanged in both *Cinderella* and *Pretty Woman*. The
latter uses current fashions and artifacts and ignores the older sexual taboos,
thus giving the film a modern appearance. Despite this, *Pretty Woman* does
not illustrate any major changes in gender expectations and is unaffected by
any form of feminist ideology.

Cinderella could not be expected to be a feminist film. Disney chose to   13
use the Perrault story and adapted that to the rhetoric of an era firmly

anchored in the feminine mystique. The characters are ranked and segregated by sex. Traditional gender stereotypes and not personal choice determine the behavior, life courses, and dreams that are shown in the cartoon. The same may be said of *Pretty Woman*, and, in addition, there is more ambivalence concerning the family and friendship and more acceptance of the traditional male values of competition and revenge than in the Disney film.

In both *Cinderella* and *Pretty Woman* the male sex is ranked higher in   14
wealth, occupation, and status than the female sex. A class society prevailed in the earlier time period of the cartoon. The Prince's family is not only wealthy but royal, making him the future king and future ruler of his country. He therefore has the highest possible status. Cinderella comes from a gentry family which has financial problems due to the death of her father and the selfishness of her stepfamily. Cinderella is forced to do the work of a scullery maid. Her status can be raised only through marriage, when she will take the position of her husband.

In *Pretty Woman* Edward Lewis is the hero. He is fabulously wealthy,   15
able to indulge his every materialistic desire. Given the Yuppie generation of the 1980s, Edward's occupation as a successful and wealthy corporate raider gives him the highest possible status. Vivian Ward is the heroine of *Pretty Woman*. As the picture opens she lacks the money to pay her rent and has a pin holding up her boot. She is a prostitute, a job defined as "debasing oneself for money." Near the ending of the movie she considers raising her status herself, but she, too, chooses to marry. Edward's background is far superior to Vivian's. His father had been rich, and his mother, a trained musician. Edward is well-educated and sophisticated. His manners are impeccable, and he is accustomed to elegant places, to formal clothing, and to upper class amusements such as polo and the opera. Vivian is the product of a lower class family from a small town in Georgia. She is intelligent but uneducated, reaching only the eleventh grade in school. She throws her gum on the sidewalk, is ignorant of table manners and how to dress, loves television, movies and popular songs, and calls an orchestra "a band."

In *Cinderella* the hero and heroine are equal at least in manners, and edu-   16
cation is not mentioned. In *Pretty Woman* education and manners help to determine status, and Vivian ranks far below Edward. The gender stereotypes in popular romances give heroes a higher status than their heroines. This is found to be true in both of these films.

In addition, gender clearly determines occupations and activities.   17
Obtaining money is not a problem for the Prince, and he hunts and travels. Cinderella remains at home and does housework, which is properly feminine but is also dirty, physically demanding and demeaning. Life is even sex-differentiated for the mice. The males go to obtain food and have exciting adventures. When a male mouse wants to help make Cinderella's dress for the ball, a female mouse says, "Leave the sewing to the women; You go get the trimmin'."

Edward is a businessman working with male executives, lawyers, bankers   18
and senators. Of course his telephone operator is female. Vivian provides female services for men. Lacking job skills she is unable to support herself by

any other kind of work open to her, and she must struggle to keep some control over her own body and out of the hands of male pimps. The hotel and store managers are men; the sales clerks are women. The expectations presented are that women are supposed to work, but that men are to hold the superior and better-paying jobs.

In both movies males have much more power and are the rescuers of females. In *Cinderella* the King has the power of life or death. Granted, Disney sentimentalizes the scenes with the King's imaginary grandchildren. The male desire to see his line and name carried on is a traditional one, however. Although the Disney cartoon ends with the marriage of the Prince and Cinderella, presumably they will have the children to fulfill the King's hopes. Males are seen as rescuers; females are more passive. The male mice and dog free Cinderella from her locked room. By marrying her the Prince saves Cinderella from her family's abuse and from her domestic chores. Even the stepsisters hope to be rescued from their daily routine by husbands.

Women who have power are presented in the Disney film as either evil or silly. The wicked stepmother controls her household and the three young women in her charge. The true nature of the stepmother was revealed only after the death of Cinderella's father, whose authority presumably restrained the stepmother's behavior. The fairy godmother has enormous magical power. This is trivialized by her silliness, her song Bibbidi Bobbidi Boo, and by her absentmindedness: she can't find her wand, or remember her magic words, or even notice that Cinderella needs a dress to wear to the ball.

The hero of *Pretty Woman* also has the power of life and death, at least over the continuance of various corporations and over the jobs of the people working there. He is able to set up a billion dollar deal to take over Morse Industries. Borrowing a necklace worth a quarter of a million dollars is a minor transaction in his life. Edward can influence Senate committees and bank officials. Because of his enormous financial power, he has only to ask to receive the services he desires. Vivian has neither power nor identity. Abandoned by the man who brought her to Los Angeles, she could not support herself. Her friend Kit talked her into becoming a prostitute. Vivian cried but was powerless to do anything else. Her feisty personality indicates counterphobia, a fear of being helpless, rather than independence. She lacks identity in repeatedly being ready to be called by any name a man likes or by being ready to do anything a man asks of her. Crying "Nobody will help me," she is unable to buy a dress by herself. She has to be rescued by Barney Thompson, the hotel manager, or by Edward and his credit card. In addition, Edward saves Vivian from being raped by Phil, his lawyer. She is also helped by Mr. Morse, the elevator man, and the hotel chauffeur.

Interestingly, the women in *Pretty Woman* have even less power than those in *Cinderella*. The snobbish salesladies have some control. They can order Vivian to leave the store. Later they are punished by losing commissions, and their roles are small. More significantly, the part of the fairy godmother is transformed into a male role. Not a woman but a man enables the Cinderella character to achieve her dreams. Barney helps Vivian to get her first ladylike dress, teaches her the table manners she needs to know, and finally unites the couple by informing Edward that the chauffeur knows where Vivian lives, and that Edward is making a mistake. Barney tactfully says, "It must be difficult to let go of something so beautiful." Ostensibly he is talking about the necklace, but they both know he is referring to Vivian. The latter does give advice and financial aid to her friend but is simply passing on Edward's words and money—his power and not hers.

Thus in neither movie do females partake of any of the stereotypical   23
male behavior. It is the men who rank higher in wealth, occupation, status, power and action. What of the women? Once again the stereotypes prevail. Traditionally women are to be beautiful, feminine, dependent, devoid of negative emotions but fully expressive of all positive ones. Females exist to fulfill male needs.

Both heroines are beautiful, but both need the right clothing to make   24
them marriageable. When Cinderella is dressed like a princess, the prince only has to see her to fall in love. An item of apparel, her glass slipper, identifies her as the woman the Prince really wants to marry. Clothing has the same powerful effect on Vivian. When she is dressed like a hooker, she can be one. Given elegant and ladylike clothing, Vivian feels cheap when propositioned and eventually decides to give up her life on the streets.

Both heroines are seen as very feminine. Femininity includes beauty and   25
appearance, the aforementioned dependence and helplessness, and also emotions. Traditionally anger and censoriousness are not feminine. The negative characters can express anger. The ugly stepsisters fight with each other and tear Cinderella's dress to shreds. Fear, sadness and self-pity are permissible for good women, as are the positive emotions of compassion, friendship, love and happiness.

Given the situations of both heroines, anger and resentment would   26
appear to be logical reactions. This is not portrayed in either film. Cinderella is obedient to her stepfamily but lives in dreams merely saying, "Well, they can't order me to stop dreaming." Unable to attend the ball, she can cry in self-pity, "It's just no use . . . I can't believe any more." Hope and dreams are restored by her fairy godmother's magic, however. At a later time when there is more openness to emotions, Vivian's anger also seems very restrained. Finding her rent money gone, she is forced to sneak out of her building to avoid the rent collector. All she says to Kit, who took the money, is "I can't believe you bought drugs with our rent money." Edward reveals to Phil that Vivian is a hooker, and although she is ready to walk out, refusing her pay, she stays, saying only, "You hurt me . . . Don't do it again." Her feeling of self-pity in Barney's office is much clearer than her resentment.

Cinderella is usually portrayed with positive emotions. She is kind, help-   27
ful, sympathetic, and loving, and by implication, pure and good. She is concerned with relationships, a real female value, even trying to persuade Bruno, the dog, and Lucifer, the evil cat, to get along together. These qualities, plus her beauty, youth, restraint, and lovely singing voice will make her a good enough wife for a future king.

The Prince, unlike Cinderella, is vulnerable internally. He is cut off from   28
his feelings. She is outwardly oppressed, kept from the ball and locked in her

room by her family and thus must be rescued by another. Nevertheless, Cinderella can fulfill the Prince's needs. He wants a wife and an escape from his boredom. Cinderella's appearance and her adoration of him activate his feelings and involve him in a love relationship. He has found a female to complement himself—she has the emotions that he lacks. Cinderella has a man to give her an identity (she is his wife), the love she has always been dreaming of to compensate for her victimization, and someone to take care of her for the rest of her life. We are told that "they lived happily ever after." *Cinderella,* therefore, clearly defines the male and female stereotypes, and pictures a successful conclusion to both male and female dreams.

Vivian, also, is usually presented with positive emotions. She is helpful, 29 ready to run and answer the door for Edward; grateful, making a point of thanking Barney; sympathetic, expressing concern and compassion for Edward and Morse; and loving, especially to Kit and to Edward. She is good to the extent of being honest and generous with her friends, wanting to pay her bills, and not using drugs. Phil clearly sees her as having a moral influence on Edward, a traditional female stereotype.

Where *Pretty Woman* is modernized is in the openness toward sex. 30 Nevertheless, there is some ambiguity. Sexuality in 1950 was covertly implied in the thought of having children within marriage. With a heroine who is a prostitute, sex in the 1990 film can be blatant. Most scenes are erotic. Vivian can be sexy and at the same time shown as anxious to leave the red light district and to become a proper wife, the traditional female goal.

Amy Kaminsky, in her study of two Argentinean women authors, makes 31 some comments that seem to be applicable to *Pretty Woman*. Agreeing with Simone de Beauvoir that the prostitute "exists as a projection of male fantasy," Kaminsky points out that the male perceptions of paid sexual encounters are of eroticism and pleasure (119). The prostitutes on the other hand, see the interaction as "devoid of sexual content, the better to demonstrate that prostitution is more about humiliation and submission to power than it is about sex" (130). Both views are found in the film. Obviously, the sexual relationship of the two central characters is supposed to be wonderful. Vivian also says, "I just do it. I'm like a robot," and this is after sexual encounters with Edward. The scenes between Vivian and Phil support the idea that prostitution is about abasement and power and not sensuality.

There are other modernizations. Edward is even more inwardly vulnera- 32 ble than the Prince. The hero of *Pretty Woman* is a compulsive worker who is unable to get in touch with his own feelings. Spending 10,000 dollars on therapy has enabled Edward to express his anger toward his father. His fear of heights, his incapacity to maintain personal relationships, and his inability to share his musical gifts with others or to take the time to relax and enjoy his life all indicate additional emotional problems. Vivian lacks the education, knowledge and background to help herself, but she can give to Edward everything he needs. She can laugh out loud; she can be spontaneous; she knows about taking days off; she is able to have fun; she can "veg-out" and relax. Despite Kit's coaching in how not to feel, Vivian allows herself to kiss Edward on the mouth and to fall in love with him. He is slower in his response, but he does begin to enjoy himself, to feel and to care, and, finally, to love. Like Cinderella and her Prince, Vivian succeeds in awakening Edward's dormant emotions.

The movies include a number of sex-segregated fantasies. There is the 33 male dream of making all the money a man could want and of winning out over all competitors. There is the fantasy of the beautiful, willing, submissive woman, as when Vivian says, "Baby, I'm going to treat you so nice you'll never want to let me go." There is the vision of great sex with a beautiful woman, with no responsibilities beyond financial ones. An old theme in popular literature and the theater is that of the rich, royal, or upper class man who wants to be loved for himself alone. None of Edward's friends (the people he "spends time with") really care, but Vivian cannot help herself. She falls in love with Edward despite all her resolves never to mix business and pleasure.

Vivian's fantasies are also stereotypical. The heroine being treated to all 34 the new clothes that she wants is a common theme in modern romances. Perhaps the male apology for having hurt the woman is a female dream. The prostitute's fantasy of a rich, good-looking, non-twisted client merges into Vivian's childhood dream of a knight on a white horse coming to rescue her from her locked tower. She, like Cinderella, wants a man to give her identity, proof that she is loved, and protection/marriage.

Respect for both sexes and the family may be found in feminist works. If 35 the family is criticized, alternatives are suggested. In *Cinderella* all of the human characters are bumbling and ridiculous or greedy and evil. The stepmother and stepsisters have no love for Cinderella, only jealousy and hatred. Her family abuses Cinderella. The King is willing to push his son into any marriage. These ideas are even more emphatic in *Pretty Woman*. In the opening scene Phil puts his wife down. "My wife went to a lot of trouble [for this party]—she called a caterer." Despite 10,000 dollars worth of therapy, Edward was not there when his father died. They had not spoken in 14 years. Little information is given about Vivian's family, but her mother does not sound nurturing. She often locked her daughter in the attic, despite the fact that it did not change Vivian's behavior. Her mother also called her daughter "a bum magnet," which may have been a self-fulfilling prophesy. Only the hero and heroine in *Cinderella* are attractive characters. In *Pretty Woman* Barney and Mr. Morse perhaps provide the "good" father figures that neither Vivian nor Edward had. In both films the family is denigrated, while, ironically, only heterosexual love and marriage are offered as a solution to the problems of life caused by families.

Recent academic work has stressed the importance of sisterhood for 36 women. This topic does not appear in *Cinderella*. Instead, women are shown as competing for men. Cinderella's friends, who often help her, are all birds and animals, which in a hierarchical society are of an even lower rank than herself. Vivian and Kit, her friend, do keep saying, "Take care of you," another modernization. Kit still doesn't seem to be a very good friend. She steers Vivian into prostitution, urges her to deny her feelings, which increases anxiety, and takes the rent money for cocaine. Although they may be thrown out of their apartment, and Vivian actually has the rent money, it takes Kit three days to come and collect it. Vivian is loving, but Kit is irresponsible and uncaring in her behavior. She sees no reason to leave the red light district, even after the dead body of Skinny Marie is found in a dumpster.

Revenge is not a feminist idea. The only revenge displayed in *Cinderella*   37 is between animals. Although the wicked cat torments everyone, it is the dog who is responsible for Lucifer's death. Revenge is more common in *Pretty Woman*. Vivian tells the snobbish salesladies of the commissions they lost. Edward repaid his father for leaving his mother by destroying his father's corporation. Phil loves "the kill." He blames Vivian for his losing a great deal of money and tries to rape her in retaliation.

Two scenes raise the question of feminism. Vivian explains to Kit that she   38 is going to a different city to finish school, find a good job and establish a life for herself. As in Keohane's definition, Vivian seems ready to "pursue her own visions" and "prepare herself to realize her own ambitions and to define her own identity" (23). Unfortunately, such ideas disappear instantly when Edward climbs up her fire escape to rescue her. In a final scene Edward asks about the ending of her dream, what the Princess did after the Knight rescued her. Vivian replies, "She rescued him right back." This *sounds* like a peer relationship, the equality of feminism, but it is not. Both the Knight, the Prince, and Edward have real power. The Princess, Cinderella, and Vivian do not. They have the capacity to have children, and they possess their sexuality, which can stir repressed emotions. As has often been said, men are human beings; women are females. This is reiterated in both films.

Cinderella expresses the gender expectations of the 1950s. *Pretty Woman*   39 demonstrates that feminist ideas are not necessary in a popular movie of the 1990s. Both movies start with the concept of dreams; both promise that dreams can come true. The question is, do we really want all of those same old tired dreams?

WORKS CITED

Bettelheim, Bruno. *The Uses of Enchantment: The Meaning and Importance of Fairy Tales*. New York: Vintage, 1977.

Bottigheimer, Ruth B. *Grimms' Bad Girls and Bold Boys: The Moral and Social Vision of the Tales*. New Haven: Yale UP, 1987.

Cinderella. Dirs. Wilfred Jackson, Hamilton Luske, and Clyde Geronimi. Disney, 1949.

Cox, Marian Roalfe. *Cinderella: Three Hundred and Forty-five Variants*. London: Nutt, 1893.

Dowling, Colette. *The Cinderella Complex: Women's Hidden Fear of Independence*. New York: Pocket, 1981.

The Greatest Movies of All Times. Blockbuster Video. 2nd. ed. N.p.: Blockbuster Entertainment, 1991.

Kaminsky, Amy. "Women Writing about Prostitution." *The Image of the Prostitute in Modern Literature.* Eds. Pierre L. Horn and Mary Beth Pringle. New York: Ungar, 1984.

Keohane, Nannerl O. "Dear Alumnae and Friends of the College." *Wellesley* Fall 1990: 23–24.

Pretty Woman. Dir. Garry Marshall. With Richard Gere and Julia Roberts. Touchstone, 1990.

Shearer, Lloyd. "Intelligence Report." *The Lubbock Avalanche Journal* 24 Feb. 1991. *Parade Magazine:* 24.

Waelti-Walters, Jennifer. *Fairy Tales and the Female Imagination.* Montreal: Eden, 1982.

Zipes, Jack. *Fairy Tales and the Art of Subversion: The Classical Genre for Children and the Process of Civilization.* New York: Wildman, 1983.

■ ■ ■

Review Questions

1. With what key question does Kelley begin her comparative analysis of *Cinderella* and *Pretty Woman?*
2. How does Kelley answer this question? What is her thesis?
3. What is a "Cinderella Complex?"
4. In paragraphs 6–11, Kelley refers to the work of several feminist writers: Keohane, Downing, Waelti-Walters, Zipes, and Bottigheimer. What purposes do these references serve? From these references, to what topic does Kelley make a transition?
5. What are some key similarities between Disney's *Cinderella* and *Pretty Woman?*
6. What are some key differences between Disney's *Cinderella* and *Pretty Woman?*

Discussion and Writing Suggestions

1. Outline Kelley's article, sketching its main sections. Pay especially close attention to the location of her thesis. How does Kelley lead up to the thesis? How does she organize her discussion after the thesis?
2. Reread Nannerl Keohane's definition of feminism in paragraph 6. Observe how Kelley introduces the definition early in the selection and then refers to it in paragraph 38. Read Colette Downing's discussion of the Cinderella complex in paragraph 8; again, observe Kelley's reference back to Downing in paragraph 21, where she describes Vivian's behavior as an example of "counterphobia." Explain Kelley's strategy in using Keohane's and Downing's material in this way.

3. To understand Kelley's comparative analysis fully, the reader needs to view both Disney's *Cinderella* and *Pretty Woman*. Arrange to see both movies, which are readily available in video rental stores. Then reread Kelley's selection and write a response. Is her analysis fair and accurate? Do you agree with her specific points of comparison and contrast? More broadly, do you agree with Kelley's conclusion?
4. Assume that Kelley is correct in the similarities she finds between views on the role of women 40 years ago and views today, as expressed in popular movies. Do these similarities surprise you? Why would we *not* see changes concerning gender roles in a movie like *Pretty Woman* but then see changes in the work of academic writers?
5. Kelley identifies as pivotal the scene in *Pretty Woman* in which Edward climbs a fire escape to "rescue" Vivian, who was planning to move to another city and become respectably self-sufficient. Kelley (paragraph 38) argues that Vivian is *not* Edward's equal even though the movie tries to argue that she is. Assuming you've seen *Pretty Woman*, respond to Kelley's analysis of the scene.
6. Kelley is critiquing two movies, only. Can you think of recent movies that feature strong heroines with minds of their own—movies that provide counter examples to or that cast doubt on Kelley's conclusion about Hollywood's attitude toward women? (Consider, for example, *Ever After* and some of the more recent Disney movies such as *Beauty and the Beast, Pocahontas*, and *Mulan*.)

Cinderella's Stepsisters

TONI MORRISON

Toni Morrison (b. 1931), an African American novelist of such acclaimed works as The Bluest Eye *(1970),* Song of Solomon *(1977),* Tar Baby *(1981), Pulitzer-prize winning* Beloved *(1987),* Jazz *(1992), and* Paradise *(1998), received the Nobel Prize for literature in 1993. Critics have hailed her work as being at once both mythic, in its themes and characters, and intensely realistic in its depictions of the sorrows, struggles, and hopes of black people. The selection that follows is excerpted from an address Morrison delivered at Barnard College. In it, she exhorts her women listeners to treat their "stepsisters" more humanely than Cinderella's stepsisters treated her.*

Let me begin by taking you back a little. Back before the days at college. To nursery school, probably, to a once-upon-a-time time when you first heard, or read, or, I suspect, even saw "Cinderella." Because it is Cinderella that I want to talk about; because it is Cinderella who causes me a feeling of urgency. What is unsettling about that fairy tale is that it is essentially the story of household—a world, if you please—of women gathered together   1 and held together in order to abuse another woman. There is, of course, a rather vague absent father and a nick-of-time prince with a foot fetish. But neither has much personality. And there are the surrogate "mothers," of course (god- and step-), who contribute both to Cinderella's grief and to her release and happiness. But it is her stepsisters who interest me. How crippling it must have been for those young girls to grow up with a mother, to watch and imitate that mother, enslaving another girl.

I am curious about their fortunes after the story ends. For contrary to recent adaptations, the stepsisters were not ugly, clumsy, stupid girls with out-size feet. The Grimm collection describes them as "beautiful and fair in appearance." When we are introduced to them they are beautiful, elegant, women of status. and clearly women of power. Having watched and partici-pated in the violent dominion of another woman, will they be any less cruel when it comes their turn to enslave other children, or even when they are required to take care of their own mother?   2

It is not a wholly medieval problem. It is quite a contemporary one: fem-inine power when directed at other women has historically been wielded in what has been described as a "masculine" manner. Soon you will be in a posi-tion to do the very same thing. Whatever your background—rich or poor—whatever the history of education in your family—five generations or one—you have taken advantage of what has been available to you at Barnard and you will therefore have both the economic and social status of the step-sisters *and* you will have their power.   3

I want not to *ask* you but to *tell* you not to participate in the oppression of your sisters. Mothers who abuse their children are women, and another woman, not an agency, has to be willing to stay their hands. Mothers who set fire to school buses are women, and another woman, not an agency, has to tell them to stay their hands. Women who stop the promotion of other women in careers are women, and another woman must come to the victim's aid. Social and welfare workers who humiliate their clients may be women, and other women colleagues have to deflect their anger.   4

I am alarmed by the violence that women do to each other: professional violence, competitive violence, emotional violence. I am alarmed by the will-ingness of women to enslave other women. I am alarmed by a growing absence of decency on the killing floor of professional women's worlds. You are the women who will take your place in the world where *you* can decide who shall flourish and who shall wither; you will make distinctions between the deserving poor and the undeserving poor; where you can yourself deter-mine which life is expendable and which is indispensable. Since you will have the power to do it, you may also be persuaded that you have the right to do it. As educated women the distinction between the two is first-order business.   5

I am suggesting that we pay as much attention to our nurturing sensibil-ities as to our ambition. You are moving in the direction of freedom and the function of freedom is to free somebody else. You are moving toward self-fulfillment, and the consequences of that fulfillment should be to discover that there is something just as important as you are and that just-as-important thing may be Cinderella—or your stepsister.   6

In your rainbow journey toward the realization of personal goals, don't   7
make choices based only on your security and your safety. Nothing is safe.
That is not to say that anything ever was, or that anything worth achieving
ever should be. Things of value seldom are. It is not safe to have a child. It is
not safe to challenge the status quo. It is not safe to choose work that has not
been done before. Or to do old work in a new way. There will always be
someone there to stop you. But in pursuing your highest ambitions, don't let
your personal safety diminish the safety of your stepsister. In wielding the
power that is deservedly yours, don't permit it to enslave your stepsisters. Let
your might and your power emanate from that place in you that is nurturing
and caring.

Women's rights is not only an abstraction, a cause; it is also a personal   8
affair. It is not only about "us"; it is also about me and you. Just the two of us.

■   ■   ■

Discussion and Writing Suggestions

1. Cinderella "is essentially the story of household—a world, if you please—
   of women gathered together and held together in order to abuse another woman." Do you agree with Morrison's characterization of the story?
2. Morrison finds *Cinderella* to be a story that teaches girls unhealthy ways
   of treating other girls—their "stepsisters." The assumption is that fairy
   tales, heard while young, can have a lasting influence on attitudes later in
   life. Do you accept the assumption?
3. In paragraph 5, Morrison writes: "Since you will have the power to
   [wield influence over others], you may also be persuaded that you have
   the right to do it." What is the difference between having the power to
   take an action and assuming that you have the right to take that action?
   Specifically, in the terms of this essay, what does Morrison mean?
4. Morrison writes that she is "alarmed by the violence that women do to each
   other: professional violence, competitive violence, emotional violence." Is
   it your sense that the "violence" women do to one another is different in
   degree or kind than the violence they do to men—or that men do to men?
5. Morrison suggests an opposition between women's ambition and their
   "nurturing sensibilities." First, what are "nurturing sensibilities?" Are
   they learned (from fairy tales, for instance)? Are they inborn? What is the
   difference between ambition and nurturing sensibilities? How might this
   difference manifest itself in the workplace? In the Perrault version of
   Cinderella? In the Grimm version?
6. In Morrison's view, female power differs from male power. How so?
7. Why should women be any less likely "to participate in the oppression"
   of other women than they are in the oppression of men? Do women
   owe it to other women to show special consideration? Why?
8. What is your response to this address, delivered at Barnard College? If
   you're a woman, what do you take from this selection? If you're a man,

what do you take? Do you suppose that responses to the address will differ along gender lines? Explain.

■ SYNTHESIS ACTIVITIES

1. In 1910, Antti Aarne published one of the early classifications of folk-tale types as an aid to scholars who were collecting tales and needed an efficient means for telling where, and with what changes, similar tales had appeared. In 1927, folklorist Stith Thompson, translating and enlarging Aarne's study, produced a work that is now a standard reference for folklorists the world over. We present the authors' description of type 510 and its two forms 510A ("Cinderella") and 510B. Use this description as a basis on which to compare and contrast any three versions of "Cinderella."

510.   *Cinderella and Cap o'Rushes.*
   I.   *The Persecuted Heroine.* (a) The heroine is abused by her stepmother and stepsisters, or (b) flees in disguise from her father who wants to marry her, or (c) is cast out by him because she has said that she loved him like salt, or (d) is to be killed by a servant.
  II.   *Magic Help.* While she is acting as servant (at home or among strangers) she is advised, provided for, and fed (a) by her dead mother, (b) by a tree on the mother's grave, or (c) a supernatural being, (d) by birds, or (e) by a goat, a sheep, or a cow. When the goat is killed, there springs up from her remains a magic tree.
 III.   *Meeting with Prince.* (a) She dances in beautiful clothing several times with a prince who seeks in vain to keep her, or she is seen by him in church. (b) She gives hints of the abuse she has endured, as servant girl, or (c) she is seen in her beautiful clothing in her room or in the church.
  IV.   *Proof of Identity.* (a) She is discovered through the slipper-test, or (b) through a ring which she throws into the prince's drink or bakes in his bread. (c) She alone is able to pluck the gold apple desired by the knight.
   V.   *Marriage with the Prince.*
  VI.   *Value of Salt.* Her father is served unsalted food and thus learns the meaning of her earlier answer.

Two forms of the type follow.

A. *Cinderella.* The two stepsisters. The stepdaughter at the grave of her own mother, who helps her (milks the cow, shakes the apple tree, helps the old man). Threefold visit to church (dance). Slipper test.

B. *The Dress of Gold, of Silver, and of Stars. (Cap o' Rushes).* Present of the father who wants to marry his own daughter. The maiden as servant of the prince, who throws various objects at her. The three-fold visit to the church and the forgotten shoe. Marriage.

2. Speculate on the reasons folktales are made and told. As you develop a theory, rely first on your own hunches regarding the origins and functions of folktale literature. You might want to recall your experiences as a child listening to tales so that you can discuss their effects on you. Rely as well on the variants of "Cinderella," which you should regard as primary sources (just as scholars do). And make use of the critical pieces you've read—Thompson, Bettelheim, Kelley, and Morrison—selecting pertinent points from each that will help clarify your points. *Remember:* Your own speculation should dominate the paper. Use sources to help you make *your* points.

3. At the conclusion of his article, Stith Thompson writes:

> Literary critics, anthropologists, historians, psychologists, and aestheticians are all needed if we are to hope to know why folktales are made, how they are invented, what art is used in their telling, how they grow and change and occasionally die.

What is your opinion of the critical work you've read on "Cinderella"? Writing from various perspectives, authors in this chapter have analyzed the tale. To what extent have the analyses illuminated "Cinderella" for you? (Have the analyses in any way "ruined" your ability to enjoy "Cinderella"?) To what extent do you find the analyses off the mark? Are the attempts at analysis inappropriate for a children's story? In your view, what place do literary critics, anthropologists, historians, and psychologists have in discussing folktales?

In developing a response to these questions, you might begin with Thompson's quotation and then follow directly with a statement of your thesis. In one part of your paper, critique the work of Bettelheim, Kelley, and/or Morrison as a way of demonstrating which analyses of folktales (if any) seem worthwhile to you. In another section of the paper (or, perhaps, woven into the critiques), you'll refer directly to the variants of "Cinderella." For the sake of convenience, you might refer to a single variant. If so, state as much to the reader and explain your choice of variant.

4. Review the variants of "Cinderella" and select two you would read to your child. In an essay, justify your decision. Which of the older European variants do you prefer: Grimm? Perrault? How do the recent versions by Sexton, Lee, and Disney affect you? And what of the Chinese, African, and Algonquin versions—are they recognizably "Cinderella"?

You might justify the variants you've selected by defining your criteria for selection and then analyzing the stories separately. (Perhaps you will use Aarne and Thompson's classification—see Synthesis

Activity 1.) You might justify your choices negatively—that is, by defining your criteria and then *eliminating* certain variants because they don't meet the criteria. In concluding the paper, you might explain how the variants you've selected work as a pair. How do they complement each other? (Or, perhaps, they *don't* complement each other and this is why you've selected them.)

5. Try writing a version of "Cinderella" and setting it on a college campus. For your version of the story to be an authentic variant, you'll need to retain certain defining features, or motifs. See Aarne and Thompson—Synthesis Activity 1. As you consider the possibilities for your story, recall Thompson's point that the teller of a folktale borrows heavily on earlier versions; the virtue of telling is not in rendering a new story but in retelling an old one and *adapting* it to local conditions and needs. Unless you plan to write a commentary "Cinderella," as Sexton's poem is, you should retain the basic motifs of the old story and add details that will appeal to your particular audience: your classmates.

6. In her 1981 book *The Cinderella Complex*, Colette Dowling wrote:

> It is the thesis of this book that personal, psychological dependency—the deep wish to be taken care of by others—is the chief force holding women down today. I call this "The Cinderella Complex"—a network of largely repressed attitudes and fears that keep women in a kind of half-light, retreating from the full use of their minds and creativity. Like Cinderella, women today are still waiting for something external to transform their lives.

    In an essay, respond to Dowling's thesis. First, apply her thesis to a few of the variants of "Cinderella." Does the thesis hold in each case? Next, respond to her view that "the chief force holding women down today" is psychological dependency, or the need for "something external" (i.e., a Prince) to transform their lives. In your experience, have you observed a Cinderella complex at work?

7. Discuss the process by which Cinderella falls in love in these tales. The paper that you write will be an extended comparison and contrast in which you observe this process at work in the variants and then discuss similarities and differences. (In structuring your paper, you'll need to make some choices: Which variants will you discuss and in what order?) At the conclusion of your extended comparison and contrast, try to answer the "so what" question. That is, pull your observations together and make a statement about Cinderella's falling in love. What is the significance of what you've learned? Share this significance with your readers.

8. Write an explanatory synthesis in which you attempt to define a feminist perspective on "Cinderella" as this is expressed by Sexton, Kelley, and Morrison. If you are feeling ambitious, you can write a second part to this essay by *applying* that definition to one variant.

Essentially, you would be writing a critique of that variant, based on the principles defined in the opening section of your essay. Conclude by giving your assessment of the variant, based on the feminist principles you have defined.

▇ RESEARCH ACTIVITIES

1. Research the fairy-tale literature of your ancestors, both the tales and any critical commentary that you can find on them. Once you have read the material, talk with older members of your family to hear any tales they have to tell. (Seek, especially, oral versions of stories you have already read.) In a paper, discuss the role that fairy-tale literature has played, and continues to play, in your family.

2. Locate the book *Morphology of the Folktale* (1958), by Russian folklorist Vladimir Propp. Use the information you find there to analyze the elements of any three fairy tales of your choosing. In a paper, report on your analysis and evaluate the usefulness of Propp's system of classifying the key elements of fairy-tale literature.

3. Bruno Bettelheim's *Uses of Enchantment* (1975) generated a great deal of reaction on its publication. Read Bettelheim and locate as many reviews of his work as possible. Based on your own reactions and on your reading of the reviews, write an evaluation in which you address Bettelheim's key assumption that fairy-tale literature provides important insights into the psychological life of children.

4. Locate and study multiple versions of any fairy tale other than "Cinderella." For a new version of "Little Red Riding Hood" see "The Company of Wolves" by Angela Carter, in this text ("The Beast Within"). Having read the versions, identify—and write your paper on—what you feel are the defining elements that make the tales variants of a single story. See if you can find the tale listed as a "type" in Aarne and Thompson, *The Types of Folk-Tales*. If you wish, argue that one version of the tale is preferable to others.

5. Various critics, such as Madonna Kolbenshchlag and Jack Zipes, author of *Breaking the Magic Spell* (1979), have taken the approach that fairy tales are far from innocuous children's stories; rather, they inculcate the unsuspecting with the value systems of the dominant culture. Write a paper in which you evaluate an interpretation of fairy-tale literature. In your paper, explicitly address the assumption that fairy tales are not morally or politically neutral but, rather, imply a distinct set of values.

6. Write a children's story. Decide on the age group that you will address, and then go to a local public library and find several books directed to the same audience. (1) Analyze these books and write a brief paper in which you identify the story elements that seem especially important for your intended audience. (2) Then attempt your

own story. (3) When you have finished, answer this question: What values are implicit in your story? What will children who read or hear the story learn about themselves and their world? Plan to submit your brief analytical paper, your story, and your final comment.

7. Videotape, and then study, several hours of Saturday morning cartoons. Then locate and read a collection of Grimm's fairy tales. In a comparative analysis, examine the cartoons and the fairy tales along any four or five dimensions that you think are important. The point of your comparisons and contrasts will be to determine how well the two types of presentations stack up against each other. Which do you find more entertaining? Illuminating? Ambitious? Useful? (These criteria are suggestions only. You should generate your own criteria as part of your research.)

8. Arrange to read to your favorite young person a series of fairy tales. Based on your understanding of the selections in this chapter, develop a list of questions concerning the importance or usefulness of fairy-tale literature to children. Read to your young friend on several occasions and, if possible, talk about the stories after you read them (or while you are reading). Then write a paper on your experience, answering as many of your initial questions as possible. (Be sure in your paper to provide a profile of the child with whom you worked; to review your selection of stories; and to list the questions you wanted to explore.)

You, the Jury

ALICE MORE: While you talk, he's gone!

THOMAS MORE: And go he should, if he was the Devil himself, until he broke the law!

WILLIAM ROPER: So now you'd give the Devil benefit of law!

MORE: Yes. What would you do? Cut a great road through the law to get after the Devil?

ROPER: I'd cut down every law in England to do that!

MORE: Oh? And when the last law was down, and the Devil turned round on you—where would you hide, Roper, the laws all being flat? This country's planted thick with laws from coast to coast—man's laws, not God's—and if you cut them down—and you're just the man to do it—d'you really think you could stand upright in the winds that would blow then? [*Quietly.*] Yes, I'd give the Devil benefit of law, for my own safety's sake.

—Robert Bolt, *A Man for All Seasons*

The above lines indicate one way of looking at the law, but clearly, many people take a different view of the legal profession. One of Shakespeare's characters declares, "The first thing we do, let's kill all the lawyers" (*Henry VI*, Pt II). Never mind that while playing off the public's perennial resentment of lawyers, Shakespeare intended this line as a sardonic commentary on mob mentality. Still, everyone loves a good lawyer joke. ("Why didn't the shark eat the lawyer who fell out of his boat? Professional courtesy.") Of course, in these litigious times, the same people who tell lawyer jokes hurry to get their own after they slip on the ice in their neighbor's driveway or when they're arrested on a drunk driving charge.

In Robert Bolt's play, Thomas More views the law as civilized society's first line of defense against chaos and anarchy. Without the law, he argues, we would have no protection against "the winds that would blow" in a lawless society. But even if we don't accept this exalted view of the law, it's certainly true that all of us, at some points in our lives, will have dealings with the law (not necessarily as a defendant, we hasten to add), and that as citizens of society, most of us rely upon the law to protect us against those who would violate our rights and to impose damages upon those who have injured us. (Those who don't rely on the law often rely instead on their own private arsenals to repel invaders and predators.)

If the average citizen is not the plaintiff or the defendant in a court case, then her or his most common direct experience with the law may be as a juror. Chosen at random from a cross-section of the population, jurors may be called upon to render a verdict in a civil case (a case of product liability, for example, or negligence, or libel) or in a criminal case (such as robbery or murder). After the lawyers on both sides have presented their witnesses and their evidence, after they have made their arguments and rebutted their opponents, and after the judge has explained the law to the jury in language they can understand, it falls to the jury to apply the law to the facts of the particular case. They must decide whether or not a rule has been violated, and if it has, the price the defendant must pay—perhaps a fine, perhaps a jail term, perhaps even the forfeiture of his or her life.

Underlying this chapter is the assumption that you are a jury member (or perhaps a judge) in a particular case. You will be presented with the facts of the case. You will also be presented with the relevant law. It is now your task to study the issues, to render a verdict either for the plaintiff or for the defendant, and—most importantly, for our purposes—to explain your reasoning. Don't worry about becoming tangled in the thickets of the law (and some of these thickets are very dense indeed). We will assume no previous legal knowledge, and for each case we will present enough facts and enough statements about the law to enable you to make an educated judgment, just as if you were a member of a jury.

Don't worry, either, about making the "right" choice. The most important thing is not that you come out on the correct side or even the side that actually prevailed in the end. (Keep in mind that through the appeals process, a higher court can reverse the ruling of a lower court—saying, in effect, that the lower court was wrong.) What is important is that you carefully analyze the case, that you go through the reasoning process systematically and logically, in a manner consistent with the facts.

In one sense, this chapter previews a particular situation in which you might one day find yourself—fulfilling your civic duty as a juror in an actual case. More generally, it will provide you with some interesting cases through which you can practice a very fundamental intellectual task in the academic and professional worlds: the task of applying a general rule or principle to a particular case or circumstance. Obviously, this is a process that doesn't happen only in law. As a student in a sociology course, for example, you might show how some principles relating to the ways that individuals obey authority apply in particular cases (for example, the suicides in the Heaven's Gate cult) and even allow you to make certain broad predictions about behavior. As a film student, you might show how the general features of the typical *film noir* operate in particular films, such as *The Big Sleep* or *A Touch of Evil*.

Besides exercising your intellectual faculties, you'll see that it's often fascinating to plunge into legal battles. After all, legal cases are, at heart, conflicts, and conflicts are inherently interesting. That's why we like to read books or watch TV shows or movies that are set in the courtroom.

We begin our chapter with a number of civil cases (that is, cases of private wrongs), starting with "The Maiden and the Pot of Gold: A Case of Emotional Distress," in which a woman sues some men who tricked her into believing that she had recovered a pot of gold from a field. Following are three selections that will help orient you to the legal system and legal reasoning. In

"The American Legal System" attorney David Hricik explains where the law comes from and describes the process of the typical lawsuit. In "How to Present Your Case Systematically and Logically," Veda R. Charrow, Myra K. Erhardt, and Robert P. Charrow describe legal thinking and legal writing, focusing particularly on the important IRAC (issue, rule, application, conclusion) technique. In "*Venezia v. Miller Brewing Company:* A Defective Beer Bottle?" writing instructor Ruthi Erdman offers a model analysis, in IRAC format, of a case in which parents sued a brewer when their young son was injured after shattering a beer bottle against a telephone pole.

"The Ridiculed Employee" deals with an additional case of emotional distress upon which you, as a jury member, can deliberate. (Can a man collect damages from a supervisor who repeatedly makes fun of his stuttering?) This selection is followed by "Assault and Battery on the Gridiron: A Case of Reckless Disregard of Safety," an unusual case in which one football player sues another for injuries sustained on the playing field. "Of Accidents and Injuries" deals with several cases of negligence, two involving spilled coffee and another two involving subway accidents. (You may remember the famous McDonald's coffee spill and the woman who collected millions for it.) In "Urban War Zone: A Case of Public Nuisance" you will consider opposing viewpoints on whether a city has a constitutional right to restrict gang activities—both criminal and noncriminal—in its neighborhoods.

The next part of the chapter deals with criminal cases. In "The Felled Stop Signs," you will decide the legal responsibility of some teenagers who pulled down highway signs, including a stop sign—a piece of "fun" that resulted in a fatal accident. In "Drag Racing and Death: Some Cases of Manslaughter," you will consider the question of how seriously the law should deal with someone who participates in a fatal drag race, even though he may not have driven the car actually involved in the accident. On a somewhat lighter note, we offer a rare case of official judicial humor: "*Chevrolet v. Tree:* A Case of Poetic Justice." Next, as a guide to the entire chapter, we offer "A Glossary of Legal Terms" to help you understand the unfamiliar legal language you will encounter while working with these cases. Finally, an expanded section on "Research Activities" shows how to conduct respectable legal research without actually being enrolled in law school.

Each selection dealing with a particular case consists of two elements. The first element presents the "Facts of the Case," as written by the panel of appeals court judges who ruled upon the case. With only a few exceptions, all of the cases you will read in this chapter are cases that have been appealed by either the plaintiff or the defendant to an appeals court after the original jury verdict. The second element presents the "Statements of the Law," statements that you will apply to the facts of the case, just as if you were following the judge's instructions. In some selections, these statements do consist of the kind of instructions that a judge would give to a jury in such cases. In others, they will be the actual statutes that may or may not have been violated. You may also read excerpts from case law—judicial opinions from previous cases dealing with similar issues that may have bearing upon the case you are currently considering.

What you will not find, however, as you consider these cases, is the ultimate outcome. If you know the outcome in advance, you are likely to be unduly swayed in your reasoning, attempting to bring it in line with the arguments of the side that prevailed. As we suggested earlier, which side won is less important for our purposes than the process of logically applying general principles to specific cases. Nevertheless, if you have to know which side won, ask your instructor; she or he will be able to consult the *Instructor's Manual*.

Occasionally, however, it will be difficult or even impossible to find out which side ultimately won. That's because some cases are sent back by the appeals court to the trial court, and most trial court cases are not published—though photocopied transcripts are available (for a hefty fee) from the clerk of the court—and the more newsworthy cases are covered by reporters. Also, a good many civil cases, after going up and down through the appeals process, are ultimately settled out of court—and frequently, the terms of the settlement are not publicly available.

This chapter offers considerable opportunities for group work. After all, work on a jury is a collective enterprise, and before a jury arrives at a verdict, unanimous or otherwise, its individual members must engage in a good deal of discussion, perhaps even argument. In some cases, your papers may be written collectively by the group; but even when individually written, they could reflect the views of more than one viewpoint. In fact, as you will see in the Charrow/Erhardt selection, the IRAC format, used widely in legal writing, should include a consideration and a rebuttal of opposing arguments.

A Note on Synthesis Activities

Because of the special nature of legal reasoning, we include synthesis activities, where appropriate, as part of the Discussion and Writing Suggestions following some of the grouped case selections, rather than at the end of the chapter.

Lawyers synthesize cases as a matter of course, but only when they are closely related, in order to point out legal precedents. We do include a few closely related cases in this chapter (for example, *Nickerson v. Hodges* and *Harris v. Jones*, both in the "emotional distress" selection and *Liebeck v. McDonalds* and *Greene v. Hardees* in the "negligence" selection); but for the most part, the cases we have selected are too different in facts and legal issues to be usefully synthesized.

The Maiden and the Pot of Gold: A Case of Emotional Distress
(NICKERSON V. HODGES)

You may have heard the phrase "emotional distress" in connection with a lawsuit and wondered how such a vague term could possibly have legal meaning. After all, people are always doing things that distress other people. Bosses inflict distress on their employees, teachers distress students, lovers distress each other. Undoubtedly, your parents drove you to emotional distress (and vice versa) yet few children sue their parents—though that has happened.

Still, there's emotional distress and there's emotional distress; some people seem to go out of their way to maliciously and outrageously distress others, and the distress they occasion sometimes is particularly severe. In these cases, we feel that the perpetrators should be legally liable—meaning that they should be forced to pay financial damages to their victims. But plaintiffs must do more than claim that they have suffered emotional distress at the hands of the defendants. They must prove such a claim, by showing how the legal definition of emotional distress applies to their particular case, or by showing how their particular case is similar, if not identical, to one or more previous cases of proven emotional distress.

The following passage presents one such case: it is part of an opinion by the Supreme Court of Louisiana in 1920. First, we present the "Facts of the Case" as summarized by the panel of judges who wrote the opinion. (Their ruling itself and the reasoning behind it are not presented here; these are for you to decide. Your instructor, however, will be able to consult the Instructor's Manual *and tell you how the case turned out.) Following the facts of the case, we offer a set of instructions that the judge might give to the jury before they begin deliberating in a case involving emotional distress. Strictly speaking, these instructions are anachronistic, since they were written in the latter part of the century (and are intended for California juries). Nonetheless, they embody the same essential assumptions about liability for emotional distress that were considered by the judges who decided the case of* Nickerson v. Hodges.

Note: In civil (as opposed to criminal) cases, such as this one, a jury will render a verdict of either of either "liable" or "not liable" (as opposed to "guilty or "not guilty").

NICKERSON ET AL. v. HODGES ET AL.
(Supreme Court of Louisiana. Feb. 2, 1920)

The Facts of the Case*　　　　　　　　　　　　　　　　　　　　　　　1

Miss Carrie E. Nickerson brought this suit against H. R. Hayes, William or "Bud" Baker, John W. Smith, Mrs. Fannie Smith, Miss Minnie Smith, A. J. Hodges, G. G. Gatling, R. M. Coyle, Sam P. D. Coyle, and Dr. Charles Coyle, claiming $15,000 as damages, alleged to have been caused in the form of financial outlay, loss in business, mental and physical suffering, humiliation, and injury to reputation and social standing, all growing out of an alleged malicious deception and conspiracy with respect to the finding of a supposed pot of gold. Subsequent to the filing of the petition, and before the trial, the said Miss Nickerson died, and her legal heirs, some 10 in number, were made parties plaintiff, and now prosecute this suit.

　　Miss Nickerson was a kinswoman of Burton and Lawson Deck, the　　2
exact degree of relationship not being fully shown by the record, and there

---

* *Nickerson v. Hodges.* 84 So. 37 (1920).

had been, in the family, a tradition that these two gentlemen, who died many years ago, had, prior to their deaths, buried a large amount of gold coin on the place now owned by the defendant John W. Smith, or on another near by. She was employed by the California Perfume Company to solicit orders for their wares in the towns, villages, etc., in Webster and other parishes, and on the occasion of a visit to the city of Shreveport seems to have interviewed a fortune teller, who told her that her said relatives had buried the gold, and gave her what purported to be a map or plat showing its location on the property of Smith.

Thereafter, with the help of some three or four other persons, principally relatives, and one Bushong, she spent several months digging, at intervals, around the house and on the premises of Smith, who seems to have extended them a cordial welcome, and to have permitted them to dig almost without limit as to time and place, and in addition boarded the fortune hunters, while so engaged, without charge. We assume that this was due, perhaps, to the fact that he, too, had a slight hope that they might find something, and he was to receive a part thereof for his concessions. At any rate, the diggers pursued their course with such persistence and at such lengths, digging around the roots of shade trees, the pillars of his house, etc. until finally, his daughter, the said Minnie Smith, William or "Bud" Baker, and H. R. Hayes conceived the idea of themselves providing a "pot of gold" for the explorers to find.

Accordingly they obtained an old copper kettle or bucket, filled it with rocks and wet dirt, and buried it in an old chimney seat on the adjoining place, where the searchers had been or were intending to also prospect for the supposed treasure. Two lids or tops were placed on the pot, the first being fastened down with hay wire; then a note was written by Hayes, dated, according to some, July 1, 1884, and, as to others, 1784, directing whoever should find the pot not to open it for three days, and to notify all the heirs. This note was wrapped in tin, placed between the first and second lids, and the latter was also securely fastened down with hay wire. This took place some time toward the latter part of March, and, according to these three defendants, was to have been an April fool; but plans miscarried somewhat, and the proper opportunity for the "find" did not present itself until April 14th.

On that day Miss Nickerson and her associates were searching and digging near the point where the pot had been buried, when one Grady Hayes, a brother of H. R. Hayes, following directions from the latter, and apparently helping the explorers to hunt for the gold, dug up the pot and gave the alarm. All of those in the vicinity, of course, rushed to the spot, those who were "in" on the secret being apparently as much excited as the rest, and, after some discussion, it was decided to remove the lid. When this was done, the note was discovered, and H. R. Hayes advised Miss Nickerson that he thought it proper that its directions should be carried out, and that the bank at Cotton Valley, a few miles distant, was the best place to deposit the "gold" for safe-keeping, until the delays could run and the heirs be notified, as requested. Following this suggestion, the pot was placed in a gunny sack, tied up, and taken to the bank for deposit. Defendant Gatling was the cashier of the bank, but refused to give a receipt for the deposit as a "pot of gold," because, as he insisted, he did not know what it contained.

As might have been supposed, it did not take long for the news to spread that Miss Nickerson and her associates in the search for fortune, had found a pot of gold, and the discussion and interest in the matter became so general that defendant A. J. Hodges, vice president of the bank, went over from his place of business in Cotton Valley to the bank, and he and Gatling, after talking the matter over, decided to examine the pot, so that, in event it did contain gold, proper precautions to guard the bank might be taken, pending the return of Miss Nickerson and the appearance of those who might claim the fortune. These two undid the wire sufficiently to peep into the pot, and discovered that it apparently contained only dirt. They then replaced the lid and held their tongues until the reappearance of Miss Nickerson. However, the secret leaked out from other sources, that the whole matter was a joke, and this information too, became pretty well distributed. 6

After depositing the pot in the bank, Miss Nickerson went to Minden, La., and induced Judge R. C. Drew to agree to accompany her to Cotton Valley on the following Monday (the deposit at the bank having been made on Saturday) for the purpose of seeing that the ceremonies surrounding the opening of the treasure were properly conducted. Judge Drew swears that he had heard in some way that the matter was a joke, and so informed Miss Nickerson, warning her not to place too much faith in the idea that she was about to come into a fortune, but that finally, because of his friendly relations with and kindly feeling toward her, he consented and did go, mainly to gratify her wishes in the premises. Some half a dozen other relatives of Burton and Lawson Deck were notified, and either accompanied or preceded Miss Nickerson to Cotton Valley. 7

With the stage thus set, the parties all appeared at the bank on Monday morning at about 11 o'clock, and among the number were H. R. Hayes, one of the defendants, who seems to have been one of the guiding spirits in the scheme, and one Bushong, the latter, we infer, from intimations thrown out by witnesses in the record, being at the time either an avowed or supposed suitor of Miss Nickerson's. Judge Drew, as the spokesman for the party, approached Gatling and informed him that it was desired that the pot be produced for the purpose of opening and examining the contents for the benefit of those thus assembled. The testimony of the witnesses varies a little as to just when the storm began; some say, as soon as the sack was brought out. Miss Nickerson discovered that the string was tied near the top, instead of down low around the pot, and immediately commenced to shout that she had been robbed; others insist that she was calm until the package was opened and the mocking earth and stones met her view. Be that as it may, she flew into a rage, threw the lid of the pot at Gatling, and for some reason, not clearly explained, turned the force of her wrath upon Hayes to such an extent that he appealed for protection, and Bushong, with another, held her arms to prevent further violence. 8

Miss Nickerson was a maiden, nearing the age of 45 years, and some 20 years before had been an inmate of an insane asylum, to the knowledge of 9 those who had thus deceived her. She was energetic and self-supporting in her chosen line of employment, as a soap drummer, until she met the fortune teller who gave her the "information" which she evidently firmly believed would ultimately enable her to find the fortune which the family tradition told her had been left hidden by her deceased relatives. The conspirators, no doubt, merely intended what they did as a practical joke, and had no willful intention of doing the lady any injury. However, the results were quite serious indeed, and the mental suffering and humiliation must have been quite unbearable, to say nothing of the disappointment and conviction, which she carried to her grave some two years later, that she had been robbed. ∎

Judge's Instructions to the Jury*

Ladies and Gentlemen of the Jury: 1

It is now my duty to instruct you on the law that applies to this case. It   2
is your duty to follow the law.

As jurors it is your duty to determine the effect and value of the evi-   3
dence and to decide all questions of fact.

You must not be influenced by sympathy, prejudice or passion.   4

The plaintiff _Carrie E. Nickerson_ seeks to recover damages based   5
upon a claim of intentional infliction of emotional distress.

The essential elements of such a claim are: 6

1. The defendant engaged in outrageous, [unprivileged] conduct;
2. [a. The] defendant intended to cause plaintiff to suffer emotional distress; [or
   [b.] [(1) The defendant engaged in the conduct with reckless disregard of the probability of causing plaintiff to suffer emotional distress;
   (2) The plaintiff was present at the time the outrageous conduct occurred; and
   (3) The defendant knew that the plaintiff was present;]
3. The plaintiff suffered severe emotional distress; and
4. Such outrageous conduct of the defendant was a cause of the emotional distress suffered by the plaintiff.

The term "emotional distress" means mental distress, mental suffering   7
or mental anguish. It includes all highly unpleasant mental reactions, such as fright, nervousness, grief, anxiety, worry, mortification, shock, humiliation and indignity, as well as physical pain.

The word "severe," in the phrase "severe emotional distress," means   8
substantial or enduring as distinguished from trivial or transitory. Severe

*California Jury Instructions, Civil: Book of Approved Jury Instructions [BAJI]. 8th ed. Prepared by The Committee on Standard Jury Instruction Civil, of the Superior Court of Los Angeles County, California. Hon. Stephen M. Lachs, Judge of the Superior Court, Chairman. Compiled and Edited by Paul G. Breckenridge, Jr. St. Paul, MN: West Publishing Co., 1994.

emotional distress is emotional distress of such substantial quantity or enduring quality that no reasonable person in a civilized society should be expected to endure it.

In determining the severity of emotional distress you should consider its intensity and duration. 9

Extreme and outrageous conduct is conduct which goes beyond all possible bounds of decency so as to be regarded as atrocious and utterly intolerable in a civilized community. 10

Extreme and outrageous conduct is not mere insults, indignities, threats, annoyances, petty oppressions or other trivialities. All persons must necessarily be expected and required to be hardened to a certain amount of rough language and to occasional acts that are definitely inconsiderate and unkind. 11

Extreme and outrageous conduct, however, is conduct which would cause an average member of the community to immediately react in outrage. 12

The extreme and outrageous character of a defendant's conduct may arise from defendant's knowledge that a plaintiff is peculiarly susceptible to emotional distress by reason of some physical or mental condition or peculiarity. Conduct may become extreme and outrageous when a defendant proceeds in the face of such knowledge, where it would not be so if defendant did not know. 13

If you find that plaintiff is entitled to a verdict against defendant, you must then award plaintiff damages in an amount that will reasonably compensate plaintiff for all loss or harm, provided that you find it was [or will be] suffered by plaintiff and was caused by the defendant's conduct. The amount of such award shall include: 14

Reasonable compensation for any fears, anxiety and other emotional distress suffered by the plaintiff. 15

No definite standard [or method of calculation] is prescribed by law by which to fix reasonable compensation for emotional distress. Nor is the opinion of any witness required as to the amount of such reasonable compensation. [Furthermore, the argument of counsel as to the amount of damages is not evidence of reasonable compensation.] In making an award for emotional distress you shall exercise your authority with calm and reasonable judgment and the damages you fix shall be just and reasonable in the light of the evidence. 16

■ ■ ■

Discussion and Writing Suggestions

1. If you were a member of the jury in the case of *Nickerson v. Hodges*, would you vote for a verdict of "liable for intentional infliction of emotional distress" against the defendants? Explain your vote, applying the

"Judge's Instructions to the Jury"—and in particular, the definitions concerning "emotional distress"—to the particular facts of this case.

2. If you vote "liable," what damages would you award the plaintiffs? Keep in mind that Miss Nickerson herself has died and the plaintiffs are now her heirs.

3. Notice that the instructions to the jury include the admonition that "All persons must necessarily be expected and required to be hardened . . . to occasional acts that are definitely inconsiderate and unkind." This is distinguished from conduct that is "[e]xtreme and outrageous." Define the conduct at issue according to one set of terms or the other, explaining your reasoning.

4. How do the particular circumstances of the plaintiff, Miss Nickerson, affect your vote on the verdict? For example, if Miss Nickerson were a different kind of person, or if the "practical joke" had been differently handled, how (if at all) would this have changed your view of the case and your view of whether the plaintiff had suffered emotional distress and was due financial damages?

5. Of the ten defendants charged, only three (Minnie Smith, William or "Bud" Baker, and H. R. Hayes) admitted to being in on the phony pot of gold scheme, but they denied "any malicious or unlawful intent." As a juror, how would you respond to this defense? How do you assess the moral and legal responsibility of some of the other figures in the case— such as the bank cashier G. G. Gatling and bank vice president A. H. Hodges?

The American Legal System

DAVID HRICIK

Where does the law come from? What is a plaintiff? Why does this country need so many different kinds of law courts? How does a case get to the Supreme Court? These basic questions about American law are addressed by David Hricik in the following selection from his book Law School Basics: A Preview of Law School and Legal Reasoning *(1996). Hricik's explanations—intended for prospective law students as an introduction to law school—will provide an important foundation for your understanding of the cases you read and write about in this chapter.*

A graduate of Northwestern University School of Law, Hricik practices at the Houston law firm of Baker and Botts. He teaches legal writing at the University of Houston Law School Center, helped create the Law School Basics *computer course at America Online, and has published articles and given lectures on topics ranging from legal ethics, to patent litigation, to judicial reform.*

Here are some basic questions: What is the "law"? Where does "law" come 1 from? What is the purpose of law?

The last question first: What is the purpose of law? 2

A. What is the Purpose of Law?

For our purposes, it is easier to begin by saying what the purpose of law is   3
not, rather than what it is. Laws are not the same as personal or individual morality. This is easy to prove: some things are legal, yet are considered immoral by some people. *See, e.g., Roe v. Wade,* 410 U.S. 113, 119 (1973) (abortion is protected by the United States Constitution). . . .[1]

Some things which are moral to some people are nonetheless always ille-   4
gal. *See, e.g., Reynolds v. United States,* 98 U.S. 145, 167 (1878) (polygamy is illegal). Some laws even require people to do things which they find utter-ly immoral. For example, Christian Scientists may be forced to accept blood transfusions, even though they believe it damns them to eternal hell. Laws are not morals—at least not an individual's or a particular group's morals. That much is clear.

There are many theories about why we have laws, about what purpose is   5
served by our explicit, institutionalized and complex legal system. Some view law as merely a tool to oppress people; others argue that laws express reason and order. Many view law as a system of rules which, when applied to facts by judges and juries, should result in rational and reasonable results to par-ticular cases—to particular facts. We will not decide who is right. As with most things, the truth no doubt lies somewhere in between.

For our purpose, we do not care too much about what the purpose of law   6
is, at least not on this fundamental level. For lawyers and law students, the law is a set of "rules" which create "duties," the breaking of which may result in "liability," usually in the form of money damages. Put at its simplest, "the law" is an expression of the social policy that people have a duty to follow the rules, and those who don't will incur liability for any harm they cause.

The "rule" is very often something so vague as having a duty to "act rea-   7
sonably under the circumstances." Or, the rule can be very specific: having to stop at a stop sign, having to drive no more than 30 miles per hour, having to do what you have agreed in a contract to do.

"Liability" for breaking a rule often comes in the form of a "judgment"   8
for money damages, which is a court's order for one person to pay money to another person. It can also take the form of an "injunction," which is a court order prohibiting someone from doing something. For example, a court could enjoin a party from selling dangerous products. (In criminal cases, "liability"

---

[1] You have just seen a case cited . . . as a lawyer would do in a brief or memorandum. A few words about case *citations* is in order here. Look at the cite for *Roe.* The words "*See, e.g.,*" mean "See, for example." "*Roe v. Wade*" means that someone named Roe is involved in a suit with someone named Wade. (You can't tell who sued whom, though, not just from the *style* of the case.) "410 U.S. 113, 119" means that the Roe versus Wade case is "reported" (*i.e.,* printed) at volume 410 of the United States Reporters, beginning at page 113, and that the specific words from the case to which I'm referring are on page 119 of that Reporter. The fact that it is in the United States Reporters means it was decided by the United States Supreme Court, as that particular reporter publishes only its decisions. The date in the parentheses is when the case was decided. The parenthetical explanation of "abortion is pro-tected by the United States Constitution" is what *I* say that the court said. It is one way to let the reader know what a case says.

can take the form of a jail or prison sentence or a fine—which is a court's order that a person pay money to the government.)

So the "purpose" of law is to have rules which create duties which, when   9
broken, result in some sort of liability to the injured party. Obviously that is
an oversimplification: for example, some of the law comprises those rules that
define *how much* someone who breaks a "rule" must pay the injured party.
But, as a general concept, law is meant to define the duties which people owe
one another.

B. Where Does "Law" Come From?

As to where this "law" comes from, it is again probably easiest to first say   10
what the law is *not*. The western world's legal systems are of two primary
kinds: common law and civil law. For our purposes, the "common law"
system which we have in the United States can be described by contrasting it
to civil law systems. By illuminating the differences, we can better see the
common law methods. Understanding how the common law system works
will help you understand why you spend so much of law school reading
cases.

Civil law jurisdictions[2] place their primary emphasis on legislation—   11
statutes or codes enacted by a parliament or similar legislative body. The governing legislatures of civil law countries try to enact comprehensive codes on
every subject. These statutes or codes provide the main source of the legal
rules. In theory, everything necessary for the legal operation of society is covered in a code or statute. Consequently, in civil law countries, decisions by
courts are not as important as those codes. The courts play a role, to be sure,
but it is comparatively less than in common law countries.

In contrast, under the common law system, like we have in the United   12
States, the society places less overall emphasis on statutes and codes. The
"common" law plays a much greater role because there are *no* statutes or
codes governing *most* legal issues. Instead, most of the "rules" are in the form
of previously-decided judicial opinions, not statutes or codes. Unlike civil
law systems, in common law countries, *judicially*-developed "rules"—that
have never been approved by any voters or elected legislative body, such as a
Congress, a state legislature, or even a city council—provide much of the governing legal framework.

The common law method means building up the law by court opinions,   13
case-by-case, as opposed to creating the law by legislative enactment. The
facts surrounding origins of the English system are illuminating:

> England had laws just as Continental countries did, even though these laws
> were not 'written' in the Romanist sense of being declared in authoritative
> texts. The rules established by general custom were declared not by a single

---

[2] An example of a civil law jurisdiction is France.

judge alone but by the whole court of the king, which represented the mag-
nates of the kingdom; *but there was no authorized version of these rules.*[3]

Under our common law system, most law comes in the form of these
judicial opinions: there is no big encyclopedia of "rules" setting out what can,
must, or should be done under any set of facts or circumstances. You will
seldom go to a "rule book" to find an "outline" of legal rules on the issue you
are researching. As will become more clear later, the common law is really a
series of *cases*—not rules—which can be applied to later fact patterns.   14

The point is so important that it bears repeating: most "law" in common
law systems is case law, decided by judges and memorialized only in written
"opinions"—not statutes, codes, or other "rule books." For instance, the
"elements" which must be alleged to effectively claim that a party was negligent in injuring another person were essentially created by the courts of
England in the sixteenth century, and were adopted by America's state courts
throughout the nineteenth century. Likewise, most contract law is primarily
found only in cases decided over hundreds of years by judges. Similarly, the
rules governing real property come from cases which were written by judges
in England long, long ago involving fee tails, fee simples, and other legal
concepts whose importance has left us, but whose labels have not.   15

Of course, there are specialized statutes in common law jurisdictions
such as the United States. Statutes provide a very comprehensive set of legal
rules for some issues. For instance, significant federal legislation, called
ERISA, governs employee benefit plans. ERISA is a complex statute, and the
government has promulgated hundreds of pages of rules and regulations
which further clarify and add to the statute. The patent statutes are comprehensive, as are some of the federal environmental statutes. Similarly, many
state legislatures have enacted very detailed state statutes on various subjects. For example, the Texas Deceptive Trade Practices Act (often called the
"DTPA"), provides a fairly complex codification of law designed to protect
consumers. There are also a *lot* of federal and state regulations which are relatively comprehensive.   16

Nonetheless, with certain exceptions, statutes play a comparatively
insignificant role in the common law system. For example, even though the
DTPA is probably one of the longer Texas statutes, the legislature left many
issues for the courts to decide by applying the statute to various facts. Those
judicial interpretations are as important—if not more so—than the words of
the DTPA statute itself.   17

The main supposed benefit of the common law system is its flexibility: a
judge can decide that the facts before him or her are different enough under
the rules so that a different *result* from an earlier case should be reached.
Courts can also create a different, new rule when needed to apply to new   18

---

[3]*Dictionary of the History of Ideas* 694 (emphasis added).

problems or social changes. The common law has an additional benefit: judges decide cases based on actual, concrete disputes, not hypotheticals. A statute cannot be written which will govern every possible fact pattern, but a court can decide what rule should apply to specific facts, and a jury can decide what result is just under all kinds of different and unforeseeable fact patterns. The common law system allows for a lot of discretion in order to achieve justice in each dispute.

Most people are surprised to learn that many, if not most, of the laws   19 that lawyers rely on in their day-to-day practice were never passed by a legislature or by Congress, but instead evolved over hundreds of years as courts developed and applied judge-made rules to the facts presented in each new dispute brought before them. That arguably makes judges very powerful. That power, in turn, means that *your* ability to effectively argue the law can shape the outcome of your client's cases. Knowing how to find the law and how to write about it will make you a more effective, and therefore a more powerful, lawyer.

To sum up, the "purpose" of law is to create duties which, if broken,   20 mean that the wrong-doer must compensate the injured party. This "set of rules," however, exists only in the form of case law; there is no "rule book," as there is in civil law countries.

C. Why Do We Have "Cases" Anyway?

Lawyers use the word "case" to refer to many very different things. "Case"   21 means a dispute: your client has been sued by IBM. That is a case. "Case" also refers to the published opinions which judges have written when they decided earlier disputes. Thus, if IBM's case against your client went to trial and the judge wrote an opinion explaining the case, that opinion is also a "case." I will refer to the latter kinds of "cases" as "opinions" whenever I think the context is confusing.

How are opinions created? As next shown a court may, when it decides   22 a case, write an opinion that will be published in a reporter. Those published opinions then become *precedent*—the law—for other courts to use when deciding later cases. To understand why opinions get written, you need to understand how lawsuits are resolved. To illustrate, I will give you something you will not get in law school: a brief and over-simplified synopsis of a lawsuit.

The *plaintiff* is the party which sues. The plaintiff files a "complaint."   23 The complaint lays out the allegations which, plaintiff claims to show, why the defendant (the party being sued) owes the plaintiff money. Put in terms of the "purpose" of law: the plaintiff alleges facts which show that the defendant owed a duty to the plaintiff, breached that duty, and injured the plaintiff. For example, in a case you will read as a 1-L,[4] the plaintiff claims that the defen-

---

[4] 1-L—the first year of law school.

dant had agreed to deliver a load of coal to the plaintiff's lumber mill; because the defendant failed to deliver the coal on time and as promised, the mill had to shut down, causing the plaintiff to lose business; because he had no coal, he could not run the mill, and so could not cut wood to sell to his customers.

After being served with the plaintiff's complaint, a defendant must file an "answer." The defendant will "deny" those allegations in the plaintiff's complaint which, the defendant contends, are not true, and will assert any "affirmative defenses" he might have. Again, for example, the defendant will deny that there was a contract to deliver coal; if there was a contract, it is legally unenforceable because it was not in writing; even if there were an enforceable contract, the damages were caused or at least exacerbated by plaintiff's failure to order coal from some other supplier. **24**

The judge will then issue a "scheduling order." Scheduling orders typically set the case for trial in a year or so, and establish certain deadlines along the way, the most important of which is a "discovery cut-off" deadline. The parties will have up to that date to take "discovery" of each other. Discovery consists of asking each other written questions (called "interrogatories"); asking each other to produce documents which are relevant to the suit (called "requests for production"); and taking each other's sworn answers to oral questions (called "depositions"). . . . **25**

Typically, at some point near the end of the discovery period, one side or the other will file a "motion for summary judgment." This motion says that the moving party is entitled to "win as a matter of law": the *movant* will argue that given the undisputed facts and under the controlling case law, it is entitled to have the court enter judgment in its favor. For example, the defendant coal supplier could file a motion for summary judgment contending that there had been no enforceable written contract, and so a judgment should be entered in the defendant's favor ordering that the plaintiff "take nothing" for the lawsuit. The other side will oppose this motion by filing a response in which it argues either that a jury must be allowed to decide the case because there are disputed facts, or, for various legal reasons, that the controlling opinions do not mean that the movant should win as a matter of law. So, the plaintiff in our coal case might contend that there really was a written contract and that a jury needs to decide whether to believe the plaintiff's story that his dog had eaten it. **26**

When the trial court judge grants or denies the motion for summary judgment, he may write an opinion which explains the facts of the case and the controlling legal principles, and then *applies* those legal principles to the facts of that particular lawsuit to explain why the court reached the result it did. Judges write opinions so that the parties understand why he ruled as he did; so that the appellate court can review whether his decision was correct (if there is a later appeal); and, in a larger sense, so that in the future other parties can conduct themselves in accordance with the law. This is one way the published opinions are created: district court judges sometimes write and publish opinions when deciding cases. **27**

If the trial judge determines that the movant is entitled to win the case as   28
a matter of law, the losing side can appeal after he writes the opinion. If the
judge denies the motion, then there must be a jury trial, after which the losing
side can still appeal. Judges sometimes write an opinion even after a jury trial,
when denying the losing party's motion for new trial or motion for judgment
as a matter of law. This is another way published opinions are created: by district judges when explaining why the result reached after a trial by jury was
correct and fair.

Any appeal will be decided by an intermediate appellate court (the exact   29
name of which depends on whether the suit is in state or federal court). The
party that *lost* in the lower court will appeal, and will be called the "appellant." The party that won will be called the "appellee." The parties will file
their *briefs* in the appellate court. After reading the briefs and perhaps allowing a short oral argument, the appellate court will write an opinion that
either *affirms* the trial court's judgment as correct, or *reverses* the trial court
because it committed some reversible error. Any appellate court opinion
which is published becomes part of the common law that can be applied by
later courts. This is another way the published opinions are created.

The loser in the court of appeals can then try to appeal to the highest   30
appellate court (usually called a supreme court). As with appellate court decisions, the published opinions of the supreme court join the common law
decision.

Thus, we have opinions because of the way by which we resolve lawsuits   31
in the common law system. The parties need to know *why* one side won. The
reviewing appellate court needs to be able to check whether the lower court
got it right. Society needs to know what the legal rules are so that in the
future, people can avoid breaking the rules. That's why we have all these
opinions.

D. The State and Federal Court Systems

The next piece of the puzzle which no one will ever *explain* to you in law   32
school is how the courts are structured. You are just supposed to already
know it, or you are supposed to figure it out from reading opinions for class.

There are at least two reasons why you need to understand the court sys-   33
tems. (System*s*, not system.) First, it will help you understand cases better
when you are preparing for class. When you read the case, and it says that the
plaintiff lost in the trial court, but won a reversal in the appellate court, you
will know that the plaintiff will be the appellee in the decision in the supreme
court. Second, the fundamental principle of legal reasoning is the doctrine of
precedent. You have to know which earlier cases are *controlling* precedent
over the particular court your case is in. In order to know which cases are
binding on your court, you have to understand how the state and federal judicial systems in the United States are structured. (You'll see why in a moment.)
The doctrine of precedent is crucial in the practice of law and in the United
States legal systems.

The fact that the United States has the federal judiciary, along with fifty   34
independent state court systems, as well as countless administrative and quasi-
judicial bodies, makes it probably the most complex judicial system in the
world. Welcome to it!

1. The Structure of the Federal Court System

The federal court system has a pyramid structure. The federal district courts,   35
of which there are about ninety, are at the base. Twelve federal appellate (or
"circuit") courts make up the middle. At the top of the judicial pyramid sits
the United States Supreme Court.

We'll study the federal judicial pyramid from the bottom up.   36

A. UNITED STATES DISTRICT COURTS As mentioned, there are about ninety   37
federal district courts. Each state has at least one, and most states are divided into several districts.

Lawsuits must originally be filed in district courts. All federal trials take   38
place in the district courts. Witnesses testify, evidence is received, and juries
reach their decisions *only* in these district courts. District courts are the only
courts which *find facts*; appellate courts cannot do so, but instead merely
apply the law to the facts as found by the district court, or determine whether
there is evidence to support the district court's fact-findings. Appellate courts
merely review the written "record" of testimony and exhibits taken in by the
trial court and apply the law to double-check whether the trial court was correct. . . .

B. UNITED STATES COURTS OF APPEAL—THE CIRCUIT COURTS Appeals from   39
district courts, with few exceptions, are heard by federal appellate courts,
called "circuit courts." The United States is divided into twelve regional cir-
cuits—the first through eleventh, plus the Court of Appeals for the District of
Columbia. (There is also the "Federal Circuit," which takes appeals from all
over the country, but only on certain issues, like patent cases.)

An appeal from a district court must go to the circuit court for that par-   40
ticular region. For example, Texas is within the Fifth Circuit. California is
within the Ninth. New York is in the Second. Illinois is in the Seventh. The
District of Columbia has its own circuit. If you look in the front of any
volume of the "F.2d's" (the Federal Second) Reporters, you'll see a map of
which states are in each circuit. So, if you lose a case in a federal district court
in Texas, you file your appeal with the Fifth Circuit. If you lose one in a
California federal district court, you appeal to the Ninth Circuit.

Whoever lost in the district court may appeal. The loser—called in the   41
appellate court the "appellant"—will file an opening brief in the circuit court
which explains why the district court's decision was wrong. Typically, the circuit courts limit appellants' briefs to fifty pages. Whoever won below will file
an appellee's brief, which is also typically fifty pages. The appellant then
usually gets a 25-page reply brief.

The appeal will be assigned to a "panel" from among the judges in that   42
particular circuit. A panel usually has three judges. These three judges then
read the briefs and sometimes permit a 30-minute (15 minute per side) oral
argument. (Oral argument is becoming rare, which—you guessed it—is [one]
reason why legal writing is so important.) Some time after oral argument, the
court will issue a written opinion explaining why the district court was right
or wrong, and so whether it is affirming or reversing the decision of the district court.

Lawsuits may not originally be filed in the appellate courts—each appel-   43
late court only *reviews* the decisions of the district courts in its circuit. As
Justice Thurgood Marshall was quoted by *The Wall Street Journal*, "such
appeals should await the outcome of the trial." It is hard to argue with that.

C. THE UNITED STATES SUPREME COURT If the loser in the court of appeals   44
wants to try, it can ask the United States Supreme Court to review the case.
Again, the United States Supreme Court sits alone at the top of the federal
judicial pyramid.

The principal way by which cases reach the Supreme Court is through the   45
writ of *certiorari*. Whoever lost in the appellate court will write a "petition for
a writ of *certiorari*," which argues why the Court should issue an order (a
"writ of *certiorari*") directing the lower court to send up records of the case
so that the Supreme Court can consider the issues which it is interested in, to
see if the result reached in the case was correct. The loser is called a "peti-
tioner" in the Supreme Court because that's what it's doing: it is petitioning
the Court for a writ of *certiorari*. The winner in the circuit court will write a
brief opposing *cert* (pronounced like the candy), arguing that either the circuit
court decided the issues correctly, or that essentially the issues are just not
important enough to warrant the Supreme Court's time, or both. The winner
below is called a "respondent" in the Supreme Court because that is what it
is doing: it is responding to a petition for a writ.

Nine justices (not, mind you, "judges") sit on the United States Supreme   46
Court. Like all federal judges, they are appointed by the President, subject to
approval by the Senate, and serve for life unless impeached. One of the nine
is appointed Chief Justice, also subject to Senate approval. He (there has
never been a female Chief Justice) presides over the Court's sessions and
determines which justice will write each opinion.

If the Court grants *cert*, then the parties write briefs, much as they did in   47
the circuit court. The Supreme Court then holds an oral argument and will
later issue an opinion deciding the case. . . .

The Supreme Court is the ultimate judicial tribunal: if you lose there, it's   48
"game over."

2. The Structures of the State Court Systems

The vast majority of cases are handled by state courts. Why? There are far   49
more state courts than federal district courts, there are far more disputes

which can be heard only in state court, there are more state laws than federal laws, and there is virtually no federal common law—only federal statutory law. Federal courts are courts of *limited jurisdiction.* Only suits which are expressly recognized by federal law may be filed in federal court. Everything else must go to state court.[5] There is very, very little federal law governing divorce, car wrecks, breach of contract, products liability, and most common disputes. Thus, most cases must go where most of the governing law subsists: in state court.

The structure of each state court system varies by state. Each state has 50 between two and four levels of courts. Generally, most states have lower courts of limited jurisdiction. Examples of this kind of court include county courts, family courts, municipal courts, JP (justice of the peace) courts, or small claims courts. The next higher level are the district or superior courts, which also act as appellate courts for cases decided by the courts of limited jurisdiction. Next up are the "true" appellate courts often thought of as intermediate appellate courts. Finally, at the top, sits a court of last resort, usually, but not always, called the state's "supreme court."

A. COURTS OF LIMITED JURISDICTION At the bottom of each state court "pyra- 51 mid" are its courts of limited jurisdiction. These can include municipal courts, JP courts, small claim courts, family courts, and the like. These courts have limited jurisdiction. This means that they have jurisdiction to handle cases involving only smaller amounts of money, or only certain kinds of cases (for example, landlord-tenant disputes). 52

Generally, these courts are informal. Parties often file suits without a lawyer; the rules of evidence may not apply; and the judges probably never write opinions that will be published in the reporters. These courts are critically important to solving the problems that confront people every day, but they generally do not add much to the common law, because they do not write opinions that are published in the reporters.

B. DISTRICT OR SUPERIOR COURTS Just above the courts of limited jurisdiction 53 are the district courts. In some states, they are called superior courts. District courts handle the bulk of the state court caseload. They also handle appeals from the courts of limited jurisdiction: the loser in a lawsuit filed in a court of limited jurisdiction can "appeal" up to the district or superior court, although usually the "appeal" takes the form of a completely new trial—"*de novo* review"—rather than the review only by written briefs which takes place in the typical appeal.

Practice before a state district court is, in broad view, much the same as 54 in a federal district court (discussed above). The procedural rules can be quite

[5] There is something called "diversity jurisdiction," which allows people to file a lawsuit in federal court only because the defendant resides in a different state than the state in which suit is brought. Even in such suits, however, state law is applied to the merits of the dispute.

different, however, and so the actual daily practice may be very different. For our purposes, however, they are quite similar: the written practice consists of pleadings and motions supported by briefs. . . .

c. INTERMEDIATE APPELLATE COURTS Intermediate appellate courts exist in 55
many states, and are much like the federal circuit courts. In most states, as a matter of right the loser in a district court can appeal and have a state court of appeals review the district court's decision for error.

   The briefing practice in state appellate courts is much as it is in the fed- 56
eral circuit courts: main brief, response; reply, followed (perhaps) by oral argument. . . .

d. COURTS OF LAST RESORT: STATE SUPREME COURTS At the top of state 57
court systems is a court of ultimate review. In a deliberate scheme to confuse you, New York calls its supreme court the "court of appeals," and Texas has *two* supreme courts—one for criminal matters and the other for civil suits. Most states, thankfully, have only one highest court, and they call it the supreme court.

   Most state supreme courts act like the United States Supreme Court, 58
taking only those cases in which they are interested and ignoring the others. They will decide whether to take your case based only on the written briefs. This means that only your *writing* can persuade the court to review your case. (Which, you guessed it, is yet another reason writing is so important.)

                              ■   ■   ■

Review Questions

   1. How does Hricik define the law?
   2. What is the difference between civil law and common law?

Discussion and Writing Suggestions

   1. Does the law as Hricik describes it—a set of rules that create duties— seem different from the way you have previously thought of the law? If so, what were your previous impressions?
   2. Based on how Hricik describes the difference between statutory law and case law, what advantages and disadvantages do you see with a legal system based largely on case law, like the one that operates in the United States?
   3. If you or someone you know has ever had experience with the legal system—particularly in terms of the way that Hricik describes the process of the typical lawsuit—describe what happened. Based on this experience, what advantages and problems did you find with the system?

How to Present Your Case
Systematically and Logically

VEDA R. CHARROW
MYRA K. ERHARDT
ROBERT P. CHARROW

The principles of effective argument, as we've discussed them in Part One of this book, apply to law no less than other disciplines and professional fields. But the special requirements of legal argument call for a more specific set of guidelines than we were able to provide earlier. The following passage, from a widely used textbook, Clear and Effective Legal Writing *by Veda R. Charrow, Myra K. Erhardt, and Robert P. Charrow, will provide some of these guidelines.*

Here, Charrow, Erhardt, and Charrow explain the IRAC (Issue, Rule, Application, Conclusion) approach to organizing legal arguments—one that has been used by generations of law students, but one whose usefulness extends beyond legal writing. Charrow and Erhardt also explain how to construct syllogisms in legal arguments and how to develop the kinds of analogies between similar cases that are basic to legal thinking.

This selection will provide an essential basis for many of the assignments that you will write in the rest of "You, the Jury."

IRAC: Organizing a Complex Legal Document

You must always impose order on your writing. Legal documents, in partic-   1
ular, demand a tight, logical structure. In other documents poor organization
may interfere with readers' comprehension, but in legal documents poor
organization can cause even greater problems. In an adversarial document, for
example, your opponents will be looking for any weak spots they can find. A
gap in your logic caused by poor organization can give your opponents an
opening for attack. In a nonadversarial document, poor organization can
make the reader believe that either your knowledge and research are not
thorough or that your thinking is not logical. . . .

Thus, the outline for a complex legal document might look like this: 2

1. Introduction providing a context
2. First claim
   a. What is the *claim* you are making? How are you proposing to resolve
      the issue or subissue? This can be further subdivided into
      i. A statement of the particular *issue* or subissue you have identified. At
         this point you may also wish to state how you believe the issue
         should be resolved.[1]
      ii. The *rule* of law that is most pertinent to the situation.
      iii. Why and how the rule should be *applied* to the facts of your case.

---

[1] This is especially important in persuasive writing, where you want to make a forceful opening statement.

iv. A *conclusion* based upon your analysis and the application of the
  law to the facts.
  (IRAC is the mnemonic for this method of organizing a claim.)
  b. What are the *objections* and counterarguments to your claim?
  c. What is your *response* to the objections and counterarguments?
  d. What is your *conclusion*? This section summarizes your reasoning
  and restates your claim.
3. Second claim
4. Conclusion

This model works well for any level of analysis, from the general analy-   3
sis of a whole problem down to the analysis of specific subissues. When you
have used this model to analyze all of the issues or subissues, you will then be
able to come to a conclusion.

1. Identifying and Presenting Issues

Your first step in setting up the structure of a complex legal document is to iden-   4
tify the important issues that you will be discussing in your document. Here is
an example of a fact situation and the issues that should be analyzed in a brief.

> Jones worked as a salesman for the Southern Corporation. His job required
> him to provide his own car and deliver perishable supplies to customers on
> his route. Jones had been told a number of times by his supervisor at
> Southern that it was extremely important that he stay on a strict time sched-
> ule with his deliveries.
>
> On March 10, Jones made a delivery during normal working hours. He
> returned to the parking lot in which he had left his car and found that Warner's
> car was blocking his car. After waiting ten minutes for Warner to return,
> Jones finally decided that he had to leave. Jones tried to move his car, but put
> a large dent in Warner's bumper and broke one of Warner's headlights in the
> process. Warner returned just as Jones broke the headlight. Warner demand-
> ed payment for the damage to his car and refused to move his car so that Jones
> could leave. Jones angrily got out of his car and moved towards Warner,
> yelling that he was already late for his deliveries and that it was Warner's fault.
> Warner angrily shook his fist at Jones and again demanded payment for the
> damage to his car. Jones, in anger, hit Warner, knocking him to the ground.
> Warner had Jones arrested.
>
> After Jones's arrest, Southern Corporation learned from the local police
> that Jones had been convicted of aggravated assault three years before
> Southern had hired him. When Southern hired Jones, the corporation did not
> inquire into his background. Warner is suing Southern for the personal
> injuries he suffered as a result of Jones's attack.
>
> *Issue 1:* Did the defendant commit an intentional tort [wrongful act]
>   when he knocked the plaintiff to the ground, or was the action priv-
>   ileged?
> *Issue 2:* Is an employer liable for injuries that its employee intentionally
>   inflicted upon the plaintiff while the employee was trying to make
>   deliveries on behalf of the employer?

Issue 3: Can the defendant employer be held liable for negligence in hiring and retaining an employee who has a criminal record for assault if the employer did not investigate the employee's background and does not know of the record?

Once you have identified the main issues, you may find that you can deal   5
with them more easily by breaking them down into smaller, more manageable subissues (or sub-subissues). For example, you might see the following subissues under Issue 1.

1. Did the act of the plaintiff in shaking his fist at the defendant place the defendant in imminent threat of physical injury?
   a. If the plaintiff's act placed the defendant in imminent threat of physical injury, did he have a duty to retreat?
   b. If the defendant did not have a duty to retreat, did he use excessive force in repelling the imminent threat?
2. Did the act of the plaintiff in refusing to move his vehicle constitute the tort of false imprisonment?
3. Did the act of the plaintiff in refusing to move his vehicle constitute the tort of trespass to chattel?

2. Presenting the Rule

The rule of law that you use in your analysis can come from case law or enact-   6
ed laws. Once you have established the applicable rule in a particular case, you should present it in a way that will make it easy to apply the law to the facts. For example, if you are discussing a particular tort or crime, or the definition of a particular legal concept, describe it by breaking it up into its elements. Thus, if the issue is whether a defendant has committed a battery, a good way to present the rule would be to take the definition from section 13 of the Restatement (Second) of Torts.

> [Section] 13   *Battery: Harmful Contact*
>> An actor is subject to liability for battery if
>> a) he *acts intending* to cause harmful or offensive contact with the person of the other or a third person, or an imminent apprehension of such a contact, and
>> b) a harmful contact with the person of the other directly or indirectly *results* (emphasis added).

If you have to synthesize the rule from case law, this will probably take   7
more time and space. This is because you will often need to go through the steps that you took and the sources that you used in your distillation of the rule.

3. Application: Analyzing Facts and Law

The next step is to examine the facts and decide whether a rule is satisfied or   8
the elements of an offense or tort are present. You should organize this section so that it follows the order of the elements of the rule. For example, you

could discuss the facts in the Jones case by applying them to the elements of battery.

> First, the defendant, Jones, *acted* when he attempted to strike the plaintiff in the parking lot. Second, the defendant *intended* to harm the plaintiff, since he spoke angrily to the plaintiff, shook his fist at the plaintiff, and then struck him. Third, the defendant struck the plaintiff and knocked the plaintiff to the ground. Thus, the defendant's act *resulted in* the harmful contact to the plaintiff.

The application section of your document is the most crucial, for it is here   9
that you have to convince your audience that your analysis is sound and that your conclusions follow logically. We have presented only the most basic application of facts to law in the example above. . . .

4. Anticipating Counterarguments

One of the best ways to ensure that you have treated an issue thoroughly is to   10
try to anticipate all possible counterarguments and defenses. Put yourself in your opponent's position: List all of the ways that you can attack or weaken your own argument. Be ruthless. After you compile the list, develop responses or rebuttals for each area of attack.

There are a number of counterarguments that the defendant might raise   11
in the battery case. The defendant might attack the way in which you applied the law to the facts; or the defendant might raise the defense that he was using reasonable force to prevent the plaintiff from committing a tort against his property (the plaintiff refused to let the defendant remove his car from the lot) or against his person (the plaintiff prevented the defendant from leaving by holding something of great value to the defendant).

5. Providing a Conclusion

The contents of your conclusion will depend upon the length and complexity   12
of the information that you have presented in the other portions of your analysis. For example, if your application section is long and intricate, then you might want to refresh your reader's memory by briefly recounting the steps in your reasoning. If the application section is short, however, you would probably not want to reiterate your reasoning. In either case, you would finish with a statement of your position or your interpretation of the facts and the law. Here is an example of a simple way to conclude the battery issue:

> Because all three elements of battery are present in the defendant's conduct, the defendant is liable for the tort of battery.

6. Organizing a Complex Legal Document: An Example

Now that we have presented and explained the different parts of the model on   13
pages 685–686, look at the following fully developed issue analysis. This analysis follows the standard IRAC—issue, rule, application, conclusion—outline.

Issue   The issue presented in this case is whether one spouse can sue the other for injuries caused by the negligence of the other spouse.

Rule   In *Sink v. Sink*, 239 P.2d 933 (1952), this court held that neither spouse may maintain an action in tort for damages against the other. Although a number of states have recently enacted legislation which allows these suits, Kansas has not joined them. This can be seen in the fact that the Kansas legislature has just enacted, in 1981, a law which authorizes any insurer to exclude coverage for any bodily injury to "any insured or any family member of an insured" in its insurance policies. Even though this law does not go into effect until January 1, 1982, it is clear that Kansas's position on interspousal tort immunity has not changed.

Application   In the present case, the plaintiff, who is the defendant's wife, was injured when the car the defendant was driving crashed into a telephone pole. The plaintiff was sitting in the passenger seat at the time of the accident. She sustained a broken leg and cuts and bruises. Although the defendant may have been negligent, the accident obviously involved injuries inflicted by one spouse upon another.

Conclusion   Therefore, this case clearly falls within the mandate of *Sink*, and the plaintiff's case should be dismissed on the basis of Kansas's very viable interspousal immunity.

Counterargument   The plaintiff has claimed that a decision upholding interspousal immunity violates logic and basic principles of justice. She notes that the new law has not yet gone into effect, so that it does not apply to the present case. She also contends that the foremost justification for immunity laws is illogical, since it is based on the premise that personal tort actions between husband and wife would disrupt the peace and harmony of the home. She cites the Restatement of the Law of Torts, which criticizes this justification by stating that it is based upon the faulty assumption that an uncompensated tort makes for peace in the family.

Response   However, it is no more logical to contend that family harmony will be better served if a husband and wife can drag each other into court and meet each other as legal adversaries. In addition, the plaintiff has overlooked a far more persuasive argument for interspousal tort immunity: under Kansas law, any recovery that the plaintiff-wife would obtain if this action were allowed to proceed would inure to the benefit of the defendant-husband. All property acquired by either spouse during the marriage is "marital property" in which each spouse has a common ownership interest. If the injured spouse (plaintiff) should die, the surviving spouse could maintain an action for wrongful death, and could share in any recovery of losses. This result would allow a negligent party to profit by his own actions. This is a result which would be truly offensive to anyone's sense of justice.

Conclusion The doctrine of interspousal immunity is as viable today as it was when initially enunciated by this court. It not only fosters family harmony, but also prevents a spouse from profiting from his or her own negligence.

For some types of documents, you will want to abbreviate or rearrange   14
the scheme presented above. For example, if you are answering an opponent's brief, you could begin by stating the opponent's objections and then follow with your own claims and conclusions. With this order, a separate "response" section may no longer be necessary, since the response may become part of your main argument. For example:

Issue The issue presented in this case is whether one spouse can sue the other for injuries caused by the negligence of the other spouse.

Subissue Does Kansas law presently require interspousal tort immunity?

The plaintiff in this case has claimed that a decision upholding interspousal immunity violates basic principles of justice and current Kansas law. She acknowledges that Kansas has enacted a law which authorizes any insurer to exclude coverage for any bodily injury to "any insured or any family member of an insured" in its insurance policies. However, she points out that this law does not establish blanket interspousal tort immunity. Also, because the law has not yet even gone into effect, it does not apply to the present case.

Rule The plaintiff's reliance on the nature and effective date of the legislation is misplaced. The law to which the plaintiff alludes is one that the Kansas legislature has just enacted, in 1981. Even though this law does not go into effect until January 1, 1982, Kansas' position on interspousal tort immunity was established long ago and has not changed. In *Sink v. Sink*, 239 P.2d

933 (1952), this court held that neither spouse may maintain an action for tort for damages against the other. Although a number of States have recently enacted legislation which explicitly allows these suits, Kansas has not joined them. In fact, the legislation mentioned by the plaintiff makes it clear that Kansas is not attempting to establish a new policy on interspousal immunity, but is merely incorporating its current policy into the laws which govern insurers.

Application   As the plaintiff has pointed out in her brief, she was injured when the car her husband was driving crashed into a telephone pole. Whether or not the defendant was negligent, the accident involved injuries inflicted by one spouse upon another. As such, Kansas' policy on interspousal tort immunity would apply.

Subissue   Is the rationale behind interspousal immunity illogical?

The plaintiff further contends that the foremost justification for immunity laws is illogical, since it is based on the premise that personal tort actions between husband and wife would disrupt family harmony. She cites the Restatement of Torts, which criticizes this justification by stating that it is based upon the faulty assumption that an uncompensated tort makes for peace in the family.

Rule   The plaintiff and the Restatement have overlooked the even greater illogic behind a premise that family harmony can be better served if a husband and wife can drag each other into court and meet as legal adversaries. In addition, the plaintiff has overlooked a far more persuasive argument for interspousal immunity: under Kansas law, any recovery that the plaintiff-wife would obtain if this action were allowed to proceed would inure to the benefit of the defendant husband.

Application   In the present case, the husband and wife could be forced to endure years as legal adversaries, waiting for an interspousal lawsuit to slowly wend its way through a complex legal system. In addition, the defendant could stand to profit by any recovery his wife receives from the couple's insurance.

Conclusion   The doctrine of interspousal immunity is as viable today as it was when initially enunciated by this court. It not only fosters family harmony, but also prevents a spouse from profiting from his or her own negligence.

SOME CAVEATS There are several caveats to consider when you use IRAC or 15 any similar outline to analyze the issues in a law school problem. Students sometimes get the impression that they have done a complete, well-rounded analysis of a question once they have taken the obvious issues through the IRAC outline. IRAC can give you a false sense of security if you mistake the thorough analysis of an issue for the thorough analysis of a whole problem or question. Once you have completed analyzing the obvious issues, make sure that you reread the problem to search for subissues or elements of issues that you might have overlooked. These are important and can influence the outcome of your problem.

IRAC is merely a framework within which to build your analysis: It 16 should not appear to your readers that you have merely plugged information into a rigid formula. Edit your writing to eliminate the mechanical effects of a series of statements that the issue is *W*, the rule is *X*, the analysis is *Y*, and that, therefore, the conclusion is *Z*. . . .

Developing a Logical Argument

In order to create a logical structure, think about what you are trying to 17 accomplish when you deal with a problem in law. You will often find that you are trying to establish that a specific set of facts fits within a well-settled rule of law. One way to do this logically and systematically is to use the principles of deductive reasoning to set up the skeleton of your legal analysis.

1. Deductive Reasoning in Law

You are probably familiar with the basic categorical syllogism. For example: 18

> *Major premise*: All men are mortal.
> *Minor premise*: Socrates is a man.
> *Conclusion*: Socrates is mortal.

Deductive reasoning is the thought process that occurs whenever you set 19 out to show that a minor premise (a specific situation, event, person, or object) fits within the class covered by a major premise (an established rule, principle, or truth) and to prove that, consequently, what applies to the class covered by the major premise must necessarily apply to the specific situation. In short, deductive reasoning allows you to prove that your particular case is covered by an established rule.

Deductive reasoning is a cornerstone of legal thought. Lawyers are often 20 called upon to decide how a rule of law applies to a given case. Since the rule is usually stated in general terms and a client's problem is generally very specific, deductive reasoning can be used to bridge the gap between the general and the specific. For example:

> *Rule of Law* (major premise): Courts have held that any agreement made in jest by one party and reasonably understood to be in jest by the other party will not be enforced as a contract.
> *Facts of our case* (minor premise): Robert agreed to paint Lee's entire house, but both Robert and Lee understood that Robert was only joking.
> *Conclusion:* Robert's agreement is not an enforceable contract.

These basic steps of deductive reasoning form the skeleton of a legal argument. In fact, the rule, application, conclusion sequence of IRAC forms a simple syllogism: The rule contains the major premise, the application contains the particular facts of the minor premise, and the conclusion sums up the information. . . .   21

2. Expanding the Syllogism into a Legal Argument

The syllogism serves as the skeleton of a legal argument. Once you have created the skeleton, you must flesh it out. For example, once you have the major premise in a particular case, you must present evidence that your specific fact situation does indeed fit within the class covered by the major premise. In the example about painting Lee's house, you would have to show that there was a promise but that both parties knew that it was made in jest, as "jest" has been interpreted by the courts.   22

In the rest of this section, we discuss techniques for expanding the different parts of a syllogism. We present the parts in the order of the standard syllogism, even though you may not always work in this order when you construct your argument.   23

A. THE MAJOR PREMISE In most cases, your major premise will either be a given (you are told what the rule of law is and you must apply it to a set of facts), or you must extract the rule from legal authorities such as constitutions, statutes, regulations, and reported cases. You must then draw the appropriate information from these authorities and present the information so that your rule is well substantiated. In addition, you must define the abstract terms in the rule in order to clarify the rule and make it easier to apply the rule to the facts in your case. . . .   24

B. THE MINOR PREMISE The most important techniques for expanding your major premise are citing authority and defining terms. The most important technique for expanding your minor premise is analogy, either to the facts of other cases or to the policies underlying other decisions.   25

Arguing by analogy: similarity of facts. When you argue by analogy, 26 you reason that if two or more situations are the same in some significant respect, they are likely to be the same in other significant respects as well, so they ought to be classified together. (If you want to *distinguish* your case from others, you show that it is *not* analogous.)

You could link the major and the minor premises of the general welfare 27 case by using the following analogy: Funding should be provided for X Auto Company because the case is similar to cases in which the Court has approved Congress's funding in the past. Here is a way you might express this.

The facts in the X Auto Company case are very similar to the facts in 28 cases that have already established the scope of "general welfare." In all of these cases, the courts agreed that

1. Private individuals or entities may receive funds from the federal government.
2. Individuals and entities may receive money that they did not personally contribute to the government.
3. Individuals and entities may receive money from the government when it helps them continue to earn money and spend money.

Arguing by analogy: similarity of policy considerations. Another way 29 to link the major and minor premises is to show that the facts of your case are covered by a particular rule because your case furthers the same social goals as other cases already covered by the rule. For example, in the X Auto Company case, you might argue that your case and the previously decided cases all fulfill the following goals, regardless of the similarities or differences in their facts.

1. They keep individuals from turning to the state for support.
2. They keep the economy balanced and functioning.
3. They show people that the government will intervene if a segment of the population is about to experience an economic crisis.

The first step in making a policy argument is to identify what the authors 30 of a rule intended when they created the rule. If you are investigating legislation, try looking at and analyzing legislative history or policy statements in the legislation itself. If you are investigating an opinion, try comparing your case with other cases that have been decided under the rule and showing that your case will help to further the same goals. You can look at any language in these opinions that sheds light on the objectives of the ruling.

Once you have established the purpose of the rule, i.e., what it was 31 intended to accomplish, you can alter your major premise to include this purpose and emphasize the specific facts in your minor premise that suit the major premise. You would then argue that the authors of the rule intended that the rule cover cases like yours and that the principles behind the rule will be dangerously eroded if the court excludes your case.

If you were arguing that by analogy to the *Steward Machine* case X   32
Auto Company should get federal funds, you might use this analogy on policy considerations:

> The courts have found that federal payments to particular groups or individuals such as the unemployed or the elderly can serve the general welfare because, in the long run, these payments benefit the entire nation. This idea is reflected in the words of Justice Cardozo in *Steward Machine* 301 U.S. 548, 586-587 (1937):
>
>> During the years 1929 to 1936, when the country was passing through a cyclical depression, the number of the unemployed mounted to unprecedented heights. . . . The fact developed quickly that the states were unable to give the requisite relief. The problem had become national in area and dimensions. There was need of help from the nation if the people were not to starve. It is too late today for the argument to be heard with tolerance that in a crisis so extreme the use of the moneys of the nation to relieve the unemployed and their dependents is a use for any purpose narrower than the promotion of the general welfare.
>
> X Auto Company employs hundreds of thousands of employees. In addition, there are thousands of other employees who work in industries that depend on X Auto Company. Even though the problems of X Auto Company are not on the scale of the problems of the Great Depression, the loss of part of a major U.S. industry would have devastating effects on the U.S. economy as a whole. If federal funds can help X Auto Company continue to employ its workers, then thousands of private individuals will continue to earn and spend money. This will help protect the health of the nation's economy.

On the other hand, you could counter an argument based on similarity of   33
policy considerations by showing that giving X Auto Company federal funds would widen the scope of the rule beyond the limits intended by those who derived the rule. This widening would have all kinds of adverse effects or troublesome consequences, such as opening the courts to a flood of frivolous litigation.

Setting up an analogy. To set up an analogy between two cases, using   34
both the facts and the policy issues, begin by making a list of similarities and differences. Here is how you might expand the general welfare example to show that one case that has already been decided involving the old-age benefit provisions of the Social Security Act is or is not analogous to the X Auto Company case.

SIMILARITIES

In both situations the recipients may receive money that they only directly paid into the system. For example, Social Security recipients may receive funds in excess of the amount they actually put into the fund. The X Auto Company will receive funds that it indirectly paid in the form of taxes, etc.

Many individuals who need support will benefit from the federal funds; employees in the case of X Auto Company, and older members of the population in the case of old-age benefits.

The X Auto Company funds will help keep the economy healthy because it will keep a major industry alive and will keep X's employees (and employees of other companies that depend on X) off of welfare and other forms of state subsidy. Similarly, the old-age benefits of Social Security assure citizens that they will have an opportunity to put money into a fund that they can draw on in their old age, provided they have worked the requisite amount of time to qualify. This keeps older people from having to turn to the state for support.

DIFFERENCES

The recipients of old-age benefits have paid into an insurance fund over the years, while the X Auto Company would be receiving money from a nonspecific tax fund that it has not contributed to. Taxes and insurance are not the same thing.

It is quite a different thing for the federal government to provide funds to a private corporation than to provide them to individuals. The government is set up to benefit members of the general population. It is not the government's purpose to benefit a large private corporation.

Giving funds to a private business may actually unbalance the economy, disturbing the free market and fair competition.

C. THE CONCLUSION After you have established and developed your major   35
and minor premises, you are ready to reach a conclusion that follows logically
from them. You may need to use a cause-and-effect argument to show *how*
you came to the conclusion.

In law you will often be required to show that there is a cause-and-effect   36
relationship between certain events or actions. . . .

Here is an example of how a cause-and-effect relationship can be estab-   37
lished within a deductive argument. First, set up the skeleton of your argument.

> *General rule* (major premise): Under the law of State *X*, the operator of
> a motor vehicle is liable for his or her wrongful act, neglect, or
> default if it causes death or injury to another person.
>
> *Specific facts* (minor premise): The plaintiff was riding in her car on the
> freeway when the defendant's car hit her from behind. Two days
> later, the plaintiff suffered severe back pains and headaches.
>
> *Conclusion:* Therefore, the defendant should be liable for the damages
> the plaintiff has suffered.

If you terminated your argument at this point, it would appear that you   38
had based your conclusion on a faulty premise or assumption: "All pain that
occurs within two days of an accident is necessarily caused by that accident."
Or your conclusion may appear to result from a *post hoc* fallacy, in which
you assert that because event *B* follows event *A* in time, event *A* has therefore
caused event *B*. To avoid the appearance that your conclusion does not follow
logically from the premises, you must articulate the causal link between
events. You could do so by beginning your conclusion with the following
information.

> There is a good deal of evidence that the plaintiff's injury was caused by the
> defendant's act of hitting the plaintiff from behind. First of all, the plaintiff's
> medical records show that the plaintiff did not have a history of back prob-
> lems or headaches, so there is no possibility that her injuries are part of a
> recurrent or chronic problem. Also, she has not engaged in any activity or suf-
> fered any other injury within the last few years that might have led to back
> pain or headaches. In addition, Dr. Jones, the plaintiff's physician, has exam-
> ined the plaintiff and will testify that the pain the plaintiff is experiencing is
> the kind that the plaintiff would be likely to feel several days after a rear-end
> collision in an automobile.

You would finish your argument by qualifying your conclusion to reflect   39
the evidence you have presented:

> Because the evidence from medical records and from an expert demonstrates
> that, in all probability, the plaintiff's injuries were caused by the defendant's
> conduct, the defendant is liable for the damage the plaintiff has suffered as a
> result of that conduct.

When you are constructing a cause-and-effect argument, keep the subject   40
matter in mind. If you are working with causation in a complex statistical
argument, you must comply with the generally accepted principles of statistical analysis. For example, you may have to adhere to a scientific definition of
causation. However, if you are writing about more common types of problems, try to appeal to your readers' sense of how the world works: Present a
cause-and-effect relationship that your readers will recognize from their own
experience. You can appeal to your readers' common sense and to the
"common wisdom of the community." Remember that judges and other

attorneys are part of the community and that they will share this sense of what probably did or did not happen in a given situation.

■ ■ ■

Discussion and Writing Suggestions

1. In what ways is the IRAC system different from the way or ways you have previously been taught to organize writing? In what ways is it similar?

2. Take an everyday situation involving a conflict between individuals, involving you or someone else you know. Discuss this situation in IRAC format, as if it were a lawsuit and one party was suing the other. Articulate the *issue* at the heart of the conflict, the *"rule"* that you believe applies (even though it is not a legal rule), the *application* of this rule to the situation at hand, your *conclusion*, a counterargument to this conclusion, your response to the counterargument, and your overall conclusion.

3. Select another situation that might provide the basis of a lawsuit, drawing upon either your own experience, the experience of someone you know, or the experience of someone in a work of fiction or film. Develop a syllogism that would apply to this situation, as if you were constructing a legal argument. Formulate the major premise and the minor premise. Develop an argument by analogy, using the double column "Similarities"-"Differences" format indicated by Charrow, Erhardt, and Charrow. Finally, write the complete argument, using IRAC format.

Venezia v. Miller Brewing Company: *A Defective Beer Bottle?*

Now that you've read how to discuss a case in IRAC format, you may be interested in having such a discussion available as a model for the kind of writing you're likely to be doing in connection with this chapter. The selection leads off, like most of the rest here, with a statement of the "Facts of the Case," followed by a section of the relevant law. More specifically, you'll consider a case in which a boy's parents sued the Miller Brewing Company when the youngster injured himself after shattering a beer bottle against a telephone pole. The relevant law in this case is the Restatement of Torts, Section 402A: *"Special Liability of Seller of Product for Physical Harm to User or Consumer." Should Miller be found liable for the boy's injuries? Does the law on product liability apply in this case? Ruthi Erdman, a writing instructor at Central Washington University, provided the following model paper for her students to use as a guide in responding to other cases in this chapter. We believe that you'll find her discussion helpful.*

*Patricia VENEZIA, Individually, and as she is next friend of
Louis Venezia, a minor, Plaintiffs, Appellants,*

v.

*MILLER BREWING COMPANY et al.,
Defendants, Appellees.*

No. 80-1036.

United States Court of Appeals,

First Circuit.

Argued May 8, 1980.

Decided July 18, 1980.

Facts of the Case*

The complaint charged Miller Brewing Company and three manufacturers of glass products with negligence, gross negligence and breach of warranty in connection with the design and manufacture of a glass bottle used as a container for Miller Beer. The complaint alleged that plaintiff, then eight years of age, was playing with friends near his home when he "found a non-returnable Miller High Life clear glass bottle" which had been "discarded by . . . persons unknown. . . ." During the course of play the "thin walled" bottle, in plaintiff's words, "came in contact with a telephone pole." Plaintiff, in his brief, has clarified this phrase, indicating that he was the party responsible for throwing the bottle against the pole. Following the impact of the glass container with the telephone pole the bottle shattered, and particles of glass entered plaintiff's eye causing severe injury. Plaintiff's basic premise is that Miller and the bottle manufacturers should have been aware of the dangers inherent in their "thin walled" "non-returnable" bottles and should have accordingly designed and marketed a product better able to safely withstand such foreseeable misuse as breakage in the course of improper handling by children. ■   1

Statements on the Law†

Restatement of Torts, Second

[SECTION] 402A. SPECIAL LIABILITY OF SELLER OF PRODUCT FOR PHYSICAL HARM TO USER OR CONSUMER

(1) One who sells any product in a defective condition unreasonably dangerous to the user or consumer or to his property is subject to liability for physical harm thereby caused to the ultimate user or consumer, or to his property if

---

Venezia v. Miller Brewing Co. 626 F.2d 188 (1980).

†*Restatement of The Law, Second: Torts 2nd*. As Adapted and Promulgated by The American Law Institute at Washington, D.C. May 25, 1963 and May 22, 1964. St. Paul, MN: West Publishing Co., 1965.

(a) the seller is engaged in the business of selling such a product, and

(b) it is expected to and does reach the user or consumer without substantial change in the condition in which it is sold.

(2) The rule stated in Subsection (1) applies although

(a) the seller has exercised all possible care in the preparation and sale of his product, and

(b) the user or consumer has not bought the product from or entered into any contractual relation with the seller. . . .

[Comment]

g. Defective condition. The rule stated in this Section applies only where 1 the product is, at the time it leaves the seller's hands, in a condition not contemplated by the ultimate consumer, which will be unreasonably dangerous to him. The seller is not liable when he delivers the product in a safe condition, and subsequent mishandling or other causes make it harmful by the time it is consumed. The burden of proof that the product was in a defective condition at the time that it left the hands of the particular seller is upon the injured plaintiff; and unless evidence can be produced which will support the conclusion that it was then defective, the burden is not sustained.

Safe condition at the time of delivery by the seller will, however, include 2 proper packaging, necessary sterilization, and other precautions required to permit the product to remain safe for a normal length of time when handled in a normal manner.

h. A product is not in a defective condition when it is safe for normal 3 handling and consumption. If the injury results from abnormal handling, as where a bottled beverage is knocked against a radiator to remove the cap, or from abnormal preparation for use, as where too much salt is added to food, or from abnormal consumption, as where a child eats too much candy and is made ill, the seller is not liable. Where, however, he has reason to anticipate that danger may result from a particular use, as where a drug is sold which is safe only in limited doses, he may be required to give adequate warning of the danger and a product sold without such warning is in a defective condition. . . .

n. Contributory negligence. Since the liability with which this Section 4 deals is not based upon negligence of the seller, but is strict liability, the rule applied to strict liability cases applies. Contributory negligence of the plaintiff is not a defense when such negligence consists merely in a failure to discover the defect in the product, or to guard against the possibility of its existence. On the other hand the form of contributory negligence which consists in voluntarily and unreasonably proceeding to encounter a known danger, and commonly passes under the name of assumption of risk, is a defense under this Section as in other cases of strict liability. If the user or consumer discovers the defect and is aware of the danger, and nevertheless proceeds unreasonably to make use of the product and is injured by it, he is barred from recovery. ■

Judge's Instructions to the Jury*

FAILURE TO WARN—ESSENTIAL ELEMENTS

The essential elements of a claim based upon an alleged defect from   1
failure to warn are:

1. The defendant was the manufacturer of a product, namely _beer bottle_ ;
2. The product was defective;   (identify the product)
3. The product defect was a cause of injury to the plaintiffs;
4. Plaintiff's injury resulted from a use of the product that was reasonably foreseeable to the defendant.

A product is defective if the use of the product in a manner that is rea-   2
sonably foreseeable by the defendant involves a substantial danger that
would not be readily recognized by the ordinary user of the product and the
manufacturer knows or should have known of the danger, but fails to give
adequate warning of such danger. ■

IRAC Essay: *Venezia vs. Miller Brewing Company: A Defective Beer Bottle?*

Facts of the Case[1]

Eight-year-old Louis Venezia was playing outside with some friends near his   1
home when he discovered a new toy: a discarded, empty beer bottle. In the
course of the play that followed, Lou threw the bottle against a telephone
pole, shattering it. Unfortunately, some particles of the splintered glass flew
into Louis's eye, leaving the little boy with severe injuries.

Now Louis's mother, Patricia Venezia, is suing the Miller Brewing   2
Company and three glass manufacturers for "negligence, gross negligence
and breach of warranty" ("*Venezia*" 699), charging her son's injuries resulted from defects in the design and manufacture of the beer bottle. According
to Mrs. Venezia, the companies involved in the bottle's manufacture should
have realized that by marketing a "thin walled" bottle which was "non-
returnable" and therefore likely to be discarded, they were creating a hazard
(699). The bottle, she claims, was inherently dangerous, as it was not designed

---

California Jury Instructions, Civil: Book of Approved Jury Instructions [BAJI]. 8th ed.
Prepared by The Committee on Standard Jury Instruction Civil, of the Superior Court of Los
Angeles County, California. Hon. Stephen M. Lachs, Judge of the Superior Court,
Chairman. Compiled and Edited by Paul G. Breckenridge, Jr. St. Paul, MN: West Publishing
Co., 1994.

[1]For the purpose of this chapter (as opposed to the purpose of a legal writing course) we recommend that the standard IRAC essay be prefaced by a statement of the "Facts of the
Case."

to "safely withstand such foreseeable misuse as breakage in the course of improper handling by children" (699).

Issue

The issue in this case is whether the defendant, who manufactured a beer   3
bottle that shattered when the plaintiff threw it against a telephone pole, severely injuring his eye from flying glass particles, should be liable for gross negligence and for breach of warranty in the design and manufacture of the bottle.

Rule

According to the law, anyone who "sells any product in a defective condi-   4
tion unreasonably dangerous to the user or consumer or to his property is subject to liability for physical harm" ("Restatement" 699). This rule applies even if "the user or consumer has not bought the product from or entered into any contractual relation with the seller" (700), so the fact that Louis Venezia did not actually buy the product is irrelevant. The law also stipu-lates that the seller is responsible only for "safe condition at the time of delivery" (700). This means that when a product "leaves the seller's hands," it must not, unbeknownst to the consumer, be in a condition "unreasonably dangerous to him" (700). It must be safe for "normal handling and con-sumption" (700).

Application

The Venezias are probably banking on the fact that safe condition at the time   5
of delivery includes "Proper packaging" (700). But was the beer sold by Miller "improperly packaged," so as to be "unreasonably dangerous" accord-ing to the accepted safety standards of the industry? What constitutes "proper packaging" for beer? True, some manufacturers of beverages such as Squeeze-it and Kool-Aid Splash package their product in soft plastic bottles that will not shatter under any circumstances. But beer is not Kool-Aid. It is intended for an entirely different consumer market consisting solely of adults, since minors cannot legally buy beer. Why should "reasonable consumer expecta-tion" require that the package for an adult beverage by unbreakable? Furthermore, even manufacturers of legal-for-kiddies beverages like Snapple and 7-up are not required to package their drinks in plastic; they use nonre-turnable glass bottles that probably would not withstand being hurled against a telephone pole.

This brings us to the question of whether Louis Venezia, in throwing the   6
bottle against the pole, contributed to the negligence that resulted in his injury. The law states, quite sensibly, that failure to discover the defect in a product is not negligence on the part of the injured consumer ("Restatement" 700). But if the consumer "voluntarily and unreasonably [proceeds] to

encounter a known danger" (700), then he is at fault, even if the product is defective. A user who "discovers the defect and is aware of the danger, and nevertheless proceeds unreasonably to make use of the product and is injured by it . . . is barred from recovery" (700)—that is, he cannot collect damages from the manufacturer.

Is it unreasonable to think that Louis Venezia was aware of the danger-   7
ous possibility that the beer bottle might shatter, and proceeded to throw it anyway? It seems unlikely that an eight-year-old child could have been *ignorant* of the shatterable nature of glass. In fact, it seems very likely that Venezia threw the bottle precisely for the thrill of making it shatter, the excitement and power of sending the glass shards flying. Why else do children hurl glass bottles against hard surfaces? Thus, the legal requirement that a product's dangerous condition must be "not readily recognized by the ordinary user" ("Instructions" 701) is not met here, and Venezia was himself negligent in "encountering a known danger," even if Miller's beer bottle was defective.

But it wasn't defective. The final case against the Venezias' suit is that   8
legally, a product is not defective as long as it is "safe for normal handling and consumption" ("Restatement" 700). The manufacturer cannot be held responsible when the consumer subjects the product to misuse:

> The seller is not liable when he delivers the product in a safe condition, and subsequent mishandling or other causes make it harmful . . . if the injury results from abnormal handling, as where a bottled beverage is knocked against a radiator to remove the cap, or from abnormal consumption, as where a child eats too much candy and is made ill, the seller is not liable. ("Restatement" 700)

Clearly, if knocking a beverage bottle against a radiator to get the cap off is not "normal handling and consumption," then neither is flinging such a bottle against a telephone pole. A bottle cannot be labeled "defective" for breaking under such misuse, even if the breakage results in painful and debilitating injury to a little boy.

Conclusion

Of course any decent person will feel sympathy for an eight-year-old boy   9
whose eye has been seriously injured, and (of course) it is natural for a traumatized, protective mother to look for someone on whom to pin the responsibility. But are the Miller Brewer Company and its glass supplies really to blame for what happened to Louis Venezia? Is a beer bottle "defective" if it shatters when thrown against a telephone pole? Surely any reasonable court will see that the Miller Company is not liable for negligence or breach of warranty and that to force it to pay damages to the Venezias would be a gross miscarriage of justice.

■ ■ ■

The Ridiculed Employee:
An Additional Case of Emotional Distress
(HARRIS V. JONES)

The first selection in this chapter, "Miss Nickerson and the Pot of Gold," presented a case of emotional distress. Now that you have had an opportunity, through the three subsequent selections, to learn more about how the law operates and how legal writing is used to formulate arguments, you are in a position to develop more knowledgeable, systematic responses to another case of emotional distress.

In Harris v. Jones, *a man sues his supervisor for repeatedly ridiculing and mimicking him. Following the facts of the case, as presented in the ruling of the appellate court, we present a number of "Statements on the Law," which help to establish the legal basis of claims for emotional distress. (Refer also the "Judge's Instructions to the Jury" in the Nickerson case, page 672.)*

WILLIAM R. HARRIS v. H. ROBERT JONES et al.
Court of Appeals of Maryland.
Dec. 9, 1977.

Facts of the Case*

The plaintiff, William R. Harris, a 26-year-old, 8-year employee of General   1
Motors Corporation (GM), sued GM and one of its supervisory employees,
H. Robert Jones, in the Superior Court of Baltimore City. The declaration
alleged that Jones, aware that Harris suffered from a speech impediment
which caused him to stutter, and also aware of Harris' sensitivity to this disability, and his insecurity because of it, nevertheless "maliciously and cruelly
ridiculed . . . [him] thus causing tremendous nervousness, increasing the physical defect itself and further injuring the mental attitude fostered by the
Plaintiff toward his problem and otherwise intentionally inflicting emotional
distress." It was also alleged in the declaration that Jones' actions occurred
within the course of his employment with GM and that GM ratified Jones'
conduct.

The evidence at trial showed that Harris stuttered throughout his entire   2
life. While he had little trouble with one syllable words, he had great difficulty
with longer words or sentences, causing him at times to shake his head up and
down when attempting to speak.

During part of 1975, Harris worked under Jones' supervision at a GM   3
automobile assembly plant. Over a five-month period, between March and
August of 1975, Jones approached Harris over 30 times at work and verbal-
ly and physically mimicked his stuttering disability. In addition, two or three

---

**Harris v. Jones.* 380 A.2d 611 (1977).

times a week during this period, Jones approached Harris and told him, in a "smart manner," not to get nervous. As a result of Jones' conduct, Harris was "shaken up" and felt "like going into a hole and hide."

On June 2, 1975, Harris asked Jones for a transfer to another depart-   4
ment; Jones refused, called Harris a "troublemaker" and chastised him for repeatedly seeking the assistance of his committeeman, a representative who handles employee grievances. On this occasion, Jones, "shaking his head up and down" to imitate Harris, mimicked his pronunciation of the word "committeeman" which Harris pronounced "mmitteeman." As a result of this incident, Harris filed an employee grievance against Jones, requesting that GM instruct Jones to properly conduct himself in the future; the grievance was marked as satisfactorily settled after GM so instructed Jones. On another occasion during the five-month period, Harris filed a similar grievance against Jones; it too was marked as satisfactorily settled after GM again instructed Jones to properly conduct himself.

Harris had been under the care of a physician for a nervous condition for   5
six years prior to the commencement of Jones' harassment. He admitted that many things made him nervous, including "bosses." Harris testified that Jones' conduct heightened his nervousness and his speech impediment worsened. He saw his physician on one occasion during the five-month period that Jones was mistreating him; the physician prescribed pills for his nerves.

Harris admitted that other employees at work mimicked his stuttering.   6
Approximately 3,000 persons were employed on each of two shifts, and Harris acknowledged the presence at the plant of a lot of "tough guys," as well as profanity, name-calling and roughhousing among the employees. He said that a bad day at work caused him to become more nervous than usual. He admitted that he had problems with supervisors other than Jones, that he had been suspended or relieved from work 10 or 12 times, and that after one such dispute, he followed a supervisor home on his motorcycle, for which he was later disciplined.

Harris' wife testified that her husband was "in a shell" at the time they   7
were married, approximately seven years prior to the trial. She said that it took her about a year to get him to associate with family and friends and that while he still had a difficult time talking, he thereafter became "calmer." Mrs. Harris testified that beginning in November of 1974, her husband became ill-tempered at home and said that he had problems at work. She said that he was drinking too much at that time, that on one occasion he threw a meat platter at her, that she was afraid of him, and that they separated for a two-week period in November of 1974. Mrs. Harris indicated that her husband's nervous condition got worse in June of 1975. She said that at a christening party held during that month Harris "got to drinking" and they argued.

On this evidence, the case was submitted to the jury after the trial court   8
denied the defendants' motions for directed verdicts; the jury awarded Harris

$3,500 compensatory damages and $15,000 punitive damages against both Jones and GM. [The verdict was then appealed by the defendant.] ■

Statements on the Law*

Restatement of Torts, Second

[SECTION] 46. OUTRAGEOUS CONDUCT CAUSING SEVERE EMOTIONAL DISTRESS

(1) One who by extreme and outrageous conduct intentionally or recklessly causes severe emotional distress to another is subject to liability for such emotional distress, and if bodily harm to the other results from it, for such bodily harm.
(2) Where such conduct is directed at a third person, the actor is subject to liability if he intentionally or recklessly causes severe emotional distress
   (a) to a member of such person's immediate family who is present at the time, whether or not such distress results in bodily harm, or
   (b) to any other person who is present at the time, if such distress results in bodily harm.

[Comment]

d. Extreme and outrageous conduct. The cases thus far decided have 1 found liability only where the defendant's conduct has been extreme and outrageous. It has not been enough that the defendant has acted with an intent which is tortious or even criminal, or that he has intended to inflict emotional distress, or even that his conduct has been characterized by "malice," or a degree of aggravation which would entitle the plaintiff to punitive damages for another tort. Liability has been found only where the conduct has been so outrageous in character, and so extreme in degree, as to go beyond all possible bounds of decency, and to be regarded as atrocious, and utterly intolerable in a civilized community. Generally, the case is one in which the recitation of the facts to an average member of the community would arouse his resentment against the actor, and lead him to exclaim, "Outrageous!"

The liability clearly does not extent to mere insults, indignities, threats, 2 annoyances, petty oppressions, or other trivialities. The rough edges of our society are still in need of a good deal of filing down, and in the meantime plaintiffs must necessarily be expected and required to be hardened to a certain amount of rough language, and to occasional acts that are definitely inconsiderate and unkind. There is no occasion for the law to intervene in every case where some one's feelings are hurt. There must still be freedom to express an unflattering opinion, and some safety valve must be left through which irascible tempers may blow off relatively harmless steam.

Restatement of The Law, Second: Torts 2nd. As Adapted and Promulgated by The American Law Institute at Washington, D.C. May 25, 1963 and May 22, 1964. St. Paul, MN: West Publishing Co., 1965.

Illustrations [liable]:

1. As a practical joke, A falsely tells B that her husband has been badly injured in an accident, and is in the hospital with both legs broken. B suffers severe emotional distress. A is subject to liability to B for her emotional distress. If it causes nervous shock and resulting illness, A is subject to liability to B for her illness.

2. A, the president of an association of rubbish collectors, summons B to a meeting of the association, and in the presence of an intimidating group of associates tells B that B has been collecting rubbish in territory which the association regards as exclusively allocated to one of its members. A demands that B pay over the proceeds of his rubbish collection, and tells B that if he does not do so the association will beat him up, destroy his truck, and put him out of business. B is badly frightened, and suffers severe emotional distress. A is subject to liability to B for his emotional distress, and if it results in illness, A is also subject to liability to B for his illness.

3. A is invited to a swimming party at an exclusive resort. B gives her a bathing suit which he knows will dissolve in water. It does dissolve while she is swimming, leaving her naked in the presence of men and women whom she has just met. A suffers extreme embarrassment, shame, and humiliation. B is subject to liability to A for her emotional distress. . . .

8. A, a creditor, seeking to collect a debt, calls on B and demands payment in a rude and insolent manner. When B says that he cannot pay, A calls B a deadbeat, and says that he will never trust B again. A's conduct, although insulting, is not so extreme or outrageous as to make A liable to B. . . .

Illustration [not liable]:

17. The same facts as Illustration 1 [above], except that B does not believe A's statement, and is only sufficiently disturbed to telephone to the hospital to find out whether it could possibly be true. A is not liable to B.

[Comment on Illustrations]

Severe emotional distress. The rule stated in this Section applies only where the emotional distress has in fact resulted, and where it is severe. Emotional distress passes under various names, such as mental suffering, mental anguish, mental or nervous shock, or the like. It includes all highly unpleasant mental reactions, such as fright, horror, grief, shame, humiliation, embarrassment, anger, chagrin, disappointment, worry, and nausea. It is only where it is extreme that the liability arises. Complete emotional tranquility is seldom attainable in this world, and some degree of transient and trivial emotional distress is a part of the price of living among people. The law intervenes only where the distress inflicted is so severe that no reasonable man could be expected to endure it. The intensity and the duration of the distress are factors to be considered in determining its severity. Severe distress must be proved; but in many cases the extreme and outrageous character of the defendant's conduct is in itself important evidence that the distress has existed. For example, the mere recital of the facts in Illustration 1 above goes far to prove that the claim is not fictitious.

The distress must be reasonable and justified under the circumstances, 9 and there is no liability where the plaintiff has suffered exaggerated and unreasonable emotional distress, unless it results from a peculiar susceptibility to such distress of which the actor has knowledge.

It is for the court to determine whether on the evidence severe emotion- 10 al distress can be found; it is for the jury to determine whether, on the evidence, it has in fact existed.

From Harris *ruling:* *

In his now classic article, *Mental and Emotional Disturbance in the Law of* 11 *Torts*, 49 Harv.L.Rev. 1033 (1936), Professor Calvert Magruder warned against imposing liability for conduct which is not outrageous and extreme; he observed at 1035 that "Against a large part of the frictions and irritations and clashing of temperaments incident to participation in a community life, a certain toughening of the mental hide is a better protection than the law could ever be," and at 1053, he said:

> "there is danger of getting into the realm of the trivial in this matter of insulting language. No pressing social need requires that every abusive outburst be converted into a tort; upon the contrary, it would be unfortunate if the law closed all the safety valves through which irascible tempers might legally blow off steam."

From Harris *ruling:* †

"In *Samms* [*v. Eccles*, 11 Utah 2d 289, 358 P.2d 344 (1961)], the 12 Supreme Court of Utah aptly stated:

> '. . . [T]he best considered view recognizes an action for severe emotional distress, though not accompanied by bodily impact or physical injury, where the defendant intentionally engaged in some conduct toward the plaintiff, (a) with the purpose of inflicting emotional distress, *or*, (b) where any reasonable person would have known that such would result; and his actions are of such a nature as to be considered outrageous and intolerable in that they offend against the generally accepted standards of decency and morality.'" 210 S.E.2d at 147-148.

13

From Harris *ruling:* ‡

The "severe emotional distress" required to support a cause of action for intentional infliction of emotional distress was discussed by the Supreme Court of Illinois in *Knierim v. Izzo*, 22 Ill.2d 73, 174 N.E.2d 157 (1961):

---

*[380 A.2d at 615]

†[380 A.2d at 614]

‡[380 A.2d at 617]

". . . not . . . every emotional upset should constitute the basis of an action. Indiscriminate allowance of actions for mental anguish would encourage neurotic overreactions to trivial hurts, and the law should aim to toughen the pysche of the citizen rather than pamper it. But a line can be drawn between the slight hurts which are the price of a complex society and the severe mental disturbances inflicted by intentional actions wholly lacking in social utility." 174 N.E.2d at 164.

Caselaw: Womack v. Eldridge*

We adopt the view that a cause of action will lie for emotional distress, unac-   14
companied by physical injury, provided four elements are shown: One, the wrongdoer's conduct was intentional or reckless. This element is satisfied where the wrongdoer had the specific purpose of inflicting emotional distress or where he intended his specific conduct and knew or should have known that emotional distress would likely result. Two, the conduct was outrageous and intolerable in that it offends against the generally accepted standards of decency and morality. This requirement is aimed at limiting frivolous suits and avoiding litigation in situations where only bad manners and mere hurt feelings are involved. Three, there was a causal connection between the wrongdoer's conduct and the emotional distress. Four, the emotional distress was severe.

■ ■ ■

Discussion and Writing Suggestions

1. Assume that you have heard the evidence in *Harris v. Jones*, as summarized in the "Facts of the Case." Assume also, that you have heard the same jury instructions as were given in the Nickerson case (pp. 672–73). Finally, assume that in asking for clarification of "emotional distress," the jury has received additional information in the form of the "Statements on the Law" presented after the "Facts of the Case."

   If you were a member of the jury deliberating on a verdict, how would you vote? Explain your reasoning, specifically referring to the particular facts of the case and to the definitions or explanations of "emotional distress." How do these definitions and explanations either support or fail to support the plaintiff's claim for damages? Emphasize those elements of the case that seemed crucial to you in reaching a determination.

2. Assume that you are an attorney *either* for the plaintiff (Harris) *or* for the defendant (Jones). Assume also, that you have researched the case and discovered a precedent, *Nickerson v. Hodges*. You believe that this precedent can support your position, owing to either its similarities to or differences from the *Harris* case. Write a brief argument to the appellate court in IRAC format explaining how the facts in *Nickerson* are similar

---

*[210 S.E.2d at 148]

to or different from those in *Harris*. (Ask your instructor for the appellate court ruling on *Nickerson*; it is included in the *Instructor's Manual*.) In developing your argument, draw upon relevant statements on the law following the facts of the case. As an IRAC model, see th "beer bottle" essay (pp. 701–03).

3. Have you (or has someone you know) ever suffered emotional distress of the type that would fit the legal definition of this term? If so, lay out the facts of the case in a manner similar to the narratives in this section. Then, using IRAC format, apply the legal standards for a judgment of emotional distress to the event or events you have described.

4. As an alternate assignment to #3 above, select a character in a story, novel, film, or TV show who has suffered emotional distress. Using IRAC format, write a brief either for the plaintiff or the defendant. For example, could Othello charge Iago with intentional infliction of emotional distress? Could "Piggy" in *Lord of the Flies* charge Jack and others?

5. *Group Assignment:* Form a jury, a group consisting of several other members of the class. (It doesn't have to have 12 members.) Choose a foreperson, someone to moderate, though not dominate, the discussion—someone who will keep the deliberations on track and keep the main issues in the forefront. Appoint someone to take notes. You may wish to tape-record the discussion.

Deliberate on the case before you: study the facts of the case; study the applicable law; apply the law to the facts of the case. Before or while you are developing your own conclusions, take account of other people's arguments. Weigh the merits of these arguments before deciding upon your vote. At the conclusion of discussion, the group will vote on a verdict. (Criminal cases require a unanimous vote; civil cases require a three-quarters majority.) If the jury is badly split, deliberate more in order to reach greater consensus.

After you arrive at a verdict, work with the foreperson as she or he prepares a report, written in IRAC format, that presents your verdict (as a conclusion), and that explains the issue, the rule, and also summarizes the main points of the discussion in the "counterargument" and "response" sections.

Assault and Battery on the Gridiron: A Case of Reckless Disregard of Safety
(Hackbart v. Cincinnati Bengals)

Should a professional football player be entitled to collect damages from another player who has injured him in the course of a game? At first, the question seems laughable: after all, if pro football is about anything, it's about organized (sometimes disorganized) violence, and players who aren't willing to run the risk of being injured, it might be argued, have no business playing the game.

Still, there must be some limits to violence, even in football. The game has rules, and one of those rules provides that: "All players are prohibited from strik- ing on the head, face or neck with the heel, back or side of the hand, wrist, fore- arm, elbow, or clasped hands."[1] Admittedly, most violations of the rules are penalized by a loss of yardage; but are there particularly extreme cases in which recourse to the law is appropriate?

In June, 1997, millions of people were outraged when Mike Tyson bit off part of Evander Holyfield's ear during a heavyweight title bout in Las Vegas. Tyson was fined $3 million and suspended indefinitely from professional boxing; some commentators noted that Holyfield could have filed a lawsuit against the offend- er. Even boxing, which is conflict at its most primal, has its rules of fair play, and Tyson clearly and egregiously violated those rules.

The case that follows deals with an incident that occurred during an NFL game played in Denver in September, 1973, between the Denver Broncos and the Cincinnati Bengals. After the initial trial, the case was appealed, first to the United States District Court in Colorado (1977), and then to the U.S. Court of Appeals, Tenth Circuit (1979).

Following the "Facts of the Case," we present a "Statement of the Law": sec- tion 500 of the Restatement of Torts, 2d., *which, the plaintiffs argued, applied to the defendant's action.*

Dale HACKBART, Plaintiff v. CINCINNATI BENGALS, INC. and Charles "Booby" Clark, Defendants.
United States District Court, D. Colorado.

Facts of the Case*

The Parties

The plaintiff, Dale Hackbart, is a citizen of Colorado who was a 35 year old   1 contract player for the Denver Broncos Football Club in the National Football League at the time of the incident. He was then 6 feet 3 inches tall and weighed 210 pounds. Mr. Hackbart had 13 years' experience as a profes- sional football player after competing in college and high school football, making a total of 21 years of experience in organized football.

The Denver game was the first regular season professional football game   2 for the defendant, Charles Clark, who was then 23 years old with a weight of 240 pounds and a height of 6 feet 1 3/4 inches. Mr. Clark was a contract player for the Cincinnati Bengals Football Club, Inc., defendant herein, which was also a member of the National Football League. Both defendants are cit- izens of states other than Colorado.

---

[1] From NFL Rules of Football: Article 1, Item 1, Subsection C, provides that: All players are prohibited from striking on the head, face or neck with the heel, back or side of the hand, wrist, forearm, elbow or clasped hands.

Hackbart v. Cincinnati Bengals. 601 F.2d 516 (1979).

The Incident

The incident which gave rise to this lawsuit occurred near the end of the first $\quad$ 3
half of the game at a time when the Denver team was leading by a score of 21
to 3. Dale Hackbart was playing a free safety position on the Broncos' defensive team and Charles Clark was playing fullback on the Bengals' offensive
team. The Cincinnati team attempted a forward pass play during which
Charles Clark ran into a corner of the north end zone as a prospective receiv-
er. That took him into an area which was the defensive responsibility of Mr.
Hackbart. The thrown pass was intercepted near the goal line by a Denver
linebacker who then began to run the ball upfield. The interception reversed
the offensive and defensive roles of the two teams. As a result of an attempt
to block Charles Clark in the end zone, Dale Hackbart fell to the ground. He
then turned and, with one knee on the ground and the other leg extended,
watched the play continue upfield. Acting out of anger and frustration, but
without a specific intent to injury, Charles Clark stepped forward and struck
a blow with his right forearm to the back of the kneeling plaintiff's head with
sufficient force to cause both players to fall forward to the ground. Both
players arose and, without comment, went to their respective teams along the
sidelines. They both returned to play during the second half of the game.

Because no official observed it, no foul was called on the disputed play $\quad$ 4
and Dale Hackbart made no report of this incident to his coaches or to
anyone else during the game. However, the game film showed very clearly
what had occurred. Mr. Hackbart experienced pain and soreness to the extent
that he was unable to play golf as he had planned on the day after the game,
he did not seek any medical attention and, although he continued to feel
pain, he played on specialty team assignments for the Denver Broncos in
games against the Chicago Bears and the San Francisco Forty-Niners on successive Sundays. The Denver Broncos then released Mr. Hackbart on waivers
and he was not claimed by any other team. After losing his employment, Mr.
Hackbart sought medical assistance, at which time it was discovered that he
had a neck injury. When that information was given to the Denver Broncos
Football Club, Mr. Hackbart received his full payment for the 1973 season
pursuant to an injury clause in his contract.

The Professional Football Industry

The claim of the plaintiff in this case must be considered in the context of $\quad$ 5
football as a commercial enterprise. The National Football League (NFL) is
an organization formed for the purpose of promoting and fostering the business of its members, the owners of professional football "clubs" with fran-
chises to operate in designated cities. . . .

Football is a recognized game which is widely played as a sport. $\quad$ 6
Commonly teams are organized by high schools and colleges and games are
played according to rules provided by associations of such schools.

The basic design of the game is the same at the high school, college and $\quad$ 7
professional levels. The differences are largely reflective of the fact that at each

level the players have increased physical abilities, improved skills and differing motivations.

Football is a contest for territory. The objective of the offensive team is   8
to move the ball through the defending team's area and across the vertical plane of the goal line. The defensive players seek to prevent that movement with their bodies. Each attempted movement involves collisions between the bodies of offensive and defensive players with considerable force and with differing areas of contact. The most obvious characteristic of the game is that all of the players engage in violent physical behavior.

The rules of play which govern the methods and style by which the NFL   9
teams compete include limitations on the manner in which players may strike or otherwise physically contact opposing players. During 1973, the rules were enforced by six officials on the playing field. The primary sanction for a violation was territorial with the amounts of yardage lost being dependent upon the particular infraction. Players were also subject to expulsion from the game and to monetary penalties imposed by the league commissioner.

The written rules are difficult to understand and, because of the speed   10
and violence of the game, their application is often a matter of subjective evaluation of the circumstances. Officials differ with each other in their rulings. The players are not specifically instructed in the interpretation of the rules, and they acquire their working knowledge of them only from the actual experience of enforcement by the game officials during contests.

Many violations of the rules do occur during each game. Ordinarily each   11
team receives several yardage penalties, but many fouls go undetected or undeclared by the officials.

Disabling injuries are also common occurrences in each contest.   12
Hospitalization and surgery are frequently required for repairs. Protective clothing is worn by all players, but it is often inadequate to prevent bodily damage. Professional football players are conditioned to "play with pain" and they are expected to perform even though they are hurt. The standard player contract imposes an obligation to play when the club physician determines that an injured player has the requisite physical ability.

The violence of professional football is carefully orchestrated. Both offen-   13
sive and defensive players must be extremely aggressive in their actions and they must play with a reckless abandonment of self-protective instincts. The coaches make studied and deliberate efforts to build the emotional levels of their players to what some call a "controlled rage."

John Ralston, the 1973 Broncos coach, testified that the pre-game psy-   14
chological preparation should be designed to generate an emotion equivalent to that which would be experienced by a father whose family had been endangered by another driver who had attempted to force the family car off the edge of a mountain road. The precise pitch of motivation for the players at the beginning of the game should be the feeling of that father when, after overtaking and stopping the offending vehicle, he is about to open the door to take revenge upon the person of the other driver.

The large and noisy crowds in attendance at the games contribute to the   15
emotional levels of the players. Quick changes in the fortunes of the teams, the

shock of violent collisions and the intensity of the competition make behavioral control extremely difficult, and it is not uncommon for players to "flare
up" and begin fighting. The record made at this trial indicates that such incidents as that which gave rise to this action are not so unusual as to be unexpected in any NFL game.

The end product of all of the organization and effort involved in the pro-   16
fessional football industry is an exhibition of highly developed individual
skills in coordinated team competition for the benefit of large numbers of
paying spectators, together with radio and television audiences. It is appropriate to infer that while some of those persons are attracted by the individual skills and precision performances of the teams, the appeal to others is the
spectacle of savagery.

Plaintiff's Theories of Liability

This case is controlled by the law of Colorado. While a theory of intentional   17
misconduct is barred by the applicable statute of limitations, the plaintiff
contends that Charles Clark's foul was so far outside of the rules of play and
accepted practices of professional football that it should be characterized as
reckless misconduct within the principles of Section 500 of the *Restatement of
Torts, 2d.* . . .

Alternatively, the plaintiff claims that his injury was at least the result of   18
a negligent act by the defendant. The difference in these contentions is but a
different in degree. Both theories are dependent upon a definition of a duty to
the plaintiff and an objective standard of conduct based upon the hypothetical reasonably prudent person. Thus, the question is what would a reasonably
prudent professional football player be expected to do under the circumstances confronting Charles Clark in this incident?

Two coaches testified at the trial of this case. Paul Brown has had 40   19
years of experience at all levels of organized football, with 20 years of coaching professional football. Both Mr. Brown and Mr. Ralston emphasized that
the coaching and instructing of professional football players did not include
any training with respect to a responsibility or even any regard for the safety
of opposing players. They both said that aggressiveness was the primary
attribute which they sought in the selection of players. Both emphasized the
importance of emotional preparation of the teams. Mr. Brown said that flare-
up fighting often occurred, even in practice sessions of his teams. ▪

Statements on the Law*

Restatement of Torts, Second

[SECTION] 500. RECKLESS DISREGARD OF SAFETY DEFINED

> The actor's conduct is in reckless disregard of the safety of another if he
> does an act or intentionally fails to do an act which it is his duty to the

---

Restatement of The Law, Second: Torts 2nd. As Adapted and Promulgated by The
American Law Institute at Washington, D.C. May 25, 1963 and May 22, 1964. St. Paul,
MN: West Publishing Co., 1965.

other to do, knowing or having reason to know of facts which would lead a reasonable man to realize, not only that his conduct creates an unreasonable risk of physical harm to another, but also that such risk is substantially greater than that which is necessary to make his conduct negligent.

Special Note: The conduct described in this Section is often called 1 "wanton or wilful misconduct" both in statutes and judicial opinions. On the other hand, this phrase is sometimes used by courts to refer to conduct intended to cause harm to another.

[Comment]

a. Types of reckless conduct. Recklessness may consist of either of two 2 different types of conduct. In one the actor knows, or has reason to know, as that term is defined in 12, of facts which create a high degree of risk of physical harm to another, and deliberately proceeds to act, or to fail to act, in conscious disregard of, or indifference to, that risk. In the other the actor has such knowledge, or reason to know, of the facts, but does not realize or appreciate the high degree of risk involved, although a reasonable man in his position would do so. An objective standard is applied to him, and he is held to the realization of the aggravated risk which a reasonable man in his place would have, although he does not himself have it.

For either type of reckless conduct, the actor must know, or have reason 3 to know, the facts which create the risk. For either, the risk must itself be an unreasonable one under the circumstances. There may be exceptional circumstances which make it reasonable to adopt a course of conduct which involves a high degree of risk of serious harm to others. While under ordinary circumstances it would be reckless to drive through heavy traffic at a high rate of speed, it may not even be negligent to do so if the driver is escaping from a bandit or carrying a desperately wounded man to the hospital for immediately necessary treatment, or if his car has been commandeered by the police for the pursuit of a fleeing felon. So too, there may be occasions in which action which would ordinarily involve so high a degree of danger as to be reckless may be better than no action at all, and therefore both reasonable and permissible. Thus one who finds another in a lonely place, and very seriously hurt, may well be justified in giving him such imperfect surgical aid as a layman can be expected to give, although it would be utterly reckless for him to meddle in the matter if professional assistance were available.

For either type of conduct, to be reckless it must be unreasonable; but to 4 be reckless, it must be something more than negligent. It must not only be unreasonable, but it must involve a risk of harm to others substantially in excess of that necessary to make the conduct negligent. It must involve an easily perceptible danger of death or substantial physical harm, and the probability that it will so result must be substantially greater than is required for ordinary negligence.

b. Perception of risk. Conduct cannot be in reckless disregard of the   5
safety of others unless the act or omission is itself intended, notwithstanding
that the actor knows of facts which would lead any reasonable man to realize the extreme risk to which it subjects the safety of others. It is reckless for
a driver of an automobile intentionally to cross a through highway in defiance
of a stop sign if a stream of vehicles is seen to be closely approaching in both
directions, but if his failure to stop is due to the fact that he has permitted his
attention to be diverted so that he does not know that he is approaching the
crossing, he may be merely negligent and not reckless. So too, if his failure to
stop is due to the fact that his brakes fail to act, he may be negligent if the bad
condition of the brakes could have been discovered by such an inspection as
it is his duty to make, but his conduct is not reckless.

c. Appreciation of extent and gravity of risk. In order that the actor's   6
conduct may be reckless, it is not necessary that he himself recognize it as
being extremely dangerous. His inability to realize the danger may be due to
his own reckless temperament, or to the abnormally favorable results of previous conduct of the same sort. It is enough that he knows or has reason to
know of circumstances which would bring home to the realization of the ordinary, reasonable man the highly dangerous character of his conduct. . . .

f. Intentional misconduct and recklessness contrasted. Reckless mis-   7
conduct differs from intentional wrongdoing in a very important particular.
While an act to be reckless must be intended by the actor, the actor does not
intend to cause the harm which results from it. It is enough that he realizes or,
from facts which he knows, should realize that there is a strong probability
that harm may result, even though he hopes or even expects that his conduct
will prove harmless. However, a strong probability is a different thing from
the substantial certainty without which he cannot be said to intend the harm
in which his act results.

g. Negligence and recklessness contrasted. Reckless misconduct differs   8
from negligence in several important particulars. It differs from that form of
negligence which consists in mere inadvertence, incompetence, unskillfulness,
or a failure to take precautions to enable the actor adequately to cope with a
possible or probable future emergency, in that reckless misconduct requires a
conscious choice of a course of action, either with knowledge of the serious
danger to others involved in it or with knowledge of facts which would disclose this danger to any reasonable man. It differs not only from the above-
mentioned form of negligence, but also from that negligence which consists in
intentionally doing an act with knowledge that it contains a risk of harm to
others, in that the actor to be reckless must recognize that his conduct involves
a risk substantially greater in amount than that which is necessary to make his
conduct negligent. The difference between reckless misconduct and conduct
involving only such a quantum of risk as is necessary to make it negligent is
a difference in the degree of the risk, but this difference of degree is so marked
as to amount substantially to a difference in kind.

Instructions to the Jury*

The plaintiff ___*Dale Hackbart*___ [also] seeks to recover damages based   1
upon a claim of reckless misconduct by a co-participant in an active sporting event.

The essential elements of such a claim are: 2

1. Plaintiff and Defendant[s] were co-participants in an active sporting
   event;
2. Defendant[s]'[s] physical conduct caused plaintiff to suffer injury;
3. The defendant intended to injure plaintiff, or was so reckless as to be
   totally outside the range of the ordinary activity involved in the sport.

[A defendant intended to inflict injury if it is established that [he] [she]   3
desired to cause such injury or knew that such an injury was substantially
certain to result from [his] [her] conduct.]

[A co-participant in an active sport is not subject to liability for an injury   4
resulting from conduct in the course of the sport that is merely accidental,
careless, or negligent.]

■ ■ ■

Discussion and Writing Suggestions

1. If you were a member of the jury deliberating on a verdict, how would
   you vote? Explain your reasoning, specifically referring to the particular
   facts of the case and to the definitions or explanations of "reckless disregard of safety" in the *Restatement of Torts*. How do these definitions
   and explanations either support or fail to support the plaintiff's claim for
   damages? Emphasize those elements of the case that seemed crucial to
   you in reaching a determination.
2. Based on the explanations in the *Restatement of Torts*, would you characterize Charles Clark's actions as "negligent" or "reckless"—or neither? Explain.
3. One judge reviewing this case (whose opinion did not necessarily prevail),
   wrote

   > It is wholly incongruous to talk about a professional football player's duty of
   > care for the safety of opposing players when he has been trained and motivat-
   > ed to be heedless of injury to himself. The character of NFL competition

California Jury Instructions, Civil: Book of Approved Jury Instructions [BAJI]. 8th ed.
Prepared by The Committee on Standard Jury Instruction Civil, of the Superior Court of Los
Angeles County, California. Hon. Stephen M. Lachs, Judge of the Superior Court,
Chairman. Compiled and Edited by Paul G. Breckenridge, Jr. St. Paul, MN: West Publishing
Co., 1994.

negates any notion that the playing conduct can be circumscribed by any standard of reasonableness. [452 F.Supp. at 356]

Another judge reviewing the case (again, whose opinion did not necessarily prevail) wrote:

> . . . it is highly questionable whether a professional football player consents or submits to injuries caused by conduct not within the rules, and there is no evidence which we have seen which shows this. [602 F.2nd. at 520]

Considering the facts of the case, which of these opinions do you find more persuasive? Explain.

4. One judge reviewing this case noted:

> The NFL rules of play are so . . . difficult of application because of the speed and violence of the play that the differences between violations which could fairly be called deliberate, reckless or outrageous and those which are "fair play" would be so small and subjective as to be incapable of articulation. The question of causation would be extremely difficult in view of the frequency of forceful collisions. [435 F.Supp. at 358]

Essentially, the judge appears to be saying that given the nature of professional football, there is no way to tell whether a violent act by one player against another is fair or not. Looking at the particular facts of this case, to what extent do you agree?

5. Have you (or has someone you know) ever been a victim of reckless disregard of safety that would fit the legal definition of this term? If so, lay out the facts of the case in a manner similar to the narratives in this section. Then, using IRAC format, apply the legal standards for a judgment of reckless disregard of safety to the event or events you have described.

6. *Group Assignment:* See Discussion and Writing Suggestion #5 in "The Ridiculed Employee" (p. 710)and apply this assignment to this case.

Of Accidents and Injuries: Some Cases of Negligence
(Liebeck v. McDonald's, Greene v. Hardees, Lucas v. New York City Transit Authority, Robinson v. NYC Transit)

One of the key concepts of law is negligence. Negligence has been defined as "the failure to exercise the standard of care that a reasonably prudent person would have exercised in the same situation" (Black's Law Dictionary). Of course, during our daily lives we're all guilty of acts of negligence; fortunately, most of these cases don't wind up in the courts. On the other hand, many other alleged acts of negligence become the basis for lawsuits or even criminal charges (for example, injuries resulting from drunk driving). In such cases, the plaintiffs have generally suffered either financial damages, injuries, or even death as a result of alleged negligence on the part of the defendants. In some cases, negligence results in the making or selling of defective products, an area of law known as product liability.

In the following selections, we focus on the question of possible negligence by one or the other or both of the parties in a number of lawsuits. (None of these cases involve criminal charges.) Probably the first case is the most notorious: a plaintiff wins a huge damage award after being severely burned by hot coffee sold to her by McDonald's. A similar case, Greene v. Hardees, *follows. Two cases follow involving injuries caused by moving New York City subway trains.*

Following each of these cases, we present "Statements on the Law" that you can use to help determine the degree to which either or both parties to the lawsuit were liable for negligence.

A Matter of Degree: How a Jury Decided That One Coffee Spill Is Worth $2.9 Million—McDonald's Callousness Was The Real Issue, Jurors Say, In Case of Burned Woman—How Hot Do You Like It?

By Andrea Gerlin, *Wall Street Journal*, Staff Reporter.*

Albuquerque, New Mexico—When a law firm here found itself defending McDonald's Corp. in a suit last year that claimed the company served dangerously hot coffee, it hired a law student to take temperatures at other local restaurants for comparison.   1

After dutifully slipping a thermometer into steaming cups and mugs all over the city, Danny Jarrett found that none came closer than about 20 degrees to the temperature that McDonald's coffee is poured, about 180 degrees Fahrenheit (82 degrees Celsius).   2

It should have been a warning.   3

But McDonald's lawyers went on to dismiss several opportunities to settle out of court, apparently convinced that no jury would punish a company for serving coffee the way customers like it. After all, its coffee's temperature helps explain why McDonald's sells a billion cups a year.   4

But now—days after a jury here awarded $2.9 million to an 81-year-old woman scalded by McDonald's coffee—some observers say the defense was naive. "I drink McDonald's coffee because it's hot, the hottest coffee around," says Robert Gregg, a Dallas defense attorney who consumes it during morning drives to the office. "But I've predicted for years that someone's going to win a suit, because I've spilled it on myself. And unlike the coffee I make at home, it's really hot. I mean, man, it hurts."   5

McDonald's, known for its fastidious control over franchisees, requires that its coffee be prepared at very high temperatures, based on recommendations of coffee consultants and industry groups that say hot temperatures   6

---

*"A Matter of Degree: How a Jury Decided That One Coffee Spill is Worth $2.9 Million." *Wall Street Journal* 2 Sep. 1994. Cacilie Rohwedder in Duesseldorf contributed to this article.

are necessary to fully extract the flavor during brewing. Before trial, McDonald's gave the opposing lawyer its operations and training manual, which says its coffee must be brewed at 195 to 205 degrees and held at 180 to 190 degrees for optimal taste. Since the verdict, McDonald's has declined to offer any comment, as have their attorneys. It is unclear if the company, whose coffee cups warn drinkers that the contents are hot, plans to change its preparation procedures.

But coffee temperature is suddenly a hot topic in the U.S. food industry. 7 The Specialty Coffee Association of America has put coffee safety on the agenda of its quarterly board meeting this month. And a spokesman for Dunkin' Donuts Inc., which sells about 500 million cups of coffee a year, says the company is looking at the verdict to see if it needs to make any changes to the way it makes coffee.

Others call it a tempest in a coffeepot. A spokesman for the National 8 Coffee Association says McDonald's coffee conforms to industry temperature standards. And a spokesman for Mr. Coffee Inc., the coffee-machine maker, says that if customer complaints are any indication, industry settings may be too low—some customers like it hotter. A spokeswoman for Starbucks Coffee Co. adds, "Coffee is traditionally a hot beverage and is served hot and I would hope that this is an isolated incident."

Coffee connoisseur William McAlpin, an importer and wholesaler in Bar 9 Harbor, Maine, who owns a coffee plantation in Costa Rica, says 175 degrees is "probably the optimum temperature, because that's when aromatics are being released. Once the aromas get in your palate, that is a large part of what makes the coffee a pleasure to drink."

Public opinion is squarely on the side of McDonald's. Polls have shown 10 a large majority of Americans—including many who typically support the little guy—to be outraged at the verdict. And radio talk-show hosts around the country have lambasted the plaintiff, her attorneys and the jurors on air. Declining to be interviewed for this story, one juror explained that he already had received angry calls from citizens around the country.

It's a reaction that many of the jurors could have understood—before 11 they heard the evidence. At the beginning of the trial, jury foreman Jerry Goens says he "wasn't convinced as to why I needed to be there to settle a coffee spill."

At that point, Mr. Goens and the other jurors knew only the basic facts: 12 that two years earlier, Stella Liebeck had bought a 49-cent cup of coffee at the drive-in window of an Albuquerque McDonald's, and while removing the lid to add cream and sugar had spilled it, causing third-degree burns of the groin, inner thighs and buttocks. Her suit, filed in state court in Albuquerque, claimed the coffee was "defective" because it was so hot.

What the jury didn't realize initially was the severity of her burns. Told 13 during the trial of Mrs. Liebeck's seven days in the hospital and of her skin grafts, and shown gruesome photographs, jurors began taking the matter more seriously. "It made me come home and tell my wife and daughters don't drink coffee in the car, at least not hot," says juror Jack Elliott.

Even more eye-opening was the revelation that McDonald's had seen such injuries many times before. Company documents showed that in the past decade McDonald's had received at least 700 reports of coffee burns ranging from mild to third degree, and had settled claims arising from scalding injuries for more than $500,000.   14

Some observers wonder why McDonald's, after years of settling coffee-burn cases, chose to take this one to trial. After all, the plaintiff was a sympathetic figure—an articulate, 81-year-old former department store clerk who said under oath that she had never filed suit before. In fact, she said, she never would have filed this one if McDonald's hadn't dismissed her request for compensation for pain and medical bills with an offer of $800.   15

Then there was the matter of Mrs. Liebeck's attorney. While recuperating from her injuries in the Santa Fe home of her daughter, Mrs. Liebeck happened to meet a pair of Texas transplants familiar with a Houston attorney who had handled a 1986 hot-coffee lawsuit against McDonald's. His name was Reed Morgan, and ever since he had deeply believed that McDonald's coffee is too hot.   16

For that case, involving a Houston woman with third-degree burns, Mr. Morgan had the temperature of coffee taken at 18 restaurants such as Dairy Queen, Wendy's and Dunkin' Donuts, and at 20 McDonald's restaurants. McDonald's, his investigator found, accounted for nine of the 12 hottest readings. Also for that case, Mr. Morgan deposed Christopher Appleton, a McDonald's quality assurance manager, who said "he was aware of this risk . . . and had no plans to turn down the heat," according to Mr. Morgan. McDonald's settled that case for $27,500.   17

Now, plotting Mrs. Liebeck's case, Mr. Morgan planned to introduce photographs of his previous client's injuries and those of a California woman who suffered second- and third-degree burns after a McDonald's employee spilled hot coffee into her vehicle in 1990, a case that was settled out of court for $230,000.   18

Tracy McGee of Rodey, Dickason, Sloan, Akin & Robb, the lawyers for McDonald's, strenuously objected. "First-person accounts by sundry women whose nether regions have been scorched by McDonald's coffee might well be worthy of Oprah," she wrote in a motion to state court Judge Robert Scott. "But they have no place in a court of law." Judge Scott did not allow the photographs nor the women's testimony into evidence, but said Mr. Morgan could mention the cases.   19

As the trial date approached, McDonald's declined to settle. At one point, Mr. Morgan says he offered to drop the case for $300,000, and was willing to accept half that amount. But McDonald's didn't bite.   20

Only days before the trial, Judge Scott ordered both sides to attend a mediation session. The mediator, a retired judge, recommended that   21

McDonald's settle for $225,00, saying a jury would be likely to award that amount. The company didn't follow his recommendation.

Instead, McDonald's continued denying any liability for Mrs. Liebeck's   22
burns. The company suggested that she may have contributed to her injuries by holding the cup between her legs and not removing her clothing immediately. And it also argued that "Mrs. Liebeck's age may have caused her injuries to have been worse than they might have been in a younger individual," since older skin is thinner and more vulnerable to injury.

The trial lasted seven sometimes mindnumbing days. Experts dueled over   23
the temperature at which coffee causes burns. A scientist testifying for McDonald's argued that any coffee hotter than 130 degrees could produce third-degree burns, so it didn't matter whether McDonald's coffee was hotter. But a doctor testifying on behalf of Mrs. Liebeck argued that lowering the serving temperature to about 160 degrees could make a big difference, because it takes less than three seconds to produce a third-degree burn at 190 degrees, about 12 to 15 seconds at 180 degrees and about 20 seconds at 160 degrees.

The testimony of Mr. Appleton, the McDonald's executive, didn't help   24
the company, jurors said later. He testified that McDonald's knew its coffee sometimes caused serious burns, but hadn't consulted burn experts about it. He also testified that McDonald's had decided not to warn customers about the possibility of severe burns, even though most people wouldn't think it possible. Finally, he testified that McDonald's didn't intend to change any of its coffee policies or procedures, saying, "There are more serious dangers in restaurants."

Mr. Elliott, the juror, says he began to realize that the case was about   25
"callous disregard for the safety of the people."

Next for the defense came P. Robert Knaff, a human-factors engineer   26
who earned $15,000 in fees from the case and who, several jurors said later, didn't help McDonald's either. Dr. Knaff told the jury that hot-coffee burns were statistically insignificant when compared to the billion cups of coffee McDonald's sells annually.

To jurors, Dr. Knaff seemed to be saying that the graphic photos they had   27
seen of Mrs. Liebeck's burns didn't matter because they were rare. "There was a person behind every number and I don't think the corporation was attaching enough importance to that," says juror Betty Farnham.

When the panel reached the jury room, it swiftly arrived at the conclusion   28
that McDonald's was liable. "The facts were so overwhelmingly against the company," says Ms. Farnham. "They were not taking care of their consumers."

Then the six men and six women decided on compensatory damages of   29
$200,000, which they reduced to $160,000 after determining that 20% of the fault belonged with Mrs. Liebeck for spilling the coffee.

The jury then found that McDonald's had engaged in willful, reckless,   30
malicious or wanton conduct, the basis for punitive damages. Mr. Morgan

had suggested penalizing McDonald's the equivalent of one to two days of companywide coffee sales, which he estimated at $1.35 million a day. During the four-hour deliberation, a few jurors unsuccessfully argued for as much as $9.6 million in punitive damages. But in the end, the jury settled on $2.7 million. McDonald's has since asked the judge for a new trial. Judge Scott has asked both sides to meet with a mediator to discuss settling the case before he rules on McDonald's request. The judge also has the authority to disregard the jury's finding or decrease the amount of damages.

One day after the verdict, a local reporter tested the coffee at the McDonald's that had served Mrs. Liebeck and found it to be a comparatively cool 158 degrees. But industry officials say they doubt that this signals any companywide change. After all, in a series of focus groups last year, customers who buy McDonald's coffee at least weekly say that "morning coffee has minimal taste requirements, but must be hot," to the point of steaming. ∎

31

Stella LIEBECK, Plaintiff, v. MCDONALD'S RESTAURANTS, P.T.S., INC. and McDonald's International, Inc., Defendants.
CV-93-02419.

District Court of New Mexico, Second Judicial District,
Bernalillo County.

Aug. 18, 1994.

Kenneth R. Wagner & Associates, P.A. by Kenneth R. Wagner,
Albuquerque, for plaintiff.

Rodey, Dickason, Sloan, Akin & Robb, P.A. by Tracy McGee,
Albuquerque, for defendants.

JUDGMENT
ROBERT H. SCOTT, District Judge.

Facts of the Case*

1 This matter came on for trial before the Court and a twelve (12) person jury on August 8, 9, 10, 11, 12, 15, 16 and 17, 1994. Defendant P.T.S., Inc. was dismissed with prejudice by stipulation of the parties entered into during trial. The issues having been duly tried and a jury having rendered its verdict against the sole remaining defendant **McDonald's** Corporation as follows:

1

1. On Plaintiff's claim for product defect, for Plaintiff;
2. On Plaintiff's claim for breach of the implied warranty of merchantability, for Plaintiff;

Liebeck v. McDonald's. 1995 WL 360309 (N.M. Dist.)

3. On Plaintiff's claim for breach of the implied warranty of fitness for particular purpose, for Plaintiff;
4. On Plaintiff's claim that Plaintiff was comparatively at fault, Plaintiff was determined to be twenty percent (20%) at fault;
5. On Plaintiff's claim for compensatory damages, Plaintiff is entitled to $200,000.00 to be reduced by $40,000.00, representing her twenty percent (20%) comparative negligence, for a net judgment of $160,000.00;
6. On Plaintiff's claim for punitive damages, punitive damages are awarded in the sum of $2,700,000.00.

It is hereby ordered, adjudged and decreed that Judgment is entered   2 solely against **McDonald's** Corporation and to Plaintiff in the amount of $160,000.00 for compensatory damages, and $2,700,000.00 to Plaintiff for punitive damages.

It is further ordered, adjudged and decreed that Plaintiff shall be award-   3 ed interest as permitted by law.

It is further ordered, adjudged and decreed that Plaintiff shall be award-   4 ed her costs to be determined upon presentation of a Cost Bill to the Court in accord with applicable law. ■

Katherine GREENE, Plaintiff, v. BODDIE-NOELL ENTERPRISES, INC., t/a Hardees, Defendant.
No. CIV. A. 97-17-B.
United States District Court,
W.D. Virginia.
June 12, 1997.

Facts of the Case*

In this products liability case, the plaintiff contends that she was badly burned   1 by hot coffee purchased from the drive-through window of a fast food restaurant, when the coffee spilled on her after it had been handed to her by the driver of the vehicle. The defendant restaurant operator moves for summary judgment on the ground that the plaintiff cannot show a prima facie case of liability.

The circumstances surrounding the accident in which the plaintiff,   2 Katherine Greene, was injured are set forth in the depositions submitted in support of the motion for summary judgment.

Greene was a passenger in a car driven by her boyfriend, Chris Blevins,   3 on the morning of December 31, 1994, when he purchased food and drink from the drive-through window of the Hardee's restaurant in Wise, Virginia,

---

Greene v. Hardees. 1997 WL 323455 W.D. Va.

operated by the defendant. Blevins paid the Hardee's employee and received an order of gravy and biscuits, a steak biscuit, juice for Greene, and coffee for himself. He immediately handed the food and beverages to Greene. The food was on a plate, and the beverages were in cups. Greene placed the plate on her lap and held a cup in each hand. According to Greene, the Styrofoam coffee cup was comfortable to hold, and had a lid on the top, although she did not notice whether the lid was fully attached.

Blevins drove out of the restaurant parking lot, and over a "bad dip" at   4 the point at which the lot meets the road. When the front tires of the car went slowly across the dip, the coffee "splashed out" on Greene, burning her legs through her clothes. Blevins remembers Greene exclaiming, "the lid came off." She did not look at the cup until the coffee burned her, and does not know whether the cup was tilted in one direction or another when the coffee spilled out.

As soon as the coffee burned her, Greene threw the food and drink to the   5 floor of the car, and in the process stepped on the coffee cup. When the cup was later retrieved from the floor of the car, the bottom of the cup was damaged, and the lid was at least partially off of the top of the cup.

After Greene was burned by the coffee, Blevins drove her to the emer-   6 gency room of a local hospital, where she was treated. She missed eleven days of work, and suffered permanent scarring to her thighs.

Both Greene and Blevins testified that they had heard of the **"McDonald's**   7 coffee case" prior to this incident and Greene testified that while she was not a coffee drinker, she had been aware that if coffee spilled on her, it would burn her. After the accident, Greene gave a recorded statement to a representative of the defendant in which she stated, "I know the lid wasn't on there good. It came off too easy."

The plaintiff filed an action against the defendant as a result of this acci-   8 dent in state court on October 21, 1996, and the defendant removed the case to this court, based on the court's diversity jurisdiction. In her suit, the plaintiff contends that the defendant impliedly warranted that the coffee sold was fit for consumption and that because of its extreme heat and improperly attached cup lid, it was not as warranted. It is also alleged that the defendant was negligent in failing to warn the plaintiff of the heat of the coffee and of the improperly attached cup lid.

From Greene *ruling:*

To prove a case of liability in Virginia, a plaintiff must show that a product   9 had a defect which rendered it unreasonably dangerous for ordinary or foreseeable use. In order to meet this burden, a plaintiff must offer proof that the product violated a prevailing safety standard, whether the standard comes from business, government or reasonable consumer expectation. Redman v. John D. Brush & Co., 111 F.3d 1174, 1178 (4th Cir.1997). ∎

Statements on the Law

*Uniform Commercial Code**

[SECTION] 2—314. IMPLIED WARRANTY: MERCHANTABILITY; USAGE OF TRADE

(1) Unless excluded or modified, a warranty that the goods shall be merchantable is implied in a contract for their sale if the seller is a merchant with respect to goods of that kind. Under this section the serving for value of food or drink to be consumed either on the premises or elsewhere is a sale.

(2) Goods to be merchantable must be at least such as

    (a) pass without objection in the trade under the contract description; and

    (b) in the case of fungible goods, are of fair average quality within the description; and

    (c) are fit for the ordinary purposes for which such goods are used; and

    (d) run, within the variations permitted by the agreement, of even kind, quality and quantity within each unit and among all units involved; and

    (e) are adequately contained, packaged, and labeled as the agreement may require; and

    (f) conform to the promises or affirmations of fact made on the container or label if any.

(3) Unless excluded or modified other implied warranties may arise from course of dealing or usage of trade. ■

Restatement of Torts, Second[†]

[SECTION] 402 A. SPECIAL LIABILITY OF SELLER OF PRODUCT FOR PHYSICAL HARM TO USER OR CONSUMER

(1) One who sells any product in a defective condition unreasonably dangerous to the user or consumer or to his property is subject to liability for physical harm thereby caused to the ultimate user or consumer, or to his property, if

    (a) the seller is engaged in the business of selling such a product, and

    (b) it is expected to and does reach the user or consumer without substantial change in the condition in which it is sold.

(2) The rule stated in Subsection (1) applies although

    (a) the seller has exercised all possible care in the preparation and sale of his product, and

    (b) the user or consumer has not bought the product from or entered into any contractual relation with the seller. . . .

Uniform Commercial Code, 9th ed. The American Law Institute, National Conference of Commissioners on Uniform State Laws. Official Text-1978, with Comments and Appendices. The American Law Institute, 4025 Chestnut Street, Philadelphia, PA 19104.

[†]*Restatement of the Law, Second: Torts, 2nd.* As Adapted and Promulgated by The American Law Institute at Washington, D.C. May 25, 1963 and May 22, 1964. St. Paul, MN: West Publishing Co., 1965.

[Comments]

    g. Defective condition. The rule stated in this Section applies only   1
where the product is, at the time it leaves the seller's hands, in a condition not
contemplated by the ultimate consumer, which will be unreasonably dangerous to him. The seller is not liable when he delivers the product in a safe condition, and subsequent mishandling or other causes make it harmful by the
time it is consumed. The burden of proof that the product was in a defective
condition at the time that it left the hands of the particular seller is upon the
injured plaintiff; and unless evidence can be produced which will support the
conclusion that it was then defective, the burden is not sustained.

    Safe condition at the time of delivery by the seller will, however, include   2
proper packaging, necessary sterilization, and other precautions required to
permit the product to remain safe for a normal length of time when handled
in a normal manner.

    h. A product is not in a defective condition when it is safe for normal   3
handling and consumption. If the injury results from abnormal handling, as
where a bottled beverage is knocked against a radiator to remove the cap, or
from abnormal preparation for use, as where too much salt is added to
food, or from abnormal consumption, as where a child eats too much candy
and is made ill, the seller is not liable. Where, however, he has reason to
anticipate that danger may result from a particular use, as where a drug is
sold which is safe only in limited doses, he may be required to give adequate
warning of the danger, and a product sold without such warning is in a
defective condition. . . .

    n. Contributory negligence. Since the liability with which this Section   4
deals is not based upon negligence of the seller, but is strict liability, the rule
applied to strict liability cases applies. Contributory negligence of the plaintiff is not a defense when such negligence consists merely in a failure to discover the defect in the product, or to guard against the possibility of its
existence. On the other hand the form of contributory negligence which consists in voluntarily and unreasonably proceeding to encounter a known
danger, and commonly passes under the name of assumption of risk, is a
defense under this Section as in other cases of strict liability. If the user or consumer discovers the defect and is aware of the danger, and nevertheless proceeds unreasonably to make use of the product and is injured by it, he is
barred from recovery. ■

Instructions to the Jury*

FAILURE TO WARN—ESSENTIAL ELEMENTS

The essential elements of a claim based upon an alleged defect from failure   1
to warn are:

California Jury Instructions, Civil: Book of Approved Jury Instructions [BAJI]. 8th ed.
Prepared by The Committee on Standard Jury Instruction Civil, of the Superior Court of Los
Angeles County, California. Hon. Stephen M. Lachs, Judge of the Superior Court,
Chairman. Compiled and Edited by Paul G. Breckenridge, Jr. St. Paul, MN: West Publishing
Co., 1994.

1. The defendant was the manufacturer of a product, namely *hot coffee* ;
(identify the product)
2. The product was defective;
3. The product defect was a cause of injury to the plaintiffs;
4. Plaintiff's injury resulted from a use of the product that was reasonably foreseeable to the defendant.

A product is defective if the use of the product in a manner that is rea- 2
sonably foreseeable by the defendant involves a substantial danger that would not be readily recognized by the ordinary user of the product and the manufacturer knows or should have known of the danger, but fails to give adequate warning of such danger.

NEGLIGENCE—ESSENTIAL ELEMENTS

The plaintiff _Katherine Greene_ seeks to recover damages based upon a 3
claim of negligence.

The essential elements of such a claim are: 4

1. The defendant was negligent;
2. Defendant's negligence was a cause of injury, damage, loss or harm to plaintiff.

Negligence is the doing of something which a reasonably prudent 5
person would not do, or the failure to do something which a reasonably prudent person would do, under circumstances similar to those shown by the evidence.

It is the failure to use ordinary or reasonable care. 6

Ordinary or reasonable care is that care which persons of ordinary pru- 7
dence would use in order to avoid injury to themselves or others under circumstances similar to those shown by the evidence.

You will note that the person whose conduct we set up as a standard is 8
not the extraordinarily cautious individual, nor the exceptionally skillful one, but a person of reasonable and ordinary prudence.

One test that is helpful in determining whether or not a person was neg- 9
ligent is to ask and answer the question whether or not, if a person of ordinary prudence had been in the same situation and possessed of the same knowledge, [he][or][she] would have foreseen or anticipated that someone might have been injured by or as a result of [his][or][her] action or inaction. If the answer to that question is "yes", and if the action or inaction reasonably could have been avoided, then not to avoid it would be negligence.

Contributory negligence is negligence on the part of a plaintiff which, 10
combining with the negligence of a defendant, contributes as a cause in bringing about the injury.

Contributory negligence, if any, on the part of the plaintiff does not bar 11
a recovery by the plaintiff against the defendant but the total amount of damages to which the plaintiff would otherwise be entitled shall be reduced in proportion to the amount of negligence attributable to the plaintiff.

PRODUCTS LIABILITY—NEGLIGENCE—COMPARATIVE FAULT

Comparative fault is negligence on the part of a plaintiff which combining [with the negligence of a defendant][or][with a defect in a product][or][with negligent or wrongful conduct of others] contributes as a cause in bringing about the injury. 12

Comparative fault, if any, on the part of plaintiff does not bar recovery by the plaintiff against the defendant but the total amount of damages to which plaintiff would otherwise be entitled shall be reduced by the percentage that plaintiff's comparative fault contributed as a cause to plaintiff's injury. 13

If you find that a cause of plaintiff's injury was [a defendant's negligence][or][a defect in the product] and that the comparative fault of the plaintiff was also a cause of said injury, you will determine the amount of damages to be awarded by you as follows: 14

First: You will determine the total amount of damages to which the plaintiff would be entitled under the court's instructions if plaintiff had not been comparatively at fault. 15

Second: You will determine what percentage of the combined causes of plaintiff's injury is attributable to plaintiff's comparative fault and what percentage of such combined causes is attributable to the [defective product][and][or][a defendant's negligence]. 16

Third: You will then reduce the total amount of plaintiff's damages by the percentage that plaintiff's comparative fault contributed as a cause to plaintiff's injury. 17

Fourth: The resulting amount, after making such reduction, will be the amount of your verdict. ▪ 18

Celestino LUCAS, Plaintiff-Respondent, v. NEW YORK CITY TRANSIT AUTHORITY, Defendant-Appellant.
Supreme Court, Appellate Division,
First Department.
July 3, 1990.

Facts of the Case*

At approximately 9:15 P.M. on May 8, 1983, George Johnson, the motorman of a nine car No. 3 train, began his approach into the 34th Street and 7th Avenue **subway** station when he saw plaintiff in the air above the tracks. Plaintiff landed feet first onto the tracks and in one continuous motion, turned to face the train, crouched down and then stretched out across the tracks. The motorman, who testified that the train was travelling at between 1

Lucas v. New York City Transit Authority. 557 N.Y.S.2d 919 (1990).

15–20 miles per hour, first observed plaintiff from 52 feet (one car length) away and immediately put the train into emergency by pulling back the emergency brake. Fifteen feet of the first car of the train passed over plaintiff before it came to a complete stop, severing his **legs** below the knee.

Plaintiff's medical experts testified that plaintiff's actions in jumping to the tracks were involuntary and the result of a postictal psychosis stemming from epilepsy. Defendant maintained that plaintiff was attempting **suicide**. Plaintiff also claimed that the motorman was negligent in failing to stop the train before contact.

Plaintiff, an epileptic, disclaimed all responsibility for the accident, arguing that his actions were involuntary and the result of a prolonged trance following a seizure suffered earlier that day. He contended that the motorman, who had sufficient opportunity to observe his conduct on the tracks, was negligent in failing to stop the train before it ran him over.

The motorman, who prior to the accident had operated trains on the IRT number three line for some thirteen years, testified that the train entered the station at a speed of less than fifteen to twenty m.p.h. This was due to a curve on the tracks ending just prior to entering the 34th Street station. According to the motorman, about one hundred fifty feet, or three car lengths, into the station, he observed plaintiff, some fifty-two feet in front of him and in midair above the tracks. He immediately pulled back the brake handle and blew the whistle, while continuing to observe plaintiff who landed on his feet, pivoted and lay down on the tracks. The train came to rest some thirteen feet, or about one-fourth car length, over plaintiff.

The record reveals that the fifty-nine year old plaintiff, who suffered from and was being treated for epilepsy, was estranged from his wife, had been unemployed since 1972, had previously attempted **suicide**, and had a psychiatric history of depression and of violent episodes. Plaintiff testified that he had only a vague recollection of his activities on the day of the accident. He recalled, however, leaving Metropolitan Hospital early that morning and drinking beer during the day. Emergency Medical Service attendants reported the smell of alcohol on plaintiff's breath following the accident.

Two neurologists retained by plaintiff offered their opinions that Lucas' leap from the platform was spurred by postictal psychosis, a trance-like state of confusion, which followed an epileptic seizure which they believe plaintiff suffered that morning and for which plaintiff was admitted to Metropolitan Hospital. The hospital records reveal that plaintiff was admitted to Metropolitan Hospital early that morning "hyperventilating and feigning [sic], comatose state without fibulation" (fibrillation) and that he walked out of the hospital at about 8:45 A.M.

A science expert called by plaintiff testified that, upon braking, before coming to rest, a train moving at fifteen m.p.h. would continue to travel about seventy-five feet, within approximately six and one-half seconds. These calculations included consideration of the motorman's approximated reaction time and of the approximate time required for the train's braking system to operate once activated. Plaintiff's expert also indicated that it would have taken plaintiff six to eight and one-half seconds to jump from the platform, whirl around and lie down. This conclusion was based upon the seventy-nine year old expert timing himself with a stop watch as he jumped off the porch of his New Jersey home.

An engineer called by the defense, with a background in the design and   8
operation of trains, testified that once thrown into emergency, the stopping distance for that nine-car train when traveling approximately fifteen m.p.h. was sixty to seventy-five feet within five to six seconds. He concluded, based upon demonstrations with several Transit Authority employees, that it would have taken plaintiff three to four seconds, once he was in mid-air, to assume his position on the tracks. . . .

Here, the evidence was undisputed that the train entered the station at   9
approximately fifteen to twenty m.p.h. Plaintiff's scientific expert testified that it would have taken between six and eight and one-half seconds for plaintiff to have jumped and positioned himself upon the tracks. He further testified that it would have taken the motorman approximately six to six and six-tenth seconds to stop the train, assuming that the train was traveling at fifteen m.p.h. Plaintiff counsel's examination of the motorman attempted to establish that the motorman's observations of plaintiff's actions on the track were so extensive that these observations must have commenced from a distance of more than fifty-two feet. However, the only evidence as to how long plaintiff was on the track reveals that the motorman could have observed all that he did and still have activated the braking system from fifty-two feet away, causing the train to stop within seventy-five feet and within six and one-half seconds. ■

Jeffrey ROBINSON, Plaintiff-Respondent, v. NEW YORK CITY TRANSIT AUTHORITY, et al., Defendants-Appellants.
Supreme Court, Appellate Division,
First Department.
Nov. 8, 1984.

Facts of the Case*

Plaintiff was severely injured when he came in contact with a subway train   1
which had just started to move out of the Parsons Boulevard station in Queens about 4:00 A.M. on November 4, 1981. Plaintiff had drunk alcoholic beverages in Manhattan two or three hours earlier. He was accompanied by his girlfriend. They got out of the train at Parsons Boulevard and plaintiff was injured when he apparently staggered into the train after the train began to move. Plaintiff's version of the accident would concededly require dismissal. His testimony indicated that he was not intoxicated; he knew where he was;

Robinson v. NYC Transit. 481 N.Y.S.2d 85 (1984).

he testified from memory as to how the accident occurred; he was standing on his own two feet and was not falling. He said he was on the platform after having left the train; he was arguing with this girlfriend; he wanted to get back into the train; she was holding his hand to restrain him. Somehow or other he broke free, slipped and apparently stepped between the already moving train and the platform. Plaintiff's case, however, was saved by testimony on deposition of the train conductor who said that he saw plaintiff on the platform staggering and appearing intoxicated. Plaintiff was accompanied by a woman (his girlfriend) who was trying to help him; plaintiff was talking to his girlfriend and shouting. At one point, plaintiff was on the opposite side of the platform from the train. The conductor closed the doors of the train and gave the signal for the train to start moving. In the meantime he had lost sight of the plaintiff behind the staircase leading from the platform. Almost immediately after the train began to move, the conductor again saw the plaintiff who by this time appeared from behind the staircase and who had staggered back into the side of the moving train.

[In addition to the following section, "Conduct of a Reasonable Man," see definitions of "Negligence" and "Comparative Fault," pp. 728–729.]

Statements on the Law

Restatement of Torts, Second *

[SECTION] 283. CONDUCT OF A REASONABLE MAN: THE STANDARD

> Unless the actor is a child, the standard of conduct to which he must conform to avoid being negligent is that of a reasonable man under like circumstances.

[Comment]

a. This Section is concerned only with the standard of conduct required of the actor to avoid being negligent. It is not concerned with the question of when he owes to another a duty to conform to that standard.   1

b. Qualities of the "reasonable man." The words "reasonable man" denote a person exercising those qualities of attention, knowledge, intelligence, and judgment which society requires of its members for the protection of their own interests and the interests of others. It enables those who are to determine whether the actor's conduct is such as to subject him to liability for harm caused thereby, to express their judgment in terms of the conduct of a human being. The fact that this judgment is personified in a "man" calls attention to the necessity of taking into account the fallibility of human beings.   2

---

*Restatement of The Law, Second: Torts, 2nd. As Adapted and Promulgated by The American Law Institute at Washington, D.C. May 25, 1963 and May 22, 1964. St. Paul, MN: West Publishing Co., 1965.

    c. Standard of the "reasonable man." Negligence is a departure from a   3
standard of conduct demanded by the community for the protection of others
against unreasonable risk. The standard which the community demands must
be an objective and external one, rather than that of the individual judgment,
good or bad, of the particular individual. It must be the same for all persons,
since the law can have no favorites; and yet allowance must be made for some
of the differences between individuals, the risk apparent to the actor, his
capacity to meet it, and the circumstances under which he must act.

    In dealing with this problem the law has made use of the standard of a   4
hypothetical "reasonable man." Sometimes this person is called a reasonable
man of ordinary prudence, or an ordinarily prudent man, or a man of average prudence, or a man of reasonable sense exercising ordinary care. It is evident that all such phrases are intended to mean very much the same thing. The
actor is required to do what this ideal individual would do in his place. The
reasonable man is a fictitious person, who is never negligent, and whose conduct is always up to standard. He is not to be identified with any real person;
and in particular he is not to be identified with the members of the jury, individually or collectively. It is therefore error to instruct the jury that the conduct of a reasonable man is to be determined by what they would themselves
have done.

    The chief advantage of this standard of the reasonable man is that it   5
enables the triers of fact who are to decide whether the actor's conduct is such
as to subject him to liability for negligence, to look to a community standard
rather than an individual one, and at the same time to express their judgment
of what that standard is in terms of the conduct of a human being. The standard provides sufficient flexibility, and leeway, to permit due allowance to be
made for such differences between individuals as the law permits to be taken
into account, and for all of the particular circumstances of the case which may
reasonably affect the conduct required, and at the same time affords a formula
by which, so far as possible, a uniform standard may be maintained.

■ ■ ■

Discussion and Writing Suggestions

1. Based on the evidence provided by Andrea Gerlin in her *Wall Street
Journal* article, and based upon the explanations of negligence and
product liability provided in the various statements on the law, to
what extent do you agree with (a) the trial jury's initial verdict in
Liebeck v. McDonald's, and (b) with the judge's decision to reduce the
damage award? Explain your reasoning, using IRAC format, as if you
were a judge of an appellate court to which this decision had been
appealed.

2. You are the District Court judge in *Greene v. Hardees*. You are familiar
with the facts of the case, as presented above. You are also familiar with

the outcome of *Liebeck v. McDonald's* and with the applicable law on negligence and product liability, as presented above. Finally, you are aware that

> [t]o prove a case of liability in Virginia, a plaintiff must show that a product had a defect which rendered it unreasonably dangerous for ordinary or foreseeable use. In order to meet this burden, a plaintiff must offer proof that the product violated a prevailing safety standard, whether the standard comes from business, government or reasonable consumer expectation.

Assume no facts about the case that are not presented in the "Statement of Facts" above. Render a verdict, and explain your reasoning, using IRAC format.

3. In *Lucas*, how would you vote on the question of liability if you were on the jury? Explain your reasoning, as if you were attempting to persuade other members of the jury. To what extent was the plaintiff responsible for his own injuries? To what extent was the motorman responsible? Focus on those facts of the case that are most crucial in forming your judgment. For example, to what extent are the speed of the train and the distance at which the motorman first saw the plaintiff crucial factors? To what extent is the plaintiff's epilepsy a crucial factor? To what extent is the fact that he appeared to have consumed alcohol before the accident a crucial factor? Assign comparative fault, if you find both parties responsible. Consider the relevant statements on the law concerning negligence and comparative fault.

4. You are either (a) the attorney for the plaintiff or (b) the attorney for the defendant in *Robinson v. New York City Transit*. You have researched the law and found *Lucas v. New York City Transit* as a precedent. Write a brief in IRAC format for your superiors in the law firm, laying out the crucial similarities and differences in the two cases and explaining how these similarities and differences will prove either *advantageous* or *disadvantageous* for your own case. Refer to relevant law, as presented in the "Statements of the Law" above.

5. *Group Assignment:* Form a jury, a group consisting of several other members of the class. (It doesn't have to have 12 members.) Choose a foreperson, someone to moderate, though not dominate, the discussion— someone who will keep the deliberations on track and keep the main issues in the forefront. Appoint someone to take notes. You may wish to tape-record the discussion.

   Deliberate on the case before you: study the facts of the case; study the applicable law; apply the law to the facts of the case. Before or while you are developing your own conclusions, take account of other people's arguments. Weigh the merits of these arguments before deciding upon your vote. At the conclusion of discussion, the group will vote on a verdict. (Criminal cases require a unanimous vote; civil cases require a three-quarters majority.) If the jury is badly split, deliberate more in order to reach greater consensus.

After you arrive at a verdict, work with the foreperson as she or he prepares a report, written in IRAC format, that presents your verdict (as a conclusion), and that explains the issue, the rule, and also summarizes the main points of the discussion in the "counterargument" and "response" sections.

"Urban War Zone": A Case of Public Nuisance
(PEOPLE V. ACUNA ET AL.)

In the summer of 1997, Los Angeles authorities obtained a court injunction against some 300 members of the notorious 18th Street Gang, centered in the largely Latino Pico-Union area of the city. According to authorities, the gang had been involved in murders, robberies, auto theft, drug dealing, and extortion. The injunction prohibited gang members from standing, sitting, walking, or gathering with one another in groups of three or more. It also imposed an 8 P.M.-to-sunrise curfew on gang members under 18 years of age.

Anti-gang injunctions are not new. Four years earlier, the city of San Jose in northern California instituted a similar injunction against the VST (Varrio Sureno Treces) gang based in the Rocksprings neighborhood. Violation of the injunction was punishable by six months in jail and a $1,000 fine. In approving the injunction, one justice observed, "Gang members threatened and intimidated residents. For example, a gang member warned a nine-year-old girl who had told police officers where some drugs were hidden that he could cut her tongue out if she ever again talked to the police. In another incident, gang members threatened a Rocksprings residence and vandalized her property after she called the police to report that some gang members urinated in her garage." While applauded by local residents, the injunction was challenged by civil libertarian groups, including the American Civil Liberties Union, which contended, "Simply because these men and women are suspected gang members, they are stripped of a variety of constitutional freedoms, the right to associate, to assemble, and the right to due process. It's guilt by association, without the City showing that the defendants themselves intended to violate the law."

With the ACLU representing the suspected gang members, the case went all the way up to the California Supreme Court. "The People," represented by San Jose City Attorney Joan R. Gallo, argued that the injunction was justified under the provisions of California's public nuisance statute. The defendants argued that the injunction was overly broad, overly vague, and violated their constitutional rights of freedom of association under the First Amendment.

Read the facts of the case, along with the relevant law and the injunction itself. Attempt to determine whether the injunction was justified. Then, formulate a position on some of the underlying issues in this legal conflict—issues concerning the rights of the community on the one hand, and the rights of individuals, on the other.

PEOPLE ex rel. GALLO, Plaintiff and Respondent, v. Carlos ACUNA et al., Defendants and Appellants.
No. S046980.
Supreme Court of California.
Jan. 30, 1997.

Facts of the Case*

At the request of the City Attorney of the City of San Jose (hereafter the City),   1
we granted review to resolve an array of challenges to two provisions of a preliminary injunction entered by the superior court against individual members
of an alleged "criminal street gang." The underlying action was instituted
under the provisions of sections 731 of the Code of Civil Procedure and 3480
of the Civil Code, the operative core of California's civil "public nuisance"
statutes.

The 48 declarations submitted by the City in support of its plea for   2
injunctive relief paint a graphic portrait of life in the community of
Rocksprings. Rocksprings is an urban war zone. The four-square-block neighborhood, claimed as the turf of a gang variously known as Varrio Sureno
Town, Varrio Sureno Treces (VST), or Varrio Sureno Locos (VSL), is an
occupied territory. Gang members, all of whom live elsewhere, congregate on
lawns, on sidewalks, and in front of apartment complexes at all hours of the
day and night. They display a casual contempt for notions of law, order, and
decency—openly drinking, smoking dope, sniffing toluene, and even snorting
cocaine laid out in neat lines on the hoods of residents' cars. The people who
live in Rocksprings are subjected to loud talk, loud music, vulgarity, profanity, brutality, fistfights and the sound of gunfire echoing in the streets. Gang
members take over sidewalks, driveways, carports, apartment parking areas,
and impede traffic on the public thoroughfares to conduct their drive-up
drug bazaar. Murder, attempted murder, drive-by shootings, assault and battery, vandalism, arson, and theft are commonplace. The community has
become a staging area for gang-related violence and a dumping ground for the
weapons and instrumentalities of crime once the deed is done. Area residents
have had their garages used as urinals; their homes commandeered as escape
routes; their walls, fences, garage doors, sidewalks, and even their vehicles
turned into a sullen canvas of gang graffiti.

The people of this community are prisoners in their own homes. Violence   3
and the threat of violence are constant. Residents remain indoors, especially
at night. They do not allow their children to play outside. Strangers wearing
the wrong color clothing are at risk. Relatives and friends refuse to visit. The
laundry rooms, the trash dumpsters, the residents' vehicles, and their parking
spaces are used to deal and stash drugs. Verbal harassment, physical intimi-

---

*"Urban War Zone": A Case of Public Nuisance." *People v. Acuna et al.* 60 Cal. Rptr.2d.

dation, threats of retaliation, and retaliation are the likely fate of anyone who complains of the gang's illegal activities or tells police where drugs may be hidden.

Among other allegations, the City's complaint asserted that the named defendants and others "[f]or more than 12 months precedent to the date of [the] complaint, continuing up to the present time . . . [have] occupied [and] used the area commonly known as 'Rocksprings' . . . in such a manner so as to constitute a public nuisance . . . injurious to the health, indecent or offensive to the senses, [and] an obstruction to the free use of property so as to interfere with the comfortable enjoyment of life or property by those persons living in the . . . neighborhood."

4

After alleging the usual requisites for equitable relief—the prospect of "great and irreparable injury" and the absence of "a plain, adequate and speedy remedy at law"—the complaint prayed for a broad and comprehensive injunction against defendants' alleged activities in Rocksprings. The superior court granted an ex parte temporary restraining order enjoining all 38 defendants named in the complaint and issued an order to show cause (OSC) why a preliminary injunction should not be entered.

5

Only five of the named defendants appeared in response to the OSC. Following a hearing, the superior court entered a preliminary injunction against the 33 defendants who had not appeared and continued the matter as to those 5 defendants who opposed entry of a preliminary injunction, leaving the temporary restraining order in force as to them. Eleven of the named defendants (the five who had originally appeared in opposition to the OSC, together with another six of the named defendants) moved to vacate the injunctions. After the matter was briefed and argued, the superior court entered a preliminary injunction. The multi-part decree, consisting of some 24 paragraphs, was the subject of an interlocutory appeal by these 11 defendants. ■

6

Statements on the Law

California Penal Code*

[SECTION] 370. PUBLIC NUISANCE DEFINED Anything which is injurious to health, or is indecent, or offensive to the senses, or an obstruction to the free use of property, so as to interfere with the comfortable enjoyment of life or property by an entire community or neighborhood, or by any considerable number of persons, or unlawfully obstructs the free passage or use, in the customary manner, of any navigable lake, or river, bay, stream, canal, or basin, or any public park, square, street, or highway, is a public nuisance.

1

*Penal Code, Annotated of the State of California, San Francisco: Bancroft-Whitney, 1985.

California Civil Code*

[SECTION] 3479. NUISANCE DEFINED Anything which is injurious to health, 　2
or is indecent or offensive to the senses, or an obstruction to the free use of
property, so as to interfere with the comfortable enjoyment of life or property, or unlawfully obstructs the free passage or use, in the customary manner,
of any navigable lake, or river, bay, stream, canal, or basin, or any public
park, square, street, or highway, is a nuisance.

[SECTION] 3480. PUBLIC NUISANCE A public nuisance is one which affects at 　3
the same time an entire community or neighborhood, or any considerable
number of persons, although the extent of the annoyance or damage inflicted upon individuals may be unequal. ■

Restatement of Torts, Second †

[SECTION] 821B. PUBLIC NUISANCE

(1) A public nuisance is an unreasonable interference with a right common
to the general public.
(2) Circumstances that may sustain a holding that an interference with a
public right is unreasonable include the following:
(a) Whether the conduct involves a significant interference with the
public health, the public safety, the public peace, the public comfort or
the public convenience, or
(b) whether the conduct is proscribed by a statute, ordinance or administrative regulation, or
(c) whether the conduct is of a continuing nature or has produced a permanent or long-lasting effect, and, as the actor knows or has reason to
know, has a significant effect upon the public right. ■

First Amendment to the U.S. Constitution

Congress shall make no law . . . abridging the freedom of speech, or of the 　1
press, or the right of the people peaceably to assemble, and to petition the
Government for a redress of grievances.

Text of Preliminary Injunction

The order granting the preliminary injunction enjoins defendants from the following acts:

"(a) Standing, sitting, walking, driving, gathering or appearing anywhere in
public view with any other defendant herein, or with any other known
'VST' (Varrio Sureno Town or Varrio Sureno Locos) member;

Civil Code, Annotated of the State of California, San Francisco: Lexis Law Publishing,
1984.
†*Restatement of The Law, Second: Torts, 2nd*. As Adapted and Promulgated by The
American Law Institute at Washington, D.C. May 25, 1963 and May 22, 1964. St. Paul,
MN: West Publishing Co., 1965.

"(b) Drinking alcoholic beverages in public excepting consumption on properly licensed premises or using drugs;

"(c) Possessing any weapons including but not limited to knives, dirks, daggers, clubs, nunchukas [*sic;* nunchakus], BB guns, concealed or loaded firearms, and any other illegal weapons as defined in the California Penal Code, and any object capable of inflicting serious bodily injury including but not limited to the following: metal pipes or rods, glass bottles, rocks, bricks, chains, tire irons, screwdrivers, hammers, crowbars, bumper jacks, spikes, razor blades, razors, sling shots, marbles, ball bearings;

"(d) Engaging in fighting in the public streets, alleys, and/or public and private property;

"(e) Using or possessing marker pens, spray paint cans, nails, razor blades, screwdrivers, or other sharp objects capable of defacing private or public property;

"(f) Spray painting or otherwise applying graffiti on any public or private property, including but not limited to the street, alley, residences, block walls, vehicles and/or any other real or personal property;

"(g) Trespassing on or encouraging others to trespass on any private property;

"(h) Blocking free ingress and egress to the public sidewalks or street, or any driveways leading or appurtenant thereto in 'Rocksprings';

"(i) Approaching vehicles, engaging in conversation, or otherwise communicating with the occupants of any vehicle or doing anything to obstruct or delay the free flow of vehicular or pedestrian traffic;

"(j) Discharging any firearms;

"(k) In any manner confronting, intimidating, annoying, harassing, threatening, challenging, provoking, assaulting and/or battering any residents or patrons, or visitors to 'Rocksprings', or any other persons who are known to have complained about gang activities, including any persons who have provided information in support of this Complaint and requests for Temporary Restraining Order, Preliminary Injunction and Permanent Injunction;

"(l) Causing, encouraging, or participating in the use, possession and/or sale of narcotics;

"(m) Owning, possessing or driving a vehicle found to have any contraband, narcotics, or illegal or deadly weapons;

"(n) Using or possessing pagers or beepers in any public space;

"(o) Possessing channel lock pliers, picks, wire cutters, dent pullers, sling shots, marbles, steel shot, spark plugs, rocks, screwdrivers, 'slim jims' and other devices capable of being used to break into locked vehicles;

"(p) Demanding entry into another person's residence at any time of the day or night;

"(q) Sheltering, concealing or permitting another person to enter into a residence not their own when said person appears to be running, hiding, or otherwise evading a law enforcement officer;

"(r) Signaling to or acting as a lookout for other persons to warn of the approach of police officers and soliciting, encouraging, employing or offering payment to others to do the same;

"(s) Climbing any tree, wall, or fence, or passing through any wall or fence by using tunnels or other holes in such structures;

"(t) Littering in any public place or place open to public view;

"(u) Urinating or defecating in any public place or place open to public view;

"(v) Using words, phrases, physical gestures, or symbols commonly known as hand signs or engaging in other forms of communication which describe or refer to the gang known as 'VST' or 'VSL' as described in this Complaint or any of the accompanying pleadings or declarations;

"(w) Wearing clothing which bears the name or letters of the gang known as 'VST' or 'VSL';

"(x) Making, causing, or encouraging others to make loud noise of any kind, including but not limited to yelling and loud music at any time of the day or night." ▪

From *Gallo* Opinion:

There are few "forms of action" in the history of Anglo-American law with   1
a pedigree older than suits seeking to restrain nuisances, whether public or private. Actions to abate private nuisances by injunction are the oldest of these apparent twins, which have almost nothing in common except the word "nuisance" itself. Unlike the private nuisance—tied to and designed to vindicate individual ownership interests in *land*—the "common" or *public* nuisance emerged from distinctly different historical origins. The public nuisance doctrine is aimed at the protection and redress of *community* interests and, at least in theory, embodies a kind of collective ideal of civil life which the courts have vindicated by equitable remedies since the beginning of the 16th century.

Originally, a public nuisance was an offense against the crown, prose-   2
cuted as a crime. The first known statute dealing with public nuisances—enacted in the 12th year of Richard II's reign—had as its subject the pollution of waters and ditches lying near settlements, and provided criminal liability for the offender. The earliest public nuisance statute thus bore a feature that marks the entire field even today: public nuisances are offenses against, or interferences with, the exercise of *rights common to the public.*

In this country, as in England, *civil* suits in equity to *enjoin* public nui-   3
sances at the instance of public law officers—typically a state's Attorney General—grew increasingly common during the course of the 19th century, a trend that was not without critics. . . . ["If a charge be of a criminal nature, or an offense against the public, and does not touch the enjoyment of property, it ought not to be brought within the direct jurisdiction of this court, which was intended to deal only in matters of civil right resting in equity. . . .' *Attorney General v. Insurance Co.*, 2 Johns. Ch. 378 . . ."].

With the publication of the Restatement Second of Torts in 1965, the law   4
of public nuisances had crystallized to such an extent that its features could be

clearly delineated. Section 821B of Restatement Second of Torts identifies five general categories of "public rights," the unreasonable interference with which may constitute a public nuisance: "the public health, the public safety, the public peace, the public comfort or the public convenience." (Rest.2d Torts, 821B, subd. (2)(a).) A "public right," according to the Restatement Second, "is one common to all members of the general public. It is collective in nature and not like the individual right that everyone has not to be assaulted or defamed or defrauded or negligently injured."

In California, the early common law categories of public nuisance, cod- 5 ified in 1872 and still applicable, define anything that is "injurious to health, or is indecent or offensive to the senses, or an obstruction to the free use of property, so as to interfere with the comfortable enjoyment of life or property, or unlawfully obstructs the free passage or use, in the customary manner, of any navigable lake, or river, bay, stream, canal, or basin, or any public park, square, street, or highway," as a nuisance. (Civ.Code, 3479.) Civil Code sections 3480 and 3481 divide the class nuisances into public and private. A public nuisance is one which "affects at the same time an entire community or neighborhood, or any considerable number of persons." (Civ.Code, 3480.) Rounding out the taxonomy of the Civil Code, section 3491 provides that "the remedies against a public nuisance are: 1. Indictment or information; 2. A civil action; or, 3. Abatement."

Section 370 of the Penal Code mirrors these civil provisions, combining 6 the characteristics of nuisances generally with a distinctly public quality: that a given activity "interfere with the comfortable enjoyment of life or property by an entire *community or neighborhood*, or by any *considerable number* of persons." (Pen. Code, [section 370], italics added.) In *People* ex rel. *Busch v. Projection Room Theater* (1976) 17 Cal.3d 42, 49, 130 Cal.Rptr. 328, 550, P.2d 600, we parsed these code provisions, remarking on "the substantial identity of definitions appearing in Penal Code section 370 and 371, and Civil Code section 3479 and 3480. . . . After quoting the text of section 370, we observed: "[T]he proscribed act may be anything which *alternatively* is injurious to health *or* is indecent, *or* offensive to the senses; the *result* of the act must interfere with the comfortable enjoyment of life *or* property; and those affected by the act may be an entire neighborhood or a considerable number of persons, and as amplified by Penal Code section 371 the extent of the annoyance or damage on the affected individuals may be unequal."

■ ■ ■

Discussion and Writing Suggestions

1. If you were a judge ruling on this anti-gang injunction, would you vote to approve it or to deny it? If you would support some of the 24 provisions, but not others, explain which ones you would support and which you would not. Put another way, which of the provisions do you find reasonable, which unreasonable? Explain.

2. One of the main objections made by defendants was that some provisions of the injunction were overly vague. What examples, if any, of vagueness do you find in the language of the injunction, and what kind of problems might such vagueness pose for its enforcement?

3. The First Amendment to the Constitution states:

> Congress shall make no law respecting an establishment of religion, or prohibiting the free exercise thereof; or abridging the freedom of speech, or of the press; or the right of the people peaceably to assemble, and to petition the Government for a redress of grievances.

Some have argued that antigang jurisdictions such as this one violate the First Amendment's guarantee of "the right of the people peaceably to assemble." One judge ruling on this case quoted an opinion by another court, as follows: "The First Amendment generally prevents government from proscribing speech, or even expressive conduct, because of disapproval of the ideas expressed."

Others have argued that the First Amendment is not absolute: the familiar example is that the right of freedom of speech does not extend to shouting "Fire!" in a crowded theater. In *Madsen v. Women's Health Center* (antiabortion demonstrators versus an abortion clinic), the Supreme Court ruled that "Freedom of association, in the sense protected by the First Amendment, 'does not extend to joining with others for the purpose of depriving third parties of their lawful rights.'"

To what extent do you believe that the antigang injunction is unconstitutional because it violates the First Amendment?

4. Commenting on this case, Justice Brown wrote:

> From Montesquieu to Locke to Madison [18th-century political philosophers], the description of the pivotal [social] compact remains unchanged: by entering society, individuals give up the unrestrained right to act as they think fit; in return, each has a positive right to society's protection. Montesquieu describes this civil liberty as "that tranquility of spirit which comes from the opinion each one has of his security, and in order for him to have this liberty the government must be such that one citizen cannot fear another citizen." ... To hold that the liberty of the peaceful, industrious residents of Rocksprings must be forfeited to preserve the illusion of freedom for those whose ill conduct is deleterious to the community as a whole is to ignore half the political promise of the Constitution and the whole of its sense. .... Preserving the peace is the first duty of government, and it is for the protection of the community from the predations of the idle, the contentious, and the brutal that government was invented.

On the other hand, Justice Mosk wrote:

> No doubt Montesquieu, Locke, and Madison would turn over in their graves when they learn they are cited in an opinion that does not enhance liberty but deprives a number of simple rights to a group of Latino youths who have not been convicted of a crime. Mindful of the admonition of another great 18th-century political philosopher, Benjamin Franklin, that

"[t]hey that can give up essential liberty to obtain a little temporary safety deserve neither liberty nor safety." . . . [Some of my colleagues] would permit our cities to close off entire neighborhoods to Latino youths who have done nothing more than dress in blue or black clothing or associate with others who do so; they would authorize criminal penalties for ordinary, nondisruptive acts of walking or driving through a residential neighborhood with a relative or friend. In my view, such a blunderbuss approach amounts to bad law and bad policy. Chief Justice [Earl] Warren warned . . . "Unfortunately, there are some who think that the way to save freedom in this country is to adopt the techniques of tyranny." [Some] here appear to embrace that misguided belief.

Summarize in two or three sentences each the ideas of Justice Brown and Justice Mosk; then explain which position is closer to your own. Draw upon both the "Facts of the Case" and the provisions of the injunction, and provide reasons for disagreeing with the opinions that you do not share.

5. One judge ruling on this injunction pointed out that only 12% of the reports of criminal activity in Rocksprings were believed by the City to be gang-related, with another 2% "possibly gang-related." How does this statistic affect your view of the justification of the San Jose injunction?

6. To what extent do you believe that injunctions such as this one are an effective way of dealing with gangs? If you do not believe they are effective, or justified, what other measures do you believe would be more effective and more justifiable? Put another way, what recourse do residents of the neighborhoods affected by gangs have if they wish to live their lives in peace and safety?

7. *Group Assignment:* See Discussion and Writing Suggestion 5 in on pp. 734–35 and apply that assignment to this case.

The Felled Stop Signs: Some Cases of Homicide
(State of Florida v. Miller, State of Utah v. Hallett)

The following selections deal with two remarkably similar cases, almost 20 years apart. In both cases, the earlier one in Utah, the later one in Florida, teenagers looking for an evening of fun pulled out or pulled down stop signs at intersections. In both cases, their actions resulted in one or more persons killed in automobile crashes. The teens were blameworthy: no one disputed that. But how blameworthy, from a legal standpoint? With what crime should they be charged? To what extent were they directly *responsible for the fatalities that occurred? You'll explore these and other issues by reading accounts of the two cases: first, the more recent case, described in an article in the* Los Angeles Times *(as of publication, no*

*appeals ruling had been issued on this case); second, the "Facts of the Case" sec-
tion of the earlier case, as described in the ruling of the Utah appellate court.
Following these accounts are two statements on the law that will provide guidelines for your deliberations: the first offers excerpts from the "Homicide" section
of the Utah Criminal Code, along with definitions of some key terms. The second
is a brief distinction (contained in a later legal opinion from an Arizona appellate
court) between "negligent homicide" and "manslaughter."*

For Fallen Stop Sign, Vandals Face Life*

Tampa, Fla.—It was a clear, dark February night when the fates collided in   1
front of Tim's Cafe at a rural intersection where a stop sign lay face-down by
the side of the road.

One of the vehicles involved was an eight-ton Mack truck loaded with   2
phosphate. The other was a white Camaro carrying three 18-year-old friends
on a one-way ride to eternity. Chances are, police said, they never knew
what hit them.

Tow trucks and sheriff's deputies were still on the scene a few hours later   3
when a fourth young man named Thomas Miller pulled up. He and a friend
had just finished working the graveyard shift at a welding shop and were
heading to Tim's for breakfast.

Miller got out of his car to see the wreckage better and, he recalled later,   4
he stood right next to the fallen stop sign.

Now, 16 months after that fatal crash, Miller and two friends stand   5
convicted on three counts of manslaughter, guilty of causing three deaths by
pulling that stop sign out of the ground days earlier.

Although Miller, 20, and his housemates, Nissa Baillie, 21, and her   6
boyfriend, Christopher Cole, 20, admitted taking about 20 road signs during
a late-night spree sometime before the fatal crash, they denied tampering
with the stop sign in front of Tim's Cafe.

But a jury did not believe them.   7

On June 19 Miller, Baillie and Cole could be sentenced to life in prison   8
in what is believed to be the first case in the United States in which the vandalism of a traffic sign has led to a multiple manslaughter conviction.

What has become known as the "stop sign case" has had a wrenching   9
effect on the families of the six young people involved, while sparking a passionate community debate on the nexus of crime and punishment.

On one side is Assistant State Atty. Leland Baldwin, who prosecuted the   10
three young people. "I have heard people ask: 'How dare you charge them
with manslaughter? This was a prank. It was an unintentional crime,'" she
said. "But this was not a prank. These were not young kids. These were
young adults. So give me a break."

On the other side is Joseph Registrato, chief assistant to the Hillsborough   11
County public defender, which represented Cole and Baillie.

---

*Mike Clary, "For Fallen Stop Sign, Vandals Face Life," *Los Angeles Times*, June 11,
1997.

"It's one thing to take a car when you're drunk and recklessly kill some- 12
body," Reigstrato said. "That law is well-understood. But in this case, they
may have committed criminal mischief and then later three people died. But
others had gone through that intersection and didn't die. So there is a serious
question about whether the [fallen] stop sign caused the deaths.

"From that they could get life in prison? It's hard to follow the ball 13
here."

Road Sign Theft Called a Commonplace Prank

About this there is no debate: The chain of events that led up to that horrific 14
crash in front of Tim's Cafe makes up a cautionary tale of sobering complexity.

Joe Episcopo figures at least half the population of America at one time 15
or another has stolen a road sign to hang on a bedroom wall, to win a scavenger hunt or just for kicks.

In fact, says Episcopo, a lawyer who represents Miller, road sign theft is 16
so common that, when potential jurors in the case against his client were
asked if they had ever taken a sign, half the pool raised a hand and three of
those who answered yes ended up being seated on the six-member panel.
"Everybody has somebody in their family who takes signs," he said.

Indeed, vandalism and theft of road signs is a problem all across the 17
country. After the trial here in the Hillsborough County courthouse was
broadcast by Court TV, public officials from as far away as Washington
state have been speaking out about the expense and danger resulting from
defaced or stolen road signs.

In Iowa, a county engineer has announced plans to use the Tampa case as 18
a springboard for a national education campaign on the issue.

Dave Krug, Hillsborough County public works department engineer, 19
estimated that 25% of all road signs ever put up in the Tampa area are damaged by vandals, knocked down or stolen. Most road sign vandalism, however, does not result in triple fatalities, attract media attention and provoke
heart-wrenching community anguish over wasted lives.

Moreover, most sign vandalism does not give rise to the sea of regrets 20
among thousands of people—including at least 11 people who testified in the
trial here—who noticed the downed stop sign during the 24 hours preceding
the crash and failed to report it.

"Well, what did you do?" Baldwin asked of one witness who noticed that 21
the stop sign was down.

"We just went back to work, got busy," the witness replied. 22

Three Target Signs 'for a Rush'

Miller, Baillie and Cole lived together in a rented $300-a-month mobile home 23
on a country road less than three miles from the intersection of Keysville and
Lithia-Pinecrest roads in eastern Hillsborough County where the fatal crash
occurred just before midnight on Feb. 7, 1996.

According to interviews they gave to a local television station and Cole's 24
testimony at trial, the three had been shopping at a nearby Wal-Mart, had
drunk a couple of beers and were headed home when one of the three suggested that they take a few railroad signs. Cole told a television reporter that
they began taking signs "for a rush."

Over a period of a couple of hours and a distance of about five miles, 25
they unbolted and pulled up railroad signs, street name signs, a "Dead End"
sign, a "Do Not Enter" sign and—from neighboring Polk County—at least
one stop sign, tossing all of them in the back of their pickup truck.

Was it fun? Cole was asked. "I suppose so, yeah," he replied. "Yeah, it 26
was fun at the time."

Night of Bowling Ends in Collision

Kevin Farr, who worked in his family's data processing business, had been 27
bowling with his father, Les, and his two older brothers on the evening of his
death. He rolled a 218 in his final league game and, as he left the bowling
alley, he shouted at one of his brothers: "Tell Mom I'll be home between
11 o'clock and 12. I don't want her to worry."

From the bowling alley Farr drove to the house of Brian Hernandez, his 28
best and oldest friend, and the pair then picked up Randall White. No one
seems to know where they were going.

June Farr said that the death of the youngest of her four children has con- 29
demned her to live day by day. "And day by day takes on a whole new meaning after something like this," she said. "Sometimes it's more like a few
minutes at a time."

The case against Miller, Cole and Baillie was circumstantial. There were 30
no fingerprints on the stop sign and no eyewitnesses who put them at the
scene. But the fallen stop sign was well within the general area of the thefts to
which the three had confessed and prosecutors presented expert testimony
that the stop sign appeared to have been pulled from the ground, not run over
by a vehicle.

The defense also had its own expert witness, a mechanical engineer who 31
testified that the stop sign had been struck by a "lateral force."

Defendants Say They Panicked Next Day

Perhaps the most damning evidence against Cole, Miller and Baillie came 32
from their own statements to police. Ron Bradish, a Sheriff's Department traffic homicide investigator, testified that Cole and Miller admitted that—during
their stealing spree—they sometimes would pull signs from the ground and, if
a car came by, leave them to pick up later.

The day after the fatal crash, the three defendants admitted to police, they 33
panicked. They gathered up most of the stolen signs from inside and outside
their mobile home and tossed them off a bridge into nearby Alafia Creek.
According to Bradish, Cole said that they got rid of the signs "so no one
would think they took the stop sign down at the crash."

Held without bail, Cole, Miller and Baillie are to be sentenced next week 34
after the judge hears from lawyers on both sides, as well as from relatives of
the convicted and those who died.

While she will not lobby for life sentences, Baldwin says, she will insist on 35
long terms. "I hope this case will be a deterrent, or, at least, somewhat
thought-provoking," she said. "Perhaps this is one of the types of cases that
have to be tried every generation to remind high school kids and others that
vandalism has consequences. And this does have an effect. Just days ago
some kids in Leon County [Tallahassee] had a stop sign in a scavenger hunt
and the media [publicity] stopped them."

Again, Registrato demurs. "This case is useless as a deterrent," he said. 36
"Send these three children to prison for life and the kids in Hillsborough
County where it happened won't have a clue about it the next day."

Episcopo and Registrato said they have prepared their clients for the 37
worst. Sentencing guidelines call for 28 years to life and Judge Bob Anderson
Mitcham has been known to use the suggested maximum as a starting point.
Last year he put a man convicted of wounding two Tampa police officers in
prison for seven consecutive life terms, ignoring guidelines that called for 14
to 24 years.

For June Farr, the sentencing decision seems straightforward. "My child 38
got the maximum penalty and he had no choice in the matter," she said.
"They knew exactly what was going to happen. They just didn't know who
the victims would be. This was not a prank. Pranks don't kill."

To those who would find life in prison too harsh a price to pay for yank- 39
ing out a stop sign, Farr responds: "They didn't have to go pick out a coffin."

Reigstrato said he would argue that Miller, Cole and Baillie could better 40
atone for their sins and better serve society by doing "a couple of years hard
time in Florida State Prison and then be required for the next 18 years to go
to high schools twice a month and tell about the consequences of criminal
mischief."

Bill Miller, Thomas Miller's father, clings to hope that his son will win a 41
retrial and be found not guilty. He acknowledged that his son, who has a
juvenile record for theft, has lied to him before. But this time, Miller said,
"Tommy says he didn't take that sign and I believe it with all my heart. We
know when he's lying."

Whatever the outcome, said Miller, 69, a retired postal worker, he knows 42
that the lives of his family, as well as the other five families involved, are forever changed.

"I was in court every day," he said, "sitting in the front row on one side, 43
across from the families of the dead boys. We didn't speak but I felt for
them. . . . They lost their children. I understand.

"Now they have to understand that I've lost mine. Win or lose, this is a 44
tragedy for both sides." ▪

STATE of Utah, Plantiff and Respondent, v. Kelly K. HALLETT and Richard James Felsch, Defendants and Appellants.
No. 15765.
Supreme Court of Utah.
Oct. 20, 1980.

Facts of the Case*

On the evening of September 24, 1977, a number of young people gathered 1
at the defendant's home in Kearns. During the evening, some of them engaged
in drinking alcoholic beverages. At about 10:30 P.M., they left the home,
apparently bent on revelry and mischief. When they got to the intersection of
5215 South and 4620 West, defendant and the codefendent Richard Felsch
(not a party to this appeal) bent over a stop sign, which faced northbound
traffic on 4620 West, until it was in a position parallel to the ground. The
group then proceeded north from the intersection, uprooted another stop
sign and placed it in the backyard of a Mr. Arlund Pope, one of the state's
witnesses. Traveling further on, defendant and his friends bent a bus stop sign
over in a similar manner.

The following morning, Sunday, September 25, 1977, at approximately 2
9:00 A.M., one Krista Limacher was driving east on 5215 South with her husband and children, en route to church. As she reached the intersection of 4620
West, the deceased, Betty Jean Carley, drove to the intersection from the
south. The stop sign was not visible, since the defendant had bent it over, and
Ms. Carley continued into the intersection. The result was that Mrs.
Limacher's vehicle struck the deceased's car broadside causing her massive
injuries which resulted in her death in the hospital a few hours later. ∎

Statements on the Law

Utah Criminal Code †

CRIMINAL HOMICIDE
Criminal homicide—elements—designations of offenses

(1) (a) A person commits criminal homicide if he intentionally, knowingly,
    recklessly, with criminal negligence, or acting with a mental state other-
    wise specified in the statute defining the offense, causes the death of
    another human being, including an unborn child.

Murder
(1) Criminal homicide constitutes murder if the actor:
    (a) intentionally or knowingly causes the death of another;

State of Utah v. Hallett. 619 P.2d 337 (1980).

†*Utah Code Unannotated*, 1996. Vol. 4. Charlottesville, VA: Michie Law Publishers, 1988-
96.

(b) intending to cause serious bodily injury to another commits an act clearly dangerous to human life that causes the death of another;

(c) acting under circumstances evidencing a depraved indifference to human life engages in conduct which creates a grave risk of death to another and thereby causes the death of another;

(d) while in the commission, attempted commission, or immediate flight from the commission or attempted commission of aggravated robbery, robbery, rate, object rape, forcible sodomy, or aggravated sexual assault, aggravated arson, arson, aggravated burglary, burglary, aggravated kidnapping, kidnapping, child kidnapping, rape of a child, object rape of a child, sodomy of a child, forcible sexual abuse, sexual abuse of a child, aggravated sexual abuse of a child, or child abuse . . . , when the victim is younger than 14 years of age, causes the death of another person . . . ; or

(e) recklessly causes the death of a peace officer while in the commission or attempted commission of:

    (i) an assault against a peace officer; or

    (ii) interference with a peace officer if the actor uses force against a peace officer.

(2) Murder is a first degree felony.   1996

Manslaughter

(1) Criminal homicide constitutes manslaughter if the actor:

    (a) recklessly causes the death of another; or

    (b) causes the death of another under the influence of extreme emotional disturbance for which there is a reasonable explanation or excuse; or

    (c) causes the death of another under circumstances where the actor reasonably believes the circumstances provide a legal justification or excuse for his conduct although the conduct is not legally justifiable or excusable under the existing circumstances.

(2) Under Subsection (1)(b), emotional disturbance does not include a condition resulting from mental illness.

(3) The reasonableness of an explanation or excuse under Subsection (1)(b), or the reasonable belief of the actor under Subsection (1)(c), shall be determined from the viewpoint of a reasonable person under the then existing circumstances.

(4) Manslaughter is a felony of the second degree.   1985

Negligent homicide

(1) Criminal homicide constitutes negligent homicide if the actor, acting with criminal negligence, causes the death of another.

(2) Negligent homicide is a class A misdemeanor.   1973

Definitions

Requirements of criminal conduct and criminal responsibility

No person is guilty of an offense unless his conduct is prohibited by law and:

(1) He acts intentionally, knowingly, recklessly, with criminal negligence, or with a mental state otherwise specified in the statute defining the offense, as the definition of the offense requires; or

(2) His acts constitute an offense involving strict liability.

Definitions of "intentionally, or with intent or willfully"; "knowingly, or with knowledge"; "recklessly, or maliciously"; and "criminal negligence or criminally negligent"

A person engages in conduct:

(1) Intentionally, or with intent or willfully with respect to the nature of his conduct or to a result of his conduct, when it is his conscious objective or desire to engage in the conduct or cause the result.

(2) Knowingly, or with knowledge, with respect to his conduct or to circumstances surrounding his conduct when he is aware of the nature of his conduct or the existing circumstances. A person acts knowingly, or with knowledge, with respect to a result of his conduct when he is aware that his conduct is reasonably certain to cause the result.

(3) Recklessly, or maliciously, with respect to circumstances surrounding his conduct or the result of his conduct when he is aware of but consciously disregards a substantial and unjustifiable risk that the circumstances exist or the result will occur. The risk must be of such a nature and degree that its disregard constitutes a gross deviation from the standard of care that an ordinary person would exercise under all the circumstances as viewed from the actor's standpoint.

(4) With criminal negligence or is criminally negligent with respect to circumstances surrounding his conduct or the result of his conduct when he ought to be aware of a substantial and unjustifiable risk that the circumstances exist or the result will occur. The risk must be of such a nature and degree that the failure to perceive it constitutes a gross deviation from the standard of care that an ordinary person would exercise in all the circumstances as viewed from the actor's standpoint.   1974

State v. Fisher*

NEGLIGENT HOMICIDE AND MANSLAUGHTER The general rule is that negligent   1
homicide is a lesser included offense of manslaughter. In *State v. Parker*, 128
Ariz. 107, 624 P.2d 304 (App. 1980), *vacated in part on other grounds*, 128
Ariz. 97, 624 P.2d 294 (1981), the Court of Appeals determined that the only
difference between manslaughter and negligent homicide is an accused's mental
state at the time of the incident. *See also State v. Montoya*, 125 Ariz. 155, 608
P.2d 92 (App. 1980). Manslaughter is established where a person, aware of a
substantial and unjustifiable risk that his or her conduct will cause the death of
another, consciously disregards that risk. Negligent homicide is established

---

State v. Fisher. 686 P.2d 750 (1984).

where a person fails to perceive the substantial and unjustifiable risk that his or her conduct will cause the death of another. The element of the greater not found in the lesser is awareness of the risk.

■ ■ ■

Discussion and Writing Suggestions

1. You are either (1) a prosecuting attorney or (2) a defense attorney involved with the Miller case. In researching precedents, you find *State of Utah v. Hallett.* For purposes of preparing either your prosecution or your defense, compare and contrast the circumstances of the *Miller* and *Hallett* cases. Consider (a) the activities of the respective defendants prior to the action being prosecuted; (b) their motivations; (c) the relationship between the defendants' actions and the automobile accidents that subsequently occurred; (d) the relative blameworthiness of the defendants; (e) with what crime, if any, the defendants should be charged; (f) any other factors you find relevant. Prepare your findings in the form of a memorandum to the District Attorney (if you are prosecuting) or the partners in your law firm (if you are defending).

2. Read the Utah Criminal Code on homicide, focusing on the distinctions drawn between murder, or manslaughter, or negligent homicide. Should Hallett and Felsch be charged with murder, or manslaughter, or negligent homicide? In a memo to the District Attorney, justify your decision. To help you with your thinking on this subject, review the definitions provided by the Utah Code of various key phrases ("intentionally or with intent or willfully," "recklessly, or maliciously," etc.) in the Code. Review also the distinction drawn between "negligent homicide" and "manslaughter" in the opinion, *State [of Arizona] v. Fisher (1984).*

3. Hallett argued that the pulling down of stop sign did not show the required *intent* to constitute negligent homicide. The Utah statute provides that a person is guilty of negligent homicide if he causes the death of another person

> with criminal negligence or is criminally negligent with respect to circumstances surrounding his conduct or the result of his conduct when he ought to be aware of a substantial and unjustifiable risk that the circumstances exist or the result will occur. The risk must be of such a nature and degree that the failure to perceive it constitutes a gross deviation from the standard of care that an ordinary person would exercise in all the circumstances as viewed from the actor's standpoint.

Based on the evidence before you and the inferences you draw from this evidence, do you believe, beyond a reasonable doubt, that the defendant's conduct met the elements of the above statute? Explain, in terms of the defendant's actions, viewed from his standpoint.

4. Hallett argued that the evidence did not support the conclusion that his acts were the *proximate cause* of Ms. Carley's death. To quote from the court's "Opinion," summarizing this argument,

> "[Defendant] starts with a uniformly recognized definition: that proximate cause is the cause which through its natural and foreseeable consequence, unbroken by any sufficient intervening cause, produces the injury which would not have occurred but for that cause. His [argument] here is that there was evidence that as the deceased approached from the south, she was exceeding the speed limit of 25 mph; and that this was subsequent intervening and proximate cause of her own death. This is based upon the fact that a motorist, who was also coming from the south, testified that he was going 25 mph and that Ms. Carley passed him some distance to the south as she approached the intersection."

Considering this argument, do you believe that the defendant's action in pulling down the stop sign was the *proximate cause* of the fatal accident? Explain your reasoning.

5. In separate opinions, two judges of the appellate court hearing *Hallett* made the following arguments concerning the defendant's degree of responsibility for the fatality:

Maughan's opinion
[W]here a party by his wrongful conduct creates a condition of peril, his action can properly be found to be the proximate cause of a resulting injury, even though later events which combined to cause the injury may also be classified as negligent, so long as the later act is something which can reasonably be expected to follow in the natural sequence of events. Moreover, when reasonable minds might differ as to whether it was the creation of the dangerous condition (defendant's conduct) which was the proximate cause, or whether it was some subsequent act (such as Ms. Carley's driving), the question is for the trier of the fact [the jury] to determine.

Reflecting upon what has been said above, we [believe] that whether the defendant's act of removing the stop sign was done in merely callous and thoughtless disregard of the safety of others, or with malicious intent, the result, which he should have foreseen, was the same: that it created a situation of peril; and that nothing that transpired thereafter should afford him relief from responsibility for the tragic consequences that did occur.

Hall's opinion
The evidence produced at trial does not discount beyond a reasonable doubt the possibility that the actions of the decedent on the morning of September 25, 1977, constituted an independent, unforeseeable intervening cause. In this regard, it is to be noted that the evidence produced at trial clearly established that the accident occurred in broad daylight and that the stop sign in question had not been removed from the intersection, but merely bent over into a position where it was still marginally visible. Moreover, the word "Stop" was clearly printed in large block letters on the pavement leading into the intersection. Even if we were to assume, however, that defendant's action in bending the stop sign over erased all indication that vehicles proceeding north on 4620 West were obliged to yield right-of-way, such would render the location of the accident an unmarked intersection. The law requires due care in approaching such intersections, with such reasonable precautions as may be necessary under the circumstances.

Evidence also appearing in the record indicates that decedent was moving at an imprudent speed when she entered the intersection. Although the exact rate of speed is disputed, it is unchallenged that she had, less than a block behind, passed a truck which, itself, was doing the legal speed limit. All parties testified that she made no attempt to slow or brake upon entering the intersection. Under such circumstances, reasonable minds must entertain a reasonable doubt that the defendant's conduct was the sole efficient legal cause of her death. . . .

I would dismiss the charge of negligent homicide.

Which argument do you find more persuasive? Explain your reasoning.

6. Try to enter into the minds of the teenagers in Florida case. One of these teens told a TV reporter that they pulled out the traffic signs "for a rush." What do you think he meant? Attempt to explain, from his point of view (to bewildered adults) why "it was fun at the time" to pull out traffic signs. What factors do you think contribute to some teenagers finding fun in such antisocial outlets? Suppose, for the sake of argument, that the teens were guilty of negligent homicide. Why would they "fail to perceive the substantial and unjustifiable risk that his or her conduct will cause the death of another"?

7. Almost certainly, you have not been involved in activities with such horrific consequences as those of the defendants in the Florida and Utah cases. Almost certainly, however, all of us have been involved in actions, which, under certain circumstances, could have resulted in very serious outcomes. And we must be prepared to deal with those outcomes. To quote a widespread slogan these days: "Actions have consequences." How do we go about determining—and dealing with—our responsibility for the consequences of our actions? To what extent are our conscious intentions a factor in our personal responsibility? Discuss these issues, drawing upon one or two specific incidents in your own life—or the life someone you know.

8. *Group Assignment:* See Discussion and Writing Suggestion 5 on pp. 734–35 and apply that assignment to one of the cases in this group.

Drag Racing and Death: Some Cases of Manslaughter
(Commonwealth of Pennsylvania v. Levin, Commonwealth of Pennsylvania v. Root, Jacobs v. State of Florida)

Negligence, as we've seen in an earlier selection this chapter, is one of the most common charges in legal cases. Negligence is defined (in Black's Law Dictionary*) as "the failure to exercise the standard of care that a reasonably prudent person would have exercised in the same situation." Such negligence is a* tort *(i.e., a private wrong),* *rather than a crime. But of course, there are degrees of negligence, depending upon the level of recklessness of the individual involved and the seriousness of the consequences. Another kind of legal negligence is "gross negligence": "a conscious, voluntary act or omission in reckless disregard of a legal duty and of the consequences to another party. . . ." Beyond that lies "criminal negligence," that is, "gross negligence so extreme that it is punishable as a crime . . . for example, involuntary manslaughter or other negligent homicide. . . ." As we've seen in the felled stop sign cases, acts that might otherwise be chargeable as lesser offenses (such as vandalism) may be chargeable as manslaughter if they result in the death of a human being.*

Of course, a jury may choose not to convict on such a charge, if it concludes that the defendant's actions do not justify a guilty verdict, or if it sees mitigating circumstances. By the same token, appeals court judges may overturn a trial court verdict if they believe that the jury's decision to convict is unsupported by the facts.

The following three cases involve drag racing. In all three cases, the races resulted in one or more fatalities. In all three cases, the defendants were convicted of involuntary manslaughter. In all three cases, the defendants appealed. As in other cases in this chapter, you will read the facts of each case, and you will read jury instructions relevant to the charge. You will also find that in two of the cases, individual judges on the appeal panel disagreed as to whether the conviction should be upheld or reversed. Once again, you are left to make your own judgment, applying the rules to the facts of the cases.

COMMONWEALTH v. Ronald LEVIN.
Superior Court of Pennsylvania.
Nov. 12, 1957.

Facts of the Case*

[2] Between five and six o'clock in the morning of May 14, 1955, appellant   1
and four other young men were together in a diner at Sixty-third and
Lancaster Avenue in the City of Philadelphia. They departed in a car owned
and operated by one of them, Robinson. At 5151 Dakota Street appellant
transferred to his own car, and drove down Dakota Street. Robinson, with his
three passengers, drove down the adjoining street. Both drivers turned right
on Fifty-first Street, appellant's car being to the rear. They then turned into
Wynnefield Avenue, going west. At Fifty-fourth and Wynnefield Avenue,
appellant attempted to pass the Robinson car. Realizing that appellant was
trying to pass, Robinson accelerated his speed. The drivers kept going faster,
appellant's car being along the side of the Robinson car to the left, in such
proximity that it could have been touched by the passengers in the Robinson
car. When the two cars arrived at Woodbine Avenue, they again bore left. As
they approached the 5700 block of Woodbine Avenue, the cars were going
approximately 80 miles per hour. One of the passengers, who was seated left
rear in the Robinson car, opened his window, and shouted to appellant to get
away. Appellant persisted in maintaining his position. The passengers called

---

*Commonwealth of Pennsylvania v. Levin. 135 A.2d 764 (1957).

to their driver, Robinson, to slow down, and he replied: "Well stop being chicken." The speed finally attained 85 to 95 miles per hour. As the cars reached Fifty-seventh Street appellant turned sharply to the right in front of Robinson, who thereupon lost control of his car, and hit a tree. One of the passengers, Klinghoffer, was thrown to the road and fatally injured. ∎

Statements on the Law*

Instructions to the Jury

INVOLUNTARY MANSLAUGHTER—DEFINED

Defendant is accused of having committed the crime of involuntary manslaughter in violation of section 192, subdivision (b) of the Penal Code.   1

    Every person who unlawfully kills a human being, without malice afore-   2 thought and without an intent to kill, is guilty of the crime of involuntary manslaughter in violation of Penal Code section 192, subdivision (b).

    A killing is unlawful within the meaning of this instruction if it occurred: 3

1. During the commission of an unlawful act [not amounting to a felony] which is dangerous to human life under the circumstances of its commission; or
2. In the commission of an act, ordinarily lawful, which involves a high degree of risk of death or great bodily harm, without due caution and circumspection.

    The commission of an unlawful act, without due caution and circum-   4 spection, would necessarily be an act that was dangerous to human life in its commission.

    In order to prove this crime, each of the following elements must be   5 proved:

1. A human being was killed; and
2. The killing was unlawful.

DUE CAUTION AND CIRCUMSPECTION—DEFINED

The term "without due caution and circumspection" refers to [a] negligent   6 act[s] which [is] [are] aggravated, reckless and flagrant and which [is] [are] such a departure from what would be the conduct of an ordinarily prudent, careful person under the same circumstances as to be contrary to a proper regard for [human life] [danger to human life] or to constitute indifference to the consequences of such act[s]. The facts must be such that the consequences of the negligent act[s] could reasonably have been foreseen. It must also appear that the [death] [danger to human life] was not the result of inattention, mistaken judgment or misadventure, but the natural and probable result of an aggravated, reckless or grossly negligent act. ∎

---

* *California Jury Instructions, Criminal: Book of Approved Jury Instructions [CALJIC]* 6th ed. Prepared by The Committee on Standard Jury Instruction Criminal, of the Superior Court of Los Angeles County, California. St. Paul, MN: West Publishing Co., 1996.

Opinion in Levin: In brief, a person is not guilty of involuntary   7
manslaughter unless his unlawful and reckless conduct was the legal cause of
the injury and death, and legal cause means conduct which is a substantial
factor in bringing about the harm.

Precedent cited in Levin: In Stark v. Rowley, 323 Pa. 522, 187 A. 509,   8
cars A and B were racing side by side. Car A finally dropped back but, in
attempting to turn behind car B, skidded across the road and collided with car
C. It was held that the driver of car B was jointly responsible with the driver
of car A for the resultant injury to the driver of car C, even though there was
no contact between car B and car C. ■

COMMONWEALTH of Pennsylvania v. Leroy W. ROOT, Appellant.
Supreme Court of Pennsylvania.
May 2, 1961.

Facts of the Case*

The testimony, which is uncontradicted in material part, discloses that, on the   1
night of the fatal accident, the defendant accepted the deceased's challenge to
engage in an automobile race; that the racing took place on a rural 3-lane
highway; that the night was clear and dry . . . ; that the speed limit on the
highway was 50 miles per hour; that, immediately prior to the accident, the
two automobiles were being operated at varying speeds of from 70 to 90 miles
per hour; that the accident occurred in a no-passing zone on the approach to
a bridge where the highway narrowed to two directionally-opposite lanes;
that, at the time of the accident, the defendant was in the lead and was proceeding in his right hand lane of travel; that the deceased, in an attempt to
pass the defendant's automobile, when a truck was closely approaching from
the opposite direction, swerved his car to the left, crossed the highway's
white dividing line and drove his automobile on the wrong side of the highway head-on into the oncoming truck with resultant fatal effect to himself.

Statements on the Law

Justice Jones in Root: This evidence would of course amply support a   2
conviction of the defendant for speeding, reckless driving and, perhaps, other
violations of The Vehicle Code of May 1, 1929, P.L. 905, as amended. In fact,
it may be noted, in passing, that the Act of January 8, 1960, P.L. (1959) 2118,
Sec. 3, 75 P.S. 1041 . . . makes automobile racing on a highway an independent crime punishable by fine or imprisonment or both up to $500 and three
years in jail. As the highway racing in the instant [present] case occurred prior

---

* *Commonwealth of Pennsylvania v. Root.* 170 A.2d 310 (1961).

to the enactment of the Act of 1960, that statute is, of course, not presently applicable.

In the case now before us, the deceased was aware of the dangerous   3
condition created by the defendant's reckless conduct in driving his automobile at an excessive rate of speed along the highway but, despite such knowledge, he recklessly chose to swerve his car to the left and into the path of an oncoming truck, thereby bringing about the head-on collision which caused his own death.

Justice Bell in Root: What is involuntary manslaughter? Involuntary   4
manslaughter is a misdemeanor and is very different from murder and from voluntary manslaughter. The prime difference between murder, voluntary manslaughter, and involuntary manslaughter may be thus summarized: Murder is an unlawful killing of another person with malice aforethought, expressed or implied. . . .

Voluntary manslaughter is the intentional killing of another person which   5
is committed under the influence of passion. . . .

Involuntary manslaughter is an unintentional and nonfelonious killing of   6
another person without malice or passion, which results from conduct by defendant which is so unlawful as to be outrageous, provided such conduct is a direct cause of the killing.

The unlawful racing by this defendant was not only unlawful, it was out-   7
rageous, but it was not a direct cause, i.e., one of the direct causes, of the killing.

Justice Eagen in Root: The opinion of the learned Chief Justice admits,   8
under the uncontradicted facts, that the defendant, at the time of the fatal accident involved, was engaged in an unlawful and reckless course of conduct. Racing an automobile at 90 miles per hour, trying to prevent another automobile going in the same direction from passing him, in a no-passing zone on a two-lane public highway, is certainly all of that. Admittedly also, there can be more than one direct cause of an unlawful death. To me, this is self-evident. But [say some of my fellow justices,] the defendant's recklessness was not a direct cause of the death. With this, I cannot agree.

If the defendant did not engage in the unlawful race and so operate his   9
automobile in such a reckless manner, this accident would never have occurred. He helped create the dangerous event. He was a vital part of it. The victim's acts were a natural reaction to the stimulus of the situation. The race, the attempt to pass the other car and forge ahead, the reckless speed, all of these factors the defendant himself helped create. He was part and parcel of them. That the victim's response was normal under the circumstances, that his reaction should have been expected and was clearly foreseeable, is to me beyond argument. That the defendant's recklessness was a substantial factor is obvious. All of this, in my opinion, makes his unlawful conduct a direct cause of the resulting collision.

The act of passing was not an "extraordinarily negligent" act, but rather   10
a "normal response" to the act of "racing." Furthermore, as Hall pulled out

to pass, Root "dropped off" his speed to 90 miles an hour. Such a move probably prevented Hall from getting back into the right-hand lane since he was
alongside of Root at the time and to brake the car at that speed would have
been fatal to both himself and Root. Moreover, the dangerous condition of
which the deceased had to become aware of before the defendant was relieved
of his direct causal connection with the ensuing accident, was not the fact that
the defendant was driving at an excessive rate of speed along the highway. He
knew that when the race began many miles and minutes earlier. *The dangerous condition necessary was an awareness of the oncoming truck and the fact
that at the rate of speed Root was traveling he couldn't safely pass him.*

   Case-law cited by Justice Eagen in Root: Wharton, Criminal Law and   11
Procedure [section] 68 (1957), speaking of causal connections, says: "A
person is only criminally liable for what he has caused, that is, there must be
a causal relationship between his act and harm sustained for which he is
prosecuted. It is not essential to the existence of a causal relationship that the
ultimate harm which has resulted was foreseen or intended by the actor. It is
sufficient that the ultimate harm is one which a reasonable man would foresee as being reasonably related to the acts of the defendant." Section 295, in
speaking about manslaughter, says: "When homicide is predicated upon the
negligence of the defendant, it must be shown that his negligence was the
proximate cause or a contributing cause of the victim's death. It must appear
that the death was not the result of misadventure, but the natural and probable result of a reckless or culpably negligent act. To render a person criminally liable for negligent homicide, the duty omitted or improperly performed
must have been his personal duty, and the negligent act from which death
resulted must have been his personal act, and not the act of another. But he
is not excused because the negligence of someone else contributed to the
result, when his act was the primary or proximate cause and the negligence of
the other did not intervene between his act and the result." ▪

M. T. Connell JACOBS, Appellant, v. STATE of Florida, Appellee.
No. G-356.
District Court of Appeal of Florida.
First District.
April 5, 1966.

Facts of the Case*

The facts are not in dispute. On the critical date appellant, together with sev-   1
eral others, engaged in a discussion regarding the relative speed of the automobiles owned by some of them. It was agreed that the Buick owned by
Kinchen, one of the participants, was the fastest of the group, but a race
would be necessary in order to determine whether the Ford owned by one

---

* *Jacobs v. State of Florida.* 184 So.2d 710 (1966).

Carter was faster than the Chevrolet owned by appellant. The group proceeded to an agreed starting point on State Road 40, a two-lane highway west of Ocala. Appellant's Chevrolet had a broken piston and Carter's Ford had a defective low gear. Because of the condition of Carter's Ford, he was given a head start in the race. Kinchen with the faster car was to go ahead of the other two and judge the winner, but at the last minute changed his mind and started last. Appellant, who left the starting line behind Carter, overtook the latter while traveling at a medium speed of about fifty-five miles an hour. All three vehicles proceeded in a westerly direction along the highway. A witness, Sands, driving along the highway in an easterly direction arrived at the crest of the hill and observed all three vehicles approaching in their correct right lane and traveling at an excessive speed. Sands saw Kinchen's Buick pull out into his left lane in order to pass the middle vehicle, and when he did Sands drove his car off the highway on to the right shoulder of the road. Another witness standing alongside the highway saw appellant's car proceeding westerly at an estimated speed of between fifty and seventy miles an hour. At the same time he observed a vehicle driven by one Buck traveling in an easterly direction at a speed of approximately twenty-five to forty miles an hour. As the Buick vehicle reached the crest of the hill, he met the two vehicles driven by Kinchen and Carter approaching him side by side traveling at an estimated speed of ninety miles an hour. The vehicle driven by Buck proceeding easterly in the south traffic lane met head-on the vehicle driven by Kinchen in a westerly direction which was also in the south traffic lane, resulting in the death of both drivers. At the time of the collision appellant was a quarter of a mile down the road ahead of the vehicles which were following him.

Under the foregoing factual situation appellant contends that the State failed to prove by any competent evidence that, as alleged in the information, he operated his vehicle in such a culpably negligent manner as to cause the collision which occurred between the vehicles operated by Kinchen and Buck. Appellant urges that the sole proximate cause of the collision was the culpable negligence of Kinchen over which appellant had no control, and for which he was not responsible. Appellant therefore concludes that the probata fails to conform to the allegata, and the court erred when it refused to direct a verdict in his favor. ■

Statements on the Law*

[SECTION] 776.011, FLORIDA STATUTES ANNOTATED
"Principle in first degree
"Whoever commits any criminal offense against the state, whether felony or misdemeanor, or aids, abets, counsels, hires, or otherwise procures such offense to be committed, is a principal in the first degree and may be charged, convicted and punished as such, whether he is or is not actually or constructively present at the commission of such offense."

---

* *West's Florida Statutes, Annotated.* St. Paul, MN: West Publishing Co., 1992.

Judge Wigginton in Jacobs: The evidence clearly shows that appellant,   3
together with others, was engaged in what is commonly known as a "drag
race" of motor vehicles on a two-lane public highway in Marion County. The
race entailed the operation of three motor vehicles traveling in the same direction at excessive and unlawful rates of speed contrary to the laws of this state.
While engaged in such unlawful activity one of the three vehicles actively participating in the race was negligently operated in such a manner as to cause
the death of the person who drove that vehicle, as well as another innocent
party who had no connection with the race. The deaths which proximately
resulted from the activities of the three persons engaged in the unlawful activity of drag racing made each of the active participants equally guilty of the
criminal act which caused the death of the innocent party. The fact that it was
the vehicle driven by the person appointed to judge the outcome of the race
which caused the death of the innocent party does not relieve appellant from
his responsibility as an active participant in the unlawful event out of which
the death arose.

In Wharton it is said: 4

". . . If each of two persons jointly engage in the commission of acts which
amount to criminal negligence, and as a result of which a third person is
killed, each may be found guilty of manslaughter even though it may be
impossible to say whose act actually caused the death."

The Supreme Court of Oregon, in the case of State v. Newberg, quoted   5
with approval from Clark & Marshall as follows:

" 'There may be principals in the second degree and accessories before the
fact to involuntary manslaughter. Thus, if two men drive separate vehicles at
a furious and dangerous speed along the highway, each inciting and abetting
the other, and one of them drives over and kills a person, the one thus causing the death is guilty of manslaughter as principal in the first degree, and the
other is guilty as principal in the second degree. . . .' "

Judge Carroll in Jacobs: I do not see how a reasonable man could law-   6
fully conclude from the evidence adduced at the trial that, beyond a reasonable doubt, the appellant was guilty either of manslaughter or of aiding and
abetting the commission of manslaughter. The culpable negligence of Willie
Kinchen, as shown by the evidence, was his attempt to pass the two racing
cars in the face of oncoming traffic. There is not a scintilla of evidence indicating that the appellant was aware of Kinchen's intention so to pass, and
hence I do not think it reasonable to hold that the appellant aided and abetted the said culpable negligence. As I view the evidence, there was no causal
relationship between the appellant's conduct in engaging in the drag race
and Kinchen's culpable negligence. The only such relationship would have to
be the discredited "if it hadn't been for" reasoning (if it hadn't been for the
race, the collision would not have occurred), but that reasoning has long

been discarded by the courts as insufficient to show proximate cause in civil cases or to show liability in criminal cases.

If the appellant is to be held criminally liable for manslaughter because he 7 participated in a race during which an act of manslaughter occurred during the race, I would think that by the extension of such reasoning the spectators lined up along the road to watch the race might be legally tried and convicted as aiders and abettors to the manslaughter, simply because the collision might not have occurred if they had not congregated and encouraged the racing. By like reasoning, also, I would think that, if the starter in a foot race at a track meet had with culpable negligence loaded his pistol with live cartridges instead of the usual blanks and shot and killed someone in the grandstand, the sprinters might be held criminally liable as aiders and abettors. Such a result, of course, would be absurd. While I recognize that these two extreme illustrations differ from the facts of the case at bar in that the appellant and the other participants may have been violating the law by engaging in a drag race, I do not think that the fact of such violation can be fairly be held to overcome the fatal deficiency in the evidence—that there was no proof of a causal connection between the acts of the appellant and the culpable negligence of Willie Kinchen that caused the death in question.

I have examined the entire transcript of trial proceedings, and, despite 8 much conflicting and confusing testimony, the following facts appear to me to be established by the testimony concerning the automobile race in question: that the defendant was to race his 1950 Chevrolet against one Charles Carter, driving his Ford, for a quarter-mile distance from Geneva's Restaurant westerly to certain railroad tracks, over a highway (one lane for westbound traffic and one for eastbound); that Willie Kinchen, owner of a 1950 Buick, was to serve as the judge to determine the winner of the race; that Carter was permitted to take off first, because his car had a defective gear; that some seconds later the defendant took off and soon passed Carter's car; that shortly after the defendant had left the starting point, Kinchen jumped into his Buick and soon arrived just behind Carter's car; that in the process of passing Carter's car Kinchen drove his Buick into the eastbound lane and crashed head-on into an oncoming Chevrolet being driven by one Buck who, along with Kinchen, was killed in the collision. There is, in my opinion, not a word of testimony in the transcript from which reasonable men could conclude that the defendant knew that Kinchen was planning to try to pass the racing cars, nor knew that Kinchen had even left the starting point for this or any other purpose, and certainly not a word that the defendant knew or had the slightest notion that Kinchen would be so reckless as to try to pass Carter's car by turning into the east lane in the face of oncoming traffic.

In view of this state of the evidence, I do not see how we can hold that the 9 evidence supported the jury's finding that the defendant was guilty of the crime of manslaughter in the killing of Buck, or that he aided and abetted in the commission of that crime.

What perturbs me particularly about this case is that I do not think that   10
the above evidence would be sufficient to hold the defendant even civilly
responsible for the death of Buck, because, even if the defendant were negligent in engaging in the race, such negligence could not be properly held to
have proximately caused Buck's death. As mentioned above, the reasoning is
not permissible in civil cases that "if it hadn't been for" a certain act the accident would not or might not have happened and hence the doer of such act is
liable for the accident. Certainly such reasoning, *a fortiori*, should not be used
to convict a person of the crime of manslaughter, and yet that's the only kind
of reasoning that links up the defendant's conduct to Kinchen's act that
resulted in the collision.

■ ■ ■

Discussion and Writing Suggestions

1. In the Levin case, the defendant argued that he was not guilty of
   manslaughter because "his car did not come into contact with the victim
   or some instrumentality which contacted the victim." Do you agree?
   Explain. If you were on the jury would you vote to convict Levin of involuntary manslaughter, taking into account the jury instructions on the definition of manslaughter and the opinion in the case itself concerning the
   requirements for a manslaughter conviction?

2. The appeals court panel in Levin offered a precedent for a verdict in this
   case. Does the precedent, *Stark v. Rowley*, support a manslaughter con-
   fiction? What are the essential similarities and differences (if any) between
   Stark v. Rowley and *Commonwealth v. Levin,* as presented here?

3. What are the key similarities and differences between *Levin* and *Root*?
   Specifically, how comparable are the actions of Levin and Root in directly causing the fatal accidents? How would you judge their relative degrees
   of responsibility? Should Root be convicted of involuntary manslaughter?
   Explain, using IRAC format.

4. Justices Jones and Bell in *Root* appear to absolve the defendant of responsibility for involuntary manslaughter (though not of reckless and unlawful driving), maintaining that Root's actions were not a *direct cause* of the
   fatal accident. Rather, it was the deceased, they maintain, who directly
   caused his own death when he recklessly pulled out into the path of an
   oncoming truck. Justice Eagen, however, disagrees with this reasoning,
   claiming that the Root was "part and parcel" of the sequence of events
   that resulted in the fatality. He also cites a well-known criminal law text
   that supports his idea that a defendant's negligence is not excused simply
   because someone else's negligence "contributed to the result." With
   whose arguments do you most agree? Explain.

5. In *Jacobs*, the defendant contended that he was not guilty of involuntary manslaughter because his vehicle was not directly involved in the fatal accident. Do you agree? Explain your verdict, using IRAC format.

6. *Jacobs* is similar to *Root* in that both involve fatal accidents resulting from one car unsuccessfully attempting to overtake another with which it was racing and then crashing directly into a third vehicle. In both cases, also, the defendant was not directly involved in the crash. To what extent do you see significant differences in the two cases? How do these differences affect your judgment of the two defendants' relative degrees of criminal responsibility?

7. In *Jacobs*, Judge Wigginton appears to take a similar position to Justice Eagen in *Root*, maintaining that a defendant who willingly participates in a drag race cannot escape responsibility for a resulting fatality simply because he was not driving the vehicle directly involved in the crash that killed an "innocent party." Judge Carroll, on the other hand, argues that Jacobs should not be held responsible for Kinchen's recklessness and "culpable negligence." In particular, Judge Carroll relies on the important legal concept of *proximate cause*, defined (in *Black's Law Dictionary*) as "a cause that directly produces an event and without which the event would not have occurred." In Carroll's view, since Jacobs's actions were not the proximate cause of Buck's death, he cannot be held legally responsible for it. Assess Judge Wigginton's and Judge Carroll's positions, referring specifically to *Jacobs*, and, if you choose, also to *Levin* and *Root*.

8. *Group Assignment:* See Discussion and Writing Suggestion 5 on pp. 734–35 and apply that assignment to one of the cases in this group.

Chevrolet v. Tree: *A Case of Poetic Justice*
(Fisher v. Lowe, Moffett, and State Farm Mutual Insurance)

Judges dressed up in robes and (in England) in silly-looking wigs: such unparalleled dignity, befitting the majesty of the law! Of course, not everyone is impressed. When the hero of Swift's Gulliver's Travels (1728) attempts to describe England to the leader of the Houyhnhnms (or intelligent horses), he begins with lawyers: "a Society of Men among us, bred up from their Youth in the Art of proving by Words multiplied for the Purpose, that White is Black, and Black is White, according as they are paid. To this Society all the rest of the People are Slaves." A century and a half later, in Trial By Jury, by Gilbert [a former lawyer] and Sullivan, a judge interrupts the proceedings to "tell you how I came to be a Judge." Following a song in which he reveals how, in order to get ahead, he married a rich attorney's "elderly, ugly daughter," then abandoned his wife once he became rich and successful, he declares: "And now, if you please, I'm ready to try/This Breach of Promise of Marriage!"

To their credit, judges occasionally acknowledge that they take themselves too seriously. David Hricik (see "The American Legal System," above) catalogues some examples of judicial humor. In United States v. Syufy Enterprises *(a movie theater chain), the court worked as many movie titles as it could into its opinion. In* Productos Carnic v. Central Am. Beef and Seafood Trading Co., *the opinion included numerous meat metaphors; and in* Chemical Specialties Mfg. Ass'n, Inc. v. Clark, *detergent names.*

In this all-too-meager tradition, the following is the complete text of an opinion from the Court of Appeals of Michigan concerning a suit for damages to a tree by a Chevrolet driven by the defendant. This ruling appears to support another opinion by a Seventh Circuit Court: "About half of the practice of a decent lawyer is telling would-be clients that they are damn fools and should stop."

WILLIAM L. FISHER, Plaintiff-Appellant, v. Karen LOWE, Larry Moffet and State Farm Mutual Automobile Insurance Company, Defendants-Appellees.
Docket No. 60732.
Court of Appeals of Michigan.
Submitted Nov. 3, 1982.
Decided Jan. 10, 1983.
Released for Publications May 6, 1983.*

A wayward Chevy struck a tree
Whose owner sued defendants three.
He sued car's owner, driver too,
And insurer for what was due
For his oak tree that now may bear
A lasting need for tender care.

The Oakland County Circuit Court,
John N. O'Brief, J., set forth
The judgment that defendants sought
And quickly an appeal was brought.

Court of Appeals, J.H. Gillis, J.,
Gave thought and then had this to say:
1) There is no liability
   Since No-Fault grants immunity;
2) No jurisdiction can be found
   Where process service is unsound;

Fisher v. Lowe, 122 Mich. App. 418.

And thus the judgment, as it's termed,
Is due to be, and is,
    Affirmed.

1. AUTOMOBILES
Defendant's Chevy struck a tree—
There was no liability;
The No-Fault Act comes into play
As owner and the driver say;

Barred by the Act's immunity,
No suit in tort will aid the tree;
Although the oak's in disarray,
No court can make defendants pay.
M.C.L.A. 500.3135.

2. PROCESS
No jurisdiction could be found
Where process service was unsound;
In personam jurisdiction
Was not even legal fiction
Where plaintiff failed to well comply
With rules of court that did apply.
GCR 1963, 105.4.

William L. Fisher, Troy, in pro. per. Romain, Donofrio & Kuck, P.C.
by Ernst W. Kuck, Southfield, for Defendants-Appellees.
Before BRONSON, P.J., and V.J. BRENNAN
and J.H. GILLIS, JJ.

J.H. GILLIS, JUDGE.
We thought that we would never see
A suit to compensate a tree.

A suit whose claim in tort is prest
Upon a mangled tree's behest;

A tree whose battered trunk was prest
Against a Chevy's crumpled crest;

A tree that faces each new day
With bark and limb in disarray;

A tree that may forever bear
A lasting need for tender care.

Flora lovers though we three,
We must uphold the court's decree.

Affirmed.[1]

■ ■ ■

Discussion and Writing Suggestions

1. You are a lawyer for Fisher and don't like the court's ruling. Write an appeal to the State Supreme Court—in verse. Keep it rhythmic and make sure it rhymes.
2. Do the same thing, assuming that you are a lawyer for one of the losing defendants in the "Maiden and the Pot of Gold" case (*Nickerson v. Hodges*), pp. 668–73.
3. Buy yourself another BMW and write a letter to your mother about it.

LEGAL GLOSSARY

Like every other profession (and perhaps more than most) the law has its own special language—a language often so complicated and obscure that even lawyers have difficulty understanding it. Here is a glossary of legal terms that you will encounter while reading this chapter. The definitions, for the most part, are from The Plain Language Law Dictionary, *edited by Robert E. Rothenberg. In some cases (indicated by "[Black's]" after the definition), they are taken from* Black's Law Dictionary: New Pocket Edition, *edited by Bryan A. Garner. In a very few other cases [indicated in brackets] we have provided definitions that do not appear in the dictionaries. Not included here are terms that are defined in the text itself—for example, when a statute or judicial instruction defines what is meant by "public nuisance" or "defective condition" or explains the meaning of "involuntary manslaughter."*

---

[1]Plaintiff commenced this action in tort against defendants Lowe and Moffet for damage to his "beautiful oak tree" caused when defendant Lowe struck it while operating defendant Moffet's automobile. The trial court granted summary judgment in favor of defendants pursuant to GCR 1963, 117.2(1). In addition, the trial court denied plaintiff's request to enter a default judgment against the insurer of the automobile, defendant State Farm Mutual Automobile Insurance Company. Plaintiff appeals as of right.

The trial court did not err in granting summary judgment in favor of defendants Lowe and Moffet. Defendants were immune from tort liability for damage to the tree pursuant to 3135 of the no-fault insurance act. M.C.L. 500.3135; M.S.A. 24.13135.

The trial court did not err in refusing to enter a default judgment against State Farm. Since it is undisputed that plaintiff did not serve process upon State Farm in accordance with the court rules, the court did not obtain personal jurisdiction over the insurer. GCR 1963, 105.4.

a fortiori   More effective; with greater reason. (Latin)

abettor   One who promotes or instigates the performance of a criminal act.

affidavit   A written statement of facts, sworn to and signed by a deponent before a notary public or some other authority having the power to witness an oath.

allegata   [Statements that have been declared to be true in a legal proceeding, without yet having been proven.]

alleged   Claimed; charged.

amend   To correct; to change; to alter, so as to correct defects in a document.

appeal   The request for a review by a higher court of a verdict or decision made by a lower court.

appellant   The party who appeals a case from a lower to a higher court.

appellate court   A court with the authority to review the handling and decision of a case tried in a lower court.

appellee   The respondent; the party against whom an appeal is taken.

breach   A violation.

case   A contested issue in a court of law; a controversy presented according to the rules of judicial proceedings.

civil   Of or relating to private rights and remedies that are sought by action or suit, as distinct from criminal proceedings. [Black's]

civil law   Law dealing with civil [private], rather than criminal matters.

codify   A code is a collection of laws; the published statutes governing a certain area, arranged in a systematic manner [thus, to "codify" is to render into law].

common law   1. Law declared by judges in area not controlled by government regulation, ordinances, or statutes. 2. Law originating from usage and custom, rather than from written statutes.

comparative negligence   A term that is used in a suit to recover damages, in which the negligence of the defendant is compared to that of the plaintiff. In other words, if the plaintiff was slightly negligent but the defendant was grossly negligent, the plaintiff may be awarded damages. Or, if the plaintiff was grossly negligent and the defendant only slightly negligent, no award may be granted.

compensatory damages   The precise loss suffered by a plaintiff, as distinguished from punitive damages, which are over and above the actual losses sustained.

continue   To postpone or adjourn a case pending in court to some future date.

contributory negligence   Negligence in which there has been a failure on the part of the plaintiff to exercise ordinary, proper care, thus contributing toward an accident. Such contributory negligence on the part of the plaintiff in a damage suit often constitute a defense for the defendant.

counsel   A lawyer, an attorney, a counsellor. To counsel means to advise.

court   A place where justice is administered.

criminal law   That branch of the law that deals with crimes and their punishment. In other words, this type of law concerns itself with public wrongs, such as robbery, burglary, forgery, homicide, etc.

culpable   At fault; indifferent to others' rights; blamable; worthy of censure.

decedent   A person who has died.

decision   A judgment or decree issued by a judge or jury; the deciding of a lawsuit; findings of a court.

declaration   [A statement, usually written.]

defendant   A person sued in a civil proceeding or accused in a criminal proceeding. [Black's]

deposition   The written testimony of a witness, given under oath. Such a statement may be presented in a trial, before a trial, at a hearing, or in response to written questions put to a witness. A deposition is also called an affidavit or a statement under oath. *Deponent:* One who gives a deposition.

directed verdict   A situation in which a judge tells the jury what its verdict must be [because the evidence is so compelling that only one decision can reasonably follow—Black's].

discovery   Compulsory disclosure by a party to an action, at another party's request, of facts or documents relevant to the action; the primary discovery devices are interrogatories, depositions, requests for admissions, and requests for production [Black's].

diversity jurisdiction   The exercise of federal court authority over cases involving parties from different states and amounts in controversy greater than $50,000. [Black's]

duty   A legal obligation.

enjoin   To forbid; to issue an injunction, thus restraining someone from carrying out a specific act; a court order demanding that someone not do, or do, something.

evidence   Anything that is brought into court in a trial in an attempt to prove or disprove alleged facts. Evidence includes the introduction of exhibits, records, documents, objects, etc., plus the testimony of witnesses, for the purpose of proving one's case. The jury or judge considers the evidence and decides in favor of one party or the other.

ex parte   For the benefit of one party. (Latin) An *ex parte* procedure is one carried out in court for the benefit of one party only, without a challenge from an opposing party.

fact   Something that took place; an act; something actual and real; an incident that occurred; an event.

felony   A major crime, as distinguished from a minor one, or misdemeanor. Felonies include robberies, burglaries, felonious assault, murder, etc.

finding of fact   A conclusion reached by a court after due consideration; a determination of the truth after consideration of statements made by the opposing parties in a suit.

findings   The result of the deliberations of a court or jury; the decisions expressed by a judicial authority after consideration of all the facts.

forms of action   Various kinds of suits brought in the common law.

fungible   A thing that can be replaced readily by another similar thing. For example, a sack of potatoes can easily be replaced by another sack of potatoes.

grand jury   A group of citizens whose duties include inquiring into crimes in their area for the purpose of determining the probability of guilt of a party or parties. Should a grand jury conclude that there is a good probability of guilt, it will recommend an indictment of the suspects.

highest court   A court of last resort; a court whose decision is final and cannot be appealed because there is no higher court to consider the matter.

impanel   To make a list of those selected for jury duty.

indictment   An accusation by a grand jury, made after thorough investigation, that someone should be tried for a crime. When an indictment is handed down, the accused must stand trial for the alleged offense, but the indictment in itself does not necessarily mean that the accused will be found guilty.

injunction   A restraining order issued by a judge that a person or persons can or cannot do a particular thing. . . . Injunctions may be temporary or permanent.

interlocutory   Temporary; not final or conclusive, as an interlocutory decree of divorce or an interlocutory judgment.

interrogatories   A set of written questions presented to a witness in order to obtain his written testimony (deposition) while he is under oath to tell the truth. Interrogatories are part of the right of discovery that a party in a suit has of obtaining facts from his adversary. They often take place prior to the commencement of the trial.

judge   A public official, appointed or elected, authorized to hear and often to decide cases brought before a court of law.

judicial   Anything related to the administration of justice; anything that has to do with a court of justice.

jurisdiction   The power and right to administer justice; the geographic area in which a judge or a court has the right to try and decide a case.

jury   A specified number of men and/or women who are chosen and sworn to look into matters of fact and, therefore, to determine and render a decision upon the evidence presented to them.

justice   The attempt by judicial means to be fair and to give each party his due, under the law.

law   The rules, regulations, ordinances, and statutes, created by the legislative bodies of government, under which people are expected to live. The law is interpreted by the nature, and our experiences in living.

lawsuit   A dispute between two or more parties brought into court for a solution; a suit; a cause; an action.

liability   Legal responsibility; the obligation to do or not do something; an obligation to pay a debt; the responsibility to behave in a certain manner.

litigation   A lawsuit; a legal action; a suit.

lower court   A trial court, or one from which an appeal may be taken, as distinguished from a court from which no appeal can be taken.

malice   Hatred; ill will; the intentional carrying out of a hurtful act without cause; hostility of one individual toward another.

matter   The subject of a legal dispute or lawsuit; the substance of the issues being litigated; the facts that go into the prosecution or defense of a claim.

negligence   Failure to do what a reasonable, careful, conscientious person is expected to do; doing something that a reasonable, careful, conscientious person would not do. *Contributory negligence:* Negligence in which there has been a failure on the part of the plaintiff to exercise ordinary, proper care, thus contributing toward an accident. *Criminal negligence:* Negligence of such a nature that it is punishable as a crime. *Gross negligence:* Conscious disregard of one's duties, resulting in injury or damage to another. Gross negligence exists when an individual, by exercising ordinary good conduct, could have prevented injury or damage. *Ordinary negligence:* Negligence that could have been avoided if only one had exercised ordinary, reasonable, proper care. Ordinary negligence is not wishful or purposeful, but rather "unthinking." *Willful negligence:* Conscious, knowing neglect of duty, with knowledge that such conduct will result in injury or damage to another.

oath   A pledge to tell the truth; a sworn promise to perform a duty; a calling on God to witness a statement.

obligation   Something a person is bound to do or bound not to do; a moral or legal duty. Penalties may be imposed upon people who fail in their obligations.

ordinance   A local law; a law passed by a legislative body of a city or township or other local government; a statute; a rule.

party   1. A person engaged in a lawsuit, either a plaintiff or a defendant. 2. A person who has taken part in a transaction, such as a party to an agreement or contract.

plaintiff The party who is bringing a lawsuit against a defendant; the person or persons who are suing.

prejudice, with Indicates a matter has been settled without possibility of appeal.

probata (*probatum*) Something proved or conclusively established; proof (Latin).[Black's]

proximate cause The immediate cause of an injury or accident; the legal cause; the real cause; a direct cause; [A cause that directly produces an event and without which the event would not have occurred.[Black's]]

punitive damages An award to a plaintiff beyond actual possible loss. Such damages are by way of punishing the defendant for his act.

question of fact The question of the truth, such question to be decided after hearing evidence from both sides in a case. It is the judge's or jury's function to decide questions of fact.

question of law A matter for the courts to decide, based on interpretation of existing laws pertaining to the matter at hand.

reasonable man Someone who acts with common sense and has the mental capacity of the average, normal sensible human being, as distinguished from an emotionally unstable, erratic, compulsive individual. In determining whether negligence exists, the court will attempt to decide whether the defendant was a reasonable person.

rebuttal The presentation of facts to a court demonstrating that testimony given by witnesses is not true.

reckless Careless; indifferent to the outcome of one's actions; heedless; negligent; acting without due caution.

recovery The award of money given by a court to the person or persons who win the lawsuit.

redress The receiving of satisfaction for an injury one has sustained.

requisite [Required; necessary.]

Restatement of Torts [A codification of the common law relating to torts (private wrongs) compiled by legal practitioners and scholars; most jurisdictions accept the Restatements as the equivalent of law, even though states have often passed their own laws on matters covered by the Restatements. The first series of Restatements (Restatement First) was begun in 1923; the second (Restatement Second) was begun in 1953. Restatements have been written in many other areas of civil law, such as contracts, property, and trusts.]

restraining order An order issued by the court without notice to the opposing party, usually granted temporarily to restrain him until the court decides whether an injunction should be ordered. In actuality, a restraining order is a form of an injunction.

reversal   The annulment or voiding or a court's judgment or decision. Such reversal usually results from a higher court overruling a lower court's action or decision.

review   1. To re-examine, consider. 2. The consideration by a higher (appellate) court of a decision made by a lower (inferior) court.

ruling   The outcome of a court's decision either on some point of law or on the case as a whole. [Black's]

statute   A law passed by the legislative branch of a government.

stipulation   An agreement between the opposing parties in a lawsuit in respect to some matters or matters that are connected to the suit. Such stipulations are made in order to avoid delays in the conducting of the trial. Many stipulations consist of the admission of facts to which both parties agree.

strict liability   Liability that does not depend on actual negligence or intent to harm, but is based on the breach of an absolute duty to make something safe.

summary judgment   A means of obtaining the court's decision without resorting to a formal trial by jury. Such judgments are sought when the opposing parties are in agreement on the facts in the dispute but wish to obtain a ruling as to the question of law that is involved.

testimony   Evidence given under oath by a witness, as distinguished from evidence derived from written documents.

tort   A wrong committed by one person against another; a civil, not a criminal wrong; a wrong not arising out of a contract; a violation of a legal duty that one person has toward another. Every tort is composed of a legal obligation, a breach of that obligation, and damage as a result of the breach of the obligation. *Tort-feasor:* a wrongdoer.

tortious   Hurtful; harmful; wrongful; injurious; in the nature of a tort.

vacate   To cancel; to annul; to set aside.

verdict   The finding or decision of a jury, duly sworn and impaneled, after careful consideration, reported to and accepted by the court.

witness   1. An individual who testifies under oath at a trial, a hearing, or before a legislative body. 2. To see or hear something take place. 3. To be present, and often to sign, a legal document, such as a will or deed.

writ   A formal order of a court, ordering someone who is out of court to do something.

▨ RESEARCH ACTIVITIES

Legal Research

Unless the institution you are attending has a law school, it will likely not have the resources you need to do genuine legal research, except at the secondary source level—i.e., general books and periodical articles dealing with legal matters. If you do not have access to a law school library, but are in or near a city that serves as the county seat, you may be able to use the law library at the county courthouse. The public does have access to these libraries, which should contain the basic tools you need to conduct research—legal encyclopedias and dictionaries, legal periodicals and indexes, style manuals, and a set of state, regional, and federal case reporters, and state and federal statutes and codes.

Many college libraries will have a set of Supreme Court decisions (in *United States Reports*), even if they do not have collections of state-level cases in regional or state case reporters, such as the *Pacific Reporter* or the *California Reports*. Supreme Court cases also are available on the web; see below. Thus, you should be able to conduct research on cases, such as *Roe v. Wade*, 410 U.S. 113 (1973), that reached the Supreme Court. (This citation means volume 410 of *United States Reports*, beginning on p. 113. To refer to a statement on a particular page, insert "at" before the page number; thus, 410 U.S. at 125).

Legal research has been transformed by the computer revolution, and vast legal databases are now available both online and on CD-ROM, through LEXIS-NEXIS and WESTLAW. If you do not have special access to online sources, however, legal research on the internet is hit or miss. America Online, for example, does have a good site on the law, though it is not comprehensive enough to allow you to conduct systematic research on cases. You will find resources, however, on various federal, state, and local statutes, as well as a number of specialized sites on such issues as constitutional law, and poverty/legal assistance. Some states have placed their statutes online: for example, you may find the complete California penal and civil codes on the World Wide Web at

<http://www.findlaw.com/california/ca01_codes/cacode.html>.

The U.S. House of Representatives maintains a law library site at

<http://law.house.gov/>.

To find other legal information, try going to the home web page of a law school library and following the links. For example, the Cornell University Law School Library site (with a link to its Legal Information Institute) is at:

<http://www.law.cornell.edu/admit/library.htm>.

The Law section of the World Wide Web Virtual Library, maintained by the Indiana University Law School, is at

<http://www.law.indiana.edu/law/v-lib/lawindex.html>.

The Emory University Law Library Electronic Reference Desk is at

<http://www.law.emory.edu/LAW/refdesk/toc.html>.

The Chicago-Kent College of Law (Illinois Institute of Technology) site is at

<http://www.kentlaw.edu/legal_resources/>.

The Harvard University Law School Library is at

<http://www.law.harvard.edu/Library>.

The University of California at Berkeley's Law School Library is at

<http://www.law.berkeley.edu/library/library.html>.

The UCLA Law School's site:

<http://www.law.ucla.edu/Research/>.

Other useful web sites for law:

FindLaw: <http://www.findlaw.com>
Law on the Web (Saint Louis University School of Law):
   <http://lawlib.slu.edu/misc/topical.htm>
Georgia State University College of Law:<http://gsulaw.gsu.edu/
      metaindex> (Meta-Index for U.S. Legal Research)
Washburn University School of Law: <http://www.washlaw.edu/>
RefLaw, the Virtual Law Library Reference Desk:
   <http://lawlib.wuacc.edu/washlaw/reflaw>

Note: The FindLaw site offers a searchable database of all Supreme Court opinions since 1893. Go to: <http://www.findlaw.com/casecode/supreme.html>.

FindLaw also offers access to Federal Circuit Court cases and state codes and cases, though only for recent years. Searchability for these cases varies from state to state.

Federal Circuit Court cases:
   <http://www.findlaw.com/casecode/courts/index.html>
State codes and cases:
   <http://www.findlaw.com/casecode/state.html>

Using an electronic legal database such as LEXIS-NEXIS or WESTLAW is similar to using any other database: you conduct a systematic search, using key terms. If you wanted to conduct research on tobacco cases, and particularly on the issue of the liability of tobacco manufacturers for deaths resulting from their products, your search terms would include the words "tobacco" and "manufacturer" and "death" and "liability" and the appropriate connectors ("and" "or," etc.). Following the search, the WESTLAW system would provide citations to all cases, within the time and regional boundaries you specify, that include these terms. (You can find the same citations, of course, by using printed indexes, such as *West's California Digest.* Such searches will take more time because printed indexes are less flexible than electronic ones that search by combinations of individual terms, and because you have to search the various printed supplements, as well as the base indexes, to make sure your research is up-to-date.) Be forewarned that you may be charged a fee to use electronic search services.

Although a comprehensive guide to legal research is beyond the scope of this book, the list below includes some of the most useful sources you will need:

LEGAL ENCYCLOPEDIAS
> *Corpus Juris Secundum* (includes case annotations)
> *American Jurisprudence 2d* (includes case annotations)
> *The Guide to American Law*

DICTIONARIES
> *Words and Phrases* (includes definitions and case annotations)
> *Black's Law Dictionary*
> *Ballentine's Law Dictionary*

ANNOTATED DECISIONS INDEXED BY LEGAL TOPIC
> *ALR (American Law Reports) Digest of Decisions and Annotations* (extensive annotated cases on selected legal issues)
> *West's [State] Digests* (index to legal issues with case annotations)

PERIODICAL INDEXES
> *Index to Legal Periodicals and Books*
> *Current Law Index*
> *Current Index to Legal Periodicals* (also in microfilm, online, and on CD-ROM)

ELECTRONIC LEGAL PERIODICAL INDEXES
> *LEXIS-NEXIS* (includes *Index to Legal Periodicals and Books* and *Legal Resource Index*)
> *LegalTrac* (CD-ROM) (part of the InfoTrac library)

MODEL CODES AND STATUTES
> *Restatement of the Law, 2d* (covers areas of civil law, such as torts and contracts)
> *Model Penal Code*

FEDERAL CASE REPORTERS (COLLECTIONS OF CASE OPINIONS, IN CHRONOLOGICAL ORDER OF DECISION)
> *United States Reports (Supreme Court)*
> *Supreme Court Reports, Lawyer's Edition*
> *Federal Supplement* (decisions of Federal District Courts)
> *Federal Reporter* (decisions of Federal Circuit courts)
> *West's Supreme Court Reporter*

REGIONAL AND STATE REPORTERS
> *Pacific Reporter* (covers Alaska, Arizona, California, Colorado, Hawaii, Idaho, Kansas, Montana, Nevada, New Mexico, Oklahoma, Oregon, Utah, Washington, Wyoming)
> *North Eastern Reporter* (Illinois, Indiana, Massachusetts, New York, Ohio)

North Western Reporter (Iowa, Michigan, Minnesota, Nebraska, North
     Dakota, South Dakota, Wisconsin)
Atlantic Reporter (Connecticut, Delaware, Maine, Maryland, New
     Hampshire, New Jersey, Pennsylvania, Rhode Island, Vermont)
South Western Reporter (Arkansas, Kentucky, Missouri, Tennessee, Texas)
South Eastern Reporter (Georgia, North Carolina, South Carolina,
     Virginia, West Virginia)
Southern (Alabama, Florida, Louisiana, Mississippi)
(*state reporters*)

STATUTES, CONSTITUTIONS, CODES
     United States Code (U.S.C.)
     United States Codes Annotated (U.C.S.A.)
     United States Code Service (U.S.C.S.)
     (*state and local statutes and codes*)

COMPUTER-ASSISTED LEGAL RESEARCH
     LEXIS-NEXIS
     WESTLAW

CITATORS (CITATION GUIDES)
     Shepard's Citations (indicates if the case, statute, article, etc., you want to
          cite as authority has been cited in other cases, statutes, articles,
          etc. The process of conducting such searches is known as
          "Shepardizing.")

To give you an idea of how you can find particular cases on particular legal
issues, below is a page from West Publishing Company's *Words and Phrases*.
Suppose you want to see how the concept of "malice" has been used in libel
cases. The entry on "malice" begins with a series of cross references to related topics, then presents a long series of legal statements on malice that have
appeared in legal opinions. Following the "general" category that begins most
entries, you can look for the particular area in which you are interested—in
this case, libel and slander.

MALICE

     See, also,
          Civil Action When Malice is not Gist of Action.
          Common-Law Malice.
          Constructive or Implied Malice.
          Deliberate Malice.
          Doctrine of Universal Malice.
          Fraud or Malice.
          Implied Malice.
          Inferred Malice.
          New York Times Malice.
          Presumed Malice.
          Secrecy and Malice.

Times Malice.
Willfulness and Malice.
With Malice.
With Malice and Unjustified in Law.

In general

In the context of intentional torts, "malice" is defined under Massachusetts law as arising from improper motive or means, including age discrimination. Galdauckas v. Interstate Hotels Corp. No. 16, D.Mass., 901 F.Supp. 454, 465.

"Malice," in context of peer review, means recklessness of consequences and mind regardless of social duty. Cooper v. Delaware Valley Medical Center, 654 A.2d 547, 553, 539 Pa. 620.

"Malice" is wickedness of disposition, hardness of heart, cruelty, recklessness of consequences and mind regardless of social duty. Green v. Pennsylvania Bd. Of Probation and Parole, Pa.Cmwlth., 664 A.2d 677, 679.

"Malice," in defamation cases, means that the defendant knows that the statement is false or that he has reckless disregard for determining whether it is true. Century Management, Inc. v. Spring, Mo. App.W.D., 905 S.W.2d 109, 113.

Libel and slander

Evidence supported jury's finding that veterinarian's inquiry of coworker as to whether former employee had drug or alcohol problem were slander per se, and were made out of "malice," rather than in "good faith," and thus were not protected by privilege; imputation of substance abuse reflected on former employee's capacity to perform duties of veterinary assistant, and veterinarian denied asking question when confronted by former employee, but during trial he claimed former employee had become unreliable. Lara v. Thomas, Iowa, 512 N.W.2d 777, 785.

In libel action arising from employer and employee relationship, actual "malice" means publication of statement with knowledge that it is false or with reckless disregard for whether it is false, and falsity coupled with negligence, failure to investigate truth or falsity of statement, and failure to act as reasonably prudent person are insufficient to show malice. Maewal v. Adventist Health Systems/Sunbelt, Inc., Tex.App.-Fort Worth, 868 S.W.2d 886, 893.

"Malice," sufficient to overcome qualified privilege in defamation action, requires showing that defendant acted with knowledge of, or in reckless disregard of, falsity of publicized matter, that is that defendant in fact entertained serious doubts about truth of publication. Mitre v. La Plaza Mall, Tex. App.-Corpus Christi, 857 S.W.2d 752, 754.

"Malice" necessary to overcome qualified privilege in defamation action may be proven by evidence of personal ill feeling, exaggerated language or extent of publication. Strauss v. Thorne, Minn. App., 490 N.W.2d 908, 912.

Essence of "malice" in libel context is not lack of prudence, but actual awareness of probable falsity of published statement. Weinel v. Monkey, 5 Dist., 481 N.E.2d 776, 778, 89 Ill.Dec. 933, 935, 134 Ill.App.3d 1039.

Other West indexes also provide references to relevant articles in legal periodicals. Don't hesitate to ask librarians for assistance in using legal indexes to find cases, articles, and other sources.

Some excellent books for teaching novice legal researchers to find cases, statutes, and articles by topic include:

Cohen, Morris, Robert C. Berring, Kent C. Olson. *How to Find the Law.* 9th ed. St. Paul, MN: Westlaw, 1989. (See also Berring's abridged version of this book, entitled *Finding the Law.*)
Jacobstein, J. Myron, Roy M. Mersky, Donald J. Dunn. *Fundamentals of Legal Research.* 6th ed. Wesbury, NY: Foundation Press, 1994.

Citations for Cases Covered in this Chapter

If you would like to follow up on cases covered in this chapter, here are the references. (See Hricik on reading legal citations.)

The Maiden and the Pot of Gold: A Case of Emotional Distress
Nickerson v. Hodges. 84 So. 37 (1920).

Venezia v. Miller Brewing Co.: A Case of Products Liability?
Venezia v. Miller Brewing Co. 626 F.2d 188 (1980).

The Ridiculed Employee: Another Case of Emotional Distress
Harris v. Jones. 380 A.2d 611 (1977).

Assault and Battery on the Gridiron: A Case of Reckless Disregard of Safety
Hackbart v. Cincinnati Bengals. 601 F.2d 516 (1979)

Of Accidents and Injuries: Some Cases of Negligence
Lieck v. McDonald's. 1995 WL 360309 (N.M. Dist)
Greene v. Hardees. 1997 WL 323455 W.D. Va.
Lucas v. New York City Transit Authority. 557 N.Y.S.2d 919 (1990).
Robinson v. NYC Transit. 481 N.Y.S.2d 85 (1984).

"Urban War Zone": A Case of Public Nuisance
People v. Acuna et al. 60 Cal. Rptr.2d 277 (1997).

The Felled Stop Signs: Some Cases of Homicide
State of Florida v. Miller. (This case had not been decided by an appeals court by publication date.)
State of Utah v. Hallett. 619 P.2d 337 (1980).

Drag Racing and Death: Some Cases of Manslaughter
Commonwealth of Pennsylvania v. Levin. 135 A.2d 764 (1957).

> *Commonwealth of Pennsylvania v. Root.* 170 A.2d 310
> (1961).
> *Jacobs v. State of Florida.* 184 So.2d 710 (1966).

Research Topics

1. Select a particular legal issue dealt with in this chapter (for example, emotional distress or drag racing) and research the book and periodical indexes to find some interesting recent cases. Use an index to legal periodicals if the library has one. Select one of these cases and report on its progress. Describe the facts of the case, identify the legal issues involved, describe and analyze the arguments on both sides, and discuss the case's outcome.

2. Using some of the internet legal sites mentioned above, browse the web until you find a topic that interests you (for example tobacco lawsuits). Then, using the hyperlinks, research the topic as fully as you are able, online. (Remember to write down, electronically copy, or bookmark important URLs, so that you can easily return to them.) Write a report *on the progress of your research*, rather than on the topic itself. Focus on what you were able to find, using web resources, and what you were unable to find. Explain your frustrations, as well as your high points of discovery. Indicate what other information—whether available online or in print—you would need to find before being able to complete a report on the topic.

3. Visit the county courthouse (if one is nearby) and sit in for a period of time on one or more trials. Report on your observations. Describe what you have seen and analyze the various aspects of the case or cases: the prosecution and defense lawyers, the defendant, the witnesses, the judge, the jury. What conclusions, from this limited observation, can you make about the legal process? What recommendations would you make to better achieve justice—or, at least, a higher standard of fairness or efficiency?

4. Research the legal system in a country other than the United States. Based upon your own experience or knowledge and upon what you have learned in this chapter, how does the process of criminal or civil cases in this other country compare to that in the United States? Which aspects of the other country's legal system appear superior to those of the United States? Which seems inferior? In your discussion refer to specific cases tried in the other country's legal system. You may choose to focus partially on offenses (such as criticizing the government) that are not crimes in the United States, but are in some other countries; however, focus primarily upon the ways that the legal system *works*.

5. Many feature films focus on courtroom drama and other legal matters. Examples: *Young Mr. Lincoln* (1939), *Adam's Rib* (1949), *The Caine Mutiny* (1954), *12 Angry Men* (1957), *Witness for the Prosecution*

(1957), *Anatomy of a Murder* (1961), *Inherit the Wind* (1960), *Judgment at Nuremberg* (1961), *To Kill a Mockingbird* (1962), *The Paper Chase* (1973), *The Verdict* (1982), *True Believer* (1989), *Class Action* (1991), *Ghosts of Mississippi* (1996).

View one or more of these films, then report on and draw conclusions from your observations. Using inductive reasoning, *infer* points of law and rules of courtroom procedure from what you see. Point out similarities and differences, where appropriate. For example, *The Caine Mutiny* deals (partially) with a court martial, where the rules of procedure are somewhat different from those in civilian courts. *Judgment at Nuremberg* deals with war crimes tribunals in postwar Germany. *12 Angry Men* deals with jury room deliberations, rather than with the trial itself. *Paper Chase* deals with a tyrannical law professor attacking the "skullsful of mush" in his students' heads and goading them to "think like a lawyer!"

12

The Beast Within: Perspectives on the Horror Film

The ego represents what we call reason and sanity, in contrast to the id, which contains the passions. . . . [T]he ego has the task of bringing the external world to bear upon the id and its tendencies, and endeavors to substitute the reality-principle for the pleasure-principle which reigns supreme in the id.

—Sigmund Freud, "The Ego and the Id"

In the climactic sequence of West Craven's *Scream* (1997), the terrified heroine flees from a knife-wielding fiend in a Halloween cloak and mask, finding protection in the arms of a friend, himself grievously wounded. They briefly open the door of the remote farmhouse to admit a panicked young man, who cries, "Stu has gone mad!" The friend, a crazed half-smile on his face, intones, "We all go a little mad sometimes!" He raises his gun, shoots the other young man, and the heroine realizes in horror that the person she has trusted is a murderous psychopath. In the scene that follows, blood spills upon gore, with the heroine at one point turning the tables upon her attacker by donning the Halloween gear, bursting out of a closet, and impaling the killer with the sharp end of an umbrella. (Of course, he's far from finished.)

The sequence is noteworthy for several reasons. First, much of its dramatic impact derives from one of the most enduring motifs in the horror genre: the psychopathic monster who, at least part of the time, looks and acts like a normal person. Sometimes the monster can control his transformation; sometimes he can't. The implication, of course, is that much of the time you can't tell monsters from normal people because their true nature is concealed beneath a civilized facade. Second, after the psychopath says, "We all go a little mad sometimes," he credits the line to Anthony Perkins in *Psycho*. He also admits that the "blood" on his shirt is corn syrup, just like the pig's blood in *Carrie*. The characters in *Scream* are aware that they're in a horror film, and as the action develops, they tick off the various conventions of the genre. When the killer lies lifeless on the floor, the young man warns the heroine to be careful because "This is the moment where the supposedly dead killer comes back to life for one last scare." ("Not in my movie!" retorts the heroine, after finishing off the killer.) In other words, let's not take the situation too seriously, folks, because we're just playing out an established formula. Our clever twist is that we know it and we're hip about it.

Scream is therefore a film about the monstrous nature of apparently ordinary people, but it's also a film about horror films; it relies upon the audience's awareness of typical situations and plot patterns in the genre. It is a genre that has been fascinating audiences since the silent film era. Early examples include F. W. Murnau's vampire film *Nosferatu* (1922) and Robert Wiene's celebrated expressionist classic, *The Cabinet of Dr. Caligari* (1919). Tod Browning's *Dracula* (1931) with Bela Lugosi, though not the first Dracula film, popularized the vampire motif and inspired an endless string of sequels. James Whale's *Frankenstein* (1931)—with Boris Karloff as the monster, was also followed by a host of sequels, most notably *The Bride of Frankenstein* (1935), composed of equal parts of horror, wit, and pathos. Karloff was also the first bandaged monster in a series of *Mummy* films.

The original werewolf film, *The Werewolf of London* (1935), was followed by the more well-known *The Wolf Man* (1941) with Lon Chaney, Jr., who reprised his role in a series of lesser sequels. Shameless producers milked the genre to its limit by creating such unnatural hybrids as *Frankenstein Meets the Wolf Man* (1943) and *Abbott and Costello Meet Frankenstein* (1948). Another horror classic, *The Invisible Man* (1933), with Claude Rains, was fortunate in spawning only one sequel. *Dr. Jekyll and Mr. Hyde* had many incarnations, though these were not sequels but remakes. In more recent years, prestigious directors have made expensive remakes of the horror classics: Francis Ford Coppola (*The Godfather*) made *Bran Stoker's Dracula* (1992); Kenneth Branagh (*Hamlet*) made *Mary Shelley's Frankenstein* (1994); Mike Nichols (*The Graduate*) made *Wolf* (1994).

Horror films have more commonly been "B" movies, however, and the kind of film that Wes Craven's *Scream* is both recreating and mocking draws upon the pulp genre represented by *The Thing* (1951), *The Invasion of the Body Snatchers* (1956), *The Night of the Living Dead* (1968), *The Texas Chainsaw Massacre* (1974), *Halloween* (1978), *Friday the Thirteenth* (1980), and Craven's own *Nightmare on Elm Street* (1985). Most of these films—and their sequels—updated the classic horror movie into the contemporary "slasher" subgenre, in which a group of helpless, isolated victims is systematically stalked and dispatched by a fiendish killer.

But why are horror films so enduringly popular? Why should a significant portion of the moviegoing public pay money to be terrified? And why should horror movies be worth studying in a college course?

Actually, the first question begins to answer to the last one. The fact that so many people in our society enjoy horror films raises interesting questions about popular culture and about the psychology of entertainment—questions that are taken up by some of the authors in this chapter. For now, we can suggest that any phenomenon that engages so many people in a culture can reveal significant aspects of that culture, can provide clues about its values, its professed ideals, its deepest fears. On a psychological level, the horror film dramatizes our nightmares, so that we can confront them and—from the safety of a darkened theater—laugh at them. So we get a thrill out of being scared (some of us, anyway!) as long as we know that as spectators we'll be perfectly safe.

One of the most popular of the horror subgenres is what some have called the "transformation" film and what we call the motif of "the beast within." James Iaccino, drawing upon the work of psychoanalyst Carl Jung, calls it the "shadow archetype." The shadow represents the dark side of our nature. As Iaccino notes, the "giant monsters, from massive insects to huge dinosaurs and even incredibly sized aliens, are all reflections of the shadow blown up to outrageous proportions." In a narrower sense (one without external monsters), the shadow represents the bestial, primeval instincts that lurk just beneath our civilized, law-abiding facades, instincts that sometimes break to the surface in irrational and murderous fury. Werewolf films are a prime example of the shadow archetype, as are the numerous Dr. Jekyll and Mr. Hyde films.

Of course, the horror genre is not confined to movies. The fertile imagination of novelists and dramatists has long provided a wide variety of approaches to the motif of "the beast within." In *Midsummer Night's Dream* (1594–95) and in *The Tempest* (1610–11), Shakespeare shows us men transformed into beasts. The gothic novelists of the eighteenth century supplied British readers with hearty portions of horror, chains rattling in the attic, and screams in the night. In *Heart of Darkness* (1899) Joseph Conrad creates a physical, spiritual, and psychological journey into the heart of darkness in each of us—epitomized in a highly educated European, Kurtz, who reverts to savagery in the jungle after being long isolated from civilization. In William Golding's *Lord of the Flies* (1954), civilized British schoolboys stranded on an island after their plane crashes turn into savages within a few short weeks, intent on killing all who refuse to join their tribe. Whether transmitted orally by storytellers, through the writing of novelists, or through the lens of filmmakers, the horror story has entertained—and terrified—its audiences.

We begin by considering the psychological dimensions of the horror film and then narrow our focus to the motif of transformation. We'll focus on werewolf films—and two in particular, *Company of Wolves* (1984) and *Wolf* (1994)—along with several of the Jekyll and Hyde films. Along the way, we'll also look at *Forbidden Planet*—a kind of psychoanalytic updating of Shakespeare's *Tempest*.

The chapter begins with an essay by horror novelist Stephen King, who asks why we should be so drawn to such horrible stuff. His starting point: "I think that we're all mentally ill. . . ." Next, Tim Dirks provides a brief historical survey of horror films, including a list of the greatest examples of the genre. Stanley Solomon examines the distinctive and characteristic features of "The Nightmare World," drawing distinctions between good and bad examples of the genre. In "Horror and Science Fiction—The Sleep of Reason" psychoanalyst Harvey M. Greenberg explores both the conscious and unconscious aspects of the tortured protagonists of films such as *Cat People*, *The Wolf Man*, *Dr. Jekyll and Mr. Hyde*, and *Forbidden Planet*. Joyce Salisbury then provides a historical dimension for our exploration in "Metamorphosis: Humans into Animals," a survey of stories from the Middle Ages involving transformations of people into animals.

In the second half of the chapter, we narrow the focus to particular "beast within" films. First, we'll consider feminist Angela Carter's rewriting of the Little Red Riding Hood story, "The Company of Wolves." She later adapted her story into a screenplay, collaborating with Neil Jordan, who directed the film version. You'll read an interview with Jordan, who discusses the making of *Company of Wolves*, and you'll consider two reviews of this film. The chapter continues with three reviews of *Wolf*, Mike Nichols' recent contribution to the subgenre of werewolf films. It concludes with two chapters from Robert Louis Stevenson's novella, *Dr. Jekyll and Mr. Hyde* and a selection of reviews of three films based upon Stevenson's story, including the recent *Mary Reilly*.

Why We Crave Horror Movies

STEPHEN KING

To think of modern horror fiction is to summon the name of Stephen King. Author of such best-selling novels as Carrie: A Novel of a Girl with a Frightening Power *(1974),* The Shining *(1977),* Pet Sematary *(1983), and* Misery *(1987), King has devoted a career to exploring our nightmares and making them come alive. His novels sell in the millions; the movie adaptations based on them play to packed (screaming) houses—all testament to King's mastery of a form that prompts a simple but mystifying question: Why do people pay good money to be scared? Over his career, in various interviews and essays, King has observed that we seek out and respond to horror in fiction as a strategy for contending with the horrors and insanity of our daily lives. In the essay that follows, he observes how a good horror story lets us keep the "alligators" lurking in our psyches fed. The premise is clear: each of us maintains both a civilized, public face and then something altogether nastier that we keep hidden but must nonetheless "feed." Good horror stories and movies do just that.*

I think that we're all mentally ill; those of us outside the asylums only hide it 1
a little better—and maybe not all that much better, after all. We've all known people who talk to themselves, people who sometimes squinch their faces into horrible grimaces when they believe no one is watching, people who have some hysterical fear—of snakes, the dark, the tight place, the long drop . . . and, of course, those final worms and grubs that are waiting so patiently underground.

When we pay our four or five bucks and seat ourselves at tenth-row 2
center in a theater showing a horror movie, we are daring the nightmare.

Why? Some of the reasons are simple and obvious. To show that we can, 3
that we are not afraid, that we can ride this roller coaster. Which is not to say that a really good horror movie may not surprise a scream out of us at some point, the way we may scream when the roller coaster twists through a complete 360 or plows through a lake at the bottom of the drop. And horror

movies, like roller coasters, have always been the special province of the young; by the time one turns 40 or 50, one's appetite for double twists or 360-degree loops may be considerably depleted.

We also go to re-establish our feelings of essential normality; the horror 4 movie is innately conservative, even reactionary. Freda Jackson as the horrible melting woman in *Die, Monster, Die!* confirms for us that no matter how far we may be removed from the beauty of a Robert Redford or a Diana Ross, we are still light-years from true ugliness.

And we go to have fun. 5

Ah, but this is where the ground starts to slope away, isn't it? Because this 6 is a very peculiar sort of fun indeed. The fun comes from seeing others menaced—sometimes killed. One critic has suggested that if pro football has become the voyeur's version of combat, then the horror film has become the modern version of the public lynching.

It is true that the mythic, "fairytale" horror film intends to take away the 7 shades of gray. . . . It urges us to put away our more civilized and adult penchant for analysis and to become children again, seeing things in pure blacks and whites. It may be that horror movies provide psychic relief on this level because this invitation to lapse into simplicity, irrationality and even outright madness is extended so rarely. We are told we may allow our emotions a free rein . . . or no rein at all.

If we are all insane, then sanity becomes a matter of degree. If your 8 insanity leads you to carve up women like Jack the Ripper or the Cleveland Torso Murderer, we clap you away in the funny farm (but neither of those two amateur-night surgeons was ever caught, heh-heh-heh); if, on the other hand your insanity leads you only to talk to yourself when you're under stress or to pick your nose on the morning bus, then you are left alone to go about your business . . . though it is doubtful that you will ever be invited to the best parties.

The potential lyncher is in almost all of us (excluding saints, past and pre- 9 sent; but then, most saints have been crazy in their own ways), and every now and then, he has to be let loose to scream and roll around in the grass. Our emotions and our fears form their own body, and we recognize that it demands its own exercise to maintain proper muscle tone. Certain of these emotional muscles are accepted—even exalted—in civilized society; they are, of course, the emotions that tend to maintain the status quo of civilization itself. Love, friendship, loyalty, kindness—these are all the emotions that we applaud, emotions that have been immortalized in the couplets of Hallmark cards and in the verses (I don't dare call it poetry) of Leonard Nimoy.

When we exhibit these emotions, society showers us with positive rein- 10 forcement; we learn this even before we get out of diapers. When, as children, we hug our rotten little puke of a sister and give her a kiss, all the aunts and uncles smile and twit and cry, "Isn't he the sweetest little thing?" Such coveted treats as chocolate-covered graham crackers often follow. But if we deliberately slam the rotten little puke of a sister's fingers in the door, sanctions follow—angry remonstrance from parents, aunts and uncles; instead of a chocolate-covered graham cracker, a spanking.

But anticivilization emotions don't go away, and they demand periodic   11
exercise. We have such "sick" jokes as, "What's the difference between a
truckload of bowling balls and a truckload of dead babies?" (You can't
unload a truckload of bowling balls with a pitchfork . . . a joke, by the way,
that I heard originally from a ten-year-old.) Such a joke may surprise a laugh
or a grin out of us even as we recoil, a possibility that confirms the thesis: If
we share a brotherhood of man, then we also share an insanity of man. None
of which is intended as a defense of either the sick joke or insanity but merely
as an explanation of why the best horror films, like the best fairy tales,
manage to be reactionary, anarchistic, and revolutionary all at the same time.

The mythic horror movie, like the sick joke, has a dirty job to do. It delib-   12
erately appeals to all that is worst in us. It is morbidity unchained, our most
base instincts let free, our nastiest fantasies realized . . . and it all happens, fit-
tingly enough, in the dark. For those reasons, good liberals often shy away
from horror films. For myself, I like to see the most aggressive of them—
Dawn of the Dead, for instance—as lifting a trap door in the civilized fore-
brain and throwing a basket of raw meat to the hungry alligators swimming
around in that subterranean river beneath.

Why bother? Because it keeps them from getting out, man. It keeps them   13
down there and me up here. It was Lennon and McCartney who said that all
you need is love, and I would agree with that.

As long as you keep the gators fed.   14

■ ■ ■

Review Questions

1. What relationship does the statement "we're all mentally ill" have, in
   King's view, to the appeal that horror movies hold for us?
2. Why do we go to horror movies, according to King?
3. In what ways might horror movies offer "psychic relief"?

Discussion and Writing Suggestions

1. Do you agree with the initial proposition that "we're all mentally ill"?
2. What does King mean when he writes that by going to horror movies,
   "we are daring the nightmare"? What *is* the nightmare?
3. Does King's discussion of how horror films act upon us reflect your own
   experience in both watching and enjoying horror films? Explain your
   response, focusing upon one or more particular examples of films that
   you think were especially effective in keeping "the gators fed."
4. How can nightmares "manage to be reactionary, anarchistic, and revolutionary all at the same time"? [A "reactionary" view is one that values
   an old, well-known (if flawed) system over present-day systems; an

"anarchistic" view is one that rebels against any system or order; a "revolutionary" view is one that seeks to replace the current system or order with a new one.]

5. King asserts (as have others, including Freud) that being civilized exacts its psychological toll. In your own life, have you seen this to be true? What have you sacrificed in order to play by the rules and be praised? At what cost? Do you see any relationship between the parts of yourself you are denying and the way you respond to horror movies?

6. King claims that "the potential lyncher is in almost all of us." Do you agree? If you're skeptical, see the chapter on Obedience to Authority in this text for more on this theme. In explaining how ordinary people could carry out Hitler's "Final Solution" and kill millions of innocent people, psychologist Stanley Milgram offers much the same analysis as King. (Milgram very carefully re-creates the conditions that lead the so-called normal person to commit acts of atrocity.)

Horror Films

TIM DIRKS

In the following selection Tim Dirks provides a useful historical survey of horror films since the silent era, and offers a list of the most important examples of the genre. He begins his discussion by focusing upon some of the key features of horror films.

Dirks, author and manager of an award-winning website, "The Greatest Films" <http://www.filmsite.org/>, which includes reviews and commentaries of many classic American movies, has been watching and studying films his entire adult life. Formerly a history teacher, Dirks currently serves as online course manager at a technology training center in the Bay Area of Northern California.

Horror films are designed to frighten and to invoke our hidden fears, often in 1
a terrifying, shocking finale, while captivating and entertaining us at the same time in a cathartic experience. Horror films effectively center on the dark side of life, the forbidden, and strange and alarming events. They deal with our most primal nature and its fears: our nightmares, our vulnerability, our alienation, our terror of the unknown, our fear of death, loss of identity, or fear of sexuality.

Whatever dark, primitive, and revolting traits that simultaneously attract 2
and repel us are featured in the horror genre. Horror films are often combined with science fiction when the menace or monster is related to a corruption of technology, or when Earth is threatened by aliens. The fantasy and supernatural film genres are not synonymous with the horror genre.

Horror films, when done well and with less reliance on horrifying special 3
effects, can be extremely potent film forms, tapping into our dream states and

the horror of the irrational and unknown, and the horror within man himself. In horror films, the irrational forces of chaos or horror invariably need to be defeated, and often these films end with a return to normalcy and victory over the monstrous.

Of necessity, horror films are generally set in spooky old mansions or fog-   4
shrouded, dark locales, with "unknown," supernatural or grotesque creatures, ranging from vampires, madmen, devils, unfriendly ghosts, monsters, "Frankensteins," demons, zombies, evil spirits, arch fiends, satanic villains, the "possessed," werewolves and freaks, even the unseen, diabolical presence of evil.

Horror films developed out of the tradition of Gothic novels from Europe   5
by way of Mary Shelley or Bram Stoker. The first Frankenstein monster film (a 10-minute version) in the US was made as early as 1910 by the Edison Studios, starring Charles Ogle as the monster. The earliest horror pictures, now-forgotten "vamp" pictures (films featuring devilish captivating ladies) in one-reel or full length features, were produced in the US from 1909 to the early 1920s, making the horror genre one of the oldest and most basic. The first genuine vampire picture was produced in Europe—F. W. Murnau's *Nosferatu* (1922), a film adaptation from Bram Stoker's novel *Dracula*.

Other European filmmakers contributed to the genre, producing a   6
number of horror films based upon old folktales, fables, and myths. One of the more memorable of the early films was Germany's silent expressionistic classic, *The Cabinet of Dr. Caligari* (1919). The shadowy, disturbing, nightmarish quality of "Caligari" was brought to Hollywood in the 1920s, and continued into the classic period of horror films in the 1930s. Before then, Hollywood was reluctant to experiment with the themes of true horror films. Instead, the studios took popular stage plays and emphasized their mystery genre features, providing rational explanations for all the supernatural and occult elements.

One actor who helped pave the way for the change in outlook and accep-   7
tance of the genre was Lon Chaney, known as "the man of a thousand faces." He starred in numerous silent horror films beginning in 1913, including the early *The Hunchback of Notre Dame* (1924) and his most memorable portrayal of Erik, the disfigured bitter composer of the Paris Opera in the groundbreaking, vividly-frightening film, *The Phantom of the Opera* (1925).

Many of these early silent classics would be remade during the talkies era.   8
For example, John Barrymore starred in the first version of the Jekyll/Hyde story, a silent film titled *Dr. Jekyll and Mr. Hyde* (1920). It was later remade in two noteworthy versions: Fredric March's Oscar-winning portrayal of the transformed scientist in director Rouben Mamoulian's *Dr. Jekyll and Mr. Hyde* (1932), and Victor Fleming's MGM production of *Dr. Jekyll and Mr. Hyde* (1941), starring Spencer Tracy in the title role and Ingrid Bergman as the "wicked" girlfriend.

By the early 1930s, horror entered into its classic phase in Hollywood—   9
the Dracula and Frankenstein Eras. The studios took tales of European vampires and undead aristocrats, mad scientists, and invisible men and created

some of the most archetypal creatures and monsters ever known for the screen. The studio best known for its pure horror films and its classic horror stars, Bela Lugosi and Boris Karloff, was Universal Pictures.

With Tod Browning's direction, Universal produced a film version of Lugosi's Broadway success about a blood-sucking vampire named *Dracula* (1931), released early in the year. The film adaptation of Bram Stoker's novel played upon fears of sexuality, blood, and the nebulous period between life and death. The first Dracula film was followed closely by James Whale's masterful monster/horror film of Mary Shelley's novel, *Frankenstein* (1931), the quintessential combination of science fiction and horror in a "mad doctor" thriller. Boris Karloff's poignant portrayal of the Monster's plight gave a personality to the outcast, uncomprehending creature. 10

Without resorting to an existing literary horror figure, such as Frankenstein, Dracula, Dr. Jekyll and Mr. Hyde, or The Invisible Man, Universal also created a new and "original" creature—the werewolf—in two films. The first werewolf film was *The Werewolf of London* (1935). The second and most famous was the excellent B-grade film *The Wolf Man* (1941), with Lon Chaney, Jr. in his first appearance. The "transformation" scene from man-to-wolf, involving complicated cosmetic/makeup artistry, is remarkably realistic. Unfortunately, the Wolf Man role hopelessly typecast Chaney, Jr. for life—he was forced to star in a series of very poor sequels, teamed up with other Universal horror stars in B-grade films including *Frankenstein Meets the Wolfman* (1943), and in two films adding Dracula to the mix: *House of Frankenstein* (1944) and *House of Dracula* (1945). The worst ignominy suffered by Chaney, Jr. was in Universal-International's comedy *Abbott and Costello Meet Frankenstein* (1948). 11

Other classic horror films of the 1930s and early 1940s include Tod Browning's unusual *Freaks* (1932), Claude Rains as *The Invisible Man* (1933) in Universal's critically acclaimed film version of H.G. Wells' novel, Charles Laughton as the horribly deformed bellringer in the excellent *The Hunchback of Notre Dame* (1939), and Claude Rains again in the remake of *Phantom of the Opera* (1943). Notable films with living dead, "zombie" plots included Universal's classic *The Mummy* (1932) with Boris Karloff in the title role—his second Monster role success (and Lon Chaney, Jr., in the title role in 40s sequels), Bela Lugosi's performance in *White Zombie* (1932) and Val Lewton's B-masterpiece production *I Walked With a Zombie* (1943) (see below). One of the best adventure/horror films of all time is the "beauty and the beast" classic *King Kong* (1933). 12

Dracula films and sequels, although more common, were less successful than many of the superb Frankenstein sequels. Universal Studios churned out more Dracula sagas in the 30s and 40s, including the first sequel *Dracula's Daughter* (1936) featuring a female vampire, and Robert Siodmak's *Son of Dracula* (1943), with Lon Chaney, Jr. in the starring role as the vampire. Britain's Hammer Studios, as they did with Frankenstein sequels in the 50s, reinvigorated the Bram Stoker novel by remaining faithful to the material in a spectacular Technicolor sequel. Talented director Terence Fisher (with 13

Christopher Lee as the reclusive Count Dracula and Peter Cushing as Dr. Van Helsing) created the classic *The Horror of Dracula* (1958).

The witty Frankenstein sequel, *Bride of Frankenstein* (1935), directed by   14
James Whale, outdid the original—it was a marvelous mixture of humor, classic terror, and unforgettable images—including Elsa Lanchester as the spectacular bride. Together, Lugosi and Karloff starred in three films together, the best being *The Black Cat* (1934). Karloff's last film as Frankenstein's Monster was Son of Frankenstein (1939)—it was one of the best sequels before many inferior creations in the 1940s and 50s, such as *The Ghost of Frankenstein* (1942), starring Lon Chaney, Jr. as the Monster, or the campy *I Was a Teenage Frankenstein* (1957).

The first of six installments of Frankenstein sequels from Britain's   15
Hammer Studios (pairing actor Peter Cushing in the starring role as Baron von Frankenstein with director Terence Fisher), *The Curse of Frankenstein* (1957), was soon followed by *The Revenge of Frankenstein* (1958) and *The Evil of Frankenstein* (1964). The fourth and best of the Peter Cushing/ Frankenstein movies was *Frankenstein Created Woman* (1967).

Val Lewton, using a more subtle, suggestive, eerie approach in a number   16
of atmospheric, sophisticated horror/suspense films, produced eleven low-budget films for RKO Studios in the 1940s, directed first by Jacques Tourneur, and then by Mark Robson and Robert Wise. Lewton's first film, directed by Tourneur in his feature-film debut, was the suspenseful horror classic *The Cat People* (1942), possibly the first horror film to never show its monster. Through 1948, Tourneur also contributed *I Walked With a Zombie* (1943), *The Seventh Victim* (1943), *Ghost Ship* (1943), *Bedlam* (1945), and *Isle of the Dead* (1945). (Years later, Tourneur returned only once to the horror genre with *Curse of the Demon* (1957), a film which demonstrated Lewton's influence. Tourneur is most famous for the film noir classic, *Out of the Past* (1947).) The most influential of Lewton's directors was Robert Wise, who created such classics as *The Curse of the Cat People* (1944) and *The Body Snatcher* (1945), and then later in his career directed *The Haunting* (1963). One of the best ghost/supernatural films ever made is *The Uninvited* (1944).

Many of the films in the horror genre from the mid-1930s to the late   17
1950s were B-grade movies, inferior sequels, or atrocious low-budget gimmick films. In the atomic age of the 1950s, most of the monster films were cheaply made, drive-in, grade-Z films. A few American-made monster/horror films of the time, however, effectively capitalized on terrorizing threats that were extraterrestrial powers, such as the alien found in the Arctic in *The Thing (From Another World)* (1951), the aberrant or alien threat in Don Siegel's classic *Invasion of the Body Snatchers* (1956), or the unusual monsters in *The Creature From the Black Lagoon* (1954), a film originally shown in 3-D, *The Blob* (1958) and *The Fly* (1958).

Horror films branched out in all different directions in the 1960s and   18
after, especially as the Production Code disappeared and film censorship was

on the decline. Horror could be found in the dark shadows of the human soul itself as in the psychopathic Bates Motel operator in *Psycho* (1960), in the modern gothic thriller starring two aging Hollywood actresses, *What Ever Happened to Baby Jane?* (1962), in the preacher with "love" and "hate" tattooed on his hands in *The Night of the Hunter* (1955), in writer Stephen King's story of a schoolgirl possessed with telekinetic powers in director Brian de Palma's film *Carrie* (1976), or in the crazed husband in a hotel closed and snowbound for the winter in another Stephen King tale, *The Shining* (1980), masterfully directed by Stanley Kubrick. Horrible conflicts could occur with supernatural monsters as in *Alien* (1979) necessitating a superhuman power or effort to destroy the threatening evil. Roman Polanski's *Rosemary's Baby* (1968) dared to show the struggle of a young pregnant woman against witches and the forces of the devil, culminating in her delivery and mothering of the devil's child. Some of the better devil-possession sequels include: *The Omen* (1976), *The Amityville Horror* (1979), and *Poltergeist* (1982).

The horror genre has recently been subject to violence, sadism, brutality, victims of possession, and blood-and-gore tales. Some of the most effective box-office successes include George Romero's unrelenting, low-budget cult classic, *Night of the Living Dead* (1968), the camp classic *It's Alive!* (1974), Tobe Hooper's exploitative cult film, *The Texas Chainsaw Massacre* (1974), the manipulative *The Exorcist* (1973) with a devil-possessed young girl, *Halloween* (1978), Brian DePalma's suspenseful, Hitchcock-like *Dressed to Kill* (1980), *Friday the 13th* (1980) (which produced seven more sequels), and Wes Craven's *A Nightmare on Elm Street* (1985). Many of these films told tales of a vengeful murderer motivated by some past misdeed or sexual perversity. [19]

These successful horror films spawned many inferior, sickening slasher films which highlight shock, violence, and usually a homicidal male psycho who commits a string of gruesome murders of female victims (where brutal killing/slashing/hacking metaphorically substitutes for a rape). Examples include *Mother's Day* (1980), *Motel Hell* (1980), *Prom Night* (1980), *He Knows You're Alone* (1981), *I Spit On Your Grave* (1981), *My Bloody Valentine* (1981), the comedy parody *Student Bodies* (1981), *Sorority House Massacre* (1986), and all the *Halloween*, *Poltergeist*, and *A Nightmare on Elm Street* sequels. [20]

SELECTION OF GREATEST HORROR FILMS
GREATEST EARLY CLASSIC HORROR FILMS:
The Phantom of the Opera (1925)
Dracula (1931)
Frankenstein (1931)
Dr. Jekyll and Mr. Hyde (1932)
Freaks (1932)
The Mummy (1932)

The Old Dark House (1932)
White Zombie (1932)
The Invisible Man (1933)
King Kong (1933)
The Black Cat (1934)
Bride of Frankenstein (1935)
The Hunchback of Notre Dame (1939)

OTHER GREATEST HORROR FILMS:
The Wolf Man (1941)
The Cat People (1942)
I Walked With a Zombie (1943)
Phantom of the Opera (1943)
The Uninvited (1944)
The Body Snatcher (1945)
The Picture of Dorian Gray (1945)
The Thing (From Another World) (1951)
House of Wax (1953)
Creature From the Black Lagoon (1954)
The Night of the Hunter (1955)
Invasion of the Body Snatchers (1956)
The Fly (1958)
Psycho (1960)
The Innocents (1961)
What Ever Happened to Baby Jane? (1962)
The Birds (1963)
The Haunting (1963)
Repulsion (1965)
Night of the Living Dead (1968)
Rosemary's Baby (1968)
The Exorcist (1973)
It's Alive! (1974)
The Texas Chainsaw Massacre (1974)
Jaws (1975)
Carrie (1976)
Halloween (1978)
Alien (1979)
Dressed to Kill (1980)
Friday the 13th (1980)
The Shining (1980)
The Howling (1981)
The Evil Dead (1982)
Poltergeist (1982)
Gremlins (1984)
A Nightmare on Elm Street (1985)
The Fly (1986)
Evil Dead 2: Dead by Dawn (1987)
Beetlejuice (1988)
Misery (1990)
The People Under the Stairs (1991)
Buffy the Vampire Slayer (1992)
Body Snatchers (1994)
Scream (1996)

■ ■ ■

Review Questions

1. How do science fiction films differ from horror films, according to Dirks?
2. What is the literary origin of the horror film genre?

Discussion and Writing Suggestions

1. In the first part of his discussion, Dirks focuses on the power of horror films to both frighten and entertain us. "They deal with our most primal nature and its fears," he writes, "our vulnerability, our alienation, our terror of the unknown, our fear of death, loss of identity, or fear of sexuality." To what extent does this conclusion—and other parts of Dirks's discussion—accurately describe your own experience with horror films? Refer to particular films and particular scenes in these films, and explain how they derive their power.
2. Select one or two films that did not make Dirks's list of great horror films (or which were made too recently to make the list) and explain why you believe they should be added to the list. What, in your view, makes a great horror film—as opposed to a merely good or competent one? As an alternative to this assignment, select one or two films that did make Dirks's list, but shouldn't have, in your opinion. Explain your reasoning.
3. Rent and view one of the films listed as a classic by Dirks. Then, critically review it, focusing in particular upon how it works (or does not work) its power. Try to cast your discussion in the terms used by Dirks in the first three paragraphs of his essay. For example, what kind of "vulnerabilities" in us does a film such as *Invasion of the Body Snatchers* or *The Fly* target? How does a film such as *Rosemary's Baby* tap into "the horror within man himself"?

The Nightmare World

STANLEY J. SOLOMON

In "The Nightmare World," Stanley J. Solomon defines the horror film as a safe environment in which to confront the violence and fear that pervade our lives. A film scholar and professor of English, Solomon provides a careful overview of the horror genre, defining its principal elements and distinguishing it from science fiction cinema—with which it shares some similarities. Like Stephen King and others in this chapter, though from an entirely different perspective, Solomon speaks to the dueling impulses in each of us. Horror movies give us a chance to recognize these impulses; in The Wolf Man, *for instance, we see ourselves in the character who, on the rising of the full moon, becomes a werewolf. This selection appeared originally in Solomon's book-length study of cinema,* Beyond Formula: American Film Genres *(1976).*

[T]he horror genre, ultimately, is a major genre because major artists of our   1
time have worked seriously in it and produced notable films that range beyond the depiction of the horrific event to probe the nightmare world hidden in all of us. The conjuring up of monsters of the mind and the objectifying of them in the cinema is a symbolic form of exorcism, which very likely the general public intuitively grasped from the genre long before William Friedkin's *The Exorcist* (1973) popularized the subject. In an era that intellectually gives little credence to devils, witches, and monsters, but lives continuously with massive violence, perversion, and nihilism, the horror film provides us with a protected access to a nightmare world otherwise shunted outside of civilization by the twentieth-century forces of sophistication, science, and sociology.

The cinema of horror concretizes this nightmare world—our abstract fears   2
of destruction and death. The midnight visits of vampires, the laboratory-induced reincarnations, the skull deformities, the murders in the fog—these visual images of the genre may be the symbols of our fears rather than the psychological source of them, but terror without a body is terror deprived of a means of menacing us. Nevertheless, it is lamentable that along with the whole modern movement toward cinematic explicitness in all genres, the horror genre should in recent years have lost much of its suggestive power. The giant shark rising from the ocean in Steven Spielberg's *Jaws* (1975) is merely a familiar creature of the sea, and the havoc it creates confined to the physical world and subject to the laws of nature; it will not leave the beach with us. In contrast, Carl Dreyer's Danish film *Vampyr* (1932), a tour de force of implicit horror, seems only a remote ancestor of the blood-lust films of the seventies. However, the genre is still open to creative talents who can give form to the explicit materials demanded by producers for financial success, and still suggest the unlimited terrors lurking in the recesses of our nightmare world.

If the depiction of archetypal fears is one aspect of the genre, the process   3
whereby these fears become dramatic incidents in a film reveals at least two other genre traits: the degree of unpreparedness on the part of the endangered victim, and the vitality or strength of the source of horror. The source is never, for instance, merely a human murderer. It may turn out to be so later in the film, but when it strikes, it is either supernaturally empowered (psychotics always have great energy in the cinema and usually the strength of several men), or simply a supernatural creature, a Frankenstein monster, a zombie, an immortal force likely to return for another killing (or worse, a film sequel). As for the characteristic of unpreparedness, Hitchcock[1] himself has elaborated on

---

[1] *Hitchcock:* Alfred Hitchcock (1899–1980), the "master of suspense" who directed such film classics as *The Lady Vanishes* (1938), *Notorious* (1946), *Strangers on a Train* (1951), *North by Northwest* (1957), *Vertigo* (1958), *Psycho* (1960), and *Frenzy* (1972).

the distinction between the kind of suddenness typical of ordinary films and his own brand of suspense, which plays on the gradual development of the potential horror in a situation—known to the audience, but beyond the film character's awareness. And certainly Hitchcock is right in the psychological sense, as well as in the esthetic sense: murder in a dark alley, which he has often discounted, is less effective than murder in a crowded, well-lit U.N. Building. But even so, we will always have ordinary films with us, and if film-makers cannot pull off the Master's style of suspense, mere shock will be used instead. Often the duration of an incident designed to shock is prolonged fool-ishly past the point where the audience fully expects it; for example, the never-exhausted use of the situation of the innocent young woman exploring the darkened, murder-filled house (which originated in the eighteenth-century gothic novel in England and was so overused even then that Jane Austen, in the 1790s, wrote one of her early novels parodying it). In such sequences our common sense tells us of the immediate danger of which the woman seems entirely unaware.

It is worth reflecting on the motif of exploration in the house of horrors.   4
There are two types of exploration in such situations; one is the relatively log-ical procedure involved when the searcher does not know that some horror is lurking in the house. In this aspect of the search motif, the levels of irony rein-force the element of terror in the sequence. A second type of exploration far more common in the genre occurs when the character actually is aware of great danger, even when the threat is ambiguous. This intrusion into the haunted house by a fearful yet determined figure, often a defenseless woman, almost always establishes an identity between the searcher and the audience; we may not know exactly what evil will befall the searcher, but we sympa-thize with him or her at each turn of the perilous corridors and at the open-ing of each squeaking door (in many low budget horror films, one can of oil would convert all the eccentric mansions into normal houses).

Yet if we sympathize with the irrational pursuit of the nightmare—when   5
a telephone call to the police station or waiting until daylight would diffuse the inherent terror of the place—what does this say about our own involve-ment in the situation? It does not seem to be some insatiable curiosity, for that could be satisfied by the characters' examining the threatening situation.

It seems that as frightened as we are of the dark horrors ahead of the   6
searcher, we must force ourselves to explore them, to continue on toward that confrontation with whatever ultimate form the nightmare can take. But it perhaps goes even further than that. The final horror is extremely limited in its possibilities. And do we not know in advance what the worst of these pos-sibilities are? An unusually brutal man, halfman, or full monster with a knife, either lunging at our back or jumping from the shadows at our face. There are some other alternatives, ghosts of indescribable forms, but essentially, for the horror to be as unbearable as we hope it is when we purchase our tickets, it has to represent death—the death of the searcher, and indeed the death of our surrogate self. Perhaps the ultimate irrationality of this typical moment of horror in the nightmare film represents our own subconscious desire to con-front our inevitable dread: to meet death before we really die. Or looked at

another way, such moments of horror are cathartic, symbolic suicides, speaking directly to our hidden wish to attempt everything and to survive unaltered, to get murdered without being murdered.

THE CINEMA OF REASON AND NIGHTMARE

The nightmare world, with which we all have a personal and very private   7
acquaintance, derives from the suppressed fears within every individual and differs for each of us, at least in its details. Some very clever illustrators and makeup artists design movie monsters that are effective in capturing some universal idea of horror but of course strike us as original all the same. A monster readily visualized by everyone is probably not very monstrous, though there do seem to be a few images derived from certain real "monstrosities" that have permeated the unconsciousness of the human race (prehistoric animals and huge spiders, rats, bats, roaches, and so on). Nevertheless, the depiction of the horrific represents a major challenge to filmmakers, for by its nature the cinema objectifies and externalizes abstract concepts so that they take on a visual embodiment. If the horror film is to succeed, some care must be taken that the essence of whatever is supposed to be the horrible object remains suggestively terrifying. A monster once seen becomes rather quickly assimilable into the environment of the film and correspondingly less intimidating. Its mere physical appearance will not do for long.

This is the basic reason for the lack of success of so many films that con-   8
cern the threat of some outside force such as a monster or a creature from another planet. Once the force is visualized, we feel that it then can be handled and destroyed sooner or later, and during the process the threat loses its initial impact. Science fiction films differ from true horror films, though they both frequently employ monsters, in that the implicit danger in the former is supposed to originate in the outer world and to be dealt with accordingly, whereas the dangers in the world of the horror film are symbols of our nightmares, projections of our inner reality—even though the necessity of the cinematic form requires, in most cases, some overtly corporeal menace. The horror film aims at psychological effects, the science fiction film at logical possibilities. Many aspects of both genres overlap, certainly, since the minor examples of both aim for sensational depictions of terror with little regard for the sense of good science fiction or the sensibility of the real horror film.

When worked out properly, the science fiction film is premised on   9
people's ability to handle things that intrude into their comfortable physical reality. For example, in the Howard Hawks-Christian Nyby science fiction film *The Thing* (1951), the strange vegetable monster is destroyed by electrocution (that is, it is fried), and even though the film ends with a warning that earth may be repeatedly invaded by other monsters or civilizations, we can hardly worry about that possibility as long as we have electricity. But in the nightmare world, dreams recur; fears sometimes take on new shapes but seldom disappear entirely (if they did, so would the practice of psychiatry). The stake is inevitably thrust into Dracula's heart—over and over again. Dracula returns, not merely for crass commercial reasons, but because he has

become rooted in the psychology of modern moviegoing society. The monsters that spring from our own psyche are either the zombies we constantly recreate or symbolic archetypal figures of evil. At the end of a science fiction film, order is restored—the spaceship crew or earth itself is saved, permanently. When we awaken from the nightmare world, we have only a temporary reprieve; another dream may follow on the next night. In that case, all that has happened has been an evaporation of a monster, which simply returns to its spiritual or disembodied form, to be picked up by our brainwaves and re-embodied sometime in another film.

The nightmare genre is thus not entirely suited to rational explanations, 10 since its primary thrust is toward the exploration of emotional states—horror and the more or less irrational response to it. If the source of the horror were itself entirely rational (for instance, an escaped lion on a city street), an irrational response to it would reveal no more than outrage or cowardice, but rational plot patterns run counter to the basics of the genre. It is necessary, in those horror films where at least a rational explanation is offered, to postpone that logical moment until all the usual effects of the genre have been achieved. But it is not at all necessary—though it usually does happen—that the source of the horror be logically categorized by the end of the film. The critical dumbfoundedness that greeted Hitchcock's *The Birds* (1963) resulted from the filmmaker's failure to provide any ultimate explanation of the bird attacks. Had Hitchcock been working in the realm of science fiction, some explanation would have been needed to finish the film, but such a requirement is irrelevant to the horror genre, even if it could have been supplied. Hitchcock reveals no interest in how the situation came about; what matters is the depiction of the rebellion of birds, a usually pleasant aspect of nature. Surely this is not a sensible theme for us to ponder in the way that we might ponder the possibilities of an invasion of flying saucers. We might be invaded by inhabitants of another planet—that is within the realm of scientific possibility; but to speculate about disruptions of nature is to engage in nightmares with an unlimited scope of possibilities beyond the laws of science and the evidence of our senses. *The Birds* is a masterpiece of another type, a probing into the response of various people to a reversal of the natural order. It is beyond the issue of plausibility.

ROMANTIC ISOLATION

Eventually the zombies of the mind can be battered down, and if not perma- 11 nently laid to rest, at least buried in crypts that might remain sealed for decades to come. But there are other fears engendered by the horror genre that do not readily subside because they are by nature nothing more than an extension or alteration of the hero. This type of horror film usually gains its peculiar effectiveness by making the hero into a monster and eventually leading us to relate to the monstrous condition, which points toward the hero's inevitable doom. This type of film relies almost equally on our underlying pity as well as on our usual fears.

The werewolf is perhaps the best representative of this ambivalent placing   12
of the beast within the body of the hero, though the actual American appearances of the character have not been notably successful (such as Stuart Walker's
The Werewolf of London [1935], George Wagner's *The Wolf Man* [1941], Eric
Kenton's *House of Frankenstein* [1944]). The werewolf, a good man who
turns periodically into a creature of violence, cannot prevent himself from
killing when, under the influence of the full moon, he becomes a huge deadly
wolf. Considered from a psychological perspective, the werewolf is just the
archetypal schizophrenic man, with uncontrollable impulses toward evil. We
share with him these impulses, but watching him on screen we undergo a
purgative experience as he acts out for us the process of inevitable doom await-
ing the person who loses control, who destroys in a moment of madness or passion. He is a cousin to Dr. Jekyll, the difference typically being that the doctor
(that is, the mad scientist) willingly brings about his own downfall by his over-
weening scientific pride or curiosity. Turning into Mr. Hyde, he becomes temporarily a mad monster, his lucidity restored for shorter and shorter lengths of
time when he can revert to his normal self. The Jekyll-Hyde category of the
horror genre is rich in attempts to devise new insights into this simple Robert
Louis Stevenson story of the split personality within all of us, and it has attracted filmmakers from Jean Renoir to Jerry Lewis.

Werewolves and Hydes are also related to a larger group of horror   13
films that deal with the obsessed maniac, but in most cases the maniac is so
depraved we cannot identify with him. Psychotic killers can hardly be
expected to pass as acceptable members of society even when their need to
kill has been temporarily satisfied. For this reason, the werewolf turned
back into his normal self, the urbane Count Dracula (in the daytime) and
Dr. Jekyll, are far more frightening figures of the nightmare world than their
more realistic kin, the diabolical murderer. Although the monster may have
chemical or physiological causes for his murders, we can often interpret his
motives as a kind of temporary insanity, though not in the legal sense. On the
surface he murders because as a monster he has to, but on another level—
not really a disguised level either—he kills because he finds it gratifying. We
in the audience never yield to the equivalent temptation, yet we note how
often the first murder committed on screen is against a somewhat unsym-
pathetic character. Viewers are thus led toward plausible identification with
the monster, even though as the crimes increase all pretense toward moral
sympathy on a rational plane disappears. We remain horrified, but we persist in feeling sympathetic toward the monster as he succumbs to his terrifying worse self.

In a relatively few but memorable instances, the nightmare genre has been   14
able to achieve a sense of the pathetic as strong or stronger than a sense of the
terrifying. It might seem that the combination of pathos and horror would not
work, but we should remember that the genre as we know it today derives
from a branch of nineteenth-century literary romanticism that was much
more at home with pathos than with horror. The theme of the savage or misfit
or monster in romantic literature is not easily duplicated in film today because
the physical appearance of the movie monster would probably need to be

toned down to generate sympathy, thereby becoming more human and less horrible. Nevertheless, the existence of some classic portrayals of pathetic monsters indicates that the nightmare world is much broader and more complex than it appears in the majority of its films which present a horror lurking somewhere "out there." Watching Dr. Frankenstein's laboratory-created monster, the audience identifies with the pursued creature driven to destruction by a frenzied mob.

James Whale's *Frankenstein* (1931) is usually among the first films that   15
come to mind when this aspect of the genre is discussed, along with his *The Bride of Frankenstein* (1935), Tod Browning's *Dracula* (1930), Ernest Schoedsack and Merian C. Cooper's *King Kong* (1933), and a number of other masterful contributions of the 1930s. *Frankenstein* is one of the most romantic films Hollywood ever turned out, and Whale might well have achieved major status as a filmmaker had he directed films with more normal, respectable surfaces. But below the surface of Whale's expressionistic fantasies, yet there in the most palpable way, are the themes of isolation and the desire to be loved, material that often seems the stuff of films that have greater pretensions to art, though few films of the era had greater claims to cinematic art. Boris Karloff's impersonation of the monster is so filled with humanity that despite the creature's clumsiness and a temper readily provoked to violence, there is no point at which we do not feel for the monster and oppose his persecutors, the townspeople, who in their uncomprehending fear chase and destroy the creature without communicating with him or learning of his gigantic potential for goodness. Though unnamed in the film, the monster has been from that time on named after his creator, Dr. Frankenstein, by the general public. The banal framing story of the overambitious scientist creating a living thing that goes out of control, escapes, and in various ways punishes the scientist for trying to be a god, was less important than the brief biography of the monster. Left to himself, the monster seeks only to establish some human contact—that is, to be loved on the level of his understanding, which is that of a big pet dog. He is, for thematic purposes, less the creation of the laboratory than the "natural man," a large, lumbering animal that fights only when he is cornered or tormented. He cannot speak in the film, though he learns to do so in the sequel, *The Bride of Frankenstein*. In the latter film he finally forms his sole friendship—with a blind hermit—though that too is doomed by interlopers who represent society and civilization. But for most of both films, the monster himself is the most frightened character.

With *Frankenstein* the motif of romantic isolation almost immediately   16
became a dominant influence in the development of the genre—though it had appeared in at least one classic instance as early as 1925 in Rupert Julian's *Phantom of the Opera*. In this film the disfigured madman lives a subterranean existence because of his terrifying face, emerging only because he has fallen in love with a woman he determines to abduct. After *Frankenstein*, numerous films depicted humans or monsters isolated in an alien environment, though the motives for that existence varied with the horror figure's degree of intelligence. In 1933, for example, *King Kong* followed directly the *Frankenstein* pattern of an innocent creature destroyed by a world that will

not respond with understanding at a moment of implicit danger. In the same year, Whale turned out another classic of the genre in *The Invisible Man*, which features a scientist who has taken a drug that produces not only his invisibility but a growing insanity that leads him to try to conquer the world. And in Michael Curtiz's *Mystery of the Wax Museum* (1933) we find another sort of archetypal figure of romantic isolation: the artist. In this case, the artist has been driven insane by a fire that ruined his wax statues and made his face hideous. Designing a mask for himself, he is able to exist within society in an outwardly unremarkable way, but nursing a desire for revenge and committing murders; he is a variant on both the *Phantom of the Opera* motif and the Jekyll-Hyde split personality.

■ ■ ■

Review Questions

1. Reread the selection's first paragraph and identify Solomon's thesis, or claim. Paraphrase this sentence.
2. Identify three traits of the horror film genre.
3. "It seems that as frightened as we are of the dark horrors ahead of the searcher, we must force ourselves to explore them." What two reasons does Solomon offer for our desire to search (as the character in the film searches) the haunted house?
4. What qualities must a monster maintain, once it is shown on the screen, if it is to remain horrifying?
5. What is the key difference between a science fiction movie and a horror movie, according to Solomon?
6. Solomon calls the werewolf "the archetypal schizophrenic man" in whose downfall we (ordinary theater goers) find a "purgative experience." What does Solomon mean, and how is the werewolf related to Dr. Jekyll and Mr. Hyde?
7. Why are movie monsters of the werewolf/Dracula/Jekyll-Hyde type more sympathetic to us than movies about psychotic killers?

Discussion and Writing Suggestions

1. Discuss Solomon's assertion that our era gives "little credence to devils, witches, and monsters, but lives continuously with massive violence, perversion, and nihilism." First, do you agree with his assessment about our era? Solomon means to contrast, or set up a tension between, our apparent disbelief in devils (for instance) and our daily exposure to violence. Explain this contrast or tension.
2. Solomon suggests that the horror film's objectifying—making objects out of—our inner demons on the screen "exorcises" these demons. What is your experience in watching horror films? Do you feel in any way relieved on leaving?

3. Think of a horror film you've seen—one that scared you. Was there a "search" scene, in which the main character must search through a haunted house (ship, hotel, . . .)? What was the search scene's effect on you? If the search made you tense, why did you watch? (Does Solomon's explanation—see Review Question #3, above—satisfy you?)

4. Solomon suggests that we all have suppressed fears that give rise to a "nightmare" world and, moreover, that this nightmare world is highly specific: different people are horrified by different thoughts and images. Is this generalization true for you?

5. Recall a horror movie that, momentarily at least, terrified you. What, in fact, was so terrifying about the monster? How well does Solomon's account of how horror movies affect us explain your reactions to the movie? For instance, in retrospect, did you find that the movie in any way gave you "protected access to a nightmare world otherwise shunted outside of civilization"?

6. What is your reaction to the serious study of horror films as a genre, or distinctive type of film? Solomon, for instance, is a scholar of the horror genre, as are many others who write articles and books. To what extent, in your view, do horror movies justify such scholarly attention? Is there in these movies the substance needed for serious study?

7. Solomon asserts that we identify with the werewolf and with the Jekyll/Hyde character. Do you find these movie monsters sympathetic? Why?

Blowing the Lid Off the Id

HARVEY GREENBERG

As a psychoanalyst, Harvey Greenberg attributes outward behavior and feelings to interior states. The view that there are subconscious and unconscious aspects to personality that determine conscious thought and action derives, in modern times, from Sigmund Freud. Freud believed in mental processes that are not directly accessible to consciousness. Some of these mental processes are instincts, urges, or desires (the "id") that have been repressed from the conscious mind (the "ego") by the "censor" (the "superego") because they are shameful or antisocial. It is in this Freudian context that Greenberg writes of horror movies "Blowing the Lid Off the Id"—of giving direct access, at least during the course of a particular movie, to our usually repressed and shameful impulses.

Here, Greenberg applies the principles of psychoanalysis (which he does for a living in New York City) not to human patients but to an artifact of human culture: movies—and, in this section of his book Movies on Your Mind *(1975), the horror film. Greenberg writes of interior "beasts" just as others do in this chapter. As you contemplate the connections among the chapter's fiction writers (Carter, King, and Stevenson), the film historian and theorist (Solomon), the historian (Salisbury), the various film critics, and the psychoanalyst (Greenberg), you might ask: are the interior states—the beasts—that these writers describe identical? Do you recognize these states in yourself? in others? Are these interior states elements of human personality that we can even acknowledge consciously?*

When he heard I wanted to become a psychoanalyst, an old general practitioner vehemently warned—"Son, stay away from the crap—when you stir a stink, all you get is a bigger stink!" The ancient injunction against stirring up the seething cauldron of the unconscious (cf., Pandora, Oedipus and other mythic meddlers with the psychic peace) rests squarely upon the anxiety we feel before the often alarming strength of our own emotions.   1

It is written that in a certain African tribe, when an individual falls ill, his relatives and friends are forced on pain of death to reveal their dreams to the shaman. If evil intent towards the afflicted one be discerned therein, the dreamer is labeled a witch, and cast out into the wilderness. To the primitive, the child and many neurotics, intense aggressive and sexual feelings are particularly reprehensible, carrying as much weight as an actual criminal deed such feelings might motivate, and laying the guilty party open to the retribution of the gods, the tribal Judges, or the remorseless Superego.   2

We are repeatedly admonished in weird cinema that even the gentlest of men may bare fangs and bay at the moon when his passions are kindled. The movie monster thus represents the destructive forces unleashed when reason and civilized morality are overthrown by our unruly instincts. The mutable lycanthrope is but another version of Hobbesian man, the naked ape bellowing in the wilderness, Fred C. Dobbs[1] in Wolf Man's Clothing!   3

Weird cinema often lays the blame for blowing the lid off the Id within the unquiet spirit of the candidate for monsterdom, and/or upon malignant outside spirits. . . . The heroine of Val Lewton's 1942 film *Cat People* (played by the memorably feline Simone Simon) has emigrated from her obscurely Transylvanian origins. She marries an apple-pie and ice-cream American oaf; when her husband develops an "innocent" relationship with a female coworker as square as he, her jealousy turns into rank paranoia, and she turns into a panther. The film is noteworthy for its xenophobia: we are led to believe that hubby bedded an alluring pussycat from across the sea, and got a tiger in his tank[2] instead.   4

---

[1] *Fred C. Dobbs:* The prospector (portrayed by Humphrey Bogart) in John Huston's *Treasure of the Sierra Madre* (1948), who, after finding gold in the mountains of Mexico, becomes crazed with greed and murderous paranoia as he suspects his partners of trying to rob him.

[2] *tiger in his tank:* In the 1960s, an ad campaign by Exxon Oil featured a cartoon "tiger in your tank" to dramatize the power of its gasoline.

On closer scrutiny, the husband proves far from innocent. He provokes   5
the incipient cat lady with stinging allusions to the charm and competence of
his "pal," while the latter, despite her demonstrations of queasy solicitude
about her rival's tenuous emotional state, is palpably out to break up the marriage. Hollywood's characteristic disguise of an immoral reality places the
responsibility for infidelity, seduction and the taunting unto madness of a vulnerable waif upon the festering rage of the attained foreigner.[3]

In Universal's *The Wolf Man* (1941), another guiltless *naif*, Lawrence   6
Talbott, loses his humanity with the eruption of his jealousy. Like the cat-
woman, Talbott is a rejected outsider, returning to the English village of his
birth after years of self-imposed exile (never explained) in America. He is
called back by his aristocrat father after his obviously preferred older brother's death. The cruel father treats him like Cain, with ill-disguised hostility
even after their formal reconciliation.

While wandering on the moors, Talbott slays a werewolf, but is bitten in   7
the fight. Later, at a village carnival, he meets the young woman he has been
wooing unsuccessfully, with her fiancé. The two men compete at a shooting
gallery. Talbott performs well until he freezes at the toy image of a wolf. His
adversary contemptuously blasts it down. "You win," Talbott groans.
Subsequently he catches the girl alone, tries clumsily to tell her of his love. She
rebuffs him, and directly thereafter he changes into a werewolf, howling out
his pain on the lonely moors. Talbott has lost an implicit Oedipal battle—the
Oedipal motif appears virtually undisguised later in the film, when the father,
after persistently denying his son's lycanthropy, is responsible for Talbott's
escape. Father then encounters son changed to Wolf Man, about to assault his
lost love on the moor. The father kills him with the same silver-headed cane
which Talbott wielded against the werewolf that infected him! (I shall have
more to say about the monster as adolescent Oedipus presently.)

The Pandora's box of the unconscious is frequently opened by the "mad"   8
scientist, a misguided humanitarian or a demented egomaniac seeking
vengeance against the world that has derided his genius. By tampering with
the natural order, the good/bad doctor inadvertently releases the Id-monster
within himself, like Dr. Henry Jekyll (*Dr. Jekyll and Mr. Hyde*), Dr. Janos
Rukh (*The Invisible Ray*), or Dr. Morbius (*Forbidden Planet*).

Dr. Jekyll and Mr. Hyde has been brought to the screen more often than   9
any other weird tale. The persona of Jekyll actually changes little from one

---

[3] Which does not, of course, diminish *Cat People's* shock value. Lewton was one of those
gifted directors who could scare an audience witless by altering the substance of the ordinary into pure menace. Take the famous sequence in which the heroine changes into her
panther persona at a hotel swimming pool, where the other woman treads water, alone and
achingly vulnerable. The quiet lapping of the wavelets, the confused lights, shadows and
echoes rebounding off the tiled walls combine to produce an atmosphere of exceptional dis-
quiet. One longs for this subtlety at a time when the horror film, caught up in pervasive cinematic sadism, so frequently leaves the sensibilities glutted with gory surfeit. [Greenberg]

film to the next: thoroughly dedicated, genteel and priggish, Jekyll remains the essence of the repressed Victorian. But Hyde's gargantuan appetite for evil has elicited a wider range of interpretation: it is, once again, the old story of Lucifer being more interesting than God! The rarely exhibited Rouben Mamoulian version (1932) remains the favorite of most critics, myself included. The fabulous transformation scene, to the accompaniment of Mamoulian's own recorded muffled heartbeat, has never been equalled. The director steadfastly refused to reveal the lighting and makeup effects that turned Frederic March's handsome features into a brutish parody of humanity. I prize the film especially for its tasteful, yet pointed evocation of Hyde's exuberant carnality (elsewhere it is Hyde's non-sexual sadism that is emphasized). Violence and eroticism are skillfully blended when Hyde lures a young barmaid into his web, goads her into a frenzy of lubricious terror, then strangles her off-camera in what is clearly intended to be an orgiastic substitute.

In Universal's *The Invisible Ray* (1933) a latter-day Jekyll, Dr. Janos   10
Rukh (Boris Karloff out of monster drag) ignores his beautiful young wife to search for "Radium X," a meteoric element with mysterious curative powers thought to have fallen to earth eons ago. Rukh recovers the lost substance in Africa, but after exposure to its intense radioactivity, develops the ability to kill at a touch or a glance. He drops out of sight and is presumed dead. Within a few years a colleague has mastered the dangers of Radium X, reaps fame and honor, while Rukh's wife falls in love with a younger man. Then Rukh resurfaces; the radioactivity seething in his brain has driven him mad, and he commences murdering everyone connected with his humiliation. Before he can kill his wife and complete the cycle of his vengeance, his strength ebbs. His older mother crushes the vial containing the antiserum that maintains his fragile hold on life, and the glowing Rukh hurls himself out a window, to be instantly reduced to ashes by the unchecked poison raging within him.

In real life, no Radium X would be required to catalyze Rukh's obses-   11
sional tendencies into a full-blown paranoid state. I have elsewhere indicated that paranoids often provoke the very maltreatment and rejection they fear. The clinician marks Rukh as chronically afraid of closeness, more at home with his grandiose fantasies than the small pleasures of genuine intimacy. Men like Rukh often sicken in their declining years, when the earlier promise of success has not been fulfilled, and death no longer seems a distance possibility. They drive themselves into emotional exile, thrusting away those who might love them with their coldness, nagging and jealous tantrums. Like Rukh, they end up as mad isolates, consumed by bitterness and envy. One notes that Rukh's mother is his executioner. She reproaches him for his misdeeds and failures, and the film implies that she has a legitimate right to do so: actually, the mothers of these obsessional-paranoid types are wont to blame and shame their sons to death with no justification save their own rancor.

As Hyde is to Jekyll, so the radioactive Rukh is to his former rational self.   12
Either the mad scientist converts his ego into the horrid image of his lustful, envious Id, or he constructs a fearful projection of his "monstrous" desires

and sets it loose to burn and pillage, often consciously unaware that the monster is the agent of his repressed wishes. The monster may thus be likened to the delinquent who is covertly encouraged to act out one parent or another's unconscious antisocial impulses. The parent in these cases has *superego lacunae*, i.e., a conscience as full of holes as a Swiss cheese. The adult projects his or her disavowed criminality upon the child, who can then be "safely" labeled as the bad seed! While the law may fail to recognize this subtle brand of complicity, at least in the movies the chickens always come home to roost. However noble or craven his conscious motivation, the mad scientist's complicity in the misdeeds of this "offspring" is acknowledged and punished when monster turns upon master and destroys both.

The mad scientist's Id-monster usually appears disguised in fur and claws   13
or encased in metal, but there is one remarkable film in which the Freudian Id itself is the Technicolor monster bred out of is creator's bad dreams—MGM's 1956 science fiction extravaganza, *Forbidden Planet.*

An interstellar space ship lands on the planet Altair IV to recover sur-   14
vivors of an ill-fated colonizing expedition. Only two of the original group remain: Morbius, a philologist of formidable intellect, and his naive, overripe daughter, Altaira. Morbius explains to the intrepid Commander John Adams that he and his family care to cherish life on Altair IV, whereas the other members of the expedition could not adjust, and were either torn limb from limb by an invisible monster that prowled the night, or were vaporized with their ship on lift-off after they were unable to persuade Morbius to leave. Since then, Morbius' wife died of natural causes, he and his daughter have lived unmolested for nearly twenty years—"yet always in my mind, I seem to feel the creature is lurking somewhere close, sly and irresistible. . . ." Morbius refuses to disclose the nature of his studies on Altair IV, but he has surrounded himself with technological marvels that are obviously beyond the competence of a linguist.

He warns his would-be rescuers to go before they, too, suffer the fate of   15
his companions. Commander Adams senses something amiss, and refuses to depart. That night his ship is invaded and disabled by the planet's reawakened invisible menace. Altaira develops a crush on the handsome commander who, in the tradition of Space Opera is irritated at her innocent provocation of his men with her lush endowments until he himself takes the fall.

Morbius is pressured to reveal the secret of the forbidden planet to   16
Adams and the eggheaded ship's doctor. Millennia ago, Altair IV was the seat of a great culture—the Krel, vastly superior to man in every way. Having vanquished crime and disease, they stood poised "on the threshold of some supreme accomplishment which was to have crowned their entire history." Then, "this all but divine race perished in a single night," leaving as enigmatic legacy an enormous web of underground machinery, still monitoring and maintaining itself after 200,000 years!

With his knowledge of linguistics and an electronic I.Q. boost from the   17
Krel "plastic educator," Morbius acquired the barest fraction of their wisdom, but enough to become a scientific wizard and also inflate his ego

beyond mortal bounds. He proposes to release the results of his research in his own godlike good time. Adams objects that mankind is entitled to the Krel data without Morbius' regency. As Morbius waxes angrier at his daughter's infatuation and the intruders' insistence that he return to Earth, the depredations of the invisible monster escalate; during one attack, Morbius is discovered stirring in a troubled slumber at his desk (Morbius = Morpheus!) while the Krel machinery registers an astronomical power drain. Here is the only instance when *Forbidden Planet*'s impressive special effects falter by violating a central canon of weird cinema—never show the audience too much. Caught in the beams of the spacemens' blasters, the Id-monster looks like a cartoon fugitive from Disneyland. Better to have left it forever unseen![4]

18   The egghead doctor slips into the Krel laboratory, and uses the plastic educator to match his wits with Morbius. He is mortally injured, but manages to warn Adams before he dies: ". . . the big machine . . . no instrumentality, true creation, but the Krel forgot one thing . . . monsters, John, monsters from the Id!" And Adams realizes that *Morbius* is the predator of the forbidden planet! The Krel machine enabled that proud race to transcend the need for physical tools, to change thought instantly into force and matter. But just as the benevolent ego of each Krel was linked to their fantastic creation, so was the Id of each, with its primitive lust and hatred. In one night, every Id-monster of the Krel summoned up the machine's illimitable power, and the race literally self-destructed.

19   But still the machine carried on. Morbius unwittingly entered into the mindlock that had blown the lid off the collective Id of the Krel. While he slept, Morbius' Id savaged his companions because they wanted him to leave Altair IV. And twenty years later, he has sent out his inner beast against Adams, his crew, yes, even his daughter when she throws in her lot with the spacemen. In one stroke, the "mindless primitive" of the lofty-minded

---

[4] The naked face of Thanatos is best revealed sparingly. Like the dim member of repressed trauma, that which is most frightening is likely to be half-glimpsed, seized and reinvented by each viewer's uniquely personal intuition of doom, like the room in Orwell's *1984* where political prisoners were confronted with their most private fears of death. Indeed, what made the great radio horror shows so much more terrifying than the average horror flick was precisely that so much was left to the febrile imagination. I still can remember an episode of Arch Obler's *Lights Out!*, in which a giant chicken heart was swallowing up New York. The announcer yelled that it was sprouting tentacles. *Tentacles*, for God's sake!! I didn't know what they were, but trying to screw up the mind's eye to get a better look scared me out of my eighth year's growth!

Laughter is a necessary ingredient of the horror experience, but it must be carefully mixed with fear. Jury-rigged horror, like the Mexican vampire cheapies that starred popular wrestlers, or the Disneyesque Id-demon of *Forbidden Planet*, ridiculously displays its seams and stitches, and the willing suspension of disbelief is itself suspended. On the other hand, horror beyond psychological tolerance cancels enjoyment and nullifies catharsis. The film becomes a nightmare from which it is impossible to awaken after leaving the safety of the theater, an unmastered trauma that continues to plague the mind. Pictures like *The Exorcist* or *Night of the Living Dead* have been supremely effective in spawning raw panic, but they also irrevocably violate our childlike faith in the movies not to harm us.

Morbius would remove his rival and the source of their rivalry, his own flesh and blood.

At first, Morbius frantically denies what he already partly knows, but as   20
with any hallucinating psychotic, his Id bursts into his waking life. The invisible monster appears outside his citadel, smashes down one supposedly unbreachable defense after another, and begins to melt down the last barrier—"solid Krel metal, twenty-six inches thick!"

"Guilty! Guilty!!" Morbius screams, "My evil self is at that door, and I   21
have no power to stop it! I deny you! I give you up!!" Miraculously, the unseen horror recedes. Morbius is disengaged from the Krel machine. Like Prospero in *The Tempest* (*Forbidden Planet* is often compared with Shakespeare's play), he breaks his staff, buries his book. But like Faustus, that other Promethean overreacher and meddler in dangerous arcana, he must pay a mortal price for his hubris. He has been physically consumed by the gigantic mental effort expended in putting his Superego back on the ascendant. This retelling of Genesis cleaves the figure of our first ancestor in twain: Morbius, eater of the forbidden fruit of the Krel knowledge, must stay behind and die, while Commander Adams(!) will be allowed to quit the tainted Eden of Altair IV.

Morbius bids Adams take his daughter and go in peace. Rather touch-   22
ingly, he calls the Commander "son," acknowledging the psychological basis of their rivalry, and activates an atomic reactor that turns the planet into a supernova after the Earthmen have departed. Watching from deep space, Adam consoles Altaira, his new Eve:

> ADAMS: About a million years from now, the human race will have crawled up to where the Krel stood in their great moment of triumph and tragedy; your father's name will shine again, like a beacon in the galaxy . . . it's true, it will remind us that we are, after all, not gods!

In supernatural cinema, these lines—"there are secrets better for man not   23
to know!"—are usually spoken by an elder scientist surveying the havoc left by the deceased monster. Reminiscent of my old mentor who warned me away from the big stink of psychoanalysis, this venerable antique stands appropriately humbled before the inscrutable turnings of the universe, in contradistinction to his presumptuous younger colleague who has either been killed by his creation or shot down in his Id-disguise to reemerge as his better self after death, like Dr. Jekyll, or Dr. Collins in *The Invisible Man*. But whether the setting be gothic or galactic, the "secrets of nature" pursued by the mad doctor to his inevitable ruin are often metaphors for the turbulent emotions locked within the secret recesses of the troubled heart.

■ ■ ■

Review Questions

1. For Greenberg, the movie monster is not simply a monster but a representation of something inside us. What, for Greenberg, does the movie monster represent?
2. What qualities, both in terms of story line and psychology, do the Cat Woman, the Wolfman, and Dr. Jekyll and Mr. Hyde share, according to Greenberg?
3. Writing in reference to the Id-monster in *Forbidden Planet*, Greenberg offers "a central canon of weird cinema—never show the audience too much." Why offer this so-called rule? To what problem is this rule a response?
4. To what does the "stink" refer in Greenberg's opening paragraph, and what role does this stink play in horror movies?

Discussion and Writing Suggestions

1. What are some of the forces that the individual and society bring to bear to keep unconscious emotions in check—that is, *un*conscious? What is so dangerous about these emotions?
2. It is a cliché that even the most mild-mannered man or woman conceals an "animal" within—an inner beast that, once provoked, can completely overrun the mild personality. In what contexts have you seen this cliché at work? Does your experience confirm it?
3. Reread this article, focusing on Greenberg's Freudian analysis of specific movies. Freud's theories form a well-developed, complex system of thought that seeks to explain (among other things) the causes of human fear and unhappiness. Select *one* of Greenberg's Freudian critiques— preferably of a movie you have seen, and respond. How useful do you find the analysis in helping you understand and appreciate the movie?
4. Following Freud, Greenberg assumes the existence of a vast, but unconscious, sea of inner emotions. When this inner sea is confused and especially stormy, the "surface" life of a person can be disrupted and, in extreme cases, be made monstrous. Offer a competing reason for the appearance of monsters, perhaps a reason that has nothing to do with inner emotions.
5. To what extent do you accept as valid the transferring of psychoanalysis—a practice meant for application to human patients—to movies? Can movies, or characters in movies, be analyzed the same way a patient on a couch can be analyzed? Explain.

Metamorphosis: Humans into Animals

JOYCE E. SALISBURY

Joyce Salisbury, professor of history at the University of Wisconsin, Green Bay, has looked to the Middle Ages in her work for the origins of modern thought. One topic that captured her imagination was "transformations," the changing of form from animal to human and from human to animal. In the early Christian Middle Ages, she writes, transformations were thought to occur at "bestial" moments involving sex or violence. Again we see, this time from the historian's perspective, an awareness of a duality in human nature. Salisbury's research clearly shows that this awareness is not a uniquely modern one. To the contrary, the psychological underpinnings of modern horror cinema can be traced back a thousand years. The selection that follows appears in Salisbury's book-length study, The Beast Within: Animals in the Middle Ages *(1994).*

The classical world had envisioned a universe in which all elements were connected. Things were joined through connecting causes or through Platonic emanations that permeated all beings, whether human or animal. The classic myths reveal this connectedness most clearly through metamorphosis, changes in form. Transformations of humans into animals permeate the classical texts with such ease that they reveal a belief in a universe in which boundaries were much more fluid between species and categories than we have seen since.[1] The Roman poet Ovid collected many of the myths and stories and wrote the most influential work on transformations. He began his *Metamorphoses* with the concrete statement, "My purpose is to tell of bodies which have been transformed into shapes of a different kind"[2] and then proceeded to retell many tales of shape-shifting. By the time we reach the final transformation, Julius Caesar into a star, we are uncertain about the permanence of any form. This same bewildering world is visible in Apuleius's *The Golden Ass*, a story of the metamorphosis of a man named Lucius into an ass and his subsequent journey as that animal in his quest to return to his human form. In *The Golden Ass*, not only was Lucius transformed, but the story is full of rapid transformations of fortune and form that mark a world with fluid boundaries.

In these stories, metamorphosis usually occurred because people exhibited the characteristics of an animal to an extreme degree. The transformation only made the manifest the bestial nature that had been within.[3] Lucius acted like an overly curious ass before he experimented with the magic cream that turned him into one; Arachne showed her skill in weaving before she was turned into a spider to spin perpetually.

The early Christian Middle Ages also inherited the idea of metamorphosis from northern pagan tradition. For example, early Irish myths show frequent examples of shape-shifting. A beautiful woman spends every other year as a swan, and the man who loves her changes into a swan to possess her.

Another woman is impregnated by a man appearing as a bird, and another couple turns into swans to escape an irate husband.[4] These transformations link the human and animal worlds at moments of sexuality, a time when the animal side traditionally emerges. The metamorphoses into birds may also recall an ancient mythological association of women, fertility and birds.[5]

The Nordic tradition of shape-shifting that survives in myths and sagas points to another bestial side of people—violence. People in these stories most often magically turned into bears or wolves to acquire the animals' strength and luck in battle. The fiercest Scandinavian warriors, the berserks, seem to have owed their strength to their ability to take on animal characteristics, or rather to allow the animal within themselves to emerge. The name "berserk" may have derived from the wearing of bearskin, a hypothesis strengthened by the alternate name for berserks—"wolf-coats." The *Volsunga Saga* offers a dramatic example of transformations brought about by wearing wolf skins. Sigmund and his son, Sinfjotli, put on wolfskins but are unable to remove them. With the skins on, they "spoke with the voice of wolves," yet they understand each other. In this form they are fierce and invincible until they are able to remove the skins and take back their human form. Testimony in Norwegian witch trials echoes the tradition of wearing skins of animals into battle, because it tells of men and women wearing wolf belts to transform themselves into the savage animal.

These stories show an awareness of the animal that is within each of us. Sometimes the animal traits were undesirable ones—lust, cannibalism, or violence. At other times, animal traits like strength or cunning were sought out. Either way, however, pagan metamorphosis myths expressed the emergence of animal traits at the expense of the human. This perception required a belief in humans as a mingling of both animal and human, a belief in a continuum of life that linked human and animal. Early medieval thinkers were too concerned with separation of species, however, to integrate these tales into their world view.

When confronted with pagan tales of metamorphosis, early church fathers were vigorous in their denial of the possibility of such shape-shifting. As early as the second century in Roman North Africa, Tertullian rejected the possibility of Ovidian metamorphosis, saying that just because people exhibit the "habits, characters, and desires" of beasts, it does not mean they can actually turn into an animal.[6] The fourth-century doctor of the church Ambrose stated the early Christian case even more strongly: "those made after the likeness and image of God cannot be changed into the forms of beasts." He further summed up the early Christian explanation, saying that metamorphosis was impossible because "the nature of beasts [is] so opposed to that of mankind."[7] Thus, he restates the Christian paradigm of separation of species and uses it to reject the pagan vision of a more fluid world.

As with so many topics, Augustine developed the early church position most fully regarding this subject. Augustine allowed for the possibility of God in his omnipotence effecting a metamorphosis of a human into an animal. Beyond that, however, Augustine claimed it was impossible and that the pagan stories were untrue. He argued that the pagan gods, who were demons in his system, could not transform people from the form in which they had been created by God. Therefore, belief in metamorphosis was only illusion. People might imagine they had been transformed into an animal, but they were not actually changed.[8]

Augustine's position remained the prevailing Christian view throughout the Middle Ages. It was reaffirmed by Thomas Aquinas and continued through the sixteenth century with theorists of demonic possession like Henri Boguet, a judge in werewolf trials who said the "much-talked-of examples of metamorphosis, . . . were true in appearance only, but not in fact."[9] Of course, this view of metamorphosis as illusion or self-delusion continues today with psychological studies of people who believe they have been transformed into animals and act on that belief.[10] The medieval church attempted to enforce this skeptical view of metamorphosis in penitential literature from Regino to Burchard which forbad belief that a man "can be transformed into a wolf, called in German a Werewolf, or into some other form."[11] This ecclesiastical legislation influenced secular law as well such as the Norwegian law code that stated: "No man shall utter slander . . . or tell impossible tales about another. Impossible is that which cannot be true . . . like calling him a werewolf."[12] However, as we have seen throughout this book, the early medieval paradigm of the separation of humans from animals could not last.

As in so many other elements of medieval thought about animals, in the twelfth century we may see a significant turning point in medieval perceptions of metamorphosis. One clear indication of the increase in popularity of the idea of human to animal transformation is seen in the fortunes of Ovid's book, *Metamorphosis*. Before the twelfth century, there were very few copies made of this classic transformation text. Between the twelfth and the fourteenth centuries, there was an explosion of popularity of the text, shown both in the numbers of new manuscripts and in the many commentaries on the work.[13] Many of the commentators on Ovid and other metamorphosis stories interpreted the tales allegorically,[14] so that traditional stories of shape-shifting could be read as moral lessons in the same way fables and bestiary lore were read. Thus, pagan ideas of metamorphosis thus reentered European consciousness in the same way as stories of animals as human exemplars.

The growing popularity of metamorphosis literature surely contributed to a reconsideration of the possibility of shape-shifting. In addition, there was a subtle shift in the medieval mind-set that facilitated a renewed belief in metamorphosis in spite of ecclesiastical reasoning to the contrary. From the twelfth century on, people believed there were many things that were not as they seemed. For example, medieval science was preoccupied with transformations in nature, such as looking for the philosopher stone that could transform base metals into gold.[15] Even the central mystery of the church, the eucharist, was increasingly viewed as a miraculous transformation. In 1215 the church declared transubstantiation doctrine, claiming that the bread and wine were transformed into the actual body and blood of Christ. By this declaration, the church was acknowledging that things may be miraculously changed beyond human power to perceive. In the twelfth-century narrative of Gerald of Wales, we can see the way the medieval mind could link transformation of the eucharist with metamorphosis of humans. Gerald listed a series of reputed transformations from Apuleius's curious ass to people being changed to pigs and hares. He then repeated and reaffirmed Augustine's statement that demons cannot change people, but went on to say that with God's permission people can change their outward appearance, if not their essence. He concluded this section by mentioning transubstantiation, saying he chooses not to discuss it, "its comprehension being far beyond the powers of the human intellect."[16] But his acceptance of the incomprehensible miracle of the Mass was joined in his mind with an acceptance of seemingly improbably shape-shifting.

In Gerald, we can see the recovery of the belief in metamorphosis. Gerald's examples reveal, however, uniquely Christian transformations, different from those described in pagan literature. In pagan metamorphosis, an external appearance changed into that of an animal to make visible the interior animal-like characteristics. In Christian metamorphosis, the exterior changed to reveal some animal-like characteristics of the human, but the human essence, the interior, remained unchanged. This was consistent with the patristic position that humans cannot be changed into animals, so it offered a way to accept a compromise form of metamorphosis.   11

Another element in the high medieval world view that helped recover a belief in metamorphosis was people's increasing tendency to define humanity and bestiality by actions. As we saw above, people (like peasants) who were perceived to act like animals were considered bestial. The criterion of action probably more often served to suggest that a particularly smart animal was actually a person who had shifted his shape. We have seen that by the late Middle Ages animals were readily perceived as being demons in disguise. This same thinking persuaded people that an animal that showed cunning greater than one might expect from an animal was really a human.[17] After all, reason was a defining quality of humans, so an animal possessing that quality might really be human. Late medieval accounts of particularly intelligent wolves frequently raise the question of whether it actually was simply a wolf, or a human in wolf shape. This was the case in 1148 when a huge wolf killed thirty people in Geneva.[18] Presumably, such skill in killing was considered beyond normal animal capacity.   12

There seem to have been two ways to understand the behavior of extraordinary wolves. One was practical, looking backward to the early medieval world when animals were just that. A late medieval definition of "werewolf" shows this view. In a treatise on hunting, Edward the Duke of York wrote, "There be some [wolves] that have eaten children or men, . . . and they are called werewolves, for men should beware of them."[19] Here we see a definition of werewolf that is totally devoid of any supernatural context. In most of the texts of the late Middle Ages, however, the supernatural was attributed to intelligent wolves, showing the second way to understand the behavior. The *Malleus Maleficarum*, the Renaissance tract for discovering witchcraft, addressed the question of wolves that were so fierce and smart they seemed   13 unlike other wolves. The *Malleus* explained that they were wolves, indeed, but they were possessed by devils.[20] An exceptional wolf was transformed into a supernatural creature. This attempt to explain the actions of a wolf then contributed to a view in which species could blend and werewolves could exist.

Finally, perhaps the change that was most influential in the growth of   14
belief in metamorphosis was the blurring of lines between humans and animals. As people began to recognize, wonder about, and fear the beast within themselves, they began looking for this animal. Belief in metamorphosis, and particularly in werewolves, reveals a fear of the beast inside overwhelming the human qualities of rationality and spirituality, leaving only the animal appetites of lust, hunger, and rage. This fear, and the related discovery of transformed humans, reaches its high point during the Renaissance and early modern periods and is outside the scope of this study. Nevertheless, in the late Middle Ages there were more frequent references to humans as animals. These stories point to the growing discovery that we too are animals.

It seems that many of the tales of transformation from human to animal   15
reentered European literary tradition from the Celtic regions. It may be that old pagan traditions remained closer to the surface in those regions and less transformed by Christian views of humanity. We have seen above how Gerald of Wales was intrigued by the concept of transformation as he brought tales back from his travels in Wales and Ireland. He told of a beautiful woman who turned into a "hairy creature, rough and shaggy" while in the embrace of a man.[21] He also described old women in Wales, Scotland, and Ireland who changed themselves into hares so they could steal people's milk by sucking the teats of cows.[22] Gerald's most involved tale concerns a couple who are cursed and forced to become wolves every seven years. The wolf speaks to a priest, asking for last rites for his wife. When the wolf peels back the wolfskin to reveal a woman, the priest gives the woman/wolf communion. This tale caused Gerald to reflect upon what was a human and what was an animal.[23] Gerald was quite right to wonder. As soon as medieval thinkers allowed for the possibility of such shape-shifting, the early medieval paradigm was breaking down. But Gerald's werewolf also shows the new Christian view of metamorphosis in which the interior remained human while the external appearance was transformed.

A thirteenth-century chronicler, Gervaise of Tilbury, also showed a belief   16
in werewolves. He preserved a Christian perspective on metamorphosis by expressing the opinion that a person's nature could not be converted to a bestial one. However, at the same time he claimed to have known at least two British werewolves, one of whom "devoured infants," highly bestial behavior.[24] Like Gerald's, Gervais's chronicle shows the Christian compromise with shape-shifting: the externals were changed, behavior was bestial, but the essence remained human.

The historical chroniclers show the beginnings of Christian transforma-   17
tion and acceptance of metamorphosis, but writers of literature probably were more influential in forwarding this view. We saw in the last chapter how Marie of France was important in popularizing fables. She also drew from

Celtic tradition and wrote a collection of short romances, *Lais*, one of which was about a werewolf called Bisclavret. Marie tells us that "people used to say—and it often actually happened—that some men turned into werewolves and lived in the woods."[25] Marie then proceeds to tell a tale of one such were-wolf, and her story is instructive because it sheds a good deal of light on medieval views of metamorphosis.

Marie tells the tale of a man who is condemned to become a wolf and 18 spend three days of every week in the woods. This unhappy man confesses his plight to his beloved bride. The faithless woman cannot accept the beast within her husband: "She never wanted to sleep with him again."[26] She reveals the secret to a knight who wishes to be her lover. The two conspire to steal the man's clothing, which is the mechanism of his conversion back to human form, and thus condemn him to remain a wolf. While in the woods, the wolf is befriended by a king, who notices the animal's exceptional abili-ties and says, "It has the mind of a man. . . . This beast is rational—he has a mind."[27] Unlike the faithless wife who cannot see beyond the beast in the man, the wise king can see the man within the beast.

The wolf's human qualities are confirmed when he attacks the knight 19 who has taken his wife, clothing, and humanity, and when he attacks his vain wife and bites off her nose. The king forces the wife to restore the wolf's cloth-ing. The wolf becomes a man again, the wife is banished (to bear noseless daughters), and the friendship with the king continues.

Marie concluded her tale by saying that the Lay "was made so it would 20 be remembered forever."[28] What morals were implicit here that should be remembered? There was the obvious moral, of course, that one had better select one's wife wisely, and perhaps not trust a woman with a secret. Beyond this, however, we learn something about Marie's views of humans and ani-mals. The man, sympathetically as he is portrayed, has the beast within him.[29] Before his wife becomes involved in his plight, he is an animal half the time. In this we see most clearly the beginnings of the twelfth-century acceptance of an animal side of people. The animal side consumes the human through the agency of a woman, more carnal and closer to animals than even the half-wolf man. Through the woman, he loses almost all outward trace of his humani-ty actually and symbolically through the loss of his clothing. However, con-sistent with Christian belief, the wolf retains his humanity within because he does not lose his rational, human thought. Finally, he is restored to humani-ty again through the agency of a friend and lord, a higher spiritual being. Marie shows us that we are all subject to a loss of humanity if we focus on the wrong things. Faith in one's lord, a spiritual tie, should be placed above carnal attraction.

The same lessons appear in the fourteenth-century tale of Arthur and 21 Gorlagon. King Arthur, wanting to understand the female mind, is led to Gorlagon, who tells him a story of female betrayal and a werewolf. In this story, a king guards a secret sapling that broke through the ground when the king was born. This sapling has the power to convert the king to a wolf. As in Marie's story, a faithless wife discovers the secret, uses it to her advantage, and the wolf is ultimately restored through friendship with another king.[30] Once again, the man is identified with his animal potentiality through the sapling, and he is reduced to a bestial state through love of a woman. He never fully loses his interior nature, however, and it is restored through good lordship.

There were many late medieval examples of literary werewolves who like 22 these two had many fine qualities. These examples introduce a "sympathetic werewolf": the audience was led to feelings of pity for the human trapped within an animal exterior.[31] This compassion seems to have extended beyond feelings for a literary creature. People in the late Middle Ages may not have come to feeling much compassion for the real animals that shared their world. But through the animals that existed in their imagination, from half-human monsters to occasionally human werewolves, they had become aware of, feared, and found empathy for the beast they discovered within us all.

REFERENCES

1. L. Barkan, *The Gods Made Flesh: Metamorphosis and the Pursuit of Paganism* (New Haven, 1986), 2–3, discusses the permeable borders of the universe that permit metamorphosis.
2. Ovid, *Metamorphoses of Ovid*, trans. M. Innes (London, 1955), 31.
3. Barkan, *Gods Made Flesh*, 19–27.
4. J. Gantz, *Early Irish Myths and Sagas* (Hammondsworth, 1981), 111–12. 64, 67.
5. See Johnson, *Lady of the Beasts*, 7–98, for traditional associations of women with birds.
6. Tertullian, "On the Soul," in *Tertullian: Apologetical Works and Minucius Felix Octavius*, trans. Quain (New York, 1950), 255.
7. Ambrose, "On Faith in the Resurrection," *Funeral Orations by Saint Gregory Nazianzen and Saint Ambrose*, trans. L. McCauley et al. (Washington, 1953), 256–57.
8. Augustine, *City of God*, 782–84.
9. Thomas Aquinas, *On the Power of God*, trans. By English Dominican Fathers (Westminster, Md., 1952), 187. For Boguet, see C. Otten, *A Lycanthropy Reader: Werewolves in Western Culture* (Syracuse, 1986), 52–53.
10. See Otten, *Lycanthropy Reader*, 31–40, for psychological analyses of cases of modern werewolves.
11. Burchard of Worms, quoted in D. Kraatz, "Fictus Lupus: The Werewolf in Christian Thought," *Classical Folia* 30 (1976), 63.
12. L. Larson, *The Earliest Norwegian Laws: Being the Gulathing Law and the Frostating Law* (New York, 1935), 123.
13. Barkan, *Gods Made Flesh*, 104, 308 n. 17.
14. Barkan, *Gods Made Flesh*, 104.
15. See Barkan, *Gods Made Flesh*, 124–26, for the relationship between this idea and the growing popularity of metamorphosis.

16. Gerald of Wales, *The Historical Works of Giraldus Cambrensis*, ed. T. Wright (London, 1887), 84.

17. Otten, *Lycanthropy Reader*, 153.

18. Otten, *Lycanthropy Reader*, 79.

19. Edward, Duke of York, *The Master of Game*, quoted in J. Cummings, *The Hound and the Hawk* (New York: 1988), 133.

20. *"The Malleus Maleficarum,"* in Otten, *Lycanthropy Reader*, 113.

21. Gerald, *Journey Through Wales*, 116.

22. Gerald, *Topography of Ireland*, 83.

23. Gerald, *Topography of Ireland*, 79–82.

24. Kraatz, "Fictus Lupus," 60.

25. Marie of France, "Bisclavret," in R. Hanning and J. Ferrante, *The Lais of Marie de France* (Durham, N.C., 1978), 92.

26. Marie de France, "Bisclavret," 94.

27. Marie of France, "Bisclavret," 96.

28. Marie of France, "Bisclavret," 100.

29. Hanning and Ferrante point out that the whole lay is a "parable about the forces of bestiality that exist within human nature and how they should (and should not) be confronted, used, or transcended;" *Lais of Marie de France*, 101.

30. "Arthur and Gorlagon," in Otten, *Lycanthropy Reader*, 234–50.

31. See Kraatz, "Fictus Lupus," 72, for an excellent analysis of the sympathetic werewolf in literature. See also Bernheimer, *Wild Man*, 164, for a summary of the story of "Guillaume de Palerne," another sympathetic tale of transformation.

■ ■ ■

Review Questions

1. What is a "metamorphosis"?
2. With which elements in life was metamorphosis associated during the early Christian Middle Ages?
3. Briefly compare and contrast the pagan and Christian views of metamorphosis.
4. What changes regarding transformations occurred in the 12th century?
5. What is the fear of metamorphosis?
6. What is a "sympathetic werewolf"?

Discussion and Writing Suggestions

1. What is your response to learning that metamorphoses, generally, and transformations from human-to-wolf, particularly, fascinated people in the ancient and medieval worlds? Through stories of transformations, what do you imagine is your connection to people who have come before you?

2. Choose one of the tales that Salisbury summarizes toward the end of the selection—the one by Marie of France or one concerning Arthur and Gorlagon. Do you find them to be morality tales in the same way that Salisbury does? Do you agree with her interpretation of the morals?

3. Choose one of the tales that Salisbury summarizes toward the end of the selection—the one by Marie of France or one concerning Arthur and Gorlagon. Work up a one-page overview of this story for a possible screenplay. Who are the main characters? (You can extrapolate from the ones in the original tale.) What is the setting (time and place)? What are the central themes? After you complete your sketch, answer two questions: Why would—or wouldn't—this story provide a useful starting point for a film? Would you regard the project as a horror film? Explain.

4. Salisbury provides evidence that, for thousands of years, people have grappled with the animal elements of human nature. Are we in your view any clearer now than were our forebears on the subject? For instance, do you consider human beings to be part animal?

The Company of Wolves

ANGELA CARTER

Angela Carter (1940–1992), an award-winning British writer of myth- and fantasy-rich fiction, for both juveniles and adults, frequently explored feminist themes. She had a special regard for recasting old tales and reinvigorating them to heighten their impact on modern readers. Critic Susan Kennedy (of the Times Literary Supplement) *wrote of Carter's* The Fairy Tales of Charles Perrault *and* Sleeping Beauty and Other Fairy Tales *that her "retelling of European folk and fairy tales has the power, not only to cause us to think again, and deeply, . . . but to plunge us into hackle-raising speculation about aspects of our human/animal nature." Such is the case with "The Company of Wolves," Carter's retelling of* Little Red Riding Hood *in which the wolfish part of men figure prominently. Carter collaborated with director Neil Jordan on a screenplay of "Company," which Jordan later directed in a movie that, for a time, became something of a cult classic. Reviews of the film appear later in the chapter. Carter's other works include* The Magic Toyshop *(1968),* Several Perceptions *(1968), and* The Bloody Chamber and Other Stories *(1979).*

Note: *You may wish to compare "The Company of Wolves" to another modern retelling of a traditional story, Tanith Lee's "When the Clock Strikes" (pp. 607–19).*

One beast and only one howls in the woods by night.   1

The wolf is carnivore incarnate and he's as cunning as he is ferocious;   2
once he's had a taste of flesh then nothing else will do.

At night, the eyes of wolves shine like candle flames, yellowish, reddish,   3
but that is because the pupils of their eyes fatten on darkness and catch the
light from your lantern to flash it back to you—red for danger; if a wolf's eyes
reflect only moonlight, then they gleam a cold and unnatural green, a miner-
al, a piercing color. If the benighted traveler spies those luminous, terrible
sequins stitched suddenly on the black thickets, then he knows he must run,
if fear has not struck him stock-still.

But those eyes are all you will be able to glimpse of the forest assassins as   4
they cluster invisibly round your smell of meat as you go through the wood
unwisely late. They will be like shadows, they will be like wraiths, grey members of a congregation of nightmare; hark! his long, wavering howl . . . an aria
of fear made audible.

The wolfsong is the sound of the rending you will suffer, in itself a mur-   5
dering.

It is winter and cold weather. In this region of mountain and forest,   6
there is now nothing for the wolves to eat. Goats and sheep are locked up in
the byre, the deer departed for the remaining pasturage on the southern
slopes—wolves grow lean and famished. There is so little flesh on them that
you could count the starveling ribs through their pelts, if they gave you time
before they pounced. Those slavering jaws; the lolling tongue; the rime of
saliva on the grizzled chops—of all the teeming perils of the night and the
forest, ghosts, hobgoblins, ogres that grill babies upon gridirons, witches that
fatten their captives in cages for cannibal tables, the wolf is worst for he
cannot listen to reason.

You are always in danger in the forest, where no people are. Step between   7
the portals of the great pines where the shaggy branches tangle about you,
trapping the unwary traveler in nets as if the vegetation itself were in a plot
with the wolves who live there, as though the wicked trees go fishing on
behalf of their friends—step between the gateposts of the forest with the
greatest trepidation and infinite precautions, for if you stray from the path for
one instant, the wolves will eat you. They are grey as famine, they are as
unkind as plague.

The grave-eyed children of the sparse villages always carry knives with   8
them when they go to tend the little flocks of goats that provide the home-
steads with acrid milk and rank, maggoty cheese. Their knives are half as big
as they are, the blades are sharpened daily.

But the wolves have ways of arriving at your own hearthside. We try and try but sometimes we cannot keep them out. There is no winter's night the cottager does not fear to see a lean, grey, famished snout questing under the door, and there was a woman once bitten in her own kitchen as she was straining the macaroni. **9**

Fear and flee the wolf; for, worst of all, the wolf may be more than he seems. **10**

There was a hunter once, near here, that trapped a wolf in a pit. This wolf had massacred the sheep and goats; eaten up a mad old man who used to live by himself in a hut halfway up the mountain and sing to Jesus all day; pounced on a girl looking after the sheep, but she made such a commotion that men came with rifles and scared him away and tried to track him to the forest but he was cunning and easily gave them the slip. So this hunter dug a pit and put a duck in it, for bait, all alive-oh; and he covered the pit with straw smeared with wolf dung. Quack, quack! went the duck and a wolf came slinking out of the forest, a big one, a heavy one, he weighed as much as a grown man and the straw gave way beneath him—into the pit he tumbled. The hunter jumped down after him, slit his throat, cut off all his paws for a trophy. **11**

And then no wolf at all lay in front of the hunter but the bloody trunk of a man, headless, footless, dying, dead. **12**

A witch from up the valley once turned an entire wedding party into wolves because the groom had settled on another girl. She used to order them to visit her, at night, from spite, and they would sit and howl around her cottage for her, serenading her with their misery. **13**

Not so very long ago, a young woman in our village married a man who vanished clean away on her wedding night. The bed was made with new sheets and the bride lay down on it; the groom said, he was going out to relieve himself, insisted on it, for the sake of decency, and she drew the coverlet up to her chin and lay there. And she waited and she waited and then she waited again—surely he's been gone a long time? Until she jumps up in bed and shrieks to hear a howling, coming on the wind from the forest. **14**

That long-drawn, wavering howl has, for all its fearful resonance, some inherent sadness in it, as if the beasts would love to be less beastly if only they knew how and never cease to mourn their own condition. There is a vast melancholy in the canticles of the wolves, melancholy infinite as the forest, endless as these long nights of winter and yet that ghastly sadness, that mourning for their own, irremediable appetites, can never move the heart for not one phrase in it hints at the possibility of redemption; grace could not come to the wolf from its own despair, only through some external mediator, so that, sometimes, the beast will look as if he half welcomes the knife that dispatches him. **15**

The young woman's brothers searched the outhouses and the haystacks but never found any remains so the sensible girl dried her eyes and found herself another husband not too shy to piss into a pot who spent the nights indoors. She gave him a pair of bonny babies and all went right as a trivet **16** until, one freezing night, the night of the solstice, the hinge of the year when things do not fit together as well as they should, the longest night, her first good man came home again.

A great thump on the door announced him as she was stirring the soup   17 for the father of her children and she knew him the moment she lifted the latch to him although it was years since she'd worn black for him and now he was in rags and his hair hung down his back and never saw a comb, alive with lice.

'Here I am again, missus,' he said. 'Get me my bowl of cabbage and be   18 quick about it.'

Then her second husband came in with wood for the fire and when the   19 first one saw she'd slept with another man and, worse, clapped his red eyes on her little children who'd crept into the kitchen to see what all the din was about, he shouted: 'I wish I were a wolf again, to teach this whore a lesson!' So a wolf he instantly became and tore off the eldest boy's left foot before he was chopped by the hatchet they used for chopping logs. But when the wolf lay bleeding and gasping its last, the pelt peeled off again and he was just as he had been, years ago, when he ran away from his marriage bed, so that she wept and her second husband beat her.

They say there's an ointment the Devil gives you that turns you into a   20 wolf the minute you rub it on. Or, that he was born feet first and had a wolf for his father and his torso is a man's but his legs and genitals are a wolf's. And he has a wolf's heart.

Seven years is a werewolf's natural span but if you burn his human   21 clothes you condemn him to wolfishness for the rest of his life, so old wives hereabouts think it some protection to throw a hat or an apron at the were-wolf, as if clothes made the man. Yet by the eyes, those phosphorescent eyes, you know him in all his shapes; the eyes alone unchanged by metamorphosis.

Before he can become a wolf, the lycanthrope strips stark naked. If you   22 spy a naked man among the pines, you must run as if the Devil were after you.

It is midwinter and the robin, the friend of man, sits on the handle of the   23 gardener's spade and sings. It is the worst time in all the year for wolves but this strong-minded child insists she will go off through the wood. She is quite sure the wild beasts cannot harm her although, well-warned, she lays a carv-ing knife in the basket her mother has packed with cheeses. There is a bottle of harsh liquor distilled from brambles; a batch of flat oatcakes baked on the heathstone; a pot or two of jam. The girl will take these delicious gifts to a reclusive grandmother so old the burden of her years is crushing her to death. Granny lives two hours' trudge through the winter woods; the child wraps herself up in her thick shawl, draws it over her head. She steps into her stout wooden shoes; she is dressed and ready and it is Christmas Eve. The malign door of the solstice still swings upon its hinges but she has been too much loved ever to feel scared.

Children do not stay young for long in this savage country. There are no   24 toys for them to play with so they work hard and grow wise but this one, so pretty and the youngest of her family, a little late-comer, had been indulged by her mother and the grandmother who'd knitted her the red shawl that, today, has the ominous if brilliant look of blood on snow. Her breasts have just begun to swell; her hair is like lint, so fair it hardly makes a shadow on her pale forehead; her cheeks are an emblematic scarlet and white and she has just started her woman's bleeding, the clock inside her that will strike, henceforward, once a month.

She stands and moves within the invisible pentacle of her own virginity. 25 She is an unbroken egg; she is a sealed vessel; she has inside her a magic space the entrance to which is shut tight with a plug of membrane; she is a closed system; she does not know how to shiver. She has her knife and she is afraid of nothing.

Her father might forbid her, if he were home, but he is away in the 26 forest, gathering wood, and her mother cannot deny her.

The forest closed upon her like a pair of jaws. 27

There is always something to look at in the forest, even in the middle of 28 winter—the huddled mounds of birds, succumbed to the lethargy of the season, heaped on the creaking boughs and too forlorn to sing; the bright frills of the winter fungi on the blotched trunks of the trees; the cuneiform slots of rabbits and deer, the herringbone tracks of the birds, a hare as lean as a rasher of bacon streaking across the path where the thin sunlight dapples the russet brakes of last year's bracken.

When she heard the freezing howl of a distant wolf, her practised hand 29 sprang to the handle of her knife, but she saw no sign of a wolf at all, nor of a naked man, neither, but then she heard a clattering among the brushwood and there sprang on to the path a fully clothed one, a very handsome young one, in the green coat and wideawake hat of a hunter, laden with carcasses of game birds. She had her hand on her knife at the first rustle of twigs but he laughed with a flash of white teeth when he saw her and made her a comic yet flattering little bow; she'd never seen such a fine fellow before, not among the rustic clowns of her native village. So on they went, through the thickening light of the afternoon.

Soon they were laughing and joking like old friends. When he offered to 30 carry her basket, she gave it to him although her knife was in it because he told her his rifle would protect them. As the day darkened, it began to snow again; she felt the first flakes settle on her eyelashes but now there was only half a mile to go and there would be a fire, and hot tea, and a welcome, a warm one surely, for the dashing huntsman as well as for herself.

This young man had a remarkable object in his pocket. It was a compass. 31 She looked at the little round glassface in the palm of his hand and watched the wavering needle with a vague wonder. He assured her this compass had taken him safely through the wood on his hunting trip because the needle always told him with perfect accuracy where the north was. She did not believe it; she knew she should never leave the path on the way through the wood or else she would be lost instantly. He laughed at her again; gleaming trails of spittle clung to his teeth. He said, if he plunged off the path into the

forest that surrounded them, he would guarantee to arrive at her grandmother's house a good quarter of an hour before she did, plotting his way
through the undergrowth with his compass, while she trudged the long way,
along the winding path.

I don't believe you. Besides, aren't you afraid of the wolves?   32

He only tapped the gleaming butt of his rifle and grinned.   33

Is it a bet? he asked her. Shall we make a game of it? What will you give   34
me if I get to your grandmother's house before you?

What would you like? she asked disingenuously.   35

A kiss.   36

Commonplaces of a rustic seduction; she lowered her eyes and blushed.   37

He went through the undergrowth and took her basket with him but she   38
forgot to be afraid of the beasts, although now the moon was rising, for she
wanted to dawdle on her way to make sure the handsome gentleman would
win his wager.

Grandmother's house stood by itself a little way out of the village. The   39
freshly fallen snow blew in eddies about the kitchen garden and the young
man stepped delicately up the snowy path to the door as if he were reluctant
to get his feet wet, swinging his bundle of game and the girl's basket and hum-
ming a little tune to himself.

There is a faint trace of blood on his chin; he has been snacking on his   40
catch.

He rapped upon the panels with his knuckles.   41

Aged and frail, granny is three-quarters succumbed to the mortality the   42
ache in her bones promises her and almost ready to give in entirely. A boy
came out from the village to build up her hearth for the night an hour ago and
the kitchen crackles with busy firelight. She has her Bible for company, she is
a pious old woman. She is propped up on several pillows in the bed set into
the wall peasant-fashion, wrapped up in the patchwork quilt she made before
she was married, more years ago than she cares to remember. Two china
spaniels with liver-coloured blotches on their coats and black noses sit on
either side of the fireplace. There is a bright rug of woven rags on the pantiles.
The grandfather clock ticks away her eroding time.

We keep the wolves outside by living well.   43

He rapped upon the panels with his hairy knuckles.   44

It is your granddaughter, he mimicked in a high soprano.   45

Lift up the latch and walk in, my darling.   46

You can tell them by their eyes, eyes of a beast of prey, nocturnal, dev-   47
astating eyes as red as a wound; you can hurl your Bible at him and your
apron after, granny, you thought that was a sure prophylactic against these
infernal vermin . . . now call on Christ and his mother and all the angels in
heaven to protect you but it won't do you any good.

His feral muzzle is sharp as a knife; he drops his golden burden of   48
gnawed pheasant on the table and puts down your dear girl's basket, too. Oh,
my God, what have you done with her?

Off with his disguise, that coat of forest-coloured cloth, the hat with the 49 feather tucked into the ribbon; his matted hair streams down his white shirt and she can see the lice moving in it. The sticks in the hearth shift and hiss; night and the forest has come into the kitchen with darkness tangled in its hair.

He strips off his shirt. His skin is the colour and texture of vellum. A crisp 50 stripe of a hair runs down his belly, his nipples are ripe and dark as poison fruit but he's so thin you could count the ribs under his skin if only he gave you the time. He strips off his trousers and she can see how hairy his legs are. His genitals, huge. Ah! huge.

The last thing the old lady saw in all this world was a young man, eyes 51 like cinders, naked as a stone, approaching her bed.

The wolf is carnivore incarnate. 52

When he had finished with her, he licked his chops and quickly dressed 53 himself again, until he was just as he had been when he came through her door. He burned the inedible hair in the fireplace and wrapped the bones up in a napkin that he hid away under the bed in the wooden chest in which he found a clean pair of sheets. These he carefully put on the bed instead of the tell-tale stained ones he stowed away in the laundry basket. He plumped up the pillows and shook out the patchwork quilt, he picked up the Bible from the floor, closed it and laid it on the table. All was as it had been before except that grandmother was gone. The sticks twitched in the grate, the clock ticked and the young man sat patiently, deceitfully beside the bed in granny's night-cap.

Rat-a-tap-tap. 54

Who's there, he quavers in granny's antique falsetto. 55

Only your granddaughter. 56

So she came in, bringing with her a flurry of snow that melted in tears on 57 the tiles, and perhaps she was a little disappointed to see only her grand-mother sitting beside the fire. But then he flung off the blanket and sprang to the door, pressing his back against it so that she could not get out again.

The girl looked round the room and saw there was not even the inden- 58 tation of a head on the smooth cheek of the pillow and how, for the first time she'd seen it so, the Bible lay closed on the table. The tick of the clock cracked like a whip. She wanted her knife from her basket but she did not dare to reach for it because his eyes were fixed upon her—huge eyes that now seemed to shine with a unique, interior light, eyes the size of saucers, saucers full of Greek fire, diabolic phosphorescence.

What big eyes you have. 59

All the better to see you with. 60

No trace at all of the old woman except for a tuft of white hair that had 61 caught in the bark of an unburned log. When the girl saw that, she knew she was in danger of death.

Where is my grandmother? 62

There's nobody here but we two, my darling. 63

Now a great howling rose up all around them, near, very near as close as 64 the kitchen garden, the howling of a multitude of wolves; she knew the worst wolves are hairy on the inside and she shivered, in spite of the scarlet shawl she pulled more closely round herself as if it could protect her although it was as red as the blood she must spill.

Who has come to sing us carols, she said.   65

Those are the voices of my brothers, darling; I love the company of   66
wolves. Look out of the window and you'll see them.

Snow half-caked the lattice and she opened it to look into the garden. It   67
was a white night of moon and snow; the blizzard whirled round the gaunt, grey beasts who squatted on their haunches among the rows of winter cabbage, pointing their sharp snouts to the moon and howling as if their hearts would break. Ten wolves; twenty wolves—so many wolves she could not count them, howling in concert as if demented or deranged. Their eyes reflected the light from the kitchen and shone like a hundred candles.

It is very cold, poor things, she said; no wonder they howl so.   68

She closed the window on the wolves' threnody and took off her scarlet   69
shawl, the colour of poppies, the colour of sacrifices, the colour of her menses, and, since her fear did her no good, she ceased to be afraid.

What shall I do with my shawl?   70

Throw it on the fire, dear one. You won't need it again.   71

She bundled up her shawl and threw it on the blaze, which instantly con-   72
sumed it. Then she drew her blouse over her head; her small breasts gleamed as if the snow had invaded the room.

What shall I do with my blouse?   73

Into the fire with it, too, my pet.   74

The thin muslin went flaring up the chimney like a magic bird and now   75
off came her skirt, her woollen stockings, her shoes, and on to the fire they went, too, and were gone for good. The firelight shone through the edges of her skin; now she was clothed only in her untouched integument of flesh. Thus dazzling, naked she combed out her hair with her fingers; her hair looked white as the snow outside. Then went directly to the man with red eyes in whose unkempt mane the lice moved; she stood up on tiptoe and unbuttoned the collar of his shirt.

What big arms you have.   76

All the better to hug you with.   77

Every wolf in the world now howled a prothalamion outside the window   78
as she freely gave him the kiss she owed him.

What big teeth you have!   79

She saw how his jaw began to slaver and the room was full of the clam-   80
our of the forest's *Liebestod* but the wise child never flinched, even as he answered: All the better to eat you with.

The girl burst out laughing; she knew she was nobody's meat. She   81
laughed at him full in the face, she ripped off his shirt for him and flung it into the fire, in the fiery wake of her own discarded clothing. The flames danced like dead souls on Walpursignacht and the old bones under the bed set up a terrible clattering but she did not pay them any heed.

Carnivore incarnate, only immaculate flesh appeases him.   82

She will lay his fearful head on her lap and she will pick out the lice from   83
his pelt and perhaps she will put the lice into her mouth and eat them, as he
will bid her, as she would do in a savage marriage ceremony.

The blizzard will die down.   84

The blizzard died down, leaving the mountains as randomly covered   85
with snow as if a blind woman had thrown a sheet over them, the upper
branches of the forest pines limed, creaking, swollen with the fall.

Snowlight, moonlight, a confusion of paw-prints.   86

All silent, all silent.   87

Midnight; and the clock strikes. It is Christmas day, the werewolves'   88
birthday, the door of the solstice stands wide open; let them all sink through.

See! sweet and sound she sleeps in granny's bed, between the paws of the   89
tender wolf.

■   ■   ■

Discussion and Writing Suggestions

1. In what way does "Company of Wolves" qualify as a *horror* story? In considering your answer, you may want to draw a distinction between content that is shocking and content that is horrifying. What makes a story horrifying? Does "Company" qualify?

2. The title of this chapter includes the phrase "the beast within." What types of beasts (you can make a case for more than one) do you find in "Company of Wolves"? In what ways are these *interior* beasts? (You might want to consider the next question in developing your answer.)

3. Before the wolf eats Granny, we read: "We keep the wolves outside by living well." What does this mean?

4. The narrator of "Company of Wolves" addresses the reader in the second person—that is, directly as "you." What effect does this narrative device have on your reading?

5. In what ways are you aware of "Little Red Riding Hood" as the foundation for Carter's story? Make a list of the ways in which "Company of Wolves" draws directly on "Riding Hood." List, as well, Carter's departures from older folk versions. In several paragraphs, try to account for these differences.

6. Reread the "Company of Wolves" and identify images associated with sexuality—both the heroine's and the wolf's. As you recall the "Red Riding Hood" folktale, to what extent is there room for an interpretation and retelling based on the emerging sexual identity of the heroine? Ultimately, what is your view of the sexuality in "Company of Wolves?"

7. Throughout the story, and especially in the opening paragraph, how does Carter shape your view of wolves? What are the associations? Specifically, how does the opening description of wolves affect you?

8. Carter takes great care to re-create a time in which forests represented territories of danger—in no small part due to the presence of wolves. Reread the story and focus on the distinctions Carter makes between life inside the forest and life outside. What pattern emerges?

9. A follow-on to the preceding question: for most of human history, walking alone in forest areas presented real dangers from wolves. Today, forests are largely tamed places; you will not encounter wolves (unless you are hiking in remote sections of Yellowstone National park, where wolves have been reintroduced by the Forest Service). Still, the forest—and the prospect of walking alone in one—resonates for many as a place of danger. Why?

10. Writers make decisions about tense structure with great care, often attempting to match tense with elements in the story to achieve a specific effect. In the "Red Riding Hood" story, Carter shifts tenses several times, between present and past and then shifting to future to past and back to present. See, for instance, paragraphs 1–10 and the shift in paragraph 11. What do you suppose Carter is trying to achieve with these changes?

Wolf at the Door:
An Interview with Neil Jordan

Neil Jordan is perhaps best known for his film The Crying Game *(1992), an atmospheric love story (with a unique twist) about an IRA volunteer who becomes involved with the lover of a British soldier he befriends. Born in Ireland in 1950, Jordan began his career as the author of two highly regarded novels,* The Past *(1980) and* Dream of a Beast *(1983) and a collection of short stories,* Night in Tunisia *(1979), all set in his homeland. His first film was* Angel *(1982), released in the United States as* Danny Boy. Company of Wolves *followed in 1984. His other films included* Mona Lisa *(1986),* Interview with the Vampire *(1994),* Michael Collins *(1996), and* The Butcher Boy *(1998).*

In a 1990 interview with the periodical Film Comment, *Jordan observed, "I like to choose characters who are surrounded by a life that seems understandable and who slowly find themselves in situations where everything has changed, where no rules exist, and where emotions and realities are brought into play that they are not prepared for." This is a comment that certainly describes* Company of Wolves. *The film stars Angela Lansbury as Granny, David Warner as Father, Sarah Patterson as Rosaleen, and (in an uncredited cameo) Terence Stamp as the devil. The evocative sets were designed by Anton Furst, who also designed Tim Burton's brooding* Batman *(1989).*

In the following selection, which appeared in the July 1984 Monthly Film Bulletin, *Jordan, interviewed by Paul Taylor and Steve Jenkins, discusses the creation and production of* Company of Wolves.

I met Steve Woolley when he was keen to distribute *Angel* after seeing it in Cannes. He told me that Palace wanted to get into production and that he would like to see anything I was thinking of doing. Then Walter Donohue of Channel 4 commissioned a series of short films, about fifty minutes or so, one of which was an adaptation by Angela Carter of her story "The Company of Wolves." I had met Angela briefly when I won the *Guardian* prize in 1979 and she was on the jury, and then again in Dublin during a centenary week for the birth of James Joyce. So I showed her script to Steve Woolley and spoke to Angela, whom I'd already talked to about films, and we thought of ways of making it into a larger feature film. Steve then got the development money and we sat down and wrote the script quite quickly, in about two or three weeks. 1

The single most important factor that drew me to Angela's work—which to me is like nothing else—is that it's both so dramatic and so graphic. She has this iconoclastic, very steely intelligence, which I don't often find now in writers. She's an intellectual in the old sense, from the 20s and 30s. But she also has this incredibly fertile imagination and thinks very strongly in terms of imagery. The first script was full of things like "a man turns into a wolf in front of his family, he gets his head chopped off and it falls into a bucket and comes up as his own head." You just don't find that sort of thing very often in British movies. That script was quite a direct transposition of the story. If you take a short story and put the narrative down as a screenplay, you get one thing. But if you look at all the little bits in between the sentences, the atmospheres and the tiny bits of description and the references, you get other things. I was really trying to pull out these little things that Angela just hinted at, saying, "Well, couldn't this be a big sequence?" It was very instructive with regard to the way that people adapt things, which is usually scaling down rather than up, because the story is only a few pages. She says things like "It was rumored once that a witch walked into a wedding party and turned the entire village into wolves." In the film that became an entire sequence. 2

We found the shape—of stories within stories, and the portmanteau device of the girl dreaming—and then we built the script up by association. Instead of the forest meaning danger, the wolf meaning sexuality and the granny authority, we tried to let images and types of stories come to us in an associative way, and follow them for the pleasure of it. I think that the meaning emerges from the pleasure, rather than in any straightforward interpretative way. I particularly wanted to avoid that rather obvious, pedestrian approach. When I was a kid, the pleasure I got from Disney films, or from *Night of the Hunter* or *The Wizard of Oz*, was more to do with recognition than interpretation. We tried to build each set so that it reminded you of something you had seen but weren't quite sure what it was. You feel that 3 you're visiting somewhere that you've been before, like Hansel and Gretel's cottage. In that sense, I wanted the culmination of the film to be recognition that this is the story of Little Red Riding Hood. Angela had built her original story around that, and she had alluded to werewolf lore at the beginning and end of it. We also took a bit from a story of hers called "Wolf Alice," and I drew a lot of images from my novel *Dream of a Beast*, which I'd just finished; things like the little babies coming out of the eggs, some of the stranger imagery.

I also wanted to play a game with the perceptions of the audience, in the   4 sense that you are led through one sequence, and think you are at home, and then someone tells a story and you go into another world, and so on. I wanted it to be like a puzzle which people would enjoy in the way that they enjoy unraveling a thriller. It may be that people are very literal-minded nowadays and don't allow themselves to take straight sensual pleasure from things. For example, when we were doing the music with George Fenton, we tried to construct the score so that at certain points—like when the girl is running through the forest—you could just sit back and eat it up. With a lot of the sequences, we were just trying to wring the sensual pleasure out of them.

It's quite difficult to know how to end a film like this. Originally we had   5 the idea that the girl just woke from the dream and it was a proper waking up. But with this kind of fantasy film, it's a little bit boring for her just to wake up and go downstairs. Then we had another thought, that she woke up, dived through the floor, and vanished. But that was very difficult to realize in concrete terms. So then I shot the ending we have now, which is actually more in keeping with the rest of the film, with the dogs coming through the house and the wolf jumping through the painting. But if you go for the spectacle and that emotional feeling, the problem is that it does get confused. If you just go back to the Alsatian scratching at the door and the girl waking up and letting the dog in, at least people could say, "Ah, it's ended now." But I wanted to make it an ambiguous ending, with the final scream and the poem—which I'd always wanted to use—and the girl's voice to strengthen the ambiguity. I didn't want the film to end with the girl under threat; it's a liberation in a way.

All along, everybody felt that it should be a studio film. In the end it was   6 a matter of logistics. You have to play a wait and see game in that regard. I mean, if we had found an extraordinary forest. . . . I did actually look, and the only one that was close to it was down in Lyme Regis, with strange trees and pools, but then one wouldn't have been able to light it properly. The fact that you don't return to the "real" world was scripted from the start. It was written so that there were just trees leading up to a real house, and then a nightmare sequence in a fantasy forest, with large mushrooms and teddy bears and things like that. And then there was a forest which was out of a Grimm's fairy-tale, which at a push could have been real, if you had had a lot of money and it happened to snow. But in the end, when I began to work with Anton Furst, the designer, and we began to enlarge the whole thing conceptually, it was clear that he could realise things much better with the studio look than by using a combination of studio and the real thing.

I wanted to do it with a bit of cheek really. It was the feeling of, why do   7
Americans have all the fun? Why are they allowed to have people's eyebrows
pop out, and people going into space, while over here we have to film people
on the streets? I wanted to make a film that had all the production values of
those American films, but that was actually subversive, that offered a more
intelligent and perhaps more real pleasure. The question of whether it would
be commercial or not never really arose except at the level of the effects. The
effects *had* to be hugely satisfying, and they had to be things you had not seen
before. And the sets and the feeling of the forest had to be immense and full
of wonder. But if it didn't work as a story, there was something wrong.
Because if you examine the films that are actually breaking ground visually
and technically, their content is terribly depressing isn't it? Hugely clever
people like Spielberg and Lucas have brought back the story—with a beginning, a middle and an end—with such a bang. And I think that's a little bit
depressing. So I wanted the film to have the visual challenge of the American
films, but also to be narratively rich and full and adventurous.

We had no generic sense of it in terms of cinema while we were writing   8
it. I didn't want to have any sense of reference for it. When you are writing,
particularly in Ireland, everything is referenced to something else. People talk
about their influences before they've written a line. I went into making films
hoping that it was free of all that, and suddenly you find that there's even
more of this baggage to take with you. That does bother me quite a bit.
Genre is a critical way of looking at films, but it's also a way of marketing
them, and I would like this film to help free people from those straitjackets.
It's odd that nowadays every film has to belong to a genre. *Angel*, despite
what people said, wasn't a *film noir*. It was a story of revenge, but stylistically
it was very brightly lit, very colorful.

If you look at silent movies, where a lot of people came into film from   9
theatre, acting and different disciplines, they didn't really create the genres as
we know them now. That happened in the 30s and 40s. And when the cine-
literate generation came along and began to tear films apart, they did it in
terms of genre again. Godard was always referring to different types of movie.
Now they're doing it in America. Ridley Scott made a haunted house movie
in space,[1] and George Lucas made a Second World War aeroplane movie in
space,[2] and they are quite simple transpositions of things. But I think if you
got someone who knew very little about films, or who had seen only silent
films, and they made a movie, you wouldn't be able to tie it to any genre. So
for us, the early silent horror films, and the sets they used to build at UFA,
were an influence, but atmospherically rather than generically. There's a bit
of *Night of the Hunter*, but it's not a matter of references. It's just using
devices that were used there, like people being looked at by little creatures. If

---

[1] *haunted house movie in space: Alien* (1979).

[2] *aeroplane movie in space: Star Wars* (1977).

you were to make a film that referred to "Beauty and the Beast," you'd be invoking the fairy-tale rather than the Cocteau film version of it. And that was the real reference: fairy-tales.

■ ■ ■

Discussion and Writing Suggestions

1. The transformation scenes of humans into wolves are quite literal in Jordan's "Company of Wolves." How effective are these scenes in which the beast within emerges?
2. Having read Angela Carter's "Company of Wolves" and watched the film version, list two or three key similarities and differences. For example, consider this difference: Jordan describes the "shape" of the film as being one of "stories within stories, and the . . . device of the girl dreaming." Compare this shape with the shape, or structure, of the short story by Carter. How closely are the structures matched? Decide on two or three other such criteria and conduct your comparison and contrast. Discuss your findings with classmates.
3. How successfully has Jordan adapted Carter's story? In developing your response, allow that the test of a successful film adaptation is *not* a literal transcription, scene by scene, from story to film. Rather, film adaptations succeed when the director captures the spirit of the written story and translates that spirit to a new medium. Considering all the similarities *and* differences you and classmates have noted between the two versions of "Company," how successful an adaptation is Jordan's film?
4. Jordan and his designer, Anton Furst, decided to film the forest for "Company" on a set—not in an actual forest. They aimed to construct a forest of imagination, something that would tap the audience's memory of the forests of fairy tales. What is your response to the film's forest? Does its intended surrealistic feel succeed for you?
5. Jordan acknowledges that it's "quite difficult to know how to end a film like this." Reread paragraph 5 of the interview and reflect on the various endings Jordan and Carter considered for "Company of Wolves." Jordan says that he tried for an "ambiguous" ending. Based on your viewing of the film, does he succeed? How satisfying for you is the ending of "Company"?
6. Jordan intended "to make a film . . . that was actually subversive." (See paragraph 7.) Something that is meant to *subvert* is meant to undercut established values or expectations. What in the Jordan film is subversive? What values or expectations are undercut?

TWO REVIEWS OF *COMPANY OF WOLVES*

For an introduction to Neil Jordan's *Company of Wolves* and its director, see the previous selection and the headnote preceding. We've selected two of the many reviews that followed the film's release in 1984. They indicate both the positive and negative reactions evoked by Jordan's second film. Some of these diverging responses may be a result of the way the film was marketed in the United States. As a biographer of Jordan has noted (in the *1993 Current Biography Yearbook*), *The Company of Wolves*, which was extremely popular in London, was envisaged by Jordan as a poetic fantasy, but American distributors marketed it as a horror film and released it to theaters that typically screened standard exploitation films. The review by Lawrence O'Toole appeared in *Macleans*, a Canadian magazine, on May 6, 1985. J. Hoberman's review appeared in *The Village Voice* on April 30, 1985.

The Fevered Dreams of Adolescence

LAWRENCE O'TOOLE

A film about a dream, *The Company of Wolves* follows the nocturnal inner   1
ramblings of Rosaleen (Sarah Patterson), an adolescent on the verge of sexual awakening. The sleeping Rosaleen's imagination takes her to an eerie make-believe land of misty woods where wolves howl at night and danger lurks around every corner. Designer Anton Furst has created a splendid fantasy atmosphere with giant toadstools, creeping vines, thatched huts and swirls of fog evoking *Hansel and Gretel* and malevolent forces. In her fevered dream Rosaleen listens with a mixture of enthusiasm and trepidation as her grandmother (Angela Lansbury) warns her to beware of men who change into hairy beasts. Granny cautions her never to stray from the path in the woods, but Rosaleen is at an age when straying from the path—on the subconscious, sexual level—is exactly what she wants to do. That crude psychoanalytic symbolism is almost comic, spoiling the otherwise delightful horror in *The Company of Wolves*.

The script, written by director Neil Jordan and English novelist Angela   2
Carter, is an extended variation on the story of Little Red Riding Hood and, to press the point, Rosaleen wears a hooded red cape. The filmmakers transform the fairy tale into an allegory about burgeoning sexuality. Rosaleen spurns an amorous village boy (Shane Johnstone), but when she walks through the woods she is lured by the huntsman (Micha Bergese), even though his eyebrows knit together—a sign of the werewolf. Clearly, Rosaleen has become attracted to the beast in men. When the dreaming Rosaleen reaches Granny's house, the old woman—whom Lansbury plays to the enjoyable hilt—regales her with a series of tales that reflect the desires and fears beset-

ting a girl on the brink of womanhood. The disconnected episodes are weighed down by their simplistic, obvious psychological subtext but they feature enough compelling imagery to keep a viewer interested, if not enthralled. The transformation from man to wolf is often terrifyingly spectacular, as in Granny's opening tale of a werewolf groom (Stephen Rea) returning to his suspicious bride (Kathryn Pogson) after several years. The bug-eyed wife watches incredulously as her strange husband begins to sprout hair and peel off his face to reveal a bloodied, prenatal manifestation of moving sinew that reforms itself into a lupine shape. It is all extremely convincing, except for the teeth, which suggest the werewolf has been seeing a good dentist.

Other sequences are humorous as well as visually captivating. In one, a   3
wronged girl who is pregnant vengefully turns her lover's bridal party into a pack of yapping wolves—reflecting the fear of pregnancy in Rosaleen's sexual fantasies. A passage in which the devil (Terence Stamp) is chauffeured through the woods in a white Rolls Royce is equally comic. Such vignettes, as well as Lansbury's cheekily exaggerated portrayal of Granny, suggest that the makers of *The Company of Wolves* were more than aware of the humor in their material. But the film's greatest attraction is its ingenuousness: Furst has created bewitching forests where teddy bears come to life and trees threaten to walk.

Still, those occasional smirks and moments of whimsy are not enough to   4
relieve the movie of its pretentious psychoanalytic cant. And while loading the tales with heavy-handed symbolism, Jordan failed to thread them together with the gossamer stitching that often connects the fragments of a nightmare. At the end of the film, when Rosaleen awakens in a sweat and her toys all fall to the floor, the implied statement that childhood is over has all the subtlety of a bear trap. *The Company of Wolves* is further proof—as if it were needed—that overanalysed dreams lose all their fascination.

Review of The Company of Wolves

J. HOBERMAN

The Company of Wolves is being saturation-dumped as if it were just anoth-   1
er horror flick—but this entertaining, unclassifiable film is something more than a belated addition to the werewolf cycle of 1980–81. A collaboration between Irish novelist turned filmmaker Neil Jordan and English literary fabulist Angela Carter, *The Company of Wolves* is a luridly convoluted Freudian fairy tale, pitched somewhere between Joe Dante's *The Howling* and Jean Cocteau's *La Belle et la bête.*

The most tangible evidence of the vaunted British film revival since *The*   2
Draughtsman's Contract (and the most sophisticated screamer since Roman

Polanski's *Fearless Vampire Killers*), *The Company of Wolves* unpacks Carter's nine-page story of the same name, placing the action inside the fevered dream of an adolescent girl. Carter's meditation on "Little Red Riding Hood" hyped the tale's libido (and added some frissons) through the infusion of werewolfiana as poetic as it was rampant. ("That long-drawn, wavering howl has, for all its fearful resonance, some inherent sadness in it, as if the beasts would love to be less beastly if only they knew how and never cease to mourn their own condition.") What's miraculous about Jordan's film is how it literalizes Carter's conceits without making them any less lyrical.

Deep within her dream, wide-eyed Rosaleen (13-year-old Sarah   3
Patterson), pout moistened with big sister's lipstick even as she imagines herself in some ersatz Dark Age, is a rapt audience for the paranoid old wives' tales of Angela Lansbury's deliciously clucking Granny. Knitting the girl an eye-searing crimson cloak of virgin wool, Lansbury tells the grisly story of the traveling man and his innocent bride, warns her against men whose eyebrows meet or who are "hairy inside," and explains that werewolves are the bastards fathered by priests and born on Christmas Day. ("By *priests?*" little Rosaleen exclaims. "Why do you think they call them Father?" is the tart reply.)

The film isn't dreamlike per se, but it revels in (and reveals) the dreamlike   4
qualities of even the most domesticated fairy tale—the repeated injunction not to "stray from the path," the mirrors Rosaleen keeps finding (most spectacularly in an eagle's nest), the continual, showstopping metamorphoses between human and lupine. Once it finds its rhythm, the film's interlocking, Chinese-box structure is quite pleasurable: as with Otar Iosseliani's ill-fated *Favorites of the Moon* or the films of Raúl Ruiz (and as befits a project that reportedly had its genesis when Jordan and Carter met at an academic conference on Borges), there's no mistaking *The Company of Wolves* for anything but a fiction.

Jordan's first film, *Angel* (released here last year as *Danny Boy*), was a   5
Point-Blank-derived metaphysical thriller whose often stunning visuals strained and broke under the burden of religious allegory. *The Company of Wolves* is far more assured and, shot entirely in the studio, offers images as rich as compost. The film unfolds in an autumnal netherworld—a damp, fecund Oz of soft earth colors and rounded, dwarfish forms. Far more than Boorman's tinsel-tawdry *Excalibur* or even Matthew Robbins's fen-dank *Dragonslayer*, *The Company of Wolves* has the sense of a dimly remembered, prehistoric Europe.

The "real" Rosaleen lives in a big country house, but she dreams herself   6
into some Celtic outpost where the villagers are a lot closer to the caves than to the stars, and their vulnerability is tangible. The wolf-haunted woods are themselves a primal thing—sometimes outrageously so, as pythons drape themselves from the trees or toads perch upon gigantic toadstools to observe Rosaleen out for a walk with an amorous bumpkin. The outside is always wanting in. The stray marmot that sneaks into Granny's house at midnight foretells the man-wolf who arrives later. Not even the church is a sanctuary;

tarantulas drop through the nave during the priest's pious evocation of Isaiah (". . . and the wolf shall dwell with the lamb").

Despite an occasional stab at class consciousness (the gentry as ravenous   7
you-know-whats), *The Company of Wolves* so insists on itself as a metaphor for Rosaleen's sexual awakening that, like Charles Perrault's moralizing "Little Red Riding Hood" (the conclusion of which is quoted with ironic gusto over the movie's end credits), it seems to reduce the fairy tale to a single, overemphatic reading. But this is to ignore the film's heady changes in tone—from farce to poetic horror, with special effects so yucky in their wit, you have to laugh with appreciation—as it purports to peel the onion of Rosaleen's unconscious. Although the girl's dream never ends, *The Company of Wolves* winds up with an image of shattered virginity as visceral as any in the movies. At the same time, Jordan and Carter are genuinely witty about sex. (Rosaleen receives sound advice from her comely, hard-working mum: "If there's a beast in men, it meets its match in women too.") Neither a solemn art film nor a brainless teen pic, this may well be the best dating movie in town.

"Children know something they can't tell," Djuna Barnes opined in   8
Nightwood. "They like Red Riding Hood and the wolf in bed!" Barnes's overripe, phantasmagorical prose style is an obvious precursor of Carter's, and *The Company of Wolves* could well be subtitled *Nightwood*—so tangled and nocturnal is its narrative, so filled with blood and yearning its tale. A horror film as literate as it is visionary, it's great fun—and that's not a cheap thrill.

■ ■ ■

Discussion and Writing Suggestions

1. Hoberman's review of "Company" is overwhelmingly positive, while O'Toole's review is mixed, finding fault with Jordan's "heavy-handed symbolism." Which of these reviews more closely resembles your response to the movie? Explain.

2. Both reviewers see in Jordan's film a metaphorical story of an adolescent girl's sexual awakening. What are the scenes from the movie that support this interpretation? Do you see "Company of Wolves" in this light? More generally, do you find the classic versions of "Little Red Riding Hood" on which "Company" is based to be about sexual awakening?

3. Both Hoberman and O'Toole agree that set designer Anton Furst succeeded in creating an evocative world—a forest of the imagination in which Rosaleen dreams the movie. O'Toole writes that Furst created "a splendid fantasy atmosphere." Hoberman calls Furst's "images as rich as compost." How did you respond to the forest in "Company?" What

associations did this forest have for you? How successful was it as a stage on which to play out the story?

4. Write a review of *Company of Wolves*. For guidance on structuring the piece (e.g., guidance on how much of a summary to provide, how many key features to evaluate, how much of the ending to give away), reread Hoberman's and O'Toole's reviews. Note that you can find elements of a movie lacking and still conclude that the movie is worthwhile, overall. See O'Toole's, particularly, as an example of a mixed review.

5. O'Toole admires (yet shudders at) the movie's transformations of humans into wolves. What was your response to the transformations? Recall the specific scenes in which transformations occur. What are their similarities and differences—both in terms of the special effects themselves and the dramatic uses to which these effects are put?

6. Generally, do you prefer to read—or not read—movie reviews before seeing a movie? What are the advantages and disadvantages of reading the reviews before—versus after? In the case of "Company," did you read or see the movie first? With what effect? Finally, assuming that readers are going to read a review before seeing the movie, what guidelines would you suggest for reviewers so that the movie viewing is enhanced, not tarnished?

REVIEWS OF *WOLF*

As indicated in the chapter introduction, the early 1990s saw remakes of several classic horror films—in 1992, *Bram Stoker's Dracula*; in 1994, both *Mary Shelley's Frankenstein* and *Wolf*. Although remakes of monster movies are not unusual in Hollywood, what's notable about this trio is that they were all filmed by "A-list" directors. The Dracula film was made by Francis Ford Coppola, renowned director of the *Godfather* films; the Frankenstein film was made by Kenneth Branagh, director of Shakespearean films *Henry V, Much Ado About Nothing*, and *Hamlet*. And the wolf-man film was made by Mike Nichols, director of *The Graduate*. Clearly, there is something about the mythology and the psychology of these durable horror archetypes that attracts some of the best creative artists in the medium.

Mike Nichols rose to prominence through his pairing with Elaine May in the late 1950s when the two created and performed satirical sketches about male-female relationships and contemporary social pressures. After the team broke up, Nichols directed Broadway plays (including Neil Simon's *Barefoot in the Park* and *The Odd Couple*) and then movies. Among his most well-known films (in addition to *The Graduate*, 1967) are *Who's Afraid of Virginia Woolf?* (1966), *Catch-22* (1970), *Carnal Knowledge* (1971), *Silkwood* (1983), *Working Girl* (1988), *Postcards from the Edge* (1990), *Regarding Henry* (1991), *The Birdcage* (1996), and *Primary Colors* (1998).

Wolf is about a New York book editor, Will Randall (Jack Nicholson), who, after being bitten by a wolf, begins to acquire both heightened visual and auditory sensation and wolflike strength and agility. After discovering that his wife Charlotte (Kate Nelligan) has been having an affair with his protégé Stewart Swinton (James Spader), Randall begins his own affair with his boss's daughter, Laura Alden (Michelle Pfeiffer). Responding to predatory business maneuverings on the part of his boss Raymond Alden (Christopher Plummer) and Swinton, Will uses his new wolfish nature to help even the score, but, like his movie forbears, grows increasingly unable to control his "beast within."

Following are three reviews of the film. Caryn James's commentary appeared in *The New York Times* (June 19, 1994). David Denby was the film critic for *New York* magazine; his review appeared in that magazine on June 20, 1994. (He now reviews films for *The New Yorker*.) Janet Maslin is lead film critic of *The New York Times*, where her review appeared on June 17, 1994.

The Werewolf Within Dances With Abandon

CARYN JAMES

In "The Company of Wolves," Neil Jordan's deliciously dark fairy tale,   1
Granny offers her adolescent granddaughter some timeless advice. The 1984 film, based on Angela Carter's shrewd story, turns "Little Red Riding Hood" into a blatant tale of erotic awakening. To navigate the wolf-filled woods of adulthood, Granny tells the girl, "Never stray from the path; never eat a windfall apple; never trust a man whose eyebrows meet." Or, she might have added, whose eyebrows arch as demonically as Jack Nicholson's.

Granny (Angela Lansbury) would have instantly spotted the hero of   2
"Wolf" as part of a new breed of movie werewolves. Though Mike Nichols's film is being advertised with the provocative line "The animal is out," one of Granny's sentiments would have served much better. "The worst kind of wolves," she warns, "are hairy on the inside."

"Wolf" is a film that half works, and its success is all in the first half. Mr.   3
Nicholson, as a book editor named Will Randall, is bitten by a wolf on a snowy road and develops strong symptoms of rejuvenation. Eventually the film loses its grip and becomes a routine horror movie, a genre in which the director seems profoundly uninterested. Until then the emerging wolfishness of Randall's character gives the film its entertaining, satiric edge and unexpectedly revealing pop-culture soul.

"I feel as if the wolf passed something along to me, a scrap of its spirit in   4
my blood," Randall says as he begins to feel unusually good. He consults an

expert on animal possession (as he explains, that's possession *by* an animal, not the kind of ownership that leads to the veterinarian's office) who calmly informs him he is changing into a wolf, and that not everyone who is bitten has the talent for such transformation. "There must be something wild within, an analogue of the wolf," the expert explains.

Something wild within? This Nichols-Nicholson wolf is definitely out of touch with typical werewolf movies. From the classic 1941 film "The Wolf Man," starring Lon Chaney Jr. to John Landis's eerie, special-effects laden "American Werewolf in London" in 1981, werewolf films have been about growing a snout, sprouting hair on your feet and being possessed by a murderous beast.   5

But the Nicholson wolf is perfectly in tune with today's pop psychology. He is the male version of the heroines in "Women Who Run With the Wolves." Clarissa Pinkola Estes's appealing book, subtitled "Myths and Stories of the Wild Woman Archetype," has been on the best-seller list for 93 weeks.   6

In the stories Mr. Estes collects, the wolf-woman represents the essential self, powerful and benign but also informed by the natural predator in humans. Randall's "analogue of the wolf" resembles Ms. Estes's "Wild Woman soul," and his introspective werewolf is the man of the moment—a moment when we are all supposed to be looking for our inner wolf cubs.   7

In one respect this spiritual focus is responsible for a major lost opportunity in "Wolf." Werewolf stories have been adapted for hundreds of years, to cover everything from mental illness to demonic possession. But the lore has almost always involved submerged sexuality and an animal released from within a man, whether he likes it or not. The appeal of the werewolf myth— and its frightening power—has much to do with loss of control and reason.   8

Such a myth would seem perfect for the age of AIDS, when sex is supposed to be a matter of calm reason and of risks diminished by the thoughtful use of condoms. What more appropriate fantasy than a scenario in which animal desires are unleashed against one's will? ("No, he didn't use a condom. He turned into a werewolf so fast!")   9

And for a time "Wolf" seems ready to explore that part of the myth. Dr. Vijay Alezias (Om Puri), the aged Indian expert whom Randall consults, assumes the Maria Ouspenskaya role; she was the wise old Gypsy woman in "The Wolf Man" who could see in a flash that Lon Chaney Jr. was headed for a furry future. Alezias tells Randall: "It feels good to be a wolf, doesn't it? Power without guilt, love without doubt." Alluring and sensible though that idea is—the perfect fantasy of irresponsibility for an age burdened with caution—it seems left over from some other better version of the script. Bestial freedom is a minor part of the Nicholson character, though he does discreetly tryst with Michelle Pfeiffer at the Mayflower Hotel before running out to Central Park to bay at the moon.   10

His shrewd, intelligent, wolfish senses are awakened more dramatically. Mr. Nicholson is mordantly funny as he gargles in the morning, making subtle wolf sounds. His receding hairline improves and he can read without   11 his glasses. He can smell an early-morning nip of tequila on a co-worker's breath from the other side of the corridor and hear soft conversations taking place on another floor. In this neat twist on the typical horror movie, he is less a werewolf than Superman in need of a shave. And he uses his improved senses well. He sniffs his wife's dress, identifies the scent of her lover and soon bites the other man's hand before bounding up the stairs on all fours to catch his wife in the man's apartment.

Randall has the analogue of the wolf, all right, but as Alezias says, only an evil man will become an evil wolf. From the Middle ages on, werewolves—and lycanthropes, people who imagined they became wolves—were often thought to be demonically possessed. "Wolf" toys briefly with that idea, too, though it seems to come out of nowhere. "I, too, will become a demon wolf," Alezias says when he asks Randall to do him a favor and bite him. But since Randall's inner-wolf analogue is basically good, he's not feeling devilish enough to comply. What kind of wimpy, nouveau wolf is he? 12

His ancestors, those more conventional movie werewolves, traded off on the myth of the unleashed beast (different from the vampire myth of eternal life), and on special effects that reached their height in "An American Werewolf in London" and Michael Jackson's video "Thriller," also directed by John Landis. Sometimes werewolf conventions were played for laughs. Michael Landon's career was jump-started when he played the lead in "I Was a Teen-Age Werewolf" (1957), and Michael J. Fox had a hit in the updated "Teen Wolf" (1985). "The Howling" (1981) is a werewolf satire that manages to be funny and creepy. 13

They all owe their spirits to "The Wolf Man," with Chaney as Larry Talbot, the ultimate good guy doomed because he was bitten by Bela Lugosi, as a Gypsy werewolf. Since a werewolf cannot be trusted to act like a gentleman (it's no mistake that wolf is a slangy term for womanizer), Talbot must resist the woman he loves. If a man's animal side comes out, the woman dies, at least in terms of social respectability in 1941. The typical werewolf myth on screen reinforces the idea of social and sexual restraint, for loss of control carries lethal consequences. 14

Newer variations suggest the value of embracing the inner wolf (not to mention dancing with them), and "The Company of Wolves" offers the most fascinating twist on the myth. In the Carter story, even more emphatically than in the film, the Red Riding Hood character, Rosaleen, gives herself freely to a wolf man. The act suggests the acceptance of her own emerging sexuality. Still, wolves are destructive and terrifying in this tale; so is human nature, with its capacity for evil and violence. It is an ambiguous freedom that allows Rosaleen to give herself to a wolf and become one. 15

But at least she isn't reduced to wolf bait, the way Michelle Pfeiffer is in "Wolf." One of the film's most annoying throwbacks to "The Wolf Man" is that her character is a convenient cliché, the woman in danger. As "Wolf" goes on, it seems to lose its early interest in character and wit, giving in to scenes of fangy teeth, yellow eyes and the contagious spread of werewolfness. 16

If "Wolf" had combined its two parts—the clever satire and the horror   17
flick—with more assurance, Mr. Nicholson might have been a wolf for the
ages. As it is, he makes an amusing wolf for the moment, hairy inside and out.

Review of Wolf

DAVID DENBY

Horror-film buffs will be disappointed with Mike Nichols's *Wolf.* So will   1
moviegoers hoping for a delirious visual experience. *Wolf,* an urbane wolfs-
bane movie, doesn't give us much of a jolt, and although its dark-blue moonlight colors look great, Nichols and cinematographer Giuseppe Rotunno
don't liberate the visual scheme for the movie. Nichols is a director who
mocks a horror picture even as he's making one. Set in the wolf-eat-wolf
world of New York publishing, the move has a slight uneasy tone, the tone of
smart people doing something not quite natural to them. Yet a lot of it is witty
and rather touching, and until the cruddy final scenes, I enjoyed it a great
deal. Nichols and writers Jim Harrison and Wesley Strick have jettisoned the
silver bullets, the Carpathian claptrap of the old Lon Chaney Jr. cornball scare
movies. Instead, the filmmakers have seized hold of the liberationist undertones. Becoming a wolf is not just suffering; it's also an escape into freedom.

Movie-world buzz has it that Jack Nicholson is too old for his part, but   2
having seen him, I can't imagine anyone else doing it. As Will Randall, the editorial director of a small, quality-lit publishing house, Nicholson, keeping his
voice low, has somehow captured the weariness, the modulated irony and
deep-down integrity of the aging New York literary man. Nicholson doesn't
glower and pose; he sticks to his business of playing a highly controlled and
self-conscious intellectual. He has the strong forehead of a man of character.
Driving through the Vermont mountains, Will hits a wolf, and then, when he
gets out of his Volvo to check the animal's condition, he gets bitten. Right
away Mike Nichols tips us off that the movie is not quite meant to be taken
straight. The seemingly dead animal cocks a yellow eye at Nicholson before
chomping on his wrist.

When Will returns to town, he discovers, as he expected, that the bil-   3
lionaire publisher (Christopher Plummer) who has purchased the publishing
house wants to replace him. The surprise is that the replacement is his friend
and protégé (James Spader), a young marketing genius who thinks books
should "sizzle." Betrayed on all sides, Will begins sprouting tufts on his
hands, and he wakes to the pleasure of strength and potency. His senses are
sharpened: He smells more, sees more; he even reads better. (I know a few editors who could use a bite.) Becoming a wolf is not just a metaphor for sexual
arousal: Will's desire for everything in life has been aroused. The wolf bite is
his Faustian bargain. The price is that he turns savage under the moon.

Miraculously, Nicholson does most of his work without special makeup; his teeth grow a little longer, but the wolfishness is mainly physical and spiritual. Invigorated, Will takes on the publishing magnate and the slimy protégé. In part the movie is about fear of old age, and a last leap at youth.

The satirical point in all this, of course, is that wolves are all around us 4
and sometimes inside us. Christopher Plummer is a terrifyingly sophisticated magnate, a man amused by the knowledge that decency and taste are a drag on profits, and James Spader outdoes himself playing James Spader. Surely this is the culminating performance of his yuppie-creep phase. The baby-faced Spader, literally dripping with sincerity (he's moist), looks most vulnerable as he's being most vicious. And Spader pulls off a comic tour de force: In the movie's most audacious scene, Spader, bitten and himself metamorphosing, kneels and sniffs at Michelle Pfeiffer in ecstasies of obsequious lust.

Mike Nichols, that compound of talent and cynicism, has never been 5
sharper at getting the undertones of hostility in ordinary speech. For once, a sophisticated New York milieu that doesn't seem fake or strained! And yet, in many ways, *Wolf* is Nichols's gentlest movie. When Will meets Laura (Pfeiffer), the billionaire's beautiful, hard-living, and miserable daughter, Nichols establishes a lovely rueful tone—and he sustains it. Pfeiffer's Laura falls in love with the much older man because he has an aura of defeated integrity, and she feels defeated herself. A few flashes of literate and tender banter between these two struck me as almost a revelation. The sound of grownups talking! Who cares if it's in a werewolf picture? The trouble is, the tenderness is finally too tame. The relationship doesn't go wild when it should. What's the point of making a modern wolfman movie if you aren't going to have a great, snarling sex scene?

Will pursues deer through the woods and chews up muggers in Central 6
Park. He doesn't suffer as Lon Chaney Jr. did. He's almost enthralled by the wolf within. I only wish Mike Nichols had liberated the wolf inside himself as well. If he had, he might have freed the camera and made us crazy with pleasure. Nichols uses New York poorly (most of *Wolf* was shot on sets), and the movie ends flatly. The pleasures of *Wolf* are minor—but they're distinct and memorable.

Review of Wolf

JANET MASLIN

All of us experience the occasional touch of beastliness, but Will Randall's 1
case is something special. For Will, a suave, well-respected New York book

editor, it would be helpful to have an animal urge or two. Polished and civilized as he is, Will has no self-protective instincts when it comes to the laws of the jungle, professional variety. And he needs some. There are times, as the first hour of "Wolf" makes enjoyably clear, when going for the jugular is exactly the right etiquette in corporate life.

So it's almost a boon for Will when his car hits an animal in Vermont one night. Getting out to investigate, Will is bitten by a wolf, and the short-term results are remarkably salutary. He returns to his office with strange new powers nicely suited to the business world. His senses are more acute, his energy revitalized. He now has the advantage of being able to see, hear and sniff out whatever sneakiness is going on behind his back.

So long as it stays confined to the level of metaphor, as it does in the first hour of "Wolf," this idea really is irresistible. And Mike Nichols's own killer instincts as an urbane social satirist are ideally suited to this milieu. Just as he did in the opening, not-yet-sentimental sections of "Regarding Henry," Mr. Nichols knowingly captures the smooth viciousness behind his characters' great shows of sophistication.

Only later, when the wolf motif is allowed to become literal, does "Wolf" sink its paws into deep quicksand. This would have been a far better film if Jack Nicholson, who perfectly embodies the courtly New York executive as an endangered species, had never been made to sprout fangs and grow hair on his hands.

Mr. Nicholson, who actually totes a briefcase for this role and gives one of his subtlest performances in recent years, is well suited to the conversational savagery that marks "Wolf" at its best. The story pits him against two well-drawn adversaries: Raymond Alden (Christopher Plummer), an elegant tycoon who has just taken over Will's publishing house, and Stewart Swinton (James Spader), the smiling young schemer who has just talked his way into Will's job.

In the film's most extravagantly entertaining sequence, Will is invited to a soiree at Alden's estate for the express purpose of being dismissed—or, to put it more politely, reassigned to a meaningless job in Eastern Europe. True to this film's air of treacherous good taste, the ax falls during a peaceable stroll around the grounds. "You're a nice person," Alden says when it's over. "Thank God I replaced you."

Stunned by this turn of events, Will winds up near Alden's stable and is befriended by the sullen, jaded Laura (Michelle Pfeiffer), Alden's rebellious daughter. "What're you, the last civilized man?" she asks him skeptically, although that is how the film would describe him. When Laura becomes interested in Will, it makes a certain sense: not only is he an obvious father figure, but he's also just right for a tough younger woman who says she's always been attracted to the wrong men. If Laura likes danger, then a guy who goes out marauding under the full moon is a fine choice.

"Wolf" tries to circumvent the usual werewolf exposition by treating Will's condition matter-of-factly. That he doesn't hide his problem from Laura signals a certain appealing sang-froid. So it's too bad when "Wolf" becomes carried away with special effects (by Rick Baker, the master of movie werewolf tricks) and lethal escapades, none of which is brought off with much panache. Unlike Francis Ford Coppola, who revealed a surprising enthusiasm for horrific vampire tricks in "Bram Stoker's 'Dracula,'" Mr. Nichols shows no great gusto for the supernatural. Nor can he deliver the magic it would have taken to provide "Wolf" with a half-decent ending.

Some of the trouble lies in the writing: "Wolf" is credited to both the rugged novelist Jim Harrison ("Sundog," "Warlock") and the genre screen-writer Wesley Strick ("Final Analysis," "True Believer," "Arachnophobia," "Cape Fear"). Small wonder that the material is wildly inconsistent at times, with a macho streak ("It feels good to be the wolf, doesn't it?") that hardly matches its better-developed soigné side. Late in the story, the writing even takes a soggily romantic turn that doesn't suit the actors at all. Lines like "I've never loved anyone this way" and "Maybe there's happy endings even for people who don't believe in them" don't belong here. 9

In addition to Mr. Nicholson, who cocks his ears and narrows his eyes with gleeful, wolfly flair, there are admirable performances from Mr. Spader, still turning the business of being despicable into a fine art, and Kate Nelligan, as Will's deceptively brisk and efficient wife. Smaller roles (like that of Eileen Atkins, as Will's devoted secretary) have been filled with Mr. Nichols's customary attention to detail. 10

Ms. Pfeiffer's role is underwritten, but her performance is expert enough to make even diffidence compelling. Mr. Plummer, as he should, radiates a self-satisfaction so great it actually seems carnivorous. "I'd never have fired you in the first place if I'd known you were *this* ruthless," he tells Will admiringly midway through the story. "Thank you," Will modestly replies. 11

Giuseppe Rotunno's richly hued cinematography, Ann Roth's costumes (with a lot of corduroy for the newly bookish Mr. Nicholson), Sam O'Steen's crisp editing and Bo Welch's lavish production design combine to create a high gloss. But their work is overshadowed by special-effects overkill in the film's later outbursts. It is shown off best in the early scenes' sleek, decorous atmosphere, where there are predators enough. 12

■ ■ ■

Discussion and Writing Suggestions

1. Caryn James characterizes Jack Nicholson's Will Randall as an "introspective werewolf [who] is the man of the moment—a moment when we are all supposed to be looking for our inner wolf cubs." James is arguing that monster movies reflect the times. Do you agree with James's assessment of Will Randall? To what extent does *Wolf* share the qualities of classic werewolf pictures? Can such a picture share these qualities *and* reflect current cultural trends?
2. James sees a correspondence between *The Company of Wolves* and *Wolf* in that the characters embrace what is wolfish in them—as opposed to earlier cinema werewolves, who considered their predicament an afflic-

tion. What about wolfishness is appealing, both to Will Randall and to Rosaleen (of *The Company of Wolves*)? Do you find wolfishness appealing?

3. David Denby sees in *Wolf* a satire on the wolfishness of big-city, interoffice politics. Is the movie a satire? And if so, is it a horror movie as well? Explain.

4. Maslin observes that director Mike Nichols "shows no great gusto for the supernatural." He doesn't seem interested in the weird, otherworldly conventions of the wolfman genre. Do you agree? It would be especially useful to develop your answer by comparing *Wolf* to the 1941 Lon Chaney *Wolf Man*. Which seems more the classic? Why?

5. All three critics find that *Wolf* fails as a movie somewhere after the midway point, when Will Randall's inner wolf, previously suggested through dialogue and subtly changing expressions of character, becomes an outer, explicit wolf. James says that "*Wolf* is a film that half works." Denby calls the last scenes "cruddy." Maslin thinks that toward the end, the movie sinks "its paws in deep quicksand." Though the critics agree the movie is flawed, each enjoys it. What is your view of the ending? What is your overall assessment of the movie?

6. Critics are bound to disagree in their assessments of a movie (though see the question immediately above). Maslin writes that the cinematographer on *Wolf* (responsible for camera work), Giuseppe Rotunno, created shots that were "richly hued." David Denby writes that Rotunno did not "liberate the visual scheme for the movie." Watch several scenes from *Wolf*, paying careful attention to shot selection and overall visual effectiveness. What is your assessment?

The Strange Case of Dr. Jekyll and Mr. Hyde

ROBERT LOUIS STEVENSON

Robert Louis Stevenson's Dr. Jekyll and Mr. Hyde, *written in 1886 and set in Victorian London, has become a classic in suspense/psychological fiction. For over a century the names* Jekyll *and* Hyde *(even for those who have never read this brief novel) have been synonymous with what psychologists would later term "split personality": the phenomenon of an individual harboring dual selves—an upstanding, public personality and a hidden (and, in Mr. Hyde's case, beastly) one. The complex and unexpected relationship between these two selves warring within one psyche fascinated Stevenson, as it later would Freud.*

Robert Louis Stevenson, born in Edinburgh, Scotland, in 1850, was trained as a lawyer, but became one of the most popular adventure novelists of the late 19th century. His romantic imagination and rhythmic prose, in such works as Treasure Island *(1883) and* Kidnapped *(1885), have captivated generations of readers. (And listeners: the writer of this headnote fondly remembers his long-vanished childhood in England listening transfixed to a serialized radio dramatization of* Treasure Island*!) The Strange Case of Dr. Jekyll and Mr. Hyde appeared in 1886. Stevenson also wrote* A Child's Garden of Verses *(1885) and* The Master of Ballantrae *(1889). Suffering from tuberculosis, he spent much of his life traveling in an attempt to recover his health, first in Saranac, New York (site of a sanatorium), and then in Samoa, where he wrote his last, unfinished novel* Weir of Hermiston, *published posthumously. Stevenson died in 1894 at the age of 44.*

We excerpt two chapters from Dr. Jekyll and Mr. Hyde: *the first, which introduces the depraved Mr. Hyde (along with a secondary character, the lawyer Utterson) and the final chapter, "Henry Jekyll's Full Statement of the Case." We recommend that you read the novel (only 90 pages, but too long for full inclusion here). What we have excerpted will provide enough of the story to reflect on the origins of the "beast" within and the relationship between that beast and our outer, socially acceptable selves.*

STORY OF THE DOOR

Mr. Utterson the lawyer was a man of a rugged countenance, that was never   1
lighted by a smile; cold, scanty and embarrassed in discourse; backward in sentiment; lean, long, dusty, dreary, and yet somehow lovable. At friendly meetings, and when the wine was to his taste, something eminently human beaconed from his eye; something indeed which never found its way into his talk, but which spoke not only in these silent symbols of the after-dinner face, but more often and loudly in the acts of his life. He was austere with himself; drank gin when he was alone, to mortify a taste for vintages; and though he enjoyed the theatre, had not crossed the doors of one for twenty years. But he had an approved tolerance for others; sometimes wondering, almost with envy, at the high pressure of spirits involved in their misdeeds; and in any extremity inclined to help rather than to reprove. "I incline to Cain's heresy," he used to say quaintly: "I let my brother go to the devil in his own way." In this character, it was frequently his fortune to be the last reputable acquaintance and the last good influence in the lives of down-going men. And to such as these, so long as they came about his chambers, he never marked a shade of change in his demeanour.

No doubt the feat was easy to Mr. Utterson; for he was undemonstrative   2
at the best, and even his friendships seemed to be founded in a similar catholicity of good-nature. It is the mark of a modest man to accept his friendly circle ready made from the hands of opportunity; and that was the lawyer's way. His friends were those of his own blood, or those whom he had known the longest; his affections, like ivy, were the growth of time, they implied no aptness in the object. Hence, no doubt, the bond that united him to Mr. Richard Enfield, his distant kinsman, the well-known man about town. It was a nut to crack for many, what these two could see in each other, or what subject they could find in common. It was reported by those who

encountered them in their Sunday walks, that they said nothing, looked singularly dull, and would hail with obvious relief the appearance of a friend. For all that, the two men put the greatest store by these excursions, counted them the chief jewel of each week, and not only set aside occasions of pleasure, but even resisted the calls of business, that they might enjoy them uninterrupted.

It chanced on one of these rambles that their way led them down a by-street in a busy quarter of London. The street was small and what is called quiet, but it drove a thriving trade on the week-days. The inhabitants were all doing well, it seemed, and all emulously hoping to do better still, and laying out the surplus of their gains in coquetry; so that the shop fronts stood along that thoroughfare with an air of invitation, like rows of smiling saleswomen. Even on Sunday, when it veiled its more florid charms and lay comparatively empty of passage, the street shone out in contrast to its dingy neighbourhood, like a fire in a forest; and with its freshly painted shutters, well-polished brasses, and general cleanliness and gaiety of note, instantly caught and pleased the eye of the passenger.

Two doors from one corner, on the left hand going east, the line was broken by the entry of a court; and just at that point, a certain sinister block of building thrust forward its gable on the street. It was two storeys high; showed no window, nothing but a door on the lower storey and a blind forehead of discoloured wall on the upper; and bore in every feature the marks of prolonged and sordid negligence. The door, which was equipped with neither bell nor knocker, was blistered and distained. Tramps slouched into the recess and struck matches on the panels; children kept shop upon the steps; the schoolboy had tried his knife on the mouldings; and for close on a generation, no one had appeared to drive away these random visitors or to repair their ravages.

Mr. Enfield and the lawyer were on the other side of the by-street; but when they came abreast of the entry, the former lifted up his cane and pointed.

"Did you ever remark that door?" he asked; and when his companion had replied in the affirmative, "It is connected in my mind," added he, "with a very odd story."

"Indeed!" said Mr. Utterson, with a slight change of voice, "and what was that?"

"Well, it was this way," returned Mr. Enfield: "I was coming home from some place at the end of the world, about three o'clock of a black winter morning, and my way lay through a part of town where there was literally nothing to be seen but lamps. Street after street, and all the folks asleep—street after street, all lighted up as if for a procession, and all as empty as a church—till at last I got into that state of mind when a man listens and listens and begins to long for the sight of a policeman. All at once, I saw two figures: one a little man who was stumping along eastwards at a good walk, and the other a girl of maybe eight or ten who was running as hard as she was able down a cross street. Well, sir, the two ran into one another naturally enough at the corner; and then came the horrible part of the thing; for the man trampled calmly over the child's body and left her screaming on the ground. It sounds nothing to hear, but it was hellish to see. It wasn't like a man; it was like some damned Juggernaut. I gave a view halloa, took to my heels, collared my gentleman, and brought him back to where there was already quite a group about the screaming child. He was perfectly cool and made no resistance, but gave me one look, so ugly that it brought out the sweat on me like running. The people who had turned out were the girl's own family; and pretty soon the doctor, for whom she had been sent, put in his appearance. Well, the child was not much the worse, more frightened, according to the Sawbones; and there you might have supposed would be an end to it. But there was one curious circumstance. I had taken a loathing to my gentleman at first sight. So had the child's family, which was only natural. But the doctor's case was what struck me. He was the usual cut and dry apothecary, of no particular age and colour, with a strong Edinburgh accent, and about as emotional as a bagpipe. Well, sir, he was like the rest of us; every time he looked at my prisoner, I saw that Sawbones turned sick and white with the desire to kill him. I knew what was in his mind, just as he knew what was in mine; and killing being out of the question, we did the next best. We told the man we could and would make such a scandal out of this, as should make his name stink from one end of London to the other. If he had any friends or any credit, we undertook that he should lose them. And all the time, as we were pitching it in red hot, we were keeping the women off him as best we could, for they were as wild as harpies. I never saw a circle of such hateful faces; and there was the man in the middle; with a kind of black, sneering coolness— frightened too, I could see that—but carrying it off, sir, really like Satan. 'If you choose to make capital out of this accident,' said he, 'I am naturally helpless. No gentleman but wishes to avoid a scene,' says he. 'Name your figure.' Well, we screwed him up to a hundred pounds for the child's family; he would have clearly liked to stick out; but there was something about the lot of us that meant mischief, and at last he struck. The next thing was to get the money; and where do you think he carried us but to that place with the door?—whipped out a key, went in, and presently came back with the matter of ten pounds in gold and a cheque for the balance on Coutt's, drawn payable to bearer, and signed with a name that I can't mention, though it's one of the points of my story, but it was a name at least very well known and often printed. The figure was stiff; but the signature was good for more than that, if it was only genuine. I took the liberty of pointing out to my gentleman that the whole business looked apocryphal; and that a man does not, in real life, walk into a cellar door at four in the morning and come out of it with another man's cheque for close upon a hundred pounds. But he was quite easy and sneering. 'Set your mind at rest,' says he; 'I will stay with you till the banks open, and cash the cheque myself.' So we all set off, the doctor, and the child's father, and our friend and myself, and passed the rest of the night in my chambers; and next day, when we had breakfasted, went in a body to the bank. I gave in the cheque myself, and said I had every reason to believe it was a forgery. Not a bit of it. The cheque was genuine."

"Tut-tut!" said Mr. Utterson.   9

"I see you feel as I do," said Mr. Enfield. "Yes, it's a bad story. For my   10
man was a fellow that nobody could have to do with, a really damnable man;
and the person that drew the cheque is the very pink of the proprieties, celebrated too, and (what makes it worse) one of your fellows who do what they
call good. Black mail, I suppose; an honest man paying through the nose for
some of the capers of his youth. Black Mail House is what I call that place
with the door, in consequence. Though even that, you know, is far from
explaining all," he added; and with the words fell into a vein of musing.

From this he was recalled by Mr. Utterson asking rather suddenly: "And   11
you don't know if the drawer of the cheque lives there?"

"A likely place, isn't it?" returned Mr. Enfield. "But I happen to have   12
noticed his address; he lives in some square or other."

"And you never asked about—the place with the door?" said Mr.   13
Utterson.

"No, sir: I had a delicacy," was the reply. "I feel very strongly about   14
putting questions; it partakes too much of the style of the day of judgment.
You start a question, and it's like starting a stone. You sit quietly on the top
of a hill; and away the stone goes, starting others; and presently some bland
old bird (the last you would have thought of) is knocked on the head in his
own back garden, and the family have to change their name. No, sir, I make
it a rule of mine: the more it looks like Queer Street, the less I ask."

"A very good rule, too," said the lawyer.   15

"But I have studied the place for myself," continued Mr. Enfield. "It   16
seems scarcely a house. There is no other door, and nobody goes in or out of
that one, but, once in a great while, the gentleman of my adventure. There are
three windows looking on the court on the first floor; none below; the windows are always shut, but they're clean. And then there is a chimney, which
is generally smoking; so somebody must live there. And yet it's not so sure; for
the buildings are so packed together about that court, that it's hard to say
where one ends and another begins."

The pair walked on again for a while in silence; and then—"Enfield,"   17
said Mr. Utterson, "that's a good rule of yours."

"Yes, I think it is," returned Enfield.   18

"But for all that," continued the lawyer, "there's one point I want to ask: 19
I want to ask the name of that man who walked over the child."

"Well," said Mr. Enfield, "I can't see what harm it would do. It was a   20
man of the name of Hyde."

"Hm," said Mr. Utterson. "What sort of man is he to see?"   21

"He is not easy to describe. There is something wrong with his appear-   22
ance; something displeasing, something downright detestable. I never saw a
man I so disliked, and yet I scarce know why. He must be deformed somewhere; he gives a strong feeling of deformity, although I couldn't specify the
point. He's an extraordinary looking man, and yet I really can name nothing
out of the way. No, sir; I can make no hand of it; I can't describe him. And
it's not want of memory; for I declare I can see him this moment."

Mr. Utterson again walked some way in silence, and obviously under a   23
weight of consideration. "You are sure he used a key?" he inquired at last.

"My dear sir . . ." began Enfield, surprised out of himself.   24

"Yes, I know," said Utterson; "I know it must seem strange. The fact is,   25
if I do not ask you the name of the other party, it is because I know it already.
You see, Richard, your tale has gone home. If you have been inexact in any
point, you had better correct it."

"I think you might have warned me," returned the other, with a touch of   26
sullenness. "But I have been pedantically exact, as you call it. The fellow had
a key; and, what's more, he has it still. I saw him use it, not a week ago."

Mr. Utterson signed deeply, but said never a word; and the young man   27
presently resumed. "Here's another lesson to say nothing," said he. "I am
ashamed of my long tongue. Let us make a bargain never to refer to this
again."

"With all my heart," said the lawyer. "I shake hands on that, Richard."   28

• • •

HENRY JEKYLL'S FULL STATEMENT OF THE CASE

I was born in the year 18– to a large fortune, endowed besides with excellent   29
parts, inclined by nature to industry, fond of the respect of the wise and
good among my fellow-men, and thus, as might have been supposed, with
every guarantee of an honourable and distinguished future. And indeed, the
worst of my faults was a certain impatient gaiety of disposition, such as has
made the happiness of many, but such as I found it hard to reconcile with my
imperious desire to carry my head high, and wear a more than commonly
grave countenance before the public. Hence it came about that I concealed my
pleasures; and that when I reached years of reflection, and began to look
round me, and take stock of my progress and position in the world, I stood
already committed to a profound duplicity of life. Many a man would have
even blazoned such irregularities as I was guilty of; but from the high views
that I had set before me, I regarded and hid them with an almost morbid sense
of shame. It was thus rather the exacting nature of my aspirations, than any
particular degradation in my faults, that made me what I was, and, with
even a deeper trench than in the majority of men, severed in me those
provinces of good and ill which divide and compound man's dual nature. In
this case, I was driven to reflect deeply and inveterately on that hard law of
life, which lies at the root of religion, and is one of the most plentiful springs
of distress. Though so profound a double-dealer, I was in no sense a hyp-
ocrite; both sides of me were in dead earnest; I was no more myself when I
laid aside restraint and plunged in shame, than when I laboured, in the eye of
day, at the furtherance of knowledge or the relief of sorrow and suffering.
And it chanced that the direction of my scientific studies, which led wholly
towards the mystic and the transcendental, reacted and shed a strong light on
this consciousness of the perennial war among my members. With every day,

and from both sides of my intelligence, the moral and the intellectual, I thus drew steadily nearer to that truth, by whose partial discovery I have been doomed to such a dreadful shipwreck: that man is not truly one, but truly two. I say two, because the state of my own knowledge does not pass beyond that point. Others will follow, others will outstrip me on the same lines; and I hazard the guess that man will be ultimately known for a mere polity of multifarious, incongruous and independent denizens. I, for my part, from the nature of my life, advanced infallibly in one direction, and in one direction only. It was on the moral side, and in my own person, that I learned to recognize the thorough and primitive duality of man; I saw that, of the two natures that contended in the field of my consciousness, even if I could rightly be said to be either, it was only because I was radically both; and from an early date, even before the course of my scientific discoveries had begun to suggest the most naked possibility of such a miracle, I had learned to dwell with pleasure, as a beloved daydream, on the thought of the separation of these elements. If each, I told myself, could but be housed in separate identities, life would be relieved of all that was unbearable; the unjust might go his way, delivered from the aspirations and remorse of his more upright twin; and the just could walk steadfastly and securely on his upward path, doing the good things in which he found his pleasure, and no longer exposed to disgrace and penitence by the hands of his extraneous evil. It was the curse of mankind that these incongruous faggots were thus bound together—that in the agonized womb of consciousness, these polar twins should be continuously struggling. How, then, were they dissociated?

I was so far in my reflections, when, as I have said, a side light began to shine upon the subject from the laboratory table. I began to perceive more deeply than it has ever yet been stated, the trembling immateriality, the mist-like transience, of this seemingly so solid body in which we walk attired. Certain agents I found to have the power to shake and to pluck back that fleshly vestment, even as a wind might toss the curtains of a pavilion. For two good reasons, I will not enter deeply into this scientific branch of my confession. First, because I have been made to learn that the doom and burthen of our life is bound for ever on man's shoulders; and when the attempt is made to cast it off, it but returns upon us with more unfamiliar and more awful pressure. Second, because, as my narrative will make, alas! too evident, my discoveries were incomplete. Enough, then, that I not only recognized my natural body from the mere aura and effulgence of certain of the powers that made up my spirit, but managed to compound a drug by which these powers should be dethroned from their supremacy, and a second form and countenance substituted, none the less natural to me because they were the expression, and bore the stamp, of lower elements in my soul.

I hesitated long before I put this theory to the test of practice. I knew well that I risked death; for any drug that so potently controlled and shook the very fortress of identity, might by the least scruple of an overdose or at the least inopportunity in the moment of exhibition, utterly blot out that immaterial tabernacle which I looked to it to change. But the temptation of a discovery so singular and profound, at last overcame the suggestions of alarm.

I had long since prepared my tincture; I purchased at once, from a firm of wholesale chemists, a large quantity of a particular salt, which I knew, from my experiments, to be the last ingredient required; and, late one accursed night, I compounded the elements, watched them boil and smoke together in the glass and when the ebullition had subsided, with a strong glow of courage, drank off the potion.

The most racking pangs succeeded: a grinding in the bones, deadly   32 nausea, and a horror of the spirit that cannot be exceeded at the hour of birth or death. Then these agonies began swiftly to subside, and I came to myself as if out of a great sickness. There was something strange in my sensations, something indescribably new, and, from its very novelty, incredibly sweet. I felt younger, lighter, happier in body; within I was conscious of a heady recklessness, a current of disordered sensual images running like a mill race in my fancy, a solution of the bonds of obligation, an unknown but not an innocent freedom of the soul. I knew myself, at the first breath of this new life, to be more wicked, tenfold more wicked, sold a slave to my original evil; and the thought, in that moment, braced and delighted me like wine. I stretched out my hands, exulting in the freshness of these sensations; and in the act, I was suddenly aware that I had lost in stature.

There was no mirror, at that date, in my room; that which stands beside   33 me as I write was brought there later on, and for the very purpose of those transformations. The night, however, was far gone into the morning—the morning, black as it was, was nearly ripe for the conception of the day—the inmates of my house were locked in the most rigorous hours of slumber; and I determined, flushed as I was with hope and triumph, to venture in my new shape as far as to my bedroom. I crossed the yard, wherein the constellations looked down upon me, I could have thought, with wonder, the first creature of that sort that their unsleeping vigilance had yet disclosed to them; I stole through the corridors, a stranger in my own house; and coming to my room, I saw for the first time the appearance of Edward Hyde.

I must here speak by theory alone, saying not that which I know, but that   34 which I suppose to be most probable. The evil side of my nature, to which I had now transferred the stamping efficacy, was less robust and less developed than the good which I had just deposed. Again, in the course of my life, which had been, after all, nine-tenths a life of effort, virtue and control, it had been much less exercised and much less exhausted. And hence, as I think, it came about that Edward Hyde was so much smaller, slighter, and younger than Henry Jekyll. Even as good shone upon the countenance of the one, evil was written broadly and plainly on the face of the other. Evil besides (which I must still believe to be the lethal side of man) had left on that body an imprint of deformity and decay. And yet when I looked upon that ugly idol in the glass, I was conscious of no repugnance, rather of a leap of welcome. This, too, was myself. It seemed natural and human. In my eyes it bore a livelier image of the spirit, it seemed more express and single, than the imperfect and divided countenance I had been hitherto accustomed to call mine. And in so far I was doubtless right. I have observed that when I wore the semblance of

Edward Hyde, none could come near to me at first without a visible misgiving of the flesh. This, as I take it, was because all human beings, as we meet them, are commingled out of good and evil; and Edward Hyde, alone, in the ranks of mankind, was pure evil.

I lingered but a moment at the mirror: the second and conclusive experiment had yet to be attempted; it yet remained to be seen if I had lost my identity beyond redemption and must flee before daylight from a house that was no longer mine: and hurrying back to my cabinet, I once more prepared and drank the cup, once more suffered the pangs of dissolution, and came to myself once more with the character, the stature, and the face of Henry Jekyll.   35

That night I had come to the fatal cross roads. Had I approached my discovery in a more noble spirit, had I risked the experiment while under the empire of generous or pious aspirations, all must have been otherwise, and from these agonies of death and birth I had come forth an angel instead of a fiend. The drug had no discriminating action; it was neither diabolical nor divine; it but shook the doors of the prison-house of my disposition; and, like the captive of Philippi, that which stood within ran forth. At that time my virtue slumbered; my evil, kept awake by ambition, was alert and swift to seize the occasion; and the thing that was projected was Edward Hyde. Hence, although I had now two characters as well as two appearances, one was wholly evil, and the other was still the old Henry Jekyll, that incongruous compound of whose reformation and improvement I had already learned to despair. The movement was thus wholly toward the worse.   36

Even at that time, I had not yet conquered my aversion to the dryness of a life to study, I would still be merrily disposed at times; and as my pleasures were (to say the least) undignified, and I was not only well known and highly considered, but growing towards the elderly man, this incoherency of my life was daily growing more unwelcome. It was on this side that my new power tempted me until I fell in slavery. I had but to drink the cup, to doff at once the body of the noted professor, and to assume, like a thick cloak, that of Edward Hyde. I smiled at the notion; it seemed to me at the time to be humorous; and I made my preparations with the most studious care. I took and furnished that house in Soho, to which Hyde was tracked by the police; and engaged as housekeeper a creature whom I well knew to be silent and unscrupulous. On the other side, I announced to my servants that a Mr. Hyde (whom I described) was to have full liberty and power about my house in the square; and, to parry mishaps, I even called and made myself a familiar object, in my second character. I next drew up that will to which you so much objected; so that if anything befell me in the person of Dr. Jekyll, I could enter on that of Edward Hyde without pecuniary loss. And thus fortified, as I supposed, on every side, I began to profit by the strange immunities of my position.   37

Men have before hired bravos to transact their crimes, while their own person and reputation sat under shelter. I was the first that ever did so for his pleasures. I was the first that could thus plod in the public eye with a load of genial respectability, and in a moment, like a school-boy, strip off these lend-   38

ings and spring headlong into the sea of liberty. But for me, in my impene-
trable mantle, the safety was complete. Think of it—I did not even exist! Let
me but escape into my laboratory door, give me but a second or two to mix
and swallow the draught that I had always standing ready; and, whatever he
had done, Edward Hyde would pass away like the stain of breath upon a
mirror; and there in his stead, quietly at home, trimming the midnight lamp
in his study, a man who could afford to laugh at suspicion, would be Henry
Jekyll.

    The pleasures which I made haste to seek in my disguise were, as I have   39
said, undignified: I would scarce use a harder term. But in the hands of
Edward Hyde, they soon began to turn towards the monstrous. When I
would come back from these excursions, I was often plunged into a kind of
wonder at my vicarious depravity. This familiar that I called out of my own
soul, and sent forth alone to do his good pleasure, was a being inherently
malign and villainous; his every act and thought centered on self; drinking
pleasure with bestial avidity from any degree of torture to another; relentless
like a man of stone. Henry Jekyll stood at times aghast before the acts of
Edward Hyde; but the situation was apart from ordinary laws, and insidiously
relaxed the grasp of conscience. It was Hyde, after all, and Hyde alone, that
was guilty. Jekyll was no worse; he woke again to his good qualities seemingly
unimpaired; he would even make haste, where it was impossible, to undo the
evil by Hyde, and thus his conscience slumbered.

    Into the details of the infamy at which I thus connived (for even now I   40
can scarce grant that I committed it) I have no design of entering; I mean but
to point out the warnings and the successive steps with which my chastise-
ment approached. I met with one accident which, as it brought on no consequence, I shall no more than mention. An act of cruelty to a child aroused
against me the anger of a passer-by, whom I recognized the other day in the
person of your kinsman; the doctor and the child's family joined him; there
were moments when I feared for my life; and at last, in order to pacify their
too just resentment, Edward Hyde had to bring them to the door, and pay
them in a cheque drawn in the name of Henry Jekyll. But this danger was
easily eliminated from the future, by opening an account at another bank in
the name of Edward Hyde himself; and when, by sloping my own hand back-
wards, I had supplied my double with a signature, I thought I sat beyond the
reach of fate.

    Some two months before the murder of Sir Danvers, I had been out for   41
one of my adventures, had returned at a late hour, and woke the next day in
bed with somewhat odd sensations. It was in vain I looked about me; in vain
I saw the decent furniture and tall proportions of my room in the square; in
vain that I recognized the pattern of the bed curtains and the design of the
mahogany frame; something still kept insisting that I was not where I was,
that I had not wakened where I seemed to be, but in the little room in Soho
where I was accustomed to sleep in the body of Edward Hyde. I smiled to
myself, and, in my psychological way, began lazily to inquire into the elements
of this illusion, occasionally, even as I did so, dropping back into a comfort-

able morning doze. I was still so engaged when, in one of my more wakeful moments, my eye fell upon my hand. Now, the hand of Henry Jekyll (as you have often remarked) was professional in shape and size; it was large, firm, white and comely. But the hand which I now saw, clearly enough, in the yellow light of a mid-London morning, lying half shut on the bedclothes, was lean, corded, knuckly, of a dusky pallor, and thickly shaded with a swart growth of hair. It was the hand of Edward Hyde.

I must have stared upon it for near half a minute, sunk as I was in the   42 mere stupidity of wonder, before terror woke up in my breast as sudden and startling as the crash of cymbals; and bounding from my bed, I rushed to the mirror. At the sight that met my eyes, my blood was changed into something exquisitely thin and icy. Yes, I had gone to bed Henry Jekyll, I had awakened Edward Hyde. How was this to be explained? I asked myself; and then, with another bound of terror—how was it to be remedied? It was well on in the morning; the servants were up; all my drugs were in the cabinet—a long journey, down two pair of stairs, through the back passage, across the open court and through the anatomical theatre, from where I was then standing horror-struck. It might indeed be possible to cover my face; but of what use was that, when I was unable to conceal the alteration of my stature? And then, with an overpowering sweetness of relief, it came back upon my mind that the servants were already used to the coming and going of my second self. I had soon dressed, as well as I was able, in clothes of my own size; had soon passed through the house, where Bradshaw stared and drew back at seeing Mr. Hyde at such an hour and in such a strange array; and ten minutes later, Dr. Jekyll had returned to his own shape, and was sitting down, with a darkened brow, to make a feint of breakfasting.

Small indeed was my appetite. This inexplicable incident, this reversal of   43 my previous experience, seemed, like the Babylonian finger on the wall, to be spelling out the letters of my judgment; and I began to reflect more seriously than ever before on the issues and possibilities of my double existence. That part of me which I had the power of projecting had lately been much exercised and nourished; it had seemed to me of late as though the body of Edward Hyde had grown in stature, as though (when I wore that form) I were conscious of a more generous tide of blood; and I began to spy a danger that, if this were much prolonged, the balance of my nature might be permanently overthrown, the power of voluntary change be forfeited, and the character of Edward Hyde become irrevocably mine. The power of the drug had not been always equally displayed. Once, very early in my career, it had totally failed me; since then I had been obliged on more than one occasion to double, and once, with infinite risk of death, to treble the amount; and these rare uncertainties had cast hitherto the sole shadow on my contentment. Now, however, and in the light of that morning's accident, I was led to remark that whereas, in the beginning, the difficulty had been to throw off the body of Jekyll, it had of late gradually but decidedly transferred itself to the other side. All things therefore seemed to point to this: that I was slowly losing hold of my original and better self, and becoming slowly incorporated with my second and worse.

Between these two, I now felt I had to choose. My two natures had   44
memory in common, but all other faculties were most unequally shared
between them. Jekyll (who was composite) now with the most sensitive appre-
hensions, now with a greedy gusto, projected and shared in the pleasures and
adventures of Hyde; but Hyde was indifferent to Jekyll, or but remembered him
as the mountain bandit remembers the cavern in which he conceals himself
from pursuit. Jekyll had more than a father's interest; Hyde had more than a
son's indifference. To cast in my lot with Jekyll was to die to those appetites
which I had long secretly indulged and had of late begun to pamper. To cast it
in with Hyde was to die to a thousand interests and aspirations, and to become,
at a blow and for ever, despised and friendless. The bargain might appear
unequal; but there was still another consideration in the scale; for while Jekyll
would suffer smartingly in the fires of abstinence, Hyde would not be even conscious of all that he had lost. Strange as my circumstances were, the terms of this
debate are as old and commonplace as man; much the same inducements and
alarms cast the die for any tempted and trembling sinner; and it fell out with me,
as it falls with so vast a majority of my fellows, that I chose the better part, and
was found wanting in the strength to keep to it.

Yes, I preferred the elderly and discontented doctor, surrounded by   45
friends, and cherishing honest hopes; and bade a resolute farewell to the liberty, the comparative youth, the light step, leaping pulses and secret pleasures,
that I had enjoyed in the disguise of Hyde. I made this choice perhaps with
some unconscious reservation, for I neither gave up the house in Soho, nor
destroyed the clothes of Edward Hyde, which still lay ready in my cabinet. For
two months, however, I was true to my determination; for two months I led
a life of such severity as I had never before attained to, and enjoyed the com-
pensations of an approving conscience. But time began at last to obliterate the
freshness of my alarm; the praises of conscience began to grow into a thing of
course; I began to be tortured with throes and longings, as of Hyde struggling
after freedom; and at last, in an hour of moral weakness, I once again compounded and swallowed the transforming draught.

I do not suppose that when a drunkard reasons with himself upon his   46
vice, he is one out of five hundred times affected by the dangers that he runs
through his brutish physical insensibility; neither had I, long as I had considered my position, made enough allowance for the complete moral insensibility and insensate readiness to evil, which were the leading characters of
Edward Hyde. Yet it was by these that I was punished. My devil had been
long caged, he came out roaring. I was conscious, even when I took the
draught, of a more unbridled, a more furious propensity to ill. It must have
been this, I suppose, that stirred in my soul that tempest of impatience with
which I listened to the civilities of my unhappy victim; I declare at least,
before God, no man morally sane could have been guilty of that crime upon
so pitiful a provocation; and that I struck in no more reasonable spirit than
that in which a sick child may break a plaything.[1] But I had voluntarily

---

[1] *break a plaything:* Henry Jekyll is referring, here, to a murder he committed as Edward
Hyde.

stripped myself of all those balancing instincts by which even the worst of us continues to walk with some degree of steadiness among temptations; and in my case, to be tempted, however slightly, was to fall.

Instantly the spirit of hell awoke in me and raged. With a transport of glee, I mauled the unresisting body, tasting delight from every blow; and it was not till weariness had begun to succeed that I was suddenly, in the top fit of my delirium, struck through the heart by a cold thrill of terror. A mist dispersed; I saw my life to be forfeit; and fled from the scene of these excesses, at once glorifying and trembling, my lust of evil gratified and stimulated, my love of life screwed to the topmost peg. I ran to the house in Soho, and (to make assurance double sure) destroyed my papers; thence I set out through the lamplit streets, in the same divided ecstasy of mind, gloating on my crime, lightheadedly devising others in the future, and yet still hastening and still hearkening in my wake for the steps of the avenger. Hyde had a song upon his lips as he compounded the draught, and as he drank it pledged the dead man. The pangs of transformation had not done tearing him, before Henry Jekyll, with streaming tears of gratitude and remorse, had fallen upon his knees and lifted his clasped hands to God. The veil of self-indulgence was rent from head to foot, I saw my life as a whole: I followed it up from the days of childhood, when I had walked with my father's hand, and through the self-denying toils of my professional life, to arrive again and again, with the same sense of unreality, at the damned horrors of the evening. I could have screamed aloud; I sought with tears and prayers to smother down the crowd of hideous images and sounds with which my memory swarmed against me; and still, between the petitions, the ugly face of my iniquity stared into my soul. As the acuteness of this remorse began to die away, it was succeeded by a sense of joy. The problem of my conduct was solved. Hyde was thenceforth impossible; whether I would or not, I was now confined to the better part of my existence; and oh, how I rejoiced to think it! with what willing humility I embraced anew the restrictions of natural life! with what sincere renunciation I locked the door by which I had so often gone and come, and ground the key under my heel!

The next day came the news that the murder had been overlooked, that the guilt of Hyde was patent to the world, and that the victim was a man high in public estimation. It was not only a crime, it had been a tragic folly. I think I was glad to know it; I think I was glad to have my better impulses thus buttressed and guarded by the terrors of the scaffold. Jekyll was now my city of refuge; let but Hyde peep out an instant, and the hands of all men would be raised to take and slay him.

I resolved in my future conduct to redeem the past; and I can say with honesty that my resolve was fruitful of some good. You know yourself how earnestly in the last months of last year I laboured to relieve suffering; you know that much was done for others, and that the days passed quietly, almost happily for myself. Nor can I truly say that I wearied of this beneficent and innocent life; I think instead that I daily enjoyed it more completely; but I was still cursed with my duality of purpose; and as the first edge of my penitence wore off, the lower side of me, so long indulged, so recently chained down, began to growl for license. Not that I dreamed of resuscitating Hyde; the bare idea of that would startle me to frenzy: no, it was in my own person that I was once more tempted to trifle with my conscience; and it was as an ordinary secret sinner that I at last fell before the assaults of temptation.

There comes an end to all things; the most capacious measure is filled at 50 last; and this brief condescension to my evil finally destroyed the balance of my soul. And yet I was not alarmed; the fall seemed natural, like a return to the old days before I had made my discovery. It was a fine, clear January day, wet under foot where the frost had melted, but cloudless overhead; and the Regent's Park was full of winter chirrupings and sweet with spring odours. I sat in the sun on a bench; the animal within me licking the chops of memory; the spiritual side a little drowsed, promising subsequent penitence, but not yet moved to begin. After all, I reflected, I was like my neighbours; and then I smiled, comparing myself with other men, comparing my active goodwill with the lazy cruelty of their neglect. And at the very moment of that vainglorious thought, a qualm came over me, a horrid nausea and the most deadly shuddering. These passed away, and left me faint; and then as in its turn the faintness subsided, I began to be aware of a change in the temper of my thoughts, a greater boldness, a contempt of danger, a solution of the bonds of obligation. I looked down; my clothes hung formlessly on my shrunken limbs; the hand that lay on my knee was corded and hairy. I was once more Edward Hyde. A moment before I had been safe of all men's respect, wealthy, beloved—the cloth laying for me in the dining-room at home; and now I was the common quarry of mankind, hunted, houseless, a known murderer, thrall to the gallows.

My reason wavered, but it did not fail me utterly. I have more than once 51 observed that, in my second character, my faculties seemed sharpened to a point and my spirits more tensely elastic; thus it came about that, where Jekyll perhaps might have succumbed, Hyde rose to the importance of the moment. My drugs were in one of the presses of my cabinet: how was I to reach them? That was the problem that (crushing my temples in my hands) I set myself to solve. The laboratory door I had closed. If I sought to enter by the house, my own servants would consign me to the gallows. I saw I must employ another hand, and thought of Lanyon.[2] How was he to be reached? how persuaded? Supposing that I escaped capture in the streets, how was I to make my way into his presence? and how should I, an unknown and displeasing visitor, prevail on the famous physician to rifle the study of his colleague, Dr. Jekyll? Then I remembered that of my original character, one part remained to me: I could write my own hand; and once I had conceived that kindling spark, the way that I must follow became lighted up from end to end.

Thereupon, I arranged my clothes as best I could, and summoning a 52 passing hansom, drove to an hotel in Portland Street, the name of which I chanced to remember. At my appearance (which was indeed comical enough,

---

[2] *Lanyon:* Dr. Lanyon is a colleague of Jekyll's.

however tragic a fate these garments covered) the driver could not conceal his mirth. I gnashed my teeth upon him with a gust of devilish fury and the smile withered from his face—happily for him—yet more happily for myself, for in another instant I had certainly dragged him from his perch. At the inn, as I entered, I looked about me with so black a countenance as made the attendants tremble; not a look did they exchange in my presence; but obsequiously took my orders, led me to a private room, and brought me wherewithal to write. Hyde in danger of his life was a creature new to me: shaken with inordinate anger, strung to the pitch of murder, lusting to inflict pain. Yet the creature was astute; mastered his fury with a great effort of the will; composed his two important letters, one to Lanyon and one to Poole[3]; and, that he might receive actual evidence of their being posted, sent them out with directions that they should be registered.

Thenceforward, he sat all day over the fire in the private room, gnawing his nails; there he dined, sitting alone with his fears, the waiter visibly quailing before his eye; and thence, when the night was fully come, he set forth in the corner of a closed cab, and was driven to and fro about the streets of the city. He, I say—I cannot say, I. That child of Hell had nothing human; nothing lived in him but fear and hatred. And when at last, thinking the driver had begun to grow suspicious, he discharged the cab and ventured on foot, attired in his misfitting clothes, an object marked out for observation, into the midst of the nocturnal passengers, these two base passions raged within him like a tempest. He walked fast, hunted by his fears, chattering to himself, skulking through the less frequented thoroughfares, counting the minutes that still divided him from midnight. Once a woman spoke to him, offering, I think, a box of lights. He smote her in the face, and she fled.   53

When I came to myself at Lanyon's,[4] the horror of my old friend perhaps   54
affected me somewhat: I do not know; it was at least but a drop in the sea to the abhorrence with which I looked back upon these hours. A change had come over me. It was no longer the fear of the gallows, it was the horror of being Hyde that racked me. I received Lanyon's condemnation partly in a dream; it was partly in a dream that I came home to my own house and got into bed. I slept after the prostration of the day, with a stringent and profound slumber which not even the nightmare that wrung me could avail to break. I awoke in the morning, shaken, weakened, but refreshed. I still hated and feared the thought of the brute that slept within me, and I had not of course forgotten the appalling dangers of the day before; but I was once more at

---

[3] Poole: Jekyll's butler.

[4] *When I came to myself at Lanyon's*: In the presence of a horrified Dr. Lanyon, Edward Hyde drinks the potion that restores him to the form of Henry Jekyll. Hyde had sent a note to Lanyon (in Jekyll's handwriting), asking him to go to Jekyll's laboratory and retrieve the chemicals needed for the transformation.

home, in my own house and close to my drugs; and gratitude for my escape shone so strong in my soul that it almost rivalled the brightness of hope.

I was stepping leisurely across the court after breakfast, drinking the   55
chill of the air with pleasure, when I was seized again with those indescribable sensations that heralded the change; and I had but the time to gain the shelter of my cabinet, before I was once again raging and freezing with the passions of Hyde. It took on this occasion a double dose to recall me to myself; and, alas! six hours after, as I sat looking sadly in the fire, the pangs returned, and the drug had to be readministered. In short, from that day forth it seemed only by a great effort as of gymnastics, and only under the immediate stimulation of the drug, that I was able to wear the countenance of Jekyll. At all hours of the day and night I would be taken with the premonitory shudder; above all, if I slept or even dozed for a moment in my chair, it was always as Hyde that I awakened. Under the strain of this continually impending doom and by the sleeplessness to which I now condemned myself, ay, even beyond what I had thought possible to man, I became, in my own person, a creature eaten up and emptied by fever, languidly weak both in body and mind, and solely occupied by one thought: the horror of my other self. But when I slept or when the virtue of the medicine wore off, I would leap almost without transition (for the pangs of transformation grew daily less marked) into the possession of a fancy brimming with images of terror, a soul boiling with causeless hatreds, and a body that seemed not strong enough to contain the raging energies of life. The powers of Hyde seemed to have grown with the sickliness of Jekyll. And certainly the hate that now divided them was equal on each side. With Jekyll, it was a thing of vital instinct. He had now seen the full deformity of that creature that shared with him some of the phenomena of consciousness, and was co-heir with him to death: and beyond these links of community, which in themselves made the most poignant part of his distress, he thought of Hyde, for all his energy of life, as of something not only hellish but inorganic. This was the shocking thing; that the slime of the pit seemed to utter cries and voices; that the amorphous dust gesticulated and sinned; that what was dead, and had no shape, should usurp the offices of life. And this again, that that insurgent horror was knit to him closer than a wife, closer than an eye; lay caged in his flesh, where he heard it mutter and felt it struggle to be born; and at every hour of weakness, and in the confidence of slumber, prevailed against him, and deposed him out of life. The hatred of Hyde for Jekyll was of a different order. His terror of the gallows drove him continually to commit temporary suicide, and return to his subordinate station of a part instead of a person; but he loathed the necessity, he loathed the despondency into which Jekyll was now fallen, and he resented the dislike with which he was himself regarded. Hence the apelike tricks that he would play me, scrawling in my own hand blasphemies on the pages of my books, burning the letters and destroying the portrait of my father; and indeed, had it not been for his fear of death, he would long ago have ruined himself in order to involve me in the ruin. But his love of life is wonderful; I go further: I, who sicken and freeze at the mere thought of him, when I recall the abjec-

tion and passion of this attachment, and when I know how he fears my power to cut him off by suicide, I find it in my heart to pity him.

It is useless, and the time awfully fails me, to prolong this description; no one has ever suffered such torments, let that suffice; and yet even to these, habit brought—no, not alleviation—but a certain callousness of soul, a certain acquiescence of despair; and my punishment might have gone on for years, but for the last calamity which has now befallen, and which has finally severed me from my own face and nature. My provision of the salt, which had never been renewed since the date of the first experiment, began to run low. I sent out for a fresh supply, and mixed the draught; the ebullition followed, and the first change of colour, not the second; I drank it, and it was without efficiency. You will learn from Poole how I have had London ransacked; it was in vain; and I am now persuaded that my first supply was impure, and that it was that unknown impurity which lent efficacy to the draught.

About a week has passed, and I am now finishing this statement under the influence of the last of the old powders. This, then, is the last time, short of a miracle, that Henry Jekyll can think his own thoughts or see his own face (now how sadly altered!) in the glass. Nor must I delay too long to bring my writing to an end; for if my narrative has hitherto escaped destruction, it has been by a combination of great prudence and great good luck. Should the throes of change take me in the act of writing it, Hyde will tear it in pieces; but if some time shall have elapsed after I have laid it by, his wonderful selfishness and circumscription to the moment will probably save it once again from the action of his apelike sprite. And indeed the doom that is closing on us both has already changed and crushed him. Half an hour from now, when I shall again and for ever reindue that hated personality, I know how I shall sit shuddering and weeping in my chair, or continue, with the most strained and fearstruck ecstasy of listening, to pace up and down this room (my last earthly refuge) and give ear to every sound of menace. Will Hyde die upon the scaffold? or will he find the courage to release himself at the last moment? God knows; I am careless; this is my true hour of death, and what is to follow concerns another than myself. Here, then, as I lay down the pen, and proceed to seal up my confession, I bring the life of that unhappy Henry Jekyll to an end.

■ ■ ■

Discussion and Writing Suggestions

1. In your reading of "Henry Jekyll's Full Statement of the Case," to what extent do you see Mr. Hyde—the beast within Jekyll—as a separate entity? That is, do you view Jekyll and Hyde as two beings or one—or both?

2. What is so appealing about Mr. Hyde to Henry Jekyll? Why would someone held in such high esteem as Jekyll, someone of such wealth and

influence, be attracted to Hyde? In developing your answer, look for passages from "Henry Jekyll's Full Statement of the Case." You may want to devote special attention to the description of Jekyll's first conversion to Hyde. (See paragraphs 4–6.) Characterize the conversion, focusing especially on the feelings that were liberated in Jekyll as he became Edward Hyde.

3. Read the first (long) paragraph of "Henry Jekyll's Full Statement of the Case." Summarize Jekyll's justifications for his scientific studies. What, exactly, was he hoping to achieve?

4. [Questions 4, 5, and 6 form a series. If you choose one, consider choosing the others.] Read "Henry Jekyll's Full Statement of the Case" and highlight all language that suggests a "double." For instance, in paragraph 29, Jekyll refers to himself as a "double-dealer" and concludes "that man is not truly one, but truly two." Now review your highlights and attempt to make sense of them: find a pattern and offer an explanation.

5. Read the description of Utterson, the lawyer, in the first paragraph of "Story of the Door." Highlight phrases that show any evidence, if any, of a doubleness, or split personality, at work in Utterson's character. Now review your highlights and attempt to make sense of them: find a pattern and offer an explanation.

6. Consider your answers to questions 4 and 5. What comparisons can you draw, if any, between the characters of Jekyll and Utterson? Bear in mind Jekyll's observation that "man is . . . truly two."

7. In "Story of the Door," Utterson asks Enfield if he (Enfield) ever inquired about "the place with the door"—the house into which Mr. Hyde entered, only to appear moments later with a check signed by Henry Jekyll. Enfield replies that he feels "very strongly about putting questions; . . . the more it looks like Queer Street, the less I ask." Enfield is saying that he prefers not to pass judgment. In the context of *Dr. Jekyll and Mr. Hyde*, why might this be an apt philosophy?

8. At the end of his life, Dr. Jekyll is drawn to observe that "the doom and burthen of our life is bound forever on man's shoulders." With the aid of science, Jekyll tried (with some initial success) to throw off the burden on his shoulders—though eventually that burden returned in ways more awful than he could have imagined. Knowing Jekyll's intentions for his experiments, and observing his suffering, to what extent do you feel sympathy for Jekyll and his efforts? Specifically, consider these questions: Was Jekyll misguided, in your view? Was he a genius who *should* have succeeded but who worked with too immature a science? Would you encourage a modern-day Jekyll?

9. Henry Jekyll could not resist the attractions of the drug that transformed him into Mr. Hyde. Is Jekyll's attraction to this drug in any way similar

to an alcoholic's attraction to alcohol? Develop a comparison *and* contrast. In developing your answer, see especially paragraph 37.

10. On considering the heinous acts committed by his other self, Jekyll observes, "It was Hyde, after all, and Hyde alone, that was guilty. Jekyll was no worse; he woke again to his good qualities seemingly unimpaired; he would even make haste, where it was possible, to undo the evil done by Hyde. And thus his conscience slumbered." Allowing that ordinary people do not split themselves into two personalities (or persons) like Jekyll and Hyde, to what extent do you recognize in this passage the logic that explains away misdeeds and makes conscience slumber?

REVIEWS OF *JEKYLL AND HYDE* FILMS

Of all the film beasts within and without, few have been more popular than Mr. Hyde. At least 13 versions of the Jekyll and Hyde story have been made for movies and TV—seven of them in the silent period alone. This does not include such perversions as *Miss Jekyll and Madame Hyde* (1915), *Abbott and Costello Meet Dr. Jekyll and Mr. Hyde* (1953), *Dr. Jekyll and Sister Hyde* (1971), or *Dr. Jekyll vs. the Werewolf* (1971). The most well-known adaptations of Stevenson's novella are Rouben Mamoulian's 1931 version, starring Fredric March, and Victor Fleming's 1941 version, starring Spencer Tracy. Jekyll/Hyde has also been portrayed by John Barrymore (1920), Jack Palance (TV, 1968), and Kirk Douglas (1973).

More interesting than the cheap knockoffs and the lame parodies are the variants made by artists who bring a fresh take to familiar material. Included among these are Jerry Lewis's comically inventive (and insightful) *The Nutty Professor* (1963). Critics variously viewed the slick, arrogant, abusive Hyde figure, Buddy Love, in *Nutty Professor* (which, for French critics, at least, earned Lewis the status of major director) either a dark version of Lewis's former partner Dean Martin or—more Freudian—as the comedian's own true nature. *The Nutty Professor* was remade (successfully) by Eddie Murphy in 1996. Another interesting take on the Jekyll and Hyde story was *Mary Reilly*, made in 1996 by Stephen Frears, director of *My Beautiful Laundrette* (1985), *The Grifters* (1990), and *Hero* (1992). Screenwriter Christopher Hampton created the character of Mary Reilly as a servant in the house of Dr. Jekyll (John Malkovich); the familiar story unfolds from her limited point of view.

The following three reviews illustrate to a very small degree the range of critical commentary on the Dr. Jekyll and Hyde story. First, Mordaunt Hall reviews Mamoulian's 1931 film for the *New York Times*. Another *Times* review, by "T.S.," treats Fleming's 1941 film. Finally, Roger Ebert reviews *Mary Reilly* for *The Chicago Sun-Times*.

Fredric March in a Splendidly Produced Pictorial Version of "Dr. Jekyll and Mr. Hyde"

MORDAUNT HALL

What with the audibility of the screen and the masterful photography, the new pictorial transcription of Stevenson's spine-chilling work, "Dr. Jekyll and Mr. Hyde," emerges as a far more tense and shuddering affair than it was as John Barrymore's silent picture. True, the producers are not a little too zealous in their desire to spread terror among audiences, but while there are pardonable roamings from the original, there is in most instances a good excuse for making the scenes as they are in this current study.   1

Fredric March is the stellar performer in this blood-curdling shadow venture. His make-up as Hyde is not done by halves, for virtually every imaginable possibility is taken advantage of to make this creature "reflecting the lower elements of Dr. Jekyll's soul" thoroughly hideous. Instead of being undersized or smaller than Dr. Jekyll, as in the Stevenson description, this repellent thing here is broader and taller. In physiognomy this Hyde has the aspects of an ape, with protruding teeth, long eye-teeth, unkempt thick hair leaving but a scant forehead, a broad nose with large nostrils, eyes with the lower part of the sockets pulled down, thick eyebrows and hairy arms and hands—a creature that would make the hairy ape of O'Neill's play a welcome sight.   2

Rouben Mamoulian, the director of this film, has gone about his task with considerable enthusiasm, and the ways in which Jekyll changes into Hyde are pictured with an expert cunning, for it is a series of gradual exposures during which the changing face does not leave the screen. The first time the transition takes place it is effective, but it is still more so in subsequent sequences, for Hyde, who cannot return to his other self without the necessary prescription, in one episode is forced virtually to accomplish the transformation from the apish thing to his ordinary form at the point of a pistol before his friend Dr. Lanyan. It is about this time that Jekyll realizes that he assumes the frightening shape suddenly without swallowing his preparation which in the first case brought about the change.   3

Mr. March's portrayal is something to arouse admiration, even taking into consideration the camera wizardry. As Dr. Jekyll he is a charming man, and as a fiend he is alert and sensual.   4

The producers have seen fit to include both a romantic theme and a sex influence in the course of the narrative, and toward the end one is apt to think that this story is to be given a happy ending. But this does not happen, for after having committed several murders, including the slaying of Ivy Parsons, a singer in a cabaret, Hyde runs amuck, wielding a heavy stick, leaping up on desks and shelves and hurling vases at his pursuers, until a Scotland Yard sleuth sounds his death-knell with a bullet.   5

One of the many highly dramatic episodes is where Jekyll calls on his 6
fiancée, Muriel Carew. After leaving her, one of the periodical transformations takes place and he re-enters the Carew home and takes Muriel in his
arms. Once she looks upon Hyde's awful physiognomy, she screams and
faints. This results in the chase that leads to the death of the man. When
breathing his last, the fearsome creature gradually changes from Hyde to
Jekyll.

Miriam Hopkins does splendidly as the unfortunate Ivy. Rose Hobart is 7
clever as the sympathetic Muriel. Holmes Herbert delivers a pleasingly
restrained performance as Dr. Lanyan, and Halliwell Hobbe's portrayal of
Muriel's father, General Carew, is another asset to this fine film. Edgar
Norton, who plays Poole, Dr. Jekyll's faithful servant, is very much at home
in the part, inasmuch as he acted it with Richard Mansfield.

The atmosphere, that of London in Stevenson's day, is quite pleasing. 8
There are the gas lamps, old-fashioned feminine costumes and other details.
Likewise the settings enhance the scenes, particularly those of the interesting
twisted little byways.

Review of Dr. Jekyll and Mr. Hyde

"T. S."

Let's be gentle and begin by admitting that the new film version of "Dr. 1
Jekyll and Mr. Hyde" has a point or two in its favor. It has, for instance, one
Ingrid Bergman: as the luckless barmaid pursued and tortured by an evil she
could not understand, the young Swedish actress proves again that a shining
talent can sometimes lift itself above an impossibly written role. There is also
at least one superbly photographed chase of the maddened Hyde running
amok through the fog-bound London streets, his cape billowing behind him
like a vision of terror. The film has, finally, the extraordinarily polished production that only Hollywood's technical wizards can achieve. And therewith
we pay all debts to the preposterous mixture of hokum and high-flown psychological balderdash that arrived yesterday at the Astor.

For around Robert Louis Stevenson's frightening fable of good and evil, 2
John Lee Mahin, who wrote the screen play, and Victor Fleming, who directed it, have created a Grand Guignol chiller with delusions of grandeur, a
nightmare interpreted by a reader of tea leaves, a mulligan stew hidden under
an expensive soufflé.

In a daring montage or two, which must have caught the censors dozing, 3
a weary Freud is dragged in by the coat-tails. In Dr. Jekyll's classic struggle
with the devil in his own bosom the producers are warming some of the
choicer chestnuts. "Come, Jekyll, the rainbow lies ahead!" calls the fiend in
the doctor's mirror. Jekyll should have known better. Had he not been told
that "one cannot flirt with the divinity of man without being damned forever"?

A little Freudian theory is a dangerous thing. It can make a piece of   4
errant hokum dizzy with significance. Faced with the choice of creating
hokum unabashed or a psychological study of a man caught in mortal conflict
with himself, the producers have tried to do both—and failed by nearly two
hours of pompous symbolism. As a result there were a good many giggles in
the house—and at the wrong places—when Spencer Tracy, as the experimenting Dr. Jekyll, downed the bubbling elixir and, after gasping like a fish
out of water, gradually assumed the shape of the bestial Mr. Hyde.

Mr. Tracy has taken the short end of the stick by choice. Though his   5
facial changes, as he alternates between Dr. Jekyll and his evil alter ego, may
be a trifle subtler than his predecessors in the role, Mr. Tracy's portrait of
Hyde is not so much evil incarnate as it is the ham rampant. When his eyes
roll in a fine frenzy like loose marbles in his head he is more ludicrous than
dreadful. When he blows grapeskins upon the fair cheek of Miss Bergman, the
enchantress of his evil dreams, it is an affront to good taste rather than a serious, and thereby acceptable, study in sadism.

Of all the actors, only Miss Bergman has emerged with some measure of   6
honor. Lana Turner, as Dr. Jekyll's pure little fiancée; Donald Crisp, as her
stiff-spined parent; Ian Hunter, as Jekyll's bewildered friend—all these move
like well-behaved puppets around the periphery of Mr. Tracy's nightmare. But
the fault lies deeper than the performances. Out of ham and hokum the adap-
tors have tried to create a study of a man caught at bay by the devil he has
released within himself. And it doesn't come off either as hokum, significant
drama or entertainment.

Mary Reilly

ROGER EBERT

What is it, this obsession with the Gothic, with gloom and shadows, sinister   1
secrets, thick foggy nights, and creatures like Hyde, who is said to "come out
of the dark is if he was made of it"? And why must a young woman almost
always be involved, as witness and victim? The Gothic is always sexually
charged, and all of its threats come down to one, against the heroine's virtue.

"Mary Reilly" works as Gothic melodrama because it understands the   2
genre so well. The story of Jekyll and Hyde would seem to be complete in
itself, with two natures fighting for control of one man. But its weakness is
that the man is a threat primarily to himself (and to victims we care little
about). Valerie Martin's novel, which supplies the source material for this
movie, also provides the story with a point of view—an innocent, naive, vulnerable young woman, a housemaid, who can dimly sense the danger she is
in, even as she feels a powerful attraction to her employer.

"Mary Reilly" is in some ways more faithful to the spirit of Robert   3
Lewis [sic] Stevenson's original story than any of the earlier films based on it,
because it's true to the underlying horror. This film is not about makeup or
special effects, or Hyde turning into the Wolf Man. It's about a powerless
young woman who feels sympathy for one side of a man's nature, and horror
of the other.

The movie stars Julia Roberts as Mary, an Irish servant in the dark, fog-   4
bound Edinburgh of more than a century ago. John Malkovich is both Dr.
Henry Jekyll, a respected local physician, and Mr. Edward Hyde, the creature
he becomes after taking an experimental potion. What does Jekyll hope the
potion will provide? Youth? Health? Potency? In a sense, he hopes it will liberate him from Hyde—from the Hyde we all have lurking within us. In another, more frightening sense, he hopes Hyde will liberate him, to be more of an
animal, and less of what was then called a gentleman.

Stephen Frears, the director, plays most of the action on a few vast and   5
yet claustrophobic sets. We see Jekyll's library, filled with books to intimidate
the uneducated housemaid. His operating theater, a Victorian monstrosity
with tiers of seats for observers, looking down into the circles of hell. His laboratory, behind the house, usually locked, reached by a strange walkway
suspended from chains. His bedroom, which one day is covered with blood,
even on the ceiling. The servants' quarters downstairs, where the strict butler
(George Cole) is jealous of the attention the master is giving young Mary.

Why is Jekyll drawn to her? Because of her scars. He asks her about   6
them, and finally she reveals that she was beaten as a child, and locked in a
closet with rats. And yet she refuses to say she hates her father for his treatment of her. This powerfully attracts Jekyll, who already feels that the Hyde
side of his nature is beyond human acceptance. If Mary cannot hate her
father, perhaps she cannot hate Jekyll and his secret; that would make her the
only human soul with sympathy for the suffering doctor.

"Mary Reilly" is a dark, sad, frightening, gloomy story. During its film-   7
ing there were reports of battles between the filmmakers and the studio,
which wanted a more upbeat ending. Of course there can be no happy ending,
because what Hyde has done, Jekyll has done—that's the whole point, in a
way. But the movie does provide a satisfactory ending, in that Mary is able to
comprehend the nature of the man's two personalities, and to pity him.

The performances are subtle and well-controlled. We often see Roberts'   8
face illuminated in darkness. She speaks little. Most of the time she does not
understand as much of the story as we do. Malkovich is quiet but simmering
with anger. All he does to separate the two identities is to use facial hair as
Jekyll and not as Hyde. (Is Hyde one of Jekyll's grown-up wild oats? asks
Bradshaw, the footman. "They do look a bit alike!") When the two characters are speaking, they are held in large closeups; the movie is as visually intimate as a Bergman film, and avoids most of the clichés suggested by the
material.

So what is it, this fascination with the Gothic? For me, it offers the fas-   9
cination of secrets, dreads and guilts. Modern horror is too easily explained;

indeed, the real world has outrun horror, and the headlines are now worse than anything Stephen King can imagine. In the 19th century, there was belief in evil, because there was belief in good. That makes stories like this sort of optimistic, in a way.

■ ■ ■

Discussion and Writing Suggestions

1. *Dr. Jekyll and Mr. Hyde* is one of the stories most frequently adapted for the movies and for television, with at least 13 versions (the earliest in 1910) produced over a span of 75 years. What, in your view, accounts for this rich history of adaptation? Why is Stevenson's story such a good source for movies?

2. Rent and watch one of the movie adaptations of *Dr. Jekyll and Mr. Hyde* reviewed here. Write a letter to the reviewer agreeing or disagreeing with the review.

3. Watch two or more of the movie versions of *Dr. Jekyll and Mr. Hyde*. Study the lead actor's portrayal of the Jekyll/Hyde character. What qualities do you think are central to a successful portrayal? Based on your answer, whose portrayal do you think is the better one? Explain your reasons.

4. Compare and contrast the characterizations of Hyde in two or more of the movie versions of this story. While all may be considered "evil," ask yourself, "Of what does evil consist, in this particular interpretation?" What qualities does March's portrayal bring out? Tracy's? Malkovich's? To what extent, if at all, do the personalities of these individual Hydes differ? To what extent are they similar?

5. The reviewer of the Spencer Tracy *Dr. Jekyll and Mr. Hyde* objects to the director's overt psychologizing of the problem of good and evil. (The reviewer writes, "A little Freudian theory is a dangerous thing.") Roger Ebert suggests that *Mary Reilly* succeeds in part because it is "faithful to the spirit of Robert Lewis [sic] Stevenson's original story," alluding to the main character's deeply psychological (and moral) struggle with his dual nature. Stevenson's story clearly invites a psychological inquiry into an individual's capacity for good and evil. Select one film version of *Dr. Jekyll and Mr. Hyde* and determine how well it presents this inquiry. Present your conclusions in a paragraph or two.

6. The original Stevenson story of *Dr. Jekyll and Mr. Hyde* did not include a romantic interest for Jekyll, as do the movie versions reviewed here. Allowing that film adapters must have some license in translating a story from print into film, explain the consistent addition of a romantic inter-

est for Jekyll. Why should such an interest be necessary for the film to succeed if it was not necessary for Stevenson's story to succeed?

7. View two or more film versions of *Dr. Jekyll and Mr. Hyde*—the Fredric March version and at least one other. Study the special effects used in the changes of Jekyll into Hyde (and vice versa) and record your observations. Consider these questions: How violent is the change? How convincing is it? What does Hyde look like as compared to Jekyll? Why do their appearances differ? In a paragraph or two, synthesize your observations into a coherent statement.

8. View the two *Nutty Professor* films mentioned in the headnote to these reviews (Jerry Lewis, 1963, and Eddie Murphy, 1996). Compare and contrast the films, focusing on characterization, humor, dialogue, and setting. You might also compare and contrast the form of "evil" that the Hyde-like characters assume in these remakes of Stevenson's story, as well as the forms of "good."

■ SYNTHESIS ACTIVITIES

1. What "beast within" emerges in horror movies? Draw on several selections in this chapter to develop your answer into an argument synthesis. Possible sources include Solomon, King, and Greenberg. To illustrate your claim, you may want, additionally, to refer to Carter's "Company of Wolves" and/or Stevenson's "Dr. Jekyll and Mr. Hyde."

2. Develop an essay in which you explain your fondness of, or impatience with, horror movies. Consider beginning the essay with an anecdote—a description of your viewing a horror movie and your response. Follow that anecdote with an analysis that draws on two or more of the selections in this chapter.

3. One classic element of the horror genre is the "search" scene, in which a character—a likely victim—searches a house (most often) in order to find something or someone. Locate several of the movies in the "filmography" on pages 791–92. View and re-view the search scenes. Write a synthesis in which you (1) explain the elements of a "classic" horror movie search scene and (2) analyze why the search scene appears in so many horror movies. In developing this analysis you might want to draw on the article by Solomon.

4. What is horrifying about horror movies? Various authors in this chapter speak to the need we have to confront, periodically, what horror movies show us. But why is what they show horrifying? Develop your answer into an argument synthesis, drawing on the movies you have watched and on at least one article in the chapter.

5. The extent to which one believes that the "beast within" is a separate entity or simply a dark but integral part of ourselves is linked to one's

sense of individual responsibility. If some malignant force "inhabits" us, then it is that force—not us—that is responsible for our misdeeds. If the dark impulses to misconduct are part of us, then we are responsible and must pay the consequences. Consider the films you have watched and the selections you have read in the context of this chapter. What evidence do you see of one attitude or another toward the beast within? Develop your observations into an argument synthesis.

6. The article by Salisbury makes clear that ours is not the only era fascinated with tales of transformation. The notion of animals and humans changing from one form to the other, and back again, is a commonplace of ancient and medieval literature. Using Salisbury as a point of departure, write an essay in which you speculate on the idea of transformation and why it might be important to people across time. In support of your speculation, draw on the work of at least one other author in this chapter.

7. How literally do you interpret the term "beast within"? That is, do you consider humans to be animals? Partly animals? What is the relationship between our animal selves and our civilized selves? Use these questions as a springboard to an argument synthesis that draws on two or more of the selections in this chapter.

8. Reread the review of Mike Nichols's film, *Wolf*. Write a comparison-contrast synthesis in which you draw on these reviews in the service of writing your own review of the film. You should refer directly to the opinions of James, Denby, and Maslin as you side with one (or more) of them or take an independent stance. Your review should leave the reader with a definite impression of your overall assessment of *Wolf*. Note that it is possible to have serious reservations about parts of a film and still generally recommend it.

9. In his book *American Film Genres*, 2nd ed. (Chicago: Nelson-Hall, 1985), Stuart M. Kaminsky makes the following observation of the *Jekyll and Hyde* movies:

> The horror of *Dr. Jekyll and Mr. Hyde* comes, not so much from the murders Hyde commits, but from the dawning realization in Jekyll that he cannot control his transformations, that he has no power to determine the times when one part of his personality will be dominant. The horror, in short, comes from Jekyll's loss of identity, his forced submission to the totally animal part of personality. This concern with loss of control is central to many horror films. (123)

Do you agree with Kaminsky's conclusion about loss of control? Develop your response into an argument synthesis in which you draw on the movies you have watched and on the articles you have read in the context of this chapter. See especially Salisbury, King, and Greenberg.

■ RESEARCH ACTIVITIES

1. Select three or four films that comprise a subgenre of the horror film, as indicated in Tim Dirks's article—for example, *Dracula* or *Frankenstein* films, or some of the more recent "slasher" films. If you're interested in werewolf films, consider, in addition to the ones treated in this chapter and in Dirks's piece, *The Howling* (1980), *An American Werewolf in London* (1981), *Wolfen* (1981), *Ladyhawke* (1983), and *An American Werewolf in Paris* (1998).

    Rent and view these films. Then, research (1) the conventions of this particular subgenre and (2) comments by reviewers and critics. In addition to conducting a subject search of horror films in both print and electronic (web and CD-ROM) sources, you might find the following books particularly helpful: Stanley J. Solomon, *Beyond Formula* (1976), Thomas Schatz, *Hollywood Genres* (1981), Barry Keith Grant, ed. *Film Genre Reader* (1986) and *Film Genre Reader II* (1995).

    For critical commentary and reviews of individual films, see *Film Index International on CD-ROM* (covers films from 1930 to the present), *Film Review Annual* (collections of film reviews, 1981 to the present), *The New York Times Film Reviews* (1913 to the present), *International Index to Film Periodicals* (1972 to the present), *Film Literature Index* (1973 to the present), *Variety Film Reviews*, *Magill's Cinema Annual* (1982 to the present), and film review listings (alphabetically listed under "Moving Pictures" or "Motion Pictures") in the *Reader's Guide to Periodical Literature*. Three useful web sources on film include Cinemachine <www.cinemachine.com/>, Cinemania <cinemania.msn.com>, and The Internet Movie Database (IMDb) <us.imdb.com/>.

    In your paper, relate the particulars of individual films to the conventions of the genre or subgenre. Show how a particular event, or motif, for example, follows the convention or varies it. Compare and contrast what happens in one film to a corresponding event in another, giving reasons for the differences, and discussing the effects of these variants. To sharpen the focus, you may want to confine your attention to just one crucial or representative scene in each film (for example, the first appearance of the "beast" or its ultimate defeat).

2. Focus your attention on a single horror film, one covered in this chapter, or another that you particularly like, or one that you would like to see. Using some of the sources suggested in the previous exercise, research the critical reviews and commentary upon this film. Categorize the main focal points of critical comment and compose an explanatory synthesis on the critical reception of this film.

3. Select a horror film based on a novel. Read the fictional work, view the film, and write a paper comparing and contrasting the two ver-

sions of the same story. Locate some critical reviews of both fiction and film and integrate these sources into your discussion.

Examples: *Frankenstein* (novel by Mary Shelley, 1818); *Dr. Jekyll and Mr. Hyde* (novel by Robert Louis Stevenson, 1886); *Dracula* (novel by Bram Stoker, 1897); *The Invisible Man* (novel by H. G. Wlls, 1897); *Psycho* (novel by Robert Bloch, 1959); *Rosemary's Baby* (novel by Ira Levin, 1967); *The Shining* (novel by Stephen King, 1977); *The Exorcist* (novel by William Petter Blatty, 1971).

4. View at least two film adaptations of the same story—for example, the Fredric March version of *Dr. Jekyll and Mr. Hyde* (1932) and the Spencer Tracy version (1941); or James Whale's *Frankenstein* (1931) and Kenneth Branagh's (1994). Researching some of the critical commentary on these films, write a paper comparing and contrasting the two or more versions. As with Research Activity 1 above, you may want to sharpen your focus by concentrating your attention upon just one or two key sequences in each film.

5. As Dirks points out in his selection, the theme of some horror and science fiction films concerns either a misuse of scientific research—and, as a corollary, the arrogance of scientists—or a corruption of technology. Many of the early horror films include some variation of the line, "I/you have meddled in things that man should leave alone!" *Frankenstein* is the most obvious example of this motif; other films in which the scientist is the bad (or at least misguided) guy include *The Invisible Man* (1933) and in the two versions of *The Fly* (1958, 1986). The arrogant Dr. Morbius overreaches in *Forbidden Planet* (1956). An atheistical scientist is the villain in *Fantastic Voyage* (1966). Many of the monster movies of the 1950s (and most recently, the 1998 *Godzilla*) blame nuclear testing for the creation of gigantic city-stomping lizards.

Research this particular aspect of horror films—the motif of the scientist or of technology as malign, dangerous, or even blasphemous (that is, encroaching on areas that belong rightfully to the deity). Use some of the sources listed in Research Activity 1 above, focusing particularly on those that deal to some degree with the ways that horror or science fiction films imply or dramatize attitudes toward science and technology.

6. If you'd like a change from horror, select another standard film genre: for example, the Western, the detective film, the gangster film, the *film noir*, the musical, the science fiction film, the war film, the screwball comedy, the black comedy, the family drama, the social problem film. Using some of the sources suggested in Research Activity 1 above, write a paper showing how two to four examples of this genre make use of its conventions.

7. Horror films have sometimes come under attack from people who believe that they can be bad influences upon young or impressionable viewers. Objections have focused on the high level of graphic violence in many horror films, as well as the underlying rape implications

in many of the older horror films (advertising material often featured a scantily clad young woman being carried off by the beast). The 1950s saw a reaction against excessively grisly horror comic books and, to a lesser extent, horror films. Research one or more of these anti-horror campaigns and report on your findings. You may also want to look into the work of social scientists (such as Edward Donnerstein and Elizabeth Rice Allgeier) who have researched the links between violence in films and violent proclivities in males. Keep in mind that the question is not only whether horror films are likely to inspire imitation of the violent actions portrayed, but also whether repeated exposure to horror films may help foster an increased tolerance of violence as an acceptable way of releasing anger or frustration.

Credits

872

Index of Authors and Titles